Global Business Today

seventh edition

Global Business Today

Charles W. L. Hill
University of Washington

William Hernández-Requejo
University of California, Irvine

McGraw-Hill Irwin

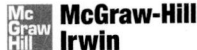

McGraw-Hill
Irwin

GLOBAL BUSINESS TODAY: GLOBAL EDITION

Published by McGraw-Hill/Irwin, a business unit of The McGraw-Hill Companies, Inc., 1221
Avenue of the Americas, New York, NY, 10020. Copyright 2011, 2009, 2008, 2006, 2004, 2001, 1998 by
The McGraw-Hill Companies, Inc. All rights reserved. No part of this publication may be reproduced or
distributed in any form or by any means, or stored in a database or retrieval system, without the prior
written consent of The McGraw-Hill Companies, Inc., including, but not limited to, in any network or
other electronic storage or transmission, or broadcast for distance learning.

Some ancillaries, including electronic and print components, may not be available to customers outside the
United States.

This book is printed on acid-free paper.

1 2 3 4 5 6 7 8 9 0 DOW/DOW 1 0 9 8 7 6 5 4 3 2 1

ISBN 978-0-07-122084-2
MHID 0-07-122084-4

For June and Mike Hill, my parents. — C. W. L. H.

To my wife and love, Martha, and to my friend and mentor, John Graham. — W. H. R.

about the authors

Charles W. L. Hill is the Hughes M. Blake Professor of International Business at the School of Business, University of Washington. Professor Hill received his Ph.D. in industrial organization economics in 1983 from the University of Manchester's Institute of Science and Technology (UMIST) in Great Britain. In addition to his position at the University of Washington, he has served on the faculties of UMIST, Texas A&M University, and Michigan State University.

Professor Hill has published some 50 articles in peer-reviewed academic journals. He has also published four college textbooks, one on strategic management, one on principles of management, and the other two on international business (one of which you are now holding). He serves on the editorial boards of several academic journals and previously served as consulting editor at the *Academy of Management Review.*

Professor Hill teaches in the MBA and executive MBA programs at the University of Washington and has received awards for teaching excellence in both programs. He has also taught on several customized executive programs. He lives in Seattle with his wife, Lane, and his children.

Born in Santa Clara, Cuba, **William Hernández-Requejo** is educated as an attorney and earned his *juris doctor* at the Georgetown University Law Center in Washington, D.C., where he specialized in international law. William is adjunct faculty at the University of California, Irvine, and numerous other institutions where he teaches classes in Global Business, International Business Transactions, Trade Regulation and the WTO, Global Negotiations, International Marketing, International Strategic Alliances, and Joint Ventures at the MBA or law school level. In addition, William is president and senior advisor in his consulting firm, Requejo Consulting, which specializes in bridging national boundaries to facilitate international commerce. William serves on the board of directors of various entities.

In collaboration with John L. Graham, William has published *Global Negotiation: The New Rules* (Palgrave Macmillan, 2008). This textbook, *Global Business Today, Global Edition,* is William's first foray into college textbook publishing. His passions are food, travel, and poetry. He lives in Irvine, California, with his wife Martha and their two children.

brief contents

contents

preface

Global Business Today is intended for the first international business course at either the undergraduate or MBA level. Our goal in writing this book has been to set a new standard for international business textbooks. We have attempted to write a book that

1. Is comprehensive and up-to-date.
2. Goes beyond an uncritical presentation and shallow explanation of the body of knowledge.
3. Maintains a tight, integrated flow between chapters.
4. Focuses on managerial implications.
5. Makes important theories accessible and interesting to students.
6. Incorporates ancillary resources that enliven the text and make it easier to teach.

Over the years, and through now seven editions, we have worked hard to adhere to these goals. It has not always been easy. An enormous amount has happened over the past decade, both in the real world of economics, politics, and business, and in the academic world of theory and empirical research. Often we have had to significantly rewrite chapters, scrap old examples, bring in new ones, incorporate new theory and evidence into the book, and phase out older theories that are increasingly less relevant to the modern and dynamic world of international business. That process continues in the current edition. As noted below, there have been significant changes in this edition, and that will no doubt continue to be the case in the future. In deciding what changes to make, we have been guided not only by our own reading, teaching, and research, but also by the invaluable feedback we receive from professors and students around the world who use the book, from reviewers, and from the editorial staff at McGraw-Hill/Irwin. Our thanks go out to all of them.

Comprehensive and Up-to-Date

To be comprehensive, an international business textbook must

- Explain how and why the world's countries differ.
- Present a thorough review of the economics and politics of international trade and investment.
- Explain the functions and form of the global monetary system.
- Examine the strategies and structures of international businesses.
- Assess the special roles of an international business's various functions.

We have always endeavored to do all of these things. Too many other texts have paid insufficient attention to the strategies and structures of international businesses and to the implications of international business for firms' various functions. This omission has been a serious deficiency. Many of the students in these international business courses will soon be working in international businesses, and they will be expected to understand the implications of international business for their organization's strategy, structure, and functions. This book pays close attention to these issues.

Comprehensiveness and relevance also require coverage of the major theories. It has always been our goal to incorporate the insights gleaned from recent academic work into the text. Consistent with this goal, over the past seven editions we have added insights from the following research:

- The new trade theory and strategic trade policy.
- The work of Nobel Prize–winning economist Amartya Sen on economic development.
- The work of Hernando de Soto on the link between property rights and economic development.
- Samuel Huntington's influential thesis on the "clash of civilizations."
- The new growth theory of economic development championed by Paul Romer and Gene Grossman.
- Empirical work by Jeffrey Sachs and others on the relationship between international trade and economic growth.
- Michael Porter's theory of the competitive advantage of nations.
- Robert Reich's work on national competitive advantage.
- The work of Nobel Prize–winner Douglas North and others on national institutional structures and the protection of property rights.
- The market imperfections approach to foreign direct investment that has grown out of Ronald Coase and Oliver Williamson's work on transaction cost economics.
- Bartlett and Ghoshal's research on the transnational corporation.
- The writings of C. K. Prahalad and Gary Hamel on core competencies, global competition, and global strategic alliances.
- Insights for international business strategy that can be derived from the resource-based view of the firm.
- Paul Samuelson's critique of free trade theory.

In addition to including leading-edge theory, in light of the fast-changing nature of the international business environment, we have made every effort to ensure that the book was as up-to-date as possible when it went to press. A significant amount has happened in the world since we first began work on this book. The Uruguay Round of GATT negotiations were successfully concluded and the World Trade Organization was established. In 2001, the WTO embarked upon another major round of talks aimed to reduce barriers to trade, the Doha Round. The European Union moved forward with its post-1992 agenda to achieve a closer economic and monetary union, including the establishment of a common currency in January 1999. The North American Free Trade Agreement passed into law, and Chile indicated its desire to become the next member of the free trade area. The Asia-Pacific Economic Cooperation forum emerged as the kernel of a possible future Asia Pacific free trade area. The former Communist states of Eastern Europe and Asia continued on the road to economic and political reform. As they did, the euphoric mood that followed the collapse of communism in 1989 was slowly replaced with a growing sense of realism about the hard path ahead for many of these countries. The global money market continued its meteoric growth. By 2007, more than $3 trillion per day was flowing across national borders. The size of such flows fueled concern about the ability of short-term speculative shifts in global capital markets to destabilize the world economy. The World Wide Web emerged from nowhere to become the backbone of an emerging global network for electronic commerce. The world continued to become more global. Several Asian Pacific economies, most notably China, continued to grow their economies at a rapid rate. Outsourcing of service functions to places such as China and India emerged as a major issue in developed Western nations. New multinationals continued to emerge from developing nations in addition to the world's established industrial powers. Increasingly, the globalization of the world economy affected a wide range of firms of all sizes, from the very large to the very small. And unfortunately, in the wake of the terrorist attacks on the United States that took place September 11, 2001, global terrorism and the attendant geopolitical risks emerged as a threat to global economic integration and activity.

New in the Seventh Edition

The success of the first six editions of *Global Business Today* was based in part upon the incorporation of leading-edge research into the text, the use of the up-to-date examples and statistics to illustrate global trends and enterprise strategy, and the discussion of current events within the context of the appropriate theory. Building on these strengths, our goals for the sixth revision have been threefold:

1. Incorporate new insights from recent scholarly research wherever appropriate.
2. Make sure the content of the text covers all appropriate issues.
3. Make sure the text is as up-to-date as possible with regard to current events, statistics, and examples.

As part of the overall revision process, *changes have been made to every chapter in the book*. All material and statistics are as up-to-date as possible as of 2009 or early 2010. We have added discussion of current events wherever appropriate. Most notably for this edition, **detailed discussion of the global financial crisis that occurred in 2008 and 2009, and its implications for international business, has been added to many chapters.** For example, Chapter 6 opens with a case that discusses the global financial crisis, the WTO, and the G20.

Elsewhere, Chapter 6 has been updated to discuss progress on the current round of talks sponsored by the WTO aimed at reducing barriers to trade, particularly in agriculture (the Doha Round). Chapter 7 now discusses the rebound in slumping foreign direct investment flows that occurred in 2008 and 2009, and explains how the global financial crisis of 2008 contributed to this. Chapter 9 discusses the weakness in the U.S. dollar between 2004 and 2008, and its paradoxical rebound in late 2008 in the midst of a severe financial crisis in United States and elsewhere.

Beyond Uncritical Presentation and Shallow Explanation

Many issues in international business are complex and thus necessitate considerations of pros and cons. To demonstrate this to students, we have adopted a critical approach that presents the arguments for and against economic theories, government policies, business strategies, organizational structures, and so on.

Related to this, we have attempted to explain the complexities of the many theories and phenomena unique to international business so the student might fully comprehend the statements of a theory or the reasons a phenomenon is the way it is. We believe that these theories and phenomena are explained in more depth in this book than they are in competing textbooks, which seem to use the rationale that a shallow explanation is little better than no explanation. In international business, a little knowledge is indeed a dangerous thing.

To help students go a step further in expanding their understanding of international business, each chapter incorporates two **globalEDGE research tasks** designed and written by Tunga Kiyak and the team at Michigan State University's globalEDGE .msu.edu site to dovetail with the content just covered.

globalEDGE Research Task

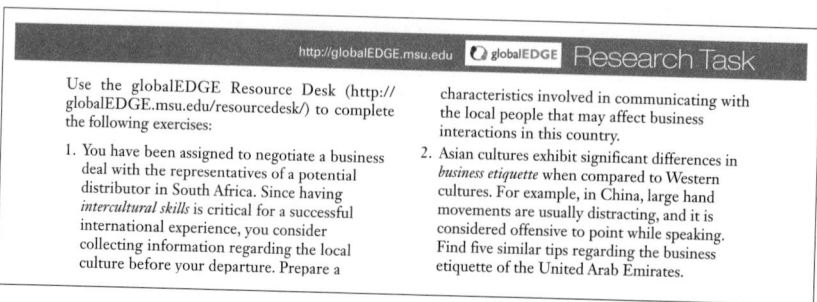

http://globalEDGE.msu.edu 🌐 globalEDGE Research Task

Use the globalEDGE Resource Desk (http://globalEDGE.msu.edu/resourcedesk/) to complete the following exercises:

1. You have been assigned to negotiate a business deal with the representatives of a potential distributor in South Africa. Since having *intercultural skills* is critical for a successful international experience, you consider collecting information regarding the local culture before your departure. Prepare a characteristics involved in communicating with the local people that may affect business interactions in this country.

2. Asian cultures exhibit significant differences in *business etiquette* when compared to Western cultures. For example, in China, large hand movements are usually distracting, and it is considered offensive to point while speaking. Find five similar tips regarding the business etiquette of the United Arab Emirates.

iGlobe is McGraw-Hill/Irwin's revolutionary Web-based video archive that incorporates international business news clips from PBS's "NewsHour." Two new clips are added every month, and teaching notes are available for you to integrate the segments with your course. Students can also subscribe for individual access (www.mhhe.com/iglobepreview).

iGLOBE

iGLOBE is McGraw-Hill/Irwin's revolutionary new Web-based video archive, incorporating international business news clips from PBS's *The NewsHour*. New clips are added every month, and teaching notes are available for you to use in integrating the segments with your classroom. Students can also subscribe for individual access. (www.mhhe.com/iglobepreview)

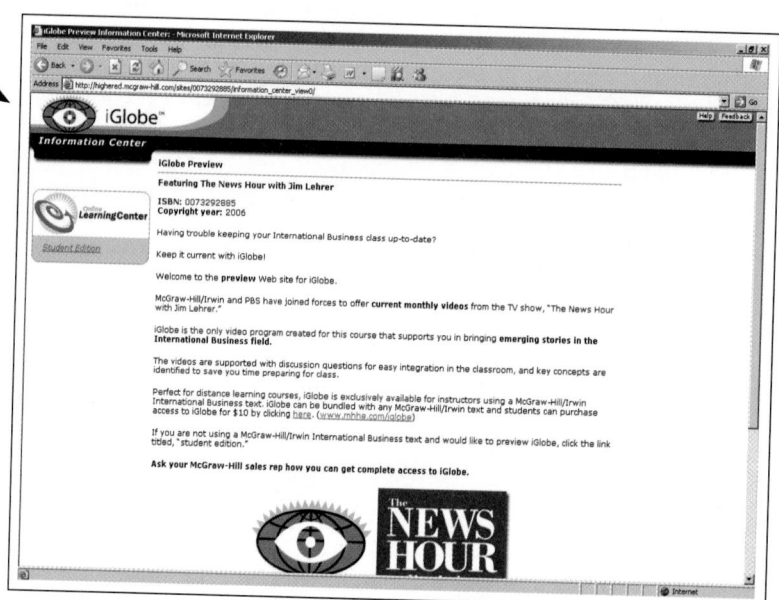

Integrated Progression of Topics

A weakness of many texts is that they lack a tight, integrated flow of topics from chapter to chapter. In Chapter 1 of this book, students will learn how the book's topics are related to each other. We've achieved integration by organizing the material so that each chapter builds on the material of the previous ones in a logical fashion.

PART ONE Chapter 1 provides an overview of the key issues to be addressed and explains the plan of the book.

PART TWO   Chapters 2 and 3 focus on national differences in political economy and culture, and Chapter 4 examines ethical issues in international business. Most international business textbooks place this material at a later point, but we believe it is vital to discuss national differences first. After all, many of the central issues in international trade and investment, the global monetary system, international business strategy and structure, and international business operations arise out of national differences in political economy and culture. To fully understand these issues, students must first appreciate the differences in countries and cultures. Ethical issues are dealt with at this juncture primarily because many ethical dilemmas flow out of national differences in political systems, economic systems, and culture.

PART THREE   Chapters 5 through 8 investigate the political economy of international trade and investment. The purpose of this part is to describe and explain the trade and investment environment in which international business occurs.

PART FOUR   Chapters 9 and 10 describe and explain the global monetary system, laying out in detail the monetary framework in which international business transactions are conducted.

PART FIVE   In Chapters 11 through 16, attention shifts from the environment to the firm. Here the book examines the strategies that firms adopt to compete effectively in the international business environment and explains how firms can perform key functions—production, marketing, R&D, human resource management, accounting, and finance—to compete and succeed in the international business environment.

Throughout the book, the relationship of new material to topics discussed in earlier chapters is pointed out to the students to reinforce their understanding of how the material comprises an integrated whole.

Focus on Managerial Implications

We have always believed that it is important to show students how the material covered in the text is relevant to the actual practice of international business. This is explicit in the later chapters of the book, which focus on the practice of international business, but it is not always obvious in the first half of the book, which considered many macro-economic and political issues, from international trade theory and foreign direct investment flows to the IMF and the influence of inflation rates on foreign exchange quotations. Accordingly, at the end of each chapter in Parts Two, Three, and Four—where the focus is on the environment of international business, as opposed to particular firms—there is a section titled "Focus on Managerial Implications." In this section, the managerial implications of the material discussed in the chapter are clearly explained.

Focus of Managerial Implications

For example, Chapter 5, "International Trade Theory," ends with a detailed discussion of the various trade theories' implications for international business management. See page 216 for the rest of this feature.

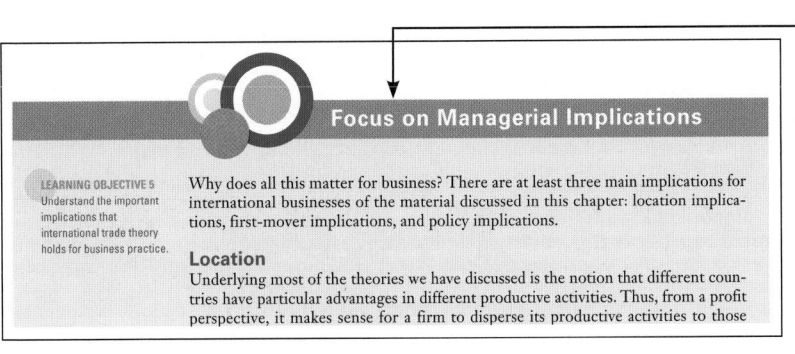

Focus on Managerial Implications

LEARNING OBJECTIVE 5
Understand the important implications that international trade theory holds for business practice.

Why does all this matter for business? There are at least three main implications for international businesses of the material discussed in this chapter: location implications, first-mover implications, and policy implications.

Location
Underlying most of the theories we have discussed is the notion that different countries have particular advantages in different productive activities. Thus, from a profit perspective, it makes sense for a firm to disperse its productive activities to those

In addition, each chapter begins with an **Opening Case** that sets the stage for the chapter content and familiarizes students with how real international companies conduct business.

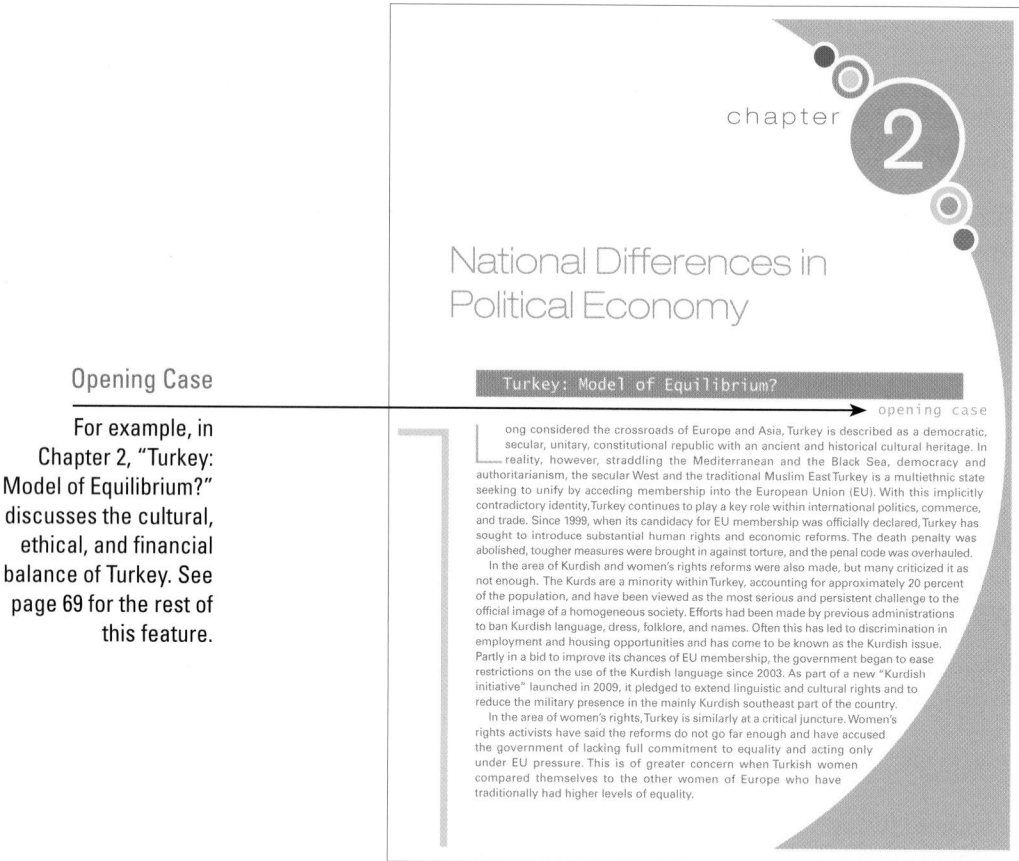

Opening Case

For example, in Chapter 2, "Turkey: Model of Equilibrium?" discusses the cultural, ethical, and financial balance of Turkey. See page 69 for the rest of this feature.

chapter 2

National Differences in Political Economy

Turkey: Model of Equilibrium?

opening case

Long considered the crossroads of Europe and Asia, Turkey is described as a democratic, secular, unitary, constitutional republic with an ancient and historical cultural heritage. In reality, however, straddling the Mediterranean and the Black Sea, democracy and authoritarianism, the secular West and the traditional Muslim East Turkey is a multiethnic state seeking to unify by acceding membership into the European Union (EU). With this implicitly contradictory identity, Turkey continues to play a key role within international politics, commerce, and trade. Since 1999, when its candidacy for EU membership was officially declared, Turkey has sought to introduce substantial human rights and economic reforms. The death penalty was abolished, tougher measures were brought in against torture, and the penal code was overhauled.

In the area of Kurdish and women's rights reforms were also made, but many criticized it as not enough. The Kurds are a minority within Turkey, accounting for approximately 20 percent of the population, and have been viewed as the most serious and persistent challenge to the official image of a homogeneous society. Efforts had been made by previous administrations to ban Kurdish language, dress, folklore, and names. Often this has led to discrimination in employment and housing opportunities and has come to be known as the Kurdish issue. Partly in a bid to improve its chances of EU membership, the government began to ease restrictions on the use of the Kurdish language since 2003. As part of a new "Kurdish initiative" launched in 2009, it pledged to extend linguistic and cultural rights and to reduce the military presence in the mainly Kurdish southeast part of the country.

In the area of women's rights, Turkey is similarly at a critical juncture. Women's rights activists have said the reforms do not go far enough and have accused the government of lacking full commitment to equality and acting only under EU pressure. This is of greater concern when Turkish women compared themselves to the other women of Europe who have traditionally had higher levels of equality.

There is also a **Closing Case** to each chapter. These cases are also designed to illustrate the relevance of chapter material for the practice of international business as well as to provide continued insight into how real companies handle those issues.

Closing Case

For example, in Chapter 2, "South Africa after the World Cup" discusses the economic and cultural challenges facing South Africa. See page 113 for the rest of this feature.

closing case

South Africa after the World Cup

For one solid month, South Africa basked on the world stage in the limelight of the World Cup. Although it is too early to assess the actual return on investment of the R33 billion (US$4.3 billion) South Africa spent on transport and telecommunications infrastructure, there is little doubt that South Africa's has reaped tremendous branding success in hosting

capita. In the largest cities, Cape Town, Port Elizabeth, Durban, and Pretoria/Johannesburg, sites of the football (soccer) games, a significant amount of economic development has taken place. Auditing firm Grant Thornton puts the overall investment at about 55 billion rand (US$7.3 billion), the equivalent of 6 percent of this year's state budget. Else-

Another tool that we have used to focus on managerial implications are **Management Focus** boxes. There is at least one Management Focus in most chapters. Like the opening cases, the purpose of these boxes is to illustrate the relevance of chapter material for the practice of international business.

Management FOCUS

Google, China, and the Free Flow of Information

Moving into China, the largest single Internet search engine market in the world made tremendous sense for Google in 2005 and was viewed by market analysts as a brilliant move. Its withdrawal in 2009 after only four years created much more controversy. Some argue that Google maintained the "high ground" and followed its motto: "Do no evil." According to Google, its security had been compromised, and certain entities within the Chinese government had obtained the e-mails of activists and dissidents without their permission. Others claimed that Google was "outfoxed" in China; a market where it held a minority market share position in the Internet search engine space to Baidu, the local search engine. The story is more complex, however.

Originally, Google had tolerated certain censorship by Chinese authorities. But, when its security systems were breached by entities within China, it exited. At that point, it began automatically re-routing traffic to Hong Kong. Now under the threat of further government sanctions, Google has stopped automatically redirecting Chinese Internet users to

its uncensored Chinese-language Web site based in Hong Kong. To continue to do so risks the license the Chinese government had recently renewed and thereby stood to potentially lose revenues from advertising in the world's largest Internet market. By way of concession, Chinese users will now have to click on a tab to reach Google's Hong Kong Web site. Doing so could cost Google more market share to Baidu.

The issues implicit in this ideological/technological confrontation go to the very nature of the deeply held Western beliefs about the free flow of information, about the relative power of a large multinational corporation, and about a burgeoning superpower. Uncensored information on the Internet is intolerable to Chinese authorities. So the current compromise appears to create a win–win situation for both Google and China. It begs the question: In this high-stakes game of publicity, corporate profit, national pride, and governmental confrontation, who really won?

Sources: D. Barboza and M. Helft, "A Compromise Allows Both China and Google to Claim Victory," *The New York Times*, July 10, 2010; and B. Acohido, "Google Quits Rerouting China's Web Traffic to Hong Kong," *USA Today*, June 30, 2010, p. 2B.

Management Focus

The Management Focus in Chapter 2, for example, looks at Google and the free flow of information in China. See page 87 for the rest of this focus.

Accessible and Interesting

The international business arena is fascinating and exciting, and we have tried to communicate our enthusiasm for it to the student. Learning is easier and better if the subject matter is communicated in an interesting, informative, and accessible manner. One technique we have used to achieve this is weaving interesting anecdotes into the narrative of the text, that is, stories that illustrate theory. The use of **Another Perspective** boxes also serves to provide additional context for the chapter topics.

Another Perspective

BYD—Innovative Dreaming

BYD stands for Build Your Dreams, and nowhere is the entrepreneurial/innovative drive better exemplified than in Asia. According to *BusinessWeek,* among the top 10 most innovative companies in the world, 6 are North American and 4 are Asian. But of the top 10, the one with the most revenue growth (42 percent from 2006 to 2009) was BYD, a company little known outside its headquarters in China.

BYD researches, produces, or supplies a virtual warehouse of rechargeable batteries, automobiles and automobile-related products, handset components, LCDs, and other electronic products. In so doing, BYD has been able to engage and interact with perhaps the hottest market sectors—namely, rechargeable batteries, smart electric automobiles, and mobile handsets. It is primed for innovative growth: It's Chinese, it's green, and Warren Buffett loves it. (Bloomberg *Businessweek,* "The 50 Most Innovative Companies 2010, April 15, 2010, http://www.businessweek.com/interactive_ reports/innovative_companies_2010.html; "BYD," *Financial Times,* March 16, 2010, p.14; and BYD Web site, www.byd.com).

Another Perspective

For example, this Another Perspective box in Chapter 2 discusses an innovative Chinese company that has cornered the market on rechargeable batteries. See page 94 for the rest of the picture.

In addition to the Management Focus feature, most chapters also have a **Country Focus** box that provides background on the political, economic, social, or cultural aspects of countries grappling with an international business issue.

Country Focus

Chapter 2, for example, discusses the concept of property rights in Vietnam. See page 96 for more details.

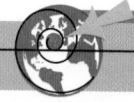

Country FOCUS

The Concept of Property Rights in Vietnam

As in most communist countries, there is no system of private property in Vietnam. In Western terms, property rights are premised on the concept of a "freehold." The individual owns the land and is free to determine its uses (with limitations). In Vietnam, the state owns all the land, and residents and investors buy and sell only the rights to use it. In this sense, it is a tenuous kind of freehold title. Unlike the stricter forms of communism found in North Korea or, to some extent, Cuba, Vietnam has evolved a system whereby land-use rights can be bought, sold, inherited, and used as collateral for a loan. The 1992 constitution granted stronger land rights to individuals, including rights over commercial and personal property as a means of spurring agricultural production. Private land use rights (LURs) may now be granted for up to 50 years. There is one caveat, however; the state can reclaim any land at any time, often with contemptuous levels of compensation.

"Use" is determined by the state. Since 2003, the Land Law permits the state to "recover" (expropriate) assigned land in any of four circumstances: (1) inefficient use or use for unassigned purposes; (2) non-use for 12 months, or project delays of 24 months or more from initial assignment; (3) intentional destruction of land; and (4) intentional failure to meet financial obligations to the state.

In Vietnam, investors and developers generally acquire land in two ways: (1) they receive an assignment of a land-use right (assignment method) or (2) they pay compensation to land users (compensation method). Only local companies may use the assignment method; both local and foreign-invested companies may use the compensation method. In terms of access to land, state-owned enterprises are at a distinct advantage to foreign companies, but recent legislation has progressively enhanced the status of foreign investors. In 2006 the Uniform Enterprise Law allowed foreign investors to form any type of company instead of only limited liability companies. Since July 1, 2004, the Land Law has allowed local private companies with long-term LURs to lease land to foreign investors.

Although all this may seem like a highly burdensome administrative task, in the World Bank's *Doing Business* report for 2009, Vietnam scored well in "registering property," ranking 40th out of 183 countries in terms of the ease with which businesses can secure rights to property. According to the report, it takes only four procedures or steps, and less than 60 days to register a property in Vietnam. In comparison with other Asia Pacific countries, Vietnam appears to be transitioning toward a more traditional concept of freehold.

Sources: *The Economist Intelligence Unit, Country Commerce 2010: Vietnam,* pp. 30–33; and D. Hare, "The Origins and Influence of Land Property Rights in Vietnam," *Development Policy Review,* 26, no. 3 (2008), pp. 339–363.

Ancillary Resources That Enliven the Text and Make It Easier to Teach

For instructors, this text offers a number of materials to help keep students active and engaged in the learning process. In addition to iGlobe resources, the **Online Learning Center** (www.mhhe.com/hill) is a one-stop place for several key instructor aids. A password-protected portion of the book's Web site will be available to adopters of *Global Business Today,* and instructors can also view student resources to make more effective supplementary assignments. The OLC includes:

- **Instructor's Manual.** The Instructor's Manual, prepared by Veronica Horton, contains course outlines; chapter teaching resources, including chapter overviews and outlines, teaching suggestions, chapter objectives, teaching suggestions for opening cases, lecture outlines, answers to critical discussion questions, teaching suggestions for the Closing Case, and two student activities (some with Internet components); and expanded Video Notes with discussion questions for each video. The answers to globalEDGE research tasks will also be included here.
- **Test Bank.** The test bank contains approximately 100 true-false, multiple-choice, and essay questions per chapter. The test bank questions are also categorized by Bloom's taxonomy levels of learning and how they meet various AACSB objectives.
- **EZ Test.** A computerized version of the test bank is available, allowing the instructor to generate random tests and to add his or her own questions.

- **PowerPoint®.** Re-created for this edition by Veronica Horton, the PowerPoint program consists of one set of slides for every chapter, featuring original materials not found in the text in addition to reproductions and illuminations of key text figures, tables, and maps. Quiz questions to keep students on their toes during classroom presentations are also included, along with instructor notes.

This book also provides rich, interactive resources to help students learn how to practice international business.

The Online Learning Center for students includes chapter quizzes, student Power-Points, and a Global Business Plan project. Students can also access interactive modules, including the following:

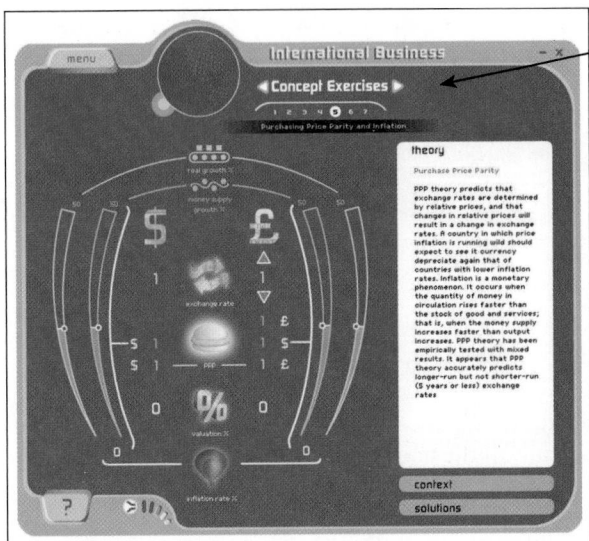

Concept Exercises

Concept Exercises help students learn how to solve realistic problems by exploring Flash modules, linked to the appropriate chapter, of the Hofstede study, absolute and comparative advantage, foreign direct investment, balance of payments, purchasing power parity and inflation, historical exchange rates, and export and import financing.

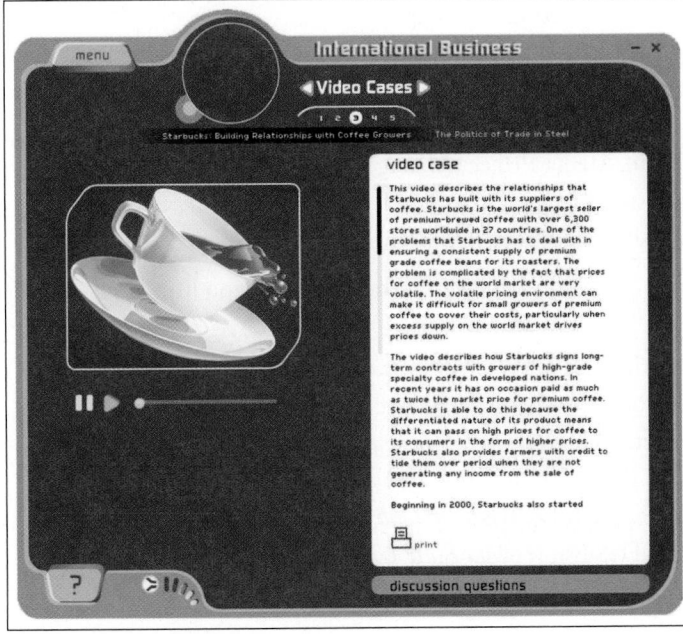

Concept Videos

The eight Concept Videos, complemented by cases and discussion questions written by Charles Hill, are also exclusive to these online activities. Students can watch and learn more when they access this activity for the appropriate chapter.

Global Business Plan

The Global Business Plan helps students take it one step further into applications, allowing them to build their own business plan one section at a time to prepare for entering a foreign market.

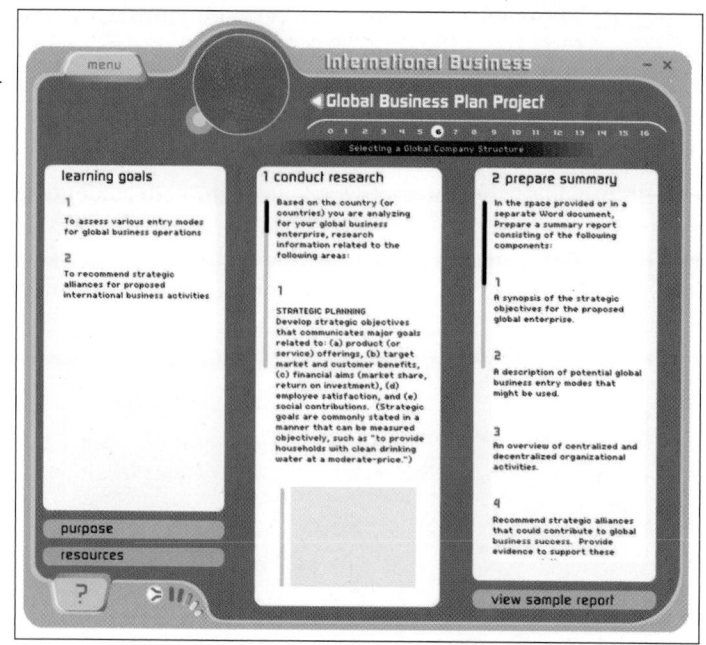

Acknowledgments

Numerous people deserve to be thanked for their assistance in preparing this book. First, we want to thank all the people at McGraw-Hill/Irwin who have worked with us on this project:

Paul Ducham, Publisher
John Weimeister, Executive Editor
Cate Rzasa, Developmental Editor
Anke Weekes, Marketing Manager
Ann Ferro, Marketing Coordinator
Jill Eccher, Project Manager
Joanne Mennemeier, Designer
Jennifer Lohn, Media Project Manager
Debra Sylvester, Production Supervisor
Jeremy Cheshareck, Photo Research

Second, thanks go to the reviewers, who provided good feedback that helped shape this edition of the book:

Ron Abernathy, *University of North Carolina–Greensboro*
John Anderson, *University of Tennessee*
David Bartlett, *University of Minnesota*
Lawrence A. Beer, *Arizona State University*
Frances DePaul, Ph.D., *Westmoreland County Community College*
Dr. Dharma DeSilva, *Wichita State University*
David J. Hrovat, *Northern Kentucky University*

Samira Hussein, *Johnson County Community College*

J. Leslie Jankovich, *San Jose State University*

Louis Nzegwu, *University of Wisconsin–Platteville*

Eydis Olsen, *Drexel University*

Andrew R. Thomas, *University of Akron*

Ronald S. Thomas, *Northeastern University*

William A. Walker, *University of Houston*

Allison D. Watts, *Shippensburg University*

David Wernick, *Florida International University*

Ross A. Wirth, *Franklin University*

Tegrity Campus: Lectures 24/7

Tegrity Campus is a service that makes class time available 24/7 by automatically capturing every lecture in a searchable format for students to review when they study and complete assignments. With a simple one-click start-and-stop process, you capture all computer screens and corresponding audio. Students can replay any part of any class with easy-to-use browser-based viewing on a PC or Mac.

Educators know that the more students can see, hear, and experience class resources, the better they learn. In fact, studies prove it. With Tegrity Campus, students quickly recall key moments by using Tegrity Campus's unique search feature. This search helps students efficiently find what they need, when they need it, across an entire semester of class recordings. Help turn all your students' study time into learning moments immediately supported by your lecture.

To learn more about Tegrity watch a 2-minute Flash demo at **http://tegritycampus .mhhe.com.**

Assurance of Learning Ready

Many educational institutions today are focused on the notion of *assurance of learning*, an important element of some accreditation standards. *Global Business Today* is designed specifically to support your assurance of learning initiatives with a simple, yet powerful solution.

Each test bank question for *Global Business Today* maps to a specific chapter learning outcome/objective listed in the text. You can use our test bank software, EZ Test and EZ Test Online to easily query for learning outcomes/objectives that directly relate to the learning objectives for your course. You can then use the reporting features of EZ Test to aggregate student results in similar fashion, making the collection and presentation of assurance of learning data simple and easy.

AACSB Statement

The McGraw-Hill Companies is a proud corporate member of AACSB International. Understanding the importance and value of AACSB accreditation, *Global Business Today*, seventh edition, recognizes the curricula guidelines detailed in the AACSB standards for business accreditation by connecting selected questions in the test bank to the six general knowledge and skill guidelines in the AACSB standards.

The statements contained in *Global Business Today*, seventh edition, are provided only as a guide for the users of this textbook. The AACSB leaves content coverage and assessment within the purview of individual schools, the mission of the school, and the faculty. While *Global Business Today*, seventh edition, and the teaching package make no claim of any specific AACSB qualification or evaluation, we have within *Global Business Today*, seventh edition, labeled selected questions according to the six general knowledge and skills areas.

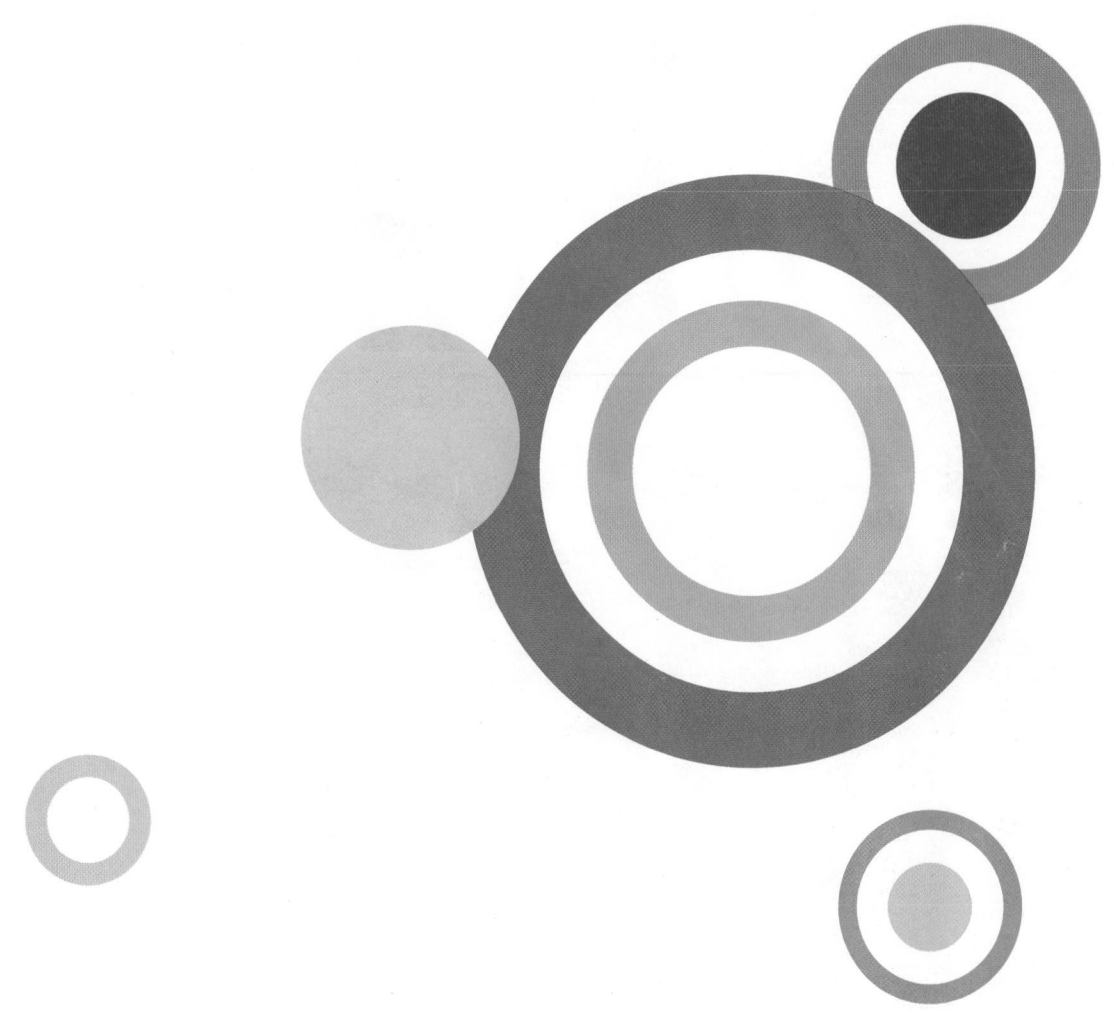

Global Business Today

part 1

Introduction and Overview

After you have read this chapter you should be able to:

1 Understand what is meant by the term *globalization*.

2 Recognize the main drivers of globalization.

3 Describe the changing nature of the global economy.

4 Explain the main arguments in the debate over the impact of globalization.

5 Understand how the process of globalization is creating opportunities and challenges for business managers.

chapter

1

Globalization

Banco Santander was founded in 1857 in the port city of Santander, Cantabria, a relatively remote area of northern Spain. At that time, the small family bank focused on the needs of the local community and the growing trade generated by the city's port. Today, Banco Santander is the one of the largest banks in the world with more than €1.111 billion in total assets and extensive operations in Europe, Latin America, Hong Kong, Singapore, Africa, and the United States. What is most impressive, however, is that much of this expansion occurred since 1999, demonstrating the many forces at work within an increasingly global environment.

The company's dynamic growth is in part a result of a visionary chief executive officer (CEO) who believed in an aggressive acquistion model to expand the business globally. Coming from the original founding family, Emilio Botín, then CEO and now current chairman of the board, put Banco Santander on a growth path of increasingly complex and sophisticated acquisitions.

The bank's buying spree began domestically and quickly went global. In 1999 Banco Santander merged with Banco Central Hispano, another Spanish bank. In 2001 it acquired Banespa, the fourth largest bank in Brazil. In 2004 the bank expanded into the United Kingdom with the purchase of Abbey National. In 2005 it initially acquired 20 percent of Sovereign Bank in the United States and in 2008 acquired the remaining shares. In 2007 Banco Santander acquired ABN. By 2008 the bank had also acquired Alliance/Leicester and Bradford and Bingley in the United Kingdom. In 2009 Banco Santander Brasil closed the world´s largest initial public offering (IPO) during the global economic downturn and the largest in Brazilian history at US$8 billion.

Although the bank's expansion may be viewed geographically—that is, the establishment of operations in various countries—the growth can also be viewed from a linguistic and cultural perspective. Each acquisition grew in complexity both in size and difficulty. Perhaps because of its seafaring traits, or because of its origins in Europe, Banco Santander recognized that if it were going to expand its reach, it would have to acquire the ability to do business not only in Spanish, but English, and more recently in Mandarin. By means of those acquisitions, and its current expansion into Asia, Banco Santander is seeking to leverage the growing trade between Asia and Latin America as the world becomes ever more interdependent.

For example, to take advantage of the growing Latin American/Asia trade, Santander Asia–Pacific was established. In January 2008 Santander opened its first Asian branch in Hong Kong. Since then it has expanded with branches and representative offices into Shanghai, Beijing, Tokyo, Seoul, and Sydney. By expanding in this manner, the bank has also acquired the ability to work and transact business in the three most active commercial languages in the world.

In this regard, the globalization of Banco Santander reflects the internalization of global knowledge and the diversification of risk. As it sought to expand into the various regions of the world, Banco Santander has evolved its corporate culture to provide its customers the multitude of financial products they require to do business in a global environment. Juan Inciarte, Santander's head of strategy, said at a recent seminar in Madrid that growth and diversification are "in the DNA" of the bank.

Banco Santander is still undergoing much change as it seeks to adapt what was once its Spanish tradition to a more cosmopolitan, diversified global force. Its global appetite for expansion continues; the 153-year-old institution is now bidding for the German consumer unit of Sweden's SEB and 300 U.K. branches of the Royal Bank of Scotland. It has recently agreed to buy back almost a quarter of its Mexican units from Bank of America for $2.5 billion, as well as purchase $3.2 billion of auto loans from Citigroup. By diversifying, Banco Santander is also mitigating its domestic and regional risk.

Banco Santander has successfully managed to avoid much of the current eurozone crisis by staying true to its diversification strategy. While many European banks focused on one particular country in Europe, Banco Santander relied on its diversified presence in various countries, including Brazil, to offset its losses elsewhere.

It will be interesting to watch how the Spanish bank grows as a global entity. Such a strong appetite for expansion requires a significant amount of digestion. ●

Sources: C. Penty, "Banco Santander Goes on a Shopping Spree," *Bloomberg BusinessWeek,* July 1, 2010, http://www.businessweek.com; S. S. Munoz and P. Kowsmann, "Santander Sole Bidder for RBS Branches," *The Wall Street Journal,* June 15, 2010, http://online.wsj.com; G. Dhungana, "Banco Santander Pushes Its Asia, China Business," www.theasset.com, October 5, 2009; and Banco Santander Annual Report 2009.

Introduction

Over the past three decades a fundamental shift has been occurring in the world economy. We have been moving away from a world in which national economies were relatively self-contained entities, isolated from each other by barriers to cross-border trade and investment; by distance, time zones, and language; and by national differences in government regulation, culture, and business systems. And we are moving toward a world in which barriers to cross-border trade and investment are declining; perceived distance is shrinking due to advances in transportation and telecommunications technology; material culture is starting to look similar the world over; and national economies are merging into an interdependent, integrated global economic system. The process by which this is occurring is commonly referred to as *globalization.*

In today's interdependent global economy, an American might drive to work in a car designed in Germany that was assembled in Mexico by Ford from components made in the United States and Japan that were fabricated from Korean steel and Malaysian rubber. She may have filled the car with gasoline at a BP service station owned by a British multinational company. The gasoline could have been made from oil pumped out of a well off the coast of Africa by a French oil company that transported it to the United States in a ship owned by a Greek shipping line. While driving to work, the American might talk to her stockbroker (using a headset) on a Nokia cell phone that was designed in Finland and assembled in Texas using chip sets produced in Taiwan that were designed by Indian engineers working for Texas Instruments. She could tell the stockbroker to purchase shares in Deutsche Telekom, a German telecommunications firm that was transformed from a former state-owned monopoly into a global company by an energetic Israeli CEO. She may turn on the car radio, which was made in Malaysia by a Japanese firm, to hear a popular hip-hop song composed by a Swede and sung by a group of Danes in English who signed a record contract with a French music company to promote their record in America. The driver might pull into a drive-through Starbucks coffee shop managed by a Korean immigrant and order a "single, tall, nonfat latte" and chocolate-covered biscotti. The coffee beans came from Costa Rica and the chocolate from Peru, while the biscotti was made locally using an old Italian recipe. After the song ends, a news announcer might inform the American listener that antiglobalization protests at a meeting of the World Economic Forum in Davos, Switzerland, have turned violent. One protester has been killed. The announcer then turns to the next item, a story about how a financial crisis that started in the U.S. banking sector may trigger a global recession and is sending stock markets down all over the world.

This is the world in which we live. It is a world where the volume of goods, services, and investment crossing national borders has expanded faster than world output for more than half a century. It is a world where more than $4 trillion in foreign exchange transactions are made every day, where $12 trillion of goods and $3.3 trillion of services were sold across national borders in 2009.[1] It is a world in which international institutions such as the World Trade Organization and gatherings of leaders from the world's most powerful economies have repeatedly called for even lower barriers to cross-border trade and investment. It is a world where the symbols of material and popular culture are increasingly global: from Coca-Cola and Starbucks to Sony PlayStations, Nokia cell phones, MTV shows, Disney films, IKEA stores, and Apple iPods and iPhones. It is a world in which products are made from inputs that come from all over the world. It is a world in which a financial crisis in America can trigger a global economic recession, which is exactly what occurred in 2008 and 2009. It is also a world in which vigorous and vocal groups protest against globalization, which they blame for a list of ills, from unemployment in developed nations to environmental degradation

and the Americanization of popular culture. And yes, these protests have on occasion turned violent.

For businesses, this process has produced many opportunities. Firms can expand their revenues by selling around the world and/or reduce their costs by producing in nations where key inputs, including labor, are cheap. The global expansion of enterprises has been facilitated by favorable political and economic trends. Since the collapse of communism at the end of the 1980s, the pendulum of public policy in nation after nation has swung toward the free market end of the economic spectrum. Regulatory and administrative barriers to doing business in foreign nations have come down, while those nations have often transformed their economies, privatizing state-owned enterprises, deregulating markets, increasing competition, and welcoming investment by foreign businesses. This has allowed businesses both large and small, from both advanced nations and developing nations, to expand internationally.

The history of Banco Santander exemplifies the opportunities that a global economy offers businesses (see the opening case). The beginnings of Banco Santander, a small family-owned bank, can be traced to its origins in a port city and the seafaring trade. After solidifying its position in Spain, the company started to expand globally in 2001. From its Iberian roots to now one of the world's largest banks with extensive global operations, Banco Santander is entrenched within the basic strategies of globalization, namely, the diversification of geography, languages, and cultures. In doing so, Banco Santander has utilized its vast international operations to offset some of the challenges inherent in expanding globally.

At the same time as it creates opportunities, globalization has also created new threats for businesses accustomed to dominating their domestic markets. Foreign companies have entered many formerly protected industries in developing nations, increasing competition and driving down prices. For three decades, U.S. automobile companies have been battling foreign enterprises, as Japanese, European, and now Korean companies have taken business from them. General Motors has seen its U.S. market share decline from more than 50 percent to less than 20 percent, while Japan's Toyota has surpassed first Ford and now GM to become the largest automobile company in the world.

As globalization unfolds, it is transforming industries and creating anxiety among those who believed their jobs were protected from foreign competition. Historically, while many workers in manufacturing industries worried about the impact foreign competition might have on their jobs, workers in service industries felt more secure. Now this too is changing. Advances in technology, lower transportation costs, and the rise of skilled workers in developing countries imply that many services no longer need to be performed where they are delivered. For example, accounting work is being outsourced from America to India. Today many individual tax returns are compiled in India. Indian accountants, trained in U.S. tax rules, perform work for U.S. accounting firms.[2] They access individual tax returns stored on computers in the United States, perform routine calculations, and save their work so that it can be inspected by a U.S. accountant, who then bills clients. As the best-selling author Thomas Friedman has argued, the world is becoming flat.[3] People living in developed nations no longer have the playing field tilted in their favor. Increasingly, enterprising individuals based in India, China, or Brazil have the same opportunities to better themselves as those living in Western Europe, the United States, or Canada.

In this book we will take a close look at the issues introduced here, and at many more besides. We will explore how changes in regulations governing international trade and investment, when coupled with changes in political systems and technology, have dramatically altered the competitive playing field confronting many businesses. We will discuss the resulting opportunities and threats and review the different strategies that managers can pursue to exploit the opportunities and counter the threats. We will consider whether globalization benefits or harms national economies. We will look at what economic theory has to say about the outsourcing of manufacturing and service jobs to places such as India and China, and at the benefits and costs of outsourcing, not just to business firms and their employees, but also to entire economies. First, though, we need to get a better overview of the nature and process of globalization, and that is the function of the current chapter.

What Is Globalization?

LEARNING OBJECTIVE 1
Understand what is meant by the term *globalization*.

As used in this book, **globalization** refers to the shift toward a more integrated and interdependent world economy. Globalization has several facets, including the globalization of markets and the globalization of production.

THE GLOBALIZATION OF MARKETS The **globalization of markets** refers to the merging of historically distinct and separate national markets into one huge global marketplace. Falling barriers to cross-border trade have made it easier to sell internationally. It has been argued for some time that the tastes and preferences of consumers in different nations are beginning to converge on some global norm, thereby helping to create a global market.[4] Consumer products such as Citigroup credit cards, Coca-Cola soft drinks, Sony PlayStation video games, McDonald's hamburgers, Starbucks coffee, and IKEA furniture are frequently held up as prototypical examples of this trend. Firms such as those just cited are more than just benefactors of this trend; they are also facilitators of it. By offering the same basic product worldwide, they help to create a global market.

A company does not have to be the size of these multinational giants to facilitate, and benefit from, the globalization of markets. In the United States, for example, nearly 90 percent of firms that export are small businesses employing less than 100 people, and their share of total U.S. exports has grown steadily over the past decade to now exceed 20 percent.[5] Firms with less than 500 employees accounted for 97 percent of all U.S. exporters and almost 30 percent of all exports by value.[6] Typical of these is Hytech, a New York-based manufacturer of solar panels that generates 40 percent of its $3 million in annual sales from exports to five countries, or B&S Aircraft Alloys, another New York company whose exports account for 40 percent of its $8 million annual revenues.[7] The situation is similar in several other nations. In Germany, for example, a staggering 98 percent of small and mid-sized companies have exposure to international markets, either via exports or international production.[8]

Despite the global prevalence of Citigroup credit cards, McDonald's hamburgers, Starbucks coffee, and IKEA stores, it is important not to push too far the view that national markets are giving way to the global market. As we shall see in later chapters, significant differences still exist among national markets along many relevant dimensions, including consumer tastes and preferences, distribution channels, culturally embedded value systems, business systems, and legal regulations. These differences frequently require companies to customize marketing strategies, product features, and operating practices to best match conditions in a particular country.

The most global markets currently are not markets for consumer products—where national differences in tastes and preferences are still often important enough to act as

Globalization
Trend away from distinct national economic units and toward one huge global market.

Globalization of Markets
Moving away from an economic system in which national markets are distinct entities, isolated by trade barriers and barriers of distance, time, and culture, and toward a system in which national markets are merging into one global market.

a brake on globalization—but markets for industrial goods and materials that serve a universal need the world over. These include the markets for commodities such as aluminum, oil, and wheat; for industrial products such as microprocessors, DRAMs (computer memory chips), and commercial jet aircraft; for computer software; and for financial assets from U.S. Treasury bills to eurobonds and futures on the Nikkei index or the Mexican peso.

In many global markets, the same firms frequently confront each other as competitors in nation after nation. Coca-Cola's rivalry with PepsiCo is a global one, as are the rivalries between Ford and Toyota, Boeing and Airbus, Caterpillar and Komatsu in earthmoving equipment, General Electric and Rolls-Royce in aero engines, and Sony, Nintendo, and Microsoft in video games. If a firm moves into a nation not currently served by its rivals, many of those rivals are sure to follow to prevent their competitor from gaining an advantage.[9] As firms follow each other around the world, they bring with them many of the assets that served them well in other national markets—including their products, operating strategies, marketing strategies, and brand names—creating some homogeneity across markets. Thus, greater uniformity replaces diversity. In an increasing number of industries, it is no longer meaningful to talk about "the German market," "the American market," "the Brazilian market," or "the Japanese market"; for many firms there is only the global market.

THE GLOBALIZATION OF PRODUCTION

Globalization of Production
Trend by individual firms to disperse parts of the productive processes to different locations around the globe to take advantage of national differences in the cost and quality of factors of production.

Factors of Production
Inputs into the productive process of a firm, including labor, management, land, capital, and technological know-how.

The **globalization of production** refers to the sourcing of goods and services from locations around the globe to take advantage of national differences in the cost and quality of **factors of production** (such as labor, energy, land, and capital). By doing this, companies hope to lower their overall cost structure or improve the quality or functionality of their product offering, thereby allowing them to compete more effectively. Consider the Boeing 777, a commercial jet airliner. Eight Japanese suppliers make parts for the fuselage, doors, and wings; a supplier in Singapore makes the doors for the nose landing gear; three suppliers in Italy manufacture wing flaps; and so on.[10] In total, some 30 percent of the 777, by value, is built by foreign companies. For its most recent jet airliner, the 787, Boeing has pushed this trend even further, with some 65 percent of the total value of the aircraft scheduled to be outsourced to foreign companies, 35 percent of which will go to three major Japanese companies.[11]

Part of Boeing's rationale for outsourcing so much production to foreign suppliers is that these suppliers are the best in the world at their particular activity. A global web of suppliers yields a better final product, which enhances the chances of Boeing winning a greater share of total orders for aircraft than its global rival Airbus. Boeing also outsources some production to foreign countries to increase the chance that it will win significant orders from airlines based in that country. For another example of a global web of activities, consider the example of Chery Automobiles profiled in the accompanying Management Focus.

Early outsourcing efforts were primarily confined to manufacturing activities, such as those undertaken by Boeing and Vizio; increasingly, however, companies are taking advantage of modern communications technology, particularly the Internet, to outsource service activities to low-cost producers in other nations. The Internet has allowed hospitals to outsource some radiology work to India, where images from MRI scans and the like are read at night while U.S. physicians sleep and the results are ready for them in the morning. Many software companies, including IBM, now use Indian engineers to perform maintenance functions on software designed in the United States. The time difference allows Indian engineers to run debugging tests on software written in the United States when U.S. engineers sleep, transmitting the

Chery Automobile and the Changing Face of Global Manufacturing

With almost an insatiable demand for automobiles, the Chinese car market is the goal of almost all automobile manufacturers. With a population of 1.3 billion and a projected annual auto sales growth rate of 9 percent, down from an astronomical rate of 25 percent, obtaining a piece of that market is the goal of any automobile executive seeking to expand sales internationally.

To focus on that market makes tremendous sense, but many Chinese automobile manufacturers are looking elsewhere as well in a bid to compete globally. Chery International, the Wuhu, Anhui–based auto manufacturer is one of these companies. Established in 1997, Chery is one of the new players on the automobile manufacturing world stage. As part of its international expansion strategy, Chery is adding six assembly plants outside of China, increasing production capabilities to 15 countries and regions.

An example of Chery's success is the A1 car, an amalgamation of Italian auto design, Austrian engineering, and a multitude of parts from two U.S. firms: Honeywell International and Visteon, the world's largest auto parts supply company. The car is assembled in one of the factories in Anhui and through a branding arrangement with Chrysler will be exported to Latin American first, then eventually to the United States and western Europe after being modified to the meet the stricter safety and environmental regulations required by these two regions.

The ambitious expansion of Chery's global network is also exemplified by the A3 and the Tiggo. The company is expanding actual production capabilities worldwide but is focusing on emerging markets. It believes that as the standard of living increases around the world, the need for affordable autos will likewise increase. Plans are currently under way to produce the A3 in Taiwan, Thailand, Syria, and Venezuela. As a compact car, the A3 is directly focused on the immediate needs of the local entry-level market. Similarly, riding the recent wave of prosperity in Brazil, Chery just recently announced plans to establish 55 dealerships throughout the country. By the end of the year, Chery hopes to produce more than 2,500 Tiggo SUVs, a collaboration with Britain's Group Lotus PLC in Brazil.

Chery's globalized vision increases the level of competition not only to the Detroit-based traditional powerhouses such as GM and Ford, but also to the other Asian manufacturers such as Toyota, Honda, and Hyundai. Although clearly not yet within the same league as BMW or Mercedes Benz, Chery seeks to eventually compete here as well by introducing and manufacturing "visionary vehicles"—"green cars"—in the growing market segment of electrical and hybrid automobiles. In this regard, Chery is establishing an early leadership position as the world seeks to become more mobile with limited resources. Has the leadership baton in auto manufacturing passed from the United States to China?

Sources: Chery International, http://www.cheryinternational.com, accessed July 19, 2010; A. Shameen, "Big Money: China as the Carmaker to the World," *The Edge Singapore*, May 25, 2009; W. Liu and H. Yeung, "China's Dynamic Industrial Sector: The Automobile Industry," *Eurasian Geography & Economics* (serial on the Internet) 49, no. 5 (September 2008), pp. 523–548 (available from Business Source Complete); and G. Fairclough, "Rating the Chery," *Wall Street Journal*, August 25, 2007, http://online.wsj.com.

corrected code back to the United States over secure Internet connections so it is ready for U.S. engineers to work on the following day. Dispersing value-creation activities in this way can compress the time and lower the costs required to develop new software programs. Other companies, from computer makers to banks, are outsourcing customer service functions, such as customer call centers, to developing nations where labor is cheaper. In another example from health care, in 2008 some 34,000 Filipinos were transcribing American medical files (such as audio files from doctors seeking approval from insurance companies for performing a procedure). More generally, some estimates suggest the outsourcing of many administrative procedures in health care, such as customer service and claims processing, could reduce health care costs in America by as much as $70 billion.[12]

Robert Reich, who served as secretary of labor in the Clinton administration, has argued that as a consequence of the trend exemplified by companies such as Boeing, IBM, and Vizio, in many cases it is becoming irrelevant to talk about American products,

Japanese products, German products, or Korean products. Increasingly, according to Reich, the outsourcing of productive activities to different suppliers results in the creation of products that are global in nature, that is, "global products."[13] But as with the globalization of markets, companies must be careful not to push the globalization of production too far. As we will see in later chapters, substantial impediments still make it difficult for firms to achieve the optimal dispersion of their productive activities to locations around the globe. These impediments include formal and informal barriers to trade between countries, barriers to foreign direct investment, transportation costs, and issues associated with economic and political risk. For example, government regulations ultimately limit the ability of hospitals to outsource the process of interpreting MRI scans to developing nations where radiologists are cheaper.

Nevertheless, the globalization of markets and production will continue. Modern firms are important actors in this trend, their very actions fostering increased globalization. These firms, however, are merely responding in an efficient manner to changing conditions in their operating environment—as well they should.

The Emergence of Global Institutions

As markets globalize and an increasing proportion of business activity transcends national borders, institutions are needed to help manage, regulate, and police the global marketplace, and to promote the establishment of multinational treaties to govern the global business system. Over the past half century, a number of important global institutions have been created to help perform these functions, including the **General Agreement on Tariffs and Trade (GATT)** and its successor, the World Trade Organization (WTO); the International Monetary Fund (IMF) and its sister institution, the World Bank; and the United Nations (UN). All these institutions were created by voluntary agreement between individual nation-states, and their functions are enshrined in international treaties.

The **World Trade Organization** (like the GATT before it) is primarily responsible for policing the world trading system and making sure nation-states adhere to the rules laid down in trade treaties signed by WTO members. As of 2010, 154 nations that collectively accounted for 97 percent of world trade were WTO members, thereby giving the organization enormous scope and influence. The WTO is also responsible for facilitating the establishment of additional multinational agreements between WTO member states. Over its entire history, and that of the GATT before it, the WTO has promoted the lowering of barriers to cross-border trade and investment. In doing so, the WTO has been the instrument of its member states, which have sought to create a more open global business system unencumbered by barriers to trade and investment between countries. Without an institution such as the WTO, the globalization of markets and production is unlikely to have proceeded as far as it has. However, as we shall see in this chapter and in Chapter 6 when we look closely at the WTO, critics charge that the organization is usurping the national sovereignty of individual nation-states.

The **International Monetary Fund** and the **World Bank** were both created in 1944 by 44 nations that met at Bretton Woods, New Hampshire. The IMF was established to maintain order in the international monetary system; the World Bank was set up to promote economic development. In the 65 years since their creation, both institutions have emerged as significant players in the global economy. The World Bank is the less controversial of the two sister institutions. It has focused on making low-interest loans to cash-strapped governments in poor nations that wish to undertake significant infrastructure investments (such as building dams or roads).

The IMF is often seen as the lender of last resort to nation-states whose economies are in turmoil and currencies are losing value against those of other nations. During the past

General Agreement on Tariffs and Trade (GATT)
International treaty that committed signatories to lowering barriers to the free flow of goods across national borders and led to the WTO.

World Trade Organization (WTO)
Organization that succeeded the General Agreement on Tariffs and Trade (GATT) as a result of the successful completion of the Uruguay Round of GATT negotiations.

International Monetary Fund (IMF)
International institution set up to maintain order in the international monetary system.

World Bank
International institution set up to promote general economic development in the world's poorer nations.

two decades, for example, the IMF has lent money to the governments of troubled states, including Argentina, Indonesia, Mexico, Russia, South Korea, Thailand, and Turkey. More recently, the IMF has taken a very proactive role in helping countries to cope with some of the effects of the 2008–2009 global financial crisis. IMF loans come with strings attached, however; in return for loans, the IMF requires nation-states to adopt specific economic policies aimed at returning their troubled economies to stability and growth. These requirements have sparked controversy. Some critics charge that the IMF's policy recommendations are often inappropriate; others maintain that by telling national governments what economic policies they must adopt, the IMF, like the WTO, is usurping the sovereignty of nation-states. We shall look at the debate over the role of the IMF in Chapter 10.

As globalization continues to expand, so will the importance of the United Nations' role in improving the living standards of the world.

The **United Nations** was established October 24, 1945, by 51 countries committed to preserving peace through international cooperation and collective security. Today nearly every nation in the world belongs to the United Nations; membership now totals 191 countries. When states become members of the United Nations, they agree to accept the obligations of the UN Charter, an international treaty that establishes basic principles of international relations. According to the charter, the UN has four purposes: to maintain international peace and security, to develop friendly relations among nations, to cooperate in solving international problems and in promoting respect for human rights, and to be a center for harmonizing the actions of nations. Although the UN is perhaps best known for its peacekeeping role, one of the organization's central mandates is the promotion of higher standards of living, full employment, and conditions of economic and social progress and development—all issues that are central to the creation of a vibrant global economy. As much as 70 percent of the work of the UN system is devoted to accomplishing this mandate. To do so, the UN works closely with other international institutions such as the World Bank. Guiding the work is the belief that eradicating poverty and improving the well-being of people everywhere are necessary steps in creating conditions for lasting world peace.[14]

United Nations
An international organization made up of 191 countries and headquartered in New York City, formed in 1945 to promote peace, security, and cooperation.

Another institution that has been in the news of late is the *G20*. Established in 1999, the G20 comprises the finance ministers and central bank governors of the 19 largest economies in the world, plus representatives from the European Union and the European Central Bank. Originally established to formulate a coordinated policy response to financial crises in developing nations, in 2008 and 2009 it became the forum through which major nations attempted to launch a coordinated policy response to the global financial crisis that started in America and then rapidly spread around the world, ushering in the first serious global economic recession since 1981.

Drivers of Globalization

Two macro factors underlie the trend toward greater globalization.[15] The first is the decline in barriers to the free flow of goods, services, and capital that has occurred since the end of World War II. The second factor is technological change, particularly the dramatic developments in recent years in communication, information processing, and transportation technologies.

LEARNING OBJECTIVE 2
Recognize the main drivers of globalization.

DECLINING TRADE AND INVESTMENT BARRIERS   During the 1920s and 30s many of the world's nation-states erected formidable barriers to international trade and foreign direct investment. **International trade** occurs when a firm exports goods or services to consumers in another country. **Foreign direct investment (FDI)** occurs when a firm invests resources in business activities outside its home country. Many of the barriers to international trade took the form of high tariffs on imports of manufactured goods. The typical aim of such tariffs was to protect domestic industries from foreign competition. One consequence, however, was "beggar thy neighbor" retaliatory trade policies, with countries progressively raising trade barriers against each other. Ultimately, this depressed world demand and contributed to the Great Depression of the 1930s.

International Trade
Occurs when a firm exports goods or services to consumers in another country.

Foreign Direct Investment (FDI)
Direct investment in business operations in a foreign country.

Having learned from this experience, the advanced industrial nations of the West committed themselves after World War II to removing barriers to the free flow of goods, services, and capital between nations.[16] This goal was enshrined in the General Agreement on Tariffs and Trade. Under the umbrella of GATT, eight rounds of negotiations among member states (now numbering 153) have worked to lower barriers to the free flow of goods and services. The most recent round of negotiations to be completed, known as the Uruguay Round, were finalized in December 1993. The Uruguay Round further reduced trade barriers; extended GATT to cover services as well as manufactured goods; provided enhanced protection for patents, trademarks, and copyrights; and established the World Trade Organization to police the international trading system.[17] Table 1.1 summarizes the impact of GATT agreements on average tariff rates for manufactured goods. As can be seen, average tariff rates have fallen significantly since 1950 and now stand at about 4 percent.

In late 2001, the WTO launched a new round of talks aimed at further liberalizing the global trade and investment framework. For this meeting, it picked the remote location of Doha in the Persian Gulf state of Qatar. At Doha, the member states of the WTO staked out an agenda. The talks were scheduled to last three years, although as of 2010 the talks are effectively stalled due to opposition from several key nations. The Doha agenda includes cutting tariffs on industrial goods, services, and agricultural products; phasing out subsidies to agricultural producers; reducing barriers to cross-border investment; and limiting the use of antidumping laws. If the Doha talks are ever completed, the biggest gain may come from discussion on agricultural products; average agricultural tariff rates are still about 40 percent, and rich nations spend some $300 billion a year in subsidies to support their farm sectors. The world's poorer nations have the most to gain from any reduction in agricultural tariffs and subsidies; such reforms would give them access to the markets of the developed world.[18]

table **1.1**

Average Tariff Rates on Manufactured Products as Percent of Value

Source: 1913–90 data are from "Who Wants to Be a Giant?" *The Economist: A Survey of the Multinationals*, June 24, 1995, pp. 3–4. Copyright © The Economist Books, Ltd. The 2008 data are from World Trade Organization, *2009 World Trade Report* (Geneva: WTO, 2009).

	1913	1950	1990	2008
France	21%	18%	5.9%	3.9%
Germany	20	26	5.9	3.9
Great Britain	—	23	5.9	3.9
Holland	5	11	5.9	3.9
Italy	18	25	5.9	3.9
Japan	30	—	5.3	2.3
Sweden	20	9	4.4	3.9
United States	44	14	4.8	3.2

In addition to reducing trade barriers, many countries have also been progressively removing restrictions to foreign direct investment. According to the United Nations, some 90 percent of the 2,600 changes made worldwide between 1992 and 2008 in the laws governing foreign direct investment created a more favorable environment for FDI.[19]

Such trends have been driving both the globalization of markets and the globalization of production. The lowering of barriers to international trade enables firms to view the world, rather than a single country, as their market. The lowering of trade and investment barriers also allows firms to base production at the optimal location for that activity. Thus, a firm might design a product in one country, produce component parts in two other countries, assemble the product in yet another country, and then export the finished product around the world.

According to WTO data, the volume of world merchandise trade has grown faster than the world economy since 1950 (see Figure 1.1).[20] From 1970 to 2008, the volume of world merchandise trade expanded more than 30-fold, outstripping the expansion of world production, which grew close to 10 times in real terms. (World merchandise trade includes trade in manufactured goods, agricultural goods, and mining products, but *not* services). But Figure 1.1 does not show that since the mid-1980s the value of international trade in services has also grown robustly. Trade in services now accounts for about 20 percent of the value of all international trade. Increasingly, international trade in services has been driven by advances in communications, which allow corporations to outsource service activities to different locations around the globe. Thus, as noted earlier, many corporations in the developed world outsource customer service functions, from software maintenance activities to customer call centers, to developing nations where labor costs are lower.

Figure 1.1 also does not show the steep drop in world trade that occurred in 2009. In 2009 the global economy contracted by 2.3 percent as the global financial crisis that began with problems in the U.S. subprime mortgage lending market reverberated around the world. The volume of merchandised trade dropped by 12.2 percent, the largest such decline since World War II. The main reason seems to have been a drop in global consumer demand, although an inability to finance international trade due to tight credit

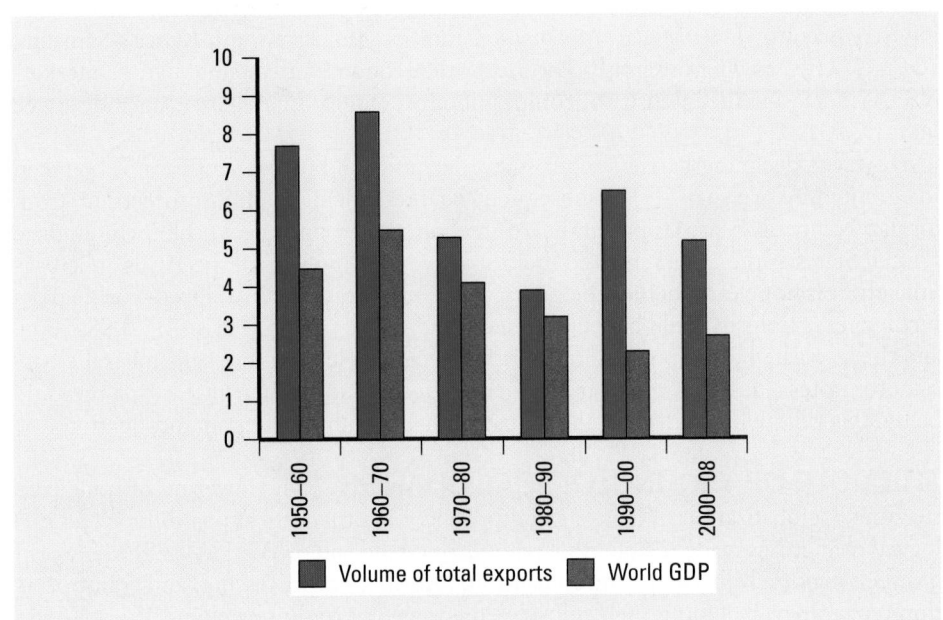

1.1 figure

Average Annual Percentage Growth in Volume of Exports and World GDP, 1950–2008

Source: Constructed by the author from World Trade Organization, *International Trade Trends and Statistics, 2009* (Geneva: WTO, 2009).

conditions may have also played a role. However, trade seemed set to rebound in 2010, with the WTO forecasting a 9.5 percent growth in volume. It would seem, therefore, that what occurred in 2009 will have no impact on the long-term trend.[21]

The data summarized in Figure 1.1 imply several things. First, more firms are doing what Boeing does with the 777 and 787: dispersing parts of their production process to different locations around the globe to drive down production costs and increase product quality. Second, the economies of the world's nation-states are becoming more intertwined. As trade expands, nations are becoming increasingly dependent on each other for important goods and services. Third, the world has become significantly wealthier since 1950, and the implication is that rising trade is the engine that has helped to pull the global economy along.

Evidence also suggests that foreign direct investment is playing an increasing role in the global economy as firms increase their cross-border investments. The average yearly outflow of FDI increased from $25 billion in 1975 to a record $1.8 trillion in 2007 (see Figure 7.1). However, FDI outflows did contract to $1.2 trillion in 2009 during the global financial crisis, although they are forecasted to recover in 2011.[22] In general, over the past 30 years the flow of FDI has accelerated faster than the growth in world trade and world output. For example, between 1992 and 2008, the total flow of FDI from all countries increased more than eightfold while world trade by value grew by some 150 percent and world output by around 45 percent.[23] As a result of the strong FDI flow, by 2009 the global stock of FDI was about $15 trillion. At least 82,000 parent companies had 810,000 affiliates in foreign markets that collectively employed more than 77 million people abroad and generated value accounting for about 11 percent of global GDP. The foreign affiliates of multinationals had over $30 trillion in global sales, higher than the value of global exports of goods and services, which stood at close to $19.9 trillion.[24]

The globalization of markets and production and the resulting growth of world trade, foreign direct investment, and imports all imply that firms are finding their home markets under attack from foreign competitors. This is true in Japan, where U.S. companies such as Kodak and Procter & Gamble are expanding their presence. It is true in the United States, where Japanese automobile firms have taken market share away from General Motors and Ford. And it is true in Europe, where the once-dominant Dutch company Philips has seen its market share in the consumer electronics industry taken by Japan's JVC, Matsushita, and Sony, and by South Korea's Samsung and LG. The growing integration of the world economy into a single, huge marketplace is increasing the intensity of competition in a range of manufacturing and service industries.

However, declining barriers to cross-border trade and investment cannot be taken for granted. As we shall see in subsequent chapters, demands for "protection" from foreign competitors are still often heard in countries around the world, including the United States. Although a return to the restrictive trade policies of the 1920s and 30s is unlikely, it is not clear whether the political majority in the industrialized world favors further reductions in trade barriers. Indeed, the global financial crisis of 2008–2009, and the associated drop in global output that occurred, led to more calls for trade barriers to protect jobs at home. If trade barriers decline no further, at least for the time being, this will put a brake upon the globalization of both markets and production.

THE ROLE OF TECHNOLOGICAL CHANGE The lowering of trade barriers made globalization of markets and production a theoretical possibility. Technological change has made it a tangible reality. Since the end of World War II, the world has seen major advances in communication, information processing, and transportation technology, including the explosive emergence of the Internet and World Wide

Web. Telecommunications is creating a global audience. Transportation is creating a global village. From Buenos Aires to Boston, and from Birmingham to Beijing, ordinary people are watching MTV, they're wearing blue jeans, and they're listening to iPods as they commute to work.

Microprocessors and Telecommunications

Perhaps the single most important innovation has been development of the microprocessor, which enabled the explosive growth of high-power, low-cost computing, vastly increasing the amount of information that can be processed by individuals and firms. The microprocessor also underlies many recent advances in telecommunications technology. Over the past 30 years, global communications have been revolutionized by developments in satellite, optical fiber, and wireless technologies, and now the Internet and the World Wide Web. These technologies rely on the microprocessor to encode, transmit, and decode the vast amount of information that flows along these electronic highways. The cost of microprocessors continues to fall, while their power increases (a phenomenon known as **Moore's law,** which predicts that the power of microprocessor technology doubles and its cost of production falls in half every 18 months).[25] As this happens, the cost of global communications plummets, which lowers the costs of coordinating and controlling a global organization. Thus, between 1930 and 1990, the cost of a three-minute phone call between New York and London fell from $244.65 to $3.32.[26] By 1998, it had plunged to just 36 cents for consumers, and much lower rates were available for businesses.[27] Indeed, by using the Internet, the cost of an international phone call is rapidly plummeting toward just a few cents per minute.

Moore's Law
The power of microprocessor technology doubles and its cost of production falls in half every 18 months.

The Internet and World Wide Web

The rapid growth of the World Wide Web is the latest expression of this development. In 1990, fewer than 1 million users were connected to the Internet. By 1995, the figure had risen to 50 million. By May 2009 the Internet had 1.6 billion users.[28] The WWW has developed into the information backbone of the global economy. In the U.S. alone, e-commerce retail sales reached $133 billion in 2008, up from almost nothing in 1998.[29] Viewed globally, the Web is emerging as an equalizer. It rolls back some of the constraints of location, scale, and time zones.[30] The Web makes it much easier for buyers and sellers to find each other, wherever they may be located and whatever their size. It allows businesses, both small and large, to expand their global presence at a lower cost than ever before.

Transportation Technology

In addition to developments in communication technology, several major innovations in transportation technology have occurred since World War II. In economic terms, the most important are probably the development of commercial jet aircraft and super-freighters and the introduction of containerization, which simplifies transshipment from one mode of transport to another. The advent of commercial jet travel, by reducing the time needed to get from one location to another, has effectively shrunk the globe. In terms of travel time, New York is now "closer" to Tokyo than it was to Philadelphia in the Colonial days.

Containerization has revolutionized the transportation business, significantly lowering the costs of shipping goods over long distances. Before the advent of containerization, moving goods from one mode of transport to another was very labor intensive, lengthy, and costly. It could take days and several hundred longshoremen to unload a ship and reload goods onto trucks and trains. With the advent of widespread containerization in the 1970s and 1980s, the whole process can now be executed by a handful of longshoremen in a couple of days. Since 1980, the world's containership fleet has more than quadrupled, reflecting in part the growing volume of international trade and in part the switch to this mode of transportation. As a result of the efficiency gains associated with

Technological advances in the area of containerization have significantly increased the efficiency of international trade.

containerization, transportation costs have plummeted, making it much more economical to ship goods around the globe, thereby helping to drive the globalization of markets and production. Between 1920 and 1990, the average ocean freight and port charges per ton of U.S. export and import cargo fell from $95 to $29 (in 1990 dollars).[31] The cost of shipping freight per ton-mile on railroads in the United States fell from 3.04 cents in 1985 to 2.3 cents in 2000, largely as a result of efficiency gains from the widespread use of containers.[32] An increased share of cargo now goes by air. Between 1955 and 1999, average air transportation revenue per ton-kilometer fell by more than 80 percent.[33] Reflecting the falling cost of airfreight, by the early 2000s air shipments accounted for 28 percent of the value of U.S. trade, up from 7 percent in 1965.[34]

Implications for the Globalization of Production

As transportation costs associated with the globalization of production declined, dispersal of production to geographically separate locations became more economical. As a result of the technological innovations discussed above, the real costs of information processing and communication have fallen dramatically in the past two decades. These developments make it possible for a firm to create and then manage a globally dispersed production system, further facilitating the globalization of production. A worldwide communications network has become essential for many international businesses. For example, Dell uses the Internet to coordinate and control a globally dispersed production system to such an extent that it holds only three days' worth of inventory at its assembly locations. Dell's Internet-based system records orders for computer equipment as they are submitted by customers via the company's Web site, then immediately transmits the resulting orders for components to various suppliers around the world, which have a real-time look at Dell's order flow and can adjust their production schedules accordingly. Given the low cost of airfreight, Dell can use air transportation to speed up the delivery of critical components to meet unanticipated demand shifts without delaying the shipment of final product to consumers. Dell also has used modern communications technology to outsource its customer service operations to India. When U.S. customers call Dell with a service inquiry, they are routed to Bangalore in India, where English-speaking service personnel handle the call.

The Internet has been a major force facilitating international trade in services. It is the Web that allows hospitals in Chicago to send MRI scans to India for analysis, accounting offices in San Francisco to outsource routine tax preparation work to accountants living in the Philippines, and software testers in India to debug code written by developers in Redmond, Washington, the headquarters of Microsoft. We are probably still in the early stages of this development. As Moore's law continues to advance and telecommunications bandwidth continues to increase, almost any work processes that can be digitalized will be, and this will allow that work to be performed wherever in the world it is most efficient and effective to do so.

The development of commercial jet aircraft has also helped knit together the worldwide operations of many international businesses. Using jet travel, an American manager need spend a day at most traveling to his or her firm's European or Asian operations. This enables the manager to oversee a globally dispersed production system.

Implications for the Globalization of Markets

In addition to the globalization of production, technological innovations have also facilitated the globalization of markets. Low-cost global communications networks such as the World Wide Web are helping to create electronic global marketplaces. As noted above, low-cost transportation has made it more economical to ship products around the world, thereby helping to create global markets. For example, due to the tumbling costs of shipping goods by air, roses grown in Ecuador can be cut and sold in New York two days later while they are still fresh. This has given rise to an industry in Ecuador that did not exist 20 years ago and now supplies a global market for roses. In addition, low-cost jet travel has resulted in the mass movement of people between countries. This has reduced the cultural distance between countries and is bringing about some convergence of consumer tastes and preferences. At the same time, global communication networks and global media are creating a worldwide culture. U.S. television networks such as CNN, MTV, and HBO are now received in many countries, and Hollywood films are shown the world over. In any society, the media are primary conveyors of culture; as global media develop, we must expect the evolution of something akin to a global culture. A logical result of this evolution is the emergence of global markets for consumer products. The first signs of this are already apparent. It is now as easy to find a McDonald's restaurant in Tokyo as it is in New York, to buy an iPod in Rio as it is in Berlin, and to buy Gap jeans in Paris as it is in San Francisco.

Despite these trends, we must be careful not to overemphasize their importance. While modern communication and transportation technologies are ushering in the "global village," significant national differences remain in culture, consumer preferences, and business practices. A firm that ignores differences between countries does so at its peril. We shall stress this point repeatedly throughout this book and elaborate on it in later chapters.

The Changing Demographics of the Global Economy

Hand in hand with the trend toward globalization has been a fairly dramatic change in the demographics of the global economy over the past 30 years. As late as the 1960s, four stylized facts described the demographics of the global economy. The first was U.S. dominance in the world economy and world trade picture. The second was U.S. dominance in world foreign direct investment. Related to this, the third fact was the dominance of large, multinational U.S. firms on the international business scene. The fourth was that roughly half the globe—the centrally planned economies of the Communist world—were off-limits to Western international businesses. As will be explained below, all four of these qualities either have changed or are now changing rapidly.

THE CHANGING WORLD OUTPUT AND WORLD TRADE PICTURE

In the early 1960s, the United States was still by far the world's dominant industrial power. In 1963 the United States accounted for 40.3 percent of world economic activity, measured by gross domestic product (GDP). By 2008, the United States accounted for 20.7 percent of world GDP, still the world's largest industrial power but down significantly in relative size since the 1960s (see Table 1.2). Nor was the United States the only developed nation to see its relative standing slip. The same occurred to Germany, France, and the United Kingdom, all nations that were among the first to industrialize. This change in the U.S. position was not an absolute decline, since the U.S. economy grew at a robust average annual rate of more than 3 percent from 1963 to 2008 (the economies of Germany, France, and the United Kingdom also grew during this time). Rather, it was a relative decline, reflecting the faster economic growth of several other economies, particularly in Asia. For example, as can be seen from Table 1.2, from 1963 to 2008, China's share of world GDP increased from a trivial amount to 11.4 percent. Other countries that markedly increased their share of world output included Japan, Thailand, Malaysia, Taiwan, and South Korea (note that GDP data in Table 1.2 are based on purchasing power parity figures, which adjust the value of GDP to reflect the cost of living in various economies).

By the end of the 1980s, the U.S. position as the world's leading exporter was threatened. Over the past 30 years, U.S. dominance in export markets has waned as Japan, Germany, and a number of newly industrialized countries such as South Korea and China have taken a larger share of world exports. During the 1960s, the United States routinely accounted for 20 percent of world exports of manufactured goods. But as Table 1.2 shows, the U.S. share of world exports of goods and services had slipped to 8.5 percent by 2009, behind China and Germany.

As emerging economies such as China, India, and Brazil continue to grow, a further relative decline in the share of world output and world exports accounted for by the United States and other long-established developed nations seems likely. By itself, this is not bad. The relative decline of the United States reflects the growing economic development and industrialization of the world economy, as opposed to any absolute

table 1.2

The Changing Demographics of World GDP and Trade

Sources: IMF, *World Economic Outlook*, October 2009. Data for 1963 are from N. Hood and J. Young, *The Economics of the Multinational Enterprise* (New York: Longman, 1973). The GDP data are based on purchasing power parity figures, which adjust the value of GDP to reflect the cost of living in various economies. Export data from WTO press release, "Trade to Expand by 9.5% in 2010," March 26, 2010.

Country	Share of World Output, 1963	Share of World GDP, 2008	Share of World Exports, 2009
United States	40.3%	20.7%	8.5%
Germany	9.7	4.2	9.0
France	6.3	3.1	3.8
Italy	3.4	2.6	3.2
United Kingdom	6.5	3.2	2.8
Canada	3.0	1.9	2.5
Japan	5.5	6.4	4.7
China	NA	11.4	9.6

decline in the health of the U.S. economy, which by many measures is stronger than ever.

Most forecasts now predict a rapid rise in the share of world output accounted for by developing nations such as China, India, Russia, Indonesia, Thailand, South Korea, Mexico, and Brazil, and a commensurate decline in the share enjoyed by rich industrialized countries such as Great Britain, Germany, Japan, and the United States. If current trends continue, the Chinese economy could ultimately be larger than that of the United States on a purchasing power parity basis, while the economy of India will approach that of Germany. The World Bank has estimated that today's developing nations may account for more than 60 percent of world economic activity by 2020, while today's rich nations, which currently account for more than 55 percent of world economic activity, may account for only about 38 percent. Forecasts are not always correct, but these suggest that a shift in the economic geography of the world is now under way, although the magnitude of that shift is not totally evident. For international businesses, the implications of this changing economic geography are clear: Many of tomorrow's economic opportunities may be found in the developing nations of the world, and many of tomorrow's most capable competitors will probably also emerge from these regions. A case in point has been the dramatic expansion of Brazil's soybean crop as profiled in the accompanying Country Focus.

Another Perspective

The Changing Face of OPEC

For decades, Saudi Arabia, as the world's leading oil producer, has been able to call the shots at the Organization of Petroleum Exporting Countries, more commonly known as OPEC. But recently Iraq put the Saudis—and the rest of OPEC—on notice. As Iraq becomes more politically stable, it is resuming oil exploration and plans to ramp up production. The government's own projections suggest that within seven years, output will rise from its current 2.5 million barrels a day to rival Saudi Arabia's daily 10 million to 12 million. Having serious competition in the oil market would change the picture for Saudi Arabia—as well as for OPEC. (Stephen Glain, "How Iraqi Oil Is Changing the World," *Foreign Policy*, March 17, 2010, www.foreignpolicy.com)

THE CHANGING FOREIGN DIRECT INVESTMENT PICTURE

Reflecting the dominance of the United States in the global economy, U.S. firms accounted for 66.3 percent of worldwide foreign direct investment flows in the 1960s. British firms were second, accounting for 10.5 percent, while Japanese firms were a distant eighth, with only 2 percent. The dominance of U.S. firms was so great that books were written about the economic threat posed to Europe by U.S. corporations.[35] Several European governments, most notably France, talked of limiting inward investment by U.S. firms.

However, as the barriers to the free flow of goods, services, and capital fell, and as other countries increased their shares of world output, non-U.S. firms increasingly began to invest across national borders. The motivation for much of this foreign direct investment by non-U.S. firms was the desire to disperse production activities to optimal locations and to build a direct presence in major foreign markets. Thus, beginning in the 1970s, European and Japanese firms began to shift labor-intensive manufacturing operations from their home markets to developing nations where labor costs were lower. In addition, many Japanese firms invested in North America and Europe—often as a hedge against unfavorable currency movements and the possible imposition of trade barriers. For example, Toyota, the Japanese automobile company, rapidly increased its investment in automobile production facilities in the United States and Europe during the late 1980s and early 1990s. Toyota executives believed that an increasingly strong Japanese yen would price Japanese automobile exports out of foreign markets; therefore, production in the most important foreign markets, as opposed to exports from Japan, made sense. Toyota also undertook these investments to head off growing political pressures in the United States and Europe to restrict Japanese automobile exports into those markets.

Country FOCUS

Brazil: Soybeans, Growth, and Politics

While much has been said about the advantages of technological change and its role in globalization, the soybean, a small legume native to East Asia, has been driving economic growth for more than 5,000 years.

The soybean is a miraculous plant used in cooking and commercial products. Having exceptional nutritional value, the soybean is found in flour, infant formula, meat and dairy substitutes, cattle feed, and a multitude of other products. Soybeans were discovered in China, Japan, and Korea, and China is the largest importer of soybeans.

Brazil is a country rich in natural resources. It is one of the largest producers and exporters of raw and processed minerals, including iron ore, bauxite, manganese, copper, tin, and gold. It has large offshore oil and gas fields that contribute to the country's reserves. And it has an abundance of highly fertile land.

Although agriculture accounts for a little less than 5 percent of Brazil's gross domestic product, its significance should not be underestimated because it is one of the largest employers in rural areas. The sector accounts for more than 20 percent of the formal jobs in the country. Most importantly, agriculture runs a large foreign trade surplus.

As the largest economy in Latin America and as the eighth-largest economy in the world, Brazil has become one of the leading producers of soybeans, second only to the United States. In so doing, Brazil has expanded it global reach to take advantage of global demands.

Brazil exports more than US$13 billion in soybean products annually, and this number is forecast to grow over the next decade. With its soybean exports, Brazil is bringing much-needed currency into the country as it continues its rapid growth. In meeting this worldwide demand for soybeans, however, Brazil has found itself facing serious global challenges as it becomes more competitive. Soybean demand has required more and more arable land that must be cleared from the jungle. In addition to the issue of deforestation, which arguably can lead to climate change and droughts, the increase in foreign investment from external multinational corporations has created even more complex issues.

The growing of soybeans has been at the cost of deforestation. The cleared land has traditionally been worked by peasants whose productivity levels are low, which has led to vast farmlands being underutilized. Brazil has more than 70 million hectares still to plow, and this fact has not gone unnoticed by large U.S. multinationals such as Archer Daniels Midland, Dow Chemical Company, DuPont, and Monsanto, which have invested heavily in this potential.

By their investment in Brazil's soybean crop, these companies are using modern agricultural methodology to increase production. This increased efficiency has come at the expense of displacing many Brazilian agricultural workers. In many rural areas this displacement has caused homelessness, political unrest, and continued calls for land reform. The Movimento Sem Terra has lead this charge. To Brazil's current administration, this continues to be a serious concern.

This issue is not new—it is based on an antiquated land system inherited from the Portuguese colonizers. Much to the world's surprise, Brazil's populist/socialist president, Luiz Ignacio Lula da Silva, has been successful appeasing the landless peasants. This is because Brazil continues to experience tremendous growth. Exports have fueled much of this economic growth. But the question must be asked: Will more exports mean more jobs for peasant workers?

Sources: Economist Intelligence Unit, Brazil Country Report, July 2010, http://www.eiu.com; M. Margolis, "Weathering the Storm," *Newsweek,* July 26, 2008, http://www.newsweek.com; B. Song et al., "Market Power and Competitive Analysis of China's Soybean Import Market," International Agricultural Trade Research Consortium (IATRC), 2007; "Land Activist Killed in Brazilian Amazon," http://news.bbc.co.uk/2/hi/americas/8600353.stm; and http://news.bbc.co.uk/2/hi/programmes/crossing_continents/3146937.stm.

Stock of Foreign Direct Investment
The total cumulative value of foreign-owned assets at a given time.

One consequence of these developments is illustrated in Figure 1.2, which shows how the stock of foreign direct investment by the world's six most important national sources—the United States, the United Kingdom, Germany, the Netherlands, France, and Japan—changed between 1980 and 2008. (The **stock of foreign direct investment** refers to the total cumulative value of foreign investments.) Figure 1.2 also shows the stock accounted for by firms from developing economies. The share of the total stock accounted for by U.S. firms declined from about 38 percent in 1980 to 19.5 percent in 2008. Meanwhile, the shares accounted for by France and the world's developing nations increased markedly. The rise in the share of FDI stock accounted for by developing nations reflects a growing trend for firms from these countries to invest outside their borders. In 2008, firms based in developing nations accounted for 14.5

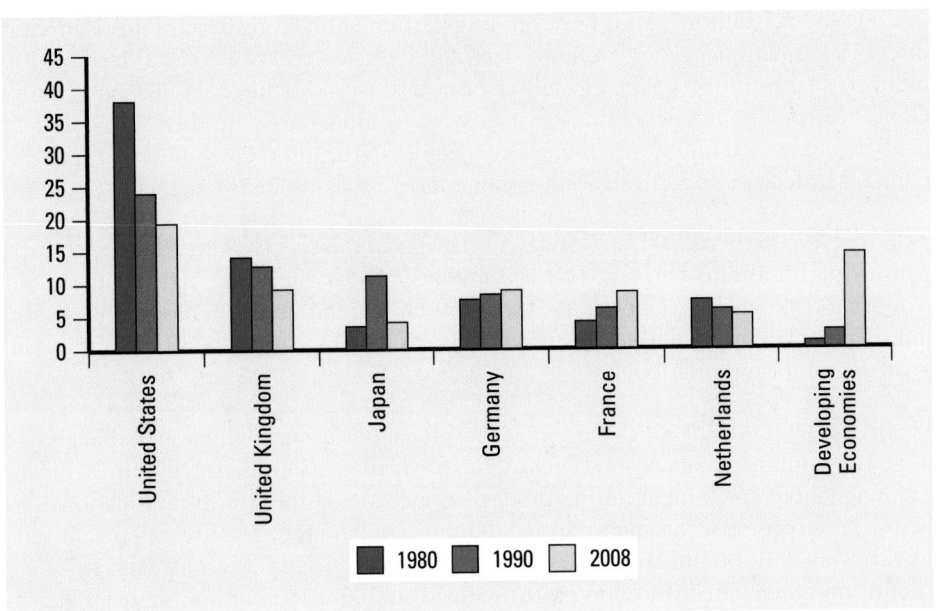

1.2 figure

Percentage Share of
Total FDI Stock,
1980–2008

Source: UNCTAD, *World Investment
Report, 2009* (Geneva: United
Nations, 2009).

percent of the stock of foreign direct investment, up from only 1.1 percent in 1980. Firms based in Hong Kong, South Korea, Singapore, Taiwan, India, and mainland China accounted for much of this investment.

Figure 1.3 illustrates two other important trends—the sustained growth in cross-border flows of foreign direct investment that occurred during the 1990s and the importance of developing nations as the destination of foreign direct investment. Throughout the 1990s, the amount of investment directed at both developed and developing nations increased dramatically, a trend that reflects the increasing internationalization of business corporations. A surge in foreign direct investment from 1998 to 2000 was followed by a slump from 2001 to 2003 associated with a slowdown in global economic activity after the collapse of the financial bubble of the late 1990s and 2000. However, the growth of foreign direct investment resumed in 2004 and continued through 2007, when it hit record levels, only to slow again in 2008 as the global financial crisis took hold (preliminary figures suggest it contracted again

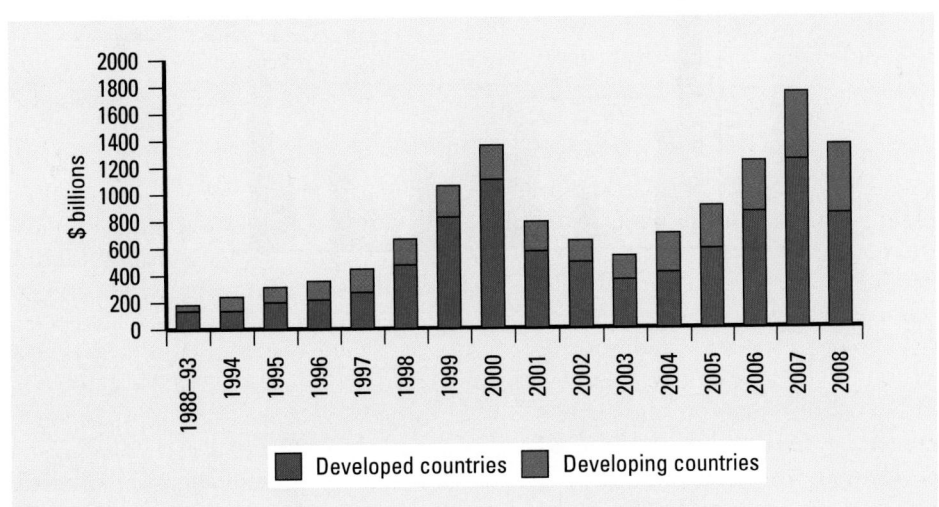

1.3 figure

FDI Inflows, 1988–2008

Sources: UNCTAD, *World
Investment Report, 2008* (Geneva:
United Nations, 2008); and "Global
Foreign Investment Now in
Decline," UNCTAD press release,
January 19, 2009.

in 2009 to $1.2 billion). Among developing nations, the largest recipient of foreign direct investment has been China, which in 2004–2009 received $60 billion to $100 billion a year in inflows. As we shall see later in this book, the sustained flow of foreign investment into developing nations is an important stimulus for economic growth in those countries, which bodes well for the future of countries such as China, Mexico, and Brazil, all leading beneficiaries of this trend.

THE CHANGING NATURE OF THE MULTINATIONAL ENTERPRISE

Multinational Enterprise (MNE)
A firm that owns business operations in more than one country.

A **multinational enterprise** (MNE) is any business that has productive activities in two or more countries. Since the 1960s, two notable trends in the demographics of the multinational enterprise have been (1) the rise of non-U.S. multinationals and (2) the growth of mini-multinationals.

Non-U.S. Multinationals

In the 1960s, global business activity was dominated by large U.S. multinational corporations. With U.S. firms accounting for about two-thirds of foreign direct investment during the 1960s, one would expect most multinationals to be U.S. enterprises. According to the data summarized in Figure 1.4, 48.5 percent of the world's 260 largest multinationals were U.S. firms in 1973. The second-largest source country was the United Kingdom, with 18.8 percent of the largest multinationals. Japan accounted for 3.5 percent of the world's largest multinationals at the time. The large number of U.S. multinationals reflected U.S. economic dominance in the three decades after World War II, while the large number of British multinationals reflected that country's industrial dominance in the early decades of the twentieth century.

By 2008 things had shifted significantly. Some 19 of the world's 100 largest nonfinancial multinationals were now U.S. enterprises; 13 were French; 13, German; 14, British; and 10, Japanese.[36] Although the 1973 data are not strictly comparable with the later data, they illustrate the trend (the 1973 figures are based on the largest 260 firms, whereas the later figures are based on the largest 100 multinationals). The globalization

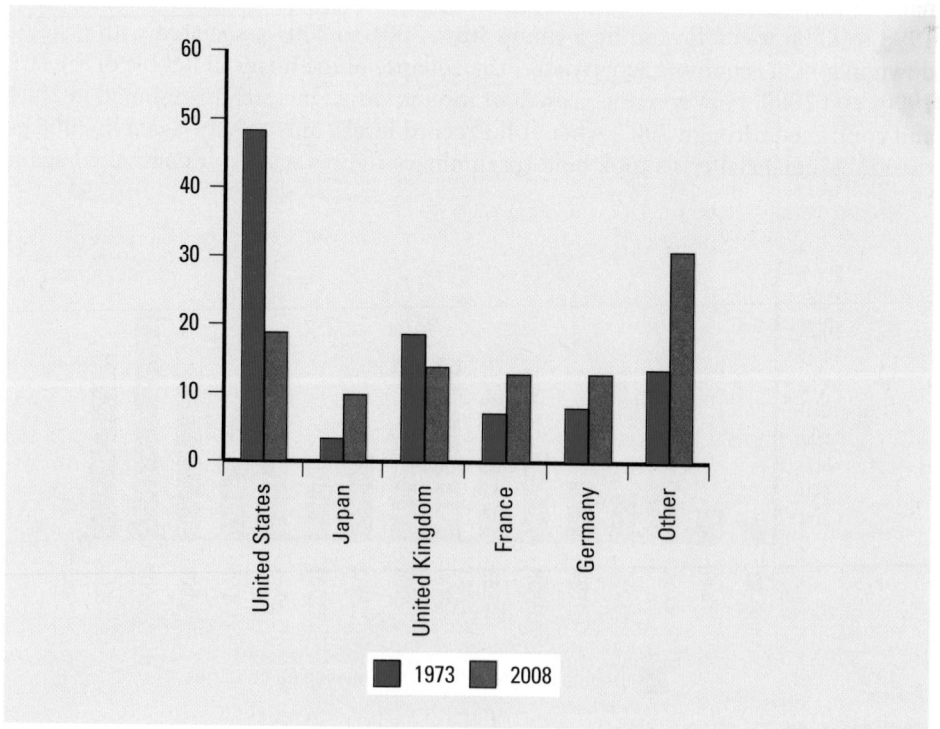

figure 1.4

National Origin of Largest Multinational Enterprises, 1973 and 2008

Source: UNCTAD, *World Investment Report, 2009* (Geneva: United Nations, 2009).

China's Haier: A Non–U.S. Multinational

In English, the term *white goods* is used to describe a large home appliance that may include refrigerators, washing machines, dishwashers, and ovens. Many of us use these products on a daily basis, and depending where you live, may be familiar with companies such as Siemens, Bosch, Fagor, Hitachi, Whirlpool Corporation, or GE. But in China, the single largest market in the world, the biggest producer of white goods is Haier.

Headquartered in Qingdao, Shandong Province, Haier was founded in 1984. In approximately 25 years Haier has grown to become the world's fourth-largest white goods manufacturer and one of China's top 100 IT companies. Haier has 240 subsidiary companies; 30 design centers, plants, and trade companies; and more than 50,000 employees throughout the world. The story of its success demonstrates the growth of many non–U.S. multinational corporations during the past quarter century.

As with other Chinese companies under the watchful eye of a centralized regime, Haier suffered from dilapidated infrastructure, poor management, and lack of quality controls until a young assistant city-manager, Zhang Ruimin, was appointed managing director.

Zhang's leadership is a story in itself. From humble beginnings, a loyal member of the Communist Party with relatively little formal education and essentially unaware of the dynamic forces at play within a global economic context, Zhang implemented aggressive managerial control over quality assurance practices at Qingdao Refrigerator Co. This began a transformation that eventually led to the creation of Haier.

With Zhang's leadership and the opening of China to the outside world, a German company, the Liebherr Group, created a joint venture with Qingdao Refrigerator Co., bringing refrigeration technology and equipment to the country. What happened next was a turnaround period that eventually led to the consolidation of many inefficient appliance manufacturers in the region.

Once established and profitable in China—with annual growth rates of 75 percent or higher—Haier sought to expand internationally with Indonesia being its first move. Through rapid succession, the company opened plants in Philippines, Malaysia, and finally in direct competition in the United States in 2000 with a production plant in South Carolina. The new millennium was a wake-up call to U.S. giants such as GE, Whirlpool, and Frigidaire.

The alarm clock never rang louder than when Haier acquired the iconic, neoclassical Greenwich Savings Bank building in New York City, firmly and symbolically placing its corporate footprint on American soil. Since then, Haier has sought to increase its presence by attempting to acquire Maytag and by expanding into such remote regions as Tunisia, Nigeria, Egypt, Algeria, South Africa, and Venezuela—specifically going where many U.S. multinationals are either hesitant or politically constrained. Furthermore, Haier is proceeding with "green product" development in countries such as India in an attempt to penetrate the second largest market in the world.

Perhaps because of the perceived direct competition with U.S. multinationals or the need to address underrepresented markets, non–U.S. multinationals are beginning to take advantage of the traditional economic dominance of U.S. multinationals. Walk into a Walmart, a Carrefour, a Tesco, or an E-Mart, and you are likely to find a Haier white good directly competing with those of the rest of the world.

Sources: Haier Web site, www.haier.com, accessed July 16, 2010; W. Mukherjee, "LG, Samsung, Godrej Plan Product Portfolio Energy-Efficient," *The Economic Times,* July 15, 2010, http://economictimes.indiatimes.com; S. H. Choe, "Wal-Mart Selling Stores and Leaving Korea," *The New York Times,* May 23, 2006; and "LG, Samsung, Godrej and Haier initiate green initiative in India," Religare Technova News, http://global.factiva.com/ha/default.aspx.

of the world economy has resulted in a relative decline in the dominance of U.S. firms in the global marketplace.

According to UN data, the ranks of the world's largest 100 multinationals are still dominated by firms from developed economies.[37] However, seven firms from developing economies had entered the UN's list of the 100 largest multinationals by 2008. The largest was Hutchison Whampoa of Hong Kong, China, which ranked 22.[38] We can reasonably expect more growth of new multinational enterprises from the world's developing nations. Firms from developing nations can be expected to emerge as important competitors in global markets, further shifting the axis of the world economy away from North America and Western Europe and threatening the long dominance of Western companies. One such rising competitor, Haier, one of China's premier manufacturers of "white goods," is profiled in the accompanying Management Focus.

The Rise of Mini-Multinationals Another trend in international business has been the growth of medium-size and small multinationals (mini-multinationals).[39] When people think of international businesses, they tend to think of firms such as Exxon, General Motors, Ford, Fuji, Kodak, Matsushita, Procter & Gamble, Sony, and Unilever—large, complex multinational corporations with operations that span the globe. Although most international trade and investment is still conducted by large firms, many medium-size and small businesses are becoming increasingly involved in international trade and investment. The rise of the Internet is lowering the barriers that small firms face in building international sales.

For example, consider Lubricating Systems, Inc., of Kent, Washington. Lubricating Systems, which manufactures lubricating fluids for machine tools, employs 25 people and generates sales of $6.5 million. It's hardly a large, complex multinational, yet more than $2 million of the company's sales are generated by exports to a score of countries, including Japan, Israel, and the United Arab Emirates. Lubricating Systems also has set up a joint venture with a German company to serve the European market.[40] Consider also Lixi, Inc., a small U.S. manufacturer of industrial X-ray equipment; 70 percent of Lixi's $4.5 million in revenues comes from exports to Japan.[41] Or take G.W. Barth, a manufacturer of cocoa-bean roasting machinery based in Ludwigsburg, Germany. Employing just 65 people, this small company has captured 70 percent of the global market for cocoa-bean roasting machines.[42] International business is conducted not just by large firms but also by medium-size and small enterprises.

THE CHANGING WORLD ORDER

Between 1989 and 1991 a series of democratic revolutions swept the Communist world. For reasons that are explored in more detail in Chapter 2, in country after country throughout Eastern Europe and eventually in the Soviet Union itself, Communist Party governments collapsed. The Soviet Union receded into history, having been replaced by 15 independent republics. Czechoslovakia divided itself into two states, while Yugoslavia dissolved into a bloody civil war among its five successor states.

Many of the former Communist nations of Europe and Asia seem to share a commitment to democratic politics and free market economics. If this continues, the opportunities for international businesses are significant. For half a century, these countries were essentially closed to Western international businesses. Now they present a host of export and investment opportunities. Just how this will play out over the next 10 to 20 years is difficult to say. The economies of many of the former Communist states are still relatively undeveloped, and their continued commitment to democracy and free market economics cannot be taken for granted. Disturbing signs of growing unrest and totalitarian tendencies continue to be seen in several Eastern European and Central Asian states, including Russia, which has shown signs of shifting back toward greater state involvement in economic activity and authoritarian government.[43] Thus, the risks involved in doing business in such countries are high, but so may be the returns.

In addition to these changes, quieter revolutions have been occurring in China, other states in Southeast Asia, and Latin America. Their implications for international businesses may be just as profound as the collapse of communism in Eastern Europe. China suppressed its own pro-democracy movement in the bloody Tiananmen Square massacre of 1989. Despite this, China continues to move progressively toward greater free market reforms. If what is occurring in China continues for two more decades, China may move from Third World to industrial superpower status even more rapidly than Japan did. If China's gross domestic product (GDP) per capita grows by an average of 6 to 7 percent, which is slower than the 8 percent growth rate achieved during the last decade, then by 2020 this nation of 1.273 billion people could boast an average income per capita of about $13,000, roughly equivalent to that of Spain's today.

The potential consequences for international business are enormous. On the one hand, with more than 1 billion people, China represents a huge and largely untapped market. Reflecting this, between 1983 and 2009, annual foreign direct investment in China increased from less than $2 billion to $100 billion annually. On the other hand, China's new firms are proving to be very capable competitors, and they could take global market share away from Western and Japanese enterprises (for example, see the Management Focus about Haier). Thus, the changes in China are creating both opportunities and threats for established international businesses.

As for Latin America, both democracy and free market reforms have been evident there too. For decades, most Latin American countries were ruled by dictators, many of whom seemed to view Western international businesses as instruments of imperialist domination. Accordingly, they restricted direct investment by foreign firms. In addition, the poorly managed economies of Latin America were characterized by low growth, high debt, and hyperinflation—all of which discouraged investment by international businesses. In the last two decades much of this had changed. Throughout most of Latin America, debt and inflation are down, governments have sold state-owned enterprises to private investors, foreign investment is welcomed, and the region's economies have expanded. Brazil, Mexico, and Chile have led the way here. These changes have increased the attractiveness of Latin America, both as a market for exports and as a site for foreign direct investment. At the same time, given the long history of economic mismanagement in Latin America, there is no guarantee that these favorable trends will continue. Indeed, in Bolivia, Ecuador, and most notably Venezuela there have been shifts back toward greater state involvement in industry, and foreign investment is now less welcome than it was during the 1990s. In these nations, the government has seized control of oil and gas fields from foreign investors and has limited the rights of foreign energy companies to extract oil and gas from their nations. Thus, as in the case of Eastern Europe, substantial opportunities are accompanied by substantial risks.

Another Perspective

How the Chinese See the World Order

Some world observers suggest there's a "push-pull" relationship among Europe, China, and the United States: When China is feuding with Europe, they say, conditions with the United States improve. Or when China and the United States are at odds, China warms up to Europe. Lately, some Chinese have perceived a shift, thanks to their nation's emerging economy while Europe and the United States are recovering slowly from the global economic downturn. They also pay close attention to recent speeches by President Barack Obama, in which he characterizes the United States as "one of the most important countries," not "the most important." (Yu Xiang, "U.S., Europe Adjust to Changing World Order," *China Post,* February 28, 2010, www.chinapost.com)

THE GLOBAL ECONOMY OF THE TWENTY-FIRST CENTURY
As discussed, the past quarter century has seen rapid changes in the global economy. Barriers to the free flow of goods, services, and capital have been coming down. The volume of cross-border trade and investment has been growing more rapidly than global output, indicating that national economies are becoming more closely integrated into a single, interdependent, global economic system. As their economies advance, more nations are joining the ranks of the developed world. A generation ago, South Korea and Taiwan were viewed as second-tier developing nations. Now they boast large economies, and their firms are major players in many global industries, from shipbuilding and steel to electronics and chemicals. The move toward a global economy has been further strengthened by the widespread adoption of liberal economic policies by countries that had firmly opposed them for two generations or more. Thus, in keeping with the normative prescriptions of liberal economic ideology, in country after country we have seen state-owned businesses privatized, widespread deregulation adopted, markets opened to more competition, and commitment increased to removing barriers to cross-border trade and investment. This suggests that over the next few

decades, countries such as the Czech Republic, Mexico, Poland, Brazil, China, India, and South Africa may build powerful market-oriented economies. In short, current trends indicate that the world is moving toward an economic system that is more favorable for international business.

But it is always hazardous to use established trends to predict the future. The world may be moving toward a more global economic system, but globalization is not inevitable. Countries may pull back from the recent commitment to liberal economic ideology if their experiences do not match their expectations. There are clear signs, for example, of a retreat from liberal economic ideology in Russia. If Russia's hesitation were to become more permanent and widespread, the liberal vision of a more prosperous global economy based on free market principles might not occur as quickly as many hope. Clearly, this would be a tougher world for international businesses.

Also, greater globalization brings with it risks of its own. This was starkly demonstrated in 1997 and 1998 when a financial crisis in Thailand spread first to other East Asian nations and then in 1998 to Russia and Brazil. Ultimately, the crisis threatened to plunge the economies of the developed world, including the United States, into a recession. We explore the causes and consequences of this and other similar global financial crises in Chapter 10. Even from a purely economic perspective, globalization is not all good. The opportunities for doing business in a global economy may be significantly enhanced, but as we saw in 1997–98, the risks associated with global financial contagion are also greater. Indeed, during 2008–09 a crisis that started in the financial sector of America, where banks had been too liberal in their lending policies to homeowners, swept around the world and plunged the global economy into its deepest recession since the early 1980s, illustrating once more that in an interconnected world a severe crisis in one region can impact the entire globe. Still, as explained later in this book, firms can exploit the opportunities associated with globalization, while at the same time reducing the risks through appropriate hedging strategies.

The Globalization Debate

Is the shift toward a more integrated and interdependent global economy a good thing? Many influential economists, politicians, and business leaders seem to think so.[44] They argue that falling barriers to international trade and investment are the twin engines driving the global economy toward greater prosperity. They say increased international trade and cross-border investment will result in lower prices for goods and services. They believe that globalization stimulates economic growth, raises the incomes of consumers, and helps to create jobs in all countries that participate in the global trading system. The arguments of those who support globalization are covered in detail in Chapters 5, 6, and 7. As we shall see, there are good theoretical reasons for believing that declining barriers to international trade and investment do stimulate economic growth, create jobs, and raise income levels. As described in Chapters 6 and 7, empirical evidence lends support to the predictions of this theory. However, despite the existence of a compelling body of theory and evidence, globalization has its critics.[45] Some of these critics have become increasingly vocal and active, taking to the streets to demonstrate their opposition to globalization. Here we look at the nature of protests against globalization and briefly review the main themes of the debate concerning the merits of globalization. In later chapters we elaborate on many of the points mentioned below.

ANTIGLOBALIZATION PROTESTS   Demonstrations against globalization date to December 1999, when more than 40,000 protesters blocked the streets of Seattle in an attempt to shut down a World Trade Organization meeting being held in the city. The demonstrators were protesting against a wide range of issues, including job losses in industries under attack from foreign competitors, downward pressure on the wage rates of unskilled workers, environmental degradation, and the cultural imperialism of global media and multinational enterprises, which was seen as being dominated by what some protesters called the "culturally impoverished" interests and values of the United States. All of these ills, the demonstrators claimed, could be laid at the feet of globalization. The World Trade Organization was meeting to try to launch a new round of talks to cut barriers to cross-border trade and investment. As such, it was seen as a promoter of globalization and a target for the antiglobalization protesters. The protests turned violent, transforming the normally placid streets of Seattle into a running battle between "anarchists" and Seattle's bemused and poorly prepared police department. Pictures of brick-throwing protesters and armored police wielding their batons were duly recorded by the global media, which then circulated the images around the world. Meanwhile, the World Trade Organization meeting failed to reach agreement, and although the protests outside the meeting halls had little to do with that failure, the impression took hold that the demonstrators had succeeded in derailing the meetings.

Emboldened by the experience in Seattle, antiglobalization protesters now turn up at almost every major meeting of a global institution. Smaller-scale protests have occurred in several countries, such as France, where antiglobalization activists destroyed a McDonald's restaurant in August 1999 to protest the impoverishment of French culture by American imperialism. (For another example, see the Country Focus on Greece and the distributive forces of antiglobalization.) While violent protests may give the antiglobalization effort a bad name, it is clear from the scale of the demonstrations that support for the cause goes beyond a core of anarchists. Large segments of the population in many countries believe that globalization has detrimental effects

Demonstrators at the WTO meeting in Seattle in December 1999 began looting and rioting in the city's downtown. Why do you think they felt that behavior was necessary?

Greece, PIIGS, and the Distributive Forces of Antiglobalization

Globalization can in many ways be viewed as an aggregational force to be met with a theoretically distributive force. To the extent that Greece sought to integrate or aggregate itself with the European Union, the believers in globalization were most certainly looking forward to benefiting from membership in a more robust economic collective. The global economic crisis, however, activated contrary distributive forces. Case in point, Greece.

Just as Greece was the cradle of European civilization, so it seems to be with regards to antiglobalization in Europe in the current fiscal crisis. In early 2010, Greece and Europe found themselves in an economic crisis that may have global consequences. It began with Greece because of the size of its sovereign debt, the scale of its budget deficit, and the sad fact that its prospects for growth are going to come at a severe price. Simply put, Greece had acquired more debt than it could pay. It stood on the verge of bankruptcy, which did not bode well for Europe. Coupled with the inability to devalue its currency, many Greeks viewed globalization and its membership in the European Union as a recipe for bad times. And its population took to the streets in protest.

In mid-summer 2010, protests continue in a stark rebuttal to the austerity programs sought by the IMF/Euro Zone rescue package. Fortunately, much of the violence characterized in the early demonstrations has abated. Many blame global capitalism, others the large multinational institutional investment banks such as Goldman Sachs for masking the true extent of Greece's debt liability. But what cannot be denied is that antiglobalization sentiments have begun to penetrate all levels of society as those austerity measures begin to be felt. And, perhaps what was most telling was how quickly a pro-integration, pro-aggregational position changed to a distributive antiglobalization position. Similarly, a recent poll suggested that 80 percent of the population were resigned to the implementation of the measures. Just like the forces of globalization, pent-up antiglobalization

sentiments cannot be contained within the boundaries of one nation-state.

In this regard, Portugal, Ireland, Italy, and Spain seem to share many of the same characteristics that made Greece falter. Collectively, the countries are called PIIGS.

In Portugal, where similar austerity programs are being implemented, signs of social unrest over the extent and severity of the fiscal adjustment are beginning to take hold. Spain, Ireland, and Italy are at the threshold of such social unrest. Collectively, the various austerity programs being implemented concurrently by numerous European governments will inevitably weigh on economic activity across the region, further highlighting the questionable benefits of globalization.

The distributive nature of antiglobalization is now being felt by those European countries forced to come to the rescue of the PIIGS. Germany, the largest exporter in Europe, with a much more stable economy, is now bearing the lion's share of the debt along with France and the IMF. Germans view this situation as unfair. This in turn has provoked political unrest. In fact, newly elected president Christian Wulff's win may be viewed as a result of the previous administration's acquiescence to the fiscal rescue package. Even France, once considered within a "safe-haven" is starting to feel the consequences of antiglobalization sentiment.

Where all this leads remains to be determined, but as Filipino economist Walden Bello points out in his book, *Deglobalization, Ideas for a New World Economy,* in the global economic crisis there appears to be "multiple crises with global capitalism." The extent to which Europe successfully manages this crisis will in many ways determine the extent to which deglobalization will take hold.

Sources: Economist Intelligence Unit, Portugal Country Report, July 2010; Economist Intelligence Unit, Greece Country Report, June 2010; B. Balzli, "How Goldman Sachs Helped Greece Mask Its True Debt," http://www.spiegel.de/international/europe/0,1518,676634,00.html; "Protesting, Wearily, Grim Resignation as Austerity Bites," http://www.huffingtonpost.com/2010/06/04/eurozone-crisis-worsens-s_n_600913.html; N. D. Schwartz and E. Dash, "Banks Bet Greece Defaults on Debt They Helped Hide," *The New York Times,* February 25, 2010; and "Domino Theory," *The Economist,* February 18, 2010.

on living standards and the environment, and the media have often fed on this fear. For example, former CNN news anchor Lou Dobbs ran TV shows that were highly critical of the trend by American companies to take advantage of globalization and "export jobs" overseas. As the world slipped into a recession in 2008, Dobbs stepped up his antiglobalization rhetoric (Dobbs left CNN in 2009).

Both theory and evidence suggest that many of these fears are exaggerated, but this may not have been communicated clearly and both politicians and business-people need to do more to counter these fears. Many protests against globalization are tapping into a general sense of loss at the passing of a world in which barriers of time and distance, and vast differences in economic institutions, political institutions, and the level of development of different nations, produced a world rich in the diversity of human cultures. This world is now passing into history. However, while the rich citizens of the developed world may have the luxury of mourning the fact that they can now see McDonald's restaurants and Starbucks coffeehouses on their vacations to exotic locations such as Thailand, fewer complaints are heard from the citizens of those countries, who welcome the higher living standards that progress brings.

GLOBALIZATION, JOBS, AND INCOME   One concern frequently voiced by globalization opponents is that falling barriers to international trade destroy manufacturing jobs in wealthy advanced economies such as the United States and Western Europe. The critics argue that falling trade barriers allow firms to move manufacturing activities to countries where wage rates are much lower.[46] Indeed, due to the entry of China, India, and states from Eastern Europe into the global trading system, along with global population growth, estimates suggest that the pool of global labor may have quadrupled between 1985 and 2005, with most of the increase taking place after 1990.[47] Other things being equal, one might conclude that this enormous expansion in the global labor force, when coupled with expanding international trade, would have depressed wages in developed nations.

This fear is supported by anecdotes. For example, D. L. Bartlett and J. B. Steele, two journalists for the *Philadelphia Inquirer* who gained notoriety for their attacks on free trade, cite the case of Harwood Industries, a U.S. clothing manufacturer that closed its U.S. operations, where it paid workers $9 per hour, and shifted manufacturing to Honduras, where textile workers receive 48 cents per hour.[48] Because of moves such as this, argue Bartlett and Steele, the wage rates of poorer Americans have fallen significantly over the past quarter of a century.

In the past few years, the same fears have been applied to services, which have increasingly been outsourced to nations with lower labor costs. The popular feeling is that when corporations such as Dell, IBM, or Citigroup outsource service activities to lower-cost foreign suppliers—as all three have done—they are "exporting jobs" to low-wage nations and contributing to higher unemployment and lower living standards in their home nations (in this case, the United States). Some lawmakers in the United States have responded by calling for legal barriers to job outsourcing.

Supporters of globalization reply that critics of these trends miss the essential point about free trade—the benefits outweigh the costs.[49] They argue that free trade will result in countries specializing in the production of those goods and services that they can produce most efficiently, while importing goods and services that they cannot produce as efficiently. When a country embraces free trade, there is always some dislocation—lost textile jobs at Harwood Industries, or lost call center jobs at Dell—but the whole economy is better off as a result. According to this view, it makes little sense for the United States to produce textiles at home when they can be produced at a lower cost in Honduras or China (which, unlike Honduras, is a major source of U.S. textile imports). Importing textiles from China leads to lower prices for clothes in the United States,

Some U.S. companies have outsourced service activities to foreign suppliers, such as this call center in India, which has drawn both criticism and support.

which enables consumers to spend more of their money on other items. At the same time, the increased income generated in China from textile exports increases income levels in that country, which helps the Chinese to purchase more products produced in the United States, such as pharmaceuticals from Amgen, Boeing jets, Intel-based computers, Microsoft software, and Cisco routers.

The same argument can be made to support the outsourcing of services to low-wage countries. By outsourcing its customer service call centers to India, Dell can reduce its cost structure, and thereby its prices for PCs. U.S. consumers benefit from this development. As prices for PCs fall, Americans can spend more of their money on other goods and services. Moreover, the increase in income levels in India allows Indians to purchase more U.S. goods and services, which helps to create jobs in the United States. In this manner, supporters of globalization argue that free trade benefits *all* countries that adhere to a free trade regime.

If the critics of globalization are correct, the evidence would show that the share of national income received by labor, as opposed to the share received by the owners of capital (e.g, stockholders and bondholders), had declined in advanced nations as a result of downward pressure on wage rates, and that decline in labor's share of national income must be due to moving production to low-wage countries, as opposed to improvement in production technology and productivity. To counter this, supporters of globalization would argue, even though labor's share of the economic pie may have declined, this does not mean lower living standards if the size of the total pie increased sufficiently to offset any decline in labor's share; in other words, evidence would show that free trade has caused economic growth and rising living standards in advanced economies to offset declines in labor's share of national income.

So what does the data say? Several recent studies shed some light.[50] First, the data suggest that over the past two decades labor's share of national income has declined. The decline in share is much more pronounced in continental Europe and Japan (about 10 percentage points) than in the United States and the United Kingdom (where it is 3 to 4 percentage points). However, detailed analysis suggests that the share of national income enjoyed by *skilled labor* has actually *increased*, suggesting that the fall in labor's share has been due to a fall in the share taken by *unskilled labor*. For illustration, a study of long-term trends in income distribution in the United States concluded:

> Nationwide, from the late 1970s to the late 1990s, the average income of the lowest-income families fell by over 6 percent after adjustment for inflation, and the average real income of the middle fifth of families grew by about 5 percent. By contrast, the average real income of the highest-income fifth of families increased by over 30 percent.[51]

Another study suggested that the earnings gap between workers in skilled and unskilled sectors has widened by 25 percent over the last two decades.[52] In sum, unskilled labor in developed nations has seen its share of national income decline over the past two decades.

However, this does not mean that the *living standards* of unskilled workers in developed nations have declined. It is possible that economic growth in developed nations has offset the fall in the share of national income enjoyed by unskilled workers, raising their living standards. Evidence suggests that real labor compensation has expanded in most developed nations since the 1980s, including the United States. A study by the Organization for Economic Cooperation and Development, whose members include the 20 richest economies in the world, noted that while the gap between the poorest and richest segments of society in some OECD countries had widened, this trend was by no means universal.[53] Contrary to the results of the study cited above, the OECD study found that in the United States, while income inequality increased from the mid-1970s to the mid-1980s, it did not widen further in the next decade. The report also notes that in almost all countries, real income levels rose over the 20-year period looked at in the study, including the incomes of the poorest segment of most OECD societies. To add to the mixed research results, a 2002 U.S. study that included data from 1990 to 2000 concluded that during those years, falling unemployment rates brought gains to low-wage workers and fairly broad-based wage growth, especially in the latter half of the 1990s. The income of the worst-paid 10 percent of the population actually rose twice as fast as that of the average worker during 1998–2000.[54] If such trends continued—and they may not have—the argument that globalization leads to growing income inequality may lose some of its punch.

As noted earlier, globalization critics argue that the decline in unskilled wage rates is due to the migration of low-wage manufacturing jobs offshore and a corresponding reduction in demand for unskilled workers. However, supporters of globalization see a more complex picture. They maintain that the apparent decline in real wage rates of unskilled workers owes far more to a technology-induced shift within advanced economies away from jobs where the only qualification was a willingness to turn up for work every day and toward jobs that require significant education and skills. They point out that many advanced economies report a shortage of highly skilled workers and an excess supply of unskilled workers. Thus, growing income inequality is a result of the wages for skilled workers being bid up by the labor market and the wages for unskilled workers being discounted. In fact, evidence suggests that technological change has had a bigger impact than globalization on the declining share of national income enjoyed by labor.[55] This indicates that to the problem of stagnant incomes among the unskilled is to be found not in limiting free trade and globalization, but in increasing society's investment in education to reduce the supply of unskilled workers.[56]

Finally, it is worth noting that the wage gap between developing and developed nations is closing as developing nations experience rapid economic growth. For example, one estimate suggests that wages in China will approach Western levels in about 30 years.[57] To the extent that this is the case, any migration of unskilled jobs to low-wage countries is a temporary phenomenon representing a structural adjustment on the way to a more tightly integrated global economy.

GLOBALIZATION, LABOR POLICIES, AND THE ENVIRONMENT
A second source of concern is that free trade encourages firms from advanced nations to move manufacturing facilities to less developed countries that lack adequate regulations to protect labor and the environment from abuse by the unscrupulous.[58] Globalization critics often argue that adhering to labor and environmental regulations significantly increases the costs of manufacturing enterprises and puts them at a competitive disadvantage in the global marketplace vis-à-vis firms based in developing nations that do not have to comply with such regulations. Firms deal with this cost disadvantage, the theory goes, by moving their production facilities to nations that do not have such burdensome regulations or that fail to enforce the regulations they have.

If this were the case, one might expect free trade to lead to an increase in pollution and result in firms from advanced nations exploiting the labor of less developed nations.[59] This argument was used repeatedly by those who opposed the 1994 formation of the North American Free Trade Agreement (NAFTA) between Canada, Mexico, and the United States. They painted a picture of U.S. manufacturing firms moving to Mexico in droves so that they would be free to pollute the environment, employ child labor, and ignore workplace safety and health issues, all in the name of higher profits.[60]

Supporters of free trade and greater globalization express doubts about this scenario. They argue that tougher environmental regulations and stricter labor standards go hand in hand with economic progress.[61] In general, as countries get richer, they enact tougher environmental and labor regulations.[62] Because free trade enables developing countries to increase their economic growth rates and become richer, this should lead to tougher environmental and labor laws. In this view, the critics of free trade have got it backward—free trade does not lead to more pollution and labor exploitation, it leads to less. By creating wealth and incentives for enterprises to produce technological innovations, the free market system and free trade could make it easier for the world to cope with pollution and population growth. Indeed, while pollution levels are rising in the world's poorer countries, they have been falling in developed nations. In the United States, for example, the concentration of carbon monoxide and sulfur dioxide pollutants in the atmosphere decreased by 60 percent between 1978 and 1997, while lead concentrations decreased by 98 percent—and these reductions have occurred against a background of sustained economic expansion.[63]

A number of econometric studies have found consistent evidence of a hump-shaped relationship between income levels and pollution levels (see Figure 1.5).[64] As an economy grows and income levels rise, initially pollution levels also rise. However, past some point, rising income levels lead to demands for greater environmental protection, and pollution levels then fall. A seminal study by Grossman and Krueger found that the turning point generally occurred before per capita income levels reached $8,000.[65]

While the hump-shaped relationship depicted in Figure 1.5 seems to hold across a wide range of pollutants—from sulfur dioxide to lead concentrations and water

figure **1.5**

Income Levels and
Environmental Pollution

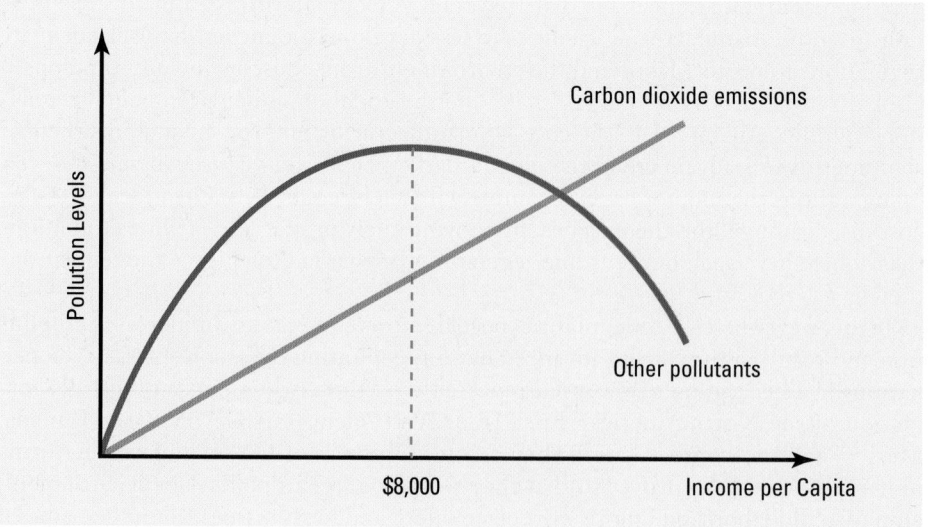

quality—carbon dioxide emissions are an important exception, rising steadily with higher income levels. Given that increased atmospheric carbon dioxide concentrations are a cause of global warming, this should be of serious concern. The solution to the problem, however, is probably not to roll back the trade liberalization efforts that have fostered economic growth and globalization, but to get the nations of the world to agree to tougher standards on limiting carbon emissions. Although UN-sponsored talks have had this as a central aim since the 1992 Earth Summit in Rio de Janeiro, there has been little success in moving toward the ambitious goals for reducing carbon emissions laid down in the Earth Summit and subsequent talks in Kyoto, Japan, in 1997 and in Copenhagen in 2009. In part this is because the largest emitters of carbon dioxide, the United States and China, have failed to reach agreements about how to proceed. China, a country whose carbon emissions are increasing at an alarming rate, has so far shown little appetite to adopt tighter pollution controls. As for the United States, political divisions in the U.S. Congress, where a strong minority sees no reason to put policies in place to limit carbon emissions, has made it difficult for even a progressive administration such as that of President Barack Obama to move forward with tight legislation on climate change.

Notwithstanding this, supporters of free trade point out that it is possible to tie free trade agreements to the implementation of tougher environmental and labor laws in less developed countries. NAFTA, for example, was passed only after side agreements had been negotiated that committed Mexico to tougher enforcement of environmental protection regulations. Thus, supporters of free trade argue that factories based in Mexico are now cleaner than they would have been without the passage of NAFTA.[66]

They also argue that business firms are not the amoral organizations that critics suggest. While there may be some rotten apples, most business enterprises are staffed by managers who are committed to behave in an ethical manner and would be unlikely to move production offshore just so they could pump more pollution into the atmosphere or exploit labor. Furthermore, the relationship between pollution, labor exploitation, and production costs may not be that suggested by critics. In general, a well-treated labor force is productive, and it is productivity rather than base wage rates that often has the greatest influence on costs. The vision of greedy managers who shift production to low-wage countries to exploit their labor force may be misplaced.

GLOBALIZATION AND NATIONAL SOVEREIGNTY   Another concern voiced by critics of globalization is that today's increasingly interdependent global economy shifts economic power away from national governments and toward supranational organizations such as the World Trade Organization, the European Union, and the United Nations. As perceived by critics, unelected bureaucrats now impose policies on the democratically elected governments of nation-states, thereby undermining the sovereignty of those states and limiting the nation's ability to control its own destiny.[67]

The World Trade Organization is a favorite target of those who attack the headlong rush toward a global economy. As noted earlier, the WTO was founded in 1994 to police the world trading system established by the General Agreement on Tariffs and Trade. The WTO arbitrates trade disputes between the 150 states that are signatories to the GATT. The arbitration panel can issue a ruling instructing a member state to change trade policies that violate GATT regulations. If the violator refuses to comply with the ruling, the WTO allows other states to impose appropriate trade sanctions on the transgressor. As a result, according to one prominent critic, U.S.

environmentalist, consumer rights advocate, and sometime presidential candidate Ralph Nader:

> Under the new system, many decisions that affect billions of people are no longer made by local or national governments but instead, if challenged by any WTO member nation, would be deferred to a group of unelected bureaucrats sitting behind closed doors in Geneva (which is where the headquarters of the WTO are located). The bureaucrats can decide whether or not people in California can prevent the destruction of the last virgin forests or determine if carcinogenic pesticides can be banned from their foods; or whether European countries have the right to ban dangerous biotech hormones in meat. . . . At risk is the very basis of democracy and accountable decision making.[68]

In contrast to Nader, many economists and politicians maintain that the power of supranational organizations such as the WTO is limited to what nation-states collectively agree to grant. They argue that bodies such as the United Nations and the WTO exist to serve the collective interests of member states, not to subvert those interests. Supporters of supranational organizations point out that the power of these bodies rests largely on their ability to persuade member states to follow a certain action. If these bodies fail to serve the collective interests of member states, those states will withdraw their support and the supranational organization will quickly collapse. In this view, real power still resides with individual nation-states, not supranational organizations.

GLOBALIZATION AND THE WORLD'S POOR   Critics of globalization argue that despite the supposed benefits associated with free trade and investment, over the past hundred years or so the gap between the rich and poor nations of the world has gotten wider. In 1870, the average income per capita in the world's 17 richest nations was 2.4 times that of all other countries. In 1990, the same group was 4.5 times as rich as the rest.[69] While recent history has shown that some of the world's poorer nations are capable of rapid periods of economic growth—witness the transformation that has occurred in some Southeast Asian nations such as South Korea, Thailand, and Malaysia—there appear to be strong forces for stagnation among the world's poorest nations. A quarter of the countries with a GDP per capita of less than $1,000 in 1960 had growth rates of less than zero from 1960 to 1995, and a third had growth rates of less than 0.05 percent.[70] Critics argue that if globalization is such a positive development, this divergence between the rich and poor should not have occurred.

Although the reasons for economic stagnation vary, several factors stand out, none of which have anything to do with free trade or globalization.[71] Many of the world's poorest countries have suffered from totalitarian governments, economic policies that destroyed wealth rather than facilitated its creation, endemic corruption, scant protection for property rights, and war. Such factors help explain why countries such as Afghanistan, Cambodia, Cuba, Haiti, Iraq, Libya, Nigeria, Sudan, Vietnam, and Zaire have failed to improve the economic lot of their citizens during recent decades. A complicating factor is the rapidly expanding populations in many of these countries. Without a major change in government, population growth may exacerbate their problems. Promoters of free trade argue that the best way for these countries to improve their lot is to lower their barriers to free trade and investment and to implement economic policies based on free market economics.[72]

Many of the world's poorer nations are being held back by large debt burdens. Of particular concern are the 40 or so "highly indebted poor countries" (HIPCs), which are home to some 700 million people. Among these countries, the average government debt burden has been has high as 85 percent of the value of the economy, as

Even as India makes strides toward economic development, it continues to carry a high budget deficit that cannot meet the needs of its soaring population.

measured by gross domestic product, and the annual costs of serving government debt consumed 15 percent of the country's export earnings.[73] Servicing such a heavy debt load leaves the governments of these countries with little left to invest in important public infrastructure projects, such as education, health care, roads, and power. The result is the HIPCs are trapped in a cycle of poverty and debt that inhibits economic development. Free trade alone, some argue, is a necessary but not sufficient prerequisite to help these countries bootstrap themselves out of poverty. Instead, large-scale debt relief is needed for the world's poorest nations to give them the opportunity to restructure their economies and start the long climb toward prosperity. Supporters of debt relief also argue that new democratic governments in poor nations should not be forced to honor debts that were incurred and mismanaged long ago by their corrupt and dictatorial predecessors.

In the late 1990s, a debt relief movement began to gain ground among the political establishment in the world's richer nations.[74] Fueled by high-profile endorsements from Irish rock star Bono (who has been a tireless and increasingly effective advocate for debt relief), the Dalai Lama, and influential Harvard economist Jeffrey Sachs, the debt relief movement was instrumental in persuading the United States to enact legislation in 2000 that provided $435 million in debt relief for HIPCs.

More important perhaps, the United States also backed an IMF plan to sell some of its gold reserves and use the proceeds to help with debt relief. The IMF and World Bank have now picked up the banner and have embarked on a systematic debt relief program.

For such a program to have a lasting effect, however, debt relief must be matched by wise investment in public projects that boost economic growth (such as education) and by the adoption of economic policies that facilitate investment and trade. The rich nations of the world also can help by reducing barriers to the importation of products from the world's poorer nations, particularly tariffs on imports of agricultural products and textiles. High tariff barriers and other impediments to trade make it difficult for poor countries to export more of their agricultural production. The World Trade Organization has estimated that if the developed nations of the world eradicated subsidies to their agricultural producers and removed tariff barriers to trade in agriculture, this would raise global economic welfare by $128 billion, with $30 billion of that going to developing nations, many of which are highly indebted. The faster growth associated with expanded trade in agriculture could reduce the number of people living in poverty by as much as 13 percent by 2015, according to the WTO.[75]

Managing in the Global Marketplace

International Business
Any firm that engages in international trade or investment.

Much of this book is concerned with the challenges of managing in an international business. An **international business** is any firm that engages in international trade or investment. A firm does not have to become a multinational enterprise, investing directly in operations in other countries, to engage in international business, although multinational enterprises are international businesses. All a firm has to do is export or import products from other countries. As the world shifts toward a truly integrated global economy, more firms, both large and small, are becoming international businesses. What does this shift toward a global economy mean for managers within an international business?

As their organizations increasingly engage in cross-border trade and investment, managers need to recognize that the task of managing an international business differs from that of managing a purely domestic business in many ways. At the most fundamental level, the differences arise from the simple fact that countries are different. Countries differ in their cultures, political systems, economic systems, legal systems, and levels of economic development. Despite all the talk about the emerging global village, and despite the trend toward globalization of markets and production, as we shall see in this book, many of these differences are very profound and enduring.

Differences between countries require that an international business vary its practices country by country. Marketing a product in Brazil may require a different approach from marketing the product in Germany; managing U.S. workers might require different skills than managing Japanese workers; maintaining close relations with a particular level of government may be very important in Mexico and irrelevant in Great Britain; the business strategy pursued in Canada might not work in South Korea; and so on. Managers in an international business must not only be sensitive to these differences, but they must also adopt the appropriate policies and strategies for coping with them. Much of this book is devoted to explaining the sources of these differences and the methods for successfully coping with them.

A further way in which international business differs from domestic business is the greater complexity of managing an international business. In addition to the problems that arise from the differences between countries, a manager in an international business is confronted with a range of other issues that the manager in a domestic business never confronts. The managers of an international business must decide where in the world to site production activities to minimize costs and to maximize value added. They must decide whether it is ethical to adhere to the lower labor and environmental standards found in many less developed nations. Then they must decide how best to coordinate and control globally dispersed production activities (which, as we shall see later in the book, is not a trivial problem). The managers in an international business also must decide which foreign markets to enter and which to avoid. They must choose the appropriate mode for entering a particular foreign country. Is it best to export its product to the foreign country? Should the firm allow a local company to produce its product under license in that country? Should the firm enter into a joint venture with a local firm to produce its product in that country? Or should the firm set up a wholly owned subsidiary to serve the market in that country? As we shall see, the choice of entry mode is critical because it has major implications for the long-term health of the firm.

Conducting business transactions across national borders requires understanding the rules governing the international trading and investment system. Managers in an international business must also deal with government restrictions on international trade and investment. They must find ways to work within the limits imposed by specific governmental interventions. As this book explains, even though many governments are nominally committed to free trade, they often intervene to regulate cross-border trade and investment. Managers within international businesses must develop strategies and policies for dealing with such interventions.

Cross-border transactions also require that money be converted from the firm's home currency into a foreign currency and vice versa. Because currency exchange rates vary in response to changing economic conditions, managers in an international business must develop policies for dealing with exchange rate movements. A firm that adopts a wrong policy can lose large amounts of money, whereas one that adopts the right policy can increase the profitability of its international transactions.

In sum, managing an international business is different from managing a purely domestic business for at least four reasons: (1) countries are different, (2) the range of problems confronted by a manager in an international business is wider and the problems themselves more complex than those confronted by a manager in a domestic business, (3) an international business must find ways to work within the limits imposed by government intervention in the international trade and investment system, and (4) international transactions involve converting money into different currencies.

In this book we examine all these issues in depth, paying close attention to the different strategies and policies that managers pursue to deal with the various challenges created when a firm becomes an international business. Chapters 2 and 3 explore how countries differ from each other with regard to their political, economic, legal, and cultural institutions. Chapter 4 takes a detailed look at the ethical issues that arise in international business. Chapters 5 to 8 look at the international trade and investment environment within which international businesses must operate. Chapters 9 to 10 review the international monetary system. These chapters focus on the nature of the foreign exchange market and the emerging global monetary system. Chapters 11 and 12 explore the strategy of international businesses. Chapters 13 to 16 look at the management of various functional operations within an international business, including production, marketing, and human relations. By the time you complete this book, you should have a good grasp of the issues that managers working within international business have to grapple with on a daily basis, and you should be familiar with the range of strategies and operating policies available to compete more effectively in today's rapidly emerging global economy.

Key Terms

Summary

This chapter sets the scene for the rest of the book. It shows how the world economy is becoming more global and reviews the main drivers of globalization, arguing that they seem to be thrusting nation-states toward a more tightly integrated global economy. We looked at how the nature of international business is changing in response to the changing global economy; we discussed some concerns raised by rapid globalization; and we reviewed implications of rapid globalization for individual managers. The chapter made the following points:

1. Over the past two decades, we have witnessed the globalization of markets and production.

2. The globalization of markets implies that national markets are merging into one huge marketplace. However, it is important not to push this view too far.

3. The globalization of production implies that firms are basing individual productive activities at the optimal world locations for the particular activities. As a consequence, it is increasingly irrelevant to talk about American products, Japanese products, or German products, since these are being replaced by "global" products.

4. Two factors seem to underlie the trend toward globalization: declining trade barriers and changes in communication, information, and transportation technologies.

5. Since the end of World War II, barriers to the free flow of goods, services, and capital have been lowered significantly. More than anything else, this has facilitated the trend toward the globalization of production and has enabled firms to view the world as a single market.

6. As a consequence of the globalization of production and markets, in the past decade world trade has grown faster than world output, foreign direct investment has surged, imports have penetrated more deeply into the world's industrial nations, and competitive pressures have increased in industry after industry.

7. The development of the microprocessor and related developments in communication and information processing technology have helped firms link their worldwide operations into sophisticated information networks. Jet air travel, by shrinking travel time, has also helped to link the worldwide operations of international businesses. These changes have enabled firms to achieve tight coordination of their worldwide operations and to view the world as a single market.

8. In the 1960s, the U.S. economy was dominant in the world, U.S. firms accounted for most of the foreign direct investment in the world economy, U.S. firms dominated the list of large multinationals, and roughly half the world—the centrally planned economies of the Communist world—was closed to Western businesses.

9. By the mid-1990s, the U.S. share of world output had been cut in half, with major shares

now being accounted for by Western European and Southeast Asian economies. The U.S. share of worldwide foreign direct investment had also fallen, by about two-thirds. U.S. multinationals were now facing competition from a large number of Japanese and European multinationals. In addition, the emergence of mini-multinationals was noted.

10. One of the most dramatic developments of the past 20 years has been the collapse of communism in Eastern Europe, which has created enormous long-run opportunities for international businesses. In addition, the move toward free market economies in China and Latin America is creating opportunities (and threats) for Western international businesses.

11. The benefits and costs of the emerging global economy are being hotly debated among businesspeople, economists, and politicians. The debate focuses on the impact of globalization on jobs, wages, the environment, working conditions, and national sovereignty.

12. Managing an international business is different from managing a domestic business for at least four reasons: (a) countries are different, (b) the range of problems confronted by a manager in an international business is wider and the problems themselves more complex than those confronted by a manager in a domestic business, (c) managers in an international business must find ways to work within the limits imposed by governments' intervention in the international trade and investment system, and (d) international transactions involve converting money into different currencies.

Critical Thinking and Discussion Questions

1. Describe the shifts in the world economy over the past 30 years. What are the implications of these shifts for international businesses based in Great Britain? North America? Hong Kong?

2. "The study of international business is fine if you are going to work in a large multinational enterprise, but it has no relevance for individuals who are going to work in small firms." Evaluate this statement.

3. How have changes in technology contributed to the globalization of markets and production? Would the globalization of production and markets have been possible without these technological changes?

4. "Ultimately, the study of international business is no different from the study of domestic business. Thus, there is no point in having a separate course on international business." Evaluate this statement.

5. How do the Internet and the associated World Wide Web affect international business activity and the globalization of the world economy?

6. If current trends continue, China may be the world's largest economy by 2020. Discuss the possible implications of such a development for (a) the world trading system, (b) the world monetary system, (c) the business strategy of today's European and U.S.-based global corporations, and (d) global commodity prices.

7. Reread the Management Focus on Chery Automobile and answer the following questions:

   a. How did Chery begin its international expansion?

   b. Who benefits from the globalization of Chery automobiles? Who are the losers?

   c. What would happen if either Europe or the United States decided to require "Made in Europe" or "Made in the USA" regulations on Chery automobiles? When thinking about the consumer, would this be good or bad?

   d. What does the Chery example teach us about competition in the global automobile arena? What does it tell us about the strategy that enterprises must develop as they seek to compete in global markets?

Use the globalEDGE Resource Desk (http://globalEDGE.msu.edu/resourcedesk/) to complete the following exercises:

Exercise 1

Your company has developed a new product that is expected to achieve high penetration rates in all the countries in which it is introduced, regardless of the average income status of the local population. Considering the costs of the product launch, the management team has decided to initially introduce the product only in countries that have a sizeable population base. Using the *Population Reference Bureau* as a resource, you are required to prepare a preliminary report with the top 10 countries of the world in terms of population size. Since growth opportunities are another major concern, the average population growth rates should be listed for management's consideration.

Exercise 2

The United Nations Conference on Trade and Development (UNCTAD) provides ranking of the largest *transnational corporations* (TNCs) in the world, including a ranking of the 100 largest financial TNCs from developing countries. Identify the largest 25 TNCs listed in the most recent ranking. What countries are these TNCs from? In what industries are they classified? Do you notice any trends in terms of the countries and industries that are represented in the ranking?

closing case

The Globalization of Real Estate

What a paradox! Nothing is more attached to a nation or a region than the land. In fact, it is by its very definition territorially limited. To own the land is to have roots. Yet the forces of globalization have manifested themselves at this most grounded level.

Although land cannot be moved, the management, improvements, and commercialization of that land can be strategically manipulated within a global context. Whether it takes on a commercial or residential aspect, the land on which an improvement occurs is potentially subject to globalization.

In the area of hotel and resort development, consider the Jumeirah Group. Their Web site proclaims they have become a hospitality industry leader by establishing a world-class portfolio of luxury hotels and resorts. Based out of Dubai in the United Arab Emirates, Jumeirah currently has hotels and resorts in Dubai, London, and New York. With expansion plans for the Americas, Asia Pacific, Middle East, and North Africa, Jumeirah is setting itself up to deliver world-class hospitality services in some of the most beautiful places on Earth. In Panama City, Panama, for example, Jumeirah manages Los Faros de Panama, a 400-room luxury hotel and Class A office space. Given its high-end clientele, Jumeirah understands that world-class hotel accommodations require access to world-class medical facilities. To address this concern, adjacent to Los Faros is the Hospital Punta Pacifica, which is affiliated with Johns Hopkins Hospital and Health System in the United States. As an example of a global real estate developer, Jumeirah is quickly acquiring a reputation.

In the area of commercial development and marketing and sales, a global strategy can make even more sense. Consider the real estate arm of PricewaterhouseCoopers (PwC). Normally viewed as one of the world's largest accounting firms, the intricate nature of holding various properties throughout the world has lead PwC to establish a real estate expertise whereby it can provide for its clients risk assessments, market reports, legal/regulatory analysis, tax implications, restructuring advice, and perhaps most importantly people—people who know the lay of the land.

Successful real estate development requires people who know the idiosyncrasies of a particular place in the world. With offices in virtually every major city around the globe and in most countries, PwC has established a network of offices and people to address virtually every real estate concern imaginable.

Many times to know the lay of the land is to live there, or at the very least visit regularly. To that extent, the globalization of residential property is manifested by a need to feel at home. Nowhere is this more exemplified than in the outskirts of Beijing, China.

Many recognize the U.S. TV show *The OC.* The OC stand for Orange County, California. Just outside of Beijing is Orange County, China. In this area, houses are identical replicas of Southern California homes, designed by Southern California architects, with model homes decorated by Los Angeles interior designers. The basement pool tables are American. Even many of the appliances are imported.

The brainchild of Zhang Bo, who lived in Orange County, California, and was influenced by the movie *Field of Dreams,* he proclaimed that "if you build it, they will come" and they did. SinoCEA—a 50–50 joint venture with China's one-party state—got to work. To date it forms part of an expansive faux Southern California zone with "Surf City"—Long Beach with a Disney theme feel. The project has sold out—not by expatriates but by local Chinese. As Weidong Yang, vice president of SinoCEA points out, "Chinese people like the image of the American lifestyle, and we are the only company building homes like this here."

But this is not without controversy. Many have viewed it as a "copy of a copy" or as one German urban-studies professor dubs Orange County, China, the "genius loci of suburbia in the age of global capitalism." By doing so they can experience a bit of Orange County and visit the Forbidden City all before lunch.

Sources: Jumeirah International Web site, www.jumeirah.com, accessed July 16, 2010; PricewaterhouseCoopers Web site, www.pwc.com, accessed July 16, 2010; Daniel Brook, "Welcome to the OC," March 22, 2008, http://www.good.is/post/welcome-to-the-oc/; and Elizabeth Rosenthal, "North of Beijing California Dreams Come True," *The New York Times,* February 3, 2003.

Case Discussion Questions

1. What are the implications of a globalized real estate market?
2. Does this lead to the homogenization of the unique characteristics and qualities of a particular place?
3. What are the cultural implications of setting up "faux residences" in some culturally distinct region? Does or can architecture influence the lifestyle of the inhabitants?
4. On balance, do you think globalization of real estate is a good thing?

part 2   Country Differences

LEARNING OBJECTIVES

After you have read this chapter you should be able to:

1 Understand how the political systems of countries differ.

2 Recognize how the economic systems of countries differ.

3 Understand how the legal systems of countries differ.

4 Explain what determines the level of economic development of a nation.

5 Identify the macro-political and economic changes taking place worldwide.

6 Describe how transition economies are moving toward market-based systems.

7 Explain the implications for management practice of national differences in political economy.

National Differences in Political Economy

Turkey: Model of Equilibrium?

Long considered the crossroads of Europe and Asia, Turkey is described as a democratic, secular, unitary, constitutional republic with an ancient and historical cultural heritage. In reality, however, straddling the Mediterranean and the Black Sea, democracy and authoritarianism, the secular West and the traditional Muslim East Turkey is a multiethnic state seeking to unify by acceding membership into the European Union (EU). With this implicitly contradictory identity, Turkey continues to play a key role within international politics, commerce, and trade. Since 1999, when its candidacy for EU membership was officially declared, Turkey has sought to introduce substantial human rights and economic reforms. The death penalty was abolished, tougher measures were brought in against torture, and the penal code was overhauled.

In the area of Kurdish and women's rights reforms were also made, but many criticized it as not enough. The Kurds are a minority within Turkey, accounting for approximately 20 percent of the population, and have been viewed as the most serious and persistent challenge to the official image of a homogeneous society. Efforts had been made by previous administrations to ban Kurdish language, dress, folklore, and names. Often this has led to discrimination in employment and housing opportunities and has come to be known as the Kurdish issue. Partly in a bid to improve its chances of EU membership, the government began to ease restrictions on the use of the Kurdish language since 2003. As part of a new "Kurdish initiative" launched in 2009, it pledged to extend linguistic and cultural rights and to reduce the military presence in the mainly Kurdish southeast part of the country.

In the area of women's rights, Turkey is similarly at a critical juncture. Women's rights activists have said the reforms do not go far enough and have accused the government of lacking full commitment to equality and acting only under EU pressure. This is of greater concern when Turkish women compared themselves to the other women of Europe who have traditionally had higher levels of equality.

After years of mounting difficulties that brought the country close to economic collapse, a tough recovery program was agreed upon with the International Monetary Fund (IMF) in 2002. Since then, Turkey has seen strong economic growth and a dramatic fall in inflation.

While the rest of Europe may not be willing to embrace Turkey as a full EU member, and as a supplicant of international aid within the financial realm, Turkey may be able to serve as a model to the rest of Europe. Over the past few years, Turkey has significantly reduced governmental costs, has limited credit to high-risk loans, and is even exporting capital. While the West is in the throes of economic crisis, Turkey seems to be weathering the storm, by itself, quite well. This is in part due to the leadership of Prime Minister Recep Tayyip Erdogan.

Not only did he instigate these reforms, Erdogan also saw a 7.3 percent growth rate during his premiership, until the global financial crisis. Under his leadership, further economic and judicial reforms and prospective EU membership are expected to continue boosting foreign direct investment.

As part of his foreign policy seeking accession into the European Union, Erdogan began a drive to demonstrate, as he pointed out, that "Turkey's accession shows that Europe is a continent where civilizations reconcile and not clash." This concerted effort at reconciliation and the improvement at relations have led to increasing volumes of trade with Asian, African, and Middle Eastern countries, as well as with Russia, helping to offset a steep decline with a recessionary Europe.

Contrast this situation with one of the other EU members: Greece. Turkey's booming exports have lowered the country's current account deficit to 2 percent compared with 15 percent for Greece. Despite the Greek government's stated determination to tackle its massive budget deficit by cutting civil service salaries and raising taxes, the market still lacks confidence in a EU bailout. And although economic contraction in Turkey was severe, Turkey's economy, notably its financial system, is proving one of the most resilient in Eurasia. Not one of the country's 49 banks needed a bailout to survive the global downturn. Partly as a result, Turkey is showing signs of a vibrant V-shaped climb out of recession. ●

Sources: BBC News; Country Profile: Turkey, accessed July 18, 2010; Padideh Ala'i, "Turkey: At the Crossroads of Secular West and Traditional East," accessed at http://ssrn.com/abstract=1615682; C. Mellow, "Anatolia Arises," *Institutional Investor-International Edition* 35, no. 3 (2010), pp. 48–81; "Economic Forecast," *Country Report: Turkey* 5 (2010), pp. 8–10; and A. Karatash, "Greek Crisis Highlights Turkey's Strength," *BusinessWeek,* March 26, 2010.

Introduction

International business is much more complicated than domestic business because countries differ in many ways. Countries have different political, economic, and legal systems. Cultural practices can vary dramatically, as can the education and skill level of the population, and countries are at different stages of economic development. All these differences can and do have major implications for the practice of international business. They have a profound impact on the benefits, costs, and risks associated with doing business in different countries; the way in which operations in different countries should be managed; and the strategy international firms should pursue in different countries. A main function of this chapter and the next is to develop an awareness of and appreciation for the significance of country differences in political systems, economic systems, legal systems, and national culture. Another function of the two chapters is to describe how the political, economic, legal, and cultural systems of many of the world's nation-states are evolving and to draw out the implications of these changes for the practice of international business.

The opening case illustrates some of the issues covered in this chapter. Throughout its long history, Turkey has had to negotiate a wide variety of influences from the East as well as the West. At the euphemistic "crossroads" of Europe and Asia, Turkey is in many ways a paradox of potentially contradictory beliefs and identities. Whether cultural or economic, it is seeking to find a balance as a modern secular European state with a traditional Muslim population. Since 1999, when its candidacy for membership in the European Union was officially declared, Turkey has undergone many of the changes necessary as a precondition of that membership. As such, Turkey has implemented a foreign policy of reconciliation that has led to reforms in human rights, increases in trade and commerce, and general economic growth. It is perhaps having to struggle and seek resolution of this paradox that has made Turkey into a potential model for how Europe, and perhaps the world, can begin to find equilibrium as it seeks to balance ever-increasing divergent influences.

More generally, this chapter focuses on how the political, economic, and legal systems of countries differ. Collectively we refer to these systems as constituting the political economy of a country. We use the term **political economy** to stress that the political, economic, and legal systems of a country are interdependent; they interact and influence each other, and in doing so they affect the level of economic well-being. In addition to reviewing these systems, we also explore how differences in political economy influence the benefits, costs, and risks associated with doing business in different countries, and how they affect management practice and strategy. In the next chapter, we will look at how differences in culture influence the practice of international business. As noted, the political economy and culture of a nation are not independent of each other. As will become apparent in Chapter 3, culture can exert an impact on political economy—on political, economic, and legal systems in a nation—and the converse can also hold true.

> **Political Economy**
> The political, economic, and legal systems of a country.

Political Systems

The political system of a country shapes its economic and legal systems.[1] As such, we need to understand the nature of different political systems before discussing economic and legal systems. By **political system** we mean the system of government in a nation. Political systems can be assessed according to two dimensions. The first is the degree to which they emphasize collectivism as opposed to individualism. The second is the degree to which they are democratic or totalitarian. These dimensions are interrelated; systems that emphasize collectivism tend toward totalitarian, whereas those that place a high value on individualism tend to be democratic. However, a large gray area exists in the middle. It is possible to have democratic societies that emphasize a mix of collectivism and individualism. Similarly, it is possible to have totalitarian societies that are not collectivist.

LEARNING OBJECTIVE 1
Understand how the political systems of countries differ.

> **Political System**
> The system of government in a nation.

COLLECTIVISM AND INDIVIDUALISM   **Collectivism** refers to a political system that stresses the primacy of collective goals over individual goals.[2] When collectivism is emphasized, the needs of society as a whole are generally viewed as being

> **Collectivism**
> A political system that emphasizes collective goals over individual goals.

more important than individual freedoms. In such circumstances, an individual's right to do something may be restricted on the grounds that it runs counter to "the good of society" or to "the common good." Advocacy of collectivism can be traced to the ancient Greek philosopher Plato (427–347 BC), who in *The Republic* argued that individual rights should be sacrificed for the good of the majority and that property should be owned in common. Plato did not equate collectivism with equality; he believed that society should be stratified into classes, with those best suited to rule (which for Plato, naturally, were philosophers and soldiers) administering society for the benefit of all. In modern times, the collectivist mantle has been picked up by socialists.

Socialism

Modern **socialism** traces its intellectual roots to Karl Marx (1818–83), although socialist thought clearly predates Marx (elements of it can be traced to Plato). Marx argued that the few benefit at the expense of the many in a capitalist society where individual freedoms are not restricted. While successful capitalists accumulate considerable wealth, Marx postulated that the wages earned by the majority of workers in a capitalist society would be forced down to subsistence levels. He argued that capitalists expropriate for their own use the value created by workers, while paying workers only subsistence wages in return. According to Marx, the pay of workers does not reflect the full value of their labor. To correct this perceived wrong, Marx advocated state ownership of the basic means of production, distribution, and exchange (i.e., businesses). His logic was that if the state owned the means of production, the state could ensure that workers were fully compensated for their labor. Thus, the idea is to manage state-owned enterprise to benefit society as a whole, rather than individual capitalists.[3]

In the early twentieth century, the socialist ideology split into two broad camps. The **communists** believed that socialism could be achieved only through violent revolution and totalitarian dictatorship, whereas the **social democrats** committed themselves to achieving socialism by democratic means, turning their backs on violent revolution and dictatorship. Both versions of socialism waxed and waned during the twentieth century. The communist version of socialism reached its high point in the late 1970s, when the majority of the world's population lived in communist states. The countries under Communist Party rule at that time included the former Soviet Union; its Eastern European client nations (e.g., Poland, Czechoslovakia, Hungary); China; the Southeast Asian nations of Cambodia, Laos, and Vietnam; various African nations (e.g., Angola and Mozambique); and the Latin American nations of Cuba and Nicaragua. By the mid-1990s, however, communism was in retreat worldwide. The Soviet Union had collapsed and had been replaced by a collection of 15 republics, many of which were at least nominally structured as democracies. Communism was swept out of Eastern Europe by the largely bloodless revolutions of 1989. Although China is still nominally a communist state with substantial limits to individual political freedom, in the economic sphere the country has moved sharply away from strict adherence to communist ideology. Other than China, communism hangs on only in a handful of small fringe states, such as North Korea and Cuba.

Social democracy also seems to have passed a high-water mark, although the ideology may prove to be more enduring than communism. Social democracy has had perhaps its greatest influence in a number of democratic Western nations, including Australia, France, Germany, Great Britain, Norway, Spain, and Sweden, where Social Democratic parties have often held political power. Other countries where social democracy has had an important influence include India and Brazil. Consistent with their Marxists roots, many social democratic governments after World War II nationalized private companies in certain industries, transforming them into state-owned enterprises to be run for the "public good rather than private profit." In Great Britain by the end of the 1970s, for example, state-owned companies had a monopoly in the telecommunications, electricity, gas, coal, railway, and shipbuilding industries, as well as substantial interests in the oil, airline, auto, and steel industries.

However, experience demonstrated that state ownership of the means of production ran counter to the public interest. In many countries, state-owned companies performed poorly. Protected from competition by their monopoly position and guaranteed government financial support, many became increasingly inefficient. Individuals paid for the luxury of state ownership through higher prices and higher taxes. As a consequence, a number of Western democracies voted many Social Democratic parties out of office in the late 1970s and early 1980s. They were succeeded by political parties, such as Britain's Conservative Party and Germany's Christian Democratic Party, that were more committed to free market economics. These parties sold state-owned enterprises to private investors (a process referred to as **privatization**). Even where Social Democratic parties regained the levers of power, as in Great Britain in 1997 when the left-leaning Labor Party won control of the government, they too now seem committed to continued private ownership.

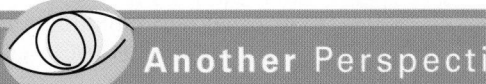

Another Perspective

Kyrgyzstan: The Difficulties of Change

Since its independence in 1991, Kyrgyzstan, the ex-Soviet republic, has been undergoing many of the challenges inherent in transitioning from a collective to an individual system. In 1990, 98 percent of all exports from Kyrgyzstan went to other parts of the Soviet Union. With the final collapse of the Soviet Union, Kyrgyzstan suffered worse than the vast majority of other former Soviet republics. Factories and state farms collapsed with the disappearance of its traditional markets. To a large extent, the integration of central Asian republics into global production networks will depend on the ability of countries such as Kyrgyzstan to integrate into the production networks controlled by multinational corporations. Many times, the transition from collectivism passes through individualism back to a different collectivist association. [M. Myant and J. Drahokoupil, "International Integration and the Structure of Exports in Central Asian Republics," *Eurasian Geography & Economics* 49, no. 5 (2008), pp. 604–622.]

Privatization
The sale of state-owned enterprises to private investors.

Individualism   The opposite of collectivism, **individualism** refers to a philosophy that an individual should have freedom in his or her economic and political pursuits. In contrast to collectivism, individualism stresses that the interests of the individual should take precedence over the interests of the state. Like collectivism, individualism can be traced to an ancient Greek philosopher, in this case Plato's disciple Aristotle (384–322 BC). In contrast to Plato, Aristotle argued that individual diversity and private ownership are desirable. In a passage that might have been taken from a speech by contemporary politicians who adhere to a free market ideology, he argued that private property is more highly productive than communal property and will thus stimulate progress. According to Aristotle, communal property receives little care, whereas property that is owned by an individual will receive the greatest care and therefore be most productive.

Individualism was reborn as an influential political philosophy in the Protestant trading nations of England and the Netherlands during the sixteenth century. The philosophy was refined in the work of a number of British philosophers, including David Hume (1711–76), Adam Smith (1723–90), and John Stuart Mill (1806–73). Individualism exercised a profound influence on those in the American colonies who sought independence from Great Britain. Indeed, the concept underlies the ideas expressed in the Declaration of Independence. In the twentieth century, several Nobel Prize–winning economists, including Milton Friedman, Friedrich von Hayek, and James Buchanan, have championed the philosophy.

Individualism is built on two central tenets. The first is an emphasis on the importance of guaranteeing individual freedom and self-expression. As John Stuart Mill put it,

Individualism
An emphasis on the importance of guaranteeing individual freedom and self-expression.

> The sole end for which mankind are warranted, individually or collectively, in interfering with the liberty of action of any of their number is self-protection. . . .
> The only purpose for which power can be rightfully exercised over any member

of a civilized community, against his will, is to prevent harm to others. His own good, either physical or moral, is not a sufficient warrant. . . . The only part of the conduct of any one, for which he is amenable to society, is that which concerns others. In the part which merely concerns himself, his independence is, of right, absolute. Over himself, over his own body and mind, the individual is sovereign.[4]

The second tenet of individualism is that the welfare of society is best served by letting people pursue their own economic self-interest, as opposed to some collective body (such as government) dictating what is in society's best interest. Or as Adam Smith put it in a famous passage from *The Wealth of Nations*, an individual who intends his own gain is

> led by an invisible hand to promote an end which was no part of his intention. Nor is it always worse for the society that it was no part of it. By pursuing his own interest he frequently promotes that of the society more effectually than when he really intends to promote it. I have never known much good done by those who effect to trade for the public good.[5]

The central message of individualism, therefore, is that individual economic and political freedoms are the ground rules on which a society should be based. This puts individualism in conflict with collectivism. Collectivism asserts the primacy of the collective over the individual; individualism asserts the opposite. This underlying ideological conflict shaped much of the recent history of the world. The Cold War, for example, was in many respects a war between collectivism, championed by the former Soviet Union, and individualism, championed by the United States.

In practical terms, individualism translates into an advocacy for democratic political systems and free market economics, which in general creates a more favorable environment for international businesses to operate in. From the late 1980s until around 2005, the waning of collectivism was matched by the ascendancy of individualism. Democratic ideals and free market economics swept away socialism and communism in many states. The changes of this period went beyond the revolutions in Eastern Europe and the former Soviet Union to include a move toward greater individualism in Latin America and many of the social democratic states of the West (e.g., Great Britain and Sweden). However, from 2005 onward there have been signs of a swing back toward left-leaning socialist ideas in several countries, including several Latin America nations such as Venezuela, Bolivia, and Paraguay, along with Russia. The global financial crisis of 2008–2009 might cause some to reevaluate the trends of the past two decades, and perhaps the pendulum will tilt back the other way for a while.

Democracy
Political system in which government is by the people, exercised either directly or through elected representatives.

Totalitarianism
Form of government in which one person or political party exercises absolute control over all spheres of human life and prohibits opposing political parties.

DEMOCRACY AND TOTALITARIANISM

Democracy and totalitarianism are at different ends of a political dimension. **Democracy** refers to a political system in which government is by the people, exercised either directly or through elected representatives. **Totalitarianism** is a form of government in which one person or political party exercises absolute control over all spheres of human life and prohibits opposing political parties. The democratic–totalitarian dimension is not independent of the collectivism–individualism dimension. Democracy and individualism go hand in hand, as do the communist version of collectivism and totalitarianism. However, gray areas exist; it is possible to have a democratic state in which collective values predominate, and it is possible to have a totalitarian state that is hostile to collectivism and in which some degree of individualism—particularly in the economic sphere—is encouraged. For example, China has seen a move toward greater individual freedom in the

Country FOCUS

The Kingdom of Saudi Arabia

As the largest country in the Middle East, the Kingdom of Saudi Arabia is an Islamic absolute monarchy. The *Basic Law of Government* adopted in 1992 declared that Saudi Arabia is a monarchy ruled by the sons and grandsons of the first king, Abd Al Aziz Al Saud. It also claims the Qu'ran as the constitution of the State and is premised on Islamic law *(Sharia)*. According to the Economist's Democracy Index it ranks as the 9th most authoritarian regime in a ranking of 167 countries. Representing 20 percent of the world's oil reserves and housing the holiest sites in Islam, Saudi Arabia plays a critical role within global politics and commerce and is on the verge of new leadership.

King Abdullah is the present reigning monarch. From this family line, the Abul-Aziz, all successive kings and the majority of government official establish their place within the country. Known as the "Custodian of the Two Holy Mosques" King Abdullah bin Abdul-Aziz acceded to the throne after the death of King Fahd on August 1, 2005. From this position, it should be noted that the King's only codified restraint of power is Islamic law.

Premised on the dictates of the Qu'ran or *fatwas,* and foreign to many in the Western world, the "Kingdom" faces many challenges as a closed society. Much of the criticism that has been levied has focused on its criminal justice system and its treatment of women. In this regard, Saudi Arabia remains very conservative. Under *Sharia,* capital punishment or corporal punishment, including amputations of hands and feet for certain crimes such as murder, robbery, rape, drug smuggling, homosexual activity, and adultery, is permissible. Women do not have the same status as men. In fact, Saudi Arabia is the only country in the world where women are banned from driving on public roads. In many ways they are treated as second-class citizens. The freedom of women is seriously restricted inside Saudi Arabia. For example, in addition to restrictions on driving, women are not allowed to travel without the permission of their closest male relative. According to *Sharia,* women who are divorced are required to return to their father's house where he in turn has final word as to their mobility. This at times had lead to convoluted reasoning where the relationship may be established by blood or breast-milk. This has led recently to women suggesting that they could give breast-milk to the chofers so as to comply with the fatwas.

Yet the trend has been toward a gradual loosening of strictures and opening of minds, although literacy is gender biased. The literacy rate for males is substantially higher at 84.7 percent in comparison with the 70.8 percent for females. In the past five years alone, new government programs have sent close to 200,000 Saudi students overseas, more than were sent in the previous 20 years.

As Saudi Arabia becomes more integrated into the global economy through its membership in the World Trade Organization, and as the country remains in the black due to continued high levels of oil revenue, more national companies are likely to expand internationally and would in turn subject themselves to external competition. Both of these factors have increased the pressure for higher standards of corporate governance and accountability.

As a way of reaching out, Saudi Arabia is planning four Economic Cities in order to spur technology transfers, develop the Kingdom's infrastructure, and facilitate foreign investment: King Abdullah Economic City in Rabigh, Prince Abdul Aziz bin Musaed Economic City in Hail, the Knowledge Economic City in Madinah, and Jizan Economic City in Jizan. SAGIA (Saudi Arabian General Investment Authority) expects these cities to attract $80 billion (SR300 billion) in investments and contribute $150 billion (SR562 billion) to the country's gross domestic product (GDP) by 2020. The hope is that the new cities will go far in spreading wealth around the country, rather than concentrating it in Riyadh, Jeddah, and Medina.

How this will be carried out actually falls in the hands of the Crowned Prince; however, the Crowned Prince Sultan is only one year younger than the 86-year-old King Abdullah and is in bad health. That is, the line of succession is not clear. Many suspect that the next in line will be Prince Nayef, one of the Sultan's half brothers, a conservative minister who has not traveled extensively and is generally not well received by those who seek to modernize the Kingdom.

What will happen is anyone's guess. Although most princes do not want to be king, there are a few that do. Of these, Nayef's 73-year-old full brother, Salman, the governor of Riyadh, and Prince Muqrin, aged 64, a former fighter pilot who is now head of intelligence, are among the top contenders. But, there are a growing number of Saudis who resent having no say in such matters. Many are calling for the transformation of the Kingdom to a constitutional monarchy. This is pitting the hard-core fundamentalists against the Western-educated liberals. As long as the oil revenues continue, Saudi society can expect to continue a privileged lifestyle, especially for the men.

Sources: *The Economist,* Democracy Index, http://www.economist.com/media/pdf/democracy_index_2007_v3.pdf; "Saudi Arabia: Political Structure," *EIU ViewsWire,* 2010; J. Gorvett, "Saudi Arabia Aims High," *Middle East 399* (2009), pp. 42–45; A. Hossain, "What's Up Saudi? The Kingdom Insists on Keeping Women in the Stone Age," June 24, 2010, http://www.huffingtonpost.com/anushay-hossain/whats-up-saudi-the-kingdo_b_624262.html; and "When Kings and Princes Grow Old," *The Economist,* July 15, 2010, http://www.economist.com/node/16588422?story_id=16588422.

economic sphere, but the country is still ruled by a totalitarian dictatorship that constrains political freedom.

Democracy
The pure form of democracy, as originally practiced by several city-states in ancient Greece, is based on a belief that citizens should be directly involved in decision making. In complex, advanced societies with populations in the tens or hundreds of millions this is impractical. Most modern democratic states practice **representative democracy.** In a representative democracy, citizens periodically elect individuals to represent them. These elected representatives then form a government, whose function is to make decisions on behalf of the electorate. In a representative democracy, elected representatives who fail to perform this job adequately will be voted out of office at the next election.

To guarantee that elected representatives can be held accountable for their actions by the electorate, an ideal representative democracy has a number of safeguards that are typically enshrined in constitutional law. These include (1) an individual's right to freedom of expression, opinion, and organization; (2) a free media; (3) regular elections in which all eligible citizens are allowed to vote; (4) universal adult suffrage; (5) limited terms for elected representatives; (6) a fair court system that is independent from the political system; (7) a nonpolitical state bureaucracy; (8) a nonpolitical police force and armed service; and (9) relatively free access to state information.[6]

Totalitarianism
In a totalitarian country, all the constitutional guarantees on which representative democracies are built—an individual's right to freedom of expression and organization, a free media, and regular elections—are denied to the citizens. In most totalitarian states, political repression is widespread, free and fair elections are lacking, media are heavily censored, basic civil liberties are denied, and those who question the right of the rulers to rule find themselves imprisoned, or worse.

Four major forms of totalitarianism exist in the world today. Until recently, the most widespread was **communist totalitarianism.** Communism, however, is in decline worldwide, and most of the Communist Party dictatorships have collapsed since 1989. Exceptions to this trend (so far) are China, Vietnam, Laos, North Korea, and Cuba, although most of these states exhibit clear signs that the Communist Party's monopoly on political power is retreating. In many respects, the governments of China, Vietnam, and Laos are communist in name only since those nations now adhere to market-based economic reforms. They remain, however, totalitarian states that deny many basic civil liberties to their populations. On the other hand, there are signs of a swing back toward communist totalitarian ideas in some states, such as Venezuela where the government of Hugo Chavez is starting to display totalitarian tendencies.

A second form of totalitarianism might be labeled **theocratic totalitarianism.** Theocratic totalitarianism is found in states where political power is monopolized by a party, group, or individual that governs according to religious principles. The most common form of theocratic totalitarianism is based on Islam and is exemplified by states such as Iran and Saudi Arabia. These states limit freedom of political and religious expression with laws based on Islamic principles (see the Country Focus).

A third form of totalitarianism might be referred to as **tribal totalitarianism.** Tribal totalitarianism has arisen from time to time in African countries such as Zimbabwe, Tanzania, Uganda, and Kenya. The borders of most African states reflect the administrative boundaries drawn by the old European colonial powers rather than tribal realities. Consequently, the typical African country contains a number of tribes. Tribal totalitarianism occurs when a political party that represents the interests of a particular tribe (and not always the majority tribe) monopolizes power. Such one-party states still exist in Africa.

Communist totalitarianism is still the political system in Vietnam, where red banners in the Hanoi marketplace remind citizens and visitors of the government's control.

A fourth major form of totalitarianism might be described as **right-wing totalitarianism.** Right-wing totalitarianism generally permits some individual economic freedom but restricts individual political freedom, frequently on the grounds that it would lead to the rise of communism. A common feature of many right-wing dictatorships is an overt hostility to socialist or communist ideas. Many right-wing totalitarian governments are backed by the military, and in some cases the government may be made up of military officers. The fascist regimes that ruled Germany and Italy in the 1930s and 1940s were right-wing totalitarian states. Until the early 1980s, right-wing dictatorships, many of which were military dictatorships, were common throughout Latin America. They were also found in several Asian countries, particularly South Korea, Taiwan, Singapore, Indonesia, and the Philippines. Since the early 1980s, however, this form of government has been in retreat. Most Latin American countries are now genuine multiparty democracies. Similarly, South Korea, Taiwan, and the Philippines have all become functioning democracies, as has Indonesia.

Right-Wing Totalitarianism
A political system in which political power is monopolized by a party, group, or individual that generally permits individual economic freedom but restricts individual political freedom, including free speech, frequently on the grounds that it would lead to the rise of communism.

Economic Systems

It should be clear from the previous section that political ideology and economic systems are connected. In countries where individual goals are given primacy over collective goals, we are more likely to find free market economic systems. In contrast, in countries where collective goals are given preeminence, the state may have taken control over many enterprises; markets in such countries are likely to be restricted rather than free. We can identify three broad types of economic systems—a market economy, a command economy, and a mixed economy.

LEARNING OBJECTIVE 2
Recognize how the economic systems of countries differ.

MARKET ECONOMY In a pure **market economy,** all productive activities are privately owned, as opposed to being owned by the state. The goods and services that a country produces are not planned by anyone. Production is determined by the interaction of supply and demand and signaled to producers through the price system. If demand for a product exceeds supply, prices will rise, signaling producers to produce more. If supply exceeds demand, prices will fall, signaling producers to produce less. In

Market Economy
An economic system in which the interaction of supply and demand determines the quantity in which goods and services are produced.

this system consumers are sovereign. The purchasing patterns of consumers, as signaled to producers through the mechanism of the price system, determine what is produced and in what quantity.

For a market to work in this manner, supply must not be restricted. A supply restriction occurs when a single firm monopolizes a market. In such circumstances, rather than increase output in response to increased demand, a monopolist might restrict output and let prices rise. This allows the monopolist to take a greater profit margin on each unit it sells. Although this is good for the monopolist, it is bad for the consumer, who has to pay higher prices. It also is probably bad for the welfare of society. Since a monopolist has no competitors, it has no incentive to search for ways to lower production costs. Rather, it can simply pass on cost increases to consumers in the form of higher prices. The net result is that the monopolist is likely to become increasingly inefficient, producing high-priced, low-quality goods, and society suffers as a consequence.

Given the dangers inherent in monopoly, the role of government in a market economy is to encourage vigorous free and fair competition between private producers. Governments do this by outlawing monopolies and restrictive business practices designed to monopolize a market (antitrust laws serve this function in the United States). Private ownership also encourages vigorous competition and economic efficiency. Private ownership ensures that entrepreneurs have a right to the profits generated by their own efforts. This gives entrepreneurs an incentive to search for better ways of serving consumer needs. That may be through introducing new products, by developing more efficient production processes, by pursuing better marketing and after-sale service, or simply through managing their businesses more efficiently than their competitors. In turn, the constant improvement in product and process that results from such an incentive has been argued to have a major positive impact on economic growth and development.[7]

Command Economy

An economic system in which the government plans the goods and services that a country produces, the quantity in which they are produced, and the prices at which they are sold.

COMMAND ECONOMY   In a pure **command economy,** the government plans the goods and services that a country produces, the quantity in which they are produced, and the prices at which they are sold. Consistent with the collectivist ideology, the objective of a command economy is for government to allocate resources for "the good of society." In addition, in a pure command economy, all businesses are state owned, the rationale being that the government can then direct them to make investments that are in the best interests of the nation as a whole rather than in the interests of private individuals. Historically, command economies were found in Communist countries where collectivist goals were given priority over individual goals. Since the demise of communism in the late 1980s, the number of command economies has fallen dramatically. Some elements of a command economy were also evident in a number of democratic nations led by socialist-inclined governments. France and India both experimented with extensive government planning and state ownership, although government planning has fallen into disfavor in both countries.

While the objective of a command economy is to mobilize economic resources for the public good, the opposite seems to have occurred. In a command economy, state-owned enterprises have little incentive to control costs and be efficient, because they cannot go out of business. Also, the abolition of private ownership means there is no incentive for individuals to look for better ways serve consumer needs; hence, dynamism and innovation are absent from command economies. Instead of growing and becoming more prosperous, such economies tend to stagnate.

MIXED ECONOMY   Between market economies and command economies can be found mixed economies. In a mixed economy, certain sectors of the economy are left to private ownership and free market mechanisms while other sectors have significant state ownership and government planning. Mixed economies were once common throughout much of the world, although they are becoming much less so. Until the 1980s, Great Britain, France, and Sweden were mixed economies, but extensive privatization has reduced state ownership of businesses in all three nations. A similar trend occurred in many other countries where there was once a large state sector, such as Brazil, Italy, and India (in India, however, the state sector remains large, still accounting for 38 percent of nonfarm output).

In mixed economies, governments also tend to take into state ownership troubled firms whose continued operation is thought to be vital to national interests. Consider, for example, the French automobile company Renault. The government took over the company when it ran into serious financial problems. The French government reasoned that the social costs of the unemployment that might result if Renault collapsed were unacceptable, so it nationalized the company to save it from bankruptcy. Renault's competitors weren't thrilled by this move because they had to compete with a company whose costs were subsidized by the state. Similarly, in 2008 and early 2009, the U.S. government took an 80 percent stake in AIG to stop that financial institution from collapsing, the theory being that if AIG did collapse, it would have very serious consequences for the entire financial system. The government of the United States usually prefers market-oriented solutions to economic problems, and in the AIG case the intention is to sell the institution back to private investors as soon as possible. The government also took similar action with respect to a number of other financial institutions, including Citigroup, and General Motors. In all of these cases, the government stake was seen as nothing more than a short-term action designed to stave of economic collapse by injecting capital into troubled enterprises, and as soon as it has been able to, the government has sold these stakes (in early 2010, for example, it sold its stake in Citigroup—for a profit).

Legal Systems

The **legal system** of a country refers to the rules, or laws, that regulate behavior along with the processes by which the laws are enforced and through which redress for grievances is obtained. The legal system of a country is of immense importance to international business. A country's laws regulate business practice, define the manner in which business transactions are to be executed, and set down the rights and obligations of those involved in business transactions. The legal environments of countries differ in significant ways. As we shall see, differences in legal systems can affect the attractiveness of a country as an investment site or market.

Like the economic system of a country, the legal system is influenced by the prevailing political system (although it is also strongly influenced by historical tradition). The government of a country defines the legal framework within which firms do business—and often the laws that regulate business reflect the rulers' dominant political ideology. For example, collectivist-inclined totalitarian states tend to enact laws that severely restrict private enterprise, whereas the laws enacted by governments in democratic states where individualism is the dominant political philosophy tend to be pro-private enterprise and pro-consumer.

Here we focus on several issues that illustrate how legal systems can vary—and how such variations can affect international business. First, we look at some basic differences in legal systems. Next we look at contract law. Third, we look at the laws governing property rights with particular reference to patents, copyrights, and trademarks. Then we discuss protection of intellectual property. Finally, we look at laws covering product safety and product liability.

DIFFERENT LEGAL SYSTEMS   There are three main types of legal systems— or legal tradition—in use around the world: common law, civil law, and theocratic law.

LEARNING OBJECTIVE 3
Understand how the legal systems of countries differ.

Legal System
System of rules that regulate behavior and the processes by which the laws are enforced and through which redress of grievances is obtained.

Common Law

Common law
A system of law based on tradition, precedent, and custom.

The common law system evolved in England over hundreds of years. It is now found in most of Great Britain's former colonies, including the United States. **Common law** is based on tradition, precedent, and custom. *Tradition* refers to a country's legal history, *precedent* to cases that have come before the courts in the past, and *custom* to the ways in which laws are applied in specific situations. When law courts interpret common law, they do so with regard to these characteristics. This gives a common law system a degree of flexibility that other systems lack. Judges in a common law system have the power to interpret the law so that it applies to the unique circumstances of an individual case. In turn, each new interpretation sets a precedent that may be followed in future cases. As new precedents arise, laws may be altered, clarified, or amended to deal with new situations.

Civil Law

Civil Law System
A system of law based on a detailed set of written laws and codes.

A **civil law system** is based on a detailed set of laws organized into codes. When law courts interpret civil law, they do so with regard to these codes. More than 80 countries, including Germany, France, Japan, and Russia, operate with a civil law system. A civil law system tends to be less adversarial than a common law system, since the judges rely upon detailed legal codes rather than interpreting tradition, precedent, and custom. Judges under a civil law system have less flexibility than those under a common law system. Judges in a common law system have the power to interpret the law, whereas judges in a civil law system have the power only to apply the law.

Theocratic Law

Theocratic Law System
A system of law based on religious teachings.

A **theocratic law system** is one in which the law is based on religious teachings. Islamic law is the most widely practiced theocratic legal system in the modern world, although usage of both Hindu and Jewish law persisted into the twentieth century. Islamic law is primarily a moral rather than a commercial law and is intended to govern all aspects of life.[8] The foundation for Islamic law is the holy book of Islam, the Koran, along with the Sunnah, or decisions and sayings of the Prophet Muhammad, and the writings of Islamic scholars who have derived rules by analogy from the principles established in the Koran and the Sunnah. Because the Koran and Sunnah are holy documents, the basic foundations of Islamic law cannot be changed. However, in practice Islamic jurists and scholars are constantly debating the application of Islamic law to the modern world. In reality, many Muslim countries have legal systems that are a blend of Islamic law and a common or civil law system.

Although Islamic law is primarily concerned with moral behavior, it has been extended to cover certain commercial activities. An example is the payment or receipt of interest, which is considered usury and outlawed by the Koran. To the devout Muslim, acceptance of interest payments is seen as a grave sin; the giver and the taker are equally damned. This is not just a matter of theology; in several Islamic states it has also become a matter of law. In the 1990s, for example, Pakistan's Federal Shariat Court, the highest Islamic lawmaking body in the country, pronounced interest to be un-Islamic and therefore illegal and demanded that the government amend all financial laws accordingly. In 1999, Pakistan's Supreme Court ruled that Islamic banking methods should be used in the country after July 1, 2001.[9] By 2008, some 500 Islamic financial institutions in the world collectively managed more than $500 billion in assets. In addition to Pakistan, Islamic financial institutions are found in many of the Gulf states, Egypt, and Malaysia.[10]

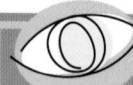

Another Perspective

Sharia Compliance — Islamic Banking

In the world of international finance, Islamic Law *(Sharia)* is playing a most interesting role. Flush with oil revenues, Arab states are using their wealth to drive financial transactions worldwide. In a system where interest *(riba* in Arabic) is not permitted, Western banks are being forced to comply with Islamic banking rules if they seek to participate in the growing number of transactions that Arab states are creating. As an example, remember the Country Focus on Saudi Arabia and the development of its Economic Cities? This is requiring a shift in the traditional conceptualization of risk. Under *Sharia,* banks are now required to share the risk. See Chapter 3 for more on this point.

DIFFERENCES IN CONTRACT LAW

The difference between common law and civil law systems can be illustrated by the approach of each to contract law (remember, most theocratic legal systems also have elements of common or civil law). A **contract** is a document that specifies the conditions under which an exchange is to occur and details the rights and obligations of the parties involved. Some form of contract regulates many business transactions. **Contract law** is the body of law that governs contract enforcement. The parties to an agreement normally resort to contract law when one party feels the other has violated either the letter or the spirit of an agreement.

Because common law tends to be relatively ill specified, contracts drafted under a common law framework tend to be very detailed with all contingencies spelled out. In civil law systems, however, contracts tend to be much shorter and less specific because many of the issues are already covered in a civil code. Thus, it is more expensive to draw up contracts in a common law jurisdiction, and resolving contract disputes can be very adversarial in common law systems. But common law systems have the advantage of greater flexibility and allow for judges to interpret a contract dispute in light of the prevailing situation. International businesses need to be sensitive to these differences; approaching a contract dispute in a state with a civil law system as if it had a common law system may backfire, and vice versa.

When contract disputes arise in international trade, there is always the question of which country's laws to apply. To resolve this issue, a number of countries, including the United States, have ratified the **United Nations Convention on Contracts for the International Sale of Goods (CIGS).** The CIGS establishes a uniform set of rules governing certain aspects of the making and performance of everyday commercial contracts between sellers and buyers who have their places of business in different nations. By adopting the CIGS, a nation signals to other adopters that it will treat the convention's rules as part of its law. The CIGS applies automatically to all contracts for the sale of goods between different firms based in countries that have ratified the convention, unless the parties to the contract explicitly opt out. One problem with the CIGS, however, is that fewer than 70 nations have ratified the convention (the CIGS went into effect in 1988).[11] Many of the world's larger trading nations, including Japan and the United Kingdom, have not ratified the CIGS.

When firms do not wish to accept the CIGS, they often opt for arbitration by a recognized arbitration court to settle contract disputes. The most well known of these courts is the International Court of Arbitration of the International Chamber of Commerce in Paris which handles more than 500 requests per year for arbitration typically from over 100 countries.[12]

PROPERTY RIGHTS AND CORRUPTION

In a legal sense, the term *property* refers to a resource over which an individual or business holds a legal title; that is, a resource that it owns. Resources include land, buildings, equipment, capital, mineral rights, businesses, and intellectual property (ideas, which are protected by patents, copyrights, and trademarks). **Property rights** refer to the legal rights over the use to which a resource is put and over the use made of any income that may be derived from that resource.[13] Countries differ in the extent to which their legal systems define and protect property rights. Almost all countries now have laws on their books that protect property rights. Even China, still nominally a Communist state despite its booming market economy, finally enacted a law to protect the rights of private property holders in 2007 (the law gives individuals the same legal protection for their property as the state).[14] However, in many countries these laws are not enforced by the authorities and property rights are violated. Property rights can be violated in two ways—through private action and through public action.

Contract
A document that specifies the conditions under which an exchange is to occur and details the rights and obligations of the parties involved.

Contract Law
The body of law that governs contract enforcement.

United Nations Convention on Contracts for the International Sale of Goods (CIGS)
A set of rules governing certain aspects of the making and performance of commercial contracts between sellers and buyers who have their places of business in different nations.

Property Rights
The bundle of legal rights over the use to which a resource is put and over the use made of any income that may be derived from that resource.

Private Action

In this context, **private action** refers to theft, piracy, blackmail, and the like by private individuals or groups. Although theft occurs in all countries, a weak legal system allows for a much higher level of criminal action in some than in others. For example, in Russia in the chaotic period following the collapse of communism, an outdated legal system, coupled with a weak police force and judicial system, offered both domestic and foreign businesses scant protection from blackmail by the "Russian Mafia." Successful business owners in Russia often had to pay "protection money" to the Mafia or face violent retribution, including bombings and assassinations (about 500 contract killings of businessmen occurred in 1995 and again in 1996).[15]

Russia is not alone in having Mafia problems (and the situation in Russia has improved significantly since the mid-1990s). The Mafia has a long history in the United States (Chicago in the 1930s was similar to Moscow in the 1990s). In Japan, the local version of the Mafia, known as the *yakuza*, runs protection rackets, particularly in the food and entertainment industries.[16] However, there was a big difference between the magnitude of such activity in Russia in the 1990s and its limited impact in Japan and the United States. This difference arose because the legal enforcement apparatus, such as the police and court system, was so weak in Russia following the collapse of communism. Many other countries from time to time have had problems similar to or even greater than those experienced by Russia.

Public Action and Corruption

Public action to violate property rights occurs when public officials, such as politicians and government bureaucrats, extort income, resources, or the property itself from property holders. This can be done through legal mechanisms such as levying excessive taxation, requiring expensive licenses or permits from property holders, taking assets into state ownership without compensating the owners, or redistributing assets without compensating the prior owners. It can also be done through illegal means, or corruption, by demanding bribes from businesses in return for the rights to operate in a country, industry, or location.[17]

Corruption has been well documented in every society, from the banks of the Congo River to the palace of the Dutch royal family, from Japanese politicians to Brazilian bankers, and from Indonesian government officials to the New York City Police Department. The government of the late Ferdinand Marcos in the Philippines was famous for demanding bribes from foreign businesses wishing to set up operations in that country.[18] The same was true of government officials in Indonesia under the rule of former president Suharto. No society is immune to corruption. However, there are systematic differences in the extent of corruption. In some countries, the rule of law minimizes corruption. Corruption is seen and treated as illegal, and when discovered, violators are punished by the full force of the law. In other countries, the rule of law is weak and corruption by bureaucrats and politicians is rife. Corruption is so endemic in some countries that politicians and bureaucrats regard it as a perk of office and openly flout laws against corruption.

According to Transparency International, an independent nonprofit organization dedicated to exposing and fighting corruption, businesses and individuals spend some $400 billion a year worldwide on bribes related to government procurement contracts alone.[19] Transparency International has also measured the level of corruption among public officials in different countries.[20] As can be seen in Figure 2.1, the organization rated countries such as Finland and New Zealand as clean; it rated others, such as Russia, India, and Indonesia as corrupt. Somalia ranked last out of all 180 countries in the survey (the country is often described as a "failed state").

Economic evidence suggests that high levels of corruption significantly reduce the foreign direct investment, level of international trade, and economic growth rate in a country.[21] By siphoning off profits, corrupt politicians and bureaucrats reduce the returns to business investment and, hence, reduce the incentive of both domestic and

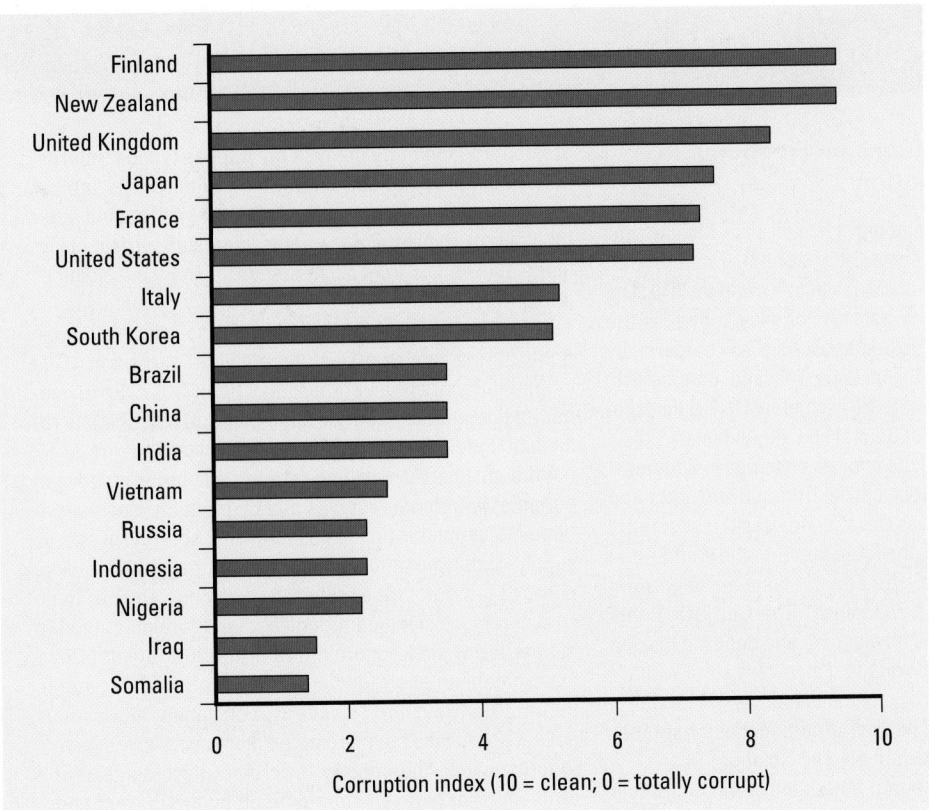

2.1 figure

Ranking of Corruption by Country, 2009

Source: Constructed by the author from raw data in Transparency International, *Global Corruption Report, 2009.*

foreign businesses to invest in that country. The lower level of investment that results hurts economic growth. Thus, we would expect countries such as Indonesia, Nigeria, and Russia to have a much lower rate of economic growth than might otherwise have been the case. A detailed example of the negative effect that corruption can have on economic progress is given in the accompanying Country Focus, which looks at the impact of corruption on economic growth in Myanmar.

Foreign Corrupt Practices Act   In the 1970s, the United States passed the **Foreign Corrupt Practices Act** following revelations that U.S. companies had bribed government officials in foreign countries in an attempt to win lucrative contracts. This law makes it illegal to bribe a foreign government official to obtain or maintain business over which that foreign official has authority, and it requires all publicly traded companies (whether or not they are involved in international trade) to keep detailed records that would reveal whether a violation of the act has occurred. Along the same lines, in 1997 trade and finance ministers from the member states of the Organization for Economic Cooperation and Development (OECD), an association of the world's 30 most powerful economies, adopted the Convention on Combating Bribery of Foreign Public Officials in International Business Transactions.[22] The convention obliges member states to make the bribery of foreign public officials a criminal offense.

However, both the U.S. law and OECD convention include language that allows for exceptions known as facilitating or expediting payments (also called *grease payments* or *speed money*), the purpose of which is to expedite or to secure the performance of a routine governmental action.[23] For example, they allow for small payments made to speed up the issuance of permits or licenses, process paperwork, or just get vegetables off the dock and on their way to market. The explanation for this exception to general

Foreign Corrupt Practices Act
U.S. law regulating behavior regarding the conduct of international business in the taking of bribes and other unethical actions.

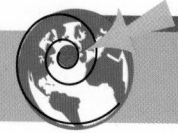

Myanmar—Restrictions on Freedoms, Poverty, and Corruption

Also known as Burma, as though it had an alias, Myanmar is, according to Transparency International, ranked third among the most corrupt countries in the world in 2010. The Union of Myanmar, as the name is formally known, is the largest country in mainland Southeast Asia. It is bordered by the People's Republic of China, Laos, Thailand, Bangladesh, and India. It has more than 1, 930 kilometers (1,1990 miles) of coastline facing the Bay of Bengal and the Andaman Sea.

Myanmar is also one of the poorest countries in Southeast Asia, but this was not always true. During British rule and administration, Burma was the second-wealthiest country in Southeast Asia. It was the "rice bowl" to the world—the largest producer of rice. The country was considered on the "fast-track" toward development. Then, in 1948, Prime Minister U Nu centralized all planning and decision making and attempted to make Burma into a welfare state with disastrous consequences. Almost immediately, rice exports collapsed. Since then it has suffered decades of stagnation, mismanagement, corruption, and isolation.

As seem to be the case throughout the world, there is a direct correlation among personal freedoms, poverty, and corruption. Although passing efforts have been made to bring about reform, governmental clampdowns, poverty, and corruption are still ubiquitous. The Union of Myanmar is ruled by the State Peace and Development Council (SPDC). This military government is the de facto government of the country. Myanmar's human rights record is dismally appalling and appears to have worsened in recent years. Many of the human rights abuses have been linked to the SPDC and other paramilitary groups. Citizens do not have the right to change their government. The military government controls virtually all aspects of life, at times forcibly, including the freedoms of speech, press, assembly, association, movement, and religion. Privacy rights are subjective. Security forces—"military intelligence"—are known to monitor the personal conversations and movements of private citizens. Incidents of forcible relocation without just cause or just compensation for land or property have little or no legal recourse.

Although many religions are practiced in Burma, the majority of the population is Buddhist. Discrimination against Muslims, Christians, and other religious and ethnic minorities appears to be almost sanctioned by the government. In particular, the government tightly controls the nation's Muslim population. Ethnic armed groups, such as the Karen National Union (KNU), the Karenni National Progressive Party (KNPP), and the Shan State Army–South (SSA), also commit human rights abuses in various regions.

Many killings, rapes, forced labor conditions, and the conscription of child soldiers have been reported throughout the country and particularly in the capital Yangon. International human rights and charitable organizations are severely restricted. If they are able to obtain visas and enter the country, they often face harassment and threats of violence many times from plain-clothed "military intelligence" and governmental authorities. The country continues to fail to comply with many of the international arena's human rights norms and laws. One of the major figures who have helped to raise the awareness has been Nobel Prize winner and democracy activist Aung San Suu Kyi. She has remained under house arrest 14 out of the last 20 years.

Although blessed with huge energy resources in terms of potential petroleum reserves and hydroelectric power potential, Myanmar is facing an increasing shortfall in energy supply. Simply put, the country does not have the requisite energy infrastructure to satisfy its growing demand. To do so will require significant domestic and foreign capital to initiate large-scale energy infrastructure projects. However, obtaining such funding is extremely difficult due to the fact that Myanmar's poverty, corruption, and serious political problems have prompted most overseas investors to look beyond the country for project development. The problem is made even more difficult by the current sanctions being levied on Burma by the United States.

One of the few glimmering hopes continues to be rice. The hope is to reestablish a vibrant rice industry that can underpin broader economic growth, as it has in Thailand and Vietnam, the world's largest rice exporters. But few buyers are willing to purchase Burmese rice, which is grown from low-quality seeds, stored in insect-infested silos, and milled in rusted factories. To turn this around will require significant investment in agricultural infrastructure. Few are willing to do so under the current conditions.

Thus a vicious cycle has been created. The two areas of potential development, energy and agriculture, will require increased foreign investment, which is not forthcoming quickly enough because of the endemic corruption and U.S. economic sanctions. While the SPDC leadership under Than Shwe appears intent on boosting agricultural development, it is unlikely that they will order a sharp crackdown on corruption as it would risk aggravating internal splits within the regime and the army. As it presently stands, the outlook continues to look difficult at best.

Sources: "Belt, Braces and Army Boots," *The Economist,* March 11, 2010, p. 46; Burma (Myanmar) Needs to Fill Its Rice Bowl," *Christian Science Monitor,* July 6, 2010; "What Stigma? Burma (Myanmar) Draws Energy-Hungry Neighbors," *Christian Science Monitor,* July 2, 2010; "Corruption Key Threat to Agricultural Reform," *Asia Monitor: South East Asia Monitor* 1, no. 21.2 (2010), pp. 1–7; "Lost Hope: Once Glittering, Yangon Is Now a Ramshackle City of Fear; Despair and Neglect in Myanmar's Old Capital; Locals See Spies on Every Corner," *The Wall Street Journal* (Eastern Edition), June 21, 2008; D. L. Steinberg, *Burma: The State of Myanmar* (Washington DC: Georgetown University Press, 2002); and "Myanmar Faces Energy Crisis Despite Potential," *Oil & Gas Journal* 97, no. 35 (August 31, 1999), p. 42.

antibribery provisions is that while grease payments are, technically, bribes, they are distinguishable from (and, apparently, less offensive than) bribes used to obtain or maintain business, because they merely facilitate performance of duties that the recipients are already obligated to perform.

THE PROTECTION OF INTELLECTUAL PROPERTY

Intellectual property refers to property that is the product of intellectual activity, such as computer software, a screenplay, a music score, or the chemical formula for a new drug. Patents, copyrights, and trademarks establish ownership rights over intellectual property. A **patent** grants the inventor of a new product or process exclusive rights for a defined period to the manufacture, use, or sale of that invention. **Copyrights** are the exclusive legal rights of authors, composers, playwrights, artists, and publishers to publish and disperse their work as they see fit. **Trademarks** are designs and names, often officially registered, by which merchants or manufacturers designate and differentiate their products (e.g., Christian Dior clothes). In the high-technology "knowledge" economy of the twenty-first century, intellectual property has become an increasingly important source of economic value for businesses. Protecting intellectual property has also become increasingly problematic, particularly if it can be rendered in a digital form and then copied and distributed at very low cost via pirated CDs or over the Internet (e.g., computer software, music and video recordings).[24]

The philosophy behind intellectual property laws is to reward the originator of a new invention, book, musical record, clothes design, restaurant chain, and the like, for his or her idea and effort. Such laws stimulate innovation and creative work. They provide an incentive for people to search for novel ways of doing things, and they reward creativity. For example, consider innovation in the pharmaceutical industry. A patent will grant the inventor of a new drug a 20-year monopoly in production of that drug. This gives pharmaceutical firms an incentive to undertake the expensive, difficult, and time-consuming basic research required to generate new drugs (it can cost $800 million in R&D and take 12 years to get a new drug on the market). Without the guarantees provided by patents, companies would be unlikely to commit themselves to extensive basic research.[25]

The protection of intellectual property rights differs greatly from country to country. Although many countries have stringent intellectual property regulations on their books, the enforcement of these regulations has often been lax. This has been the case even among many of the 183 countries that are now members of the **World Intellectual Property Organization,** all of which have signed international treaties designed to protect intellectual property, including the oldest such treaty, the **Paris Convention for the Protection of Industrial Property,** which dates to 1883 and has been signed by some 170 nations. Weak enforcement encourages the piracy (theft) of intellectual property. China and Thailand have recently been among the worst offenders in Asia. Pirated computer software is widely available in China. Similarly, the streets of Bangkok, Thailand's capital, are lined with stands selling pirated copies of Rolex watches, Levi Strauss jeans, videotapes, and computer software.

Piracy in music recordings is rampant. The International Federation of the Phonographic Industry claims that about one-third of all recorded music products sold worldwide are pirated (illegal) copies, suggesting that piracy costs the industry more than $4.5 billion annually.[26] The computer software industry also suffers from lax enforcement of intellectual property rights. Estimates suggest that violations of intellectual property rights cost personal computer software firms revenues equal to $53 billion in 2008.[27] According to the Business Software Alliance, a software industry association, in 2008 some 41 percent of all software applications used in the world were pirated. The worst region was Central and Eastern Europe where the piracy rate was 66 percent (see Figure 2.2). One of the worst countries was China, where the piracy rate in 2008 ran at

Intellectual Property
Products of the mind, such as computer software, a screenplay, a music score, or the chemical formula for a new drug; can be protected by patents, copyrights, and trademarks.

Patent
Grants the inventor of a new product or process exclusive rights for a defined period to the manufacture, use, or sale of that invention.

Copyright
The exclusive legal rights of authors, composers, playwrights, artists, and publishers to publish and disperse their work as they see fit.

Trademark
Designs and names, often officially registered, by which merchants or manufacturers designate and differentiate their products.

World Intellectual Property Organization
An international organization whose members sign treaties designed to protect intellectual property.

Paris Convention for the Protection of Industrial Property
International agreement to protect intellectual property; dates to 1883 and has been signed by some 170 nations.

The software piracy rate in China in 2008 ran at 80 percent and cost the industry more than $6.7 billion in lost sales.

80 percent and cost the industry more than $6.7 billion in lost sales, up from $444 million in 1995. The piracy rate in the United States was much lower at 20 percent; however, the value of sales lost was more significant because of the size of the U.S. market, reaching an estimated $9.1 billion in 2008.[28]

International businesses have a number of possible responses to violations of their intellectual property. They can lobby their respective governments to push for international agreements to ensure that intellectual property rights are protected and that the law is enforced. Partly as a result of such actions, international laws are being strengthened. As we shall see in Chapter 6, the most recent world trade agreement, signed in 1994, for the first time extends the scope of the General Agreement on Tariffs and Trade to cover intellectual property. Under the new agreement, known as the Trade Related Aspects of Intellectual Property Rights (or TRIPS), as of 1995 a council of the World Trade Organization is overseeing enforcement of much stricter intellectual property regulations. These regulations oblige WTO members to grant and enforce patents lasting at least 20 years and copyrights lasting 50 years. Rich countries had to comply with the rules within a year. Poor countries, in which such protection generally was much weaker, had five years of grace, and the very poorest have 10 years.[29] (For further details of the TRIPS agreement, see Chapter 6.)

In addition to lobbying governments, firms can file lawsuits on their behalf. Firms may also choose to stay out of countries where intellectual property laws are lax or information is censored by government agencies (see the accompanying Management Focus for details). Firms also need to be on alert to ensure that pirated copies of their products produced in countries with weak intellectual property laws don't turn up in their home market or in Third World countries. For example, U.S. computer software giant Microsoft discovered that pirated Microsoft software, produced illegally in Thailand, was being sold worldwide as the real thing.

PRODUCT SAFETY AND PRODUCT LIABILITY

Product safety laws set certain safety standards to which a product must adhere. **Product liability** involves holding a firm and its officers responsible when a product causes injury, death, or damage. Product liability can be much greater if a product does not conform to required safety standards. Both civil and criminal product liability laws exist. Civil laws call for payment and monetary damages. Criminal liability laws result in fines or imprisonment. Both civil and criminal liability laws are probably more extensive in the United States than in any

Product Safety Laws
Set certain safety standards to which a product must adhere.

Product Liability
Involves holding a firm and its officers responsible when a product causes injury, death, or damage.

figure

Regional Piracy Rates for Computer Software, 2008

Source: Business Software Alliance, "Sixth Annual BSA and IDC Global Software Piracy Study," May 2009, www.bsa.org, accessed April 5, 2010.

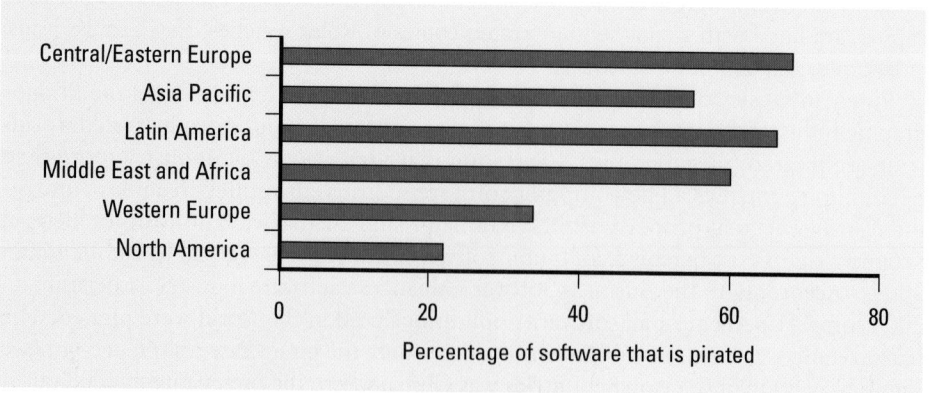

Management FOCUS

Google, China, and the Free Flow of Information

Moving into China, the largest single Internet search engine market in the world made tremendous sense for Google in 2005 and was viewed by market analysts as a brilliant move. Its withdrawal in 2009 after only four years created much more controversy. Some argue that Google maintained the "high ground" and followed its motto: "Do no evil." According to Google, its security had been compromised, and certain entities within the Chinese government had obtained the e-mails of activists and dissidents without their permission. Others claimed that Google was "outfoxed" in China; a market where it held a minority market share position in the Internet search engine space to Baidu, the local search engine. The story is more complex, however.

Originally, Google had tolerated certain censorship by Chinese authorities. But, when its security systems were breached by entities within China, it exited. At that point, it began automatically re-routing traffic to Hong Kong. Now under the threat of further government sanctions, Google has stopped automatically redirecting Chinese Internet users to

its uncensored Chinese-language Web site based in Hong Kong. To continue to do so risks the license the Chinese government had recently renewed and thereby stood to potentially lose revenues from advertising in the world's largest Internet market. By way of concession, Chinese users will now have to click on a tab to reach Google's Hong Kong Web site. Doing so could cost Google more market share to Baidu.

The issues implicit in this ideological/technological confrontation go to the very nature of the deeply held Western beliefs about the free flow of information, about the relative power of a large multinational corporation, and about a burgeoning superpower. Uncensored information on the Internet is intolerable to Chinese authorities. So the current compromise appears to create a win–win situation for both Google and China. It begs the question: In this high-stakes game of publicity, corporate profit, national pride, and governmental confrontation, who really won?

Sources: D. Barboza and M. Helft, "A Compromise Allows Both China and Google to Claim Victory," *The New York Times,* July 10, 2010; and B. Acohido, "Google Quits Rerouting China's Web Traffic to Hong Kong," *USA Today,* June 30, 2010, p. 2B.

---

other country, although many other Western nations also have comprehensive liability laws. Liability laws are typically least extensive in less developed nations. A boom in product liability suits and awards in the United States resulted in a dramatic increase in the cost of liability insurance. Many business executives argue that the high costs of liability insurance make American businesses less competitive in the global marketplace.

In addition to the competitiveness issue, country differences in product safety and liability laws raise an important ethical issue for firms doing business abroad. When product safety laws are tougher in a firm's home country than in a foreign country or when liability laws are more lax, should a firm doing business in that foreign country follow the more relaxed local standards or should it adhere to the standards of its home country? While the ethical thing to do is undoubtedly to adhere to home-country standards, firms have been known to take advantage of lax safety and liability laws to do business in a manner that would not be allowed at home.

The Determinants of Economic Development

LEARNING OBJECTIVE 4
Explain what determines the level of economic development of a nation.

The political, economic, and legal systems of a country can have a profound impact on the level of economic development and hence on the attractiveness of a country as a possible market or production location for a firm. Here we look first at how countries differ in their level of development. Then we look at how political economy affects economic progress.

DIFFERENCES IN ECONOMIC DEVELOPMENT Different countries have dramatically different levels of economic development. One common measure of economic development is a country's **gross national income (GNI)** per head of population.

Gross National Income (GNI)
The yardstick for measuring the economic activity of a country; it measures the total annual income received by a nation's residents.

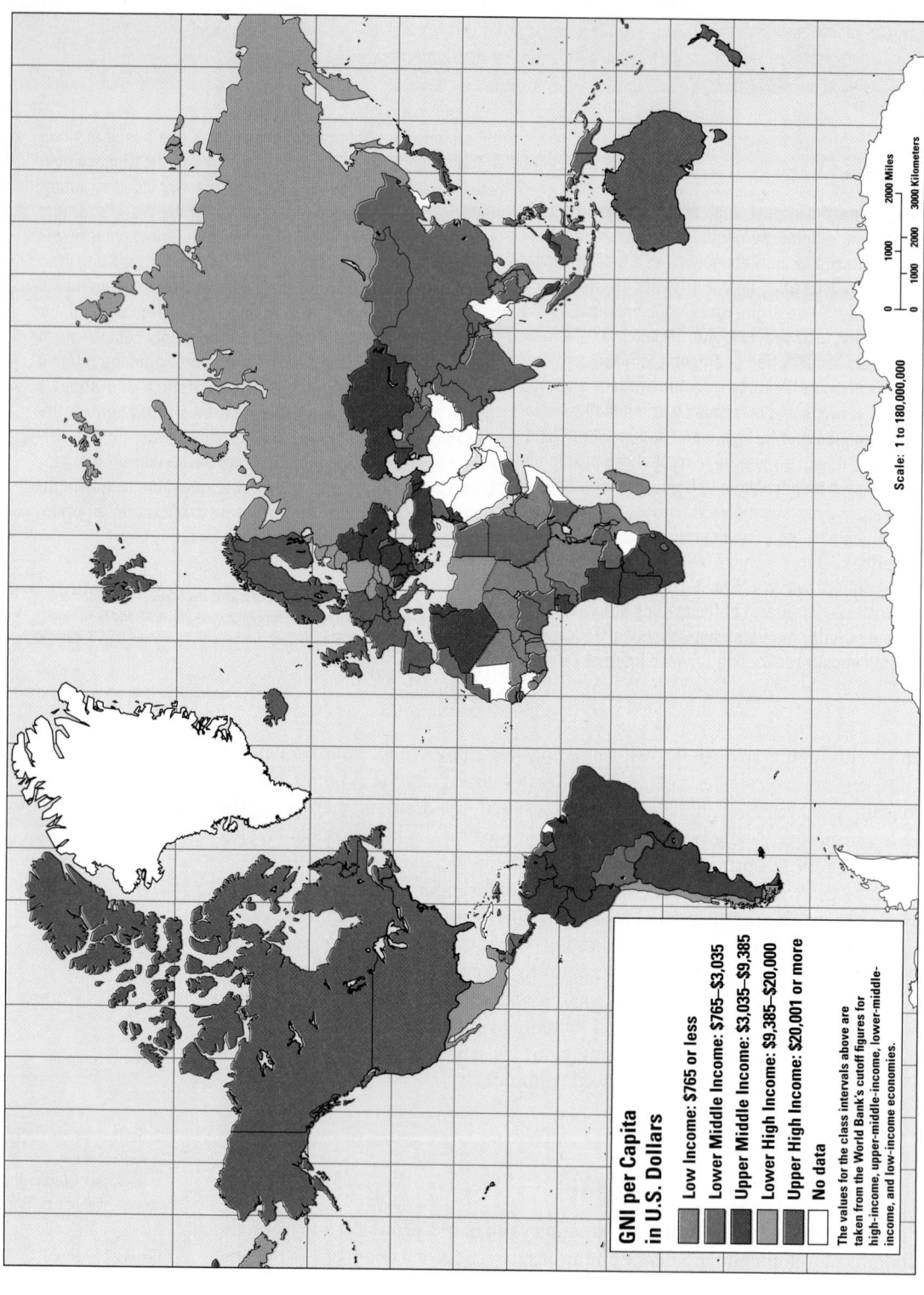

GNI per Capita in U.S. Dollars

Low Income: $765 or less

Lower Middle Income: $765–$3,035

Upper Middle Income: $3,035–$9,385

Lower High Income: $9,385–$20,000

Upper High Income: $20,001 or more

No data

The values for the class intervals above are taken from the World Bank's cutoff figures for high-income, upper-middle-income, lower-middle-income, and low-income economies.

Scale: 1 to 180,000,000

0   1000   2000 Miles

0   1000   2000   3000 Kilometers

2.1 map Gross National Income per Capita, 2008

Source: Data from World Bank, "World Development Indicators Online, 2010." Reprinted by permission from the International Bank for Reconstruction and Development. ©2010 by the World Bank.

GNI is regarded as a yardstick for the economic activity of a country; it measures the total annual income received by residents of a nation. Map 2.1 summarizes the GNI per capita of the world's nations in 2008. As can be seen, countries such as Japan, Sweden, Switzerland, and the United States are among the richest on this measure, whereas the large countries of China and India are among the poorest. Japan, for example, had a 2008 GNI per capita of $38,210, but China achieved only $2,940 and India just $1,070.[30]

GNI per person figures can be misleading because they don't consider differences in the cost of living. For example, although the 2008 GNI per capita of Switzerland at $65,330 exceeded that of the United States, which was $47,580, the higher cost of living in Switzerland meant that U.S. citizens could actually afford more goods and services than Swiss citizens. To account for differences in the cost of living, one can adjust GNI per capita by purchasing power. Referred to as a **purchasing power parity (PPP)** adjustment, it allows for a more direct comparison of living standards in different countries. The base for the adjustment is the cost of living in the United States. The PPP for different countries is then adjusted (up or down) depending upon whether the cost of living is lower or higher than in the United States. For example, in 2008 the GNI per capita for China was $2,940, but the PPP per capita was $6,020, suggesting that the cost of living was lower in China and that $2,940 in China would buy as much as $6,020 in the United States. Table 2.1 gives the GNI per capita measured at PPP in 2008 for a selection of countries, along with their GNI per capita and their growth rate in gross domestic product (GDP) from 1998 to 2008. Map 2.2 summarizes the GNI PPP per capita in 2008 for the nations of the world.

As can be seen, there are striking differences in the standards of living between countries. Table 2.1 suggests that the average Indian citizen can afford to consume only around 6 percent of the goods and services consumed by the average U.S. citizen on a PPP basis. Given this, one might conclude that, despite having a population of 1.1 billion, India is unlikely to be a very lucrative market for the consumer products produced by many Western international businesses. However, this would be incorrect because India has a fairly wealthy middle class of close to 200 million people, despite its large number of very poor. In absolute terms, the Indian economy now rivals that of Brazil and Russia (see Table 2.1).

Purchasing Power Parity (PPP)
An adjustment in gross domestic product per capita to reflect differences in the cost of living.

Country	GNI per Capita, 2008	GNI PPP per Capita, 2008	GDP Growth Rate, 1999–2008	Size of Economy GDP, 2007 (billions)
Brazil	$7,350	$10,070	3.33%	$1,612
China	2,940	6,020	9.75	4,326
Germany	42,440	35,940	1.47	3,653
India	950	2,960	7.22	1,218
Japan	37,670	35,220	1.31	4,909
Nigeria	1,070	1,940	5.54	213
Poland	11,880	17,310	4.20	527
Russia	9,620	15,630	6.99	1,608
Switzerland	65,330	46,460	1.94	488
United Kingdom	45,390	36,130	2.58	2,646
United States	46,580	46,970	2.58	1,420

 **2.1 table**

Economic Data for Select Countries

Source: World Bank, "World Development Indicators Online, 2010."

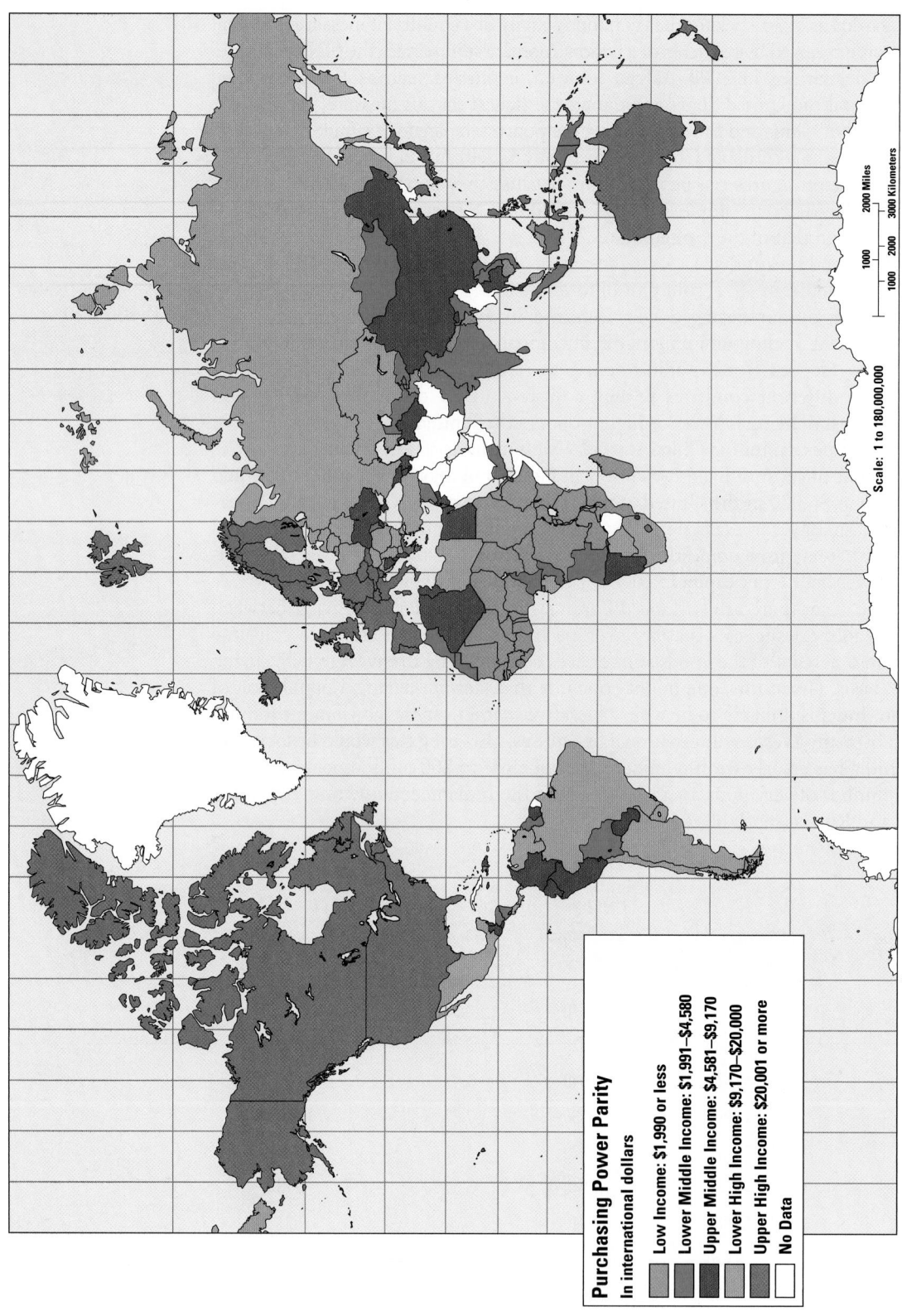

Purchasing Power Parity

In international dollars

- Low Income: $1,990 or less
- Lower Middle Income: $1,991–$4,580
- Upper Middle Income: $4,581–$9,170
- Lower High Income: $9,170–$20,000
- Upper High Income: $20,001 or more
- No Data

2.2 map Gross National Income PPP per Capita, 2008

Source. Data from World Bank, "World Development Indicators Online, 2010." Reprinted by permission from the International Bank for Reconstruction and Development. © 2010 by the World Bank.

Scale: 1 to 180,000,000

2000 Miles

3000 Kilometers

The GNI and PPP data give a static picture of development. They tell us, for example, that China is much poorer than the United States, but they do not tell us if China is closing the gap. To assess this, we have to look at the economic growth rates achieved by countries. Table 2.1 gives the rate of growth in gross domestic product (GDP) achieved by a number of countries between 1999 and 2008. Map 2.3 summarizes the growth rate in GDP from 1999 to 2008. Although countries such as China and India are currently poor, their economies are large in absolute terms and growing more rapidly than those of many advanced nations. They are already huge markets for the products of international businesses. If it maintains its growth rates, China in particular will be larger than all but that of the United States within a decade, and India too will be among the largest economies in the world. Given that potential, many international businesses are trying to gain a foothold in these markets now. Even though their current contributions to an international firm's revenues might be relatively small, their future contributions could be much larger.

BROADER CONCEPTIONS OF DEVELOPMENT: AMARTYA SEN

The Nobel Prize–winning economist Amartya Sen has argued that development should be assessed less by material output measures such as GNI per capita and more by the capabilities and opportunities that people enjoy.[31] According to Sen, development should be seen as a process of expanding the real freedoms that people experience. Hence, development requires the removal of major impediments to freedom: poverty as well as tyranny, poor economic opportunities as well as systematic social deprivation, neglect of public facilities as well as the intolerance of repressive states. In Sen's view, development is not just an economic process, but it is a political one too, and to succeed requires the "democratization" of political communities to give citizens a voice in the important decisions made for the community. This perspective leads Sen to emphasize basic health care, especially for children, and basic education, especially for women. Not only are these factors desirable for their instrumental value in helping to achieve higher income levels, but they are also beneficial in their own right. People cannot develop their capabilities if they are chronically ill or woefully ignorant.

Sen's influential thesis has been picked up by the United Nations, which has developed the **Human Development Index (HDI)** to measure the quality of human life in different nations. The HDI is based on three measures: life expectancy at birth (a function of health care), educational attainment (measured by a combination of the adult literacy rate and enrollment in primary, secondary, and tertiary education), and whether average incomes, based on PPP estimates, are sufficient to meet the basic needs of life in a country (adequate food, shelter, and health care).

As such, the HDI comes much closer to Sen's conception of how development should be measured than narrow economic measures such as GNI per capita—although Sen's thesis suggests that political freedoms should also be included in the index, and they are not. The HDI is scaled from 0 to 1. Countries scoring less than 0.5 are classified as having low human development (the quality of life is poor); those scoring from 0.5 to 0.8 are classified as having medium human development; and those that score above 0.8 are classified as having high human development. Map 2.4 summarizes the HDI scores for 2007, the most recent year for which data are available.

Human Development Index (HDI)
An attempt by the UN to assess the impact of a number of factors on the quality of human life in a country.

Another Perspective

If We Were a Community of 100 People
To get a good sense of the scale of economic and demographic measures that this chapter describes, if we were a community of 100, 61 of us would be Asian, 12 European, 13 North and South American, 13 African, and 1 Australian. Six of us would own 59 percent of the community's wealth. Thirteen would be hungry or malnourished, 14 could not read, and 7 would be educated (secondary level). Thirty would have bank accounts and 53 would live on $2.00 a day or less. To learn more and to see the video that offers these meaningful metrics, visit www.miniature-earth.com.

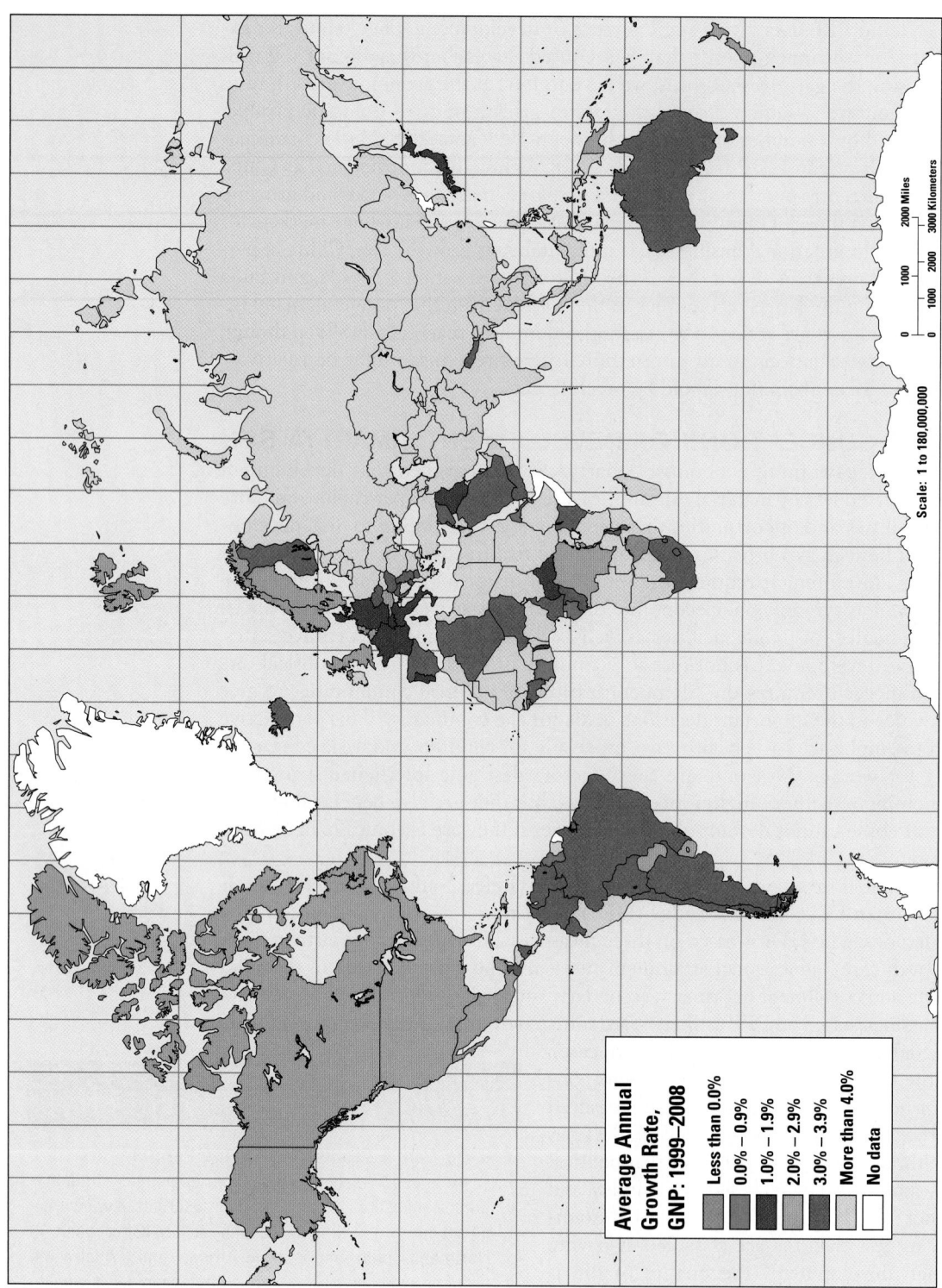

2.3 map Growth Rate in GDP per Capita, 1999–2008

Average Annual
Growth Rate,
GNP: 1999–2008

Less than 0.0%
0.0% – 0.9%
1.0% – 1.9%
2.0% – 2.9%
3.0% – 3.9%
More than 4.0%
No data

Scale: 1 to 180,000,000

0   1000   2000 Miles
0 1000 2000 3000 Kilometers

Source: Data from World Bank, "World Development Indicators Online, 2010." Reprinted by permission from the International Bank for Reconstruction and Development. © 2010 by the World Bank.

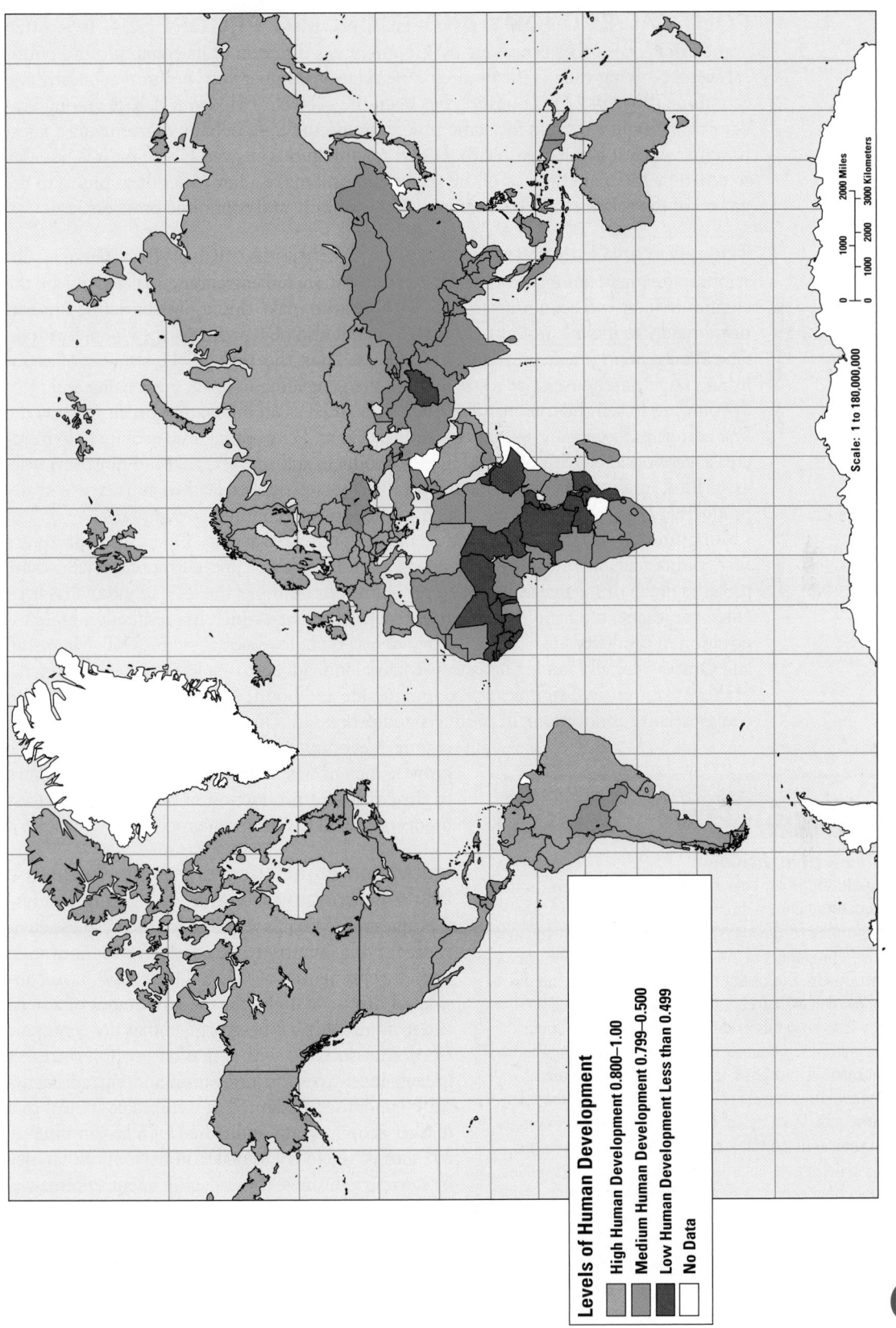

Levels of Human Development

High Human Development 0.800–1.00

Medium Human Development 0.799–0.500

Low Human Development Less than 0.499

No Data

Scale: 1 to 180,000,000

0	1000	2000 Miles
0	1000 2000	3000 Kilometers

2.4 map Human Development Index, 2007

Source: Data from United Nations, *Human Development Report, 2007, Human Development Index, 2007.*

POLITICAL ECONOMY AND ECONOMIC PROGRESS It is often argued that a country's economic development is a function of its economic and political systems. What then is the nature of the relationship between political economy and economic progress? This question has been the subject of vigorous debate among academics and policy makers for some time. Despite the long debate, this remains a question for which it is not possible to give an unambiguous answer. However, it is possible to untangle the main threads of the arguments and make a few generalizations as to the nature of the relationship between political economy and economic progress.

Innovation and Entrepreneurship Are the Engines of Growth

There is substantial agreement among economists that innovation and entrepreneurial activity are the engines of long-run economic growth.[32] Those who make this argument define **innovation** broadly to include not just new products but also new processes, new organizations, new management practices, and new strategies. Thus, the Toys "R" Us strategy of establishing large warehouse-style toy stores and then engaging in heavy advertising and price discounting to sell the merchandise can be classified as an innovation because it was the first company to pursue this strategy. Innovation and entrepreneurial activity help to increase economic activity by creating new products and markets that did not previously exist. Plus, innovations in production and business processes lead to an increase in the productivity of labor and capital, which further boosts economic growth rates.[33]

Innovation
Development of new products, processes, organizations, management practices, and strategies.

Innovation is also seen as the product of entrepreneurial activity. Often, **entrepreneurs** first commercialize innovative new products and processes, and entrepreneurial activity provides much of the dynamism in an economy. For example, the U.S. economy has benefited greatly from a high level of entrepreneurial activity, which has resulted in rapid innovation in products and process. Firms such as Google, Cisco Systems, Dell, Microsoft, and Oracle were all founded by entrepreneurial individuals to exploit new technology. All of these firms created significant economic value and boosted productivity by helping to commercialize innovations in products and processes. Thus, one can conclude that if a country's economy is to sustain long-run economic growth, the business environment must be conducive to the consistent production of product and process innovations and to entrepreneurial activity.

Entrepreneurs
Those who first commercialize innovations.

Another Perspective

BYD—Innovative Dreaming

BYD stands for Build Your Dreams, and nowhere is the entrepreneurial/innovative drive better exemplified than in Asia. According to *BusinessWeek,* among the top 10 most innovative companies in the world, 6 are North American and 4 are Asian. But of the top 10, the one with the most revenue growth (42 percent from 2006 to 2009) was BYD, a company little known outside its headquarters in China.

BYD researches, produces, or supplies a virtual warehouse of rechargeable batteries, automobiles and automobile-related products, handset components, LCDs, and other electronic products. In so doing, BYD has been able to engage and interact with perhaps the hottest market sectors—namely, rechargeable batteries, smart electric automobiles, and mobile handsets. It is primed for innovative growth: It's Chinese, it's green, and Warren Buffett loves it. (Bloomberg *Businessweek,* "The 50 Most Innovative Companies 2010, April 15, 2010, http://www.businessweek.com/interactive_reports/innovative_companies_2010.html; "BYD," *Financial Times,* March 16, 2010, p.14; and BYD Web site, www.byd.com).

Innovation and Entrepreneurship Require a Market Economy

This leads logically to a further question: What is required for the business environment of a country to be conducive to innovation and entrepreneurial activity? Those who have considered this issue highlight the advantages of a market economy.[34] It has been argued that the economic freedom associated with a market economy creates greater incentives for innovation and entrepreneurship than either a planned or a mixed economy. In a market economy, any individual who has an innovative idea is free to try to make money out of that idea by starting a business (by engaging in entrepreneurial activity). Similarly, existing businesses are free to improve their operations through innovation. To the extent that they are successful, both individual entrepreneurs and established businesses can reap rewards in the form of high profits. Thus, market economies contain enormous incentives to develop innovations.

In a planned economy, the state owns all means of production. Consequently, entrepreneurial individuals have few economic incentives to develop valuable new innovations, because it is the state, rather than the individual, that captures most of the gains. The lack of economic freedom and incentives for innovation was probably a main factor in the economic stagnation of many former Communist states and led ultimately to their collapse at the end of the 1980s. Similar stagnation occurred in many mixed economies in those sectors where the state had a monopoly (such as coal mining and telecommunications in Great Britain). This stagnation provided the impetus for the widespread privatization of state-owned enterprises that we witnessed in many mixed economies during the mid-1980s and is still going on today (*privatization* refers to the process of selling state-owned enterprises to private investors).

A study of 102 countries over a 20-year period provided evidence of a strong relationship between economic freedom (as provided by a market economy) and economic growth.[35] The study found that the more economic freedom a country had between 1975 and 1995, the more economic growth it achieved and the richer its citizens became. The six countries that had persistently high ratings of economic freedom from 1975 to 1995 (Hong Kong, Switzerland, Singapore, the United States, Canada, and Germany) were also all in the top 10 in terms of economic growth rates. In contrast, no country with persistently low economic freedom achieved a respectable growth rate. In the 16 countries for which the index of economic freedom declined the most during 1975 to 1995, gross domestic product fell at an annual rate of 0.6 percent.

Innovation and Entrepreneurship Require Strong Property Rights

Strong legal protection of property rights is another requirement for a business environment to be conducive to innovation, entrepreneurial activity, and hence economic growth.[36] Both individuals and businesses must be given the opportunity to profit from innovative ideas. Without strong property rights protection, businesses and individuals run the risk that the profits from their innovative efforts will be expropriated, either by criminal elements or by the state. The state can expropriate the profits from innovation through legal means, such as excessive taxation, or through illegal means, such as demands from state bureaucrats for kickbacks in return for granting an individual or firm a license to do business in a certain area (i.e., corruption). According to the Nobel Prize–winning economist Douglass North, throughout history many governments have displayed a tendency to engage in such behavior. Inadequately enforced property rights reduce the incentives for innovation and entrepreneurial activity—because the profits from such activity are "stolen"—and hence reduce the rate of economic growth.

The influential Peruvian development economist Hernando de Soto has argued that much of the developing world will fail to reap the benefits of capitalism until property rights are better defined and protected.[37] De Soto's arguments are interesting because he claims that the key problem is not the risk of expropriation but the chronic inability of property owners to establish legal title to the property they own. As an example of the scale of the problem, he cites the situation in Haiti where individuals must take 176 steps over 19 years to own land legally. Because most property in poor countries is informally "owned," the absence of legal proof of ownership means that property holders cannot convert their assets into capital, which could then be used to finance business ventures. Banks will not lend money to the poor to start businesses because the poor possess no proof that they own property, such as farmland, that can be used as collateral for a loan. By de Soto's calculations, the total value of real estate held by the poor in Third World and former Communist states amounted to more than $9.3 trillion in 2000. If those assets could be converted into capital, the result could be an economic revolution that would allow the poor to bootstrap their way out of poverty. Interestingly enough, the Vietnamese seem to have taken de Soto's arguments to heart. Despite

Country FOCUS

The Concept of Property Rights in Vietnam

As in most communist countries, there is no system of private property in Vietnam. In Western terms, property rights are premised on the concept of a "freehold." The individual owns the land and is free to determine its uses (with limitations). In Vietnam, the state owns all the land, and residents and investors buy and sell only the rights to use it. In this sense, it is a tenuous kind of freehold title. Unlike the stricter forms of communism found in North Korea or, to some extent, Cuba, Vietnam has evolved a system whereby land-use rights can be bought, sold, inherited, and used as collateral for a loan. The 1992 constitution granted stronger land rights to individuals, including rights over commercial and personal property as a means of spurring agricultural production. Private land use rights (LURs) may now be granted for up to 50 years. There is one caveat, however; the state can reclaim any land at any time, often with contemptuous levels of compensation.

"Use" is determined by the state. Since 2003, the Land Law permits the state to "recover" (expropriate) assigned land in any of four circumstances: (1) inefficient use or use for unassigned purposes; (2) non-use for 12 months, or project delays of 24 months or more from initial assignment; (3) intentional destruction of land; and (4) intentional failure to meet financial obligations to the state.

In Vietnam, investors and developers generally acquire land in two ways: (1) they receive an assignment of a land-use right (assignment method) or (2) they pay compensation to land users (compensation method). Only local companies may use the assignment method; both local and foreign-invested companies may use the compensation method. In terms of access to land, state-owned enterprises are at a distinct advantage to foreign companies, but recent legislation has progressively enhanced the status of foreign investors. In 2006 the Uniform Enterprise Law allowed foreign investors to form any type of company instead of only limited liability companies. Since July 1, 2004, the Land Law has allowed local private companies with long-term LURs to lease land to foreign investors.

Although all this may seem like a highly burdensome administrative task, in the World Bank's *Doing Business* report for 2009, Vietnam scored well in "registering property," ranking 40th out of 183 countries in terms of the ease with which businesses can secure rights to property. According to the report, it takes only four procedures or steps, and less than 60 days to register a property in Vietnam. In comparison with other Asia Pacific countries, Vietnam appears to be transitioning toward a more traditional concept of freehold.

Sources: *The Economist Intelligence Unit,* Country Commerce 2010: Vietnam, pp. 30-33; and D. Hare, "The Origins and Influence of Land Property Rights in Vietnam," *Development Policy Review,* 26, no. 3 (2008), pp. 339–363.

still being officially a Communist country, since 1992 the Vietnamese government has passed a series of laws that have given certain property rights to local and foreign individuals and corporations the ability to use the land as collateral for loans, for inheritances, and investments in leases (see the accompanying Country Focus for details).

The Required Political System   Much debate surrounds which kind of political system best achieves a functioning market economy with strong protection for property rights.[38] People in the West tend to associate a representative democracy with a market economic system, strong property rights protection, and economic progress. Building on this, we tend to argue that democracy is good for growth. However, some totalitarian regimes have fostered a market economy and strong property rights protection and have experienced rapid economic growth. Five of the fastest-growing economies of the past 30 years—China, South Korea, Taiwan, Singapore, and Hong Kong—had one thing in common at the start of their economic growth: undemocratic governments. At the same time, countries with stable democratic governments, such as India, experienced sluggish economic growth for long periods. In 1992, Lee Kuan Yew, Singapore's leader for many years, told an audience, "I do not believe that democracy necessarily leads to development. I believe that a country needs to develop discipline more than democracy. The exuberance of democracy leads to undisciplined and disorderly conduct which is inimical to development."[39]

However, those who argue for the value of a totalitarian regime miss an important point: If dictators made countries rich, then much of Africa, Asia, and Latin America should have been growing rapidly during 1960 to 1990, and this was not the case. Only a totalitarian regime that is committed to a market system and strong protection of property rights is capable of promoting economic growth. Also, there is no guarantee that a dictatorship will continue to pursue such progressive policies. Dictators are rarely benevolent. Many are tempted to use the apparatus of the state to further their own private ends, violating property rights and stalling economic growth. Given this, it seems likely that democratic regimes are far more conducive to long-term economic growth than are dictatorships, even benevolent ones. Only in a well-functioning, mature democracy are property rights truly secure.[40] Nor should we forget Amartya Sen's arguments that we reviewed earlier. Totalitarian states, by limiting human freedom, also suppress human development and therefore are detrimental to progress.

Economic Progress Begets Democracy   While it is possible to argue that democracy is not a necessary precondition for a free market economy in which property rights are protected, subsequent economic growth often leads to establishment of a democratic regime. Several of the fastest-growing Asian economies, including South Korea and Taiwan, adopted more democratic governments during the past three decades. Thus, although democracy may not always be the cause of initial economic progress, it seems to be one consequence of that progress.

A strong belief that economic progress leads to adoption of a democratic regime underlies the fairly permissive attitude that many Western governments have adopted toward human rights violations in China. Although China has a totalitarian government in which human rights are violated, many Western countries have been hesitant to criticize the country too much for fear that this might hamper the country's march toward a free market system. The belief is that once China has a free market system, greater individual freedoms and democracy will follow. Whether this optimistic vision comes to pass remains to be seen.

GEOGRAPHY, EDUCATION, AND ECONOMIC DEVELOPMENT   While a country's political and economic systems are probably the big engine driving its rate of economic development, other factors are also important. One that has received attention recently is geography.[41] But the belief that geography can influence economic policy, and hence economic growth rates, goes back to Adam Smith. The influential Harvard University economist Jeffrey Sachs argues:

> throughout history, coastal states, with their long engagements in international trade, have been more supportive of market institutions than landlocked states, which have tended to organize themselves as hierarchical (and often military) societies. Mountainous states, as a result of physical isolation, have often neglected market-based trade. Temperate climes have generally supported higher densities of population and thus a more extensive division of labor than tropical regions.[42]

Sachs's point is that by virtue of favorable geography, certain societies were more likely to engage in trade than others and were thus more likely to be open to and develop market-based economic systems, which in turn would promote faster economic growth. He also argues that, irrespective of the economic and political institutions a country adopts, adverse geographical conditions, such as the high rate of disease, poor soils, and hostile climate that afflict many tropical countries, can have a negative impact on development. Together with colleagues at Harvard's Institute for International Development, Sachs tested for the impact of geography on a country's economic growth rate between 1965 and 1990. He found that landlocked countries grew more slowly than coastal economies and that being entirely landlocked reduced a country's growth rate by roughly 0.7 percent per year. He also found that tropical countries grew 1.3 percent more slowly each year than countries in the temperate zone.

Education emerges as another important determinant of economic development (a point that Amartya Sen emphasizes). The general assertion is that nations that invest more in education will have higher growth rates because an educated population is a more productive population. Anecdotal comparisons suggest this is true. In 1960, Pakistanis and South Koreans were on equal footing economically. However, just 30 percent of Pakistani children were enrolled in primary schools, while 94 percent of South Koreans were. By the mid-1980s, South Korea's GNP per person was three times that of Pakistan's.[43] A survey of 14 statistical studies that looked at the relationship between a country's investment in education and its subsequent growth rates concluded investment in education did have a positive and statistically significant impact on a country's rate of economic growth.[44] Similarly, the work by Sachs discussed above suggests that investments in education help explain why some countries in Southeast Asia, such as Indonesia, Malaysia, and Singapore, have been able to overcome the disadvantages associated with their tropical geography and grow far more rapidly than tropical nations in Africa and Latin America.

States in Transition

LEARNING OBJECTIVE 5
Identify the macro-political and economic changes taking place worldwide.

The political economy of many of the world's nation-states has changed radically since the late 1980s. Two trends have been evident. First, during the late 1980s and early 1990s, a wave of democratic revolutions swept the world. Totalitarian governments collapsed and were replaced by democratically elected governments that were typically more committed to free market capitalism than their predecessors had been. Second, there has been a strong move away from centrally planned and mixed economies and toward a more free market economic model. We shall look first at the spread of democracy and then turn our attention to the spread of free market economics.

THE SPREAD OF DEMOCRACY   One notable development of the past 20 years has been the spread of democracy (and, by extension, the decline of totalitarianism). Map 2.5 reports on the extent of totalitarianism in the world as determined by Freedom House.[45] This map charts political freedom in 2009, grouping countries into three broad groupings—free, partly free, and not free. In "free" countries, citizens enjoy a high degree of political and civil freedoms. "Partly free" countries are characterized by some restrictions on political rights and civil liberties, often in the context of corruption, weak rule of law, ethnic strife, or civil war. In "not free" countries, the political process is tightly controlled and basic freedoms are denied.

Freedom House classified 89 countries as free in 2009, accounting for some 46 percent of the world's nations. These countries respect a broad range of political rights. Another 58 countries accounting for 30 percent of the world's nations were classified as partly free, while 47 countries representing 24 percent of the world's nations were classified as not free. The number of democracies in the world has increased from 69 nations in 1987 to 116 in 2009, slightly below the 2006 total of 123. But not all democracies are free, according to Freedom House, because some democracies still restrict certain political and civil liberties. For example, Russia was rated "not free." According to Freedom House,

> Russia's step backwards into the Not Free category is the culmination of a growing trend . . . to concentrate political authority, harass and intimidate the media, and politicize the country's law-enforcement system.[46]

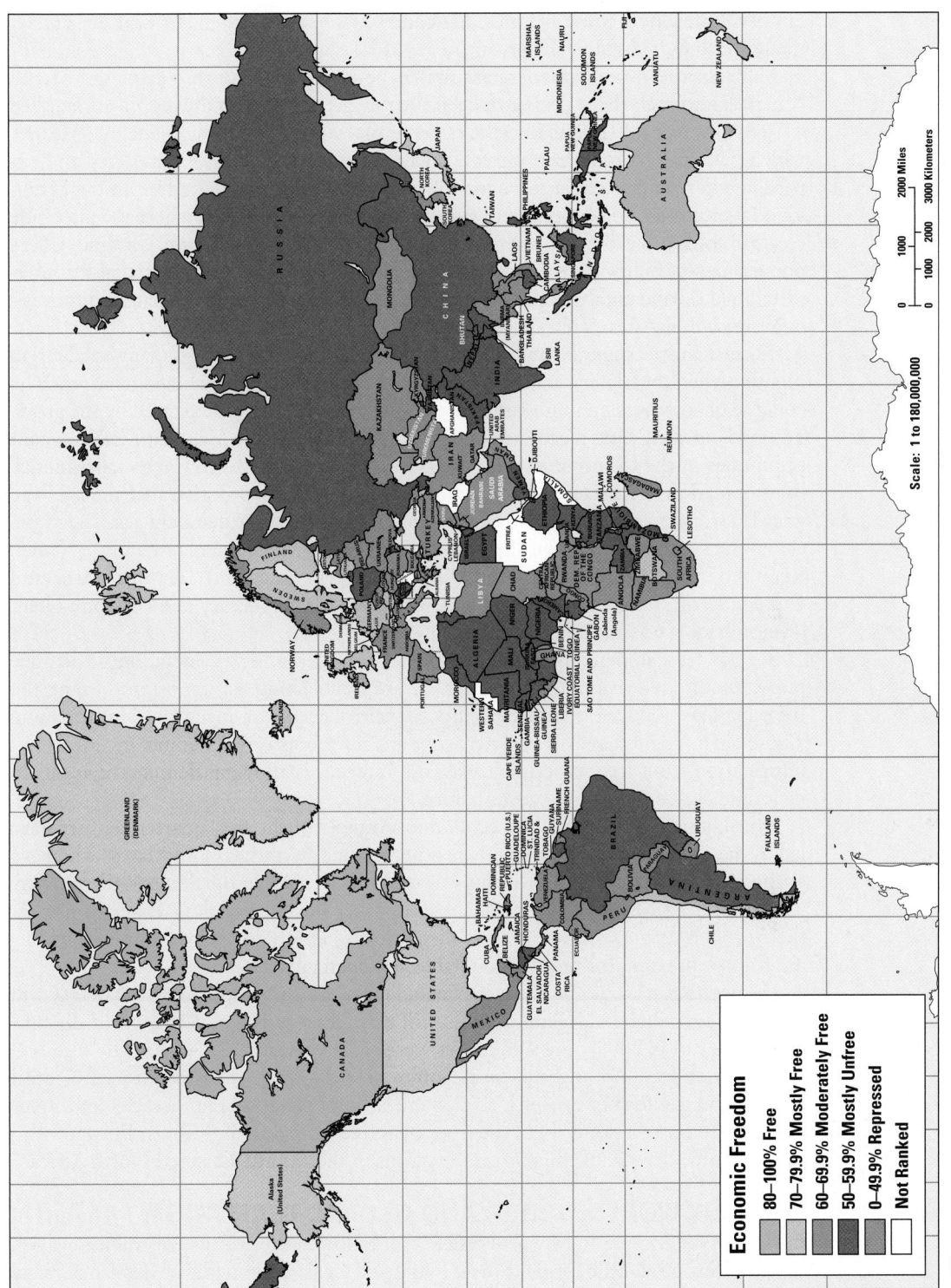

2.5 map Political Freedom in 2009

Economic Freedom
- 80–100% Free
- 70–79.9% Mostly Free
- 60–69.9% Moderately Free
- 50–59.9% Mostly Unfree
- 0–49.9% Repressed
- Not Ranked

Scale: 1 to 180,000,000

Source: Map data from Freedom House. *Freedom in the World, 2010: The Annual Survey of Political Rights and Civil Liberties*, www.freedomhouse.org. Reprinted with permission.

Similarly, Freedom House argues that democracy is being restricted in Venezuela under the leadership of Hugo Chavez.

Many of the newer democracies are to be found in Eastern Europe and Latin America, although there also have been notable gains in Africa during this time, such as in South Africa. Entrants into the ranks of the world's democracies include Mexico, which held its first fully free and fair presidential election in 2000 after free and fair parliamentary and state elections in 1997 and 1998; Senegal, where free and fair presidential elections led to a peaceful transfer of power; Yugoslavia, where a democratic election took place despite attempted fraud by the incumbent; and Ukraine, where popular unrest following widespread ballot fraud in the 2004 presidential election resulted in a second election, the victory of a reform candidate, and a marked improvement in civil liberties.

Three main reasons account for the spread of democracy.[47] First, many totalitarian regimes failed to deliver economic progress to the vast bulk of their populations. The collapse of communism in Eastern Europe, for example, was precipitated by the growing gulf between the vibrant and wealthy economies of the West and the stagnant economies of the Communist East. In looking for alternatives to the socialist model, the populations of these countries could not have failed to notice that most of the world's strongest economies were governed by representative democracies. Today, the economic success of many of the newer democracies, such as Poland and the Czech Republic in the former Communist bloc, the Philippines and Taiwan in Asia, and Chile in Latin America, has strengthened the case for democracy as a key component of successful economic advancement.

Second, new information and communication technologies, including shortwave radio, satellite television, fax machines, desktop publishing, and, most important, the Internet, have reduced the state's ability to control access to uncensored information. These technologies have created new conduits for the spread of democratic ideals and information from free societies. Today, the Internet is allowing democratic ideals to penetrate closed societies as never before.[48]

Third, in many countries the economic advances of the past quarter century have led to the emergence of increasingly prosperous middle and working classes who have pushed for democratic reforms. This was certainly a factor in the democratic transformation of South Korea. Entrepreneurs and other business leaders, eager to protect their property rights and ensure the dispassionate enforcement of contracts, are another force pressing for more accountable and open government.

Despite this, it would be naive to conclude that the global spread of democracy will continue unchallenged. Democracy is still rare in large parts of the world. In sub-Saharan Africa in 2009, only 9 countries were considered free, 23 were partly free, and 16 were not free. Among the post-Communist countries in Eastern and Central Europe and the former Soviet Union, 8 are still not electoral democracies and Freedom House classifies only 14 of these states as free (primarily in Eastern Europe). And there is only 1 free state among the 17 nations of the Middle East and North Africa.

THE NEW WORLD ORDER AND GLOBAL TERRORISM The end of the Cold War and the "new world order" that followed the collapse of communism in Eastern Europe and the former Soviet Union, taken together with the demise of many authoritarian regimes in Latin America, have given rise to intense speculation about the future shape of global geopolitics. Author Francis Fukuyama has argued, "We may be witnessing . . . the end of history as such: that is, the end point of mankind's ideological evolution and the universalization of Western liberal democracy as the final form of human government."[49] Fukuyama goes on to say that the war of ideas may be at an end and that liberal democracy has triumphed.

Others question Fukuyama's vision of a more harmonious world dominated by a universal civilization characterized by democratic regimes and free market capitalism. In a controversial book, the influential political scientist Samuel Huntington argues that there is no "universal" civilization based on widespread acceptance of Western liberal democratic ideals.[50] Huntington maintains that while many societies may be modernizing—they are adopting the material paraphernalia of the modern world, from automobiles to Coca-Cola and MTV—they are not becoming more Western. On the contrary, Huntington theorizes that modernization in non-Western societies can result in a retreat toward the traditional, such as the resurgence of Islam in many traditionally Muslim societies. He writes,

> The Islamic resurgence is both a product of and an effort to come to grips with modernization. Its underlying causes are those generally responsible for indigenization trends in non-Western societies: urbanization, social mobilization, higher levels of literacy and education, intensified communication and media consumption, and expanded interaction with Western and other cultures. These developments undermine traditional village and clan ties and create alienation and an identity crisis. Islamist symbols, commitments, and beliefs meet these psychological needs, and Islamist welfare organizations, the social, cultural, and economic needs of Muslims caught in the process of modernization. Muslims feel a need to return to Islamic ideas, practices, and institutions to provide the compass and the motor of modernization.[51]

Thus, the rise of Islamic fundamentalism is portrayed as a response to the alienation produced by modernization.

In contrast to Fukuyama, Huntington sees a world that is split into different civilizations, each of which has its own value systems and ideology. In addition to Western civilization, Huntington predicts the emergence of strong Islamic and Sinic (Chinese) civilizations, as well as civilizations based on Japan, Africa, Latin America, Eastern Orthodox Christianity (Russian), and Hinduism (Indian). Huntington also sees the civilizations as headed for conflict, particularly along the "fault lines" that separate them, such as Bosnia (where Muslims and Orthodox Christians have clashed), Kashmir (where Muslims and Hindus clash), and the Sudan (where a bloody war between Christians and Muslims has persisted for decades). Huntington predicts conflict between the West and Islam and between the West and China. He bases his predictions on an analysis of the different value systems and ideology of these civilizations, which in his view tend to bring them into conflict with each other. While some commentators originally dismissed Huntington's thesis, in the aftermath of the terrorist attacks on the United States on September 11, 2001, Huntington's views received new attention.

If Huntington's views are even partly correct, they have important implications for international business. They suggest many countries may be increasingly difficult places in which to do business, either because they are shot through with violent conflicts or because they are part of a civilization that is in conflict with an enterprise's home country. Huntington's views are speculative and controversial. It is not clear that his predictions will come to pass. More likely is the evolution of a global political system that is positioned somewhere between Fukuyama's universal global civilization based on liberal democratic ideals and Huntington's vision of a fractured world. That would still be a world, however, in which geopolitical forces periodically limit the ability of business enterprises to operate in certain foreign countries.

In Huntington's thesis, global terrorism is a product of the tension between civilizations and the clash of value systems and ideology. Others point to terrorism's roots in long-standing conflicts that seem to defy political resolution, the Palestinian, Kashmir, and Northern Ireland conflicts being obvious examples. It should also be noted that a substantial amount of terrorist activity in some parts of the world, such as Colombia, has been interwoven with the illegal drug trade. The attacks of September 11, 2001, created the impression that global terror is on the rise, although accurate statistics on this are hard to come by. What we do know is that according to data from the U.S. Department of State, in 2008 there were some 11,770 terrorist attacks worldwide, about the same as in 2005 and a decline from 14,507 in 2007. These attacks resulted in 15,765 deaths. The Middle East accounted for 40 percent of the attacks and 35 percent of the fatalities.[52] Other global hot spots for terrorist incidents in 2007 included the Sudan, Nigeria, and Afghanistan. As former U.S. Secretary of State Colin Powell has maintained, terrorism represents one of the major threats to world peace and economic progress in the twenty-first century.[53]

THE SPREAD OF MARKET-BASED SYSTEMS

Paralleling the spread of democracy since the 1980s has been the transformation from centrally planned command economies to market-based economies. More than 30 countries that were in the former Soviet Union or the Eastern European Communist bloc have changed their economic systems. A complete list of countries where change is now occurring also would include Asian states such as China and Vietnam, as well as African countries such as Angola, Ethiopia, and Mozambique.[54] There has been a similar shift away from a mixed economy. Many states in Asia, Latin America, and Western Europe have sold state-owned businesses to private investors (privatization) and deregulated their economies to promote greater competition.

The rationale for economic transformation has been the same the world over. In general, command and mixed economies failed to deliver the kind of sustained economic performance that was achieved by countries adopting market-based systems, such as the United States, Switzerland, Hong Kong, and Taiwan. As a consequence, even more states have gravitated toward the market-based model. Map 2.6, based on data from the Heritage Foundation, a politically conservative U.S. research foundation, gives some idea of the degree to which the world has shifted toward market-based economic systems. The Heritage Foundation's index of economic freedom is based on 10 indicators, such as the extent to which the government intervenes in the economy, trade policy, the degree to which property rights are protected, foreign investment regulations, and taxation rules. A country can score between 1 (most free) and 5 (least free) on each of these indicators. The lower a country's average score across all 10 indicators, the more closely its economy represents the pure market model. According to the 2009 index, which is summarized in Map 2.6, the world's freest economies are (in rank order) Hong Kong, Singapore, Australia, New Zealand, Ireland, Switzerland, Canada, United States, Denmark, and Chile. Japan came in at 19; Mexico at 41; France at 64; Brazil, 113; India, 124; China 140; and Russia, 143. The economies of Cuba, Laos, Iran, Venezuela, and North Korea are to be found near the bottom of the rankings.[55]

Another Perspective

Latin America's Two Lefts

Two lefts don't necessarily make a right. In a 2006 article, Jorge Castañeda, the ex-Mexican Foreign Minister, describes a tendency toward a leftist Latin America but further clarifies that there are "two lefts." As he claims: "One has radical roots but is now open-minded and modern; the other is close-minded and stridently populist." Today the argument can be made in reference to Cuba, Venezuela, Brazil, Argentina, Ecuador, Bolivia, and Paraguay. Many of the leaders have seriously questioned the benefits of a complete adherence to the concept of capitalism. Why have the governments of Brazil, Chile, and Uruguay pursued moderate, gradual change, whereas their counterparts in Venezuela, Bolivia, and Ecuador have proceeded with considerable economic and political radicalism? Must it be a situation of "Capitalism—Take It or Leave It"? (J.E. Castañeda, "Latin America's Left Turn," *Foreign Affairs*, May/June 2006.)

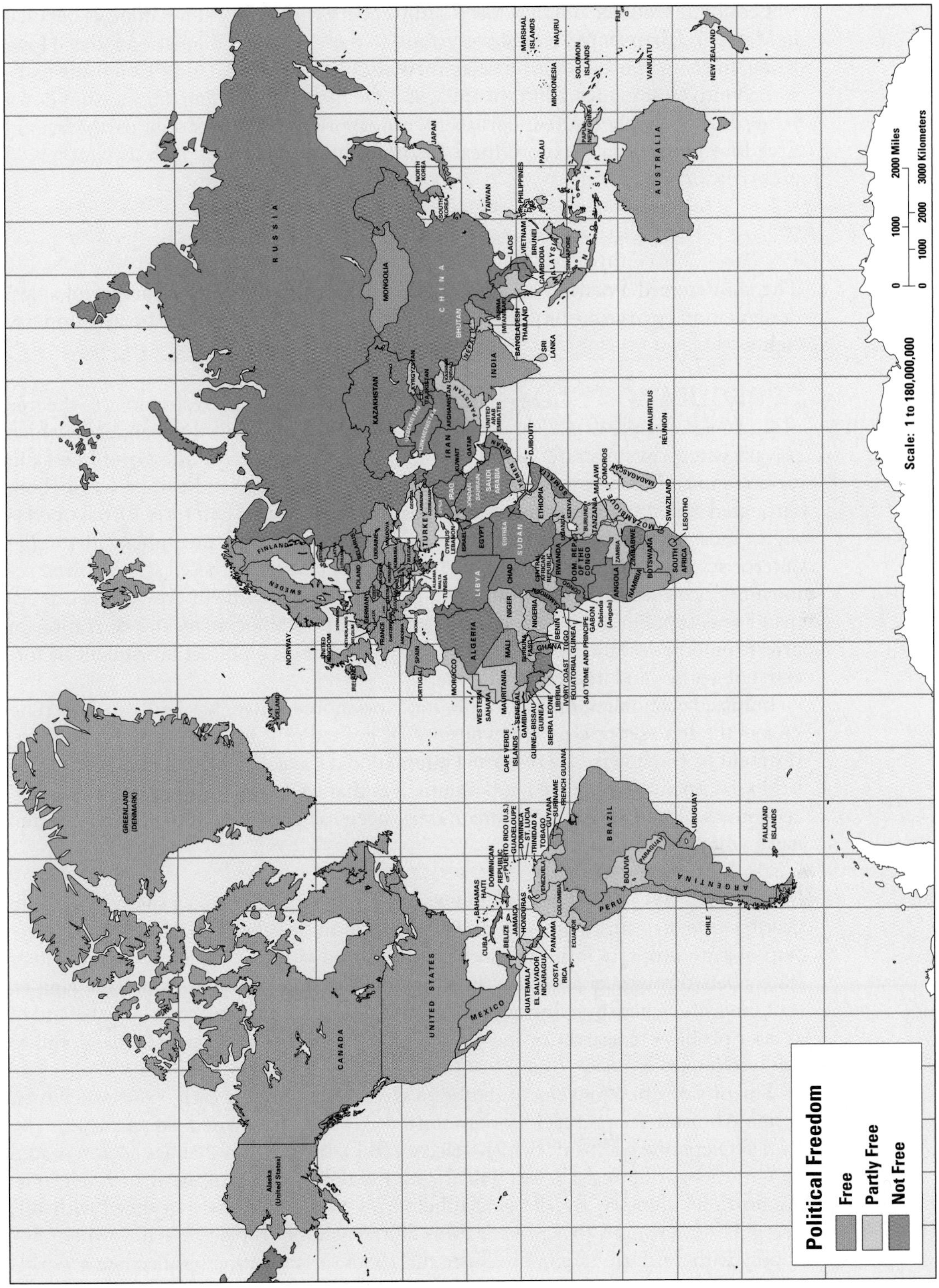

Political Freedom
- Free
- Partly Free
- Not Free

2.6 map Distribution of Economic Freedom, 2009

Source: Heritage Foundation, www.heritage.org/index/.

Scale: 1 to 180,000,000

Economic freedom does not necessarily equate with political freedom, as detailed in Map 2.6. For example, the two top states in the Heritage Foundation index, Hong Kong and Singapore, cannot be classified as politically free. Hong Kong was reabsorbed into Communist China in 1997, and the first thing Beijing did was shut down Hong Kong's freely elected legislature. Singapore is ranked as only partly free on Freedom House's index of political freedom due to practices such as widespread press censorship.

The Nature of Economic Transformation

LEARNING OBJECTIVE 6
Describe how transition economies are moving toward market-based systems.

The shift toward a market-based economic system often entails a number of steps: deregulation, privatization, and creation of a legal system to safeguard property rights.[56]

Deregulation

Removal of government restrictions concerning the conduct of business.

DEREGULATION   **Deregulation** involves removing legal restrictions to the free play of markets, the establishment of private enterprises, and the manner in which private enterprises operate. Before the collapse of communism, the governments in most command economies exercised tight control over prices and output, setting both through detailed state planning. They also prohibited private enterprises from operating in most sectors of the economy, severely restricted direct investment by foreign enterprises, and limited international trade. Deregulation in these cases involved removing price controls, thereby allowing prices to be set by the interplay between demand and supply; abolishing laws regulating the establishment and operation of private enterprises; and relaxing or removing restrictions on direct investment by foreign enterprises and international trade.

In mixed economies, the role of the state was more limited; but here too, in certain sectors the state set prices, owned businesses, limited private enterprise, restricted investment by foreigners, and restricted international trade. For these countries, deregulation has involved the same kind of initiatives that we have seen in former command economies, although the transformation has been easier because these countries often had a vibrant private sector.

PRIVATIZATION   Hand in hand with deregulation has come a sharp increase in privatization. Privatization, as we discussed earlier in this chapter, transfers the ownership of state property into the hands of private individuals, frequently by the sale of state assets through an auction.[57] Privatization is seen as a way to stimulate gains in economic efficiency by giving new private owners a powerful incentive—the reward of greater profits—to search for increases in productivity, to enter new markets, and to exit losing ones.[58]

The privatization movement started in Great Britain in the early 1980s when then Prime Minister Margaret Thatcher started to sell state-owned assets such as the British telephone company, British Telecom (BT). In a pattern that has been repeated around the world, this sale was linked with the deregulation of the British telecommunications industry. By allowing other firms to compete head-to-head with BT, deregulation ensured that privatization did not simply replace a state-owned monopoly with a private monopoly. Since the 1980s, privatization has become a worldwide phenomenon. More than 8,000 acts of privatization were completed around the world between 1995 and 1999.[59] Some of the most dramatic privatization programs occurred in the economies of the former Soviet Union and its Eastern European satellite states. In the Czech Republic, for example, three-quarters of all state-owned enterprises were privatized between 1989 and 1996, helping to push the share of gross domestic product accounted for by the private sector up from 11 percent in 1989 to 60 percent in 1995.[60]

As privatization has proceeded around the world, it has become clear that simply selling state-owned assets to private investors is not enough to guarantee economic growth. Studies of privatization in central Europe have shown that the process often fails to deliver predicted benefits if the newly privatized firms continue to receive subsidies from the state and if they are protected from foreign competition by barriers to international trade and foreign direct investment.[61] In such cases, the newly privatized firms are sheltered from competition and continue acting like state monopolies. When these circumstances prevail, the newly privatized entities often have little incentive to restructure their operations to become more efficient. For privatization to work, it must also be accompanied by a more general deregulation and opening of the economy. Thus, when Brazil decided to privatize the state-owned telephone monopoly, Telebras Brazil, the government also split the company into four independent units that were to compete with each other and removed barriers to foreign direct investment in telecommunications services. This action ensured that the newly privatized entities would face significant competition and thus would have to improve their operating efficiency to survive.

The ownership structure of newly privatized firms also is important.[62] Many former command economies, for example, lack the legal regulations regarding corporate governance that are found in advanced Western economies. In advanced market economies, boards of directors are appointed by shareholders to make sure managers consider the interests of shareholders when making decisions and try to manage the firm in a manner that is consistent with maximizing the wealth of shareholders. However, some former Communist states still lack laws requiring corporations to establish effective boards. In such cases, managers with a small ownership stake can often gain control over the newly privatized entity and run it for their own benefit, while ignoring the interests of other shareholders. Sometimes these managers are the same Communist bureaucrats who ran the enterprise before privatization. Because they have been schooled in the old ways of doing things, they often hesitate to take drastic action to increase the efficiency of the enterprise. Instead, they continue to run the firm as a private fiefdom, seeking to extract whatever economic value they can for their own betterment (in the form of perks that are not reported) while doing little to increase the economic efficiency of the enterprise so that shareholders benefit. Such developments seem less likely to occur, however, if a foreign investor takes a stake in the newly privatized entity. The foreign investor, who usually is a major provider of capital, is often able to use control over a critical resource (money) to push through needed change.

LEGAL SYSTEMS   As noted earlier in this chapter, a well-functioning market economy requires laws protecting private property rights and providing mechanisms for contract enforcement. Without a legal system that protects property rights, and without the machinery to enforce that system, the incentive to engage in economic activity can be reduced substantially by private and public entities, including organized crime, that expropriate the profits generated by the efforts of private-sector entrepreneurs. When communism collapsed, many of these countries lacked the legal structure required to protect property rights, all property having been held by the state. Although many nations have made big strides toward instituting the required system, it will be many more years before the legal system is functioning as smoothly as it does in the West. For example, in most Eastern European nations, the title to urban and agricultural property is often uncertain because of incomplete and inaccurate records, multiple pledges on the same property, and unsettled claims resulting from demands for restitution from owners in the pre-Communist era. Also, although most countries have improved their commercial codes, institutional weaknesses still undermine contract enforcement. Court capacity is often inadequate, and procedures for resolving contract disputes out of court are often lacking or poorly developed.[63] Nevertheless, progress is being made. In 2004, for example, China amended its constitution to state that "private property was not to be encroached upon," and in 2007 it enacted a new law on property rights that gave private property holders many of the same protections as those enjoyed by the state.[64]

Implications of Changing Political Economy

LEARNING OBJECTIVE 7
Explain the implications for management practice of national differences in political economy.

The global changes in political and economic systems discussed above have several implications for international business. The long-standing ideological conflict between collectivism and individualism that defined the twentieth century is less in evidence today. The West won the Cold War, and Western ideology is now widespread. Although command economies remain and totalitarian dictatorships can still be found around the world, the tide has been running in favor of free markets and democracy. It remains to be seen, however, whether the global financial crisis of 2008–2009, and the recession that followed, will lead to a retrenchment. Certainly many commentators have blamed the problems that led to this crisis on a lack of regulation, and in so far as this has been the case, some reassessment of Western political ideology seems likely.

Notwithstanding the crisis of 2008–2009, the implications for business of the trends of the past two decades are enormous. For nearly 50 years, half of the world was off-limits to Western businesses. Now much of that has changed. Many of the national markets of Eastern Europe, Latin America, Africa, and Asia may still be undeveloped and impoverished, but they are potentially enormous. With a population of more than 1.2 billion, the Chinese market alone is potentially bigger than that of the United States, the European Union, and Japan combined. Similarly India, with its nearly 1.1 billion people, is a potentially huge market. Latin America has another 400 million potential consumers. It is unlikely that China, Russia, Vietnam, or any of the other states now moving toward a market system will attain the living standards of the West soon. Nevertheless, the upside potential is so large that companies need to consider making inroads now. For example, if China and Japan continue to grow at the rate they did during 1996–2008, China will surpass Japan and become the world's second-largest national economy behind the United States by 2020.

Just as the potential gains are large, so are the risks. There is no guarantee that democracy will thrive in many of the world's newer democratic states, particularly if these states have to grapple with severe economic setbacks. Totalitarian dictatorships could return, although they are unlikely to be of the communist variety. Although the bipolar world of the Cold War era has vanished, it may be replaced by a multipolar world dominated by a number of civilizations. In such a world, much of the economic promise inherent in the global shift toward market-based economic systems may stall in the face of conflicts between civilizations. While the long-term potential for economic gain from investment in the world's new market economies is large, the risks associated with any such investment are also substantial. It would be foolish to ignore these. The financial system in China, for example, is not transparent, and many suspect that Chinese banks hold a high proportion of nonperforming loans on their books. If true, these bad debts could trigger a significant financial crisis during the next decade in China, which would dramatically lower growth rates.

The material discussed in this chapter has two broad implications for international business. First, the political, economic, and legal systems of a country raise important ethical issues that have implications for the practice of international business. For example, what ethical implications are associated with doing business in totalitarian countries where citizens are denied basic human rights, corruption is rampant, and bribes are necessary to gain permission to do business? Is it right to operate in such a setting? A full discussion of the ethical implications of country differences in political economy is reserved for Chapter 4, where we explore ethics in international business in much greater depth.

Second, the political, economic, and legal environments of a country clearly influence the attractiveness of that country as a market or investment site. The benefits, costs, and risks associated with doing business in a country are a function of that country's political, economic, and legal systems. The overall attractiveness of a country as a market or investment site depends on balancing the likely long-term benefits of doing business in that country against the likely costs and risks. Below we consider the determinants of benefits, costs, and risks.

Benefits

In the most general sense, the long-run monetary benefits of doing business in a country are a function of the size of the market, the present wealth (purchasing power) of consumers in that market, and the likely future wealth of consumers. While some markets are very large when measured by number of consumers (e.g., China and India), low living standards may imply limited purchasing power and therefore a relatively small market when measured in economic terms. International businesses need to be aware of this distinction, but they also need to keep in mind the likely future prospects of a country. In 1960, South Korea was viewed as just another impoverished Third World nation. By 2008 it was the world's 11th-largest economy, measured in terms of GDP. International firms that recognized South Korea's potential in 1960 and began to do business in that country may have reaped greater benefits than those that wrote off South Korea.

By identifying and investing early in a potential future economic star, international firms may build brand loyalty and gain experience in that country's business practices. These will pay back substantial dividends if that country achieves sustained high economic growth rates. In contrast, late entrants may find that they lack the brand loyalty and experience necessary to achieve a significant presence in the market. In the language of business strategy, early entrants into potential future economic stars may be able to reap substantial first-mover advantages, while late entrants may fall victim to late-mover disadvantages.[65] (**First-mover advantages** are the advantages that accrue to early entrants into a market. **Late-mover disadvantages** are the handicaps that late entrants might suffer.) This kind of reasoning has been driving significant inward investment into China, which may become the world's second-largest economy by 2020 if it continues growing at current rates (China is already the world's fourth-largest national economy). For more than a decade, China has been the largest recipient of foreign direct investment in the developing world as international businesses including General Motors, Volkswagen, Coca-Cola, and Unilever try to establish a sustainable advantage in this nation.

A country's economic system and property rights regime are reasonably good predictors of economic prospects. Countries with free market economies in which property rights are protected tend to achieve greater economic growth rates than command economies or economies where property rights are poorly protected. It follows that a country's

First-Mover Advantages
Advantages that accrue to the first to enter a market.

Late-Mover Disadvantages
Handicaps experienced by being a late entrant into a market.

economic system, property rights regime, and market size (in terms of population) probably constitute reasonably good indicators of the potential long-run benefits of doing business in a country. In contrast, countries where property rights are not well respected and where corruption is rampant tend to have lower levels of economic growth. One must be careful about generalizing too much from this, however, since both China and India have achieved high growth rates despite relatively weak property rights regimes and high levels of corruption. In both countries, the shift toward a market-based economic system has produced large gains despite weak property rights and endemic corruption.

Costs

A number of political, economic, and legal factors determine the costs of doing business in a country. With regard to political factors, a company may have to pay off politically powerful entities in a country before the government allows it to do business there. The need to pay what are essentially bribes is greater in closed totalitarian states than in open democratic societies where politicians are held accountable by the electorate (although this is not a hard-and-fast distinction). Whether a company should actually pay bribes in return for market access should be determined on the basis of the legal and ethical implications of such action. We discuss this consideration in Chapter 4, when we look closely at the issue of business ethics.

With regard to economic factors, one of the most important variables is the sophistication of a country's economy. It may be more costly to do business in relatively primitive or undeveloped economies because of the lack of infrastructure and supporting businesses. At the extreme, an international firm may have to provide its own infrastructure and supporting business, which obviously raises costs. When McDonald's decided to open its first restaurant in Moscow, it found that to serve food and drink indistinguishable from that served in McDonald's restaurants elsewhere, it had to vertically integrate backward to supply its own needs. The quality of Russian-grown potatoes and meat was too poor. Thus, to protect the quality of its product, McDonald's set up its own dairy farms, cattle ranches, vegetable plots, and food processing plants within Russia. This raised the cost of doing business in Russia, relative to the cost in more sophisticated economies where high-quality inputs could be purchased on the open market.

As for legal factors, it can be more costly to do business in a country where local laws and regulations set strict standards with regard to product safety, safety in the workplace, environmental pollution, and the like (since adhering to such regulations is costly). It can also be more costly to do business in a country like the United States, where the absence of a cap on damage awards has meant spiraling liability insurance rates. It can be more costly to do business in a country that lacks well-established laws for regulating business practice (as is the case in many of the former Communist nations). In the absence of a well-developed body of business contract law, international firms may find no satisfactory way to resolve contract disputes and, consequently, routinely face large losses from contract violations. Similarly, local laws that fail to adequately protect intellectual property can lead to the theft of an international business's intellectual property and lost income.

Risks

Political Risk
The likelihood that political forces will cause drastic changes in a country's business environment that will adversely affect the profit and other goals of a business enterprise.

As with costs, the risks of doing business in a country are determined by a number of political, economic, and legal factors. **Political risk** has been defined as the likelihood that political forces will cause drastic changes in a country's business environment that adversely affect the profit and other goals of a business enterprise.[66] So defined, political risk tends to be greater in countries experiencing social unrest and disorder or in countries where the underlying nature of a society increases the likelihood of social unrest. Social unrest typically finds expression in strikes, demonstrations, terrorism, and violent conflict. Such unrest is more likely to be found in countries that contain more than one ethnic nationality, in countries where competing ideologies are battling for political control, in countries where economic mismanagement has created high inflation and falling living standards, or in countries that straddle the "fault lines" between civilizations.

Social unrest can result in abrupt changes in government and government policy or, in some cases, in protracted civil strife. Such strife tends to have negative economic implications for the profit goals of business enterprises. For example, in the aftermath of the 1979 Islamic revolution in Iran, the Iranian assets of numerous U.S. companies were seized by the new Iranian government without compensation. Similarly, the violent disintegration of the Yugoslavian federation into warring states, including Bosnia, Croatia, and Serbia, precipitated a collapse in the local economies and in the profitability of investments in those countries.

More generally, a change in political regime can result in the enactment of laws that are less favorable to international business. In Venezuela, for example, the populist socialist politician Hugo Chavez won power in 1998, was reelected as president in 2000, and was reelected in 2006. Chavez has declared himself to be a "Fidelista," a follower of Cuba's Fidel Castro. He has pledged to improve the lot of the poor in Venezuela through government intervention in private business and has frequently railed against American imperialism, all of which is of concern to Western enterprises doing business in the country. Among other actions, he increased the royalties foreign oil companies operating in Venezuela have to pay the government from 1 to 30 percent of sales.

Other risks may arise from a country's mismanagement of its economy. An **economic risk** can be defined as the likelihood that economic mismanagement will cause drastic changes in a country's business environment that hurt the profit and other goals of a particular business enterprise. Economic risks are not independent of political risk. Economic mismanagement may give rise to significant social unrest and hence political risk. Nevertheless, economic risks are worth emphasizing as a separate category because there is not always a one-to-one relationship between economic mismanagement and social unrest. One visible indicator of economic mismanagement tends to be a country's inflation rate. Another is the level of business and government debt in the country.

In Asian states such as Indonesia, Thailand, and South Korea, businesses increased their debt rapidly during the 1990s, often at the bequest of the government, which was encouraging them to invest in industries deemed to be of "strategic importance" to the country. The result was overinvestment, with more industrial (factories) and commercial capacity (office space) being built than could be justified by demand conditions. Many of these investments turned out to be uneconomic. The borrowers failed to generate the profits necessary to service their debt payment obligations. In turn, the banks that had lent money to these businesses suddenly found that they had rapid increases in nonperforming loans on their books. Foreign investors, believing that many local companies and banks might go bankrupt, pulled their money out of these countries, selling local stock, bonds, and currency. This action precipitated the 1997–98 financial crises in Southeast Asia. The crisis included a precipitous decline in the value of Asian stock markets, which in some cases exceeded 70 percent; a similar collapse in the value of many Asian currencies against the U.S. dollar; an implosion of local demand; and a severe economic recession that will affect many Asian countries for years to come. In short, economic risks were rising throughout Southeast Asia during the 1990s. Astute foreign businesses and investors limited their exposure in this part of the world. More naive businesses and investors lost their shirts.

On the legal front, risks arise when a country's legal system fails to provide adequate safeguards in the case of contract violations or to protect property rights. When legal safeguards are weak, firms are more likely to break contracts or steal intellectual property if they perceive it as being in their interests to do so. Thus, a **legal risk** can be

Economic Risk
The likelihood that events, including economic mismanagement, will cause drastic changes in a country's business environment that hurt the profit and other goals of a particular business enterprise.

Legal Risk
The likelihood that a trading partner will opportunistically break a contract or expropriate property rights.

defined as the likelihood that a trading partner will opportunistically break a contract or expropriate property rights. When legal risks in a country are high, an international business might hesitate entering into a long-term contract or joint-venture agreement with a firm in that country. For example, in the 1970s when the Indian government passed a law requiring all foreign investors to enter into joint ventures with Indian companies, U.S. companies such as IBM and Coca-Cola closed their investments in India. They believed that the Indian legal system did not provide for adequate protection of intellectual property rights, creating the very real danger that their Indian partners might expropriate the intellectual property of the American companies—which for IBM and Coca-Cola amounted to the core of their competitive advantage.

Overall Attractiveness

The overall attractiveness of a country as a potential market or investment site for an international business depends on balancing the benefits, costs, and risks associated with doing business in that country (see Figure 2.3). Generally, the costs and risks associated with doing business in a foreign country are typically lower in economically advanced and politically stable democratic nations and greater in less developed and politically unstable nations. The calculus is complicated, however, because the potential long-run benefits are dependent not only upon a nation's current stage of economic development or political stability but also on likely future economic growth rates. Economic growth appears to be a function of a free market system and a country's capacity for growth (which may be greater in less developed nations). This leads one to conclude that, other things being equal, the benefit–cost–risk trade-off is likely to be most favorable in politically stable developed and developing nations that have free market systems and no dramatic upsurge in either inflation rates or private-sector debt. It is likely to be least favorable in politically unstable developing nations that operate with a mixed or command economy or in developing nations where speculative financial bubbles have led to excess borrowing.

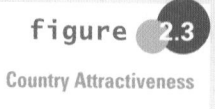

figure 2.3

Country Attractiveness

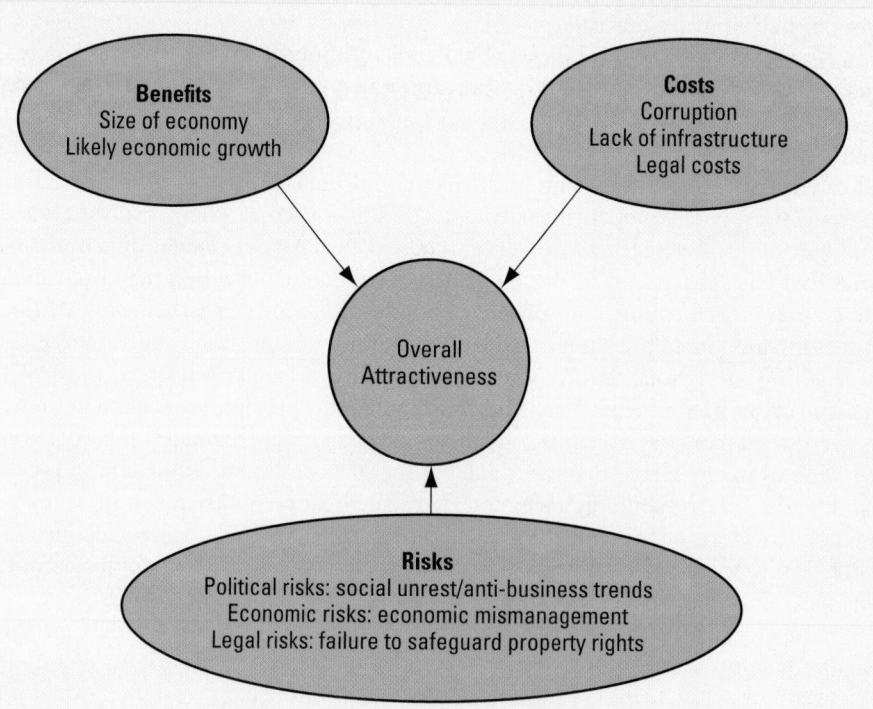

political economy, p. 71

political system, p. 71

collectivism, p. 71

socialism, p. 72

communists, p. 72

social democrats, p. 72

privatization, p. 73

individualism, p. 73

democracy, p. 74

totalitarianism, p. 74

representative democracy, p. 76

communist totalitarianism, p. 76

theocratic totalitarianism, p. 76

tribal totalitarianism, p. 76

right-wing totalitarianism, p. 77

market economy, p. 77

command economy, p. 78

legal system, p. 79

common law, p. 80

civil law system, p. 80

theocratic law system, p. 80

contract, p. 81

contract law, p. 81

United Nations Convention on Contracts for the International Sale of Goods (CIGS), p. 81

property rights, p. 81

private action, p. 82

public action, p. 82

Foreign Corrupt Practices Act, p. 83

intellectual property, p. 85

patent, p. 85

copyright, p. 85

trademark, p. 85

World Intellectual Property Organization, p. 85

Paris Convention for the Protection of Industrial Property, p. 85

product safety laws, p. 86

product liability, p. 86

gross national income (GNI), p. 87

purchasing power parity (PPP), p. 89

Human Development Index (HDI), p. 91

innovation, p. 94

entrepreneurs, p. 94

deregulation, p. 104

first-mover advantages, p. 107

late-mover disadvantages, p. 107

political risk, p. 108

economic risk, p. 109

legal risk, p. 109

Summary

This chapter has reviewed how the political, economic, and legal systems of countries vary. The potential benefits, costs, and risks of doing business in a country are a function of its political, economic, and legal systems. The chapter made the following points:

1. Political systems can be assessed according to two dimensions: the degree to which they emphasize collectivism as opposed to individualism, and the degree to which they are democratic or totalitarian.

2. Collectivism is an ideology that views the needs of society as being more important than the needs of the individual. Collectivism translates into an advocacy for state intervention in economic activity and, in the case of communism, a totalitarian dictatorship.

3. Individualism is an ideology that is built on an emphasis of the primacy of individual's freedoms in the political, economic, and cultural realms. Individualism translates into an advocacy for democratic ideals and free market economics.

4. Democracy and totalitarianism are at different ends of the political spectrum. In a representative democracy, citizens periodically elect individuals to represent them and political freedoms are guaranteed by a constitution. In a totalitarian state, political power is monopolized by a party, group, or individual, and basic political freedoms are denied to citizens of the state.

5. There are three broad types of economic systems: a market economy, a command economy, and a mixed economy. In a market economy, prices are free of controls and private ownership is predominant. In a command economy, prices are set by central planners, productive assets are owned by the state, and private ownership is forbidden. A mixed economy has elements of both a market economy and a command economy.

6. Differences in the structure of law between countries can have important implications for the practice of international business.

The degree to which property rights are protected can vary dramatically from country to country, as can product safety and product liability legislation and the nature of contract law.

7. The rate of economic progress in a country seems to depend on the extent to which that country has a well-functioning market economy in which property rights are protected.

8. Many countries are now in a state of transition. There is a marked shift away from totalitarian governments and command or mixed economic systems and toward democratic political institutions and free market economic systems.

9. The attractiveness of a country as a market and/or investment site depends on balancing the likely long-run benefits of doing business in that country against the likely costs and risks.

10. The benefits of doing business in a country are a function of the size of the market (population), its present wealth (purchasing power), and its future growth prospects. By investing early in countries that are currently poor but are nevertheless growing rapidly, firms can gain first-mover advantages that will pay back substantial dividends in the future.

11. The costs of doing business in a country tend to be greater where political payoffs are required to gain market access, where supporting infrastructure is lacking or underdeveloped, and where adhering to local laws and regulations is costly.

12. The risks of doing business in a country tend to be greater in countries that are politically unstable, subject to economic mismanagement, and lacking a legal system to provide adequate safeguards in the case of contract or property rights violations.

Critical Thinking and Discussion Questions

1. Free market economies stimulate greater economic growth, whereas state-directed economies stifle growth. Discuss.

2. A democratic political system is an essential condition for sustained economic progress. Discuss.

3. What is the relationship between corruption in a country (i.e., bribe taking by government officials) and economic growth? Is corruption always bad?

4. The Nobel Prize–winning economist Amartya Sen argues that the concept of development should be broadened to include more than just economic development. What other factors does Sen think should be included in an assessment of development? How might adoption of Sen's views influence government policy? Do you think Sen is correct that development is about more than just economic development? Explain.

5. You are the CEO of a company that has to choose between making a $100 million investment in Russia or the Czech Republic. Both investments promise the same long-run return, so your choice is driven by risk considerations. Assess the various risks of doing business in each of these nations. Which investment would you favor and why?

6. Read the Country Focus on The Kingdom of Saudi Arabia, then answer the following questions:

   a. Under King Abdullah's leadership, how would you characterize Saudi Arabia's political system? What kind of judicial criminal system has been put in place?

   b. Although a closed society, many Saudis are traveling and experiencing the world. Do you think this will result in women being treated differently in the Kingdom?

   c. What do you think of King Abdullah's planned Economic Cities?

   d. What do you think is the long-term prognosis for Saudi Arabia after the death of King Abdullah? What interests must be taken into consideration?

   e. Will Saudi Arabia continue to attract foreign investment if it maintains its society closed to the rest of the world?

Use the globalEDGE Resource Desk (http://globalEDGE.msu.edu/resourcedesk/) to complete the following exercises:

Exercise 1

You work for a manufacturing company that has operations in the United States and Western Europe. However, increasing competition has prompted the firm to examine the option of shifting production to a lower-cost location. You have narrowed the list of potential countries to Taiwan, South Africa, and Argentina. Based on political and economic *risk ratings*, how would you rate the attractiveness of these three countries for your company? Prepare a brief report summarizing your assessment, including a detailed evaluation of risks for your top country choice.

Exercise 2

The *Market Potential Index* (MPI) is an indexing study conducted by the Michigan State University Center for International Business Education and Research (MSU-CIBER) to compare emerging markets on a variety of dimensions. Provide a description of the indicators used in the indexing procedure. Which of the indicators should have greater importance for a company that markets cellular telephones? Considering the MPI rankings, which five developing countries would you advise a company selling laptops to enter first?

closing case

South Africa after the World Cup

For one solid month, South Africa basked on the world stage in the limelight of the World Cup. Although it is too early to assess the actual return on investment of the R33 billion (US$4.7 billion) South Africa spent on transport and telecommunications infrastructure, there is little doubt that South Africa's has reaped tremendous branding success in hosting football in front of a television audience of billions of people. On average, 500 million spectators around the world have been estimated to have tuned in to watch each of the 64 matches. Nearly half a million foreign fans visited the country, many for the first time, to watch the tournament. But perhaps most importantly was the unifying effect that the games had among the various people. South African whites and blacks were very proud of their achievement.

With a population of slightly more than 49 million, South Africa ranks just above Spain, the World Cup champions. But, unlike Spain, with essentially three or four Iberian cultures and languages, the South African constitution officially recognizes 11 languages with 80 percent of the population being black; 9 percent white; and the rest a mixture of "colored," Indian, or Asian ethnicities.

It is precisely this diversity, and especially between the blacks and the rest—a reality of South African demographics and legacy of Apartheid—that is the root of many of South Africa's challenges. South Africa has a rural/urban economy with high levels of unemployment and low GDP per capita. In the largest cities, Cape Town, Port Elizabeth, Durban, and Pretoria/Johannesburg, sites of the football (soccer) games, a significant amount of economic development has taken place. Auditing firm Grant Thornton puts the overall investment at about 55 billion rand (US$7.3 billion), the equivalent of 6 percent of this year's state budget. Elsewhere, however, in the more rural areas, poverty is prevalent. In some ways it resembles Brazil with its income disparity.

In fact, a recent Organization for Economic Cooperation and Development (OECD) report comparing South Africa with Brazil, India, China, and Indonesia claims that "few if any countries have seen such high sustained levels of open unemployment." Whereas, most of the developing countries are able to provide employment to 65 percent of the population, South Africa is struggling to reach 40 percent employment. According to the report, the most worrisome thing is that among the young black male population, those between 15 and 24 years of age (football age), the situation appears to be worsening. It was during the period of Apartheid that poor, disaffected, young males played a pivotal, many times violent, role in anti-government demonstrations. The report describes a "growing dualism" that harkens back to the Apartheid era in labor markets and a "low level of entrepreneurialism among the black population," despite various government efforts. Labor strikes and potential social unrest are being threatened.

In addition, there is a growing concern. Rumors have been circulating of renewed violence against African immigrants, most from Zimbabwe. They remember back to the xenophobic attacks of 2008 that left 62 dead and the country in shock. Accused of stealing South African jobs and women, the African immigrants have begun to suffer sporadic attacks again. The army is being deployed alongside the police in hot spots in the Western Cape. Hundreds of black foreigners are fleeing back to their own countries. In an attempt to address the unemployment concern, pressure is being placed on the government to create job search assistance, training-based wage subsidies, age-differentiated minimum wages, and an extended probationary period for young workers.

Now that the games are over, however, a graphic reality awakening is imposing itself once again on one of the most promising yet culturally sensitive countries in the world. Much like other developing countries, poverty and unemployment continue to challenge South Africa. Can the unifying, positive economic effects of the World Cup be replicated in an Olympic event?

Sources: "Midyear Population Estimates: 2010," *Statistics South Africa,* accessed July 21, 2010; "Is There a Lot More to Come?" *The Economist,* July 15, 2010; "You're Nicked," *The Economist,* July 8, 2010; R. Lapper, "OECD on South Africa: Mission Far from Accomplished," *Financial Times,* July 20, 2010; S. Rubenfeld, "OECD South Africa Should Be More Proactive against Bribery," *Dow Jones Newswire,* July 20 2010; and OECD, "Economic Survey of South Africa," July 19, 2010.

Case Discussion Questions

1. How would you describe the World Cup effect on South Africa? Was it just a summer game or the beginning of a new era?

2. Do you believe that a marked increase in employment will reduce most of South Africa's cultural tensions?

3. What are some of the ways South Africa is addressing the disproportionate unemployment rate among the young black population?

4. Considering the success of the World Cup, should South Africa seek the Olympic Games in 2020 or 2024? What are the advantages and disadvantages?

LEARNING OBJECTIVES

After you have read this chapter you should be able to:

1 Explain what is meant by the culture of a society.

2 Identify the forces that lead to differences in social culture.

3 Identify the business and economic implications of differences in culture.

4 Recognize how differences in social culture influence values in the workplace.

5 Demonstrate an appreciation for the economic and business implications of cultural change.

Differences in Culture

Doing Business in Russia

opening case

I n the Western world, many relationships are established and business is conducted on the golf course. In other parts of the world, business happens in the *banya*. Whether the Finnish sauna or the Turkish *hammam,* in Russia, the *banya* or bathhouse is a time-honored tradition. In mid-December with an outside temperature below freezing, at the Sandunovskiye Banya, Moscow's oldest and most famous bathhouse, Nathan Jacobson, president of Toronto, Canada–based West Group knew this tradition as he prepared with his staff for a series of meetings with oil, gas, and aluminum executives. He knew about the *banyas* from years of challenging, at times successful, experiences working in the Russian Byzantine system of official and unofficial business barriers.

Right after *perestroika,* the business climate was very difficult in Russia. As the country transitioned from a command economy to a more liberal open-market economy, finding a way to get business done in Russia was critical.

In Russia, it was not uncommon for regional governors to be killed and protection rackets to thrive, where a corrupt police force and a questionable judicial system made official recourse difficult at best, where commercial credit is almost unknown, and where the customs service is renowned for extortion, not only Russian businesspeople, but foreign executives such as Nathan Jacobson depend on powerful relationships, pursued in the *banyas,* while hunting, or in the sharing of a meal to get business done. As a testament to the savviness of working internationally, the West Group eventually grew to become the largest Canadian company in the former Soviet Union.

This example illustrates one aspect of the differences between doing business in the West and doing business in Russia. In the West, heavy reliance is placed on a well-established legal/regulatory system to structure and resolve many of the challenges facing businesspeople as they conduct various transactions. Western business practices resort to corporate and contract law as the basis of such interaction. When a dispute arises, a solution is sought within the judicial system. In Russia, and in many other countries, this approach does not necessarily work. Reliance on the legal/regulatory framework is just not possible. As in China, in Russia personal power, relationships, and connections—many established in the *banyas* rather than in the judicial system—are the key to getting things done. And the key to understanding this process is *blat.*

There is a saying, "International work is interpersonal work." Whether *guanxi* in China, *wasta* in the Middle East, or *amiguismo* in Cuba, *blat* as it is known in Russia not only means "connections" but also denotes the use of informal agreements—the exchange of services or favors, contacts, or black market deals to achieve a predetermined result. Or simply put, the use of "personal networks" to get ahead. West Group was able to get ahead during a very challenging period right after the Russian economic transition by means of recognizing acute business opportunities and by using *blat*.

The concept of *blat* had its origins in the former Soviet Union and had a criminal connotation. It has since evolved to mean business relationships where favors are exchanged. Because in the Soviet Union, the *Gosplan* (State Planning Committee) inefficiently calculated and planned various policy objectives, enterprises often had to rely on people with connections, who could then use *blat* to help fulfill these objectives. The term further evolved to connote acquainting, obtaining, or arranging. It is in a sense particularistic.

Particularism refers to the claim that a certain event is outside the scope of any rule and is unique. China and Russia are particularistic societies. In particularistic cultures, the focus is on the exceptional nature of the present situation. Rules are not as important as personal relationships. In these types of societies, people are usually divided into friends (those we know and can trust) and potentially dangerous strangers. Once a favor has been conveyed to a friend, that friend knows that it will eventually be reciprocated.

In today's Russia, the concept of *blat* has further evolved. As the West Group example illustrates, in post–Soviet Russia, a relatively high degree of uncertainty and ambiguity continues to exist. Therefore, *blat* transactions have at their core an attempt to reduce that level of uncertainty and ambiguity. That is, they are initiated by definite intention and are rationally controlled.

As one could well imagine, there is also a negative side to *blat*. The network aspects of *blat* can be very complex, even Byzantine. As a complicating phenomenon, many of the ex-Communist functionaries are now at the head of private enterprises and public administrations. This requires even more extensive *blat* relationships as the network continues to grow. And although as Russia continues its development in a market economy with its inherent commercialization and marketization, where power is exchanged for money, one would think that *blat* would be fading. This, however, is not the case.

Although significant strides have been made in Russia to establish a legal/regulatory system that permits objective structures and resolutions, much is still needed to replace *blat* transactions. This is especially true as it relates to tax authorities, customs offices, the banking sector, and regional administrations. Gaining access to good schools and universities and to high-quality medical services still requires *blat*. ●

Sources: P. Webster, "Russian Dreams," *Canadian Business* Online, February 17, 2003; S. Michailova and V. Worm, "Personal Networking in Russia and China: *Blat* and *Guanxi*," *European Management Journal* 21, no. 4 (2003), pp. 509–519; and A.V. Ledeneva, *Russia's Economy of Favours:* Blat, *Networking and Informal Exchange* (Cambridge, U.K.: Cambridge University Press, 1998), p. 1.

Introduction

In Chapter 2, we saw how national differences in political, economic, and legal systems influence the benefits, costs, and risks associated with doing business in different countries. In this chapter, we will explore how differences in culture across and within countries can affect international business. Several themes run through this chapter. The first is that business success in a variety of countries requires cross-cultural literacy. By **cross-cultural literacy,** we mean an understanding of how cultural differences across and within nations can affect the way business is practiced. In these days of global communications, rapid transportation, and worldwide markets, when the era of the global village seems just around the corner, it is easy to forget just how different various cultures really are. Underneath the veneer of modernism, deep cultural differences often remain. Take the Chinese. Increasingly, they are embracing the material products of modern society. Anyone who has visited Shanghai cannot fail to be struck by how modern the city seems, with its skyscrapers, department stores, and freeways. Yet beneath the veneer of Western modernism, long-standing cultural traditions rooted in a 2,000-year-old ideology continue to have an important influence on the way business is transacted in China. As the opening case illustrates, in Russia, *blat*, or a network of social relationships with others backed by reciprocal obligations, is central to getting business done. Firms that lack sufficient *blat* may find themselves at a disadvantage when doing business in Russia. The lesson: To succeed in Russia you have to understand and play by the Russian rules. More generally, in this chapter, we shall argue that it is important for foreign businesses to understand the culture that prevails in those countries where they do business, and that success requires a foreign enterprise to adapt to the culture of its host country.[1]

> **Cross-Cultural Literacy**
> An understanding of how cultural differences across and within nations can affect the way business is practiced.

Another theme developed in this chapter is that a relationship may exist between the culture and the cost of doing business in a country or region. Different cultures are more or less supportive of the capitalist mode of production and may increase or lower the costs of doing business. For example, some observers have argued that cultural factors lowered the costs of doing business in Japan and helped to explain Japan's rapid economic ascent during the 1960s, 70s, and 80s.[2] Similarly, cultural factors can sometimes raise the costs of doing business. Historically, class divisions were an important aspect of British culture, and for a long time, firms operating in Great Britain found it difficult to achieve cooperation between management and labor. Class divisions led to a high level of industrial disputes in that country during the 1960s and 1970s and raised the costs of doing business relative to the costs in countries such as Switzerland, Norway, Germany, or Japan, where class conflict was historically less prevalent.

The British example, however, brings us to another theme we will explore in this chapter. Culture is not static. It can and does evolve, although the rate at which culture can change is the subject of some dispute. Important aspects of British culture have changed significantly over the past 30 years, and this is reflected in weaker class distinctions and a lower level of industrial disputes. Indeed, in recent years the number of days lost due to strikes in the United Kingdom has been significantly less than in Australia, the United States, Ireland, and Canada.[3] Finally, multinational enterprises can themselves be engines of cultural change, particularly with regard to material culture. For example, Western fast-food companies such as McDonald's may help to change the dining culture in developing nations such as India, drawing people away from traditional restaurants and toward fast-food outlets.

What Is Culture?

LEARNING OBJECTIVE 1
Explain what is meant by the culture of a society.

Culture
A system of values and norms that are shared among a group of people and that when taken together constitute a design for living.

Values
Abstract ideas about what a group believes to be good, right, and desirable.

Norms
Social rules and guidelines that prescribe appropriate behavior in particular situations.

Society
A group of people who share a common set of values and norms.

Folkways
Routine conventions of everyday life.

Scholars have never been able to agree on a simple definition of *culture*. In the 1870s, the anthropologist Edward Tylor defined culture as "that complex whole which includes knowledge, belief, art, morals, law, custom, and other capabilities acquired by man as a member of society."[4] Since then hundreds of other definitions have been offered. Geert Hofstede, an expert on cross-cultural differences and management, defined culture as "the collective programming of the mind which distinguishes the members of one human group from another. . . . Culture, in this sense, includes systems of values; and values are among the building blocks of culture."[5] Another definition of culture comes from sociologists Zvi Namenwirth and Robert Weber, who see culture as a system of ideas and argue that these ideas constitute a design for living.[6]

Here we follow both Hofstede and Namenwirth and Weber by viewing **culture** as a system of values and norms that are shared among a group of people and that when taken together constitute a design for living. By **values** we mean abstract ideas about what a group believes to be good, right, and desirable. Put differently, values are shared assumptions about how things ought to be.[7] By **norms** we mean the social rules and guidelines that prescribe appropriate behavior in particular situations. We shall use the term **society** to refer to a group of people who share a common set of values and norms. While a society may be equivalent to a country, some countries harbor several societies (i.e., they support multiple cultures), and some societies embrace more than one country.

VALUES AND NORMS   Values form the bedrock of a culture. They provide the context within which a society's norms are established and justified. They may include a society's attitudes toward such concepts as individual freedom, democracy, truth, justice, honesty, loyalty, social obligations, collective responsibility, the role of women, love, sex, marriage, and so on. Values are not just abstract concepts; they are invested with considerable emotional significance. People argue, fight, and even die over values such as freedom. Values also often are reflected in the political and economic systems of a society. As we saw in Chapter 2, democratic free market capitalism is a reflection of a philosophical value system that emphasizes individual freedom.

Norms are the social rules that govern people's actions toward one another. Norms can be subdivided further into two major categories: folkways and mores. **Folkways** are the routine conventions of everyday life. Generally, folkways are actions of little moral significance. Rather, they are social conventions concerning things such as the appropriate dress code in a particular situation, good social manners, eating with the correct utensils, neighborly behavior, and the like. Although folkways define the way people are expected to behave, violation of them is not normally a serious matter. People who violate folkways may be thought of as eccentric or ill-mannered, but they are not usually considered to be evil or bad. In many countries, foreigners may initially be excused for violating folkways.

A good example of folkways concerns attitudes toward time in different countries. People are keenly aware of the passage of time in the United States and Northern European cultures such as Germany and Britain. Businesspeople are very conscious about scheduling their time and are quickly irritated when their time is wasted because a business associate is late for a meeting or if they are kept waiting. They talk about time as though it were money, as something that can be spent, saved, wasted, and lost.[8] Alternatively, in Arab, Latin, and Mediterranean cultures, time has a more elastic character. Keeping to a schedule is viewed as less important than finishing an interaction with people. For example, an American businesswoman might feel slighted if she is kept waiting for 30 minutes outside the office of a Latin American executive before a meeting, but the Latin American may simply be completing an interaction with an associate and view the information gathered from this as more important than sticking to a rigid schedule.

The Latin American executive intends no disrespect, but due to a mutual misunderstanding about the importance of time, the American may see things differently. Similarly, Saudi attitudes to time have been shaped by their nomadic Bedouin heritage, in which precise time played no real role and arriving somewhere tomorrow might mean next week. Like Latin Americans, many Saudis are unlikely to understand the American obsession with precise time and schedules, and Americans need to adjust their expectations accordingly.

Folkways include rituals and symbolic behavior. Rituals and symbols are the most visible manifestations of a culture and constitute the outward expression of deeper values. For example, upon meeting a foreign business executive, a Japanese executive will hold his business card in both hands and bow while presenting the card to the foreigner.[9] This ritual behavior is loaded with deep cultural symbolism. The card specifies the rank of the Japanese executive, which is a very important piece of information in a hierarchical society such as Japan (Japanese often have business cards with Japanese printed on one side, and English printed on the other). The bow is a sign of respect, and the deeper the angle of the bow, the greater the reverence one person shows for the other. The person receiving the card is expected to examine it carefully, which is a way of returning respect and acknowledging the card giver's position in the hierarchy. The foreigner is also expected to bow when taking the card and to return the greeting by presenting the Japanese executive with his own card, similarly bowing in the process. To not do so, and to fail to read the card that he has been given, instead casually placing it in his jacket, violates this important folkway and is considered rude.

Mores are norms that are seen as central to the functioning of a society and to its social life. They have much greater significance than folkways. Accordingly, violating mores can bring serious retribution. Mores include such factors as indictments against theft, adultery, incest, and cannibalism. In many societies, certain mores have been enacted into law. Thus, all advanced societies have laws against theft, incest, and cannibalism. However, there are also many differences between cultures. In America, for example, drinking alcohol is widely accepted, whereas in Saudi Arabia the consumption of alcohol is viewed as violating important social mores and is punishable by imprisonment (as some Western citizens working in Saudi Arabia have discovered).

Another Perspective

The Relativity of Time

And we do not necessarily refer to Einstein's theory but to the reality that various cultures view time differently. The way we perceive time, structure our time, and react to time is culturally based. Two hundred miles may make all the difference in the world. To be on time to catch a train that is scheduled to leave at 11:00 am in Italy may mean that you will arrive at 11:00 am and expect the train to actually leave at 11:20 am. To arrive at 11:00 am in Germany may mean you missed the train. In those countries such as Germany or the United States, time is conceived in a linear fashion or "monochronic." One event proceeds to the next. In other cultures, such as Italy, Mexico, or Saudi Arabia, the concept of time is "polychronic" or having multiple events that can proceed in parallel fashion. So the next time you are waiting for a meeting and the person is late, or you miss a train, or have a meal, consider where you are and adjust your time accordingly. (Various referenced countries on Executive Planet Web site, www.executiveplanet.com, accessed July 22, 2010)

Mores
Norms that are seen as central to the functioning of a society and to its social life.

CULTURE, SOCIETY, AND THE NATION-STATE
We have defined a society as a group of people that share a common set of values and norms; that is, people who are bound together by a common culture. There is not a strict one-to-one correspondence between a society and a nation-state. Nation-states are political creations. They may contain a single culture or several cultures. While the French nation can be thought of as the political embodiment of French culture, the nation of Canada has at least three cultures—an Anglo culture, a French-speaking "Quebecois" culture, and a Native American culture. Similarly, many African nations have important cultural differences between tribal groups, as exhibited in the early 1990s when Rwanda dissolved into a bloody civil war between two tribes, the Tutsis and Hutus. Africa is not alone in this regard. India is composed of many distinct cultural groups. During the first Gulf War, the prevailing view

presented to Western audiences was that Iraq was a homogenous Arab nation. However, since then we have learned that several different societies exist within Iraq, each with its own culture. The Kurds in the north do not view themselves as Arabs and have their own distinct history and traditions. There are two Arab societies: the Shiites in the South and the Sunnis who populate the middle of the country and who ruled Iraq under the regime of Saddam Hussein (the terms *Shiites* and *Sunnis* refer to different sects within the religion of Islam). Among the southern Sunnis is another distinct society of 500,000 Marsh Arabs who live at the confluence of the Tigris and Euphrates rivers, pursuing a way of life that dates back 5,000 years.[10]

At the other end of the scale are cultures that embrace several nations. Several scholars argue that we can speak of an Islamic society or culture that is shared by the citizens of many different nations in the Middle East, Asia, and Africa. As you will recall from the last chapter, this view of expansive cultures that embrace several nations underpins Samuel Huntington's view of a world that is fragmented into different civilizations, including Western, Islamic, and Sinic (Chinese).[11]

To complicate things further, it is also possible to talk about culture at different levels. It is reasonable to talk about "American society" and "American culture," but there are several societies within America, each with its own culture. One can talk about African-American culture, Cajun culture, Chinese-American culture, Hispanic culture, Indian culture, Irish-American culture, and Southern culture. The relationship between culture and country is often ambiguous. Even if a country can be characterized as having a single homogenous culture, often that national culture is a mosaic of subcultures.

LEARNING OBJECTIVE 2
Identify the forces that lead to differences in social culture.

THE DETERMINANTS OF CULTURE   The values and norms of a culture do not emerge fully formed. They are the evolutionary product of a number of factors, including the prevailing political and economic philosophies, the social structure of a society, and the dominant religion, language, and education (see Figure 3.1). We

figure **3.1**

The Determination of Culture

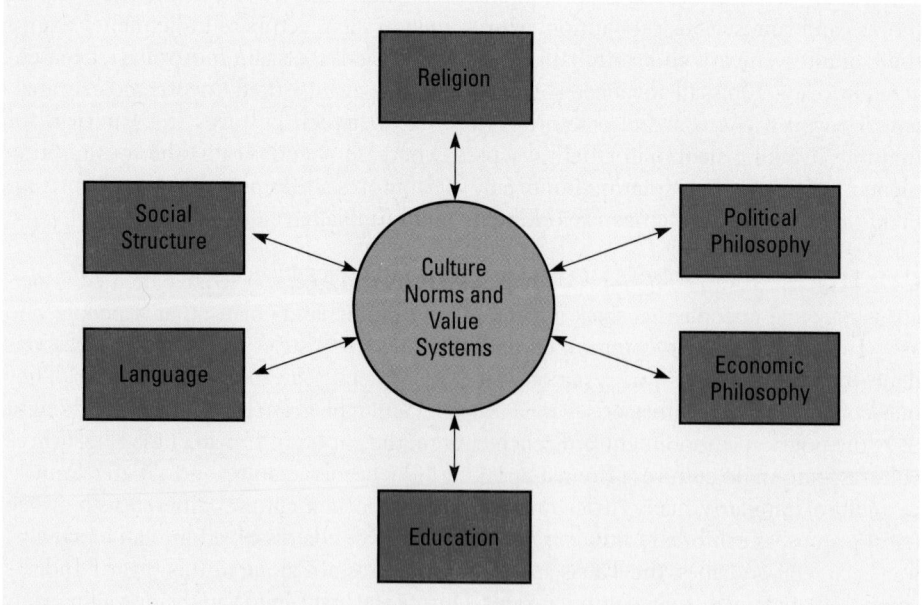

discussed political and economic philosophies at length in Chapter 2. Such philosophies clearly influence the value systems of a society. For example, the values found in Communist North Korea toward freedom, justice, and individual achievement are clearly different from the values found in the United States, precisely because each society operates according to different political and economic philosophies. Below we will discuss the influence of social structure, religion, language, and education. The chain of causation runs both ways. While factors such as social structure and religion clearly influence the values and norms of a society, the values and norms of a society can influence social structure and religion.

Social Structure

A society's **social structure** refers to its basic social organization. Although social structure consists of many different aspects, two dimensions are particularly important when explaining differences between cultures. The first is the degree to which the basic unit of social organization is the individual, as opposed to the group. In general, Western societies tend to emphasize the primacy of the individual, whereas groups tend to figure much larger in many other societies. The second dimension is the degree to which a society is stratified into classes or castes. Some societies are characterized by a relatively high degree of social stratification and relatively low mobility between strata (e.g., Indian); other societies are characterized by a low degree of social stratification and high mobility between strata (e.g., American).

Social Structure
The basic social organization of a society.

INDIVIDUALS AND GROUPS A **group** is an association of two or more individuals who have a shared sense of identity and who interact with each other in structured ways on the basis of a common set of expectations about each other's behavior.[12] Human social life is group life. Individuals are involved in families, work groups, social groups, recreational groups, and so on. However, while groups are found in all societies, societies differ according to the degree to which the group is viewed as the primary means of social organization.[13] In some societies, individual attributes and achievements are viewed as being more important than group membership; in others the reverse is true.

Group
An association of two or more individuals who have a shared sense of identity and who interact with each other in structured ways on the basis of a common set of expectations about each other's behavior.

The Individual In Chapter 2, we discussed individualism as a political philosophy. However, individualism is more than just an abstract political philosophy. In many Western societies, the individual is the basic building block of social organization. This is reflected not just in the political and economic organization of society but also in the way people perceive themselves and relate to each other in social and business settings. The value systems of many Western societies, for example, emphasize individual achievement. The social standing of individuals is not so much a function of whom they work for as of their individual performance in whatever work setting they choose.

The emphasis on individual performance in many Western societies has both beneficial and harmful aspects. In the United States, the emphasis on individual performance finds expression in an admiration of rugged individualism and entrepreneurship. One benefit of this is the high level of entrepreneurial activity in the United States and other Western societies. New products and new ways of doing business (e.g., personal computers, photocopiers, computer software, biotechnology, supermarkets, and discount retail stores) have repeatedly been created in the United States by entrepreneurial individuals. One can argue that the dynamism of the U.S. economy owes much to the philosophy of individualism.

LEARNING OBJECTIVE 3
Identify the business and economic implications of differences in culture.

Individualism also finds expression in a high degree of managerial mobility between companies, and this is not always a good thing. Although moving from company to company may be good for individual managers who are trying to build impressive résumés, it is not necessarily a good thing for American companies. The lack of loyalty and commitment to an individual company, and the tendency to move on for a better offer, can result in managers who have good general skills but lack the knowledge, experience, and network of interpersonal contacts that come from years of working within the same company. An effective manager draws on company-specific experience, knowledge, and a network of contacts to find solutions to current problems, and American companies may suffer if their managers lack these attributes. One positive aspect of high managerial mobility is that executives are exposed to different ways of doing business. The ability to compare business practices helps U.S. executives identify how good practices and techniques developed in one firm might be profitably applied to other firms.

The emphasis on individualism may also make it difficult to build teams within an organization to perform collective tasks. If individuals are always competing with each other on the basis of individual performance, it may be difficult for them to cooperate. A study of U.S. competitiveness by the Massachusetts Institute of Technology suggested that U.S. firms are being hurt in the global economy by a failure to achieve cooperation both within a company (e.g., between functions; between management and labor) and between companies (e.g., between a firm and its suppliers). Given the emphasis on individualism in the American value system, this failure is not surprising.[14] The emphasis on individualism in the United States, while helping to create a dynamic entrepreneurial economy, may raise the costs of doing business due to its adverse impact on managerial stability and cooperation.

The Group   In contrast to the Western emphasis on the individual, the group is the primary unit of social organization in many other societies. For example, in Japan, the social status of an individual is determined as much by the standing of the group to which he or she belongs as by his or her individual performance.[15] In traditional Japanese society, the group was the family or village to which an individual belonged. Today, the group has frequently come to be associated with the work team or business organization to which an individual belongs. In a now-classic study of Japanese society, Nakane noted how this expresses itself in everyday life:

> When a Japanese faces the outside (confronts another person) and affixes some position to himself socially he is inclined to give precedence to institution over kind of occupation. Rather than saying, "I am a typesetter" or "I am a filing clerk," he is likely to say, "I am from B Publishing Group" or "I belong to S company."[16]

LEARNING OBJECTIVE 3
Identify the business and economic implications of differences in culture.

Nakane goes on to observe that the primacy of the group to which an individual belongs often evolves into a deeply emotional attachment in which identification with the group becomes all-important in one's life. One central value of Japanese culture is the importance attached to group membership. This may have beneficial implications for business firms. Strong identification with the group is argued to create pressures for mutual self-help and collective action. If the worth of an individual is closely linked to the achievements of the group (e.g., firm), as Nakane maintains is the case in Japan, this creates a strong incentive for individual members of the group to work together for the common good. Some argue that the success of Japanese enterprises in the global economy has been based partly on their ability to achieve close cooperation between individuals within a company and between companies. This has found expression in the widespread diffusion of self-managing work teams within Japanese organizations, the close cooperation among different functions within Japanese companies (e.g., among manufacturing, marketing, and R&D), and the cooperation between a company and its suppliers on issues such as design, quality control, and inventory reduction.[17] In all of these cases, cooperation is driven by the need to improve the performance of the group (i.e., the business firm).

The primacy of the value of group identification also discourages managers and workers from moving from company to company. Lifetime employment in a particular company was long the norm in certain sectors of the Japanese economy (estimates suggest that between 20 and 40 percent of all Japanese employees have formal or informal lifetime employment guarantees). Over the years, managers and workers build up knowledge, experience, and a network of interpersonal business contacts. All these things can help managers perform their jobs more effectively and achieve cooperation with others.

However, the primacy of the group is not always beneficial. Just as U.S. society is characterized by a great deal of dynamism and entrepreneurship, reflecting the primacy of values associated with individualism, some argue that Japanese society is characterized by a corresponding lack of dynamism and entrepreneurship. Although the long-run consequences are unclear, the United States could continue to create more new industries than Japan and continue to be more successful at pioneering radically new products and new ways of doing business.

SOCIAL STRATIFICATION

All societies are stratified on a hierarchical basis into social categories—that is, into **social strata.** These strata are typically defined on the basis of characteristics such as family background, occupation, and income. Individuals are born into a particular stratum. They become a member of the social category to which their parents belong. Individuals born into a stratum toward the top of the social hierarchy tend to have better life chances than those born into a stratum toward the bottom of the hierarchy. They are likely to have better education, health, standard of living, and work opportunities. Although all societies are stratified to some degree, they differ in two related ways. First, they differ from each other with regard to the degree of mobility between social strata; second, they differ with regard to the significance attached to social strata in business contexts (see the Country Focus).

Social Mobility

The term **social mobility** refers to the extent to which individuals can move out of the strata into which they are born. Social mobility varies significantly from society to society. The most rigid system of stratification is a caste system. A **caste system** is a closed system of stratification in which social position is determined by the family into which a person is born, and change in that position is usually not possible during an individual's lifetime. Often a caste position carries with it a specific occupation. Members of one caste might be shoemakers, members of another might be butchers, and so on. These occupations are embedded in the caste and passed down through the family to succeeding generations. Although the number of societies with caste systems diminished rapidly during the twentieth century, one partial example still remains. India has four main castes and several thousand subcastes. Even though the caste system was officially abolished in 1949, two years after India became independent, it is still a force in rural Indian society where occupation and marital opportunities are still partly related to caste.[18]

A **class system** is a less rigid form of social stratification in which social mobility is possible. It is a form of open stratification in which the position a person has by birth can be changed through his or her own achievements or luck. Individuals born into a

LEARNING OBJECTIVE 2
Identify the forces that lead to differences in social culture.

Social Strata
Hierarchical social categories often based on family background, occupation, and income.

Social Mobility
The extent to which individuals can move out of the strata into which they are born.

Caste System
A closed system of stratification in which social position is determined by the family into which a person is born, and change in that position is usually not possible during an individual's lifetime.

Class System
A system of social stratification in which the position a person has by birth can be changed through his or her own achievements or luck.

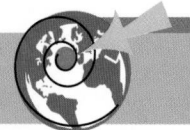

Country FOCUS

Understanding Mexico's Complexities

Mexico is a complicated country. It is mixture of history; pre-Hispanic Mesoamerican indigenous tribes; and Spanish, American, and European influences within a highly diverse geographic land. To begin to understand Mexican culture is to dwell within the thousands of years it has taken to develop this culture. To understand its history is to understand current Mexican thought and action.

Mexico can be said to have had five major indigenous civilizations: the Olmec, the Teotihuacan, the Toltec, the Mexica, and the Maya. These various societies formed the foundation upon which Spanish influence came to bear in the *mestizo* (Amerindian/European) culture.

Geographic and social stratification is prevalent in Mexico. From the northern stretches to the southern jungles, Mexican geography and its corresponding populace encompass two oceans, a variety of landscapes, and a divergent rural and urban population. These may be grouped into the following five regions: El Distrito Federal—Mexico City; El Norte—the Border Area; the Central Part—Guadalajara; the Southeast—Oaxaca, Chiapas, and Yucatan; and Baja—Tijuana and Cabo San Lucas. Each one of these regions has its own cultural strata and attributes and therefore presents unique environments in which to conduct business.

Perhaps nowhere is this best exemplified than by the differences between Mexico City and the states of Oaxaca and Chiapas. Fiercely independent, self-confident (at times culturally arrogant), and the country's capital, Mexico City *(El Distrito Federal)* is not only the center of economic and political activity but essentially the unifying metropolis of its past. As the seat of the federal government, Mexico City is cosmopolitan, sophisticated, and dynamic with many of the problems and challenges facing a world-class city. Catering to the service sector, "el DF"—as Mexico City is known—houses the largest banks, accounting and law firms, and Latin American headquarters for some of the world's largest multinational firms.

In contrast, Oaxaca and Chiapas are among the most indigenous states in Mexico. The lush mountainous jungles filled with ancient Mayan pyramids and architecture are home to the Maya culture, including the Zapotec and Mixtec people. Both states are considered among Mexico's poorest regions. This geographic, socioeconomic, and cultural contrast with Mexico City led in 2006 to social unrest and violence with human rights violations and deaths.

Known as an active port back in the 16th century, present-day tourist destination, Huatulco, located on the Pacific Coast in the state of Oaxaca, caters to an eclectic variety of Mexican, American, and European visitors. It is hoped that the town will eventually grow to rival Cancun on the Atlantic side of the country. But in these southern reaches, agriculture, particularly coffee production worked by the local population, continues to represent the economic foundation of the region. As recent attacks on activists appear to suggest, remnants of the 2006 clash lay just underneath the surface. This region's future is questionable if it is to rely primarily on this globally traded bean.

Sources: K. Bricker and E. Godoy, "Mexico: Terror Returns to Oaxaca," *Inter Press Service*, April 30, 2010, http://ipsnews.net; "North and South: Why Can't Its Stagnant Southern States Catch Up with the Rest of Mexico?" *The Economist*, April 24, 2008; and William Hernandez Requejo and John L. Graham, *Global Negotiation, The New Rules* (New York: Palgrave Macmillan, 2008), pp. 205–215.

class at the bottom of the hierarchy can work their way up; conversely, individuals born into a class at the top of the hierarchy can slip down.

While many societies have class systems, social mobility within a class system varies from society to society. For example, some sociologists have argued that Britain has a more rigid class structure than certain other Western societies, such as the United States.[19] Historically, British society was divided into three main classes: the upper class, which was made up of individuals whose families for generations had wealth, prestige, and occasionally power; the middle class, whose members were involved in professional, managerial, and clerical occupations; and the working class, whose members earned their living from manual occupations. The middle class was further subdivided into the upper-middle class, whose members were involved in important managerial occupations and the prestigious professions (e.g., lawyers, accountants, doctors), and the lower-middle class, whose members were involved in clerical work (e.g., bank tellers) and the less prestigious professions (e.g., schoolteachers).

The British class system exhibited significant divergence between the life chances of members of different classes. The upper and upper-middle classes typically sent their children to a select group of private schools, where they wouldn't mix with lower-class children, and where they picked up many of the speech accents and social norms that marked them as being from the higher strata of society. These same private schools also had close ties with the most prestigious universities, such as Oxford and Cambridge. Until fairly recently, Oxford and Cambridge guaranteed a certain number of places for the graduates of these private schools. Having been to a prestigious university, the offspring of the upper and upper-middle classes then had an excellent chance of being offered a prestigious job in companies, banks, brokerage firms, and law firms run by members of the upper and upper-middle classes.

In contrast, the members of the British working and lower-middle classes typically went to state schools. The majority left at 16, and those who went on to higher education found it more difficult to get accepted at the best universities. When they did, they found that their lower-class accent and lack of social skills marked them as being from a lower social stratum, which made it more difficult for them to get access to the most prestigious jobs.

Because of this, the class system in Britain perpetuated itself from generation to generation, and mobility was limited. Although upward mobility was possible, it could not normally be achieved in one generation. While an individual from a working-class background may have established an income level that was consistent with membership in the upper-middle class, he or she may not have been accepted as such by others of that class due to accent and background. However, by sending his or her offspring to the "right kind of school," the individual could ensure that his or her children were accepted.

According to many commentators, modern British society is now rapidly leaving this class structure behind and moving toward a classless society. However, sociologists continue to dispute this finding and present evidence that this is not the case. For example, one study reported that state schools in the London suburb of Islington, which has a population of 175,000, had only 79 candidates for university, while one prestigious private school alone, Eton, sent more than that number to Oxford and Cambridge.[20] This, according to the study's authors, implies that "money still begets money." They argue that a good school means a good university, a good university means a good job, and merit has only a limited chance of elbowing its way into this tight little circle.

The class system in the United States is less pronounced than in Britain and mobility is greater. Like Britain, the United States has its own upper, middle, and working classes. However, class membership is determined to a much greater degree by individual economic achievements, as opposed to background and schooling. Thus, an individual can, by his or her own economic achievement, move smoothly from the working class to the upper class in a lifetime. Successful individuals from humble origins are highly respected in American society.

Another society where class divisions have historically been of some importance has been China, where there has been a long-standing difference between the life chances of the rural peasantry and urban dwellers. Ironically, this historic division was strengthened during the high point of Communist rule because of a rigid system of household registration that restricted most Chinese to the place of their birth for their lifetime. Bound to collective farming, peasants were cut off from many urban privileges—compulsory education, quality schools, health care, public housing, varieties of foodstuffs, to name only a few—and they largely lived in poverty. Social mobility was thus very limited. This system crumbled following reforms of the late 1970s and early 1980s, and as a consequence, migrant peasant laborers have flooded into China's cities looking for work. Sociologists now hypothesize that a new class system is emerging in China based less on the rural-urban divide and more on urban occupation.[21]

Until the late 1970s, social mobility in China was very limited, but now sociologists believe a new class system is emerging in China based less on the rural-urban divide and more on urban occupation.

LEARNING OBJECTIVE 3
Identify the business and economic implications of differences in culture.

Class Consciousness
A tendency for people to perceive themselves in terms of their class background.

Significance   From a business perspective, the stratification of a society is significant if it affects the operation of business organizations. In American society, the high degree of social mobility and the extreme emphasis on individualism limit the impact of class background on business operations. The same is true in Japan, where most of the population perceives itself to be middle class. In a country such as Great Britain, however, the relative lack of class mobility and the differences between classes have resulted in the emergence of class consciousness. **Class consciousness** refers to a condition where people tend to perceive themselves in terms of their class background, and this shapes their relationships with members of other classes.

This has been played out in British society in the traditional hostility between upper-middle-class managers and their working-class employees. Mutual antagonism and lack of respect historically made it difficult to achieve cooperation between management and labor in many British companies and resulted in a relatively high level of industrial disputes. However, as noted earlier, the last two decades have seen a dramatic reduction in industrial disputes, which bolsters the arguments of those who claim that the country is moving toward a classless society (the level of industrial disputes in the United Kingdom is now lower than in the United States). Alternatively, as noted above, class consciousness may be reemerging in urban China, and it may ultimately prove to be significant there.

An antagonistic relationship between management and labor classes, and the resulting lack of cooperation and high level of industrial disruption, tends to raise the costs of production in countries characterized by significant class divisions. In turn, this can make it more difficult for companies based in such countries to establish a competitive advantage in the global economy.

Religious and Ethical Systems

Religion may be defined as a system of shared beliefs and rituals that are concerned with the realm of the sacred.[22] **Ethical systems** refer to a set of moral principles, or values, that are used to guide and shape behavior. Most of the world's ethical systems are the product of religions. Thus, we can talk about Christian ethics and Islamic ethics. However, there is a major exception to the principle that ethical systems are grounded in religion. Confucianism and Confucian ethics influence behavior and shape culture in parts of Asia, yet it is incorrect to characterize Confucianism as a religion.

The relationship among religion, ethics, and society is subtle and complex. Among the thousands of religions in the world today, four dominate in terms of numbers of adherents: Christianity with 1.7 billion adherents, Islam with around 1 billion adherents, Hinduism with 750 million adherents (primarily in India), and Buddhism with 350 million adherents (see Map 3.1). Although many other religions have an important influence in certain parts of the modern world (for example, Judaism, which has 18 million adherents), their numbers pale in comparison with these dominant religions (however, as the precursor of both Christianity and Islam, Judaism has an indirect influence that goes beyond its numbers). We will review these four religions, along with Confucianism, focusing on their business implications. Some scholars have argued that the most important business implications of religion center on the extent to which different religions shape attitudes toward work and entrepreneurship and the degree to which the religious ethics affect the costs of doing business in a country.

It is hazardous to make sweeping generalizations about the nature of the relationship between religion and ethical systems and business practice. While some scholars argue that there is a relationship between religious and ethical systems and business practice in a society, in a world where nations with Catholic, Protestant, Muslim, Hindu, and Buddhist majorities all show evidence of entrepreneurial activity and sustainable economic growth, it is important to view such proposed relationships with a degree of skepticism. The proposed relationships may exist, but their impact is probably small compared to the impact of economic policy. Alternatively, research by economists Robert Barro and Rachel McCleary suggests that strong religious beliefs, and particularly beliefs in heaven, hell, and an afterlife, have a positive impact on economic growth rates, irrespective of the particular religion in question.[23] Barro and McCleary looked at religious beliefs and economic growth rates in 59 countries during the 1980s and 1990s. Their conjecture was that higher religious beliefs stimulate economic growth because they help to sustain aspects of individual behavior that lead to higher productivity.

CHRISTIANITY

Christianity is the most widely practiced religion in the world. Approximately 20 percent of the world's people identify themselves as Christians. The vast majority of Christians live in Europe and the Americas, although their numbers are growing rapidly in Africa. Christianity grew out of Judaism. Like Judaism, it is a monotheistic religion (monotheism is the belief in one god). A religious division in the eleventh century led to the establishment of two major Christian organizations—the Roman Catholic Church and the Orthodox Church. Today, the Roman Catholic Church accounts for more than half of all Christians, most of whom are found in Southern Europe and Latin America. The Orthodox Church, while less influential, is still of major importance in several countries (e.g., Greece and Russia). In the sixteenth century, the Reformation led to a further split with Rome; the result was Protestantism. The nonconformist nature of Protestantism has facilitated the emergence of numerous denominations under the Protestant umbrella (e.g., Baptist, Methodist, Calvinist).

LEARNING OBJECTIVE 2
Identify the forces that lead to differences in social culture.

Religion
A system of shared beliefs and rituals that are concerned with the realm of the sacred.

Ethical Systems
A set of moral principles, or values, that are used to guide and shape behavior.

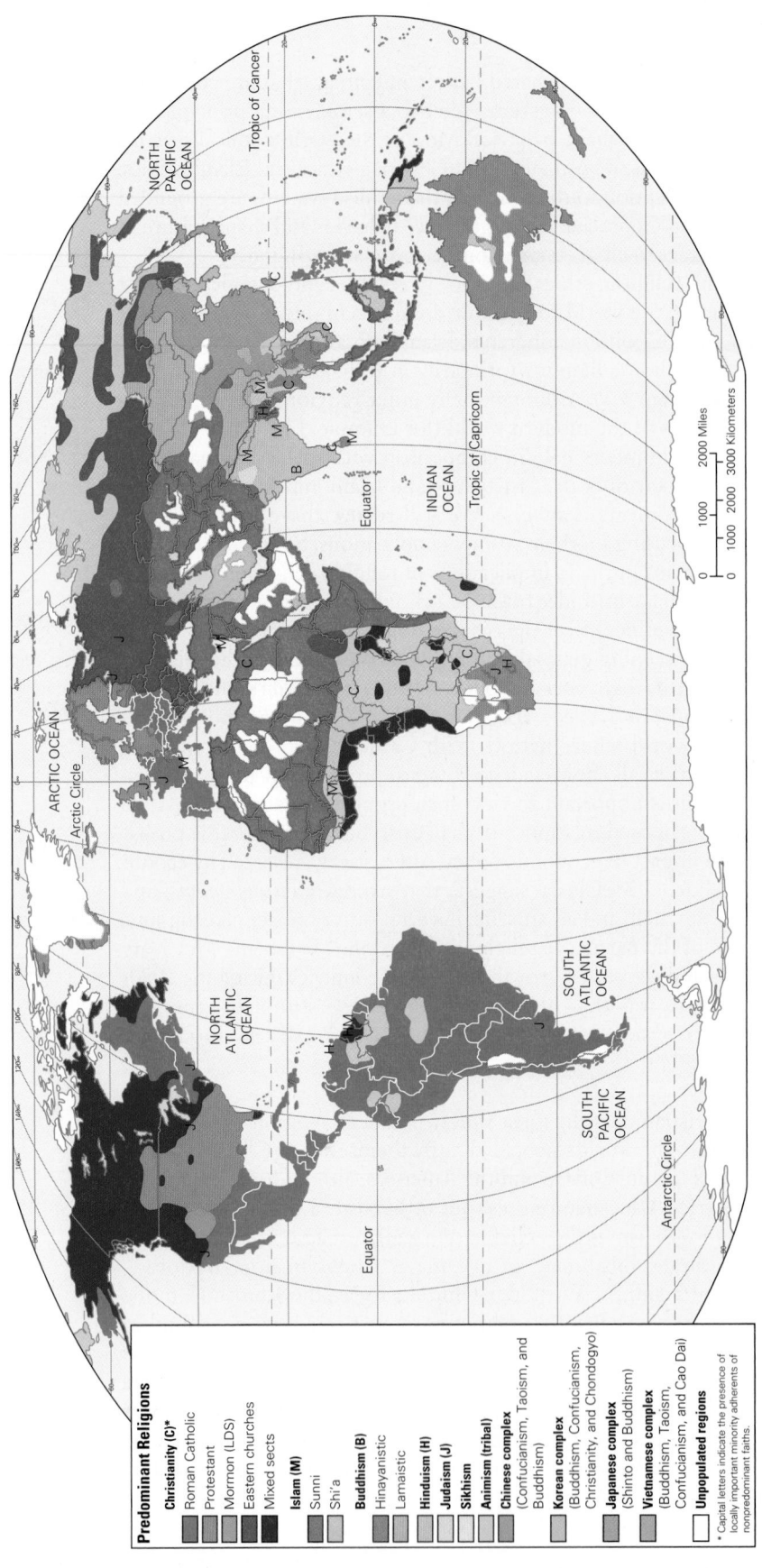

Predominant Religions

Christianity (C)*
Roman Catholic
Protestant
Mormon (LDS)
Eastern churches
Mixed sects

Islam (M)
Sunni
Shi'a

Buddhism (B)
Hinayanistic
Lamaistic

Hinduism (H)

Judaism (J)

Sikhism

Animism (tribal)

Chinese complex
(Confucianism, Taoism, and Buddhism)

Korean complex
(Buddhism, Confucianism, Christianity, and Chondogyo)

Japanese complex
(Shinto and Buddhism)

Vietnamese complex
(Buddhism, Taoism, Confucianism, and Cao Dai)

Unpopulated regions

* Capital letters indicate the presence of locally important minority adherents of nonpredominant faiths.

3.1 map World Religions

Source: John L. Allen, Student Atlas of World Politics, 7th ed. Map 8, © 2006 by the McGraw-Hill Companies, Inc. All rights reserved. Reprinted by permission of McGraw-Hill Contemporary Learning Series.

Economic Implications of Christianity: The Protestant Work Ethic   Several sociologists have argued that of the main branches of Christianity—Catholic, Orthodox, and Protestant—the latter has the most important economic implications. In 1904, a German sociologist, Max Weber, made a connection between Protestant ethics and "the spirit of capitalism" that has since become famous.[24] Weber noted that capitalism emerged in Western Europe, where

> business leaders and owners of capital, as well as the higher grades of skilled labor, and even more the higher technically and commercially trained personnel of modern enterprises, are overwhelmingly Protestant.[25]

Weber theorized that there was a relationship between Protestantism and the emergence of modern capitalism. He argued that Protestant ethics emphasize the importance of hard work and wealth creation (for the glory of God) and frugality (abstinence from worldly pleasures). According to Weber, this kind of value system was needed to facilitate the development of capitalism. Protestants worked hard and systematically to accumulate wealth. However, their ascetic beliefs suggested that rather than consuming this wealth by indulging in worldly pleasures, they should invest it in the expansion of capitalist enterprises. Thus, the combination of hard work and the accumulation of capital, which could be used to finance investment and expansion, paved the way for the development of capitalism in Western Europe and subsequently in the United States. In contrast, Weber argued that the Catholic promise of salvation in the next world, rather than this world, did not foster the same kind of work ethic.

Protestantism also may have encouraged capitalism's development in another way. By breaking away from the hierarchical domination of religious and social life that characterized the Catholic Church for much of its history, Protestantism gave individuals significantly more freedom to develop their own relationship with God. The right to freedom of form of worship was central to the nonconformist nature of early Protestantism. This emphasis on individual religious freedom may have paved the way for the subsequent emphasis on individual economic and political freedoms and the development of individualism as an economic and political philosophy. As we saw in Chapter 2, such a philosophy forms the bedrock on which entrepreneurial free market capitalism is based. Building on this, some scholars claim there is a connection between individualism, as inspired by Protestantism, and the extent of entrepreneurial activity in a nation.[26] Again, one must be careful not to generalize too much from this historical sociological view. While nations with a strong Protestant tradition such as Britain, Germany, and the United States were early leaders in the industrial revolution, nations with Catholic or Orthodox majorities show significant and sustained entrepreneurial activity and economic growth in the modern world.

ISLAM   With about 1 billion adherents, Islam is the second largest of the world's major religions. Islam dates back to AD 610 when the prophet Muhammad began spreading the word, although the Muslim calendar begins in AD 622 when, to escape growing opposition, Muhammad left Mecca for the oasis settlement of Yathrib, later known as Madina. Adherents of Islam are referred to as Muslims. Muslims constitute a majority in more than 35 countries and inhabit a nearly contiguous stretch of land from the northwest coast of Africa, through the Middle East, to China and Malaysia in the Far East.

Islam has roots in both Judaism and Christianity (Islam views Jesus Christ as one of God's prophets). Like Christianity and Judaism, Islam is a monotheistic religion. The central principle of Islam is that there is but the one true omnipotent God. Islam requires unconditional acceptance of the uniqueness, power, and authority of God and the understanding that the objective of life is to fulfill the dictates of his will in the hope of admission to paradise. According to Islam, worldly gain and temporal power are an illusion. Those who pursue riches on earth may gain them, but those who forgo worldly ambitions to seek the favor of Allah may gain the greater treasure—entry into paradise. Other major principles of Islam include (1) honoring and respecting parents, (2) respecting the rights of others, (3) being generous but not a squanderer, (4) avoiding killing except for justifiable causes, (5) not committing adultery, (6) dealing justly and equitably with others, (7) being of pure heart and mind, (8) safeguarding the possessions of orphans, and (9) being humble and unpretentious.[27] Obvious parallels exist with many of the central principles of both Judaism and Christianity.

Islam is an all-embracing way of life governing the totality of a Muslim's being.[28] As God's surrogate in this world, a Muslim is not a totally free agent but is circumscribed by religious principles—by a code of conduct for interpersonal relations—in social and economic activities. Religion is paramount in all areas of life. The Muslim lives in a social structure that is shaped by Islamic values and norms of moral conduct. The ritual nature of everyday life in a Muslim country is striking to a Western visitor. Among other things, orthodox Muslim ritual requires prayer five times a day (business meetings may be put on hold while the Muslim participants engage in their daily prayer ritual), requires that women should be dressed in a certain manner, and forbids the consumption of pork and alcohol.

Islamic Fundamentalism The past three decades have witnessed the growth of a social movement often referred to as Islamic fundamentalism.[29] In the West, Islamic fundamentalism is associated in the media with militants, terrorists, and violent upheavals, such as the bloody conflict occurring in Algeria, the killing of foreign tourists in Egypt, and the September 11, 2001, attacks on the World Trade Center and Pentagon in the United States. This characterization is misleading. Just as Christian fundamentalists are motivated by sincere and deeply held religious values firmly rooted in their faith, so are Islamic fundamentalists. The violence that the Western media

The rise of Islamic fundamentalism as a reaction against globalization and the prevalence of Western cultural ideas has sent many scrambling to try to understand Muslim culture and promote greater dialogue.

associates with Islamic fundamentalism is perpetrated by a small minority of radical "fundamentalists" who have hijacked the religion to further their own political and violent ends. (Some Christian "fundamentalists" have done exactly the same, including Jim Jones and David Koresh.) The vast majority of Muslims point out that Islam teaches peace, justice, and tolerance, not violence and intolerance, and that Islam explicitly repudiates the violence that a radical minority practices.

The rise of fundamentalism has no one cause. In part, it is a response to the social pressures created in traditional Islamic societies by the move toward modernization and by the influence of Western ideas, such as liberal democracy, materialism, equal rights for women, and attitudes toward sex, marriage, and alcohol. In many Muslim countries, modernization has been accompanied by a growing gap between a rich urban minority and an impoverished urban and rural majority. For the impoverished majority, modernization has offered little in the way of tangible economic progress, while threatening the traditional value system. Thus, for a Muslim who cherishes his or her traditions and believes that his or her identity is jeopardized by the encroachment of alien Western values, Islamic fundamentalism has become a cultural anchor.

Fundamentalists demand commitment to traditional religious beliefs and rituals. The result has been a marked increase in the use of symbolic gestures that confirm Islamic values. In areas where fundamentalism is strong, women have resumed wearing floor-length, long-sleeved dresses and covering their hair; religious studies have increased in universities; the publication of religious tracts has increased; and public religious orations have risen.[30] Also, the sentiments of some fundamentalist groups are often anti-Western. Rightly or wrongly, Western influence is blamed for a range of social ills, and many fundamentalists' actions are directed against Western governments, cultural symbols, businesses, and even individuals.

In several Muslim countries, fundamentalists have gained political power and have used this to try to make Islamic law (as set down in the Koran, the bible of Islam) the law of the land. There are good grounds for this in Islam. Islam makes no distinction between church and state. It is not just a religion; Islam is also the source of law, a guide to statecraft, and an arbiter of social behavior. Muslims believe that every human endeavor is within the purview of the faith—and this includes political activity—because the only purpose of any activity is to do God's will.[31] (Some Christian fundamentalists also share this view.) Muslim fundamentalists have been most successful in Iran, where a fundamentalist party has held power since 1979, but they also have had an influence in many other countries, such as Algeria, Afghanistan (where the Taliban established an extreme fundamentalist state until removed by the U.S.-led coalition in 2002), Egypt, Pakistan, the Sudan, and Saudi Arabia.

Economic Implications of Islam The Koran establishes some explicit economic principles, many of which are pro-free enterprise.[32] The Koran speaks approvingly of free enterprise and of earning legitimate profit through trade and commerce (the prophet Mohammed was once a trader). The protection of the right to private property is also embedded within Islam, although Islam asserts that all property is a favor from Allah (God), who created and so owns everything. Those who hold property are regarded as trustees rather than owners in the Western sense of the word. As trustees they are entitled to receive profits from the property but are admonished to use it in a righteous, socially beneficial, and prudent manner. This reflects Islam's concern with social justice. Islam is critical of those who earn profit through the exploitation of others. In the Islamic view of the world, humans are part of a collective in which the wealthy and successful have obligations to help the disadvantaged. Put simply, in Muslim countries, it is fine to earn a profit, so long as that

LEARNING OBJECTIVE 3
Identify the business and economic implications of differences in culture.

Country FOCUS

Dubai—A Crisis in Islamic Finance

For many years, Dubai, one of the seven emirates of the United Arab Emirates (UAE), a Muslim country lead by Mohammed bin Rashid Al Maktoum, experienced unprecedented economic growth. Although oil and natural gas production supported most of Dubai's early economic development, today it accounts for only 6 percent of the region's GDP. Today, trade, tourism, service sectors, logistics, and financial services and industries account for the vast majority of the GDP.

Through Dubai World, the government's flag bearer and investment company, a wide variety of industry segments and "mega-projects" were developed, including real estate developments such as The Palm Islands and The World. This development was financed on appreciating real estate prices and sovereign debt; a testament to the effective integration of traditional global financial markets and strict dictates of the Quran and Islamic finance. In this regard, Dubai represented a model by which the world's Muslims could participate in an integrated, globalized economy.

Then on November 25, 2009, Dubai (through Dubai World) shocked the financial world by threatening to default on $4.5 billion *sukuk*, or Islamic bonds, and delay the payment for six months on an additional $26 billion. The implications of this potential default sent the world's financial markets into crisis. Issues relating to the role of sovereign debt in overall global development, the imperfections of Islamic banking, and the contagion effect became obvious.

Although technically a purely commercial matter, Dubai World's potential default would normally not count as a national or sovereign debt default, but because of its direct links to the emirate and the ruling families, it was interpreted as such. That is, Dubai World's debt was supposedly guaranteed by the nation and the ruling families. This fact was not clear, however. This in turn led to speculation

and fears as to other sovereign debts such as Greece and the Ukraine.

Similarly, the Dubai World debt crisis lead to issues regarding the role Islamic banking is playing within a global context. Issues of transparency and full disclosure became immediately relevant. As became quickly clear when Dubai World first announced its debt troubles, however, there was no legal sovereign guarantee. The problem was in the fact that the lines between state ownership, and consequently state guarantees, were dubious because of the different structuring methodologies required by Islamic law.

As the Middle East continues to reap the profits from oil and gas production, and as it diversifies into other sectors, it will continue to attract capital. Islamic and non-Islamic banking institutions will seek to utilize that capital not only at home but throughout the world.

Fortunately Dubai World has reached a preliminary agreement with its core group of creditors, which represents 60 percent of the debt owed to lenders. With the additional information provided, creditors will have more time to mull over their options before accepting (or not) the terms of the proposal. Although still under the auspices of *Sharia* law, Islamic companies, such as Dubai World, are finding themselves in the position of private borrowers who have to renegotiate the terms of their contracts without government support, under a great deal of public scrutiny. While currently viewed as a "parallel banking system" continued activity between Islamic and non-Islamic banks will only increase the amount of economic integration. As it restructures its debt, Dubai may continue to serve as a model.

Sources: B. Plamondon and S. Gunduzler, "Dubai World Meets with Creditors, Restructuring Plan to Be Finalized Soon," *IHS Global Insight Daily Analysis*, July 23, 2010; "Sukuk It Up," *The Economist* April 2010, pp. 82–83; and "Finding the Ripcord. Dubai Reveals How It Wants to Restructure Its Debt," *The Economist*, May 25, 2010.

profit is justly earned and not based on the exploitation of others for one's own advantage. It also helps if those making profits undertake charitable acts to help the poor. Furthermore, Islam stresses the importance of living up to contractual obligations, of keeping one's word, and of abstaining from deception. For a closer look at how Islam, capitalism, and globalization are forced to coexist, see the accompanying Country Focus on Dubai.

Given the Islamic proclivity to favor market-based systems, Muslim countries are likely to be receptive to international businesses as long as those businesses behave in a manner that is consistent with Islamic ethics. Businesses that are perceived as making an unjust profit through the exploitation of others, by deception, or by breaking contractual obligations are unlikely to be welcomed in an Islamic country. In addition, in Islamic countries where fundamentalism is on the rise, hostility toward Western-owned businesses is likely to increase.

In the previous chapter, we noted that one economic principle of Islam prohibits the payment or receipt of interest, which is considered usury. This is not just a matter of theology; in several Islamic states, it is also a matter of law. The Koran clearly condemns interest, which is called *riba* in Arabic, as exploitative and unjust. For many years, banks operating in Islamic countries conveniently ignored this condemnation, but about 30 years ago, starting with the establishment of an Islamic bank in Egypt, Islamic banks began to appear in predominantly Muslim countries. By 2008, more than 200 Islamic financial institutions worldwide managed more than $700 billion in assets.[33] Even conventional banks are entering the market—both Citigroup and HSBC, two of the world's largest financial institutions, now offer Islamic financial services. While only Iran and the Sudan enforce Islamic banking conventions, in an increasing number of countries, customers can choose between conventional banks and Islamic banks.

Conventional banks make a profit on the spread between the interest rate they have to pay to depositors and the higher interest rate they charge borrowers. Because Islamic banks cannot pay or charge interest, they must find a different way of making money. Islamic banks have experimented with two different banking methods—the *mudarabah* and the *murabaha*.[34]

A *mudarabah* contract is similar to a profit-sharing scheme. Under *mudarabah*, when an Islamic bank lends money to a business, rather than charging that business interest on the loan, it takes a share in the profits that are derived from the investment. Similarly, when a business (or individual) deposits money at an Islamic bank in a savings account, the deposit is treated as an equity investment in whatever activity the bank uses the capital for. Thus, the depositor receives a share in the profit from the bank's investment (as opposed to interest payments) according to an agreed-on ratio. Some Muslims claim this is a more efficient system than the Western banking system, since it encourages both long-term savings and long-term investment. However, there is no hard evidence of this, and many believe that a *mudarabah* system is less efficient than a conventional Western banking system.

The second Islamic banking method, the *murabaha* contract, is the most widely used among the world's Islamic banks, primarily because it is the easiest to implement. In a *murabaha* contract, when a firm wishes to purchase something using a loan—let's say a piece of equipment that costs $1,000—the firm tells the bank after having negotiated the price with the equipment manufacturer. The bank then buys the equipment for $1,000, and the borrower buys it back from the bank at some later date for, say, $1,100, a price that includes a $100 markup for the bank. A cynic might point out that such a markup is functionally equivalent to an interest payment, and it is the similarity between this method and conventional banking that makes it so much easier to adopt.

HINDUISM Hinduism has approximately 750 million adherents, most of them on the Indian subcontinent. Hinduism began in the Indus Valley in India more than 4,000 years ago, making it the world's oldest major religion. Unlike Christianity and Islam, its founding is not linked to a particular person. Nor does it have an officially sanctioned sacred book such as the Bible or the Koran. Hindus believe that a moral force in society requires the acceptance of certain responsibilities, called *dharma*. Hindus believe in reincarnation, or rebirth into a different body, after death. Hindus also believe in *karma*, the spiritual progression of each person's soul. A person's karma is affected by the way he or she lives. The moral state of an individual's karma determines the challenges he or she will face in the next life. By perfecting the soul in each new life, Hindus believe that an individual can eventually achieve *nirvana*, a state of

LEARNING OBJECTIVE 2
Identify the forces that lead to differences in social culture.

complete spiritual perfection that renders reincarnation no longer necessary. Many Hindus believe that the way to achieve nirvana is to lead a severe ascetic lifestyle of material and physical self-denial, devoting life to a spiritual rather than material quest.

One of the interesting aspects of Hindu culture is the reverence for the cow, which Hindus see as a gift of the gods to the human race. The sacred status of the cow created some unique problems for McDonald's when it entered India in the 1990s, since devout Hindus do not eat beef (and many are also vegetarians).

LEARNING OBJECTIVE 3
Identify the business and economic implications of differences in culture.

Economic Implications of Hinduism

Max Weber, famous for expounding on the Protestant work ethic, also argued that the ascetic principles embedded in Hinduism do not encourage the kind of entrepreneurial activity in pursuit of wealth creation that we find in Protestantism.[35] According to Weber, traditional Hindu values emphasize that individuals should be judged not by their material achievements but by their spiritual achievements. Hindus perceive the pursuit of material well-being as making the attainment of nirvana more difficult. Given the emphasis on an ascetic lifestyle, Weber thought that devout Hindus would be less likely to engage in entrepreneurial activity than devout Protestants.

Mahatma Gandhi, the famous Indian nationalist and spiritual leader, was certainly the embodiment of Hindu asceticism. It has been argued that the values of Hindu asceticism and self-reliance that Gandhi advocated had a negative impact on the economic development of postindependence India.[36] But one must be careful not to read too much into Weber's arguments. Modern India is a very dynamic entrepreneurial society, and millions of hardworking entrepreneurs form the economic backbone of the country's rapidly growing economy.

Historically, Hinduism also supported India's caste system. The concept of mobility between castes within an individual's lifetime makes no sense to traditional Hindus. Hindus see mobility between castes as something that is achieved through spiritual progression and reincarnation. An individual can be reborn into a higher caste in his or her next life if he or she achieves spiritual development in this life. Although the caste system has been abolished in India, it still casts a long shadow over Indian life, according to many observers. In so far as the caste system limits individuals' opportunities to adopt positions of responsibility and influence in society, the economic consequences of this religious belief are somewhat negative. For example, within a business organization, the most able individuals may find their route to the higher levels of the organization blocked simply because they come from a lower caste. By the same token, individuals may get promoted to higher positions within a firm as much because of their caste background as because of their ability.

LEARNING OBJECTIVE 2
Identify the forces that lead to differences in social culture.

BUDDHISM

Buddhism was founded in India in the sixth century BC by Siddhartha Gautama, a Nepalese prince who renounced his wealth to pursue an ascetic lifestyle and spiritual perfection. Siddhartha achieved nirvana but decided to remain on earth to teach his followers how they too could achieve this state of spiritual enlightenment. Siddhartha became known as the Buddha (which means "the awakened one"). Today, Buddhism has 350 million followers, most of whom are found in Central and Southeast Asia, China, Korea, and Japan. According to Buddhism, suffering originates in people's desires for pleasure. Cessation of suffering can be achieved by following a path for transformation. Siddhartha offered the Noble Eightfold Path as a route for transformation. This emphasizes right seeing, thinking, speech, action, living, effort, mindfulness, and meditation. Unlike Hinduism, Buddhism does not support the caste system. Nor does Buddhism advocate the kind of extreme ascetic behavior that is encouraged by Hinduism. Nevertheless, like Hindus, Buddhists stress the afterlife and spiritual achievement rather than involvement in this world.

Economic Implications of Buddhism   The emphasis on wealth creation that is embedded in Protestantism is not found in Buddhism. Thus, in Buddhist societies, we do not see the same kind of historical cultural stress on entrepreneurial behavior that Weber claimed could be found in the Protestant West. But unlike Hinduism, the lack of support for the caste system and extreme ascetic behavior suggests that a Buddhist society may represent a more fertile ground for entrepreneurial activity than a Hindu culture.

LEARNING OBJECTIVE 3
Identify the business and economic implications of differences in culture.

CONFUCIANISM   Confucianism was founded in the fifth century BC by K'ung-Fu-tzu, more generally known as Confucius. For more than 2,000 years until the 1949 Communist revolution, Confucianism was the official ethical system of China. While observance of Confucian ethics has been weakened in China since 1949, more than 200 million people still follow the teachings of Confucius, principally in China, Korea, and Japan. Confucianism teaches the importance of attaining personal salvation through right action. Although not a religion, Confucian ideology has become deeply embedded in the culture of these countries over the centuries and, through that, has an impact on the lives of many millions more. Confucianism is built around a comprehensive ethical code that sets guidelines for relationships with others. High moral and ethical conduct and loyalty to others are central to Confucianism. Unlike religions, Confucianism is not concerned with the supernatural and has little to say about the concept of a supreme being or an afterlife.

LEARNING OBJECTIVE 2
Identify the forces that lead to differences in social culture.

Economic Implications of Confucianism   Some scholars maintain that Confucianism may have economic implications as profound as those Weber argued were to be found in Protestantism, although they are of a different nature.[37] Their basic thesis is that the influence of Confucian ethics on the culture of China, Japan, South Korea, and Taiwan, by lowering the costs of doing business in those countries, may help explain their economic success. In this regard, three values central to the Confucian system of ethics are of particular interest: loyalty, reciprocal obligations, and honesty in dealings with others.

LEARNING OBJECTIVE 3
Identify the business and economic implications of differences in culture.

In Confucian thought, loyalty to one's superiors is regarded as a sacred duty—an absolute obligation. In modern organizations based in Confucian cultures, the loyalty that binds employees to the heads of their organization can reduce the conflict between management and labor that we find in more class-conscious societies. Cooperation between management and labor can be achieved at a lower cost in a culture where the virtue of loyalty is emphasized in the value systems.

However, in a Confucian culture, loyalty to one's superiors, such as a worker's loyalty to management, is not blind loyalty. The concept of reciprocal obligations is important. Confucian ethics stress that superiors are obliged to reward the loyalty of their subordinates by bestowing blessings on them. If these "blessings" are not forthcoming, then neither will be the loyalty. This Confucian ethic is central to the Chinese concept of *guanxi*, which refers to relationship networks supported by reciprocal obligations.[38] As discussed in the opening case, *guanxi* means relationships, although in business settings it can be better understood as

Another Perspective

The Rise of Chinese Buddhism

Once-atheist, China is becoming not only supportive but encouraging of Chinese Buddhists. The new attitude has economic as well as religious reasons. While tensions remain between the Chinese government and Tibetan Buddhism (the Dalai Lama is considered a separatist), the Chinese form of Buddhism is not seen as problematic. As a charitable institution, Buddhism is making a significant social impact in China. As people have more disposable income, donations are growing. These donations in turn help improve living conditions in the less-developed areas of China. Cash-strapped local governments welcome the help. The Chinese also support Chinese Buddhism as a means of counteracting the influences of Christianity and Protestantism, which has exploded. (L. Lim, "Beijing Finds Common Cause with Chinese Buddhists," *National Public Radio*, July 22, 2010. www.npr.org, accessed July 23, 2010)

DMG-Shanghai

In 1993, New Yorker Dan Mintz moved to China as a free-lance film director with no contacts, no advertising experience, and no Mandarin. By 2006, the company he had founded in China, DMG, had emerged as one of China's fastest-growing advertising agencies with a client list that included Budweiser, Unilever, Sony, Nabisco, Audi, Volkswagen, China Mobile, and dozens of other Chinese brands. Mintz attributes his success in part to what the Chinese call *guanxi*.

In a society that lacks a strong rule-based legal tradition, and thus legal ways of redressing wrongs such as violations of business agreements, *guanxi* is an important mechanism for building long-term business relationships and getting business done in China. There is a tacit acknowledgment that if you have the right *guanxi*, legal rules can be broken, or at least bent.

Mintz, who is now fluent in Mandarin, cultivated his *guanxiwang* by going into business with two young Chinese who had connections, Bing Wu and Peter Xiao. Bing Wu, who works on the production side of the business, was a former national gymnastics champion, which translates into prestige and access to business and government officials. Peter Xiao comes from a military family with major political connections. Together, these three have been able to open doors that long-established Western advertising agencies have not. They have done it in

large part by leveraging the contacts of Wu and Xiao, and by backing up their connections with what the Chinese call *Shi li*, the ability to do good work.

A case in point was DMG's campaign for Volkswagen, which helped the German company to become ubiquitous in China. The ads used traditional Chinese characters, which had been banned by Chairman Mao during the cultural revolution in favor of simplified versions. To get permission to use the characters in film and print ads—a first in modern China—the trio had to draw on high-level government contacts in Beijing. They won over officials by arguing that the old characters should be thought of not as "characters" but as art. Later, they shot TV spots for the ad on Shanghai's famous Bund, a congested boulevard that runs along the waterfront of the old city. Drawing again on government contacts, they were able to shut down the Bund to make the shoot. Steven Spielberg had been able to close only a portion of the street when he filmed *Empire of the Sun* there in 1986. DMG has also filmed inside Beijing's Forbidden City, even though it is against the law to do so. Using his contacts, Mintz persuaded the government to lift the law for 24 hours. As Mintz has noted, "We don't stop when we come across regulations. There are restrictions everywhere you go. You have to know how get around them and get things done."

Sources: J. Bryan, "The Mintz Dynasty," *Fast Company*, April 2006, pp. 56–62; and M. Graser, "Featured Player," *Variety*, October 18, 2004, p. 6.

connections. Today, Chinese will often cultivate a *guanxiwang*, or "relationship network," for help. Reciprocal obligations are the glue that holds such networks together. If those obligations are not met—if favors done are not paid back or reciprocated—the reputation of the transgressor is tarnished and the person will be less able to draw on his or her *guanxiwang* for help in the future. Thus, the implicit threat of social sanctions is often sufficient to ensure that favors are repaid, obligations are met, and relationships are honored. In a society that lacks a rule-based legal tradition, and thus legal ways of redressing wrongs such as violations of business agreements, *guanxi* is an important mechanism for building long-term business relationships and getting business done in China. For an example of the importance of *guanxi*, read the Management Focus on DMG-Shanghai.

A third concept found in Confucian ethics is the importance attached to honesty. Confucian thinkers emphasize that, although dishonest behavior may yield short-term benefits for the transgressor, dishonesty does not pay in the long run. The importance attached to honesty has major economic implications. When companies can trust each other not to break contractual obligations, the costs of doing business are lowered. Expensive lawyers are not needed to resolve contract disputes. In a Confucian society, people may be less hesitant to commit substantial resources to cooperative ventures than in a society where honesty is less pervasive. When companies adhere to Confucian ethics, they can trust each other not to violate the terms of cooperative agreements. Thus, the costs of achieving cooperation between companies may be lower in societies such as Japan relative to societies where trust is less pervasive.

For example, it has been argued that the close ties between the automobile companies and their component parts suppliers in Japan are facilitated by a combination of trust and reciprocal obligations. These close ties allow the auto companies and their suppliers to work together on a range of issues, including inventory reduction, quality control, and design. The competitive advantage of Japanese auto companies such as Toyota may in part be explained by such factors.[39] Similarly, the combination of trust and reciprocal obligations is central to the workings and persistence of *guanxi* networks in China. Someone seeking and receiving help through a *guanxi* network is then obligated to return the favor and faces social sanctions if that obligation is not reciprocated when it is called upon. If the person does not return the favor, his or her reputation will be tarnished and he or she will be unable to draw on the resources of the network in the future. It is claimed that these relationship-based networks can be more important in helping to enforce agreements between businesses than the Chinese legal system. Some claim that *guanxi* networks are a substitute for the legal system.[40]

Language

One obvious way in which countries differ is language. By language, we mean both the spoken and the unspoken means of communication. Language is one of the defining characteristics of a culture.

LEARNING OBJECTIVE 2
Identify the forces that lead to differences in social culture.

SPOKEN LANGUAGE Language does far more than just enable people to communicate with each other. The nature of a language also structures the way we perceive the world. The language of a society can direct the attention of its members to certain features of the world rather than others. The classic illustration of this phenomenon is that whereas the English language has but one word for snow, the language of the Inuit (Eskimos) lacks a general term for it. Instead, because distinguishing different forms of snow is so important in the lives of the Inuit, they have 24 words that describe different types of snow (e.g., powder snow, falling snow, wet snow, drifting snow).[41]

Because language shapes the way people perceive the world, it also helps define culture. Countries with more than one language often have more than one culture. Canada has an English-speaking culture and a French-speaking culture. Tensions between the two can run quite high, with a substantial proportion of the French-speaking minority demanding independence from a Canada "dominated by English speakers." The same phenomenon can be observed in many other countries. Belgium is divided into Flemish and French speakers, and tensions between the two groups exist; in Spain, a Basque-speaking minority with its own distinctive culture has been agitating for independence from the Spanish-speaking majority for decades; on the Mediterranean island of Cyprus, the culturally diverse Greek- and Turkish-speaking populations of the island engaged in open conflict in the 1970s, and the island is now partitioned into two parts. While it does not necessarily follow that language differences create differences in culture and, therefore, separatist pressures (e.g., witness the harmony in Switzerland, where four languages are spoken), there certainly seems to be a tendency in this direction.[42]

Chinese is the mother tongue of the largest number of people, followed by English and Hindi, which is spoken in India. However, the most widely spoken language in the world is English, followed by French, Spanish, and Chinese (i.e., many people speak English as a second language). English is increasingly becoming the language of international business. When a Japanese and a German businessperson get together

LEARNING OBJECTIVE 3
Identify the business and economic implications of differences in culture.

When You Can't Find the Right Words
Trying to find the correct words to express your heartfelt condolences is difficult in any culture. In some high-context cultures it is made much easier. When someone dies in Japan it is customary to slightly bow and give the next of kin an envelope (*koden* or *reizen* depending on the religion) with $20 or $30 dollars to show your condolences. It is as though you were saying, "I am sorry for the death of your husband. Please accept this envelope as a token of my condolence. It must be very difficult and I hope this small token can help." In actuality, all you are saying is "Please accept this envelope." The rest is completely understood. (A. Reed, Journal Entry for May 25, 2007, in www.discovernikkei.org/en/journal/2007/5/25/jet-tales/, accessed July 23, 2010; and Japanese Acknowledgement of Condolences, http://www.japan-guide.com/forum/quereadisplay.html?0+47280, accessed July 23, 2010)

to do business, it is almost certain that they will communicate in English. However, although English is widely used, learning the local language yields considerable advantages. Most people prefer to converse in their own language, and being able to speak the local language can build rapport, which may be very important for a business deal. International businesses that do not understand the local language can make major blunders through improper translation. For example, the Sunbeam Corporation used the English words for its "Mist-Stick" mist-producing hair curling iron when it entered the German market, only to discover after an expensive advertising campaign that *mist* means excrement in German. General Motors was troubled by the lack of enthusiasm among Puerto Rican dealers for its new Chevrolet Nova. When literally translated into Spanish, *nova* means star. However, when spoken it sounds like "no va," which in Spanish means "it doesn't go." General Motors changed the name of the car to Caribe.[43]

LEARNING OBJECTIVE 2
Identify the forces that lead to differences in social culture.

UNSPOKEN LANGUAGE   Unspoken language refers to nonverbal communication. We all communicate with each other by a host of nonverbal cues. The raising of eyebrows, for example, is a sign of recognition in most cultures, while a smile is a sign of joy. Many nonverbal cues, however, are culturally bound. A failure to understand the nonverbal cues of another culture can lead to a communication failure. For example, making a circle with the thumb and the forefinger is a friendly gesture in the United States, but it is a vulgar sexual invitation in Greece and Turkey. Similarly, while most Americans and Europeans use the thumbs-up gesture to indicate that "it's all right," in Greece the gesture is obscene.

Another aspect of nonverbal communication is personal space, which is the comfortable amount of distance between you and someone you are talking with. In the United States, the customary distance apart adopted by parties in a business discussion is five to eight feet. In Latin America, it is three to five feet. Consequently, many North Americans unconsciously feel that Latin Americans are invading their personal space and can be seen backing away from them during a conversation. Indeed, the American may feel that the Latin is being aggressive and pushy. In turn, the Latin American may interpret such backing away as aloofness. The result can be a regrettable lack of rapport between two businesspeople from different cultures.

Education

LEARNING OBJECTIVE 2
Identify the forces that lead to differences in social culture.

Formal education plays a key role in a society. Formal education is the medium through which individuals learn many of the language, conceptual, and mathematical skills that are indispensable in a modern society. Formal education also supplements the family's role in socializing the young into the values and norms of a society. Values and norms are taught both directly and indirectly. Schools generally teach basic facts about the social and political nature of a society. They also focus on the fundamental obligations of citizenship. Cultural norms are also taught indirectly at school. Respect for others, obedience to authority, honesty, neatness, being on time, and so on, are all part of the hidden curriculum of schools. The use of a grading system also teaches children the value of personal achievement and competition.[44]

From an international business perspective, one important aspect of education is its role as a determinant of national competitive advantage.[45] The availability of a pool of skilled and educated workers seems to be a major determinant of the likely economic success of a country. In analyzing the competitive success of Japan since 1945, for example, Michael Porter notes that after the war, Japan had almost nothing except for a pool of skilled and educated human resources.

> With a long tradition of respect for education that borders on reverence, Japan possessed a large pool of literate, educated, and increasingly skilled human resources. . . . Japan has benefited from a large pool of trained engineers. Japanese universities graduate many more engineers per capita than in the United States. . . . A first-rate primary and secondary education system in Japan operates based on high standards and emphasizes math and science. Primary and secondary education is highly competitive. . . . Japanese education provides most students all over Japan with a sound education for later education and training. A Japanese high school graduate knows as much about math as most American college graduates.[46]

Porter's point is that Japan's excellent education system is an important factor explaining the country's postwar economic success. Not only is a good education system a determinant of national competitive advantage, but it is also an important factor guiding the location choices of international businesses. The recent trend to outsource information technology jobs to India, for example, is partly due to the presence of significant numbers of trained engineers in India, which in turn is a result of the Indian education system. By the same token, it would make little sense to base production facilities that require highly skilled labor in a country where the education system was so poor that a skilled labor pool wasn't available, no matter how attractive the country might seem on other dimensions. It might make sense to base production operations that require only unskilled labor in such a country.

The general education level of a country is also a good index of the kind of products that might sell in a country and of the type of promotional material that should be used. For example, a country where more than 70 percent of the population is illiterate is unlikely to be a good market for popular books. Promotional material containing written descriptions of mass-marketed products is unlikely to have an effect in a country where almost three-quarters of the population cannot read. It is far better to use pictorial promotions in such circumstances.

Culture and the Workplace

Of considerable importance for an international business with operations in different countries is how a society's culture affects the values found in the workplace. Management process and practices may need to vary according to culturally determined work-related values. For example, if the cultures of the United States and France result in different work-related values, an international business with operations in both countries should vary its management process and practices to account for these differences.

Probably the most famous study of how culture relates to values in the workplace was undertaken by Geert Hofstede.[47] As part of his job as a psychologist working for IBM, Hofstede collected data on employee attitudes and values for more than 100,000 individuals from 1967 to 1973. These data enabled him to compare dimensions of culture across 40 countries. Hofstede isolated four dimensions that he claimed summarized different cultures—power distance, uncertainty avoidance, individualism versus collectivism, and masculinity versus femininity.

Hofstede's **power distance** dimension focused on how a society deals with the fact that people are unequal in physical and intellectual capabilities. According to Hofstede, high power distance cultures were found in countries that let inequalities grow over time into inequalities of power and wealth. Low power distance cultures were found in societies that tried to play down such inequalities as much as possible.

The **individualism versus collectivism** dimension focused on the relationship between the individual and his or her fellows. In individualistic societies, the ties between individuals were loose and individual achievement and freedom were highly valued. In societies where collectivism was emphasized, the ties between individuals were tight. In such societies, people were born into collectives, such as extended families, and everyone was supposed to look after the interests of his or her collective.

Hofstede's **uncertainty avoidance** dimension measured the extent to which different cultures socialized their members into accepting ambiguous situations and tolerating uncertainty. Members of high uncertainty avoidance cultures placed a premium on job security, career patterns, retirement benefits, and so on. They also had a strong need for rules and regulations; the manager was expected to issue clear instructions, and subordinates' initiatives were tightly controlled. Lower uncertainty avoidance cultures were characterized by a greater readiness to take risks and less emotional resistance to change.

Hofstede's **masculinity versus femininity** dimension looked at the relationship between gender and work roles. In masculine cultures, sex roles were sharply differentiated and traditional "masculine values," such as achievement and the effective exercise of power, determined cultural ideals. In feminine cultures, sex roles were less sharply distinguished, and little differentiation was made between men and women in the same job.

Hofstede created an index score for each of these four dimensions that ranged from 0 to 100 and scored high for high individualism, high power distance, high uncertainty avoidance, and high masculinity. He averaged the score for all employees from a given country. Table 3.1 summarizes these data for 20 selected countries. Western nations such as the United States, Canada, and Britain score high on the individualism scale and low on the power distance scale. At the other extreme are a group of Latin American and Asian countries that emphasize collectivism over individualism and score high on the power distance scale. Table 3.1 also reveals that Japan's culture has strong uncertainty avoidance and high masculinity. This characterization fits the standard stereotype of Japan as a country that is male dominant and where uncertainty avoidance exhibits itself in the institution of lifetime employment. Sweden and Denmark stand out as countries that have both low uncertainty avoidance and low masculinity (high emphasis on "feminine" values).

Hofstede's results are interesting for what they tell us in a very general way about differences between cultures. Many of Hofstede's findings are consistent with standard Western stereotypes about cultural differences. For example, many people believe Americans are more individualistic and egalitarian than the Japanese (they have a lower power distance), who in turn are more individualistic and egalitarian than Mexicans. Similarly, many might agree that Latin countries such as Mexico place a higher emphasis on masculine value—they are machismo cultures—than the Nordic countries of Denmark and Sweden.

However, one should be careful about reading too much into Hofstede's research. It has been criticized on a number of points.[48] First, Hofstede assumes there is a one-to-one correspondence between culture and the nation-state, but as we saw earlier,

	Power Distance	Uncertainty Avoidance	Individualism	Masculinity
Argentina	49	86	46	56
Australia	36	51	90	61
Brazil	69	76	38	49
Canada	39	48	80	52
Denmark	18	23	74	16
France	68	86	71	43
Germany (F.R.)	35	65	67	66
Great Britain	35	35	89	66
Indonesia	78	48	14	46
India	77	40	48	56
Israel	13	81	54	47
Japan	54	92	46	95
Mexico	81	82	30	69
Netherlands	38	53	80	14
Panama	95	86	11	44
Spain	57	86	51	42
Sweden	31	29	71	5
Thailand	64	64	20	34
Turkey	66	85	37	45
United Sates	40	46	91	62

3.1 table

Work-Related Values for 20 Selected Countries

Source: G. Hofstede, *Culture's Consequences.* © 1980, Sage Publications. Cited in G. Hofstede, "The Cultural Relativity of Organizational Practices and Theories," *Journal of International Business Studies* 14 (Fall 1983), pp. 75–89. Reprinted by permission of Geert Hofstede.

many countries have more than one culture. Hofstede's results do not capture this distinction. Second, the research may have been culturally bound. The research team was composed of Europeans and Americans. The questions they asked of IBM employees and their analysis of the answers may have been shaped by their own cultural biases and concerns. So it is not surprising that Hofstede's results confirm Western stereotypes, because it was Westerners who undertook the research.

Third, Hofstede's informants worked not only within a single industry, the computer industry, but also within one company, IBM. At the time, IBM was renowned for its own strong corporate culture and employee selection procedures, making it possible that the employees' values were different in important respects from the values of the cultures from which those employees came. Also, certain social classes (such as unskilled manual workers) were excluded from Hofstede's sample. A final caution is that Hofstede's work is now beginning to look dated. Cultures do not stand still; they evolve, albeit slowly. What was a reasonable characterization in the 1960s and 1970s may not be so today.

Still, just as it should not be accepted without question, Hofstede's work should not be dismissed either. It represents a starting point for managers trying to figure out how cultures differ and what that might mean for management practices. Also, several other scholars have found strong evidence that differences in culture affect values and practices in the workplace, and Hofstede's basic results have been replicated using more diverse samples of individuals in different settings.[49] Still, managers should use the results with caution, for they are not necessarily accurate.

Hofstede subsequently expanded his original research to include a fifth dimension that he argued captured additional cultural differences not brought out in his earlier work.[50] He referred to this dimension as "Confucian dynamism" (sometimes called *long-term orientation*). According to Hofstede, **Confucian dynamism** captures attitudes toward time, persistence, ordering by status, protection of face, respect for tradition, and reciprocation of gifts and favors. The label refers to these "values" being derived from Confucian teachings. As might be expected, East Asian countries such as Japan, Hong Kong, and Thailand scored high on Confucian dynamism, while nations such as the United States and Canada scored low. Hofstede and his associates went on to argue that their evidence suggested that nations with higher economic growth rates scored high on Confucian dynamism and low on individualism—the implication being Confucianism is good for growth. However, subsequent studies have shown that this finding does not hold up under more sophisticated statistical analysis.[51] During the past decade countries with high individualism and low Confucian dynamics such as the United States have attained high growth rates, while some Confucian cultures such as Japan have had stagnant economic growth. In reality, while culture might influence the economic success of a nation, it is just one of many factors, and while its importance should not be ignored, it should not be overstated either. The factors discussed in Chapter 2—economic, political, and legal systems—are probably more important than culture in explaining differential economic growth rates over time.

Confucian Dynamism
Theory that Confucian teachings affect attitudes toward time, persistence, ordering by status, protection of face, respect for tradition, and reciprocation of gifts and favors.

Cultural Change

LEARNING OBJECTIVE 5
Demonstrate the economic and business implications of cultural change.

Culture is not a constant; it evolves over time.[52] Changes in value systems can be slow and painful for a society. In the 1960s, for example, American values toward the role of women, love, sex, and marriage underwent significant changes. Much of the social turmoil of that time reflected these changes. Change can often be quite profound. For example, at the beginning of the 1960s, the idea that women might hold senior management positions in major corporations was not widely accepted. Many scoffed at the idea. Today, it is a reality, and few in the mainstream of American society question the development or the capability of women in the business world. American culture has changed (although it is still more difficult for women to gain senior management positions than men). Similarly, the value systems of many ex-communist states, such as Russia, are undergoing significant changes as those countries move away from values that emphasize collectivism and toward those that emphasize individualism. While social turmoil is an inevitable outcome of such a shift, the shift will still probably occur.

Similarly, some claim that a major cultural shift has been occurring in Japan, with a move toward greater individualism.[53] The model Japanese office worker, or "salaryman," is characterized as being loyal to his boss and the organization to the point of giving up evenings, weekends, and vacations to serve the organization, which is the collective of which the employee is a member. However, a new

Another Perspective

Indian Airlines and the Free Market
In the mid-1990s, the average Indian air traveler was indifferent to the services that domestic government airlines were providing. Then came private airlines and Jet Airways with its higher level of services and on-time schedule. The Indian consumer could not get enough of the benefits of capitalism. But what the average Indian consumer has yet to fathom is the flip side of market forces—namely, the need to make draconian decisions that may cost jobs. And they will come. (S. Mishra, "Indians Must Learn Free Market Is Not a Fairy Tale," *Advertising Age,* November 10, 2008)

generation of office workers does not seem to fit this model. An individual from the new generation is likely to be more direct than the traditional Japanese. He acts more like a Westerner, a *gaijian*. He does not live for the company and will move on if he gets the offer of a better job. He is not keen on overtime, especially if he has a date. He has his own plans for his free time, and they may not include drinking or playing golf with the boss.[54]

Several studies have suggested that economic advancement and globalization may be important factors in societal change.[55] For example, there is evidence that economic progress is accompanied by a shift in values away from collectivism and toward individualism.[56] Thus, as Japan has become richer, the cultural emphasis on collectivism has declined and greater individualism is being witnessed. One reason for this shift may be that richer societies exhibit less need for social and material support structures built on collectives, whether the collective is the extended family or the paternalistic company. People are better able to take care of their own needs. As a result, the importance attached to collectivism declines, while greater economic freedoms lead to an increase in opportunities for expressing individualism.

The culture of societies may also change as they become richer because economic progress affects a number of other factors, which in turn influence culture. For example, increased urbanization and improvements in the quality and availability of education are both a function of economic progress, and both can lead to declining emphasis on the traditional values associated with poor rural societies. A 25-year study of values in 78 countries, known as the World Values Survey, coordinated by the University of Michigan's Institute for Social Research, has documented how values change. The study linked these changes in values to changes in a country's level of economic development.[57] According to this research, as countries get richer, a shift occurs away from "traditional values" linked to religion, family, and country, and toward "secular rational" values. Traditionalists say religion is important in their lives. They have a strong sense of national pride; they also think that children should be taught to obey and that the first duty of a child is to make his or her parents proud. They say abortion, euthanasia, divorce, and suicide are never justified. At the other end of this spectrum are secular rational values.

The MTV awards show in India demonstrates the globalization of what originally was a phenomenon in American pop culture. Do you think traditional Indian values are at risk from the importation of MTV?

Another category in the World Values Survey is quality of life attributes. At one end of this spectrum are "survival values," the values people hold when the struggle for survival is of paramount importance. These values tend to stress that economic and physical security are more important than self-expression. People who cannot take food or safety for granted tend to be xenophobic, are wary of political activity, have authoritarian tendencies, and believe that men make better political leaders than women. "Self-expression" or "well-being" values stress the importance of diversity, belonging, and participation in political processes.

As countries get richer, there seems to be a shift from "traditional" to "secular rational" values, and from "survival values" to "well-being" values. The shift, however, takes time, primarily because individuals are socialized into a set of values when they are young and find it difficult to change as they grow older. Substantial changes in values are linked to generations, with younger people typically being in the vanguard of a significant change in values.

With regard to globalization, some have argued that advances in transportation and communication technologies, the dramatic increase in trade since World War II, and the rise of global corporations such as Hitachi, Disney, Microsoft, and Levi Strauss, whose products and operations can be found around the globe, are creating conditions for the merging of cultures.[58] With McDonald's hamburgers in China, The Gap in India, iPods in South Africa, and MTV everywhere helping to foster a ubiquitous youth culture, some argue that the conditions for less cultural variation have been created. At the same time, one must not ignore important countertrends, such as the shift toward Islamic fundamentalism in several countries; the separatist movement in Quebec, Canada; or the continuing ethnic strains and separatist movements in Russia. Such countertrends in many ways are a reaction to the pressures for cultural convergence. In an increasingly modern and materialistic world, some societies are trying to reemphasize their cultural roots and uniqueness. Cultural change is not unidirectional, with national cultures converging toward some homogenous global entity. Also, while some elements of culture change quite rapidly—particularly the use of material symbols—other elements change slowly if at all. Thus, just because people the world over wear blue jeans and eat at McDonald's, one should not assume that they have also adopted American values—for more often than not, they have not.

Focus on Managerial Implications

LEARNING OBJECTIVE 3
Identify the business and economic implications of differences in culture.

International business is different from national business because countries and societies are different. In this chapter, we have seen just how different societies can be. Societies differ because their cultures vary. Their cultures vary because of profound differences in social structure, religion, language, education, economic philosophy, and political philosophy. Three important implications for international business flow from these differences. The first is the need to develop cross-cultural literacy. There is a need not only to appreciate that cultural differences exist but also to appreciate what such differences mean for international business. A second implication centers on the connection between culture and national competitive advantage. A third implication looks at the connection between culture and ethics in decision making. In this section, we will explore the first two of these issues in depth. The connection between culture and ethics is explored in the next chapter.

Cross-Cultural Literacy

One of the biggest dangers confronting a company that goes abroad for the first time is the danger of being ill-informed. International businesses that are ill-informed about the practices of another culture are likely to fail. Doing business in different cultures requires adaptation to conform with the value systems and norms of that culture. Adaptation can embrace all aspects of an international firm's operations in a foreign country. The way in which deals are negotiated, the appropriate incentive pay systems for salespeople, the structure of the organization, the name of a product, the tenor of relations between management and labor, the manner in which the product is promoted, and so on, are all sensitive to cultural differences. What works in one culture might not work in another.

To combat the danger of being ill-informed, international businesses should consider employing local citizens to help them do business in a particular culture. They must also ensure that home-country executives are cosmopolitan enough to understand how differences in culture affect the practice of international business. Transferring executives overseas at regular intervals to expose them to different cultures will help build a cadre of cosmopolitan executives. An international business must also be constantly on guard against the dangers of *ethnocentric behavior*. **Ethnocentrism** is a belief in the superiority of one's own ethnic group or culture. Hand in hand with ethnocentrism goes a disregard or contempt for the culture of other countries. Unfortunately, ethnocentrism is all too prevalent; many Americans are guilty of it, as are many French people, Japanese people, British people, and so on. Ugly as it is, ethnocentrism is a fact of life, one that international businesses must be on guard against.

Ethnocentrism
A belief in the superiority of one's own ethnic group or culture; often results in disregard or contempt for the culture of other countries.

Simple examples illustrate how important cross-cultural literacy can be. Anthropologist Edward T. Hall has described how Americans, who tend to be informal in nature, react strongly to being corrected or reprimanded in public.[59] This can cause problems in Germany, where a cultural tendency toward correcting strangers can shock and offend most Americans. For their part, Germans can be a bit taken aback by the tendency of Americans to call everyone by their first name. This is uncomfortable enough among executives of the same rank, but it can be seen as insulting when a young and junior American executive addresses an older and more senior German manager by his first name without having been invited to do so. Hall concludes it can take a long time to get on a first-name basis with a German; if you rush the process you will be perceived as overfriendly and rude, and that may not be good for business.

Hall also notes that cultural differences in attitude to time can cause a myriad of problems. He notes that in the United States, giving a person a deadline is a way of increasing the urgency or relative importance of a task. However, in the Middle East, giving a deadline can have exactly the opposite effect. The American who insists an Arab business associate make his mind up in a hurry is likely to be perceived as overly demanding and exerting undue pressure. The result may be exactly the opposite of what the American intended, with the Arab going slow as a reaction to the American's arrogance and rudeness. For his part, the American may believe that an Arab associate is being rude if he shows up late to a meeting because he met a friend in the street and stopped to talk. The American, of course, is very concerned about time and scheduling. But for the Arab, who lives in a society where social networks are a major source of information, and maintaining relationships

Social networking and the importance of communal eating are some of the collectivist values Arabs bring to business.

is important, finishing the discussion with a friend is more important than adhering to a strict schedule. Indeed, the Arab may be puzzled as to why the American attaches so much importance to time and schedule.

Culture and Competitive Advantage

One theme that continually surfaces in this chapter is the relationship between culture and national competitive advantage. Put simply, the value systems and norms of a country influence the costs of doing business in that country. The costs of doing business in a country influence the ability of firms to establish a competitive advantage in the global marketplace. We have seen how attitudes toward cooperation between management and labor, toward work, and toward the payment of interest are influenced by social structure and religion. It can be argued that the class-based conflict between workers and management in class-conscious societies, when it leads to industrial disruption, raises the costs of doing business in that society. Similarly, we have seen how some sociologists have argued that the ascetic "other-worldly" ethics of Hinduism may not be as supportive of capitalism as the ethics embedded in Protestantism and Confucianism. Also, Islamic laws banning interest payments may raise the costs of doing business by constraining a country's banking system.

Japan presents an interesting case study of how culture can influence competitive advantage. Some scholars have argued that the culture of modern Japan lowers the costs of doing business relative to the costs in most Western nations. Japan's emphasis on group affiliation, loyalty, reciprocal obligations, honesty, and education all boost the competitiveness of Japanese companies. The emphasis on group affiliation and loyalty encourages individuals to identify strongly with the companies in which they work. This tends to foster an ethic of hard work and cooperation between management and labor "for the good of the company." Similarly, reciprocal obligations and honesty help foster an atmosphere of trust between companies and their suppliers. This encourages them to enter into long-term relationships with each other to work on inventory reduction, quality control, and design—all of which have been shown to improve an organization's competitiveness. This level of cooperation has often been lacking in the West, where the relationship between a company and its suppliers tends to be a short-term one structured around competitive bidding rather than one based on long-term mutual commitments. In addition, the availability of a pool of highly skilled labor, particularly engineers, has helped Japanese enterprises develop cost-reducing process innovations that have boosted their productivity.[60] Thus, cultural factors may help explain the competitive advantage enjoyed by many Japanese businesses in the global marketplace. The rise of Japan as an economic power during the second half of the twentieth century may be in part attributed to the economic consequences of its culture.

It also has been argued that the Japanese culture is less supportive of entrepreneurial activity than, say, American society. In many ways, entrepreneurial activity is a product of an individualistic mind-set, not a classic characteristic of the Japanese. This may explain why American enterprises, rather than Japanese corporations, dominate industries where entrepreneurship and innovation are highly valued, such as computer software and biotechnology. Of course, obvious and significant exceptions to this generalization exist. Masayoshi Son recognized the potential of software far faster than any of Japan's corporate giants; set up his company, Softbank, in 1981; and has since built it into Japan's top software distributor. Similarly, dynamic entrepreneurial individuals established major Japanese companies such as Sony and Matsushita (now know as Panasonic). But these examples may be the exceptions that prove the rule, for as yet there has been no surge in entrepreneurial high-technology enterprises in Japan equivalent to what has occurred in the United States.

For the international business, the connection between culture and competitive advantage is important for two reasons. First, the connection suggests which countries are likely to produce the most viable competitors. For example, one might argue that U.S. enterprises are likely to see continued growth in aggressive, cost-efficient competitors from those Pacific Rim nations where a combination of free market economics, Confucian ideology, group-oriented social structures, and advanced education systems can all be found (e.g., South Korea, Taiwan, Japan, and, increasingly, China).

Second, the connection between culture and competitive advantage has important implications for the choice of countries in which to locate production facilities and do business. Consider a hypothetical case when a company has to choose between two countries, A and B, for locating a production facility. Both countries are characterized by low labor costs and good access to world markets. Both countries are of roughly the same size (in terms of population) and both are at a similar stage of economic development. In country A, the education system is undeveloped, the society is characterized by a marked stratification between the upper and lower classes, and there are six major linguistic groups. In country B, the education system is well developed, social stratification is lacking, group identification is valued by the culture, and there is only one linguistic group. Which country makes the best investment site?

Country B probably does. In country A, conflict between management and labor, and between different language groups, can be expected to lead to social and industrial disruption, thereby raising the costs of doing business.[61] The lack of a good education system also can be expected to work against the attainment of business goals.

The same kind of comparison could be made for an international business trying to decide where to push its products, country A or B. Again, country B would be the logical choice because cultural factors suggest that in the long run, country B is the nation most likely to achieve the greatest level of economic growth.

But as important as culture is, it is probably less important than economic, political, and legal systems in explaining differential economic growth between nations. Cultural differences are significant, but we should not overemphasize their importance in the economic sphere. For example, earlier we noted that Max Weber argued that the ascetic principles embedded in Hinduism do not encourage entrepreneurial activity. While this is an interesting academic thesis, recent years have seen an increase in entrepreneurial activity in India, particularly in the information technology sector where India is rapidly becoming an important global player. The ascetic principles of Hinduism and caste-based social stratification have apparently not held back entrepreneurial activity in this sector.

Key Terms

cross-cultural literacy, p. 119

culture, p. 120

values, p. 120

norms, p. 120

society, p. 120

folkways, p. 120

mores, p. 121

social structure, p. 123

group, p. 123

social strata, p. 125

social mobility, p. 125

caste system, p. 125

class system, p. 125

class consciousness, p. 128

religion, p. 129

ethical systems, p. 129

power distance, p. 142

individualism versus collectivism, p. 142

uncertainty avoidance, p. 142

masculinity versus femininity, p. 142

Confucian dynamism, p. 144

ethnocentrism, p. 147

Summary

We have looked at the nature of social culture and studied some implications for business practice. The chapter made the following points:

1. Culture is a complex whole that includes knowledge, beliefs, art, morals, law, customs, and other capabilities acquired by people as members of society.

2. Values and norms are the central components of a culture. Values are abstract ideals about what a society believes to be good, right, and desirable. Norms are social rules and guidelines that prescribe appropriate behavior in particular situations.

3. Values and norms are influenced by political and economic philosophy, social structure, religion, language, and education.

4. The social structure of a society refers to its basic social organization. Two main dimensions along which social structures differ are the individual–group dimension and the stratification dimension.

5. In some societies, the individual is the basic building block of social organization. These societies emphasize individual achievements above all else. In other societies, the group is the basic building block of social organization. These societies emphasize group membership and group achievements above all else.

6. All societies are stratified into different classes. Class-conscious societies are characterized by low social mobility and a high degree of stratification. Less class-conscious societies are characterized by high social mobility and a low degree of stratification.

7. Religion may be defined as a system of shared beliefs and rituals that is concerned with the realm of the sacred. Ethical systems refer to a set of moral principles, or values, that are used to guide and shape behavior. The world's major religions are Christianity, Islam, Hinduism, and Buddhism. Although not a religion, Confucianism has an impact on behavior that is as profound as that of many religions. The value systems of different religious and ethical systems have different implications for business practice.

8. Language is one defining characteristic of a culture. It has both spoken and unspoken dimensions. In countries with more than one spoken language, we tend to find more than one culture.

9. Formal education is the medium through which individuals learn skills and are socialized into the values and norms of a society. Education plays an important role in the determination of national competitive advantage.

10. Geert Hofstede studied how culture relates to values in the workplace. He isolated four dimensions that he claimed summarized different cultures: power distance, uncertainty avoidance, individualism versus collectivism, and masculinity versus femininity.

11. Culture is not a constant; it evolves. Economic progress and globalization seem to be two important engines of cultural change.

12. One danger confronting a company that goes abroad for the first time is being ill-informed. To develop cross-cultural literacy, international businesses need to employ host-country nationals, build a cadre of cosmopolitan executives, and guard against the dangers of ethnocentric behavior.

13. The value systems and norms of a country can affect the costs of doing business in that country.

Critical Thinking and Discussion Questions

1. Outline why the culture of a country might influence the costs of doing business in that country. Illustrate your answer with examples.

2. Do you think that business practices in an Islamic country are likely to differ from business practices in the United States? If so, how?

3. What are the implications for international business of differences in the dominant religion or ethical system of a country?

4. Choose two countries that appear to be culturally diverse. Compare the cultures of those countries and then indicate how cultural

differences influence (*a*) the costs of doing business in each country, (*b*) the likely future economic development of that country, and (*c*) business practices.

5. Reread the Country Focus about Islam, capitalism, and globalization in Dubai. Then answer the following questions:

   a. How does Islam change the nature of international banking?

   b. For what purposes did Dubai and Dubai World use Islamic banking in their development?

   c. What are the advantages and disadvantages of Dubai counting on the traditional banking system? What does Dubai's integration into the global banking system teach us?

6. Reread the Management Focus on DMG-Shanghai and answer the follow questions:

   a. Why do you think that it is so important to cultivate *guanxi* and *guanxiwang* in China?

   b. What does the experience of DMG tells us about the way things work in China? What would likely happen to a business that obeyed all of the rules and regulations, rather than trying to find a way around them as Dan Mintz apparently did?

   c. What are the ethical issues that might arise when drawing upon *guanxiwang* to get things done in China? What does this suggest about the limits of using *guanxiwang* for a Western business committed to high ethical standards?

---

http://globalEDGE.msu.edu 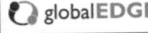 globalEDGE Research Task

Use the globalEDGE Resource Desk (http://globalEDGE.msu.edu/resourcedesk/) to complete the following exercises:

1. You have been assigned to negotiate a business deal with the representatives of a potential distributor in South Africa. Since having *intercultural skills* is critical for a successful international experience, you consider collecting information regarding the local culture before your departure. Prepare a short description of the most striking cultural characteristics involved in communicating with the local people that may affect business interactions in this country.

2. Asian cultures exhibit significant differences in *business etiquette* when compared to Western cultures. For example, in China, large hand movements are usually distracting, and it is considered offensive to point while speaking. Find five similar tips regarding the business etiquette of the United Arab Emirates.

---

closing case

Anheuser-Busch InBev: Global versus Local Culture

In Jupille, Belgium, beer has been a way of life for hundreds of years. As in other parts of Belgium, life is lived in the local pubs, and beer has been the social identity. In this town of 10,000 nestled in the heartland of a beer drinking culture, Anheuser-Busch Inbev, the world's largest brewer, established a brewery. For a while, centuries old artisanal beer drinking tradition "bellied up to the bar" with "global beer."

Headquartered in the medieval town of Leuven, Belgium, not too far from Jupille, Anheuser-Busch InBev, AB Inbev for short, employs approximately 116,000 people in 23 countries around the world. The company works through six operational zones: North America, Latin America North and Latin America South, Western Europe, Central and Eastern Europe, and Asia Pacific. With more than 200 brands, AB Inbev produces not only the well-known Budweiser, Stella Artois, and Beck's brands, but "multi-country brands," such as Leffe and Hoegaarden, and "local brews," such as Bud Light, Skol, Brahma, Quilmes, Michelob, Harbin, Sedrin, Klinskoye,

Sibirskaya Korona, Chernigivske, and Jupiler, which is brewed in Jupille. The once strictly Belgian brewer that served the local Belgian pub clientele is now catering to the beer palate of most of the world.

How this came about is a testament to the global forces that change culture. From its early beginnings at the Den Hoorn brewery in Leuven in 1366, through a series of acquisitions, AB InBev is the end product of the merger between Anheuser Busch & Co. from St. Louis, Missouri, USA and AmBev, a combination of two Brazilian brewers, Antartica and Brahma. When the two largest Belgian brewers merged forming Interbrew, AmBev and Interbrew merged to form InBev. Subsequent acquisitions have given AB InBev production capabilities in China and South America. The integration of these various companies and cultures into a cohesive whole is a story unto itself, but with AB InBev consolidation came a change in corporate culture.

Although Belgians drink 20 gallons of beer per capita and rank seventh in the world, Belgian beer consumption has declined 19 percent in the last decade. In fact, the sales for many western European beer brands have become stagnant. Within competitive global capitalism, and lead by Carlos Brito, the Brazilian CEO, AB InBev instituted a culture that is seeking to develop world-class efficiencies and reduce 10 percent of its 8,000-strong workforce in western Europe. Preferring to focus more on the growing global markets while at the same time maintaining its historical "cache" of being a Belgian beer company, AB InBev is applying its corporate culture on a global scale.

As discussed on AB InBev's Web site, www.ab-inbev. com, "Developing world-class efficiency" is among its "Four Pillars of Strategy." By that the company means doing business the "InBev Way": seeking optimization of plant production and network brewing capabilities on a global scale. The other three pillars include "Our Winning Brand Portfolio," "Targeted External Growth," and "Winning at the Point of Connection." AB InBev explains the "point of connection" is when the customer or consumer chooses to purchase or consume an AB InBev product. It describes this as seeking to utilize sales, merchandizing, and distribution.

A reduction in presence means a loss of jobs—263 jobs in Belgium. Although AB InBev employs more than 3,000 in Belgium, the Belgians did not take the job loss sitting down. In essence, it represented a culture change; pitting beer-brewing tradition against global efficiency. The proposed reductions led to protests. In 2006 the company tried to close its Hoegaarden brewery but failed. In the latest attempts at cutbacks by AB InBev, labor union workers blocked the entrances to three breweries for three weeks, preventing raw materials from entering and beer from leaving. Local politicians and newspapers criticized AB InBev for cutting jobs during a recession while making profits—more than $3 billion in the first nine months of 2009. Sales for Stella Artois, the most purchased beer, plummeted in what was described as a "psychological reaction" to AB InBev. Dewandeleer, the owner of The Black Sheep, a Brussels café, explained that the company was losing its identity by buying so many foreign breweries and taking its focus off Belgium. He complained, "We are waking up to realize that Belgian beer isn't Belgian anymore."

Micro- and midsize breweries took advantage. Haacht, a midsize brewery that employs more than 450 people with annual sales of $139 million, promoted itself as being " a truly Belgian beer." Local culture was pitted against the multinational company.

AB InBev currently controls more than 57 percent of the Belgian market and three of Belgium's most popular brands, Jupiler, Hoegaarden, and Leffe. In the short term, it is doubtful that Belgians will stop drinking beer and hanging out in pubs. In the interim, AB Inbev will continue its global expansion, permitting local Belgian breweries to maintain the "truly Belgian tradition."

Sources: Anheuser-Busch Inbev Web site, www.ab-inbev.com, accessed July 26, 2010; Haacht Brewery Web site, www.haacht.com, accessed July 26, 2010; J. W. Miller, "Big Beer Gets Belgian Emotion Flowing," *The Wall Street Journal,* February 23, 2010; and "AB InBev Consults over Swathe of Job Cuts in Western EU," *The Grocer,* January 16, 2010, www.thegrocer.co.uk.

Case Discussion Questions

1. How did the various mergers and acquisitions by AB InBev change the way Belgian beer was brewed?

2. Is the company's strategy used in Belgium correct? Do you think this will eventually alienate the "average" Belgian?

3. What future do you see for small and midsize breweries in Belgium? Will they have the capabilities to compete efficiently with AB InBev?

4. Will the average Belgian beer drinker accept the dominance of AB InBev with its "international" culture, or will he or she look to maintain his or her cultural identity elsewhere?

5. Do you see this conflict happening in other industries where cultural identity is closely associated with a product or service? Say, for example, within the automobile, watch, or perfume industries? Can you think of any others?

part 2 Country Differences

LEARNING OBJECTIVES

After you have read this chapter you should be able to:

1   Understand the ethical issues faced by international businesses.

2   Recognize an ethical dilemma.

3   Identify the causes of unethical behavior by managers.

4   Describe the different philosophical approaches to ethics.

5   Explain how managers can incorporate ethical considerations into their decision making.

chapter

4

Ethics in International Business

According to global capitalism, labor will seek out its most efficient expression. For many years the "most efficient expression" was found in the cheap labor pools of China. Recently, however, as China's currency, the renminbi, appreciates, and wage demands of factory workers in China continue to rise, many companies such as Walmart, H&M, Zara, and others are turning to Bangladesh to find cheaper sources of labor.

Li & Fung, a Hong Kong company that handles sourcing and apparel manufacturing for companies like Walmart and Liz Claiborne, reported that Bangladesh is becoming very competitive. Its production in Bangladesh jumped 20 percent last year, while China, its biggest supplier, slid 5 percent. This is because wages within the garment sector in Bangladesh are the lowest in the world. Currently the minimum wage in Bangladesh is 1662 taka, approximately $20 per month (or $0.14 cents per hour) versus the minimum wages in China's industrial coastal provinces, which can range from $117 to $147 per month.

According to Bangladeshi government sources, the country's ability to compete with China is good. The textile/garment sector represents 80 percent of the country's $18 billion export earnings. It has permitted much of the recent growth and more importantly an influx of hard currency.

But the economics of the garment industry are harsh. Of the approximately 3 million people who work in the garment industry, 80 percent are women. Many women work 14 to 16 hours a day, seven days a week. Some are also required to work a 19-hour shift at least twice a week. That calls for being at the factory 110 hours a week, with just one day off every two or three months. As an example, at the production level, typical factory management gives the workers a total of 28 minutes to sew a men's long sleeved denim shirt (size large) destined for Walmart stores. Based on the highest wages paid in most of these factories, it calculates to 21 cents an hour, the direct labor cost to sew the shirt is just 10 cents! (28 minutes = 46.66% of an hour; 46.66% × $0.21 = $0.097999—i.e., 10 cents).

In the area of Ashulia, Dhaka, the center of the garment district, recent protests seeking an increase in the minimum wage to 5,000 taka per month ($43) suggest that these economics cannot continue. According to labor unions, the current minimum wages do not permit a subsistence existence. Even the country's prime minister described the current minimum wage as "inhumanely low." In response to this economic reality, factory workers have begun walking off their jobs and turning to the streets in the hundreds of thousands. More than 200 factories shut down to prevent property damage during the protests. Police and workers have clashed, at times violently. Cumulatively, this is crippling production and leading to an increase in political instability. Ironically, this situation may have dire consequences for future foreign direct investment. Everyone questions the efficiency of continuing to work in this type of environment. ●

Sources: J. Melik, "The Human Cost of Cheap Clothing," BBC World Service, Business Daily, July 25, 2010, accessed at www.bbc.co.uk/new/business; "With Lower Garment-worker Pay, Bangladesh Moves in on China," Manila Bulletin, 2010; OECD Guidelines for Multinational Enterprises, 2001, accessed at www.oecd.org/daf/investment/guidelines July 27, 2010; "For Bangladesh, an Economic Door Opens; Rising Costs in China Have Manufacturers Looking Elsewhere," International Herald Tribune, 2010, S. Alam, "Bangladesh Hikes Wages for Protesting Garment Workers." Agence France Presse, July 27, 2010; C. Barton, "Crunch Time for Bangladesh Garment Industry," Agence France Presse, July 27, 2010; National Labor Committee website, www.nlcnet.org, accessed July 27, 2010; J. Alam, "Bangladesh Prime Minister Says Wages Paid to Country's Garment Workers Are Inhumanly Low," Associated Press Newswires, 2010, and "Roundup: 200 Apparel Factories in Bangladesh Shut after Labor Unrest over Wage Hike," Xinhua News Agency, June 22, 2010.

Introduction

The opening case describes awful working conditions and very low pay for workers in Bangladesh's garment factories. No doubt work is contracted out to these factories because costs are so low. However, the description of the working conditions and the wages paid to workers raises the question of whether it is ethical to outsource production to such factories, and, what, if anything, companies that use such suppliers should do about this issue. The situation presents companies that use these factories as suppliers with an ethical problem. Understanding the nature of ethical problems, and deciding what course of action to pursue when confronted with one, is a central theme in this chapter. As we shall see repeatedly in this chapter, ethical problems occur frequently in international business.

The term *ethics* refers to accepted principles of right or wrong that govern the conduct of a person, the members of a profession, or the actions of an organization. **Business ethics** are the accepted principles of right or wrong governing the conduct of businesspeople, and an **ethical strategy** is a strategy, or course of action, that does not violate these accepted principles. This chapter looks at how ethical issues should be incorporated into decision making in an international business. Next, we review the reasons for poor ethical decision making. Then we discuss different philosophical

Business Ethics
The accepted principles of right or wrong governing the conduct of businesspeople.

Ethical Strategy
A strategy, or course of action, that does not violate the accepted principles of right or wrong governing the conduct of businesspeople.

approaches to business ethics. We close the chapter by reviewing the different processes that managers can adopt to make sure that ethical considerations are incorporated into decision making in an international business firm.

Ethical Issues in International Business

Many of the ethical issues in international business are rooted in the fact that political systems, law, economic development, and culture vary significantly from nation to nation. What is considered normal practice in one nation may be considered unethical in another. Because they work for an institution that transcends national borders and cultures, managers in a multinational firm need to be particularly sensitive to these differences. In the international business setting, the most common ethical issues involve employment practices, human rights, environmental regulations, corruption, and the moral obligation of multinational corporations.

LEARNING OBJECTIVE 1
Understand the ethical issues faced by international businesses.

EMPLOYMENT PRACTICES When work conditions in a host nation are clearly inferior to those in a multinational's home nation, what standards should be applied: those of the home nation, those of the host nation, or something in between? While few would suggest that pay and work conditions should be the same across nations, how much divergence is acceptable? For example, while 12-hour workdays, extremely low pay, and a failure to protect workers against toxic chemicals may be common in some developing nations, does this mean that it is OK for a multinational to tolerate such working conditions in its subsidiaries there, or to condone it by using local subcontractors (the opening case gives an example of such a situation)?

In the 1990s Nike found itself at the center of a storm of protests when news reports revealed that working conditions at many of its subcontractors were very poor. Typical of the allegations were those detailed in a *48 Hours* program that aired on CBS-TV in 1996. The report painted a picture of young women at a Vietnamese subcontractor who worked with toxic materials six days a week in poor conditions for only 20 cents an hour. The report also stated that a living wage in Vietnam was at least $3 a day, an income that could not be achieved at the subcontractor without working substantial overtime. Nike and its subcontractors were not breaking any laws, but this report, and others like it, raised questions about the ethics of using sweatshop labor to make what were essentially fashion accessories. It may have been legal, but was it ethical to use subcontractors who by Western standards clearly exploited their workforce? Nike's critics thought not, and the company found itself the focus of a wave of demonstrations and consumer boycotts. These exposés surrounding Nike's use of subcontractors forced the company to reexamine its policies. Realizing that, even though it was breaking no law, its subcontracting policies were perceived as unethical, Nike's management established a code of conduct for Nike subcontractors and instituted annual monitoring by independent auditors of all subcontractors.[1]

As the Nike case demonstrate, a strong argument can be made that it is not OK for a multinational firm to tolerate poor working conditions in its foreign operations or those of its subcontractors. However, this still leaves unanswered the question of what standards should be applied. We shall return to and

It may have been legal for a Vietnamese contractor to allow employees to work with toxic materials six days a week in poor conditions for 20 cents an hour at a Nike factory. But was it ethical for Nike to use subcontractors who by Western standards clearly exploited their workers?

Management FOCUS

NLC: Your Company's International Labor Policy Compliance Officers?

Nonprofit, nongovernmental organizations (NGOs) play a significant role within international business, especially in their ability to enhance the public's awareness of labor injustices. Global managers increasingly have to deal with such entities as they seek to maintain a competitive edge.

As an NGO, the National Labor Committee (NLC) was founded in 1981 to combat sweatshops throughout the world. Traditionally NLC has directly focused on those large multinational firms that have immediate name recognition in its reports on labor rights violations. So it came as somewhat of a surprise that in a 2010 report the NLC sponsored an investigation into working practices not of a large multinational corporation but rather the Guangzhou, China, factories of the Tampa Bay, Florida–based Jabil Circuit. The NLC report alleges that at Jabil's Guangzhou factory, 6,000 employees are pitted against many illegal temporary workers, stand for 12-hour shifts with few bathroom breaks, live in six-person dorm rooms, are paid below subsistence wages, and are controlled so closely by private security that it resembles a "minimum-security prison." The plant, only 1 of 18 Jabil operates in China, makes high-tech products for such clients as Whirlpool, HP, IBM, Intel, and Cisco, the report says. Interestingly enough, it was the focus on this smaller, lower-profile international manufacturer and not on its customers directly and management's response that merits a closer look.

The entry of U.S. companies into China supposedly represented the establishment of higher standards and an increased respect for human, women's, and worker's rights. Many of these standards are reflected in the domestic labor policies of these companies. In an apparent attempt to drive the point further, the NLC is now attempting to work at the next level down within the value chain. The focus on Jubil is consistent with the international notoriety caused by the recent suicides at Apple's supplier Foxconn and the egregious labor conditions at KYE Systems, Microsoft's mouse manufacturer.

At Foxconn Technology Group, a Taiwanese company, 10 workers committed suicide because of working conditions. Foxconn had a previous history of systematic labor abuses at the factories that made Apple iPods and other products. Foxconn's response at the behest of Apple brought about significant changes. To the extent it was premised on extremely low wages, Foxconn partially resolved the issue by increasing wages. But the impact had a lasting impression. After the incident, perhaps to avoid any further public criticism, Foxconn shut down its India plant when as many as 250 workers got sick. Pesticide inhalation was suspected. The plant remained closed until there were assurances that the contaminant was no longer present. Prior to the publicized deaths, such precautions were essentially unheard of.

Similarly, when KYE Systems Corporation, also a Taiwanese-based manufacturer, came under NLC scrutiny for working condition violations, including the hiring of children, claims of working under a "military-style system" where workers were regularly subjected to searches, and extreme working conditions lasting up to $16\frac{1}{2}$ hour shifts, management immediately came out to the factories to inspect and conduct audits. This has lead to Microsoft's "on-premise" inspection personnel playing a more important role. Can or should the NLC or other NGOs play the role of a company's international labor policy compliance officers?

Sources: National Labor Committee, www.nlcnet.org; R. Trigaux, "Jabil Sends Managers to China Factory to Check Worker Conditions Cited in a Labor Rights Report," *St. Petersburg Times,* July 1, 2010; Associated Press, "Foxconn Shuts India Plant after Workers Get Sick," *Bloomberg Businessweek* July 26, 2010, accessed at www.businessweek.com/ap/financialnews/D9H74AGOO.htm.

consider this issue in more detail later in the chapter. For now, note that establishing minimal acceptable standards that safeguard the basic rights and dignity of employees, auditing foreign subsidiaries and subcontractors on a regular basis to make sure those standards are met, and taking corrective action if they are not, is a good way to guard against ethical abuses. Another Western company, Levi Strauss, has long taken such an approach. The company terminated a long-term contract with one of its large suppliers, the Tan family, after it discovered the Tans were allegedly forcing 1,200 Chinese and Filipino women to work 74 hours per week in guarded compounds on the Mariana Islands.[2] For another example of problems with working practices among suppliers, see the accompanying Management Focus that looks at working conditions in three companies and the role that NGOs are beginning to play.

HUMAN RIGHTS   Questions about human rights can arise in international business. Basic human rights still are not respected in many nations. Rights that we take for granted in developed nations, such as freedom of association, freedom of speech, freedom of assembly, freedom of movement, freedom from political repression, and so on, are by no means universally accepted (see Chapter 2 for details). One of the most obvious historic examples was South Africa during the days of white rule and apartheid, which did not end until 1994. The apartheid system denied basic political rights to the majority nonwhite population of South Africa, mandated segregation between whites and nonwhites, reserved certain occupations exclusively for whites, and prohibited blacks from being placed in positions where they would manage whites. Despite the odious nature of this system, Western businesses operated in South Africa. By the 1980s, however, many questioned the ethics of doing so. They argued that inward investment by foreign multinationals, by boosting the South African economy, supported the repressive apartheid regime.

Several Western businesses started to change their policies in the late 1970s and early 1980s.[3] General Motors, which had significant activities in South Africa, was at the forefront of this trend. GM adopted what came to be called the *Sullivan principles*, named after Leon Sullivan, a black Baptist minister and a member of GM's board of directors. Sullivan argued that it was ethically justified for GM to operate in South Africa so long as two conditions were fulfilled. First, the company should not obey the apartheid laws in its own South African operations (a form of passive resistance). Second, the company should do everything within its power to promote the abolition of apartheid laws. Sullivan's principles were widely adopted by U.S. firms operating in South Africa. Their violation of the apartheid laws was ignored by the South African government, which clearly did not want to antagonize important foreign investors.

However, after 10 years, Leon Sullivan concluded that simply following the principles was not sufficient to break down the apartheid regime and that any American company, even those adhering to his principles, could not ethically justify their continued presence in South Africa. Over the next few years, numerous companies divested their South African operations, including Exxon, General Motors, Kodak, IBM, and Xerox. At the same time, many state pension funds signaled they would no longer hold stock in companies that did business in South Africa, which helped to persuade several companies to divest their South African operations. These divestments, coupled with the imposition of economic sanctions from the U.S. and other governments, contributed to the abandonment of white minority rule and apartheid in South Africa and the introduction of democratic elections in 1994. Thus, adopting an ethical stance was argued to have helped improve human rights in South Africa.[4]

Although change has come in South Africa, many repressive regimes still exist in the world. Is it ethical for multinationals to do business in them? It is often argued that inward investment by a multinational can be a force for economic, political, and social progress that ultimately improves the rights of people in repressive regimes. This position was first discussed in Chapter 2, when we noted that economic progress in a nation could create pressure for democratization. In general, this belief suggests it is ethical for a multinational to do business in nations that lack the democratic structures and

Another Perspective

To Be "Dangerous" in Havana

In 2006 when Fidel Castro turned over power to his brother Raul, the international community hoped that a new era would begin in Cuba that would deal with human rights abuse and political repression. In November 2009, Human Rights Watch, the international NGO that conducts research and advocacy on human rights, issued a report saying that the repressive system appears to be intact and that a new "legal" device has been put in place to permit the arresting of dissenters, critics of the state, and individuals for "dangerousness." *Dangerousness* was defined to include failing to attend pro-government rallies, not belonging to official party organizations, "anti-social" behavior, and being unemployed. (Human Rights Watch, "New Castro, Same Cuba," November 2009, http://www.hrw.org/en/node/86549/ section/2, accessed July 26, 2010) human rights records of developed nations. Investment in China, for example, is frequently justified on the grounds that although China's human rights record is often questioned by human rights groups, and although the country is not a democracy, continuing inward investment will help boost economic growth and raise living standards. These developments will ultimately create pressures from the Chinese people for more participative government, political pluralism, and freedom of expression and speech.

However, there is a limit to this argument. As in the case of South Africa, some regimes are so repressive that investment cannot be justified on ethical grounds. Another example would be Myanmar (formally known as Burma). Ruled by a military dictatorship for more than 45 years, Myanmar has one of the worst human rights records in the world. Beginning in the mid-1990s, many Western companies exited Myanmar, judging the human rights violations to be so extreme that doing business there cannot be justified on ethical grounds. The accompanying Management Focus looks at two companies' decision to work in Eritrea, where human rights violations are common. A cynic might note that Eritrea has a small economy and that divestment carries no great economic penalty for Western firms, unlike, for example, divestment from China.

Nigeria is another country where serious questions have arisen over the extent to which foreign multinationals doing business in the country have contributed to human rights violations. Most notably, the largest foreign oil producer in the country, Royal Dutch Shell, has been repeatedly criticized.[5] In the early 1990s, several ethnic groups in Nigeria, which was ruled by a military dictatorship, protested against foreign oil companies for causing widespread pollution and failing to invest in the communities from which they extracted oil. Shell reportedly requested the assistance of Nigeria's Mobile Police Force (MPF) to quell the demonstrations. According to the human rights group Amnesty International, the results were bloody. In 1990, the MPF put down protests against Shell in the village of Umuechem, killing 80 people and destroying 495 homes. In 1993, following protests in the Ogoni region of Nigeria that were designed to stop contractors from laying a new pipeline for Shell, the MPF raided the area to quell the unrest. In the chaos that followed, it has been alleged that 27 villages were razed, 80,000 Ogoni people displaced, and 2,000 people killed.

Critics argued that Shell shouldered some of the blame for the massacres. Shell never acknowledged this, and the MPF probably used the demonstrations as a pretext for punishing an ethnic group that had been agitating against the central government for some time. Nevertheless, these events did prompt Shell to look at its own ethics and to set up internal mechanisms to ensure that its subsidiaries acted in a manner that was consistent with basic human rights.[6] More generally, the question remains, what is the responsibility of a foreign multinational when operating in a country where basic human rights are trampled on? Should the company be there at all, and if it is there, what actions should it take to avoid the situation Shell found itself in?

ENVIRONMENTAL POLLUTION   Ethical issues arise when environmental regulations in host nations are inferior to those in the home nation. Many developed nations have substantial regulations governing the emission of pollutants, the dumping of toxic chemicals, the use of toxic materials in the workplace, and so on. Those regulations are often lacking in developing nations, and according to critics, the result can be higher levels of pollution from the operations of multinationals than would be allowed at home. For example, consider again the case of foreign oil companies in Nigeria. According to a 1992 report prepared by environmental activists in Nigeria, in the Niger Delta region:

> Apart from air pollution from the oil industry's emissions and flares day and night, producing poisonous gases that are silently and systematically wiping out vulnerable airborne biota and endangering the life of plants, game, and man

Management FOCUS

Gold Mining in Eritrea

According to Amnesty International, Eritrea consistently ranks among the poorest countries in Africa with the highest incidence of human rights violations. Eritrea has a population of only 5 million people, an illiteracy rate of more than 60 percent, and a highly repressive authoritarian government. This same government prohibits independent journalism, opposition parties, unregistered religious organizations, and virtually all civil society activity. Perceived dissidents, deserters, those evading mandatory military service, and other critics of the government and their families are regularly punished and harassed. Many have languished in prison cells since 2008. Some government critics from registered religions, including Islam and the Eritrean Orthodox Church, also remain in detention. Conditions were so bad that the UN mission recently withdrew from the country, stating that the Eritrean government was obstructing its operations. Yet, with large gold and mineral deposits, Eritrea is attracting multinational mining corporations.

In 2007, Nevsun Resources Ltd.—the publicly traded Toronto, Canada, mining concern—got final approval to mine gold, copper, and zinc at the Bisha mine in Eritrea. Although small by global standards, Nevsun is big in Eritrea. The Bisha mine is expected to go into production in late 2010. By the first quarter of 2011, the company expects to produce more than 100,000 ounces of gold at a cost of less than $250 per ounce. At the current world price of $1,123 per ounce, Nevsun stands to make a good profit.

Similarly, Sunridge Gold Corp., also a Canadian mining firm, has partnered with majority stakeholder Antofagasta Minerals S.A., the Chilean mining company, to explore mineral deposit potentials in the Asmara Project area of Eritrea. Initial estimates are encouraging, potentially 1.28 billion pounds of copper, 2.5 billion pounds of zinc, 1.05 million ounces of gold, and 31.2 million ounces of silver may be extracted. With a total investment of $15 million, Antofagasta's investment is approximately the same as the nation's exports, which in 2009 totaled $17 million.

Mining is an environmentally and culturally high-impact activity in any country. The Bisha mine is no different. The open pit project is 60 percent owned by Nevsun and 40 percent by the state-owned Eritrean National Mining Corporation. The potential impact is addressed in the "Environmental and Social Management Plans" being proposed. This plan seeks to control and monitor the impact of various factors from noise, to topsoil erosion, to wastewater treatment, to social and community management procedures. The Social Management Plan addresses the "Cultural Heritage" of the site. Neither plan adequately addresses the inherent issues involved in dealing with the Eritrean government.

The Bisha mine will hire approximately 358 workers, 90 percent of whom will be Eritrean. Politically speaking, this is an important number. In an environment such as Eritrea with a high unemployment rate, who gets hired is going to be important. The plan specifically states: "Lists of 'Preferred Individuals' will not be accepted (e.g., lists provided by non-BMSC personnel to seek favor for certain individuals outside of the formal recruitment process)." As the largest investment in Eritrea during the past decade, how this mining process is carried out when specific governmental interests come to bear will be very interesting to watch.

Sources: "Environmental Management Plan," Nevsun Resources Ltd. Web site www.nevsun.com, accessed July 27, 2010; Sunridge Gold Corporation Web site www.sunridgegold.com, accessed July 27, 2010; Antofagasta Minerals S.A. Web site www.antofagasta.co.uk, accessed July 27, 2010; "Sunridge Gold Final Report for Strategic Production Study for the Asmara Project, Eritrea," *African Business News*, July 22, 2010, accessed at www.mbendi.com/a_sndmsg/news_view.asp?I=109262&PG=35.

himself, we have widespread water pollution and soil/land pollution that results in the death of most aquatic eggs and juvenile stages of the life of fin fish and shell fish on the one hand, whilst, on the other hand, agricultural land contaminated with oil spills becomes dangerous for farming, even where they continue to produce significant yields."[7]

The implication inherent in this description is that pollution controls applied by foreign companies in Nigeria were much laxer than those in developed nations.

Should a multinational feel free to pollute in a developing nation? (To do so hardly seems ethical.) Is there a danger that amoral management might move production to a developing nation precisely because costly pollution controls are not required, and the company is therefore free to despoil the environment and perhaps endanger local people in its quest to lower production costs and gain a competitive advantage? What is the right and moral thing to do in such circumstances—pollute to gain an economic advantage, or make sure that foreign subsidiaries adhere to common standards regarding pollution controls?

These questions take on added importance because some parts of the environment are a public good that no one owns, but anyone can despoil. No one owns the atmosphere or the oceans, but polluting both, no matter where the pollution originates, harms all.[8] The atmosphere and oceans can be viewed as a global commons from which everyone benefits but for which no one is specifically responsible. In such cases, a phenomenon known as the *tragedy of the commons* becomes applicable. The tragedy of the commons occurs when a resource held in common by all, but owned by no one, is overused by individuals, resulting in its degradation. The phenomenon was first named by Garrett Hardin when describing a particular problem in sixteenth-century England. Large open areas, called commons, were free for all to use as pasture. The poor put out livestock on these commons and supplemented their meager incomes. It was advantageous for each to put out more and more livestock, but the social consequence was far more livestock than the commons could handle. The result was overgrazing, degradation of the commons, and the loss of this much-needed supplement.[9]

In the modern world, corporations can contribute to the global tragedy of the commons by moving production to locations where they are free to pump pollutants into the atmosphere or dump them in oceans or rivers, thereby harming these valuable global commons. While such action may be legal, is it ethical? Again, such actions seem to violate basic societal notions of ethics and social responsibility. This issue is taking on greater importance as concerns about human-induced global warming move to center stage. Most climate scientists argue that (*a*) human industrial and commercial activity is increasing the amount of carbon dioxide in the atmosphere; (*b*) carbon dioxide is a greenhouse gas, which reflects heat back to the earth's surface, warming the globe; and (*c*) as a result, the average temperature of the earth is increasing. The accumulated scientific evidence supports this argument.[10] Given this, societies around the world are starting to restrict the amount of carbon dioxide that can be emitted into the atmosphere as a by-product of industrial and commercial activity. However, regulations differ from nation to nation. Given this, is it ethical for a company to try to escape tight emission limits by moving production to a country with lax regulations, given that doing so will contribute to global warming? Again, many would argue that doing so violates basic ethical principles.

A marketplace in Myanmar/Burma. Many activists question Unocal's continued involvement in Myanmar/Burma because the state's dictatorship harshly punishes proponents of democracy.

CORRUPTION   As noted in Chapter 2, corruption has been a problem in almost every society in history, and it continues to be one today.[11] There always have been and always will be corrupt government officials. International businesses can and have gained economic advantages by making payments to those officials. A classic example concerns a well-publicized incident in the 1970s. Carl Kotchian, the president of Lockheed, made a $12.5 million payment to Japanese agents and government officials to secure a large order for Lockheed's TriStar jet from Nippon Air. When the payments were discovered, U.S. officials charged Lockheed with falsification of its records and tax violations. Although such payments were supposed to be an accepted business practice in Japan (they might be viewed as an exceptionally lavish form of gift giving), the revelations created a scandal there too. The government ministers in question were criminally charged, one committed suicide, the government fell in disgrace, and the Japanese people were outraged. Apparently, such a payment was not an accepted way of doing business in Japan! The payment was nothing more than a bribe, paid to corrupt officials, to secure a large order that might otherwise have gone to another manufacturer, such as Boeing. Kotchian clearly engaged in unethical behavior, and to argue that the payment was an "acceptable form of doing business in Japan" was self-serving and incorrect.

The Lockheed case was the impetus for the 1977 passage of the **Foreign Corrupt Practices Act** in the United States, which we first discussed in Chapter 2. The act outlawed the paying of bribes to foreign government officials to gain business. Some U.S. businesses immediately objected that the act would put U.S. firms at a competitive disadvantage (there is no evidence that subsequently occurred).[12] The act was subsequently amended to allow for "facilitating payments." Sometimes known as speed money or grease payments, facilitating payments are *not* payments to secure contracts that would not otherwise be secured and nor are they payments to obtain exclusive preferential treatment. Rather they are payments to ensure receiving the standard treatment that a business ought to receive from a foreign government, but might not due to the obstruction of a foreign official.

In 1997, the trade and finance ministers from the member states of the Organization for Economic Cooperation and Development (OECD) followed the U.S. lead and adopted the **Convention on Combating Bribery of Foreign Public Officials in International Business Transactions.**[13] The convention, which went into force in 1999, obliges member states and other signatories to make the bribery of foreign public officials a criminal offense. The convention excludes facilitating payments made to expedite routine government action from the convention.

While facilitating payments, or speed money, are excluded from both the Foreign Corrupt Practices Act and the OECD convention on bribery, the ethical implications of making such payments are unclear. In many countries, payoffs to government officials in the form of speed money are a part of life. One can argue that not investing because government officials demand speed money ignores the fact that such investment can bring substantial benefits to the local populace in terms of income and jobs. From a pragmatic standpoint, giving bribes, although a little evil might be the price that must be paid to do a greater good (assuming the investment creates jobs where none existed and assuming the practice is not illegal). Several economists advocate this reasoning, suggesting that in the context of pervasive and cumbersome regulations in developing countries, corruption may improve efficiency and help growth! These economists theorize that in a country where preexisting political structures distort or limit the workings of the market mechanism, corruption in the form of black marketeering, smuggling, and side payments to government bureaucrats to "speed up" approval for business investments may enhance welfare.[14] Arguments such as this persuaded the U.S. Congress to exempt facilitating payments from the Foreign Corrupt Practices Act.

In contrast, other economists have argued that corruption reduces the returns on business investment and leads to low economic growth.[15] In a country where corruption is common, unproductive bureaucrats who demand side payments for granting the enterprise permission to operate may siphon off the profits from a business activity. This reduces businesses' incentive to invest and may retard a country's economic growth rate. One study of the connection between corruption and economic growth in 70 countries found that corruption had a significant negative impact on a country's growth rate.[16]

Foreign Corrupt Practices Act
A U.S. law regulating behavior regarding the conduct of international business in the taking of bribes and other unethical actions.

Convention on Combating Bribery of Foreign Public Officials in International Business Transactions
OECD convention that obliges member states to make the bribery of foreign public officials a criminal offense.

In addition to a commitment to introduce cleaner fuels and renewable energy, BP also supports urban renewal programs, art sponsorships, literacy drives, and conservation programs.

Given the debate and the complexity of this issue, one again might conclude that generalization is difficult and the demand for speed money creates a genuine ethical dilemma. Yes, corruption is bad, and yes, it may harm a country's economic development, but yes, there are also cases where side payments to government officials can remove the bureaucratic barriers to investments that create jobs. However, this pragmatic stance ignores the fact that corruption tends to corrupt both the bribe giver and the bribe taker. Corruption feeds on itself, and once an individual starts down the road of corruption, pulling back may be difficult if not impossible. This argument strengthens the ethical case for never engaging in corruption, no matter how compelling the benefits might seem.

Many multinationals have accepted this argument. The large oil multinational, BP, for example, has a zero-tolerance approach toward facilitating payments. Other corporations have a more nuanced approach. For example, consider the following from the code of ethics at Dow Corning:

> Dow Corning employees will not authorize or give payments or gifts to government employees or their beneficiaries or anyone else in order to obtain or retain business. Facilitating payments to expedite the performance of routine services are strongly discouraged. In countries where local business practice dictates such payments and there is no alternative, facilitating payments are to be for the minimum amount necessary and must be accurately documented and recorded.[17]

This statement allows for facilitating payments when "there is no alternative," although they are strongly discouraged.

MORAL OBLIGATIONS Multinational corporations have power that comes from their control over resources and their ability to move production from country to country. Although that power is constrained not only by laws and regulations, but also by the discipline of the market and the competitive process, it is nevertheless substantial. Some moral philosophers argue that with power comes the social responsibility for multinationals to give something back to the societies that enable them to prosper and grow. The concept of **social responsibility** refers to the idea that businesspeople should consider the social consequences of economic actions when making business decisions, and that there should be a presumption in favor of decisions that have both good economic and social consequences.[18] In its purest form, social responsibility can be supported for its own sake simply because it is the right way for a business to behave. Advocates of this approach argue that businesses, particularly large successful businesses, need to recognize their *noblesse oblige* and give something back to the societies that have made their success possible. *Noblesse oblige* is a French term that refers to honorable and benevolent behavior considered the responsibility of people of high (noble) birth. In a business setting, it is taken to mean benevolent behavior that is the responsibility of *successful* enterprises. This has long been recognized by many businesspeople, resulting in a substantial and venerable history of

Social Responsibility
The idea that businesspeople should consider the social consequences of economic actions when making business decisions.

Management FOCUS

News Corp.'s Dealings in China

Rupert Murdoch built News Corporation into one of the largest media conglomerates in the world with interests that include newspapers, publishing, and television broadcasting. According to critics, however, Murdoch abused his power to gain preferential access to the Chinese media market by systematically suppressing media content that was critical of China and by publishing material designed to ingratiate the company with the Chinese leadership.

In 1994, News Corporation excluded BBC news broadcasts from Star TV coverage in the region after it had become clear that Chinese politicians were unhappy with the BBC's continual reference to repression in China, and most notably, the 1989 massacre of student protesters for democracy in Beijing's Tiananmen Square. In 1995, News Corporation's book publishing subsidiary, HarperCollins, published a flattering biography of Deng Xiaoping, the former leader of China, written by his daughter. Then in 1998, HarperCollins dropped plans to publish the memoirs of Chris Patten, the last governor of Hong Kong before its transfer to the Chinese. Patten, a critic of Chinese leaders, had aroused their wrath by attempting to introduce a degree of democracy into the administration of the old British territory before its transfer back to China in 1997.

In a 1998 interview in *Vanity Fair,* Murdoch took another opportunity to ingratiate himself with the Chinese leadership when he described the Dalai Lama, the exiled leader of Chinese-occupied Tibet, as "a very political old monk shuffling around in Gucci shoes." On the heels of this, in 2001 Murdoch's son James, who was in charge of running Star TV, made disparaging remarks about Falun Gong, a spiritual movement involving breathing exercises and meditation that had become so popular in China that the Communist regime regarded it as a political threat and suppressed its activities. According to James Murdoch, Falun Gong was a "dangerous," "apocalyptic cult" that "clearly does not have the success of China at heart."

Critics argued that these events were all part of a deliberate effort on the part of News Corporation to curry favor with the Chinese. The company received its reward in 2001 when Star TV struck an agreement with the Chinese government to launch a Mandarin-language entertainment channel for the affluent southern coastal province of Guangdong. Earlier that year, China's leader, Jiang Zemin, had publicly praised Murdoch and Star TV for their efforts "to present China objectively and to cooperate with the Chinese press."

Once in China, News Corporation was soon tugging at the constraints imposed on it by the Chinese government. Starting in 2002, News Corp set up shell companies, owned by News Corp employees, which resold News Corp programming to local cable TV networks throughout China, in direct violation of Chinese regulations. Payments, sometimes in the form of briefcases stuffed with cash, were channeled to News Corp through the shell companies. One such deal involved selling News Corp programming through a shell company known as Runde Investments to a nationwide satellite TV channel, Qinghai Satellite, based in the remote Qinghai province of China. Runde was partly owned by the son of former hard-line Communist Party propaganda minister Ding Guangen. If News Corp was hoping that its political connections would help it to get away with these actions, it was badly disappointed. In 2005, Chinese authorities raided News Corp headquarters and seized documents and equipment. They also quickly terminated the deal with Qinghai Satellite.

Sources: J. Kahn, "Murdoch's Dealings in China: It's Business, and It's Personal," *New York Times,* Asia Edition, June 26, 2007; M. Forney, "Testing Beijing's Limits," *Time,* September 5, 2005; and Daniel Litvin, *"Empires of Profit* (New York: Texere, 2003).

corporate giving to society and in businesses making social investments designed to enhance the welfare of the communities in which they operate.

However, there are examples of multinationals that have abused their power for private gain. The most famous historic example relates to one of the earliest multinationals, the British East India Company. Established in 1600, the East India Company grew to dominate the entire Indian subcontinent in the nineteenth century. At the height of its power, the company deployed over 40 warships, possessed the largest standing army in the world, was the de facto ruler of India's 240 million people, and even hired its own church bishops, extending its dominance into the spiritual realm.[19]

Power itself is morally neutral; how power is used is what matters. It can be used in a positive way to increase social welfare, which is ethical, or it can be used in a manner that is ethically and morally suspect. Consider the case of News Corporation, one of the largest media conglomerates in the world, which is profiled in the accompanying Management Focus. The power of media companies derives from their ability to shape public perceptions by the material they choose to publish. News Corporation founder and CEO Rupert Murdoch has long considered China to be one of the most promising media markets in the world and has sought permission to expand News Corporation's operations in China, particularly the satellite broadcasting operations of Star TV. Some critics believe that Murdoch used the power of News Corporation in an unethical way to attain this objective.

Some multinationals have acknowledged a moral obligation to use their power to enhance social welfare in the communities where they do business. BP, one of the world's largest oil companies, has made it part of the company policy to undertake "social investments" in the countries where it does business.[20] In Algeria, BP has been investing in a major project to develop gas fields near the desert town of Salah. When the company noticed the lack of clean water in Salah, it built two desalination plants to provide drinking water for the local community and distributed containers to residents so they could take water from the plants to their homes. There was no economic reason for BP to make this social investment, but the company believes it is morally obligated to use its power in constructive ways. The action, while a small thing for BP, is a very important thing for the local community.

Ethical Dilemmas

LEARNING OBJECTIVE 2
Recognize an ethical dilemma.

The ethical obligations of a multinational corporation toward employment conditions, human rights, corruption, environmental pollution, and the use of power are not always clear-cut. There may be no agreement about accepted ethical principles. From an international business viewpoint, some argue that what is ethical depends upon one's cultural perspective.[21] In the United States, it is considered acceptable to execute murderers, but in many cultures this is not acceptable; execution is viewed as an affront to human dignity and the death penalty is outlawed. Many Americans find this attitude very strange, but many Europeans find the American approach barbaric. For a more business-oriented example, consider the practice of "gift giving" between the parties to a business negotiation. While this is considered right and proper behavior in many Asian cultures, some Westerners view the practice as a form of bribery, and therefore unethical, particularly if the gifts are substantial.

Managers often confront very real ethical dilemmas where the appropriate course of action is not clear. For example, imagine that a visiting American executive finds that a foreign subsidiary in a poor nation has hired a 12-year-old girl to work on a factory floor. Appalled to find that the subsidiary is using child labor in direct violation of the company's own ethical code, the American instructs the local manager to replace the child with an adult. The local manager dutifully complies. The girl, an orphan, who is the only breadwinner for herself and her 6-year-old brother, is unable to find another job, so in desperation she turns to prostitution. Two years later she dies of AIDS. Meanwhile, her brother takes up begging. He encounters the American while begging outside the local McDonald's. Oblivious that this was the man responsible for his fate, the boy begs him for money. The American quickens his pace and walks rapidly past the outstretched hand into the restaurant, where he orders a quarter-pound cheeseburger with fries and a cold milk shake. A year later, the boy contracts tuberculosis and dies.

Had the visiting American understood the gravity of the girl's situation, would he still have requested her replacement? Perhaps not! Would it have been better, therefore, to stick with the status quo and allow the girl to continue working? Probably not, because that would have violated the reasonable prohibition against child labor found in the company's own ethical code. What then would have been the right thing to do? What was the obligation of the executive given this ethical dilemma?

There is no easy answer to these questions. That is the nature of **ethical dilemmas**—they are situations in which none of the available alternatives seems ethically acceptable.[22] In this case, employing child labor was not acceptable, but given that she was employed, neither was denying the child her only source of income. What the American executive needed, what all managers need, was a moral compass, or perhaps an ethical algorithm, that would guide him through such an ethical dilemma to find an acceptable solution. Later we will outline what such a moral compass, or ethical algorithm, might look like. For now, it is enough to note that ethical dilemmas exist because many real-world decisions are complex; difficult to frame; and involve first-, second-, and third-order consequences that are hard to quantify. Doing the right thing, or even knowing what the right thing might be, is often far from easy.[23]

Ethical Dilemma
A situation in which none of the available alternatives seems ethically acceptable.

The Roots of Unethical Behavior

As we have seen, examples abound of managers behaving in a manner that might be judged unethical in an international business setting. Why do managers behave in an unethical manner? There is no simple answer to this question, for the causes are complex, but some generalizations can be made (see Figure 4.1).[24]

PERSONAL ETHICS   Business ethics are not divorced from *personal ethics*, which are the generally accepted principles of right and wrong governing the conduct of individuals. As individuals, we are typically taught that it is wrong to lie and cheat—it is unethical—and that it is right to behave with integrity and honor, and to stand up for what we believe to be right and true. This is generally true across societies. The personal ethical code that guides our behavior comes from a number of sources, including our parents, our schools, our religion, and the media. Our personal ethical code exerts a profound influence on the way we behave as businesspeople. An individual with a strong sense of personal ethics is less likely to behave in an unethical manner in a business setting. It follows that the first step to establishing a strong sense of business ethics is for a society to emphasize strong personal ethics.

Home-country managers working abroad in multinational firms (expatriate managers) may experience more than the usual degree of pressure to violate their personal

LEARNING OBJECTIVE 3
Identify the causes of unethical behavior by managers.

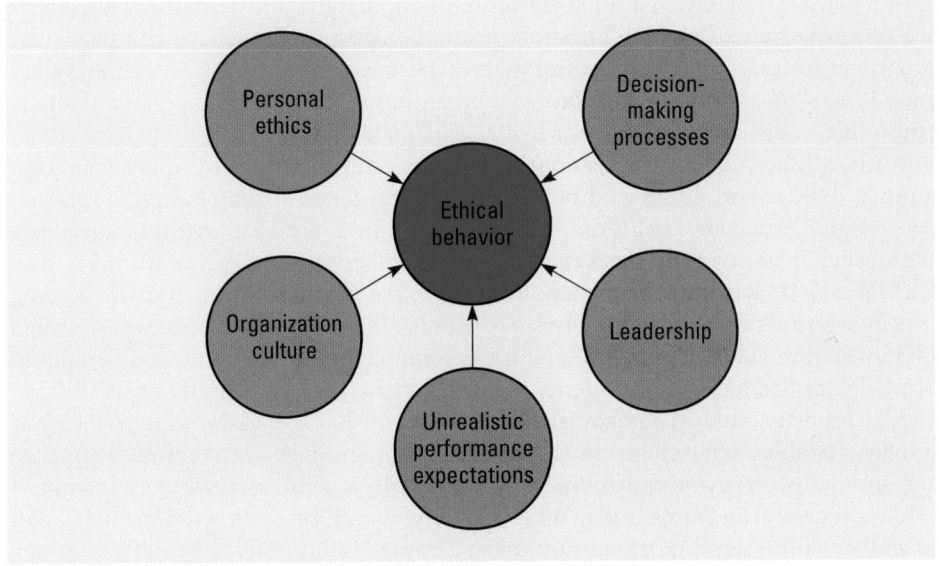

4.1 figure

Determinants of Ethical Behavior

ethics. They are away from their ordinary social context and supporting culture, and they are psychologically and geographically distant from the parent company. They may be based in a culture that does not place the same value on ethical norms important in the manager's home country, and they may be surrounded by local employees who have less rigorous ethical standards. The parent company may pressure expatriate managers to meet unrealistic goals that can only be fulfilled by cutting corners or acting unethically. For example, to meet centrally mandated performance goals, expatriate managers might give bribes to win contracts or might implement working conditions and environmental controls that are below minimal acceptable standards. Local managers might encourage the expatriate to adopt such behavior. Due to its geographical distance, the parent company may be unable to see how expatriate managers are meeting goals, or may choose not to see how they are doing so, allowing such behavior to flourish and persist.

DECISION-MAKING PROCESSES   Several studies of unethical behavior in a business setting have concluded that businesspeople sometimes do not realize they are behaving unethically, primarily because they simply fail to ask, "Is this decision or action ethical?"[25] Instead, they apply a straightforward business calculus to what they perceive to be a business decision, forgetting that the decision may also have an important ethical dimension. The fault lies in processes that do not incorporate ethical considerations into business decision making. This may have been the case at Nike when managers originally made subcontracting decisions (see the earlier discussion). Those decisions were probably made based on good economic logic. Subcontractors were probably chosen based on business variables such as cost, delivery, and product quality, and the key managers simply failed to ask, "How does this subcontractor treat its workforce?" If they thought about the question at all, they probably reasoned that it was the subcontractor's concern, not theirs.

ORGANIZATION CULTURE   The climate in some businesses does not encourage people to think through the ethical consequences of business decisions. This brings us to the third cause of unethical behavior in businesses—an organizational culture that deemphasizes business ethics, reducing all decisions to the purely economic. The term **organization culture** refers to the values and norms that are shared among employees of an organization. You will recall from Chapter 3 that *values* are abstract ideas about what a group believes to be good, right, and desirable, while *norms* are the social rules and guidelines that prescribe appropriate behavior in particular situations. Just as societies have cultures, so do business organizations. Together, values and norms shape the culture of a business organization, and that culture has an important influence on the ethics of business decision making.

Organization Culture
The values and norms shared among an organization's employees.

Author Robert Bryce has explained how the organization culture at now-bankrupt multinational energy company Enron was built on values that emphasized greed and deception.[26] According to Bryce, the tone was set by top managers who engaged in self-dealing to enrich themselves and their own families. Bryce tells how former Enron CEO Kenneth Lay made sure his own family benefited handsomely from Enron. Much of Enron's corporate travel business was handled by a travel agency part owned by Lay's sister. When an internal auditor recommended that the company could do better by using another travel agency, the auditor soon found himself out of a job. In 1997, Enron acquired a company owned by Kenneth Lay's son, Mark Lay, which was trying to establish a business trading paper and pulp products. At the time, Mark Lay and another company he controlled were targets of a federal criminal investigation of bankruptcy fraud and embezzlement. As part of the deal, Enron hired Mark Lay as an executive with a three-year contract that guaranteed him at least $1 million in pay over that period, plus options to purchase about 20,000 shares of Enron. Bryce also details how Lay's grown daughter used an Enron jet to transport her king-sized bed to France. With Kenneth Lay as an example, it is perhaps not surprising that self-dealing soon became endemic at Enron. The most notable example was Chief Financial Officer Andrew Fastow, who set up "off balance sheet" partnerships that not only hid Enron's true financial condition from investors, but also paid tens of millions of dollars directly to Fastow. (Fastow was subsequently indicted by the government for criminal fraud and went to jail.)

Former investment firm owner Bernard Madoff walks past the media in New York. Madoff was convicted of running a financial scheme that left his clients with little money to show for their investment. His unethical behavior affected banks and businesses worldwide.

UNREALISTIC PERFORMANCE EXPECTATIONS A fourth cause of unethical behavior has already been hinted at—it is pressure from the parent company to meet unrealistic performance goals that can be attained only by cutting corners or acting in an unethical manner. Again, Bryce discusses how this may have occurred at Enron. Lay's successor as CEO, Jeff Skilling, put a performance evaluation system in place that weeded out 15 percent of underperformers every six months. This created a pressure-cooker culture with a myopic focus on short-run performance, and some executives and energy traders responded to that pressure by falsifying their performance—inflating the value of trades, for example—to make it look as if they were performing better than was actually the case.

The lesson from the Enron debacle is that an organizational culture can legitimize behavior that society would judge as unethical, particularly when this is mixed with a focus on unrealistic performance goals, such as maximizing short-term economic performance, no matter what the costs. In such circumstances, there is a greater than average probability that managers will violate their own personal ethics and engage in unethical behavior. Conversely, an organization culture can do just the opposite and reinforce the need for ethical behavior. At Hewlett-Packard, for example, Bill Hewlett and David Packard, the company's founders, propagated a set of values known as The HP Way. These values, which shape the way business is conducted both within and by the corporation, have an important ethical component. Among other things, they stress the need for confidence in and respect for people, open communication, and concern for the individual employee.

LEADERSHIP The Enron and Hewlett-Packard examples suggest a fifth root cause of unethical behavior—leadership. Leaders help to establish the culture of an organization, and they set the example that others follow. Other employees in a business often take their cue from business leaders, and if those leaders do not behave in an ethical manner, they might not either. It is not what leaders say that matters, but what they do. Enron, for example, had a code of ethics that Kenneth Lay himself often referred to, but Lay's own actions to enrich family members spoke louder than any words.

Philosophical Approaches to Ethics

We shall look at several different approaches to business ethics here, beginning with some that can best be described as straw men, which either deny the value of business ethics or apply the concept in a very unsatisfactory way. After discussing, and dismissing, the straw men, we then move on to consider approaches that are favored by most

LEARNING OBJECTIVE 4
Describe the different philosophical approaches to ethics.

moral philosophers and form the basis for current models of ethical behavior in international businesses.

STRAW MEN   Straw men approaches to business ethics are raised by business ethics scholars primarily to demonstrate that they offer inappropriate guidelines for ethical decision making in a multinational enterprise. Four such approaches to business ethics are commonly discussed in the literature. These approaches can be characterized as the Friedman doctrine, cultural relativism, the righteous moralist, and the naive immoralist. All of these approaches have some inherent value, but all are unsatisfactory in important ways. Nevertheless, sometimes companies adopt these approaches.

The Friedman Doctrine

The Nobel Prize-winning economist Milton Friedman wrote an article in 1970 that has since become a classic straw man that business ethics scholars outline only to then tear down.[27] Friedman's basic position is that the only social responsibility of business is to increase profits, so long as the company stays within the rules of law. He explicitly rejects the idea that businesses should undertake social expenditures beyond those mandated by the law and required for the efficient running of a business. For example, his arguments suggest that improving working conditions beyond the level required by the law *and* necessary to maximize employee productivity will reduce profits and are therefore not appropriate. His belief is that a firm should maximize its profits because that is the way to maximize the returns that accrue to the owners of the firm, its stockholders. If stockholders then wish to use the proceeds to make social investments, that is their right, according to Friedman, but managers of the firm should not make that decision for them.

Although Friedman is talking about social responsibility, rather than business ethics per se, many business ethics scholars equate social responsibility with ethical behavior and thus believe Friedman is also arguing against business ethics. However, the assumption that Friedman is arguing against ethics is not quite true, for Friedman does state,

> There is one and only one social responsibility of business—to use its resources and engage in activities designed to increase its profits so long as it stays within the rules of the game, which is to say that it engages in open and free competition without deception or fraud.[28]

In other words, Friedman states that businesses should behave in an ethical manner and not engage in deception and fraud.

Nevertheless, Friedman's arguments do break down under examination. This is particularly true in international business where the "rules of the game" are not well established and differ from country to county. Consider again the case of sweatshop labor. Child labor may not be against the law in a developing nation, and maximizing productivity may not require that a multinational firm stop using child labor in that country, but it is still immoral to use child labor because the practice conflicts with widely held views about what is the right and proper thing to do. Similarly, there may be no rules against pollution in a developed nation and spending money on pollution control may reduce the profit rate of the firm, but generalized notions of morality would hold that it is still unethical to dump toxic pollutants into rivers or foul the air with gas releases. In addition to the local consequences of such pollution, which may have serious health effects for the surrounding population, there is also a global consequence as pollutants degrade those two global commons so important to us all—the atmosphere and the oceans.

Cultural Relativism
The belief that ethics are culturally determined and that firms should adopt the ethics of the cultures in which they operate.

Cultural Relativism

Another straw man often raised by business ethics scholars is **cultural relativism,** which is the belief that ethics are nothing more than the reflection of a culture—all ethics are culturally determined—and that accordingly, a firm should adopt the ethics of the culture in which it is operating.[29] This approach is often summarized by the maxim *when in Rome do as the Romans*. As with Friedman's approach, cultural relativism does not stand up to a closer look. At its extreme, cultural relativism suggests that if a culture supports slavery, it is OK to use slave labor in a country. Clearly, it is not! Cultural relativism implicitly rejects the idea that universal notions of morality transcend different cultures, but, as we shall argue later in the chapter, some universal notions of morality are found across cultures.

While dismissing cultural relativism in its most sweeping form, some ethicists argue there is residual value in this approach.[30] As we noted in Chapter 3, societal values and norms do vary from culture to culture, customs do differ, so it might follow that certain business practices are ethical in one country, but not another. Indeed, the facilitating payments allowed in the Foreign Corrupt Practices Act can be seen as an acknowledgment that in some countries, the payment of speed money to government officials is necessary to get business done, and if not ethically desirable, it is at least ethically acceptable.

However, not all ethicists or companies agree with this pragmatic view. As noted earlier, oil company BP explicitly states it will not make facilitating payments, no matter what the prevailing cultural norms are. BP has enacted a zero-tolerance policy for facilitation payments, primarily on the basis that such payments are a low-level form of corruption, and thus cannot be justified because corruption corrupts both the bribe giver and the bribe taker, and perpetuates the corrupt system. As BP notes on its Web site, because of its zero-tolerance policy:

> Some oil product sales in Vietnam involved inappropriate commission payments to the managers of customers in return for placing orders with BP. These were stopped during 2002 with the result that BP failed to win certain tenders with potential profit totaling $300k. In addition, two sales managers resigned over the issue. The business, however, has recovered using more traditional sales methods and has exceeded its targets at year-end.[31]

BP's experience suggests that companies should not use cultural relativism as an argument for justifying behavior that is clearly based upon suspect ethical grounds, even if that behavior is both legal and routinely accepted in the country where the company is doing business.

The Righteous Moralist

Righteous moralism contends that a multinational's home-country standards of ethics are the appropriate ones for companies to follow in foreign countries. This approach is typically associated with managers from developed nations. While this seems reasonable at first blush, the approach can create problems. Consider the following example: An American bank manager was sent to Italy and was appalled to learn that the local branch's accounting department recommended grossly underreporting the bank's profits for income tax purposes.[32] The manager insisted that the bank report its earnings accurately, American style. When he was called by the Italian tax department to the firm's tax hearing, he was told the firm owed three times as much tax as it had paid, reflecting the department's standard assumption that each

Righteous Moralism
The belief that a multinational's home-country standards of ethics are the appropriate ones for companies to follow in foreign countries.

firm underreports its earnings by two-thirds. Despite his protests, the new assessment stood. In this case, the righteous moralist has run into a problem caused by the prevailing cultural norms in the country where he is doing business. How should he respond? The righteous moralist would argue for maintaining the position, while a more pragmatic view might be that in this case, the right thing to do is to follow the prevailing cultural norms, since there is a big penalty for not doing so.

The main criticism of the righteous moralist approach is that its proponents go too far. While there are some universal moral principles that should not be violated, it does not always follow that the appropriate thing to do is adopt home-country standards. For example, U.S. laws set strict guidelines with regard to minimum wage and working conditions. Does this mean it is ethical to apply the same guidelines in a foreign country, paying people the same as they are paid in the United States, providing the same benefits and working conditions? Probably not, because doing so might nullify the reason for investing in that country and therefore deny locals the benefits of inward investment by the multinational. Clearly, a more nuanced approach is needed.

Naïve Immoralism
The belief that if a manager of a multinational sees that firms from other nations are not following ethical norms in a host nation, that manager should not either.

The Naive Immoralist   **Naive immoralism** asserts that if a manager of a multinational sees that firms from other nations are not following ethical norms in a host nation, that manager should not either. The classic example to illustrate the approach is known as the drug lord problem. In one variant of this problem, an American manager in Colombia routinely pays off the local drug lord to guarantee that his plant will not be bombed and that none of his employees will be kidnapped. The manager argues that such payments are ethically defensible because everyone is doing it.

The objection is twofold. First, to say that an action is ethically justified if everyone is doing it is not sufficient. If firms in a country routinely employ 12-year-olds and make them work 10-hour days, is it therefore ethically defensible to do the same? Obviously not, and the company does have a clear choice. It does not have to abide by local practices, and it can decide not to invest in a country where the practices are particularly odious. Second, the multinational must recognize that it does have the ability to change the prevailing practice in a country. It can use its power for a positive moral purpose. This is what BP is doing by adopting a zero-tolerance policy with regard to facilitating payments. BP is stating that the prevailing practice of making facilitating payments is ethically wrong, and it is incumbent upon the company to use its power to try to change the standard. While some might argue that such an approach smells of moral imperialism and a lack of cultural sensitivity, if it is consistent with widely accepted moral standards in the global community, it may be ethically justified.

To return to the drug lord problem, an argument can be made that it is ethically defensible to make such payments, not because everyone else is doing so but because not doing so would cause greater harm (i.e., the drug lord might seek retribution and engage in killings and kidnappings). Another solution to the problem is to refuse to invest in a country where the rule of law is so weak that drug lords can demand protection money. This solution, however, is also imperfect, for it might mean denying the law-abiding citizens of that country the benefits associated with inward investment by the multinational (i.e., jobs, income, greater economic growth and welfare). Clearly, the drug lord problem constitutes one of those intractable ethical dilemmas where there is no obvious right solution, and managers need a moral compass to help them find an acceptable solution to the dilemma.

UTILITARIAN AND KANTIAN ETHICS   In contrast to the straw men just discussed, most moral philosophers see value in utilitarian and Kantian approaches to business ethics. These approaches were developed in the eighteenth and nineteenth centuries and although they have been largely superseded by more modern approaches, they form part of the tradition upon which newer approaches have been constructed.

The utilitarian approach to business ethics dates to philosophers such as David Hume (1771–1776), Jeremy Bentham (1784–1832), and John Stuart Mill (1806–1873). **Utilitarian approaches** to ethics hold that the moral worth of actions or practices is determined by their consequences.[33] An action is judged desirable if it leads to the best possible balance of good consequences over bad consequences. Utilitarianism is committed to the maximization of good and the minimization of harm. Utilitarianism recognizes that actions have multiple consequences, some of which are good in a social sense and some of which are harmful. As a philosophy for business ethics, it focuses attention on the need to weigh carefully all of the social benefits and costs of a business action and to pursue only those actions where the benefits outweigh the costs. The best decisions, from a utilitarian perspective, are those that produce the greatest good for the greatest number of people.

Utilitarian Approaches
These approaches to ethics hold that the moral worth of actions or practices is determined by their consequences.

Many businesses have adopted specific tools such as cost-benefit analysis and risk assessment that are firmly rooted in a utilitarian philosophy. Managers often weigh the benefits and costs of an action before deciding whether to pursue it. An oil company considering drilling in the Alaskan wildlife preserve must weigh the economic benefits of increased oil production and the creation of jobs against the costs of environmental degradation in a fragile ecosystem. An agricultural biotechnology company such as Monsanto must decide whether the benefits of genetically modified crops that produce natural pesticides outweigh the risks. The benefits include increased crop yields and reduced need for chemical fertilizers. The risks include the possibility that Monsanto's insect-resistant crops might make matters worse over time if insects evolve a resistance to the natural pesticides engineered into Monsanto's plants, rendering the plants vulnerable to a new generation of super bugs.

For all of its appeal, utilitarian philosophy does have some serious drawbacks as an approach to business ethics. One problem is measuring the benefits, costs, and risks of a course of action. In the case of an oil company considering drilling in Alaska, how does one measure the potential harm done to the region's ecosystem? In the Monsanto example, how can one quantify the risk that genetically engineered crops might ultimately result in the evolution of super bugs that are resistant to the natural pesticide engineered into the crops? In general, utilitarian philosophers recognize that the measurement of benefits, costs, and risks is often not possible due to limited knowledge.

The second problem with utilitarianism is that the philosophy omits the consideration of justice. The action that produces the greatest good for the greatest number of people may result in the unjustified treatment of a minority. Such action cannot be ethical, precisely because it is unjust. For example, suppose that in the interests of keeping down health insurance costs, the government decides to screen people for the HIV virus and deny insurance coverage to those who are HIV positive. By reducing health costs, such action might produce significant benefits for a large number of people, but the action is unjust because it discriminates unfairly against a minority.

Kantian ethics are based on the philosophy of Immanuel Kant (1724–1804). **Kantian ethics** hold that people should be treated as ends and never purely as *means* to the ends of others. People are not instruments, like a machine. People have dignity and need to be respected as such. Employing people in sweatshops, making them work long hours for low pay in poor work conditions, is a violation of ethics, according to Kantian philosophy, because it treats people as mere cogs in a machine and not as conscious moral beings that have dignity. Although contemporary moral

Kantian ethics
The belief that people should be treated as ends and never as means to the ends of others.

philosophers tend to view Kant's ethical philosophy as incomplete—for example, his system has no place for moral emotions or sentiments such as sympathy or caring—the notion that people should be respected and treated with dignity still resonates in the modern world.

RIGHTS THEORIES

Developed in the twentieth century, **rights theories** recognize that human beings have fundamental rights and privileges that transcend national boundaries and cultures. Rights establish a minimum level of morally acceptable behavior. One well-known definition of a fundamental right construes it as something that takes precedence over or "trumps" a collective good. Thus, we might say that the right to free speech is a fundamental right that takes precedence over all but the most compelling collective goals and overrides, for example, the interest of the state in civil harmony or moral consensus.[34] Moral theorists argue that fundamental human rights form the basis for the *moral compass* that managers should navigate by when making decisions that have an ethical component. More precisely, they should not pursue actions that violate these rights.

The notion that there are fundamental rights that transcend national borders and cultures was the underlying motivation for the United Nations **Universal Declaration of Human Rights,** which has been ratified by almost every country on the planet and lays down basic principles that should always be adhered to irrespective of the culture in which one is doing business.[35] Echoing Kantian ethics, Article 1 of this declaration states:

> Article 1: All human beings are born free and equal in dignity and rights. They are endowed with reason and conscience and should act towards one another in a spirit of brotherhood.

Article 23 of this declaration, which relates directly to employment, states:

> Everyone has the right to work, to free choice of employment, to just and favorable conditions of work, and to protection against unemployment.
>
> Everyone, without any discrimination, has the right to equal pay for equal work.
>
> Everyone who works has the right to just and favorable remuneration ensuring for himself and his family an existence worthy of human dignity, and supplemented, if necessary, by other means of social protection.
>
> Everyone has the right to form and to join trade unions for the protection of his interests.

Clearly, the rights to "just and favorable work conditions," "equal pay for equal work," and remuneration that ensures an "existence worthy of human dignity" embodied in Article 23 imply that it is unethical to employ child labor in sweatshop settings and pay less than subsistence wages, even if that happens to be common practice in some countries. These are fundamental human rights that transcend national borders.

It is important to note that along with *rights* come *obligations*. Because we have the right to free speech, we are also obligated to make sure that we respect the free speech of others. The notion that people have obligations is stated in Article 29 of the Universal Declaration of Human Rights:

> Article 29: Everyone has duties to the community in which alone the free and full development of his personality is possible.

Within the framework of a theory of rights, certain people or institutions are obligated to provide benefits or services that secure the rights of others. Such obligations also fall upon more than one class of moral agent (a moral agent is any person or institution that is capable of moral action such as a government or corporation).

For example, to escape the high costs of toxic waste disposal in the West, in the late 1980s several firms shipped their waste in bulk to African nations, where it was disposed of at a much lower cost. In 1987, five European ships unloaded toxic waste containing dangerous poisons in Nigeria. Workers wearing sandals and shorts unloaded the barrels for $2.50 a day and placed them in a dirt lot in a residential area. They were not told about the contents of the barrels.[36] Who bears the obligation for protecting the rights of workers and residents to safety in a case like this? According to rights theorists, the obligation rests not on the shoulders of one moral agent, but on the shoulders of all moral agents whose actions might harm or contribute to the harm of the workers and residents. Thus, it was the obligation not just of the Nigerian government but also of the multinational firms that shipped the toxic waste to make sure it did no harm to residents and workers. In this case, both the government and the multinationals apparently failed to recognize their basic obligation to protect the fundamental human rights of others.

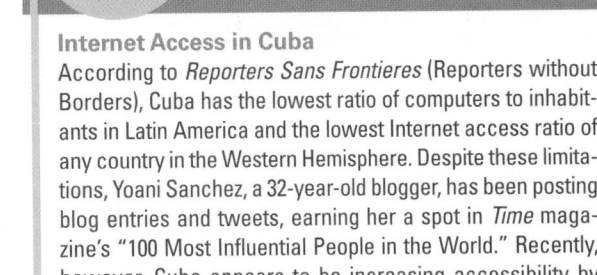

Another Perspective

Internet Access in Cuba

According to *Reporters Sans Frontieres* (Reporters without Borders), Cuba has the lowest ratio of computers to inhabitants in Latin America and the lowest Internet access ratio of any country in the Western Hemisphere. Despite these limitations, Yoani Sanchez, a 32-year-old blogger, has been posting blog entries and tweets, earning her a spot in *Time* magazine's "100 Most Influential People in the World." Recently, however, Cuba appears to be increasing accessibility by means of the "Telecentro." Combined with new fiberoptic cables from Venezuela, a Brazilian import, "telecentros" are public computer labs that use open source software and provide free Internet access for poor and underserved communities. Whether this will in fact increase access remains to be seen. (Reporters Sans Frontieres Web site, http://en.rsf. org/; A. Nelson, "Will 'Telecentros' Transform Cuba's Internet Access?" April 14, 2010, http://www.pbs.org/mediashift/ 2010/04/will-telecentros-transform-cubas-internet-access104.html, accessed July 28, 2010)

JUSTICE THEORIES   Justice theories focus on the attainment of a just distribution of economic goods and services. A **just distribution** is one that is considered fair and equitable. There is no one theory of justice, and several theories of justice conflict with each other in important ways.[37] Here we shall focus on one particular theory of justice that is both very influential and has important ethical implications. The theory is attributed to philosopher John Rawls.[38] Rawls argues that all economic goods and services should be distributed equally except when an unequal distribution would work to everyone's advantage.

According to Rawls, valid principles of justice are those with which all persons would agree if they could freely and impartially consider the situation. Impartiality is guaranteed by a conceptual device that Rawls calls the *veil of ignorance*. Under the veil of ignorance, everyone is imagined to be ignorant of all of his or her particular characteristics, for example, race, sex, intelligence, nationality, family background, and special talents. Rawls then asks what system people would design under a veil of ignorance. Under these conditions, people would unanimously agree on two fundamental principles of justice.

The first principle is that each person be permitted the maximum amount of basic liberty compatible with a similar liberty for others. Rawls takes these to be political liberty (e.g., the right to vote), freedom of speech and assembly, liberty of conscience and freedom of thought, the freedom and right to hold personal property, and freedom from arbitrary arrest and seizure.

The second principle is that once equal basic liberty is assured, inequality in basic social goods—such as income and wealth distribution, and opportunities—is to be allowed *only* if such inequalities benefit everyone. Rawls accepts that inequalities can be just if the system that produces inequalities is to the advantage of everyone. More precisely, he formulates what he calls the *difference principle*, which is that inequalities are justified if they benefit the position of the least-advantaged person. So, for example,

Just Distribution
A distribution of economic goods and services that is considered fair and equitable.

wide variations in income and wealth can be considered just if the market-based system that produces this unequal distribution also benefits the least-advantaged members of society. One can argue that a well-regulated, market-based economy and free trade, by promoting economic growth, benefit the least-advantaged members of society. In principle at least, the inequalities inherent in such systems are therefore just (in other words, the rising tide of wealth created by a market-based economy and free trade lifts all boats, even those of the most disadvantaged).

In the context of international business ethics, Rawls's theory creates an interesting perspective. Managers could ask themselves whether the policies they adopt in foreign operations would be considered just under Rawls's veil of ignorance. Is it just, for example, to pay foreign workers less than workers in the firm's home country? Rawls's theory would suggest it is, so long as the inequality benefits the least-advantaged members of the global society (which is what economic theory suggests). Alternatively, it is difficult to imagine that managers operating under a veil of ignorance would design a system where foreign employees were paid subsistence wages to work long hours in sweatshop conditions and where they were exposed to toxic materials. Such working conditions are clearly unjust in Rawls's framework, and therefore, it is unethical to adopt them. Similarly, operating under a veil of ignorance, most people would probably design a system that imparts some protection from environmental degradation to important global commons, such as the oceans, atmosphere, and tropical rain forests. To the extent that this is the case, it follows that it is unjust, and by extension unethical, for companies to pursue actions that contribute toward extensive degradation of these commons. Thus, Rawls's veil of ignorance is a conceptual tool that contributes to the moral compass that managers can use to help them navigate through difficult ethical dilemmas.

Focus on Managerial Implications

LEARNING OBJECTIVE 5
Explain how managers can incorporate ethical considerations into their decision making.

What then is the best way for managers in a multinational firm to make sure that ethical considerations figure into international business decisions? How do managers decide upon an ethical course of action when confronted with decisions pertaining to working conditions, human rights, corruption, and environmental pollution? From an ethical perspective, how do managers determine the moral obligations that flow from the power of a multinational? In many cases, there are no easy answers to these questions, for many of the most vexing ethical problems arise because there are very real dilemmas inherent in them and no obvious correct action. Nevertheless, managers can and should do many things to make sure that basic ethical principles are adhered to and that ethical issues are routinely inserted into international business decisions.

Here we focus on five things that an international business and its managers can do to make sure ethical issues are considered in business decisions. These are (1) favor hiring and promoting people with a well-grounded sense of personal ethics; (2) build an organizational culture that places a high value on ethical behavior; (3) make sure that leaders within the business not only articulate the rhetoric of ethical behavior, but also act in a manner that is consistent with that rhetoric; (4) put decision-making processes in place that require people to consider the ethical dimension of business decisions; and (5) develop moral courage.

Hiring and Promotion

It seems obvious that businesses should strive to hire people who have a strong sense of personal ethics and would not engage in unethical or illegal behavior. Similarly, you would not expect a business to promote people, and perhaps to fire people, whose behavior does not match generally accepted ethical standards. However, actually doing so is very difficult. How do you know that someone has a poor sense of personal ethics? In our society, we have an incentive to hide a lack of personal ethics from public view. Once people realize that you are unethical, they will no longer trust you.

Is there anything that businesses can do to make sure they do not hire people who subsequently turn out to have poor personal ethics, particularly given that people have an incentive to hide this from public view (indeed, the unethical person may lie about his or her nature)? Businesses can give potential employees psychological tests to try to discern their ethical predisposition, and they can check with prior employees regarding someone's reputation (e.g., by asking for letters of reference and talking to people who have worked with the prospective employee). The latter is common and does influence the hiring process. Promoting people who have displayed poor ethics should not occur in a company where the organization culture values the need for ethical behavior and where leaders act accordingly.

Not only should businesses strive to identify and hire people with a strong sense of personal ethics, but it also is in the interests of prospective employees to find out as much as they can about the ethical climate in an organization. Who wants to work at a multinational such as Enron, which ultimately entered bankruptcy because unethical executives had established risky partnerships that were hidden from public view and that existed in part to enrich those same executives? Table 4.1 lists questions job seekers might want to ask a prospective employer.

Some probing questions to ask about a prospective employer:

1. Is there a formal code of ethics? How widely is it distributed? Is it reinforced in other formal ways such as through decision-making systems?
2. Are workers at all levels trained in ethical decision making? Are they also encouraged to take responsibility for their behavior or to question authority when asked to do something they consider wrong?
3. Do employees have formal channels available to make their concerns known confidentially? Is there a formal committee high in the organization that considers ethical issues?
4. Is misconduct disciplined swiftly and justly within the organization?
5. Is integrity emphasized to new employees?
6. How are senior managers perceived by subordinates in terms of their integrity? How do such leaders model ethical behavior?

4.1 table

A Job Seeker's Ethics Audit

Source: Linda K. Trevino, chair of the Department of Management and Organization, Smeal College of Business, Pennsylvania State University. Reported in K. Maher, "Career Journal. Wanted: Ethical Employer," *The Wall Street Journal,* July 9, 2002, p. B1.

Organization Culture and Leadership

To foster ethical behavior, businesses need to build an organization culture that values ethical behavior. Three things are particularly important in building an organization culture that emphasizes ethical behavior. First, the businesses must explicitly articulate values that emphasize ethical behavior. Many companies now do this by drafting a **code of ethics,** which is a formal statement of the ethical priorities a business adheres to. Often, the code of ethics draws heavily upon documents such as the UN Universal Declaration of Human Rights, which itself is grounded in Kantian and rights-based theories of moral philosophy. Others have incorporated ethical statements into documents that articulate the values or mission of the business. For example, the food and consumer products multinational Unilever has a code of ethics that includes the following points:[39]

Employees: Unilever is committed to diversity in a working environment where there is mutual trust and respect and where everyone feels responsible for the performance and reputation of our company. We will recruit, employ, and promote employees on the sole basis of the qualifications and abilities needed for the work to be performed. We are committed to safe and healthy working conditions for all employees. We will not use any form of forced, compulsory, or child labor. We are committed to working with employees to develop and enhance each individual's skills and capabilities. We respect the dignity of the individual and the right of employees to freedom of association. We will maintain good communications with employees through company-based information and consultation procedures.

Business Integrity: Unilever does not give or receive, whether directly or indirectly, bribes or other improper advantages for business or financial gain. No employee may offer, give, or receive any gift or payment which is, or may be construed as being, a bribe. Any demand for, or offer of, a bribe must be rejected immediately and reported to management. Unilever accounting records and supporting documents must accurately describe and reflect the nature of the underlying transactions. No undisclosed or unrecorded account, fund, or asset will be established or maintained.

It is clear from these principles, that among other things, Unilever will not tolerate substandard working conditions, use child labor, or give bribes under any circumstances. Note also the reference to respecting the dignity of employees, a statement that is grounded in Kantian ethics. Unilever's principles send a very clear message about appropriate ethics to managers and employees.

Having articulated values in a code of ethics or some other document, leaders in the business must give life and meaning to those words by repeatedly emphasizing their importance *and then acting on them.* This means using every relevant opportunity to stress the importance of business ethics and making sure that key business decisions not only make good economic sense but also are ethical. Many companies have gone a step further, hiring independent auditors to make sure they are behaving in a manner consistent with their ethical codes. Nike, for example, has hired independent

Another Perspective

Is "Fair Trade" Free Trade?
Although it has increased in popularity over the past decades, the concept of "fair trade" has been criticized from both ends of the political spectrum. Traditional, right-wing economists view it as a subsidy causing price distortion within the concept of free trade. The progressives, on the left, view it as not adequately challenging the free trade system. To the extent it promotes market access to more marginalized producers in developing nations by reducing the number of intermediaries, "fair trade" may be said to increase market accessibility, thereby promoting free trade. But if forced to comply with a process that certifies products have been produced, traded, processed, and packaged in accordance with specific standards, hasn't the producer essentially changed from one regulated environment to another? How about fair trade in the highly regulated world of vodka? (Kathryn Roethel, "New Vodka Shakes Up Scene with Fair Trade, " *San Francisco Chronicle* July 22, 2010; "Fair Trade," accessed at www.wikipedia.com)

auditors to make sure subcontractors used by the company are living up to Nike's code of conduct.

Finally, building an organization culture that places a high value on ethical behavior requires incentive and reward systems, including promotions that reward people who engage in ethical behavior and sanction those who do not. At General Electric, for example, the former CEO Jack Welch has described how he reviewed the performance of managers, dividing them into several groups. These included over-performers who displayed the right values and were singled out for advancement and bonuses and over-performers who displayed the wrong values and were let go. Welch was not willing to tolerate leaders within the company who did not act in accordance with the central values of the company, even if they were in all other respects skilled managers.[40]

Decision-Making Processes

In addition to establishing the right kind of ethical culture in an organization, business-people must be able to think through the ethical implications of decisions in a systematic way. To do this, they need a moral compass, and both rights theories and Rawls's theory of justice help to provide such a compass. Beyond these theories, some experts on ethics have proposed a straightforward practical guide—or ethical algorithm—to determine whether a decision is ethical.[41] According to these experts, a decision is acceptable on ethical grounds if a businessperson can answer yes to each of these questions:

- Does my decision fall within the accepted values or standards that typically apply in the organizational environment (as articulated in a code of ethics or some other corporate statement)?
- Am I willing to see the decision communicated to all stakeholders affected by it—for example, by having it reported in newspapers or on television?
- Would the people with whom I have a significant personal relationship, such as family members, friends, or even managers in other businesses, approve of the decision?

Others have recommended a five-step process to think through ethical problems (this is another example of an ethical algorithm).[42] In step one, businesspeople should identify which stakeholders a decision would affect and in what ways. A firm's **stakeholders** are individuals or groups that have an interest, claim, or stake in the company, in what it does, and in how well it performs.[43] They can be divided into internal stakeholders and external stakeholders. **Internal stakeholders** are individuals or groups who work for or own the business. They include all employees, the board of directors, and stockholders. **External stakeholders** are all other individuals and groups that have some claim on the firm. Typically, this group comprises customers, suppliers, lenders, governments, unions, local communities, and the general public.

All stakeholders are in an exchange relationship with the company. Each stakeholder group supplies the organization with important resources (or contributions), and in exchange each expects its interests to be satisfied (by inducements).[44] For example, employees provide labor, skills, knowledge, and time and in exchange expect commensurate income, job satisfaction, job security, and good working conditions. Customers provide a company with its revenues and in exchange they want quality products that represent value for money. Communities provide businesses with local infrastructure and in exchange they want businesses that are responsible citizens and seek some assurance that the quality of life will be improved as a result of the business firm's existence.

Stakeholder analysis involves a certain amount of what has been called *moral imagination.*[45] This means standing in the shoes of a stakeholder and asking how a proposed decision might impact that stakeholder. For example, when considering outsourcing to

Stakeholders The individuals or groups that have an interest, stake, or claim in the actions and overall performance of a company.

Internal Stakeholders People who work for or own the business, such as employees, directors, and stockholders.

External Stakeholders The individuals and groups that have some claim on the firm, such as customers, suppliers, and unions.

subcontractors, managers might need to ask themselves how it might feel to be working under substandard health conditions for long hours.

Step two involves judging the ethics of the proposed strategic decision, given the information gained in step one. Managers need to determine whether a proposed decision would violate the *fundamental rights* of any stakeholders. For example, we might argue that the right to information about health risks in the workplace is a fundamental entitlement of employees. Similarly, the right to know about potentially dangerous features of a product is a fundamental entitlement of customers (something tobacco companies violated when they did not reveal to their customers what they knew about the health risks of smoking). Managers might also want to ask themselves whether they would allow the proposed strategic decision if they were designing a system under Rawls's veil of ignorance. For example, if the issue under consideration was whether to outsource work to a subcontractor with low pay and poor working conditions, managers might want to ask themselves whether they would allow such action if they were considering it under a veil of ignorance, where they themselves might ultimately be the ones to work for the subcontractor.

The judgment at this stage should be guided by various moral principles that should not be violated. The principles might be those articulated in a corporate code of ethics or other company documents. In addition, certain moral principles that we have adopted as members of society—for instance, the prohibition on stealing—should not be violated. The judgment at this stage will also be guided by the decision rule that is chosen to assess the proposed strategic decision. Although maximizing long-run profitability is the decision rule that most businesses stress, it should be applied subject to the constraint that no moral principles are violated—that the business behaves in an ethical manner.

Step three requires managers to establish moral intent. This means the business must resolve to place moral concerns ahead of other concerns in cases where either the fundamental rights of stakeholders or key moral principles have been violated. At this stage, input from top management might be particularly valuable. Without the proactive encouragement of top managers, middle-level managers might tend to place the narrow economic interests of the company before the interests of stakeholders. They might do so in the (usually erroneous) belief that top managers favor such an approach.

Step four requires the company to engage in ethical behavior. Step five requires the business to audit its decisions, reviewing them to make sure they were consistent with ethical principles, such as those stated in the company's code of ethics. This final step is critical and often overlooked. Without auditing past decisions, businesspeople may not know if their decision process is working and if changes should be made to ensure greater compliance with a code of ethics.

Ethics Officers

To make sure that a business behaves in an ethical manner, a number of firms now have ethics officers. These individuals are responsible for making sure that all employees are trained to be ethically aware, that ethical considerations enter the business decision-making process, and that the company's code of ethics is followed. Ethics officers may also be responsible for auditing decisions to make sure they are consistent with this code. In many businesses, ethics officers act as an internal ombudsperson with responsibility for handling confidential inquiries from employees, investigating complaints from employees or others, reporting findings, and making recommendations for change.

For example, United Technologies, a multinational aerospace company with worldwide revenues of more than $30 billion, has had a formal code of ethics since 1990.[46] United Technologies has some 160 business practice officers (this is the company's name for ethics officers). They are responsible for making sure the code is followed. United Technologies also established an ombudsperson program in

United Technologies, the maker of Sikorsky helicopters, demonstrates its commitment to ethical behavior by employing over 160 business practices officers.

1986 that lets employees inquire anonymously about ethics issues. The program has received some 60,000 inquiries since 1986, and over 10,000 cases have been handled by an ombudsperson.

Moral Courage

Finally, it is important to recognize that employees in an international business may need significant *moral courage*. Moral courage enables managers to walk away from a decision that is profitable, but unethical. Moral courage gives an employee the strength to say no to a superior who instructs her to pursue actions that are unethical. Moral courage gives employees the integrity to go public to the media and blow the whistle on persistent unethical behavior in a company. Moral courage does not come easily; there are well-known cases where individuals have lost their jobs because they blew the whistle on corporate behaviors they thought unethical, telling the media about what was occurring.[47]

However, companies can strengthen the moral courage of employees by committing themselves to not retaliate against employees who exercise moral courage, say no to superiors, or otherwise complain about unethical actions. For example, consider the following extract from Unilever's code of ethics:

> Any breaches of the Code must be reported in accordance with the procedures specified by the Joint Secretaries. The Board of Unilever will not criticize management for any loss of business resulting from adherence to these principles and other mandatory policies and instructions. The Board of Unilever expects employees to bring to their attention, or to that of senior management, any breach or suspected breach of these principles. Provision has been made for employees to be able to report in confidence and no employee will suffer as a consequence of doing so.[48]

This statement gives permission to employees to exercise moral courage. Companies can also set up ethics hotlines, which allow employees to anonymously register a complaint with a corporate ethics officer.

Summary of Decision-Making Steps

All of the steps discussed here—hiring and promoting people based upon ethical considerations as well as more traditional metrics of performance, establishing an ethical culture in the organization, instituting ethical decision-making processes, appointing ethics officers, and creating an environment that facilitates moral courage—can help to make sure that when making business decisions, managers are cognizant of the ethical implications and do not violate basic ethical prescripts. At the same time, it must be recognized that not all ethical dilemmas have a clean and obvious solution—that is why they are dilemmas. There are clearly things that international businesses should not do and there are things that they should do but there are also actions that present managers with true dilemmas. In these cases, a premium is placed on managers' ability to make sense out of complex situations and make balanced decisions that are as just as possible.

Key Terms

business ethics, p. 156

ethical strategy, p. 156

Foreign Corrupt Practices Act, p. 163

Convention on Combating Bribery of Foreign Public Officials in International Business Transactions, p. 163

social responsibility, p. 164

ethical dilemma, p. 167

organization culture, p. 168

cultural relativism, p. 170

righteous moralism, p. 171

naïve immoralism, p. 172

utilitarian approaches, p. 173

Kantian ethics, p. 173

rights theories, p. 174

Universal Declaration of Human Rights, p. 174

just distribution, p. 175

code of ethics, p. 178

stakeholders, p. 179

internal stakeholders, p. 179

external stakeholders, p. 179

Summary

This chapter has discussed the source and nature of ethical issues in international businesses, the different philosophical approaches to business ethics, and the steps managers can take to ensure that ethical issues are respected in international business decisions. The chapter made the following points:

1. The term *ethics* refers to accepted principles of right or wrong that govern the conduct of a person, the members of a profession, or the actions of an organization. Business ethics are the accepted principles of right or wrong governing the conduct of businesspeople, and an ethical strategy is one that does not violate these accepted principles.

2. Ethical issues and dilemmas in international business are rooted in the variations among political systems, law, economic development, and culture from nation to nation.

3. The most common ethical issues in international business involve employment practices, human rights, environmental

regulations, corruption, and the moral obligation of multinational corporations.

4. Ethical dilemmas are situations in which none of the available alternatives seems ethically acceptable.

5. Unethical behavior is rooted in poor personal ethics, the psychological and geographical distances of a foreign subsidiary from the home office, a failure to incorporate ethical issues into strategic and operational decision making, a dysfunctional culture, and failure of leaders to act in an ethical manner.

6. Moral philosophers contend that approaches to business ethics such as the Friedman doctrine, cultural relativism, the righteous moralist, and the naive immoralist are unsatisfactory in important ways.

7. The Friedman doctrine states that the only social responsibility of business is to increase profits, as long as the company stays within the rules of law. Cultural relativism contends that

one should adopt the ethics of the culture in which one is doing business. The righteous moralist monolithically applies home-country ethics to a foreign situation, while the naive immoralist believes that if a manager of a multinational sees that firms from other nations are not following ethical norms in a host nation, that manager should not either.

8. Utilitarian approaches to ethics hold that the moral worth of actions or practices is determined by their consequences, and the best decisions are those that produce the greatest good for the greatest number of people.

9. Kantian ethics state that people should be treated as ends and never purely as *means* to the ends of others. People are not instruments, like a machine. People have dignity and need to be respected as such.

10. Rights theories recognize that human beings have fundamental rights and privileges that transcend national boundaries and cultures.

These rights establish a minimum level of morally acceptable behavior.

11. The concept of justice developed by John Rawls suggests that a decision is just and ethical if people would allow for it when designing a social system under a veil of ignorance.

12. To make sure that ethical issues are considered in international business decisions, managers should (*a*) favor hiring and promoting people with a well-grounded sense of personal ethics; (*b*) build an organization culture that places a high value on ethical behavior; (*c*) make sure that leaders within the business not only articulate the rhetoric of ethical behavior, but also act in a manner that is consistent with that rhetoric; (*d*) put decision-making processes in place that require people to consider the ethical dimension of business decisions; and (*e*) be morally courageous and encourage others to do the same.

Critical Thinking and Discussion Questions

1. A visiting American executive finds that a foreign subsidiary in a poor nation has hired a 12-year-old girl to work on a factory floor, in violation of the company's prohibition on child labor. He tells the local manager to replace the child and tell her to go back to school. The local manager tells the American executive that the child is an orphan with no other means of support, and she will probably become a street child if she is denied work. What should the American executive do?

2. Drawing upon John Rawls's concept of the veil of ignorance, develop an ethical code that will (*a*) guide the decisions of a large oil multinational toward environmental protection, and (*b*) influence the policies of a clothing company to outsourcing of the manufacturing process.

3. Under what conditions is it ethically defensible to outsource production to the developing world where labor costs are lower when such actions also involve laying off long-term employees in the firm's home country?

4. Are facilitating payments ethical?

5. A manager from a developing country is overseeing a multinational's operations in a country where drug trafficking and lawlessness are rife. One day, a representative of a local "big man" approaches the manager and asks for a "donation" to help the "big man" provide housing for the poor. The representative tells the manager that in return for the donation, the "big man" will make sure that the manager has a productive stay in his country. No threats are made, but the manager is well aware that the "big man" heads a criminal organization that is engaged in drug trafficking. He also knows that the big man does indeed help the poor in the run-down neighborhood of the city where he was born. What should the manager do?

6. Reread the Management Focus on Gold Mining in Eritrea and answer the following questions:

   a. Was it ethical for Nevsun to enter into a partnership with Eritrea's authoritarian government?

   b. Nevsun has outlined a social management plan that provides Eritrean workers with many of the same rights given to its Canadian workers. Do you foresee a problem with the way this policy is viewed in Eritrea?

Use the globalEDGE Resource Desk (http://globalEDGE.msu.edu/resourcedesk/) to complete the following exercises:

1. The Organization for Economic Cooperation and Development (OECD) *Guidelines for Multinational Enterprises* is a set of voluntary principles and standards for responsible business conduct addressed by governments for multinational enterprises. The guidelines provide recommendations in a number of areas including labor relations, the environment, bribery, competition, and taxation. Find the text of the guidelines and prepare an outline of the guidelines in the area of employment and industrial relations.

2. The *Corruption Perceptions Index* (CPI) is a comparative assessment of integrity performance in a variety of countries. Provide a description of this index and its ranking. Identify the five countries with the lowest and the highest CPI scores. Do you notice any trends or similarities among the countries listed?

closing case

Rio Tinto Bribery Scandal: Iron-Ore Complexities

In the Shanghai No. 1 Intermediate People's Court, behind closed doors, Stern Hu, head of Rio Tinto's China sales force, and three others, confessed to taking bribes and stealing commercial secrets. The court sentenced Mr. Hu to 10 years imprisonment and fines. The others got between 7 and 14 years. They confessed to having steered iron-ore shipments to more than a dozen Chinese steelmakers in exchange for bribes valued in the hundreds of thousands of dollars each. Originally they had been accused of "violating state secrets"— spying. Once having defended them, the Anglo-Australian mining giant quickly "dismissed" the employees, claiming there was "clear evidence" they had violated Chinese law and the Rio Tinto Code of Business. But accepting the validity of the verdict, which was contrary to Rio Tinto's own internal investigation, speaks more to the complex nature of iron-ore extraction in China than to whether they were actually guilty of the confessed crime.

Complex legal, commercial, and political strategies appear to be involved in this case. To the sales executives, the legal strategy to confess was premised on the opaque and sometimes puzzling nature of the Chinese legal system. The confession was considered part of a legal strategy in a judicial system that favors admissions of guilt in exchange for lighter sentences. At times conducted behind closed doors, issues remained as to whether payments made were legitimate commissions on iron-ore sales or whether they were illegal bribes. Some analysts also suggested that prosecution might have been politically motivated in retaliation for what Chinese officials perceived as excessive profits obtained by Rio Tinto in the mining of iron ore in China.

For Rio Tinto, China is its most important client. Approximately 24 percent of its $10.69 billion in global revenues come from China. Continuing its operations in China was critical to the company's continued success. But Rio Tinto is "enmeshed" in a political situation in China that goes beyond a case of "corrupt" employees. All along, it was in Rio Tinto's best interest that the ex-employees also confessed. In fact, by confessing their "immoral wrongdoings," these ex-employees helped Rio Tinto's relations with China to actually improve. The government could gain face by apparently upholding its judicial system. Often criticized for turning a blind eye to corruption, the Chinese were seeking to establish that they are aggressively pursuing a policy of anti-corruption by means of their judicial system. By separating themselves from the criminal actions of a few employees, Rio Tinto could claim the case was closed and move on to repairing ties which had been strained not only by the corruption case but by the ongoing issues related to iron-ore extraction in China.

Rio Tinto's relationship with China had been strained because of the way it treated the Chinese steel industry in 2009, when the mining company resisted steelmakers' demands for a 45 percent cut in benchmark iron-ore prices; the way it abandoned plans for a £19.5 billion capital injection from Chinalco, a Chinese state-owned miner, which led to a loss of face for the Chinese government; and the manner in which it had partnered with BHP Billiton, another very large Australian iron-ore mining company, so as to change the traditional method of annual negotiations for pricing iron ore. In fact, steelmakers around the world are concerned that these two big producers can influence, perhaps control, prices by combining operations. Various antitrust authorities around the world are reviewing the proposed venture, and many are watching to see whether China's Ministry of Commerce launches its own investigation.

While the soon to be ex-employees were confessing, Rio Tinto's Chief Executive Officer Tom Albanese met with Premier Wen Jiabao. The two men shook hands, and Mr. Albanese exclaimed: "I want to look to the future."

Sources: Rio Tinto Website," The Way We Work—Our Global Code of Business Conduct," www.riotinto.com; J. T. Areddy, "Rio Tinto China Employees Get Jail Terms for Bribery," *The Wall Street Journal,* March 30, 2010, accessed at http://www.onlinewsj.com; J. T. Areddy, "World News: Rio Tinto Officials Admit Taking Bribes–Surprising Move Opens Chinese Trial, But Its Meaning Remains Uncertain," *The Wall Street Journal,* March 23, 2010, accessed at http://www.onlinewsj.com; and W. MacNamara, and P. Waldmeir, "Rio Tinto Courts China as Bribery Trial Begins, " *Financial Times* March 22, 2010.

Case Discussion Questions

1. What does the sales executives' confession represent to the Chinese? Were they the "fall guys" to a larger more political scheme?

2. What are Rio Tinto's interests in China? Why would Rio Tinto seek to partner with BHP Billiton? What threat does this pose to the Chinese or to other developing nations?

3. Did either Rio Tinto or the Chinese engage in any corrupt behavior? If so, how?

4. How do the concepts of justice, face, and relationship manifest themselves in this case?

LEARNING OBJECTIVES

After you have read this chapter you should be able to:

1 Understand why nations trade with each other.

2 Summarize the different theories explaining trade flows between nations.

3 Recognize why many economists believe that unrestricted free trade between nations will raise the economic welfare of countries that participate in a free trade system.

4 Explain the arguments of those who maintain that government can play a proactive role in promoting national competitive advantage in certain industries.

5 Understand the important implications that international trade theory holds for business practice.

chapter 5

International Trade Theory

Having overcome one political, macroeconomic, and business challenge after another, Brazil is now a globalization success story. When President Luiz Inácio Lula da Silva, "Lula" as he is affectionately known, took office in 2002, he embarked on a series of pro-market reforms; safeguarded the central bank's independence, controlled the budget deficit, and effectively began to exploit the country's vast natural resources. This led to a period of sustained growth and economic welfare that has catapulted Brazil into one of the world's leading emerging markets.

Contrary to what many feared when he took office, the leftist leaning, populist president, who once used to shine shoes, has progressively moved to the center with an internationally focused expansion foreign policy. Finally utilizing its agricultural prowess and abundant natural resources, Brazil's exports have more than tripled on rising world demand for soybeans, iron-ore, beef, and automobiles. Under President Lula's trade diversification policy, the biggest change has been in the expansion of trade and investment with China. China has become Brazil's largest export and import partner and provides investment and finance to secure supplies of key minerals. Brazil has also continued to develop trade with the rest of Latin America, other Asian countries, the Middle East, and Africa, especially in agriculture. Domestically, President Lula also increased investment in the creation and repair of roads and railways, in the simplification and reduction of taxation, and in the modernization of the country's energy production to avoid further shortages. After decades as the largest foreign debtor among emerging economies, Brazil became a net creditor for the first time in January 2008.

This prosperity can be seen everywhere. Skyscrapers are going up along the boulevards of São Paolo. Automobile and computer sales are booming. Formal sector jobs are being created at a rapid rate. Many analysts forecast growth in 2010 will be 7 percent—the highest rate since 1986. The 2014 World Cup and the 2016 Olympics are in the near future with US$18.7 billion in planned new investment and financing for infrastructures for the events. The future looks bright. In a recent report by the Economist Intelligence Unit, 536 senior executives worldwide were surveyed and share in a general optimism about Brazil's prospects.

Yet many "deep-seated problems" remain. Perhaps most importantly, Brazil is home to some of the world's greatest wealth disparities. As the 2002 film *Cidade de Deus (City of God)* graphically depicted, poverty remains a huge problem and threatens the country's future stability. As Brazil continues its development, it will have to deal with an inadequate educational system, extreme bureaucracy, corruption, the lack of infrastructure, and fractious politics—just to name a few. But signs continue to be encouraging. The same area of Rio de Janeiro depicted in the *City of God* has undergone a dramatic transformation—in part because of more efficient policing, better city government, and the positive impact a strong economy has had on the poorer sections of the country. The largest economy in Latin America, with the most abundant natural resources—the perpetual "country of tomorrow"—may be changing to an "opportunity of a lifetime." ●

Sources: "Brazil Unbound: How Investors See Brazil and Brazil Sees the World," *The Economist Intelligence Unit,* July 27, 2010; M. Gunther, "The World's New Economic Landscape," *Fortune,* July 8, 2010, accessed at http://money.cnn.com/2010; "A Magic Moment for the City of God," *The Economist,* June 10, 2010; "Flying Too High for Safety," *The Economist,* May 20, 2010; Gray, "Brazil, India and Turkey Emerge," *Fortune,* June 4, 2010, accessed at http://money.cnn.com/2010; and G. Parra-Bernal and L. Pimentel, "Brazil Became Net Creditor for First Time in January (Update4)" *Bloomberg,* February 21, 2008, accessed at http://www.bloomberg.com/apps/news?pid=newsarchive&sid=aPLYQJIG_Re8.

Introduction

The success of Brazil over the past eight years is a striking example of the benefits of free trade, globalization, and good leadership. By expanding trade, especially into China, Brazil not only found a market for its goods but an investment partner. Focusing on trade diversification has enabled Brazil to exploit its large labor force, its natural resources, and its role as the largest economy in Latin America. The income trade generated has in turn been used for domestic improvements. But, as we have seen, great wealth disparity continues to be a problem. Whether Brazil, by continuing the policy of trade diversification, will be able to bridge the gap between the rich and the poor remains to be seen and is one of the topics of this chapter.

In the world of international trade, there are always winners and losers, but as economists have long argued, the benefits to the winners outweigh the costs born by the losers, resulting in a net gain to society. Economists argue that in the long-run, free trade stimulates economic growth and raises living standards across the board. The economic arguments surrounding the benefits and costs of free trade in goods and services are not abstract academic ones. International trade theory has shaped the economic policy of many nations for the past 50 years. It was the driver behind the formation of the World Trade Organization and regional trade blocs such as the European Union and the North American Free Trade Agreement (NAFTA). The 1990s, in particular, saw a global move toward greater free trade. Therefore, it is crucially important to understand these theories and why they have been so successful in shaping the economic policy of so many nations and the competitive environment in which international businesses compete.

This chapter has two goals that go to the heart of the debate over the benefits and costs of free trade. The first is to review a number of theories that explain why it is beneficial for a country to engage in international trade. The second goal is to explain the pattern of international trade that we observe in the world economy. With regard to the pattern of trade, we will be primarily concerned with explaining the pattern of exports and imports of goods and services between countries. The pattern of foreign direct investment between countries is discussed in Chapter 7.

An Overview of Trade Theory

We open this chapter with a discussion of mercantilism. Propagated in the sixteenth and seventeenth centuries, mercantilism advocated that countries should simultaneously encourage exports and discourage imports. Although mercantilism is an old and largely discredited doctrine, its echoes remain in modern political debate and in the trade policies of many countries. Next, we will look at Adam Smith's theory of absolute advantage. Proposed in 1776, Smith's theory was the first to explain why unrestricted free trade is beneficial to a country. **Free trade** refers to a situation where a government does not attempt to influence through quotas or duties what its citizens can buy from another country, or what they can produce and sell to another country. Smith argued that the invisible hand of the market mechanism, rather than government policy, should determine what a country imports and what it exports. His arguments imply that such a laissez-faire stance toward trade was in the best interests of a country. Building on Smith's work are two additional theories that we shall review. One is the theory of comparative advantage, advanced by the nineteenth century English economist David Ricardo. This theory is the intellectual basis of the modern argument for unrestricted free trade. In the twentieth century, Ricardo's work was refined by two Swedish economists, Eli Heckscher and Bertil Ohlin, whose theory is known as the Heckscher-Ohlin theory.

Free Trade
The absence of government barriers to the free flow of goods and services between countries.

THE BENEFITS OF TRADE   The great strength of the theories of Smith, Ricardo, and Heckscher-Ohlin is that they identify with precision the specific benefits of international trade. Common sense suggests that some international trade is beneficial. For example, nobody would suggest that Iceland should grow its own oranges. Iceland can benefit from trade by exchanging some of the products that it can produce at a low cost (fish) for some products that it cannot produce at all (oranges). Thus, by engaging in international trade, Icelanders are able to add oranges to their diet of fish.

LEARNING OBJECTIVE 1
Understand why nations trade with each other.

The theories of Smith, Ricardo, and Heckscher-Ohlin go beyond this common-sense notion, however, to show why it is beneficial for a country to engage in international trade *even for products it is able to produce for itself*. This is a difficult concept for people to grasp. For example, many people in the United States believe that American consumers should buy products made in the United States by American companies whenever possible to help save American jobs from foreign competition. The same kind of nationalistic sentiments can be observed in many other countries.

However, the theories of Smith, Ricardo, and Heckscher-Ohlin tell us that a country's economy may gain if its citizens buy certain products from other nations that could be produced at home. The gains arise because international trade allows a country to specialize in the manufacture and export of products that can be produced most efficiently in that country, while importing products that can be produced more efficiently in other countries. Thus, it may make sense for the United States to specialize in the production and export of commercial jet aircraft, since the efficient production of commercial jet aircraft requires resources that are abundant in the United States, such as a highly skilled labor force and cutting-edge technological know-how. On the other hand, it may make sense for the United States to import textiles from China since the efficient production of textiles requires a relatively cheap labor force—and cheap labor is not abundant in the United States.

Of course, this economic argument is often difficult for segments of a country's population to accept. With their future threatened by imports, U.S. textile companies and their employees have tried hard to persuade the government to limit the importation of textiles by demanding quotas and tariffs. Although such import controls may benefit particular groups, such as textile businesses and their employees, the theories of Smith, Ricardo, and Heckscher-Ohlin suggest that the economy as a whole is hurt by such action. Limits on imports are often in the interests of domestic producers, but not domestic consumers.

THE PATTERN OF INTERNATIONAL TRADE The theories of Smith, Ricardo, and Heckscher-Ohlin help to explain the pattern of international trade that we observe in the world economy. Some aspects of the pattern are easy to understand. Climate and natural resource endowments explain why Ghana exports cocoa, Brazil exports coffee, Saudi Arabia exports oil, and China exports crawfish. However, much of the observed pattern of international trade is more difficult to explain. For example, why does Japan export automobiles, consumer electronics, and machine tools? Why does Switzerland export chemicals, pharmaceuticals, watches, and jewelry? Why does Bangladesh export garments? David Ricardo's theory of comparative advantage offers an explanation in terms of international differences in labor productivity. The more sophisticated Heckscher-Ohlin theory emphasizes the interplay between the proportions in which the factors of production (such as land, labor, and capital) are available in different countries and the proportions in which they are needed for producing particular goods. This explanation rests on the assumption that countries have varying endowments of the various factors of production. Tests of this theory, however, suggest that it is a less powerful explanation of real-world trade patterns than once thought.

One early response to the failure of the Heckscher-Ohlin theory to explain the observed pattern of international trade was the product life-cycle theory. Proposed by Raymond Vernon, this theory suggests that early in their life cycle, most new products are produced in and exported from the country in which they were developed. As a new product becomes widely accepted internationally, however, production starts in other countries. As a result, the theory suggests, the product may ultimately be exported back to the country of its original innovation.

In a similar vein, during the 1980s economists such as Nobel Prize winner Paul Krugman developed what has come to be known as the new trade theory. **New trade theory** (for which Krugman won the Nobel Prize in 2008) stresses that in some cases countries specialize in the production and export of particular products not because of underlying differences in factor endowments, but because in certain industries the world market can support only a limited number of firms. (This is argued to be the case for the commercial aircraft industry.) In such industries, firms that enter the market first are able to build a competitive advantage that is subsequently difficult to challenge. Thus, the observed pattern of trade between nations may be due in part to the ability of firms within a given nation to capture first-mover advantages. The United States is a major exporter of commercial jet aircraft because American firms such as Boeing were first movers in the world market. Boeing built a competitive advantage that has subsequently been difficult for firms from countries with equally favorable factor endowments to challenge (although Europe's Airbus Industries has succeeded in doing that). In a work related to the new trade theory, Michael Porter developed a theory, referred to as the theory of national competitive advantage. This attempts to explain why particular nations achieve international success in particular industries. In addition to factor endowments, Porter points out the importance of country factors such as domestic demand and domestic rivalry in explaining a nation's dominance in the production and export of particular products.

TRADE THEORY AND GOVERNMENT POLICY Although all these theories agree that international trade is beneficial to a country, they lack agreement in their recommendations for government policy. Mercantilism makes a crude case for government involvement in promoting exports and limiting imports. The theories of Smith, Ricardo, and Heckscher-Ohlin form part of the case for unrestricted free trade. The argument for unrestricted free trade is that both import controls and export incentives (such as subsidies) are self-defeating and result in wasted resources. Both the new trade theory and Porter's theory of national competitive advantage can be interpreted as justifying some limited government intervention to support the development of certain export-oriented industries. We will discuss the pros and cons of this argument, known as strategic trade policy, as well as the pros and cons of the argument for unrestricted free trade, in Chapter 6.

Mercantilism

The first theory of international trade, mercantilism, emerged in England in the mid-sixteenth century. The principle assertion of mercantilism was that gold and silver were the mainstays of national wealth and essential to vigorous commerce. At that time, gold and silver were the currency of trade between countries; a country could earn gold and silver by exporting goods. Conversely, importing goods from other countries would result in an outflow of gold and silver to those countries. The main tenet of **mercantilism** was that it was in a country's best interests to maintain a trade surplus, to export more than it imported. By doing so, a country would accumulate gold and silver and, consequently, increase its national wealth, prestige, and power. As the English mercantilist writer Thomas Mun put it in 1630:

> The ordinary means therefore to increase our wealth and treasure is by foreign trade, wherein we must ever observe this rule: to sell more to strangers yearly than we consume of theirs in value.[1]

New Trade Theory
Theory that sometimes countries specialize in the production and export of particular products not because of underlying differences in factor endowments, but because in certain industries the world market can support only a limited number of firms.

LEARNING OBJECTIVE 2
Summarize the different theories explaining trade flows between nations.

Mercantilism
An economic philosophy advocating that countries should simultaneously encourage exports and discourage imports.

Country FOCUS

Singapore: Knowledge-Based Economy

Singapore is a small island country/city-state in Southeast Asia, with a decreasing population of approximately 3.2 million people. It does not have natural resources, and it cannot compete with low-cost labor from China or Bangladesh. Yet, Singapore has a highly developed and successful free-market economy. It enjoys a remarkably open and corruption-free environment, stable prices, and a per capita GDP higher than most developed countries. As a testament to its competitiveness, Singapore regularly ranks among the most competitive countries in the world, according to the World Economic Forum's *Global Competitiveness Report 2009–2010*.

To remain competitive, Singapore has chosen to pursue a knowledge-based economy, a preferred hub for the exchange of value-added information and knowledge. Whereas many countries focus on traditional factors of production, land, labor, and capital to sustain development, Singapore has chosen to focus on knowledge and skills as the only source of comparative advantage. It views knowledge or intellectual property as a source of value and wealth creation. In this regard, the government plays a critical role.

In a knowledge-based economy, productivity and growth are, to a large extent, determined by the rate of technical progress, the accumulation of knowledge, and a network or system that can efficiently distribute knowledge and information. In this type of economy, the sciences, technology, industry, and education are the cornerstones. Innovation fostered by an infrastructure that encourages investments in research and training is the goal. It is based on knowledge production and knowledge transference.

In the year 2000, the Singaporean government initiated IT2000, seeking to transform Singapore into an "Intelligent Island" by integrating information technology into every aspect of society to develop Singapore into a global hub, boost the economic engine, enhance the potential of the individual, link communities locally and globally, and improve the quality of life. In so doing, the government has focused on the knowledge infrastructure and human and intellectual capital. The acquisition of Internet broadband capabilities and a "life-long learning" philosophy were crucial.

Now 10 years later, the government is moving to further liberalize the economy (particularly financial services, telecommunications, and power), to emphasize technology and innovation in the educational system, and to enhance the country's physical infrastructure. It is also providing financial incentives to investors and working to improve legislation and regulations to encourage research and development, as well as fostering entrepreneurship in technology-intensive arenas. Singapore is also encouraging multinational companies to establish knowledge-intensive manufacturing and service operations. What is unclear, however, is whether the knowledge being gained is "internalized" or whether it is capable of being moved—much the same way the other factors of production are mobile.

Sources: World Economic Forum, *Global Competitiveness Report, 2009–2010,* accessed at www.weforum.org; C. Lay Lek and S. Al-Hawamdeh, "Government Initiatives and the Knowledge Economy: Case of Singapore," in W. Kim et al. (eds.): *Human.Society@Internet 2001, Lecture Notes in Computer Science* (Berlin: Springer), pp. 19–32.

Consistent with this belief, the mercantilist doctrine advocated government intervention to achieve a surplus in the balance of trade. The mercantilists saw no virtue in a large volume of trade. Rather, they recommended policies to maximize exports and minimize imports. To achieve this, imports were limited by tariffs and quotas, while exports were subsidized.

The classical economist David Hume pointed out an inherent inconsistency in the mercantilist doctrine in 1752. According to Hume, if England had a balance-of-trade surplus with France (it exported more than it imported) the resulting inflow of gold and silver would swell the domestic money supply and generate inflation in England. In France, however, the outflow of gold and silver would have the opposite effect. France's money supply would contract, and its prices would fall. This change in relative prices between France and England would encourage the French to buy fewer English goods (because they were becoming more expensive) and the English to buy more French goods (because they were becoming cheaper). The result would be a deterioration in the English balance of trade and an improvement in France's trade balance, until the English surplus was eliminated. Hence, according to Hume, in the long run no country could sustain a surplus on the balance of trade and so accumulate gold and silver as the mercantilists had envisaged.

The flaw with mercantilism was that it viewed trade as a zero-sum game. (A **zero-sum game** is one in which a gain by one country results in a loss by another.) It was left to Adam Smith and David Ricardo to show the shortsightedness of this approach and to demonstrate that trade is a positive-sum game, or a situation in which all countries can benefit. Unfortunately, the mercantilist doctrine is by no means dead. Neo-mercantilists equate political power with economic power and economic power with a balance-of-trade surplus. Critics argue that many nations have adopted a neo-mercantilist strategy that is designed to simultaneously boost exports and limit imports. For example, critics charge that China is pursuing a neo-mercantilist policy, deliberately keeping its currency value low against the U.S. dollar in order to sell more goods to the United States, and thus amass a trade surplus and foreign exchange reserves.[2]

Absolute Advantage

In his 1776 landmark book *The Wealth of Nations*, Adam Smith attacked the mercantilist assumption that trade is a zero-sum game. Smith argued that countries differ in their ability to produce goods efficiently. In his time, the English, by virtue of their superior manufacturing processes, were the world's most efficient textile manufacturers. Due to the combination of favorable climate, good soils, and accumulated expertise, the French had the world's most efficient wine industry. The English had an *absolute advantage* in the production of textiles, while the French had an *absolute advantage* in the production of wine. Thus, a country has an **absolute advantage** in the production of a product when it is more efficient than any other country in producing it.

According to Smith, countries should specialize in the production of goods for which they have an absolute advantage and then trade these for goods produced by other countries. In Smith's time, this suggested that the English should specialize in the production of textiles while the French should specialize in the production of wine. England could get all the wine it needed by selling its textiles to France and buying wine in exchange. Similarly, France could get all the textiles it needed by selling wine to England and buying textiles in exchange. Smith's basic argument, therefore, is that a country should never produce goods at home that it can buy at a lower cost from other countries. Smith demonstrates that, by specializing in the production of goods in which each has an absolute advantage, both countries benefit by engaging in trade.

Consider the effects of trade between two countries, Ghana and South Korea. The production of any good (output) requires resources (inputs) such as land, labor, and capital. Assume that Ghana and South Korea both have the same amount of resources and that these resources can be used to produce either rice or cocoa. Assume further that 200 units of resources are available in each country. Imagine that in Ghana it takes 10 resources to produce one ton of cocoa and 20 resources to produce one ton of rice. Thus, Ghana could produce 20 tons of cocoa and no rice, 10 tons of rice and no cocoa, or some combination of rice and cocoa between these two extremes. The different combinations that Ghana could produce are represented by the line GG' in Figure 5.1. This is referred to as Ghana's *production possibility frontier* (PPF). Similarly, imagine that in South Korea it takes 40 resources to produce one ton of cocoa and 10 resources to produce one ton of rice. Thus, South Korea could produce 5 tons of cocoa and no rice, 20 tons of rice and no cocoa, or

Zero-Sum Game
A situation in which an economic gain by one country results in an economic loss by another.

LEARNING OBJECTIVE 2
Summarize the different theories explaining trade flows between nations.

Absolute Advantage
A country has an absolute advantage in the production of a product when it is more efficient than any other country in producing it.

figure 5.1

The Theory of Absolute
Advantage

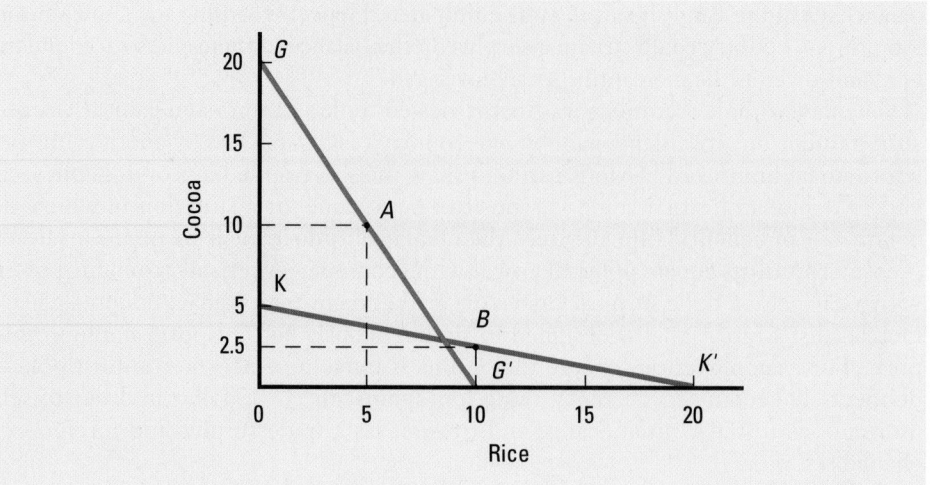

some combination between these two extremes. The different combinations avail-able to South Korea are represented by the line KK' in Figure 5.1, which is South Korea's PPF. Clearly, Ghana has an absolute advantage in the production of cocoa. (More resources are needed to produce a ton of cocoa in South Korea than in Ghana.) By the same token, South Korea has an absolute advantage in the produc-tion of rice.

Now consider a situation in which neither country trades with any other. Each coun-try devotes half of its resources to the production of rice and half to the production of cocoa. Each country must also consume what it produces. Ghana would be able to produce 10 tons of cocoa and 5 tons of rice (point A in Figure 5.1), while South Korea would be able to produce 10 tons of rice and 2.5 tons of cocoa (point B in Figure 5.1). Without trade, the combined production of both countries would be 12.5 tons of cocoa (10 tons in Ghana plus 2.5 tons in South Korea) and 15 tons of rice (5 tons in Ghana and 10 tons in South Korea). If each country were to specialize in producing the good for which it had an absolute advantage and then trade with the other for the good it lacks, Ghana could produce 20 tons of cocoa, and South Korea could produce 20 tons of rice. Thus, by specializing, the production of both goods could be increased. Production of cocoa would increase from 12.5 tons to 20 tons, while production of rice would increase from 15 tons to 20 tons. The increase in production that would result from specialization is therefore 7.5 tons of cocoa and 5 tons of rice. Table 5.1 summarizes these figures.

By engaging in trade and swapping one ton of cocoa for one ton of rice, producers in both countries could consume more of both cocoa and rice. Imagine that Ghana and South Korea swap cocoa and rice on a one-to-one basis; that is, the price of one ton of cocoa is equal to the price of one ton of rice. If Ghana decided to export 6 tons of cocoa to South Korea and import 6 tons of rice in return, its final consumption after trade would be 14 tons of cocoa and 6 tons of rice. This is 4 tons more cocoa than it could have consumed before specialization and trade and 1 ton more rice. Similarly, South Korea's final consumption after trade would be 6 tons of cocoa and 14 tons of rice. This is 3.5 tons more cocoa than it could have consumed before specialization and trade and 4 tons more rice. Thus, as a result of specialization and trade, output of both cocoa and rice would be increased, and consumers in both nations would be able to consume more. Thus, we can see that trade is a positive-sum game; it produces net gains for all involved.

Resources Required to Produce 1 Ton of Cocoa and Rice		
	Cocoa	**Rice**
Ghana	10	20
South Korea	40	10
Production and Consumption without Trade		
	Cocoa	**Rice**
Ghana	10.0	5.0
South Korea	2.5	10.0
Total production	12.5	15.0
Production with Specialization		
	Cocoa	**Rice**
Ghana	20.0	0.0
South Korea	0.0	20.0
Total production	20.0	20.0
Consumption after Ghana Trades 6 Tons of Cocoa for 6 Tons of South Korean Rice		
	Cocoa	**Rice**
Ghana	14.0	6.0
South Korea	6.0	14.0
Increase in Consumption as a Result of Specialization and Trade		
	Cocoa	**Rice**
Ghana	4.0	1.0
South Korea	3.5	4.0

5.1 table

Absolute Advantage
and the Gains
from Trade

Comparative Advantage

David Ricardo took Adam Smith's theory one step further by exploring what might happen when one country has an absolute advantage in the production of all goods.[3] Smith's theory of absolute advantage suggests that such a country might derive no benefits from international trade. In his 1817 book *Principles of Political Economy*, Ricardo showed that this was not the case. According to Ricardo's theory of comparative advantage, it makes sense for a country to specialize in the production of those goods that it produces most efficiently and to buy the goods that it produces less efficiently from other countries, even if this means buying goods from other countries that it could produce more efficiently itself.[4] While this may seem counterintuitive, the logic can be explained with a simple example.

LEARNING OBJECTIVE 2
Summarize the different
theories explaining trade
flows between nations.

figure 5.2

The Theory of
Comparative Advantage

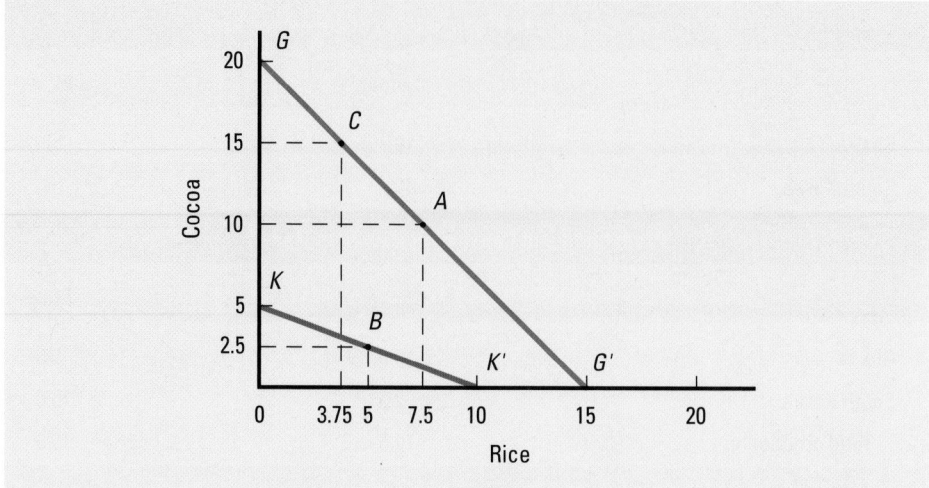

Assume that Ghana is more efficient in the production of both cocoa and rice; that is, Ghana has an absolute advantage in the production of both products. In Ghana it takes 10 resources to produce one ton of cocoa and 13⅓ resources to produce one ton of rice. Thus, given its 200 units of resources, Ghana can produce 20 tons of cocoa and no rice, 15 tons of rice and no cocoa, or any combination in between on its PPF (the line GG' in Figure 5.2). In South Korea it takes 40 resources to produce one ton of cocoa and 20 resources to produce one ton of rice. Thus, South Korea can produce 5 tons of cocoa and no rice, 10 tons of rice and no cocoa, or any combination on its PPF (the line KK' in Figure 5.2). Again assume that without trade, each country uses half of its resources to produce rice and half to produce cocoa. Thus, without trade, Ghana will produce 10 tons of cocoa and 7.5 tons of rice (point A in Figure 5.2), while South Korea will produce 2.5 tons of cocoa and 5 tons of rice (point B in Figure 5.2).

In light of Ghana's absolute advantage in the production of both goods, why should it trade with South Korea? Although Ghana has an absolute advantage in the production of both cocoa and rice, it has a comparative advantage only in the production of cocoa: Ghana can produce 4 times as much cocoa as South Korea, but only 1.5 times as much rice. Ghana is *comparatively* more efficient at producing cocoa than it is at producing rice.

Without trade the combined production of cocoa will be 12.5 tons (10 tons in Ghana and 2.5 in South Korea), and the combined production of rice will also be 12.5 tons (7.5 tons in Ghana and 5 tons in South Korea). Without trade each country must consume what it produces. By engaging in trade, the two countries can increase their combined production of rice and cocoa, and consumers in both nations can consume more of both goods.

THE GAINS FROM TRADE Imagine that Ghana exploits its comparative advantage in the production of cocoa to increase its output from 10 tons to 15 tons. This uses 150 units of resources, leaving the remaining 50 units of resources to use in producing 3.75 tons of rice (point C in Figure 5.2). Meanwhile, South Korea specializes in the production of rice, producing 10 tons. The combined output of both cocoa and rice has now increased. Before specialization, the combined output was 12.5 tons of cocoa and 12.5 tons of rice. Now it is 15 tons of cocoa and 13.75 tons of rice (3.75 tons in Ghana and 10 tons in South Korea). The source of the increase in production is summarized in Table 5.2.

Resources Required to Produce 1 Ton of Cocoa and Rice		
	Cocoa	**Rice**
Ghana	10	13.33
South Korea	40	20
Production and Consumption without Trade		
	Cocoa	**Rice**
Ghana	10.0	7.5
South Korea	2.5	5.0
Total production	12.5	12.5
Production with Specialization		
	Cocoa	**Rice**
Ghana	15.0	3.75
South Korea	0.0	10.0
Total production	15.0	13.75
Consumption after Ghana Trades 4 Tons of Cocoa for 4 Tons of South Korean Rice		
	Cocoa	**Rice**
Ghana	11.0	7.75
South Korea	4.0	6.0
Increase in Consumption as a Result of Specialization and Trade		
	Cocoa	**Rice**
Ghana	1.0	0.25
South Korea	1.5	1.0

5.2 table

Comparative Advantage and the Gains from Trade

Not only is output higher, but both countries also can now benefit from trade. If Ghana and South Korea swap cocoa and rice on a one-to-one basis, with both countries choosing to exchange 4 tons of their export for 4 tons of the import, both countries are able to consume more cocoa and rice than they could before specialization and trade (see Table 5.2). Thus, if Ghana exchanges 4 tons of cocoa with South Korea for 4 tons of rice, it is still left with 11 tons of cocoa, which is 1 ton more than it had before trade. The 4 tons of rice it gets from South Korea in exchange for its 4 tons of cocoa, when added to the 3.75 tons it now produces domestically, leaves it with a total of 7.75 tons of rice, which is .25 of a ton more than it had before specialization. Similarly, after swapping 4 tons of rice with Ghana, South Korea still ends up with 6 tons of rice, which is more than it had before specialization. In addition, the 4 tons of cocoa it receives in exchange is 1.5 tons more than it produced before trade. Thus, consumption of cocoa and rice can increase in both countries as a result of specialization and trade.

LEARNING OBJECTIVE 3
Recognize why many
economists believe that
unrestricted free trade
between nations will raise
the economic welfare of
countries that participate in
a free trade system.

The basic message of the theory of comparative advantage is that *potential world production is greater with unrestricted free trade than it is with restricted trade*. Ricardo's theory suggests that consumers in all nations can consume more if there are no restrictions on trade. This occurs even in countries that lack an absolute advantage in the production of any good. In other words, to an even greater degree than the theory of absolute advantage, *the theory of comparative advantage suggests that trade is a positive-sum game in which all countries that participate realize economic gains*. As such, this theory provides a strong rationale for encouraging free trade. So powerful is Ricardo's theory that it remains a major intellectual weapon for those who argue for free trade.

QUALIFICATIONS AND ASSUMPTIONS The conclusion that free trade is universally beneficial is a rather bold one to draw from such a simple model. Our simple model includes many unrealistic assumptions:

1. We have assumed a simple world in which there are only two countries and two goods. In the real world, there are many countries and many goods.
2. We have assumed away transportation costs between countries.
3. We have assumed away differences in the prices of resources in different countries. We have said nothing about exchange rates, simply assuming that cocoa and rice could be swapped on a one-to-one basis.
4. We have assumed that resources can move freely from the production of one good to another within a country. In reality, this is not always the case.
5. We have assumed constant returns to scale; that is, that specialization by Ghana or South Korea has no effect on the amount of resources required to produce one ton of cocoa or rice. In reality, both diminishing and increasing returns to specialization exist. The amount of resources required to produce a good might decrease or increase as a nation specializes in production of that good.
6. We have assumed that each country has a fixed stock of resources and that free trade does not change the efficiency with which a country uses its resources. This static assumption makes no allowances for the dynamic changes in a country's stock of resources and in the efficiency with which the country uses its resources that might result from free trade.
7. We have assumed away the effects of trade on income distribution within a country.

Given these assumptions, can the conclusion that free trade is mutually beneficial be extended to the real world of many countries, many goods, positive transportation costs, volatile exchange rates, immobile domestic resources, non-constant returns to specialization, and dynamic changes? Although a detailed extension of the theory of comparative advantage is beyond the scope of this book, economists have shown that the basic result derived from our simple model can be generalized to a world composed of many countries producing many different goods.[5] Despite the shortcomings of the Ricardian model, research suggests that the basic proposition that countries will export the goods that they are most efficient at producing is borne out by the data.[6]

However, once all the assumptions are dropped, the case for unrestricted free trade, while still positive, has been argued by some economists associated with the "new trade theory" to lose some of its strength.[7] We return to this issue later in this chapter and in the next when we discuss the new trade theory. Moreover, in a recent and widely discussed analysis, the Nobel Prize winning economist Paul Samuelson argued that contrary to the standard interpretation, in certain circumstances the theory of comparative advantage predicts that a rich country might actually be *worse* off by switching to a free trade regime with a poor nation.[8] We will consider Samuelson's critique in the next section.

EXTENSIONS OF THE RICARDIAN MODEL   Let us explore the effect of relaxing three of the assumptions identified above in the simple comparative advantage model. Below we relax the assumptions that resources move freely from the production of one good to another within a country, that there are constant returns to scale, and that trade does not change a country's stock of resources or the efficiency with which those resources are utilized.

Immobile Resources   In our simple comparative model of Ghana and South Korea, we assumed that producers (farmers) could easily convert land from the production of cocoa to rice, and vice versa. While this assumption may hold for some agricultural products, resources do not always shift quite so easily from producing one good to another. A certain amount of friction is involved. For example, embracing a free trade regime for an advanced economy such as the United States often implies that the country will produce less of some labor-intensive goods, such as textiles, and more of some knowledge-intensive goods, such as computer software or biotechnology products. Although the country as a whole will gain from such a shift, textile producers will lose. A textile worker in South Carolina is probably not qualified to write software for Microsoft. Thus, the shift to free trade may mean that she becomes unemployed or has to accept another less attractive job, such as working at a fast-food restaurant.

Resources do not always move easily from one economic activity to another. The process creates friction and human suffering too. While the theory predicts that the benefits of free trade outweigh the costs by a significant margin, this is of cold comfort to those who bear the costs. Accordingly, political opposition to the adoption of a free trade regime typically comes from those whose jobs are most at risk. In the United States, for example, textile workers and their unions have long opposed the move toward free trade precisely because this group has much to lose from free trade. Governments often ease the transition toward free trade by helping to retrain those who lose their jobs as a result. The pain caused by the movement toward a free trade regime is a short-term phenomenon, while the gains from trade once the transition has been made are both significant and enduring.

Diminishing Returns   The simple comparative advantage model developed above assumes constant returns to specialization. By **constant returns to specialization** we mean the units of resources required to produce a good (cocoa or rice) are assumed to remain constant no matter where one is on a country's production possibility frontier (PPF). Thus, we assumed that it always took Ghana 10 units of resources to produce one ton of cocoa. However, it is more realistic to assume diminishing returns to specialization. Diminishing returns to specialization occurs when more units of resources are required to produce each additional unit. While 10 units of resources may be sufficient to increase Ghana's output of cocoa from 12 tons to 13 tons, 11 units of resources may be needed to increase output from 13 to 14 tons, 12 units of resources to increase output from 14 tons to 15 tons, and so on. Diminishing returns implies a convex PPF for Ghana (see Figure 5.3), rather than the straight line depicted in Figure 5.2.

It is more realistic to assume diminishing returns for two reasons. First, not all resources are of the same quality. As a country tries to increase its output of a certain good, it is increasingly likely to draw on more marginal resources whose productivity is not as great as those initially employed. The result is that it requires ever more resources to produce an equal increase in output. For example, some land is more productive than other land. As Ghana tries to expand its output of cocoa, it might have to utilize increasingly marginal land that is less fertile than the land it originally used. As yields per acre decline, Ghana must use more land to produce one ton of cocoa.

Constant Returns to Specialization
The units of resources required to produce a good are assumed to remain constant no matter where one is on a country's production possibility frontier.

figure 5.3

Ghana's PPF under
Diminishing Returns

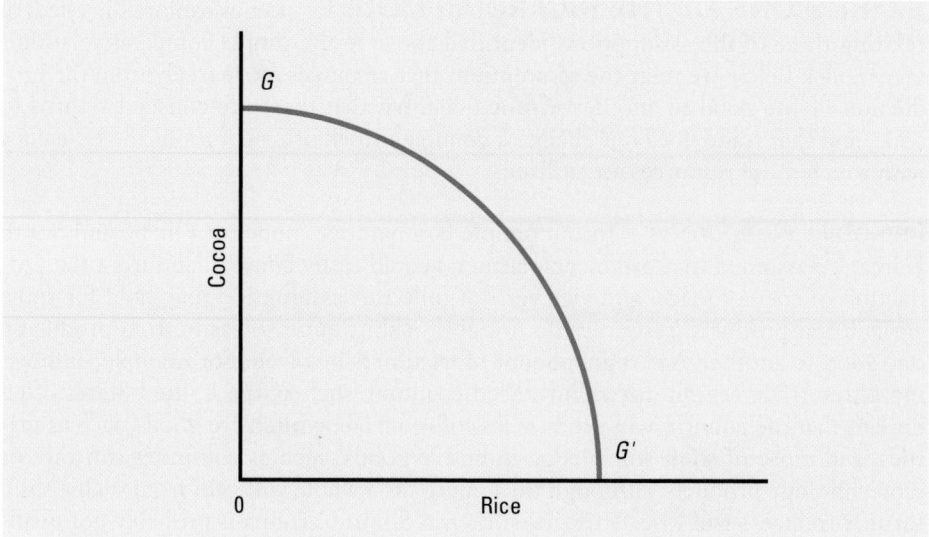

A second reason for diminishing returns is that different goods use resources in different proportions. For example, imagine that growing cocoa uses more land and less labor than growing rice, and that Ghana tries to transfer resources from rice production to cocoa production. The rice industry will release proportionately too much labor and too little land for efficient cocoa production. To absorb the additional resources of labor and land, the cocoa industry will have to shift toward more labor-intensive methods of production. The effect is that the efficiency with which the cocoa industry uses labor will decline, and returns will diminish.

Diminishing returns show that it is not feasible for a country to specialize to the degree suggested by the simple Ricardian model outlined earlier. Diminishing returns to specialization suggest that the gains from specialization are likely to be exhausted before specialization is complete. In reality, most countries do not specialize, but instead, produce a range of goods. However, the theory predicts that it is worthwhile to specialize until that point where the resulting gains from trade are outweighed by diminishing returns. Thus, the basic conclusion that unrestricted free trade is beneficial still holds, although because of diminishing returns, the gains may not be as great as suggested in the constant returns case.

LEARNING OBJECTIVE 3
Recognize why many
economists believe that
unrestricted free trade
between nations will raise
the economic welfare of
countries that participate
in a free trade system.

Dynamic Effects and Economic Growth   The simple comparative advantage model assumed that trade does not change a country's stock of resources or the efficiency with which it utilizes those resources. This static assumption makes no allowances for the dynamic changes that might result from trade. If we relax this assumption, it becomes apparent that opening an economy to trade is likely to generate dynamic gains of two sorts.[9] First, free trade might increase a country's stock of resources as increased supplies of labor and capital from abroad become available for use within the country. For example, this has been occurring in Eastern Europe since the early 1990s, with many Western businesses investing significant capital in the former Communist countries.

Second, free trade might also increase the efficiency with which a country uses its resources. Gains in the efficiency of resource utilization could arise from a number of factors. For example, economies of large-scale production might become available as trade expands the size of the total market available to domestic firms. Trade might make better technology from abroad available to domestic firms; better technology can increase labor productivity or the productivity of land. (The so-called green revolution had this effect on agricultural outputs in developing countries.) Also, opening an economy to foreign competition might stimulate domestic producers to look for ways to increase their efficiency. Again, this phenomenon has arguably been occurring in the once-protected markets of Eastern Europe, where many former state monopolies have had to increase the efficiency of their operations to survive in the competitive world market.

Dynamic gains in both the stock of a country's resources and the efficiency with which resources are utilized will cause a country's PPF to shift outward. This is illustrated in Figure 5.4, where the shift from PPF_1 to PPF_2 results from the dynamic gains that arise from free trade. As a consequence of this outward shift, the country in Figure 5.4 can produce more of both goods than it did before introduction of free trade. The theory suggests that opening an economy to free trade not only results in static gains of the type discussed earlier, but also results in dynamic gains that stimulate economic growth. If this is so, then one might think that the case for free trade becomes stronger still, and in general it does. However, as noted above, in a recent article one of the leading economic theorists of the twentieth century, Paul Samuelson, argued that in some circumstances, dynamic gains can lead to an outcome that is not so beneficial.

The Samuelson Critique   Paul Samuelson's critique looks at what happens when a rich country—the United States—enters into a free trade agreement with a poor country—China—that rapidly improves its productivity after the introduction of a free trade regime (i.e., there is a dynamic gain in the efficiency with which resources are used in the poor country). Samuelson's model suggests that in such cases, the lower prices that U.S. consumers pay for goods imported from China following the introduction of a free trade regime *may* not be enough to produce a net gain to for the U.S. economy if the dynamic effect of free trade is to lower real wage rates in the United States. As he stated in a *New York Times* interview, "Being able to purchase groceries 20 percent cheaper at Walmart (due to international trade) does not necessarily make up for the wage losses (in America)."[10]

Samuelson goes on to note that he is particularly concerned about the ability to offshore service jobs that traditionally were not internationally mobile, such as software debugging, call center jobs, accounting jobs, and even medical diagnosis of MRI scans (see the accompanying Country Focus for details). Recent advances in communications

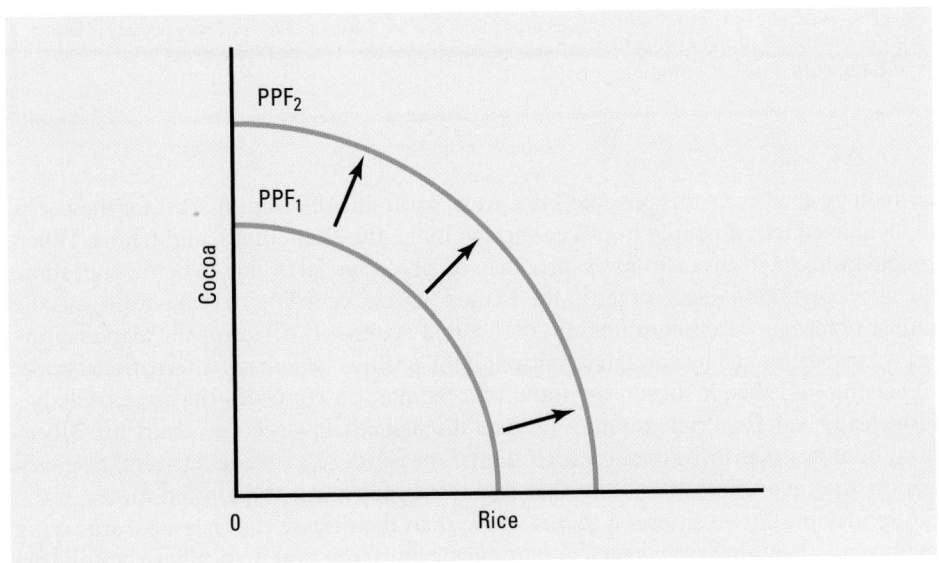

 figure

The Influence of Free Trade on the PPF

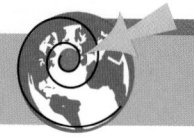
The Mobility of White-Collar Jobs

Economists have long argued that free trade produces gains for all countries that participate in a free trading system, but as the next wave of globalization sweeps through the U.S. economy, many people are wondering if this is true, particularly those who stand to lose their jobs because of this wave of globalization. In the popular imagination for much of the past quarter century, free trade was associated with the movement of low-skill, blue-collar manufacturing jobs out of rich countries such as the United States and toward low-wage countries—textiles to Costa Rica, athletic shoes to the Philippines, steel to Brazil, electronic products to Malaysia, and so on. While many observers bemoaned the "hollowing out" of U.S. manufacturing, economists stated that high-skilled and high-wage white-collar jobs associated with the knowledge-based economy would stay in the United States. Computers might be assembled in Malaysia, so the argument went, but they would continue to be designed in Silicon Valley by high-skilled U.S. engineers.

Recent developments have some people questioning this assumption. As the global economy slowed after 2000 and corporate profits fell, many American companies responded by moving white-collar "knowledge-based" jobs to developing nations where they could be performed for a fraction of the cost. During the long economic boom of the 1990s, Bank of America had to compete with other organizations for the scarce talents of information technology specialists, driving annual salaries to more than $100,000. However, with business under pressure, the bank cut nearly 5,000 jobs from its 25,000-strong U.S.-based IT workforce. Some of these jobs were transferred to India, where work that costs $100 an hour in the United States can be done for $20 an hour.

One beneficiary of Bank of America's downsizing is Infosys Technologies Ltd., a Bangalore, India, information technology firm where 250 engineers now develop IT applications for the bank. Other Infosys employees are busy processing home loan applications for Greenpoint Mortgage of Novato, California. Nearby in the offices of another Indian firm, Wipro Ltd., five radiologists interpret 30 CT scans a day for Massachusetts General Hospital that are sent over the Internet. At yet another Bangalore business, engineers earn $10,000 a year designing leading-edge semiconductor chips for Texas Instruments. Nor is India the only beneficiary of these changes. Accenture, a large U.S. management consulting and information technology firm, moved 5,000 jobs in software development and accounting to the Philippines. Also in the Philippines, Procter & Gamble employs 650 professionals who prepare the company's global tax returns. The work used to be done in the United States, but now it is done in Manila, with just final submission to local tax authorities in the United States and other countries handled locally.

Even McGraw-Hill, the publisher of this textbook, has outsourced many of its production processes to India in an attempt to be more competitive in the face of severe job cuts in the United States. As part of a corporate re-organization, McGraw-Hill in 2008 announced significant job cuts (more than 600) and a change of more than $40 million as part of a strategic shift toward more digital products. This shift facilitated the outsourcing of many functions that were at one time done in the United States. The majority of those cuts came from McGraw's Education Division.

Sources: "McGraw-Hill Cutting over 600 Jobs, More Than Half in Education Division," *Education Week,* 27, no. 19 (2008), p. 5; P. Engardio, A. Bernstein, and M. Kripalani, "Is Your Job Next?" *BusinessWeek,* February 3, 2003, pp. 50–60; "America's Pain, India's Gain," *The Economist,* January 11, 2003, p. 57; and M. Schroeder and T. Aeppel, "Skilled Workers Mount Opposition to Free Trade, Swaying Politicians," *The Wall Street Journal,* October 10, 2003, pp. A1, A11.

technology have made this possible, effectively expanding the labor market for these jobs to include educated people in places such as India, the Philippines, and China. When coupled with rapid advances in the productivity of foreign labor due to better education, the effect on middle-class wages in the United States, according to Samuelson, may be similar to mass inward migration into the United States—it will lower the market clearing wage rate, *perhaps* by enough to outweigh the positive benefits of international trade.

Having said this, it should be noted that Samuelson concedes that free trade has historically benefited rich counties (as data discussed below seem to confirm). Moreover, he notes that introducing protectionist measures (e.g., trade barriers) to guard against the theoretical possibility that free trade may harm the United States in the future may produce a situation that is worse than the disease the measures are trying to prevent. To quote Samuelson: "Free trade may turn out pragmatically to be still best for each region in comparison to lobbyist-induced tariffs and quotas which involve both a perversion of democracy and non-subtle deadweight distortion losses."[11]

Some economists have been quick to dismiss Samuelson's fears.[12] While not questioning his analysis, they note that developing nations are unlikely to be able to upgrade the skill level of their workforce rapidly enough to give rise to the situation in Samuelson's model. In other words, the countries will quickly run into diminishing returns. To quote one such rebuttal: "The notion that India and China will quickly educate 300 million of their citizens to acquire sophisticated and complex skills at stake borders on the ludicrous. The educational sectors in these countries face enormous difficulties."[13] Notwithstanding such rebuttals, however, Samuelson's stature is such that his work will undoubtedly be debated for some time.

Evidence for the Link between Trade and Growth   Many economic studies have looked at the relationship between trade and economic growth.[14] In general, these studies suggest that, as predicted by the standard theory of comparative advantage, countries that adopt a more open stance toward international trade enjoy higher growth rates than those that close their economies to trade (the opening case provides evidence of the link between trade and growth). Jeffrey Sachs and Andrew Warner created a measure of how "open" to international trade an economy was and then looked at the relationship between "openness" and economic growth for a sample of more than 100 countries from 1970 to 1990.[15] Among other findings, they reported:

LEARNING OBJECTIVE 3
Recognize why many economists believe that unrestricted free trade between nations will raise the economic welfare of countries that participate in a free trade system.

> We find a strong association between openness and growth, both within the group of developing and the group of developed countries. Within the group of developing countries, the open economies grew at 4.49 percent per year, and the closed economies grew at 0.69 percent per year. Within the group of developed economies, the open economies grew at 2.29 percent per year, and the closed economies grew at 0.74 percent per year.[16]

A study by Wacziarg and Welch updated the Sachs and Warner data through the late 1990s. They found that from 1950 to 1998, countries that liberalized their trade regimes experienced, on average, increases in their annual growth rates of 1.5 percent compared to preliberalization times.[17]

The message of these studies seems clear: Adopt an open economy and embrace free trade, and your nation will be rewarded with higher economic growth rates. Higher growth will raise income levels and living standards. This last point has been confirmed by a study that looked at the relationship between trade and growth in incomes. The study, undertaken by Jeffrey Frankel and David Romer, found that on average, a one percentage point increase in the ratio of a country's trade to its gross domestic product increases income per person by at least one-half percent.[18] For every 10 percent increase in the importance of international trade in an economy, average income levels will rise by at least 5 percent. Despite the short-term adjustment costs associated with adopting a free trade regime, trade would seem to produce greater economic growth and higher living standards in the long run, just as the theory of Ricardo would lead us to expect.[19]

Heckscher-Ohlin Theory

Ricardo's theory stresses that comparative advantage arises from differences in productivity. Thus, whether Ghana is more efficient than South Korea in the production of cocoa depends on how productively it uses its resources. Ricardo stressed labor productivity and argued that differences in labor productivity between nations underlie the notion of comparative advantage. Swedish economists Eli Heckscher (in 1919)

LEARNING OBJECTIVE 2
Summarize the different theories explaining trade flows between nations.

Factor Endowments
The extent to which a country is endowed with such resources as land, labor, and capital.

and Bertil Ohlin (in 1933) put forward a different explanation of comparative advantage. They argued that comparative advantage arises from differences in national factor endowments.[20] By **factor endowments** they meant the extent to which a country is endowed with such resources as land, labor, and capital. Nations have varying factor endowments, and different factor endowments explain differences in factor costs; specifically, the more abundant a factor, the lower its cost. The Heckscher-Ohlin theory predicts that countries will export those goods that make intensive use of factors that are locally abundant, while importing goods that make intensive use of factors that are locally scarce. Thus, the Heckscher-Ohlin theory attempts to explain the pattern of international trade that we observe in the world economy. Like Ricardo's theory, the Heckscher-Ohlin theory argues that free trade is beneficial. Unlike Ricardo's theory, however, the Heckscher-Ohlin theory argues that the pattern of international trade is determined by differences in factor endowments, rather than differences in productivity.

The Heckscher-Ohlin theory has commonsense appeal. For example, the United States has long been a substantial exporter of agricultural goods, reflecting in part its unusual abundance of arable land. In contrast, China excels in the export of goods produced in labor-intensive manufacturing industries, such as textiles and footwear. This reflects China's relative abundance of low-cost labor. The United States, which lacks abundant low-cost labor, has been a primary importer of these goods. Note that it is relative, not absolute, endowments that are important; a country may have larger absolute amounts of land and labor than another country, but be relatively abundant in one of them.

THE LEONTIEF PARADOX

The Heckscher-Ohlin theory has been one of the most influential theoretical ideas in international economics. Most economists prefer the Heckscher-Ohlin theory to Ricardo's theory because it makes fewer simplifying assumptions. Because of its influence, the theory has been subjected to many empirical tests. Beginning with a famous study published in 1953 by Wassily Leontief (winner of the Nobel Prize in economics in 1973), many of these tests have raised questions about the validity of the Heckscher-Ohlin theory.[21] Using the Heckscher-Ohlin theory, Leontief postulated that since the United States was relatively abundant in capital compared to other nations, the United States would be an exporter of capital-intensive goods and an importer of labor-intensive goods. To his surprise, however, he found that U.S. exports were less capital intensive than U.S. imports. Since this result was at variance with the predictions of the theory, it has become known as the Leontief paradox.

No one is quite sure why we observe the Leontief paradox. One possible explanation is that the United States has a special advantage in producing new products or goods made with innovative technologies. Such products may be less capital intensive than products whose technology has had time to mature and become suitable for mass production. Thus, the United States may be exporting goods that heavily use skilled labor and innovative entrepreneurship, such as computer software, while importing heavy manufacturing products that use large amounts of capital. Some empirical studies tend to confirm this.[22] Still, tests of the Heckscher-Ohlin theory using data for a large number of countries tend to confirm the existence of the Leontief paradox.[23]

This leaves economists with a difficult dilemma. They prefer the Heckscher-Ohlin theory on theoretical grounds, but it is a relatively poor predictor of real-world international trade patterns. On the other hand, the theory they regard as being too limited, Ricardo's theory of comparative advantage, actually predicts trade patterns with greater accuracy. The best solution to this dilemma may be to return to the Ricardian idea that trade patterns are largely driven by international differences in productivity.

Thus, one might argue that the United States exports commercial aircraft and imports textiles not because its factor endowments are especially suited to aircraft manufacture and not suited to textile manufacture, but because the United States is relatively more efficient at producing aircraft than textiles. A key assumption in the Heckscher-Ohlin theory is that technologies are the same across countries. This may not be the case. Differences in technology may lead to differences in productivity, which in turn, drives international trade patterns.[24] Thus, Japan's success in exporting automobiles since the 1970s has been not just because of the relative abundance of capital, but also because of its development of innovative manufacturing technology that enabled it to achieve higher productivity levels in automobile production than other countries that also had abundant capital. More recent empirical work suggests that this theoretical explanation may be correct.[25] The new research shows that once differences in technology across countries are controlled for, countries do indeed export those goods that make intensive use of factors that are locally abundant, while importing goods that make intensive use of factors that are locally scarce. In other words, once the impact of differences of technology on productivity is controlled for, the Heckscher-Ohlin theory seems to gain predictive power.

The Product Life-Cycle Theory

Raymond Vernon initially proposed the product life-cycle theory in the mid-1960s.[26] Vernon's theory was based on the observation that for most of the twentieth century a very large proportion of the world's new products had been developed by U.S. firms and sold first in the U.S. market (e.g., mass-produced automobiles, televisions, instant cameras, photocopiers, personal computers, and semiconductor chips). To explain this, Vernon argued that the wealth and size of the U.S. market gave U.S. firms a strong incentive to develop new consumer products. In addition, the high cost of U.S. labor gave U.S. firms an incentive to develop cost-saving process innovations.

LEARNING OBJECTIVE 2
Summarize the different theories explaining trade flows between nations.

Just because a new product is developed by a U.S. firm and first sold in the U.S. market, it does not follow that the product must be produced in the United States. It could be produced abroad at some low-cost location and then exported back into the United States. However, Vernon argued that most new products were initially produced in America. Apparently, the pioneering firms believed it was better to keep production facilities close to the market and to the firm's center of decision making, given the uncertainty and risks inherent in introducing new products. Also, the demand for most new products tends to be based on non-price factors. Consequently, firms can charge relatively high prices for new products, which obviates the need to look for low-cost production sites in other countries.

Vernon went on to argue that early in the life cycle of a typical new product, while demand is starting to grow rapidly in the United States, demand in other advanced countries is limited to high-income groups. The limited initial demand in other advanced countries does not make it worthwhile for firms in those countries to start producing the new product, but it does necessitate some exports from the United States to those countries.

Over time, demand for the new product starts to grow in other advanced countries (e.g., Great Britain, France, Germany, and Japan). As it does, it becomes worthwhile for foreign producers to begin producing for their home markets. In addition, U.S. firms might set up production facilities in those advanced countries where demand is growing. Consequently, production within other advanced countries begins to limit the potential for exports from the United States.

As the market in the United States and other advanced nations matures, the product becomes more standardized, and price becomes the main competitive weapon. As this occurs, cost considerations start to play a greater role in the competitive process. Producers based in advanced countries where labor costs are lower than in the United States (e.g., Italy, Spain) might now be able to export to the United States. If cost pressures become intense, the process might not stop there. The cycle by which the United States lost its advantage to other advanced countries might be repeated once more, as developing countries (e.g., Thailand) begin to acquire a production advantage over advanced countries. Thus, the locus of global production initially switches from the United States to other advanced nations and then from those nations to developing countries.

The consequence of these trends for the pattern of world trade is that over time the United States switches from being an exporter of the product to an importer of the product as production becomes concentrated in lower-cost foreign locations. Figure 5.5 shows the growth of production and consumption over time in the United States, other advanced countries, and developing countries.

EVALUATING THE PRODUCT LIFE-CYCLE THEORY   Historically, the product life-cycle theory seems to be an accurate explanation of international trade patterns. Consider photocopiers; the product was first developed in the early 1960s by Xerox in the United States and sold initially to U.S. users. Originally Xerox exported photocopiers from the United States, primarily to Japan and the advanced countries of Western Europe. As demand began to grow in those countries, Xerox entered into joint ventures to set up production in Japan (Fuji-Xerox) and Great Britain (Rank-Xerox). In addition, once Xerox's patents on the photocopier process expired, other foreign competitors began to enter the market (e.g., Canon in Japan, Olivetti in Italy). As a consequence, exports from the United States declined, and U.S. users began to buy some of their photocopiers from lower-cost foreign sources, particularly Japan. More recently, Japanese companies have found that manufacturing costs are too high in their own country, so they have begun to switch production to developing countries such as Singapore and Thailand. Thus, initially the United States and now other advanced countries (e.g., Japan and Great Britain) have switched from being exporters of photocopiers to importers. This evolution in the pattern of international trade in photocopiers is consistent with the predictions of the product life-cycle theory that mature industries tend to go out of the United States and into low-cost assembly locations.

However, the product life-cycle theory is not without weaknesses. Viewed from an Asian or European perspective, Vernon's argument that most new products are developed and introduced in the United States seems ethnocentric and increasingly dated. Although it may be true that during U.S. dominance of the global economy (from 1945 to 1975), most new products were introduced in the United States, there have always been important exceptions. These exceptions appear to have become more common in recent years. Many new products are now first introduced in Japan (e.g., videogame consoles) or Europe (new wireless phones). Moreover, with the increased globalization and integration of the world economy discussed in Chapter 1, a growing number of new products (e.g., laptop computers, compact disks, and digital cameras) are now introduced simultaneously in the United States, Japan, and the advanced European nations. This may be accompanied by globally dispersed production, with particular components of a new product being produced in those locations around the globe where the mix of factor costs and skills is most favorable (as predicted by the theory of comparative advantage). In sum, although Vernon's theory may be useful for explaining the pattern of international trade during the brief period of American global dominance, its relevance in the modern world seems more limited.

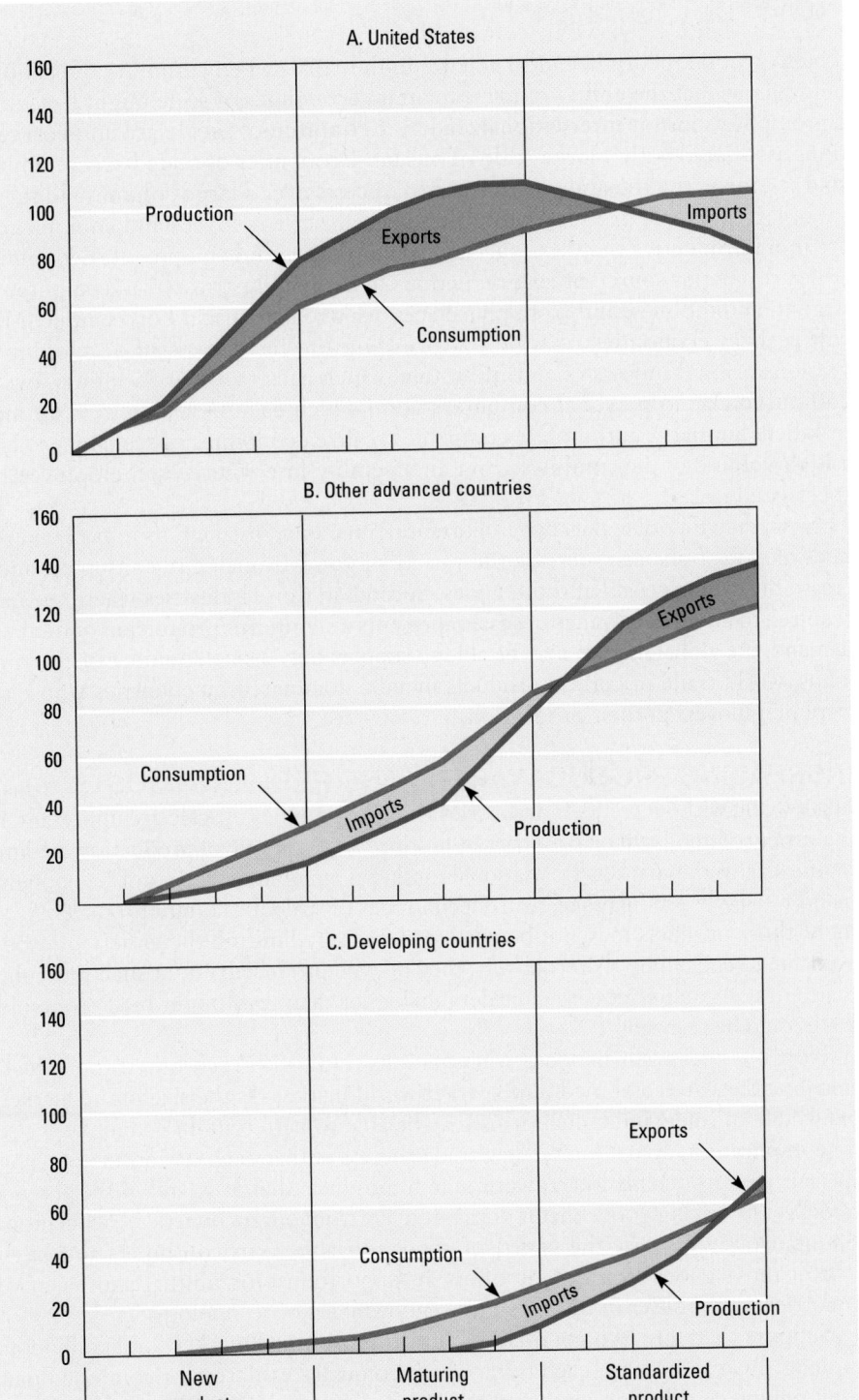

5.5 figure

The Product Life-Cycle Theory

Source: Adapted from R. Vernon and L. T. Wells, *The Economic Environment of International Business.* 4th ed., © 1986. Reprinted by permission of Pearson Education, Inc. Upper Saddle River, N.J.

A. United States

Production

Exports

Consumption

Imports

B. Other advanced countries

Consumption

Imports

Production

Exports

C. Developing countries

Consumption

Imports

Production

Exports

New product

Maturing product

Standardized product

Stages of product development

New Trade Theory

LEARNING OBJECTIVE 2
Summarize the different theories explaining trade flows between nations.

Economies of Scale
Cost advantages associated with large-scale production.

The new trade theory began to emerge in the 1970s when a number of economists pointed out that the ability of firms to attain economies of scale might have important implications for international trade.[27] **Economies of scale** are unit cost reductions associated with a large scale of output. Economies of scale have a number of sources, including the ability to spread fixed costs over a large volume, and the ability of large-volume producers to utilize specialized employees and equipment that are more productive than less-specialized employees and equipment. Economies of scale are a major source of cost reductions in many industries, from computer software to automobiles, and from pharmaceuticals to aerospace. For example, Microsoft realizes economies of scale by spreading the fixed costs of developing new versions of its Windows operating system, which runs to about $5 billion, over the 250 million or so personal computers upon which each new system is ultimately installed. Similarly, automobile companies realize economies of scale by producing a high volume of automobiles from an assembly line where each employee has a specialized task.

New trade theory makes two important points: First, through its impact on economies of scale, trade can increase the variety of goods available to consumers and decrease the average costs of those goods. Second, in those industries where the output required to attain economies of scale represents a significant proportion of total world demand, the global market may be able to support only a small number of enterprises. Thus, world trade in certain products may be dominated by countries whose firms were first movers in their production.

LEARNING OBJECTIVE 3
Recognize why many economists believe that unrestricted free trade between nations will raise the economic welfare of countries that participate in a free trade system.

INCREASING PRODUCT VARIETY AND REDUCING COSTS

Imagine first a world without trade. In industries where economies of scale are important, both the variety of goods that a country can produce and the scale of production are limited by the size of the market. If a national market is small, there may not be enough demand to enable producers to realize economies of scale for certain products. Accordingly, those products may not be produced, thereby limiting the variety of products available to consumers. Alternatively, they may be produced, but at such low volumes that unit costs and prices are considerably higher than they might be if economies of scale could be realized.

Now consider what happens when nations trade with each other. Individual national markets are combined into a larger world market. As the size of the market expands due to trade, individual firms may be able to better attain economies of scale. The implication, according to new trade theory, is that each nation may be able to specialize in producing a narrower range of products than it would in the absence of trade, yet by buying goods that it does not make from other countries, each nation can simultaneously increase the *variety* of goods available to its consumers and *lower the costs* of those goods—thus trade offers an opportunity for mutual gain even when countries do not differ in their resource endowments or technology.

Suppose there are two countries, each with an annual market for 1 million automobiles. By trading with each other, these countries can create a combined market for 2 million cars. In this combined market, due to the ability to better realize economies of scale, more varieties (models) of cars can be produced, and cars can be produced at a lower average cost, than in either market alone. For example, demand for a sports car may be limited to 55,000 units in each national market, while a total output of at least 100,000 per year may be required to realize significant scale economies. Similarly, demand for a minivan may be 80,000 units in each national market, and again a total output of at least 100,000 per year may be required to realize significant scale economies. Faced with limited domestic market demand, firms in each nation may decide not to produce a sports car, since the costs of doing so at such low volume are too great. Although they may produce minivans, the cost of doing so will be higher, as will prices, than if significant economies of scale had been attained. Once the two countries decide to trade, however, a firm in one nation may specialize in producing sports cars, while a firm in the other nation may produce minivans. The combined demand for 110,000 sports cars and 160,000 minivans allows each firm to realize scale economies. Consumers in this case benefit from having access to a product (sports cars) that was not available before international trade and from the lower price for a product (minivans) that could not be produced at the most efficient scale before international trade. Trade is thus mutually beneficial because it allows for the specialization of production, the realization of scale economies, the production of a greater variety of products, and lower prices.

ECONOMIES OF SCALE, FIRST MOVER ADVANTAGES AND THE PATTERN OF TRADE

A second theme in new trade theory is that the pattern of trade we observe in the world economy may be the result of economies of scale and first-mover advantages. **First-mover advantages** are the economic and strategic advantages that accrue to early entrants into an industry.[28] The ability to capture scale economies ahead of later entrants, and thus benefit from a lower cost structure, is an important first-mover advantage. New trade theory argues that for those products where economies of scale are significant and represent a substantial proportion of world demand, the first movers in an industry can gain a scale-based cost advantage that later entrants find almost impossible to match. Thus, the pattern of trade that we observe for such products may reflect first-mover advantages. Countries may dominate in the export of certain goods because economies of scale are important in their production and because firms located in those countries were the first to capture scale economies, giving them a first-mover advantage.

First-Mover Advantages
Advantages accruing to the first to enter a market.

For example, consider the commercial aerospace industry, where substantial scale economies come from the ability to spread the fixed costs of developing a new jet aircraft over a large number of sales. It has cost Airbus some $15 billion to develop its new super-jumbo jet, the 550-seat A380. To recoup those costs and break even, Airbus will have to sell at least 250 A380 planes. If Airbus can sell over 350 A380 planes, it will apparently be a profitable venture. Total demand over the next 20 years for this class of aircraft is estimated to be somewhere between 400 and 600 units. Thus, the global market can probably profitably support only one producer of jet aircraft in the super-jumbo category. It follows that the European Union might come to dominate in the export of very large jet aircraft, primarily because a European-based firm, Airbus, was the first to produce a super-jumbo jet and realize scale economies. Other potential producers, such as Boeing, might be shut out of the market because they will lack the scale economies that Airbus will enjoy. By pioneering this market category, Airbus may have captured a first-mover advantage based on scale economies that will be difficult for rivals to match, and that will result in the European Union becoming the leading exporter of very large jet aircraft. (Boeing does not believe the market to be large enough to profitably support even one producer, hence its decision not to build a similar aircraft, and instead focus on its super-efficient 787.)

IMPLICATIONS OF NEW TRADE THEORY

New trade theory has important implications. The theory suggests that nations may benefit from trade even when they do not differ in resource endowments or technology. Trade allows a nation to specialize in the production of certain products, attaining scale economies and lowering

LEARNING OBJECTIVE 3
Recognize why many economists believe that unrestricted free trade between nations will raise the economic welfare of countries that participate in a free trade system.

The European Union may come to dominate in the export of super-jumbo jets primarily because Airbus, a European-based firm, was the first to produce a 550-seat aircraft and realize economies of scale.

the costs of producing those products, while buying products that it does not produce from other nations that specialize in the production of those products. By this mechanism, the variety of products available to consumers in each nation is increased, while the average costs of those products should fall, as should their price, freeing resources to produce other goods and services.

The theory also suggests that a country may predominate in the export of a good simply because it was lucky enough to have one or more firms among the first to produce that good. Because they are able to gain economies of scale, the first movers in an industry may get a lock on the world market that discourages subsequent entry. First movers' ability to benefit from increasing returns creates a barrier to entry. In the commercial aircraft industry, the fact that Boeing and Airbus are already in the industry and have the benefits of economies of scale discourages new entry and reinforces the dominance of America and Europe in the trade of midsized and large jet aircraft. This dominance is further reinforced because global demand may not be sufficient to profitably support another producer of midsized and large jet aircraft in the industry. So although Japanese firms might be able to compete in the market, they have decided not to enter the industry but to ally themselves as major subcontractors with primary producers (e.g., Mitsubishi Heavy Industries is a major subcontractor for Boeing on the 777 and 787 programs).

New trade theory is at variance with the Heckscher-Ohlin theory, which suggests that a country will predominate in the export of a product when it is particularly well endowed with those factors used intensively in its manufacture. New trade theorists argue that the United States is a major exporter of commercial jet aircraft not because it is better endowed with the factors of production required to manufacture aircraft, but because one of the first movers in the industry, Boeing, was a U.S. firm. The new trade theory is not at variance with the theory of comparative advantage. Economies of scale increase productivity. Thus, the new trade theory identifies an important source of comparative advantage.

This theory is quite useful in explaining trade patterns. Empirical studies seem to support the predictions of the theory that trade increases the specialization of production within an industry, increases the variety of products available to consumers, and results in lower average prices.[29] With regard to first-mover advantages and international trade, a study by Harvard business historian Alfred Chandler suggests the existence of first-mover advantages is an important factor in explaining the dominance of firms from certain nations in specific industries.[30] The number of firms is very limited in many global industries, including the chemical industry, the heavy construction-equipment industry, the heavy truck industry, the tire industry, the consumer electronics industry, the jet engine industry, and the computer software industry.

Perhaps the most contentious implication of the new trade theory is the argument that it generates for government intervention and strategic trade policy.[31] New trade theorists stress the role of luck, entrepreneurship, and innovation in giving a firm first-mover advantages. According to this argument, the reason Boeing was the first mover in commercial jet aircraft manufacture—rather than firms such as Great Britain's DeHavilland and Hawker Siddeley, or Holland's Fokker, all of which could have been—was that Boeing was both lucky and innovative. One way Boeing was lucky is that DeHavilland's Comet jet airliner, introduced two years earlier than Boeing's first jet airliner, the 707, was found to be full of serious technological flaws. Had DeHavilland not made serious technological mistakes, Great Britain might have become the world's leading exporter of commercial jet aircraft. Boeing's innovativeness was demonstrated by its independent development of the technological know-how required to build a commercial jet airliner. Several new trade theorists have pointed out, however, that Boeing's R&D was largely paid for by the U.S. government; the 707 was a spin-off from a government-funded military program (the entry of Airbus into the industry was also supported by significant government subsidies). Herein is a rationale for government intervention; by the sophisticated and judicious use of subsidies, could a government increase the chances of its domestic firms becoming first movers in newly emerging industries, as the U.S. government apparently did with Boeing (and the European Union did with Airbus)? If this is possible, and the new trade theory suggests it might be, we have an economic rationale for a proactive trade policy that is at variance with the free trade prescriptions of the trade theories we have reviewed so far. We will consider the policy implications of this issue in Chapter 6.

LEARNING OBJECTIVE 4
Explain the arguments of those who maintain that government can play a proactive role in promoting national competitive advantage in certain industries.

National Competitive Advantage: Porter's Diamond

In 1990 Michael Porter of the Harvard Business School published the results of an intensive research effort that attempted to determine why some nations succeed and others fail in international competition.[32] Porter and his team looked at 100 industries in 10 nations. Like the work of the new trade theorists, Porter's work was driven by a belief that existing theories of international trade told only part of the story. For Porter, the essential task was to explain why a nation achieves international success in a particular industry. Why does Japan do so well in the automobile industry? Why does Switzerland excel in the production and export of precision instruments and pharmaceuticals? Why do Germany and the United States do so well in the chemical industry? These questions cannot be answered easily by the Heckscher-Ohlin theory, and the theory of comparative advantage offers only a partial explanation. The theory of comparative advantage would say that Switzerland excels in the production and export of precision instruments because it uses its resources very productively in these industries. Although this may be correct, this does not explain why Switzerland

LEARNING OBJECTIVE 2
Summarize the different theories explaining trade flows between nations.

figure 5.6

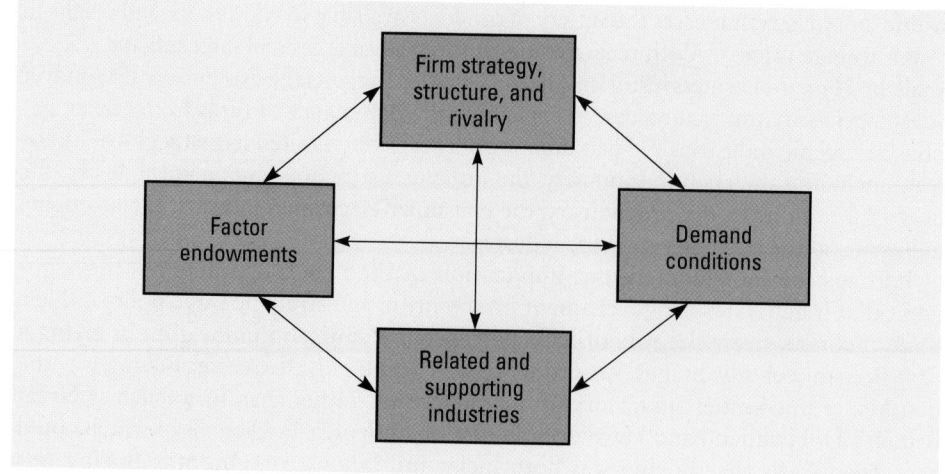

is more productive in this industry than Great Britain, Germany, or Spain. Porter tries to solve this puzzle.

Porter theorizes that four broad attributes of a nation shape the environment in which local firms compete, and these attributes promote or impede the creation of competitive advantage (see Figure 5.6). These attributes are

- *Factor endowments*—a nation's position in factors of production such as skilled labor or the infrastructure necessary to compete in a given industry.
- *Demand conditions*—the nature of home demand for the industry's product or service.
- *Relating and supporting industries*—the presence or absence of supplier industries and related industries that are internationally competitive.
- *Firm strategy, structure, and rivalry*—the conditions governing how companies are created, organized, and managed and the nature of domestic rivalry.

Porter speaks of these four attributes as constituting the *diamond.* He argues that firms are most likely to succeed in industries or industry segments where the diamond is most favorable. He also argues that the diamond is a mutually reinforcing system. The effect of one attribute is contingent on the state of others. For example, Porter argues favorable demand conditions will not result in competitive advantage unless the state of rivalry is sufficient to cause firms to respond to them.

Porter maintains that two additional variables can influence the national diamond in important ways: chance and government. Chance events, such as major innovations, can reshape industry structure and provide the opportunity for one nation's firms to supplant another's. Government, by its choice of policies, can detract from or improve national advantage. For example, regulation can alter

Another Perspective

Renewable Energy: Emerging Opportunities
Global investments in renewable energy are expected to reach $653.35 billion by the year 2015. China, India, and Brazil are key hot spots. Demand is fueling this investment. The rapid economic growth and energy needs of these countries require an expansion in power generation. Although conventional forms of energy, such as coal, oil, and gas, will still prevail, many countries will be looking to wind, solar, biomass, and hydropower as alternatives to satisfy this need. Companies that can recognize this opportunity stand to benefit from the shift in production. ("Green Energy in Emerging Economies: Renewable Investment, Capacity Growth, and Future Outlook," *PR Newswire,* March 4, 2010, accessed at http://www.prnewswire.com; "Research and Markets; This Essential Report on Renewable Energy Investment in India, China and Brazil Is Now Available," *Journal of India,* August 3, 2010)

home demand conditions, antitrust policies can influence the intensity of rivalry within an industry, and government investments in education can change factor endowments.

FACTOR ENDOWMENTS

Factor endowments lie at the center of the Heckscher-Ohlin theory. While Porter does not propose anything radically new, he does analyze the characteristics of factors of production. He recognizes hierarchies among factors, distinguishing between *basic factors* (e.g., natural resources, climate, location, and demographics) and *advanced factors* (e.g., communication infrastructure, sophisticated and skilled labor, research facilities, and technological know-how). He argues that advanced factors are the most significant for competitive advantage. Unlike the naturally endowed basic factors, advanced factors are a product of investment by individuals, companies, and governments. Thus, government investments in basic and higher education, by improving the general skill and knowledge level of the population and by stimulating advanced research at higher education institutions, can upgrade a nation's advanced factors.

The relationship between advanced and basic factors is complex. Basic factors can provide an initial advantage that is subsequently reinforced and extended by investment in advanced factors. Conversely, disadvantages in basic factors can create pressures to invest in advanced factors. An obvious example of this phenomenon is Japan, a country that lacks arable land and mineral deposits and yet through investment has built a substantial endowment of advanced factors. Porter notes that Japan's large pool of engineers (reflecting a much higher number of engineering graduates per capita than almost any other nation) has been vital to Japan's success in many manufacturing industries.

DEMAND CONDITIONS

Porter emphasizes the role home demand plays in upgrading competitive advantage. Firms are typically most sensitive to the needs of their closest customers. Thus, the characteristics of home demand are particularly important in shaping the attributes of domestically made products and in creating pressures for innovation and quality. Porter argues that a nation's firms gain competitive advantage if their domestic consumers are sophisticated and demanding. Such consumers pressure local firms to meet high standards of product quality and to produce innovative products. Porter notes that Japan's sophisticated and knowledgeable buyers of cameras helped stimulate the Japanese camera industry to improve product quality and to introduce innovative models. A similar example can be found in the energy industry, where sophisticated and demanding local customers in several European countries helped push Siemens to invest in green technology, including renewable energy and wind power. The case of Siemens is discussed in more depth in the accompanying Management Focus.

RELATED AND SUPPORTING INDUSTRIES

The third broad attribute of national advantage in an industry is the presence of suppliers or related industries that are internationally competitive. The benefits of investments in advanced factors of production by related and supporting industries can spill over into an industry,

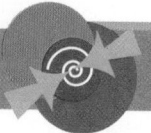

Siemens and the Rise of Germany's Renewable Energy

As the recent Deepwater Horizon oil spill in the Gulf of Mexico suggests, alternative sources of clean, renewable energy must be considered. Indeed, according to Siemens AG President and CEO Peter Loscher, "The world economy is undergoing a 'paradigm shift' toward sustainability and green technology. " Siemens appears to be leading much of the change. Despite the current economic crisis, Loscher is asking companies and governments to remain focused on the broad trends of "climate change, demographic change, urbanization and globalization." As head of Europe's largest engineering conglomerate, Loscher is in the unique position to influence the paradigm.

Siemens' position essentially coincides with Germany's. For many, at the country level, Germany has served as the model to be replicated elsewhere. Although it can easily be attributed to the increase in oil prices and the oil spill crisis, the story actually goes back more than two decades. Premised more on historical events that reinforced one another, renewable energy proponents were able to establish Germany's renewable energy model based on two events. The first event was the Chernobyl disaster, which discredited nuclear energy. This event opened a window of opportunity for renewable energy, which policy entrepreneurs in the German parliament were eager to exploit and which did not depend upon volatile energy prices.

The second event was Germany's admittance to the European Union. Until such time, coal provided more than 50 percent of Germany's electricity production. But Germany is the biggest producer of brown coal. Brown coal mining is expensive and had only been sustained by massive governmental subsidies. These subsidies were eventually ruled illegal by the European Union. The other factor that has undermined the political support for coal is the fast-growing movement against global warming. Thus, the aversion to nuclear power and the desire to reduce CO_2 emissions opened an opportunity for renewable energy, especially in the area of electricity generation. Siemens saw the opportunity and reacted.

Since then, Siemens has focused on solar, biomass, small hydroelectric, and wind power generation in Germany and throughout Europe as part of the "paradigm shift." In particular, Siemens' Wind Power division is leading much of the charge. When started in 2004, it accounted for a very small percentage of the overall renewable energy division. Now as a "grown-up member" of the Siemens family of companies, it is contributing to the bottom line. It is striving to be the wind turbine provider to the world.

Located in Denmark, Siemens Wind Power is manufacturing wind turbines for onshore, coastal, and offshore wind sites. But the offshore wind sites are where management sees growing opportunities. In this niche sector within renewable energies, Siemens Wind Power is number 1. Using years of experience working with German and European utility companies such as E.ON and Dong, Siemens now exploits these offshore projects to increase renewable energy sales by 55 percent to $3.4 billion. Focusing on "direct-drive" technology (in offshore work, moving parts present reliability problems), Siemens is leveraging its time and knowledge of the market to continue its commitment to sustainable, green technology. If imitation is the best form of flattery, then GE, one of Siemens' most fierce competitors, is copying Siemens when it bought Norway's ScanWind so as to diversify from its US-based wind generation business and acquire "direct-drive" offshore technology.

Sources: M. Frondel, N. Ritter, C. M. Schmidt, and C. Vance, "Economic Impacts from the Promotion of Renewable Energy Technologies: The German Experience," *Energy Policy,* 38, no. 8 (2010), pp. 4048–4056; J. Ewing, "Siemens Rides the Offshore Winds," *BusinessWeek,* November 25, 2009, accessed at http://www.businessweek.com/articles/; S. Minter, "Siemens Sees Green Tech Driving Economic Growth." *Industry Week,* July 22, 2009, accessed at http://www.industryweek.com/articles/; and F. N. Laird and C. Stefes, "The Diverging Paths of German and United States Policies for Renewable Energy," *Energy Policy,* 37, no. 7 (2009), pp. 619–2629.

thereby helping it achieve a strong competitive position internationally. Swedish strength in fabricated steel products (e.g., ball bearings and cutting tools) has drawn on strengths in Sweden's specialty steel industry. Technological leadership in the U.S. semiconductor industry provided the basis for U.S. success in personal computers and several other technically advanced electronic products. Similarly, Switzerland's success in pharmaceuticals is closely related to its previous international success in the technologically related dye industry.

One consequence of this process is that successful industries within a country tend to be grouped into clusters of related industries. This was one of the most pervasive findings of Porter's study. One such cluster Porter identified was in the German textile and apparel sector, which included high-quality cotton, wool, synthetic fibers, sewing machine needles, and a wide range of textile machinery. Such clusters are important because valuable knowledge can flow between the firms within a geographic cluster, benefiting all within that cluster. Knowledge flows occur when employees move between firms within a region and when national industry associations bring employees from different companies together for regular conferences or workshops.[33]

FIRM STRATEGY, STRUCTURE, AND RIVALRY   The fourth broad attribute of national competitive advantage in Porter's model is the strategy, structure, and rivalry of firms within a nation. Porter makes two important points here. First, different nations are characterized by different management ideologies, which either help them or do not help them to build national competitive advantage. For example, Porter noted the predominance of engineers in top management at German and Japanese firms. He attributed this to these firms' emphasis on improving manufacturing processes and product design. In contrast, Porter noted a predominance of people with finance backgrounds leading many U.S. firms. He linked this to U.S. firms' lack of attention to improving manufacturing processes and product design. He argued that the dominance of finance led to an overemphasis on maximizing short-term financial returns. According to Porter, one consequence of these different management ideologies was a relative loss of U.S. competitiveness in those engineering-based industries where manufacturing processes and product design issues are all-important (e.g., the automobile industry).

Porter's second point is that there is a strong association between vigorous domestic rivalry and the creation and persistence of competitive advantage in an industry. Vigorous domestic rivalry induces firms to look for ways to improve efficiency, which makes them better international competitors. Domestic rivalry creates pressures to innovate, to improve quality, to reduce costs, and to invest in upgrading advanced factors. All this helps to create world-class competitors. Porter cites the case of Japan:

> Nowhere is the role of domestic rivalry more evident than in Japan, where it is all-out warfare in which many companies fail to achieve profitability. With goals that stress market share, Japanese companies engage in a continuing struggle to outdo each other. Shares fluctuate markedly. The process is prominently covered in the business press. Elaborate rankings measure which companies are most popular with university graduates. The rate of new product and process development is breathtaking.[34]

EVALUATING PORTER'S THEORY   Porter contends that the degree to which a nation is likely to achieve international success in a certain industry is a function of the combined impact of factor endowments, domestic demand conditions, related and supporting industries, and domestic rivalry. He argues that the presence of all four components is usually required for this diamond to boost competitive performance (although there are exceptions). Porter also contends that government can influence each of the four components of the diamond—either

LEARNING OBJECTIVE 4
Explain the arguments of those who maintain that government can play a proactive role in promoting national competitive advantage in certain industries.

positively or negatively. Factor endowments can be affected by subsidies, policies toward capital markets, policies toward education, and so on. Government can shape domestic demand through local product standards or with regulations that mandate or influence buyer needs. Government policy can influence supporting and related industries through regulation and influence firm rivalry through such devices as capital market regulation, tax policy, and antitrust laws.

If Porter is correct, we would expect his model to predict the pattern of international trade that we observe in the real world. Countries should be exporting products from those industries where all four components of the diamond are favorable, while importing in those areas where the components are not favorable. Is he correct? We simply do not know. Porter's theory has not been subjected to detailed empirical testing. Much about the theory rings true, but the same can be said for the new trade theory, the theory of comparative advantage, and the Heckscher-Ohlin theory. It may be that each of these theories, which complement each other, explains something about the pattern of international trade.

Focus on Managerial Implications

LEARNING OBJECTIVE 5
Understand the important implications that international trade theory holds for business practice.

Why does all this matter for business? There are at least three main implications for international businesses of the material discussed in this chapter: location implications, first-mover implications, and policy implications.

Location

Underlying most of the theories we have discussed is the notion that different countries have particular advantages in different productive activities. Thus, from a profit perspective, it makes sense for a firm to disperse its productive activities to those countries where, according to the theory of international trade, they can be performed most efficiently. If design can be performed most efficiently in France, that is where design facilities should be located; if the manufacture of basic components can be performed most efficiently in Singapore, that is where they should be manufactured; and if final assembly can be performed most efficiently in China, that is where final assembly should be performed. The result is a global web of productive activities, with different activities being performed in different locations around the globe depending on considerations of comparative advantage, factor endowments, and the like. If the firm does not do this, it may find itself at a competitive disadvantage relative to firms that do.

Consider the production of a laptop computer, a process with four major stages: (1) basic research and development of the product design, (2) manufacture of standard electronic components (e.g., memory chips), (3) manufacture of advanced components (e.g., flat-top color display screens and microprocessors), and (4) final assembly. Basic R&D requires a pool of highly skilled and educated workers with good backgrounds in microelectronics. The two countries with a comparative advantage in basic microelectronics R&D and design are Japan and the United States, so most producers of laptop computers locate their R&D facilities in one, or both, of these countries. (Apple, IBM, Motorola, Texas Instruments, Toshiba, and Sony all have major R&D facilities in both Japan and the United States.)

The manufacture of standard electronic components is a capital-intensive process requiring semiskilled labor, and cost pressures are intense. The best locations for such activities today are places such as Taiwan, Malaysia, and South Korea. These countries have pools of relatively skilled, moderate-cost labor. Thus, many producers of laptop computers have standard components, such as memory chips, produced at these locations.

The manufacture of advanced components such as microprocessors is a capital-intensive process requiring skilled labor. Because cost pressures are not so intense at this stage, these components can be—and are—manufactured in countries with high labor costs that also have pools of highly skilled labor (e.g. Japan and the United States).

Finally, assembly is a relatively labor-intensive process requiring only low-skilled labor, and cost pressures are intense. As a result, final assembly may be carried out in a country such as Mexico, which has an abundance of low-cost, low-skilled labor. A laptop computer produced by a U.S. manufacturer may be designed in California, have its standard components produced in Taiwan and Singapore, its advanced components produced in Japan and the United States, its final assembly in Mexico, and be sold in the United States or elsewhere in the world. By dispersing production activities to different locations around the globe, the U.S. manufacturer is taking advantage of the differences between countries identified by the various theories of international trade.

First-Mover Advantages

According to the new trade theory, firms that establish a first-mover advantage with regard to the production of a particular new product may subsequently dominate global trade in that product. This is particularly true in industries where the global market can profitably support only a limited number of firms, such as the aerospace market, but early commitments also seem to be important in less concentrated industries such as the market for manufacturing wind turbines (see the Management Focus on Siemens). For the individual firm, the clear message is that it pays to invest substantial financial resources in trying to build a first-mover, or early-mover, advantage, even if that means several years of losses before a new venture becomes profitable. The idea is to preempt the available demand, gain cost advantages related to volume, build an enduring brand ahead of later competitors, and, consequently, establish a long-term sustainable competitive advantage. Although the details of how to achieve this are beyond the scope of this book, many publications offer strategies for exploiting first-mover advantages, and for avoiding the traps associated with pioneering a market (first-mover disadvantages).[35]

Government Policy

The theories of international trade also matter to international businesses because firms are major players on the international trade scene. Business firms produce exports, and business firms import the products of other countries. Because of their pivotal role in international trade, businesses can exert a strong influence on government trade policy, lobbying to promote free trade or trade restrictions. The theories of international trade claim that promoting free trade is generally in the best interests of a country, although it may not always be in the best interest of an individual firm. Many firms recognize this and lobby for open markets.

For example, when the U.S. government announced its intention to place a tariff on Japanese imports of liquid-crystal display (LCD) screens in the 1990s, IBM and Apple Computer protested strongly. Both IBM and Apple pointed out that (1) Japan was the lowest-cost source of LCD screens, (2) they used these screens in their own laptop computers, and (3) the proposed tariff, by increasing the cost of LCD screens, would increase the cost of laptop computers produced by IBM and Apple, thus making them less competitive in the world market. In other words, the tariff, designed to protect U.S. firms, would be self-defeating. In response to these pressures, the U.S. government reversed its posture.

Unlike IBM and Apple, however, businesses do not always lobby for free trade. In the United States, for example, restrictions on imports of steel are the result of direct pressure by U.S. firms on the government. In some cases, the government has responded to pressure by getting foreign companies to agree to "voluntary" restrictions on their imports, using the implicit threat of more comprehensive formal trade barriers to get them to adhere to these agreements (historically, this has occurred in the automobile industry). In other cases, the government used what are called "antidumping" actions to justify tariffs on imports from other nations (these mechanisms will be discussed in detail in the next chapter).

As predicted by international trade theory, many of these agreements have been self-defeating, such as the voluntary restriction on machine tool imports agreed to in 1985. Due to limited import competition from more efficient foreign suppliers, the prices of machine tools in the United States rose to higher levels than would have prevailed under free trade. Because machine tools are used throughout the manufacturing industry, the result was to increase the costs of U.S. manufacturing in general, creating a corresponding loss in world market competitiveness. Shielded from international competition by import barriers, the U.S. machine tool industry had no incentive to increase its efficiency. Consequently, it lost many of its export markets to more efficient foreign competitors. Because of this misguided action, the U.S. machine tool industry shrunk during the period when the agreement was in force. For anyone schooled in international trade theory, this was not surprising.[36] A similar scenario unfolded in the U.S. steel industry, where tariff barriers erected by the government in 2001 raised the cost of steel to important U.S. users, such as automobile companies and appliance makers, making their products more uncompetitive.

Finally, Porter's theory of national competitive advantage also contains policy implications. Porter's theory suggests that it is in the best interest of business for a firm to invest in upgrading advanced factors of production; for example, to invest in better training for its employees and to increase its commitment to research and development. It is also in the best interests of business to lobby the government to adopt policies that have a favorable impact on each component of the national diamond. Thus, according to Porter, businesses should urge government to increase investment in education, infrastructure, and basic research (since all these enhance advanced factors) and to adopt policies that promote strong competition within domestic markets (since this makes firms stronger international competitors, according to Porter's findings).

Key Terms

free trade, p. 189

new trade theory, p. 191

mercantilism, p. 191

zero-sum game, p. 193

absolute advantage, p. 193

constant returns to specialization, p. 199

factor endowments, p. 204

economies of scale, p. 208

first-mover advantages, p. 209

This chapter has reviewed a number of theories that explain why it is beneficial for a country to engage in international trade and has explained the pattern of international trade observed in the world economy. We have seen how the theories of Smith, Ricardo, and Heckscher-Ohlin all make strong cases for unrestricted free trade. In contrast, the mercantilist doctrine and, to a lesser extent, the new trade theory can be interpreted to support government intervention to promote exports through subsidies and to limit imports through tariffs and quotas.

In explaining the pattern of international trade, the second objective of this chapter, we have seen that with the exception of mercantilism, which is silent on this issue, the different theories offer largely complementary explanations. Although no one theory may explain the apparent pattern of international trade, taken together, the theory of comparative advantage, the Heckscher-Ohlin theory, the product life-cycle theory, the new trade theory, and Porter's theory of national competitive advantage do suggest which factors are important. Comparative advantage tells us that productivity differences are important; Heckscher-Ohlin tells us that factor endowments matter; the product life-cycle theory tells us that where a new product is introduced is important; the new trade theory tells us that increasing returns to specialization and first-mover advantages matter; and Porter tells us that all these factors may be important insofar as they impact the four components of the national diamond. The chapter made these major points:

1. Mercantilists argued that it was in a country's best interests to run a balance-of-trade surplus. They viewed trade as a zero-sum game, in which one country's gains cause losses for other countries.

2. The theory of absolute advantage suggests that countries differ in their ability to produce goods efficiently. The theory suggests that a country should specialize in producing goods in areas where it has an absolute advantage and import goods in areas where other countries have absolute advantages.

3. The theory of comparative advantage suggests that it makes sense for a country to specialize in producing those goods that it can produce most efficiently, while buying goods that it can produce relatively less efficiently from other

countries—even if that means buying goods from other countries that it could produce more efficiently itself.

4. The theory of comparative advantage suggests that unrestricted free trade brings about increased world production; that is, that trade is a positive-sum game.

5. The theory of comparative advantage also suggests that opening a country to free trade stimulates economic growth, which creates dynamic gains from trade. The empirical evidence seems to be consistent with this claim.

6. The Heckscher-Ohlin theory argues that the pattern of international trade is determined by differences in factor endowments. It predicts that countries will export those goods that make intensive use of locally abundant factors and will import goods that make intensive use of factors that are locally scarce.

7. The product life-cycle theory suggests that trade patterns are influenced by where a new product is introduced. In an increasingly integrated global economy, the product life-cycle theory seems to be less predictive than it once was.

8. New trade theory states that trade allows a nation to specialize in the production of certain goods, attaining scale economies and lowering the costs of producing those goods, while buying goods that it does not produce from other nations that are similarly specialized. By this mechanism, the variety of goods available to consumers in each nation is increased, while the average costs of those goods should fall.

9. New trade theory also states that in those industries where substantial economies of scale imply that the world market will profitably support only a few firms, countries may predominate in the export of certain products simply because they had a firm that was a first mover in that industry.

10. Some new trade theorists have promoted the idea of strategic trade policy. The argument is that government, by the sophisticated and judicious use of subsidies, might be able to increase the chances of domestic firms becoming first movers in newly emerging industries.

11. Porter's theory of national competitive advantage suggests that the pattern of trade is influenced

by four attributes of a nation: (*a*) factor endowments, (*b*) domestic demand conditions, (*c*) relating and supporting industries, and (*d*) firm strategy, structure, and rivalry.

12. Theories of international trade are important to an individual business firm primarily because they can help the firm decide where to locate its various production activities.

13. Firms involved in international trade can and do exert a strong influence on government policy toward trade. By lobbying government, business firms can promote free trade or trade restrictions.

Critical Thinking and Discussion Questions

1. Mercantilism is a bankrupt theory that has no place in the modern world. Discuss.

2. Is free trade fair? Discuss.

3. Unions in developed nations often oppose imports from low-wage countries and advocate trade barriers to protect jobs from what they often characterize as "unfair" import competition. Is such competition "unfair"? Do you think that this argument is in the best interests of (*a*) the unions, (*b*) the people they represent, and/or (*c*) the country as a whole?

4. What are the potential costs of adopting a free trade regime? Do you think governments should do anything to reduce these costs? What?

5. Reread the Country Focus on Singapore and then answer the following questions:
   a. Why did Singapore choose to change from a manufacturing economy to a knowledge economy?
   b. What role does the government play within Singapore's knowledge economy? Is this significantly different than the role it would play within a more "traditional" economy?
   c. The last sentence uses the word "internalized." Given the mobile nature of knowledge, do you think there is any way that Singapore can retain the knowledge it is acquiring?

6. Reread the Country Focus "The Mobility of White-Collar Jobs."
   a. Who benefits from the outsourcing of skilled white-collar jobs to developing nations? Who are the losers?
   b. Will developing nations like the United States suffer from the loss of high-skilled and high-paying jobs?
   c. Is there a difference between the transference of high-paying white-collar jobs, such as computer programming and accounting, to developing nations and low-paying blue-collar jobs? If so, what is the difference, and should government do anything to stop the flow of white-collar jobs out of the country to countries such as India?

7. Drawing upon the new trade theory and Porter's theory of national competitive advantage, outline the case for government policies that would build national competitive advantage in biotechnology. What kinds of policies would you recommend that the government adopt? Are these policies at variance with the basic free trade philosophy?

8. The world's poorest countries are at a competitive disadvantage in every sector of their economies. They have little to export. They have no capital; their land is of poor quality; they often have too many people given available work opportunities; and they are poorly educated. Free trade cannot possibly be in the interests of such nations! Discuss.

Research Task 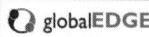 globalEDGE   http://globalEDGE.msu.edu

Use the globalEDGE Resource Desk (http://globalEDGE.msu.edu/resourcedesk/) to complete the following exercises:

1. You work for a telecommunications company and your current project is to determine the five African countries that, in your estimation, should have an advantage in telecommunications infrastructure. Use a resource that tracks *statistics on economic factors* such as Internet use of each country. Develop a list and brief report on the

top five African countries in telecommunications infrastructure. Were you surprised by any countries listed? Why (or, why not)?

2. Your coffee firm is seeking new locations to source coffee from to sustain its growth as it internationalizes. Currently, your company only purchases green coffee beans from South America and is hoping to begin purchasing coffee from the Central American countries of Costa Rica, El Salvador, Guatemala, Honduras, and Panama. Applying the most current information from *FAOSTAT*, a UN agency Web site that gathers data on food and agricultural trade flows, determine which three countries have the highest export value of green coffee as well as growth of export value over the most recent year of data available.

Born Global

The internationalization of a company usually takes many years. Organizations generally expand into new geographic markets or develop new areas of business slowly and gradually, following an evolutionary pattern. This usually happens by means of a progressively more complex international expansion strategy, starting at home and then expanding into "closed markets." Many times that begins with exporting, passing through licensing, strategic alliances, and then foreign direct investments in the form of offshore operations by means of mergers and/or acquisitions. Some firms, however, bypass this "natural evolution" and are "born global."

Born global firms undergo a very early and very rapid *internationalization* process. The term was originally coined by McKinsey and Company in 1993 to describe early internationalizing firms in Australia. Today the term is more commonly used to describe those small to medium enterprises (SMEs) that because of globalization and advances in technology permit them to compete on a global scale. The appearance of born global firms is revolutionizing concepts of competition within the global economy.

In their insightful book, *Born Global Firms: A New International Enterprise,* S. Tamer Cavusgil and Gary Knight point out that born global firms are usually highly active internationally from the earliest moments, usually have limited financial and tangible resources, and are to be found across a wide variety of industries. Managers of born global firms tend to be entrepreneurial and international in their outlook; they tend to emphasize differential and superior product quality strategies, utilize state of the art communications technologies, and use intermediaries for their specific "on-the-ground" needs such as distribution.

According to Cavusgil and Knight, there are certain internationalization triggers that engender born global firms. These include an export push and pull, a worldwide monopoly position, product and marketing positions that require international involvement, superior product offerings, global network of relationships, and a clear global niche market. When found, these triggers tend to facilitate the decision to go global rapidly.

Born global firms come from many sectors and are found in many countries. In fact, in a study of 500 "hidden champions," highly successful international niche players from Europe and North America, the authors found that more than one-third had begun to sell their products in foreign markets in their first year of business. But the propensity to become a born global firm is not equally found in all sectors and in all countries. Some sectors "naturally" lend themselves to born global firms.

In Brazil, for example, all software firms are not necessarily born Brazilian. Software firms, because of the very nature of product they are developing, are capable of being born global if management so chooses. Rather than focusing on the market-penetrating characteristics of the product (software), many are looking at the interactive language, namely, Portuguese, English, Spanish, or others, as the determining factor. To write software code that permits interactivity in English, Spanish, and Portuguese immediately places the firm within an international context. The distribution of the product is only limited by the specific infrastructure capabilities of a particular market. In this regard, the Internet serves as a channel for born global companies.

In another example, Logitech, the computer peripheral company headquartered in Switzerland, in many ways exemplifies the concept of "born global." From its early beginnings in 1981, Logitech recognized that the mice, keyboards, and low-cost video-cams it produced had a worldwide market and demand. Founded by two Italians and a Swiss, the company generated more than $2.2 billion in sales in 2009 with products sold in nearly every country of the world. This success was built from a very early beginning with regard to the way the company configured its global value chain to lower production costs while maintaining the value of the innovative assets that lead to differentiation.

Although much R&D still comes out of Switzerland, most corporate functions, including marketing, finance, and logistical operations, are now out of Fremont, California. Opening a factory in Taiwan shortly thereafter in order to deliver high volume and low costs, Logitech sought out its most prestigious OEM customers—Apple and IBM. From there, the company expanded into China to increase its production capacity.

Sources: Luis Antonio Dib, Angela da Rocha, and Jorge Ferreira da Silva, "The Internationalization Process of Brazilian Software Firms and the Born Global Phenomenon: Examining Firm, Network, and Entrepreneur Variables," *Springer Science + Business Media*, February 17, 2010; S. Tamer Cavusgil and Gary Knight, *Born Global Firms: A New International Enterprise* (New York: Business Expert Press, 2009); and Logitech International Website, accessed at http://www.logitech.com.

Case Discussion Questions

1. How does a "born global firm" differ from a firm that undergoes a traditional international expansion strategy?

2. What are some of the managerial characteristics of a born global firm? How are these distinguishable from those of a traditional firm that seeks to expand with a more traditional evolutionary process?

3. What unique characteristics of Brazilian software firms make them ideal candidates for born global status?

4. Do traditional theories of absolute advantage or comparative advantage theories apply to born global firms? Why would companies such as Logitech retain R&D in Switzerland, house corporate functions in California, and produce products in Taiwan and China?

5. Why do you think Logitech decided to shift its corporate headquarters from Switzerland to California?

6. Does Porter's diamond help explain the unique nature of born global firms?

7. As the world becomes more globalized, do you think that born global firms will be more common? Will large multinational firms be able to compete internationally with highly innovative born global firms? What are some of the potential disadvantages associated with born global firms?

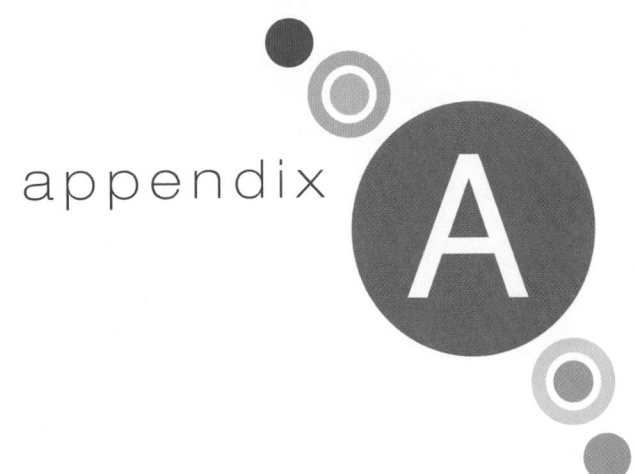

appendix A

International Trade and the Balance of Payments

International trade involves the sale of goods and services to residents in other countries (exports) and the purchase of goods and services from residents in other countries (imports). A country's **balance-of-payments accounts** keep track of the payments to and receipts from other countries for a particular time period. These include payments to foreigners for imports of goods and service, and receipts from foreigners for goods and services exported to them. A summary copy of the U.S. balance-of-payments accounts for 2008 is given in Table A.1. Any transaction resulting in a payment to other countries is entered in the balance-of-payments accounts as a debit and given a negative (−) sign. Any transaction resulting in a receipt from other countries is entered as a credit and given a positive (+) sign. In this appendix we briefly describe the form of the balance-of-payments accounts, and we discuss whether a current account deficit, often a cause of much concern in the popular press, is something to worry about.

Balance-of-Payments Accounts
National accounts that track both payments to and receipts from foreigners.

Balance of Payments Accounts

Balance-of-payments accounts are divided into three main sections: the current account, the capital account, and the financial account (to confuse matters, what is now called the *capital account* was until recently part of the current account, and the financial account use to be called the capital account). The **current account** records transactions that pertain to three categories, all of which can be seen in Table A.1. The first category, *goods*, refers to the export or import of physical goods (e.g., agricultural foodstuffs, autos, computers, chemicals). The second category is the export or import of *services* (e.g., intangible products such as banking and insurance services). The third category, *income receipts and payments*, refers to income from foreign investments and payments that have to be made to foreigners investing in a country. For example, if a U.S. citizen owns a share of a Finnish company and receives a dividend payment of $5, that payment shows up on the U.S. current account as the receipt of $5 of investment income. Also included in the current account are unilateral current transfers, such as U.S. government grants to foreigners (including foreign aid), and private payments to foreigners (such as when a foreign worker in the United States sends money to his or her home country).

Current Account
In the balance of payments, records transactions involving the export or import of goods and services.

table

U.S. Balance of
Payments Accounts,
2008 ($ millions)

Source: Bureau of Economic
Analysis

CURRENT ACCOUNT	$ Millions
Exports of Goods, Services, and Income Receipts	**$ 2,591,233**
Goods	1,276,994
Services	549,602
Income Receipts	764,637
Imports of Goods, Services, and Income Payments	**−3,168,938**
Goods	−2,117,245
Services	−405,287
Income Payments	−646,406
Unilateral current transfers (net)	**−128,363**
Current Account Balance	**−706,068**
CAPITAL ACCOUNT	
Capital Account Transactions (net)	**953**
FINANCIAL ACCOUNT	
U.S.-Owned Assets Abroad, net	**−106**
U.S. Official Reserve Assets	−4,848
U.S. Government Assets	−529,615
U.S. Private Assets	534,357
Foreign-Owned Assets in the United States	**534,071**
Foreign Official Assets in the United States	487,021
Other Foreign Assets in the United States	47,050
Statistical Discrepancy	**200,055**

Current Account Deficit
Occurs when a country imports more good, services, and income than it exports.

Current Account Surplus
Occurs when a country exports more goods, services, and income than it imports.

A **current account deficit** occurs when a country imports more goods, services, and income than it exports. A **current account surplus** occurs when a country exports more goods, services, and income than it imports. Table A.1 shows that in 2008 the United States ran a current account deficit of $706 billion. This is often a headline-grabbing figure and is widely reported in the news media. In recent years the U.S. current account deficit has been getting steadily larger, primarily because America imports far more physical goods than it exports (you will notice that America actually runs a surplus on trade in services and is close to balance on income payments).

The 2006 current account deficit of $803 billion was the largest on record and was equivalent to about 6.5 percent of the country's GDP. The deficit shrank a little in 2007 and 2008, and provisional estimates suggested it would fall to about $450 billion in 2009. Many people find these figures disturbing, the common assumption being that high imports of goods displaces domestic production, causes unemployment, and reduces the growth of the U.S. economy. For example, *The New York Times* responded to the record current account deficit in 2006 by stating:

> A growing trade deficit acts as a drag on overall economic growth. Economists said that they expect that, in light of the new numbers, the government will have to revise its estimate of the nation's fourth quarter gross domestic product to show slightly slower expansion.[37]

However, the issue is somewhat more complex than implied by statements like this. Fully understanding the implications of a large and persistent deficit requires that we look at the rest of the balance-of-payments accounts.

The **capital account** records onetime changes in the stock of assets. As noted above, until recently this item was included in the current account. The capital account includes capital transfers, such as debt forgiveness and migrants' transfers (the goods and financial assets that accompany migrants as they enter or leave the country). In the big scheme of things, this is a relatively small figure amounting to $953 million in 2008.

Capital Account
Records onetime changes in the stock of assets.

The **financial account** (formally the capital account) records transactions that involve the purchase or sale of assets. Thus, when a German firm purchases stock in a U.S. company, or buys a U.S. bond, the transaction enters the U.S. balance of payments as a credit on the capital account. This is because capital is flowing into the country. When capital flows out of the United States, it enters the capital account as a debit.

Financial Account
Records transactions that involve the purchase or sale of assets.

The financial account is comprised of a number of elements. The net change in U.S.-owned assets abroad includes the change in assets owned by the U.S. government (U.S. official reserve assets and U.S. government assets) and the change in assets owned by private individuals and corporations. As can be seen from Table A.1, in 2008 there was a –$106 million reduction in U.S. assets owned abroad, primarily due to a $529 billion fall in the amount of foreign assets owned by the U.S. government. In other words, the government was selling foreign assets, such as foreign bonds and currencies, during 2008. On the other hand, there was a $534 billion increase in the amount of foreign assets owned by private entities, indicating that U.S.-owned enterprises and private individuals were net buyers of foreign assets in 2008, including foreign stocks, bonds, and real estate.

Also included in the financial account are foreign-owned assets in the United States. These are divided into assets owned by foreign governments (foreign official assets) and assets owed by other foreign entities such as corporations and individuals (other foreign assets in the United States). As can be seen, in 2008 foreigners increased their holdings of U.S. assets, including treasury bills, corporate stocks and bonds, and direct investments in the United States, by $534 billion. Some $487 billion of this was due to an increase in the holding of U.S. assets by foreign governments, with the remainder being due to investments by private corporations and individuals in U.S. assets.

It is important at this point to understand that a basic principle of balance-of-payments accounting is double-entry bookkeeping. Every international transaction automatically enters the balance of payments twice—once as a credit and once as a debit. Imagine that you purchase a car produced in Japan by Toyota for $20,000. Since your purchase represents a payment to another country for goods, it will enter the balance of payments as a debit on the current account. Toyota now has the $20,000 and must do something with it. If Toyota deposits the money at a U.S. bank, Toyota has purchased a U.S. asset—a bank deposit worth $20,000—and the transaction will show up as a $20,000 credit on the financial account. Or Toyota might deposit the cash in a Japanese bank in return for Japanese yen. Now the Japanese bank must decide what to do with the $20,000. Any action that it takes will ultimately result in a credit for the U.S. balance of payments. For example, if the bank lends the $20,000 to a Japanese firm that uses it to import personal computers from the United States, then the $20,000 must be credited to the U.S. balance-of-payments current account. Or the Japanese bank might use the $20,000 to purchase U.S. government bonds, in which case it will show up as a credit on the U.S. balance-of-payments financial account.

Thus, any international transaction automatically gives rise to two offsetting entries in the balance of payments. Because of this, *the sum of the current account balance, the capital account, and the financial account balance should always add up to zero.* In practice, this does not always occur due to the existence of "statistical discrepancies," the source of which need not concern us here (in 2008 the statistical discrepancy amounted to $200 billion).

Does the Current Account Deficit Matter?

As discussed above, there is some concern when a country is running a deficit on the current account of its balance of payments.[38] In recent years a number of rich countries, including most notably the United States, have run persistent and growing current account deficits. When a country runs a current account deficit, the money that flows to other countries can then be used by those countries to purchase assets in the deficit country. Thus, when the United States runs a trade deficit with China, the Chinese use the money that they receive from U.S. consumers to purchase U.S. assets such as stocks, bonds, and the like. Put another way, a deficit on the current account is financed by selling assets to other countries; that is, by a surplus on the financial account. Thus, the persistent U.S. current account deficit is being financed by a steady sale of U.S. assets (stocks, bonds, real estate, and whole corporations) to other countries. In short, countries that run current account deficits become net debtors.

For example, as a result of financing its current account deficit through asset sales, the United States must deliver a stream of interest payments to foreign bondholders, rents to foreign landowners, and dividends to foreign stockholders. One might argue that such payments to foreigners drain resources from a country and limit the funds available for investment within the country. Since investment within a country is necessary to stimulate economic growth, a persistent current account deficit can choke off a country's future economic growth. This is the basis of the argument that persistent deficits are bad for an economy.

However, things are not this simple. For one thing, in an era of global capital markets money is efficiently directed toward its highest value uses, and over the past quarter of a century many of the highest value uses of capital have been in the United States. So even though capital is flowing out of the United States in the form of payments to foreigners, much of that capital finds its way right back into the country to fund productive investments in the United States. In short, it is not clear that the current account deficit chokes off U.S. economic growth. In fact, notwithstanding the 2008–2009 recession, the U.S. economy has grown at an impressive rate over the past 25 years, despite running a persistent current account deficit, and despite financing that deficit by selling U.S. assets to foreigners. This is precisely because foreigners reinvest much of the income earned from U.S. assets, and from exports to the United States, right back into the United States. This revisionist view, which has gained in popularity in recent years, suggests that a persistent current account deficit might not be the drag on economic growth it was once thought to be.[39]

Having said this, there is still a nagging fear that at some point the appetite that foreigners have for U.S. assets might decline. If foreigners suddenly reduce their investments in the United States, what would happen? In short, instead of reinvesting the dollars that they earn from exports and investment in the United States back into the country, they would sell those dollars for another currency, European euros, Japanese yen, or Chinese yuan, for example, and invest in euro-, yen- and yuan-denominated assets instead. This would lead to a fall in the value of the dollar on foreign exchange markets, and that in turn would increase the price of imports, and lower the price of U.S. exports making them more competitive, which should reduce the overall level of the current account deficit. Thus, in the long run the persistent U.S.

current account deficit could be corrected via a reduction in the value of the U.S. dollar. The concern is that such adjustments may not be smooth. Rather than a controlled decline in the value of the dollar, the dollar might suddenly lose a significant amount of its value in a very short time, precipitating a "dollar crisis."[40] Since the U.S. dollar is the world's major reserve currency, and is held by many foreign governments and banks, any dollar crisis could deliver a body blow to the world economy and at the very least trigger a global economic slowdown. That would not be a good thing.

Key Terms

balance-of-payments accounts, p. 223

current account, p. 223

current account deficit, p. 224

current account surplus, p. 224

capital account, p. 225

financial account, p. 225

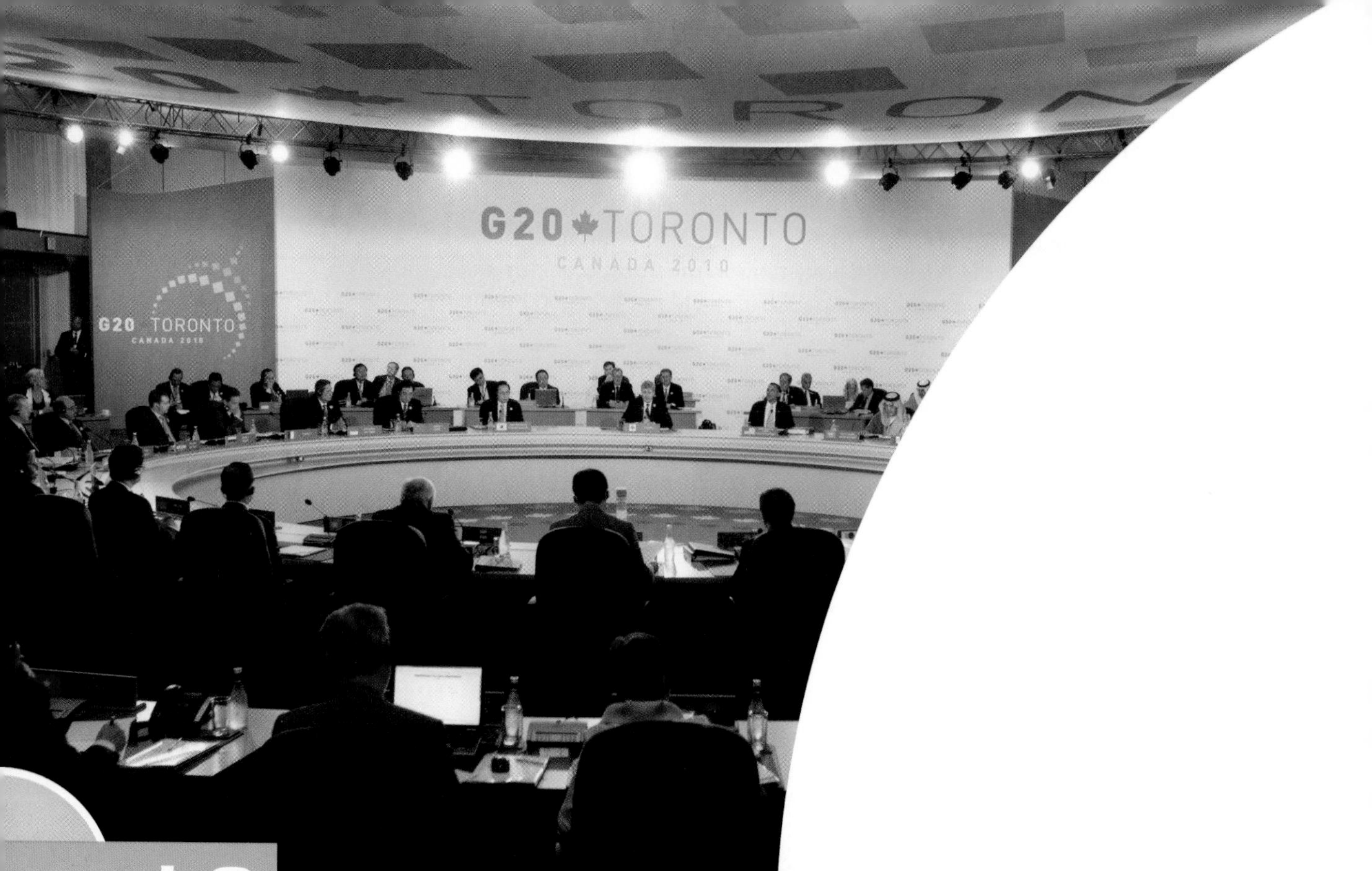
G20 TORONTO
CANADA 2010
G20 TORONTO
CANADA 2010

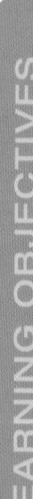

part 3 Cross-Border Trade and Investment

LEARNING OBJECTIVES

After you have read this chapter you should be able to:

1. Identify the policy instruments used by governments to influence international trade flows.
2. Understand why governments sometimes intervene in international trade.
3. Summarize and explain the arguments against strategic trade policy.
4. Describe the development of the world trading system and the current trade issues.
5. Explain the implications for managers of developments in the world trading system.

The Political Economy of International Trade

Over the past 25 years, two facts have characterized trade. First, the volume of world trade has grown every single year, creating an increasingly interdependent global economy, and second, barriers to international trade have been progressively reduced. Between 1990 and 2007, international trade grew by 6 percent per annum compounded, while import tariffs on goods fell from an average of 26 percent in 1986 to 8.8 percent in 2007. In the wake of the global financial crisis that started in the United States in 2008 and quickly spread around the world, this has now changed.

As global demand slumped and financing for international trade dried up in the wake of tight credit conditions, so did the volume of international trade. The volume of world trade fell by 2 percent in 2008, the first decline since 1982, and an additional 9 percent in 2009. In times of economic trouble, nations have a tendency to protect themselves by adhering to a trade protectionist policy. It is a self-preservation mechanism.

This contraction is alarming because, in the past, sharp declines in trade have been followed by calls for greater protectionism from foreign competition as governments try to protect jobs at home in the wake of declining demand. This occurred in the 1930s, when shrinking trade was followed quickly by increases in trade barriers. This actually made the situation far worse and led to the Great Depression in the United States.

Today, regional and multilateral trade agreements such as NAFTA, ASEAN, and the WTO, and international coordinating bodies, such as the Group of 20 (G20), the International Monetary Fund, and the World Bank, now limit the ability of national governments to raise trade barriers and address, in a more coordinated manner, the financial issues associated with international trade and development.

Most notably, World Trade Organization (WTO) rules in theory constrain the ability of countries to implement significant increases in trade barriers. But WTO rules are not perfect, and evidence shows that countries raised barriers to international trade as a result of the recent financial crisis. Under WTO rules, countries may raise some tariffs, and, according to the World Bank, in 2008 and 2009, they were doing just that. For example, Ecuador increased duties on 600 goods. Russia increased import tariffs on used cars, while India placed tariffs on some steel imports. According to the World Bank, however, two-thirds of the protectionist measures taken in 2008 and 2009 were various kinds of "nontariff" barriers designed to get around WTO rules. Indonesia, Argentina, and India implemented various forms of subsidies in an attempt to circumvent WTO rules in a protectionist posture. But the rise in these tariffs, antidumping duties, and subsidies explain less than one-fiftieth of the collapse in world trade during the crisis. The fall in trade reflected more of a drop in demand and a lack of trade finance.

In fact, there is even some evidence that activity has rebalanced. There appears to be a growing import demand from emerging economies that have weathered the economic crisis better. According to IMF figures, of nine emerging markets in the G20, seven got a higher share of their imports from rich countries in 2009 than they did a year earlier.

In this regard, the G20, the group of developed and emerging economies, has played a significant coordinating role in avoiding the protectionist mentality that characterized previous global crises. Whether viewed as an "improvised crisis committee" or a "steering committee" to the world, the G20 represents one of the ongoing global coordinating efforts as the global financial crisis is addressed. What the global economic crisis clearly highlighted was the need for global leadership and economic cooperation among countries. ●

Sources: "Defying Gravity and History," *The Economist,* August 5, 2010; A. F. Cooper, "The G20 as an Improvised Crisis Committee and/or a Contested 'Steering Committee' for the World," *International Affairs* 86, no. 3 (May 2010), pp. 741–757, accessed at http://onlinelibrary.wiley.com; "The Nuts and Bolts Come Apart," *The Economist,* March 28, 2009, pp. 79–81; "Barriers to Entry," *The Economist,* December 20, 2008, p. 121; and "Beyond Doha," *The Economist,* October 11, 2008, pp. 30–33.

Introduction

Free Trade
The absence of government barriers to the free flow of goods and services between countries.

Our review of the classical trade theories of Smith, Ricardo, and Heckscher-Ohlin in Chapter 5 showed us that in a world without trade barriers, trade patterns are determined by the relative productivity of different factors of production in different countries. Countries will specialize in products that they can make most efficiently, while importing products that they can produce less efficiently. Chapter 5 also laid out the intellectual case for free trade. Remember, **free trade** refers to a situation in which a government does not attempt to restrict what its citizens can buy from or sell to another country. As we saw in Chapter 5, the theories of Smith, Ricardo, and Heckscher-Ohlin predict that the consequences of free trade include both static economic gains (because free trade supports a higher level of domestic consumption and more efficient utilization of resources) and dynamic economic gains (because free trade stimulates economic growth and the creation of wealth).

In this chapter, we look at the political reality of international trade. Although many nations are nominally committed to free trade, they tend to intervene in international trade to protect the interests of politically important groups or promote the interests of key domestic producers. As the opening case illustrates, global financial crises are increasingly being addressed by global organizations, whether the WTO or the G20. And although countries may respond by raising tariffs and nontariff barriers in an attempt to protect domestic producers and hold onto jobs, a growing trend in a more coordinated global response appears to be overriding such nationalistic tendencies. While such actions are understandable from a political perspective, international trade theory teaches us that they are self-defeating. Ultimately, protecting inefficient producers raises the price of goods and services and results in lower economic growth.

In this chapter, we explore the political and economic reasons that governments have for intervening in international trade. When governments intervene, they often do so by restricting imports of goods and services into their nation, while adopting policies that promote domestic production and exports. As in 2008 and 2009, normally their motives are to protect domestic producers. In recent years, social issues have intruded into the decision-making calculus. In the United States, for example, a movement is growing to ban imports of goods from countries that do not abide by the same labor, health, and environmental regulations as the United States.

We start this chapter by describing the range of policy instruments that governments use to intervene in international trade. This is followed by a detailed review of the various political and economic motives that governments have for intervention. In the third section of this chapter, we consider how the case for free trade stands up in view of the various justifications given for government intervention in international trade. Then we look at the emergence of the modern international trading system, which is based on the General Agreement on Tariffs and Trade and its successor, the WTO. The GATT and WTO are the creations of a series of multinational treaties. The most recent was completed in 1995, involved more than 120 countries, and resulted in the creation of the WTO. The purpose of these treaties has been to lower barriers to the free flow of goods and services between nations. Like the GATT before it, the WTO promotes free trade by limiting the ability of national governments to adopt policies that restrict imports into their nations. In the final section of this chapter, we discuss the implications of this material for management practice.

Instruments of Trade Policy

Trade policy uses seven main instruments: tariffs, subsidies, import quotas, voluntary export restraints, local content requirements, administrative policies, and antidumping duties. Tariffs are the oldest and simplest instrument of trade policy. As we shall see later in this chapter, they are also the instrument that the GATT and WTO have

LEARNING OBJECTIVE 1
Identify the policy instruments used by governments to influence international trade flows.

been most successful in limiting. A fall in tariff barriers in recent decades has been accompanied by a rise in nontariff barriers, such as subsidies, quotas, voluntary export restraints, and antidumping duties.

TARIFFS

A **tariff** is a tax levied on imports (or exports). Tariffs fall into two categories. **Specific tariffs** are levied as a fixed charge for each unit of a good imported (for example, $3 per barrel of oil). **Ad valorem tariffs** are levied as a proportion of the value of the imported good. In most cases, tariffs are placed on imports to protect domestic producers from foreign competition by raising the price of imported goods. However, tariffs also produce revenue for the government. Until the income tax was introduced, for example, the U.S. government received most of its revenues from tariffs.

The important thing to understand about an import tariff is who suffers and who gains. The government gains, because the tariff increases government revenues. Domestic producers gain, because the tariff affords them some protection against foreign competitors by increasing the cost of imported foreign goods. Consumers lose because they must pay more for certain imports. For example, in 2002 the U.S. government placed an ad valorem tariff of 8 percent to 30 percent on imports of foreign steel. The idea was to protect domestic steel producers from cheap imports of foreign steel. The effect, however, was to raise the price of steel products in the United States between 30 and 50 percent. A number of U.S. steel consumers, ranging from appliance makers to automobile companies, objected that the steel tariffs would raise their costs of production and make it more difficult for them to compete in the global marketplace. Whether the gains to the government and domestic producers exceed the loss to consumers depends on various factors such as the amount of the tariff, the importance of the imported good to domestic consumers, the number of jobs saved in the protected industry, and so on. In the steel case, many argued that the losses to steel consumers apparently outweighed the gains to steel producers. In November 2003, the World Trade Organization declared that the tariffs represented a violation of the WTO treaty, and the United States removed them in December of that year.

In general, two conclusions can be derived from economic analysis of the effect of import tariffs.[1] First, tariffs are pro-producer and anti-consumer. While they protect producers from foreign competitors, this restriction of supply also raises domestic prices. For example, a study by Japanese economists calculated that tariffs on imports of foodstuffs, cosmetics, and chemicals into Japan cost the average Japanese consumer about $890 per year in the form of higher prices.[2] Almost all studies find that import tariffs impose significant costs on domestic consumers in the form of higher prices.[3]

Second, import tariffs reduce the overall efficiency of the world economy. They reduce efficiency because a protective tariff encourages domestic firms to produce products at home that, in theory, could be produced more efficiently abroad. The consequence is an inefficient utilization of resources. For example, tariffs on the importation of rice into South Korea have led to an increase in rice production in that country; however, rice farming is an unproductive use of land in South Korea. It would make more sense for the

South Koreans to purchase their rice from lower-cost foreign producers and to utilize the land now employed in rice production in some other way, such as growing foodstuffs that cannot be produced more efficiently elsewhere or for residential and industrial purposes.

Sometimes tariffs are levied on exports of a product from a country. Export tariffs are far less common than import tariffs. In general, export tariffs have two objectives: first, to raise revenue for the government, and second, to reduce exports from a sector, often for political reasons. For example, in 2004 China imposed a tariff on textile exports. The primary objective was to moderate the growth in exports of textiles from China, thereby alleviating tensions with other trading partners.

SUBSIDIES

A **subsidy** is a government payment to a domestic producer. Subsidies take many forms, including cash grants, low-interest loans, tax breaks, and government equity participation in domestic firms. By lowering production costs, subsidies help domestic producers in two ways: (1) competing against foreign imports and (2) gaining export markets. According to the World Trade Organization, in the mid-2000s countries spent some $300 billion on subsidies, $250 billion of which was spent by 21 developed nations.[4] As noted in the opening case, between mid-2008 and mid-2009 some developed nations gave $45 billion in subsidies to their automobile makers. While the purpose of the subsidies was to help them survive a very difficult economic climate, one of the consequences was to give subsidized companies an unfair competitive advantage in the global auto industry.

> **Subsidy**
> Government financial assistance to a domestic producer.

Agriculture tends to be one of the largest beneficiaries of subsidies in most countries. In the mid-2000s, the European Union was paying about €44 billion annually ($55 billion) in farm subsidies. Not to be outdone, in May 2002 President George W. Bush signed into law a bill that contained subsidies of more than $180 billion for U.S. farmers spread out over 10 years. This was followed in 2007 by a farm bill that contained $286 billion in subsidies for the next 10 years. The Japanese also have a long history of supporting inefficient domestic producers with farm subsidies.

Nonagricultural subsidies are much lower, but they are still significant. For example, subsidies historically were given to Boeing and Airbus to help them lower the cost of developing new commercial jet aircraft. In Boeing's case, subsides came in the form of tax credits for R&D spending or Pentagon money that was used to develop military technology, which then was transferred to civil aviation projects. In the case of Airbus, subsidies took the form of government loans at below-market interest rates. See the Management Focus on page 238 about Boeing and Airbus.

The main gains from subsidies accrue to domestic producers, whose international competitiveness is increased as a result. Advocates of strategic trade policy (which, as you will recall from Chapter 5, is an outgrowth of the new trade theory) favor subsidies to help domestic firms achieve a dominant position in those industries in which economies of scale are important and the world market is not large enough to profitably support more than a few firms (aerospace and semiconductors are two such industries). According to this argument, subsidies can help a firm achieve a first-mover advantage in an emerging industry (just as U.S. government subsidies, in the form of substantial R&D grants, allegedly helped Boeing). If this is achieved, further gains to the domestic economy arise from the employment and tax revenues that a major global company can generate. However, government subsidies must be paid for, typically by taxing individuals and corporations.

Whether subsidies generate national benefits that exceed their national costs is debatable. In practice, many subsidies are not that successful at increasing the international competitiveness of domestic producers. Rather, they tend to protect the inefficient and promote excess production. One study estimated that if advanced

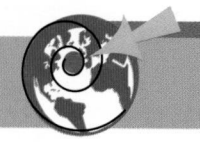

Country FOCUS

Globally Integrated Vietnam

Forty years ago, Vietnam was a different country. Caught in the "American War," Vietnam was struggling to survive. Ten years ago, Saigon's streets were filled with bicycles. Today, with real GDP growth expected to reach 6.4 percent in 2010 and 6.9 percent in 2011, Vietnamese traffic is congested with mopeds and scooters and the occasional Toyota. Vietnam has turned to capitalism and international trade to sustain economic growth. It is in the process of integrating into the global economy.

Over the past 20 years and since implementing *Moi Doi* reforms, the government of Vietnam has experienced much growth. The plan has been to emulate the growth of other Southeast Asian countries and improve living standards. Manufactured exports are replacing agriculture as the most important sector of the Vietnamese economy. Foreign investment in the textile, steel, and light manufacturing sectors has increased significantly.

Much of the change has been led by the *Viet Kieu,* the ethnic Vietnamese who have returned home after having grown up overseas. The *Viet Kieu* own and operate many of the local food and beverage chains that seem to be popping up all over Vietnam. The *Viet Kieu* are also serving as a bridge between the local Vietnamese and the rest of the world. Take, for example, Than Trong Phuc, the Vietnam country manager for U.S. chipmaker Intel. Phuc's life story is the stuff of corporate legend. As a youngster, he was one of the last people to climb aboard a helicopter before the fall of Saigon. He returned to Vietnam as the lead man for one of the biggest engines of global capitalism. That return has been a big success story. Since Phuc's return, Intel's chips have ended up in most computers found in Vietnam,

and he was instrumental in establishing one of the world's first citywide Wi-Fi networks.

Vietnam's integration into the global economy has continued by its inclusion to the World Trade Organization in 2007. Similarly, Vietnam and the European Union have begun bilateral negotiations in the hopes of establishing a free trade agreement. Not only does this represent an ongoing trend toward globalization but, more importantly, it represents for Vietnam an opportunity to tap into the $15 trillion European market—the world's largest economy. In courting the European market, Vietnam is hoping to attract manufacturing that would otherwise go to China or India. As a result, investor confidence is increasing. Vietnam's growth saw acceleration in the first half of 2010 as the economy went up 6.16 percent year-on-year, boosting investor confidence in the Southeast Asian $100 billion economy. Problems still remain, however, especially in the areas of basic infrastructure including electricity and roads. As International Strategic Analysis highlights in its country report, foreign investment in Vietnam's manufacturing sector will continue to drive high rates of industrial production growth. Given the potential for instability in other areas of Southeast Asia, especially Thailand, Vietnam has the potential, through continued economic integration and foreign investment, to become the region's next great industrial center.

Sources: International Strategic Analysis, Vietnam, accessed August 14, 2010, http://www.isa-world.com/isareports/; "Interview: Vietnam's Growth Accelerates, Reinforces Investor Confidence: Economists," *Xinhua News Agency — CEIS,* July 2, 2010; J. W. Miller and P. Barta, "EU, Vietnam Plan Trade Talks," *The Wall Street Journal,* March 3, 2010, http://online.wsj.com; J. Chaffin, "Europe to Enter Vietnam Talks." *Financial Times,* March 3, 2010; and Daniel Altman., "Managing Globalization: What Works in Vietnam," *International Herald Tribune,* June 20, 2007.

countries abandoned subsidies to farmers, global trade in agricultural products would be 50 percent higher and the world as a whole would be better off by $160 billion.[5] Another study estimated that removing all barriers to trade in agriculture (both subsidies and tariffs) would raise world income by $182 billion.[6] Some countries, however, are shifting from subsidies to foreign investment. In an effort to integrate itself into the global economy, Vietnam has changed its agricultural focus to seeking foreign investment for its manufacturing sector (see the Country Focus).

IMPORT QUOTAS AND VOLUNTARY EXPORT RESTRAINTS An

Import Quota
A direct restriction on the quantity of some good that may be imported into a country.

import quota is a direct restriction on the quantity of some good that may be imported into a country. The restriction is usually enforced by issuing import licenses to a group of individuals or firms. For example, the United States has a quota on cheese imports. The only firms allowed to import cheese are certain trading companies, each of which is allocated the right to import a maximum number of

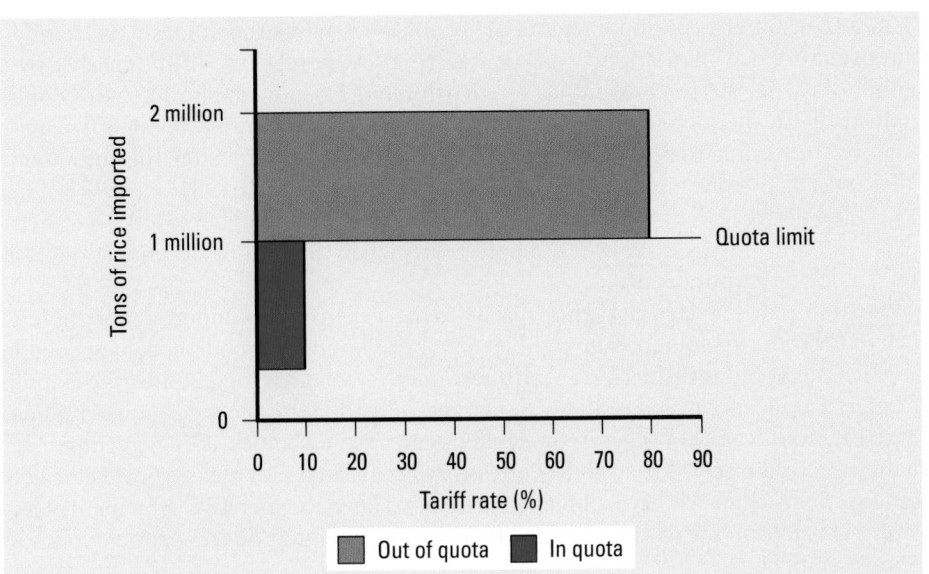

pounds of cheese each year. In some cases, the right to sell is given directly to the governments of exporting countries. Historically this is the case for sugar and textile imports in the United States. However, the international agreement governing the imposition of import quotas on textiles, the Multi-Fiber Agreement, expired in December 2004.

A common hybrid of a quota and a tariff is known as a tariff rate quota. Under a **tariff rate quota,** a lower tariff rate is applied to imports within the quota than those over the quota. For example, as illustrated in Figure 6.1, an ad valorem tariff rate of 10 percent might be levied on rice imports into South Korea of 1 million tons, after which an out-of-quota rate of 80 percent might be applied. Thus, South Korea might import 2 million tons of rice, 1 million at a 10 percent tariff rate and another 1 million at an 80 percent tariff. Tariff rate quotas are common in agriculture, where their goal is to limit imports over quota. For an example, see the Country Focus that looks at how Japan uses the combination of a tariff rate quota and subsidies to protect inefficient Japanese wheat farmers from foreign competition.

A variant on the import quota is the voluntary export restraint. A **voluntary export restraint (VER)** is a quota on trade imposed by the exporting country, typically at the request of the importing country's government. One of the most famous historical examples is the limitation on auto exports to the United States enforced by Japanese automobile producers in 1981. A response to direct pressure from the U.S. government, this VER limited Japanese imports to no more than 1.68 million vehicles per year. The agreement was revised in 1984 to allow 1.85 million Japanese vehicles per year. The agreement was allowed to lapse in 1985, but the Japanese government indicated its intentions at that time to continue to restrict exports to the United States to 1.85 million vehicles per year.[7] Foreign producers agree to VERs because they fear more damaging punitive tariffs or import quotas might follow if they do not. Agreeing to a VER is seen as a way to make the best of a bad situation by appeasing protectionist pressures in a country.

As with tariffs and subsidies, both import quotas and VERs benefit domestic producers by limiting import competition. As with all restrictions on trade, quotas do not

Tariff Rate Quota
The process of applying a lower tariff rate to imports within the quota than those over the quota.

Voluntary Export Restraint (VER)
A quota on trade imposed by the exporting country, typically at the request of the importing country's government.

benefit consumers. An import quota or VER always raises the domestic price of an imported good. When imports are limited to a low percentage of the market by a quota or VER, the price is bid up for that limited foreign supply. The automobile industry VER mentioned above increased the price of the limited supply of Japanese imports. According to a study by the U.S. Federal Trade Commission, the automobile VER cost U.S. consumers about $1 billion per year between 1981 and 1985. That $1 billion per year went to Japanese producers in the form of higher prices.[8] The extra profit that producers make when supply is artificially limited by an import quota is referred to as a **quota rent.**

Quota Rent
The extra profit producers make when supply is artificially limited by an import quota.

If a domestic industry lacks the capacity to meet demand, an import quota can raise prices for *both* the domestically produced and the imported good. This happened in the U.S. sugar industry, in which a tariff rate quota system has long limited the amount foreign producers can sell in the U.S. market. According to one study, import quotas have caused the price of sugar in the United States to be as much as 40 percent greater than the world price.[9] These higher prices have translated into greater profits for U.S. sugar producers, which have lobbied politicians to keep the lucrative agreement. They argue U.S. jobs in the sugar industry will be lost to foreign producers if the quota system is scrapped.

Local Content Requirement
A requirement that some specific fraction of a good be produced domestically.

LOCAL CONTENT REQUIREMENTS

A **local content requirement** is a requirement that some specific fraction of a good be produced domestically. The requirement can be expressed either in physical terms (e.g., 75 percent of component parts for this product must be produced locally) or in value terms (e.g., 75 percent of the value of this product must be produced locally). Local content regulations have been widely used by developing countries to shift their manufacturing base from the simple assembly of products whose parts are manufactured elsewhere into the local manufacture of component parts. They have also been used in developed countries to try to protect local jobs and industry from foreign competition. For example, a little-known law in the United States, the Buy America Act, specifies that government agencies must give preference to American products when putting contracts for equipment out to bid unless the foreign products have a significant price advantage. The law specifies a product as "American" if 51 percent of the materials by value are produced domestically. This amounts to a local content requirement. If a foreign company, or an American one for that matter, wishes to win a contract from a U.S. government agency to provide some equipment, it must ensure that at least 51 percent of the product by value is manufactured in the United States.

Local content regulations provide protection for a domestic producer of parts in the same way an import quota does: by limiting foreign competition. The aggregate economic effects are also the same; domestic producers benefit, but the restrictions on imports raise the prices of imported components. In turn, higher prices for imported components are passed on to consumers of the final product in the form of higher final prices. So as with all trade policies, local content regulations tend to benefit producers and not consumers.

Administrative Trade Policies
Bureaucratic rules designed to make it difficult for imports to enter a country.

ADMINISTRATIVE POLICIES

In addition to the formal instruments of trade policy, governments of all types sometimes use informal or administrative policies to restrict imports and boost exports. **Administrative trade policies** are bureaucratic rules designed to make it difficult for imports to enter a country. It has been argued that the Japanese are the masters of this trade barrier. In recent decades,

Japan's formal tariff and nontariff barriers have been among the lowest in the world. However, critics charge that the country's informal administrative barriers to imports more than compensate for this. For example, at one point the Netherlands exported tulip bulbs to almost every country in the world except Japan. In Japan, customs inspectors insisted on checking every tulip bulb by cutting it vertically down the middle, and even Japanese ingenuity could not put them back together. Federal Express also initially had a tough time expanding its global express shipping services into Japan because Japanese customs inspectors insist on opening a large proportion of express packages to check for pornography, a process that delayed an "express" package for days. Japan is not the only country that engages in such policies. France once required that all imported videotape recorders arrive through a small customs entry point that was both remote and poorly staffed. The resulting delays kept Japanese VCRs out of the French market until a VER agreement was negotiated.[10] As with all instruments of trade policy, administrative instruments benefit producers and hurt consumers, who are denied access to possibly superior foreign products.

ANTIDUMPING POLICIES   In the context of international trade, **dumping** is variously defined as selling goods in a foreign market at below their costs of production or as selling goods in a foreign market at below their "fair" market value. There is a difference between these two definitions; the fair market value of a good is normally judged to be greater than the costs of producing that good because the former includes a "fair" profit margin. Dumping is viewed as a method by which firms unload excess production in foreign markets. Some dumping may be the result of predatory behavior, with producers using substantial profits from their home markets to subsidize prices in a foreign market with a view to driving indigenous competitors out of that market. Once this has been achieved, so the argument goes, the predatory firm can raise prices and earn substantial profits.

An alleged example of dumping occurred in 1997, when two South Korean manufacturers of semiconductors, LG Semicon and Hyundai Electronics, were accused of selling dynamic random access memory chips (DRAMs) in the U.S. market at below their costs of production. This action occurred in the middle of a worldwide glut of chip-making capacity. It was alleged that the firms were trying to unload their excess production in the United States.

Antidumping policies are designed to punish foreign firms that engage in dumping. The ultimate objective is to protect domestic producers from unfair foreign competition. Although antidumping policies vary somewhat from country to country, the majority are similar to those used in the United States. If a domestic producer believes that a foreign firm is dumping production in the U.S. market, it can file a petition with two government agencies, the Commerce Department and the International Trade Commission. In the Korean DRAM case, Micron Technology, a U.S. manufacturer of DRAMs, filed the petition. The government agencies then investigate the complaint. If a complaint has merit, the Commerce Department may impose an antidumping duty on the offending foreign imports (antidumping duties are often called **countervailing duties**). These duties, which represent a special tariff, can be fairly substantial and stay in place for up to five years. For example, after reviewing Micron's complaint, the Commerce Department imposed 9 percent and 4 percent countervailing duties on LG Semicon and Hyundai DRAM chips, respectively.

Dumping
selling goods in a foreign market at below their costs of production or below their "fair" market value.

Antidumping Policies
Policies designed to punish foreign firms that engage in dumping and thus protect domestic producers from unfair foreign competition.

Countervailing Duties
Antidumping duties.

"The Subsidized Skies"

In the highly competitive $3 trillion global commercial airplane-manufacturing sector, governmental subsidies play a large role. For example, the World Trade Organization ruled that four European governments had provided illegal subsidies over the past 40 years for every jet Airbus has launched to the detriment of Boeing. The ruling claims that Airbus benefited from more than $20 billion in illegal subsidies. After years of complaining, Boeing appears to have won, but the dispute is far from over. When Airbus and Boeing were the only two real competitors in the airplane-manufacturing sector, the issues were fairly clear. However, as emerging countries with their own airline-manufacturing companies enter the competitive field, the stakes are beginning to change. Sometimes the subsidy takes the form of loan guarantees by means of export-credit financing. Export credits have risen dramatically over the past years and have provided a new form of finance for start-up airplane manufacturers.

An export credit is mainly loan guarantees offered by a government to support foreign buyers of the country's products or services. The export credit is used in a wide variety of sectors. For example, India's central bank extended its 2 percent subsidy scheme for export credit to now include credit to exporters of leather and leather products, jute manufacturing, engineering goods, and textiles.

In the airplane-manufacturing sector, governments from most countries that produced jetliners in 2007 had agreed on a set of terms for export-credit financing, called the Aviation Sector Understanding (ASU). The ASU is unclear, however, as to domestic financing. Such financing last year was responsible for approximately $20 billion in jetliner sales worldwide, including some 30 percent of Airbus and Boeing deliveries. These loan guarantees played a crucial role in maintaining profitability at near-record levels, despite the global economic crisis.

Under such terms, the government promises that an airline will repay a loan to buy planes. If the carrier fails to pay, the export-credit agency covers the loan and repossesses the plane. As may be expected, such guarantees can lower the cost of an airplane by several million dollars compared with those financed by commercial lenders. These improved funding terms also allow airlines to buy more planes and expand more quickly. Nowhere is this more relevant than in airplane-producing countries such as Europe, the United States, Brazil, Canada, Japan, United Arab Emirates (UAE), and others.

Originally, the export credit was established to assist weak carriers in emerging markets. Developed countries' airline carriers could arrange commercial loans at rates below the cost of government-backed financing. Recently, however, wealthy countries, such as the UAE, Norway, and Japan, have used the export credit to the competitive advantage of their airplane makers. Europe and the United States argue they are disadvantaged. Airbus and Boeing specifically cannot "export fund" in their home-country sales. The issue is further aggravated by the global economic crisis and limited commercial financing programs. The secret to remaining competitive in the capital-intensive and risky business of commercial aircraft development is to know how to tap into governmental funds in compliance with international trade agreements.

Sources: D. Michaels and M. Trottman, "World News: US Airlines Will Oppose Export Credit Expansion," *The Wall Street Journal Europe,* August 13, 2010; "India to Extend Export Credit Subsidy to More Sectors—Central Bank," *Dow Jones Business News,* August 10, 2010; L. Blumenthal, "Illegal Airbus Subsidies Hurt U.S. Airline Industry, WTO Says." *McClatchy—Tribune News Service,* June 30, 2010; and M. Unnikrishnan, "Who Is the Real Winner in the WTO Subsidy Cases?" *Aviation Week & Space Technology,* 172.24 (2010), p. 14.

The Case for Government Intervention

LEARNING OBJECTIVE 2
Understand why governments sometimes intervene in international trade.

Now that we have reviewed the various instruments of trade policy that governments can use, it is time to look at the case for government intervention in international trade. Arguments for government intervention take two paths: political and economic. Political arguments for intervention are concerned with protecting the interests of certain groups within a nation (normally producers), often at the expense of other groups (normally consumers), or with achieving some political objective that lies outside the sphere of economic relationships, such as protecting the environment or human rights. Economic arguments for intervention are typically concerned with boosting the overall wealth of a nation (to the benefit of all, both producers and consumers).

POLITICAL ARGUMENTS FOR INTERVENTION

Political arguments for government intervention cover a range of issues, including preserving jobs, protecting industries deemed important for national security, retaliating against unfair foreign competition, protecting consumers from "dangerous" products, furthering the goals of foreign policy, and advancing the human rights of individuals in exporting countries.

Protecting Jobs and Industries

Perhaps the most common political argument for government intervention is that it is necessary for protecting jobs and industries from unfair foreign competition. The tariffs placed on imports of foreign steel by President George W. Bush in 2002 were designed to do this. (Many steel producers were located in states that Bush needed to win reelection in 2004.) A political motive also underlay establishment of the Common Agricultural Policy (CAP) by the European Union. The CAP was designed to protect the jobs of Europe's politically powerful farmers by restricting imports and guaranteeing prices. However, the higher prices that resulted from the CAP have cost Europe's consumers dearly. This is true of many attempts to protect jobs and industries through government intervention. For example, the imposition of steel tariffs in 2002 raised steel prices for American consumers, such as automobile companies, making them less competitive in the global marketplace.

National Security

Countries sometimes argue that it is necessary to protect certain industries because they are important for national security. Defense-related industries often get this kind of attention (e.g., aerospace, advanced electronics, semiconductors, etc.). Although not as common as it used to be, this argument is still made. Those in favor of protecting the U.S. semiconductor industry from foreign competition, for example, argue that semiconductors are now such important components of defense products that it would be dangerous to rely primarily on foreign producers for them. In 1986, this argument helped persuade the federal government to support Sematech, a consortium of 14 U.S. semiconductor companies that accounted for 90 percent of the U.S. industry's revenues. Sematech's mission was to conduct joint research into manufacturing techniques that can be parceled out to members. The government saw the venture as so critical that Sematech was specially protected from antitrust laws. Initially, the U.S. government provided Sematech with $100 million per year in subsidies. By the mid-1990s, however, the U.S. semiconductor industry had regained its leading market position, largely through the personal computer boom and demand for microprocessor chips made by Intel. In 1994, the consortium's board voted to seek an end to federal funding, and since 1996 the consortium has been funded entirely by private money.[11]

Retaliation

Some argue that governments should use the threat to intervene in trade policy as a bargaining tool to help open foreign markets and force trading partners to "play by the rules of the game." The U.S. government has used the threat of punitive trade sanctions to try to get the Chinese government to enforce its intellectual property laws. Lax enforcement of these laws had given rise to massive copyright infringements in China that had been costing U.S. companies such as Microsoft hundreds of millions of dollars per year in lost sales revenues. After the United States threatened to impose 100 percent tariffs on a range of Chinese imports, and after harsh words between officials from the two countries, the Chinese agreed to tighter enforcement of intellectual property regulations.[12]

If it works, such a politically motivated rationale for government intervention may liberalize trade and bring with it resulting economic gains. It is a risky strategy, however. A country that is being pressured may not back down and instead may respond to the imposition of punitive tariffs by raising trade barriers of its own. This is exactly what the Chinese government threatened to do when pressured by the United States, although it ultimately did back down. If a government does not back down, however, the results could be higher trade barriers all around and an economic loss to all involved.

Protecting Consumers   Many governments have long had regulations to protect consumers from unsafe products. The indirect effect of such regulations often is to limit or ban the importation of such products. For example, in 2003 several countries, including Japan and South Korea, decided to ban imports of American beef after a single case of mad cow disease was found in Washington State. The ban was motivated to protect consumers from what was seen to be an unsafe product. Together, Japan and South Korea accounted for about $2 billion of U.S. beef sales, so the ban had a significant impact on U.S. beef producers. After two years, both countries lifted the ban, although they placed stringent requirements on U.S. beef imports to reduce the risk of importing beef that might be tainted by mad cow disease (for example, Japan required that all beef must come from cattle under 21 months of age).[13]

The accompanying Country Focus describes how the European Union banned the sale and importation of hormone-treated beef. The ban was motivated by a desire to protect European consumers from the possible health consequences of eating meat from animals treated with growth hormones. The conflict over the importation of hormone-treated beef into the EU may prove to be a taste of things to come. In addition to the use of hormones to promote animal growth and meat production, biotechnology has made it possible to genetically alter many crops so that they resist common herbicides, produce proteins that are natural insecticides, grow dramatically improved yields, or withstand inclement weather conditions. A new breed of genetically modified tomatoes has an antifreeze gene inserted into its genome and

A genetically engineered cotton seed that protects against three common insects has been met with resistance in Europe due to a fear that these genetically altered seeds could potentially be harmful to humans.

Biotechnology and Trade

In the 1970s, scientists discovered how to synthesize certain hormones and use them to accelerate the growth rate of livestock animals, reduce the fat content of meat, and increase milk production. Bovine somatotropin (BST), a growth hormone produced by cattle, was first synthesized by the biotechnology firm Genentech. Injections of BST could be used to supplement an animal's own hormone production and increase its growth rate. These hormones soon became popular among farmers, who found that they could cut costs and help satisfy consumer demands for leaner meat. Although these hormones occurred naturally in animals, consumer groups in several countries soon raised concerns about the practice. They argued that the use of hormone supplements was unnatural and that the health consequences of consuming hormone-treated meat were unknown but might include hormonal irregularities and cancer.

The European Union responded to these concerns in 1989 by banning the use of growth-promoting hormones in the production of livestock and the importation of hormone-treated meat. The ban was controversial because a reasonable consensus existed among scientists that the hormones posed no health risk. Although the EU banned hormone-treated meat, many other countries did not, including big meat-producing countries such as Australia, Canada, New Zealand, and the United States. The use of hormones soon became widespread in these countries. According to trade officials outside the EU, the European ban constituted an unfair restraint on trade. As a result of this ban, exports of meat to the EU fell. For example, U.S. red meat exports to the EU declined from $231 million in 1988 to $98 million in 1994. The complaints of meat exporters were bolstered in 1995 when Codex Alimentarius, the international food standards body of the UN's Food and Agriculture Organization and the World Health Organization, approved the use of growth hormones. In making this decision, Codex reviewed the scientific literature and found no evidence of a link between the consumption of hormone-treated meat and human health problems, such as cancer.

Fortified by such decisions, in 1995 the United States pressed the EU to drop the import ban on hormone-treated beef. The EU refused, citing "consumer concerns about food safety." In response, both Canada and the United States independently filed formal complaints with the World Trade Organization. The United States was joined in its complaint by a number of other countries, including Australia and New Zealand. The WTO created a trade panel of three independent experts. After reviewing evidence and hearing from a range of experts and representatives of both parties, the panel in May 1997 ruled that the EU ban on hormone-treated beef was illegal because it had no scientific justification. The EU immediately indicated it would appeal the finding to the WTO court of appeals. The WTO court heard the appeal in November 1997 and in February 1998 agreed with the findings of the trade panel that the EU had not presented any scientific evidence to justify the hormone ban.

This ruling left the EU in a difficult position. Legally, the EU had to lift the ban or face punitive sanctions, but the ban had wide public support in Europe. The EU feared that lifting the ban could produce a consumer backlash. Instead the EU did nothing, so in February 1999 the United States asked the WTO for permission to impose punitive sanctions on the EU. The WTO responded by allowing the United States to impose punitive tariffs valued at $120 million on EU exports to the United States. The EU decided to accept these tariffs rather than lift the ban on hormone-treated beef, and as of 2010, the ban and punitive tariffs were still in place. To offset the ban, the United States has begun to focus on China and India as new growth markets for genetically modified corn and hormone-treated beef.

Sources: S. Kilman, "U.S. to Adopt New Export Strategy," *The Wall Street Journal,* March 5, 2010, http://online.wsj.com; C. Southey, "Hormones Fuel a Meaty EU Row," *Financial Times,* September 7, 1995, p. 2; E. L. Andrews, "In Victory for U.S., European Ban on Treated Beef Is Ruled Illegal," *The New York Times,* May 9, 1997, p. A1; F. Williams and G. de Jonquieres, "WTO's Beef Rulings Give Europe Food for Thought," *Financial Times,* February 13, 1998, p. 5; R. Baily, "Food and Trade: EU Fearmongers' Lethal Harvest," *Los Angeles Times,* August 18, 2002, p. M3; "The US-EU Dispute over Hormone-Treated Beef," *The Kiplinger Agricultural Letter,* January 10, 2003; and Scott Miller, "EU Trade Sanctions Have Duel Edge," *The Wall Street Journal,* February 26, 2004, p. A3.

can thus be grown in colder climates than hitherto possible. Another example is a genetically engineered cotton seed produced by Monsanto. The seed has been engineered to express a protein that protects against three common insect pests: the cotton bollworm, tobacco budworm, and pink bollworm. Use of this seed reduces or eliminates the need for traditional pesticide applications for these pests.

As enticing as such innovations sound, they have met with intense resistance from consumer groups, particularly in Europe. The fear is that the widespread use of genetically altered seed corn could have unanticipated and harmful effects on human health and may result in "genetic pollution." (An example of genetic pollution would be when the widespread use of crops that produce natural pesticides stimulates the evolution of "superbugs" that are resistant to those pesticides.) Such concerns have led Austria and Luxembourg to outlaw the importation, sale, or use of genetically altered organisms. Sentiment against genetically altered organisms also runs strong in several other European countries, most notably Germany and Switzerland. It seems likely, therefore, that the World Trade Organization will be drawn into the conflict between those that want to expand the global market for genetically altered organisms, such as Monsanto, and those that want to limit it, such as Austria and Luxembourg.[14]

Furthering Foreign Policy Objectives

Governments sometimes use trade policy to support their foreign policy objectives.[15] A government may grant preferential trade terms to a country with which it wants to build strong relations. Trade policy has also been used several times to pressure or punish "rogue states" that do not abide by international law or norms. Iraq labored under extensive trade sanctions after the UN coalition defeated the country in the 1991 Gulf War until the 2003 invasion of Iraq by U.S.-led forces. The theory is that such pressure might persuade the rogue state to mend its ways, or it might hasten a change of government. In the case of Iraq, the sanctions were seen as a way of forcing that country to comply with several UN resolutions. The United States has maintained long-running trade sanctions against Cuba. Their principal function is to impoverish Cuba in the hope that the resulting economic hardship will lead to the downfall of Cuba's Communist government and its replacement with a more democratically inclined (and pro-U.S.) regime. The United States also has had trade sanctions in place against Libya and Iran, both of which it accuses of supporting terrorist action against U.S. interests and building weapons of mass destruction. In late 2003, the sanctions against Libya seemed to yield some returns when that country announced it would terminate a program to build nuclear weapons, and the U.S. government responded by relaxing those sanctions.

Other countries can undermine unilateral trade sanctions. The U.S. sanctions against Cuba, for example, have not stopped other Western countries from trading with Cuba. The U.S. sanctions have done little more than help create a vacuum into which other trading nations, such as Canada and Germany, have stepped. In an attempt to halt this and further tighten the screws on Cuba, in 1996 the U.S. Congress passed the **Helms-Burton Act.** This act allows Americans to sue foreign firms that use property in Cuba confiscated from them after the 1959 revolution. Later in 1996, Congress passed a similar law, the **D'Amato Act,** aimed at Libya and Iran.

The passage of Helms-Burton elicited protests from America's trading partners, including the European Union, Canada, and Mexico, all of which claim the law violates their sovereignty and is illegal under World Trade Organization rules. For example, Canadian companies that have been doing business in Cuba for years see no reason they should suddenly be sued in U.S. courts when Canada does not restrict trade with Cuba. They are not violating Canadian law, and they are not U.S. companies, so why should they be subject to U.S. law? Despite such protests, the law is still on the books in the United States, although the U.S. government has not enforced this act—probably because it is unenforceable.

Protecting Human Rights

Protecting and promoting human rights in other countries is an important element of foreign policy for many democracies. Governments sometimes use trade policy to try to improve the human rights policies of trading partners. For years, the most obvious example of this was the annual debate in the United States over whether to grant most favored nation (MFN) status to China.

Helms-Burton Act
Act passed in 1996 that allowed Americans to sue foreign firms that use Cuban property confiscated from them after the 1959 revolution.

D'Amato Act
Act passed in 1996, similar to the Helms-Burton Act, aimed at Libya and Iran.

MFN status allows countries to export goods to the United States under favorable terms. Under MFN rules, the average tariff on Chinese goods imported into the United States was 8 percent. If China's MFN status were rescinded, tariffs could have risen to about 40 percent. Trading partners who are signatories of the World Trade Organization, as most are, automatically receive MFN status. However, China did not join the WTO until 2001, so historically the decision of whether to grant MFN status to China was a real one. The decision was made more difficult by the perception that China had a poor human rights record. As indications of the country's disregard for human rights, critics of China often point to the 1989 Tiananmen Square massacre, China's continuing subjugation of Tibet (which China occupied

Beijing's Tiananmen Square, a tangible reminder of China's history of human rights abuses.

in the 1950s), and the squashing of political dissent in China.[16] These critics argue that it was wrong for the United States to grant MFN status to China, and that instead, the United States should withhold MFN status until China showed measurable improvement in its human rights record. The critics argue that trade policy should be used as a political weapon to force China to change its internal policies toward human rights.

Others contend that limiting trade with such countries would make matters worse, not better. They argue that the best way to change the internal human rights stance of a country is to engage it through international trade. At its core, the argument is simple: Growing bilateral trade raises the income levels of both countries, and as a state becomes richer, its people begin to demand, and generally receive, better treatment with regard to their human rights. This is a variant of the argument in Chapter 2 that economic progress begets political progress (if political progress is measured by the adoption of a democratic government that respects human rights). This argument ultimately won the day in 1999 when the Clinton administration blessed China's application to join the WTO and announced that trade and human rights issues should be decoupled.

Protecting the Environment   Protecting the environment has become an important policy objective of many nations. Increasingly, environmental interest groups such as Friends of the Earth and the Sierra Club have been pressuring governments to regulate international trade in a way the protects the environment. The growing concern over global warming has added an important dimension to this debate.

One argument frequently made by environmental organizations is that there is a strong relationship between income levels and environmental pollution and degradation (i.e., industrial development leads to more pollution). Thus, to the extent that international trade leads to higher income levels, it can also be expected to lead to a decline in environmental quality. Organizations such as the Sierra Club argue that as a consequence, strong environmental safeguards need to be part of any trade agreements, and governments should be allowed to restrict trade if doing so benefits the environment.

As noted in Chapter 1, the empirical evidence suggests the relationship between income levels and pollution is not a linear one—rather it is an inverted U-shaped relationship (see Figure 1.5).[17] To begin with, as countries start to climb the ladder of economic progress, pollution levels do increase, but past some threshold, they start to decline. The reason being that as societies get richer, citizens lobby for environmental protections, and governments tend to respond. We can see this process starting to unfold today in China. China has had an awful reputation for pollution, but in the last few years the Chinese government has been working hard to improve the air quality in its major cities (although the country still has a considerable way to go). In developed nations such as the United States and United Kingdom, the air is much cleaner that it was half a century ago. This data suggests that international trade, and the growth that results from it, may not be damaging to the environment.

There is a very important exception to these trends, however, and that is emissions of carbon dioxide. Carbon dioxide emissions do rise with income levels. Thus, the country with the highest income per capita, the United States, also produces the greatest carbon dioxide emissions per capita. The reason is that carbon dioxide emissions are a by-product of energy use (i.e., oil, gas, or coal burning). Richer societies are more energy intensive, and to the extent that they use hydrocarbons to produce that energy, this leads to higher carbon dioxide emissions.

Carbon dioxide is the greenhouse gas at the center of concerns over global warming. These concerns can be stated simply.[18] First, the burning of fossil fuels to produce energy also releases carbon dioxide into the atmosphere (and atmospheric carbon dioxide concentrations have steadily increased since preindustrial times). Second, carbon dioxide absorbs heat radiated from the earth, warming the atmosphere. Third, as a consequence, average global temperatures will increase. Indeed, estimates suggest that average global temperatures increased by 0.7 degree centigrade during the past century, and they are forecasted to rise by between 1.1 and 6.4 degrees centigrade this century.[19] Fourth, as global temperatures increase, there will be environmental dislocation, ice caps will melt and sea levels will rise, flooding low-lying costal areas; weather patterns will change; the frequency of violent storms will increase; tropical diseases (such as malaria) will move northward; species will go extinct; and so on.

Of course, the global climate varies naturally due too, for example, changes in solar radiation connected with the well-known sun spot cycle, volcanic activity (which can inject large amounts of sulfur dioxide particles into the atmosphere, temporarily cooling it), changes in the circulation of ocean currents, and long-term changes in the orbit of the earth and the tilt of its axis. Human-induced global warming is overlaid on these natural variations. Thus, a natural cooling trend might be moderated by greater atmospheric carbon dioxide concentrations, and a natural warming trend exacerbated by them.

Although there is debate over the precise relationship between carbon dioxide concentrations and the extent of future global warming, the vast majority of climate scientists have concluded that unless we take rapid action, we face a rate of warming that in unprecedented during the history of our civilization and may cause major environmental dislocation.[20] Given this, they advocate restricting greenhouse gas emissions, particularly carbon dioxide. The first international agreement to limit global warming, the Kyoto Protocol, was signed in 1997, although its impact was reduced by the failure of two of the world's largest producers of carbon dioxide, the United States and China, to sign. A second international agreement was reached in Copenhagen in 2009, this time with the participation of the United States and China.

What does this have to do with international trade? So far, there has been little direct connection between the global warming debate and international trade. However, looking forward, adherence to targets regarding carbon emissions might start to factor into trade agreements. Specifically, if countries do not meet their targets for reducing carbon emissions specified in international treaties, they may find themselves the targets of retaliatory action. The EU, for example, might respond to the failure of the United States to meet its treaty commitments by placing a carbon tariff on the import of certain goods from the United States. Ten years ago this was a remote possibility. Ten years from now it may be a significant factor in the international trade environment.

A second argument made with regard to environmental regulations is that, to save money, corporations will move production to countries where environmental regulations are lax. Thus, for example, if tight environmental standards in the United States raise costs, a manufacturing firm might move production to a pollution haven such as Mexico where environmental standards are weaker. To protect against this possibility, environmental organizations argue that governments should place tariffs or other limitations on goods imported from countries where environmental regulations are lax.

Economists have studied this issue but have found little evidence that firms do move production in response to changes in pollution regulations.[21] Their findings suggest that pollution abatement costs are a relatively small component of the cost structure of most enterprises, and that other factors, such as labor productivity, access to technological know-how, and transportation costs are far more important in determining location decisions. It is also worth noting that migrating to a pollution haven would violate the ethical principles of many (but not all) organizations (see Chapter 4 for details).

In sum, although environmental concerns have not figured significantly in trade treaties to date, there is a good chance that they will do so in the future, particularly with regard to the emission of carbon dioxide and other greenhouse gases.

ECONOMIC ARGUMENTS FOR INTERVENTION   With the development of the new trade theory and strategic trade policy (see Chapter 5), the economic arguments for government intervention have undergone a renaissance in recent years. Until the early 1980s, most economists saw little benefit in government intervention and strongly advocated a free trade policy. This position has changed at the margins with the development of strategic trade policy, although as we will see in the next section, there are still strong economic arguments for sticking to a free trade stance.

The Infant Industry Argument

The **infant industry argument** is by far the oldest economic argument for government intervention. Alexander Hamilton proposed it in 1792. According to this argument, many developing countries have a potential comparative advantage in manufacturing, but new manufacturing industries cannot initially compete with established industries in developed countries. To allow manufacturing to get a toehold, the argument is that governments should temporarily support new industries (with tariffs, import quotas, and subsidies) until they have grown strong enough to meet international competition.

This argument has had substantial appeal for the governments of developing nations during the past 50 years, and the GATT has recognized the infant industry argument as a legitimate reason for protectionism. Nevertheless, many economists remain critical of this argument for two main reasons. First, protection of manufacturing from foreign competition does no good unless the protection helps make the industry efficient. In case after case, however, protection seems to have done little more than foster the development of inefficient industries that have little hope of ever competing in the world market. Brazil, for example, built the world's tenth-largest auto industry behind tariff barriers and quotas. Once those barriers were removed in the late 1980s, however, foreign imports soared, and the industry was forced to face up to the fact that after 30 years of protection, the Brazilian industry was one of the world's most inefficient.[22]

Second, the infant industry argument relies on an assumption that firms are unable to make efficient long-term investments by borrowing money from the domestic or international capital market. Consequently, governments have been required to

Infant Industry Argument
New industries in developing countries must be temporarily protected from international competition to help them reach a position where they can compete on world markets with the firms of developed nations.

subsidize long-term investments. Given the development of global capital markets over the past 20 years, this assumption no longer looks as valid as it once did. Today, if a developing country has a potential comparative advantage in a manufacturing industry, firms in that country should be able to borrow money from the capital markets to finance the required investments. Given financial support, firms based in countries with a potential comparative advantage have an incentive to endure the necessary initial losses in order to make long-run gains without requiring government protection. Many Taiwanese and South Korean firms did this in industries such as textiles, semiconductors, machine tools, steel, and shipping. Thus, given efficient global capital markets, the only industries that would require government protection would be those that are not worthwhile.

Strategic Trade Policy Some new trade theorists have proposed the strategic trade policy argument.[23] We reviewed the basic argument in Chapter 5 when we considered the new trade theory. The new trade theory argues that in industries in which the existence of substantial economies of scale implies that the world market will profitably support only a few firms, countries may predominate in the export of certain products simply because they had firms that were able to capture first-mover advantages. The long-term dominance of Boeing in the commercial aircraft industry has been attributed to such factors.

Strategic Trade Policy
Government policy aimed at improving the competitive position of a domestic industry or domestic firm in the world market.

The **strategic trade policy** argument has two components. First, it is argued that by appropriate actions, a government can help raise national income if it can somehow ensure that the firm or firms that gain first-mover advantages in an industry are domestic rather than foreign enterprises. Thus, according to the strategic trade policy argument, a government should use subsidies to support promising firms that are active in newly emerging industries. Advocates of this argument point out that the substantial R&D grants that the U.S. government gave Boeing in the 1950s and 1960s probably helped tilt the field of competition in the newly emerging market for passenger jets in Boeing's favor. (Boeing's first commercial jet airliner, the 707, was derived from a military plane.) Similar arguments have been made with regard to Japan's dominance in the production of liquid crystal display screens (used in laptop computers). Although these screens were invented in the United States, the Japanese government, in cooperation with major electronics companies, targeted this industry for research support in the late 1970s and early 1980s. The result was that Japanese firms, not U.S. firms, subsequently captured first-mover advantages in this market.

The second component of the strategic trade policy argument is that it might pay a government to intervene in an industry by helping domestic firms overcome the barriers to entry created by foreign firms that have already reaped first-mover advantages. This argument underlies government support of Airbus, Boeing's major competitor. Formed in 1966 as a consortium of four companies from Great Britain, France, Germany, and Spain, Airbus had less than 5 percent of the world commercial aircraft market when it began production in the mid-1970s. By 2009, it had increased its share to 45 percent, threatening Boeing's long-term dominance of the market. How did Airbus achieve this? According to the U.S. government, the answer is a $15 billion subsidy from the governments of Great Britain, France, Germany, and Spain.[24] Without this subsidy, Airbus would never have been able to break into the world market.

If these arguments are correct, they support a rationale for government intervention in international trade. Governments should target technologies that may be important in the future and use subsidies to support development work aimed at commercializing those technologies. Furthermore, government should provide export subsidies until the domestic firms have established first-mover advantages in the world market. Government support may also be justified if it can help domestic firms overcome the first-mover advantages enjoyed by foreign competitors and emerge as viable competitors in the world market (as in the Airbus and semiconductor examples). In this case, a combination of home-market protection and export-promoting subsidies may be needed.

The Revised Case for Free Trade

LEARNING OBJECTIVE 3
Summarize and explain the arguments against strategic trade policy.

The strategic trade policy arguments of the new trade theorists suggest an economic justification for government intervention in international trade. This justification challenges the rationale for unrestricted free trade found in the work of classic trade theorists such as Adam Smith and David Ricardo. In response to this challenge to economic orthodoxy, a number of economists—including some of those responsible for the development of the new trade theory, such as Paul Krugman—point out that although strategic trade policy looks appealing in theory, in practice it may be unworkable. This response to the strategic trade policy argument constitutes the revised case for free trade.[25]

RETALIATION AND TRADE WAR Krugman argues that a strategic trade policy aimed at establishing domestic firms in a dominant position in a global industry is a beggar-thy-neighbor policy that boosts national income at the expense of other countries. A country that attempts to use such policies will probably provoke retaliation. In many cases, the resulting trade war between two or more interventionist governments will leave all countries involved worse off than if a hands-off approach had been adopted in the first place. If the U.S. government were to respond to the Airbus subsidy by increasing its own subsidies to Boeing, for example, the result might be that the subsidies would cancel each other out. In the process, both European and U.S. taxpayers would end up supporting an expensive and pointless trade war, and both Europe and the United States would be worse off.

Krugman may be right about the danger of a strategic trade policy leading to a trade war. The problem, however, is how to respond when one's competitors are already being supported by government subsidies; that is, how should Boeing and the United States respond to the subsidization of Airbus? According to Krugman, the answer is probably not to engage in retaliatory action but to help establish rules of the game that minimize the use of trade-distorting subsidies. This is what the World Trade Organization seeks to do.

DOMESTIC POLICIES Governments do not always act in the national interest when they intervene in the economy; politically important interest groups often influence them. The European Union's support for the Common Agricultural Policy (CAP), which arose because of the political power of French and German farmers, is an example. The CAP benefited inefficient farmers and the politicians who relied on the farm vote, but not consumers in the EU, who end up paying more for their foodstuffs. Thus, a further reason for not embracing strategic trade policy, according to Krugman, is that such a policy is almost certain to be captured by special-interest groups within the economy, who will distort it to their own ends. Krugman concludes that in the United States,

> To ask the Commerce Department to ignore special-interest politics while formulating detailed policy for many industries is not realistic: To establish a blanket policy of free trade, with exceptions granted only under extreme pressure, may not be the optimal policy according to the theory but may be the best policy that the country is likely to get.[26]

Development of the World Trading System

Strong economic arguments support unrestricted free trade. While many governments have recognized the value of these arguments, they have been unwilling to unilaterally lower their trade barriers for fear that other nations might not follow suit. Consider the problem that two neighboring countries, say, Brazil and Argentina, face when deciding whether to lower trade barriers between them. In principle, the government of Brazil might favor lowering trade barriers, but it might be unwilling to do so for fear that Argentina will not do the same. Instead, the government might fear that the Argentineans will take advantage of Brazil's low barriers to enter the Brazilian market, while at the same time continuing to shut Brazilian products out of their market through high trade barriers. The Argentinean government might believe that it faces the same dilemma. The essence of the problem is a lack of trust. Both governments recognize that their respective nations will benefit from lower trade barriers between them, but neither government is willing to lower barriers for fear that the other might not follow.[27]

Such a deadlock can be resolved if both countries negotiate a set of rules to govern cross-border trade and lower trade barriers. But who is to monitor the governments to make sure they are playing by the trade rules? And who is to impose sanctions on a government that cheats? Both governments could set up an independent body to act as a referee. This referee could monitor trade between the countries, make sure that no side cheats, and impose sanctions on a country if it does cheat in the trade game.

While it might sound unlikely that any government would compromise its national sovereignty by submitting to such an arrangement, since World War II an international trading framework has evolved that has exactly these features. For its first 50 years, this framework was known as the General Agreement on Tariffs and Trade. Since 1995, it has been known as the World Trade Organization. Here we look at the evolution and workings of the GATT and WTO.

FROM SMITH TO THE GREAT DEPRESSION   As noted in Chapter 5, the theoretical case for free trade dates to the late eighteenth century and the work of Adam Smith and David Ricardo. Free trade as a government policy was first officially embraced by Great Britain in 1846, when the British Parliament repealed the Corn Laws. The Corn Laws placed a high tariff on imports of foreign corn. The objectives of the Corn Laws tariff were to raise government revenues and to protect British corn producers. There had been annual motions in Parliament in favor of free trade since the 1820s when David Ricardo was a member. However, agricultural protection was withdrawn only as a result of a protracted debate when the effects of a harvest failure in Great Britain were compounded by the imminent threat of famine in Ireland. Faced with considerable hardship and suffering among the populace, Parliament narrowly reversed its long-held position.

During the next 80 years or so, Great Britain, as one of the world's dominant trading powers, pushed the case for trade liberalization; but the British government was a voice in the wilderness. Its major trading partners did not reciprocate the British policy of unilateral free trade. The only reason Britain kept this policy for so long was that as the world's largest exporting nation, it had far more to lose from a trade war than did any other country.

By the 1930s, the British attempt to stimulate free trade was buried under the economic rubble of the Great Depression. The Great Depression had roots in the failure of the world economy to mount a sustained economic recovery after the end of World War I in 1918. Things got worse in 1929 with the U.S. stock market collapse and the subsequent run on the U.S. banking system. Economic problems were compounded in 1930 when the U.S. Congress passed the Smoot-Hawley tariff. Aimed at avoiding rising unemployment by protecting domestic industries and diverting consumer demand away from foreign products, the **Smoot-Hawley Act** erected an enormous wall of tariff barriers. Almost every industry was rewarded with its "made-to-order" tariff. A particularly odd aspect of the Smoot-Hawley tariff-raising binge was that the United States was running a balance-of-payment surplus at the time and it was the world's largest creditor nation. The Smoot-Hawley Act had a damaging effect on employment abroad. Other countries reacted to the U.S. action by raising their own tariff barriers. U.S. exports tumbled in response, and the world slid further into the Great Depression.[28]

Smoot-Hawley Act
Enacted in 1930 by the U.S. Congress, this tariff erected a wall of barriers against imports into the United States.

1947–1979: GATT, TRADE LIBERALIZATION, AND ECONOMIC GROWTH

Economic damage caused by the beggar-thy-neighbor trade policies that the Smoot-Hawley Act ushered in exerted a profound influence on the economic institutions and ideology of the post–World War II world. The United States emerged from the war both victorious and economically dominant. After the debacle of the Great Depression, opinion in the U.S. Congress had swung strongly in favor of free trade. Under U.S. leadership, the GATT was established in 1947.

The GATT was a multilateral agreement whose objective was to liberalize trade by eliminating tariffs, subsidies, import quotas, and the like. From its foundation in 1947 until it was superseded by the WTO, the GATT's membership grew from 19 to more than 120 nations. The GATT did not attempt to liberalize trade restrictions in one fell swoop; that would have been impossible. Rather, tariff reduction was spread over eight rounds. The last, the Uruguay Round, was launched in 1986 and completed in December 1993. In these rounds, mutual tariff reductions were negotiated among all members, who then committed themselves not to raise import tariffs above negotiated rates. GATT regulations were enforced by a mutual monitoring mechanism. If a country believed that one of its trading partners was violating a GATT regulation, it could ask the Geneva-based bureaucracy that administered the GATT to investigate. If GATT investigators found the complaints to be valid, member countries could be asked to pressure the offending party to change its policies. In general, such pressure was sufficient to get an offending country to change its policies. If it were not, the offending country could be expelled from the GATT.

In its early years, the GATT was by most measures very successful. For example, the average tariff declined by nearly 92 percent in the United States between the Geneva Round of 1947 and the Tokyo Round of 1973–79. Consistent with the theoretical arguments first advanced by Ricardo and reviewed in Chapter 5, the move toward free trade under the GATT appeared to stimulate economic growth. From 1953 to 1963, world trade grew at an annual rate of 6.1 percent, and world income grew at an annual rate of 4.3 percent. Performance from 1963 to 1973 was even better; world trade grew at 8.9 percent annually, and world income grew at 5.1 percent annually.[29]

1980–1993: PROTECTIONIST TRENDS

During the 1980s and early 1990s, the world trading system erected by the GATT came under strain as pressures for greater protectionism increased around the world. Three reasons caused the rise in such pressures during the 1980s. First, the economic success of Japan strained the world trading system. Japan was in ruins when the GATT was created. By the early 1980s, however, it had become the world's second-largest economy and its largest exporter. Japan's success in such industries as automobiles and semiconductors might have been enough to strain the world trading system. Things were made worse by the widespread perception in the West that despite low tariff rates and subsidies, Japanese markets were closed to imports and foreign investment by administrative trade barriers.

Second, the world trading system was strained by the persistent trade deficit in the world's largest economy, the United States. Although the deficit peaked in 1987 at more than $170 billion, by the end of 1992 the annual rate was still running about $80 billion. From a political perspective, the matter was worsened in 1992 by the $45 billion U.S. trade deficit with Japan, a country perceived as not playing by the rules. The consequences of the U.S. deficit included painful adjustments in industries such as automobiles, machine tools, semiconductors, steel, and textiles, where domestic producers steadily lost market share to foreign competitors. The resulting unemployment gave rise to renewed demands in the U.S. Congress for protection against imports.

A third reason for the trend toward greater protectionism was that many countries found ways to get around GATT regulations. Bilateral voluntary export restraints, or VERs, circumvent GATT agreements, because neither the importing country nor the exporting country complain to the GATT bureaucracy in Geneva—and without a complaint, the GATT bureaucracy can do nothing. Exporting countries agree to VERs to avoid more damaging punitive tariffs. One of the best-known examples is the automobile VER between Japan and the United States, under which Japanese producers promised to limit their auto imports into the United States as a way of defusing growing trade tensions. According to a World Bank study, 13 percent of the imports of industrialized countries in 1981 were subjected to nontariff trade barriers such as VERs. By 1986, this figure had increased to 16 percent. The most rapid rise was in the United States, where the value of imports affected by nontariff barriers (primarily VERs) increased by 23 percent between 1981 and 1986.[30]

THE URUGUAY ROUND AND THE WORLD TRADE ORGANIZATION

Against the background of rising pressures for protectionism, in 1986 GATT members embarked on their eighth round of negotiations to reduce tariffs, the Uruguay Round (so named because it occurred in Uruguay). This was the most difficult round of negotiations yet, primarily because it was also the most ambitious. Until then, GATT rules had applied only to trade in manufactured goods and commodities. In the Uruguay Round, member countries sought to extend GATT rules to cover trade in services. They also sought to write rules governing the protection of intellectual property, to reduce agricultural subsidies, and to strengthen the GATT's monitoring and enforcement mechanisms.

The Uruguay Round dragged on for seven years before an agreement was reached December 15, 1993. It went into effect July 1, 1995. The Uruguay Round contained the following provisions:

1. Tariffs on industrial goods were to be reduced by more than one-third, and tariffs were to be scrapped on more than 40 percent of manufactured goods.
2. Average tariff rates imposed by developed nations on manufactured goods were to be reduced to less than 4 percent of value, the lowest level in modern history.
3. Agricultural subsidies were to be substantially reduced.
4. GATT fair trade and market access rules were to be extended to cover a wide range of services.
5. GATT rules also were to be extended to provide enhanced protection for patents, copyrights, and trademarks (intellectual property).
6. Barriers on trade in textiles were to be significantly reduced over 10 years.
7. The World Trade Organization was to be created to implement the GATT agreement.

Services and Intellectual Property   In the long run, the extension of GATT rules to cover services and intellectual property may be particularly significant. Until 1995, GATT rules applied only to industrial goods (i.e., manufactured goods and commodities). In 2007, world trade in services amounted to $3.260 billion (compared to world trade in goods of $13,570 billion).[31] Ultimately, extension of GATT rules to this important trading arena could significantly increase both the total share of world trade accounted for by services and the overall volume of world trade. The extension of GATT rules to cover intellectual property will make it much easier for high-technology companies to do business in developing nations where intellectual property rules historically have been poorly enforced (see Chapter 2 for details).

The World Trade Organization   The clarification and strengthening of GATT rules and the creation of the World Trade Organization also hold out the promise of more effective policing and enforcement of GATT rules. The WTO acts as an umbrella organization that encompasses the GATT along with two new sister bodies, one on services and the other on intellectual property. The WTO's General Agreement on Trade in Services (GATS) has taken the lead to extending free trade agreements to services. The WTO's Agreement on Trade-Related Aspects of Intellectual Property Rights (TRIPS) is an attempt to narrow the gaps in the way intellectual property rights are protected around the world and to bring them under common international rules. WTO has taken over responsibility for arbitrating trade disputes and monitoring the trade policies of member countries. While the WTO operates on the basis of consensus as the GATT did, in the area of dispute settlement, member countries are no longer able to block adoption of arbitration reports. Arbitration panel reports on trade disputes between member countries are automatically adopted by the WTO unless there is a consensus to reject them. Countries that have been found by the arbitration panel to violate GATT rules may appeal to a permanent appellate body, but its verdict is binding. If offenders fail to comply with the recommendations of the arbitration panel, trading partners have the right to compensation or, in the last resort, to impose (commensurate) trade sanctions. Every stage of the procedure is subject to strict time limits. Thus, the WTO has something that the GATT never had—teeth.[32]

WTO: Experience to Date   By 2010, the WTO had 153 members, including China, which joined at the end of 2001, who collectively account for 97 percent of world trade. Another 25 countries, including the Russian Federation, were negotiating for membership. Since its formation, the WTO has remained at the forefront of efforts to promote global free trade. Its creators expressed the hope that the enforcement mechanisms granted to the WTO would make it more effective than the GATT had been at policing global trade rules. The great hope was that the WTO might emerge as an effective advocate and facilitator of future trade deals, particularly in areas such as services. The experience so far has been encouraging, although the collapse of WTO talks in Seattle in late 1999, slow progress with the next round of trade talks (the Doha Round), and a shift back toward some limited protectionism in 2008–2009 have raised a number of questions about the future direction of the WTO.

WTO as Global Police   The first decade in the life of the WTO suggests that its policing and enforcement mechanisms are having a positive effect.[33] Between 1995 and early 2010 more than 400 trade disputes between member countries were brought to the WTO.[34] This record compares with a total of 196 cases handled by the GATT over almost half a century. Of the cases brought to the WTO, three-fourths had been resolved by informal consultations between the disputing countries. Resolving the remainder has involved more formal procedures, but these have been largely successful.

In general, countries involved have adopted the WTO's recommendations. The fact that countries are using the WTO represents an important vote of confidence in the organization's dispute resolution procedures.

Expanding Trade Agreements

As explained above, the Uruguay Round of GATT negotiations extended global trading rules to cover trade in services. The WTO was given the role of brokering future agreements to open global trade in services. The WTO was also encouraged to extend its reach to encompass regulations governing foreign direct investment, something the GATT had never done. Two of the first industries targeted for reform were the global telecommunication and financial services industries.

In February 1997, the WTO brokered a deal to get countries to agree to open their telecommunication markets to competition, allowing foreign operators to purchase ownership stakes in domestic telecommunication providers and establishing a set of common rules for fair competition. Under the pact, 68 countries accounting for more than 90 percent of world telecommunication revenues pledged to start opening their markets to foreign competition and to abide by common rules for fair competition in telecommunications. Most of the world's biggest markets, including the United States, European Union, and Japan, were fully liberalized by January 1, 1998, when the pact went into effect. All forms of basic telecommunication service are covered, including voice telephony, data and fax transmissions, and satellite and radio communications. Many telecommunication companies responded positively to the deal, pointing out that it would give them a much greater ability to offer their business customers one-stop shopping—a global, seamless service for all their corporate needs and a single bill.[35]

This was followed in December 1997 with an agreement to liberalize cross-border trade in financial services.[36] The deal covers more than 95 percent of the world's financial services market. Under the agreement, which took effect at the beginning of March 1999, 102 countries pledged to open to varying degrees their banking, securities, and insurance sectors to foreign competition. In common with the telecommunication deal, the accord covers not just cross-border trade but also foreign direct investment. Seventy countries agreed to dramatically lower or eradicate barriers to foreign direct investment in their financial services sector. The United States and the European Union, with minor exceptions, are fully open to inward investment by foreign banks, insurance, and securities companies. As part of the deal, many Asian countries made important concessions that allow significant foreign participation in their financial services sectors for the first time.

WTO protesters gather in front of the Niketown store at Fifth Avenue and Pike Street in downtown Seattle before the opening of the WTO session in 1999.

The WTO in Seattle: A Watershed?

At the end of November 1999, representatives from the WTO's member states met in Seattle, Washington. The goal of the meeting was to launch a new round of talks—dubbed "the millennium round"—aimed at further reducing barriers to cross-border trade and investment. Prominent on the agenda was an attempt to get the assembled countries to agree to work toward the reduction of barriers to cross-border trade in agricultural products and trade and investment in services.

These expectations were dashed on the rocks of a hard and unexpected reality. The talks ended

December 3, 1999, without any agreement being reached. Inside the meeting rooms, the problem was an inability to reach consensus on the primary goals for the next round of talks. A major stumbling block was friction between the United States and the European Union over whether to endorse the aim of ultimately eliminating subsidies to agricultural exporters. The United States wanted the elimination of such subsidies to be a priority. The EU, with its politically powerful farm lobby and long history of farm subsidies, was unwilling to take this step. Another stumbling block was related to efforts by the United States to write "basic labor rights" into the law of the world trading system. The United States wanted the WTO to allow governments to impose tariffs on goods imported from countries that did not abide by what the United States saw as fair labor practices. Representatives from developing nations reacted angrily to this proposal, suggesting it was simply an attempt by the United States to find a legal way of restricting imports from poorer nations.

While the disputes inside the meeting rooms were acrimonious, it was events outside that captured the attention of the world press. The WTO talks proved to be a lightning rod for a diverse collection of organizations from environmentalists and human rights groups to labor unions. For various reasons, these groups oppose free trade. All these organizations argued that the WTO is an undemocratic institution that was usurping the national sovereignty of member states and making decisions of great importance behind closed doors. They took advantage of the Seattle meetings to voice their opposition, which the world press recorded.

Environmentalists expressed concern about the impact that free trade in agricultural products might have on the rate of global deforestation. They argued that lower tariffs on imports of lumber from developing nations will stimulate demand and accelerate the rate at which virgin forests are logged, particularly in nations such as Malaysia and Indonesia. They also pointed to the adverse impact that some WTO rulings have had on environmental policies. For example, the WTO had blocked a U.S. rule that ordered shrimp nets be equipped with a device that allows endangered sea turtles to escape. The WTO found the rule discriminated against foreign importers who lacked such nets.[37] Environmentalists argued that the rule was necessary to protect the turtles from extinction.

Human rights activists see WTO rules as outlawing the ability of nations to stop imports from countries where child labor is used or working conditions are hazardous. Similarly, labor unions oppose trade laws that allow imports from low-wage countries and result in a loss of jobs in high-wage countries. They buttress their position by arguing that American workers are losing their jobs to imports from developing nations that do not have adequate labor standards.

Supporters of the WTO and free trade dismiss these concerns. They have repeatedly pointed out that the WTO exists to serve the interests of its member states, not subvert them. The WTO lacks the ability to force any member nation to take an action to which it is opposed. The WTO can allow member nations to impose retaliatory tariffs on countries that do not abide by WTO rules, but that is the limit of its power. Furthermore, supporters argue, it is rich countries that pass strict environmental laws and laws governing labor standards, not poor ones. In their view, free trade, by raising living standards in developing nations, will be followed by the passage of such laws in these nations. Using trade regulations to try to impose such practices on developing nations, they believe, will produce a self-defeating backlash.

Many representatives from developing nations, which make up about 70 percent of the WTO's members, also reject the position taken by environmentalists and advocates of human and labor rights. Poor countries, which depend on exports to boost their economic growth rates and work their way out of poverty, fear that rich countries will use environmental concerns, human rights, and labor-related issues to erect barriers to the products of the developing world. They believe that attempts to incorporate language about the environment or labor standards in future trade agreements will amount to little more than trade barriers by another name.[38] If this were to occur, they argue that the effect would be to trap the developing nations of the world in a grinding cycle of poverty and debt.

These pro-trade arguments fell on deaf ears. As the WTO representatives gathered in Seattle, environmentalists, human rights activists, and labor unions marched in the streets. Some of the more radical elements in these organizations, together with groups of anarchists who were philosophically opposed to "global capitalism" and "the rape of the world by multinationals," succeeded not only in shutting down the opening ceremonies of the WTO but also in sparking violence in the normally peaceful streets of Seattle. A number of demonstrators damaged property and looted; and the police responded with tear gas, rubber bullets, pepper spray, and baton charges. When it was over, 600 demonstrators had been arrested, millions of dollars in property had been damaged in downtown Seattle, and the global news media had their headline: "WTO Talks Collapse amid Violent Demonstrations."

What happened in Seattle is notable because it may have been a watershed of sorts. In the past, previous trade talks were pursued in relative obscurity with only interested economists, politicians, and businesspeople paying much attention. Seattle demonstrated that the issues surrounding the global trend toward free trade have moved to center stage in the popular consciousness, and they have remained there since. The debate on the merits of free trade and globalization has become mainstream. Whether further liberalization occurs, therefore, may depend on the importance that popular opinion in countries such as the United States attaches to issues such as human rights and labor standards, job security, environmental policies, and national sovereignty. It will also depend on the ability of advocates of free trade to articulate in a clear and compelling manner the argument that, in the long run, free trade is the best way of promoting adequate labor standards, of providing more jobs, and of protecting the environment.

THE FUTURE OF THE WTO: UNRESOLVED ISSUES AND THE DOHA ROUND

Much remains to be done on the international trade front. Four issues at the forefront of the current agenda of the WTO are the increase in antidumping policies, the high level of protectionism in agriculture, the lack of strong protection for intellectual property rights in many nations, and continued high tariff rates on nonagricultural goods and services in many nations. We shall look at each in turn before discussing the latest round of talks between WTO members aimed at reducing trade barriers, the Doha Round, which began in 2001 and were still ongoing as of 2010.

Antidumping Actions

Antidumping actions proliferated during the 1990s. WTO rules allow countries to impose antidumping duties on foreign goods that are being sold cheaper than at home, or below their cost of production, when domestic producers can show that they are being harmed. Unfortunately, the rather vague definition of what constitutes "dumping" has proved to be a loophole that many countries are exploiting to pursue protectionism.

Between 1995 and 2008, WTO members had reported implementation of some 3,427 antidumping actions to the WTO. India initiated the largest number of antidumping actions, some 564; the EU initiated 391 over the same period, and the United States 418 (see Figure 6.2). Antidumping actions seem to be concentrated in certain sectors of the economy such as basic metal industries (e.g., aluminum and steel), chemicals, plastics, and machinery and electrical equipment.[39] These sectors account

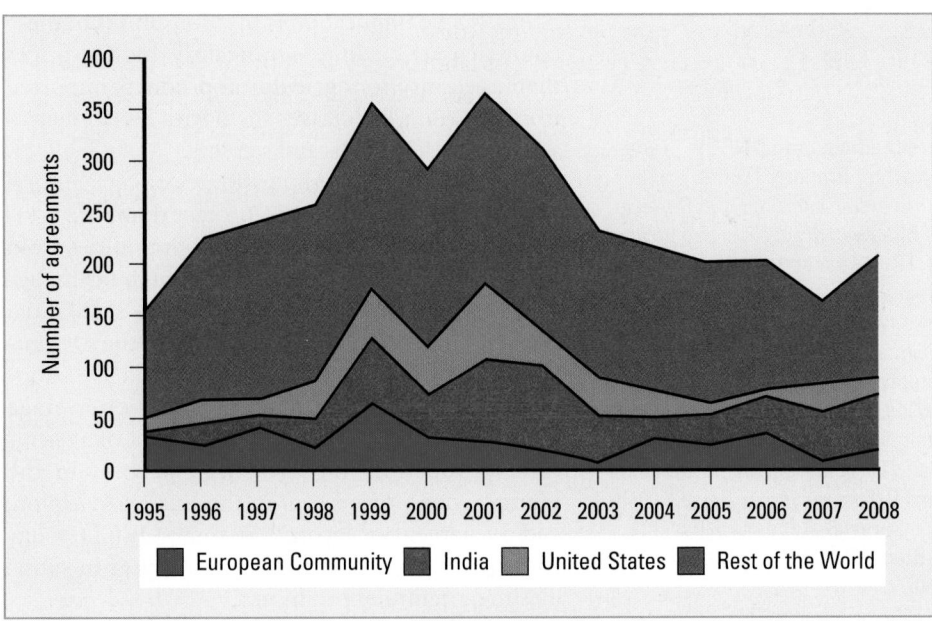

6.2 figure

Antidumping Actions, 1995–2008

Source: Constructed by author from WTO data.

for some 70 percent of all antidumping actions reported to the WTO. These four sectors since 1995 have been characterized by periods of intense competition and excess productive capacity, which have led to low prices and profits (or losses) for firms in those industries. It is not unreasonable, therefore, to hypothesize that the high level of antidumping actions in these industries represents an attempt by beleaguered manufacturers to use the political process in their nations to seek protection from foreign competitors, who they claim are engaging in unfair competition. While some of these claims may have merit, the process can become very politicized as representatives of businesses and their employees lobby government officials to "protect domestic jobs from unfair foreign competition," and government officials, mindful of the need to get votes in future elections, oblige by pushing for antidumping actions. The WTO is clearly worried by this trend, suggesting that it reflects persistent protectionist tendencies and pushing members to strengthen the regulations governing the imposition of antidumping duties.

Figure 6.2 suggests that antidumping actions peaked in the 1999-2001 time period and declined thereafter. However, the WTO reported a rise in antidumping actions in 2008 and 2009 as the global financial crisis took hold (the 2009 data are not included in Figure 6.2, since at the time of writing the data had not been finalized). Many of these actions seem to have been a direct response to the decline in global demand that followed the financial crisis and suggest that countries were using antidumping actions as a means of protecting domestic producers. The most frequent target of these actions was China.

Protectionism in Agriculture   Another recent focus of the WTO has been the high level of tariffs and subsidies in the agricultural sector of many economies. Tariff rates on agricultural products are generally much higher than tariff rates on manufactured products or services. For example, in the mid-2000s the average tariff rates on nonagricultural products were 4.2 percent for Canada, 3.8 percent for the European Union, 3.9 percent for Japan, and 4.4 percent for the United States. On agricultural products, however, the average tariff rates were 21.2 percent for Canada, 15.9 percent for the European Union, 18.6 percent for Japan, and 10.3 percent for the United

The TRIPs Controversy

To developing nations, academics, and NGOs, Trade-Related Aspects of Intellectual Property (TRIPs) are becoming increasingly controversial. In his book, *In Defense of Globalization,* Jagdish Bhagwati argues it is bad policy. Bhagwati argues that TRIPs essentially establish a wealth redistribution mechanism. It moves money from developing countries to developed countries—namely, those that pay for copyright and patents to the owners of those copyrights and patents. In particular, the argument goes, TRIPs make accessibility to medicines for developing countries more difficult. This issue is being negotiated in the Doha Round of the WTO. [J. Bhagwati, *In Defense of Globalization* [New York: Oxford University Press, 2004]; B. Pecoul, "Fighting for Survival Access to Essential Medicines in Poor Countries," *Harvard International Review* 23, no. 3 (2001), p. 60]

States.[40] The implication is that consumers in these countries are paying significantly higher prices than necessary for agricultural products imported from abroad, which leaves them with less money to spend on other goods and services.

The historically high tariff rates on agricultural products reflect a desire to protect domestic agriculture and traditional farming communities from foreign competition. In addition to high tariffs, agricultural producers also benefit from substantial subsidies. According to estimates from the Organization for Economic Cooperation and Development (OECD), government subsidies on average account for some 17 percent of the cost of agricultural production in Canada, 21 percent in the United States, 35 percent in the European Union, and 59 percent in Japan.[41] In total, OECD countries spend more than $300 billion a year in subsidies to agricultural producers.

Not surprising, the combination of high tariff barriers and significant subsidies introduces significant distortions into the production of agricultural products and international trade of those products. The net effect is to raise prices to consumers, reduce the volume of agricultural trade, and encourage the overproduction of products that are heavily subsidized (with the government typically buying the surplus). Because global trade in agriculture currently amounts to 10.5 percent of total merchandized trade, or about $750 billion per year, the WTO argues that removing tariff barriers and subsidies could significantly boost the overall level of trade, lower prices to consumers, and raise global economic growth by freeing consumption and investment resources for more productive uses. According to estimates from the International Monetary Fund, removal of tariffs and subsidies on agricultural products would raise global economic welfare by $128 billion annually.[42] Others suggest gains as high as $182 billion.[43]

The biggest defenders of the existing system have been the advanced nations of the world, which want to protect their agricultural sectors from competition by low-cost producers in developing nations. In contrast, developing nations have been pushing hard for reforms that would allow their producers greater access to the protected markets of the developed nations. Estimates suggest that removing all subsidies on agricultural production alone in OECD countries could return to the developing nations of the world three times more than all the foreign aid they currently receive from the OECD nations.[44] In other words, free trade in agriculture could help to jump-start economic growth among the world's poorer nations and alleviate global poverty.

Protecting Intellectual Property   Another issue that has become increasingly important to the WTO has been protecting intellectual property. The 1995 Uruguay agreement that established the WTO also contained an agreement to protect intellectual property (the Trade-Related Aspects of Intellectual Property Rights, or TRIPS, agreement). The TRIPS regulations oblige WTO members to grant and enforce patents lasting at least 20 years and copyrights lasting 50 years. Rich countries had to comply with the rules within a year. Poor countries, in which such protection generally was much weaker, had five years' grace, and the very poorest had 10 years. The basis for this agreement was a strong belief among signatory nations that the protection of intellectual property through patents, trademarks, and copyrights must be an essential element of the international trading system. Inadequate protections for intellectual property reduce the incentive for innovation. Because innovation is a central engine of economic growth and rising living standards, the argument has been that a multilateral agreement is needed to protect intellectual property.

Without such an agreement it is feared that producers in a country, let's say India, might market imitations of patented innovations pioneered in a different country, say the United States. This can affect international trade in two ways. First, it reduces the export opportunities in India for the original innovator in the United States. Second, to the extent that the Indian producer is able to export its pirated imitation to additional countries, it also reduces the export opportunities in those countries for the U.S. inventor. Also, one can argue that because the size of the total world market for the innovator is reduced, its incentive to pursue risky and expensive innovations is also reduced. The net effect would be less innovation in the world economy and less economic growth.

Something very similar to this has been occurring in the pharmaceutical industry, with Indian drug companies making copies of patented drugs discovered elsewhere. In 1970, the Indian government stopped recognizing product patents on drugs, but it elected to continue respecting process patents. This permitted Indian companies to reverse-engineer Western pharmaceuticals without paying licensing fees. As a result, foreigners' share of the Indian drug market fell from 75 percent in 1970 to 30 percent in 2000. For example, an Indian company sells a version of Bayer's patented antibiotic Cipro for $0.12 a pill, versus the $5.50 it costs in the United States. Under the WTO TRIPS agreement, India agreed to adopt and enforce the international drug patent regime by 2005.[45]

As noted in Chapter 2, intellectual property rights violation is also an endemic problem in several other industries, most notably computer software and music. The WTO believes that reducing piracy rates in areas such as drugs, software, and music recordings would have a significant impact on the volume of world trade and increase the incentive for producers to invest in the creation of intellectual property. A world without piracy would have more new drugs, computer software, and music recordings produced every year. In turn, this would boost economic and social welfare, and global economic growth rates. It is thus in the interests of WTO members to make sure that intellectual property rights are respected and enforced. While the 1995 Uruguay agreement that created the WTO did make headway with the TRIPS agreement, some believe these requirements do not go far enough and further commitments are necessary.

Market Access for Nonagricultural Goods and Services   Although the WTO and the GATT have made big strides in reducing the tariff rates on nonagricultural products, much work remains. Although most developed nations have brought their tariff rates on industrial products down to an *average* of 3.8 percent of value, exceptions still remain. In particular, while average tariffs are low, high tariff rates persist on certain imports into developed nations, which limit market access and economic growth. For example, Australia and South Korea, both OECD countries, still have bound tariff rates of 15.1 percent and 24.6 percent, respectively, on imports of transportation equipment (*bound tariff rates* are the highest rate that can be charged, which is often, but not always, the rate that is charged). In contrast, the bound tariff rates on imports of transportation equipment into the United States, EU, and Japan are 2.7 percent, 4.7 percent, and 0 percent, respectively (see Table 6.1). A particular area for concern is high tariff rates on imports of selected goods from developing nations into developed nations.

table 6.1

Bound Tariffs on Select Industrial Products (simple averages)

Source: WTO.

Country	Metals	Transportation Equipment	Electric Machinery
Canada	2.8%	6.8%	5.2%
United States	1.8	2.7	2.1
Brazil	33.4	33.6	31.9
Mexico	34.7	35.8	34.1
European Union	1.6	4.7	3.3
Australia	4.5	15.1	13.3
Japan	0.9	0.0	0.2
South Korea	7.7	24.6	16.1

In addition, tariffs on services remain higher than on industrial goods. The average tariff on business and financial services imported into United States, for example, is 8.2 percent, into the EU it is 8.5 percent, and into Japan it is 19.7 percent.[46] Given the rising value of cross-border trade in services, reducing these figures can be expected to yield substantial gains.

The WTO would like to bring down tariff rates still further and reduce the scope for the selective use of high tariff rates. The ultimate aim is to reduce tariff rates to zero. Although this might sound ambitious, 40 nations have already moved to zero tariffs on information technology goods, so a precedent exists. Empirical work suggests that further reductions in average tariff rates toward zero would yield substantial gains. One estimate by economists at the World Bank suggests that a broad global trade agreement coming out of the current Doha negotiations could increase world income by $263 billion annually, of which $109 billion would go to poor countries.[47] Another estimate from the OECD suggests a figure closer to $300 billion annually.[48] See the accompanying Country Focus about Nigeria and what it would take for the country to become a significant factor in the global trade environment.

Looking further out, the WTO would like to bring down tariff rates on imports of nonagricultural goods into developing nations. Many of these nations use the infant industry argument to justify the continued imposition of high tariff rates; however, ultimately these rates need to come down for these nations to reap the full benefits of international trade. For example, the bound tariff rates of 53.9 percent on imports of transportation equipment into India and 33.6 percent on imports into Brazil, by raising domestic prices, help to protect inefficient domestic producers and limit economic growth by reducing the real income of consumers who must pay more for transportation equipment and related services.

A New Round of Talks: Doha   Antidumping actions, trade in agricultural products, better enforcement of intellectual property laws, and expanded market access were four of the issues the WTO wanted to tackle at the 1999 meetings in Seattle, but those meetings were derailed. In late 2001, the WTO tried again to launch a new round of talks between member states aimed at further liberalizing the global trade and investment framework. For this meeting, it picked the remote location of Doha in the Persian Gulf state of Qatar, no doubt with an eye on the difficulties that antiglobalization protesters would have in getting there. Unlike the Seattle meetings, at Doha, the member states of the WTO agreed to launch a new round of talks and staked out an agenda. The talks were originally scheduled to last

Nigeria: The Next BRIC?

In 2005, Goldman Sachs identified 11 countries (the "Next 11" or N-11) that have a high potential of becoming the world's largest economies in the 21st century along with the BRICs. Nigeria was one of them.

In comparison to Asian and Latin American countries, Nigeria has not benefited as much from globalization and integration into the world economy. Membership in multinational organizations such as the WTO, IMF, and World Bank does not guarantee economic integration. Indeed, much of the African continent has been marginalized from such benefits. Among African countries, however, Nigeria is one of two major African countries, the other being South Africa, with strong potential to harness the opportunities and meet the challenges that the global economy could provide.

Nigeria in particular has some key advantages. It has the largest population in the continent and has been growing rapidly, due in part to gains from economic reforms and oil revenues. Nigeria is the eighth most populous country in the world, with a population in excess of 150 million people, and the seventh largest oil exporter in the world, with the 10th largest oil reserves.

Nigeria's integration into the global economy, however, has been below potential. Under President Obasanjo, two key objectives were pursued: (1) to finalize the transition to civilian rule and end the military's direct involvement in politics and (2) to put the Nigerian economy on the road to recovery. Until his death, President Yar'Adua maintained the policies of economic reform and corruption reduction that were enacted by his predecessor. While it has improved its global rankings on indicators of competitiveness, business climate, and productivity in the past five years, Nigeria still ranks below most of its peer group (Mexico, Brazil, China, India) on these indicators. Between 2000 and 2008, GDP growth averaged more than 7.5 percent annually. There was particularly strong growth in telecommunications (where Nigeria now has in excess of 70 million mobile phone subscribers), the banking sector, and agriculture. And yet Nigeria remains among the poorest countries and consistently ranks among the most corrupt countries, despite or as a result of its oil wealth. Further integration into the global economy would require sustained policy reforms, improved governance, and public–private investments in social, human, and physical infrastructure besides membership in multilateral trade organizations.

Sources: J. O'Neill, D. Wilson, R. Purushothaman, and A. Stupnytska, Global Economics Paper, No. 134, Goldman Sachs, GS Global Economic Web site, Economic Research from the GS Institutional Portal at https://portal.gs.com; F. Beddington, "Nigeria: A BRIC in the Making," *Global Investor*, 227 (2009), pp. 19–21; and T. Oshikoya, "Nigeria in the Global Economy," *Business Economics*, 43, no. 1 (2008), pp. 31–43.

three years, although they have already gone on longer and may not be concluded for a while.

The agenda includes cutting tariffs on industrial goods and services, phasing out subsidies to agricultural producers, reducing barriers to cross-border investment, and limiting the use of antidumping laws. Some difficult compromises were made to reach agreement on this agenda. The EU and Japan had to give significant ground on the issue of agricultural subsidies, which are used extensively by both entities to support politically powerful farmers. The United States bowed to pressure from virtually every other nation to negotiate revisions of antidumping rules, which the United States has used extensively to protect its steel producers from foreign competition. Europe had to scale back its efforts to include environmental policy in the trade talks, primarily because of pressure from developing nations that see environmental protection policies as trade barriers by another name. Excluded from the agenda was any language pertaining to attempts to tie trade to labor standards in a country.

Countries with big pharmaceutical sectors acquiesced to demands from African, Asian, and Latin American nations on the issue of drug patents. Specifically, the language in the agreement declares that WTO regulation on intellectual property "does not and should not prevent members from taking measures to protect public health." This language was meant to assure the world's poorer nations that they can make or buy generic equivalents to fight such killers as AIDS and malaria.

Clearly, it is one thing to agree to an agenda and quite another to reach a consensus on a new treaty. Nevertheless, if an agreement is reached there are some clear potential winners. These include low-cost agricultural producers in the developing world and developed nations such as Australia and the United States. If the talks are successful, agricultural producers in these nations will ultimately see the global markets for their goods expand. Developing nations also gain from the lack of language on labor standards, which many saw as an attempt by rich nations to erect trade barriers. The sick and poor of the world also benefit from guaranteed access to cheaper medicines. There are also clear losers in this agreement, including EU and Japanese farmers, U.S. steelmakers, environmental activists, and pharmaceutical firms in the developed world. These losers can be expected to lobby their governments hard during the ensuing years to make sure that the final agreement is more in their favor.[49] In general, though, if ultimately successful, the Doha Round of negotiations could significantly raise global economic welfare. As noted above, estimates suggest that a successful Doha Round would raise global incomes by as much as $300 billion annually, with 60 percent of the gain going to the world's poorer nations, which would help to pull 150 million people out of poverty.[50]

The talks are currently ongoing, and as seems normal in these cases, they are characterized by halting progress punctuated by significant setbacks and missed deadlines. A September 2003 meeting in Cancun, Mexico, broke down, primarily because there was no agreement on how to proceed with reducing agricultural subsidies and tariffs; the EU, United States, and India, among others, proved less than willing to reduce tariffs and subsidies to their politically important farmers, while countries such as Brazil and certain West African nations wanted free trade as quickly as possible. In 2004, both the United States and the EU made a determined push to start the talks again. However, since then little progress has been made and the talks are in deadlock, primarily because of disagreements over how deep the cuts in subsidies to agricultural produces should be. As of early 2010, the goal was to reduce tariffs for manufactured and agricultural goods by 60 to 70 percent, and to cut subsidies to half of their current level, but getting nations to agree to these goals was proving exceedingly difficult.

Focus on Managerial Implications

LEARNING OBJECTIVE 5
Explain the implications for managers of developments in the world trading system.

What are the implications of all this for business practice? Why should the international manager care about the political economy of free trade or about the relative merits of arguments for free trade and protectionism? There are two answers to this question. The first concerns the impact of trade barriers on a firm's strategy. The second concerns the role that business firms can play in promoting free trade or trade barriers.

Trade Barriers and Firm Strategy

To understand how trade barriers affect a firm's strategy, consider first the material in Chapter 5. Drawing on the theories of international trade, we discussed how it makes sense for the firm to disperse its various production activities to those countries around the globe where they can be performed most efficiently. Thus, it may make sense for a firm to design and engineer its product in one country, to manufacture components in another, to perform final assembly operations in yet another country, and then export the finished product to the rest of the world.

Clearly, trade barriers constrain a firm's ability to disperse its productive activities in such a manner. First and most obvious, tariff barriers raise the costs of exporting products to a country (or of exporting partly finished products between countries). This may put the firm at a competitive disadvantage to indigenous competitors in that country. In response, the firm may then find it economical to locate production facilities in that country so that it can compete on an even footing. Second, quotas may limit a firm's ability to serve a country from locations outside of that country. Again, the response by the firm might be to set up production facilities in that country—even though it may result in higher production costs. Such reasoning was one of the factors behind the rapid expansion of Japanese automaking capacity in the United States during the 1980s and 1990s. This followed the establishment of a VER agreement between the United States and Japan that limited U.S. imports of Japanese automobiles.

Third, to conform to local content regulations, a firm may have to locate more production activities in a given market than it would otherwise. Again, from the firm's perspective, the consequence might be to raise costs above the level that could be achieved if each production activity was dispersed to the optimal location for that activity. And finally, even when trade barriers do not exist, the firm may still want to locate some production activities in a given country to reduce the threat of trade barriers being imposed in the future.

All these effects are likely to raise the firm's costs above the level that could be achieved in a world without trade barriers. The higher costs that result need not translate into a significant competitive disadvantage relative to other foreign firms, however, if the countries imposing trade barriers do so to the imported products of all foreign firms, irrespective of their national origin. But when trade barriers are targeted at exports from a particular nation, firms based in that nation are at a competitive disadvantage to firms of other nations. The firm may deal with such targeted trade barriers by moving production into the country imposing barriers. Another strategy may be to move production to countries whose exports are not targeted by the specific trade barrier.

Finally, the threat of antidumping action limits the ability of a firm to use aggressive pricing to gain market share in a country. Firms in a country also can make strategic use of antidumping measures to limit aggressive competition from low-cost foreign producers. For example, the U.S. steel industry has been very aggressive in bringing antidumping actions against foreign steelmakers, particularly in times of weak global demand for steel and excess capacity. In 1998 and 1999, the United States faced a surge in low-cost steel imports as a severe recession in Asia left producers there with excess capacity. The U.S. producers filed several complaints with the International Trade Commission. One argued that Japanese producers of hot rolled steel were selling it at below cost in the United States. The ITC agreed and levied tariffs ranging from 18 percent to 67 percent on imports of certain steel products from Japan (these tariffs are separate from the steel tariffs discussed earlier).[51]

Policy Implications

As noted in Chapter 5, business firms are major players on the international trade scene. Because of their pivotal role in international trade, firms can and do exert a strong influence on government policy toward trade. This influence can encourage protectionism or it can encourage the government to support the WTO and push for open markets and freer trade among all nations. Government policies with regard to international trade can have a direct impact on business.

Consistent with strategic trade policy, examples can be found of government intervention in the form of tariffs, quotas, antidumping actions, and subsidies helping firms and industries establish a competitive advantage in the world economy. In general, however, the arguments contained in this chapter and in Chapter 5 suggest that government intervention has three drawbacks. Intervention can be self-defeating because it tends to protect the inefficient rather than help firms become efficient global competitors. Intervention is dangerous; it may invite retaliation and trigger a trade war. Finally, intervention is unlikely to be well executed, given the opportunity for such a policy to be captured by special-interest groups. Does this mean that business should simply encourage government to adopt a laissez-faire free trade policy?

Most economists would probably argue that the best interests of international business are served by a free trade stance, but not a laissez-faire stance. It is probably in the best long-run interests of the business community to encourage the government to aggressively promote greater free trade by, for example, strengthening the WTO. Business probably has much more to gain from government efforts to open protected markets to imports and foreign direct investment than from government efforts to support certain domestic industries in a manner consistent with the recommendations of strategic trade policy.

This conclusion is reinforced by a phenomenon we touched on in Chapter 1—the increasing integration of the world economy and internationalization of production that has occurred over the past two decades. We live in a world where many firms of all national origins increasingly depend for their competitive advantage on globally dispersed production systems. Such systems are the result of freer trade. Freer trade has brought great advantages to firms that have exploited it and to consumers who benefit from the resulting lower prices. Given the danger of retaliatory action, business firms that lobby their governments to engage in protectionism must realize that by doing so they may be denying themselves the opportunity to build a competitive advantage by constructing a globally dispersed production system. By encouraging their governments to engage in protectionism, their own activities and sales overseas may be jeopardized if other governments retaliate. This does not mean a firm should never seek protection in the form of antidumping actions and the like, but it should review its options carefully and think through the larger consequences.

Key Terms

free trade, p. 230

tariff, p. 232

specific tariff, p. 232

ad valorem tariff, p. 232

subsidy, p. 233

import quota, p. 234

tariff rate quota, p. 235

voluntary export restraint (VER), p. 235

quota rent, p. 236

local content requirement, p. 236

administrative trade policies, p. 236

dumping, p. 237

antidumping policies, p. 237

countervailing duties, p. 237

Helms-Burton Act, p. 242

D'Amato Act, p. 242

infant industry argument, p. 245

strategic trade policy, p. 246

Smoot-Hawley Act, p. 249

The goal of this chapter was to describe how the reality of international trade deviates from the theoretical ideal of unrestricted free trade reviewed in Chapter 5. In this chapter, we have reported the various instruments of trade policy, reviewed the political and economic arguments for government intervention in international trade, reexamined the economic case for free trade in light of the strategic trade policy argument, and looked at the evolution of the world trading framework. While a policy of free trade may not always be the theoretically optimal policy (given the arguments of the new trade theorists), in practice it is probably the best policy for a government to pursue. In particular, the long-run interests of business and consumers may be best served by strengthening international institutions such as the WTO. Given the danger that isolated protectionism might escalate into a trade war, business probably has far more to gain from government efforts to open protected markets to imports and foreign direct investment (through the WTO) than from government efforts to protect domestic industries from foreign competition. The chapter made the following points:

1. Trade policies, such as tariffs, subsidies, antidumping regulations, and local content requirements tend to be pro-producer and anti-consumer. Gains accrue to producers (who are protected from foreign competitors), but consumers lose because they must pay more for imports.

2. There are two types of arguments for government intervention in international trade: political and economic. Political arguments for intervention are concerned with protecting the interests of certain groups, often at the expense of other groups, or with promoting goals with regard to foreign policy, human rights, consumer protection, and the like. Economic arguments for intervention are about boosting the overall wealth of a nation.

3. A common political argument for intervention is that it is necessary to protect jobs. However, political intervention often hurts consumers and it can be self-defeating. Countries sometimes argue that it is important to protect certain industries for reasons of national security. Some argue that government should use the threat to intervene in trade policy as a bargaining tool to open foreign markets. This can be a risky policy; if it fails, the result can be higher trade barriers.

4. The infant industry argument for government intervention contends that to let manufacturing get a toehold, governments should temporarily support new industries. In practice, however, governments often end up protecting the inefficient.

5. Strategic trade policy suggests that with subsidies, government can help domestic firms gain first-mover advantages in global industries where economies of scale are important. Government subsidies may also help domestic firms overcome barriers to entry into such industries.

6. The problems with strategic trade policy are twofold: (*a*) such a policy may invite retaliation, in which case all will lose, and (*b*) strategic trade policy may be captured by special-interest groups, which will distort it to their own ends.

7. The GATT was a product of the postwar free trade movement. The GATT was successful in lowering trade barriers on manufactured goods and commodities. The move toward greater free trade under the GATT appeared to stimulate economic growth.

8. The completion of the Uruguay Round of GATT talks and the establishment of the World Trade Organization have strengthened the world trading system by extending GATT rules to services, increasing protection for intellectual property, reducing agricultural subsidies, and enhancing monitoring and enforcement mechanisms.

9. Trade barriers act as a constraint on a firm's ability to disperse its various production activities to optimal locations around the globe. One response to trade barriers is to establish more production activities in the protected country.

10. Business may have more to gain from government efforts to open protected markets to imports and foreign direct investment than from government efforts to protect domestic industries from foreign competition.

1. Do you think governments should consider human rights when granting preferential trading rights to countries? What are the arguments for and against taking such a position?

2. Whose interests should be the paramount concern of government trade policy—the interests of producers (businesses and their employees) or those of consumers?

3. Given the arguments relating to the new trade theory and strategic trade policy, what kind of trade policy should business be pressuring government to adopt?

4. You are an employee of a U.S. firm that produces personal computers in Thailand and then exports them to the United States and other countries for sale. The personal computers were originally produced in Thailand to take advantage of relatively low labor costs and a skilled workforce. Other possible locations considered at the time were Malaysia and Hong Kong. The U.S. government decides to impose punitive 100 percent ad valorem tariffs on imports of computers from Thailand to punish the country for administrative trade barriers that restrict U.S. exports to Thailand. How should your firm respond? What does this tell you about the use of targeted trade barriers?

5. Reread the Management Focus "The Subsidized Skies." Does subsidization help or hinder international air traffic? How do subsidies help developed nations as opposed to developing nations? As developing countries become more competitive, will they be able to learn from the mistakes of the developed countries?

 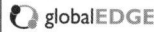

Use the globalEDGE Resource Desk (http://globalEDGE.msu.edu/resourcedesk/) to complete the following exercises:

1. Your company is considering exporting its pharmaceutical products to Japan, but management's current knowledge of the country's trade policies and barriers for this sector is limited. Conduct the appropriate level of research in a *trade barriers database* to identify any information on Japan's current standards and technical requirements for pharmaceutical products. Prepare an executive summary of your findings.

2. You work for a national chain of clothing stores that is considering importing textiles from India into the United States. You want to determine whether the goods are subject to import quotas. Using information provided by the *U.S. Customs and Border Protections*, prepare a report highlighting the elements that determine whether a shipment is subject to this type of trade restriction.

closing case

International Slave Trade

International slave trade, the involuntary trafficking of human beings across borders, is big business. Although accurate figures are hard to determine, human trafficking generates more than $30 billion annually and enslaves between 12 and 27 million people around the globe, half of them children under the age of 18. The UN estimates that human traffickers earn around $10 billion per year and that the average sale price for a slave is approximately $12,500. Because operating costs (for transportation and false documents) are estimated to be approximately $3,000 for each slave, human traffickers can earn nearly $10,000 per victim. Yearning to leave poverty and harsh economic conditions behind, the victims usually become indebted by "taking out a loan" that must be repaid with servitude to the "employer" for a specified period of time. Human trafficking is a product of the same political, technological, and economic forces that have fueled globalization. It is premised on the mobility of labor and the efficiency of production, the very foundations of the global economy. Its victims are mostly women and children.

Modern slavery typically involves women and children being forced into servitude through violence, deception, and deprivation. According to the United Nations' International Labor Organization (ILO), most slave laborers work in agriculture, mining, and prostitution. Approximately 80 percent of slaves are women, and approximately 50 percent are younger than 18. Most of the slaves come from countries such as Albania, Belarus, China, Romania, Russia, and Thailand and reside in Asia, Africa, Latin America, and the Caribbean. Particularly large slave populations exist in Venezuela, Algeria, Sudan, North Korea, Persian Gulf states, Uzbekistan, Argentina, Russia, China, Indochina, and India. Most trafficking is national or regional in nature; that is, the nationality of the trafficker is usually the same as the victim. The most victims from the widest range of origin end up in Europe, whereas victims from Asia are trafficked to the widest range of destinations.

The global economy demands inexpensive labor, and this demand is driving much of the slave trade. Some of the more controversial activists contend that multinational companies purchase materials produced in developing countries by slave laborers. According to the ILO, forced laborers generate more than $30 billion in profits annually. Moreover, the increasing mobility of the population as a whole, and the accessibility of transportation in general, are facilitating human trafficking. The ILO estimates that approximately two-and-a-half million people are trafficked across national borders annually. The modern global slave trade generally involves the use of deception and coercion to induce victims to cross national borders in search of new jobs. Once the target has arrived in a foreign country, he or she is then forced into some form of labor bondage.

As reprehensible as it may seem, advanced industrial states have failed to take much action to address the issue. While many developed countries have implemented specific laws to curtail illegal trafficking of human beings, little has been done at the less-developed country level. At the supranational level, the United Nations has sought to take the lead through its Office of Drugs and Crime. Part of the problem has been the definition of "human trafficking."

Since being enacted in the United States, the Trafficking Victims Protection Act (TVPA) of 2000 has resulted in the prosecution of many slave traffickers. But the United States does not typically pursue and punish the countries involved. In these other countries, human trafficking violations are rarely prosecuted. Economic sanctions are rarely used to curtail such behavior. According to the United Nations, these victims span the globe, being trafficked "from 127 countries to be exploited in 137 countries." Particularly disturbing is the use of child slaves as soldiers. In Africa, children are often forced to serve as soldiers in ongoing armed conflicts, but relatively little is known about this type of traffic in this region. In fact, there is only a partial understanding of the international slave trade. There are no standardized international data available, unlike the illegal drug trade, which is highly documented. Perhaps the greatest irony is that slavery today seems to thrive in some parts of the world because of economic growth, not despite it.

Sources: United Nations, *Global Report on the Trafficking of Humans,* UN Global Initiative to Fight Human Trafficking. February 2009, accessed at www.unodc.org/documents/human-trafficking/Global_Report_on_TIP.pdf; D. Batstone, *Not for Sale, The Return of Global Slave Trade and How We Can Fight It.* (San Francisco: Harper, 2007); and E. B. Kapstein, "The New Global Slave Trade," *Foreign Affairs* 85, no. 6 (2006), pp. 103–115.

Case Discussion Questions

1. Who benefits from slave trade? Besides the trafficker, do governments? Multinational corporations?

2. Should we change our conception of the mobility of labor and the efficiency of production as part of the global economy?

3. What can be done to stop the enslavement of people? If there is a demand for cheap labor and if people are willing to "take out loans" that need to be repaid, does this constitute "human trafficking"?

LEARNING OBJECTIVES

After you have read this chapter you should be able to:

1. Recognize current trends regarding foreign direct investment in the world economy.

2. Explain the different theories of foreign direct investment.

3. Understand how political ideology shapes a government's attitudes toward FDI.

4. Describe the benefits and costs of FDI to home and host countries.

5. Explain the range of policy instruments that governments use to influence FDI.

6. Identify the implications for management practice of the theory and government policies associated with FDI.

Foreign Direct Investment

Carrefour in India

India is a complicated, highly fragmented retail market. Millions of tiny *kiranas* or "mom & pop" shops account for as much as 95 percent of the $450 billion retail market. These are "unorganized," very small retailers with limited inventory and inefficient distribution channels. Encouraged by the successes in Latin America and other parts of Asia, large "organized" retailers (supermarkets, hypermarkets, and department stores) such as Tesco, Walmart, and Carrefour are now looking to cash in on what A. T. Kearney, the global management consultancy, last year called "the leading emerging retail market." Spurred by rapid economic growth, a fast-expanding middle class, and "mushrooming malls," plus a more liberal foreign direct investment climate, the large retailers are expanding their presence in India quickly.

One of the latest retail giants to arrive, Carrefour, opened its first wholesale outlet in Delhi in July 2010 and has plans to open more shops in other Indian cities this year. The French firm follows Walmart, the world's biggest retailer, which last year opened its doors in Amritsar, in northern India. This expansion into India was not possible until very recently.

Opening up the retail sector has long been a benchmark for economic reform in India. Since the early 1990s, the Indian government had imposed a number of restrictions to foreign direct investment in general and to the retail sector in particular. The government had kept foreign retailers at arm's length in an effort to protect millions of *kiranas,* the tiny shopkeepers, and their suppliers. At present, the country only permits 100 percent foreign direct investment in cash-and-carry stores (wholesale) that sell to other retailers; single-brand retail outlets are allowed foreign ownership of 51 percent. Any further liberalization has been politically complicated because the domestic retail market, the *kiranas,* employs 33.1 million people and represents a large voting constituency for governments to easily displease. Displeasure was manifest when protests erupted across the country in 2007 when Reliance Industries, India's biggest company, tried to set up a network of supermarkets.

In an attempt to better understand the displeasure, ICRIER (Indian Council for Research in International Economic Relations), a nationally recognized think-tank, was retained to gauge the impact of the organized retail sector on the *kiranas.* It found that the arrival of a formal organized retailer caused sales in nearby *kiranas* to drop by 23 percent within one year. But from five years on, the small shops were generally back where they had started. Furthermore, there were indications that the presence of organized retailers improved access to better-quality products. This has been attributed to better distribution channels brought about by the organized retailers. For the country as a whole, the ICRIER report projected that the total retail market would grow by 13 percent a year, from $322 billion in 2006–2007 to $590 billion in 2011–2012. The unorganized retail sector was expected to grow by about 10 percent a year, from $309 billion in 2006–2007 to $496 billion in 2011–2012, while the organized retail sector was likely to grow by 45 to 50 percent a year and to expand from 4 percent of India's retail sector to 16 percent by the end of 2011–2012. Drawing on this report, the Department of Industrial Policy and Promotion (DIPP) recommended a calibrated opening of multi-brand retailing to foreign firms. Although India allows foreign retailers to sell directly to other retailers or institutions, it bars them from selling to individuals (consumers). Foreign investment is currently prohibited in multi-brand retailing.

This is evident in a comparison of the Indian penetration strategy between Walmart and Carrefour. Walmart has partnered with Bharti Enterprises in order to circumvent this restrictive foreign direct investment legislation. Both Walmart and Bharti have a 50–50 joint venture for wholesale cash-and-carry and back-end supply chain management. Carrefour, the world's second largest retailer by revenue and the first worldwide franchiser, has confirmed that it remains committed to entering both the wholesale and consumer retail sectors. Over the past few years, it has attempted to find a partner that would enable it to go after the "*kirana*-bound" customer. After several attempts, it has yet to find such a partner. In the meantime, Carrefour will be limited to a cash-and-carry model (wholesale), selling to hotels and restaurants. If recent DIPP gestures are any indication, this may soon change, at which point Carrefour will be well positioned to take advantage of the foreign direct investment opportunities in India. ●

Sources: Economist Intelligence Unit, *India Country Report,* August 2010; "Carrefour in India; a Wholesale Invasion," *The Economist,* May 20, 2010; P. Lapoule, "Carrefour and Its Competitors in India," *Management Decision,* 48, no. 3 (2010), pp. 396–402; and J. Elliott, "Wal-Mart Must Wait," *Fortune,* 153, no. 10 (2006), pp. 37–40.

Introduction

Foreign direct investment (FDI) occurs when a firm invests directly in facilities to produce or market a product in a foreign country. According to the U.S. Department of Commerce, in the United States FDI occurs whenever a U.S. citizen, organization, or affiliated group takes an interest of 10 percent or more in a foreign business entity. Once a firm undertakes FDI, it begins down a path eventually leading to a *multinational enterprise.* One of the more advanced forms is evident in the opening case: Carrefour in India.

As one of the largest global retailers with retail outlets throughout the world, Carrefour typifies a truly multinational enterprise.

FDI takes on two main forms. The first is a **greenfield investment,** which involves the establishment of a new operation in a foreign country. The second involves acquiring or merging with an existing firm in the foreign country (Walmart's entry into Japan was in the form of an acquisition). Acquisitions can be a minority (where the foreign firm takes a 10 percent to 49 percent interest in the firm's voting stock), majority (foreign interest of 50 percent to 99 percent), or full outright stake (foreign interest of 100 percent).[1]

We begin this chapter by looking at the importance of foreign direct investment in the world economy. Next, we review the theories that have been used to explain foreign direct investment. The chapter then moves on to look at government policy toward foreign direct investment and closes with a section on implications for business.

Foreign Direct Investment in the World Economy

When discussing foreign direct investment, it is important to distinguish between the flow of FDI and the stock of FDI. The **flow of FDI** refers to the amount of FDI undertaken over a given time period (normally a year). The **stock of FDI** refers to the total accumulated value of foreign-owned assets at a given time. We also talk of **outflows of FDI,** meaning the flow of FDI out of a country, and **inflows of FDI,** the flow of FDI into a country.

TRENDS IN FDI   The past 30 years have seen a marked increase in both the flow and stock of FDI in the world economy. The average yearly outflow of FDI increased from $25 billion in 1975 to a record $1.8 trillion in 2007 (see Figure 7.1). However, FDI outflows did contract to $1.2 trillion in 2009 in the wake of the global financial crisis, although they are forecasted to recover in 2011.[2] In general, however, over the past three decades the flow of FDI has accelerated faster than the growth in world trade and world output. For example, between 1992 and 2008, the total flow of FDI from all countries increased more than eightfold while world trade by value grew by some 150 percent and world output by around 45 percent.[3] As a result of the strong FDI flow, by 2009 the global stock of FDI was about $15 trillion. At least 82,000 parent companies had 810,000 affiliates in foreign markets that collectively employed more than 77 million people abroad and generated value accounting for about 11 percent of global GDP. The foreign affiliates of multinationals had over $30 trillion in global sales, higher than the value of global exports of goods and services, which stood at close to $19.9 trillion.[4]

FDI has grown more rapidly than world trade and world output for several reasons. First, despite the general decline in trade barriers over the past 30 years, business firms still fear protectionist pressures. Executives see FDI as a way of circumventing future trade barriers. Second, much of the increase in FDI has been driven by the political and economic changes that have been occurring in many of the world's developing nations. The general shift toward democratic political institutions and free market economies that we discussed in Chapter 2 has encouraged FDI. Across much of Asia, Eastern Europe, and Latin America, economic growth, economic deregulation, privatization programs that are open to foreign investors, and removal of many restrictions on FDI have made these countries more attractive to foreign multinationals. According to the United Nations, some 90 percent of the 2,600 changes made worldwide between 1992 and 2008 in the laws governing foreign direct investment created a more favorable environment for FDI (see Figure 7.2).[5] However, since 2002, the number of regulations that are less favorable toward FDI has increased, suggesting the pendulum may be starting to

Greenfield Investment
Establishing a new operation in a foreign country.

LEARNING OBJECTIVE 1
Recognize current trends regarding foreign direct investment in the world economy.

Flow of FDI
The amount of FDI undertaken over a given time period (normally a year).

Stock of FDI
The total accumulated value of foreign-owned assets at a given time.

Outflows of FDI
The flow of FDI out of a country.

Inflows of FDI
The flow of FDI into a country.

figure 7.1

FDI Outflows, 1982–2009
($ billion)

Source: Constructed by the author
from data in United Nations, *World
Investment Report, 2009* (New York
and Geneva: United Nations, 2009).

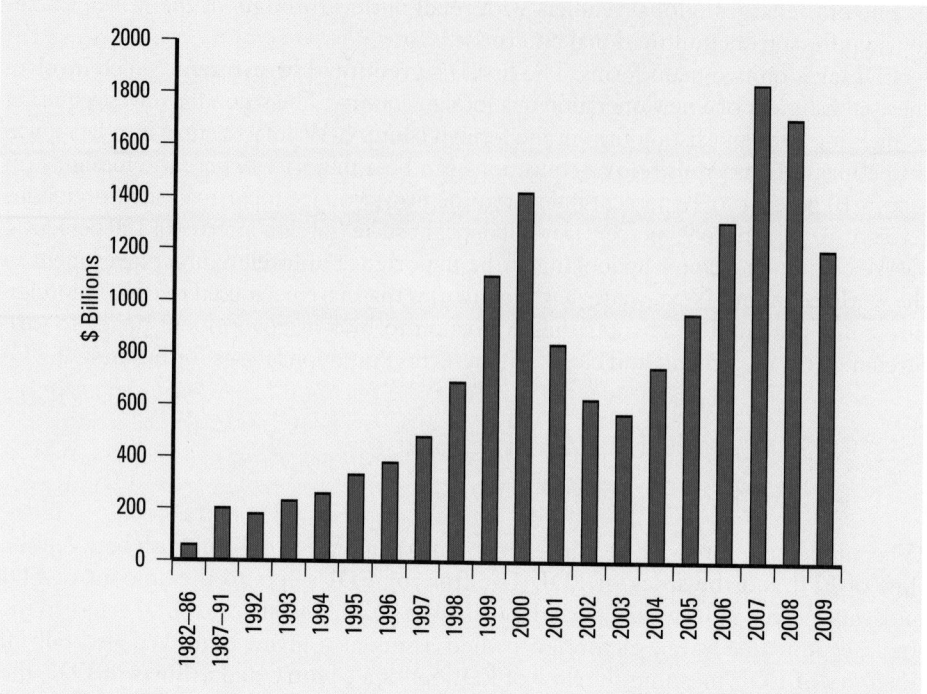

figure 7.2

National Regulatory
Changes Governing FDI,
1992–2008

Source: Constructed by the author
from data in United Nations, *World
Investment Report, 2009* (New York
and Geneva: United Nations, 2009).

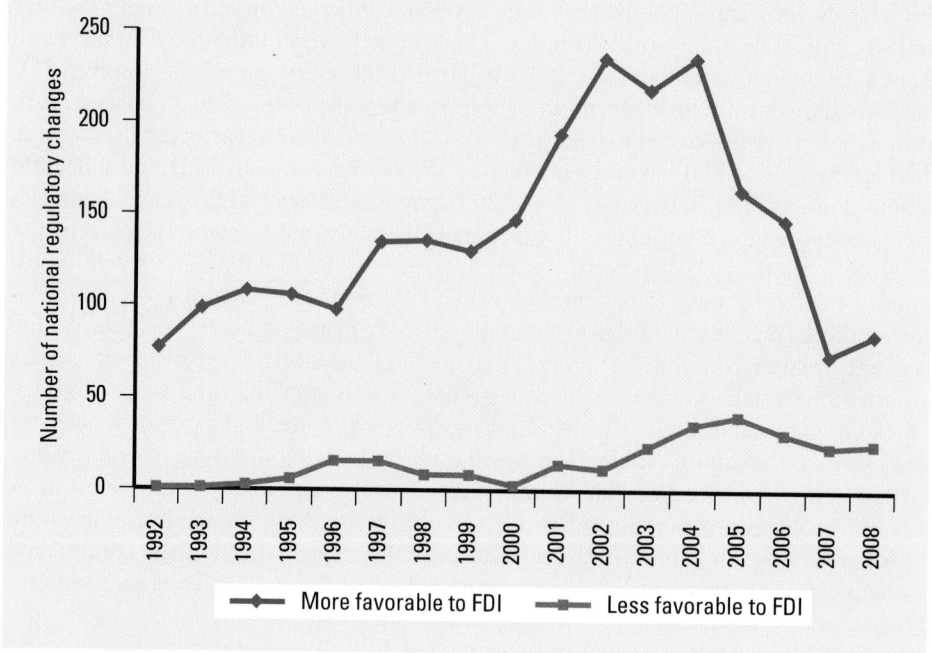

swing the other way. Latin America, in particular, has seen an increase in regulations that
are less favorable to FDI; two-thirds of the reported changes in 2005 and 2008 made the
environment for direct investment less welcome there. Most of these unfavorable
changes were focused on extractive industries, such as oil and gas, where governments
seem focused on limiting FDI and capturing more of the economic value from FDI
through, for example, higher taxes and royalty rates applied to foreign enterprises.

Notwithstanding recent adverse developments in some nations, the general desire of governments to facilitate FDI also has been reflected in a sharp increase in the number of bilateral investment treaties designed to protect and promote investment between two countries. As of 2009, 2,676 such treaties involved more than 180 countries, a 12-fold increase from the 181 treaties that existed in 1980.[6]

The globalization of the world economy is also having a positive impact on the volume of FDI. Many firms (such as Carrefour profiled in the opening case) now see the whole world as their market, and they are undertaking FDI in an attempt to make sure they have a significant presence in many regions. For reasons that we shall explore later in this book, many firms now believe it is important to have production facilities based close to their major customers. This, too, creates pressure for greater FDI.

THE DIRECTION OF FDI Historically, most FDI has been directed at the developed nations of the world as firms based in advanced countries invested in the others' markets (see Figure 7.3). During the 1980s and 1990s, the United States was often the favorite target for FDI inflows. The United States has been an attractive target for FDI because of its large and wealthy domestic markets, its dynamic and stable economy, a favorable political environment, and the openness of the country to FDI. Investors include firms based in Great Britain, Japan, Germany, Holland, and France. Inward investment into the United States remained high during the 2000s, totaling $271 billion in 2007 and $316 billion in 2008. The developed nations of the European Union have also been recipients of significant FDI inflows, principally from U.S. and Japanese enterprises and from other member states of the EU. In 2007, inward investment into the EU reached a record $842 billion, although it fell to $503 billion in 2008. The United Kingdom and France were the largest national recipients. Some $280 billion was invested in the United Kingdom in 2007 and 2008 combined, and $275 billion in France.[7]

Even though developed nations still account for the largest share of FDI inflows, FDI into developing nations has increased (see Figure 7.3). From 1985 to 1990, the annual

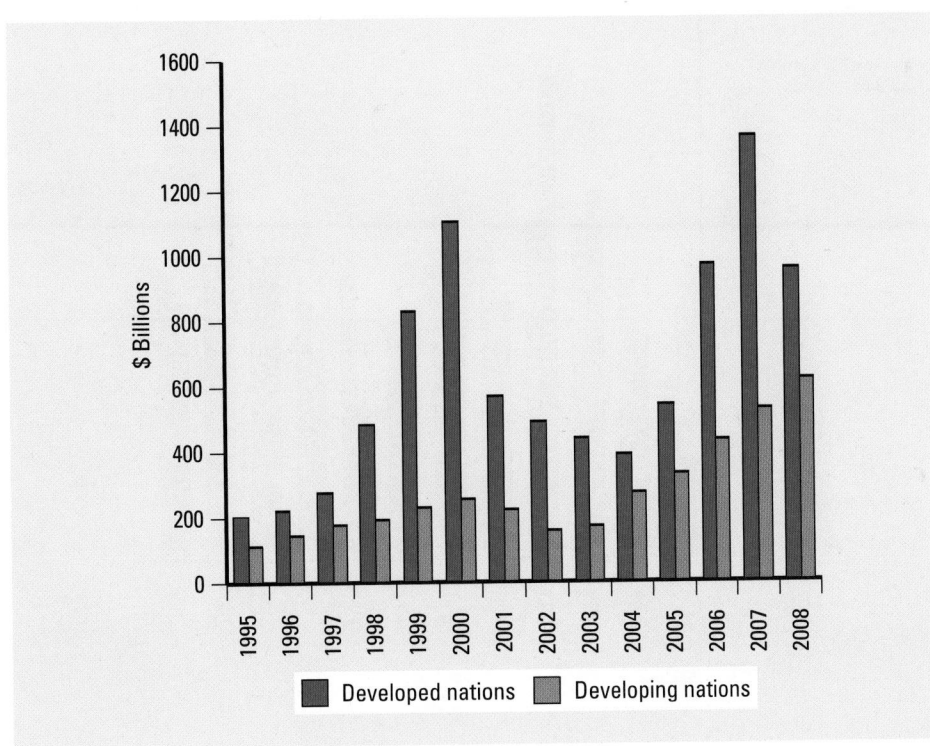

7.3 figure

FDI Inflows by Region, 1995–2008 ($ billion)

Source: Constructed by the author from data in United Nations, *World Investment Report, 2009* (New York and Geneva: United Nations, 2009).

inflow of FDI into developing nations averaged $27.4 billion, or 17.4 percent of the total global flow. In the mid- to late 1990s, the inflow into developing nations was generally between 35 and 40 percent of the total, before falling back to account for about 25 percent of the total in the 2000–2002 period and then rising to 31 to 40 percent between 2004 and 2008. Most recent inflows into developing nations have been targeted at the emerging economies of South, East, and Southeast Asia. Driving much of the increase has been the growing importance of China as a recipient of FDI, which attracted around $60 billion of FDI in 2004 and rose steadily to hit $108 billion in 2008.[8] By way of comparison, the strong flow of investment into Indonesia is discussed in the accompanying Country Focus.

Latin America emerged as the next most important region in the developing world for FDI inflows. In 2008, total inward investments into this region reached about $144 billion. Mexico and Brazil have historically been the two top recipients of inward FDI in Latin America, a trend that continued in 2008. At the other end of the scale, Africa has long received the smallest amount of inward investment, although the continent did receive a record $87 billion in 2008. In recent years, Chinese enterprises have emerged as major investors in Africa, particularly in extraction industries where they seem to be trying to assure future supplies of valuable raw materials. The inability of Africa to attract greater investment is in part a reflection of the political unrest, armed conflict, and frequent changes in economic policy in the region.[9]

Another way of looking at the importance of FDI inflows is to express them as a percentage of gross fixed capital formation. **Gross fixed capital formation** summarizes the total amount of capital invested in factories, stores, office buildings, and the like. Other things being equal, the greater the capital investment in an economy, the more favorable its future growth prospects are likely to be. Viewed this way, FDI can be seen as an important source of capital investment and a determinant of the future growth rate of an economy. Figure 7.4 summarizes inward flows of FDI as a percentage of gross fixed capital

Gross Fixed Capital Formation
Summarizes the total amount of capital invested in factories, stores, office buildings, and the like.

figure 7.4

Inward FDI as a Percentage of Gross Fixed Capital Formation, 1992–2008

Source: Constructed by the author from data in United Nations, *World Investment Report, 2009* (New York and Geneva: United Nations, 2009).

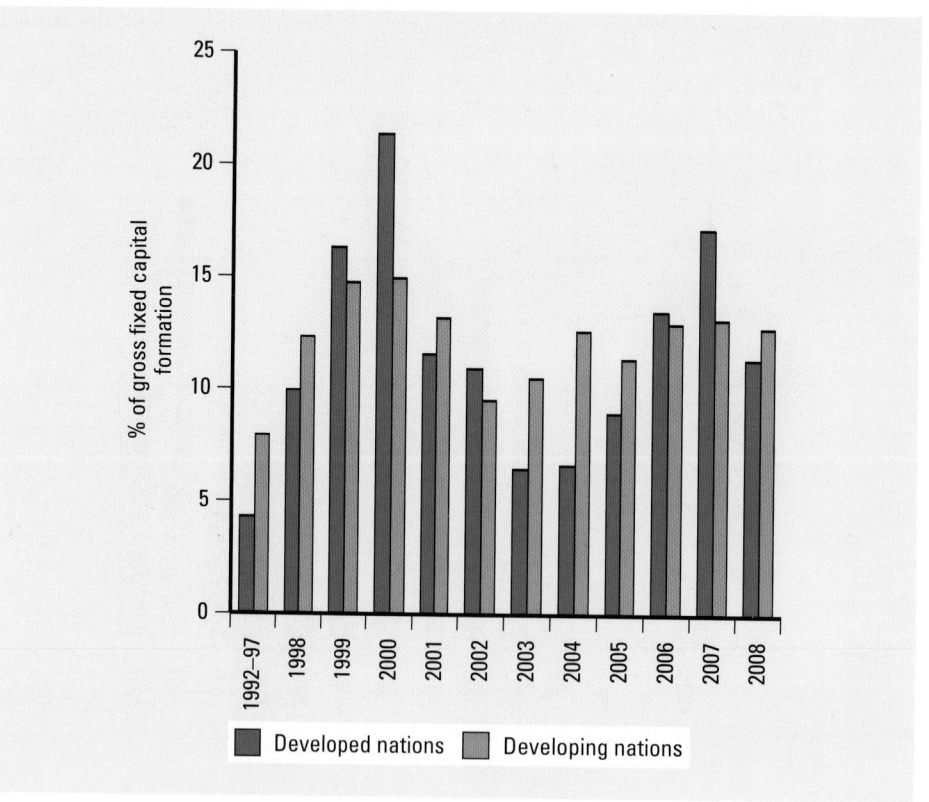

Country FOCUS

Foreign Direct Investment in Indonesia

Things are happening in Indonesia. The gross domestic product growth accelerated to 5.7 percent on an annualized basis in the first quarter of 2010, its highest level since mid-2008. Exports soared in early 2010, rising by 36 percent year-on-year in May 2010. The country's inflation rate rose to 5.1 percent year-on-year in June 2010, but Indonesia's unemployment rate fell to 7.6 percent in March 2010 and is forecast to continue to decline over the near term. In May 2010, Finance Minister Sri Mulyani Indrawati resigned after she was appointed to be the new managing director of the World Bank. She had been increasingly critical of the country's old guard politicians who had blocked economic reforms that she had supported. In June 2010, President Susilo Bambang Yudhoyono, Indonesia's first-ever directly elected president, imposed a two-year moratorium on deforestation in an attempt to combat climate change and vowed to eliminate corruption and poverty. This has not gone unnoticed by the foreign investment community.

Drawn to the country's more stable political climate and growing consumer demand, Gita Wrjawan, head of the Investment Coordinating Board, Indonesia's official investment regulatory body, predicted a 25 percent increase in foreign direct investment in 2010, claiming it could hit $13.14 billion compared to $10.5 billion last year. Among the biggest foreign direct investors was Singapore, with $1.6 billion investments in the transportation, telecommunication, and warehousing sectors. Adding to this dynamic process, and looking toward the future, the Indonesian government has announced it will offer tax incentives on renewable energy projects to help cut the country's dependency on fossil fuels. Finance minister Sri Mulyani Indrawati signed a decree earlier in the year that will reduce the net tax base by 5 percent annually for the next six years on the total investment in renewable energy initiatives. Foreign investors will also receive a lower tax rate on all dividend payments. Companies involved in construction will not be charged value-added tax or import duty on machinery and equipment used for such projects. Indonesia is seeking to produce 30 percent of its energy from gas, 20 percent from oil-based fuels, 30 percent from coal, and the rest from a combination of solar power and geothermal renewable sources.

But things are not as rosy as they first appeared. Indonesia has one of the world's highest political risk ratings. Indonesia is a group of more than 17,000 islands with a population of around 230 million people. This diverse geographic expanse has historically represented a wide variety of challenges. Most importantly, the unity of the country as a whole has been consistently questioned. Separatist forces are constantly tugging at that unity. The greatest risk remains the potential for conflict throughout the country, particularly in areas farther away from the dominant island of Java. Nowhere is this more obvious than in the potential conflict with East Timor.

East Timor achieved its independence from Indonesia in 2002 after 27 years of occupation. From 1975 to 2002, 200,000 people were killed during Indonesia's suppression of rebel groups in East Timor. Indonesia's support for rampant militias favoring integration resulted in thousands of more deaths. In addition, terrorism is a growing risk and has already caused much damage to Indonesia and its reputation.

Indonesia has the largest Muslim population in the world. Although Indonesia is officially a secular state, a society tolerant of a moderate form of Islam, radical Islamists began to gain momentum. Since the October 2002 Bali bombings, in which more than 200 people were killed, many of them tourists, the government appears to have taken a more active role in controlling the pro-Al Qaeda forces linked to bombings.

Since 2004, foreign investment has grown in Indonesia, but confusion with regard to the restrictions could slow this growth once again. Case in point, the government of Indonesia has been accused of "sending mixed messages" with regard to its investment policy. For example, the Finance Minister announced that Qatar Telecom will be allowed to buy a 65 percent share of Indonesia's second largest mobile phone operator, Indosat, despite previously being limited to a 49 percent stake. Under laws passed last year, foreigners are allowed to own only 49 percent of fixed-line telecom companies and 65 percent of mobile operators. The "official" explanation was that the government had previously limited foreign ownership of Indosat to 49 percent because, despite being primarily a mobile operator, the company also has a fixed-line business. Other issues have also hindered sustained foreign investment. These include the lack of central authority, corruption, and foreign competition from China and Vietnam.

Indonesia still has a long way to go to attract the level of foreign investment that is needed to boost long-term economic growth in the region. Foreign direct investments into Southeast Asia are growing at unprecedented levels. Indonesia is struggling to attract this investment.

Source: "Boom & Gloom; Indonesia Predicts 25% Foreign Investment Jump as Bourse Stays Buoyant," *The Strait Times* (Singapore) July 29, 2010; G. Brownell, "Regions: Asia –Indonesia Signs Green Initiative," *Foreign Direct Investment,* April 15, 2010; "Regions: Asia–Indonesia Makes U-turn on Ownership," *Foreign Direct Investment,* (2009); and "Terrorism Haven: Indonesia," Council on Foreign Relations, December 2005, accessed at http://www.cfr.org/publication/9361/terrorism_havens.html.

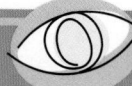
formation for developed and developing economies for 1992–2008. During 1992–1997, FDI flows accounted for about 4 percent of gross fixed capital formation in developed nations and 8 percent in developing nations. By 2006–2008, the figure was 14 percent worldwide, suggesting that FDI had become an increasingly important source of investment in the world's economies.

These gross figures hide important individual country differences. For example, in 2008, inward FDI accounted for some 47 percent of gross fixed capital formation in Sweden and 21 percent in the United Kingdom, but 2.3 percent in Venezuela and 2.2 percent in Japan—suggesting that FDI is an important source of investment capital, and thus economic growth, in the first two countries but not the latter two. These differences can be explained by several factors, including the perceived ease and attractiveness of investing in a nation. To the extent that burdensome regulations limit the opportunities for foreign investment in countries such as Japan and Venezuela, these nations may be hurting themselves by limiting their access to needed capital investments (see the opening case for more details on Japan).

THE SOURCE OF FDI   Since World War II, the United States has been the largest source country for FDI, a position it retained during the late 1990s and early 2000s. Other important source countries include the United Kingdom, France, Germany, the Netherlands, and Japan. Collectively, these six countries accounted for 56 percent of all FDI outflows for the 1998–2008 period and 61 percent of the total global stock of FDI in 2008 (see Figure 7.5). As might be expected, these countries also predominate in rankings of the world's largest multinationals.[10] These nations dominate primarily because they were the most developed nations with the largest economies during much of the postwar period and therefore home

figure 7.5

Cumulative FDI Outflows, 1998–2008 ($ billions)

Note: Share accounted for by the United States would have been larger were it not for significant one-time investment inflows in 2005 due to changes in U.S. tax laws.

Source: Constructed by the author from data in United Nations, *World Investment Report, 2009* (New York and Geneva: United Nations, 2009).

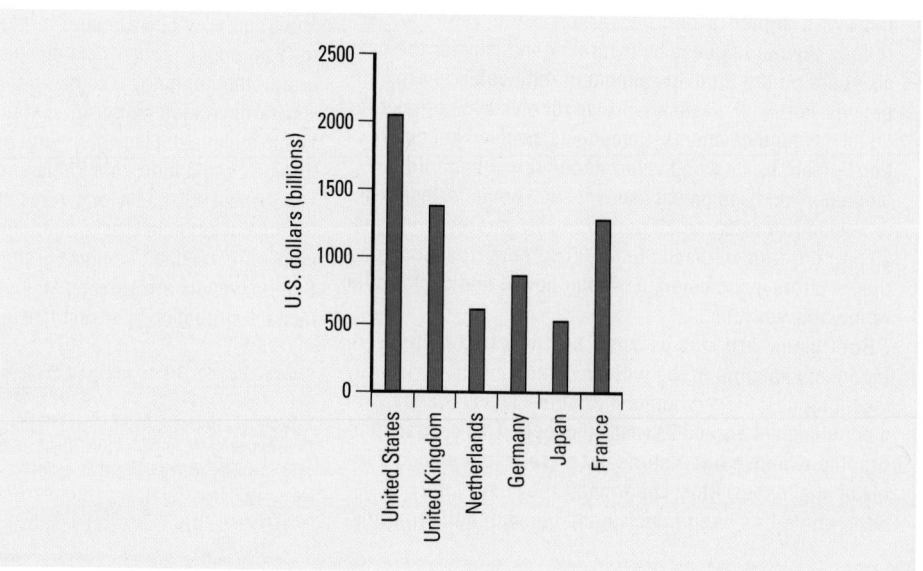

to many of the largest and best-capitalized enterprises. Many of these countries also had a long history as trading nations and naturally looked to foreign markets to fuel their economic expansion. Thus, it is no surprise that enterprises based there have been at the forefront of foreign investment trends.

THE FORM OF FDI: ACQUISITIONS VERSUS GREENFIELD INVESTMENTS

FDI can take the form of a greenfield investment in a new facility or an acquisition of or a merger with an existing local firm. The data suggest the majority of cross-border investment is in the form of mergers and acquisitions rather than greenfield investments. UN estimates indicate that some 40 to 80 percent of all FDI inflows per annum were in the form of mergers and acquisitions between 1998 and 2008. In 2001, for example, mergers and acquisitions accounted for some 78 percent of all FDI inflows. In 2004, the figure was 59 percent, while in 2008 it was 40 percent.[11]

When you see a BP gas station as you are driving down the road, do you realize that the company is British owned? BP = British Petroleum.

However, FDI flows into developed nations differ markedly from those into developing nations. In the case of developing nations, only about one-third of FDI is in the form of cross-border mergers and acquisitions. The lower percentage of mergers and acquisitions may simply reflect the fact that there are fewer target firms to acquire in developing nations.

When contemplating FDI, why do firms apparently prefer to acquire existing assets rather than undertake greenfield investments? We shall consider it in greater depth in Chapter 12; for now we will make only a few basic observations. First, mergers and acquisitions are quicker to execute than greenfield investments. This is an important consideration in the modern business world where markets evolve very rapidly. Many firms apparently believe that if they do not acquire a desirable target firm, then their global rivals will. Second, foreign firms are acquired because those firms have valuable strategic assets, such as brand loyalty, customer relationships, trademarks or patents, distribution systems, production systems, and the like. It is easier and perhaps less risky for a firm to acquire those assets than to build them from the ground up through a greenfield investment. Third, firms make acquisitions because they believe they can increase the efficiency of the acquired unit by transferring capital, technology, or management skills. However, there is evidence that many mergers and acquisitions fail to realize their anticipated gains.[12]

Theories of Foreign Direct Investment

In this section, we review several theories of foreign direct investment. These theories approach the various phenomena of foreign direct investment from three complementary perspectives. One set of theories seeks to explain why a firm will favor direct investment as a means of entering a foreign market when two other alternatives, exporting and licensing, are open to it. Another set of theories seeks to explain why firms in the same industry often undertake foreign direct investment at the same time, and why they favor certain locations over others as targets for foreign direct investment. Put differently, these theories attempt to explain the observed *pattern* of foreign direct

LEARNING OBJECTIVE 2
Explain the different theories of foreign direct investment.

investment flows. A third theoretical perspective, known as the **eclectic paradigm,** attempts to combine the two other perspectives into a single holistic explanation of foreign direct investment (this theoretical perspective is *eclectic* because the best aspects of other theories are taken and combined into a single explanation).

WHY FOREIGN DIRECT INVESTMENT?

Why do firms go to all of the trouble of establishing operations abroad through foreign direct investment when two alternatives, exporting and licensing, are available for exploiting the profit opportunities in a foreign market? **Exporting** involves producing goods at home and then shipping them to the receiving country for sale. **Licensing** involves granting a foreign entity (the licensee) the right to produce and sell the firm's product in return for a royalty fee on every unit sold. The question is important, given that a cursory examination of the topic suggests that foreign direct investment may be both expensive and risky compared with exporting and licensing. FDI is expensive because a firm must bear the costs of establishing production facilities in a foreign country or of acquiring a foreign enterprise. FDI is risky because of the problems associated with doing business in a different culture where the rules of the game may be very different. Relative to indigenous firms, there is a greater probability that a foreign firm undertaking FDI in a country for the first time will make costly mistakes due to its ignorance. When a firm exports, it need not bear the costs associated with FDI, and it can reduce the risks associated with selling abroad by using a native sales agent. Similarly, when a firm allows another enterprise to produce its products under license, the licensee bears the costs or risks. So why do so many firms apparently prefer FDI over either exporting or licensing? The answer can be found by examining the limitations of exporting and licensing as means for capitalizing on foreign market opportunities.

Limitations of Exporting

The viability of an exporting strategy is often constrained by transportation costs and trade barriers. When transportation costs are added to production costs, it becomes unprofitable to ship some products over a large distance. This is particularly true of products that have a low value-to-weight ratio and that can be produced in almost any location. For such products, the attractiveness of exporting decreases, relative to either FDI or licensing. This is the case, for example, with cement. Thus, Cemex, the large Mexican cement maker, has expanded internationally by pursuing FDI, rather than exporting (see the Management Focus feature on Cemex). For products with a high value-to-weight ratio, however, transportation costs are normally a minor component of total landed cost (e.g., electronic components, personal computers, medical equipment, computer software, etc.) and have little impact on the relative attractiveness of exporting, licensing, and FDI.

Transportation costs aside, some firms undertake foreign direct investment as a response to actual or threatened trade barriers such as import tariffs or quotas. By placing tariffs on imported goods, governments can increase the cost of exporting relative to foreign direct investment and licensing. Similarly, by limiting imports through quotas, governments increase the attractiveness of FDI and licensing. For example, the wave of FDI by Japanese auto companies in the United States during the 1980s and 1990s was partly driven by protectionist threats from Congress and by quotas on the importation of Japanese cars. For Japanese auto companies, these factors decreased the profitability of exporting and increased that of foreign direct investment. In this context, it is important to understand that trade barriers do not have to be physically in place for FDI to be favored over exporting. Often, the desire to reduce the threat that trade barriers might be imposed is enough to justify foreign direct investment as an alternative to exporting.

Foreign Direct Investment by Cemex

In little more than a decade, Mexico's largest cement manufacturer, Cemex, has transformed itself from a primarily Mexican operation into the third-largest cement company in the world behind Holcim of Switzerland and Lafarge Group of France. Cemex has long been a powerhouse in Mexico and currently controls more than 60 percent of the market for cement in that country. Cemex's domestic success has been based in large part on an obsession with efficient manufacturing and a focus on customer service that is tops in the industry.

Cemex is a leader in using information technology to match production with consumer demand. The company sells ready-mixed cement that can survive for only about 90 minutes before solidifying, so precise delivery is important. But Cemex can never predict with total certainty what demand will be on any given day, week, or month. To better manage unpredictable demand patterns, Cemex developed a system of seamless information technology, including truck-mounted global positioning systems, radio transmitters, satellites, and computer hardware, that allows it to control the production and distribution of cement like no other company can, responding quickly to unanticipated changes in demand and reducing waste. The results are lower costs and superior customer service, both differentiating factors for Cemex.

The company also pays lavish attention to its distributors—some 5,000 in Mexico alone—who can earn points toward rewards for hitting sales targets. The distributors can then convert those points into Cemex stock. High-volume distributors can purchase trucks and other supplies through Cemex at significant discounts. Cemex also is known for its marketing drives that focus on end users, the builders themselves. For example, Cemex trucks drive around Mexican building sites, and if Cemex cement is being used, the construction crews win soccer balls, caps, and T-shirts.

Cemex's international expansion strategy was driven by a number of factors. First, the company wished to reduce its reliance on the Mexican construction market, which was characterized by very volatile demand. Second, the company realized there was tremendous demand for cement in many developing countries, where significant construction was being undertaken or needed. Third, the company believed that it understood the needs of construction businesses in developing nations better than the established multinational cement companies, all of which were from developed nations. Fourth, Cemex believed that it could create significant value by acquiring inefficient cement companies in other markets and transferring its skills in customer service, marketing, information technology, and production management to those units.

The company embarked in earnest on its international expansion strategy in the early 1990s. Initially, Cemex targeted other developing nations, acquiring established cement makers in Venezuela, Colombia, Indonesia, the Philippines, Egypt, and several other countries. It also purchased two stagnant companies in Spain and turned them around. Bolstered by the success of its Spanish ventures, Cemex began to look for expansion opportunities in developed nations. In 2000, Cemex purchased Houston-based Southland, one of the largest cement companies in the United States, for $2.5 billion. Following the Southland acquisition, Cemex had 56 cement plants in 30 countries, most of which were gained through acquisitions. In all cases, Cemex devoted great attention to transferring its technological, management, and marketing know-how to acquired units, thereby improving their performance.

In 2004, Cemex made another major foreign investment move, purchasing RMC of Great Britain for $5.8 billion. RMC was a huge multinational cement firm with sales of $8.0 billion, only 22 percent of which were in the United Kingdom, and operations in more than 20 other nations, including many European nations where Cemex had no presence. Finalized in March 2005, the RMC acquisition has transformed Cemex into a global powerhouse in the cement industry with more than $15 billion in annual sales and operations in 50 countries. Only about 15 percent of the company's sales are now generated in Mexico. Following the acquisition of RMC, Cemex found that the RMC plant in Rugby was running at only 70 percent of capacity, partly because repeated production problems kept causing a kiln shutdown. Cemex brought in an international team of specialists to fix the problem and quickly increased production to 90 percent of capacity. Going forward, Cemex has made it clear that it will continue to expand and is eyeing opportunities in the fast-growing economies of China and India where currently it lacks a presence, and where its global rivals are already expanding.

Sources: C. Piggott, "Cemex's Stratospheric Rise," *Latin Finance,* March 2001, p. 76; J. F. Smith, "Making Cement a Household Word," *Los Angeles Times,* January 16, 2000, p. C1; D. Helft, "Cemex Attempts to Cement Its Future," *The Industry Standard,* November 6, 2000; Diane Lindquist, "From Cement to Services," *Chief Executive,* November 2002, pp. 48–50; "Cementing Global Success," *Strategic Direct Investor,* March 2003, p. 1; M. T. Derham, "The Cemex Surprise," *Latin Finance,* November 2004, pp. 1–2; "Holcim Seeks to Acquire Aggregate," *The Wall Street Journal,* January 13, 2005, p. 1; J. Lyons, "Cemex Prowls for Deals in Both China and India," *The Wall Street Journal,* January 27, 2006, p. C4; and S. Donnan, "Cemex Sells 25 Percent Stake in Semen Gresik," *FT.com,* May 4, 2006, p. 1.

Internalization Theory
The argument that firms prefer FDI over licensing to retain control over know-how, manufacturing, marketing, and strategy or because some firm capabilities are not amenable to licensing; also known as the market imperfections approach.

Limitations of Licensing

A branch of economic theory known as **internalization theory** seeks to explain why firms often prefer foreign direct investment over licensing as a strategy for entering foreign markets (this approach is also known as the market imperfections approach).[13] According to internalization theory, licensing has three major drawbacks as a strategy for exploiting foreign market opportunities. First, *licensing may result in a firm's giving away valuable technological know-how to a potential foreign competitor.* For example, in the 1960s, RCA licensed its leading-edge color television technology to a number of Japanese companies, including Matsushita and Sony. At the time, RCA saw licensing as a way to earn a good return from its technological know-how in the Japanese market without the costs and risks associated with foreign direct investment. However, Matsushita and Sony quickly assimilated RCA's technology and used it to enter the U.S. market to compete directly against RCA. As a result, RCA is now a minor player in its home market, while Matsushita and Sony have a much bigger market share.

A second problem is that *licensing does not give a firm the tight control over manufacturing, marketing, and strategy in a foreign country that may be required to maximize its profitability.* With licensing, control over manufacturing, marketing, and strategy is granted to a licensee in return for a royalty fee. However, for both strategic and operational reasons, a firm may want to retain control over these functions. The rationale for wanting control over the strategy of a foreign entity is that a firm might want its foreign subsidiary to price and market very aggressively as a way of keeping a foreign competitor in check. Unlike a wholly owned subsidiary, a licensee would probably not accept such an imposition, because it would likely reduce the licensee's profit, or it might even cause the licensee to take a loss.

The rationale for wanting control over the operations of a foreign entity is that the firm might wish to take advantage of differences in factor costs across countries, producing only part of its final product in a given country, while importing other parts from elsewhere where they can be produced at lower cost. Again, a licensee would be unlikely to accept such an arrangement, since it would limit the licensee's autonomy. Thus, for these reasons, when tight control over a foreign entity is desirable, foreign direct investment is preferable to licensing.

A third problem with licensing arises when the firm's competitive advantage is based not as much on its products as on the management, marketing, and manufacturing capabilities that produce those products. The problem here is that *such capabilities are often not amenable to licensing.* While a foreign licensee may be able to physically reproduce the firm's product under license, it often may not be able to do so as efficiently as the firm could itself. As a result, the licensee may not be able to fully exploit the profit potential inherent in a foreign market.

For example, consider Toyota, a company whose competitive advantage in the global auto industry is acknowledged to come from its superior ability to manage the overall process of designing, engineering, manufacturing, and selling automobiles; that is, from its management and organizational capabilities. Indeed, Toyota is credited with pioneering the development of a new production process, known as *lean production*, that enables it to produce higher-quality automobiles at a lower cost than its global rivals.[14] Although Toyota could license certain products, its real competitive advantage comes from its management and process capabilities. These kinds of skills are difficult to articulate or codify; they certainly cannot be written down in a simple licensing contract. They are organizationwide and have been developed over the years. They are not embodied in any one individual but instead are widely dispersed throughout the company. Put another way, Toyota's skills are embedded in its organizational culture, and culture is something that cannot be licensed. Thus, if Toyota were to allow a foreign entity to produce its cars under license, the chances are that the entity could not do so anywhere near as efficiently as could Toyota. In turn, this would limit the ability of the foreign entity to fully develop the market potential of that product. Such reasoning underlies Toyota's preference for direct investment in foreign markets, as opposed to allowing foreign automobile companies to produce its cars under license.

All of this suggests that when one or more of the following conditions holds, markets fail as a mechanism for selling know-how and FDI is more profitable than licensing: (1) when the firm has valuable know-how that cannot be adequately protected by a licensing contract; (2) when the firm needs tight control over a foreign entity to maximize its market share and earnings in that country; and (3) when a firm's skills and know-how are not amenable to licensing.

Advantages of Foreign Direct Investment   It follows that a firm will favor foreign direct investment over exporting as an entry strategy when transportation costs or trade barriers make exporting unattractive. Furthermore, the firm will favor foreign direct investment over licensing (or franchising) when it wishes to maintain control over its technological know-how, or over its operations and business strategy, or when the firm's capabilities are simply not amenable to licensing, as may often be the case.

THE PATTERN OF FOREIGN DIRECT INVESTMENT   Observation
suggests that firms in the same industry often undertaken foreign direct investment about the same time. There also is a clear tendency for firms to direct their investment activities toward certain locations. The two theories we consider in this section attempt to explain the patterns that we observe in FDI flows.

Strategic Behavior   One theory is based on the idea that FDI flows are a reflection of strategic rivalry between firms in the global marketplace. An early variant of this argument was expounded by F. T. Knickerbocker, who looked at the relationship between FDI and rivalry in oligopolistic industries.[15] An **oligopoly** is an industry composed of a limited number of large firms (e.g., an industry in which four firms control 80 percent of a domestic market would be defined as an oligopoly). A critical competitive feature of such industries is interdependence of the major players: What one firm does can have an immediate impact on the major competitors, forcing a response in kind. By cutting prices, one firm in an oligopoly can take market share away from its competitors, forcing them to respond with similar price cuts to retain their market share. Thus, the interdependence between firms in an oligopoly leads to imitative behavior; rivals often quickly imitate what a firm does in an oligopoly.

Oligopoly
An industry composed of a limited number of large firms.

Imitative behavior can take many forms in an oligopoly. One firm raises prices, the others follow; one expands capacity, and the rivals imitate lest they be left at a disadvantage in the future. Knickerbocker argued that the same kind of imitative behavior characterizes FDI. Consider an oligopoly in the United States in which three firms—A, B, and C—dominate the market. Firm A establishes a subsidiary in France. Firms B and C decide that if successful, this new subsidiary may knock out their export business to France and give firm A a first-mover advantage. Furthermore, firm A might discover some competitive asset in France that it could repatriate to the United States to torment firms B and C on their native soil. Given these possibilities, firms B and C decide to follow firm A and establish operations in France.

Studies that looked at FDI by U.S. firms during the 1950s and 60s show that firms based in oligopolistic industries tended to imitate each other's FDI.[16] The same phenomenon has been observed with regard to FDI undertaken by Japanese firms during the 1980s.[17] For example, Toyota and Nissan responded to investments by Honda in the United States and Europe by undertaking their own FDI in the United States and Europe. More recently, research has shown that models of strategic behavior in a global oligopoly can explain the pattern of FDI in the global tire industry.[18]

Multipoint Competition

Arises when two or more enterprises encounter each other in different regional markets, national markets, or industries.

Knickerbocker's theory can be extended to embrace the concept of multipoint competition. **Multipoint competition** arises when two or more enterprises encounter each other in different regional markets, national markets, or industries.[19] Economic theory suggests that rather like chess players jockeying for advantage, firms will try to match each other's moves in different markets to try to hold each other in check. The idea is to ensure that a rival does not gain a commanding position in one market and then use the profits generated there to subsidize competitive attacks in other markets. Kodak and Fuji Photo Film Co., for example, compete against each other around the world. If Kodak enters a particular foreign market, Fuji will not be far behind. Fuji feels compelled to follow Kodak to ensure that Kodak does not gain a dominant position in the foreign market that it could then leverage to gain a competitive advantage elsewhere. The converse also holds, with Kodak following Fuji when the Japanese firm is the first to enter a foreign market.

Although Knickerbocker's theory and its extensions can help to explain imitative FDI behavior by firms in oligopolistic industries, it does not explain why the first firm in an oligopoly decides to undertake FDI rather than to export or license. Internalization theory addresses this phenomenon. The imitative theory also does not address the issue of whether FDI is more efficient than exporting or licensing for expanding abroad. Again, internalization theory addresses the efficiency issue. For these reasons, many economists favor internalization theory as an explanation for FDI, although most would agree that the imitative explanation tells an important part of the story.

The Product Life Cycle

Raymond Vernon's product life-cycle theory, described in Chapter 5, also is used to explain FDI. Vernon argued that often the same firms that pioneer a product in their home markets undertake FDI to produce a product for consumption in foreign markets. Thus, Xerox introduced the photocopier in the United States, and it was Xerox that set up production facilities in Japan (Fuji Xerox) and Great Britain (Rank Xerox) to serve those markets. Vernon's view is that firms undertake FDI at particular stages in the life cycle of a product they have pioneered. They invest in other advanced countries when local demand in those countries grows large enough to support local production (as Xerox did). They subsequently shift production to developing countries when product standardization and market saturation give rise to price competition and cost pressures. Investment in developing countries, where labor costs are lower, is seen as the best way to reduce costs.

Vernon's theory has merit. Firms do invest in a foreign country when demand in that country will support local production, and they do invest in low-cost locations (e.g., developing countries) when cost pressures become intense.[20] However, Vernon's theory fails to explain why it is profitable for a firm to undertake FDI at such times, rather than continuing to export from its home base or licensing a foreign firm to produce its product. Just because demand in a foreign country is large enough to support local production, it does not necessarily follow that local production is the most profitable option. It may still be more profitable to produce at home and export to that country (to realize the economies of scale that arise from serving the global market from one location). Alternatively, it may be more profitable for the firm to license a foreign company to produce its product for sale in that country. The product life-cycle theory ignores these options and, instead, simply argues that once a foreign market is large enough to support local production, FDI will occur. This limits its explanatory power and its usefulness to business in that it fails to identify when it is profitable to invest abroad.

THE ECLECTIC PARADIGM

The eclectic paradigm has been championed by the British economist John Dunning.[21] Dunning argues that in addition to the various factors discussed above, location-specific advantages are also of considerable importance in explaining both the rationale for and the direction of foreign direct investment. By **location-specific advantages,** Dunning means the advantages that arise from utilizing resource endowments or assets that are tied to a particular foreign location and that a firm finds valuable to combine with its own unique assets (such as the firm's technological, marketing, or management capabilities). Dunning accepts the argument of internalization theory that it is difficult for a firm to license its own unique capabilities and know-how. Therefore, he argues that combining location-specific assets or resource endowments with the firm's own unique capabilities often requires foreign direct investment. That is, it requires the firm to establish production facilities where those foreign assets or resource endowments are located.

An obvious example of Dunning's arguments are natural resources, such as oil and other minerals, which are by their character specific to certain locations. Dunning suggests that to exploit such foreign resources, a firm must undertake FDI. Clearly, this explains the FDI undertaken by many of the world's oil companies, which have to invest where oil is located to combine their technological and managerial capabilities with this valuable location-specific resource. Another obvious example are valuable human resources, such as low-cost, highly skilled labor. The cost and skill of labor varies from country to country. Since labor is not internationally mobile, according to Dunning it makes sense for a firm to locate production facilities in those countries where the cost and skills of local labor is most suited to its particular production processes.

However, Dunning's theory has implications that go beyond basic resources such as minerals and labor. Consider Silicon Valley, which is the world center for the computer and semiconductor industry. Many of the world's major computer and semiconductor companies, such as Apple Computer, Hewlett-Packard, and Intel, are located close to each other in the Silicon Valley region of California. As a result, much of the cutting-edge research and product development in computers and semiconductors occurs there. According to Dunning's arguments, there is knowledge being generated in Silicon Valley with regard to the design and manufacture of computers and semiconductors that is available nowhere else in the world. To be

sure, as it is commercialized that knowledge diffuses throughout the world, but the leading edge of knowledge generation in the computer and semiconductor industries is to be found in Silicon Valley. In Dunning's language, this means that Silicon Valley has a *location-specific advantage* in the generation of knowledge related to the computer and semiconductor industries. In part, this advantage comes from the sheer concentration of intellectual talent in this area, and in part it arises from a network of informal contacts that allows firms to benefit from each others' knowledge generation. Economists refer to such knowledge "spillovers" as **externalities,** and a well-established theory suggests that firms can benefit from such externalities by locating close to their source.[22]

In so far as this is the case, it makes sense for foreign computer and semiconductor firms to invest in research and, perhaps, production facilities so they too can learn about and utilize valuable new knowledge before those based elsewhere, thereby giving them a competitive advantage in the global marketplace.[23] Evidence suggests that European, Japanese, South Korean, and Taiwanese computer

Location-Specific Advantages
Advantages that arise from utilizing resource endowments or assets that are tied to a particular foreign location and that a firm finds valuable to combine with its own unique assets (such as the firm's technological, marketing, or management capabilities).

Externalities
Knowledge spillovers.

Silicon Valley has long been known as the epicenter of the computer and semiconductor industry.

and semiconductor firms are investing in the Silicon Valley region, precisely because they wish to benefit from the externalities that arise there.[24] Others have argued that direct investment by foreign firms in the U.S. biotechnology industry has been motivated by desires to gain access to the unique location-specific technological knowledge of U.S. biotechnology firms.[25] Dunning's theory, therefore, seems to be a useful addition to those outlined above, for it helps explain how location factors affect the direction of FDI.[26]

Political Ideology and Foreign Direct Investment

LEARNING OBJECTIVE 3
Understand how political ideology shapes a government's attitudes toward FDI.

Historically, political ideology toward FDI within a nation has ranged from a dogmatic radical stance that is hostile to all inward FDI at one extreme to an adherence to the noninterventionist principle of free market economics at the other. Between these two extremes is an approach that might be called *pragmatic nationalism*.

THE RADICAL VIEW   The radical view traces its roots to Marxist political and economic theory. Radical writers argue that the multinational enterprise (MNE) is an instrument of imperialist domination. They see the MNE as a tool for exploiting host countries to the exclusive benefit of their capitalist-imperialist home countries. They argue that MNEs extract profits from the host country and take them to their home country, giving nothing of value to the host country in exchange. They note, for example, that key technology is tightly controlled by the MNE, and that important jobs in the foreign subsidiaries of MNEs go to home-country nationals rather than to citizens of the host country. Because of this, according to the radical view, FDI by the MNEs of advanced capitalist nations keeps the less developed countries of the world relatively backward and dependent on advanced capitalist nations for investment, jobs, and technology. Thus, according to the extreme version of this view, no country should ever permit foreign corporations to undertake FDI, since they can never be instruments of economic development, only of economic domination. Where MNEs already exist in a country, they should be immediately nationalized.[27]

From 1945 until the 1980s, the radical view was very influential in the world economy. Until the collapse of communism between 1989 and 1991, the countries of Eastern Europe were opposed to FDI. Similarly, communist countries elsewhere, such as China, Cambodia, and Cuba, were all opposed in principle to FDI (although in practice the Chinese started to allow FDI in mainland China in the 1970s). Many socialist countries, particularly in Africa where one of the first actions of many newly independent states was to nationalize foreign-owned enterprises, also embraced the radical position. Countries whose political ideology was more nationalistic than socialistic further embraced the radical position. This was true in Iran and India, for example, both of which adopted tough policies restricting FDI and nationalized many foreign-owned enterprises. Iran is a particularly interesting case because its Islamic government, while rejecting Marxist theory, has essentially embraced the radical view that FDI by MNEs is an instrument of imperialism.

By the end of the 1980s, the radical position was in retreat almost everywhere. There seem to be three reasons for this: (1) the collapse of communism in Eastern Europe; (2) the generally abysmal economic performance of those countries that embraced the radical position, and a growing belief by many of these countries that FDI can be an important source of technology and jobs and can stimulate economic growth; and (3) the strong economic performance of those developing countries that embraced capitalism rather than radical ideology (e.g., Singapore, Hong Kong, and Taiwan).

THE FREE MARKET VIEW The free market view traces its roots to classical economics and the international trade theories of Adam Smith and David Ricardo (see Chapter 5). The intellectual case for this view has been strengthened by the internalization explanation of FDI. The free market view argues that international production should be distributed among countries according to the theory of comparative advantage. Countries should specialize in the production of those goods and services that they can produce most efficiently. Within this framework, the MNE is an instrument for dispersing the production of goods and services to the most efficient locations around the globe. Viewed this way, FDI by the MNE increases the overall efficiency of the world economy.

Imagine that Dell decided to move assembly operations for many of its personal computers from the United States to Mexico to take advantage of lower labor costs in Mexico. According to the free market view, moves such as this can be seen as increasing the overall efficiency of resource utilization in the world economy. Mexico, due to its lower labor costs, has a comparative advantage in the assembly of PCs. By moving the production of PCs from the United States to Mexico, Dell frees U.S. resources for use in activities in which the United States has a comparative advantage (e.g., the design of computer software, the manufacture of high-value-added components such as microprocessors, or basic R&D). Also, consumers benefit because the PCs cost less than they would if they were produced domestically. In addition, Mexico gains from the technology, skills, and capital that the PC company transfers with its FDI. Contrary to the radical view, the free market view stresses that such resource transfers benefit the host country and stimulate its economic growth. Thus, the free market view argues that FDI is a benefit to both the source country and the host country.

For reasons explored earlier in this book (see Chapter 2), the free market view has been ascendant worldwide in recent years, spurring a global move toward the removal of restrictions on inward and outward foreign direct investment. However, in practice no country has adopted the free market view in its pure form (just as no country has adopted the radical view in its pure form). Countries such as Great Britain and the United States are among the most open to FDI, but the governments of these countries both have still reserved the right to intervene. Britain does so by reserving the right to block foreign takeovers of domestic firms if the takeovers are seen as "contrary to national security interests" or if they have the potential for "reducing competition." (In practice, the British government has rarely exercised this right.) U.S. controls on FDI are more limited and largely informal. For political reasons, the United States will occasionally restrict U.S. firms from undertaking FDI in certain countries (e.g., Cuba and Iran). In addition, inward FDI meets some limited restrictions. For example, foreigners are prohibited from purchasing more than 25 percent of any U.S. airline or from acquiring a controlling interest in a U.S. television broadcast network. Since 1988, the government has had the right to review the acquisition of a U.S. enterprise by a foreign firm on the grounds of national security. However, of the 1,500 bids reviewed by the Committee on Foreign Investment in the United States under this law by 2008, only one has been nullified: the sale of a Seattle-based aircraft parts manufacturer to a Chinese enterprise in the early 1990s.[28]

PRAGMATIC NATIONALISM In practice, many countries have adopted neither a radical policy nor a free market policy toward FDI, but instead a policy that can best be described as pragmatic nationalism.[29] The pragmatic nationalist view is that FDI has both benefits and costs. FDI can benefit a host country by bringing capital, skills, technology, and jobs, but those benefits come at a cost. When a foreign company rather than a domestic company produces products, the profits from that investment go abroad. Many countries are also concerned that a foreign-owned manufacturing plant may import many components from its home country, which has negative implications for the host country's balance-of-payments position.

Recognizing this, countries adopting a pragmatic stance pursue policies designed to maximize the national benefits and minimize the national costs. According to this view, FDI should be allowed so long as the benefits outweigh the costs. Japan offers an example of pragmatic nationalism. Until the 1980s, Japan's policy was probably one of the most restrictive among countries adopting a pragmatic nationalist stance. This was due to Japan's perception that direct entry of foreign (especially U.S.) firms with ample managerial resources into the Japanese markets could hamper the development and growth of their own industry and technology.[30] This belief led Japan to block the majority of applications to invest in Japan. However, there were always exceptions to this policy. Firms that had important technology were often permitted to undertake FDI if they insisted that they would neither license their technology to a Japanese firm nor enter into a joint venture with a Japanese enterprise. IBM and Texas Instruments were able to set up wholly owned subsidiaries in Japan by adopting this negotiating position. From the perspective of the Japanese government, the benefits of FDI in such cases—the stimulus that these firms might impart to the Japanese economy—outweighed the perceived costs.

Another aspect of pragmatic nationalism is the tendency to aggressively court FDI believed to be in the national interest by, for example, offering subsidies to foreign MNEs in the form of tax breaks or grants. The countries of the European Union often seem to be competing with each other to attract U.S. and Japanese FDI by offering large tax breaks and subsidies. Britain has been the most successful at attracting Japanese investment in the automobile industry. Nissan, Toyota, and Honda now have major assembly plants in Britain and use the country as their base for serving the rest of Europe—with obvious employment and balance-of-payments benefits for Britain.

SHIFTING IDEOLOGY   Recent years have seen a marked decline in the number of countries that adhere to a radical ideology. Although few countries have adopted a pure free market policy stance, an increasing number of countries are gravitating toward the free market end of the spectrum and have liberalized their foreign investment regime. This includes many countries that less than two decades ago were firmly in the radical camp (e.g., the former communist countries of Eastern Europe and many of the socialist countries of Africa) and several countries that until recently could best be described as pragmatic nationalists with regard to FDI (e.g., Japan, South Korea, Italy, Spain, and most Latin American countries). One result has been the surge in the volume of FDI worldwide, which, as we noted earlier, has been growing twice as fast as the growth in world trade. Another result has been an increase in the volume of FDI directed at countries that have recently liberalized their FDI regimes, such as China, India, and Vietnam.

As a counterpoint, there is recent evidence of the beginnings of what might become a shift to a more hostile approach to foreign direct investment. Venezuela and Bolivia have become increasingly hostile to foreign direct investment. In 2005 and 2006, the governments of both nations unilaterally rewrote contracts for oil and gas exploration, raising the royalty rate that foreign enterprises had to pay the government for oil and gas extracted in their territories. Bolivian President Evo Morales in 2006 nationalized the nation's gas fields and stated he would evict foreign firms unless they agreed to pay about 80 percent of their revenues to the state and relinquish production oversight. In some developed nations, too, there is increasing evidence of hostile reactions to inward FDI. In Europe in 2006, there was a hostile political reaction to the attempted takeover of Europe's largest steel company, Arcelor, by Mittal Steel, a global company controlled by the Indian entrepreneur Lakshmi Mittal. In mid-2005 China National Offshore Oil Company withdrew a takeover bid for Unocal of the United States after highly negative reaction in Congress about the proposed takeover of a "strategic asset" by a Chinese company. Similarly, in 2006 a Dubai-owned company withdrew its planned takeover of some operations at six U.S. ports after negative political reactions. So far, these countertrends are nothing more

Management FOCUS

Lessons Learned from an Ill-fated International Expansion

Seeking to become a leading global financial services conglomerate, former CEO Rolf Huppi led the Swiss-based Zurich Financial Services on a highly aggressive expansion plan in the 1990s. He began acquiring asset management and investment capabilities, and he expanded into the United States. In 1995, Huppi acquired Kemper Corp. for $2 billion, and 70 percent of the mutual fund manager Scudder, Stevens and Clark for $1.6 billion two years later. Then in 1998, Zurich spent $18.6 billion to acquire the financial division of British-American Tobacco, which included the Eagle Star group of insurance companies and mutual funds in the United Kingdom and Farmers Group, the third largest personal-lines property and casualty insurer in the United States.

By 2002, Zurich was bleeding with $3.4 billion in losses. Unable to manage the unwieldy nature of such vast corporate growth, Huppi was replaced with James Schiro, an American executive who immediately went on a cost-cutting campaign, shedding all but the core insurance business. Some analysts attribute the lack of success to a wide variety of integration issues inherent in such rapid acquisitions, particularly when acquiring foreign entities.

Under Shapiro, the company had rebounded to post net income of $2.1 billion by 2003. Since then, and with subsequent leadership, the company has turned a healthy profit. Normally, this would be the end of the story. But it was precisely this corrective step that permitted Zurich to weather the global crisis that affected most, if not all, of the insurance companies worldwide.

Taking advantage of the global economic crisis, and using the lessons learned in the early part of the millennium, Zurich "got back on the horse" and acquired AIG's U.S. Personal Auto Group, an entity that includes 21st Century Insurance Co., which insures more than 4 million vehicles, paying only $1.9 billion for the company. The deal made Zurich the third largest auto insurer in the United States behind State Farm and Allstate, with 7.4 percent of the market. In comparison, property and casualty insurance accounted for 57 percent of Zurich's gross written premiums and fees last year, compared with 43 percent for life insurance. As demonstrated by the AIG acquisition, what expansion has occurred has been carefully controlled. The profits are fairly well distributed. Western Europe generated 38 percent of premiums and fees, the United States provided 28 percent, and Asia chipped in just 2 percent. The company gets the remainder of its revenues from the rest of the Americas, Eastern Europe, the Middle East, and Africa. Zurich's next international push appears to be in Asia. When the moment is right, we can expect another acquisition. Will the company be able to continue to apply the lessons learned?

Sources: J. Kandell, "Zurich Financial Rebounds from Insurance Industry Crisis," *Institutional Investor-International Edition,* June 2010, accessed at http://www.institutionalinvestor.com/Article.aspx?ArticleID=2585802; and E. Holm, "Zurich Acquisition of AIG Unit May Spark More Deals (Update1)," April 17, 2009, http://www.bloomberg.com/apps/news?pid=newsarchive&sid=asjWoouElmCM.

than isolated incidents, but if they become more widespread, the 30-year movement toward lower barriers to cross-border investment could be in jeopardy. As detailed in the accompanying Management Focus, Zurich Financial Services went on an aggressive global buying spree in the mid-1990s that caused the company great financial distress.

Benefits and Costs of FDI

To a greater or lesser degree, many governments can be considered pragmatic nationalists when it comes to FDI. Accordingly, their policy is shaped by a consideration of the costs and benefits of FDI. Here we explore the benefits and costs of FDI, first from the perspective of a host (receiving) country, and then from the perspective of the home (source) country. In the next section, we look at the policy instruments governments use to manage FDI.

LEARNING OBJECTIVE 4
Describe the benefits and costs of FDI to home and host countries.

HOST-COUNTRY BENEFITS   The main benefits of inward FDI for a host country arise from resource-transfer effects, employment effects, balance-of-payments effects, and effects on competition and economic growth.

Resource-Transfer Effects   Foreign direct investment can make a positive contribution to a host economy by supplying capital, technology, and management resources

that would otherwise not be available and thus boost that country's economic growth rate (as the opening case makes clear, the Japanese government has recently come around to this view and has adopted a more permissive attitude to inward investment).[31]

With regard to capital, many MNEs, by virtue of their large size and financial strength, have access to financial resources not available to host-country firms. These funds may be available from internal company sources, or, because of their reputation, large MNEs may find it easier to borrow money from capital markets than host-country firms would.

As for technology, you will recall from Chapter 2 that technology can stimulate economic development and industrialization. Technology can take two forms, both of which are valuable. Technology can be incorporated in a production process (e.g., the technology for discovering, extracting, and refining oil) or it can be incorporated in a product (e.g., personal computers). However, many countries lack the research and development resources and skills required to develop their own indigenous product and process technology. This is particularly true in less developed nations. Such countries must rely on advanced industrialized nations for much of the technology required to stimulate economic growth, and FDI can provide it.

Research supports the view that multinational firms often transfer significant technology when they invest in a foreign country.[32] For example, a study of FDI in Sweden found that foreign firms increased both the labor and total factor productivity of Swedish firms that they acquired, suggesting that significant technology transfers had occurred (technology typically boosts productivity).[33] Also, a study of FDI by the Organization for Economic Cooperation and Development (OECD) found that foreign investors invested significant amounts of capital in R&D in the countries in which they had invested, suggesting that not only were they transferring technology to those countries, but they may also have been upgrading existing technology or creating new technology in those countries.[34]

Foreign management skills acquired through FDI may also produce important benefits for the host country. Foreign managers trained in the latest management techniques can often help to improve the efficiency of operations in the host country, whether those operations are acquired or greenfield developments. Beneficial spin-off effects may also arise when local personnel who are trained to occupy managerial, financial, and technical posts in the subsidiary of a foreign MNE leave the firm and help to establish indigenous firms. Similar benefits may arise if the superior management skills of a foreign MNE stimulate local suppliers, distributors, and competitors to improve their own management skills.

Employment Effects Another beneficial employment effect claimed for FDI is that it brings jobs to a host country that would otherwise not be created there. The effects of FDI on employment are both direct and indirect. Direct effects arise when a foreign MNE employs a number of host-country citizens. Indirect effects arise when jobs are created in local suppliers as a result of the investment and when jobs are created because of increased local spending by employees of the MNE. The indirect employment effects are often as large as, if not larger than, the direct effects. For example,

Another Perspective

Rwanda's Recovery: Africa's Turnaround

Many of us remember the 1994 genocide that Rwanda suffered. Afterward, *The Economist* named Africa "the hopeless continent." Since then, and between 2000 and 2008, Africa's annual output grew by 4.9 percent (adjusted for purchasing-power parity), twice as fast as in the 1980s and 1990s and faster than the global average of 3.8 percent. During that same period, foreign direct investment increased from $10 billion to $88 billion—more than India ($42 billion) and, even more remarkably, catching up with China ($108 billion). Perhaps nowhere was that turnaround more dramatic than in Rwanda. Government authorities are trying to position Rwanda as a trading and services hub in the region. As an example, Rwanda is now selling coffee to Costco, the U.S. wholesale grocer. Furthermore, the United States is investing in Rwandan infrastructure. U.S.-based railroad, Burlington Northern–Santa Fe, is seeking to take advantage of this growth opportunity. ("Uncaging the Lions: Business is Transforming Africa for the Better," *The Economist*, June 10, 2010; *The Economist Intelligence Unit*, Rwanda Country Report, August 2010) when Toyota decided to open a new auto plant in France, estimates suggested the plant would create 2,000 direct jobs and perhaps another 2,000 jobs in support industries.[35]

Cynics argue that not all the "new jobs" created by FDI represent net additions in employment. In the case of FDI by Japanese auto companies in the United States, some argue that the jobs created by this investment have been more than offset by the jobs lost in U.S.-owned auto companies, which have lost market share to their Japanese competitors. As a consequence of such substitution effects, the net number of new jobs created by FDI may not be as great as initially claimed by an MNE. The issue of the likely net gain in employment may be a major negotiating point between an MNE wishing to undertake FDI and the host government.

When FDI takes the form of an acquisition of an established enterprise in the host economy as opposed to a greenfield investment, the immediate effect may be to reduce employment as the multinational tries to restructure the operations of the acquired unit to improve its operating efficiency. However, even in such cases, research suggests that once the initial period of restructuring is over, enterprises acquired by foreign firms tend to grow their employment base at a faster rate than domestic rivals. For example, an OECD study found that foreign firms created new jobs at a faster rate than their domestic counterparts.[36] In America, the workforce of foreign firms grew by 1.4 percent per year, compared with 0.8 percent per year for domestic firms. In Britain and France, the workforce of foreign firms grew at 1.7 percent per year, while employment at domestic firms fell by 2.7 percent. The same study found that foreign firms tended to pay higher wage rates than domestic firms, suggesting that the quality of employment was better. Another study looking at FDI in Eastern European transition economies found that although employment fell following the acquisition of an enterprise by a foreign firm, often those enterprises were in competitive difficulties and would not have survived if they had not been acquired. Also, after an initial period of adjustment and retrenchment, employment downsizing was often followed by new investments, and employment either remained stable or increased.[37]

Balance-of-Payments Effects

FDI's effect on a country's balance-of-payments accounts is an important policy issue for most host governments. A country's **balance-of-payments accounts** track both its payments to and its receipts from other countries. Governments normally are concerned when their country is running a deficit on the current account of their balance of payments. The **current account** tracks the export and import of goods and services. A current account deficit, or trade deficit as it is often called, arises when a country is importing more goods and services than it is exporting. Governments typically prefer to see a current account surplus rather than a deficit. The only way in which a current account deficit can be supported in the long run is by selling assets to foreigners (for a detailed explanation of why this is the case, see the appendix to Chapter 5). For example, the persistent U.S. current account deficit since the 1980s has been financed by a steady sale of U.S. assets (stocks, bonds, real estate, and whole corporations) to foreigners. Since national governments invariably dislike seeing the assets of their country fall into foreign hands, they prefer their nation to run a current account surplus. There are two ways in which FDI can help a country to achieve this goal.

First, if the FDI is a substitute for imports of goods or services, the effect can be to improve the current account of the host country's balance of payments. Much of the FDI by Japanese automobile companies in the United States and Europe, for example, can be seen as substituting for imports from Japan. Thus, the current account of the U.S. balance of payments has improved somewhat because many Japanese companies are now supplying the U.S. market from production facilities in the United States, as opposed to facilities in Japan. Insofar as this has reduced the need to finance a current account deficit by asset sales to foreigners, the United States has clearly benefited.

Balance-of-Payments Accounts
National accounts that track both payments to and receipts from other countries.

Current Account
In the balance of payments, records transactions involving the export and import of goods and services.

A second potential benefit arises when the MNE uses a foreign subsidiary to export goods and services to other countries. According to a UN report, inward FDI by foreign multinationals has been a major driver of export-led economic growth in a number of developing and developed nations over the last decade.[38] For example, in China exports increased from $26 billion in 1985 to more than $250 billion by 2001 and to $969 billion in 2006. Much of this dramatic export growth was due to the presence of foreign multinationals that invested heavily in China during the 1990s. The subsidiaries of foreign multinationals accounted for 50 percent of all exports from that country in 2001, up from 17 percent in 1991. In mobile phones, for example, the Chinese subsidiaries of foreign multinationals—primarily Nokia, Motorola, Ericsson, and Siemens—accounted for 95 percent of China's exports.

Effect on Competition and Economic Growth

Economic theory tells us that the efficient functioning of markets depends on an adequate level of competition between producers. When FDI takes the form of a greenfield investment, the result is to establish a new enterprise, increasing the number of players in a market and thus consumer choice. In turn, this can increase the level of competition in a national market, thereby driving down prices and increasing the economic welfare of consumers. Increased competition tends to stimulate capital investments by firms in plant, equipment, and R&D as they struggle to gain an edge over their rivals. The long-term results may include increased productivity growth, product and process innovations, and greater economic growth.[39] Such beneficial effects seem to have occurred in the South Korean retail sector following the liberalization of FDI regulations in 1996. FDI by large Western discount stores, including Walmart, Costco, Carrefour, and Tesco, seems to have encouraged indigenous discounters such as E-Mart to improve the efficiency of their own operations. The results have included more competition and lower prices, which benefit South Korean consumers.

FDI's impact on competition in domestic markets may be particularly important in the case of services, such as telecommunications, retailing, and many financial services, where exporting is often not an option because the service has to be produced where it is delivered.[40] For example, under a 1997 agreement sponsored by the World Trade Organization, 68 countries accounting for more than 90 percent of world telecommunications revenues pledged to start opening their markets to foreign investment and competition and to abide by common rules for fair competition in telecommunications. Before this agreement, most of the world's telecommunications markets were closed to foreign competitors, and in most countries the market was monopolized by a single carrier, which was often a state-owned enterprise. The agreement has dramatically increased the level of competition in many national telecommunications markets producing two major benefits. First, inward investment has increased competition and stimulated investment in the modernization of telephone networks around the world, leading to better service. Second, the increased competition has resulted in lower prices.

HOST-COUNTRY COSTS

Three costs of FDI concern host countries. They arise from possible adverse effects on competition within the host nation, adverse effects on the balance of payments, and the perceived loss of national sovereignty and autonomy.

Adverse Effects on Competition

Host governments sometimes worry that the subsidiaries of foreign MNEs may have greater economic power than indigenous competitors. If it is part of a larger international organization, the foreign MNE may be able to draw on funds generated elsewhere to subsidize its costs in the host market, which could drive indigenous companies out of business and allow the firm to monopolize the market. Once the market is monopolized, the foreign MNE could raise prices above those that would prevail in competitive markets, with harmful effects on the economic welfare of the host nation. This concern tends to be greater in countries that have few large firms of their own (generally less developed countries). It tends to be a relatively minor concern in most advanced industrialized nations.

In general, while FDI in the form of greenfield investments should increase competition, it is less clear that this is the case when the FDI takes the form of acquisition of an established enterprise in the host nation, as was the case when Cemex acquired RMC is Britain (see the Management Focus, "Foreign Direct Investment by Cemex"). Because an acquisition does not result in a net increase in the number of players in a market, the effect on competition may be neutral. When a foreign investor acquires two or more firms in a host country, and subsequently merges them, the effect may be to reduce the level of competition in that market, create monopoly power for the foreign firm, reduce consumer choice, and raise prices. For example, in India, Hindustan Lever Ltd., the Indian subsidiary of Unilever, acquired its main local rival, Tata Oil Mills, to assume a dominant position in the bath soap (75 percent) and detergents (30 percent) markets. Hindustan Lever also acquired several local companies in other markets, such as the ice cream makers Dollops, Kwality, and Milkfood. By combining these companies, Hindustan Lever's share of the Indian ice cream market went from zero in 1992 to 74 percent in 1997.[41] However, although such cases are of obvious concern, there is little evidence that such developments are widespread. In many nations, domestic competition authorities have the right to review and block any mergers or acquisitions that they view as having a detrimental impact on competition. If such institutions are operating effectively, this should be sufficient to make sure that foreign entities do not monopolize a country's markets.

Adverse Effects on the Balance of Payments   The possible adverse effects of FDI on a host country's balance-of-payments position are twofold. First, set against the initial capital inflow that comes with FDI must be the subsequent outflow of earnings from the foreign subsidiary to its parent company. Such outflows show up as capital outflow on balance of payments accounts. Some governments have responded to such outflows by restricting the amount of earnings that can be repatriated to a foreign subsidiary's home country. A second concern arises when a foreign subsidiary imports a substantial number of its inputs from abroad, which results in a debit on the current account of the host country's balance of payments. One criticism leveled against Japanese-owned auto assembly operations in the United States, for example, is that they tend to import many component parts from Japan. Because of this, the favorable impact of this FDI on the current account of the U.S. balance-of-payments position may not be as great as initially supposed. The Japanese auto companies responded to these criticisms by pledging to purchase 75 percent of their component parts from U.S.-based manufacturers (but not necessarily U.S.-owned manufacturers). When the Japanese auto company Nissan invested in the United Kingdom, Nissan responded to concerns about local content by pledging to increase the proportion of local content to 60 percent and subsequently raising it to more than 80 percent.

National Sovereignty and Autonomy   Some host governments worry that FDI is accompanied by some loss of economic independence. The concern is that key decisions that can affect the host country's economy will be made by a foreign parent that has no real commitment to the host country, and over which the host country's government has no real control. Most economists dismiss such concerns as groundless and irrational. Political scientist Robert Reich has noted that such concerns are the product of outmoded thinking because they fail to account for the growing interdependence of the world economy.[42] In a world in which firms from all advanced nations are increasingly investing in each other's markets, it is not possible for one country to hold another to "economic ransom" without hurting itself.

HOME-COUNTRY BENEFITS

The benefits of FDI to the home (source) country arise from three sources. First, the home country's balance of payments benefits from the inward flow of foreign earnings. FDI can also benefit the home country's balance of payments if the foreign subsidiary creates demands for home-country exports of capital equipment, intermediate goods, complementary products, and the like.

Second, benefits to the home country from outward FDI arise from employment effects. As with the balance of payments, positive employment effects arise when the foreign subsidiary creates demand for home-country exports. Thus, Toyota's investment in auto assembly operations in Europe has benefited both the Japanese balance-of-payments position and employment in Japan, because Toyota imports some component parts for its European-based auto assembly operations directly from Japan.

Third, benefits arise when the home-country MNE learns valuable skills from its exposure to foreign markets that can subsequently be transferred back to the home country. This amounts to a reverse resource-transfer effect. Through its exposure to a foreign market, an MNE can learn about superior management techniques and superior product and process technologies. These resources can then be transferred back to the home country, contributing to the home country's economic growth rate.[43] For example, one reason General Motors and Ford invested in Japanese automobile companies (GM owned part of Isuzu, and Ford owns part of Mazda) was to learn about their production processes. If GM and Ford are successful in transferring this know-how back to their U.S. operations, the result may be a net gain for the U.S. economy.

HOME-COUNTRY COSTS

Against these benefits must be set the apparent costs of FDI for the home (source) country. The most important concerns center on the balance-of-payments and employment effects of outward FDI. The home country's balance of payments may suffer in three ways. First, the balance of payments suffers from the initial capital outflow required to finance the FDI. This effect, however, is usually more than offset by the subsequent inflow of foreign earnings. Second, the current account of the balance of payments suffers if the purpose of the foreign investment is to serve the home market from a low-cost production location. Third, the current account of the balance of payments suffers if the FDI is a substitute for direct exports. Thus, insofar as Toyota's assembly operations in the United States are intended to substitute for direct exports from Japan, the current account position of Japan will deteriorate.

With regard to employment effects, the most serious concerns arise when FDI is seen as a substitute for domestic production. This was the case with Toyota's investments in the United States and Europe. One obvious result of such FDI is reduced home-country employment. If the labor market in the home country is already tight, with little unemployment, this concern may not be that great. However, if the home country is suffering from unemployment, concern about the export of jobs may arise. For example, one objection frequently raised by U.S. labor leaders to the free trade pact between the United States, Mexico, and Canada (see the next chapter) is that the United States will lose hundreds of thousands of jobs as U.S. firms invest in Mexico to take advantage of cheaper labor and then export back to the United States.[44]

INTERNATIONAL TRADE THEORY AND FDI   When assessing the costs and benefits of FDI to the home country, keep in mind the lessons of international trade theory (see Chapter 5). International trade theory tells us that home-country concerns about the negative economic effects of offshore production may be misplaced. The term **offshore production** refers to FDI undertaken to serve the home market. Far from reducing home-country employment, such FDI may actually stimulate economic growth (and hence employment) in the home country by freeing home-country resources to concentrate on activities where the home country has a comparative advantage. In addition, home-country consumers benefit if the price of the particular product falls as a result of the FDI. Also, if a company were prohibited from making such investments on the grounds of negative employment effects while its international competitors reaped the benefits of low-cost production locations, it would undoubtedly lose market share to its international competitors. Under such a scenario, the adverse long-run economic effects for a country would probably outweigh the relatively minor balance-of-payments and employment effects associated with offshore production.

> **Offshore Production**
> FDI undertaken to serve the home market.

Government Policy Instruments and FDI

We have now reviewed the costs and benefits of FDI from the perspective of both home country and host country. We now turn our attention to the policy instruments that home (source) countries and host countries can use to regulate FDI.

> **LEARNING OBJECTIVE 5**
> Explain the range of policy instruments that governments use to influence FDI.

HOME-COUNTRY POLICIES   Through their choice of policies, home countries can both encourage and restrict FDI by local firms. We look at policies designed to encourage outward FDI first. These include foreign risk insurance, capital assistance, tax incentives, and political pressure. Then we will look at policies designed to restrict outward FDI.

Encouraging Outward FDI

Many investor nations now have government-backed insurance programs to cover major types of foreign investment risk. The types of risks insurable through these programs include the risks of expropriation (nationalization), war losses, and the inability to transfer profits back home. Such programs are particularly useful in encouraging firms to undertake investments in politically unstable countries.[45] In addition, several advanced countries also have special funds or banks that make government loans to firms wishing to invest in developing countries. As a further incentive to encourage domestic firms to undertake FDI, many countries have eliminated double taxation of foreign income (i.e., taxation of income in both the host country and the home country). Last, and perhaps most significant, a number of investor countries (including the United States) have used their political influence to persuade host countries to relax their restrictions on inbound FDI. For example, in response to direct U.S. pressure, Japan relaxed many of its formal restrictions on inward FDI in the 1980s. Now, in response to further U.S. pressure, Japan moved toward relaxing its informal barriers to inward FDI. One beneficiary of this trend has been Toys "R" Us, which, after five years of intensive lobbying by company and U.S. government officials, opened its first retail stores in Japan in December 1991. By 2009, Toys "R" Us had more 170 stores in Japan, and its Japanese operation, in which Toys "R" Us retained a controlling stake, had a listing on the Japanese stock market.

Restricting Outward FDI

Virtually all investor countries, including the United States, have exercised some control over outward FDI from time to time. One policy has been to limit capital outflows out of concern for the country's balance of payments. From the early 1960s until 1979, for example, Britain had exchange-control regulations that limited the amount of capital a firm could take out of the country. Although the main intent of such policies was to improve the British balance of payments, an important secondary intent was to make it more difficult for British firms to undertake FDI.

In addition, countries have occasionally manipulated tax rules to try to encourage their firms to invest at home. The objective behind such policies is to create jobs at home rather than in other nations. At one time, Britain adopted such policies. The British advance corporation tax system taxed British companies' foreign earnings at a higher rate than their domestic earnings. This tax code created an incentive for British companies to invest at home.

Finally, countries sometimes prohibit national firms from investing in certain countries for political reasons. Such restrictions can be formal or informal. For example, formal U.S. rules prohibited U.S. firms from investing in countries such as Cuba and Iran, whose political ideology and actions are judged to be contrary to U.S. interests. Similarly, during the 1980s, informal pressure was applied to dissuade U.S. firms from investing in South Africa. In this case, the objective was to pressure South Africa to change its apartheid laws, which happened during the early 1990s.

HOST-COUNTRY POLICIES Host countries adopt policies designed both to restrict and to encourage inward FDI. As noted earlier in this chapter, political ideology has determined the type and scope of these policies in the past. In the last decade of the twentieth century, many countries moved quickly away from a situation where they adhered to some version of the radical stance and prohibited much FDI and toward a situation where a combination of free market objectives and pragmatic nationalism took hold.

Encouraging Inward FDI It is common for governments to offer incentives to foreign firms to invest in their countries. Such incentives take many forms, but the most common are tax concessions, low-interest loans, and grants or subsidies. Incentives are motivated by a desire to gain from the resource-transfer and employment effects of FDI. They are also motivated by a desire to capture FDI away from other potential host countries. For example, in the mid-1990s, the governments of Britain and France competed with each other on the incentives they offered Toyota to invest in their respective countries. In the United States, state governments often compete with each other to attract FDI. For example, Kentucky offered Toyota an incentive package worth $112 million to persuade it to build its U.S. automobile assembly plants there. The package included tax breaks, new state spending on infrastructure, and low-interest loans.[46]

Restricting Inward FDI Host governments use a wide range of controls to restrict FDI in one way or another. The two most common are ownership restraints and performance requirements. Ownership restraints can take several forms. In some countries, foreign companies are excluded from specific fields. They are excluded from tobacco and mining in Sweden and from the development of certain natural resources in Brazil, Finland, and Morocco. In other industries, foreign ownership may be permitted although a significant proportion of the equity of the subsidiary must be

Often governments provide incentives to attract foreign firms. For example, Kentucky offered Toyota an incentive package worth $112 million to build its assembly plant there.

owned by local investors. Foreign ownership is restricted to 25 percent or less of an airline in the United States. In India, foreign firms were prohibited from owning media businesses until 2001, when the rules were relaxed, allowing foreign firms to purchase up to 26 percent of a newspaper.[47]

The rationale underlying ownership restraints seems to be twofold. First, foreign firms are often excluded from certain sectors on the grounds of national security or competition. Particularly in less developed countries, the feeling seems to be that local firms might not be able to develop unless foreign competition is restricted by a combination of import tariffs and controls on FDI. This is a variant of the infant industry argument discussed in Chapter 6.

Second, ownership restraints seem to be based on a belief that local owners can help to maximize the resource-transfer and employment benefits of FDI for the host country. Until the early 1980s, the Japanese government prohibited most FDI but allowed joint ventures between Japanese firms and foreign MNEs if the MNE had a valuable technology. The Japanese government clearly believed such an arrangement would speed up the subsequent diffusion of the MNE's valuable technology throughout the Japanese economy.

Performance requirements can also take several forms. Performance requirements are controls over the behavior of the MNE's local subsidiary. The most common performance requirements are related to local content, exports, technology transfer, and local participation in top management. As with certain ownership restrictions, the logic underlying performance requirements is that such rules help to maximize the benefits and minimize the costs of FDI for the host country. Many countries employ some form of performance requirements when it suits their objectives. However, performance requirements tend to be more common in less developed countries than in advanced industrialized nations.[48]

INTERNATIONAL INSTITUTIONS AND THE LIBERALIZATION OF FDI

Until the 1990s, there was no consistent involvement by multinational institutions in the governing of FDI. This changed with the formation of the World Trade Organization in 1995. The WTO embraces the promotion of international trade in services. Since many services have to be produced where they are sold, exporting is not an option (for example, one cannot export McDonald's hamburgers or consumer banking services). Given this, the WTO has become involved in regulations governing FDI. As might be expected for an institution created to promote free trade, the thrust of the WTO's efforts has been to push for the liberalization of regulations governing FDI, particularly in services. Under the auspices of the WTO, two extensive multinational agreements were reached in 1997 to liberalize trade in telecommunications and financial services. Both these agreements contained detailed clauses that require signatories to liberalize their regulations governing inward FDI, essentially opening their markets to foreign telecommunications and financial services companies.

The WTO has had less success trying to initiate talks aimed at establishing a universal set of rules designed to promote the liberalization of FDI. Led by Malaysia and India, developing nations have so far rejected efforts by the WTO to start such discussions. In an attempt to make some progress on this issue, the OECD in 1995 initiated talks between its members. The aim of the talks was to draft a multilateral agreement on investment (MAI) that would make it illegal for signatory states to discriminate against foreign investors. This would liberalize rules governing FDI between OECD states.

These talks broke down in early 1998, primarily because the United States refused to sign the agreement. According to the United States, the proposed agreement contained too many exceptions that would weaken its powers. For example, the proposed agreement would not have barred discriminatory taxation of foreign-owned companies, and it would have allowed countries to restrict foreign television programs and music in the name of preserving culture. Environmental and labor groups also campaigned against the MAI, criticizing the proposed agreement because it contained no binding environmental or labor agreements. Despite such setbacks, negotiations on a revised MAI treaty might restart in the future. As noted earlier, many individual nations have continued to liberalize their policies governing FDI to encourage foreign firms to invest in their economies.[49]

Focus on Managerial Implications

LEARNING OBJECTIVE 6
Identify the implications for management practice of the theory and government policies associated with FDI.

Several implications for business are inherent in the material discussed in this chapter. In this section, we deal first with the implications of the theory and then turn our attention to the implications of government policy.

The Theory of FDI

The implications of the theories of FDI for business practice are straightforward. First, it is worth noting that the location-specific advantages argument associated with John Dunning does help explain the *direction* of FDI. However, the location-specific advantages argument does not explain *why* firms prefer FDI to licensing or to exporting. In this regard, from both an explanatory and a business perspective perhaps the most useful theories are those that focus on the limitations of exporting and licensing; that is, internalization theories. These theories are useful because they identify with some precision how the relative profitability of foreign direct investment, exporting, and licensing vary with circumstances. The theories suggest that exporting is preferable to licensing and FDI so long as transportation costs are minor and trade barriers are trivial. As transportation costs or trade barriers increase, exporting becomes unprofitable, and the choice is between FDI and licensing. Since FDI is more costly and more risky than licensing, other things being equal, the theories argue that licensing is preferable to FDI. Other things are seldom equal, however. Although licensing may work, it is not an attractive option when one or more of the following conditions exist: (*a*) the firm has valuable know-how that cannot be adequately protected by a licensing contract, (*b*) the firm needs tight control over a foreign entity to maximize its market share and earnings in that country, and (*c*) a firm's skills and capabilities are not amenable to licensing. Figure 7.6 presents these considerations as a decision tree.

Firms for which licensing is not a good option tend to be clustered in three types of industries:

1. High-technology industries in which protecting firm-specific expertise is of paramount importance and licensing is hazardous.
2. Global oligopolies, in which competitive interdependence requires that multinational firms maintain tight control over foreign operations so that they have the ability to launch coordinated attacks against their global competitors.
3. Industries in which intense cost pressures require that multinational firms maintain tight control over foreign operations (so that they can disperse manufacturing to locations around the globe where factor costs are most favorable in order to minimize costs).

Although empirical evidence is limited, the majority of the evidence seems to support these conjectures.[50] In addition, licensing is not a good option if the competitive advantage of a firm is based upon managerial or marketing knowledge that is embedded

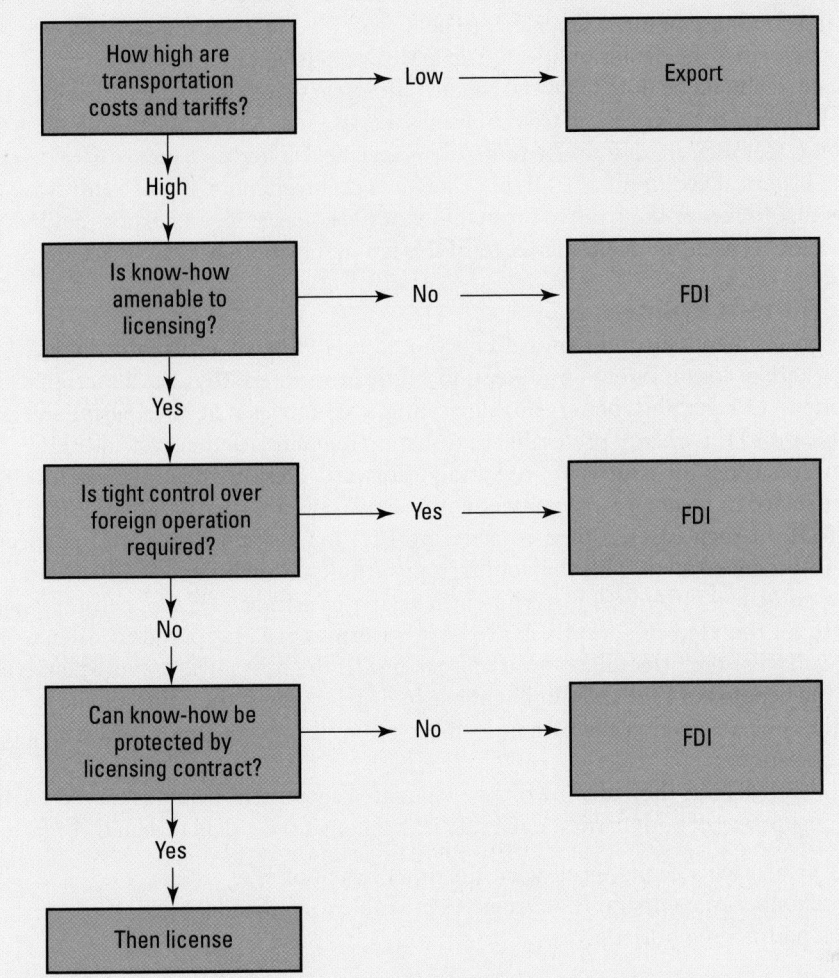

figure
A Decision Framework

in the routines of the firm or the skills of its managers, and that is difficult to codify in a "book of blueprints." This would seem to be the case for firms based in a fairly wide range of industries.

Firms for which licensing is a good option tend to be in industries whose conditions are opposite to those specified above. That is, licensing tends to be more common, and more profitable, in fragmented, low-technology industries in which globally dispersed manufacturing is not an option. A good example is the fast-food industry. McDonald's has expanded globally by using a franchising strategy. Franchising is essentially the service-industry version of licensing, although it normally involves much longer-term commitments than licensing. With franchising, the firm licenses its brand name to a foreign firm in return for a percentage of the franchisee's profits. The franchising contract specifies the conditions that the franchisee must fulfill if it is to use the franchisor's brand name. Thus McDonald's allows foreign firms to use its brand name so long as they agree to run their restaurants on exactly the same lines as McDonald's restaurants elsewhere in the world. This strategy makes sense for McDonald's because (*a*) like many services, fast food cannot be exported; (*b*) franchising economizes the costs and risks associated with opening up foreign markets; (*c*) unlike technological know-how, brand names are relatively easy to protect using a contract; (*d*) there is no compelling reason for McDonald's to have tight control over franchisees; and (*e*) McDonald's know-how, in terms of how to run a fast-food restaurant, is amenable to being specified in a written contract (e.g., the contract specifies the details of how to run a McDonald's restaurant).

Finally, it should be noted that the product life-cycle theory and Knickerbocker's theory of FDI tend to be less useful from a business perspective. The problem with these two theories is that they are descriptive rather than analytical. They do a good job of describing the historical evolution of FDI, but they do a relatively poor job of identifying the factors that influence the relative profitability of FDI, licensing, and exporting. Indeed, the issue of licensing as an alternative to FDI is ignored by both of these theories.

Government Policy

A host government's attitude toward FDI should be an important variable in decisions about where to locate foreign production facilities and where to make a foreign direct investment. Other things being equal, investing in countries that have permissive policies toward FDI is clearly preferable to investing in countries that restrict FDI.

However, often the issue is not this straightforward. Despite the move toward a free market stance in recent years, many countries still have a rather pragmatic stance toward FDI. In such cases, a firm considering FDI must often negotiate the specific terms of the investment with the country's government. Such negotiations center on two broad issues. If the host government is trying to attract FDI, the central issue is likely to be the kind of incentives the host government is prepared to offer to the MNE and what the firm will commit in exchange. If the host government is uncertain about the benefits of FDI and might choose to restrict access, the central issue is likely to be the concessions that the firm must make to be allowed to go forward with a proposed investment.

To a large degree, the outcome of any negotiated agreement depends on the relative bargaining power of both parties. Each side's bargaining power depends on three factors:

- The value each side places on what the other has to offer.
- The number of comparable alternatives available to each side.
- Each party's time horizon.

From the perspective of a firm negotiating the terms of an investment with a host government, the firm's bargaining power is high when the host government places a high value on what the firm has to offer, the number of comparable alternatives open to the firm is greater, and the firm has a long time in which to complete the negotiations. The converse also holds. The firm's bargaining power is low when the host government places a low value on what the firm has to offer, the number of comparable alternatives open to the firm is fewer, and the firm has a short time in which to complete the negotiations.[51]

Key Terms

The objectives of this chapter were to review theories that attempt to explain the pattern of FDI between countries and to examine the influence of governments on firms' decisions to invest in foreign countries. The following points were made:

1. Any theory seeking to explain FDI must explain why firms go to the trouble of acquiring or establishing operations abroad, when the alternatives of exporting and licensing are available to them.

2. High transportation costs or tariffs imposed on imports help explain why many firms prefer FDI or licensing over exporting.

3. Firms often prefer FDI to licensing when (*a*) a firm has valuable know-how that cannot be adequately protected by a licensing contract, (*b*) a firm needs tight control over a foreign entity in order to maximize its market share and earnings in that country, and (*c*) a firm's skills and capabilities are not amenable to licensing.

4. Knickerbocker's theory suggests that much FDI is explained by imitative behavior by rival firms in an oligopolistic industry.

5. Vernon's product life-cycle theory suggests that firms undertake FDI at particular stages in the life cycle of products they have pioneered. However, Vernon's theory does not address the issue of whether FDI is more efficient than exporting or licensing for expanding abroad.

6. Dunning has argued that location-specific advantages are of considerable importance in explaining the nature and direction of FDI. According the Dunning, firms undertake FDI to exploit resource endowments or assets that are location specific.

7. Political ideology is an important determinant of government policy toward FDI. Ideology ranges from a radical stance that is hostile to FDI to a noninterventionist, free market stance. Between the two extremes is an approach best described as pragmatic nationalism.

8. Benefits of FDI to a host country arise from resource transfer effects, employment effects, and balance-of-payments effects.

9. The costs of FDI to a host country include adverse effects on competition and balance of payments and a perceived loss of national sovereignty.

10. The benefits of FDI to the home (source) country include improvement in the balance of payments as a result of the inward flow of foreign earnings, positive employment effects when the foreign subsidiary creates demand for home-country exports, and benefits from a reverse resource-transfer effect. A reverse resource-transfer effect arises when the foreign subsidiary learns valuable skills abroad that can be transferred back to the home country.

11. The costs of FDI to the home country include adverse balance-of-payments effects that arise from the initial capital outflow and from the export substitution effects of FDI. Costs also arise when FDI exports jobs abroad.

12. Home countries can adopt policies designed to both encourage and restrict FDI. Host countries try to attract FDI by offering incentives and try to restrict FDI by dictating ownership restraints and requiring that foreign MNEs meet specific performance requirements.

Critical Thinking and Discussion Questions

1. In 2004, inward FDI accounted for some 24 percent of gross fixed capital formation in Ireland, but only 0.6 percent in Japan. What do you think explains this difference in FDI inflows into the two countries?

2. Compare and contrast these explanations of FDI: internalization theory, Vernon's product life-cycle theory, and Knickerbocker's theory of FDI. Which theory do you think offers the best explanation of the historical pattern of FDI? Why?

3. Read the Management Focus on Cemex and then answer the following questions:
   a. Which theoretical explanation, or explanations, of FDI best explains Cemex's FDI?
   b. What is the value that Cemex brings to the host economy? Can you see any potential drawbacks of inward investment by Cemex in an economy?
   c. Cemex has a strong preference for acquisitions over greenfield ventures as an entry mode. Why?
   d. Why is majority control so important to Cemex?

4. You are the international manager of a U.S. business that has just developed a revolutionary new personal computer that can perform the same functions as existing PCs but costs only half as much to manufacture. Several patents protect the unique design of this computer. Your CEO has asked you to formulate a recommendation for how to expand into Western Europe. Your options are (a) to export from the United States, (b) to license a European firm to manufacture and market the computer in Europe, or (c) to set up a wholly owned subsidiary in Europe. Evaluate the pros and cons of each alternative and suggest a course of action to your CEO.

Use the globalEDGE Resource Desk (http://globalEDGE.msu.edu/resourcedesk/) to complete the following exercises:

1. You are working for a company that is considering investing in a foreign country. Management has requested a report regarding the attractiveness of alternative countries based on the potential return of FDI. Accordingly, the ranking of the top 10 countries in terms of FDI attractiveness is a crucial ingredient for your report. A colleague mentioned a potentially useful tool called the *FDI Confidence Index*, which is updated periodically. Find this index and provide additional information regarding how the index is constructed.

2. Your company is considering opening a new factory in Latin America, and management is evaluating the specific country locations for this direct investment. The pool of candidate countries has been narrowed to Argentina, Brazil, and Mexico. Prepare a short report comparing the foreign direct investment climate and regulations of these three countries, using the *Country Commercial Guides* prepared by the U.S. Department of Commerce.

closing case

Foreign Direct Investment in Africa

Many claim that the solution to Africa's problems is foreign direct investment (FDI). This position has been espoused by the United Nations Economic Commission for Africa in its Economic Report on Africa. Other global institutions, such as the International Monetary Fund and the World Bank, also have suggested that attracting large inflows of foreign investment will lead to economic development. Sub-Saharan African governments have been generally eager to follow the advice.

In Africa, FDI is generally seen by various country governments as a means of overcoming scarce resources, such as capital and entrepreneurship; as providing access to foreign markets; as source of efficient managerial techniques; as vehicle for the transference of technology and innovation; and perhaps most importantly as employment generation. These obviously may differ within different regions and sectors and between the economic/financial policy of a particular country. However, as part of the strategic objectives of the African Union and in an attempt to organize this intent, South African economics ministers are seeking to establish a "free trade zone" that stretches from "Cape Horn to Cairo." Under the proposal, the "trade route" would include the South African Development Community (SADC), the Common Market for Eastern and Southern Africa (CMESA), and the East African Community (EAC). The goal is to make it easier for foreign investors to move capital, goods, and services among African nations.

Part of the linking process is demonstrated by a series of multinational telecommunications groups that are moving into Africa as the continent continues to liberalize its FDI policies. In 2009, in the face of one of the harshest economic periods, telecoms have substantially invested in Africa. According to the London publication, *Foreign Direct Investment*, 36 investment projects were closed in 2009, the same number as in 2008, but in capital expenditures the growth was more than fivefold. Capital expenditure in 2009 was almost $10 billion compared with $1.86 billion in 2008.

One of those investors was the Indian cellular service provider Bharti Airtel, which acquired Kuwait-based mobile telecom group Zain. Zain has a physical presence in 25 countries across Africa and the Middle East, with an estimated 60 percent of its customers coming from Africa. This acquisition prompted MTN, the South African competitor to Bharti Airtel, to enter into talks to purchase Egypt's OrascomTelecom. MTN has also opened a new headquarters in Ghana's capital, Accra, which will act as its head office for west and central Africa. As the most active telecom investor in Africa, MTN has, over the past year, developed five greenfield projects. From the European side, since 2003, Nokia has made the most investments in the region, with 13 projects totaling $58.74 billion. Interestingly enough, there are rumors that MTN and Bharti are in discussions over a potential merger. Such a union between the two companies would create a telecom powerhouse with access to the Indian, African, and Gulf markets.

Other companies potentially looking to expand into Africa include Vodacom, Millicom International Cellular, Portugal Telecom, and Orange. In preparation for a possible investment, Vodacom has established a string of communication centers in Tanzania. This telecommunications capability is permitting further investments.

Among the various African IT sectors, the one receiving the most investment in recent years has been information communications technology and Internet infrastructure, with 59 projects since 2003 totaling $26.3 billion. Whether Africa will be able to establish the free trade zone in combination with the African Union efforts will be challenging.

Sources: S. Anderson, "Regions: Middle East & Africa—Telecom Firms Rush to Africa," *Foreign Direct Investment*, June 1, 2010; "Regions: Middle East & Africa—Ministers Seek Africa Trade Zone," *Foreign Direct Investment*, June 1, 2010; and N. Mwilima, *Foreign Direct Investment in Africa*, Africa Labour Research Network, Labour Resource and Research Institute (LaRRI), September 2003.

Case Discussion Questions

1. What are some of the benefits FDI could bring to Africa?

2. Why have the African economics ministers sought to establish a "free trade zone." Are there any disadvantages in such an organizing structure?

3. Why do you suspect that the telecommunication companies are entering Africa? Are they the first movers in a unifying attempt? Are there other sectors that serve that same function? If so, which are they and what function do they serve?

4. After reading this closing case and the other sections of the textbook, in your judgment does foreign direct investment benefit a host nation? Explain your reasoning.

After you have read this chapter you should be able to:

1 Describe the different levels of regional economic integration.

2 Understand the economic and political arguments for regional economic integration.

3 Understand the economic and political arguments against regional economic integration.

4 Explain the history, current scope, and future prospects of the world's most important regional economic agreements.

5 Understand the implications for business that are inherent in regional economic integration agreements.

chapter

8

Regional Economic Integration

opening case

When the North American Free Trade Agreement (NAFTA) went into effect in 1994, the treaty specified that by 2000 trucks from each nation would be allowed to cross each other's borders and deliver goods to their ultimate destination. The argument was that such a policy would lead to great efficiencies. Before NAFTA, Mexican trucks stopped at the border, and goods had to be unloaded and reloaded onto American trucks, a process that took time and cost money. It was also argued that greater competition from Mexican trucking firms would lower the price of road transportation within NAFTA. Given that two-thirds of cross-border trade within NAFTA goes by road, supporters argued that the savings could be significant.

This provision was vigorously opposed by the Teamsters Union in the United States, which represents truck drivers. The union argued that Mexican truck drivers had poor safety records, and that Mexican trucks did not adhere to the strict safety and environmental standards of the United States. To quote James Hoffa, the president of the Teamsters: "Mexican trucks are older, dirtier and more dangerous than American trucks. American truck drivers are taken off the road if they commit a serious traffic violation in their personal vehicle. That's not so in Mexico. Limits on the hours a driver can spend behind the wheel are ignored in Mexico."

Although they did not state so explicitly, the Teamsters were also clearly motivated by a desire to protect the pay and employment opportunities for American truck drivers.

Under pressure from the Teamsters, the United States dragged its feet on implementation of the trucking agreement. Ultimately the Teamsters sued to stop implementation. An American court rejected the union's arguments and stated the country must honor the treaty. So did a NAFTA dispute settlement panel. This panel ruled in 2001 that the United States was violating the NAFTA treaty and gave Mexico the right to impose retaliatory tariffs.

Mexico decided not to do that, instead giving the United States a chance to honor its commitment. The Bush administration tried to do just that, but was thwarted by opposition in Congress, which approved a measure setting 22 new safety standards that Mexican trucks would have to meet before entering the United States.

In an attempt to break the stalemate, in 2007 the U.S. government set up a pilot program under which trucks from some 100 Mexican transportation companies could enter the United States, provided they passed American safety inspections. The Mexican trucks were tracked, and after 18 months, that program showed that the Mexican carriers actually had a slightly better safety record than their U.S. counterparts. The Teamsters immediately lobbied Congress to kill the pilot program. In March 2009 an amendment attached to a large spending bill did just that.

This time the Mexican government did not let the United States off the hook. As allowed to under the terms of the NAFTA agreement, Mexico immediately placed tariffs on some $2.4 billion of goods shipped from the United States to Mexico. California, an important exporter of agricultural products to Mexico, was hit hard. Table grapes now faced a 45 percent tariff, while wine, almonds, and juices will pay a 20 percent tariff. Pears, which primarily come from Washington State, faced a 20 percent tariff (4 out of 10 pears that the United States exports go to Mexico). Other products hit with the 20 percent tariff include exports of personal hygiene products and jewelry from New York, tableware from Illinois, and oil seeds from North Dakota. The U.S. Chamber of Commerce has estimated that the current situation costs some 25,600 U.S. jobs. The U.S. government said it would try to come up with a new program that both addressed the "legitimate concerns" of Congress and honored its commitment to the NAFTA treaty. What that agreement will be, however, remains to be seen, and as of early 2010, there was no agreement in sight. ●

Sources: J. Giermanski, "Mexican Trucking, Tariffs, Security, and Safety," *CSO Online,* August 25, 2010, http://www.csoonline.com/article/605215/mexican-trucking-tariffs-security-and-safety?page=1; "Don't Keep on Trucking," *The Economist,* March 21, 2009, p. 39; "Mexico Retaliates," *The Wall Street Journal,* March 19, 2009, p. A14; J. P. Hoffa, "Keep Mexican Trucks Out," *USA Today,* March 1, 2009, p. 10; "The Mexican-American War of 2009," *Washington Times,* March 24, 2009, p. A18; and J. Moreno, "In NAFTA Rift, Profits Take a Hit," *HoustonChronical.com,* November 12, 2009.

Introduction

In this chapter we will take a close look at the arguments for regional economic integration through the establishment of trading blocs such as the European Union and the North American Free Trade Agreement. We will discuss the difficult process of forming such blocks and using them as an institutional means for lowering the barriers to cross-border trade and investment between member states. The opening case illustrates some of the promise and problems associated with integrating the economies of different nations into regional trading blocs. The NAFTA provision to remove barriers to trucking across borders was meant to encourage greater efficiencies, with the lower costs benefitting the citizens of all three signatory countries. However, as described in the case, political opposition has stymied any attempt to implement this aspect of NAFTA. By 2009 Mexico was imposing retaliatory tariffs on imports of U.S. goods, as allowed for by the treaty, in an attempt to get the Americans to honor their commitment. Doing so will not be easy, however, given the strong opposition from the well-connected Teamsters Union in the United States.

By **regional economic integration** we mean agreements among countries in a geographic region to reduce, and ultimately remove, tariff and nontariff barriers to the free flow of goods, services, and factors of production between each other. The past two decades have witnessed an unprecedented proliferation of regional trade blocs that promote regional economic integration. World Trade Organization members are required to notify the WTO of any regional trade agreements in which they participate. By 2010, nearly all of the WTO's members had notified the organization of participation in one or more regional trade agreements. The total number of regional trade agreements currently in force is around 400.[1]

Regional Economic Integration
Agreements among countries in a geographic region to reduce, and ultimately remove, tariff and nontariff barriers to the free flow of goods, services, and factors of production between each other.

Consistent with the predictions of international trade theory and particularly the theory of comparative advantage (see Chapter 5) agreements designed to promote freer trade within regions are believed to produce gains from trade for all member countries. As we saw in Chapter 6, the General Agreement on Tariffs and Trade and its successor, the World Trade Organization, also seek to reduce trade barriers. With 153 member states, the WTO has a worldwide perspective. By entering into regional agreements, groups of countries aim to reduce trade barriers more rapidly than can be achieved under the auspices of the WTO.

Nowhere has the movement toward regional economic integration been more successful than in Europe. On January 1, 1993, the European Union (EU) formally removed many barriers to doing business across borders within the EU in an attempt to create a single market with 340 million consumers. However, the EU did not stop there. The member states of the EU have launched a single currency, the euro; they are moving toward a closer political union. On May 1, 2004, the EU expanded from 15 to 25 countries and in 2007 two more countries joined, Bulgaria and Romania, making the total 27. Today, the EU has a population of almost 500 million and a gross domestic product of €11 trillion, making it larger than the United States in economic terms.

Similar moves toward regional integration are being pursued elsewhere in the world. Canada, Mexico, and the United States have implemented the North American Free Trade Agreement (NAFTA). Ultimately, this promises to remove all barriers to the free flow of goods and services between the three countries. While the implementation of NAFTA has resulted in job losses in some sectors of the American economy, in aggregate and consistent with the predications of international trade theory, most economists argue that

Another Perspective

The Origins of "Economic Integration"
Evidence of economic integration goes as far back as the early Roman Empire, whereby economic historians have suggested that a centralized trading system was characterized more by voluntary locally networked markets working within a mutually beneficial exchange system. Interestingly enough, and to a large extent, the modern conceptualization of economic integration is a result of the work of Canadian economist Jacob Viner. In the 1950s, Viner considered trade flows between two states prior and after their unification and then in relation to the rest of the world and its subsequent summary by Hungarian economist Béla Balassa in the 1960s. Balassa believed that supranational common markets, with their free movement of economic factors across national borders, naturally generate demand for further integration, not only economically (via monetary unions) but also politically—and, thus, that economic communities naturally evolve into political unions over time. (P. Temin, "Market Economy in the Early Roman Empire," University of Oxford, Discussion Papers in Economic and Social History, No. 39, March 2001; A. Leitch, "Viner, Jacob," in *A Princeton Companion* [Princeton, NJ: Princeton University Press, 1978]; and K. Polanyi, *The Livelihood of Man* [New York; Academic Press, 1977])

the benefits of greater regional trade outweigh any costs. South America, too, has moved toward regional integration. In 1991, Argentina, Brazil, Paraguay, and Uruguay implemented an agreement known as Mercosur to start reducing barriers to trade between each other, and although progress within Mercosur has been halting, the institution is still in place. There are also active attempts at regional economic integration in Central America, the Andean region of South America, Southeast Asia, and parts of Africa.

While the move toward regional economic integration is generally seen as a good thing, some observers worry that it will lead to a world in which regional trade blocs compete against each other. In this possible future scenario, free trade will exist within each bloc, but each bloc will protect its market from outside competition with high tariffs. The specter of the EU and NAFTA turning into economic fortresses that shut out foreign producers with high tariff barriers is worrisome to those who believe in unrestricted free trade. If such a situation were to materialize, the resulting decline in trade between blocs could more than offset the gains from free trade within blocs.

With these issues in mind, this chapter will explore the economic and political debate surrounding regional economic integration, paying particular attention to the economic and political benefits and costs of integration; review progress toward regional economic integration around the world; and map the important implications of regional economic integration for the practice of international business. Before tackling these objectives, we first need to examine the levels of integration that are theoretically possible.

Levels of Economic Integration

LEARNING OBJECTIVE 1
Describe the different levels of regional economic integration.

Several levels of economic integration are possible in theory (see Figure 8.1). From least integrated to most integrated, they are a free trade area, a customs union, a common market, an economic union, and, finally, a full political union.

In a **free trade area**, all barriers to the trade of goods and services among member countries are removed. In the theoretically ideal free trade area, no discriminatory

figure 8.1

Levels of Economic Integration

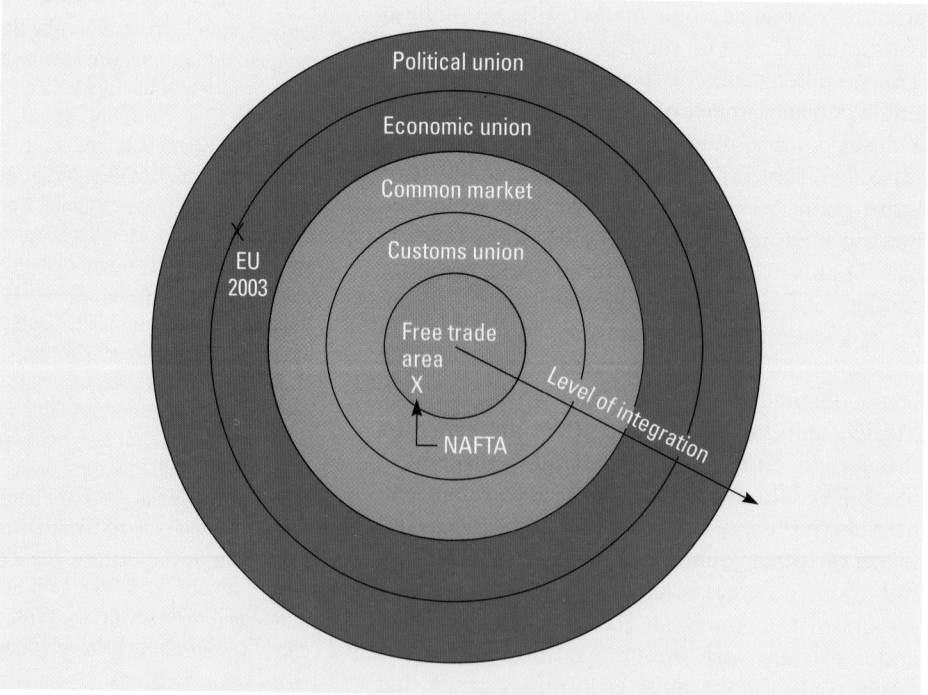

tariffs, quotas, subsidies, or administrative impediments are allowed to distort trade between members. Each country, however, is allowed to determine its own trade policies with regard to nonmembers. Thus, for example, the tariffs placed on the products of nonmember countries may vary from member to member. Free trade agreements are the most popular form of regional economic integration, accounting for almost 90 percent of regional agreements.[2]

The most enduring free trade area in the world is the **European Free Trade Association (EFTA).** Established in January 1960, EFTA currently joins four countries—Norway, Iceland, Liechtenstein, and Switzerland—down from seven in 1995 (three EFTA members, Austria, Finland, and Sweden, joined the EU on January 1, 1996). EFTA was founded by those Western European countries that initially decided not to be part of the European Community (the forerunner of the EU). Its original members included Austria, Great Britain, Denmark, Finland, and Sweden, all of which are now members of the EU. The emphasis of EFTA has been on free trade in industrial goods. Agriculture was left out of the arrangement, each member being allowed to determine its own level of support. Members are also free to determine the level of protection applied to goods coming from outside EFTA. Other free trade areas include the North American Free Trade Agreement, which we shall discuss in depth later in the chapter.

The customs union is one step farther along the road to full economic and political integration. A **customs union** eliminates trade barriers between member countries and adopts a common external trade policy. Establishment of a common external trade policy necessitates significant administrative machinery to oversee trade relations with nonmembers. Most countries that enter into a customs union desire even greater economic integration down the road. The EU began as a customs union, but has now moved beyond this stage. Other customs unions around the world include the current version of the Andean Community (formally known as the Andean Pact) between Bolivia, Colombia, Ecuador, Peru, and Venezuela. The Andean Community established free trade between member countries and imposes a common tariff, of 5 to 20 percent, on products imported from outside.[3]

The next level of economic integration, a **common market** has no barriers to trade between member countries, includes a common external trade policy, and allows factors of production to move freely between members. Labor and capital are free to move because there are no restrictions on immigration, emigration, or cross-border flows of capital between member countries. Establishing a common market demands a significant degree of harmony and cooperation on fiscal, monetary, and employment policies. Achieving this degree of cooperation has proven very difficult. For years, the European Union functioned as a common market, although it has now moved beyond this stage. Mercosur, the South American grouping of Argentina, Brazil, Paraguay, and Uruguay (Venezuela has also applied to join), hopes to eventually establish itself as a common market.

An economic union entails even closer economic integration and cooperation than a common market. Like the common market, an **economic union** involves the free flow of products and factors of production between member countries and the adoption of a common external trade policy, but it also requires a common currency, harmonization of members' tax rates, and a common monetary and fiscal policy. Such a high degree of integration demands a coordinating bureaucracy and the sacrifice of significant amounts of national sovereignty to that bureaucracy. The EU is an economic union, although an imperfect one since not all members of the EU have adopted the euro, the currency of the EU; differences in tax rates and regulations across countries still remain; and some markets, such as the market for energy, are still not fully deregulated.

Free Trade Area
A group of countries committed to removing all barriers to the free flow of goods and services between each other, but pursuing independent external trade policies.

European Free Trade Association (EFTA)
A free trade association including Norway, Iceland, Liechtenstein, and Switzerland.

Customs Union
A group of countries committed to (1) removing all barriers to the free flow of goods and services between each other and (2) the pursuit of a common external trade policy.

Common Market
A group of countries committed to (1) removing all barriers to the free flow of goods, services, and factors of production between each other and (2) the pursuit of a common external trade policy.

Economic Union
A group of countries committed to (1) removing all barriers to the free flow of goods, services, and factors of production; (2) the adoption of a common currency; (3) the harmonization of tax rates; and (4) the pursuit of a common external trade policy.

The move toward economic union raises the issue of how to make a coordinating bureaucracy accountable to the citizens of member nations. The answer is through **political union** in which a central political apparatus coordinates the economic, social, and foreign policy of the member states. The EU is on the road toward at least partial political union. The European Parliament, which is playing an ever more important role in the EU, has been directly elected by citizens of the EU countries since the late 1970s. In addition, the Council of Ministers (the controlling, decision-making body of the EU) is composed of government ministers from each EU member. The United States provides an example of even closer political union; in the United States, independent states are effectively combined into a single nation. Ultimately, the EU may move toward a similar federal structure.

The Case for Regional Integration

The case for regional integration is both economic and political. The case for integration is typically not accepted by many groups within a country, which explains why most attempts to achieve regional economic integration have been contentious and halting. In this section, we examine the economic and political cases for integration and two impediments to integration. In the next section, we look at the case against integration.

THE ECONOMIC CASE FOR INTEGRATION

The economic case for regional integration is straightforward. We saw in Chapter 5 how economic theories of international trade predict that unrestricted free trade will allow countries to specialize in the production of goods and services that they can produce most efficiently. The result is greater world production than would be possible with trade restrictions. That chapter also revealed how opening a country to free trade stimulates economic growth, which creates dynamic gains from trade. Chapter 7 detailed how foreign direct investment (FDI) can transfer technological, marketing, and managerial know-how to host nations. Given the central role of knowledge in stimulating economic growth, opening a country to FDI also is likely to stimulate economic growth. In sum, economic theories suggest that free trade and investment is a positive-sum game, in which all participating countries stand to gain.

Given this, the theoretical ideal is an absence of barriers to the free flow of goods, services, and factors of production among nations. However, as we saw in Chapters 6 and 7, a case can be made for government intervention in international trade and FDI. Because many governments have accepted part or all of the case for intervention, unrestricted free trade and FDI have proved to be only an ideal. Although international institutions such as the WTO have been moving the world toward a free trade regime, success has been less than total. In a world of many nations and many political ideologies, it is very difficult to get all countries to agree to a common set of rules.

Against this background, regional economic integration can be seen as an attempt to achieve additional gains from the free flow of trade and investment between countries beyond those attainable under international agreements such as the WTO. It is easier to establish a free trade and investment regime among a limited number of adjacent

---

Another Perspective

Economic Integration and Aggregation Theory
Based on the concept of aggregation, economic integration not only facilitates the factors of production—namely, the mobility of labor, capital, and technology—but also highlights the underlying principle that "the sums of its parts are more than the whole"; that is, using Aristotle's logic, $1 + 1 + 1 > 3$. This aggregation theory is used throughout global business; it serves as a premise for strategic alliances and mergers, for consolidations and organizational design. It is also one of the underlying principles for globalization. As noted earlier, integration facilitates efficiencies that many times are difficult to quantify.

countries than among the world community. Coordination and policy harmonization problems are largely a function of the number of countries that seek agreement. The greater the number of countries involved, the more perspectives that must be reconciled, and the harder it will be to reach agreement. Thus, attempts at regional economic integration are motivated by a desire to exploit the gains from free trade and investment.

THE POLITICAL CASE FOR INTEGRATION The political case for regional economic integration also has loomed large in several attempts to establish free trade areas, customs unions, and the like. Linking neighboring economies and making them increasingly dependent on each other creates incentives for political cooperation between the neighboring states and reduces the potential for violent conflict. In addition, by grouping their economies, the countries can enhance their political weight in the world.

These considerations underlay the 1957 establishment of the European Community (EC), the forerunner of the EU. Europe had suffered two devastating wars in the first half of the 20th century, both arising out of the unbridled ambitions of nation-states. Those who have sought a united Europe have always had a desire to make another war in Europe unthinkable. Many Europeans also believed that after World War II, the European nation-states were no longer large enough to hold their own in world markets and politics. The need for a united Europe to deal with the United States and the politically alien Soviet Union loomed large in the minds of many of the EC's founders.[4] A long-standing joke in Europe is that the European Commission should erect a statue to Joseph Stalin, for without the aggressive policies of the former dictator of the old Soviet Union, the countries of Western Europe may have lacked the incentive to cooperate and form the EC.

IMPEDIMENTS TO INTEGRATION Despite the strong economic and political arguments in support, integration has never been easy to achieve or sustain for two main reasons. First, although economic integration aids the majority, it has its costs. While a nation as a whole may benefit significantly from a regional free trade agreement, certain groups may lose. Moving to a free trade regime involves painful adjustments. For example, due to the 1994 establishment of NAFTA, some Canadian and U.S. workers in such industries as textiles, which employ low-cost, low-skilled labor, lost their jobs as Canadian and U.S. firms moved production to Mexico. The promise of significant net benefits to the Canadian and U.S. economies as a whole is little comfort to those who lose as a result of NAFTA. Such groups have been at the forefront of opposition to NAFTA and will continue to oppose any widening of the agreement. Thus, as we saw in the opening case, the Teamsters Union in the United States has vigorously opposed the implementation of a trucking agreement in the treaty.

A second impediment to integration arises from concerns over national sovereignty. For example, Mexico's concerns about maintaining control of its oil interests resulted in an agreement with Canada and the United States to exempt the Mexican oil industry from any liberalization of foreign investment regulations achieved under NAFTA. Concerns about national sovereignty arise because close economic integration demands that countries give up some degree of control over such key issues as monetary policy, fiscal policy (e.g., tax policy), and trade policy. This has been a major stumbling block in the EU. To achieve full economic union, the EU introduced a common currency, the euro, controlled by a central EU bank. Although most member states have signed on, Great Britain remains an important holdout. A politically important segment of public opinion in that country opposes a common currency on the grounds that it would require relinquishing control of the country's monetary policy to the EU, which many British perceive as a bureaucracy run by foreigners. In 1992, the British won the right to opt out of any single currency agreement, and as of 2010, the British government had yet to reverse its decision, nor did it seem likely to.

The Case Against Regional Integration

LEARNING OBJECTIVE 3
Understand the economic and political arguments against regional economic integration.

Trade Creation
Trade created due to regional economic integration; occurs when high-cost domestic producers are replaced by low-cost foreign producers in a free trade area.

Trade Diversion
Trade diverted due to regional economic integration; occurs when low-cost foreign suppliers outside a free trade area are replaced by higher-cost foreign suppliers in a free trade area.

Although the tide has been running in favor of regional free trade agreements in recent years, some economists have expressed concern that the benefits of regional integration have been oversold, while the costs have often been ignored.[5] They point out that the benefits of regional integration are determined by the extent of trade creation, as opposed to trade diversion. **Trade creation** occurs when high-cost domestic producers are replaced by low-cost producers within the free trade area. It may also occur when higher-cost external producers are replaced by lower-cost external producers within the free trade area. **Trade diversion** occurs when lower-cost external suppliers are replaced by higher-cost suppliers within the free trade area. A regional free trade agreement will benefit the world only if the amount of trade it creates exceeds the amount it diverts.

Suppose the United States and Mexico imposed tariffs on imports from all countries, and then they set up a free trade area, scrapping all trade barriers between themselves but maintaining tariffs on imports from the rest of the world. If the United States began to import textiles from Mexico, would this change be for the better? If the United States previously produced all its own textiles at a higher cost than Mexico, then the free trade agreement has shifted production to the cheaper source. According to the theory of comparative advantage, trade has been created within the regional grouping, and there would be no decrease in trade with the rest of the world. Clearly, the change would be for the better. If, however, the United States previously imported textiles from Costa Rica, which produced them more cheaply than either Mexico or the United States, then trade has been diverted from a low-cost source—a change for the worse.

In theory, WTO rules should ensure that a free trade agreement does not result in trade diversion. These rules allow free trade areas to be formed only if the members set tariffs that are not higher or more restrictive to outsiders than the ones previously in effect. However, as we saw in Chapter 6, GATT and the WTO do not cover some nontariff barriers. As a result, regional trade blocs could emerge whose markets are protected from outside competition by high nontariff barriers. In such cases, the trade diversion effects might outweigh the trade creation effects. The only way to guard against this possibility, according to those concerned about this potential, is to increase the scope of the WTO so it covers nontariff barriers to trade. There is no sign that this is going to occur anytime soon, however; so the risk remains that regional economic integration will result in trade diversion.

Regional Economic Integration in Europe

LEARNING OBJECTIVE 4
Explain the history, current scope, and future prospects of the world's most important regional economic agreements.

European Union
An economic group of 27 European nations; established as a customs union, it is moving toward economic union; formerly the European Community.

Europe has two trade blocs—the European Union and the European Free Trade Association. Of the two, the EU is by far the more significant, not just in terms of membership (the EU currently has 27 members; the EFTA has 4), but also in terms of economic and political influence in the world economy. Many now see the EU as an emerging economic and political superpower of the same order as the United States. Accordingly, we will concentrate our attention on the EU.[6]

EVOLUTION OF THE EUROPEAN UNION   The **European Union** (EU) is the product of two political factors: (1) the devastation of Western Europe during two world wars and the desire for a lasting peace, and (2) the European nations' desire to hold their own on the world's political and economic stage. In addition, many Europeans were aware of the potential economic benefits of closer economic integration of the countries.

The forerunner of the EU, the European Coal and Steel Community was formed in 1951 by Belgium, France, West Germany, Italy, Luxembourg, and the Netherlands. Its objective was to remove barriers to intragroup shipments of coal, iron, steel, and scrap metal. With the signing of the **Treaty of Rome** in 1957, the European Community was established. The name changed again in 1994 when the European Community became the European Union following the ratification of the Maastricht Treaty (discussed later).

Treaty of Rome
The 1957 treaty that established the European Community.

The Treaty of Rome provided for the creation of a common market. Article 3 of the treaty laid down the key objectives of the new community, calling for the elimination of internal trade barriers and the creation of a common external tariff and requiring member states to abolish obstacles to the free movement of factors of production among the members. To facilitate the free movement of goods, services, and factors of production, the treaty provided for any necessary harmonization of the member states' laws. Furthermore, the treaty committed the EC to establish common policies in agriculture and transportation.

The community grew in 1973, when Great Britain, Ireland, and Denmark joined. These three were followed in 1981 by Greece, in 1986 by Spain and Portugal, and in 1996 by Austria, Finland, and Sweden, bringing the total membership to 15 (East Germany became part of the EC after the reunification of Germany in 1990). Another 10 countries joined the EU on May 1, 2004, 8 of them from Eastern Europe plus the small Mediterranean nations of Malta and Cyprus. Bulgaria and Romania joined in 2007, bringing the total number of member states to 27 (see Map 8.1). With a population of almost 500 million and a GDP of €11 trillion, larger than that of the United States, the EU through these enlargements has become a global superpower.[7]

European Commission
Body responsible for proposing EU legislation, implementing it, and monitoring compliance.

POLITICAL STRUCTURE OF THE EUROPEAN UNION The economic policies of the EU are formulated and implemented by a complex and still-evolving political structure. The four main institutions in this structure are the European Commission, the Council of the European Union, the European Parliament, and the Court of Justice.[8]

The **European Commission** is responsible for proposing EU legislation, implementing it, and monitoring compliance with EU laws by member states. Headquartered in Brussels, Belgium, the commission has more than 24,000 employees. It is run by a group of commissioners appointed by each member country for five-year renewable terms. There are 27 commissioners, one from each member state. A president of the commission is chosen by member states, and the president then chooses other members in consultation with the states. The entire commission has to be approved by the European Parliament before it can begin work. The commission has a monopoly in proposing European Union legislation. The commission makes a proposal, which goes to the Council of the European Union and then to the European Parliament. The council

L'Oreal Chief Executive Officer Lindsay Owen-Jones and L'Oreal Deputy Chief Executive Officer Jean-Paul Agon attend a press conference to announce that L'Oreal was buying Body Shop International, renowned for its ethical hair and skin products. L'Oreal, the world's leading cosmetics company, bought Body Shop for £652 million pounds (€940 million; $1.143 billion). The European Commission reviews acquisitions such as this between competitors.

map **8.1**

Member States of the European Union in 2010

Source: The European Union; http://europa.eu/abc/european_countries/index_en.htm.

cannot legislate without a commission proposal in front of it. The commission is also responsible for implementing aspects of EU law, although in practice much of this must be delegated to member states. Another responsibility of the commission is to monitor member states to make sure they are complying with EU laws. In this policing role, the commission will normally ask a state to comply with any EU laws that are being broken. If this persuasion is not sufficient, the commission can refer a case to the Court of Justice.

The European Commission's role in competition policy has become increasingly important to business in recent years. Since 1990 when the office was formally assigned a role in competition policy, the EU's competition commissioner has been steadily gaining influence as the chief regulator of competition policy in the member nations of the EU. As with antitrust authorities in the United States, which include the Federal Trade Commission and the Department of Justice, the role of the competition commissioner is to ensure that no one enterprise uses its market power to drive out competitors and monopolize markets. The commissioner also reviews proposed mergers and acquisitions to

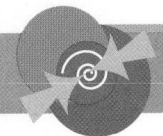

Management FOCUS

The European Commission: Limitations on Economic Integration?

Within an integrated economy, not all efforts at integration are viewed similarly, let alone favorably, especially when they appear to stifle competition. Consider the most recent case of the proposed acquisition of Sara Lee by Unilever.

Unilever is actually two companies. One is Dutch, the other British. Unilever N.V. and Unilever PLC, together with their group companies, constitute a global food, personal care, and household products powerhouse. The company's vast portfolio of products includes Hellmann's (mayonnaise), Knorr (soups), Lipton (tea), Dove and Lux (soaps), and Sure and Degree (antiperspirants). Unilever's consumer goods are sold in more than 170 countries. The company was the world's #1 consumer products maker until Procter & Gamble purchased Gillette in 2005. Based in England, Unilever PLC trades on the London and New York stock exchanges.

In an attempt to maintain the competitive edge lost to Procter & Gamble, Unilever is now seeking to acquire several divisions of Sara Lee, including its personal care unit and its European detergents business. The hope is that the $1.65 billion acquisition will strengthen its operations in Western Europe and Asia, adding Brylcreem and Radox to its portfolio. The proposed acquisition, however, is coming under scrutiny.

The European Commission, the European Union's executive arm and Europe's highest antitrust authority, and "the competition watchdog," is concerned with the transaction. Although only two mergers have been rejected in the past six years—Ryanair Holdings PLC's bid for Ireland's Aer Lingus Group PLC and a tie-up in the Portuguese electricity market—this one has come under the Commission's watchful eye, and they have instigated an investigation.

The reason for the investigation is because an initial market inquiry suggests that there may be a series of products that raise potential antitrust issues. The European Commission is concerned about "several product markets, including deodorants, skin cleansing and fabric products." Joaquin Almunia, the EU competition commissioner, said: "This merger creates significant overlaps in a number of products used by consumers on an everyday basis. We need to make sure that if there are competition concerns, they are duly addressed."

If the proposed transaction were permitted, Unilever would stand to acquire more than 90 brands across different product categories in 19 European countries, which resulted in sales of more than 750 million euros (more than $1 billion dollars) in 2009. Antitrust is one of the forces that work against economic integration. Based on the concept of monopoly and fair competition, the European Union is careful to make sure that a competitive environment is maintained. As usually happens, Unilever may not be able to acquire all of Sara Lee's companies and all their products. By limiting the acquisition, the European Commission hopes to maintain the competitive environment within the European Union.

Sources: L. Vitorovich and P. Kiviniemi, "EU Voices Concerns over Unilever's Deal with Sara Lee," *The Wall Street Journal,* August 19, 2010, http://online.wsj.com/article/NA_WSJ_PUB:SB100014240527487; A. White and S. Bodoni, "Unilever's Acquisition of Sara Lee Detergents Business Faces EU Objections," http://www.bloomberg.com/news/2010-08-19/unilever-s-planned-acquisition-of-sara-lee-faces-eu-antitrust-objection.html; and James Thompson, "Unilever Faces Probe over Sara Lee." *The Independent,* June 2, 2010, http://www.independent.co.uk/news/business/news/unilever-faces-probe-over-sara-lee-1988706.html.

make sure they do not create a dominant enterprise with substantial market power.[9] For example, in 2000 a proposed merger between Time Warner of the United States and EMI of the United Kingdom, both music recording companies, was withdrawn after the commission expressed concerns that the merger would reduce the number of major record companies from five to four and create a dominant player in the $40 billion global music industry. Similarly, the commission blocked a proposed merger between two U.S. telecommunication companies, WorldCom and Sprint, because their combined holdings of Internet infrastructure in Europe would give the merged companies so much market power that the commission argued the combined company would dominate that market. Another example of the commission's influence over business combinations is given in the accompanying Management Focus, which looks at the commission's role in shaping mergers and joint ventures in the personal care and household products industries.

The **European Council** represents the interests of member states. It is clearly the ultimate controlling authority within the EU since draft legislation from the commission can become EU law only if the council agrees. The council is composed of one representative from the government of each member state. The membership,

European Council
The ultimate controlling authority within the EU.

however, varies depending on the topic being discussed. When agricultural issues are being discussed, the agriculture ministers from each state attend council meetings; when transportation is being discussed, transportation ministers attend, and so on. Before 1993, all council issues had to be decided by unanimous agreement between member states. This often led to marathon council sessions and a failure to make progress or reach agreement on commission proposals. In an attempt to clear the resulting logjams, the Single European Act formalized the use of majority voting rules on issues "which have as their object the establishment and functioning of a single market." Most other issues, however, such as tax regulations and immigration policy, still require unanimity among council members if they are to become law. The votes that a country gets in the council are related to the size of the country. For example, Britain, a large country, has 29 votes, whereas Denmark, a much smaller state, has 7 votes.

European Parliament
Elected EU body that consults on issues proposed by the European Commission.

The **European Parliament,** which now has 732 members, is directly elected by the populations of the member states. The parliament, which meets in Strasbourg, France, is primarily a consultative rather than legislative body. It debates legislation proposed by the commission and forwarded to it by the council. It can propose amendments to that legislation, which the commission and ultimately the council are not obliged to take up but often will. The power of the parliament recently has been increasing, although not by as much as parliamentarians would like. The European Parliament now has the right to vote on the appointment of commissioners as well as veto some laws (such as the EU budget and single-market legislation).

One major debate waged in Europe over the past few years is whether the council or the parliament should ultimately be the most powerful body in the EU. Some in Europe expressed concern over the democratic accountability of the EU bureaucracy. One side argued that the answer to this apparent democratic deficit lay in increasing the power of the parliament, while others think that true democratic legitimacy lies with elected governments, acting through the Council of the European Union.[10] After significant debate, in December 2007 the member states signed a new treaty, the **Treaty of Lisbon,** under which the power of the European Parliament is increased. Ratified by all member states by the end of 2009, the treaty makes the European Parliament the co-equal legislator for almost all European laws.[11] The Treaty of Lisbon also creates a new position, a president of the European Council, who will serve a 30-month term and represent the nation-states that make up the European Union. Under the treaty, the European Commission will be reduced to 18 members, with a rotation system that ensures that every member state has regular and equal membership.

The Treaty of Lisbon
Treaty signed in 2007 that made the European Parliament the co-equal legislator for almost all European laws and also created the position of the president of the European Council.

Court of Justice
Supreme appeals court for EU law.

The **Court of Justice,** which is comprised of one judge from each country, is the supreme appeals court for EU law. Like commissioners, the judges are required to act as independent officials, rather than as representatives of national interests. The commission or a member country can bring other members to the court for failing to meet treaty obligations. Similarly, member countries, companies, or institutions can bring the commission or council to the court for failure to act according to an EU treaty.

Single European Act
A 1987 act, adopted by members of the European Community, that committed member countries to establishing an economic union.

THE SINGLE EUROPEAN ACT

Two revolutions occurred in Europe in the late 1980s. The first was the collapse of communism in Eastern Europe. The second revolution was much quieter, but its impact on Europe and the world may have been just as profound as the first. It was the adoption of the **Single European Act** by the member nations of the European Community (EC) in 1987. This act committed member countries to work toward establishment of a single market by December 31, 1992.

The Single European Act was born of a frustration among members that the community was not living up to its promise. By the early 1980s, it was clear that the EC had fallen short of its objectives to remove barriers to the free flow of trade and investment between member countries and to harmonize the wide range of technical and legal standards for doing business. Against this background, many of the EC's prominent businesspeople mounted an energetic campaign in the early 1980s to end the EC's economic divisions. The EC responded by creating the Delors Commission. Under the chairmanship of Jacques Delors, the commission proposed that all impediments to the formation of a single market be eliminated by December 31, 1992. The result was the Single European Act, which was independently ratified by the parliaments of each member country and became EC law in 1987.

The Objectives of the Act   The purpose of the Single European Act was to have one market in place by December 31, 1992. The act proposed the following changes:[12]

- Remove all frontier controls between EC countries, thereby abolishing delays and reducing the resources required for complying with trade bureaucracy.
- Apply the principle of "mutual recognition" to product standards. A standard developed in one EC country should be accepted in another, provided it meets basic requirements in such matters as health and safety.
- Open public procurement to nonnational suppliers, reducing costs directly by allowing lower-cost suppliers into national economies and indirectly by forcing national suppliers to compete.
- Lift barriers to competition in the retail banking and insurance businesses, which should drive down the costs of financial services, including borrowing, throughout the EC.
- Remove all restrictions on foreign exchange transactions between member countries by the end of 1992.
- Abolish restrictions on cabotage—the right of foreign truckers to pick up and deliver goods within another member state's borders—by the end of 1992. Estimates suggested this would reduce the cost of haulage within the EC by 10 to 15 percent.

All those changes were predicted to lower the costs of doing business in the EC, but the single-market program was also expected to have more complicated supply-side effects. For example, the expanded market was predicted to give EC firms greater opportunities to exploit economies of scale. In addition, it was thought that the increase in competitive intensity brought about by removing internal barriers to trade and investment would force EC firms to become more efficient. To signify the importance of the Single European Act, the European Community also decided to change its name to the European Union once the act took effect.

Impact   The Single European Act has had a significant impact on the EU economy.[13] The act provided the impetus for the restructuring of substantial sections of European industry. Many firms have shifted from national to pan-European production and distribution systems in an attempt to realize scale economies and better compete in a single market.

Creation of a single financial services market in the European Union has taken longer than expected due to member states' differing regulations and the significant amount of inertia involved in getting people to accept this change.

EU's Single Financial Services Not Yet a Reality

The European Union in 1999 embarked upon an ambitious action plan to create a single market in financial services by January 1, 2005. Launched a few months after the euro, the EU's single currency, the goal was to dismantle barriers to cross-border activity in financial services, creating a continent-wide market for banking service, insurance services, and investment products. In this vision of a single Europe, a citizen of France might use a German firm for basic banking services, borrow a home mortgage from an Italian institution, buy auto insurance from a Dutch enterprise, and keep her savings in mutual funds managed by a British company. Similarly, an Italian firm might raise capital from investors across Europe, using a German firm as its lead underwriter to issue stock for sale through stock exchanges in London and Frankfurt.

One main benefit of a single market, according to its advocates, would be greater competition for financial services, which would give consumers more choices, lower prices, and require financial service firms in the EU to become more efficient, thereby increasing their global competitiveness. Another major benefit would be the creation of a single European capital market. The increased liquidity of a larger capital market would make it easier for firms to borrow funds, lowering their cost of capital (the price of money) and stimulating business investment in Europe, which would create more jobs. A European Commission study suggested that the creation of a single market in financial services would increase the EU's gross domestic product by 1.1 percent a year, creating an additional €130 billion in wealth over a decade. Total business investment would increase by 6 percent annually in the long run, private consumption by 0.8 percent, and total employment by 0.5 percent a year.

Creating a single market has been anything but easy. The financial markets of different EU member states have historically been segmented from each other, and each has its own regulatory framework. In the past, EU financial services firms rarely did business across national borders because of a host of different national regulations with regard to taxation, oversight, accounting information, cross-border takeovers, and the like, all of which had to be harmonized.

To complicate matters, long-standing cultural and linguistic barriers complicated the move toward a single market. While in theory an Italian might benefit by being able to purchase homeowners' insurance from a British company, in practice he might be predisposed to purchase it from a local enterprise, even if the price were higher.

By 2010 the EU had made significant progress. More than 40 measures designed to create a single market in financial services had become EU law and others were in the pipeline. The new rules embraced issues as diverse as the conduct of business by investment firms, stock exchanges, and banks; disclosure standards for listing companies on public exchanges; and the harmonization of accounting standards across nations. However, there had also been significant setbacks. Most notably, legislation designed to make it easier for firms to make hostile cross-border acquisitions was defeated, primarily due to opposition from German members of the European Parliament, making it more difficult for financial service firms to build pan-European operations. In addition, national governments have still reserved the right to block even friendly cross-border mergers between financial service firms. For example, Italian banking law still requires the governor of the Bank of Italy to give permission to any foreign enterprise that wishes to purchase more than 5 percent of an Italian bank—and no foreigners have yet to acquire a majority position in an Italian bank, primarily, say critics, due to nationalistic concerns on the part of the Italians.

The critical issue now is enforcement of the rules that have been put in place. Some believe that it will be at least another decade before the benefits of the new regulations become apparent. In the meantime, the changes may impose significant costs on financial institutions as they attempt to deal with the new raft of regulations.

Sources: European Commission: The EU Single Market, http://ec.europa.eu/internal_market/top_layer/index_24_en.htm, accessed August 25, 2010; C. Randzio-Plath, "Europe Prepares for a Single Financial Market," *Intereconomic,* May–June 2004, pp. 142–46; T. Buck, D. Hargreaves, and P. Norman, "Europe's Single Financial Market," *Financial Times,* January 18, 2005, p. 17; "The Gate-keeper," *The Economist,* February 19, 2005, p. 79; P. Hofheinz, "A Capital Idea: The European Union Has a Grand Plan to Make Its Financial Markets More Efficient," *The Wall Street Journal,* October 14, 2002, p. R4; and "Banking on McCreevy: Europe's Single Market," *The Economist,* November 26, 2005, p. 91.

The results have included faster economic growth than would otherwise have been the case.

However, nearly two decades after the formation of a single market, the reality still falls short of the ideal. For example, as described in the accompanying Country Focus, it has been hard work to establish a fully functioning single market for financial services in the EU. Thus, although the EU is undoubtedly moving toward a single marketplace, established legal, cultural, and language differences between nations mean that implementation has been uneven.

THE ESTABLISHMENT OF THE EURO

In December 1991, EC members signed a treaty (the **Maastricht Treaty**) that committed them to adopting a common currency by January 1, 1999.[14] The euro is now used by 16 of the 27 member states of the European Union; these 16 states are members of what is often referred to as the euro zone. It encompasses 330 million EU citizens and includes the powerful economies of Germany and France. Many of the countries that joined the EU on May 1, 2004, and the two that joined in 2007, will adopt the euro when they fulfill certain economic criteria—a high degree of price stability, a sound fiscal situation, stable exchange rates, and converged long-term interest rates. The current members had to meet the same criteria.

Maastricht Treaty
Treaty agreed to in 1991, but not ratified until January 1, 1994, that committed the 12 member states of the European Community to adopt a common currency.

Establishment of the euro has rightly been described as an amazing political feat with few historical precedents. Establishing the euro required participating national governments not only to give up their own currencies, but also to give up control over monetary policy. Governments do not routinely sacrifice national sovereignty for the greater good, indicating the importance that the Europeans attach to the euro. By adopting the euro, the EU has created the second most widely traded currency in the world after that of the U.S. dollar. Some believe that ultimately the euro could come to rival the dollar as the most important currency in the world.

Three long-term EU members, Great Britain, Denmark, and Sweden, are still sitting on the sidelines. The countries agreeing to the euro locked their exchange rates against each other January 1, 1999. Euro notes and coins were not actually issued until January 1, 2002. In the interim, national currencies circulated in each of the 12 countries. However, in each participating state, the national currency stood for a defined amount of euros. After January 1, 2002, euro notes and coins were issued and the national currencies were taken out of circulation. By mid-2002, all prices and routine economic transactions within the euro zone were in euros.

Benefits of the Euro

Europeans decided to establish a single currency in the EU for a number of reasons. First, they believe that businesses and individuals will realize significant savings from having to handle one currency, rather than many. These savings come from lower foreign exchange and hedging costs. For example, people going from Germany to France no longer have to pay a commission to a bank to change German deutsche marks into French francs. Instead, they use euros. According to the European Commission, such savings amount to 0.5 percent of the European Union's GDP, or about $55 billion a year.

Second, and perhaps more importantly, the adoption of a common currency makes it easier to compare prices across Europe. This has been increasing competition because it has become easier for consumers to shop around. For example, if a German finds that cars sell for less in France than Germany, he may be tempted to purchase from a French car dealer rather than his local car dealer. Alternatively, traders may engage in arbitrage to exploit such price differentials, buying cars in France and reselling them in Germany. The only way that German car dealers will be able to hold on to business in the face of such competitive pressures will be to reduce the prices they charge for cars. As a consequence of such pressures, the introduction of a common currency has led to lower prices, which translates into substantial gains for European consumers.

Third, faced with lower prices, European producers have been forced to look for ways to reduce their production costs to maintain their profit margins. The introduction of a common currency, by increasing competition, has produced long-run gains in the economic efficiency of European companies.

Fourth, the introduction of a common currency has given a boost to the development of a highly liquid pan-European capital market. Over time, the development of such a capital market should lower the cost of capital and lead to an increase in both the level of investment and the efficiency with which investment funds are allocated. This could be especially helpful to smaller companies that have historically had difficulty borrowing money from domestic banks. For example, the capital market of Portugal is very small and illiquid, which makes it extremely difficult for bright Portuguese entrepreneurs with a good idea to borrow money at a reasonable price. However, in theory, such companies can now tap a much more liquid pan-European capital market.

Finally, the development of a pan-European, euro-denominated capital market will increase the range of investment options open to both individuals and institutions. For example, it will now be much easier for individuals and institutions based in, let's say, Holland to invest in Italian or French companies. This will enable European investors to better diversify their risk, which again lowers the cost of capital, and should also increase the efficiency with which capital resources are allocated.[15]

Costs of the Euro   The drawback, for some, of a single currency is that national authorities have lost control over monetary policy. Thus, it is crucial to ensure that the EU's monetary policy is well managed. The Maastricht Treaty called for establishment of the independent European Central Bank (ECB), similar in some respects to the U.S. Federal Reserve, with a clear mandate to manage monetary policy so as to ensure price stability. The ECB, based in Frankfurt, is meant to be independent from political pressure—although critics question this. Among other things, the ECB sets interest rates and determines monetary policy across the euro zone.

The implied loss of national sovereignty to the ECB underlies the decision by Great Britain, Denmark, and Sweden to stay out of the euro zone for now. Many in these countries are suspicious of the ECB's ability to remain free from political pressure and to keep inflation under tight control.

In theory, the design of the ECB should ensure that it remains free of political pressure. The ECB is modeled on the German Bundesbank, which historically has been the most independent and successful central bank in Europe. The Maastricht Treaty prohibits the ECB from taking orders from politicians. The executive board of the bank, which consists of a president, vice president, and four other members, carries out policy by issuing instructions to national central banks. The policy itself is determined by the governing council, which consists of the executive board plus the central bank governors from the 17 euro zone countries. The governing council votes on interest rate changes. Members of the executive board are appointed for eight-year nonrenewable terms, insulating them from political pressures to get reappointed. Nevertheless, the jury is still out on the issue of the ECB's independence, and it will take some time for the bank to establish its credentials.

Optimal Currency Area
One where similarities in the underlying structure of economic activity make it feasible to adopt a single currency.

According to critics, another drawback of the euro is that the EU is not what economists would call an optimal currency area. In an **optimal currency area,** similarities in the underlying structure of economic activity make it feasible to adopt a single currency and use a single exchange rate as an instrument of macroeconomic policy. Many of the European economies in the euro zone, however, are very dissimilar. For example, Finland and Portugal have different wage rates, tax regimes, and business cycles, and they may react very differently to external economic shocks. A change in the euro exchange rate that helps Finland may hurt Portugal. Obviously, such differences complicate macroeconomic policy. For example, when euro economies are not growing in unison, a common monetary policy may mean that interest rates are too high for depressed regions and too low for booming regions. It will be interesting to see how the European Union copes with the strains caused by such divergent economic performance.

One way of dealing with such divergent effects within the euro zone might be for the EU to engage in fiscal transfers, taking money from prosperous regions and pumping it into depressed regions. Such a move, however, would open a political can of worms. Would the citizens of Germany forgo their "fair share" of EU funds to create jobs for underemployed Portuguese workers?

Some critics believe that the euro puts the economic cart before the political horse. In their view, a single currency should follow, not precede, political union. They argue that the euro will unleash enormous pressures for tax harmonization and fiscal transfers from the center, both policies that cannot be pursued without the appropriate political structure. The most apocalyptic vision that flows from these negative views is that far from stimulating economic growth, as its advocates claim, the euro will lead to lower economic growth and higher inflation within Europe. To quote one critic:

> Imposing a single exchange rate and an inflexible exchange rate on countries that are characterized by different economic shocks, inflexible wages, low labor mobility, and separate national fiscal systems without significant cross-border fiscal transfers will raise the overall level of cyclical unemployment among EMU members. The shift from national monetary policies dominated by the (German) Bundesbank within the European Monetary System to a European Central Bank governed by majority voting with a politically determined exchange rate policy will almost certainly raise the average future rate of inflation.[16]

The Experience to Date   Since its establishment January 1, 1999, the euro has had a volatile trading history against the world's major currency, the U.S. dollar. After starting life in 1999 at €1 = $1.17, the euro steadily fell until it reached a low of €1 = $0.83 in October 2000, leading critics to claim the euro was a failure. A major reason for the fall in the euro's value was that international investors were investing money in booming U.S. stocks and bonds and taking money out of Europe to finance this investment. In other words, they were selling euros to buy dollars so that they could invest in dollar-denominated assets. This increased the demand for dollars and decreased the demand for the euro, driving the value of the euro down.

The fortunes of the euro began improving in late 2001 when the dollar weakened, and the currency stood at a robust all-time high of €1 = $1.54 in early March 2008. One reason for the rise in the value of the euro was that the flow of capital into the United States had stalled as the U.S. financial markets fell.[17] Many investors were now taking money out of the United States, selling dollar-denominated assets such as U.S. stocks and bonds, and purchasing euro-denominated assets. Falling demand for U.S. dollars and rising demand for euros translated into a fall in the value of the dollar against the euro. Furthermore, in a vote of confidence in both the euro and the ability of the ECB to manage monetary policy within the euro zone,

 **Another** Perspective

Saving the PIIGS
PIIGS is the acronym for Portugal, Italy, Ireland, Greece, and Spain. It has been coined to reflect much of the euro zone crisis and the financial integrity of the European Union. During the global financial crisis of 2007–2010, the term was used more extensively, and with a perceived offensive connotation, with regard to the sovereign debt issues that each country faced after a decade of reckless spending. What to do with these countries has furthermore been interpreted as, "What will Germany and France do?" In this regard, both countries, but Germany in particular has been viewed as bearing the most responsibility in saving the euro and the PIIGS. (T. Kalwarski, "Finding Investing Pearls in PIIGS Countries," *Bloomberg Businessweek*, February 25, 2010, http://www.businessweek.com/magazine/content/10_10/b4169072685376.htm and M. Moran, "Opinion: Europe Hopes PIIGS Will Fly," *Global Post*, January 26, 2010, http://www.globalpost.com/dispatch/worldview/100122/european-union-greece-economy.

Crisis in the Euro Zone

When the euro was established, some critics worried that free-spending countries in the euro zone (such as Italy) might borrow excessively, running up large public-sector deficits that they could not finance. This would then rock the value of the euro, requiring their more sober brethren, such as Germany or France, to step in and bail out the profligate nation. In early 2010, this worry was fast becoming a reality as a financial crisis in Greece rocked the value of the euro.

The financial crisis had its roots in a decade of free spending by the Greek government. The government ran up a high level of debt to finance extensive spending in the public sector. Much of the increase in spending could be characterized as an attempt by the government to buy off powerful interest groups in Greek society, from teachers and farmers to public employees, rewarding them with high pay and extensive benefits. To make matters worse, the government misled the international community about the level of its indebtedness. In October 2009 a new government took power and quickly announced that the 2009 deficit, which had been projected to be around 5 percent, would actually be around 12.7 percent. The previous government had apparently been cooking the books.

This shattered any faith that international investors might have had in the Greek economy. Interest rates on Greek government debt soared to 7.1 percent, about 4 percentage points higher than the rate on German bonds.

Two of the three international rating agencies also cut their ratings on Greek bonds and warned that further downgrades were likely. The main concern now was that the Greek government might not be able to refinance some €20 billion of debt that matured in April or May 2010. A further concern was that the Greek government might lack the political willpower to make the large cuts in public spending necessary to bring down the deficit and restore investor confidence. This raised the specter that either the IMF, or the European Central Bank with the support of Germany and France, would have to step in and bail out the Greek government, imposing fiscal discipline on the country in return for loans that would keep the country from defaulting on its debt.

Nor was Greece alone in having large public-sector deficits. Three other euro zone countries—Spain, Portugal, and Ireland—also all had large debt loads, and interest rates on their bonds also surged as investors sold out. This raised the specter of financial contagion, with large-scale defaults among the weaker members of the euro zone. If this did occur, the EU and IMF would most certainly have to step in and rescue the troubled nations. With this possibility, once considered very remote, investors started to move money out of euros, and the value of the euro started to fall on the foreign exchange market.

Sources: "A very European Crisis," *The Economist,* February 6, 2010, pp. 75–77; and L. Thomas, "Is Debt Trashing the Euro?" *The New York Times,* February 7, 2010, pp. 1, 7.

many foreign central banks added more euros to their supply of foreign currencies. In the first three years of its life, the euro never reached the 13 percent of global reserves made up by the deutsche mark and other former euro zone currencies. The euro didn't jump that hurdle until early 2002, but by 2004 it made up 20 percent of global reserves. Currency specialists expected the growing U.S. current account deficit, which reached 7 percent of GDP in 2005, to drive the dollar down further, and the euro still higher over the next two to four years.[18] In 2007 this started to occur, with the euro appreciating steadily against the dollar from 2005 until early 2008. Since the euro has weakened somewhat, reflecting concerns over slow economic growth and growing budget deficits among several EU member states, particularly Greece, Portugal and Spain (see the accompanying Country Focus for more details). Nevertheless, in early 2010 the exchange rate, which stood at €1 = $1.35, was still strong compared to the exchange rate in the early 2000s. While the strong euro has been a source of pride for Europeans, it does make it harder for euro zone exporters to sell their goods abroad.

ENLARGEMENT OF THE EUROPEAN UNION
A major issue facing the EU over the past few years has been that of enlargement. Enlargement of the EU into Eastern Europe has been a possibility since the collapse of communism at the end of

the 1980s, and by the end of the 1990s, 13 countries had applied to become EU members. To qualify for EU membership the applicants had to privatize state assets, deregulate markets, restructure industries, and tame inflation. They also had to enshrine complex EU laws into their own systems, establish stable democratic governments, and respect human rights.[19] In December 2002, the EU formally agreed to accept the applications of 10 countries, and they joined May 1, 2004. The new members include the Baltic countries, the Czech Republic, and the larger nations of Hungary and Poland. The only new members not in Eastern Europe are the Mediterranean island nations of Malta and Cyprus. Their inclusion in the EU expanded the union to 25 states, stretching from the Atlantic to the borders of Russia; added 23 percent to the landmass of the EU; brought 75 million new citizens into the EU, building an EU with a population of 450 million people; and created a single continental economy with a GDP of close to €11 trillion. In 2007, Bulgaria and Romania joined, bringing total member ship to 27 nations.

The new members were not able to adopt the euro until at least 2007 (and 2010 in the case of the latest entrants), and free movement of labor between the new and existing members was not allowed until then. Consistent with theories of free trade, the enlargement should create added benefits for all members. However, given the small size of the Eastern European economies (together they amount to only 5 percent of the GDP of current EU members) the initial impact will probably be small. The biggest notable change might be in the EU bureaucracy and decision-making processes, where budget negotiations among 27 nations are bound to prove more problematic than negotiations among 15 nations.

Left standing at the door is Turkey. Turkey, which has long lobbied to join the union, presents the EU with some difficult issues. The country has had a customs union with the EU since 1995, and about half of its international trade is already with the EU. However, full membership has been denied because of concerns over human rights issues (particularly Turkish policies toward its Kurdish minority). In addition, some on the Turk side suspect the EU is not eager to let a primarily Muslim nation of 66 million people, which has one foot in Asia, join the EU. The European Union formally indicated in December 2002 that it would allow the Turkish application to proceed with no further delay in December 2004 if the country improved its human rights record to the satisfaction of the EU. In 2004 the EU agreed to allow Turkey to start accession talks in October 2005, but those talks are not moving along rapidly, and the nation will not join until 2013, if at all.

Regional Economic Integration in the Americas

No other attempt at regional economic integration comes close to the EU in its boldness or its potential implications for the world economy, but regional economic integration is on the rise in the Americas. The most significant attempt is the North American Free Trade Agreement. In addition to NAFTA, several other trade blocs are in the offing in the Americas (see Map 8.2), the most significant of which appear to be the Andean Community and Mercosur. Also, negotiations are under way to establish a hemisphere-wide Free Trade Area of the Americas (FTAA), although currently they seem to be stalled.

LEARNING OBJECTIVE 4
Explain the history, current scope, and future prospects of the world's most important regional economic agreements.

THE NORTH AMERICAN FREE TRADE AGREEMENT The governments of the United States and Canada in 1988 agreed to enter into a free trade agreement, which took effect January 1, 1989. The goal of the agreement was to eliminate

map 8.2

Economic Integration in the Americas

Source: *The Economist*, April 21, 2001, p. 20. Copyright © 2001 The Economist Newspaper Ltd. All rights reserved. Reprinted with permission. Further reproduction prohibited. www.economist.com

Continental Commerce

- NAFTA
- MERCOSUR
- Andean community
- Central America
- Caribbean community

all tariffs on bilateral trade between Canada and the United States by 1998. This was followed in 1991 by talks among the United States, Canada, and Mexico aimed at establishing a **North American Free Trade Agreement** for the three countries. The talks concluded in August 1992 with an agreement in principle, and the following year the agreement was ratified by the governments of all three countries. The agreement became law January 1, 1994.[20]

North American Free Trade Agreement (NAFTA)
Free trade area between Canada, Mexico, and the United States.

NAFTA'S Contents   The contents of NAFTA include the following:

- Abolition by 2004 of tariffs on 99 percent of the goods traded between Mexico, Canada, and the United States.
- Removal of most barriers on the cross-border flow of services, allowing financial institutions, for example, unrestricted access to the Mexican market by 2000.
- Protection of intellectual property rights.

- Removal of most restrictions on foreign direct investment between the three member countries, although special treatment (protection) will be given to Mexican energy and railway industries, American airline and radio communications industries, and Canadian culture.
- Application of national environmental standards, provided such standards have a scientific basis. Lowering of standards to lure investment is described as being inappropriate.
- Establishment of two commissions with the power to impose fines and remove trade privileges when environmental standards or legislation involving health and safety, minimum wages, or child labor are ignored.

The Case for NAFTA   Proponents of NAFTA have argued that the free trade area should be viewed as an opportunity to create an enlarged and more efficient productive base for the entire region. Advocates acknowledge that one effect of NAFTA would be that some U.S. and Canadian firms would move production to Mexico to take advantage of lower labor costs. (In 2004, the average hourly labor cost in Mexico was still one-tenth of that in the United States and Canada.) Movement of production to Mexico, they argued, was most likely to occur in low-skilled, labor-intensive manufacturing industries where Mexico might have a comparative advantage. Advocates of NAFTA argued that many would benefit from such a trend. Mexico would benefit from much-needed inward investment and employment. The United States and Canada would benefit because the increased incomes of the Mexicans would allow them to import more U.S. and Canadian goods, thereby increasing demand and making up for the jobs lost in industries that moved production to Mexico. U.S. and Canadian consumers would benefit from the lower prices of products made in Mexico. In addition, the international competitiveness of U.S. and Canadian firms that move production to Mexico to take advantage of lower labor costs would be enhanced, enabling them to better compete with Asian and European rivals.

The Case against NAFTA   Those who opposed NAFTA claimed that ratification would be followed by a mass exodus of jobs from the United States and Canada into Mexico as employers sought to profit from Mexico's lower wages and less strict environmental and labor laws. According to one extreme opponent, Ross Perot, up to 5.9 million U.S. jobs would be lost to Mexico after NAFTA in what he famously characterized as a "giant sucking sound." Most economists, however, dismissed these numbers as being absurd and alarmist. They argued that Mexico would have to run a bilateral trade surplus with the United States of close to $300 billion for job loss on such a scale to occur—and $300 billion was the size of Mexico's GDP. In other words, such a scenario seemed implausible.

More sober estimates of the impact of NAFTA ranged from a net creation of 170,000 jobs in the United States (due to increased Mexican demand for U.S. goods and services) and an increase of $15 billion per year to the joint U.S. and Mexican GDP, to a net loss of 490,000 U.S. jobs. To put these numbers in perspective, employment in the U.S. economy was predicted to grow by 18 million from 1993 to 2003. As most economists repeatedly stressed, NAFTA would have a small impact on both Canada and the United States. It could hardly be any other way, since the Mexican economy was only 5 percent of the size of the U.S. economy. Signing NAFTA required the largest leap of economic faith from Mexico rather than Canada or the United States. Falling trade barriers would expose Mexican firms to highly efficient U.S. and Canadian competitors that, when compared to the average Mexican firm, had

Many workers in the United States initially believed that NAFTA would take away their jobs as employers looked for cheaper labor in Mexico. However, a 1996 study by researchers at the University of California–Los Angeles concluded the impact on jobs was a net gain of 3,000 for the United States in the first two years of the NAFTA regime.

far greater capital resources, access to highly educated and skilled workforces, and much greater technological sophistication. The short-run outcome was likely to be painful economic restructuring and unemployment in Mexico. But advocates of NAFTA claimed there would be long-run dynamic gains in the efficiency of Mexican firms as they adjusted to the rigors of a more competitive marketplace. To the extent that this occurred, they argued, Mexico's economic growth rate would accelerate, and Mexico might become a major market for Canadian and U.S. firms.[21]

Environmentalists also voiced concerns about NAFTA. They pointed to the sludge in the Rio Grande River and the smog in the air over Mexico City and warned that Mexico could degrade clean air and toxic waste standards across the continent. They pointed out that the lower Rio Grande was the most polluted river in the United States, and that with NAFTA, chemical waste and sewage would increase along its course from El Paso, Texas, to the Gulf of Mexico.

There was also opposition in Mexico to NAFTA from those who feared a loss of national sovereignty. Mexican critics argued that their country would be dominated by U.S. firms that would not really contribute to Mexico's economic growth, but instead would use Mexico as a low-cost assembly site, while keeping their high-paying, high-skilled jobs north of the border.

NAFTA: The Results Studies of NAFTA's impact to date suggest its initial effects were at best muted, and both advocates and detractors may have been guilty of exaggeration.[22] On average, studies indicate that NAFTA's overall impact has been small but positive.[23] From 1993 to 2005, trade between NAFTA's partners grew by 250 percent.[24] Canada and Mexico are now the number one and two trade partners of the United States, suggesting the economies of the three NAFTA nations have become more closely integrated. In 1990, U.S. trade with Canada and Mexico accounted for about a quarter of total U.S. trade. By 2005, the figure was close to one-third. Canada's trade with its NAFTA partners increased from about 70 percent to more than 80 percent of all Canadian foreign trade between 1993 and 2005, while Mexico's trade with NAFTA increased from 66 percent to 80 percent over the same period. All three countries also experienced strong productivity growth over this period. In Mexico, labor productivity has increased by 50 percent since 1993, and the passage of NAFTA may have contributed to this. However, estimates suggest that employment effects of NAFTA have been small. The most pessimistic estimates suggest the United States lost 110,000 jobs per year due to NAFTA between 1994 and 2000—and many economists dispute this figure—which is tiny compared to the more than 2 million jobs a year created in the United States during the same period. Perhaps the most significant impact of NAFTA has not been economic, but political. Many observers credit NAFTA with helping to create the background for increased political stability in Mexico. Mexico is now viewed as a stable democratic nation with a steadily growing economy, something that is beneficial to the United States, which shares a 2,000-mile border with the country.[25]

Enlargement   One issue confronting NAFTA is that of enlargement. A number of other Latin American countries have indicated their desire to eventually join NAFTA. The governments of both Canada and the United States are adopting a wait-and-see attitude with regard to most countries. Getting NAFTA approved was a bruising political experience, and neither government is eager to repeat the process soon. Nevertheless, the Canadian, Mexican, and U.S. governments began talks in 1995 regarding Chile's possible entry into NAFTA. As of 2008, however, these talks had yielded little progress, partly because of political opposition in the U.S. Congress to expanding NAFTA. In December 2002, however, the United States and Chile did sign a bilateral free trade pact.

THE ANDEAN COMMUNITY

THE ANDEAN COMMUNITY   Bolivia, Chile, Ecuador, Colombia, and Peru signed an agreement in 1969 to create the Andean Pact. The **Andean Pact** was largely based on the EU model, but was far less successful at achieving its stated goals. The integration steps begun in 1969 included an internal tariff reduction program, a common external tariff, a transportation policy, a common industrial policy, and special concessions for the smallest members, Bolivia and Ecuador.

> **Andean Pact**
> A 1969 agreement between Bolivia, Chile, Ecuador, Colombia, and Peru to establish a customs union.

By the mid-1980s, the Andean Pact had all but collapsed and had failed to achieve any of its stated objectives. There was no tariff-free trade between member countries, no common external tariff, and no harmonization of economic policies. Political and economic problems seem to have hindered cooperation between member countries. The countries of the Andean Pact have had to deal with low economic growth, hyperinflation, high unemployment, political unrest, and crushing debt burdens. In addition, the dominant political ideology in many of the Andean countries during this period tended toward the radical/socialist end of the political spectrum. Since such an ideology is hostile to the free market economic principles on which the Andean Pact was based, progress toward closer integration could not be expected.

The tide began to turn in the late 1980s when, after years of economic decline, the governments of Latin America began to adopt free market economic policies. In 1990, the heads of the five current members of the Andean Community—Bolivia, Ecuador, Peru, Colombia, and Venezuela—met in the Galápagos Islands. The resulting Galápagos Declaration effectively relaunched the Andean Pact, which was renamed the Andean Community in 1997. The declaration's objectives included the establishment of a free trade area by 1992, a customs union by 1994, and a common market by 1995. This last milestone has not been reached. A customs union was implemented in 1995, although until 2003 Peru opted out and Bolivia received preferential treatment. The Andean Community now operates as a customs union. In December 2003, it signed an agreement with Mercosur to restart stalled negotiations on the creation of a free trade area between the two trading blocs. Those negotiations are currently proceeding at a slow pace. In late 2006, Venezuela withdrew from the Andean Community as part of that country's attempts to join Mercosur.

Mercosur
Pact between Argentina, Brazil, Paraguay, and Uruguay to establish a free trade area.

MERCOSUR

Mercosur originated in 1988 as a free trade pact between Brazil and Argentina. The modest reductions in tariffs and quotas accompanying this pact reportedly helped bring about an 80 percent increase in trade between the two countries in the late 1980s.[26] This success encouraged the expansion of the pact in March 1990 to include Paraguay and Uruguay. In 2006, Venezuela signed a membership agreement, although this has yet to be ratified and it may take years for Venezuela to become a full member.

The initial aim of Mercosur was to establish a full free trade area by the end of 1994 and a common market sometime thereafter. In December 1995, Mercosur's members agreed to a five-year program under which they hoped to perfect their free trade area and move toward a full customs union—something that has yet to be achieved.[27] For its first eight years or so, Mercosur seemed to be making a positive contribution to the economic growth rates of its member states. Trade between Mercosur's four core members quadrupled between 1990 and 1998. The combined GDP of the four member states grew at an annual average rate of 3.5 percent between 1990 and 1996, a performance that is significantly better than the four attained during the 1980s.[28]

However, Mercosur had its critics, including Alexander Yeats, a senior economist at the World Bank, who wrote a stinging critique of the pact.[29] According to Yeats, the trade diversion effects of Mercosur outweigh its trade creation effects. Yeats pointed out that the fastest-growing items in intra-Mercosur trade were cars, buses, agricultural equipment, and other capital-intensive goods that are produced relatively inefficiently in the four member countries. In other words, Mercosur countries, insulated from outside competition by tariffs that run as high as 70 percent of value on motor vehicles, are investing in factories that build products that are too expensive to sell to anyone but themselves. The result, according to Yeats, is that Mercosur countries might not be able to compete globally once the group's external trade barriers come down. In the meantime, capital is being drawn away from more efficient enterprises. In the near term, countries with more efficient manufacturing enterprises lose because Mercosur's external trade barriers keep them out of the market.

Mercosur hit a significant roadblock in 1998, when its member states slipped into recession and intrabloc trade slumped. Trade fell further in 1999 following a financial crisis in Brazil that led to the devaluation of the Brazilian real, which immediately made the goods of other Mercosur members 40 percent more expensive in Brazil, their largest export market. At this point, progress toward establishing a full customs union all but stopped. Things deteriorated further in 2001 when Argentina, beset by economic stresses, suggested the customs union be temporarily suspended. Argentina wanted to suspend Mercosur's tariff so that it could abolish duties on imports of capital equipment, while raising those on consumer goods to 35 percent (Mercosur had established a 14 percent import tariff on both sets of goods). Brazil agreed to this request, effectively halting Mercosur's quest to become a fully functioning customs union.[30] Hope for a revival arose in 2003 when new Brazilian President Lula da Silva announced his support for a revitalized and expanded Mercosur modeled after the

EU with a larger membership, a common currency, and a democratically elected parliament.[31] As of 2010, however, little progress had been made in moving Mercosur down that road, and critics felt that the customs union was, if anything, becoming more imperfect over time.[32]

CENTRAL AMERICAN COMMON MARKET, CAFTA, AND CARICOM

Two other trade pacts in the Americas have not made much progress. In the early 1960s, Costa Rica, El Salvador, Guatemala, Honduras, and Nicaragua attempted to set up a **Central American Common Market.** It collapsed in 1969 when war broke out between Honduras and El Salvador after a riot at a soccer match between teams from the two countries. Since then the six member countries have made some progress toward reviving their agreement (the five founding members were joined by the Dominican Republic). The proposed common market was given a boost in 2003 when the United States signaled its intention to enter into bilateral free trade negotiations with the group. These cumulated in a 2005 agreement to establish a free trade agreement between the six countries and the United States. Known as the **Central America Free Trade Agreement,** or CAFTA, the aim is to lower trade barriers between the United States and the six countries for most goods and services.

A customs union was to have been created in 1991 between the English-speaking Caribbean countries under the auspices of the Caribbean Community. Referred to as **CARICOM,** it was established in 1973. However, it repeatedly failed to progress toward economic integration. A formal commitment to economic and monetary union was adopted by CARICOM's member states in 1984, but since then little progress has been made. In October 1991, the CARICOM governments failed, for the third consecutive time, to meet a deadline for establishing a common external tariff. Despite this, CARICOM expanded to 15 members by 2005. In early 2006, six CARICOM members established the **Caribbean Single Market and Economy (CSME).** Modeled on the EU's single market, the goal of CSME is to lower trade barriers and harmonize macroeconomic and monetary policy between member states.[33]

FREE TRADE AREA OF THE AMERICAS

At a hemisphere-wide Summit of the Americas in December 1994, a Free Trade Area of the Americas (FTAA) was proposed. It took more than three years for the talks to start, but in April 1998, 34 heads of state traveled to Santiago, Chile, for the second Summit of the Americas where they formally inaugurated talks to establish an FTAA by January 1, 2005—something that didn't occur. The continuing talks have addressed a wide range of economic, political, and environmental issues related to cross-border trade and investment. Although both the United States and Brazil were early advocates of the FTAA, support from both countries seems to be mixed at this point. Because the United States and Brazil have the largest economies in North and South America, respectively, strong U.S. and Brazilian support is a precondition for establishment of the free trade area.

The major stumbling blocks so far have been twofold. First, the United States wants its southern neighbors to agree to tougher enforcement of intellectual property rights and lower manufacturing tariffs, which they do not seem to be eager to embrace. Second, Brazil and Argentina want the United States to reduce its subsidies to U.S. agricultural producers and scrap tariffs on agricultural imports, which the U.S. government does not seem inclined to do. For progress to be made, most observers agree that the United States and Brazil have to first reach an agreement on these crucial issues.[34] If the FTAA is eventually established, it will have major implications for

Central American Common Market
A trade pact between Costa Rica, El Salvador, Guatemala, Honduras, and Nicaragua, which began in the early 1960s but collapsed in 1969 due to war.

Central America Free Trade Agreement (CAFTA)
The agreement of the member states of the Central American Common Market joined by the Dominican Republic to trade freely with the United States.

CARICOM
An association of English-speaking Caribbean states that are attempting to establish a customs union.

Caribbean Single Market and Economy (CSME)
Unites six CARICOM members in agreeing to lower trade barriers and harmonize macroeconomic and monetary policies.

cross-border trade and investment flows within the hemisphere. The FTAA would open a free trade umbrella over 850 million people who accounted for some $18 trillion in GDP in 2008.

Currently, however, FTAA is very much a work in progress, and the progress has been slow. The most recent attempt to get talks going again, in November 2005 at a summit of 34 heads of state from North and South America, failed when opponents, led by Venezuela's populist president, Hugo Chavez, blocked efforts by the Bush administration to set an agenda for further talks on FTAA. In voicing his opposition, Chavez condemned the U.S. free trade model as a "perversion" that would unduly benefit the United States, to the detriment of poor people in Latin America whom Chavez claims have not benefited from free trade details.[35] Such views make it unlikely that there will be much progress on establishing a FTAA in the near term.

Regional Economic Integration Elsewhere

LEARNING OBJECTIVE 4
Explain the history, current scope, and future prospects of the world's most important regional economic agreements.

Numerous attempts at regional economic integration have been tried throughout Asia and Africa. However, few exist in anything other than name. Perhaps the most significant is the Association of Southeast Asian Nations (ASEAN). In addition, the Asia-Pacific Economic Cooperation (APEC) forum has recently emerged as the seed of a potential free trade region.

Association of Southeast Asian Nations (ASEAN)
An attempt to establish a free trade area between Brunei, Cambodia, Indonesia, Laos, Malaysia, Myanmar, Philippines, Singapore, Thailand, and Vietnam.

ASSOCIATION OF SOUTHEAST ASIAN NATIONS

Formed in 1967, the **Association of Southeast Asian Nations (ASEAN)** includes Brunei, Cambodia, Indonesia, Laos, Malaysia, Myanmar, Philippines, Singapore, Thailand, and Vietnam. Laos, Myanmar, Vietnam, and Cambodia have all joined recently, creating a regional grouping of 500 million people with a combined GDP of some $740 billion (see Map 8.3). The basic objective of ASEAN is to foster freer trade between member countries and to achieve cooperation in their industrial policies. Progress so far has been limited, however.

Until recently only 5 percent of intra-ASEAN trade consisted of goods whose tariffs had been reduced through an ASEAN preferential trade arrangement. This may be changing. In 2003, an ASEAN Free Trade Area (AFTA) between the six original members of ASEAN came into full effect. The AFTA has cut tariffs on manufacturing and agricultural products to less than 5 percent. However, there are some significant exceptions to this tariff reduction. Malaysia, for example, refused to bring down tariffs on imported cars until 2005 and then agreed to only lower the tariff to 20 percent, not the 5 percent called for under the AFTA. Malaysia wanted to protect Proton, an inefficient local carmaker, from foreign competition. Similarly, the Philippines has refused to lower tariff rates on petrochemicals, and rice, the largest agricultural product in the region, will remain subject to higher tariff rates until at least 2020.[36]

Notwithstanding such issues, ASEAN and AFTA are at least progressing toward establishing a free trade zone. Vietnam joined the AFTA in 2006, Laos and Myanmar in 2008, and Cambodia in 2010. The goal was to reduce import tariffs among the six original members to zero by 2010, and to do so by 2015 for the newer members (although important exceptions to that goal, such as tariffs on rice, will persist).

ASEAN also recently signed a free trade agreement with China. This went into effect January 1, 2010. Trade between China and ASEAN members more than tripled during the first decade of the 21st century, and this agreement should spur further growth. The agreement between ASEAN and China removes tariffs on 90 percent of traded goods.[37]

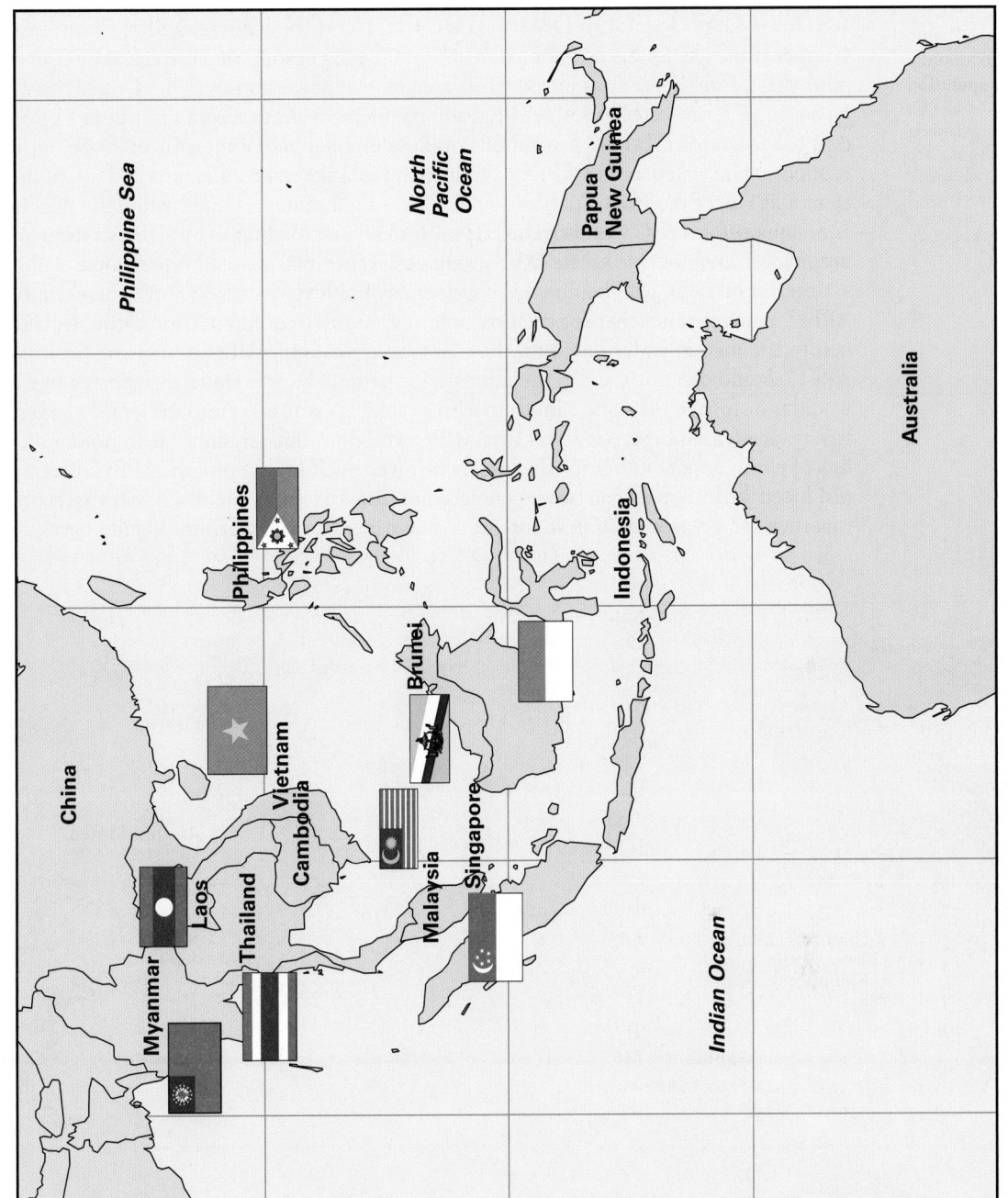

North Pacific Ocean

Papua New Guinea

Australia

Philippine Sea

Indonesia

Philippines

Brunei

China

Vietnam

Cambodia

Singapore

Laos

Malaysia

Thailand

Myanmar

Indian Ocean

8.3 map   ASEAN Countries

Source: www.aseansec.org.

Asia-Pacific Economic Cooperation (APEC)

Made up of 21 member states whose goal is to increase multilateral cooperation in view of the economic rise of the Pacific nations.

ASIA-PACIFIC ECONOMIC COOPERATION

Asia-Pacific Economic Cooperation (APEC) was founded in 1990 at the suggestion of Australia. APEC currently has 21 member states including such economic powerhouses as the United States, Japan, and China (see Map 8.4). Collectively, the member states account for about 55 percent of the world's GNP, 49 percent of world trade, and much of the growth in the world economy. The stated aim of APEC is to increase multilateral cooperation in view of the economic rise of the Pacific nations and the growing interdependence within the region. U.S. support for APEC was also based on the belief that it might prove a viable strategy for heading off any moves to create Asian groupings from which it would be excluded.

Interest in APEC was heightened considerably in November 1993 when the heads of APEC member states met for the first time at a two-day conference in Seattle. Debate before the meeting speculated on the likely future role of APEC. One view was that APEC should commit itself to the ultimate formation of a free trade area. Such a move would transform the Pacific Rim from a geographical expression into the world's largest free trade area. Another view was that APEC would produce no more than hot air and lots of photo opportunities for the leaders involved. As it turned out, the APEC meeting produced little more than some vague commitments from member states to work together for greater economic integration and a general lowering of trade barriers.

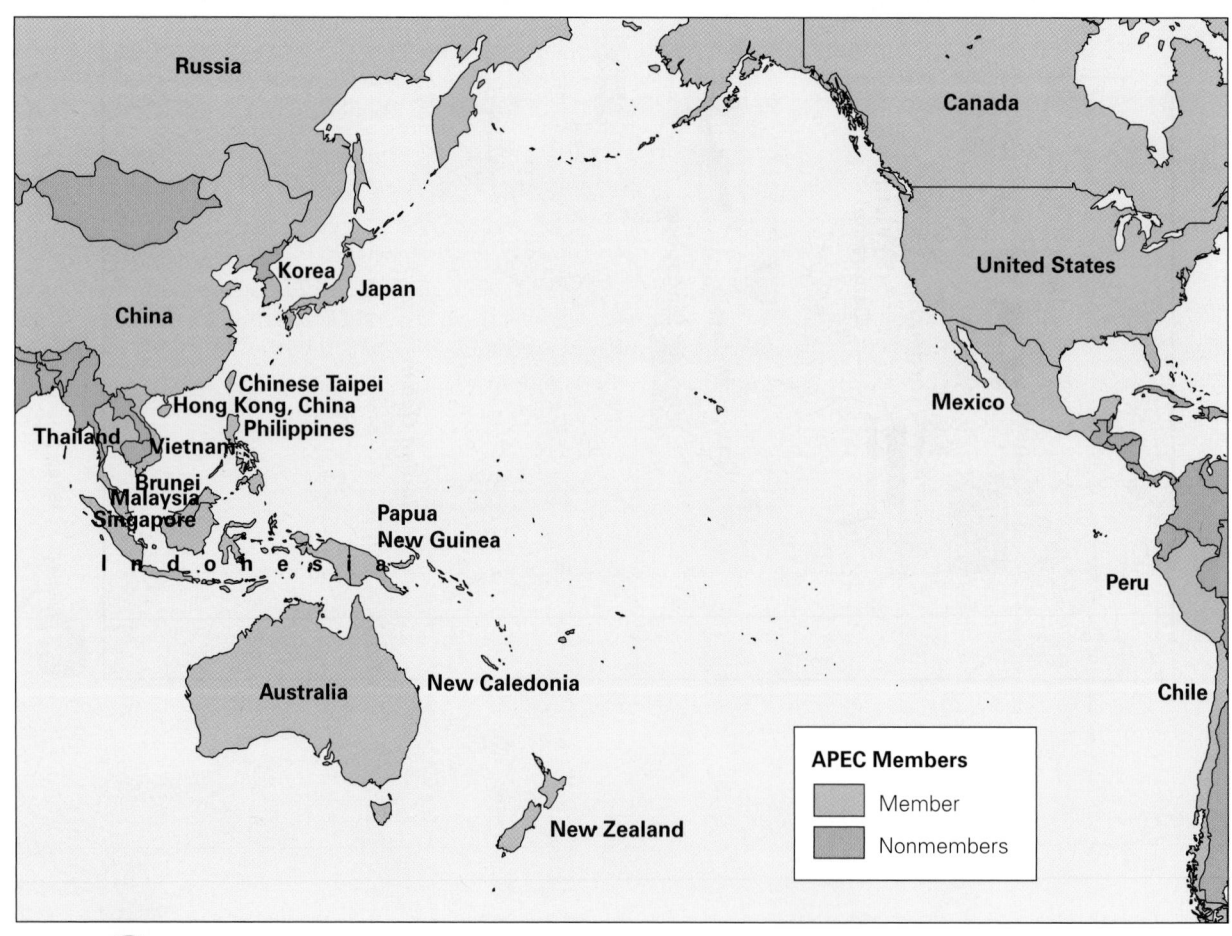

map 8.4

APEC Members

However, significantly, member states did not rule out the possibility of closer economic cooperation in the future.[38]

The heads of state have met again on a number of occasions. At a 1997 meeting, member states formally endorsed proposals designed to remove trade barriers in 15 sectors, ranging from fish to toys. However, the vague plan committed APEC to doing no more than holding further talks, which is all that they have done to date. Commenting on the vagueness of APEC pronouncements, the influential Brookings Institution, a U.S.-based economic policy institution, noted that APEC "is in grave danger of shrinking into irrelevance as a serious forum." Despite the slow progress, APEC is worth watching. If it eventually does transform itself into a free trade area, it will probably be the world's largest.[39]

REGIONAL TRADE BLOCS IN AFRICA   African countries have been experimenting with regional trade blocs for half a century. There are now nine trade blocs on the African continent. Many countries are members of more than one group. Although the number of trade groups is impressive, progress toward the establishment of meaningful trade blocs has been slow.

Many of these groups have been dormant for years. Significant political turmoil in several African nations has persistently impeded any meaningful progress. Also, deep suspicion of free trade exists in several African countries. The argument most frequently heard is that because these countries have less developed and less diversified economies, they need to be "protected" by tariff barriers from unfair foreign competition. Given the prevalence of this argument, it has been hard to establish free trade areas or customs unions.

The most recent attempt to reenergize the free trade movement in Africa occurred in early 2001, when Kenya, Uganda, and Tanzania, member states of the East African Community (EAC), committed themselves to relaunching their bloc, 24 years after it collapsed. The three countries, with 80 million inhabitants, intend to establish a customs union, regional court, legislative assembly, and, eventually, a political federation.

Their program includes cooperation on immigration, road and telecommunication networks, investment, and capital markets. However, while local business leaders welcomed the relaunch as a positive step, they were critical of the EAC's failure in practice to make progress on free trade. At the EAC treaty signing in November 1999, members gave themselves four years to negotiate a customs union, with a draft slated for the end of 2001. But that fell far short of earlier plans for an immediate free trade zone, shelved after Tanzania and Uganda, fearful of Kenyan competition, expressed concerns that the zone could create imbalances similar to those that contributed to the breakup of the first community.[40] Nevertheless, in 2005 the EAC did start to implement a customs union, although many tariffs remained in place until 2010. In 2007, Burundi and Rwanda joined the EAC.

Focus on Managerial Implications

LEARNING OBJECTIVE 5
Understand the implications for business that are inherent in regional economic integration agreements.

Currently the most significant developments in regional economic integration are occurring in the European Union and NAFTA. Although some of the Latin American trade blocs, ASEAN, and the proposed FTAA may have economic significance in the future, the EU and NAFTA currently have more profound and immediate implications for business practice. Accordingly, in this section we will concentrate on the business implications of those two groups. Similar conclusions, however, could be drawn with regard to the creation of a single market anywhere in the world.

Opportunities

The creation of a single market through regional economic integration offers significant opportunities because markets that were formerly protected from foreign competition are increasingly open. For example, in Europe before 1992 the large French and Italian markets were among the most protected. These markets are now much more open to foreign competition in the form of both exports and direct investment. Nonetheless, to fully exploit such opportunities, it may pay non-EU firms to set up EU subsidiaries. Many major U.S. firms have long had subsidiaries in Europe. Those that do not would be advised to consider establishing them now, lest they run the risk of being shut out of the EU by nontariff barriers.

Additional opportunities arise from the inherent lower costs of doing business in a single market—as opposed to 27 national markets in the case of the EU or 3 national markets in the case of NAFTA. Free movement of goods across borders, harmonized product standards, and simplified tax regimes make it possible for firms based in the EU and the NAFTA countries to realize potentially significant cost economies by centralizing production in those EU and NAFTA locations where the mix of factor costs and skills is optimal. Rather than producing a product in each of the 27 EU countries or the 3 NAFTA countries, a firm may be able to serve the whole EU or North American market from a single location. This location must be chosen carefully, of course, with an eye on local factor costs and skills.

For example, in response to the changes created by EU after 1992, the St. Paul, Minnesota-based 3M Company consolidated its European manufacturing and distribution facilities to take advantage of economies of scale. Thus, a plant in Great Britain now produces 3M's printing products and a German factory its reflective traffic control materials for all of the EU. In each case, 3M chose a location for centralized production after carefully considering the likely production costs in alternative locations within the EU. The ultimate goal of 3M is to dispense with all national distinctions, directing R&D, manufacturing, distribution, and marketing for each product group from an EU headquarters.[41] Similarly, Unilever, one of Europe's largest companies, began rationalizing its production in advance of 1992 to attain scale economies. Unilever concentrated its production of dishwashing powder for the EU in one plant, bath soap in another, and so on.[42]

Even after the removal of barriers to trade and investment, enduring differences in culture and competitive practices often limit the ability of companies to realize cost economies by centralizing production in key locations and producing a standardized product for a single multi-country market. Consider the case of Atag Holdings NV, a Dutch maker of kitchen appliances.[43] Atag thought it was well placed to benefit from the single market, but found it tough going. Atag's plant is just one mile from the German border and near the center of the EU's population. The company thought it could cater to both the "potato" and "spaghetti" belts—marketers' terms for consumers in Northern and Southern Europe—by producing two main product lines and selling these standardized "euro-products" to "euro-consumers." The main benefit of doing so is the economy of scale derived from mass production of a standardized range of products. Atag quickly discovered that the "euro-consumer" was a myth. Consumer preferences vary much more across nations than Atag had thought. Consider ceramic cooktops; Atag planned to market just 2 varieties throughout the EU but has found it needs 11. Belgians, who cook in huge pots, require extra-large burners. Germans like oval pots and burners to fit. The French need small burners and very low temperatures for simmering sauces and broths. Germans like oven knobs on the top; the French want them on the front. Most Germans and French prefer black and white ranges; the British demand a range of colors including peach, pigeon blue, and mint green.

Threats

Just as the emergence of single markets creates opportunities for business, it also presents a number of threats. For one thing, the business environment within each grouping will become more competitive. The lowering of barriers to trade and investment between countries is likely to lead to increased price competition throughout the EU and NAFTA. For example, before 1992 a Volkswagen Golf cost 55 percent more in Great Britain than in Denmark and 29 percent more in Ireland than in Greece.[44] Over time, such price differentials will vanish in a single market. This is a direct threat to any firm doing business in EU or NAFTA countries. To survive in the tougher single-market environment, firms must take advantage of the opportunities offered by the creation of a single market to rationalize their production and reduce their costs. Otherwise, they will be at a severe disadvantage.

A further threat to firms outside these trading blocs arises from the likely long-term improvement in the competitive position of many firms within the areas. This is particularly relevant in the EU, where many firms have historically been limited by a high cost structure in their ability to compete globally with North American and Asian firms. The creation of a single market and the resulting increased competition in the EU is beginning to produce serious attempts by many EU firms to reduce their cost structure by rationalizing production. This is transforming many EU companies into efficient global competitors. The message for non-EU businesses is that they need to prepare for the emergence of more capable European competitors by reducing their own cost structures.

Another threat to firms outside of trading areas is the threat of being shut out of the single market by the creation of a "trade fortress." The charge that regional economic integration might lead to a fortress mentality is most often leveled at the EU. Although the free trade philosophy underpinning the EU theoretically argues against the creation of any fortress in Europe, occasional signs indicate the EU may raise barriers to imports and investment in certain "politically sensitive" areas, such as autos. Non-EU firms might be well advised, therefore, to set up their own EU operations. This could also occur in the NAFTA countries, but it seems less likely.

Finally, the emerging role of the European Commission in competition policy suggests the EU is increasingly willing and able to intervene and impose conditions on companies proposing mergers and acquisitions. This is a threat insofar as it limits the ability of firms to pursue the corporate strategy of their choice. The commission may require significant concessions from businesses as a precondition for allowing proposed mergers and acquisitions to proceed. While this constrains the strategic options for firms, it should be remembered that in taking such action, the commission is trying to maintain the level of competition in Europe's single market, which should benefit consumers.

Key Terms

regional economic integration, p. 303

free trade area, p. 305

European Free Trade Association (EFTA), p. 305

customs union, p. 305

common market, p. 305

economic union, p. 305

political union, p. 306

trade creation, p. 308

trade diversion, p. 308

Summary

This chapter pursued three main objectives: to examine the economic and political debate surrounding regional economic integration; to review the progress toward regional economic integration in Europe, the Americas, and elsewhere; and to distinguish the important implications of regional economic integration for the practice of international business. The chapter made the following points:

1. A number of levels of economic integration are possible in theory. In order of increasing integration, they include a free trade area, a customs union, a common market, an economic union, and full political union.

2. In a free trade area, barriers to trade between member countries are removed, but each country determines its own external trade policy. In a customs union, internal barriers to trade are removed and a common external trade policy is adopted. A common market is similar to a customs union, except that a common market also allows factors of production to move freely between countries. An economic union involves even closer integration, including the establishment of a common currency and the harmonization of tax rates. A political union is the logical culmination of attempts to achieve ever closer economic integration.

3. Regional economic integration is an attempt to achieve economic gains from the free flow of trade and investment between neighboring countries.

4. Integration is not easily achieved or sustained. Although integration brings benefits to the

majority, it is never without costs for the minority. Concerns over national sovereignty often slow or stop integration attempts.

5. Regional integration will not increase economic welfare if the trade creation effects in the free trade area are outweighed by the trade diversion effects.

6. The Single European Act sought to create a true single market by abolishing administrative barriers to the free flow of trade and investment between EU countries.

7. Sixteen EU members now use a common currency, the euro. The economic gains from a common currency come from reduced exchange costs, reduced risk associated with currency fluctuations, and increased price competition within the EU.

8. Increasingly, the European Commission is taking an activist stance with regard to competition policy, intervening to restrict mergers and acquisitions that it believes will reduce competition in the EU.

9. Although no other attempt at regional economic integration comes close to the EU in terms of potential economic and political significance, various other attempts are being made in the world. The most notable include NAFTA in North America, the Andean Pact and Mercosur in Latin America, ASEAN in Southeast Asia, and perhaps APEC.

10. The creation of single markets in the EU and North America means that many markets that were formerly protected from foreign competition are now more open. This creates

major investment and export opportunities for firms within and outside these regions.

11. The free movement of goods across borders, the harmonization of product standards, and the simplification of tax regimes make it possible for firms based in a free trade area to realize potentially enormous cost economies by centralizing production in those locations

within the area where the mix of factor costs and skills is optimal.

12. The lowering of barriers to trade and investment between countries within a trade group will probably be followed by increased price competition.

Critical Thinking and Discussion Questions

1. NAFTA has produced significant net benefits for the Canadian, Mexican, and U.S. economies. Discuss.

2. What are the economic and political arguments for regional economic integration? Given these arguments, why don't we see more substantial examples of integration in the world economy?

3. What effect is creation of a single market and a single currency within the EU likely to have on competition within the EU? Why?

4. Do you think it is correct for the European Commission to restrict mergers between American companies that do business in Europe? (For example, the European Commission vetoed the proposed merger between WorldCom and Sprint, both U.S. companies, and it carefully reviewed the merger between AOL and Time Warner, again both U.S. companies.)

5. How should a U.S. firm that currently exports only to ASEAN countries respond to the creation of a single market in this regional grouping?

6. How should a firm with self-sufficient production facilities in several ASEAN countries respond to the creation of a single market? What are the constraints on its ability to respond in a manner that minimizes production costs?

7. After a promising start, Mercosur, the major Latin American trade agreement, has faltered and made little progress since 2000. What problems are hurting Mercosur? What can be done to solve these problems?

8. Would establishment of a Free Trade Area of the Americas (FTAA) be good for the two most advanced economies in the hemisphere, the United States and Canada? How might the establishment of the FTAA impact the strategy of North American firms?

9. Reread the Management Focus, "The European Commission: Limitations on Economic Integration," then answer the following questions:

   a. What is the reasoning behind the acquisition of Sara Lee by Unilever? Is the proposed acquisition the best response to the perceived increase in competition by P&G?

   b. Why would the European Commission seek to restrict Unilever's purchase of Sara Lee? Isn't this contrary to the overall goal of economic integration?

   c. From a critical thinking position, what role does competition play within the concept of economic integration? How do you believe antitrust laws fit within the concept of economic integration?

http://globalEDGE.msu.edu  Research Task

Use the globalEDGE Resource Desk (http://global EDGE.msu.edu/resourcedesk/) to complete the following exercises:

1. The enlargement of the European Union into Eastern Europe has brought together countries

with different levels of economic development. Choose two long-term EU member countries and two newer members. Compare and contrast the macroeconomic situation in these countries by analyzing each country's primary economic indicators available from the most recent version of *Eurostatistics Data for Short-Term Economic Analysis*, a statistical book published periodically by *Eurostat*. Prepare a short report describing the similarities and differences between the two groups of countries.

2. The establishment of the Free Trade Area of the Americas could be a threat as well as an opportunity for your company. Identify the countries participating in the negotiations for the *FTAA*. Are there any countries in the Americas not participating in the negotiations? What are the main issues covered in the negotiation process?

The European Energy Market

For several years now the European Union, the largest regional trading bloc in the world, has been trying to liberalize its energy market, replacing the markets of its 27 member states with a single continent-wide market for electricity and gas. The first phase of liberalization went into effect in June 2007. When fully implemented, the ability of energy producers to sell electricity and gas across national borders will increase competition. The road toward the creation of a single EU energy market, however, has been anything but easy. Many national markets are dominated by a single enterprise, often a former state-owned utility. Electricitie de France, for example, has an 87 percent share of that country's electricity market. Injecting competition into such concentrated markets will prove difficult.

To complicate matters, most of these utilities are vertically integrated, producing, transmitting, and selling power. These vertically integrated producers have little interest in letting other utilities use their transmission grids to sell power to end users, or in buying power from other producers. For the full benefits of competition to take hold, the EU recognizes that utilities need to be split into generation, transmission, and marketing companies so that the business of selling energy can be separated from the businesses of producing it and transmitting it. Only then, so the thinking goes, will independent power marketing companies be able to buy energy from the cheapest source, whether it is within national borders or elsewhere in the EU, and resell it to consumers, thereby promoting competition.

For now, efforts to mandate the de-integration of utilities are some way off. Indeed, in February 2007 national energy ministers from the different EU states rejected a call from the European Commission, the top competition body in the EU, to break apart utilities. Instead the energy ministers asked the commission for more details about what such a move would accomplish, thereby effectively delaying any attempt to de-integrate national power companies. In mid-2008, they reached a compromise that fell short of mandating the unbundling, or de-integration, of national energy companies due to powerful opposition from France and Germany among others (both nations have large vertically integrated energy companies).

The response of established utilities to the creation of a single continent-wide market for energy has been to try to acquire utilities in other EU nations in an effort to build systems that serve more than one country. The underlying logic is that larger utilities should be able to realize economies of scale, and this would enable them to compete more effectively in a liberalized market. However, some cross-border takeover bids have run into fierce opposition from local politicians who resent their "national energy companies" being taken over by foreign entities. Most notably, when E.ON, the largest German utility, made a bid to acquire Endesa, Spain's largest utility, in 2006, Spanish politicians sought to block the acquisition and keep ownership of Endesa in Spanish hands, imposing conditions on the deal that were designed to stop the Germans from acquiring the Spanish company. In response to this outburst of nationalism, the European Commission took the Spanish government to the European Union's highest court, arguing that Madrid had violated the commission's exclusive powers within the EU to scrutinize and approve big cross-border mergers in Europe. Subsequently, Enel, Italy's biggest power company, stepped in and purchased Endesa.

Sources: "Power Struggles: European Utilities," *The Economist*, December 2, 2006, p. 74; "Anger Management in Brussels," *Petroleum Economist*, April 2006, pp. 1–3; R. Bream, "Liberalization of EU Market Accelerates Deal-making," *Financial Times*, February 28, 2007, p. 4; "Twists and Turns: Energy Liberalization in Europe," *The Economist*, December 8, 2007, p. 76; and "Better than Nothing?" *The Economist*, June 14, 2008, p. 80.

Case Discussion Questions

1. What do you think are the economic benefits of liberalizing the EU energy market? Who stands to gain the most from liberalization?

2. What are the implications of liberalization for energy producers in the EU? How will the environment they face change post-liberalization. What actions will they have to take?

3. Why is the de-integration of large energy companies seen as such an important part of any attempt to liberalize the EU energy market?

4. Why do you think progress toward the liberalization of the EU energy market has been fairly slow so far?

The Foreign Exchange Market

Chinese Yuan and Economic Balance

Much of the spectacular growth China has experienced over the past two decades has been attributed to the value of the yuan or renminbi (RMB) in comparison to other currencies, especially the U.S. dollar. To the Chinese, an undervalued yuan facilitates the exportation of goods and services. Chinese goods are cheaper when the yuan is cheap. Growth has been maintained by selling to foreign markets. To others, this "artificial" valuation causes imbalances within the global economy. Some claim the yuan is as much as 50 percent undervalued; that suggests that China is unfairly subsidizing its exporters with cheap currency. As becomes obvious, the issue is one of balancing domestic growth and global interests. As might be expected, each perspective has its critics.

During periods of economic expansion and growth by other countries, little attention was given to the yuan and its relative foreign value. When rich countries, such as the United States and Europe, had low unemployment rates, the outsourcing of manufacturing capabilities to China was not considered problematic. But as soon as this began to cause trade imbalances and as the global crisis hit, critics not only in the United States and Europe but elsewhere as well, began to view the dollar/yuan exchange under new light.

As the central bank, the People's Bank of China establishes the foreign exchange policy. Historically, the RMB has been pegged to the U.S. dollar. Shortly after the "opening" of China in the 1980s, the yuan was devalued in order to improve the competitiveness of Chinese exports. The official USD/RMB exchange rate dropped from 1.5 yuan to the dollar to 8.62 in 1984, the lowest level on record. In July 2005, China officially lifted the peg and did a one-off devaluation to 8.11 yuan. In June 2010, just before the meeting of the G20, a meeting specifically set to address the global financial crisis, in a statement written in both Mandarin and English, China's central bank acquiesced somewhat.

As summer 2010 began, China's central bank said it would again allow the yuan to move more freely against a basket of currencies, ruling out as unwarranted a "one-off revaluation." This came to be viewed as a "managed unpegging." By allowing a more "flexible" (stronger) yuan, China hopes to cool its economy and tame inflation. A stronger yuan would cut the costs of imported goods and has the added benefit of liberating China's interest-rate policy.

Quick results should not be expected, however, as long as the yuan is permitted to float in relation to a basket of currencies. The basket of currencies consists of the U.S. dollar, euro, Japanese yen, and South Korean won, with a smaller proportion made up of the British pound, Thai baht, Russian ruble, Australian dollar, Canadian dollar, and Singapore dollar. For example, as long as the euro (and potentially other currencies in the future) continues its decline, it will bring the overall value of the basket down as well as lessening any downward adjustment to the dollar. A lot will depend on how fast the yuan is allowed to appreciate. Some China-watchers argue that it will be more measured as long as it continues to be valued within a basket of currencies. Others view the situation in more complex terms. Although arguably a stronger yuan would make exports less profitable and give consumers more spending power, displaced workers would have to find jobs elsewhere. In contrast, a sharp rise in the yuan may create massive unemployment, not an increase in Chinese consumption. Multiple changes will need to be developed if an economic balance is to be achieved, not only in China but around the globe. ●

Sources: "The Long March," *The Economist,* June 26, 2010, accessed at http://www.economist.com/node/16425904?story_id=16425904; L. Fitzgeorge-Parker, "China: Caution Is Key for PBoC," *Euromoney,* 41, no. 495 (2010), p. 34; and People's Bank of China, "Further Reform of the RMB Exchange Rate Regime and Enhance the RMB Exchange Rate Flexibility," June 19, 2010, accessed at http://www.pbc.gov.cn/english/detail.asp?col=6400&id=1488 http://www.pbc.gov.cn/english/detail.asp?col=6400&id=1488. See also, http://www.chinanews.com.cn/news/2005/2005-08-10/26/610367.shtml.

Introduction

Like many enterprises in the global economy, manufacturing and service sector companies are affected by changes in the value of currencies on the foreign exchange markets. As detailed in the opening case, regardless of whether a company happens to be in the manufacturing or service sector, a depreciating or appreciating currency will affect sales, survivability, and/or profitability. Whether based on the sterling pound, the U.S. or Canadian dollar, the Thai baht, or the Chinese yuan, careful management of exchange risk will result in a higher likelihood of business success.

What happens in the foreign exchange market can have a fundamental impact on the sales, profits, and strategy of an enterprise. Accordingly, it is very important for managers to understand the working of the foreign exchange market, and what the impact of changes in currency exchange rates might be for their enterprise. With this in mind, the current chapter has three main objectives. The first is to explain how the foreign exchange market works. The second is to examine the forces that determine exchange rates, and to discuss the degree to which it is possible to predict future exchange rate movements. The third objective is to map the implications for international business of exchange rate movements. This chapter is the first of two that deal with the international monetary system and its relationship to international business. In the next chapter, we will explore the institutional structure of the international monetary system. The institutional structure is the context within which the foreign exchange market functions. As we shall see, changes in the institutional structure of the international monetary system can exert a profound influence on the development of foreign exchange markets.

The **foreign exchange market** is a market for converting the currency of one country into that of another country. An **exchange rate** is simply the rate at which one currency is converted into another. For example, Billabong uses the foreign exchange market to convert the dollars it earns from selling surf wear in the United States into Australian dollars. Without the foreign exchange market, international trade and international investment on the scale that we see today would be impossible; companies would have to resort to barter. The foreign exchange market is the lubricant that enables companies based in countries that use different currencies to trade with each other.

We know from earlier chapters that international trade and investment have their risks. Some of these risks exist because future exchange rates cannot be perfectly predicted. The rate at which one currency is converted into another can change over time. For example, at the start of 2001 one U.S. dollar bought 1.065 euros, but by the start of 2010, one U.S. dollar bought only 0.74 euro. The dollar had fallen sharply in value against the euro. This made American goods cheaper in Europe, boosting export sales. At the same time, it made European goods more expensive in the United States, which hurt the sales and profits of European companies that sold goods and services to the United States.

One function of the foreign exchange market is to provide some insurance against the risks that arise from such volatile changes in exchange rates, commonly referred to as foreign exchange risk. Although the foreign exchange market offers some insurance against foreign exchange risk, it cannot provide complete insurance. It is not unusual for international businesses to suffer losses because of unpredicted changes in exchange rates. Currency fluctuations can make seemingly profitable trade and investment deals unprofitable, and vice versa.

We begin this chapter by looking at the functions and the form of the foreign exchange market. This includes distinguishing among spot exchanges, forward exchanges, and currency swaps. Then we will consider the factors that determine exchange rates. We will also look at how foreign trade is conducted when a country's currency cannot be exchanged for other currencies; that is, when its currency is not convertible. The chapter closes with a discussion of these things in terms of their implications for business.

The Functions of the Foreign Exchange Market

The foreign exchange market serves two main functions. The first is to convert the currency of one country into the currency of another. The second is to provide some insurance against **foreign exchange risk,** by which we mean the adverse consequences of unpredictable changes in exchange rates.[1]

Foreign Exchange Market
A market for converting the currency of one country into that of another country.

Exchange Rate
The rate at which one currency is converted into another.

LEARNING OBJECTIVE 1
Describe the functions of the foreign exchange market.

Foreign Exchange Risk
The risk that changes in exchange rates will hurt the profitability of a business deal.

CURRENCY CONVERSION   Each country has a currency in which the prices of goods and services are quoted. In the United States, it is the dollar ($); in Great Britain, the pound (£); in France, Germany, and other members of the euro zone it is the euro (€); in Japan, the yen (¥); and so on. In general, within the borders of a particular country, one must use the national currency. A U.S. tourist cannot walk into a store in Edinburgh, Scotland, and use U.S. dollars to buy a bottle of Scotch whisky. Dollars are not recognized as legal tender in Scotland; the tourist must use British pounds. Fortunately, the tourist can go to a bank and exchange her dollars for pounds. Then she can buy the whisky.

When a tourist changes one currency into another, she is participating in the foreign exchange market. The exchange rate is the rate at which the market converts one currency into another. For example, an exchange rate of €1 = $1.30 specifies that one euro buys $1.30 U.S. dollars. The exchange rate allows us to compare the relative prices of goods and services in different countries. Our U.S. tourist wishing to buy a bottle of Scotch whisky in Edinburgh may find that she must pay £30 for the bottle, knowing that the same bottle costs $45 in the United States. Is this a good deal? Imagine the current pound/dollar exchange rate is £1.00 = $2.00 (i.e., one British pound buys $2.00). Our intrepid tourist takes out her calculator and converts £30 into dollars. (The calculation is 30 × 2). She finds that the bottle of Scotch costs the equivalent of $60. She is surprised that a bottle of Scotch whisky could cost less in the United States than in Scotland (alcohol is taxed heavily in Great Britain).

Tourists are minor participants in the foreign exchange market; companies engaged in international trade and investment are major ones. International businesses have four main uses of foreign exchange markets. First, the payments a company receives for its exports, the income it receives from foreign investments, or the income it receives from licensing agreements with foreign firms may be in foreign currencies. To use those funds in its home country, the company must convert them to its home country's currency. Consider the Scotch distillery that exports its whisky to the United States. The distillery is paid in dollars, but since those dollars cannot be spent in Great Britain, they must be converted into British pounds. Similarly, an Australian company sells its products in the United States for dollars; it must convert the U.S. dollars it receives into Australian dollars to use them in Australia.

Second, international businesses use foreign exchange markets when they must pay a foreign company for its products or services in its country's currency. For example, Dell buys many of the components for its computers from Malaysian firms. The Malaysian companies must be paid in Malaysia's currency, the ringgit, so Dell must convert money from dollars into ringgit to pay them.

Third, international businesses also use foreign exchange markets when they have spare cash that they wish to invest for short terms in money markets. For example, consider a U.S. company that has $10 million it wants to invest for three months. The best interest rate it can earn on these funds in the United States may be 4 percent. Investing in a South Korean money market account, however, may earn 12 percent. Thus, the company may change its $10 million into Korean won and invest it in South Korea. Note, however, that the rate of return it earns on this investment depends not only on the Korean interest rate, but also on the changes in the value of the Korean won against the dollar in the intervening period.

Currency speculation is another use of foreign exchange markets. **Currency speculation** typically involves the short-term movement of funds from one currency to another in the hopes of profiting from shifts in exchange rates. Consider again a U.S. company with $10 million to invest for three months. Suppose the company suspects that the U.S. dollar is overvalued against the Japanese yen. That is, the company expects the value of the dollar to depreciate (fall) against that of the yen. Imagine the current dollar/yen exchange rate is $1 = ¥120. The company exchanges its $10 million into yen, receiving ¥1.2 billion ($10 million × 120 = ¥1.2 billion). Over the next three months, the value of the dollar depreciates against the yen until $1 = ¥100. Now the company exchanges its ¥1.2 billion back into dollars and finds that it has $12 million. The company has made a $2 million profit on currency speculation in three months on an initial investment of $10 million! In general, however, companies should beware, for speculation by definition is a very risky business. The company cannot know for sure what will happen to exchange rates. While a speculator may profit handsomely if his speculation about future currency movements turns out to be correct, he can also lose vast amounts of money if it turns out to be wrong.

A kind of speculation that has become more common in recent years is known as the **carry trade.** The carry trade involves borrowing in one currency where interest rates are low, and then using the proceeds to invest in another currency where interest rates are high. For example, if the interest rate on borrowings in Japan is 1 percent, but the interest rate on deposits in American banks is 6 percent, it can make sense to borrow in Japanese yen, then convert the money into U.S. dollars and deposit it in an American bank. The trader can make a 5 percent margin by doing so, minus the transaction costs associated with changing one currency into another. The speculative element of this trade is that its success is based upon a belief that there will be no adverse movement in exchange rates (or interest rates for that matter) that will make the trade unprofitable. However, if the yen were to rapidly increase in value against the dollar, then it would take more U.S. dollars to repay the original loan, and the trade could fast become unprofitable. The dollar-yen carry trade was actually very significant during the mid-2000s, peaking at over $1 trillion in 2007, when some 30 percent of trade on the Tokyo foreign exchange market was related to the carry trade.[2] This carry trade declined in importance during 2008–09 precisely because the Japanese yen was increasing in value against the dollar, making the trade riskier (in addition, interest rate differentials were falling as U.S. rates came down, making the trade less profitable even if exchange rates were stable).

INSURING AGAINST FOREIGN EXCHANGE RISK
A second function of the foreign exchange market is to provide insurance against foreign exchange risk, which is the possibility that unpredicted changes in future exchange rates will have adverse consequences for the firm. When a firm insures itself against foreign exchange risk, we say that is it engaging in **hedging.** To explain how the market performs this function, we must first distinguish among spot exchange rates, forward exchange rates, and currency swaps.

Spot Exchange Rates
When two parties agree to exchange currency and execute the deal immediately, the transaction is referred to as a spot exchange. Exchange rates governing such "on the spot" trades are referred to as spot exchange rates. The **spot exchange rate** is the rate at which a foreign exchange dealer converts one currency into another currency on a particular day. Thus, when our U.S. tourist in Edinburgh goes to a bank to convert her dollars into pounds, the exchange rate is the spot rate for that day.

Currency Speculation
Involves the short-term movement of funds from one currency to another in the hopes of profiting from shifts in exchange rates.

Carry Trade
Involves borrowing in one currency where interest rates are low, and then using the proceeds to invest in another currency where interest rates are high.

Hedging
The process of insuring one's business against foreign exchange risk by using forward exchanges or currency swaps.

LEARNING OBJECTIVE 2
Understand what is meant by spot exchange rates.

Spot Exchange Rate
The exchange rate at which a foreign exchange dealer will convert one currency into another currency on a particular day.

Using insurance to protect against forward exchange rates helps companies hedge against financial risk.

Spot exchange rates are reported on a real-time basis on many financial Web sites. Table 9.1 shows the exchange rates for a selection of currencies traded in the New York foreign exchange market as of 1:11 p.m. February 18, 2009. An exchange rate can be quoted in two ways: as the amount of foreign currency one U.S. dollar will buy, or as the value of a dollar for one unit of foreign currency. Thus, one U.S. dollar bought €0.7954 on February 18, 2009, and one euro bought $1.2572 U.S. dollars.

Spot rates change continually, often on a minute-by-minute basis (although the magnitude of changes over such short periods is usually small). The value of a currency is determined by the interaction between the demand and supply of that currency relative to the demand and supply of other currencies. For example, if lots of people want U.S. dollars and dollars are in short supply, and few people want British pounds and pounds are in plentiful supply, the spot exchange rate for converting dollars into pounds will change. The dollar is likely to appreciate against the pound (or the pound will depreciate against the dollar). Imagine the spot exchange rate is £1 = $2.00 when the market opens. As the day progresses, dealers demand more dollars and fewer pounds. By the end of the day, the spot exchange rate might be £1 = $1.98. Each pound now buys fewer dollars than at the start of the day. The dollar has appreciated, and the pound has depreciated.

LEARNING OBJECTIVE 3
Recognize the role that forward exchange rates play in insuring against foreign exchange risk.

Forward Exchange Rates   Changes in spot exchange rates can be problematic for an international business. For example, a U.S. company that imports laptop computers from Japan knows that in 30 days it must pay yen to a Japanese supplier when a shipment arrives. The company will pay the Japanese supplier ¥200,000 for each laptop computer, and the current dollar/yen spot exchange rate is $1 = ¥120. At this rate, each computer costs the importer $1,667 (i.e., 1,667 = 200,000/120). The importer knows

Major Currency Cross Rates							
Currency Last Trade	U.S. $ N/A	¥en 1:22pm ET	Euro 1:22pm ET	Can $ 1:22pm ET	U.K. £ 1:22pm ET	AU $ 1:20pm ET	Swiss Franc 1:22pm ET
1 U.S. $ =	1	92.3550	0.7954	1.2641	0.7034	1.5736	1.1736
1 ¥en =	0.0108	1	0.0086	0.0137	0.0076	0.0170	0.0127
1 Euro =	1.2572	116.114	1	1.5893	0.8843	1.9784	1.4755
1 Can $ =	0.7911	73.0599	0.6292	1	0.5564	1.2448	0.9284
1 U.K. £ =	1.4217	131.290	1.1308	1.7971	1	2.2371	1.6685
1 AU $ =	0.6355	58.6903	0.5055	0.8033	0.4470	1	0.7458
1 Swiss Franc =	0.8521	78.6938	0.6777	1.0771	0.5994	1.3408	1

table

Value of the U.S. Dollar against other Currencies, February 18, 2009

Source: Yahoo! Finance.

she can sell the computers the day they arrive for $2,000 each, which yields a gross profit of $333 on each computer ($2,000 − $1,667). However, the importer will not have the funds to pay the Japanese supplier until the computers have been sold. If over the next 30 days the dollar unexpectedly depreciates against the yen, say, to $1 = ¥95, the importer will still have to pay the Japanese company ¥200,000 per computer, but in dollar terms that would be equivalent to $2,105 per computer, which is more than she can sell the computers for. A depreciation in the value of the dollar against the yen from $1 = ¥120 to $1 = ¥95 would transform a profitable deal into an unprofitable one.

To *insure* or *hedge* against this risk, the U.S. importer might want to engage in a forward exchange. A **forward exchange** occurs when two parties agree to exchange currency and execute the deal at some specific date in the future. Exchange rates governing such future transactions are referred to as **forward exchange rates.** For most major currencies, forward exchange rates are quoted for 30 days, 90 days, and 180 days into the future. In some cases, it is possible to get forward exchange rates for several years into the future. Returning to our computer importer example, let us assume the 30-day forward exchange rate for converting dollars into yen is $1 = ¥110. The importer enters into a 30-day forward exchange transaction with a foreign exchange dealer at this rate and is guaranteed that she will have to pay no more than $1,818 for each computer (1,818 = 200,000/110). This guarantees her a profit of $182 per computer ($2,000 − $1,818). She also insures herself against the possibility that an unanticipated change in the dollar/yen exchange rate will turn a profitable deal into an unprofitable one.

Forward Exchange
When two parties agree to exchange currency and execute the deal at some specific date in the future.

Forward Exchange Rate
The exchange rate governing forward exchange transactions.

In this example, the spot exchange rate ($1 = ¥120) and the 30-day forward rate ($1 = ¥110) differ. Such differences are normal; they reflect the expectations of the foreign exchange market about future currency movements. In our example, the fact that $1 bought more yen with a spot exchange than with a 30-day forward exchange indicates foreign exchange dealers expected the dollar to depreciate against the yen in the next 30 days. When this occurs, we say the dollar is selling at a discount on the 30-day forward market (i.e., it is worth less than on the spot market). Of course, the opposite can also occur. If the 30-day forward exchange rate were $1 = ¥130, for example, $1 would buy more yen with a forward exchange than with a spot exchange. In such a case, we say the dollar is selling at a premium on the 30-day forward market. This reflects the foreign exchange dealers' expectations that the dollar will appreciate against the yen over the next 30 days.

In sum, when a firm enters into a forward exchange contract, it is taking out insurance against the possibility that future exchange rate movements will make a transaction unprofitable by the time that transaction has been executed. Although many firms routinely enter into forward exchange contracts to hedge their foreign exchange risk, there are some spectacular examples of what happens when firms don't take out this insurance. There are other factors that may influence foreign currency exchange. For example, consider the accompanying Management Focus, which explains how macro economic and commercial environments affect exchange rates.

Currency Swaps
The discussion of spot and forward exchange rates might lead you to conclude that the option to buy forward is very important to companies engaged in international trade—and you would be right. By April 2007, the latest date for which information is available, forward instruments accounted for some 69 percent of all foreign exchange transactions, while spot exchanges accounted for 31 percent.[3] However, the vast majority of these forward exchanges were not forward exchanges of the type we have been discussing, but rather a more sophisticated instrument known as currency swaps.

A **currency swap** is the simultaneous purchase and sale of a given amount of foreign exchange for two different value dates. Swaps are transacted between international businesses and their banks, between banks, and between governments when it is

Currency Swap
Simultaneous purchase and sale of a given amount of foreign exchange for two different value dates.

Competition and Exchange Rates

Perhaps one of the most competitive rivalries in global business has been between the two giants of aerospace: EADS and Boeing. In addition to the inherent competition between their aeronautical products, a fierce rivalry may be said to exist between the euro (EADS) and the dollar (Boeing), and its relative exchange rate.

Based out of Leiden, Netherlands, European Aeronautic Defense and Space Co. (EADS), the largest European aerospace corporation and makers of civil and military aircraft (including Airbus as well as communications systems, missiles, space rockets, satellites, and related systems) reported that first quarter profits for 2010 had fallen 39 percent on deteriorating currency hedges and costs associated with the development of the Airbus A380. Along with U.S.-based Boeing, EADS is one of the largest exporters in the world. In that role, its exposure to currency fluctuations is high.

According to investment reports, exchange rate fluctuations shaved 300 million euros ($372 million) off EADS earnings before interest and tax in the first quarter of 2010, partly due to "out-of-the-money" currency hedges. At the end of the first quarter, March 2010, EADS had a hedge portfolio equivalent to $66.2 billion at an average euro/dollar rate of $1.39. As an example of how quickly things can change, a decline of more than 20 percent in the value of the euro against the U.S. dollar is once again bolstering the competitiveness of Airbus, while eroding a pricing advantage that a weak dollar has provided to Boeing.

In a demonstration of how macroeconomic and commercial environments affect exchange rates, concerns about the financial health of Greece and other members of the 16-country euro zone pushed the currency below $1.20—its lowest level in more than four years—down from $1.50 in late 2009. A stronger U.S. currency benefits Airbus, which sells its jets in dollars but incurs about half its expenses in euros. Furthermore, according to industry analysts, the recent decline of the euro will allow Airbus to lower the price of a new jet by 10 percent and command the same profit it did when the euro was equivalent to $1.50. That gives the European aircraft giant the flexibility to be more aggressive when it competes with Boeing for airline orders.

Ironically, the same hedging strategy that mitigates negative currency swings also mitigates positive swings. The competitive advantage of a weaker euro won't become evident immediately. In the near-term, the benefits of a lower euro will be limited for many European contractors because they have hedged their dollar costs. Those hedges, secured as protection when the euro was soaring in value against the dollar, have locked them into paying above-market exchange rates. At current rates, the hedges EADS held represent an estimated $2 billion drag on profits. Senior EADS executives do not expect to see the full benefit of the euro's decline until some time in the 2012–2014 time frame.

Boeing would not be competitive, however, if it were to assume that the euro's recent weakness will be short lived. Concerns that the financial crisis may yet spread to Eastern Europe have economists predicting the currency could fall to parity with the dollar—an unthinkable notion just a few months ago. Couple that with some of the recent efficiency drives at EADS that cut €3 billion in costs, and Boeing is facing a more formidable competitor.

But while the euro has slumped 18 percent from its November 2009 peak to a four-year low of $1.24 amid jitters over the creditworthiness of Greece and other heavily indebted euro zone countries, existing hedges mean EADS won't start to benefit from the weaker euro until 2012. It has $13.4 billion of hedges for the rest of this year, at an average of $1.37 to the euro, and $16.9 billion in 2011, at a rate of $1.39.

Chief Executive Louis Gallois said he is "cautiously optimistic" that the aerospace industry is slowly recovering from last year's downturn. EADS booked 14.38 billion euros of new orders in the January-to-March period, up 54 percent from a year earlier, reflecting increased orders for A350 and A330 wide-bodied planes made by its wholly owned Airbus subsidiary. The value of Airbus's order backlog swelled by €26.4 billion to €366.1 billion, chiefly due to the dollar's appreciation.

Sources: "EADS Reports Half-Year 2010 Results," August 3, 2010, accessed at http://www.ameinfo.com/239348.html; D. Pearson, "Airbus Parent's Income Falls on Currency-Hedging Costs," *The Wall Street Journal*, May 15, 2010, accessed at http://online.wsj.com/article/NA_WSJ_PUB: SB10001424052748703460404575243540897928112.html; and EADS Web site at www.eads.com.

desirable to move out of one currency into another for a limited period without incurring foreign exchange risk. A common kind of swap is spot against forward. Consider a company such as Apple Computer. Apple assembles laptop computers in the United States, but the screens are made in Japan. Apple also sells some of the finished laptops in Japan. So, like many companies, Apple both buys from and sells to Japan. Imagine Apple needs to change $1 million into yen to pay its supplier of laptop screens today. Apple knows that in 90 days it will be paid ¥120 million by the Japanese importer that buys its finished laptops. It will want to convert these yen into dollars for use in the United States. Let us say today's spot exchange rate is $1 = ¥120 and the 90-day forward exchange rate is $1 = ¥110. Apple sells $1 million to its bank in return for ¥120 million. Now Apple can pay its Japanese supplier. At the same time, Apple enters into a 90-day forward exchange deal with its bank for converting ¥120 million into dollars. Thus, in 90 days Apple will receive $1.09 million (¥120 million/110 = $1.09 million). Since the yen is trading at a premium on the 90-day forward market, Apple ends up with more dollars than it started with (although the opposite could also occur). The swap deal is just like a conventional forward deal in one important respect: It enables Apple to insure itself against foreign exchange risk. By engaging in a swap, Apple knows today that the ¥120 million payment it will receive in 90 days will yield $1.09 million.

Another Perspective

Key into Exchange Rate Language

The language used to describe exchange rates can be confusing, even though the ideas themselves are simple. Here's why: Any given observation describes a changing relationship (the movement in the currencies) that itself describes two relationships (the exchange rates for both currencies). The important thing to remember is that an exchange rate is described in terms of other exchange rates.

The language we use to describe these moving phenomena works in a similar, dual way: The euro gains against the dollar, so the euro is strengthening, or becoming dearer, from a dollar perspective. Meanwhile, the same observation indicates its mirror image, that the dollar is weakening, becoming cheaper against the euro, from a euro perspective.

The Nature of the Foreign Exchange Market

The foreign exchange market is not located in any one place. It is a global network of banks, brokers, and foreign exchange dealers connected by electronic communications systems. When companies wish to convert currencies, they typically go through their own banks rather than entering the market directly. The foreign exchange market has been growing at a rapid pace, reflecting a general growth in the volume of cross-border trade and investment (see Chapter 1). In March 1986, the average total value of global foreign exchange trading was about $200 billion per day. According to the tri-annual survey by the Bank of International Settlements, by April 1995, it was more than $1,200 billion per day, by April 2004 it reached $1.8 trillion per day, and by April 2007 it had surged to $3.21 trillion per day.[4] The most important trading centers are London (34 percent of activity), New York (16 percent of activity), and Zurich, Tokyo, and Singapore (all with around 6 percent of activity).[5] Major secondary trading centers include Frankfurt, Paris, Hong Kong, and Sydney.

London's dominance in the foreign exchange market is due to both history and geography. As the capital of the world's first major industrial trading nation, London had become the world's largest center for international banking by the end of the nineteenth century, a position it has retained. Today London's central position between Tokyo and Singapore to the east and New York to the west has made it the critical link between the East Asian and New York markets. Due to the particular differences in time zones, London opens soon after Tokyo closes for the night and is still open for the first few hours of trading in New York.[6]

Two features of the foreign exchange market are of particular note. The first is that the market never sleeps. Tokyo, London, and New York are all shut for only 3 hours out of every 24. During these three

Even though the British pound has declined in its importance as a vehicle currency, London remains the key location for global foreign exchange.

hours, trading continues in a number of minor centers, particularly San Francisco and Sydney, Australia. The second feature of the market is the integration of the various trading centers. High-speed computer linkages between trading centers around the globe have effectively created a single market. The integration of financial centers implies there can be no significant difference in exchange rates quoted in the trading centers. For example, if the yen/dollar exchange rate quoted in London at 3 p.m. is ¥120 = $1, the yen/dollar exchange rate quoted in New York at the same time (10 a.m. New York time) will be identical. If the New York yen/dollar exchange rate were ¥125 = $1, a dealer could make a profit through **arbitrage,** buying a currency low and selling it high. For example, if the prices differed in London and New York as given, a dealer in New York could take $1 million and use that to purchase ¥125 million. She could then immediately sell the ¥125 million for dollars in London, where the transaction would yield $1.046666 million, allowing the trader to book a profit of $46,666 on the transaction. If all dealers tried to cash in on the opportunity, however, the demand for yen in New York would rise, resulting in an appreciation of the yen against the dollar such that the price differential between New York and London would quickly disappear. Because foreign exchange dealers are always watching their computer screens for arbitrage opportunities, the few that arise tend to be small, and they disappear in minutes.

> **Arbitrage**
> The purchase of securities in one market for immediate resale in another to profit from a price discrepancy.

Another feature of the foreign exchange market is the important role played by the U.S. dollar. Although a foreign exchange transaction can involve any two currencies, most transactions involve dollars on one side. This is true even when a dealer wants to sell a nondollar currency and buy another. A dealer wishing to sell Korean won for Brazilian real, for example, will usually sell the won for dollars and then use the dollars to buy real. Although this may seem a roundabout way of doing things, it is actually cheaper than trying to find a holder of real who wants to buy won. Because the volume of international transactions involving dollars is so great, it is not hard to find dealers who wish to trade dollars for won or real.

Due to its central role in so many foreign exchange deals, the dollar is a vehicle currency. In 2007, 86 percent of all foreign exchange transactions involved dollars on one side of the transaction. After the dollar, the most important vehicle currencies were the euro (37 percent), the Japanese yen (16.5 percent), and the British pound (15 percent)—reflecting the importance of these trading entities in the world economy. The euro has replaced the German mark as the world's second most important vehicle currency. The British pound used to be second in importance to the dollar as a vehicle currency, but its importance has diminished in recent years. Despite this, London has retained its leading position in the global foreign exchange market.

Economic Theories of Exchange Rate Determination

> **LEARNING OBJECTIVE 4**
> Understand the different theories explaining how currency exchange rates are determined and their relative merits.

At the most basic level, exchange rates are determined by the demand and supply of one currency relative to the demand and supply of another. For example, if the demand for dollars outstrips the supply of them and if the supply of Japanese yen is greater than the demand for them, the dollar/yen exchange rate will change. The dollar will appreciate against the yen (or the yen will depreciate against the dollar). However, while differences in relative demand and supply explain the determination of exchange rates, they do so only in a superficial sense. This simple explanation does not tell us what factors underlie the demand for and supply of a currency. Nor does it tell us when the demand for dollars will exceed the supply (and vice versa) or when the supply of Japanese yen will exceed demand for them (and vice versa). Neither does it tell us under what conditions a currency is in demand or under what conditions it is not demanded. In this section, we will review economic theory's answers to these questions. This will give us a deeper understanding of how exchange rates are determined.

If we understand how exchange rates are determined, we may be able to forecast exchange rate movements. Because future exchange rate movements influence export opportunities, the profitability of international trade and investment deals, and the price competitiveness of foreign imports, this is valuable information for an international business. Unfortunately, there is no simple explanation. The forces that determine exchange rates are complex, and no theoretical consensus exists, even among academic economists who study the phenomenon every day. Nonetheless, most economic theories of exchange rate movements seem to agree that three factors have an important impact on future exchange rate movements in a country's currency: the country's price inflation, its interest rate, and market psychology.[7]

PRICES AND EXCHANGE RATES   To understand how prices are related to exchange rate movements, we first need to discuss an economic proposition known as the law of one price. Then we will discuss the theory of purchasing power parity (PPP), which links changes in the exchange rate between two countries' currencies to changes in the countries' price levels.

The Law of One Price   The **law of one price** states that in competitive markets free of transportation costs and barriers to trade (such as tariffs), identical products sold in different countries must sell for the same price when their price is expressed in terms of the same currency.[8] For example, if the exchange rate between the British pound and the dollar is £1 = $2.00, a jacket that retails for $80 in New York should sell for £40 in London (since $80/2.00 = £40). Consider what would happen if the jacket cost £30 in London ($60 in U.S. currency). At this price, it would pay a trader to buy jackets in London and sell them in New York (an example of *arbitrage*). The company initially could make a profit of $20 on each jacket by purchasing it for £30 ($60) in London and selling it for $80 in New York (we are assuming away transportation costs and trade barriers). However, the increased demand for jackets in London would raise their price in London, and the increased supply of jackets in New York would lower their price there. This would continue until prices were equalized. Thus, prices might equalize when the jacket cost £35 ($70) in London and $70 in New York (assuming no change in the exchange rate of £1 = $2.00).

> **Law of One Price**
> In competitive markets free of transportation costs and barriers to trade, identical products sold in different countries must sell for the same price when their price is expressed in terms of the same currency.

Purchasing Power Parity   If the law of one price were true for all goods and services, the purchasing power parity (PPP) exchange rate could be found from any individual set of prices. By comparing the prices of identical products in different currencies, it would be possible to determine the "real" or PPP exchange rate that would exist if markets were efficient. (An **efficient market** has no impediments to the free flow of goods and services, such as trade barriers, and prices reflect all available public information.)

A less extreme version of the PPP theory states that given relatively efficient markets—that is, markets in which few impediments to international trade exist—the price of a "basket of goods" should be roughly equivalent in each country. To express the PPP theory in symbols, let P$ be the U.S. dollar price of a basket of particular goods and P¥ be the price of the same basket of goods in Japanese yen. The PPP theory predicts that the dollar/yen exchange rate, E$/¥, should be equivalent to:

> **Efficient Market**
> A market which has no impediments to the free flow of goods and services, such as trade barriers, and prices reflect all available public information.

$$E_{\$/¥} = P_{\$}/P_{¥}$$

Thus, if a basket of goods costs $200 in the United States and ¥20,000 in Japan, PPP theory predicts that the dollar/yen exchange rate should be $200/¥20,000 or $0.01 per Japanese yen (i.e., $1 = ¥100).

Every year, the newsmagazine *The Economist* publishes its own version of the PPP theorem, which it refers to as the "Big Mac Index." *The Economist* has selected McDonald's Big Mac as a proxy for a "basket of goods" because it is produced according to more or less the same recipe in about 120 countries. The Big Mac PPP is the exchange rate that would have hamburgers costing the same in each country. According to *The Economist*, comparing a country's actual exchange rate with the one predicted by the PPP theorem based on relative prices of Big Macs is a test on whether a currency is undervalued or not. This is not a totally serious exercise, as *The Economist* admits, but it does provide us with a useful illustration of the PPP theorem.

Relative currency values according to the Big Mac index for January 6, 2010, are reproduced in Table 9.2. To calculate the index *The Economist* converts the price of a Big Mac in a country into dollars at current exchange rates and divides that by the average price of a Big Mac in America (which was $3.58). According to the PPP theorem, the prices should be the same. If they are not, it implies that the currency is either overvalued against the dollar or undervalued. For example, the average price of a Big Mac in the euro area was $4.84 at the euro/dollar exchange rate prevailing in early 2010. Dividing this by the average price of a Big Mac in the United States gives 1.35 (i.e., 4.84/3.58), which suggests that the euro was overvalued by 35 percent against the U.S. dollar.

The next step in the PPP theory is to argue that the exchange rate will change if relative prices change. For example, imagine there is no price inflation in the United States, while prices in Japan are increasing by 10 percent a year. At the beginning of the year, a basket of goods costs $200 in the United States and ¥20,000 in Japan, so the dollar/yen exchange rate, according to PPP theory, should be $1 = ¥100. At the end of the year, the basket of goods still costs $200 in the United States, but it costs ¥22,000 in Japan. PPP theory predicts that the exchange rate should change as a result. More precisely, by the end of the year:

$$E_{\$/¥} = \$200/¥22,000$$

Thus, ¥1 = $0.0091 (or $1 = ¥110). Because of 10 percent price inflation, the Japanese yen has depreciated by 10 percent against the dollar. One dollar will buy 10 percent more yen at the end of the year than at the beginning.

Money Supply and Price Inflation

In essence, PPP theory predicts that changes in relative prices will result in a change in exchange rates. Theoretically, a country in which price inflation is running wild should expect to see its currency depreciate against that of countries in which inflation rates are lower. If we can predict what a country's

9.2 table

The Big Mac Index,
January 6, 2010

Source: *The Economist*, January 6,
2010, http://www.economist.com/
daily/chartgallery/displaystory.
cfm?story_id=15210330.

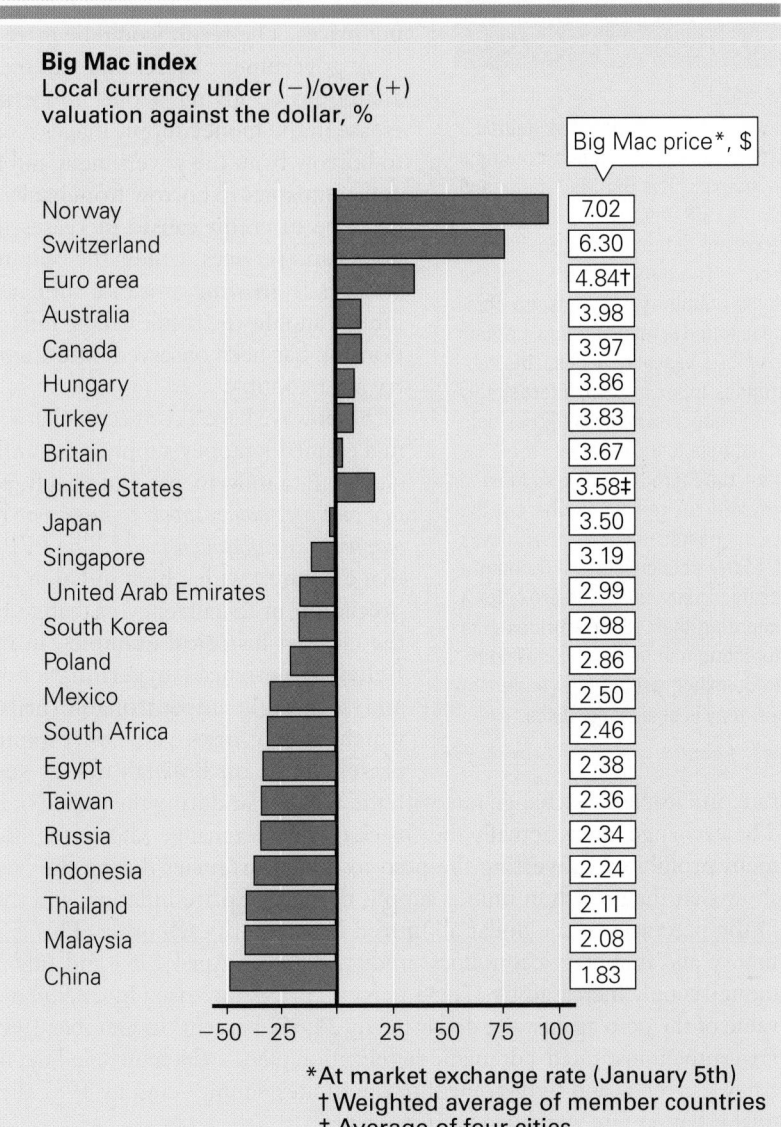

Big Mac index
Local currency under (−)/over (+)
valuation against the dollar, %

	Big Mac price*, $
Norway	7.02
Switzerland	6.30
Euro area	4.84†
Australia	3.98
Canada	3.97
Hungary	3.86
Turkey	3.83
Britain	3.67
United States	3.58‡
Japan	3.50
Singapore	3.19
United Arab Emirates	2.99
South Korea	2.98
Poland	2.86
Mexico	2.50
South Africa	2.46
Egypt	2.38
Taiwan	2.36
Russia	2.34
Indonesia	2.24
Thailand	2.11
Malaysia	2.08
China	1.83

−50 −25 25 50 75 100

*At market exchange rate (January 5th)
†Weighted average of member countries
‡ Average of four cities

Source: *The Economist* using McDonald's price data

future inflation rate is likely to be, we can also predict how the value of its currency relative to other currencies—its exchange rate—is likely to change. The growth rate of a country's money supply determines its likely future inflation rate.[9] Thus, in theory at least, we can use information about the growth in money supply to forecast exchange rate movements.

Inflation is a monetary phenomenon. It occurs when the quantity of money in circulation rises faster than the stock of goods and services; that is, when the money supply increases faster than output increases. Imagine what would happen if everyone in the country was suddenly given $10,000 by the government. Many people would rush out to spend their extra money on those things they had always wanted—new cars, new furniture, better clothes, and so on. There would be a surge in demand for goods and services. Car dealers, department stores, and other providers of goods and services

would respond to this upsurge in demand by raising prices. The result would be price inflation.

A government increasing the money supply is analogous to giving people more money. An increase in the money supply makes it easier for banks to borrow from the government and for individuals and companies to borrow from banks. The resulting increase in credit causes increases in demand for goods and services. Unless the output of goods and services is growing at a rate similar to that of the money supply, the result will be inflation. This relationship has been observed time after time in country after country.

So now we have a connection between the growth in a country's money supply, price inflation, and exchange rate movements. Put simply, *when the growth in a country's money supply is faster than the growth in its output, price inflation is fueled.* The PPP theory tells us that a country with a high inflation rate will see depreciation in its currency exchange rate. In one of the clearest historical examples, in the mid-1980s, Bolivia experienced hyperinflation—an explosive and seemingly uncontrollable price inflation in which money loses value very rapidly. Table 9.3 presents data on Bolivia's money supply, inflation rate, and its peso's exchange rate with the U.S. dollar during the period of hyperinflation. The exchange rate is actually the "black market" exchange rate, as the Bolivian government prohibited converting the peso to other currencies during the period. The data show that the growth in money supply, the rate of price inflation, and the depreciation of the peso against the dollar all moved in step with each other. This is just what PPP theory and monetary economics predict. Between April 1984 and July 1985, Bolivia's money supply increased by 17,433 percent, prices increased by 22,908 percent, and the value of the peso against the dollar fell by 24,662 percent! In October 1985, the Bolivian government instituted a dramatic stabilization plan—which included the introduction of a new currency and tight control of the money supply—and by 1987 the country's annual inflation rate was down to 16 percent.[10]

Another way of looking at the same phenomenon is that an increase in a country's money supply, which increases the amount of currency available, changes the relative demand and supply conditions in the foreign exchange market. If the U.S. money supply is growing more rapidly than U.S. output, dollars will be relatively more plentiful than the currencies of countries where monetary growth is closer to output growth. As a result of this relative increase in the supply of dollars, the dollar will depreciate on the foreign exchange market against the currencies of countries with slower monetary growth.

Government policy determines whether the rate of growth in a country's money supply is greater than the rate of growth in output. A government can increase the money supply simply by telling the country's central bank to issue more money. Governments tend to do this to finance public expenditure (building roads, paying government workers, paying for defense, etc.). A government could finance public expenditure by raising taxes, but since nobody likes paying more taxes and since politicians do not like to be unpopular, they have a natural preference for expanding the money supply. Unfortunately, there is no magic money tree. The inevitable result of excessive growth

Month	Money Supply (billions of pesos)	Price Level Relative to 1982 (average = 1)	Exchange Rate (pesos per dollar)
1984			
April	270	21.1	3,576
May	330	31.1	3,512
June	440	32.3	3,342
July	599	34.0	3,570
August	718	39.1	7,038
September	889	53.7	13,685
October	1,194	85.5	15,205
November	1,495	112.4	18,469
December	3,296	180.9	24,515
1985			
January	4,630	305.3	73,016
February	6,455	863.3	141,101
March	9,089	1,078.6	128,137
April	12,885	1,205.7	167,428
May	21,309	1,635.7	272,375
June	27,778	2,919.1	481,756
July	47,341	4,854.6	885,476
August	74,306	8,081.0	1,182,300
September	103,272	12,647.6	1,087,440
October	132,550	12,411.8	1,120,210

9.3 table

Macroeconomic Data for Bolivia, April 1984 to October 1985

Source: Juan-Antino Morales, "Inflation Stabilization in Bolivia," in *Inflation Stabilization: The Experience of Israel, Argentina, Brazil, Bolivia, and Mexico*, ed. Michael Bruno et al. (Cambridge, MA: MIT Press, 1988).

in money supply is price inflation. However, this has not stopped governments around the world from expanding the money supply, with predictable results. If an international business is attempting to predict future movements in the value of a country's currency on the foreign exchange market, it should examine that country's policy toward monetary growth. If the government seems committed to controlling the rate of growth in money supply, the country's future inflation rate may be low (even if the current rate is high) and its currency should not depreciate too much on the foreign exchange market. If the government seems to lack the political will to control the rate of growth in money supply, the future inflation rate may be high, which is likely to cause its currency to depreciate. Historically, many Latin American governments have fallen into this latter category, including Argentina, Bolivia, and Brazil. More recently, many of the newly democratic states of Eastern Europe made the same mistake.

Empirical Tests of PPP Theory   PPP theory predicts that exchange rates are determined by relative prices, and that changes in relative prices will result in a change in exchange rates. A country in which price inflation is running wild should expect to see its currency depreciate against that of countries with lower inflation rates. This is intuitively appealing, but is it true in practice? There are several good examples of the connection between a country's price inflation and exchange rate position (such as Bolivia). However, extensive empirical testing of PPP theory has yielded mixed results.[11] While PPP theory seems to yield relatively accurate predictions in the long run, it does not appear to be a strong predictor of short-run movements in exchange rates covering time spans of five years or less.[12] In addition, the theory seems to best predict exchange rate changes for countries with high rates of inflation and underdeveloped capital markets. The theory is less useful for predicting short-term exchange rate movements between the currencies of advanced industrialized nations that have relatively small differentials in inflation rates.

The failure to find a strong link between relative inflation rates and exchange rate movements has been referred to as the purchasing power parity puzzle. Several factors may explain the failure of PPP theory to predict exchange rates more accurately.[13] PPP theory assumes away transportation costs and barriers to trade. In practice, these factors are significant and they tend to create significant price differentials between countries. Transportation costs are certainly not trivial for many goods. Moreover, as we saw in Chapter 6, governments routinely intervene in international trade, creating tariff and nontariff barriers to cross-border trade. Barriers to trade limit the ability of traders to use arbitrage to equalize prices for the same product in different countries, which is required for the law of one price to hold. Government intervention in cross-border trade, by violating the assumption of efficient markets, weakens the link between relative price changes and changes in exchange rates predicted by PPP theory.

In addition, the PPP theory may not hold if many national markets are dominated by a handful of multinational enterprises that have sufficient market power to be able to exercise some influence over prices, control distribution channels, and differentiate their product offerings between nations.[14] In fact, this situation seems to prevail in a number of industries. In the detergent industry, two companies, Unilever and Procter & Gamble, dominate the market in nation after nation. In heavy earthmoving equipment, Caterpillar Inc. and Komatsu are global market leaders. In the market for semiconductor equipment, Applied Materials has a commanding market share lead in almost every important national market. Microsoft dominates the market for personal computer operating systems and applications systems around the world, and so on. In such cases, dominant enterprises may be able to exercise a degree of pricing power, setting different prices in different markets to reflect varying demand conditions. This is referred to as price discrimination. For price discrimination to work, arbitrage must be limited. According to this argument, enterprises with some market power may be able to control distribution channels and therefore limit the unauthorized resale (arbitrage) of products purchased in another national market. They may also be able to limit resale (arbitrage) by differentiating otherwise identical products among nations along some line, such as design or packaging.

For example, even though the version of Microsoft Office sold in China may be less expensive than the version sold in the United States, the use of arbitrage to equalize prices may be limited because few Americans would want a version that was based on Chinese characters. The design differentiation between Microsoft Office for China and for the United States means that the law of one price would not work for Microsoft Office, even if transportation costs were trivial and tariff barriers between the United States and China did not exist. If the inability to practice arbitrage were widespread enough, it would break the connection between changes in relative prices and exchange rates predicted by the PPP theorem and help explain the limited empirical support for this theory.

Another factor of some importance is that governments also intervene in the foreign exchange market in attempting to influence the value of their currencies. We will look at why and how they do this in Chapter 10. For now, the important thing to note is that governments regularly intervene in the foreign exchange market, and this further weakens the link between price changes and changes in exchange rates. One more factor explaining the failure of PPP theory to predict short-term movements in foreign exchange rates is the impact of investor psychology and other factors on currency purchasing decisions and exchange rate movements. We will discuss this issue in more detail later in this chapter.

INTEREST RATES AND EXCHANGE RATES Economic theory tells us that interest rates reflect expectations about likely future inflation rates. In countries where inflation is expected to be high, interest rates also will be high, because investors want compensation for the decline in the value of their money. This relationship was first formalized by economist Irvin Fisher and is referred to as the Fisher effect. The **Fisher effect** states that a country's "nominal" interest rate (i) is the sum of the required "real" rate of interest (r) and the expected rate of inflation over the period for which the funds are to be lent (I). More formally,

$$i = r + I$$

For example, if the real rate of interest in a country is 5 percent and annual inflation is expected to be 10 percent, the nominal interest rate will be 15 percent. As predicted by the Fisher effect, a strong relationship seems to exist between inflation rates and interest rates.[15]

We can take this one step further and consider how it applies in a world of many countries and unrestricted capital flows. When investors are free to transfer capital between countries, real interest rates will be the same in every country. If differences in real interest rates did emerge between countries, arbitrage would soon equalize them. For example, if the real interest rate in Japan was 10 percent and only 6 percent in the United States, it would pay investors to borrow money in the United States and invest it in Japan. The resulting increase in the demand for money in the United States would raise the real interest rate there, while the increase in the supply of foreign money in Japan would lower the real interest rate there. This would continue until the two sets of real interest rates were equalized.

It follows from the Fisher effect that if the real interest rate is the same worldwide, any difference in interest rates between countries reflects differing expectations about inflation rates. Thus, if the expected rate of inflation in the United States is greater than that in Japan, U.S. nominal interest rates will be greater than Japanese nominal interest rates.

Since we know from PPP theory that there is a link (in theory at least) between inflation and exchange rates, and since interest rates reflect expectations about inflation, it follows that there must also be a link between interest rates and exchange rates. This link is known as the international Fisher effect (IFE). The **international Fisher effect** states that for any two countries, the spot exchange rate should change in an equal amount but in the opposite direction to the difference in nominal interest rates between the two countries. Stated more formally, the change in the spot exchange rate between the United States and Japan, for example, can be modeled as follows:

$$[(S_1 - S_2)/S_2] \times 100 = i_\$ - i_¥$$

where $i_\$$ and $i_¥$ are the respective nominal interest rates in the United States and Japan, S_1 is the spot exchange rate at the beginning of the period, and S_2 is the spot exchange rate at the end of the period. If the U.S. nominal interest rate is higher than Japan's, reflecting greater expected inflation rates, the value of the dollar against the yen should fall by that interest rate differential in the future. So if the interest rate in the

George Soros, whose Quantum Fund has been fantastically successful in managing hedge funds, has been criticized by world leaders for being able to cause huge changes in currency markets by his actions.

United States is 10 percent and in Japan it is 6 percent, we would expect the value of the dollar to depreciate by 4 percent against the Japanese yen.

Do interest rate differentials help predict future currency movements? The evidence is mixed; as in the case of PPP theory, in the long run, there seems to be a relationship between interest rate differentials and subsequent changes in spot exchange rates. However, considerable short-run deviations occur. Like PPP, the international Fisher effect is not a good predictor of short-run changes in spot exchange rates.[16]

INVESTOR PSYCHOLOGY AND BANDWAGON EFFECTS

Empirical evidence suggests that neither PPP theory nor the international Fisher effect are particularly good at explaining short-term movements in exchange rates. One reason may be the impact of investor psychology on short-run exchange rate movements. Evidence accumulated over the past decade reveals that various psychological factors play an important role in determining the expectations of market traders as to likely future exchange rates.[17] In turn, expectations have a tendency to become self-fulfilling prophecies.

A famous example of this mechanism occurred in September 1992 when the famous international financier George Soros made a huge bet against the British pound. Soros borrowed billions of pounds, using the assets of his investment funds as collateral, and immediately sold those pounds for German deutsche marks (this was before the advent of the euro). This technique, known as short selling, can earn the speculator enormous profits if he can subsequently buy back the pounds he sold at a much better exchange rate, and then use those pounds, purchased cheaply, to repay his loan. By selling pounds and buying deutsche marks, Soros helped to start pushing down the value of the pound on the foreign exchange markets. More importantly, when Soros started shorting the British pound, many foreign exchange traders, knowing Soros's reputation, jumped on the bandwagon and did likewise. This triggered a classic **bandwagon effect** with traders moving as a herd in the same direction at the same time. As the bandwagon effect gained momentum, with more traders selling British pounds and purchasing deutsche marks in expectation of a decline in the pound, their expectations became a self-fulfilling prophecy. Massive selling forced down the value of the pound against the deutsche mark. In other words, the pound declined in value not so much because of any major shift in macroeconomic fundamentals, but because investors followed a bet placed by a major speculator, George Soros.

According to a number of studies, investor psychology and bandwagon effects play a major role in determining short-run exchange rate movements.[18] However, these effects can be hard to predict. Investor psychology can be influenced by political factors and by microeconomic events, such as the investment decisions of individual firms, many of which are only loosely linked to macroeconomic fundamentals, such as relative inflation rates. Also, bandwagon effects can be both triggered and exacerbated by the idiosyncratic behavior of politicians. Something like this seems to have occurred in Southeast Asia during 1997 when, one after another, the currencies of Thailand, Malaysia, South Korea, and Indonesia lost between 50 percent and 70 percent of their value against the U.S. dollar in a few months. For a detailed look at what occurred in South Korea, see the accompanying Country Focus. The collapse in the value of the Korean currency did not occur because South Korea had a higher inflation rate than the United States. It occurred because of an excessive buildup of dollar-denominated debt among South Korean firms. By mid-1997 it was clear that these companies were

Bandwagon Effect
When traders move like a herd, all in the same direction and at the same time, in response to each others' perceived actions.

Anatomy of a Currency Crisis

In early 1997, South Korea could look back with pride on a 30-year "economic miracle" that had raised the country from the ranks of the poor and given it the world's 11th-largest economy. By the end of 1997, the Korean currency, the won, had lost a staggering 67 percent of its value against the U.S. dollar, the South Korean economy lay in tatters, and the International Monetary Fund was overseeing a $55 billion rescue package. This sudden turn of events had its roots in investments made by South Korea's large industrial conglomerates, or *chaebol,* during the 1990s, often at the bequest of politicians. In 1993, Kim Young-Sam, a populist politician, became president of South Korea. Mr. Kim took office during a mild recession and promised to boost economic growth by encouraging investment in export-oriented industries. He urged the *chaebol* to invest in new factories. South Korea enjoyed an investment-led economic boom in 1994–1995, but at a cost. The *chaebol,* always reliant on heavy borrowing, built up massive debts that were equivalent, on average, to four times their equity.

As the volume of investments ballooned during the 1990s, the quality of many of these investments declined significantly. The investments often were made on the basis of unrealistic projections about future demand conditions. This resulted in significant excess capacity and falling prices. An example is investments made by South Korean *chaebol* in semiconductor factories. Investments in such facilities surged in 1994 and 1995 when a temporary global shortage of dynamic random access memory chips (DRAMs) led to sharp price increases for this product. However, supply shortages had disappeared by 1996 and excess capacity was beginning to make itself felt, just as the South Koreans started to bring new DRAM factories on stream. The results were predictable; prices for DRAMs plunged and the earnings of South Korean DRAM manufacturers fell by 90 percent, which meant it was difficult for them to make scheduled payments on the debt they had acquired to build the extra capacity. The risk of corporate bankruptcy increased significantly, and not just in the semiconductor industry. South Korean companies were also investing heavily in a wide range of other industries, including automobiles and steel.

Matters were complicated further because much of the borrowing had been in U.S. dollars, as opposed to Korean won. This had seemed like a smart move at the time. The dollar/won exchange rate had been stable at around $1 = won 850. Interest rates on dollar borrowings were two to three percentage points lower than rates on borrowings in Korean won. Much of this borrowing was in the form of short-term, dollar-denominated debt that had to be paid back to the lending institution within one year. While the borrowing strategy seemed to make sense, it involved risk. If the won were to depreciate against the dollar, the size of the debt burden that South Korean companies would have to service would increase when measured in the local currency. Currency depreciation would raise borrowing costs, depress corporate earnings, and increase the risk of bankruptcy. This is exactly what happened.

By mid-1997, foreign investors had become alarmed at the rising debt levels of South Korean companies, particularly given the emergence of excess capacity and plunging prices in several areas where the companies had made huge investments, including semiconductors, automobiles, and steel. Given increasing speculation that many South Korean companies would not be able to service their debt payments, foreign investors began to withdraw their money from the Korean stock and bond markets. In the process, they sold Korean won and purchased U.S. dollars. The selling of won accelerated in mid-1997 when two of the smaller chaebol filed for bankruptcy, citing their inability to meet scheduled debt payments. The increased supply of won and the increased demand for U.S. dollars pushed down the price of won in dollar terms from around won 840 = $1 to won 900 = $1.

At this point, the South Korean central bank stepped into the foreign exchange market to try to keep the exchange rate above won 1,000 = $1. It used dollars that it held in reserve to purchase won. The idea was to try to push up the price of the won in dollar terms and restore investor confidence in the stability of the exchange rate. This action, however, did not address the underlying debt problem faced by South Korean companies. Against a backdrop of more corporate bankruptcies in South Korea, and the government's stated intentions to take some troubled companies into state ownership, Standard & Poor's, the U.S. credit rating agency, downgraded South Korea's sovereign debt. This caused the Korean stock market to plunge 5.5 percent, and the Korean won to fall to won 930 = $1. According to S&P, "The downgrade of . . . ratings reflects the escalating cost to the government of supporting the country's ailing corporate and financial sectors."

The S&P downgrade triggered a sharp sale of the Korean won. In an attempt to protect the won against what was fast becoming a classic bandwagon effect, the South Korean central bank raised short-term interest rates to over 12 percent, more than double the inflation rate. The bank also stepped up its intervention in the currency exchange markets, selling dollars and purchasing won in an attempt to keep the exchange rate above won 1,000 = $1.

(continued)

The main effect of this action, however, was to rapidly deplete South Korea's foreign exchange reserves. These stood at $30 billion on November 1, but fell to only $15 billion two weeks later. With its foreign exchange reserves almost exhausted, the South Korean central bank gave up its defense of the won November 17. Immediately, the price of won in dollars plunged to around won 1,500 = $1, effectively increasing by 60 to 70 percent the amount of won heavily indebted Korean companies had to pay to meet scheduled payments on their dollar-denominated debt. These losses, due to adverse changes in foreign exchange rates, depressed the profits of many firms. South Korean firms suffered foreign exchange losses of more than $15 billion in 1997.

Sources: J. Burton and G. Baker, "The Country That Invested Its Way into Trouble," *Financial Times*, January 15, 1998, p. 8; J. Burton, "South Korea's Credit Rating Is Lowered," *Financial Times*, October 25, 1997, p. 3; J. Burton, "Currency Losses Hit Samsung Electronics," *Financial Times*, March 20, 1998, p. 24; and "Korean Firms' Foreign Exchange Losses Exceed US $15 Billion," *Business Korea*, February 1998, p. 55.

having trouble servicing this debt. Foreign investors, fearing a wave of corporate bankruptcies, took their money out of the country, exchanging won for U.S. dollars. As this began to depress the exchange rate, currency traders jumped on the bandwagon and speculated against the won (selling it short), and it was this that produced a collapse in the value of the won.

SUMMARY OF EXCHANGE RATE THEORIES   Relative monetary growth, relative inflation rates, and nominal interest rate differentials are all moderately good predictors of long-run changes in exchange rates. They are poor predictors of short-run changes in exchange rates, however, perhaps because of the impact of psychological factors, investor expectations, and bandwagon effects on short-term currency movements. This information is useful for an international business. Insofar as the long-term profitability of foreign investments, export opportunities, and the price competitiveness of foreign imports are all influenced by long-term movements in exchange rates, international businesses would be advised to pay attention to countries' differing monetary growth, inflation, and interest rates. International businesses that engage in foreign exchange transactions on a day-to-day basis could benefit by knowing some predictors of short-term foreign exchange rate movements. Unfortunately, short-term exchange rate movements are difficult to predict.

Exchange Rate Forecasting

LEARNING OBJECTIVE 5
Identify the merits of different approaches toward exchange rate forecasting.

A company's need to predict future exchange rate variations raises the issue of whether it is worthwhile for the company to invest in exchange rate forecasting services to aid decision making. Two schools of thought address this issue. The efficient market school argues that forward exchange rates do the best possible job of forecasting future spot exchange rates, and, therefore, investing in forecasting services would be a waste of money. The other school of thought, the inefficient market school, argues that companies can improve the foreign exchange market's estimate of future exchange rates (as contained in the forward rate) by investing in forecasting services. In other words, this school of thought does not believe the forward exchange rates are the best possible predictors of future spot exchange rates.

THE EFFICIENT MARKET SCHOOL   Forward exchange rates represent market participants' collective predictions of likely spot exchange rates at specified future dates. If forward exchange rates are the best possible predictor of future spot rates, it would make no sense for companies to spend additional money trying to forecast short-run exchange rate movements. Many economists believe the foreign exchange market is efficient at setting forward rates.[19] As mentioned earlier, an efficient market is one in which prices reflect all available public information. (If forward rates reflect all available information about likely future changes in exchange rates, a company cannot beat the market by investing in forecasting services.)

If the foreign exchange market is efficient, forward exchange rates should be unbiased predictors of future spot rates. This does not mean the predictions will be accurate in any specific situation. It means inaccuracies will not be consistently above or below future spot rates; they will be random. Many empirical tests have addressed the efficient market hypothesis. Although most of the early work seems to confirm the hypothesis (suggesting that companies should not waste their money on forecasting services) some recent studies have challenged it.[20] There is some evidence that forward rates are not unbiased predictors of future spot rates, and that more accurate predictions of future spot rates can be calculated from publicly available information.[21]

THE INEFFICIENT MARKET SCHOOL

Citing evidence against the efficient market hypothesis, some economists believe the foreign exchange market is inefficient. An **inefficient market** is one in which prices do not reflect all available information. In an inefficient market, forward exchange rates will not be the best possible predictors of future spot exchange rates.

Inefficient Market
One in which prices do not reflect all available information.

If this is true, it may be worthwhile for international businesses to invest in forecasting services (as many do). The belief is that professional exchange rate forecasts might provide better predictions of future spot rates than forward exchange rates do. However, the track record of professional forecasting services is not that good.[22] For example, forecasting services did not predict the 1997 currency crisis that swept through Southeast Asia, nor did they predict the rise in the value of the dollar that occurred during late 2008, a period when the United States fell into a deep financial crisis that some thought would lead to a decline in the *value* of the dollar (it appears that the dollar rose because it was seen as a relatively safe currency in a time when many nations were experiencing economic trouble).

APPROACHES TO FORECASTING

Assuming the inefficient market school is correct that the foreign exchange market's estimate of future spot rates can be improved, on what basis should forecasts be prepared? Here again, there are two schools of thought. One adheres to fundamental analysis, while the other uses technical analysis.

Fundamental Analysis

Fundamental analysis draws on economic theory to construct sophisticated econometric models for predicting exchange rate movements. The variables contained in these models typically include those we have discussed, such as relative money supply growth rates, inflation rates, and interest rates. In addition, they may include variables related to balance-of-payments positions.

Fundamental Analysis
Draws on economic theory to construct sophisticated econometric models for predicting exchange rate movements.

Running a deficit on a balance-of-payments current account (a country is importing more goods and services than it is exporting) creates pressures that may result in the depreciation of the country's currency on the foreign exchange market.[23] Consider what might happen if the United States was running a persistent current account balance-of-payments deficit (as in fact, it has been). Since the United States would be importing more than it was exporting, people in other countries would be increasing their holdings of U.S. dollars. If these people were willing to hold their dollars, the dollar's exchange rate would not be influenced. However, if these people converted their dollars into other currencies, the supply of dollars in the foreign exchange market would increase (as would demand for the other currencies). This shift in demand

and supply would create pressures that could lead to the depreciation of the dollar against other currencies.

This argument hinges on whether people in other countries are willing to hold dollars. This depends on such factors as U.S. interest rates, the return on holding other dollar-denominated assets such as stocks in U.S. companies, and, most importantly, inflation rates. So, in a sense, the balance-of-payments situation is not a fundamental predictor of future exchange rate movements. For example, between 1998 and 2001, the U.S. dollar appreciated against most major currencies despite a growing balance-of-payments deficit. Relatively high real interest rates in the United States, coupled with low inflation and a booming U.S. stock market that attracted inward investment from foreign capital, made the dollar very attractive to foreigners, so they did not convert their dollars into other currencies. On the contrary, they converted other currencies into dollars to invest in U.S. financial assets, such as bonds and stocks, because they believed they could earn a high return by doing so. Capital flows into the United States fueled by foreigners who wanted to buy U.S. stocks and bonds kept the dollar strong despite the current account deficit. But what makes financial assets such as stocks and bonds attractive? The answer is prevailing interest rates and inflation rates, both of which affect underlying economic growth and the real return to holding U.S. financial assets. Given this, we are back to the argument that the fundamental determinants of exchange rates are monetary growth, inflation rates, and interest rates.

Technical Analysis

Technical analysis uses price and volume data to determine past trends, which are expected to continue into the future. This approach does not rely on a consideration of economic fundamentals. Technical analysis is based on the premise that there are analyzable market trends and waves and that previous trends and waves can be used to predict future trends and waves. Since there is no theoretical rationale for this assumption of predictability, many economists compare technical analysis to fortune-telling. Despite this skepticism, technical analysis has gained favor in recent years.[24]

Currency Convertibility

Until this point we have invalidly assumed that the currencies of various countries are freely convertible into other currencies. Due to government restrictions, a significant number of currencies are not freely convertible into other currencies. A country's currency is said to be **freely convertible** when the country's government allows both residents and nonresidents to purchase unlimited amounts of a foreign currency with it. A currency is said to be **externally convertible** when only nonresidents may convert it into a foreign currency without any limitations. A currency is **nonconvertible** when neither residents nor nonresidents are allowed to convert it into a foreign currency.

Free convertibility is not universal. Many countries place some restrictions on their residents' ability to convert the domestic currency into a foreign currency (a policy of external convertibility). Restrictions range from the relatively minor (such as restricting the amount of foreign currency they may take with them out of the country on trips) to the major (such as restricting domestic businesses' ability to take foreign currency out of the country). External convertibility restrictions can limit domestic companies' ability to invest abroad, but they present few problems for foreign companies wishing to do business in that country. For example, even if the Japanese government tightly controlled the ability of its residents to convert the yen into U.S. dollars, all U.S. businesses with deposits in Japanese banks may at any time convert all their yen into dollars and take them out of the country. Thus, a U.S. company with a subsidiary

To deal with nonconvertibility problems, companies will barter instead. Venezuela traded iron ore for Caterpillar construction equipment. Caterpillar sold the iron ore to Romania for farm products, which it then sold on international markets for dollars.

in Japan is assured that it will be able to convert the profits from its Japanese operation into dollars and take them out of the country.

Serious problems arise, however, under a policy of nonconvertibility. This was the practice of the former Soviet Union, and it continued to be the practice in Russia for several years after the collapse of the Soviet Union. When strictly applied, nonconvertibility means that although a U.S. company doing business in a country such as Russia may be able to generate significant ruble profits, it may not convert those rubles into dollars and take them out of the country. Obviously this is not desirable for international business.

Governments limit convertibility to preserve their foreign exchange reserves. A country needs an adequate supply of these reserves to service its international debt commitments and to purchase imports. Governments typically impose convertibility restrictions on their currency when they fear that free convertibility will lead to a run on their foreign exchange reserves. This occurs when residents and nonresidents rush to convert their holdings of domestic currency into a foreign currency—a phenomenon generally referred to as **capital flight.** Capital flight is most likely to occur when the value of the domestic currency is depreciating rapidly because of hyperinflation, or when a country's economic prospects are shaky in other respects. Under such circumstances, both residents and nonresidents tend to believe that their money is more likely to hold its value if it is converted into a foreign currency and invested abroad. Not only will a run on foreign exchange reserves limit the country's ability to service its international debt and pay for imports, but it will also lead to a precipitous depreciation in the exchange rate as residents and nonresidents unload their holdings of domestic currency on the foreign exchange markets (thereby increasing the market supply of the country's currency). Governments fear that the rise in import prices

Capital Flight
Residents convert domestic currency into a foreign currency.

resulting from currency depreciation will lead to further increases in inflation. This fear provides another rationale for limiting convertibility.

Countertrade
The trade of goods and services for other goods and services.

Companies can deal with the nonconvertibility problem by engaging in countertrade. **Countertrade** refers to a range of barter-like agreements by which goods and services can be traded for other goods and services. Countertrade can make sense when a country's currency is nonconvertible. For example, consider the deal that General Electric struck with the Romanian government when that country's currency was nonconvertible. When General Electric won a contract for a $150 million generator project in Romania, it agreed to take payment in the form of Romanian goods that could be sold for $150 million on international markets. In a similar case, the Venezuelan government negotiated a contract with Caterpillar under which Venezuela would trade 350,000 tons of iron ore for Caterpillar heavy construction equipment. Caterpillar subsequently traded the iron ore to Romania in exchange for Romanian farm products, which it then sold on international markets for dollars.[25] Similarly, in a 2003 deal the government of Indonesia entered into a countertrade with Libya under which Libya agreed to purchase $540 million in Indonesian goods, including textiles, tea, coffee, electronics, plastics, and auto parts, in exchange for 50,000 barrels per day of Libyan crude oil.[26]

How important is countertrade? Twenty years ago, a large number of nonconvertible currencies existed in the world, and countertrade was quite significant. However, in recent years many governments have made their currencies freely convertible, and the percentage of world trade that involves countertrade is probably significantly below 10 percent.[27]

Focus on Managerial Implications

This chapter contains a number of clear implications for business. First, it is critical that international businesses understand the influence of exchange rates on the profitability of trade and investment deals. Adverse changes in exchange rates can make apparently profitable deals unprofitable. As noted, the risk introduced into international business transactions by changes in exchange rates is referred to as foreign exchange risk. Foreign exchange risk is usually divided into three main categories: transaction exposure, translation exposure, and economic exposure.

Transaction Exposure

LEARNING OBJECTIVE 6
Compare and contrast the differences between translation, transaction, and economic exposure, and explain what managers can do to manage each type of exposure.

Transaction Exposure
Extent to which income from individual transactions is affected by fluctuations in foreign exchange values.

Transaction exposure is the extent to which the income from individual transactions is affected by fluctuations in foreign exchange values. Such exposure includes obligations for the purchase or sale of goods and services at previously agreed prices and the borrowing or lending of funds in foreign currencies. For example, suppose in 2004 an American airline agreed to purchase 10 Airbus 330 aircraft for €120 million each for a total price of €1.20 billion, with delivery scheduled for 2005 and payment due then. When the contract was signed in 2001 the dollar/euro exchange rate stood at $1 = €1.10 so the American airline anticipated paying $1.1 billion for the 10 aircraft when they were delivered (€1.2 billion/1.1 = $1.09 billion). However, imagine that the value of the dollar depreciates against the euro over the intervening period, so that one dollar buys only €0.80 in 2008 when payment is due ($1 = €0.80). Now the total cost in U.S. dollars is $1.5 billion (€1.2 billion/0.80 = $1.5 billion), an increase of $0.41 billion! The transaction exposure here is $0.41 billion, which is the money lost due to an adverse movement in exchange rates between the time when the deal was signed and when the aircraft were paid for.

Translation Exposure

Translation exposure is the impact of currency exchange rate changes on the reported financial statements of a company. Translation exposure is concerned with the present measurement of past events. The resulting accounting gains or losses are said to be unrealized—they are "paper" gains and losses—but they are still important. Consider a U.S. firm with a subsidiary in Mexico. If the value of the Mexican peso depreciates significantly against the dollar this would substantially reduce the dollar value of the Mexican subsidiary's equity. In turn, this would reduce the total dollar value of the firm's equity reported in its consolidated balance sheet. This would raise the apparent leverage of the firm (its debt ratio), which could increase the firm's cost of borrowing and potentially limit its access to the capital market. Similarly, if an American firm has a subsidiary in the European Union, and if the value of the euro depreciates rapidly against that of the dollar over a year, this will reduce the dollar value of the euro profit made by the European subsidiary, resulting in negative translation exposure. In fact, many U.S. firms suffered from significant negative translation exposure in Europe during 2000, precisely because the euro did depreciate rapidly against the dollar. In 2002–2007, the euro rose in value against the dollar. This positive translation exposure boosted the dollar profits of American multinationals with significant operations in Europe.

Economic Exposure

Economic exposure is the extent to which a firm's future international earning power is affected by changes in exchange rates. Economic exposure is concerned with the long-run effect of changes in exchange rates on future prices, sales, and costs. This is distinct from transaction exposure, which is concerned with the effect of exchange rate changes on individual transactions, most of which are short-term affairs that will be executed within a few weeks or months. Consider the effect of wide swings in the value of the dollar on many U.S. firms' international competitiveness. The rapid rise in the value of the dollar on the foreign exchange market in the 1990s hurt the price competitiveness of many U.S. producers in world markets. U.S. manufacturers that relied heavily on exports (such as Caterpillar) saw their export volume and world market share decline. The reverse phenomenon occurred in 2000–2009, when the dollar declined against most major currencies. The fall in the value of the dollar helped increase the price competitiveness of U.S. manufacturers in world markets.

Reducing Translation and Transaction Exposure

A number of tactics can help firms minimize their transaction and translation exposure. These tactics primarily protect short-term cash flows from adverse changes in exchange rates. We have already discussed two of these tactics at length in the chapter, entering into forward exchange rate contracts and buying swaps. In addition to buying forward and using swaps, firms can minimize their foreign exchange exposure through leading and lagging payables and receivables—that is, paying suppliers and collecting payment from customers early or late depending on expected exchange rate movements. A **lead strategy** involves attempting to collect foreign currency receivables (payments from customers) early when a foreign currency is expected to depreciate and paying foreign currency payables (to suppliers) before they are due when a currency is expected to appreciate. A **lag strategy** involves delaying collection of foreign currency receivables if that currency is expected to appreciate and delaying payables if the currency is expected to depreciate. Leading and lagging involves accelerating payments from weak-currency to strong-currency countries and delaying inflows from strong-currency to weak-currency countries.

Taking Advantage of a Rising or Declining Currency: Diversification

In August 2000, 1 USD = 0.9045 euro. Ten years later, in August 2010, 1 USD = 1.27 euro. The ten-year difference amounts to approximately 30 percent. What is not immediately obvious is that in July 2008 it got to be 1.5887 and in June 2010 it dropped to 1.19. There are advantages as well as disadvantages, depending from which perspective one wishes to see the corresponding rise or fall of a particular currency.

For example, simple advice dictates that when the euro is plummeting, you should sell shares of U.S. manufacturers that sell in Europe and buy shares of, say, German, French, and Dutch competitors that sell in the United States. The weakening euro, after all, makes their goods cheaper in the United States, boosting sales and market share. The reciprocal would be true for a rising euro. If only things were so simple.

In a more globalized world, such simplified currency exposure is rare. For example, many multinational corporations establish manufacturing and operations precisely to take advantage of currency fluctuations. As part of an overall currency risk strategy that may include hedging vehicles, multinational corporations such as Caterpillar, Coca-Cola, and 3M diversify their global operations.

Based out of Peoria, Illinois, in the United States, Caterpillar makes construction and mining machinery and is one of the largest U.S. exporters. It has manufacturing plants worldwide, including euro zone countries such as Germany, France, and the Netherlands. Except for giant trucks that can carry up to 380 tons of debris, few machines are made exclusively in the United States; rather they are an amalgamation of multiple countries' manufacturing capabilities. The goal has been to manufacture as close as possible to the point of delivery. Therefore, for Caterpillar, regional sales should be used to determine how evenly the company's currency exposure is spread.

Coca-Cola takes a somewhat similar tack. Coca-Cola seeks to spread its sales even more finely by region. Having done business in 71 countries last year, Coca-Cola represents one of the most geographically diversified companies in the world. Over the long term, such diversification protects the company from currency swings. In recent years, Coca-Cola has seen rapid sales growth in emerging markets. According to the company, it plans to invest $2 billion to expand its distribution in China over the next three years.

Still other companies, such as 3M, diversify via product lines. The St. Paul, Minnesota, conglomerate has a product portfolio that includes everything from touch screens to dog chews. Last year, 3M collected 37 percent of its sales in the United States; 27 percent in Asia Pacific countries; 26 percent in Europe, the Middle East, and Africa; and the rest in Latin America and Canada. In fact, 3M now generates so much free cash that it can reinvest it at a rising rate in emerging markets to bolster future growth there.

Sources: Historical currency quotes, accessed at http://www.google.com/finance?hl=en&q=CURRENCY:EURUSD; and J. Hough, "Playing the Plunging Euro," *The Wall Street Journal*, May 22, 2010, accessed at http://online.wsj.com/article/NA_WSJ_PUB:SB10001424052748704167704575258600742192026.html.

Lead and lag strategies can be difficult to implement, however. The firm must be in a position to exercise some control over payment terms. Firms do not always have this kind of bargaining power, particularly when they are dealing with important customers who are in a position to dictate payment terms. Also, because lead and lag strategies can put pressure on a weak currency, many governments limit leads and lags. For example, some countries set 180 days as a limit for receiving payments for exports or making payments for imports.

Reducing Economic Exposure

Reducing economic exposure requires strategic choices that go beyond the realm of financial management. The key to reducing economic exposure is to distribute the firm's productive assets to various locations so the firm's long-term financial well-being is not severely affected by adverse changes in exchange rates. This is a strategy that firms both large and small sometimes pursue. For example, fearing that the euro will continue to strengthen against the U.S. dollar, some European firms who do significant business in the United States have set up local production facilities in that market to ensure that a rising euro does not put them at a competitive disadvantage relative to their local rivals. Similarly, Toyota has production plants distributed around the world in part to make sure that a rising Yen does not price Toyota cars out of local markets. Caterpillar has also pursued this strategy, setting up factories around the world that can act as a hedge against the possibility that a strong dollar will price Caterpillar's exports out of foreign markets. In 2008 and 2009, this real hedge proved to be very useful. The accompanying Management Focus discusses how three multinational corporations reduced their currency risk exposure.

Other Steps for Managing Foreign Exchange Risk

The firm needs to develop a mechanism for ensuring it maintains an appropriate mix of tactics and strategies for minimizing its foreign exchange exposure. Although there is no universal agreement as to the components of this mechanism, a number of common themes stand out.[28] First, central control of exposure is needed to protect resources efficiently and ensure that each subunit adopts the correct mix of tactics and strategies. Many companies have set up in-house foreign exchange centers. Although such centers may not be able to execute all foreign exchange deals—particularly in large, complex multinationals where myriad transactions may be pursued simultaneously—they should at least set guidelines for the firm's subsidiaries to follow.

Second, firms should distinguish between, on one hand, transaction and translation exposure and, on the other, economic exposure. Many companies seem to focus on reducing their transaction and translation exposure and pay scant attention to economic exposure, which may have more profound long-term implications.[29] Firms need to develop strategies for dealing with economic exposure. For example, Black & Decker, the maker of power tools, has a strategy for actively managing its economic risk. The key to Black & Decker's strategy is flexible sourcing. In response to foreign exchange movements, Black & Decker can move production from one location to another to offer the most competitive pricing. Black & Decker manufactures in more than a dozen locations around the world—in Europe, Australia, Brazil, Mexico, and Japan. More than 50 percent of the company's productive assets are based outside North America. Although each of Black & Decker's factories focuses on one or two products to achieve economies of scale, there is considerable overlap. On average, the company runs its factories at no more than 80 percent capacity, so most are able to switch rapidly from producing one product to producing another or to add a product. This allows a factory's production to be changed in response to foreign exchange movements. For example, if the dollar depreciates against other currencies, the amount of imports into the United States from overseas subsidiaries can be reduced and the amount of exports from U.S. subsidiaries to other locations can be increased.[30]

Third, the need to forecast future exchange rate movements cannot be overstated, though, as we saw earlier in the chapter, this is a tricky business. No model comes close to perfectly predicting future movements in foreign exchange rates. The best that can be said is that in the short run, forward exchange rates provide the best predictors of exchange rate movements, and in the long run, fundamental economic factors—particularly relative inflation rates—should be watched because they influence exchange rate movements. Some firms attempt to forecast exchange rate movements in-house; others rely on outside forecasters. However, all such forecasts are imperfect attempts to predict the future.

Fourth, firms need to establish good reporting systems so the central finance function (or in-house foreign exchange center) can regularly monitor the firm's exposure positions. Such reporting systems should enable the firm to identify any exposed accounts, the exposed position by currency of each account, and the time periods covered.

Finally, on the basis of the information it receives from exchange rate forecasts and its own regular reporting systems, the firm should produce monthly foreign exchange exposure reports. These reports should identify how cash flows and balance sheet elements might be affected by forecasted changes in exchange rates. The reports can then be used by management as a basis for adopting tactics and strategies to hedge against undue foreign exchange risks.

Surprisingly, some of the largest and most sophisticated firms don't take such precautionary steps, exposing themselves to very large foreign exchange risks. However, as we have seen in the case of Caterpillar, Coca-Cola, and 3M, some global firms have taken such precautions to avoid foreign exchange risks.

Key Terms

Summary

This chapter explained how the foreign exchange market works, examined the forces that determine exchange rates, and then discussed the implications of these factors for international business. Given that changes in exchange rates can dramatically alter the profitability of foreign trade and investment deals, this is an area of major interest to international business. The chapter made the following points:

1. One function of the foreign exchange market is to convert the currency of one country into the currency of another. A second function of the foreign exchange market is to provide insurance against foreign exchange risk.

2. The spot exchange rate is the exchange rate at which a dealer converts one currency into another currency on a particular day.

3. Foreign exchange risk can be reduced by using forward exchange rates. A forward exchange rate is an exchange rate governing future transactions. Foreign exchange risk can also be reduced by engaging in currency swaps. A swap is the simultaneous purchase and sale of a given amount of foreign exchange for two different value dates.

4. The law of one price holds that in competitive markets that are free of transportation costs and barriers to trade, identical products sold in different countries must sell for the same price when their price is expressed in the same currency.

5. Purchasing power parity (PPP) theory states the price of a basket of particular goods should be roughly equivalent in each country. PPP theory predicts that the exchange rate will change if relative prices change.

6. The rate of change in countries' relative prices depends on their relative inflation rates. A

country's inflation rate seems to be a function of the growth in its money supply.

7. The PPP theory of exchange rate changes yields relatively accurate predictions of long-term trends in exchange rates, but not of short-term movements. The failure of PPP theory to predict exchange rate changes more accurately may be due to transportation costs, barriers to trade and investment, and the impact of psychological factors such as bandwagon effects on market movements and short-run exchange rates.

8. Interest rates reflect expectations about inflation. In countries where inflation is expected to be high, interest rates also will be high.

9. The international Fisher effect states that for any two countries, the spot exchange rate should change in an equal amount but in the opposite direction to the difference in nominal interest rates.

10. The most common approach to exchange rate forecasting is fundamental analysis. This relies on variables such as money supply growth, inflation rates, nominal interest rates, and balance-of-payments positions to predict future changes in exchange rates.

11. In many countries, the ability of residents and nonresidents to convert local currency into a foreign currency is restricted by government policy. A government restricts the convertibility of its currency to protect the country's foreign exchange reserves and to halt any capital flight.

12. Problematic for international business is a policy of nonconvertibility, which prohibits residents and nonresidents from exchanging local currency for foreign currency. Nonconvertibility makes it very difficult to engage in international trade and investment in the country. One way of coping with the nonconvertibility problem is to engage in countertrade—to trade goods and services for other goods and services.

13. The three types of exposure to foreign exchange risk are transaction exposure, translation exposure, and economic exposure.

14. Tactics that insure against transaction and translation exposure include buying forward, using currency swaps, leading and lagging payables and receivables, manipulating transfer prices, using local debt financing, accelerating dividend payments, and adjusting capital budgeting to reflect foreign exchange exposure.

15. Reducing a firm's economic exposure requires strategic choices about how the firm's productive assets are distributed around the globe.

16. To manage foreign exchange exposure effectively, the firm must exercise centralized oversight over its foreign exchange hedging activities, recognize the difference between transaction exposure and economic exposure, forecast future exchange rate movements, establish good reporting systems within the firm to monitor exposure positions, and produce regular foreign exchange exposure reports that can be used as a basis for action.

Critical Thinking and Discussion Questions

1. The interest rate on South Korean government securities with one-year maturity is 4 percent, and the expected inflation rate for the coming year is 2 percent. The interest rate on U.S. government securities with one-year maturity is 7 percent, and the expected rate of inflation is 5 percent. The current spot exchange rate for Korean won is $1 = W1,200. Forecast the spot exchange rate one year from today. Explain the logic of your answer.

2. Two countries, Great Britain and the United States, produce just one good: beef. Suppose the price of beef in the United States is $2.80 per pound and in Britain it is £3.70 per pound.
   a. According to PPP theory, what should the dollar/pound spot exchange rate be?
   b. Suppose the price of beef is expected to rise to $3.10 in the United States and to £4.65 in Britain. What should the one-year forward dollar/pound exchange rate be?
   c. Given your answers to parts a and b, and given that the current interest rate in the United States is 10 percent, what would you expect the current interest rate to be in Britain?

3. Reread the Management Focus "Competition and Exchange Rates," then answer the following questions:

   a. What are the positive and negative aspects of hedging in general?

   b. What are some of the advantages for EADS of a weaker euro? What effect would a stronger euro have on EADS?

   c. Apart from hedging through the foreign exchange market, what else can EADS do to reduce its exposure to future declines in the value of the U.S. dollar against the euro?

4. You manufacture wine goblets. In mid-June you receive an order for 10,000 goblets from Japan. Payment of ¥400,000 is due in mid-December. You expect the yen to rise from its present rate of $1 = ¥130 to $1 = ¥100 by December. You can borrow yen at 6 percent a year. What should you do?

5. You are the CFO of a U.S. firm whose wholly owned subsidiary in Mexico manufactures component parts for your U.S. assembly operations. The subsidiary has been financed by bank borrowings in the United States. One of your analysts told you that the Mexican peso is expected to depreciate by 30 percent against the dollar on the foreign exchange markets over the next year. What actions, if any, should you take?

Research Task    globalEDGE   http://globalEDGE.msu.edu

Use the globalEDGE Resource Desk (http://globalEDGE.msu.edu/resourcedesk/) to complete the following exercises:

1. You are assigned the duty of ensuring the availability of 100 million Japanese yen for a payment scheduled for tomorrow. Your company possesses only U.S. dollars, so you must identify a Web site that provides *real-time exchange rates* and find the spot exchange rate for Japanese yen. How many dollars do you have to spend to acquire the amount of yen required?

2. Your company imports olive oil from Italy to sell in the United States. As expected, the exchange rate has changed from the previous year has impacted your bottom line. In preparing an annual report for your company, you would like to include a one-year *currency chart* showing the monthly movement of the U.S. dollar versus the euro. Download the relevant data indicating the exchange rate between these two currencies once per month for the past year. Then, analyze the data and describe the pattern you see. Over the past year, has the dollar gained or lost ground versus the euro?

closing case

The Yen and Exports: Japan's Continued Recovery

After years of little economic growth, Japan is beginning to recover, even in the face of a global recession. According to Nikkei, the Japanese financial information provider, profits at Japan's largest companies rose by 46 percent, or $44 billion (¥3.8 trillion), during the second quarter of 2010, which represented a fourfold increase from a year ago. Compared to the previous year when many Japanese firms lost money, this surge in exports was wonderful news.

At Toyota, the automobile maker, quarterly operating profit increased to ¥212 billion, having lost ¥195 billion the previous year. This in part was due to strong demand coming from Asia. Similarly, Sony, the electronics firm, posted a robust ¥79 billion profit during the same quarter, reversing a pretax loss of ¥33 billion a year ago. Specifically, its revenue from emerging markets grew by about 40 percent; sales in Brazil nearly doubled. Many are concerned, however, that the increase in exports was a result of the relative strength of the yen to other currencies and may be short lived.

Both Toyota and Sony hedged their expectations (profitability) by establishing the yen/dollar ratio at ¥ = 90 and the euro at ¥ = 125. If the yen continues to appreciate, however, such spectacular growth is going to be curtailed. As of the end of August 2010, the yen/dollar ratio was ¥ = 84 and the yen/euro ratio was 107. The strong yen is problematic for Japanese exporters because it makes their products more expensive overseas and eats into overseas sales sent back to Japan.

This critical relationship between the yen and other currencies is best demonstrated by Canon, the maker of digital cameras, and a competitor to Sony. When Canon started the year, it said each drop of ¥ = 1 in the euro's average foreign exchange rate for the full year would cost the company ¥ = 6.4 billion ($80.7 million) in annual sales and ¥ = 4.6 billion in operating profits. Canon officials said it planned to offset the impact with more aggressive cost cuts.

Similarly, the Japanese currency has continued to surge against the dollar, which has been weighed down by weak U.S. economic indicators and falling Treasury yields. At ¥ = 83.57, the yen is at its strongest levels in 15 years. This is putting tremendous pressure on the Japanese government to intervene, which it has not done since 2004 when the yen/dollar ratio was ¥ = 109.

Besides using traditional hedging vehicles, Japanese companies are also strategically, and operationally, hedging these risks by adapting to foreign markets. Whereas Japan had traditionally focused its manufacturing in Japan, producing products specifically for the Japanese market, the country is now developing offshore capabilities as a means of producing cheaper goods and adapting those products to the local market.

Panasonic, another electronics firm, is using foreign engineers to develop products. Now only 10 to 20 percent of the products it sells overseas are "Japanese products." As another example of adaptation, Panasonic is altering the configuration of its refrigerators to the Indonesian market. As it turns out, Indonesians need more space to accommodate large two-liter bottles of water. Indonesians boil water in the morning and put the bottles in the refrigerator to cool.

In India, where power outages are to be expected, Panasonic is developing air conditioners that operate with little energy, reducing the overall burden on the grid. And because Indians tend to run the air conditioners 24 hours a day, the motors are designed to be quiet.

In the most recent quarter, emerging-market sales helped Panasonic post a profit of ¥84 billion, reversing a ¥52 billion loss in the same period a year earlier. The firm expects revenue for electronics and appliances from emerging markets to increase from 25 percent of its total today to 31 percent in 2012.

A strong yen makes exports more expensive, but it makes mergers and acquisitions cheaper. Recognizing this fact, Japanese firms have spent more than $11 billion on deals in developing countries so far this year, according to Dealogic, already surpassing the total in 2009. By shifting production abroad and sourcing locally, we can expect Japanese companies to maintain their competitiveness within the global market.

Sources: "The New Frontier for Corporate Japan," *The Economist*, August 5, 2010, accessed at http://www.economist.com/node/16743435?story_id=16743435&CFID=145012086&CFTOKEN=20798347; D. Wakabayashi, Y. Takahashi, "Strong Yen Puts Japan's Export-led Recovery at Growing Risk," *The Australian*, 2010, p. 27; Y. Hayashi, "Exports to Asia Power Japan's Growth Spurt," *The Wall Street Journal*, May 20, 2010, accessed at http://online.wsj.com/article/NA_WSJ_PUB:SB10001424052748703559004575256292145790152.html.

Case Discussion Questions

1. Why have exports increased in Japan over the past two years? Was it due exclusively to the yen?

2. Why do you think companies set expectations on the relative value of the yen in relation to the dollar or euro?

3. Besides traditional hedging, what other means of mitigating the risk of a rising yen do companies have at their disposal? Are these consistent with some of the larger issues implicit in globalization?

part 4   Global Money System

10

The International Monetary System

opening case

Asians in general, but Chinese in particular, love to gamble. Except for the lottery, however, gambling is illegal on the mainland of China. So where do the Chinese go to gamble? Macau. And so does most of Southeast Asia.

Macau (also known as Macao) is one of the two special administrative regions (SARs) of the People's Republic of China, the other being Hong Kong. Located on the western side of the Pearl River Delta, Macau borders Guangdong Province to the north and faces the South China Sea on the east and south. Macau was originally a Portuguese colony, and since 1847 gambling has been legalized to generate income for the government. The industry experienced its next major breakthrough in 1962, when the government granted the *Sociedade de Turismo e Diversões de Macau* (STDM), a syndicate jointly formed by Hong Kong's Stanley Ho and Macau businessmen, the monopoly rights to all forms of gambling. Since then, Las Vegas casino operators, the Wynn Resorts, and the "Sands China," for example, have entered the market, and business is booming.

"The Monte Carlo of the Orient" is moving a lot of money. Macau is heavily dependent on gambling. Some contend overly so. In 2009, the island's 30-odd casinos generated income of around $15 billion. According to industry specialists, its overall gambling revenue in that year rose by nearly 10 percent, whereas North America's fell by 7 percent and Europe's by 12 percent.

In Macau, the unit of currency is the "pataca," which is currently pegged to the Hong Kong dollar at a rate of HK$1 = MOP1.02. Very much like Hong Kong, Macau has been an advocate of free trade policy for a long time, and its legal tender, the pataca, has long been pegged to the Hong Kong dollar. The name *pataca* comes from a Portuguese word applied to the Mexican dollar, which was commonly circulated in the region during the 19th century. The Hong Kong dollar in turn is pegged to the U.S. dollar; therefore, the pataca is indirectly pegged to the U.S. dollar.

Interestingly enough, one country (China) has to contend with three systems and three currencies. As the Chinese renminbi (RMB) has appreciated in relation to the U.S. dollar, there has been a drop in value of the pataca. And, since most of Macau's food and commodities are imported from the Chinese mainland, the price of these goods has become more and more expensive. The pegging of the pataca to the HK dollar is now being questioned as being inflationary.

On the other side of the equation, the fact that the pataca is pegged (indirectly) to the U.S. dollar represents a positive aspect to the service industry (gambling and tourism). According to the Macanese Monetary Authority, however, there is no obvious correlation between the exchange rate of the pataca and inflation, because the exchange rate index that gauges the strength of the pataca has remained stable from the beginning of this year (2010) until now, and its exchange rate against the RMB has only slid by 1 percent. Official figures indicated that tourism-related sectors account for more than 50 percent of Macau's employed population, and the revenues contributed by service exports amount to more than 140 billion patacas (US$17.5 billion) every year. Furthermore, Macau's Monetary Authority claims that all this has indicated that the existing exchange rate system has been an important factor in maintaining the stability of Macau's financial system, and "the SAR government does not deem the deviation from a policy to peg the pataca to the Hong Kong dollar as an indispensable measure to combat inflation."

The competitive advantage of the exchange rate regime may be short lived, however. What is not apparent was the growing gambling competition from other Southeast Asian countries such as Singapore, Cambodia, and Vietnam. Singapore in particular is quickly moving into the gaming world with its Genting Singapore's Resorts World Sentosa. And the fate of the pataca, and the Hong Kong dollar for that matter, may be questioned. If the renmimbi is finally allowed to float, or even if it is not, the future of the pataca appears questionable at best. ●

Sources: S. Holmes, "Singapore Casinos Could Rival Las Vegas by 2012," *The Wall Street Journal* Online, August 18, 2010, http://online.wsj.com/article/SB10001424052748703649004575436743057042602.html?mod=googlewsj; "The Dragon's Gambling Den," *The Economist,* July 8, 2010, http://www.economist.com/node/16507748; "Macau Economy: Policy Outlook for 2010–11," *EIU ViewsWire,* January 27, 2010; "Macau to Keep Pegging Pataca to HK Dollar Despite Inflation," *Asia Pulse,* 2010; and "Pataca Faces Extinction," *Asiamoney* 10, no. 7 (September 1999), p. 96.

Introduction

International Monetary System
Institutional arrangements countries adopt to govern exchange rates.

In this chapter we look at the international monetary system, and its role in determining exchange rates. The **international monetary system** refers to the institutional arrangements that govern exchange rates. In Chapter 9 we assumed the foreign exchange market was the primary institution for determining exchange rates, and the impersonal market forces of demand and supply determined the relative value of any two currencies (i.e., their exchange rate). Furthermore, we explained that the demand

and supply of currencies is influenced by their respective countries' relative inflation rates and interest rates. When the foreign exchange market determines the relative value of a currency, we say that the country is adhering to a **floating exchange rate** regime. Four of the world's major trading currencies—the U.S. dollar, the European Union's euro, the Japanese yen, and the British pound—are all free to float against each other. Thus, their exchange rates are determined by market forces and fluctuate against each other day to day, if not minute to minute. However, the exchange rates of many currencies are not determined by the free play of market forces; other institutional arrangements are adopted.

Many of the world's developing nations peg their currencies, primarily to the dollar or the euro. A **pegged exchange rate** means the value of the currency is fixed relative to a reference currency, such as the U.S. dollar, and then the exchange rate between that currency and other currencies is determined by the reference currency exchange rate. Macau, for example, has pegged its exchange rate to the Hong Kong dollar, which in turn is pegged to the U.S. dollar (see opening case). Similarly, many of the states around the Gulf of Arabia have long pegged their currencies to the dollar.

Other countries, while not adopting a formal pegged rate, try to hold the value of their currency within some range against an important reference currency such as the U.S. dollar, or a "basket" of currencies. This is often referred to as a **dirty float.** It is a float because in theory, the value of the currency is determined by market forces, but it is a *dirty float* (as opposed to a clean float) because the central bank of a country will intervene in the foreign exchange market to try to maintain the value of its currency if it depreciates too rapidly against an important reference currency. This has been the policy adopted by the Chinese since July 2005. The value of the Chinese currency, the yuan, has been linked to a basket of other currencies, including the dollar, yen, and euro, and it is allowed to vary in value against individual currencies, but only within tight limits. As discussed in Chapter 5, some believe that the Chinese are deliberately holding down the value of their currency to promote exports.

Still other countries have operated with a **fixed exchange rate,** in which the values of a set of currencies are fixed against each other at some mutually agreed on exchange rate. Before the introduction of the euro in 2000, several member states of the European Union operated with fixed exchange rates within the context of the **European Monetary System (EMS).** For a quarter of a century after World War II, the world's major industrial nations participated in a fixed exchange rate system. Although this system collapsed in 1973, some still argue that the world should attempt to reestablish it.

In this chapter, we will explain how the international monetary system works and point out its implications for international business. To understand how the system works, we must review its evolution. We will begin with a discussion of the gold standard and its breakup during the 1930s. Then we will discuss the 1944 Bretton Woods conference. This established the basic framework for the post–World War II international monetary system. The Bretton Woods system called for fixed exchange rates against the U.S. dollar. Under this fixed exchange rate system, the value of most currencies in terms of U.S. dollars was fixed for long periods and allowed to change only under a specific set of circumstances. The Bretton Woods conference also created two major international institutions that play a role in the international monetary system—the International Monetary Fund (IMF) and the World Bank. The IMF was given the task of maintaining order in the international monetary system; the World Bank's role was to promote development.

Today, both these institutions continue to play major roles in the world economy and in the international monetary system. In 1997 and 1998, for example, the IMF helped

Floating Exchange Rate
A system under which the exchange rate for converting one currency into another is continuously adjusted depending on the laws of supply and demand.

Pegged Exchange Rate
Currency value is fixed relative to a reference currency.

Dirty Float
A system under which a country's currency is nominally allowed to float freely against other currencies, but in which the government will intervene, buying and selling currency, if it believes that the currency has deviated too far from its fair value.

Fixed Exchange Rate
A system under which the exchange rate for converting one currency into another is fixed.

European Monetary System (EMS)
A system to regulate fixed exchange rates before the introduction of the euro.

several Asian countries deal with the dramatic decline in the value of their currencies that occurred during the Asian financial crisis that started in 1997. In 2010 the IMF had programs in 68 countries, the majority in the developing world, and had some $175 billion in loans to nations.[1] At times of financial crisis, such as that which unfolded in 2008 and 2009, these loan amounts can spike much higher. The role of the IMF and to a lesser extent the World Bank and the appropriateness of their policies for many developing nations has been vigorously debated. Several prominent critics claim that in some cases, IMF policies make things worse, not better. The debate over the role of the IMF took on new urgency given the institution's extensive involvement in the economies of developing countries during the late 1990s and early 2000s. Accordingly, we shall discuss the issue in some depth.

The Bretton Woods system of fixed exchange rates collapsed in 1973. Since then, the world has operated with a mixed system in which some currencies are allowed to float freely, but many are either managed by government intervention or pegged to another currency. We will explain the reasons for the failure of the Bretton Woods system as well as the nature of the present system. We will also discuss how pegged exchange rate systems work. More than three decades after the breakdown of the Bretton Woods system, the debate continues over what kind of exchange rate regime is best for the world. Some economists advocate a system in which major currencies are allowed to float against each other. Others argue for a return to a fixed exchange rate regime similar to the one established at Bretton Woods. This debate is intense and important, and we will examine the arguments of both sides.

Finally, we will discuss the implications of all this material for international business. We will see how the exchange rate policy adopted by a government can have an important impact on the outlook for business operations in a given country. We will also look at how the policies adopted by the IMF can have an impact on the economic outlook for a country and, accordingly, on the costs and benefits of doing business in that country.

The Gold Standard

LEARNING OBJECTIVE 1
Describe the historical development of the modern global monetary system.

The gold standard had its origin in the use of gold coins as a medium of exchange, unit of account, and store of value—a practice that dates to ancient times. When international trade was limited in volume, payment for goods purchased from another country was typically made in gold or silver. However, as the volume of international trade expanded in the wake of the Industrial Revolution, a more convenient means of financing international trade was needed. Shipping large quantities of gold and silver around the world to finance international trade seemed impractical. The solution adopted was to arrange for payment in paper currency and for governments to agree to convert the paper currency into gold on demand at a fixed rate.

MECHANICS OF THE GOLD STANDARD Pegging currencies to gold and guaranteeing convertibility is known as the **gold standard.** By 1880, most of the world's major trading nations, including Great Britain, Germany, Japan, and the United States, had adopted the gold standard. Given a common gold standard, the value of any currency in units of any other currency (the exchange rate) was easy to determine.

Gold Standard
The practice of pegging currencies to gold and guaranteeing convertibility.

For example, under the gold standard, one U.S. dollar was defined as equivalent to 23.22 grains of "fine" (pure) gold. Thus, one could, in theory, demand that the U.S. government convert that one dollar into 23.22 grains of gold. Since there are 480 grains in an ounce, one ounce of gold cost $20.67 (480/23.22). The amount of a currency needed to purchase one ounce of gold was referred to as the **gold par value.** The British pound was valued at 113 grains of fine gold. In other words, one ounce of gold cost £4.25 (480/113). From the gold par values of pounds and dollars, we can calculate what the exchange rate was for converting pounds into dollars; it was £1 = $4.87 (i.e., $20.67/£4.25).

Gold Par Value
The amount of currency needed to purchase one ounce of gold.

STRENGTH OF THE GOLD STANDARD The great strength claimed for the gold standard was that it contained a powerful mechanism for achieving balance-of-trade equilibrium by all countries.[2] A country is said to be in **balance-of-trade equilibrium** when the income its residents earn from exports is equal to the money its residents pay to other countries for imports (the current account of its balance of payments is in balance). Suppose there are only two countries in the world, Japan and the United States. Imagine Japan's trade balance is in surplus because it exports more to the United States than it imports from the United States. Japanese exporters are paid in U.S. dollars, which they exchange for Japanese yen at a Japanese bank. The Japanese bank submits the dollars to the U.S. government and demands payment of gold in return. (This is a simplification of what would occur, but it will make our point.)

Balance-of-Trade Equilibrium
Reached when the income a country's residents earn from exports equals the money residents pay for imports.

Under the gold standard, when Japan has a trade surplus, there will be a net flow of gold from the United States to Japan. These gold flows automatically reduce the U.S. money supply and swell Japan's money supply. As we saw in Chapter 9, there is a close connection between money supply growth and price inflation. An increase in money supply will raise prices in Japan, while a decrease in the U.S. money supply will push U.S. prices downward. The rise in the price of Japanese goods will decrease demand for these goods, while the fall in the price of U.S. goods will increase demand for these goods. Thus, Japan will start to buy more from the United States, and the United States will buy less from Japan, until a balance-of-trade equilibrium is achieved.

This adjustment mechanism seems so simple and attractive that even today, almost 70 years after the final collapse of the gold standard, some people believe the world should return to a gold standard.

THE PERIOD BETWEEN THE WARS: 1918–1939 The gold standard worked reasonably well from the 1870s until the start of World War I in 1914, when it was abandoned. During the war, several governments financed part of their massive military expenditures by printing money. This resulted in inflation, and by the war's end in 1918, price levels were higher everywhere. The United States returned to the gold standard in 1919, Great Britain in 1925, and France in 1928.

Great Britain returned to the gold standard by pegging the pound to gold at the pre-war gold parity level of £4.25 per ounce, despite substantial inflation between 1914 and 1925. This priced British goods out of foreign markets, which pushed the country into a deep depression. When foreign holders of pounds lost confidence in Great Britain's commitment to maintaining its currency's value, they began converting their holdings of pounds into gold. The British government saw that it could not satisfy the demand for gold without seriously depleting its gold reserves, so it suspended convertibility in 1931.

The United States followed suit and left the gold standard in 1933 but returned to it in 1934, raising the dollar price of gold from $20.67 per ounce to $35 per ounce. Since more dollars were needed to buy an ounce of gold than before, the implication was that the dollar was worth less. This effectively amounted to a devaluation of the dollar relative to other currencies. Thus, before the devaluation, the pound/dollar exchange rate was £1 = $4.87, but after the devaluation it was £1 = $8.24. By reducing the price of U.S. exports and increasing the price of imports, the government was trying to create employment in the United States by boosting output (the U.S. government was basically using the exchange rate as an instrument of trade policy—something it now accuses China of doing). However, a number of other countries adopted a similar tactic, and in the cycle of competitive devaluations that soon emerged, no country could win.

The net result was the shattering of any remaining confidence in the system. With countries devaluing their currencies at will, one could no longer be certain how much gold a currency could buy. Instead of holding onto another country's currency, people often tried to change it into gold immediately, lest the country devalue its currency in the intervening period. This put pressure on the gold reserves of various countries, forcing them to suspend gold convertibility. By the start of World War II in 1939, the gold standard was dead.

The Bretton Woods System

LEARNING OBJECTIVE 2
Explain the role played by the World Bank and the IMF in the international monetary system.

In 1944, at the height of World War II, representatives from 44 countries met at Bretton Woods, New Hampshire, to design a new international monetary system. With the collapse of the gold standard and the Great Depression of the 1930s fresh in their minds, these statesmen were determined to build an enduring economic order that would facilitate postwar economic growth. There was consensus that fixed exchange rates were desirable. In addition, the conference participants wanted to avoid the senseless competitive devaluations of the 1930s, and they recognized that the gold standard would not assure this. The major problem with the gold standard as previously constituted was that no multinational institution could stop countries from engaging in competitive devaluations.

The agreement reached at Bretton Woods established two multinational institutions—the International Monetary Fund (IMF) and the World Bank. The task of the IMF would be to maintain order in the international monetary system and that of the World Bank would be to promote general economic development. The Bretton Woods agreement also called for a system of fixed exchange rates that would be policed by the IMF. Under the agreement, all countries were to fix the value of their currency in terms of gold but were not required to exchange their currencies for gold. Only the dollar remained convertible into gold—at a price of $35 per ounce. Each country decided

In 1944, at the height of World War II, representatives from 44 countries met at Bretton Woods, New Hampshire, to design a new international monetary system. Pictured here is Henry Morgenthau, then secretary of the Treasury, addressing the opening meeting of the conference where the IMF and the World Bank were established.

what it wanted its exchange rate to be vis-à-vis the dollar and then calculated the gold par value of the currency based on that selected dollar exchange rate. All participating countries agreed to try to maintain the value of their currencies within 1 percent of the par value by buying or selling currencies (or gold) as needed. For example, if foreign exchange dealers were selling more of a country's currency than demanded, that country's government would intervene in the foreign exchange markets, buying its currency in an attempt to increase demand and maintain its gold par value.

Another aspect of the Bretton Woods agreement was a commitment not to use devaluation as a weapon of competitive trade policy. However, if a currency became too weak to defend, a devaluation of up to 10 percent would be allowed without any formal approval by the IMF. Larger devaluations required IMF approval.

THE ROLE OF THE IMF
The IMF Articles of Agreement were heavily influenced by the worldwide financial collapse, competitive devaluations, trade wars, high unemployment, hyperinflation in Germany and elsewhere, and general economic disintegration that occurred between the two world wars. The aim of the Bretton Woods agreement, of which the IMF was the main custodian, was to try to avoid a repetition of that chaos through a combination of discipline and flexibility.

Discipline
A fixed exchange rate regime imposes discipline in two ways. First, the need to maintain a fixed exchange rate puts a brake on competitive devaluations and brings stability to the world trade environment. Second, a fixed exchange rate regime imposes monetary discipline on countries, thereby curtailing price inflation. For example, consider what would happen under a fixed exchange rate regime if Great Britain rapidly increased its money supply by printing pounds. As explained in Chapter 9, the increase in money supply would lead to price inflation. Given fixed exchange rates, inflation would make British goods uncompetitive in world markets, while the prices of imports would become more attractive in Great Britain. The result would be a widening trade deficit in Great Britain, with the country importing more than it exports. To correct this trade imbalance under a fixed exchange rate regime, Great Britain would be required to restrict the rate of growth in its money supply to bring price inflation back under control. Thus, fixed exchange rates are seen as a mechanism for controlling inflation and imposing economic discipline on countries.

Flexibility
Although monetary discipline was a central objective of the Bretton Woods agreement, it was recognized that a rigid policy of fixed exchange rates would be too inflexible. It would probably break down just as the gold standard had. In some cases, a country's attempts to reduce its money supply growth and correct a persistent balance-of-payments deficit could force the country into recession and create high unemployment. The architects of the Bretton Woods agreement wanted to avoid high unemployment, so they built limited flexibility into the system. Two major features of the IMF Articles of Agreement fostered this flexibility: IMF lending facilities and adjustable parities.

The IMF stood ready to lend foreign currencies to members to tide them over during short periods of balance-of-payments deficits, when a rapid tightening of monetary or fiscal policy would hurt domestic employment. A pool of gold and currencies contributed by IMF members provided the resources for these lending operations. A persistent balance-of-payments deficit can lead to a depletion of a country's reserves of foreign currency, forcing it to devalue its currency. By providing deficit-laden countries with short-term foreign currency loans, IMF funds would buy time for countries to bring down their inflation rates and reduce their balance-of-payments deficits. The belief was that such loans would reduce pressures for devaluation and allow for a more orderly and less painful adjustment.

Countries were to be allowed to borrow a limited amount from the IMF without adhering to any specific agreements. However, extensive drawings from IMF funds would require a country to agree to increasingly stringent IMF supervision of its macroeconomic policies. Heavy borrowers from the IMF must agree to monetary and fiscal conditions set down by the IMF, which typically included IMF-mandated targets on domestic money supply growth, exchange rate policy, tax policy, government spending, and so on.

The system of adjustable parities allowed for the devaluation of a country's currency by more than 10 percent if the IMF agreed that a country's balance of payments was in "fundamental disequilibrium." The term *fundamental disequilibrium* was not defined in the IMF's Articles of Agreement, but it was intended to apply to countries that had suffered permanent adverse shifts in the demand for their products. Without devaluation, such a country would experience high unemployment and a persistent trade deficit until the domestic price level had fallen far enough to restore a balance-of-payments equilibrium. The belief was that devaluation could help sidestep a painful adjustment process in such circumstances.

THE ROLE OF THE WORLD BANK   The official name for the World Bank is the International Bank for Reconstruction and Development (IBRD). When the Bretton Woods participants established the World Bank, the need to reconstruct the war-torn economies of Europe was foremost in their minds. The bank's initial mission was to help finance the building of Europe's economy by providing low-interest loans. As it turned out, the World Bank was overshadowed in this role by the Marshall Plan, under which the United States lent money directly to European nations to help them rebuild. So the bank turned its attention to "development" and began lending money to Third World nations. In the 1950s, the bank concentrated on public-sector projects. Power stations, road building, and other transportation investments were much in favor. During the 1960s, the bank also began to lend heavily in support of agriculture, education, population control, and urban development.

The bank lends money under two schemes. Under the IBRD scheme, money is raised through bond sales in the international capital market. Borrowers pay what the bank calls a market rate of interest—the bank's cost of funds plus a margin for expenses. This "market" rate is lower than commercial banks' market rate. Under the IBRD scheme, the bank offers low-interest loans to risky customers whose credit rating is often poor, such as the governments of underdeveloped nations.

A second scheme is overseen by the International Development Association (IDA), an arm of the bank created in 1960. Resources to fund IDA loans are raised through subscriptions from wealthy members such as the United States, Japan, and Germany. IDA loans go only to the poorest countries. Borrowers have 50 years to repay at an interest rate of 1 percent a year. The world's poorest nations receive grants and no-interest loans.

The Collapse of the Fixed Exchange Rate System

LEARNING OBJECTIVE 1
Describe the historical development of the modern global monetary system.

The system of fixed exchange rates established at Bretton Woods worked well until the late 1960s, when it began to show signs of strain. The system finally collapsed in 1973, and since then we have had a managed-float system. To understand why the system collapsed, one must appreciate the special role of the U.S. dollar in the system. As the only currency that could be converted into gold, and as the currency that served as the reference point for all others, the dollar occupied a central place in the system. Any pressure on the dollar to devalue could wreak havoc with the system, and that is what occurred.

Most economists trace the breakup of the fixed exchange rate system to the U.S. macroeconomic policy package of 1965–1968.[3] To finance both the Vietnam conflict and his welfare programs, President Lyndon Johnson backed an increase in U.S. government spending that was not financed by an increase in taxes. Instead, it was financed by an increase in the money supply, which led to a rise in price inflation from less than 4 percent in 1966 to close to 9 percent by 1968. At the same time, the rise in government spending had stimulated the economy. With more money in their pockets, people spent more—particularly on imports—and the U.S. trade balance began to deteriorate.

The increase in inflation and the worsening of the U.S. foreign trade position gave rise to speculation in the foreign exchange market that the dollar would be devalued. Things came to a head in the spring of 1971 when U.S. trade figures showed that for the first time since 1945, the United States was importing more than it was exporting. This set off massive purchases of German deutsche marks in the foreign exchange market by speculators who guessed that the mark would be revalued against the dollar. On a single day, May 4, 1971, the Bundesbank (Germany's central bank) had to buy $1 billion to hold the dollar/deutsche mark exchange rate at its fixed exchange rate given the great demand for deutsche marks. On the morning of May 5, the Bundesbank purchased another $1 billion during the first hour of foreign exchange trading! At that point, the Bundesbank faced the inevitable and allowed its currency to float.

In the weeks following the decision to float the deutsche mark, the foreign exchange market became increasingly convinced that the dollar would have to be devalued. However, devaluation of the dollar was no easy matter. Under the Bretton Woods provisions, any other country could change its exchange rates against all currencies simply by fixing its dollar rate at a new level. But as the key currency in the system, the dollar could be devalued only if all countries agreed to simultaneously revalue against the dollar. Many countries did not want this, because it would make their products more expensive relative to U.S. products.

To force the issue, President Nixon announced in August 1971 that the dollar was no longer convertible into gold. He also announced that a new 10 percent tax on imports would remain in effect until U.S. trading partners agreed to revalue their currencies against the dollar. This brought the trading partners to the bargaining table, and in December 1971 an agreement was reached to devalue the dollar by about 8 percent against foreign currencies. The import tax was then removed.

The problem was not solved, however. The U.S. balance-of-payments position continued to deteriorate throughout 1972, while the nation's money supply continued to expand at an inflationary rate. Speculation continued to grow that the dollar was still overvalued and that a second devaluation would be necessary. In anticipation, foreign exchange dealers began converting dollars to deutsche marks and other currencies. After a massive wave of speculation in February 1972, which culminated with European central banks spending $3.6 billion on March 1 to try to prevent their currencies from appreciating against the dollar, the foreign exchange market was closed. When the foreign exchange market reopened March 19, the currencies of Japan and most European countries were floating against the dollar, although many developing countries continued to peg their currency to the dollar, and many do to this day. At that time, the switch to a

Another Perspective

United States off the Gold Standard
When President Nixon took the United States off the gold standard in 1971, his decision established the dollar as the standard against which other currencies would be measured. The U.S. gold reserves, which in 1945 had held 80 percent of all gold reserves worldwide, had been under serious pressure since France, under the leadership of Charles De Gaulle, had demanded to convert the French dollar reserves to gold in 1965, the first of many central bank requests. Nixon's decision set up the dollar to be the de facto standard of the new floating system, and it continues that way today.

floating system was viewed as a temporary response to unmanageable speculation in the foreign exchange market. But it is now nearly 40 years since the Bretton Woods system of fixed exchange rates collapsed, and the temporary solution looks permanent.

The Bretton Woods system had an Achilles' heel: The system could not work if its key currency, the U.S. dollar, was under speculative attack. The Bretton Woods system could work only as long as the U.S. inflation rate remained low and the United States did not run a balance-of-payments deficit. Once these things occurred, the system soon became strained to the breaking point.

The Floating Exchange Rate Regime

LEARNING OBJECTIVE 1
Describe the historical development of the modern global monetary system.

The floating exchange rate regime that followed the collapse of the fixed exchange rate system was formalized in January 1976 when IMF members met in Jamaica and agreed to the rules for the international monetary system that are in place today.

THE JAMAICA AGREEMENT   The Jamaica meeting revised the IMF's Articles of Agreement to reflect the new reality of floating exchange rates. The main elements of the Jamaica agreement include the following:

- Floating rates were declared acceptable. IMF members were permitted to enter the foreign exchange market to even out "unwarranted" speculative fluctuations.
- Gold was abandoned as a reserve asset. The IMF returned its gold reserves to members at the current market price, placing the proceeds in a trust fund to help poor nations. IMF members were permitted to sell their own gold reserves at the market price.
- Total annual IMF quotas—the amount member countries contribute to the IMF—were increased to $41 billion. (Since then they have been increased to $300 billion while the membership of the IMF has been expanded to include 184 countries. In 2009, the IMF was seeking to increase its funding to help with the global financial crisis). Non-oil-exporting, less developed countries were given greater access to IMF funds.

EXCHANGE RATES SINCE 1973   Since March 1973, exchange rates have become much more volatile and less predictable than they were between 1945 and 1973.[4] This volatility has been partly due to a number of unexpected shocks to the world monetary system, including:

- The oil crisis in 1971, when the Organization of Petroleum Exporting Countries (OPEC) quadrupled the price of oil. The harmful effect of this on the U.S. inflation rate and trade position resulted in a further decline in the value of the dollar.
- The loss of confidence in the dollar that followed a sharp rise in the U.S. inflation rate in 1977–1978.
- The oil crisis of 1979, when OPEC once again increased the price of oil dramatically—this time it was doubled.
- The unexpected rise in the dollar between 1980 and 1985, despite a deteriorating balance-of-payments picture.
- The rapid fall of the U.S. dollar against the Japanese yen and German deutsche mark between 1985 and 1987, and against the yen between 1993 and 1995.
- The partial collapse of the European Monetary System in 1992.
- The 1997 Asian currency crisis, when the Asian currencies of several countries, including South Korea, Indonesia, Malaysia, and Thailand, lost between 50 percent and 80 percent of their value against the U.S. dollar in a few months.
- The decline in the value of the U.S. dollar from 2001 to 2009.

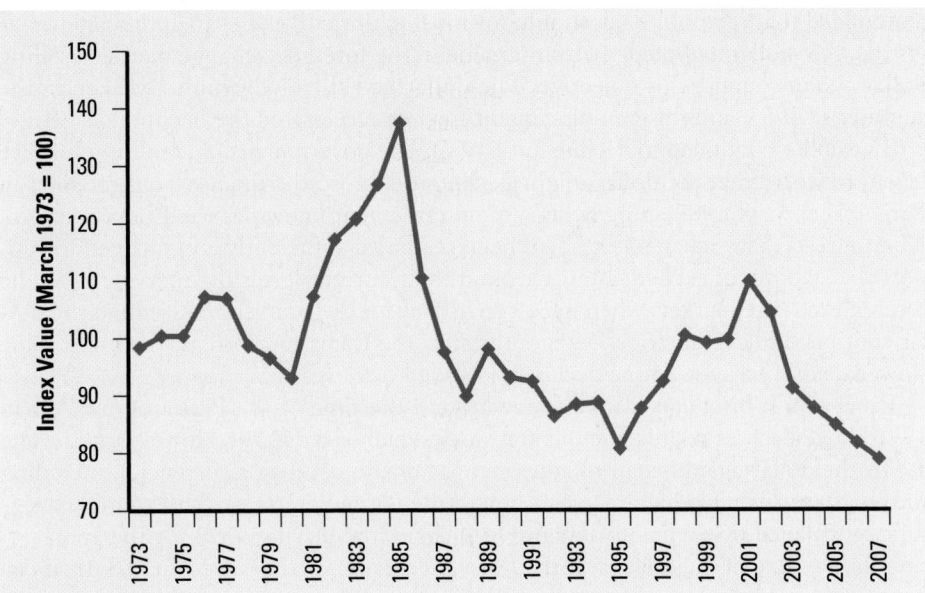

10.1 figure

Major Currencies
Dollar Index, 1973–2009

Source: Constructed by the author
from Federal Reserve Board
statistics at www.federalreserve
.gov/releases/H10/summary/.

Figure 10.1 summarizes how the value of the U.S. dollar has fluctuated against an index of major trading currencies between 1973 and 2009. (The index, which was set equal to 100 in March 1973, is a weighted average of the foreign exchange values of the U.S. dollar against currencies that circulate widely outside the country of issue.) An interesting phenomenon in Figure 10.1 is the rapid rise in the value of the dollar between 1980 and 1985 and its subsequent fall between 1985 and 1988. A similar, though less pronounced, rise and fall in the value of the dollar occurred between 1995 and 2009. We will briefly discuss the rise and fall of the dollar during these periods, since this tells us something about how the international monetary system has operated in recent years.[5]

The rise in the value of the dollar between 1980 and 1985 occurred when the United States was running a large and growing trade deficit, importing substantially more than it exported. Conventional wisdom would suggest that the increased supply of dollars in the foreign exchange market as a result of the trade deficit should lead to a reduction in the value of the dollar, but as shown in Figure 10.1 it increased in value. Why?

A number of favorable factors overcame the unfavorable effect of a trade deficit. Strong economic growth in the United States attracted heavy inflows of capital from foreign investors seeking high returns on capital assets. High real interest rates attracted foreign investors seeking high returns on financial assets. At the same time, political turmoil in other parts of the world, along with relatively slow economic growth in the developed countries of Europe, helped create the view that the United States was a good place to invest. These inflows of capital increased the demand for dollars in the foreign exchange market, which pushed the value of the dollar upward against other currencies.

The fall in the value of the dollar between 1985 and 1988 was caused by a combination of government intervention and market forces. The rise in the dollar, which priced U.S. goods out of foreign markets and made imports relatively cheap, had contributed to a dismal trade picture. In 1985, the United States posted a record-high trade deficit of more than $160 billion. This led to growth in demands for protectionism in the United States. In September 1985, the finance ministers and central bank governors of the so-called Group of Five major industrial countries (Great Britain, France, Japan, Germany, and the United States) met at the Plaza Hotel in New York and reached what was later referred to as the Plaza Accord. They announced that it would be desirable for most major currencies to appreciate vis-à-vis the U.S. dollar and pledged to intervene in the foreign exchange markets, selling dollars, to encourage this objective. The dollar had already begun to weaken in the summer of 1985, and this announcement further accelerated the decline.

The dollar continued to decline until 1987. The governments of the Group of Five began to worry that the dollar might decline too far, so the finance ministers met in Paris in February 1987 and reached a new agreement known as the Louvre Accord. They agreed that exchange rates had been realigned sufficiently and pledged to support the stability of exchange rates around their current levels by intervening in the foreign exchange markets when necessary to buy and sell currency. Although the dollar continued to decline for a few months after the Louvre Accord, the rate of decline slowed, and by early 1988 the decline had ended.

Except for a brief speculative flurry around the time of the Persian Gulf War in 1991, the dollar was relatively stable for the first half of the 1990s. However, in the late 1990s the dollar again began to appreciate against most major currencies, including the euro after its introduction, even though the United States was still running a significant balance-of-payments deficit. Once again, the driving force for the appreciation in the value of the dollar was that foreigners continued to invest in U.S. financial assets, primarily stocks and bonds, and the inflow of money drove up the value of the dollar on foreign exchange markets. The inward investment was due to a belief that U.S. financial assets offered a favorable rate of return.

By 2002, however, foreigners had started to lose their appetite for U.S. stocks and bonds, and the inflow of money into the United States slowed. Instead of reinvesting dollars earned from exports to the United States in U.S. financial assets, they exchanged those dollars for other currencies, particularly euros, to invest them in non-dollar-denominated assets. One reason for this was the continued growth in the U.S. trade deficit, which hit a record $767 billion in 2005 (by 2009 it had fallen to $381 billion). Although the U.S. trade deficits had been hitting records for decades, this deficit was the largest ever when measured as a percentage of the country's GDP (7 percent of GDP in 2005).

The record deficit meant that ever more dollars were flowing out of the United States into foreign hands, and those foreigners were less inclined to reinvest those dollars in the United States at a rate required to keep the dollar stable. This growing reluctance of foreigners to invest in the United States was due to several factors. First, there was a slowdown in U.S. economic activity during 2001–2002, and a somewhat slow recovery thereafter, which made U.S. assets less attractive. Second, the U.S. government's budget deficit expanded rapidly after 2001, hitting a record $318 billion in 2005 before falling back to $158 billion in 2007, and then surging again to $1.4 trillion in 2009 due to government stimulus plans and bailouts in the midst of a deep financial crisis. This led to fears that ultimately the budget deficit would be financed by an expansionary monetary policy that could lead to higher price inflation. Since inflation would reduce the value of the dollar, foreigners decided to hedge against this risk by holding fewer dollar assets in their investment portfolios. Third, from 2003 onward U.S. government officials began to "talk down" the value of the dollar, in part because the administration believed that a cheaper dollar would increase exports and reduce imports,

 **Another** Perspective

"Petrodollars" and OPEC

In the early 1970s, dollars became the currency of choice for oil trades through an agreement between the United States and OPEC. This commitment of OPEC to dollar sales was made secretly by the United States and Saudi Arabia, first, then the United States and other OPEC countries. The impact of "petrodollars" (U.S. dollars earned through the sale of petroleum) is huge. Petrodollars lead oil-producing nations to invest their dollar surpluses in the United States. In fact, OPEC dollar surpluses help to fund the U.S. trade deficit. Iraq, Iran, and Venezuela have at times initiated a push to move trading in oil to the euro, attempting to create the "petroeuro." So far, OPEC has stayed with the dollar. (P. D. Scott, *Drugs, Oil, and War: The United States in Afghanistan, Colombia, and Indochina* [Lanham: MD: Rowman & Littlefield, 2003], pp. 41–42)

Country FOCUS

The U.S. Dollar, Oil Prices, and Recycling Petrodollars

Between 2004 and 2008 global oil prices surged. They peaked at over $170 a barrel in 2008, up from about $20 in 2001, before falling sharply back to the mid-$30 range by early 2009. The rise in oil prices was due to a combination of greater than expected demand for oil, particularly from rapidly developing giants such as China and India; tight supplies; and perceived geopolitical risks in the Middle East, the world's largest oil-producing region.

The surge in oil prices was a windfall for oil-producing countries. Collectively they earned around $700 billion in oil revenues in 2005, and well over $1 trillion in 2007 and 2008, some 64 percent of which went to members of OPEC. Saudi Arabia, the world's largest oil producer, reaped a major share. Since oil is priced in U.S. dollars, the rise in oil prices has translated into a substantial increase in the dollar holdings of oil producers (the dollars earned from the sale of oil are often referred to as *petrodollars*). In essence, rising oil prices represent a net transfer of dollars from oil consumers in countries such as the United States to oil producers in Russia, Saudi Arabia, and Venezuela. What did they do with those dollars?

One option for producing countries was to spend their petrodollars on public-sector infrastructure, such as health services, education, roads, and telecommunications systems. Among other things, this could boost economic growth in those countries, and pull in foreign imports, which would help to balance the trade surpluses enjoyed by oil producers and support global economic growth. Spending did pick up in many oil-producing countries. However, according to the IMF, OPEC members spent only around 40 percent of their windfall profits from higher oil prices in 2002–2007 (an exception was Venezuela, where President Hugo Chavez was on a spending spree). The last time oil prices increased sharply in 1979, oil producers significantly ramped up spending on infrastructure, only to find themselves saddled with excessive debt when oil prices collapsed a few years later. This time they were more cautious—an approach that now seems wise given the rapid collapse in oil prices during late 2008.

Another option was for oil producers to invest a good chunk of the dollars they earned from oil sales in dollar-denominated assets, such as U.S. bonds, stocks, and real estate. This did happen. OPEC members funneled dollars back into U.S. assets, mostly low-risk government bonds. The implication is that by recycling their petrodollars, oil producers helped to finance the large and growing current account deficit of the United States, enabling it to pay its large oil import bill.

A third possibility for oil producers was to invest in non-dollar-denominated assets, including European and Japanese bonds and stocks. This too happened. Some OPEC investors have purchased not just small equity positions, but entire companies. In 2005, for example, Dubai International Capital purchased the Tussauds Group, a British theme-park firm, and DP World of Dubai purchased P&O, Britain's biggest port and ferries group. Despite examples such as these, between 2005 and 2008, the bulk of petrodollars appear to have been recycled into dollar-denominated assets. In part this was because U.S. interest rates increased throughout 2004–2007. However, if the flow of petrodollars should dry up, with oil-rich countries investing in other currencies, such as euro-denominated assets, the dollar could fall sharply.

One final point on petrodollars: They are also facilitating the boom in Islamic banking. Islamic finance is playing an increasing role in global finance with the use of petrodollars. In these countries, the largest players insist on Islamic banking. Muslim and non-Muslim countries are willing to accommodate the large capital flows petrodollars permit. This sector will continue to grow as long as petrodollar can be recycled. "Expanding Horizons," *Islamic Finance Asia*, 2010;

Sources: "Recycling the Petrodollars; Oil Producers' Surpluses," *The Economist,* November 12, 2005, pp. 101–02; S. Johnson, "Dollar's Rise Aided by OPEC Holdings," *Financial Times,* December 5, 2005, p. 17; and "The Petrodollar Puzzle," *The Economist,* June 9, 2007, p. 86.

thereby improving the U.S. balance of trade position.[6] Foreigners saw this as a signal that the U.S. government would not intervene in the foreign exchange markets to prop up the value of the dollar, which increased their reluctance to reinvest dollars earned from export sales in U.S. financial assets. As a result of these factors, demand for dollars weakened and the value of the dollar slid on the foreign exchange markets, hitting an index value of 80.19 in December 2004, the lowest value since the index began in 1973. Although the dollar strengthened a little in 2005 and 2006, many commentators believed that it would resume its fall if large holders of U.S. dollars, such as oil-producing states, decided to diversify their foreign exchange holdings (see the accompanying Country Focus). Indeed, the dollar's fall resumed in 2007, and by February 2010 the dollar index against major currencies stood at 76.1, down from 102.5 in November 2002.

Interestingly, from mid-2008 through early 2009 the dollar staged a moderate rally against major currencies, despite the fact that the American economy was suffering from a serious financial crisis. The reason seems to be that despite America's problems, things were even worse in many other countries, and foreign investors saw the dollar has a safe haven and put their money in low-risk U.S. assets, particularly low-yielding U.S. government bonds. This rally faltered in mid-2009 as investors became worried about the level of U.S. indebtedness.

In sum, we see that in recent history the value of the dollar has been determined by both market forces and government intervention. Under a floating exchange rate regime, market forces have produced a volatile dollar exchange rate. Governments have sometimes responded by intervening in the market—buying and selling dollars—in an attempt to limit the market's volatility and to correct what they see as overvaluation (in 1985) or potential undervaluation (in 1987) of the dollar. In addition to direct intervention, the value of the dollar has frequently been influenced by statements from government officials. The dollar may not have declined by as much as it did in 2004, for example, had not U.S. government officials publicly ruled out any action to stop the decline. Paradoxically, a signal not to intervene can affect the market. The frequency of government intervention in the foreign exchange market explains why the current system is sometimes thought of as a **managed-float system** or a dirty-float system.

Managed-Float System
System under which some currencies are allowed to float freely, but the majority are either managed by government intervention or pegged to another currency.

Fixed versus Floating Exchange Rates

LEARNING OBJECTIVE 3
Compare and contrast the differences between a fixed and a floating exchange rate system.

The breakdown of the Bretton Woods system has not stopped the debate about the relative merits of fixed versus floating exchange rate regimes. Disappointment with the system of floating rates in recent years has led to renewed debate about the merits of fixed exchange rates. In this section, we review the arguments for fixed and floating exchange rate regimes.[7] We will discuss the case for floating rates before discussing why many commentators are disappointed with the experience under floating exchange rates and yearn for a system of fixed rates.

THE CASE FOR FLOATING EXCHANGE RATES   The case in support of floating exchange rates has two main elements: monetary policy autonomy and automatic trade balance adjustments.

Monetary Policy Autonomy   It is argued that under a fixed system, a country's ability to expand or contract its money supply as it sees fit is limited by the need to maintain exchange rate parity. Monetary expansion can lead to inflation, which puts downward pressure on a fixed exchange rate (as predicted by the PPP theory; see Chapter 9). Similarly, monetary contraction requires high interest rates (to reduce the demand for money). Higher interest rates lead to an inflow of money from abroad, which puts upward pressure on a fixed exchange rate. Thus, to maintain exchange rate parity under a fixed system, countries were limited in their ability to use monetary policy to expand or contract their economies.

Advocates of a floating exchange rate regime argue that removal of the obligation to maintain exchange rate parity would restore monetary control to a government. If a government faced with unemployment wanted to increase its money supply to stimulate domestic demand and reduce unemployment, it could do so unencumbered by the need to maintain its exchange rate. While monetary expansion might lead to inflation, this would lead to a depreciation in the country's currency. If PPP theory is correct, the resulting currency depreciation on the foreign exchange markets should offset the effects of inflation. Although under a floating exchange rate regime, domestic inflation would have an impact on the exchange rate, it should have no impact on businesses' international cost competitiveness due to exchange rate depreciation. The rise in domestic costs should be exactly offset by the fall in the value of the country's currency on the foreign exchange markets. Similarly, a government could use monetary policy to contract the economy without worrying about the need to maintain parity.

Trade Balance Adjustments   Under the Bretton Woods system, if a country developed a permanent deficit in its balance of trade (importing more than it exported) that could not be corrected by domestic policy, this would require the IMF to agree to a currency devaluation. Critics of this system argue that the adjustment mechanism works much more smoothly under a floating exchange rate regime. They argue that if a country is running a trade deficit, the imbalance between the supply and demand of that country's currency in the foreign exchange markets (supply exceeding demand) will lead to depreciation in its exchange rate. In turn, by making its exports cheaper and its imports more expensive, an exchange rate depreciation should correct the trade deficit.

THE CASE FOR FIXED EXCHANGE RATES   The case for fixed exchange rates rests on arguments about monetary discipline, speculation, uncertainty, and the lack of connection between the trade balance and exchange rates.

Monetary Discipline   We have already discussed the nature of monetary discipline inherent in a fixed exchange rate system when we discussed the Bretton Woods system. The need to maintain a fixed exchange rate parity ensures that governments do not expand their money supplies at inflationary rates. While advocates of floating rates argue that each country should be allowed to choose its own inflation rate (the monetary autonomy argument), advocates of fixed rates argue that governments all too often give in to political pressures and expand the monetary supply far too rapidly, causing unacceptably high price inflation. A fixed exchange rate regime would ensure that this does not occur.

Speculation   Critics of a floating exchange rate regime also argue that speculation can cause fluctuations in exchange rates. They point to the dollar's rapid rise and fall during the 1980s, which they claim had nothing to do with comparative inflation rates and the U.S. trade deficit, but everything to do with speculation. They argue that when foreign exchange dealers see a currency depreciating, they tend to sell the currency in the expectation of future depreciation regardless of the currency's longer-term prospects. As more traders jump on the bandwagon, the expectations of depreciation are realized. Such destabilizing speculation tends to accentuate the fluctuations around the exchange rate's long-run value. It can damage a country's economy by distorting export and import prices. Thus, advocates of a fixed exchange rate regime argue that such a system will limit the destabilizing effects of speculation.

Uncertainty   Speculation also adds to the uncertainty surrounding future currency movements that characterizes floating exchange rate regimes. The unpredictability of exchange rate movements in the post–Bretton Woods era has made business planning difficult, and it adds risk to exporting, importing, and foreign investment activities. Given a volatile exchange rate, international businesses do not know how to react to the changes—and often they do not react. Why change plans for exporting, importing, or foreign investment after a 6 percent fall in the dollar this month, when the dollar may rise 6 percent next month? This uncertainty, according to the critics, dampens the growth of international trade and investment. They argue that a fixed exchange rate, by eliminating such uncertainty, promotes the growth of international trade and investment. Advocates of a floating system reply that the forward exchange market insures against the risks associated with exchange rate fluctuations (see Chapter 9), so the adverse impact of uncertainty on the growth of international trade and investment has been overstated.

Trade Balance Adjustments

Those in favor of floating exchange rates argue that floating rates help adjust trade imbalances. Critics question the closeness of the link between the exchange rate and the trade balance. They claim trade deficits are determined by the balance between savings and investment in a country, not by the external value of its currency.[8] They argue that depreciation in a currency will lead to inflation (due to the resulting increase in import prices). This inflation will wipe out any apparent gains in cost competitiveness that arise from currency depreciation. In other words, a depreciating exchange rate will not boost exports and reduce imports, as advocates of floating rates claim; it will simply boost price inflation. In support of this argument, those who favor fixed rates point out that the 40 percent drop in the value of the dollar between 1985 and 1988 did not correct the U.S. trade deficit. In reply, advocates of a floating exchange rate regime argue that between 1985 and 1992, the U.S. trade deficit fell from more than $160 billion to about $70 billion, and they attribute this in part to the decline in the value of the dollar.

WHO IS RIGHT?

Which side is right in the vigorous debate between those who favor a fixed exchange rate and those who favor a floating exchange rate? Economists cannot agree. Business, as a major player on the international trade and investment scene, has a large stake in the resolution of the debate. Would international business be better off under a fixed regime, or are flexible rates better? The evidence is not clear.

We do, however, know that a fixed exchange rate regime modeled along the lines of the Bretton Woods system will not work. Speculation ultimately broke the system, a phenomenon that advocates of fixed rate regimes claim is associated with floating exchange rates! Nevertheless, a different kind of fixed exchange rate system might be more enduring and might foster the stability that would facilitate more rapid growth in international trade and investment. In the next section, we look at potential models for such a system and the problems with such systems.

Exchange Rate Regimes in Practice

LEARNING OBJECTIVE 4
Identify the exchange rate regimes that are used in the world today and why countries adopt different exchange rate regimes.

Governments around the world pursue a number of different exchange rate policies. These range from a pure "free float" where the exchange rate is determined by market forces to a pegged system that has some aspects of the pre-1973 Bretton Woods system of fixed exchange rates. Figure 10.2 summarizes the exchange rate policies adopted by member states of the IMF. Some 14 percent of the IMF's members allow their currency to float freely. Another 26 percent intervene in only a limited way (the so-called managed float). A further 28 percent of IMF members now have no separate

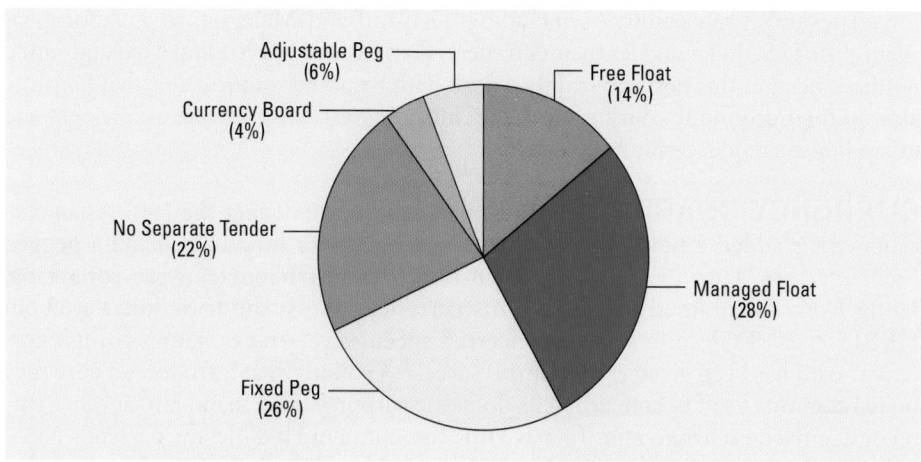

10.2 figure

Exchange Rate
Policies, IMF
Members, 2006

Source: Constructed by the author
from IMF data.

legal tender of their own. These include the European Union countries that have adopted the euro, and effectively given up their own currencies, along with smaller states mostly in Africa or the Caribbean that have no domestic currency and have adopted a foreign currency as legal tender within their borders, typically the U.S. dollar or the euro. The remaining countries use more inflexible systems, including a fixed peg arrangement (26 percent) under which they peg their currencies to other currencies, such as the U.S. dollar or the euro, or to a basket of currencies. Other countries have adopted a system under which their exchange rate is allowed to fluctuate against other currencies within a target zone (an adjustable peg system). In this section, we will look more closely at the mechanics and implications of exchange rate regimes that rely on a currency peg or target zone.

PEGGED EXCHANGE RATES   Under a pegged exchange rate regime, a country will peg the value of its currency to that of a major currency so that, for example, as the U.S. dollar rises in value, its own currency rises too. Pegged exchange rates are popular among many of the world's smaller nations. As with a full fixed exchange rate regime, the great virtue claimed for a pegged exchange rate is that it imposes monetary discipline on a country and leads to low inflation. For example, if Belize pegs the value of the Belizean dollar to that of the U.S. dollar so that US$1 = B$1.97, then the Belizean government must make sure the inflation rate in Belize is similar to that in the United States. If the Belizean inflation rate is greater than the U.S. inflation rate, this will lead to pressure to devalue the Belizean dollar (i.e., to alter the peg). To maintain the peg, the Belizean government would be required to rein in inflation. Of course, for a pegged exchange rate to impose monetary discipline on a country, the country whose currency is chosen for the peg must also pursue sound monetary policy.

   Evidence shows that adopting a pegged exchange rate regime moderates inflationary pressures in a country. An IMF study concluded that countries with pegged exchange rates had an average annual inflation rate of 8 percent, compared with 14 percent for intermediate regimes and 16 percent for floating regimes.[9] However, many countries operate with only a nominal peg and in practice are willing to devalue their currency rather than pursue a tight monetary policy. It can be very difficult for a smaller country to maintain a peg against another currency if capital is flowing out of the country and foreign exchange traders are speculating against the currency. Something like this occurred in 1997 when a combination of adverse capital flows and currency speculation forced several Asian countries, including Thailand and Malaysia, to abandon pegs against the U.S. dollar and let their currencies float freely. Malaysia and Thailand would not have been in this position had they dealt with a number of problems that began to arise in their economies during the 1990s, including excessive private-sector debt and expanding current account trade deficits.

CURRENCY BOARDS Hong Kong's experience during the 1997 Asian currency crisis added a new dimension to the debate over how to manage a pegged exchange rate. During late 1997 when other Asian currencies were collapsing, Hong Kong maintained the value of its currency against the U.S. dollar at about HK$15 = $7.80 despite several concerted speculative attacks. Hong Kong's currency board has been given credit for this success. A country that introduces a **currency board** commits itself to converting its domestic currency on demand into another currency at a fixed exchange rate. To make this commitment credible, the currency board holds reserves of foreign currency equal at the fixed exchange rate to at least 100 percent of the domestic currency issued. The system used in Hong Kong means its currency must be fully backed by the U.S. dollar at the specified exchange rate. This is still not a true fixed exchange rate regime, because the U.S. dollar, and by extension the Hong Kong dollar, floats against other currencies, but it has some features of a fixed exchange rate regime.

> **Currency Board**
> Means of controlling a country's currency.

Under this arrangement, the currency board can issue additional domestic notes and coins only when there are foreign exchange reserves to back it. This limits the ability of the government to print money and, thereby, create inflationary pressures. Under a strict currency board system, interest rates adjust automatically. If investors want to switch out of domestic currency into, for example, U.S. dollars, the supply of domestic currency will shrink. This will cause interest rates to rise until it eventually becomes attractive for investors to hold the local currency again. In the case of Hong Kong, the interest rate on three-month deposits climbed as high as 20 percent in late 1997, as investors switched out of Hong Kong dollars and into U.S. dollars. The dollar peg held, however, and interest rates declined again.

Since its establishment in 1983, the Hong Kong currency board has weathered several storms, including the latest. This success persuaded several other countries in the developing world to consider a similar system. Argentina introduced a currency board in 1991 (but abandoned it in 2002) and Bulgaria, Estonia, and Lithuania have all gone down this road in recent years (seven IMF members have currency boards). Despite interest in the arrangement, however, critics are quick to point out that currency boards have their drawbacks.[10] If local inflation rates remain higher than the inflation rate in the country to which the currency is pegged, the currencies of countries with currency boards can become uncompetitive and overvalued (this is what happened in the case of Argentina which had a currency board; see the closing case). Also, under a currency board system, government lacks the ability to set interest rates. Interest rates in Hong Kong, for example, are effectively set by the U.S. Federal Reserve. In addition, economic collapse in Argentina in 2001 and the subsequent decision to abandon its currency board dampened much of the enthusiasm for this mechanism of managing exchange rates.

Crisis Management by the IMF

LEARNING OBJECTIVE 5
Understand the debate surrounding the role of the IMF in the management of financial crises.

Many observers initially believed that the collapse of the Bretton Woods system in 1973 would diminish the role of the IMF within the international monetary system. The IMF's original function was to provide a pool of money from which members could borrow, short term, to adjust their balance-of-payments position and maintain their exchange rate. Some believed the demand for short-term loans would be considerably diminished under a floating exchange rate regime. A trade deficit would presumably lead to a decline in a country's exchange rate, which would help reduce imports and boost exports. No temporary IMF adjustment loan would be needed. Consistent with this, after 1973, most industrialized countries tended to let the foreign exchange market determine exchange rates in response to demand and supply. No major industrial country has borrowed funds from the IMF since the mid-1970s, when Great Britain and Italy did. Since the early 1970s, the rapid development of global capital markets has allowed developed countries such as Great Britain and the United States to finance their deficits by borrowing private money, as opposed to drawing on IMF funds. Despite these developments, the activities of the IMF have expanded over the past 30 years. By 2010, the IMF had 186 members, 54 of which had some kind of IMF program in place. In 1997, the institution

Another Perspective

IMF and the World Bank
Although both are products of the Bretton Woods System, the IMF and the World Bank actually serve two distinct functions. The IMF's mandate promotes international monetary cooperation and provides policy advice and technical assistance to help countries build and maintain strong economies. According to the IMF's Web site, the Fund also makes loans and helps countries design policy programs to solve balance of payments or currency problems when sufficient financing on affordable terms cannot be obtained to meet net international payments. The World Bank's mandate promotes longer-term economic development and poverty reduction by providing technical and financial support to help countries reform particular sectors or implement specific projects—for example, building schools and health centers, providing water and electricity, fighting disease, and protecting the environment. The two institutions collaborate to assist member countries. (IMF Web site, www.imf.org, accessed August 30, 2010)

implemented its largest rescue packages until that date, committing more than $110 billion in short-term loans to three troubled Asian countries—South Korea, Indonesia, and Thailand. This was followed by additional IMF rescue packages in Turkey, Russia, Argentina, and Brazil. IMF loans increased again in late 2008 as the global financial crisis took hold. In late 2008 and early 2009 the IMF made some $50 billion in loans to troubled emerging economies. In April 2009, in response to the growing financial crisis, major IMF members agreed to triple the institution's resources from $250 billion to $750 billion, thereby giving the IMF the financial leverage to act aggressively in times of global financial crisis.

The IMF's activities have expanded because periodic financial crises have continued to hit many economies in the post-Bretton Woods era, particularly among the world's developing nations. The IMF has repeatedly lent money to nations experiencing financial crises, requesting in return that the governments enact certain macroeconomic policies. Critics of the IMF claim these policies have not always been as beneficial as the IMF might have hoped and in some cases may have made things worse. Following the IMF loans to several Asian economies, these criticisms reached new levels and a vigorous debate was waged as to the appropriate role of the IMF. In this section, we shall discuss some of the main challenges the IMF has had to deal with over the past quarter of a century and review the ongoing debate over the role of the IMF.

Currency Crisis
Occurs when a speculative attack on the exchange value of a currency results in a sharp depreciation in the value of the currency or forces authorities to expend large volumes of international currency reserves and sharply increase interest rates to defend the prevailing exchange rate.

FINANCIAL CRISES IN THE POST-BRETTON WOODS ERA   A number of broad types of financial crises have occurred over the past 30 years, many of which have required IMF involvement. A **currency crisis** occurs when a speculative attack on the exchange value of a currency results in a sharp depreciation in the value of the currency or forces authorities to expend large volumes of international currency reserves and sharply increase interest rates to defend the prevailing exchange rate. This is what happened in Brazil in 2002, and the IMF stepped in to help stabilize the value of the Brazilian currency on foreign exchange markets. A **banking crisis** refers to a loss of confidence in the banking system that leads to a run on

Banking Crisis
A loss of confidence in the banking system that leads to a run on banks, as individuals and companies withdraw their deposits.

banks, as individuals and companies withdraw their deposits. A **foreign debt crisis** is a situation in which a country cannot service its foreign debt obligations, whether private-sector or government debt.

These crises tend to have common underlying macroeconomic causes: high relative price inflation rates, a widening current account deficit, excessive expansion of domestic borrowing, and asset price inflation (such as sharp increases in stock and property prices).[11] At times, elements of currency, banking, and debt crises may be present simultaneously, as in the 1997 Asian crisis, the 2000–2002 Argentinean crisis and the 2008 crisis in Latvia.

To assess the frequency of financial crises, the IMF looked at the macroeconomic performance of a group of 53 countries from 1975 to 1997 (22 of these countries were developed nations, and 31 were developing countries).[12] The IMF found there had been 158 currency crises, including 55 episodes in which a country's currency declined by more than 25 percent. There were also 54 banking crises. The IMF's data suggest that developing nations were more than twice as likely to experience currency and banking crises as developed nations. It is not surprising, therefore, that most of the IMF's loan activities since the mid-1970s have been targeted toward developing nations.

Here we look at two crises that have been of particular significance in terms of IMF involvement since the early 1990s—the 1995 Mexican currency crisis and the 1997 Asian financial crisis. These crises were the result of excessive foreign borrowings, a weak or poorly regulated banking system, and high inflation rates. These factors came together to trigger simultaneous debt and currency crises. Checking the resulting crises required IMF involvement.

MEXICAN CURRENCY CRISIS OF 1995

The Mexican peso had been pegged to the dollar since the early 1980s when the International Monetary Fund made it a condition for lending money to the Mexican government to help bail the country out of a 1982 financial crisis. Under the IMF-brokered arrangement, the peso had been allowed to trade within a tolerance band of plus or minus 3 percent against the dollar. The band was also permitted to "crawl" down daily, allowing for an annual peso depreciation of about 4 percent against the dollar. The IMF believed that the need to maintain the exchange rate within a fairly narrow trading band would force the Mexican government to adopt stringent financial policies to limit the growth in the money supply and contain inflation.

Until the early 1990s, it looked as if the IMF policy had worked. However, the strains were beginning to show by 1994. Since the mid-1980s, Mexican producer prices had risen 45 percent more than prices in the United States, and yet there had not been a corresponding adjustment in the exchange rate. By late 1994, Mexico was running a $17 billion trade deficit, which amounted to some 6 percent of the country's gross domestic product, and there had been an uncomfortably rapid expansion in public- and private-sector debt. Despite these strains, Mexican government officials had been stating publicly that they would support the peso's dollar peg at around $1 = 3.5 pesos by adopting appropriate monetary policies and by intervening in the currency markets if necessary. Encouraged by such statements, $64 billion of foreign investment money poured into Mexico between 1990 and 1994 as corporations and money managers sought to take advantage of the booming economy.

However, many currency traders concluded the peso would have to be devalued, and they began to dump pesos on the foreign exchange market. The government tried to hold the line by buying pesos and selling dollars, but it lacked the foreign currency reserves required to halt the speculative tide (Mexico's foreign exchange reserves fell from $6 billion at the beginning of 1994 to less than $3.5 billion at the end of the year). In mid-December 1994, the Mexican government abruptly announced a devaluation. Immediately, much of the short-term investment money that had flowed into Mexican stocks and bonds over the previous year reversed its course, as foreign investors bailed out of peso-denominated financial assets. This exacerbated the sale of the peso and contributed to the rapid 40 percent drop in its value.

The IMF stepped in again, this time arm in arm with the U.S. government and the Bank for International Settlements. Together the three institutions pledged close to $50 billion to help Mexico stabilize the peso and to redeem $47 billion of public- and private-sector debt that was set to mature in 1995. Of this amount, $20 billion came from the U.S. government and another $18 billion came from the IMF (which made Mexico the largest recipient of IMF aid up to that point). Without the aid package, Mexico would probably have defaulted on its debt obligations, and the peso would have gone into free fall. As is normal in such cases, the IMF insisted on tight monetary policies and further cuts in public spending, both of which helped push the country into a deep recession. However, the recession was relatively short-lived, and by 1997 the country was once more on a growth path, had pared down its debt, and had paid back the $20 billion borrowed from the U.S. government ahead of schedule.[13]

THE ASIAN CRISIS   The financial crisis that erupted across Southeast Asia during the fall of 1997 emerged as the biggest challenge to date for the IMF. Holding the crisis in check required IMF loans to help the shattered economies of Indonesia, Thailand, and South Korea stabilize their currencies. In addition, although they did not request IMF loans, the economies of Japan, Malaysia, Singapore, and the Philippines were also hurt by the crisis.

The seeds of this crisis were sown during the previous decade when these countries were experiencing unprecedented economic growth. Although there were and remain important differences between the individual countries, a number of elements were common to most. Exports had long been the engine of economic growth in these countries. From 1990 to 1996, the value of exports from Malaysia had grown by 18 percent annually, Thai exports had grown by 16 percent per year, Singapore's by 15 percent, Hong Kong's by 14 percent, and those of South Korea and Indonesia by 12 percent annually.[14]

The nature of these exports had also shifted in recent years from basic materials and products such as textiles to complex and increasingly high-technology products, such as automobiles, semiconductors, and consumer electronics.

The Investment Boom   The wealth created by export-led growth helped fuel an investment boom in commercial and residential property, industrial assets, and infrastructure. The value of commercial and residential real estate in cities such as Hong Kong and Bangkok started to soar. This fed a building boom the likes of which had never been seen in Asia. Heavy borrowing from banks financed much of this construction. As for industrial assets, the success of Asian exporters encouraged them to make bolder investments in industrial capacity. This was exemplified most clearly by South Korea's giant diversified conglomerates, or *chaebol*, many of which had ambitions to build a major position in the global automobile and semiconductor industries.

An added factor behind the investment boom in most Southeast Asian economies was the government. In many cases, the governments had embarked on huge infrastructure projects. In Malaysia, for example, a new government administrative center was being constructed in Putrajaya for M$20 billion (U.S. $8 billion at the pre-July 1997 exchange rate), and the government was funding the development of a massive high-technology communications corridor and the huge Bakun dam, which at a cost of M$13.6 billion was to be the most expensive power-generation plant in the country.[15] Throughout the region, governments also encouraged private businesses to invest in certain sectors of the economy in accordance with "national goals" and "industrialization strategy." In South Korea, long a country where the government played a proactive role in private-sector investments, President Kim Young-Sam urged the *chaebol* to invest in new factories as a way of boosting economic growth. South Korea enjoyed an investment-led economic boom in 1994–1995, but at a cost. The *chaebol*, always reliant on heavy borrowings, built up massive debts that were equivalent, on average, to four times their equity.[16]

In Indonesia, President Suharto had long supported investments in a network of an estimated 300 businesses owned by his family and friends in a system known as "crony capitalism." Many of these businesses were granted lucrative monopolies by the president. For example, Suharto announced in 1995 that he had decided to manufacture a national car, built by a company owned by one of his sons, Hutomo Mandala Putra, in association with Kia Motors of South Korea. To support the venture, a consortium of Indonesian banks was "ordered" by the government to offer almost $700 million in start-up loans to the company.[17]

By the mid-1990s, Southeast Asia was in the grips of an unprecedented investment boom, much of it financed with borrowed money. Between 1990 and 1995, gross domestic investment grew by 16.3 percent annually in Indonesia, 16 percent in Malaysia, 15.3 percent in Thailand, and 7.2 percent in South Korea. By comparison, investment grew by 4.1 percent annually over the same period in the United States and 0.8 percent in all high-income economies.[18] And the rate of investment accelerated in 1996. In Malaysia, for example, spending on investment accounted for a remarkable 43 percent of GDP in 1996.[19]

Excess Capacity   As the volume of investments ballooned during the 1990s, often at the bequest of national governments, the quality of many of these investments declined significantly. The investments often were made on the basis of unrealistic projections about future demand conditions. The result was significant excess capacity. For example, South Korean *chaebol* investments in semiconductor factories surged in 1994 and 1995 when a temporary global shortage of dynamic random access memory chips (DRAMs) led to sharp price increases for this product. However, supply shortages had disappeared by 1996 and excess capacity was beginning to make itself felt, just as the South Koreans started to bring new DRAM factories on stream. The results were predictable; prices for DRAMs plunged, and the earnings of South Korean DRAM manufacturers fell by 90 percent, which meant it was difficult for them to make scheduled payments on the debt they had taken on to build the extra capacity.[20]

In another example, a building boom in Thailand resulted in excess capacity in residential and commercial property. By early 1997, an estimated 365,000 apartment units were unoccupied in Bangkok. With another 100,000 units scheduled to be completed in 1997, years of excess demand in the Thai property market had been replaced by excess supply. By one estimate, Bangkok's building boom had produced enough excess space by 1997 to meet its residential and commercial needs for five years.[21]

The Debt Bomb   By early 1997 what was happening in the South Korean semiconductor industry and the Bangkok property market was being played out elsewhere in the region. Massive investments in industrial assets and property had created excess capacity and plunging prices, while leaving the companies that had made the investments groaning under huge debt burdens that they were now finding it difficult to service.

To make matters worse, much of the borrowing had been in U.S. dollars, as opposed to local currencies. This had originally seemed like a smart move. Throughout the region, local currencies were pegged to the dollar, and interest rates on dollar borrowings were generally lower than rates on borrowings in domestic currency. Thus, it often made economic sense to borrow in dollars if the option was available. However, if the governments could not maintain the dollar peg and their currencies started to depreciate against the dollar, this would increase the size of the debt burden when measured in the local currency. Currency depreciation would raise borrowing costs and could result in companies defaulting on their debt obligations.

Expanding Imports   A final complicating factor was that by the mid-1990s, although exports were still expanding across the region, imports were too. The investments in infrastructure, industrial capacity, and commercial real estate were sucking in foreign goods at unprecedented rates. To build infrastructure, factories, and office buildings, Southeast Asian countries were purchasing capital equipment and materials from America, Europe, and Japan. Many Southeast Asian states saw the current accounts of their balance of payments shift strongly into the red during the mid-1990s. By 1995, Indonesia was running a current account deficit that was equivalent to 3.5 percent of its GDP, Malaysia's was 5.9 percent, and Thailand's was 8.1 percent.[22] With deficits like these, it was increasingly difficult for the governments of these countries to maintain their currencies against the U.S. dollar. If that peg could not be held, the local currency value of dollar-denominated debt would increase, raising the specter of large-scale default on debt service payments. The scene was now set for a potentially rapid economic meltdown.

The Crisis   The Asian meltdown began in mid-1997 in Thailand when it became clear that several key Thai financial institutions were on the verge of default. These institutions had been borrowing dollars from international banks at low interest rates and lending Thai baht at higher interest rates to local property developers. However, due to speculative over-building, these developers could not sell their commercial and residential property, forcing them to default on their debt obligations. In turn, the Thai financial institutions seemed increasingly likely to default on their dollar-denominated debt obligations to international banks. Sensing the beginning of the crisis, foreign investors fled the Thai stock market, selling their positions and converting them into U.S. dollars. The increased demand for dollars and increased supply of Thai baht, pushed down the dollar/Thai baht exchange rate, while the stock market plunged.

Seeing these developments, foreign exchange dealers and hedge funds started speculating against the baht, selling it short. For the previous 13 years, the Thai baht had been pegged to the U.S. dollar at an exchange rate of about $1 = Bt25. The Thai government tried to defend the peg, but only succeeded in depleting its foreign exchange reserves. On July 2, 1997, the Thai government abandoned its defense and announced it would allow the baht

By 1997, years of excess demand in the Thai property market resulted in enough excess space to meet its residential and commercial needs for five years.

to float freely against the dollar. The baht started a slide that would bring the exchange rate down to $1 = Bt55 by January 1998. As the baht declined, the Thai debt bomb exploded. The 55 percent decline in the value of the baht against the dollar doubled the amount of baht required to serve the dollar-denominated debt commitments taken on by Thai financial institutions and businesses. This increased the probability of corporate bankruptcies and further pushed down the battered Thai stock market. The Thailand Set stock market index ultimately declined from 787 in January 1997 to a low of 337 in December of that year, on top of a 45 percent decline in 1996.

On July 28, the Thai government called in the International Monetary Fund. With its foreign exchange reserves depleted, Thailand lacked the foreign currency needed to finance its international trade and service debt commitments and desperately needed the capital the IMF could provide. It also needed to restore international confidence in its currency and needed the credibility associated with gaining access to IMF funds. Without IMF loans, the baht likely would increase its free fall against the U.S. dollar and the whole country might go into default. The IMF agreed to provide the Thai government with $17.2 billion in loans, but the conditions were restrictive.[23] The IMF required the Thai government to increase taxes, cut public spending, privatize several state-owned businesses, and raise interest rates—all steps designed to cool Thailand's overheated economy. The IMF also required Thailand to close illiquid financial institutions. In December 1997, the government shut 56 financial institutions, laying off 16,000 people and further deepening the recession that now gripped the country.

Following the devaluation of the Thai baht, wave after wave of speculation hit other Asian currencies. One after another in a period of weeks, the Malaysian ringgit, Indonesian rupiah, and the Singaporean dollar were all marked sharply lower. With its foreign exchange reserves down to $28 billion, Malaysia let the ringgit float on July 14, 1997. Before the devaluation, the ringgit was trading at $1 = 2.525 ringgit. Six months later it had declined to $1 = 4.15 ringgit. Singapore followed on July 17, and the Singaporean dollar quickly dropped in value from $1 = S$1.495 before the devaluation to $1 = S$2.68 a few days later. Next up was Indonesia, whose rupiah was allowed to float August 14. For Indonesia, this was the beginning of a precipitous decline in the value of its currency, which was to fall from $1 = 2,400 rupiah in August 1997 to $1 = 10,000 rupiah on January 6, 1998, a loss of 76 percent.

With the exception of Singapore, whose economy is probably the most stable in the region, these devaluations were driven by factors similar to those behind the earlier devaluation of the Thai baht—a combination of excess investment; high borrowings, much of it in dollar-denominated debt; and a deteriorating balance-of-payments position. Although both Malaysia and Singapore were able to halt the slide in their currencies and stock markets without the help of the IMF, Indonesia was not. Indonesia was struggling with a private-sector, dollar-denominated debt of close to $80 billion. With the rupiah sliding precipitously almost every day, the cost of servicing this debt was exploding, pushing more Indonesian companies into technical default.

On October 31, 1997, the IMF announced it had assembled a $37 billion rescue deal for Indonesia in conjunction with the World Bank and the Asian Development Bank. In return, the Indonesian government agreed to close a number of troubled banks, reduce public spending, remove government subsidies on basic foodstuffs and energy, balance the budget, and unravel the crony capitalism that was so widespread in Indonesia. But the government of President Suharto appeared to backtrack several times on commitments made to the IMF. This precipitated further declines in the Indonesian currency and stock markets. Ultimately, Suharto removed costly government subsidies, only to see the country dissolve into chaos as the populace took to the streets to protest the resulting price increases. This unleashed a chain of events that led to Suharto's removal from power in May 1998.

The final domino to fall was South Korea. During the 1990s, South Korean companies had built up huge debt loads as they invested heavily in new industrial capacity. Now they found they had too much industrial capacity and could not generate the income required to service their debt. South Korean banks and companies had also made the mistake of borrowing in dollars, much of it in the form of short-term loans that would come due within a year. Thus, when the Korean won started to decline in the fall of 1997 in sympathy with the problems elsewhere in Asia, South Korean companies saw their debt obligations balloon. Several large companies were forced to file for bankruptcy. This triggered a decline in the South Korean currency and stock market that was difficult to halt. The South Korean central bank tried to keep the dollar/won exchange rate above $1 = W1,000 but found that this only depleted its foreign exchange reserves. On November 17, the South Korean central bank gave up the defense of the won, which quickly fell to $1 = W1,500.

With its economy on the verge of collapse, the South Korean government on November 21 requested $20 billion in standby loans from the IMF. As the negotiations progressed, it became apparent that South Korea was going to need far more than $20 billion. Among other problems, the country's short-term foreign debt was found to be twice as large as previously thought at close to $100 billion, while the country's foreign exchange reserves were down to less than $6 billion. On December 3, 1997, the IMF and South Korean government reached a deal to lend $55 billion to the country. The agreement with the IMF called for the South Koreans to open their economy and banking system to foreign investors. South Korea also pledged to restrain the *chaebol* by reducing their share of bank financing and requiring them to publish consolidated financial statements and undergo annual independent external audits. On trade liberalization, the IMF said South Korea would comply with its commitments to the World Trade Organization to eliminate trade-related subsidies and restrictive import licensing and would streamline its import certification procedures, all of which should open the South Korean economy to greater foreign competition.[24]

EVALUATING THE IMF'S POLICY PRESCRIPTIONS   By 2009, the IMF was committing loans to some 54 countries that were struggling with economic and currency crises. A detailed example and a variation of one such program are discussed in the accompanying Country Focus, which looks at IMF loans to Greece. All IMF loan packages come with conditions attached. Until very recently, the IMF has insisted on a combination of tight macroeconomic policies, including cuts in public spending, higher interest rates, and tight monetary policy. It has also often pushed for the deregulation of sectors formerly protected from domestic and foreign competition, privatization of state-owned assets, and better financial reporting from the banking sector. These policies are designed to cool overheated economies by reining in inflation and reducing government spending and debt. Recently, this set of policy prescriptions has come in for tough criticisms from many observers, and the IMF itself has started to change its approach.[25]

Inappropriate Policies   One criticism is that the IMF's traditional policy prescriptions represent "one-size-fits-all" approach to macroeconomic policy that is inappropriate for many countries. In the case of the Asian crisis, critics argue that the tight macroeconomic policies imposed by the IMF are not well suited to countries that are suffering not from excessive government spending and inflation, but from a private-sector debt crisis with deflationary undertones.[26] In South Korea, for example, the government had been running a budget surplus for years (it was 4 percent of South Korea's GDP in 1994–1996) and inflation was low at about 5 percent. South Korea had the second strongest financial position of any country in the Organization for Economic Cooperation and Development. Despite this, critics say, the IMF insisted on applying the same policies that it applies to countries suffering from high inflation. The IMF required South Korea to maintain an inflation rate of 5 percent. However, given the collapse in the value of its currency and the subsequent rise in price for imports such as oil, critics claimed inflationary pressures would inevitably increase in South Korea. So to hit a 5 percent inflation rate, the South Koreans would be forced to apply an unnecessarily tight monetary policy. Short-term interest rates in South Korea did jump from 12.5 percent to 21 percent immediately after the country signed its initial deal with the IMF. Increasing interest rates made it even more difficult for companies to service their already excessive short-term debt obligations, and critics used this as evidence to argue that the cure prescribed by the IMF may actually increase the probability of widespread corporate defaults, not reduce them.

At the time, the IMF rejected this criticism. According to the IMF, the central task was to rebuild confidence in the won. Once this was achieved, the won would recover from its oversold levels, reducing the size of South Korea's dollar-denominated debt burden when expressed in won, making it easier for companies to service their debt. The IMF also argued that by requiring South Korea to remove restrictions on foreign direct investment, foreign capital would flow into the country to take advantage of cheap assets. This, too, would increase demand for the Korean currency and help to improve the dollar/won exchange rate.

Korea did recover fairly quickly from the crisis, supporting the position of the IMF. While the economy contracted by 7 percent in 1998, by 2000 it had rebounded and grew at a 9 percent rate (measured by growth in GDP). Inflation, which peaked at 8 percent in 1998, fell to 2 percent by 2000, and unemployment fell from 7 percent to 4 percent over the same period. The won hit a low of $1 = W1,812 in early 1998, but by 2000 was back to an exchange rate of around $1 = W1,200, at which it seems to have stabilized.

Moral Hazard Arises when people behave recklessly because they know they will be saved if things go wrong.

Moral Hazard   A second criticism of the IMF is that its rescue efforts are exacerbating a problem known to economists as moral hazard. **Moral hazard** arises when people behave recklessly because they know they will be saved if things go wrong. Critics point out that many Japanese and Western banks were far too willing to lend large amounts of capital to overleveraged Asian companies during the boom years of the 1990s. These critics argue that the banks should now be forced to pay the price for their rash lending policies, even if that means some banks must close.[27] Only by taking such drastic action, the argument goes, will banks learn the error of their ways and not engage in rash lending in the future. By providing support to these countries, the IMF is reducing the probability of debt default and in effect bailing out the banks whose loans gave rise to this situation.

This argument ignores two critical points. First, if some Japanese or Western banks with heavy exposure to the troubled Asian economies were forced to write off their loans due to widespread debt default, the impact would have been difficult to contain. The failure of large Japanese banks, for example, could have triggered a meltdown in the Japanese financial markets. That would almost inevitably lead to a serious decline in stock markets around the world, which was the very risk the IMF was trying to avoid by stepping in with financial support. Second, it is incorrect to imply that some banks have not had to pay the price for rash lending policies. The IMF has insisted on the closure of banks in South Korea, Thailand, and Indonesia. Foreign banks with short-term loans outstanding to South Korean enterprises have been forced by circumstances to reschedule those loans at interest rates that do not compensate for the extension of the loan maturity.

Lack of Accountability   The final criticism of the IMF is that it has become too powerful for an institution that lacks any real mechanism for accountability.[28] The IMF has determined macroeconomic policies in those countries, yet according to critics such as noted economist Jeffrey Sachs, the IMF, with a staff of less than 1,000, lacks the expertise required to do a good job. Evidence of this, according to Sachs, can be found in the fact that the IMF was singing the praises of the Thai and South Korean governments only months before both countries lurched into crisis. Then the IMF put together a draconian program for South Korea without having deep knowledge of the country. Sachs' solution to this problem is to reform the IMF so it makes greater use of outside experts and its operations are open to greater outside scrutiny.

Observations   As with many debates about international economics, it is not clear which side is correct about the appropriateness of IMF policies. There are cases where one can argue that IMF policies have been counterproductive, or only had limited success. But the IMF can also point to some notable accomplishments, including its success in containing the Asian crisis, which could have rocked the global international monetary system to its core, and its actions in 2008 and 2009 to contain the global financial crisis, quickly stepping in to rescues countries such as Iceland and Latvia. Similarly, many observers give the IMF credit for its deft handling of politically difficult situations, such as the Mexican peso crisis, and for successfully promoting a free market philosophy.

Several years after the IMF's intervention, the economies of Asia and Mexico recovered. Certainly they all averted the kind of catastrophic implosion that might have occurred had the IMF not stepped in, and although some countries still faced considerable problems, it is not clear that the IMF should take much blame for this. The IMF cannot force countries to adopt the policies required to correct economic mismanagement. While a government may commit to taking corrective action in return for an IMF loan, internal political problems may make it difficult for a government to act on that commitment. In such cases, the IMF is caught between a rock and a hard place, for if it decided to withhold money, it might trigger financial collapse and the kind of contagion that it seeks to avoid.

Finally, it is notable that in recent years the IMF has started to change its policies. Specifically, in response to the global financial crisis of 2008–2009 the IMF began to urge countries to adopt policies that included fiscal stimulus and monetary easing—the direct opposite of what the fund traditionally advocated. Some economists in the fund are also now arguing that higher inflation rates might be a good thing, if the consequence is greater growth in aggregate demand, which would help to pull nations out of recessionary conditions. The IMF, in other words, is starting to display the very flexibility in policy responses that its critics claim it lacks. While the traditional policy of tight controls on fiscal policy and tight monetary policy targets might be appropriate for countries suffering from high inflation rates, the Asian economic crisis and the 2008–2000 global financial crisis were caused not by high inflation rates, but by excessive debt, and the IMF's "new approach" seems tailored to deal with this.[29]

Country FOCUS

The Greek Debt Crisis, the European Union, and the IMF

In January 2001, Greece became the 12th member to join the European Union (EU) and changed its currency to the euro. It had done so after years of cutting inflation and interest rates, and the country had finally brought the drachma into conformity with the euro. In 2004, under close scrutiny, however, Greece's budget figures showed that the country had not actually met euro-zone currency conditions. One of the conditions demanded by the EU was that Greece's deficit was to be below 3 percent, and Greece had never complied.

In March 2005, with the right-wing New Democracy government in place, Greece embarked on an austerity program of cutting the budget deficit, increasing the value-added tax (VAT) to 19 percent, and raising taxes on alcohol and tobacco in an attempt to get public finances back on track after hosting the 2004 Summer Olympics. By spring 2006, the austerity program appeared to be working, and Greece experienced an increase of 4.1 percent in the first quarter of 2006. Recovery appeared to be in sight.

But, by October 2009, just as socialist George Papandreou became prime minister, the Greek economy had contracted 0.3 percent, and the national debt had risen to €262 billion, from €168 billion in 2004. The government projected that the 2009 deficit would reach 6 percent. Toward the end of 2009, Papandreou declared that Greece was in need of "intensive care" as the country's deficit mounted. In December 2009, Fitch, the country investor rating service, dropped Greece's long-term debt to BBB+ from A−. This was the first time in a decade that Greece did not have an A rating and pushed up the country's cost of borrowing.

Right before Christmas 2009, the Greek government announced radical reforms in an attempt to put "the house back in order." Riots broke out in Athens, and thousands of workers took to the streets. Standard & Poor's, another credit rating agency, also lowered the creditworthiness of Greece. Investors worldwide believed that Greece, a member of the EU with the euro as its national currency, might default.

In 2010, Greece announced a wider austerity package, including a freeze on public sector pay and higher taxes for low- and middle-income households. More riots broke out with tear gas used to control striking public-sector workers. Papandreou again sought help from the EU. European ministers convened to determine whether a rescue package for Greece would be possible. Germany, which had voiced doubts about allowing less-developed nations into the EU euro zone back in 2001, opposed the financial rescue package, saying that the country should tackle its debt problems by itself. Tangentially, Goldman Sachs, the global investment bank, was accused of helping to cause the crisis by using derivatives contracts to disguise how much Greece was borrowing. An austerity program has been implemented by Greece, cutting bonus pay and raising taxes. As a result, the Greek government issued 10-year bonds, and the investment community responded favorably with a €16 billion bid. The final response, however, was weak. By March 2010, the financial markets began to lose faith in Greece's ability to service the debt. In mid-April, after weeks of negotiations, the EU agreed to a €35 billion rescue package. With €16 billion maturing in May 2010, Greece acknowledged it will need help not only from the EU but from the IMF as well and asked for a €45 billion rescue package. Standard & Poor's lowered Greece's credit rating to junk bond status, and stock markets plummetted worldwide.

Analysts and politicians warned that €45 billion simply would not be enough to sort out the Greek crisis, with Goldman Sachs predicting that the country may need a €150 billion rescue package. EU and IMF officials convinced Angela Merkel, the German prime minister, that Germany must participate. Germany reluctantly agreed. Merkel acknowledged that having allowed Greece to enter the EU may have been a mistake.

In early May 2010, after much negotiations, the EU, IMF, and the European Central Bank finally agreed on a €110 billion "bailout." Sensing the level of "belt-tightening" that this bailout would provoke, Greece once again experienced riots, this time with protesters taking the Acropolis. Stock markets continued to fall, and gold reached record levels as questions remained whether this bailout package would solve Greece's problems.

Since then, the actual Greek bailout has risen to €140 billion, with the IMF lending €38 billion, but such large figures represent only a fraction of the €1 trillion package that Europe has set aside for the continent's overall financial crisis. Like Greece, other countries, such as Portugal, Spain, Ireland, Italy, and Belgium, found themselves in potentially similar circumstances. The extent of the "contagion" questioned the continued viability of the euro as the EU's currency.

The €1 trillion package also forced alliances that had not been utilized until now. Namely, for the first time, the EU found itself in a lending predicament without experience and brought in the IMF to assist in the overall structure. For the first time, a "supranational" organization, the European Union, collaborated with an international institution, the IMF, and a specific country, Greece, to avoid a global financial meltdown. The question that remains is whether

(continued)

Greece can endure the restructuring and the hardships this financial crisis entails.

We can expect the European Commission—which enforces the policies of the EU—and the IMF—in a rare minority role—to carefully monitor Greece's budget. If Greece complies, the rescue package will guarantee financial support until 2012. As the Greeks reluctantly accept their fate, violence should abate for the time being. However, if the situation does not appear better, 2012 looms as another potential crisis period. Expect the EU to look to the IMF for experience in how to handle that crisis should it occur.

Sources: N. Ferguson, "Euro Trashed," *Newsweek,* May 31, 2010; G. Wearden, "Greece Debt Crisis: Timeline," May 5, 2010, accessed at http://www.guardian.co.uk/business/2010/may/05/greece-debt-crisis-timeline; S. Rastello, M. Petrakis, and J. Stearns. "Now It's Up to the IMF to Make Greece Shape Up," *Bloomberg Businessweek,* April 26, 2010; and "High Stakes: What Has the Fund Got Itself into by Participating in Europe's Bailout?" *The Economist,* http://www.economist.com/node/16116929?story_id=16116929.

Focus on Managerial Implications

The implications for international businesses of the material discussed in this chapter fall into three main areas: currency management, business strategy, and corporate–government relations.

LEARNING OBJECTIVES 6
Explain the implications of the global monetary system for currency management and business strategy.

Currency Management

An obvious implication with regard to currency management is that companies must recognize that the foreign exchange market does not work quite as depicted in Chapter 9. The current system is a mixed system in which a combination of government intervention and speculative activity can drive the foreign exchange market. Companies engaged in significant foreign exchange activities need to be aware of this and to adjust their foreign exchange transactions accordingly. For example, the currency management unit of Caterpillar claims it made millions of dollars in the hours following the announcement of the Plaza Accord by selling dollars and buying currencies that it expected to appreciate on the foreign exchange market following government intervention.

Under the present system, speculative buying and selling of currencies can create very volatile movements in exchange rates (as exhibited by the rise and fall of the dollar during the 1980s and the Asian currency crisis of the late 1990s). Contrary to the predictions of the purchasing power parity theory (see Chapter 9), exchange rate movements during the 1980s and 1990s often did not seem to be strongly influenced by relative inflation rates. Insofar as volatile exchange rates increase foreign exchange risk, this is not good news for business. On the other hand, as we saw in Chapter 9, the foreign exchange market has developed a number of instruments, such as the forward market and swaps, that can help to insure against foreign exchange risk. Not surprisingly, use of these instruments has increased markedly since the breakdown of the Bretton Woods system in 1973.

Business Strategy

The volatility of the present global exchange rate regime presents a conundrum for international businesses. Exchange rate movements are difficult to predict, and yet their movement can have a major impact on a business's competitive position. For a detailed example, see the accompanying Management Focus on German automakers

German Automobiles and the Chinese Yuan

Mercedes Benz, BMW, and Volkswagen are experiencing tremendous growth as they come off two years of economic downturn. China has been driving much of that growth. Among Germany's premium car makers—BMW AG, Daimler AG's Mercedes-Benz, and Volkswagen AG's Audi—individual car sales to China have soared between 63 and 132 percent so far this year (2010). Such growth has fueled a surge in profits, pushing operating margins to record levels, despite weak sales in their home markets of Europe and stuttering growth in the United States.

Behind the windfall is a confluence of factors. Chinese luxury-car drivers are gravitating toward pricier, higher-end vehicles with much bigger engines and more options than such buyers in the three automakers' more mature markets. The euro's roughly 15 percent slide against the dollar and the Chinese yuan in the first half of 2010 added another boost to profit margins on cars imported from Germany or elsewhere. As a result, analysts estimate that German automakers, particularly BMW and Mercedes, may have been reaping as much as 30,000 euros ($38,613) in profit per car exported to and sold in China, roughly 10 times the amount they typically do in Europe.

At BMW, for example, Chinese profitability may have contributed as much as 90 percent of the carmaker's 1.3 billion euros in second-quarter operating profit from its auto segment. BMW AG, its official name, had net profits skyrocket as a result of this booming demand for luxury cars in China. But particularly interesting was the fact that exchange-rate fluctuations worked in favor of BMW. With the euro weaker against the dollar, earnings generated in China are inflated when converted to the euro. Financially, BMW views the Chinese yuan as effectively pegged to the dollar. Its strategy has been to fully hedge against unfavorable currency fluctuations in 2010 and expect its full-year earnings to benefit from exchange rates. Chief Financial Officer Friedrich Eichiner described BMW's currency hedging for 2011 as "very solid," but he didn't elaborate during an analyst conference call. He noted, however, that BMW has already started to hedge its exposure in 2012.

Similarly, since 1973 Volkswagen has been using sophisticated international business practices by relying more on currency hedging as a means of increasing its profitability. Since then, Volkswagen and its sister company, Audi, have been significantly increasing their hedging from an original 40 percent net currency exposure of $5.6 billion in 2003 to more than 75 percent more recently. VW's gross currency exposure is currently at more than $12 billion. It should be mentioned that half of that was "naturally" hedged by producing cars locally such as in Brazil, Mexico, and China. Carmakers typically use local production—such as BMW AG's plant in Spartanburg, South Carolina, and Daimler AG's plant in Vance, Alabama—as a hedge against currency swings.

Sources: V. Fuhrmans, "China Cultivates Taste for German Cars," *The Wall Street Journal,* August 19, 2010; C. Rauwald, "Luxury Demand Drives BMW Results," *The Wall Street Journal,* August 3, 2010; G. Reinking, D. Kurylko, and J. Snyder, "Currency Chills U.S.-made Audi," *Automotive News,* June 28, 2010, accessed at http://www.autoweek.com/article/20100628/carnews/100629898; and U. Harnischfeger, "VW Increases Its Currency Hedging," *Financial Times,* 2003, p. 29.

and their surging profits doing business in China. Faced with uncertainty about the future value of currencies, firms can utilize the forward exchange market. However, the forward exchange market is far from perfect as a predictor of future exchange rates (see Chapter 9). It is also difficult if not impossible to get adequate insurance coverage for exchange rate changes that might occur several years in the future. The forward market tends to offer coverage for exchange rate changes a few months—not years— ahead. Given this, it makes sense to pursue strategies that will increase the company's strategic flexibility in the face of unpredictable exchange rate movements—that is, to pursue strategies that reduce the economic exposure of the firm (which we first discussed in Chapter 9).

Maintaining strategic flexibility can take the form of dispersing production to different locations around the globe as a real hedge against currency fluctuations. Consider the case of Daimler-Benz, Germany's export-oriented automobile and aerospace company. In June 1995, the company stunned the German business community when it announced it expected to post a severe loss in 1995 of about $720 million. The cause was Germany's strong currency, which had appreciated by 4 percent against a basket of major currencies since the beginning of 1995 and had risen by more than 30 percent against the U.S. dollar since late 1994. By mid-1995, the exchange rate against the dollar stood at $1 = DM1.38. Daimler's management believed it could not make money with an exchange rate under $1 = DM1.60. Daimler's senior managers concluded that the appreciation of the mark against the dollar was probably permanent, so they decided to move substantial production outside of Germany and increase purchasing of foreign components. The idea was to reduce the vulnerability of the company to future exchange rate movements. Even before it acquired Chrysler Corporation in 1998, the Mercedes-Benz division planned to produce 10 percent of its cars outside of Germany by 2000, mostly in the United States.[30] Similarly, the move by Japanese automobile companies to expand their productive capacity in the United States and Europe can be seen in the context of the increase in the value of the yen between 1985 and 1995, which raised the price of Japanese exports. For the Japanese companies, building production capacity overseas is a hedge against continued appreciation of the yen (as well as against trade barriers).

Another way of building strategic flexibility and reducing economic exposure involves contracting out manufacturing. This allows a company to shift suppliers from country to country in response to changes in relative costs brought about by exchange rate movements. However, this kind of strategy may work only for low-value-added manufacturing (e.g., textiles), in which the individual manufacturers have few if any firm-specific skills that contribute to the value of the product. It may be less appropriate for high-value-added manufacturing, in which firm-specific technology and skills add significant value to the product (e.g., the heavy equipment industry) and in which switching costs are correspondingly high. For high-value-added manufacturing, switching suppliers will lead to a reduction in the value that is added, which may offset any cost gains arising from exchange rate fluctuations.

The roles of the IMF and the World Bank in the present international monetary system also have implications for business strategy. Increasingly, the IMF has been acting as the macroeconomic police of the world economy, insisting that countries seeking significant borrowings adopt IMF-mandated macroeconomic policies. These policies typically include anti-inflationary monetary policies and reductions in government spending. In the short run, such policies usually result in a sharp contraction of demand. International businesses selling or producing in such countries need to be aware of this and plan accordingly. In the long run, the kind of policies imposed by the IMF can promote economic growth and an expansion of demand, which create opportunities for international business.

Corporate–Government Relations

As major players in the international trade and investment environment, businesses can influence government policy toward the international monetary system. For example, intense government lobbying by U.S. exporters helped convince the U.S. government that intervention in the foreign exchange market was necessary. With this in mind, business can and should use its influence to promote an international monetary system that facilitates the growth of international trade and investment. Whether a fixed or floating regime is optimal is a subject for debate. However, exchange rate volatility such as the world experienced during the 1980s and 1990s creates an environment less conducive to international trade and investment than one with more stable exchange rates. Therefore, it would seem to be in the interests of international business to promote an international monetary system that minimizes volatile exchange rate movements, particularly when those movements are unrelated to long-run economic fundamentals.

Key Terms

international monetary system, p. 370

floating exchange rate, p. 371

pegged exchange rate, p. 371

dirty float, p. 371

fixed exchange rate, p. 371

European Monetary System (EMS), p. 371

gold standard, p. 372

gold par value, p. 373

balance-of-trade equilibrium, p. 373

managed-float system, p. 382

currency board, p. 386

currency crisis, p. 387

banking crisis, p. 387

foreign debt crisis, p. 388

moral hazard, p. 394

Summary

This chapter explained the workings of the international monetary system and pointed out its implications for international business. The chapter made the following points:

1. The gold standard is a monetary standard that pegs currencies to gold and guarantees convertibility to gold. It was thought that the gold standard contained an automatic mechanism that contributed to the simultaneous achievement of a balance-of-payments equilibrium by all countries. The gold standard broke down during the 1930s as countries engaged in competitive devaluations.

2. The Bretton Woods system of fixed exchange rates was established in 1944. The U.S. dollar was the central currency of this system; the value of every other currency was pegged to its value. Significant exchange rate devaluations were allowed only with the permission of the IMF. The role of the IMF was to maintain order in the international monetary system (*a*) to avoid a repetition of the competitive devaluations of the 1930s and (*b*) to control price inflation by imposing monetary discipline on countries.

3. The fixed exchange rate system collapsed in 1973, primarily due to speculative pressure on the dollar following a rise in U.S. inflation and a growing U.S. balance-of-trade deficit.

4. Since 1973 the world has operated with a floating exchange rate regime, and exchange rates have become more volatile and far less predictable. Volatile exchange rate movements have helped reopen the debate over the merits of fixed and floating systems.

5. The case for a floating exchange rate regime claims (*a*) such a system gives countries autonomy regarding their monetary policy and (*b*) floating exchange rates facilitate smooth adjustment of trade imbalances.

6. The case for a fixed exchange rate regime claims (*a*) the need to maintain a fixed exchange rate imposes monetary discipline on a country, (*b*) floating exchange rate regimes are vulnerable to speculative pressure, (*c*) the uncertainty that accompanies floating exchange rates dampens the growth of international trade and investment, and (*d*) far from correcting trade imbalances, depreciating a currency on the foreign exchange market tends to cause price inflation.

7. In today's international monetary system, some countries have adopted floating exchange rates, some have pegged their currency to another currency such as the U.S. dollar, and some have pegged their currency to a basket of other currencies, allowing their currency to fluctuate within a zone around the basket.

8. In the post–Bretton Woods era, the IMF has continued to play an important role in helping countries navigate their way through financial crises by lending significant capital to embattled governments and by requiring them to adopt certain macroeconomic policies.

9. An important debate is occurring over the appropriateness of IMF-mandated macroeconomic policies. Critics charge that the IMF often imposes inappropriate conditions on developing nations that are the recipients of its loans.

10. The present managed-float system of exchange rate determination has increased the importance of currency management in international businesses.

11. The volatility of exchange rates under the present managed-float system creates both opportunities and threats. One way of responding to this volatility is for companies to build strategic flexibility and limit their economic exposure by dispersing production to different locations around the globe by contracting out manufacturing (in the case of low-value-added manufacturing) and other means.

Critical Thinking and Discussion Questions

1. Why did the gold standard collapse? Is there a case for returning to some type of gold standard? What is it?

2. What opportunities might current IMF lending policies to developing nations create for international businesses? What threats might they create?

3. Do you think the standard IMF policy prescriptions of tight monetary policy and reduced government spending are always appropriate for developing nations experiencing a currency crisis? How might the IMF change its approach? What would the implications be for international businesses?

4. Debate the relative merits of fixed and floating exchange rate regimes. From the perspective of an international business, what are the most important criteria in a choice between the systems? Which system is the more desirable for an international business?

5. Imagine that Canada, the United States, and Mexico decide to adopt a fixed exchange rate system. What would be the likely consequences of such a system for (*a*) international businesses and (*b*) the flow of trade and investment among the three countries?

6. Reread the Country Focus on the U.S. dollar, oil prices, and recycling petrodollars, then answer the following questions:

   a. What will happen to the value of the U.S. dollar if oil producers decide to invest most of their earnings from oil sales in domestic infrastructure projects?

   b. What factors determine the relative attractiveness of dollar-, euro-, and yen-denominated assets to oil producers flush with petrodollars? What might lead them to direct more funds toward non-dollar-denominated assets?

   c. What will happen to the value of the U.S. dollar if OPEC members decide to invest more of their petrodollars toward non-dollar-denominated assets, such as euro-denominated stocks and bonds?

   d. In addition to oil producers, China is also accumulating a large stock of dollars, currently estimated to total $1.4 trillion. What would happen to the value of the dollar if China and oil-producing nations all shifted out of dollar-denominated assets at the same time? What would be the consequence for the U.S. economy?

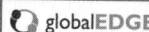
Use the globalEDGE Resource Desk (http://global EDGE.msu.edu/resourcedesk/) to complete the following exercises:

1. While Latvia has been a member state of the European Union since 2004, it has not completed the third stage of the European Monetary Union and therefore still uses its own currency, the Latvian lats. Visit the site of the *Bank of Latvia* to get more information about the current monetary policy in Latvia. How is the value of lats determined? Why?

2. The International Capital Markets division of the International Monetary Fund (IMF) publishes the *Global Financial Stability Report*, a semiannual report that provides an assessment of global financial markets. Find the Global Financial Stability Map in the most recent report. Provide a description of the indicators used to construct the map and briefly summarize what the most current map illustrates in terms of changes in financial stability risks.

closing case

Hungary's Monetary Crisis

According to many economists, Hungary is facing a Greek-style financial meltdown. Unlike Greece, however, Hungary joined the European Union but did not take on the euro and maintained its own currency, the forint.

Hungary has had one of the most successful economies in Central Europe and has experienced steady economic growth since 1997. As an ex-Soviet bloc country, Hungary has transitioned from a one-party centrally planned economy to a multi-party market economy. Although Hungary enjoyed one of the most liberal and economically advanced economies of the former Eastern bloc, it was not until the 1990s that Hungary underwent full-fledged market liberalization and began the development that led to its membership in the European Union in 2004. Hungary's development during this period was based on the influx of foreign investment through a fairly extensive privatization program. In fact, since 1998, Hungary has received 25 percent of all the foreign direct investment going to Central and Eastern Europe. It has been the darling of Central Europe. Nevertheless, the privatization that played a major role in this economic growth has aroused significant national passions. Interestingly enough, it has been the leftist Hungarian governments that have espoused the benefits of such privatization. Because it has not yet complied with the Maastricht treaties criteria for the adoption of the euro, Hungary still uses its national currency, the forint, which has been a symbol of nationalist pride and independence.

In April 2010, the Fidesz, the center right political party lead by Prime Minister Viktor Orban, won parlimentary elec-

tions in a landslide victory, unseating the minority Socialist government that had implemented painful austerity measures to regain investor confidence. Although Hungary's debt to gross domestic product ratio is the highest in the region at around 80 percent, the country is different from Greece. While this may be viewed as a detriment, it has also given Hungary a certain level of flexibility that other European countries, such as Greece, do not enjoy.

Whereas Greece has been forced into a bailout with the help of the European Union and the IMF, Hungary now has the option of not necessarily accepting a loan. In 2008, Hungary received an emergency loan package, a standby credit line of $25.1 billion from the IMF and the European Union when the country was hit hard by the economic crisis. This loan helped the country avert insolvency. When Hungary drew on the line, both bodies imposed austerity measures. Since then, however, Hungary has decided not to draw any further on the loan and has decided to finance itself from the international bond market. In so doing, Hungary has taken on its own fate without an externally imposed austerity program. In a contrarian posture, the Orban government has favored growth policies over austerity and refused to assume the obligations to reduce its budget deficit to 3 percent of GDP, as mandated by EU and IMF agreements.

In the interim, the forint has gone through bouts of volatility in May, June, and July 2010, first owing to the aftermath of Greece's fiscal woes, and subsequently to the suspension of talks between Hungary and the IMF. In early August 2010, the forint appeared to be settling at a lower level. Hungary's fundamental economic indicators remain relatively weak, and concerns over its ability to finance massive external debt especially after 2011 will remain strong. This will be so at least until the government shows that it can bring public finances sustainably under control, and until the country's large imbalances narrow substantially.

Continued uncertainty in global markets also poses a risk of further attacks on the forint. In the aftermath of the financial crisis that engulfed peripheral members of the euro area in late 2009, international bond investors will place increased scrutiny on the assets of vulnerable EU members such as Hungary. According to currency forecasters, the forint is therefore likely to average about Ft277 to €1 in 2010 as the economy remains in recession, before appreciating slightly in 2011 as GDP growth picks up. How economic growth will be obtained will not be known until after the October 2010 municipal elections, when the Orban administration will issue its economic program.

Sources: G. Fairclough, "Hungary Goes It Alone on Economic Agenda," *The Wall Street Journal,* August 2, 2010, accessed at http://online.wsj.com/article/SB20001424052748703314904575399231189704608.html;

"Hungary Vows to Avert Greece-Like Crisis," *The Wall Street Journal,* June 5, 2010; V. Gulyas, "Update: Hungary to Maintain Ties with IMF," *Dow Jones Business News,* September 3, 2010; "Hungary Will Choose Its Own Debt Service Path—PM," *Reuters News,* 2010; and "Hungary: Future of the Forint," *The Economist Intelligence Unit— Executive Briefing,* September 3, 2010.

Case Discussion Questions

1. In the Country Focus on the Greek Debt Crisis, the European Union, and the IMF, we came to appreciate the anatomy of the Greek crisis and its role in the global financial crisis. How does Hungary differ from Greece in its response to the financial crisis?

2. Do you think now that the European Union has assisted lesser-developed countries in Europe such as Greece, that it will look at countries such as Hungary under a different set of principles prior to admittance in the euro zone?

3. What do you think lies ahead for the forint?

4. What are the advantages and disadvantages of a nation-state maintaining its own currency? Was it to the benefit of Hungary's population not to have assumed the euro?

LEARNING OBJECTIVES

After you have read this chapter you should be able to:

1   Explain the concept of strategy.

2   Recognize how firms can profit by expanding globally.

3   Understand how pressures for cost reductions and pressures for local responsiveness influence strategic choice.

4   Identify the different strategies for competing globally and their pros and cons.

5   Explain the pros and cons of using strategic alliances to support global strategies.

chapter 11

The Strategy of International Business

AXA

Originally founded in 1816 as *Mutuelle de L'assurance contre L'incendie* (the *Ancienne Mutuelle*) and through subsequent acquisition in 1978 of *Compagnie Parisienne de Garantie,* the French insurance company became *Mutuelles Unies.* Seeking to become a global insurance conglomerate after acquiring the Dourot Group in 1982, then Chairman and CEO Claude Bébéar hired an outside consultant to conduct a computer-generated search for a new name for the company. The selection criteria consisted of a short and snappy name to convey vitality; a name that begins with the letter A so that it would appear near the top of all lists; and something that could be pronounced easily in every language, consistent with the group's desire for an international presence. In 1985, Mr. Bébéar chose the name AXA for the company.

As one of the world's largest insurance conglomerates, AXA is actually an amalgamation of independently run businesses, operated according to the laws and regulations of many different countries. Groupe AXA, as known in Europe, is engaged in life, health, and other forms of insurance as well as investment management. As the parent company, Groupe AXA exercises a limited influence on the independently run business units because of the unique insurance/investment regulatory environment of the various units.

AXA's focus has been primarily in Western Europe, North America, Asia Pacific, and the Middle East. The company has five separate business units: Life & Savings, Property & Casualty, International Insurance, Asset Management, and Other Services. It is ranked as the ninth largest company in the world. From its headquarters in the 8th arrondissement of Paris, AXA coordinates the efforts of more than 128,000 employees and agents who service 96 million clients around the world.

As was to be expected, the global financial crisis hurt many financial institutions, especially insurance companies. One need only recall the American Insurance Group (AIG) catastrophe. Although not as dire,

AXA's financial standing was not immune to the effects of the economic downturn. How the company responded, however, is a testament to the complex nature of international finance strategy.

In 2008, at the height of the financial crisis, AXA announced that its earnings would suffer significantly and that its 2012 projections, essentially doubling its 2005 income, would be scrapped. In so doing, AXA simultaneously let it be known that it was looking for acquisitions in the South Korea and Hong Kong markets. While acknowledging the economic downturn, AXA focused on possible opportunities that the AIG fiasco had generated. AXA's overall strategy was to focus on growing emerging markets. As with other financial institutions, the company believed that the emerging markets had become the new competitive grounds. As part of that strategy, AXA was looking at AIG's Asian life insurance business. Consistent with its global emerging market strategy, in June 2008 AXA completed the acquisition of 36.7 percent of the share capital of RESO, Russia's second largest property and casualty insurer. In July of the same year, AXA completed the acquisition of Seguros ING (subsequently renamed AXA Seguros, SA de Compañia de Valores), the third largest Mexican insurer with leading positions in key markets such as motor and health and also active in the life insurance market. AXA ended the year by acquiring OYAK's 50 percent share in AXA OYAK, Turkey's largest property and casualty insurer, thereby consolidating its holdings.

In 2009, AXA announced the strengthening of its position in Central and Eastern Europe with the acquisition of minority interests held by the European Bank for Reconstruction and Development (EBRD) in AXA's Hungarian, Czech, and Polish subsidiaries, and a transaction, currently under negotiation, in which AXA would acquire 100 percent of AXA Asia-Pacific Holding's (AXA APH) Asian businesses while an Australian partner would acquire 100 percent of AXA APH's Australia and New Zealand businesses.

The changing of the name, the development of global operations in various countries, and the strategic investments in emerging markets reflect a sophisticated international business strategy that has permitted AXA to grow over the past 100 years. ●

Sources: AXA Annual Report, 2009; AXA Web site, www.axa.com.

Introduction

Our primary concern thus far in this book has been with aspects of the larger environment in which international businesses compete. As we have described it in the preceding chapters, this environment has included the different political, economic, and cultural institutions found in nations, the international trade and investment framework, and the international monetary system. Now our focus shifts from the environment to the firm itself and, in particular, to the actions managers can take to compete more effectively as an international business. In this chapter, we look at how firms can increase their profitability by expanding their operations in foreign markets. We discuss the different strategies that firms pursue when competing internationally. We consider the pros and cons of these strategies. We discuss the various factors that affect a firm's choice of strategy. We also look at why firms often enter into strategic alliances with their global competitors, and we discuss the benefits, costs, and risks of strategic alliances.

AXA, profiled in the opening case, gives us a preview of some issues that we will explore in this chapter. Like many other companies, AXA moved into other countries because it saw huge opportunities for growth. It thought it could create value by transferring AXA's financial expertise, products, and services to a large percentage of the world's markets. International business strategy many times requires a new identity. When it changed its name to AXA, the company embarked on that international strategy. As it expanded, AXA permitted each country unit to essentially operate independently of the parent. But as we will come to learn, even the best international strategies are not adequate protection for global market forces that go awry. In the case of AXA, it sought to take advantage of those that did not do as well. Some of the various reasons it may have chosen those specific acquisitions and investments in those particular countries is the subject of this chapter. As we shall see later in the chapter, many other companies, especially those within the manufacturing sector, have taken a different tact, moving from what can be characterized as *localization strategy*, where local country managers have considerable autonomy over manufacturing and marketing to *global strategy*, where the corporate center exercises more control over manufacturing, marketing, and product development decisions. As we shall see later in this chapter, many other companies have made a similar shift in the last two decades, moving from what can be characterized as a *localization strategy*, where local country managers have considerable autonomy over manufacturing and marketing, to a *global strategy*, where the corporate center exercises more control over manufacturing, marketing, and product development decisions. The tendency to make such a shift in many international businesses is a response to the globalization of markets, a phenomenon that we first discussed in Chapter 1. We shall discuss this process later in the chapter. To begin, however, we need to define exactly what we mean by strategy.

Strategy and The Firm

Before we discuss the strategies that managers in the multinational enterprise can pursue, we need to review some basic principles of strategy. A firm's **strategy** can be defined as the actions that managers take to attain the goals of the firm. For most firms, the preeminent goal is to maximize the value of the firm for its owners, its shareholders (subject to the very important constraint that this is done in a legal, ethical, and socially responsible manner—see Chapter 5 for details). To maximize the value of a firm, managers must pursue strategies that increase the *profitability* of the enterprise and its rate of *profit growth* over time (see Figure 11.1). **Profitability** can be measured in a number of ways, but for consistency, we shall define it as the rate of return that the firm makes on its invested capital (ROIC), which is calculated by dividing the net profits of the firm by

LEARNING OBJECTIVE 1
Explain the concept of strategy.

Strategy
Actions managers take to attain the firm's goals.

Profitability
A ratio or rate of return concept, calculated by dividing the net profits of the firm by total invested capital.

figure 11.1

Determinants of Enterprise Value

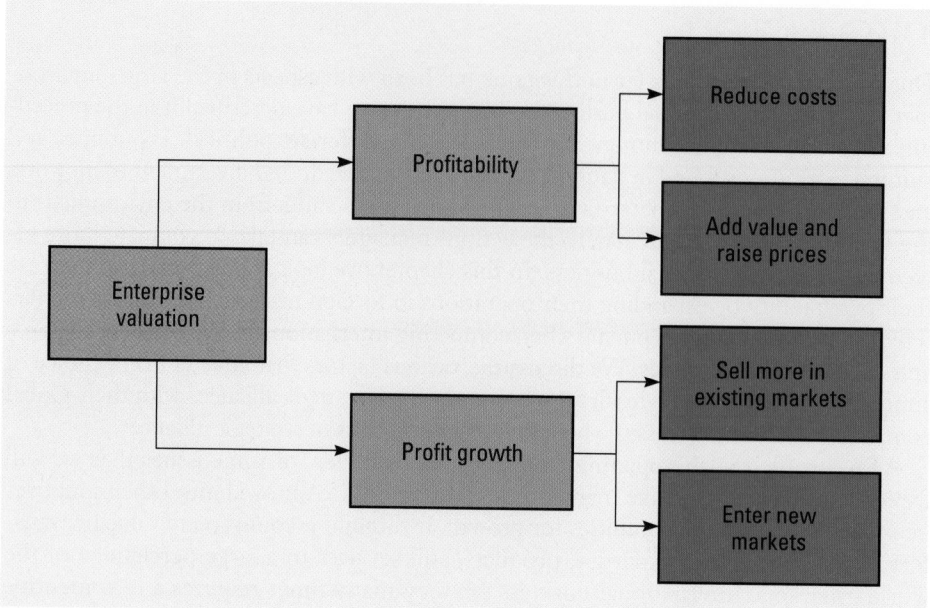

total invested capital.[1] **Profit growth** is measured by the percentage increase in net profits over time. In general, higher profitability and a higher rate of profit growth will increase the value of an enterprise and thus the returns garnered by its owners, the shareholders.[2]

Managers can increase the profitability of the firm by pursuing strategies that lower costs or by pursuing strategies that add value to the firm's products, which enables the firm to raise prices. Managers can increase the rate at which the firm's profits grow over time by pursuing strategies to sell more products in existing markets or by pursuing strategies to enter new markets. As we shall see, expanding internationally can help managers boost the firm's profitability *and* increase the rate of profit growth over time.

VALUE CREATION The way to increase the profitability of a firm is to create more value. The amount of value a firm creates is measured by the difference between its costs of production and the value that consumers perceive in its products. In general, the more value customers place on a firm's products, the higher the price the firm can charge for those products. However, the price a firm charges for a good or service is typically less than the value placed on that good or service by the customer. This is because the customer captures some of that value in the form of what economists call a consumer surplus.[3] The customer is able to do this because the firm is competing with other firms for the customer's business, so the firm must charge a lower price than it could were it a monopoly supplier. Also, it is normally impossible to segment the market to such a degree that the firm can charge each customer a price that reflects that individual's assessment of the value of a product, which economists refer to as a customer's reservation price. For these reasons, the price that gets charged tends to be less than the value placed on the product by many customers.

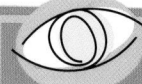

Another Perspective

Education as a Part of Your Value Chain
The concept of value chain can be used to examine the role your undergraduate education plays in your life plans. If you look closely at your personal development plans (education, internship, physical and emotional/spiritual fitness, extracurricular activities) and think about them in terms of primary and support activities, how does your choice of major fit into your personal development strategy? How do your choices of how you spend your time fit into your value chain? Do you ever spend time doing things that don't support the strategic goals of your personal value chain?

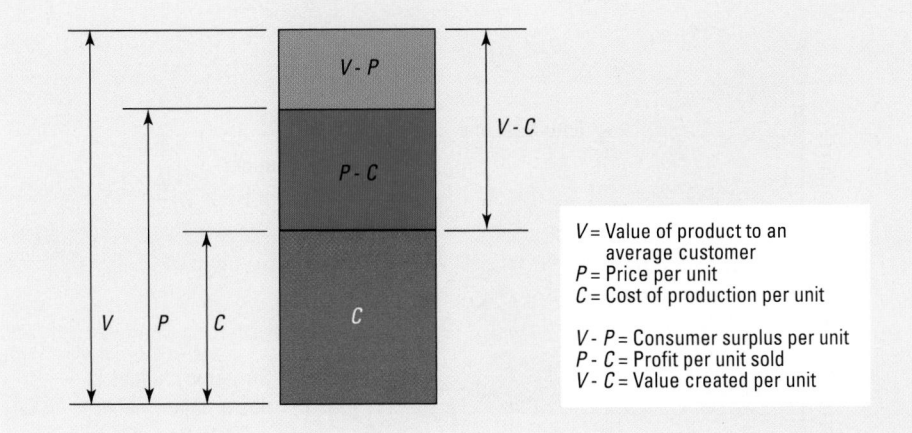

V = Value of product to an
      average customer
P = Price per unit
C = Cost of production per unit

$V - P$ = Consumer surplus per unit
$P - C$ = Profit per unit sold
$V - C$ = Value created per unit

Figure 11.2 illustrates these concepts. The value of a product to an *average* consumer is V; the average price that the firm can charge a consumer for that product given competitive pressures and its ability to segment the market is P; and the average unit cost of producing that product is C (C comprises all relevant costs, including the firm's cost of capital). The firm's profit per unit sold (π) is equal to $P - C$, while the consumer surplus per unit is equal to $V - P$ (another way of thinking of the consumer surplus is as "value for the money"; the greater the consumer surplus, the greater the value for the money the consumer gets). The firm makes a profit so long as P is greater than C, and its profit will be greater the lower C is *relative* to P. The difference between V and P is in part determined by the intensity of competitive pressure in the marketplace; the lower the intensity of competitive pressure, the higher the price charged relative to V.[4] In general, the higher the firm's profit per unit sold, the greater its profitability will be, all else being equal.

The firm's **value creation** is measured by the difference between V and C ($V - C$); a company creates value by converting inputs that cost C into a product on which consumers place a value of V. A company can create more value ($V - C$) either by lowering production costs, C, or by making the product more attractive through superior design, styling, functionality, features, reliability, after-sales service, and the like, so that consumers place a greater value on it (V increases) and, consequently, are willing to pay a higher price (P increases). This discussion suggests that *a firm has high profits when it creates more value for its customers and does so at a lower cost.* We refer to a strategy that focuses primarily on lowering production costs as a *low-cost strategy.* We refer to a strategy that focuses primarily on increasing the attractiveness of a product as a *differentiation strategy.*[5] Coca-Cola primarily focuses on the differentiation side of this equation—it tried to differentiate itself from rivals by brand-building advertisements.

Michael Porter has argued that *low cost* and *differentiation* are two basic strategies for creating value and attaining a competitive advantage in an industry.[6] According to Porter, superior profitability goes to those firms that can create superior value, and the way to create superior value is to drive down the cost structure of the business and/or differentiate the product in some way so that consumers value it more and are prepared to pay a premium price. Superior value creation relative to rivals does not necessarily require a firm to have the lowest cost structure in an industry, or to create the most valuable product in the eyes of consumers. However, it does require that the gap between value (V) and cost of production (C) be greater than the gap attained by competitors.

Value Creation
Performing activities that increase the value of goods or services to consumers.

figure **11.3**

Strategic Choice in
the International
Hotel Industry

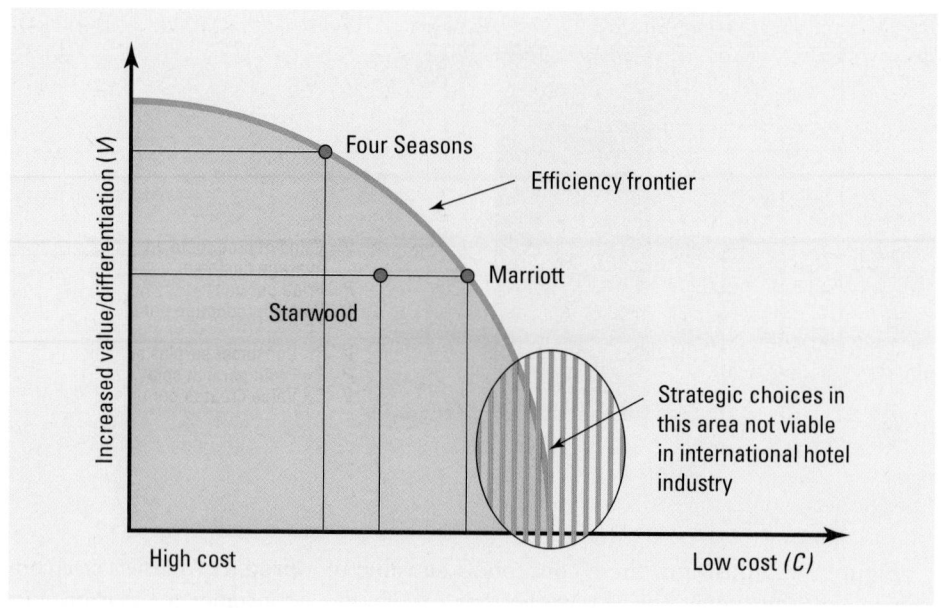

STRATEGIC POSITIONING

Porter notes that it is important for a firm to be explicit about its choice of strategic emphasis with regard to value creation (differentiation) and low cost, and to configure its internal operations to support that strategic emphasis.[7] Figure 11.3 illustrates his point. The convex curve in Figure 11.3 is what economists refer to as an efficiency frontier. The efficiency frontier shows all the different positions a firm can adopt with regard to adding value to the product (V) and lowering cost (C) assuming that its internal operations are configured efficiently to support a particular position (note that the horizontal axis in Figure 11.3 is reverse scaled—moving along the axis to the right implies lower costs). The efficiency frontier has a convex shape because of diminishing returns. Diminishing returns imply that when a firm already has significant value built into its product offering, increasing value by a relatively small amount requires significant additional costs. The converse also holds, when a firm already has a low-cost structure, it has to give up a lot of value in its product offering to get additional cost reductions.

Three hotel firms with a global presence that cater to international travelers are plotted on Figure 11.3—Four Seasons, Marriott International, and Starwood (Starwood owns the Sheraton and Westin chains). Four Seasons positions itself as a luxury chain and emphasizes the value of its product offering, which drives up its costs of operations. Marriott and Starwood are positioned more in the middle of the market. Both emphasize sufficient value to attract international business travelers, but are not luxury chains like Four Seasons. In Figure 11.3, Four Seasons and Marriott are shown to be on the efficiency frontier, indicating that their internal operations are well configured to their strategy and run efficiently. Starwood is inside the frontier, indicating that its operations are not running as efficiently as they might be, and that its costs are too high. This implies that Starwood is less profitable than Four Seasons and Marriott, and that its managers must take steps to improve the company's performance.

Porter emphasizes that it is very important for management to decide where the company wants to be positioned with regard to value (V) and cost (C), to configure operations accordingly, and to manage them efficiently to make sure the firm is operating on the efficiency frontier. However, not all positions on the efficiency frontier are viable. In the international hotel industry, for example, there might not be enough demand to support a chain that emphasizes very low cost and strips all the value out of its product offering (see Figure 11.3). International travelers are relatively affluent and expect a degree of comfort (value) when they travel.

A central tenet of the basic strategy paradigm is that to maximize its profitability, a firm must do three things: (*a*) pick a position on the efficiency frontier that is viable in the sense that there is enough demand to support that choice; (*b*) configure its internal operations, such as manufacturing, marketing, logistics, information systems, human resources, and so on, so that they support that position; and (*c*) make sure the firm has the right organization structure in place to execute its strategy. *The strategy, operations, and organization of the firm must all be consistent with each other if it is to attain a competitive advantage and garner superior profitability.* By **operations** we mean the different value creation activities a firm undertakes, which we shall review next.

Operations
The various value creation activities a firm undertakes.

OPERATIONS: THE FIRM AS A VALUE CHAIN
The operations of a firm can be thought of as a value chain composed of a series of distinct value creation activities including production, marketing and sales, materials management, R&D, human resources, information systems, and the firm infrastructure. We can categorize these value creation activities, or operations, as primary activities and support activities (see Figure 11.4).[8] As noted above, if a firm is to implement its strategy efficiently, and position itself on the efficiency frontier shown in Figure 11.3, it must manage these activities effectively and in a manner that is consistent with its strategy.

Primary Activities
Primary activities have to do with the design, creation, and delivery of the product; its marketing; and its support and after-sale service. Following normal practice, in the value chain illustrated in Figure 11.4, the primary activities are divided into four functions: research and development, production, marketing and sales, and customer service.

Research and development (R&D) is concerned with the design of products and production processes. Although we think of R&D as being associated with the design of physical products and production processes in manufacturing enterprises, many service companies also undertake R&D. For example, banks compete with each other by developing new financial products and new ways of delivering those products to customers. Online banking and smart debit cards are two examples of product development in the banking industry. Earlier examples of innovation in the banking industry included automated teller machines, credit cards, and debit cards. Through superior

11.4 figure

The Value Chain

Support activities

Company infrastructure

Information systems   Logistics   Human resources

R&D   Production   Marketing and sales   Customer service

Primary activities

product design, R&D can increase the functionality of products, which makes them more attractive to consumers (raising V). Alternatively, R&D may result in more efficient production processes, thereby cutting production costs (lowering C). Either way, the R&D function can create value.

Production is concerned with the creation of a good or service. For physical products, when we talk about production we generally mean manufacturing. Thus, we can talk about the production of an automobile. For services such as banking or health care, "production" typically occurs when the service is delivered to the customer (for example, when a bank originates a loan for a customer it is engaged in "production" of the loan). For a retailer such as Walmart, "production" is concerned with selecting the merchandise, stocking the store, and ringing up the sale at the cash register. For MTV, production is concerned with the creation, programming, and broadcasting of content, such as music videos and thematic shows. The production activity of a firm creates value by performing its activities efficiently so lower costs result (lower C) and/or by performing them in such a way that a higher-quality product is produced (which results in higher V).

The marketing and sales functions of a firm can help to create value in several ways. Through brand positioning and advertising, the marketing function can increase the value (V) that consumers perceive to be contained in a firm's product. If these create a favorable impression of the firm's product in the minds of consumers, they increase the price that can be charged for the firm's product. For example, Ford has produced a high-value version of its Ford Expedition SUV. Sold as the Lincoln Navigator and priced around $10,000 higher, the Navigator has the same body, engine, chassis, and design as the Expedition, but through skilled advertising and marketing, supported by some fairly minor features changes (e.g., more accessories and the addition of a Lincoln-style engine grille and nameplate), Ford has fostered the perception that the Navigator is a "luxury SUV." This marketing strategy has increased the perceived value (V) of the Navigator relative to the Expedition, and enables Ford to charge a higher price (P) for the car.

Marketing and sales can also create value by discovering consumer needs and communicating them back to the R&D function of the company, which can then design products that better match those needs. For example, the allocation of research budgets at Pfizer, the world's largest pharmaceutical company, is determined by the marketing function's assessment of the potential market size associated with solving unmet medical needs. Thus, Pfizer is currently directing significant monies to R&D efforts aimed at finding treatments for Alzheimer's disease, principally because marketing has identified the treatment of Alzheimer's as a major unmet medical need in nations around the world where the population is aging.

The role of the enterprise's service activity is to provide after-sale service and support. This function can create a perception of superior value (V) in the minds of consumers by solving customer problems and supporting customers after they have purchased the product. Caterpillar, the U.S.-based manufacturer of heavy earthmoving equipment, can get spare parts to any point in the world within 24 hours, thereby minimizing the amount of downtime its customers have to suffer if their Caterpillar equipment malfunctions. This is an extremely valuable capability in an industry where downtime is very expensive. It has helped to increase the value that customers associate with Caterpillar products and thus the price that Caterpillar can charge.

Support Activities   The support activities of the value chain provide inputs that allow the primary activities to occur (see Figure 11.4). In terms of attaining a competitive advantage, support activities can be as important as, if not more important than, the "primary" activities of the firm. Consider information systems; these systems refer to the electronic systems for managing inventory, tracking sales, pricing products, selling products, dealing with customer service inquiries, and so on. Information systems, when coupled with the communications features of the Internet, can alter the efficiency and effectiveness with which a firm manages its other value creation activities. Dell, for example, has used its information systems to attain a competitive advantage over rivals. When customers place an order for a Dell product over the firm's Web site, that information is immediately transmitted, via the Internet, to suppliers, who then configure their production schedules to produce and ship that product so that it arrives at the right assembly plant at the right time. These systems have reduced the amount of inventory that Dell holds at its factories to under two days, which is a major source of cost savings.

The logistics function controls the transmission of physical materials through the value chain, from procurement through production and into distribution. The efficiency with which this is carried out can significantly reduce cost (lower C), thereby creating more value. The combination of logistics systems and information systems is a particularly potent source of cost savings in many enterprise, such as Dell, where information systems tell Dell on a real-time basis where in its global logistics network parts are, when they will arrive at an assembly plant, and how production should be scheduled.

The human resource function can help create more value in a number of ways. It ensures that the company has the right mix of skilled people to perform its value creation activities effectively. The human resource function also ensures that people are adequately trained, motivated, and compensated to perform their value creation tasks. In a multinational enterprise, one of the things human resources can do to boost the competitive position of the firm is to take advantage of its transnational reach to identify, recruit, and develop a cadre of skilled managers, regardless of their nationality, who can be groomed to take on senior management positions. They can find the very best, wherever they are in the world. The senior management ranks of many multinationals are becoming increasingly diverse, as managers from a variety of national backgrounds have ascended to senior leadership positions. Japan's Sony, for example, is now headed not by a Japanese national, but by Howard Stringer, a Welshman.

The final support activity is the company infrastructure, or the context within which all the other value creation activities occur. The infrastructure includes the organizational structure, control systems, and culture of the firm. Because top management can exert considerable influence in shaping these aspects of a firm, top management should also be viewed as part of the firm's infrastructure. Through strong leadership, top management can consciously shape the infrastructure of a firm and through that the performance of all its value creation activities.

ORGANIZATION: THE IMPLEMENTATION OF STRATEGY

The strategy of a firm is implemented through its organization. For a firm to have superior ROIC, its organization must support it strategy and operations. The term **organization architecture** can be used to refer to the totality of a firm's organization, including formal organizational structure, control systems and incentives, organizational culture, processes, and people.[9] Figure 11.5 illustrates these different elements. By **organizational structure,** we mean three things: First, the formal division of the organization into subunits such as product divisions, national operations, and functions (most organizational charts display this aspect of structure); second, the location of decision-making responsibilities within that structure (e.g., centralized or decentralized); and third, the establishment of integrating mechanisms to coordinate the activities of subunits including cross functional teams and or pan-regional committees.

Organization Architecture
The totality of a firm's organization, including formal organizational structure, control systems and incentives, organizational culture, processes, and people.

Organizational Structure
The three-part structure of an organization, including its formal division into subunits such as product divisions, its location of decision-making responsibilities within that structure, and the establishment of integrating mechanisms to coordinate the activities of subunits.

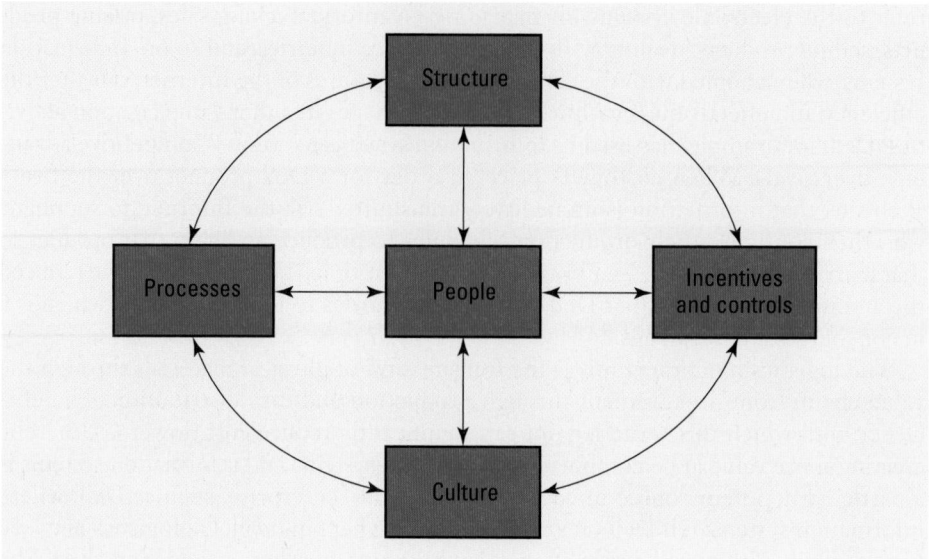

Controls

The metrics used to measure the performance of subunits and make judgments about how well managers are running those subunits.

Incentives

The devices used to reward appropriate managerial behavior.

Processes

The manner in which decisions are made and work is performed within the organization.

Organizational Culture

The norms and value systems shared among an organization's employees.

People

The employees of an organization, its recruiting, compensation, and retention strategies, and the type of people who work at the organization.

Controls are the metrics used to measure the performance of subunits and make judgments about how well managers are running those subunits. **Incentives** are the devices used to reward appropriate managerial behavior. Incentives are very closely tied to performance metrics. For example, the incentives of a manager in charge of a national operating subsidiary might be linked to the performance of that company. Specifically, she might receive a bonus if her subsidiary exceeds its performance targets.

Processes are the manner in which decisions are made and work is performed within the organization. Examples are the processes for formulating strategy, for deciding how to allocate resources within a firm, or for evaluating the performance of managers and giving feedback. Processes are conceptually distinct from the location of decision-making responsibilities within an organization, although both involve decisions. While the CEO might have ultimate responsibility for deciding what the strategy of the firm should be (i.e., the decision-making responsibility is centralized), the process he or she uses to make that decision might include the solicitation of ideas and criticism from lower-level managers.

Organizational culture is the norms and value systems that are shared among the employees of an organization. Just as societies have cultures (see Chapter 3 for details), so do organizations. Organizations are societies of individuals who come together to perform collective tasks. They have their own distinctive patterns of culture and sub-culture.[10] As we shall see, organizational culture can have a profound impact on how a firm performs. Finally, by **people** we mean not just the employees of the organization, but also the strategy used to recruit, compensate, and retain those individuals and the type of people that they are in terms of their skills, values, and orientation (discussed in depth in Chapter 16).

As illustrated by the arrows in Figure 11.5, the various components of an organization's architecture are not independent of each other: Each component shapes, and is shaped by, other components of architecture. An obvious example is the strategy regarding people. This can be used proactively to hire individuals whose internal values are consistent with those that the firm wishes to emphasize in its organization culture. Thus, the people component of architecture can be used to reinforce (or not) the prevailing culture of the organization.

If a firm is going to maximize its profitability, it must pay close attention to opportunities between the various components of its internal architecture and the external opportunity at hand. For illustration, again consider AXA. To take advantage of the global process occurring early on and the subsequent global recession, then CEO Claude Bébéar and subsequent leadership found that they had to not only improve the global "look" by changing the name but also recognize and pursue the opportunities in emerging markets. In other words, they had to change the structure and organization of AXA so that it matched the new realities of the global crisis.

IN SUM: STRATEGIC FIT   In sum, as we have repeatedly stressed, for a firm to attain superior performance and earn a high return on capita, its strategy (as captured by its desired strategic position on the efficiency frontier) must make sense given market conditions (there must be sufficient demand to support that strategic choice). The operations of the firm must be configured in a way that supports the strategy of the firm, and the organization architecture of the firm must match the operations and strategy of the firm. In other words, as illustrated in Figure 11.6, market conditions, strategy, operations, and organization must all be consistent with each other, or fit each other, for superior performance to be attained.

Of course, the issue is more complex than illustrated in Figure 11.6. For example, the firm can influence market conditions through its choice of strategy—it can create demand by leveraging core skills to create new market opportunities. In addition, shifts in market conditions caused by new technologies, government action such as deregulation, demographics, or social trends can mean that the strategy of the firm no longer fits the market. In such circumstances, the firm must change its strategy, operations, and organization to fit the new reality, which can be extraordinarily difficult. And last but by no means least, international expansion adds an additional layer of complexity to the strategic challenges facing the firm. We shall now consider this.

11.6 figure

Strategic Fit

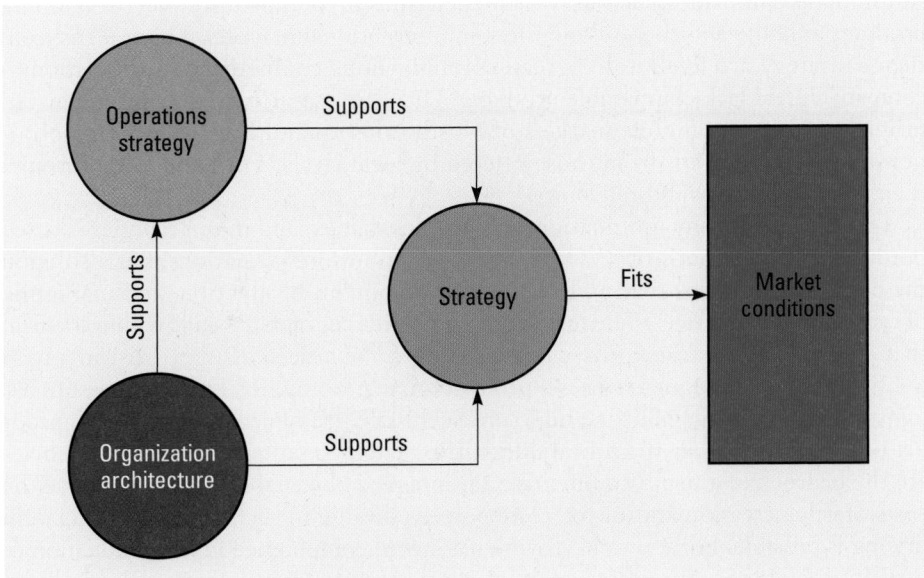

Global Expansion, Profitability, and Profit Growth

LEARNING OBJECTIVE 2
Recognize how firms can profit by expanding globally.

Expanding globally allows firms to increase their profitability and rate of profit growth in ways not available to purely domestic enterprises.[11] Firms that operate internationally are able to:

1. Expand the market for their domestic product offerings by selling those products in international markets.
2. Realize location economies by dispersing individual value creation activities to those locations around the globe where they can be performed most efficiently and effectively.
3. Realize greater cost economies from experience effects by serving an expanded global market from a central location, thereby reducing the costs of value creation.
4. Earn a greater return by leveraging any valuable skills developed in foreign operations and transferring them to other entities within the firm's global network of operations.

As we will see, however, a firm's ability to increase its profitability and profit growth by pursuing these strategies is constrained by the need to customize its product offering, marketing strategy, and business strategy to differing national conditions; that is, by the imperative of localization.

EXPANDING THE MARKET: LEVERAGING PRODUCTS AND COMPETENCIES

A company can increase its growth rate by taking goods or services developed at home and selling them internationally. Almost all multinationals started out doing just this. For example, Procter & Gamble developed most of its best-selling products such as Pampers disposable diapers and Ivory soap in the United States, and subsequently then sold them around the world. Likewise, although Microsoft developed its software in the United States, from its earliest days the company has always focused on selling that software in international markets. Automobile companies such as Volkswagen and Toyota also grew by developing products at home and then selling them in international markets. The returns from such a strategy are likely to be greater if indigenous competitors in the nations a company enters lack comparable products. Thus, Toyota increased its profits by entering the large automobile markets of North America and Europe, offering products that were different from those offered by local rivals (Ford and GM) through their superior quality and reliability.

Core Competence
A firm's skills that competitors cannot easily match or imitate.

The success of many multinational companies that expand in this manner is based not just upon the goods or services that they sell in foreign nations, but also upon the core competencies that underlie the development, production, and marketing of those goods or services. The term **core competence** refers to skills within the firm that competitors cannot easily match or imitate.[12] These skills may exist in any of the firm's value creation activities—production, marketing, R&D, human resources, logistics, general management, and so on. Such skills are typically expressed in product offerings that other firms find difficult to match or imitate. Core competencies are the bedrock of a firm's competitive advantage. They enable a firm to reduce the costs of value creation and/or to create perceived value in such a way that premium pricing is possible. For example, Toyota has a core competence in the production of cars. It is able to produce high-quality, well-designed cars at a lower delivered cost than any other firm in the world. The competencies that enable Toyota to do this seem to reside primarily in the firm's production and logistics functions.[13] McDonald's has a core competence in managing fast-food operations (it seems to be one of the most skilled firms in the world in this industry); Procter & Gamble has a core competence in developing and marketing name brand consumer products (it is one of the most skilled firms in the world in this business); Starbucks has a core competence in the management of retail outlets selling high volumes of freshly brewed coffee-based drinks.

Since core competencies are by definition the source of a firm's competitive advantage, the successful global expansion by manufacturing companies such as Toyota and P&G was based not just on leveraging products and selling them in foreign markets, but also on the transfer of core competencies to foreign markets where indigenous competitors lacked them. The same can be said of companies engaged in the service sectors of an economy, such as financial institutions, retailers, restaurant chains, and hotels. Expanding the market for their services often means replicating their business model in foreign nations (albeit with some changes to account for local differences, which we will discuss in more detail soon). Starbucks, for example, is expanding rapidly outside of the United States by taking the basic business model it developed at home and using that as a blueprint for establishing international operations. Similarly, McDonald's is famous for its international expansion strategy, which has taken the company into more than 120 nations that collectively generate over half of the company's revenues.

LOCATION ECONOMIES   We know from earlier chapters that countries differ along a range of dimensions, including the economic, political, legal, and cultural, and that these differences can either raise or lower the costs of doing business in a country. The theory of international trade also teaches us that due to differences in factor costs, certain countries have a comparative advantage in the production of certain products. Japan might excel in the production of automobiles and consumer electronics; the United States in the production of computer software, pharmaceuticals, biotechnology products, and financial services; Switzerland in the production of precision instruments and pharmaceuticals; South Korea in the production of semiconductors; and China in the production of apparel.[14]

For a firm that is trying to survive in a competitive global market, this implies that *trade barriers and transportation costs* permitting, the firm will benefit by basing each value creation activity it performs at that location where economic, political, and cultural conditions, including relative factor costs, are most conducive to the performance of that activity. Thus, if the best designers for a product live in France, a firm should base its design operations in France. If the most productive labor force for assembly operations is in Mexico, assembly operations should be based in Mexico. If the best marketers are in the United States, the marketing strategy should be formulated in the United States. And so on.

Firms that pursue such a strategy can realize what we refer to as **location economies,** which are the economies that arise from performing a value creation activity in the optimal location for that activity, wherever in the world that might be (transportation costs and trade barriers permitting). Locating a value creation activity in the optimal location for that activity can have one of two effects. *It can lower the costs of value creation and help the firm to achieve a low-cost position, and/or it can enable a firm to differentiate its product offering from those of competitors.* In terms of Figure 11.2, it can lower C and/or increase V (which in general supports higher pricing), both of which boost the profitability of the enterprise.

For an example of how this works in an international business, consider Clear Vision, a manufacturer and distributor of eyewear. Started in the 1980s by David Glassman, the

Location Economies
Cost advantages from performing a value creation activity in the optimal location for that activity.

firm now generates annual gross revenues of more than \$100 million. Not exactly small, but no corporate giant either, Clear Vision is a multinational firm with production facilities on three continents and customers around the world. Clear Vision began its move toward becoming a multinational in the 1980s. The strong dollar at that time made U.S.-based manufacturing very expensive. Low-priced imports were taking an ever-larger share of the U.S. eyewear market, and Clear Vision realized it could not survive unless it also began to import. Initially the firm bought from independent overseas manufacturers, primarily in Hong Kong. However, the firm became dissatisfied with these suppliers' product quality and delivery. As Clear Vision's volume of imports increased, Glassman decided the best way to guarantee quality and delivery was to set up Clear Vision's own manufacturing operation overseas. Accordingly, Clear Vision found a Chinese partner, and together they opened a manufacturing facility in Hong Kong, with Clear Vision being the majority shareholder.

The choice of the Hong Kong location was influenced by its combination of low labor costs, a skilled workforce, and tax breaks given by the Hong Kong government. The firm's objective at this point was to lower production costs by locating value creation activities at an appropriate location. After a few years, however, the increasing industrialization of Hong Kong and a growing labor shortage had pushed up wage rates to the extent that it was no longer a low-cost location. In response, Glassman and his Chinese partner moved part of their manufacturing to a plant in mainland China to take advantage of the lower wage rates there. Again, the goal was to lower production costs. The parts for eyewear frames manufactured at this plant are shipped to the Hong Kong factory for final assembly and then distributed to markets in North and South America. The Hong Kong factory now employs 80 people and the China plant between 300 and 400.

At the same time, Clear Vision was looking for opportunities to invest in foreign eyewear firms with reputations for fashionable design and high quality. Its objective was not to reduce production costs but to launch a line of high-quality differentiated, "designer" eyewear. Clear Vision did not have the design capability in-house to support such a line, but Glassman knew that certain foreign manufacturers did. As a result, Clear Vision invested in factories in Japan, France, and Italy, holding a minority shareholding in each case. These factories now supply eyewear for Clear Vision's Status Eye division, which markets high-priced designer eyewear.[15]

Thus, to deal with a threat from foreign competition, Clear Vision adopted a strategy intended to lower its cost structure (lower C): shifting its production from a high-cost location, the United States, to a low-cost location, first Hong Kong and later China. Then Clear Vision adopted a strategy intended to increase the perceived value of its product (increase V) so it could charge a premium price (P). Reasoning that premium pricing in eyewear depended on superior design, its strategy involved investing capital in French, Italian, and Japanese factories that had reputations for superior design. In sum, Clear Vision's strategies included some actions intended to reduce its costs of creating value and other actions intended to add perceived value to its product through differentiation. The overall goal was to increase the value created by Clear Vision and thus the profitability of the enterprise. To the extent that these strategies were successful, the firm should have attained a higher profit margin and greater profitability than if it had remained a U.S.-based manufacturer of eyewear.

Global Web
When different stages of the value chain are dispersed to those locations around the globe where value added is maximized or where costs of value creation are minimized.

Creating a Global Web
Generalizing from the Clear Vision example, one result of this kind of thinking is the creation of a **global web** of value creation activities, with different stages of the value chain being dispersed to those locations around

the globe where perceived value is maximized or where the costs of value creation are minimized.[16] Consider Lenovo's ThinkPad laptop computers (Lenovo is the Chinese computer company that purchased IBM's personal computer operations in 2005).[17] This product is designed in the United States by engineers because Lenovo believes that the United States is the best location in the world to do the basic design work. The case, keyboard, and hard drive are made in Thailand; the display screen and memory in South Korea; the built-in wireless card in Malaysia; and the microprocessor in the United States. In each case, these components are manufactured and sourced from the optimal location given current factor costs. These components are than shipped to an assembly operation in Mexico, where the product is assembled before being shipped to the United States for final sale. Lenovo assembles the ThinkPad in Mexico because managers have calculated that due to low labor costs, the costs of assembly can be minimized there. The marketing and sales strategy for North America is developed by Lenovo personnel in the United States, primarily because managers believe that due to their knowledge of the local marketplace, U.S. personnel add more value to the product through their marketing efforts than personnel based elsewhere.

In theory, a firm that realizes location economies by dispersing each of its value creation activities to its optimal location should have a competitive advantage vis-à-vis a firm that bases all of its value creation activities at a single location. It should be able to better differentiate its product offering (thereby raising perceived value, V) and lower its cost structure (C) than its single-location competitor. In a world where competitive pressures are increasing, such a strategy may become an imperative for survival.

Some Caveats   Introducing transportation costs and trade barriers complicates this picture. Due to favorable factor endowments, New Zealand may have a comparative advantage for automobile assembly operations, but high transportation costs would make it an uneconomical location from which to serve global markets. Another caveat concerns the importance of assessing political and economic risks when making location decisions. Even if a country looks very attractive as a production location when measured against all the standard criteria, if its government is unstable or totalitarian, the firm might be advised not to base production there. (Political risk is discussed in Chapter 2.) Similarly, if the government appears to be pursuing inappropriate economic policies that could lead to foreign exchange risk, that might be another reason for not basing production in that location, even if other factors look favorable.

EXPERIENCE EFFECTS   The **experience curve** refers to systematic reductions in production costs that have been observed to occur over the life of a product.[18] A number of studies have observed that a product's production costs decline by some quantity about each time *cumulative* output doubles. The relationship was first observed in the aircraft industry, where each time cumulative output of airframes was doubled, unit costs typically declined to 80 percent of their previous level.[19] Thus, production cost for the fourth airframe would be 80 percent of production cost for the second airframe, the eighth airframe's production costs 80 percent of the fourth's, the sixteenth's 80 percent of the eighth's, and so on. Figure 11.7 illustrates this experience curve relationship between unit production costs and *cumulative* output (the relationship is for *cumulative* output over time, and *not* output in any one period, such as a year). Two things explain this: learning effects and economies of scale.

Experience Curve
Systematic production cost reductions that occur over the life of a product.

figure **11.7**

The Experience Curve

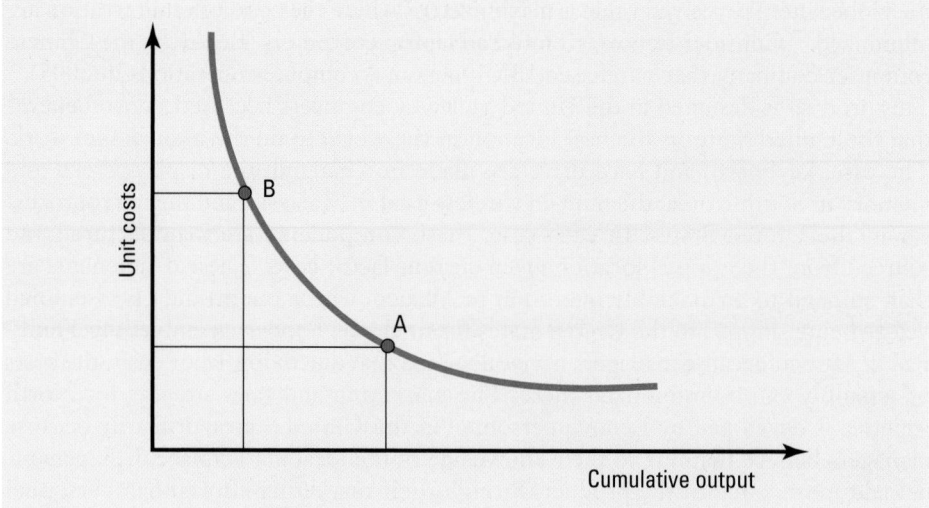

Learning Effects

Learning Effects Cost savings from learning by doing.

Learning Effects **Learning effects** refer to cost savings that come from learning by doing. Labor, for example, learns by repetition how to carry out a task, such as assembling airframes, most efficiently. Labor productivity increases over time as individuals learn the most efficient ways to perform particular tasks. Equally important, in new production facilities, management typically learns how to manage the new operation more efficiently over time. Hence, production costs decline due to increasing labor productivity and management efficiency, which increases the firm's profitability.

Learning effects tend to be more significant when a technologically complex task is repeated, because there is more that can be learned about the task. Thus, learning effects will be more significant in an assembly process involving 1,000 complex steps than in one of only 100 simple steps. No matter how complex the task, however, learning effects typically disappear after a while. It has been suggested that they are important only during the start-up period of a new process and that they cease after two or three years.[20] Any decline in the experience curve after such a point is due to economies of scale.

Economies of Scale

Economies of Scale Cost advantages associated with large-scale production.

Economies of Scale **Economies of scale** refer to the reductions in unit cost achieved by producing a large volume of a product. Attaining economies of scale lowers a firm's unit costs and increases its profitability. Economies of scale have a number of sources. One is the ability to spread fixed costs over a large volume.[21] Fixed costs are the costs required to set up a production facility, develop a new product, and the like. They can be substantial. For example, the fixed cost of establishing a new production line to manufacture semiconductor chips now exceeds $1 billion. Similarly, according to one estimate, developing a new drug and bringing it to market costs about $800 million and takes about 12 years.[22] The only way to recoup such high fixed costs may be to sell the product worldwide, which reduces average unit costs by spreading fixed costs over a larger volume. The more rapidly that cumulative sales volume is built up, the more rapidly fixed costs can be amortized over a large production volume, and the more rapidly unit costs will fall.

Second, a firm may not be able to attain an efficient scale of production unless it serves global markets. In the automobile industry, for example, an efficiently scaled factory is one designed to produce about 200,000 units a year. Automobile firms would prefer to produce a single model from each factory since this eliminates the costs associated with switching production from one model to another. If domestic demand for a particular model is only 100,000 units a year, the inability to attain a 200,000-unit output will drive up average unit costs. By serving international markets as well, however, the firm may be able to push production volume up to 200,000 units a year, thereby reaping greater scale economies, lowering unit costs, and boosting profitability. By serving domestic and international markets from its production facilities a firm may be able to utilize those facilities more intensively. For example, if Intel sold microprocessors only in the United States, it may only be able to keep its factories open for one shift, five days a week. By serving international markets from the same factories, Intel can utilize its productive assets more intensively, which translates into higher capital productivity and greater profitability.

Finally, as global sales increase the size of the enterprise, so its bargaining power with suppliers increases, which may allow it to attain economies of scale in purchasing, bargaining down the cost of key inputs and boosting profitability that way. For example, Walmart has been able to use its enormous sales volume as a lever to bargain down the price it pays suppliers for merchandise sold through its stores.

Strategic Significance   The strategic significance of the experience curve is clear. Moving down the experience curve allows a firm to reduce its cost of creating value (to lower C in Figure 11.2) and increase its profitability. The firm that moves down the experience curve most rapidly will have a cost advantage vis-à-vis its competitors. Firm A in Figure 11.7, because it is farther down the experience curve, has a clear cost advantage over firm B.

Many of the underlying sources of experience-based cost economies are plant based. This is true for most learning effects as well as for the economies of scale derived by spreading the fixed costs of building productive capacity over a large output, attaining an efficient scale of output, and utilizing a plant more intensively. Thus, one key to progressing downward on the experience curve as rapidly as possible is to increase the volume produced by a single plant as rapidly as possible. Because global markets are larger than domestic markets, a firm that serves a global market from a single location is likely to build accumulated volume more quickly than a firm that serves only its home market or that serves multiple markets from multiple production locations. Thus, serving a global market from a single location is consistent with moving down the experience curve and establishing a low-cost position. In addition, to get down the experience curve rapidly, a firm may need to price and market aggressively so demand will expand rapidly. It will also need to build sufficient production capacity for serving a global market. Also, the cost advantages of serving the world market from a single location will be even more significant if that location is the optimal one for performing the particular value creation activity.

Once a firm has established a low-cost position, it can act as a barrier to new competition. Specifically, an established firm that is well down the experience curve, such as firm A in Figure 11.7, can price so that it is still making a profit while new entrants, which are farther up the curve, are suffering losses.

The classic example of the successful pursuit of such a strategy concerns the Japanese consumer electronics company Matsushita. Along with Sony and Philips, Matsushita was in the race to develop a commercially viable videocassette recorder in the 1970s. Although Matsushita initially lagged behind Philips and Sony, it was able to get its VHS format accepted as the world standard and to reap enormous experience curve-based cost economies in the process. This cost advantage subsequently constituted a formidable barrier to new competition. Matsushita's strategy was to build global volume as rapidly as possible. To ensure it could accommodate worldwide demand, the firm increased its production capacity 33-fold from 205,000 units in 1977 to 6.8 million units by 1984. By serving the world market from a single location in Japan, Matsushita was able to realize significant learning effects and economies of scale. These allowed Matsushita to drop its prices 50 percent within five years of selling its first VHS-format VCR. As a result, Matsushita was the world's major VCR producer by 1983, accounting for about 45 percent of world production and enjoying a significant cost advantage over its competitors. The next largest firm, Hitachi, accounted for only 11.1 percent of world production in 1983.[23] Today, firms such as Intel are the masters of this kind of strategy. The costs of building a state-of-the-art facility to manufacture microprocessors are so large (now in excess of $2 billion) that to make this investment pay Intel *must* pursue experience curve effects, serving world markets from a limited number of plants to maximize the cost economies that derive from scale and learning effects.

LEVERAGING SUBSIDIARY SKILLS   Implicit in our earlier discussion of core competencies is the idea that valuable skills are developed first at home and then transferred to foreign operations. However, for more mature multinationals that have already established a network of subsidiary operations in foreign markets, the development of valuable skills can just as well occur in foreign subsidiaries.[24] Skills can be created anywhere within a multinational's global network of operations, wherever people have the opportunity and incentive to try new ways of doing things. The creation of skills that help to lower the costs of production, or to enhance perceived value and support higher product pricing, is not the monopoly of the corporate center.

Leveraging the skills created within subsidiaries and applying them to other operations within the firm's global network may create value. McDonald's increasingly is finding that its foreign franchisees are a source of valuable new ideas. Faced with slow growth in France, its local franchisees experimented not only with the menu, but also with the layout and theme of restaurants. Gone are the ubiquitous golden arches, gone too are many of the utilitarian chairs and tables and other plastic features of the fast-food giant. Many McDonald's restaurants in France now have hardwood floors, exposed brick walls, and even armchairs. Half of the 930 or so outlets in France have been upgraded to a level that would make them unrecognizable to an American. The menu, too, was changed to include premier sandwiches, such as chicken on focaccia bread, priced some 30 percent higher than the average hamburger. The strategy worked. Following the change, increases in same-store sales rose from 1 percent annually to 3.4 percent. Impressed with the impact, McDonald's executives considered similar changes at other McDonald's restaurants in markets where same-store sales growth was sluggish, including the United States.[25]

For the managers of the multinational enterprise, this phenomenon creates important new challenges. First, they must have the humility to recognize that valuable skills that lead to competencies can arise anywhere within the firm's global network, not just at the corporate center. Second, they must establish an incentive system that encourages local employees to acquire new skills. This is not as easy as it sounds. Creating new skills involves a degree of risk. Not all new skills add value. For every valuable idea created by a McDonald's subsidiary in a foreign country, there may be several failures. The management of the multinational must install incentives that encourage employees to take the necessary risks. The company must reward people for successes and not sanction them unnecessarily for taking risks that did not pan out. Third, managers must have a process for identifying when valuable new skills have been created in a subsidiary. And finally, they need to act as facilitators, helping to transfer valuable skills within the firm.

PROFITABILITY AND PROFIT GROWTH SUMMARY   We have seen how firms that expand globally can increase their profitability and profit growth by entering new markets where indigenous competitors lack similar competencies, by lowering costs and adding value to their product offering through the attainment of location economies, by exploiting experience curve effects, and by transferring valuable skills between their global network of subsidiaries. Strategies that increase profitability may also expand a firm's business, and thus enable it to attain a higher rate of profit growth. For example, by simultaneously realizing location economies and experience effects a firm may be able to produce a more highly valued product at a lower unit cost, thereby boosting profitability. The increase in the perceived value of the product may also attract more customers, thereby growing revenues and profits as well. Furthermore, rather than raising prices to reflect the higher perceived value of the product, the firm's managers may elect to hold prices low in order to increase global market share and attain greater scale economies (in other words, they may elect to offer consumers better "value for money"). Such a strategy could increase the firm's rate of profit growth even further, since consumers will be attracted by prices that are low relative to value. The strategy might also increase profitability if the scale economies that result from market share gains are substantial. In sum, managers need to keep in mind the complex relationship between profitability and profit growth when making strategic decisions about pricing.

Cost Pressures and Pressures for Local Responsiveness

Firms that compete in the global marketplace typically face two types of competitive pressures that affect their ability to realize location economies and experience effects, to leverage products and transfer competencies and skills within the enterprise. They face *pressures for cost reductions* and *pressures to be locally responsive* (see Figure 11.8).[26] These competitive pressures place conflicting demands on a firm. Responding to pressures for cost reductions requires that a firm try to minimize its unit costs. But

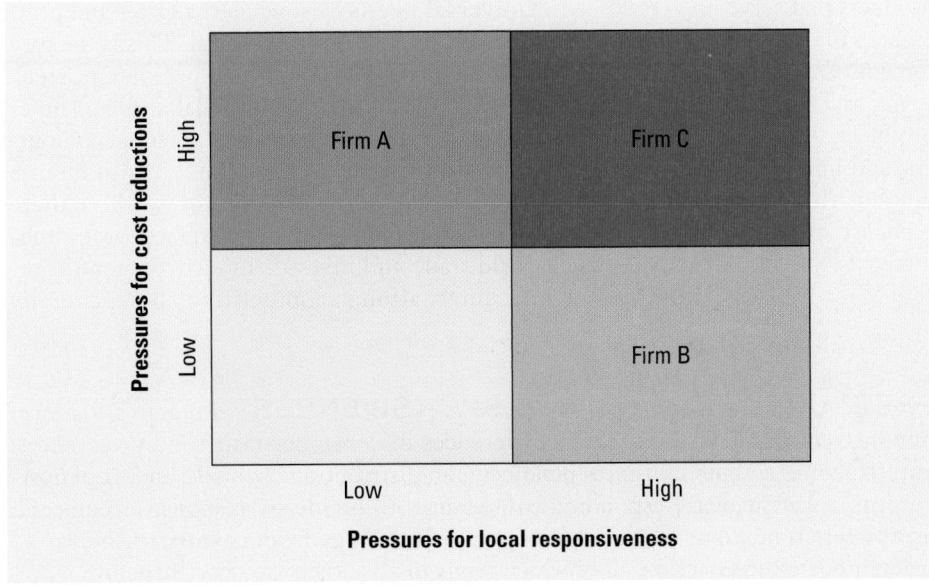

 figure

Pressures for Cost Reductions and Local Responsiveness

responding to pressures to be locally responsive requires that a firm differentiate its product offering and marketing strategy from country to country in an effort to accommodate the diverse demands arising from national differences in consumer tastes and preferences, business practices, distribution channels, competitive conditions, and government policies. Because differentiation across countries can involve significant duplication and a lack of product standardization, it may raise costs.

While some enterprises, such as firm A in Figure 11.8, face high pressures for cost reductions and low pressures for local responsiveness, and others, such as firm B, face low pressures for cost reductions and high pressures for local responsiveness, many companies are in the position of firm C. They face high pressures for *both* cost reductions and local responsiveness. Dealing with these conflicting and contradictory pressures is a difficult strategic challenge, primarily because being locally responsive tends to raise costs.

PRESSURES FOR COST REDUCTIONS
In competitive global markets, international businesses often face pressures for cost reductions. Responding to pressures for cost reduction requires a firm to try to lower the costs of value creation. A manufacturer, for example, might mass-produce a standardized product at the optimal location in the world, wherever that might be, to realize economies of scale, learning effects, and location economies. Alternatively, a firm might outsource certain functions to low-cost foreign suppliers in an attempt to reduce costs. Thus, many computer companies have outsourced their telephone-based customer service functions to India, where qualified technicians who speak English can be hired for a lower wage rate than in the United States. In the same manner, a retailer such as Walmart might push its suppliers (manufacturers) to do the same. (The pressure that Walmart has placed on its suppliers to reduce prices has been cited as a major cause of the trend among North American manufacturers to shift production to China.[27]) A service business such as a bank might respond to cost pressures by moving some back-office functions, such as information processing, to developing nations where wage rates are lower.

Pressures for cost reduction can be particularly intense in industries producing commodity-type products where meaningful differentiation on nonprice factors is difficult and price is the main competitive weapon. This tends to be the case for products that serve universal needs. **Universal needs** exist when the tastes and preferences of consumers in different nations are similar if not identical. This is the case for conventional commodity products such as bulk chemicals, petroleum, steel, sugar, and the like. It also tends to be the case for many industrial and consumer products; for example, handheld calculators, semiconductor chips, personal computers, and liquid crystal display screens. Pressures for cost reductions are also intense in industries where major competitors are based in low-cost locations, where there is persistent excess capacity, and where consumers are powerful and face low switching costs. The liberalization of the world trade and investment environment in recent decades, by facilitating greater international competition, has generally increased cost pressures.[28]

PRESSURES FOR LOCAL RESPONSIVENESS
Pressures for local responsiveness arise from national differences in consumer tastes and preferences, infrastructure, accepted business practices, and distribution channels, and from host-government demands. Responding to pressures to be locally responsive requires a firm to differentiate its products and marketing strategy from country to country to accommodate these factors, all of which tends to raise the firm's cost structure.

Differences in Customer Tastes and Preferences

Strong pressures for local responsiveness emerge when customer tastes and preferences differ significantly between countries, as they often do for deeply embedded historic or cultural reasons. In such cases, a multinational's products and marketing message have to be customized to appeal to the tastes and preferences of local customers. This typically creates pressure to delegate production and marketing responsibilities and functions to a firm's overseas subsidiaries.

For example, the automobile industry in the 1980s and early 1990s moved toward the creation of "world cars." The idea was that global companies such as General Motors, Ford, and Toyota would be able to sell the same basic vehicle the world over, sourcing it from centralized production locations. If successful, the strategy would have enabled automobile companies to reap significant gains from global scale economies. However, this strategy frequently ran aground upon the hard rocks of consumer reality. Consumers in different automobile markets seem to have different tastes and preferences, and demanded different types of vehicles. North American consumers show a strong demand for pickup trucks. This is particularly true in the South and West where many families have a pickup truck as a second or third car. But in European countries, pickup trucks are seen purely as utility vehicles and are purchased primarily by firms rather than individuals. As a consequence, the product mix and marketing message needs to be tailored to consider the different nature of demand in North America and Europe.

Some commentators have argued that customer demands for local customization are on the decline worldwide.[29] According to this argument, modern communications and transport technologies have created the conditions for a convergence of the tastes and preferences of consumers from different nations. The result is the emergence of enormous global markets for standardized consumer products. The worldwide acceptance of McDonald's hamburgers, Coca-Cola, Gap clothes, Nokia cell phones, and Sony PlayStations, all of which are sold globally as standardized products, are often cited as evidence of the increasing homogeneity of the global marketplace.

However, this argument seems somewhat naïve in many consumer goods markets. Significant differences in consumer tastes and preferences still exist across nations and cultures. Managers in international businesses do not yet have the luxury of being able to ignore these differences, and they may not for a long time to come. Even in a modern industry such as the cell phone business, important national differences in consumer usage patterns can be observed. Until recently, for example, Americans, tended to think of cell phones primarily as devices for talking, and not as devices that can also send e-mails and browse the Web. Consequently, when

Americans in the South and West may use pickup trucks as a second or third car, but in Europe, pickups are seen purely as utility vehicles, which affects the marketing message being sent.

Banking for the Poor: A Contagious International Strategy

In 1976 Professor Muhammad Yunus, head of the Rural Economics Program at the University of Chittagong, had a brilliant idea. He sought to create a research project exploring whether a credit-delivery system could be established to service the poorest of the poor in Bangladesh. Exploring the idea, Professor Yunus developed the concept of Grameen Bank. Grameen is derived from the Bengla word for "village" or "rural." In so doing, he created a "bank" unlike any other. Strategically he sought not only to extend banking facilities to poor men and women, but among his objectives he wanted to create opportunities for employment and assist women who were confined to the household by giving them the ability to pursue opportunities. Most importantly, he wanted to reverse the age-old vicious circle of "low income, low saving, and low investment," into a virtuous circle of "low income, injection of credit, investment, more income, more savings, more investment, more income."

The first test was done in Jobra (a village adjacent to Chittagong University) and some of the neighboring villages during 1976–1979. With the sponsorship of the central bank of Bangladesh and the support of the nationalized commercial banks, the project was extended to the Tangail district (a district north of Dhaka, the capital city of Bangladesh) in 1979. With the success in Tangail, the project was extended to several other districts in the country. In October 1983, the Grameen Bank Project was transformed into an independent bank by government legislation. Today, Grameen Bank is owned by the rural poor whom it serves. Borrowers of the bank own 90 percent of its shares, while the remaining 10 percent is owned by the government. For his efforts, Professor Yunus and Grameen Bank were awarded the Nobel Peace Prize in 2006. Good strategies are borderless.

According to the World Bank, more than 1.1 billion people live on $1 dollar per day; the ability to provide financial opportunity that fosters development to these people has engendered the concept of socially responsible investment (SCI). Not only viewed for the financial return on the investment, SCI also considers the social, environmental, and ethical consequences of that investment. Since its inception, "microfinance" or "community development bank" has grown into more than $25 billion in loans to the poor. Unlike top-down development initiatives such as debt forgiveness or international aid, microfinance stands out for its bottom-up approach.

Among the top microfinance institutions are ASA, VBSP, BRAC, and BRI, representing more than 25 million borrowers, not only in Bangladesh where it has established a good foothold, but in Vietnam and Indonesia as well. Interestingly, this approach is drawing the attention of some of the largest financial institutions around the globe. Deutsche Bank, for example, is beginning to recognize not only the potential financial returns of microfinance but also the social value. Ironically, the poorest of the poor may be teaching and perhaps competing with the richest of the rich.

Sources: Grameen Bank Web site, www.grameen-info.org; and "Microfinance: An Emerging Investment Opportunity, Uniting Social Investment and Financial Returns," Deutsche Bank Research, December 19, 2007, accessed at http://www.dbresearch.com/PROD/DBR_INTERNET_EN-PROD/PROD0000000000219174.pdf.

selling to U.S. consumers, cell phone manufacturers focused more on slim good looks and less on advanced functions and features. This was in direct contrast to Asia and Europe, where text messaging and Web browsing were much more widely embraced by the early 2000s. A cultural issue seems to be at work here. People in Europe and Asia often have more time to browse the Web on their phones because they spend more time commuting on trains, while Americans tend to spend more time in cars, where their hands are occupied.[30] However, it is now clear that key technological innovations in the United States, and particularly the development of the iPhone by Apple, are changing this.

Differences in Infrastructure and Traditional Practices
Pressures for local responsiveness arise from differences in infrastructure or traditional practices among countries, creating a need to customize products accordingly. Fulfilling this need may require the delegation of manufacturing and production functions to foreign subsidiaries. For example, in North America, consumer electrical systems are based on 110 volts, whereas in some European countries, 240-volt systems are standard. Thus, domestic electrical appliances have to be customized for this difference in infrastructure. Traditional practices also often vary across nations. For example, in Britain, people

drive on the left-hand side of the road, creating a demand for right-hand-drive cars, whereas in France (and the rest of Europe), people drive on the right-hand side of the road and therefore want left-hand-drive cars. Obviously, automobiles have to be customized to accommodate this difference in traditional practice.

Although many national differences in infrastructure are rooted in history, some are quite recent. For example, in the wireless telecommunications industry, different technical standards exist in different parts of the world. A technical standard known as GSM is common in Europe, and an alternative standard, CDMA, is more common in the United States and parts of Asia. Equipment designed for GSM will not work on a CDMA network, and vice versa. Thus, companies such as Nokia, Motorola, and Ericsson, which manufacture wireless handsets and infrastructure such as switches, need to customize their product offering according to the technical standard prevailing in a given country.

Differences in Distribution Channels   A firm's marketing strategies may have to be responsive to differences in distribution channels among countries, which may necessitate the delegation of marketing functions to national subsidiaries. In the pharmaceutical industry, for example, the British and Japanese distribution systems are radically different from the U.S. system. British and Japanese doctors will not accept or respond favorably to a U.S.-style high-pressure sales force. Thus, pharmaceutical companies have to adopt different marketing practices in Britain and Japan compared with the United States—soft sell versus hard sell. Similarly, Poland, Brazil and Russia all have similar per capita income on a purchasing power parity basis, but there are big differences in distribution systems across the three countries. In Brazil, supermarkets account for 36 percent of food retailing, in Poland for 18 percent, and in Russia for less than 1 percent.[31] These differences in channels require that companies adapt their own distribution and sales strategy.

Host Government Demands   Economic and political demands imposed by host-country governments may require local responsiveness. For example, pharmaceutical companies are subject to local clinical testing, registration procedures, and pricing restrictions, all of which make it necessary that the manufacturing and marketing of a drug should meet local requirements. Because governments and government agencies control a significant proportion of the health care budget in most countries, they are in a powerful position to demand a high level of local responsiveness.

More generally, threats of protectionism, economic nationalism, and local content rules (which require that a certain percentage of a product should be manufactured locally) dictate that international businesses manufacture locally. For example, consider Bombardier, the Canadian-based manufacturer of railcars, aircraft, jet boats, and snowmobiles. Bombardier has 12 railcar factories across Europe. Critics of the company argue that the resulting duplication of manufacturing facilities leads to high costs and helps explain why Bombardier makes lower profit margins on its railcar operations than on its other business lines. In reply, managers at Bombardier argue that in Europe, informal rules with regard to local content favor people who use local workers. To sell railcars in Germany, they claim, you must manufacture in Germany. The same goes for Belgium, Austria, and France. To try to address its cost structure in Europe, Bombardier has centralized its engineering and purchasing functions, but it has no plans to centralize manufacturing.[32]

Choosing a Strategy

Pressures for local responsiveness imply that it may not be possible for a firm to realize the full benefits from economies of scale, learning effects, and location economies. It may not be possible to serve the global marketplace from a single low-cost location, producing a globally standardized product, and marketing it worldwide to attain the cost reductions

LEARNING OBJECTIVE 4
Identify the different strategies for competing globally and their pros and cons.

figure **11.9**

Four Basic Strategies

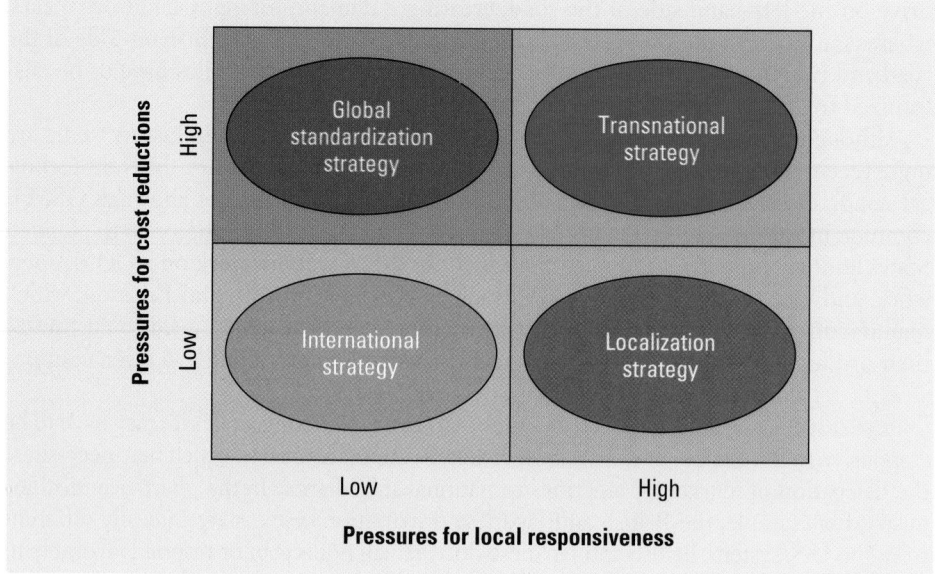

associated with experience effects. The need to customize the product offering to local conditions may work against the implementation of such a strategy. For example, automobile firms have found that Japanese, American, and European consumers demand different kinds of cars, and this necessitates producing products that are customized for local markets. In response, firms such as Honda, Ford, and Toyota are pursuing a strategy of establishing top-to-bottom design and production facilities in each of these regions so that they can better serve local demands. Although such customization brings benefits, it also limits the ability of a firm to realize significant scale economies and location economies.

In addition, pressures for local responsiveness imply that it may not be possible to leverage skills and products associated with a firm's core competencies wholesale from one nation to another. Concessions often have to be made to local conditions. Despite being depicted as "poster boy" for the proliferation of standardized global products, even McDonald's has found that it has to customize its product offerings (i.e., its menu) to account for national differences in tastes and preferences.

How do differences in the strength of pressures for cost reductions versus those for local responsiveness affect the firm's choice of strategy? Firms typically choose among four main strategic postures when competing internationally. These can be characterized as a global standardization strategy, a localization strategy, a transnational strategy, and an international strategy.[33] The appropriateness of each strategy varies given the extent of pressures for cost reductions and local responsiveness. Figure 11.9 illustrates the conditions under which each of these strategies is most appropriate.

Global Standardization Strategy
A firm focuses on increasing profitability and profit growth by reaping the cost reductions that come from economies of scale, learning effects, and location economies.

GLOBAL STANDARDIZATION STRATEGY Firms that pursue a **global standardization strategy** focus on increasing profitability and profit growth by reaping the cost reductions that come from economies of scale, learning effects, and location economies; that is, their strategic goal is to pursue a low-cost strategy on a global scale. The production, marketing, and R&D activities of firms pursuing a global standardization strategy are concentrated in a few favorable locations. Firms pursuing a global standardization strategy try not to customize their product offering and marketing strategy to local conditions because customization involves shorter production runs and the duplication of functions, which tends to raise costs. Instead, they prefer to

Management FOCUS

CCECC's Localization Strategy

Sino–African relations began in the 1950s, but it was not until 1971 that Nigeria–China relations blossomed, and a reinforcing and rewarding relationship between both countries began in earnest. Fang Yi, former Chinese Minister of Foreign Trade and Economic Cooperation, visited Nigeria in 1972, a visit that provided an opportunity for signing the first economic, scientific, and technical cooperation agreement as well as a trade agreement.

Shortly thereafter, China Civil Engineering Construction Corporation (CCECC) began working in Nigeria. Since then, CCECC has employed more than 20,000 local workers on 70 projects, building mostly roads, bridges, and railways. Rather than using more skilled Chinese expatriates, CCECC decided early on that the company and Nigeria would benefit more by localizing its labor force and focusing on those local projects that would maximize the development of the country and their pocketbooks. CCECC even took it one step further by identifying promising Nigerian workers and sending them to China to receive the most advanced training in technology and promoting them from assistants to project managers. Using this strategy gave CCECC a sense

of belonging in Nigeria. "Belonging" has translated into ongoing contract awards.

As recently as 2008, CCECC was awarded an $840 million contract for the Abuja Light Rail, with the financing secured by a $500 million loan from the Chinese government. The Abuja Light Rail project is meant to alleviate the traffic congestion in Abuja, the capital of Nigeria, and the surrounding towns.

Such localization efforts by CCECC are filtering into other Chinese sectors as well. Take the case of China National Offshore Oil Corporation (CNOOC), the state-owned oil company. Leveraging CCECC's extensive knowledge of the Nigerian political environment, CNOOC is now competing with the likes of ExxonMobil and Royal Dutch Shell for a series of blocks that are coming up for renewal.

Sources: "CCECC's Localization Strategy Pays Off in Nigeria," *Xinhua's China Economic Information Service*, August 12, 2010, accessed at http://www.chinadaily.com.cn/business/2010-08/12/content_11145866.htm; Tschang Chi-chu, "Chinese Construction Firms Leaving Region for Africa, Mid-East," *The Straits Times (Singapore)*, December 16, 2006; "Nigeria: Federal Capital Territory Signs 500m Deal with China," *BBC Monitoring Africa*, 2010; and "Nigeria: Chinese Interest in Africa's Crude Oil: Who Gains?" *Plus News Pakistan*, 2009.

market a standardized product worldwide so that they can reap the maximum benefits from economies of scale and learning effects. They also tend to use their cost advantage to support aggressive pricing in world markets.

This strategy makes most sense when there are strong pressures for cost reductions and demands for local responsiveness are minimal. Increasingly, these conditions prevail in many industrial goods industries, whose products often serve universal needs. In the semiconductor industry, for example, global standards have emerged, creating enormous demands for standardized global products. Accordingly, companies such as Intel, Texas Instruments, and Motorola all pursue a global standardization strategy. However, these conditions are not yet found in many consumer goods markets, where demands for local responsiveness remain high. The strategy is inappropriate when demands for local responsiveness are high. The experience of CCECC, which is discussed in the accompanying Management Focus, illustrates what can happen when a domestic localization strategy begins to acquire global implications.

LOCALIZATION STRATEGY A **localization strategy** focuses on increasing profitability by customizing the firm's goods or services so that they provide a good match to tastes and preferences in different national markets. Localization is most appropriate when there are substantial differences across nations with regard to consumer tastes and preferences, and where cost pressures are not too intense. By customizing the product offering to local demands, the firm increases the value of that product in the local market. On the downside, because it involves some duplication of functions and smaller production runs, customization limits the ability of the firm to capture the cost reductions associated with mass-producing a standardized product for

Localization Strategy
Increasing profitability by customizing the firm's goods or services so that they provide a good match to tastes and preferences in different national markets.

global consumption. The strategy may make sense, however, if the added value associated with local customization supports higher pricing, which enables the firm to recoup its higher costs, or if it leads to substantially greater local demand, enabling the firm to reduce costs through the attainment of some scale economies in the local market.

At the same time, firms still have to keep an eye on costs. Firms pursuing a localization strategy still need to be efficient and, whenever possible, to capture some scale economies from their global reach. As noted earlier, many automobile companies have found that they have to customize some of their product offerings to local market demands—for example, producing large pickup trucks for U.S. consumers and small fuel-efficient cars for Europeans and Japanese. At the same time, these multinationals try to get some scale economies from their global volume by using common vehicle platforms and components across many different models, and manufacturing those platforms and components at efficiently scaled factories that are optimally located. By designing their products in this way, these companies have been able to localize their product offering, yet simultaneously capture some scale economies, learning effects, and location economies.

TRANSNATIONAL STRATEGY   We have argued that a global standardization strategy makes most sense when cost pressures are intense and demands for local responsiveness limited. Conversely, a localization strategy makes most sense when demands for local responsiveness are high, but cost pressures are moderate or low. What happens, however, when the firm simultaneously faces both strong cost pressures and strong pressures for local responsiveness? How can managers balance the competing and inconsistent demands such divergent pressures place on the firm? According to some researchers, the answer is to pursue what has been called a transnational strategy.

Two of these researchers, Christopher Bartlett and Sumantra Ghoshal, argue that in today's global environment, competitive conditions are so intense that to survive, firms must do all they can to respond to pressures for cost reductions and local responsiveness. They must try to realize location economies and experience effects, to leverage products internationally, to transfer core competencies and skills within the company, and to simultaneously pay attention to pressures for local responsiveness.[34] Bartlett and Ghoshal note that in the modern multinational enterprise, core competencies and skills do not reside just in the home country but can develop in any of the firm's worldwide operations. Thus, they maintain that the flow of skills and product offerings should not be all one way, from home country to foreign subsidiary. Rather, the flow should also be from foreign subsidiary to home country and from foreign subsidiary to foreign subsidiary. Transnational enterprises, in other words, must also focus on leveraging subsidiary skills.

In essence, firms that pursue a **transnational strategy** are trying to simultaneously achieve low costs through location economies, economies of scale, and learning effects; differentiate their product offering across geographic markets to account for local differences; and foster a multidirectional flow of skills between different subsidiaries in the firm's global network of operations. As attractive as this may sound in theory, the strategy is not an easy one to pursue since it places conflicting demands on the company. Differentiating the product to respond to local demands in different geographic markets raises costs, which runs counter to the goal of reducing costs. Companies such as Ford and ABB (one of the

Transnational Strategy
Attempt to simultaneously achieve low costs through location economies, economies of scale, and learning effects while also differentiating product offering across geographic markets to account for local differences and fostering a multidirectional flow of skills between different subsidiaries in the firm's global network of operations.

IKEA, a worldwide retailer of home furnishings, is becoming more of a transnational company.

world's largest engineering conglomerates) have tried to embrace a transnational strategy and found it difficult to implement.

How best to implement a transnational strategy is one of the most complex questions that large multinationals are grappling with today. Few if any enterprises have perfected this strategic posture. But some clues as to the right approach can be derived from a number of companies. Consider the case of Caterpillar. The need to compete with low-cost competitors such as Komatsu of Japan forced Caterpillar to look for greater cost economies. However, variations in construction practices and government regulations across countries mean that Caterpillar also has to be responsive to local demands. Therefore, Caterpillar confronted significant pressures for cost reductions *and* for local responsiveness.

To deal with cost pressures, Caterpillar redesigned its products to use many identical components and invested in a few large-scale component manufacturing facilities, sited at favorable locations, to fill global demand and realize scale economies. At the same time, the company augments the centralized manufacturing of components with assembly plants in each of its major global markets. At these plants, Caterpillar adds local product features, tailoring the finished product to local needs. Thus, Caterpillar is able to realize many of the benefits of global manufacturing while reacting to pressures for local responsiveness by differentiating its product among national markets.[35] Caterpillar started to pursue this strategy in 1979 and by 1997 had succeeded in doubling output per employee, significantly reducing its overall cost structure in the process. Meanwhile, Komatsu and Hitachi, which are still wedded to a Japan-centric global strategy, have seen their cost advantages evaporate and have been steadily losing market share to Caterpillar.

Changing a firm's strategic posture to build an organization capable of supporting a transnational strategy is a complex and challenging task. Some would say it is too complex, because the strategy implementation problems of creating a viable organizational structure and control systems to manage this strategy are immense.

INTERNATIONAL STRATEGY   Sometimes it is possible to identify multinational firms that find themselves in the fortunate position of being confronted with low cost pressures and low pressures for local responsiveness. Many of these enterprises have pursued an **international strategy,** taking products first produced for their domestic market and selling them internationally with only minimal local customization. The distinguishing feature of many such firms is that they are selling a product that serves universal needs, but they do not face significant competitors, and thus unlike firms pursuing a global standardization strategy, they are not confronted with pressures to reduce their cost structure. Xerox found itself in this position in the 1960s after its invention and commercialization of the photocopier. The technology underlying the photocopier was protected by strong patents, so for several years Xerox did not face competitors—it had a monopoly. The product serves universal needs, and it was highly valued in most developed nations. Thus, Xerox was able to sell the same basic product the world over, charging a relatively high price for that product. Since Xerox did not face direct competitors, it did not have to deal with strong pressures to minimize its cost structure.

Enterprises pursuing an international strategy have followed a similar developmental pattern as they expanded into foreign markets. They tend to centralize product development functions such as R&D at home. However, they also tend to establish manufacturing and marketing functions in each major country or geographic region in which they do business. The resulting duplication can raise costs, but this is less of an issue if the firm does not face strong pressures for cost reductions. Although they may undertake some local customization of product offering and marketing strategy, this tends to be rather limited in scope. Ultimately, in most firms that pursue an international strategy, the head office retains fairly tight control over marketing and product strategy.

International Strategy
Trying to create value by taking products first produced for the domestic market and selling them internationally with only minimal local customization.

Other firms that have pursued this strategy include GraceKennedy and Microsoft. GraceKennedy, in particular, expanded into new markets with new products (see the accompanying Management Focus). Similarly, the bulk of Microsoft's product development work takes place in Redmond, Washington, where the company is headquartered. Although some localization work is undertaken elsewhere, this is limited to producing foreign-language versions of popular Microsoft programs.

THE EVOLUTION OF STRATEGY   The Achilles' heel of the international strategy is that over time, competitors inevitably emerge, and if managers do not take proactive steps to reduce their firm's cost structure, it will be rapidly outflanked by efficient global competitors. This is exactly what happened to Xerox. Japanese companies such as Canon ultimately invented their way around Xerox's patents, produced their own photocopiers in very efficient manufacturing plants, priced them below Xerox's products, and rapidly took global market share from Xerox. In the final analysis, Xerox's demise was not due to the emergence of competitors, for ultimately that was bound to occur, but due to its failure to proactively reduce its cost structure in advance of the emergence of efficient global competitors. The message in this story is that an international strategy may not be viable in the long term, and to survive, firms need to shift toward a global standardization strategy or a transnational strategy in advance of competitors (see Figure 11.10).

The same can be said about a localization strategy. Localization may give a firm a competitive edge, but if it is simultaneously facing aggressive competitors, the company will also have to reduce its cost structure, and the only way to do that may be to shift toward a transnational strategy. This is what GraceKennedy has done (see the Management Focus). Thus, as competition intensifies, international and localization strategies tend to become less viable, and managers need to orientate their companies toward either a global standardization strategy or a transnational strategy.

figure 11.10

Changes in Strategy over Time

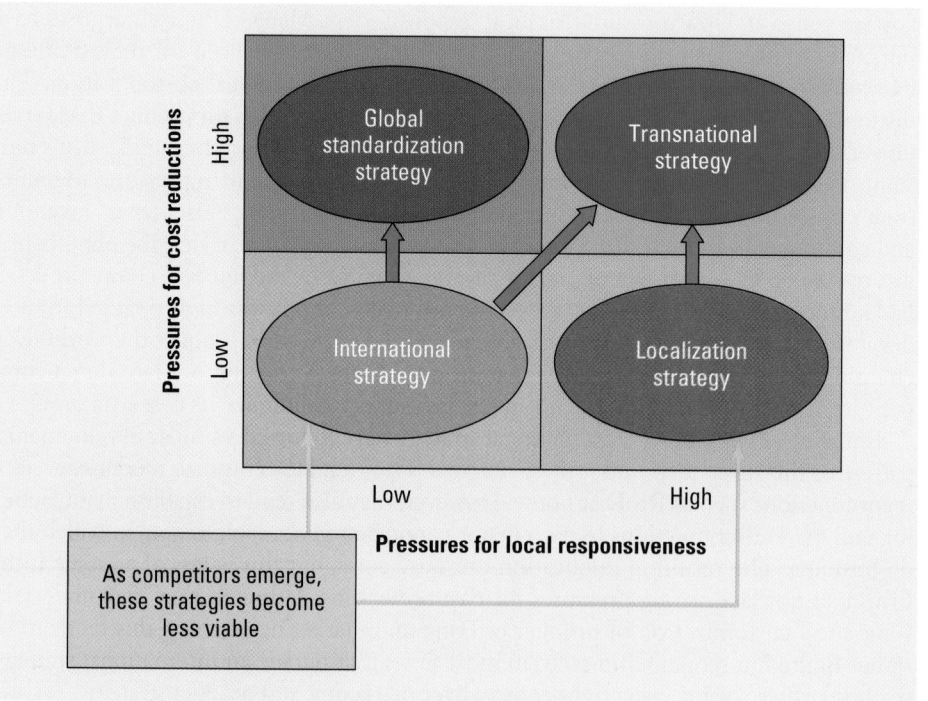

Evolution of GraceKennedy

Founded in 1922, Kingston, Jamaica-based GraceKennedy has evolved to become one of the Caribbean's largest and most diversified corporate entities. Having started as a small trading and wharf operator, GraceKennedy has grown to a varied network of 60 subsidiaries and affiliated companies in the Caribbean, North and Central America, and the United Kingdom. It has grown from a privately held enterprise to a publicly traded conglomerate, with operations in the areas of food processing and distribution, banking and finance, insurance and remittances services, along with building materials retailing.

The evolution may be said to have begun in 1995 with the development of "Vision 2020." Upon his appointment in 1995 as CEO, Douglas Orane set the company on a path toward international expansion, aspiring to move beyond its island roots into the international landscape. The Harvard MBA chose to benchmark GraceKennedy's expansion to the best international companies. In doing so, and as part of that expansion, GraceKennedy has pursued new ventures domestically and abroad. It built a new state-of-the-art distribution center in the outskirts of Kingston and completed one of the largest acquisitions to date in WT Foods, a British producer and distributor of ethnic food brands.

Regarded by many as the iconic Jamaican company (at one point the ex-Chairman, Carlton Alexander, was known as "Mr. Jamaica"), GraceKennedy sought to establish a more diversified strategy by expanding its international profile. GraceKennedy sought to liberate itself from the "ups and downs" of the Jamaican economy and yet remain an integral part of the Jamaican community.

Until the diversification, GraceKennedy relied on sales inside Jamaica and the expatriate community outside the country for its Afro-Caribbean food products and remittances services. The mission statement reads, "To satisfy the unmet needs of the Caribbean people wherever we live in the world." According to financial analysts, diversification has become its strength.

Food Trading International, for example, the export arm of GraceKennedy, had a particularly profitable year in 2009. This was in part due to the establishment of an inbond warehouse that facilitated the servicing of smaller markets previously unable to be adequately serviced. The company also launched a number of products in new markets, including Trinidad and Guyana. Other launches are planned for the United States, Barbados, and Canada.

On the banking and investment side, First Global Bank established a strategic alliance with International Finance Corporation, a member of the World Bank, to facilitate loans to small and medium-size enterprises. Unfortunately, unauthorized and undisclosed trading activity in U.S. Treasury bonds by a senior employee has tarnished some of the gains made within the international community. However, corrective measures have been put in place and appear to be rectifying the situation. Global remittances, one of the company's key services, were not affected, however. It saw robust growth in revenues and profits.

The strategy seems to be working. In 2008, revenues hit $700 million before dropping to $648 million in 2009 due to the financial crisis. In 2009, its stock took a beating, but, spurred by the Jamaican debt exchange, the stock once again surged and climbed 80 percent from it low in November 2009 of 42 cents to 75 cents. In fact, in 1995 GraceKennedy's market value stood at $1.29 billion; in 2009 it was at $3.7 billion.

Sources: GraceKennedy Annual Report 2009, GraceKennedy Web site, www.gracekennedy.com; and K. Collister, "Grace Under Pressure," *Latin Trade,* 18, no. 2 (2010), pp. 55–58.

Strategic Alliances

Strategic alliances refer to cooperative agreements between potential or actual competitors. In this section, we are concerned specifically with strategic alliances between firms from different countries. Strategic alliances run the range from formal joint ventures, in which two or more firms have equity stakes (e.g., Fuji–Xerox), to short-term contractual agreements, in which two companies agree to cooperate on a particular task (such as developing a new product). Collaboration between competitors is fashionable; recent decades have seen an explosion in the number of strategic alliances.

LEARNING OBJECTIVE 5
Explain the pros and cons of using strategic alliances to support global strategies.

Strategic Alliances
Cooperative agreements between two or more firms.

THE ADVANTAGES OF STRATEGIC ALLIANCES

Firms ally themselves with actual or potential competitors for various strategic purposes.[36] First, strategic alliances may facilitate entry into a foreign market. For example, many firms feel that if they are to successfully enter the Chinese market, they need a local partner who understands business conditions, and who has good connections (or *guanxi*—see Chapter 3). Thus, in 2004 Warner Brothers entered into a joint venture with two Chinese partners to produce and distribute films in China. As a foreign film company, Warner found that if it wanted to produce films on its own for the Chinese market it had to go through a complex approval process for every film, and it had to farm out distribution to a local company, which made doing business in China very difficult. Due to the participation of Chinese firms, however, the joint-venture films will go through a streamlined approval process, and the venture will be able to distribute any films it produces. Also, the joint venture will be able to produce films for Chinese TV, something that foreign firms are not allowed to do.[37]

Strategic alliances also allow firms to share the fixed costs (and associated risks) of developing new products or processes. An alliance between Boeing and a number of Japanese companies to build Boeing's 787 commercial jetliner was motivated by Boeing's desire to share the estimated $8 billion investment required to develop the aircraft. For another example of cost sharing, see the accompanying Management Focus, which discusses the strategic alliances between Cisco and Fujitsu.

Third, an alliance is a way to bring together complementary skills and assets that neither company could easily develop on its own.[38] In 2003, for example, Microsoft and Toshiba established an alliance aimed at developing embedded microprocessors (essentially tiny computers) that can perform a variety of entertainment functions in an automobile (e.g., run a back-seat DVD player or a wireless Internet connection). The processors run a version of Microsoft's Windows CE operating system. Microsoft brings its software engineering skills to the alliance and Toshiba its skills in developing microprocessors.[39] The alliance between Cisco and Fujitsu was also formed to share know-how.

Fourth, it can make sense to form an alliance that will help the firm establish technological standards for the industry that will benefit the firm. For example, in 1999 Palm Computer, the leading maker of personal digital assistants (PDAs), entered into an alliance with Sony under which Sony agreed to license and use Palm's operating system in Sony PDAs. The motivation for the alliance was in part to help establish Palm's operating system as the industry standard for PDAs, as opposed to a rival Windows-based operating system from Microsoft.[40]

THE DISADVANTAGES OF STRATEGIC ALLIANCES

The advantages we have discussed can be very significant. Despite this, some commentators have criticized strategic alliances on the grounds that they give competitors a low-cost route to new technology and markets.[41] For example, a few years ago some commentators argued that many strategic alliances between U.S. and Japanese firms were part of an implicit Japanese strategy to keep high-paying, high-value-added jobs in Japan while gaining the project engineering and production process skills that underlie the competitive success of many U.S. companies.[42] They argued that Japanese success in the

DaimlerChrysler–Mitsubishi Alliance: A Brief Anatomy of a Failed Alliance

The DaimlerChrysler–Mitsubishi alliance lasted only 69 months! It was the initiated in 2000 by Jürgen E. Schrempp, then chairman of DaimlerChrysler (DCX), and stands today as one example of a failed alliance.

Having secured the European and North American markets with the alliance between Daimler Benz and Chrysler, Schrempp sought to also gain a foothold in the Asian market with Mitsubishi. Mitsubishi was Daimler's third choice, and, after much negotiation, a deal was struck that permitted Daimler to have 34 percent of Mitsubishi. A subsequent recall of 1 million Mitsubishi autos and a dramatic drop in share price served as the marriage's rocky phase. Mitsubishi's difficulties affected DaimlerChrysler's profits. Another 1.5 million cars were recalled shortly thereafter. Eventually, the stock plummeted to one-quarter the value when DaimlerChrysler bought in. If the honeymoon and the marriage were fraught with problems, then the divorce was just as ugly.

In April 2004, DCX chose not to invest further in Mitsubishi. DCX began selling its shares and finally did so at $1.1 billion, completely terminating its investment. The eventual buyer of the shares sold by DCX was Mitsubishi itself. Controlling ownership went to the *keiretsu* itself. On the way, the failed alliance cost the jobs of Schrempp, Rolf Eckrodt, chairman and CEO of Mitsubishi; and Wolfgang Bernhard, COO of Chrysler. More than 10,000 Mitsubishi employees would be axed, and one of its four assembly plants would be closed. Ironically enough, the DaimlerChrysler alliance would also terminate prematurely.

Sources: DaimlerChrysler–Mitsubishi Alliance, www.wikipedia.com; S. Miller, and N. Shirouzu, "DaimlerChrysler, Mitsubishi Hold Talks That Could Lead to Alliance," *The Wall Street Journal—Eastern Edition*, 235, no. 48 (2000), p. A3; and J. Schmid, "For Daimler, Mitsubishi Opens Door to Asia," *The New York Times*, March 28, 2000.

machine tool and semiconductor industries was built on U.S. technology acquired through strategic alliances. And they argued that U.S. managers were aiding the Japanese by entering alliances that channel new inventions to Japan and provide a U.S. sales and distribution network for the resulting products. Although such deals may generate short-term profits, so the argument goes, in the long run the result is to "hollow out" U.S. firms, leaving them with no competitive advantage in the global marketplace.

These critics have a point; alliances have risks. Unless a firm is careful, it can give away more than it receives. But there are so many examples of apparently successful alliances between firms—including alliances between U.S. and Japanese firms—that their position seems extreme. It is difficult to see how the Microsoft–Toshiba alliance, the Boeing–Mitsubishi alliance for the 787, or the Fuji–Xerox alliance fit the critics' thesis. In these cases, both partners seem to have gained from the alliance. Why do some alliances benefit both firms while others benefit one firm and hurt the other? The next section provides an answer to this question.

MAKING ALLIANCES WORK   The failure rate for international strategic alliances seems to be high. One study of 49 international strategic alliances found that two-thirds run into serious managerial and financial troubles within two years of their formation, and that although many of these problems are solved, 33 percent are ultimately rated as failures by the parties involved.[43] The success of an alliance seems to be a function of three main factors: partner selection, alliance structure, and the manner in which the alliance is managed.

Partner Selection   One key to making a strategic alliance work is to select the right ally. A good ally, or partner, has three characteristics. First, a good partner helps the firm achieve its strategic goals, whether they are market access, sharing the costs and risks of product development, or gaining access to critical core competencies. The partner must have capabilities that the firm lacks and that it values. Second, a good partner shares the firm's vision for the purpose of the alliance. If two firms approach an alliance with radically different agendas, the chances are great that the relationship will not be harmonious, will not flourish, and will end in divorce. Third, a good partner is unlikely to try to opportunistically exploit the alliance for its own ends; that is, to expropriate the firm's technological know-how while giving away little in return. In this respect, firms with reputations for "fair play" to maintain probably make the best allies. For example, companies such as General Electric are involved in so many strategic alliances that it would not pay the company to trample over individual alliance partners.[44] This would tarnish GE's reputation of being a good ally and would make it more difficult for GE to attract alliance partners. Because IBM attaches great importance to its alliances, it is unlikely to engage in the kind of opportunistic behavior that critics highlight. Similarly, their reputations make it less likely (but by no means impossible) that such Japanese firms as Sony, Toshiba, and Fuji, which have histories of alliances with non-Japanese firms, would opportunistically exploit an alliance partner.

To select a partner with these three characteristics, a firm needs to conduct comprehensive research on potential alliance candidates. To increase the probability of selecting a good partner, the firm should:

1. Collect as much pertinent, publicly available information on potential allies as possible.
2. Gather data from informed third parties. These include firms that have had alliances with the potential partners, investment bankers who have had dealings with them, and former employees.
3. Get to know the potential partner as well as possible before committing to an alliance. This should include face-to-face meetings between senior managers (and perhaps middle-level managers) to ensure that the chemistry is right.

Alliance Structure A partner having been selected, the alliance should be structured so that the firm's risks of giving too much away to the partner are reduced to an acceptable level. First, alliances can be designed to make it difficult (if not impossible) to transfer technology not meant to be transferred. The design, development, manufacture, and service of a product manufactured by an alliance can be structured so as to wall off sensitive technologies to prevent their leakage to the other participant. In a long-standing alliance between General Electric and Snecma to build commercial aircraft engines for single-aisle commercial jet aircraft, for example, GE reduced the risk of excess transfer by walling off certain sections of the production process. The modularization effectively cut off the transfer of what GE regarded as key competitive technology, while permitting Snecma access to final assembly. Formed in 1974, the alliance has been remarkably successful, and today it dominates the market for jet engines used on the Boeing 737 and Airbus 320.[45] Similarly, in the alliance between Boeing and the Japanese to build the 767, Boeing walled off research, design, and marketing functions considered central to its competitive position, while allowing the Japanese to share in production technology. Boeing also walled off new technologies not required for 767 production.[46]

Second, contractual safeguards can be written into an alliance agreement to guard against the risk of opportunism by a partner. (Opportunism includes the theft of technology and/or markets.) For example, TRW, Inc., has three strategic alliances with large Japanese auto component suppliers to produce seat belts, engine valves, and steering gears for sale to Japanese-owned auto assembly plants in the United States. TRW has clauses in each of its alliance contracts that bar the Japanese firms from competing with TRW to supply U.S.-owned auto companies with component parts. By doing this, TRW protects itself against the possibility that the Japanese companies are entering into the alliances merely to gain access to the North American market to compete with TRW in its home market.

Third, both parties to an alliance can agree in advance to swap skills and technologies that the other covets, thereby ensuring a chance for equitable gain. Cross-licensing agreements are one way to achieve this goal. Fourth, the risk of opportunism by an alliance partner can be reduced if the firm extracts a significant credible commitment from its partner in advance. The long-term alliance between Xerox and Fuji to build photocopiers for the Asian market perhaps best illustrates this. Rather than enter into an informal agreement or a licensing arrangement (which Fuji Photo initially wanted), Xerox insisted that Fuji invest in a 50/50 joint venture to serve Japan and East Asia. This venture constituted such a significant investment in people, equipment, and facilities that Fuji Photo was committed from the outset to making the alliance work to earn a return on its investment. By agreeing to the joint venture, Fuji essentially made a credible commitment to the alliance. Given this, Xerox felt secure in transferring its photocopier technology to Fuji.[47]

Managing the Alliance   Once a partner has been selected and an appropriate alliance structure has been agreed on, the task facing the firm is to maximize its benefits from the alliance. As in all international business deals, an important factor is sensitivity to cultural differences (see Chapter 3). Many differences in management style are attributable to cultural differences, and managers need to make allowances for these in dealing with their partner. Beyond this, maximizing the benefits from an alliance seems to involve building trust between partners and learning from partners.[48]

Managing an alliance successfully requires building interpersonal relationships between the firms' managers, or what is sometimes referred to as *relational capital*.[49] This is one lesson that can be drawn from a successful strategic alliance between Ford and Mazda. Ford and Mazda set up a framework of meetings within which their managers not only discuss matters pertaining to the alliance but also have time to get to know each other better. The belief is that the resulting friendships help build trust and facilitate harmonious relations between the two firms. Personal relationships also foster an informal management network between the firms. This network can then be used to help solve problems arising in more formal contexts (such as in joint committee meetings between personnel from the two firms).

Academics have argued that a major determinant of how much acquiring knowledge a company gains from an alliance is its ability to learn from its alliance partner.[50] For example, in a five-year study of 15 strategic alliances between major multinationals, Gary Hamel, Yves Doz, and C. K. Prahalad focused on a number of alliances between Japanese companies and Western (European or American) partners.[51] In every case in which a Japanese company emerged from an alliance stronger than its Western partner, the Japanese company had made a greater effort to learn. Few Western companies studied seemed to want to learn from their Japanese partners. They tended to regard the alliance purely as a cost-sharing or risk-sharing device, rather than as an opportunity to learn how a potential competitor does business.

Consider the alliance between General Motors and Toyota constituted in 1985 to build the Chevrolet Nova. This alliance was structured as a formal joint venture, called New United Motor Manufacturing, Inc., and each party had a 50 percent equity stake. The venture owned an auto plant in Fremont, California. According to one Japanese manager, Toyota quickly achieved most of its objectives from the alliance: "We learned about U.S. supply and transportation. And we got the confidence to manage U.S. workers."[52] All that knowledge was then transferred to Georgetown, Kentucky, where Toyota opened its own plant in 1988. Possibly all GM got was a new product, the

Chevrolet Nova. Some GM managers complained that the knowledge they gained through the alliance with Toyota has never been put to good use inside GM. They believe they should have been kept together as a team to educate GM's engineers and workers about the Japanese system. Instead, they were dispersed to various GM subsidiaries.

To maximize the learning benefits of an alliance, a firm must try to learn from its partner and then apply the knowledge within its own organization. It has been suggested that all operating employees should be well briefed on the partner's strengths and weaknesses and should understand how acquiring particular skills will bolster their firm's competitive position. Hamel, Doz, and Prahalad note that this is already standard practice among Japanese companies. They made this observation:

> We accompanied a Japanese development engineer on a tour through a partner's factory. This engineer dutifully took notes on plant layout, the number of production stages, the rate at which the line was running, and the number of employees. He recorded all this despite the fact that he had no manufacturing responsibility in his own company, and that the alliance did not encompass joint manufacturing. Such dedication greatly enhances learning.[53]

For such learning to be of value, it must be diffused throughout the organization (as was seemingly not the case at GM after the GM–Toyota joint venture). To achieve this, the managers involved in the alliance should educate their colleagues about the skills of the alliance partner.

Key Terms

strategy, p. 407

profitability, p. 407

profit growth, p. 408

value creation, p. 409

operations, p. 411

organization architecture, p. 413

organizational structure, p. 413

controls, p. 414

incentives, p. 414

processes, p. 414

organizational culture, p. 414

people, p. 414

core competence, p. 416

location economies, p. 417

global web, p. 418

experience curve, p. 419

learning effects, p. 420

economies of scale, p. 420

universal needs, p. 424

global standardization strategy, p. 428

localization strategy, p. 429

transnational strategy, p. 430

international strategy, p. 431

strategic alliances, p. 433

Summary

In this chapter we reviewed basic principles of strategy and the various ways in which firms can profit from global expansion, and we looked at the strategies firms that compete globally can adopt. The chapter made the following points:

1. A strategy can be defined as the actions that managers take to attain the goals of the firm. For most firms, the preeminent goal is to maximize shareholder value. Maximizing shareholder value requires firms to focus on

increasing their profitability and the growth rate of profits over time.

2. International expansion may enable a firm to earn greater returns by transferring the product offerings derived from its core competencies to markets where indigenous competitors lack those product offerings and competencies.

3. It may pay a firm to base each value creation activity it performs at that location where factor conditions are most conducive to the

performance of that activity. We refer to this strategy as focusing on the attainment of location economies.

4. By rapidly building sales volume for a standardized product, international expansion can assist a firm in moving down the experience curve by realizing learning effects and economies of scale.

5. A multinational firm can create additional value by identifying valuable skills created within its foreign subsidiaries and leveraging those skills within its global network of operations.

6. The best strategy for a firm to pursue often depends on a consideration of the pressures for cost reductions and for local responsiveness.

7. Firms pursuing an international strategy transfer the products derived from core competencies to foreign markets, while undertaking some limited local customization.

8. Firms pursuing a localization strategy customize their product offering, marketing strategy, and business strategy to national conditions.

9. Firms pursuing a global standardization strategy focus on reaping the cost reductions that come from experience curve effects and location economies.

10. Many industries are now so competitive that firms must adopt a transnational strategy. This involves a simultaneous focus on reducing costs, transferring skills and products, and boosting local responsiveness. Implementing such a strategy may not be easy.

11. Strategic alliances are cooperative agreements between actual or potential competitors.

12. The advantage of alliances are that they facilitate entry into foreign markets, enable partners to share the fixed costs and risks associated with new products and processes, facilitate the transfer of complementary skills between companies, and help firms establish technical standards.

13. A disadvantage of a strategic alliance is that the firm risks giving away technological know-how and market access to its alliance partner in return for very little.

14. The disadvantages associated with alliances can be reduced if the firm selects partners carefully, paying close attention to the firm's reputation and the structure of the alliance so as to avoid unintended transfers of know-how.

15. Two keys to making alliances work seem to be building trust and informal communications networks between partners and taking proactive steps to learn from alliance partners.

Critical Discussion Questions

1. In a world of zero transportation costs, no trade barriers, and nontrivial differences between nations with regard to factor conditions, firms must expand internationally if they are to survive. Discuss.

2. Plot the position of the following firms on Figure 11.8: Procter & Gamble, IBM, Nokia, Coca-Cola, Dow Chemicals, US Steel, McDonald's. In each case justify your answer.

3. Reread the Management Focus, "Evolution of GraceKennedy," and then answer the following questions:

   a. What strategy was GraceKennedy pursuing when it first chose to enter foreign markets?

   b. What role does Jamaica, as a country, actually play in the international strategy of GraceKennedy? Is GraceKennedy marketing to the Jamaican people?

   c. Do you find the current strategy of GraceKennedy to be limiting? That is, what is the eventual market for GraceKennedy products and services?

4. What do you see as the main organizational problems that are likely to be associated with implementation of a transnational strategy?

5. Reread the Management Focus, "DaimlerChrysler–Mitsubishi Alliance: A Brief Anatomy of a Failed Alliance." Although brief in description, what do you suspect were the main reasons the alliance did not work? Do you think it was destined to be a failure from the beginning? If so, why?

Use the globalEDGE Resource Desk (http://global EDGE.msu.edu/resourcedesk/) to complete the following exercises:

1. Several classifications and rankings of the world's largest companies are prepared by a variety of sources. Find one such *composite ranking* system and identify the criteria that are used in ranking the top global companies. Extract the list of the highest ranked 25 companies, paying particular attention to the home countries of the companies.

2. The top management of your company, a manufacturer and marketer of laptop computers, has decided to pursue international expansion opportunities in Eastern Europe. To achieve economies of scale, management is aiming toward a strategy of minimum local adaptation. Focusing on an eastern European country of your choice, and using the "Countries" section of globalEDGE (select *Countries* at the main menu), prepare an executive summary that features those aspects of the product where standardization will simply not work and adaptation to local conditions will be essential.

Renault-Nissan-Daimler: Evolution of a Strategic Alliance

In March 1999, French automobile manufacturer Renault and Japanese car maker Nissan entered into a strategic alliance. It was the first industrial and commercial partnership of its kind involving a French and a Japanese company. Described as a "transformative alliance," Nissan was on the verge of bankruptcy, and Renault's sales were lagging. Since the formation of the alliance, Nissan has achieved a spectacular financial turnaround. Renault has bettered its operational performance and has accelerated its international development. Combining expertise and profit sharing, Nissan develops new gasoline engines, while Renault focuses on diesel engines. Within the international arena, the alliance has recently announced another alliance with Bajaj, an Indian manufacturer, to develop an ultra-low-cost vehicle in 2010 and a partnership with Russian automaker AvtoVaz. The successes to date have indeed been transformative.

Although most cross-border alliances fail, the Renault–Nissan alliance is an exception. Linked through cross-shareholding, the Renault–Nissan alliance became the third largest global automobile maker (based on sales for the year 2008) and was originally the brainchild of Louis Schweitzer, then chairman and CEO of Renault. But the actual success of the alliance has been attributed to its current CEO. So much so, that now under the legendary leadership of the French/Lebanese Carlos Ghosn, the Renault–Nissan alliance is looking for a third partner.

In June 2006, encouraged by Kirk Kerkorian, one of the largest individual shareholders of General Motors, Ghosn sought an alliance with the largest automobile manufacturer. As rumored, Renault wanted 20 percent of GM and the CEO position, essentially ousting Rick Wagoner. The negotiations ended with neither side agreeing to terms. Two years later, during the financial meltdown, GM would declare bankruptcy and subject itself to a governmental bailout.

Still looking for a third partner, Ghosn opened talks with Daimler, in an attempt to strategically address the growing smaller car market. Understanding that the demographic shifts and emissions legislation are driving demand for smaller, less-costly cars, such a partnership would better position the automakers in an area of growth but with higher costs given the need for more advanced technology. As such, the automakers are looking to cooperate in a wide range of areas, from the sharing of engines to small-car platforms. In the small-car area, Daimler has had significant challenges.

Much the same way Renault spoke with General Motors, Daimler has recognized the efficiencies inherent in an alliance. It has talked with Volkswagen, Fiat, and even its fiercest rival BMW in an attempt to acquire efficient small-car production capabilities that the company desperately needed. In the United States, for example, one of the German carmaker's largest market, Daimler has struggled with its mini Smart cars and its Mercedes Class A and B models. Over the past 12 years, Daimler has lost at least $540 million on these models. Sales of Daimler's Smart car in the United States have seen a slide from the 25,000 units sold in 2008 to less than 4,000 units in the period between January and July in 2010. An alliance with Renault–Nissan would give Daimler access to the fuel, efficient, small-engine, small-car platforms; Renault's experience in electric power trains; and perhaps most importantly, cost cutting.

For Renault–Nissan, a partnership with Daimler would give the alliance Daimler's hybrid-engine technology, electronics, and quality expertise. It may also gain access to Daimler's expertise in larger and diesel engines, plus a partner with financial security able to share investment costs associated with the development of fuel-efficient technologies.

In an industry known for its partnerships and collaboration, the potential Renault–Nissan–Daimler alliance is but one more. One need only remember the DaimlerChrysler–Mitsubishi attempt, which lasted only 69 months and cost Daimler's CEO Jürgen Schrempp his job. What is new is the successful integration of the first two partners when most cross-border alliances end up as failures. As stated in the mission statement of the Renault–Nissan alliance: "The objective is to establish a powerful automotive group and develop synergies while conserving the corporate culture and identity of each brand. The Alliance is built on values of trust and mutual respect." It remains to be determined if the addition of Daimler will continue the success story.

Sources: N. E. Boudette and V. Fuhrmans, "Daimler to Ally with Renault, Nissan on Small Cars," *The Wall Street Journal,* April 6, 2010, accessed at http://online.wsj.com/article/ SB10001424052702304017404575165973682713554.html; "Business: A Big Plan for Small Cars; Daimler and Renault-Nissan Join Forces," *The Economist,* April 8, 2010; and Renault Web site: www.renault.com.

Case Discussion Questions

1. What were some of the reasons for the Renault–Nissan alliance? What are some of the disadvantages of the relationship?

2. You will note that the original alliance between Renault and Nissan was premised on cross-shareholding; that is, where each partner would be a shareholder of the other. Do you think this was instrumental in the success of the alliance? If so, why?

3. Do you think leadership plays a significant role in the success of a strategic alliance? If so, how?

4. What do you think the three potential partners will have to do to achieve a successful strategic alliance? Will each continue with independent corporate cultures? Will each be able to integrate with the others while maintaining its individuality?

part 5   Competing in a Global Marketplace

LEARNING OBJECTIVES

After you have read this chapter you should be able to:

1   Explain the three basic decisions that firms contemplating foreign expansion must make: which markets to enter, when to enter those markets, and on what scale.

2   Compare and contrast the different modes that firms use to enter foreign markets.

3   Identify the factors that influence a firm's choice of entry mode.

4   Recognize the pros and cons of acquisitions versus greenfield ventures as an entry strategy.

chapter

12

Entering Foreign Markets

The Tata Group is the largest private corporation in India. With annual revenues of more than $70 billion, Tata Group now derives 65 percent of its sales outside of India and employs 357,000 people worldwide. Through its various companies, Tata has interests in tea, hotels, cars, steel, power generation, chemicals, and information technology, among others. Over the past 10 years, Tata has grown from a local Indian company to a multinational organization. It is now the largest employer in the United Kingdom. This meteoric climb has been premised on an international expansion strategy and a mode of entry based essentially on strategic mergers and acquisitions for large companies and a wide variety of joint ventures for smaller companies. Each is being led by specific strategic drivers.

For example, when Tata bought 30 percent of Burni, the Indonesian company, it did so to tie up a long-term supply of coal. When it bought Corus, the U.K. steel maker, it did so with the vision of becoming one of the top five steel producers in the world. The acquisition gave Tata Steel the scale that would have been virtually impossible to organically develop in India. Likewise, Tata Power Company is considering the acquisition of U.K.-based power generator InterGen NV from GMR Infrastructure. It is doing so to increase its global presence. InterGen, with generation capacity of more than 6,300 megawatts (MW), has power plants in the United Kingdom, Netherlands, Mexico, Philippines, and Australia.

Tata Motors, the automobile-manufacturing arm of the Tata Group, has undertaken a similar strategy. In 2008, Tata Motors acquired Jaguar and Land Rover for $2.3 billion, which included the use of the brand names Daimler and Lanchester. The internal development of these brands would have been virtually impossible. Elsewhere, Tata Motors expanded by means of a joint venture. In a 51–49 split, Tata Motors partnered with Marcopolo of Brazil. The joint venture was established to manufacture and assemble fully built buses and coaches targeted at developing mass rapid transportation systems in emerging markets. Similar to the development of the "Nano," the world's cheapest car, Tata Motors is branding it as the "Asian People's Car," further placing Tata among the most innovative of companies.

The expanse and reach of this strategy is being facilitated by Tata Communications, one of the world's leading providers of "wholesale global transmission" capabilities. Tata Communications has one of the most advanced and largest submarine cable networks in the world, with connectivity to more than 200 countries. Although headquartered in Mumbai, India, just like its parent company, Tata Communications has a strong international presence in Montreal, Singapore, and London.

In fact, a review of the overall expansion strategy of the Tata Group demonstrates a wide geographic reach. Over the past 10 years, the Tata Group has merged or acquired an interest in companies in the United States, United Kingdom, Spain, Morocco, China, Korea, Switzerland, Germany, South Africa, Australia, Thailand, Singapore, Russian, Czech Republic, Poland, and Sri Lanka. The sectors have ranged from automobile to telecommunications, consultancy, chemicals, and hotels. Specifically in the hotel sector, through Indian Hotels, the Tata Group has joint ventures with many of the largest most prestigious hotel groups, including Ritz Carlton and Starwood.

As mentioned by the Tata Group's general counsel, the determination of which specific mode of entry to be used was not only predicated on the business, technology, and policy integration issues that served as the fundamental drivers, but also on the intangible issues such as management. In that regard, the Tata Group has been very alert to the pre-integration and post-integration issues in those acquisitions, mergers, and joint ventures. As Tata continues its expansion, the integration of these diversified companies into a cohesive international organization will become increasingly difficult.

One critical issue within its strategic expansion will be the succession of Ratan Tata, the chairman of Tata Sons, the holding company of the Tata Group. All of this expansion has occurred during his tenure. At age 72, he has given word that he would like to retire. Up until this point, five of the past six chairmen have been, Tatas, named after the original founder. With the majority of Tata's revenues being generated abroad, it will be interesting to see who will replace such an international visionary. ●

Sources: Tata Group Web site, www.tata.com; "Tata Power in Talks to Buy Majority Stake in InterGen," *The Economic Times,* September 9, 2010; R. Evans, "Tata's Outbound Strategy," *International Financial Law Review,* 29, no. 2 (2010), pp. 30-31; and P. Beckett, "Boss Talk: Tata Chairman Doesn't Sweat the Timing on Global Expansion," *The Wall Street Journal,* November 19, 2009, p. B1.

Introduction

This chapter is concerned with two closely related topics: (1) the decision of which foreign markets to enter, when to enter them, and on what scale; and (2) the choice of entry mode. Any firm contemplating foreign expansion must first struggle with the issue of which foreign markets to enter and the timing and scale of entry. The choice of which markets to enter should be driven by an assessment of relative long-run growth and profit potential.

The choice of mode for entering a foreign market is another major issue with which international businesses must wrestle. The various modes for serving foreign markets are exporting, licensing or franchising to host-country firms, establishing joint ventures with a host-country firm, setting up a new wholly owned subsidiary in a host country to serve its market, or acquiring an established enterprise in the host nation to serve that market. Each of these options has advantages and disadvantages. The magnitude of the advantages and disadvantages associated with each entry mode is determined by a number of factors, including transport costs, trade barriers, political risks, economic risks, business risks, costs, and firm strategy. The optimal entry mode varies by situation, depending on these factors. Thus, whereas some firms may best serve a given market by exporting, other firms may better serve the market by setting up a new wholly owned subsidiary or by acquiring an established enterprise.

As discussed in the opening case, the expansion of the Tata Group has been impressive. Its primary choice of entry mode has been a combination of mergers and acquisitions along with joint ventures. This strategy has been applied through many sectors, including automobile manufacturing, power generation, telecommunications, and the hotel industry. The Tata Group has sought to establish a presence not only in specific markets but also in specific industries as it seeks to expand its footprint. Perhaps most importantly, it has been very aware of the tangible drivers—such as business, technology, and policies—that have driven that expansion but also not forgetting the intangible factors such as management. If Tata continues to address all of these factors, it will serve to demonstrate just how important it can be for a company to get its foreign market entry strategy right.

Basic Entry Decisions

A firm contemplating foreign expansion must make three basic decisions: which markets to enter, when to enter those markets, and on what scale.[1]

WHICH FOREIGN MARKETS?   The world has more than 200 nation-states. They do not all hold the same profit potential for a firm contemplating foreign expansion. Ultimately, the choice must be based on an assessment of a nation's long-run profit potential. This potential is a function of several factors, many of which we have studied in earlier chapters. In Chapter 2, we looked in detail at the economic and political factors that influence the potential attractiveness of a foreign market. There we noted that the attractiveness of a country as a potential market for an international business depends on balancing the benefits, costs, and risks associated with doing business in that country.

Chapter 2 also noted that the long-run economic benefits of doing business in a country are a function of factors such as the size of the market (in terms of demographics), the present wealth (purchasing power) of consumers in that market, and the likely future wealth of consumers, which depends upon economic growth rates. While some markets are very large when measured by number of consumers (e.g., China, India, and Indonesia), one must also look at living standards and economic growth. On this basis, China and India, while relatively poor, are growing so rapidly that

Another Perspective

Thailand's Homebuilder Enters Foreign Markets
As a child in Thailand, Thongma Vijitpongpun helped his father sell soup to day laborers, balancing twin hampers on a shoulder pole and learning the first rule of good business: deliver quality at an affordable price. Today Thongma's business, Pruksa Real Estate, uses mass-production techniques to build quality, affordable housing for low- and middle-income families. Pruksa's process has been so successful—with recent annual revenues pegged at $569 million—that the company intends to expand to other Asian countries where the need for low-cost housing is great. First on Pruksa's list are India, Vietnam, and the Maldives, with China, Indonesia, and the Philippines to follow. (Brian Mertens, "Biggest Thai Home Builder Moving Abroad to Expand Company," *Forbes.com*, February 8, 2010, www.forbes.com)

they are attractive targets for inward investment. Alternatively, weak growth in Indonesia implies that this populous nation is a far less attractive target for inward investment. As we saw in Chapter 2, likely future economic growth rates appear to be a function of a free market system and a country's capacity for growth (which may be greater in less developed nations). We also argued in Chapter 2 that the costs and risks associated with doing business in a foreign country are typically lower in economically advanced and politically stable democratic nations, and they are greater in less developed and politically unstable nations.

The discussion in Chapter 2 suggests that, other things being equal, the benefit–cost–risk trade-off is likely to be most favorable in politically stable developed and developing nations that have free market systems, and where there is not a dramatic upsurge in either inflation rates or private-sector debt. The trade-off is likely to be least favorable in politically unstable developing nations that operate with a mixed or command economy or in developing nations where speculative financial bubbles have led to excess borrowing (see Chapter 2 for further details).

Another important factor is the value an international business can create in a foreign market. This depends on the suitability of its product offering to that market and the nature of indigenous competition.[2] If the international business can offer a product that has not been widely available in that market and that satisfies an unmet need, the value of that product to consumers is likely to be much greater than if the international business simply offers the same type of product that indigenous competitors and other foreign entrants are already offering. Greater value translates into an ability to charge higher prices and/or to build sales volume more rapidly. By considering such factors, a firm can rank countries in terms of their attractiveness and long-run profit potential. Preference is then given to entering markets that rank highly. For example, Tesco, the large British grocery chain, has been aggressively expanding its foreign operations in recent years, primarily by focusing on emerging markets that lack strong indigenous competitors (see the accompanying Management Focus).

TIMING OF ENTRY

Timing of Entry
Entry is early when a firm enters a foreign market before other foreign firms and late when a firm enters after other international businesses have established themselves.

Once attractive markets have been identified, it is important to consider the **timing of entry.** We say that entry is early when an international business enters a foreign market before other foreign firms and late when it enters after other international businesses have already established themselves. The advantages frequently associated with entering a market early are commonly known as **first-mover advantages.**[3] One first-mover advantage is the ability to preempt rivals and capture demand by establishing a strong brand name. This desire has driven the rapid expansion by Tesco into developing nations (see the Management Focus). A second advantage is the ability to build sales volume in that country and ride down the experience curve ahead of rivals, giving the early entrant a cost advantage over later entrants. One could argue that this factor motivated GM to enter the Chinese automobile market in 1997 when it was still tiny. This cost advantage may enable the early entrant to cut prices below that of later entrants, thereby driving them out of the market. A third advantage is the ability of early entrants to create switching costs that tie customers into their products or services. Such switching costs make it difficult for later entrants to win business.

First-Mover Advantages
Advantages accruing to the first to enter a market.

First-Mover Disadvantages
Disadvantages associated with entering a foreign market before other international businesses.

There can also be disadvantages associated with entering a foreign market before other international businesses. These are often referred to as **first-mover disadvantages.**[4] These disadvantages may give rise to **pioneering costs,** costs that an early entrant has to bear that a later entrant can avoid. Pioneering costs arise when the business system in a foreign country is so different from that in a firm's home market that the enterprise has to devote considerable effort, time, and expense to learning the

Pioneering Costs
Costs that an early entrant has to bear that a later entrant can avoid, such as the time and effort in learning the rules, failure due to ignorance, and the liability of being a foreigner.

Management FOCUS

Tesco's International Growth Strategy

Tesco is the largest grocery retailer in the United Kingdom, with a 25 percent share of the local market. In its home market, the company's strengths are reputed to come from strong competencies in marketing and store site selection, logistics and inventory management, and its own label product offerings. By the early 1990s, these competencies had already given the company a leading position in the United Kingdom. The company was generating strong free cash flows, and senior management had to decide how to use that cash. One strategy they settled on was overseas expansion. As they looked at international markets, they soon concluded the best opportunities were not in established markets, such as those in North America and Western Europe, where strong local competitors already existed, but in the emerging markets of Eastern Europe and Asia where there were few capable competitors but strong underlying growth trends.

Tesco's first international foray was into Hungary in 1994, when it acquired an initial 51 percent stake in Global, a 43-store, state-owned grocery chain. By 2004, Tesco was the market leader in Hungary, with some 60 stores and a 14 percent market share. In 1995, Tesco acquired 31 stores in Poland from Stavia; a year later it added 13 stores purchased from Kmart in the Czech Republic and Slovakia; and the following year it entered the Republic of Ireland.

Tesco's Asian expansion began in 1998 in Thailand when it purchased 75 percent of Lotus, a local food retailer with 13 stores. Building on that base, Tesco had 64 stores in Thailand by 2004. In 1999, the company entered South Korea when it partnered with Samsung to develop a chain of hypermarkets. This was followed by entry into Taiwan in 2000, Malaysia in 2002, and China in 2004. The move into China came after three years of careful research and discussions with potential partners. Like many other Western companies, Tesco was attracted to the Chinese market by its large size and rapid growth. In the end, Tesco settled on a 50/50 joint venture with Hymall, a hypermarket chain that is controlled by Ting Hsin, a Taiwanese group, which had been operating in China for six years. Currently, Hymall has 25 stores in China, and it plans to open another 10 each year. Ting Hsin is a well-capitalized enterprise in its own right, and it will match Tesco's investments, reducing the risks Tesco faces in China.

As a result of these moves, by 2007 Tesco had more than 800 stores outside the United Kingdom, which generated £7.6 billion in annual revenues. In the United Kingdom, Tesco had some 1,900 stores, generating £30 billion. The addition of international stores has helped to make Tesco the fourth-largest company in the global grocery market behind Walmart, Carrefour of France, and Ahold of Holland. Of the four, however, Tesco may be the most successful internationally. By 2005, all of its foreign ventures were making money.

In explaining the company's success, Tesco's managers have detailed a number of important factors. First, the company devotes considerable attention to transferring its core capabilities in retailing to its new ventures. At the same time, it does not send in an army of expatriate managers to run local operations, preferring to hire local managers and support them with a few operational experts from the United Kingdom. Second, the company believes that its partnering strategy in Asia has been a great asset. Tesco has teamed with good companies that have a deep understanding of the markets in which they are participating but that lack Tesco's financial strength and retailing capabilities. Consequently, both Tesco and its partners have brought useful assets to the venture, which have increased the probability of success. As the venture becomes established, Tesco has typically increased its ownership stake in its partner. Thus, under current plans, by 2011 Tesco will own 99 percent of Homeplus, its South Korean hypermarket chain. When the venture was established, Tesco owned 51 percent. Third, the company has focused on markets with good growth potential but that lack strong indigenous competitors, which provides Tesco with ripe ground for expansion.

In 2006, Tesco took its international expansion strategy to the next level when it announced it would enter the crowded U.S. grocery market with its Tesco Express concept. Currently running in five countries, Tesco Express stores are smaller, high-quality neighborhood grocery outlets that feature a large selection of prepared and healthy foods. Tesco will initially enter on the West Coast, investing some £250 million per year, with breakeven expected in the second year of operation. Although some question the wisdom of this move, others point out that in the United Kingdom Tesco has consistently outperformed the ASDA chain, which is owned by Walmart. Also, the Tesco Express format is not something found in the United States.

Sources: P. N. Child, "Taking Tesco Global," *The McKenzie Quarterly*, no. 3 (2002); H. Keers, "Global Tesco Sets Out Its Stall in China," *Daily Telegraph*, July 15, 2004, p. 31; K. Burgess, "Tesco Spends Pounds 140m on Chinese Partnership," *Financial Times*, July 15, 2004, p. 22; J. McTaggart, "Industry Awaits Tesco Invasion," *Progressive Grocer*, March 1, 2006, pp. 8–10; and Tesco's annual reports, archived at www.tesco.com.

rules of the game. Pioneering costs include the costs of business failure if the firm, due to its ignorance of the foreign environment, makes major mistakes. A certain liability is associated with being a foreigner, and this liability is greater for foreign firms that enter a national market early.[5] Research seems to confirm that the probability of survival increases if an international business enters a national market after several other foreign firms have already done so.[6] The late entrant may benefit by observing and learning from the mistakes made by early entrants.

Pioneering costs also include the costs of promoting and establishing a product offering, including the costs of educating customers. These can be significant when the product being promoted is unfamiliar to local consumers. In contrast, later entrants may be able to ride on an early entrant's investments in learning and customer education by watching how the early entrant proceeded in the market, by avoiding costly mistakes made by the early entrant, and by exploiting the market potential created by the early entrant's investments in customer education. For example, KFC introduced the Chinese to American-style fast food, but a later entrant, McDonald's, has capitalized on the market in China.

An early entrant may be put at a severe disadvantage, relative to a later entrant, if regulations change in a way that diminishes the value of an early entrant's investments. This is a serious risk in many developing nations where the rules that govern business practices are still evolving. Early entrants can find themselves at a disadvantage if a subsequent change in regulations invalidates prior assumptions about the best business model for operating in that country.

SCALE OF ENTRY AND STRATEGIC COMMITMENTS Another issue that an international business needs to consider when contemplating market entry is the scale of entry. Entering a market on a large scale involves the commitment of significant resources and implies rapid entry. Consider the entry of the Dutch insurance company ING into the U.S. insurance market in 1999. ING had to spend several billion dollars to acquire its U.S. operations. Not all firms have the resources necessary to enter on a large scale, and even some large firms prefer to enter foreign markets on a small scale and then build slowly as they become more familiar with the market.

The consequences of entering on a significant scale—entering rapidly—are associated with the value of the resulting strategic commitments.[7] A strategic commitment has a long-term impact and is difficult to reverse. Deciding to enter a foreign market on a significant scale is a major strategic commitment. Strategic commitments, such as rapid large-scale market entry, can have an important influence on the nature of competition in a market. For example, by entering the U.S. financial services market on a significant scale, ING signaled its commitment to the market. Such a move has several effects. On the positive side, it makes it easier for the company to attract customers and distributors (such as insurance agents). The scale of entry gives both customers and distributors reasons for believing that ING will remain in the market for the long run. The scale of entry may also give other foreign institutions considering entry into the United States pause; now they would have to compete not only against indigenous institutions in the United States, but also against an aggressive and successful European institution. On the negative side, by committing itself heavily to the United States, ING would have fewer resources available to support expansion in other desirable markets, such as Japan. The commitment to the United States limits the company's strategic flexibility.

As suggested by the ING example, significant strategic commitments are neither unambiguously good nor bad. Rather, they tend to change the competitive playing field and unleash a number of changes, some of which may be desirable and some of which will not be. It is important for a firm to think through the implications of large-scale entry into a market and act accordingly. Of particular relevance is trying to identify how actual and potential competitors might react to large-scale entry into a market. Also, the large-scale entrant is more likely than the small-scale entrant to be able to capture first-mover advantages associated with demand preemption, scale economies, and switching costs.

The value of the commitments that flow from rapid large-scale entry into a foreign market must be balanced against the resulting risks and lack of flexibility associated with significant commitments. But strategic inflexibility can also have value. A famous example from military history illustrates the value of inflexibility. When Hernán Cortés landed in Mexico, he ordered his men to burn all but one of his ships. Cortés reasoned that by eliminating their only method of retreat, his men had no choice but to fight hard to win against the Aztecs—and ultimately they did.[8]

Balanced against the value and risks of the commitments associated with large-scale entry are the benefits of a small-scale entry. Small-scale entry allows a firm to learn about a foreign market while limiting the firm's exposure to that market. Small-scale entry is a way to gather information about a foreign market before deciding whether to enter on a significant scale and how best to enter. By giving the firm time to collect information, small-scale entry reduces the risks associated with a subsequent large-scale entry. But the lack of commitment associated with small-scale entry may make it more difficult for the small-scale entrant to build market share and to capture first-mover or early-mover advantages. The risk-averse firm that enters a foreign market on a small scale may limit its potential losses, but it may also miss the chance to capture first-mover advantages.

MARKET ENTRY SUMMARY   There are no "right" decisions here, just decisions that are associated with different levels of risk and reward. Entering a large developing nation such as China or India before most other international businesses in the firm's industry, and entering on a large scale, will be associated with high levels of risk. In such cases, the liability of being foreign is increased by the absence of prior foreign entrants whose experience can be a useful guide. At the same time, the potential long-term rewards associated with such a strategy are great. The early large-scale entrant into a major developing nation may be able to capture significant first-mover advantages that will bolster its long-run position in that market.[9] This was what GM hoped to do when it entered China in 1997, and as of 2010 it seems as if GM has captured a significant first-mover, or at least early-mover, advantage. In contrast, entering developed nations such as Australia or Canada after other international businesses in the firm's industry, and entering on a small scale to first learn more about those markets, will be associated with much lower levels of risk. However, the potential long-term rewards are also likely to be lower because the firm is essentially forgoing the opportunity to capture first-mover advantages and because the lack of commitment signaled by small-scale entry may limit its future growth potential.

This section has been written largely from the perspective of a business based in a developed country considering entry into foreign markets. Christopher Bartlett and Sumantra Ghoshal have pointed out the ability that businesses based in developing nations have to enter foreign markets and become global players.[10] Although such firms tend to be late entrants into foreign markets, and although their resources may be limited, Bartlett and Ghoshal argue that such late movers can still succeed against well-established global competitors by pursuing appropriate strategies. In particular, Bartlett and Ghoshal argue that companies based in developing nations should use the entry of foreign multinationals as an opportunity to learn from these competitors by benchmarking their operations and performance against them.

Furthermore, they suggest the local company may be able to find ways to differentiate itself from a foreign multinational, for example, by focusing on market niches that the multinational ignores or is unable to serve effectively if it has a standardized global product offering. Having improved its performance through learning and differentiated its product offering, the firm from a developing nation may then be able to pursue its own international expansion strategy. Even though the firm may be a late entrant into many countries, by benchmarking and then differentiating itself from early movers in global markets, the firm from the developing nation may still be able to build a strong international business presence. The accompanying Country Focus provides an example of specific market entry, which looks at Panama with its inherent risks and rewards.

Entry Modes

LEARNING OBJECTIVE 2
Compare and contrast the different modes that firms use to enter foreign markets.

Once a firm decides to enter a foreign market, the question arises as to the best mode of entry. Firms can use six different modes to enter foreign markets: exporting, turnkey projects, licensing, franchising, establishing joint ventures with a host-country firm, or setting up a new wholly owned subsidiary in the host country. Each entry mode has advantages and disadvantages. Managers need to consider these carefully when deciding which to use.[11]

EXPORTING   Many manufacturing firms begin their global expansion as exporters and only later switch to another mode for serving a foreign market. We take a close look at the mechanics of exporting in the next chapter. Here we focus on the advantages and disadvantages of exporting as an entry mode.

Exporting
Sale of products produced in one country to residents of another country.

Advantages   **Exporting** has two distinct advantages. First, it avoids the often substantial costs of establishing manufacturing operations in the host country. Second, exporting may help a firm achieve experience curve and location economies (see Chapter 11). By manufacturing the product in a centralized location and exporting it to other national markets, the firm may realize substantial scale economies from its global sales volume. This is how Sony came to dominate the global TV market, how Matsushita came to dominate the VCR market, how many Japanese automakers made inroads into the U.S. market, and how South Korean firms such as Samsung gained market share in computer memory chips.

Disadvantages   Exporting has a number of drawbacks. First, exporting from the firm's home base may not be appropriate if lower-cost locations for manufacturing the product can be found abroad (i.e., if the firm can realize location economies by moving production elsewhere). Thus, particularly for firms pursuing global or transnational strategies, it may be preferable to manufacture where the mix of factor conditions is most favorable from a value creation perspective and to export to the rest of the world from that location. This is not so much an argument against exporting as an argument against exporting from the firm's home country. Many U.S. electronics firms have moved some of their manufacturing to the Far East because of the availability of low-cost, highly skilled labor there. They then export from that location to the rest of the world, including the United States.

A second drawback to exporting is that high transport costs can make exporting uneconomical, particularly for bulk products. One way of getting around this is to

Country FOCUS

Panama: Right Place at the Right Time

For various companies and for various reasons, Panama is quickly becoming one of the key entry markets. This has been in part due to various changes in the legal/regulatory environment and the development of large infrastructure projects. In fact, since 2007 when "Ley 41," as it is known locally, permitted multinational corporations a number of operational and financial benefits, more than 21 multinational companies have entered the Panamanian market. Specifically, during the past three years, Harsco Corporation, Caterpillar, Procter & Gamble, AES, BNP Paribas, LG, Hewlett-Packard, and 3M have chosen to establish operations and/or create regional offices or headquarters in Panama. They believe it is the right place and the right time to enter the Panamanian market.

While the world was in the midst of a financial meltdown, Panama experienced a 2.8 percent increase in GDP in 2009 (as compared to 8 percent in 2008). In addition to the legal/regulatory changes mentioned, this growth was also a result of the "genesis" effect that the approval and subsequent implementation of expansion plans for the Panama Canal and the development of other mega-infrastructure projects such as the underground transportation system has had on the economy. It is no surprise that during the period 2009–2010, Panama experienced significant international market entry activity in the form of an increase operational presence in mergers and acquisitions.

For Harsco Corporation, a worldwide industrial services company, the choice was logical. It entered the Panamanian market on the piggyback of infrastructure development opportunities. By acquiring ESCO Interamerica, the leading engineering and equipment services provider to the infrastructure sector and the number one market leader in Central America and the Caribbean, Harsco Infrastructure group's America operations immediately expanded the group's existing Latin America presence in Mexico, Chile, and Peru. The company also expanded to seven additional countries, including Colombia, Costa Rica, El Salvador, Guatemala, Panama, Trinidad and Tobago, and Puerto Rico.

The timeliness of infrastructure development opportunities, and specifically the expansion of the Canal, also attracted Caterpillar. The Panama Canal was indeed in need of expansion. As the world's transportation vessels continued to grow in size, the Panama Canal became too small, forcing the larger container vessels to travel around the tip of South America. The expansion calls for a new single-lane, three-step lock system that will allow the Panama Canal to accommodate larger vessels that cannot currently pass through the Canal. The Panama Canal Authority estimates the eight-year project will cost about $5.3 billion

and will consist of six smaller projects, requiring the removal of approximately 104.6 million cubic yards (80 million cubic meters) of material. Caterpillar makes bulldozers and heavy equipment, so the Panama Canal expansion is Caterpillar's "bread and butter." Caterpillar expects to supply this need through exports from its Latin American operations.

All of this development requires power. AES Panama, the Panamanian operations of the global AES, is the largest power generator in Panama. With four hydroelectric plants, it comprises 36 percent of the total installed generation capacity for the country. The increased activity suggests that if profits continue, its presence in Panama may permit AES Panama to export to other Central American countries.

Nonconstruction sectors also gained from Ley 41 and the infrastructure development boom. In the first quarter of 2010, for example, the banking sector, which is Panama's economic stronghold, saw the purchase of BNP Paribas, SA Panama Branch's commercial and investment banking business, by the Bank of Nova Scotia. Nova Scotia has an international expansionist strategy in Latin America. Likewise, in the insurance and reinsurance business, Mapfre America SA, a Spanish-based global insurer, acquired a majority of the shares of Aseguradora Mundial SA, Mundial Desarrollo de Negocio SA, and their respective subsidiaries from Grupo Mundial Tenedora SA. To some extent, this expansion dovetailed with the expansionist efforts of Banco Santander and BBVA.

In 2007, correctly anticipating rapid growth, Procter & Gamble chose Panama for its Latin America Regional Center. As part of its thinking, the company selected the site to include all the regional business units: Household Care, Health & Well Being, Beauty & Grooming, LA Regional Management, and the Latin America Distributor Market organization that manages P&G business in Central America, Ecuador, and Bolivia. This choice was driven by its privileged location with proximity to key countries and as a strategic point of connectivity in the fastest-growing economy in Central America.

At other times, the entry mode is modest. For LG, Panama is the only country in Central America where it has a presence. From those operations, LG markets to the rest of Central America and into northern South America. If the boom continues, we can expect this initial entry to grow as well.

Sources: R. Arango and A. Rubinoff, "How Panama M&A Will Grow," *International Financial Law Review*, 29, no. 6 (2010), pp. 42–44; Caterpillar Web site, www.cat.com; Panama America, http://www.pa-digital.com.pa/; AES Corporation Web site, http://www.aes.com/aes/index?page=country&cat=PA; LG Web site, www.lg.com; and Procter & Gamble Web site, www.pg.com.

manufacture bulk products regionally. This strategy enables the firm to realize some economies from large-scale production and at the same time to limit its transport costs. For example, many multinational chemical firms manufacture their products regionally, serving several countries from one facility.

Another drawback is that tariff barriers can make exporting uneconomical. Similarly, the threat of tariff barriers by the host-country government can make it very risky. A fourth drawback to exporting arises when a firm delegates its marketing, sales, and service in each country where it does business to another company. This is a common approach for manufacturing firms that are just beginning to expand internationally. The other company may be a local agent, or it may be another multinational with extensive international distribution operations. Local agents often carry the products of competing firms and so have divided loyalties. In such cases, the local agent may not do as good a job as the firm would if it managed its marketing itself. Similar problems can occur when another multinational takes on distribution.

The way around such problems is to set up wholly owned subsidiaries in foreign nations to handle local marketing, sales, and service. By doing this, the firm can exercise tight control over marketing and sales in the country while reaping the cost advantages of manufacturing the product in a single location, or a few choice locations.

TURNKEY PROJECTS

Firms that specialize in the design, construction, and start-up of turnkey plants are common in some industries. In a **turnkey project,** the contractor agrees to handle every detail of the project for a foreign client, including the training of operating personnel. At completion of the contract, the foreign client is handed the "key" to a plant that is ready for full operation—hence, the term *turnkey.* This is a means of exporting process technology to other countries. Turnkey projects are most common in the chemical, pharmaceutical, petroleum refining, and metal refining industries, all of which use complex, expensive production technologies.

> **Turnkey Project**
> A project in which a firm agrees to set up an operating plant for a foreign client and hand over the "key" when the plant is fully operational.

Advantages
The know-how required to assemble and run a technologically complex process, such as refining petroleum or steel, is a valuable asset. Turnkey projects are a way of earning great economic returns from that asset. The strategy is particularly useful where FDI is limited by host-government regulations. For example, the governments of many oil-rich countries have set out to build their own petroleum refining industries, so they restrict FDI in their oil and refining sectors. But because many of these countries lack petroleum-refining technology, they gain it by entering into turnkey projects with foreign firms that have the technology. Such deals are often attractive to the selling firm because without them, they would have no way to earn a return on their valuable know-how in that country. A turnkey strategy can also be less risky than conventional FDI. In a country with unstable political and economic environments, a longer-term investment might expose the firm to unacceptable political and/or economic risks (e.g., the risk of nationalization or of economic collapse).

Disadvantages
Three main drawbacks are associated with a turnkey strategy. First, the firm that enters into a turnkey deal will have no long-term interest in the foreign country. This can be a disadvantage if that country subsequently proves to be

a major market for the output of the process that has been exported. One way around this is to take a minority equity interest in the operation. Second, the firm that enters into a turnkey project with a foreign enterprise may inadvertently create a competitor. For example, many of the Western firms that sold oil-refining technology to firms in Saudi Arabia, Kuwait, and other Gulf states now find themselves competing with these firms in the world oil market. Third, if the firm's process technology is a source of competitive advantage, then selling this technology through a turnkey project is also selling competitive advantage to potential and/or actual competitors.

LICENSING A **licensing agreement** is an arrangement whereby a licensor grants the rights to intangible property to another entity (the licensee) for a specified period, and in return, the licensor receives a royalty fee from the licensee.[12] Intangible property includes patents, inventions, formulas, processes, designs, copyrights, and trademarks. For example, to enter the Japanese market, Xerox, inventor of the photocopier, established a joint venture with Fuji Photo that is known as Fuji–Xerox. Xerox then licensed its xerographic know-how to Fuji–Xerox. In return, Fuji–Xerox paid Xerox a royalty fee equal to 5 percent of the net sales revenue that Fuji–Xerox earned from the sales of photocopiers based on Xerox's patented know-how. In the Fuji–Xerox case, the license was originally granted for 10 years, and it has been renegotiated and extended several times since. The licensing agreement between Xerox and Fuji–Xerox also limited Fuji–Xerox's direct sales to the Asian Pacific region (although Fuji–Xerox does supply Xerox with photocopiers that are sold in North America under the Xerox label).[13]

> **Licensing**
> Occurs when a firm (the licensor) licenses the rights to produce its product, its production processes, or its brand name or trademark to another firm (the licensee); in return, the licensor collects a royalty fee from the licensee.

Advantages In the typical international licensing deal, the licensee puts up most of the capital necessary to get the overseas operation going. Thus, a primary advantage of licensing is that the firm does not have to bear the development costs and risks associated with opening a foreign market. Licensing is very attractive for firms lacking the capital to develop operations overseas. In addition, licensing can be attractive when a firm is unwilling to commit substantial financial resources to an unfamiliar or politically volatile foreign market. Licensing is also often used when a firm wishes to participate in a foreign market but is prohibited from doing so by barriers to investment. This was one of the original reasons for the formation of the Fuji–Xerox joint venture in 1962. Xerox wanted to participate in the Japanese market but was prohibited from setting up a wholly owned subsidiary by the Japanese government. So Xerox set up the joint venture with Fuji and then licensed its know-how to the joint venture.

Finally, licensing is frequently used when a firm possesses some intangible property that might have business applications, but it does not want to develop those applications itself. For example, Bell Laboratories at AT&I originally invented the transistor circuit in the 1950s, but AT&I decided it did not want to produce transistors, so it licensed the technology to a number of other companies, such as Texas Instruments. Similarly, Coca-Cola has licensed its famous trademark to clothing manufacturers, which have incorporated the design into clothing.

Disadvantages Licensing has three serious drawbacks. First, it does not give a firm the tight control over manufacturing, marketing, and strategy that is required for realizing experience curve and location economies. Licensing typically involves each licensee setting up its own production operations. This severely limits the firm's ability to realize experience curve and location economies by producing its product in a centralized location. When these economies are important, licensing may not be the best way to expand overseas.

Second, competing in a global market may require a firm to coordinate strategic moves across countries by using profits earned in one country to support competitive

At the completion of the contract, the foreign client is handed the "key" to a plant that is ready for full operation.

attacks in another. By its very nature, licensing limits a firm's ability to do this. A licensee is unlikely to allow a multinational firm to use its profits (beyond those due in the form of royalty payments) to support a different licensee operating in another country.

A third problem with licensing is one that we encountered in Chapter 7 when we reviewed the economic theory of FDI. This is the risk associated with licensing technological know-how to foreign companies. Technological know-how constitutes the basis of many multinational firms' competitive advantage. Most firms wish to maintain control over how their know-how is used, and a firm can quickly lose control over its technology by licensing it. Many firms have made the mistake of thinking they could maintain control over their know-how within the framework of a licensing agreement. RCA Corporation, for example, once licensed its color TV technology to Japanese firms including Matsushita and Sony. The Japanese firms quickly assimilated the technology, improved on it, and used it to enter the U.S. market, taking substantial market share away from RCA.

There are ways of reducing this risk. One way is by entering into a cross-licensing agreement with a foreign firm. Under a cross-licensing agreement, a firm might license some valuable intangible property to a foreign partner, but in addition to a royalty payment, the firm might also request that the foreign partner license some of its valuable know-how to the firm. Such agreements are believed to reduce the risks associated with licensing technological know-how, since the licensee realizes that if it violates the licensing contract (by using the knowledge obtained to compete directly with the licensor), the licensor can do the same to it. Cross-licensing agreements enable firms to hold each other hostage, which reduces the probability that they will behave opportunistically toward each other.[14] Such cross-licensing agreements are increasingly common in high-technology industries. For example, the U.S. biotechnology firm Amgen licensed one of its key drugs, Nuprogene, to Kirin, the Japanese pharmaceutical company. The license gives Kirin the right to sell Nuprogene in Japan. In return, Amgen receives a royalty payment and, through a licensing agreement, gained the right to sell some of Kirin's products in the United States.

Another way of reducing the risk associated with licensing is to follow the Fuji–Xerox model and link an agreement to license know-how with the formation of a joint venture in which the licensor and licensee take important equity stakes. Such an approach aligns the interests of licensor and licensee because both have a stake in ensuring that the venture is successful. Thus, the risk that Fuji Photo might appropriate Xerox's technological know-how and then compete directly against Xerox in the global photocopier market was reduced by the establishment of a joint venture in which both Xerox and Fuji Photo had an important stake.

Franchising
A specialized form of licensing in which the franchiser sells intangible property to the franchisee and insists on rules to conduct the business.

FRANCHISING   Franchising is similar to licensing, although franchising tends to involve longer-term commitments than licensing. **Franchising** is basically a specialized form of licensing in which the franchiser not only sells intangible property (normally a trademark) to the franchisee, but also insists that the franchisee agree to abide by strict rules as to how it does business. The franchiser will also often assist the franchisee to run the business on an ongoing basis. As with licensing, the franchiser typically receives a royalty payment, which amounts to some percentage of the franchisee's revenues. Whereas licensing is pursued primarily by manufacturing firms, franchising is employed primarily by service firms.[15] McDonald's is a good example of a firm that has grown by using a franchising strategy. McDonald's strict rules as to how franchisees should operate a restaurant extend to control over the menu, cooking methods, staffing policies, and design and location. McDonald's also organizes the supply chain for its franchisees and provides management training and financial assistance.[16]

Advantages   The advantages of franchising as an entry mode are very similar to those of licensing. The firm is relieved of many of the costs and risks of opening a foreign market on its own. Instead, the franchisee typically assumes those costs and risks. This creates a good incentive for the franchisee to build a profitable operation as quickly as possible. Thus, using a franchising strategy, a service firm can build a global presence quickly and at a relatively low cost and risk, as McDonald's has.

Disadvantages   The disadvantages are less pronounced than in the case of licensing. Since franchising is often used by service companies, there is no reason to consider the need for coordination of manufacturing to achieve experience curve and location economies. But franchising may inhibit the firm's ability to take profits out of one country to support competitive attacks in another. A more significant disadvantage of franchising is quality control. The foundation of franchising arrangements is that the firm's brand name conveys a message to consumers about the quality of the firm's product. Thus, a business traveler checking in at a Four Seasons hotel in Hong Kong can reasonably expect the same quality of room, food, and service that she would receive in New York. The Four Seasons name is supposed to guarantee consistent product quality. This presents a problem in that foreign franchisees may not be as concerned about quality as they are supposed to be, and the result of poor quality can extend beyond lost sales in a particular foreign market to a decline in the firm's worldwide reputation. For example, if the business traveler has a bad experience at the Four Seasons in Hong Kong, she may never go to another Four Seasons hotel and may urge her colleagues to do likewise. The geographical distance of the firm from its foreign franchisees can make poor quality difficult to detect. In addition, the sheer numbers of franchisees—in the case of McDonald's, tens of thousands—can make quality control difficult. Due to these factors, quality problems may persist.

One way around this disadvantage is to set up a subsidiary in each country in which the firm expands. The subsidiary might be wholly owned by the company or a joint venture with a foreign company. The subsidiary assumes the rights and obligations to establish franchises throughout the particular country or region. McDonald's, for example, establishes a master franchisee in many countries. Typically, this master franchisee is a joint venture between McDonald's and a local firm. The proximity and the smaller number of franchises to oversee reduce the quality control challenge. In addition, because the subsidiary (or master franchisee) is at least partly owned by the firm, the firm can place its own managers in the subsidiary to help ensure that it is doing a good job of monitoring the franchises. This organizational arrangement has proven very satisfactory for McDonald's, KFC, and others.

JOINT VENTURES   A **joint venture** entails establishing a firm that is jointly owned by two or more otherwise independent firms. Fuji–Xerox, for example, was set up as a joint venture between Xerox and Fuji Photo. Establishing a joint venture with a foreign firm has long been a popular mode for entering a new market. The most typical joint venture is a 50/50 venture, in which each of the two parties holds a 50 percent ownership stake and contributes a team of managers to share operating control. This was the case with the Fuji–Xerox joint venture until 2001; it is now

Joint Venture
Establishing a firm that is jointly owned by two or more otherwise independent firms.

a 25/75 venture with Xerox holding 25 percent. The GM SAIC venture in China was a 50/50 venture until 2010, when it became a 51/49 venture, with SAIC holding the 51 percent stake. Some firms, however, have sought joint ventures in which they have a majority share and thus tighter control.[17]

Advantages   Joint ventures have a number of advantages. First, a firm benefits from a local partner's knowledge of the host country's competitive conditions, culture, language, political systems, and business systems. (This was one reason Tata entered into joint ventures around the world; see the opening case.) Thus, for many U.S. firms, joint ventures have involved the U.S. company providing technological know-how and products and the local partner providing the marketing expertise and the local knowledge necessary for competing in that country. Second, when the development costs and/or risks of opening a foreign market are high, a firm might gain by sharing these costs and or risks with a local partner. Third, in many countries, political considerations make joint ventures the only feasible entry mode. Research suggests joint ventures with local partners face a low risk of being subject to nationalization or other forms of adverse government interference.[18] This appears to be because local equity partners, who may have some influence on host-government policy, have a vested interest in speaking out against nationalization or government interference.

Disadvantages   Despite these advantages, joint ventures have major disadvantages. First, as with licensing, a firm that enters into a joint venture risks giving control of its technology to its partner. Thus, a proposed joint venture in 2002 between Boeing and Mitsubishi Heavy Industries to build a new wide-body jet (the 787), raised fears that Boeing might unwittingly give away its commercial airline technology to the Japanese. However, joint-venture agreements can be constructed to minimize this risk. One option is to hold majority ownership in the venture. This allows the dominant partner to exercise greater control over its technology. But it can be difficult to find a foreign partner willing to settle for minority ownership. Another option is to "wall off" from a partner technology that is central to the core competence of the firm, while sharing other technology.

A second disadvantage is that a joint venture does not give a firm the tight control over subsidiaries that it might need to realize experience curve or location economies. Nor does it give a firm the tight control over a foreign subsidiary that it might need for engaging in coordinated global attacks against its rivals. Consider the entry of Texas Instruments (TI) into the Japanese semiconductor market. When TI established semiconductor facilities in Japan, it did so for the dual purpose of checking Japanese manufacturers' market share and limiting their cash available for invading TI's global market. In other words, TI was engaging in global strategic coordination. To implement this strategy, TI's subsidiary in Japan had to be prepared to take instructions from corporate headquarters regarding competitive strategy. The strategy also required the Japanese subsidiary to run at a loss if necessary. Few if any potential joint-venture partners would have been willing to accept such conditions, since it would have necessitated a willingness to accept a negative return on investment. Indeed, many joint ventures establish a degree of autonomy that would make such direct control over strategic decisions all but impossible to establish.[19] Thus, to implement this strategy, TI set up a wholly owned subsidiary in Japan.

A third disadvantage with joint ventures is that the shared ownership arrangement can lead to conflicts and battles for control between the investing firms if their goals and objectives change or if they take different views as to what the strategy should be. This was apparently not a problem with the Fuji–Xerox joint venture. According to

Yotaro Kobayashi, currently the chairman of Fuji–Xerox, a primary reason is that both Xerox and Fuji Photo adopted an arm's-length relationship with Fuji–Xerox, giving the venture's management considerable freedom to determine its own strategy.[20] However, much research indicates that conflicts of interest over strategy and goals often arise in joint ventures. These conflicts tend to be greater when the venture is between firms of different nationalities, and they often end in the dissolution of the venture.[21] Such conflicts tend to be triggered by shifts in the relative bargaining power of venture partners. For example, in the case of ventures between a foreign firm and a local firm, as a foreign partner's knowledge about local market conditions increases, it depends less on the expertise of a local partner. This increases the bargaining power of the foreign partner and ultimately leads to conflicts over control of the venture's strategy and goals.[22] Some firms have sought to limit such problems by entering into joint ventures in which one partner has a controlling interest.

WHOLLY OWNED SUBSIDIARIES In a **wholly owned subsidiary,** the firm owns 100 percent of the stock. Establishing a wholly owned subsidiary in a foreign market can be done two ways. The firm either can set up a new operation in that country, often referred to as a greenfield venture, or it can acquire an established firm in the host nation and use that firm to promote its products.[23] For example, ING's strategy for entering the U.S. insurance market was to acquire established U.S. enterprises, rather than try to build an operation from the ground floor.

Wholly Owned Subsidiary
A subsidiary in which the firm owns 100 percent of the stock.

Advantages   There are several clear advantages of wholly owned subsidiaries. First, when a firm's competitive advantage is based on technological competence, a wholly owned subsidiary will often be the preferred entry mode because it reduces the risk of losing control over that competence. (See Chapter 7 for more details.) Many high-tech firms prefer this entry mode for overseas expansion (e.g., firms in the semiconductor, electronics, and pharmaceutical industries). Second, a wholly owned subsidiary gives a firm tight control over operations in different countries. This is necessary for engaging in global strategic coordination (i.e., using profits from one country to support competitive attacks in another).

Third, a wholly owned subsidiary may be required if a firm is trying to realize location and experience curve economies (as firms pursuing global and transnational strategies try to do). As we saw in Chapter 11, when cost pressures are intense, it may pay a firm to configure its value chain in such a way that the value added at each stage is maximized. Thus, a national subsidiary may specialize in manufacturing only part of the product line or certain components of the end product, exchanging parts and products with other subsidiaries in the firm's global system. Establishing such a global production system requires a high degree of control over the operations of each affiliate. The various operations must be prepared to accept centrally determined decisions as to how they will produce, how much they will produce, and how their output will be priced for transfer to the next operation. Because licensees or joint-venture partners are unlikely to accept such a subservient role, establishing wholly owned subsidiaries may be necessary. Finally, establishing a wholly owed subsidiary gives the firm a 100 percent share in the profits generated in a foreign market.

Disadvantages   Establishing a wholly owned subsidiary is generally the most costly method of serving a foreign market from a capital investment standpoint. Firms doing this must bear the full capital costs and risks of setting up overseas operations. The risks associated with learning to do business in a new culture are less if the firm acquires an established host-country enterprise. However, acquisitions raise additional problems, including those associated with trying to marry divergent corporate cultures. These problems may more than offset any benefits derived by acquiring an established operation. Because the choice between greenfield ventures and acquisitions is such an important one, we shall discuss it in more detail later in the chapter.

Selecting an Entry Mode

LEARNING OBJECTIVE 3
Identify the factors that influence a firm's choice of entry mode.

As the preceding discussion demonstrated, all the entry modes have advantages and disadvantages, as summarized in Table 12.1. Thus, trade-offs are inevitable when selecting an entry mode. For example, when considering entry into an unfamiliar country with a track record for discriminating against foreign-owned enterprises when awarding government contracts, a firm might favor a joint venture with a local enterprise. Its rationale might be that the local partner will help it establish operations in an unfamiliar environment and will help the company win government contracts. However, if the firm's core competence is based on proprietary technology, entering a joint venture might risk losing control of that technology to the joint-venture partner, in which case the strategy may seem unattractive. Despite the existence of such trade-offs, it is possible to make some generalizations about the optimal choice of entry mode.[24]

table **12.1**

Advantages and
Disadvantages of
Entry Modes

Entry Mode	Advantages	Disadvantages
Exporting	Ability to realize location and experience curve economies	High transport costs Trade barriers Problems with local marketing agents
Turnkey contracts	Ability to earn returns from process technology skills in countries where FDI is restricted	Creating efficient competitors Lack of long-term market presence
Licensing	Low development costs and risks	Lack of control over technology Inability to realize location and experience curve economies Inability to engage in global strategic coordination
Franchising	Low development costs and risks	Lack of control over quality Inability to engage in global strategic coordination
Joint ventures	Access to local partner's knowledge Sharing development costs and risks Politically acceptable	Lack of control over technology Inability to engage in global strategic coordination Inability to realize location and experience economies
Wholly owned subsidiaries	Protection of technology Ability to engage in global strategic coordination Ability to realize location and experience economies	High costs and risks

CORE COMPETENCIES AND ENTRY MODE   We saw in Chapter 11 that firms often expand internationally to earn greater returns from their core competencies, transferring the skills and products derived from their core competencies to foreign markets where indigenous competitors lack those skills. The optimal entry mode for these firms depends to some degree on the nature of their core competencies. A distinction can be drawn between firms whose core competency is in technological know-how and those whose core competency is in management know-how.

Technological Know-How

As was observed in Chapter 7, if a firm's competitive advantage (its core competence) is based on control over proprietary technological know-how, licensing and joint-venture arrangements should be avoided if possible to minimize the risk of losing control over that technology. Thus, if a high-tech firm sets up operations in a foreign country to profit from a core competency in technological know-how, it will probably do so through a wholly owned subsidiary. This rule should not be viewed as hard and fast, however. Sometimes a licensing or joint-venture arrangement can be structured to reduce the risk of licensees or joint-venture partners expropriating technological know-how. Another exception exists when a firm perceives its technological advantage to be only transitory, when it expects rapid imitation of its core technology by competitors. In such cases, the firm might want to license its technology as rapidly as possible to foreign firms to gain global acceptance for its technology before the imitation occurs.[25] Such a strategy has some advantages. By licensing its technology to competitors, the firm may deter them from developing their own, possibly superior, technology. Further, by licensing its technology, the firm may establish its technology as the dominant design in the industry (as Matsushita did with its VHS format for VCRs). This may ensure a steady stream of royalty payments. However, the attractions of licensing are frequently outweighed by the risks of losing control over technology and if this is a risk, licensing should be avoided.

Management Know-How

The competitive advantage of many service firms is based on management know-how (e.g., McDonald's, Starbucks). For such firms, the risk of losing control over the management skills to franchisees or joint-venture partners is not that great. These firms' valuable asset is their brand name, and brand names are generally well protected by international laws pertaining to trademarks. Given this, many of the issues arising in the case of technological know-how are of less concern here. As a result, many service firms favor a combination of franchising and subsidiaries to control the franchises within particular countries or regions. The subsidiaries may be wholly owned or joint ventures, but most service firms have found that joint ventures with local partners work best for the controlling subsidiaries. A joint venture is often politically more acceptable and brings a degree of local knowledge to the subsidiary.

PRESSURES FOR COST REDUCTIONS AND ENTRY MODE   The greater the pressures for cost reductions are, the more likely a firm will want to pursue some combination of exporting and wholly owned subsidiaries. By manufacturing in those locations where factor conditions are optimal and then exporting to the rest of the world, a firm may be able to realize substantial location and experience curve economies. The firm might then want to export the finished product to marketing subsidiaries based in various countries. These subsidiaries will typically be wholly owned and have the responsibility for overseeing distribution in their particular countries. Setting up wholly owned marketing subsidiaries is preferable to joint-venture arrangements and to using foreign marketing agents because it gives the firm tight control that might be required for coordinating a globally dispersed value chain. It also gives the firm the ability to use the profits generated in one market to improve its competitive position in another market. In other words, firms pursuing global standardization or transnational strategies tend to prefer establishing wholly owned subsidiaries.

Greenfield Venture or Acquisition?

LEARNING OBJECTIVE 4
Recognize the pros and cons of acquisitions versus greenfield ventures as an entry strategy.

A firm can establish a wholly owned subsidiary in a country by building a subsidiary from the ground up, the so-called greenfield strategy, or by acquiring an enterprise in the target market.[26] The volume of cross-border acquisitions has been growing at a rapid rate for two decades. Over the past decade, between 40 and 80 percent of all FDI inflows have been in the form of mergers and acquisitions. In 2001, for example, mergers and acquisitions accounted for 80 percent of all FDI inflows. In 2004 the figure was 51 percent, or some $381 billion. In 2008 the figure was 40 percent, or some $673 billion.[27] The relative low figure recorded in 2008 reflects the impact of the global economic crisis, which depressed equity values worldwide and made cross-border mergers and acquisitions less attractive as an entry mode.

PROS AND CONS OF ACQUISITIONS

Acquisitions have three major points in their favor. First, they are quick to execute. By acquiring an established enterprise, a firm can rapidly build its presence in the target foreign market. When the German automobile company Daimler-Benz decided it needed a bigger presence in the U.S. automobile market, it did not increase that presence by building new factories to serve the United States, a process that would have taken years. Instead, it acquired the number three U.S. automobile company, Chrysler, and merged the two operations to form DaimlerChrysler (Daimler spun off Chrysler into a private equity firm in 2007). When the Spanish telecommunications service provider Telefonica wanted to build a service presence in Latin America, it did so through a series of acquisitions, purchasing telecommunications companies in Brazil and Argentina. In these cases, the firms made acquisitions because they knew that was the quickest way to establish a sizable presence in the target market.

Second, in many cases firms make acquisitions to preempt their competitors. The need for preemption is particularly great in markets that are rapidly globalizing, such as telecommunications, where a combination of deregulation within nations and liberalization of regulations governing cross-border foreign direct investment has made it much easier for enterprises to enter foreign markets through acquisitions. Such markets may see concentrated waves of acquisitions as firms race each other to attain global scale. In the telecommunications industry, for example, regulatory changes triggered what can be called a feeding frenzy, with firms entering each other's markets via acquisitions to establish a global presence. These included the $60 billion acquisition of Air Touch Communications in the United States by the British company Vodafone, which was the largest acquisition ever; the $13 billion acquisition of One 2 One in Britain by the

Three pros to acquisitions, such as Vodafone's purchase of AirTouch, include a quick execution, preemption of the competition, and less risk than greenfield ventures.

German company Deutsche Telekom; and the $6.4 billion acquisition of Excel Communications in the United States by Teleglobe of Canada, all of which occurred in 1998 and 1999.[28] A similar wave of cross-border acquisitions occurred in the global automobile industry over the same time period, with Daimler acquiring Chrysler, Ford acquiring Volvo, and Renault acquiring Nissan.

Third, managers may believe acquisitions to be less risky than greenfield ventures. When a firm makes an acquisition, it buys a set of assets that are producing a known revenue and profit stream. In contrast, the revenue and profit stream from a greenfield venture is uncertain because it does not yet exist. When a firm makes an acquisition in a foreign market, it not only acquires a set of tangible assets, such as factories, logistics systems, customer service systems, and so on, but it also acquires valuable intangible assets including a local brand name and managers' knowledge of the business environment in that nation. Such knowledge can reduce the risk of mistakes caused by ignorance of the national culture.

Despite the arguments for making acquisitions, acquisitions often produce disappointing results.[29] For example, a study by Mercer Management Consulting looked at 150 acquisitions worth more than $500 million each that were undertaken between January 1990 and July 1995.[30] The Mercer study concluded that 50 percent of these acquisitions eroded shareholder value, while another 33 percent created only marginal returns. Only 17 percent were judged to be successful. Similarly, a study by KPMG, an accounting and management consulting company, looked at 700 large acquisitions between 1996 and 1998. The study found that while some 30 percent of these actually created value for the acquiring company, 31 percent destroyed value, and the remainder had little impact.[31] A similar study by McKenzie Co. estimated that some 70 percent of mergers and acquisitions failed to achieve expected revenue synergies.[32] In a seminal study of the post-acquisition performance of acquired companies, David Ravenscraft and Mike Scherer concluded that on average the profits and market shares of acquired companies declined following acquisition.[33] They also noted that a smaller but substantial subset of those companies experienced traumatic difficulties, which ultimately led to their being sold by the acquiring company. Ravenscraft and Scherer's evidence suggests that many acquisitions destroy rather than create value. While most of this research has looked at domestic acquisitions, the findings probably also apply to cross-border acquisitions.[34]

Why Do Acquisitions Fail?   Acquisitions fail for several reasons. First, the acquiring firms often overpay for the assets of the acquired firm. The price of the target firm can get bid up if more than one firm is interested in its purchase, as is often the case. In addition, the management of the acquiring firm is often too optimistic about the value that can be created via an acquisition and is thus willing to pay a significant premium over a target firm's market capitalization. This is called the "hubris hypothesis" of why acquisitions fail. The hubris hypothesis postulates that top managers typically overestimate their ability to create value from an acquisition, primarily because rising to the top of a corporation has given them an exaggerated sense of their own capabilities.[35] For example, Daimler acquired Chrysler in 1998 for $40 billion, a premium of 40 percent over the market value of Chrysler before the takeover bid. Daimler paid this much because it thought it could use Chrysler to help it grow market share in the United States. At the time, Daimler's management issued bold announcements about the "synergies" that would be created from combining the operations of the two companies. Executives believed they could attain greater scale economies from the global presence, take costs out of the German and U.S. operations, and boost the profitability of the combined entity. However, within a year of the acquisition, Daimler's German management was faced with a crisis at Chrysler, which was suddenly losing money due to weak sales in the United States. In retrospect, Daimler's management had been far too optimistic about the potential for future demand in the U.S. auto market and about the opportunities for creating value from "synergies." Daimler acquired Chrysler at the end of a multiyear boom in U.S. auto sales and paid a large premium over Chrysler's market value just before demand slumped (and in 2007, in an admission of failure, Daimler sold its Chrysler unit to a private equity firm).[36]

Second, many acquisitions fail because there is a clash between the cultures of the acquiring and acquired firm. After an acquisition, many acquired companies experience high management turnover, possibly because their employees do not like the acquiring company's way of doing things.[37] This happened at DaimlerChrysler; many senior managers left Chrysler in the first year after the merger. Apparently, Chrysler executives disliked the dominance in decision making by Daimler's German managers, while the Germans resented that Chrysler's American managers were paid two to three times as much as their German counterparts. These cultural differences created tensions, which ultimately exhibited themselves in high management turnover at Chrysler.[38] The loss of management talent and expertise can materially harm the performance of the acquired unit.[39] This may be particularly problematic in an international business, where management of the acquired unit may have valuable local knowledge that can be difficult to replace.

Third, many acquisitions fail because attempts to realize synergies by integrating the operations of the acquired and acquiring entities often run into roadblocks and take much longer than forecast. Differences in management philosophy and company culture can slow the integration of operations. Differences in national culture may exacerbate these problems. Bureaucratic haggling between managers also complicates the process. Again, this reportedly occurred at DaimlerChrysler, where grand plans to integrate the operations of the two companies were bogged down by endless committee meetings and by simple logistical considerations such as the six-hour time difference between Detroit and Germany. By the time an integration plan had been worked out, Chrysler was losing money, and Daimler's German managers suddenly had a crisis on their hands.

Finally, many acquisitions fail due to inadequate pre-acquisition screening.[40] Many firms decide to acquire other firms without thoroughly analyzing the potential benefits and costs. They often move with undue haste to execute the acquisition, perhaps because they fear another competitor may preempt them. After the acquisition, however, many acquiring firms discover that instead of buying a well-run business, they have purchased a troubled organization. This may be a particular problem in cross-border acquisitions because the acquiring firm may not fully understand the target firm's national culture and business system.

Reducing the Risks of Failure   These problems can all be overcome if the firm is careful about its acquisition strategy.[41] Screening of the foreign enterprise to be acquired, including a detailed auditing of operations, financial position, and management culture, can help to make sure the firm (1) does not pay too much for the acquired unit, (2) does not uncover any nasty surprises after the acquisition, and (3) acquires a firm whose organization culture is not antagonistic to that of the acquiring enterprise. It is also important for the acquirer to allay any concerns that management in the acquired enterprise might have. The objective should be to reduce unwanted management attrition after the acquisition. Finally, managers must move rapidly after an acquisition to put an integration plan in place and to act on that plan. Some people in both the acquiring and acquired units will try to slow or stop any integration efforts, particularly when losses of employment or management power are involved, and managers should have a plan for dealing with such impediments before they arise.

PROS AND CONS OF GREENFIELD VENTURES   The big advantage of establishing a greenfield venture in a foreign country is that it gives the firm a much greater ability to build the kind of subsidiary company that it wants. For example, it is much easier to build an organization culture from scratch than it is to change the culture of an acquired unit. Similarly, it is much easier to establish a set of operating routines in a new subsidiary than it is to convert the operating routines of an acquired unit. This is a very important advantage for many international businesses, where transferring products, competencies, skills, and know-how from the established operations of the firm to the new subsidiary are principal ways of creating value. For example, when Lincoln Electric, the U.S. manufacturer of arc welding equipment, first ventured overseas in the mid-1980s, it did so by acquisitions, purchasing arc welding equipment companies in Europe. However, Lincoln's competitive advantage in the United States was based on a strong organizational culture and a unique set of incentives that encouraged its employees to do everything possible to increase productivity. Lincoln found through bitter experience that it was almost impossible to transfer its organizational culture and incentives to acquired firms, which had their own distinct organizational cultures and incentives. As a result, the firm switched its entry strategy in the mid-1990s and began to enter foreign countries by establishing greenfield ventures, building operations from the ground up. While this strategy takes more time to execute, Lincoln has found that it yields greater long-run returns than the acquisition strategy.

Set against this significant advantage are the disadvantages of establishing a greenfield venture. Greenfield ventures are slower to establish. They are also risky. As with any new venture, a degree of uncertainty is associated with future revenue and profit prospects. However, if the firm has already been successful in other foreign markets and understands what it takes to do business in other countries, these risks may not be that great. For example, having already gained great knowledge about operating internationally, the risk to McDonald's of entering yet another country is probably not that great. Also, greenfield ventures are less risky than acquisitions in the sense that there is less potential for unpleasant surprises. A final disadvantage is the possibility of being preempted by more aggressive global competitors who enter via acquisitions and build a big market presence that limits the market potential for the greenfield venture.

MAKING A CHOICE   The choice between acquisitions and greenfield ventures is not an easy one. Both modes have their advantages and disadvantages. In general, the choice will depend on the circumstances confronting the firm. If the firm is seeking to enter a market where there are already well-established incumbent enterprises, and where global competitors are also interested in establishing a presence, it may pay the firm to enter via an acquisition. In such circumstances, a greenfield venture may be too slow to establish a sizable presence. However, if the firm is going to make an

 **Another** Perspective

Risk and Control Again

All agree that business is about risk. Taking the right risk determines success or failure. Yet risk is unavoidable. The other aspect of business is control. Ideally, you want to be in complete control, yet that is impossible. Therefore, successful business seeks to mitigate risk and maximize control. To a large extent, the mode of entry is one of the critical means by which to potentially mitigate risk and maximize control. To a large extent, foreign expansion has more uncontrollable factors than those that can be controlled. Consider political and legal factors, economic climate, competitors, cultural forces, geography, and the limitations on distribution, and you quickly come to the realization that you cannot control everything. But, what you will be able to control is the research. Nothing will assist more in making the correct decision about risk and control than good research.

acquisition, its management should be cognizant of the risks associated with acquisitions that were discussed earlier and consider these when determining which firms to purchase. It may be better to enter by the slower route of a greenfield venture than to make a bad acquisition.

If the firm is considering entering a country where there are no incumbent competitors to be acquired, then a greenfield venture may be the only mode. Even when incumbents exist, if the competitive advantage of the firm is based on the transfer of organizationally embedded competencies, skills, routines, and culture, it may still be preferable to enter via a greenfield venture. Things such as skills and organizational culture, which are based on significant knowledge that is difficult to articulate and codify, are much easier to embed in a new venture than they are in an acquired entity, where the firm may have to overcome the established routines and culture of the acquired firm. Thus, as our earlier examples suggest, firms such as McDonald's and Lincoln Electric prefer to enter foreign markets by establishing greenfield ventures.

Key Terms

timing of entry, p. 446
first-mover advantages, p. 446
first-mover disadvantages, p. 446
pioneering costs, p. 446

exporting, p. 450
turnkey project, p. 452
licensing, p. 453
franchising, p. 454

joint venture, p. 455
wholly owned
subsidiary, p. 457

Summary

The chapter made the following points:

1. Basic entry decisions include identifying which markets to enter, when to enter those markets, and on what scale.

2. The most attractive foreign markets tend to be found in politically stable developed and developing nations that have free market systems and where there is not a dramatic upsurge in either inflation rates or private-sector debt.

3. There are several advantages associated with entering a national market early, before other international businesses have established themselves. These advantages must be balanced against the pioneering costs that early entrants often have to bear, including the greater risk of business failure.

4. Large-scale entry into a national market constitutes a major strategic commitment that is likely to change the nature of competition in

that market and limit the entrant's future strategic flexibility. Although making major strategic commitments can yield many benefits, there are also risks associated with such a strategy.

5. The six modes of entering a foreign market are exporting, creating turnkey projects, licensing, franchising, establishing joint ventures, and setting up a wholly owned subsidiary.

6. Exporting has the advantages of facilitating the realization of experience curve economies and of avoiding the costs of setting up manufacturing operations in another country. Disadvantages include high transport costs, trade barriers, and problems with local marketing agents.

7. Turnkey projects allow firms to export their process know-how to countries where FDI might be prohibited, thereby enabling the firm

to earn a greater return from this asset. The disadvantage is that the firm may inadvertently create efficient global competitors in the process.

8. The main advantage of licensing is that the licensee bears the costs and risks of opening a foreign market. Disadvantages include the risk of losing technological know-how to the licensee and a lack of tight control over licensees.

9. The main advantage of franchising is that the franchisee bears the costs and risks of opening a foreign market. Disadvantages center on problems of quality control of distant franchisees.

10. Joint ventures have the advantages of sharing the costs and risks of opening a foreign market and of gaining local knowledge and political influence. Disadvantages include the risk of losing control over technology and a lack of tight control.

11. The advantages of wholly owned subsidiaries include tight control over technological know-how. The main disadvantage is that the firm must bear all the costs and risks of opening a foreign market.

12. The optimal choice of entry mode depends on the firm's strategy. When technological know-how constitutes a firm's core competence, wholly owned subsidiaries are preferred, since they best control technology. When management know-how constitutes a firm's core competence, foreign franchises controlled by joint ventures seem to be optimal. When the firm is pursuing a global standardization or transnational strategy, the need for tight control over operations to realize location and experience curve economies suggests wholly owned subsidiaries are the best entry mode.

13. When establishing a wholly owned subsidiary in a country, a firm must decide whether to do so by a greenfield venture strategy or by acquiring an established enterprise in the target market.

14. Acquisitions are quick to execute, may enable a firm to preempt its global competitors, and involve buying a known revenue and profit stream. Acquisitions may fail when the acquiring firm overpays for the target, when the culture of the acquiring and acquired firms clash, when there is a high level of management attrition after the acquisition, and when there is a failure to integrate the operations of the acquiring and acquired firm.

15. The advantage of a greenfield venture in a foreign country is that it gives the firm a much greater ability to build the kind of subsidiary company that it wants. For example, it is much easier to build an organization culture from scratch than it is to change the culture of an acquired unit.

Critical Thinking and Discussion Questions

1. Review the Management Focus "Tesco's International Growth Strategy." Then answer the following questions:
   a. Why did Tesco's initial international expansion strategy focus on developing nations?
   b. How does Tesco create value in its international operations?
   c. In Asia, Tesco has a long history of entering into joint-venture agreements with local partners. What are the benefits of doing this for Tesco? What are the risks? How are those risks mitigated?
   d. In March 2006 Tesco announced it would enter the United States. This represents a departure from its historic strategy of focusing on developing nations. Why do you think Tesco made this decision? How is the U.S. market different from others Tesco has entered? What are the risks here? How do you think Tesco will do?

2. Licensing proprietary technology to foreign competitors is the best way to give up a firm's competitive advantage. Discuss.

3. Discuss how the need for control over foreign operations varies with firms' strategies and core competencies. What are the implications for the choice of entry mode?

4. A small Canadian firm that has developed some valuable new medical products using its unique biotechnology know-how is trying to decide how

best to serve the European Community market. Its choices are given below. The cost of investment in manufacturing facilities will be a major one for the Canadian firm, but it is not outside its reach. If these are the firm's only options, which one would you advise it to choose? Why?

- Manufacture the product at home and let foreign sales agents handle marketing.

- Manufacture the products at home and set up a wholly owned subsidiary in Europe to handle marketing.

- Enter into an alliance with a large European pharmaceutical firm. The product would be manufactured in Europe by the 50/50 joint venture and marketed by the European firm.

Research Task 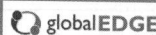 http://globalEDGE.msu.edu

Use the globalEDGE Resource Desk (http://global EDGE.msu.edu/resourcedesk/) to complete the following exercises:

1. Entrepreneur magazine annually publishes a ranking of America's top 200 *franchisers* seeking international franchisees. Provide a list of the top 10 companies that pursue franchising as a mode of international expansion. Study one of these companies in detail and provide a description of its business model, its international expansion pattern, the qualifications it looks for

in its franchisees, and the type of support and training it provides.

2. The U.S. Commercial Service prepares a series of reports titled the *Country Commercial Guide (CCG)* for each country of interest to U.S. investors. Utilize this guide to gather information on China. Imagine that your company is in agribusiness and is considering entering this country. Select the most appropriate entry method, supporting your decision with the information collected from the commercial guide.

closing case

Intel in Costa Rica

For more than a year, Intel searched the world to find the right place to establish its next semiconductor assembly and test plant. Among the choices were Indonesia, Thailand, Brazil, Argentina, Chile, Mexico, and Costa Rica. As part of its strategy Intel sought cheap, well-educated, reliable labor in a strategically located environment. Although many of these countries could have provided that cheap source of labor, Mexico in particular was a strong candidate. It is a large country and is close to the North American market and the Pacific Basin. Much to the surprise of many, however, in 1997 Intel chose Costa Rica.

Intel chose Costa Rica, the small Central American country, for various strategic reasons. In addition to the relatively location-specific advantage as compared to most of the other countries, among the most important determining factors were the favorable, already existing, corporate tax exemptions available to firms that satisfied certain conditions under the free zone scheme; the excellent educational level of the labor force; a stable political scenario; economic openness;

and a relatively corruption-free environment. As marketed to Intel, "Small is beautiful." Costa Rica's relatively small size was precisely what attracted Intel.

Intel's strategic decision-making process took more than one year and involved four phases: pre-qualification, site research, contingent announcement and delivery, and start-up.

Lead by an experienced international team, Intel began the strategic process of determining the best site. This site selection team was headed by Intel's vice president of international site selection, in collaboration with the vice president of the technology and management group; vice president of finance, tax, customs and licensing; and an international site selection analyst. The team also included functional experts from operations, environmental health and safety, human resources, legal, administration, and public relations. Understanding this process, Costa Rica was able to mobilize support in the political and business communities and respond to Intel's requests for information from these divergent departments and provide assistance in very short periods of time. It was very clear that Costa Rica also understood the magnitude of the opportunity.

Intel had every reason to be very careful in its final selection. Unlike many other manufacturing firms, for Intel the decision to expand internationally is not premised on access to foreign markets but rather to production capabilities. The costs associated with shipping silicon chips is minimal compared to the production of that chip.

Establishing silicon wafer semiconductor manufacturing capabilities is an expensive endeavor, normally ranging between $100 and $300 million. Such an investment is projected approximately two years ahead of production demand. The world of semiconductor manufacturing is fast paced. Production capabilities must be acquired quickly. Given the short product life cycle of a silicon chip, Intel recognized the need for expansion and continuously sought to expand production capabilities to meet that demand. It had done so successfully with silicon wafer manufacturing in Ireland and Israel and assembly and testing plants in Malaysia, China, and the Philippines. For Costa Rica, Intel had projected an initial $300 million investment in a greenfield development. To a small country such as Costa Rica, a $300 million investment was equivalent to 2.1 percent of the country's GDP. But, perhaps most importantly, is the derivative impact that this mode of entry had on the economy and the population in general.

The "ripple" or "genesis" effect this had on the Costa Rican economy merits discussion. Since its initial investment, subsequent investments and expansion have occurred. Until the financial crisis hit, Intel's microprocessing plant accounted for as much as 20 percent of Costa Rican exports and 5 percent of the country's GDP. According to the World Bank, Intel directly employs approximately 2,900 workers and indirectly another 2,000 from suppliers. Just as important, the wages paid are significantly above those of the agricultural sector.

For Intel, the decision to enter Costa Rica also had some unforeseen benefits. At one point, the Costa Rican plant supplied 25 percent of the chips for Intel worldwide. But, besides the special attention by the Figueres administration early on in "fast-tracking" its start-up, Intel discovered higher levels of engineering and software development capabilities that permitted expansion into more sophisticated processes. The company also found a higher level of managerial maturity that permitted it to replace costly expatriates in less than two years, quicker than the three years it had anticipated.

Approximately 12 years later, the greenfield appears to be bearing fruit. The decision to invest in Costa Rica appears to have been beneficial to both Intel and Costa Rica. Whether Costa Rica can leverage Intel as an anchor for the further development of an "electronic cluster" that would attract further investment remains to be seen.

Sources: "Impact of Intel in Costa Rica—Nine Years After the Decision to Invest," Investing in Development Series, Multilateral Investment Guarantee Agency, 2006; "Intel supone el 4.9 por ciento del PIB de Costa Rica," El Economista, June 10, 2006; "Intel Expands Operations," Latin America Monitor: Central America Monitor, 20, no. 12 (2003), p. 7; "Costa Rica Company: Intel Announces More Investment," EIU ViewsWire, 2003; and D. Spar, "Attracting High Technology Investment, Intel's Costa Rican Plant," Foreign Investment Advisory Service, Joint Facility of the International Financial Corporation and the World Bank, Occasional Paper, April 11, 1998.

Case Discussion Questions

1. Intel has consistently chosen to increase its production capabilities by means of a greenfield development. Why do you think this is the case?

2. Why do you think Intel has developed an international site selection team? Why are the various functions identified as being a necessary part of that team?

3. What are the risks that Intel must assume as it enters into the development of a silicon manufacturing plant in a foreign country?

4. As the case points out, it appears that the relationship between Intel and Costa Rica seems to be progressing well. What are some of the advantages of such goodwill between Intel and Costa Rica?

5. Although Intel has been successful in establishing production capabilities in foreign countries, what modification in strategy do you propose would make its choice even better?

chapter 13

Exporting, Importing, and Countertrade

Coficab and Tunisia

Coficab is one of the world's most successful suppliers of automotive electrical cables and wires. Tunisia has a small export-led economy. Whereas the global financial crisis hit most of the developed world, Coficab and Tunisia actually benefited. Coficab has 10 percent market share worldwide and 25 percent European share of the automobile wiring market. Much of their business is export driven. Having started in Tunis, Tunisia, with their first plant in 1992, over the past two decades Coficab has expanded into Portugal, Morocco, Germany, and Romania to facilitate the export demands of its customers. And demanding customers they are.

One need only recall the recent Toyota wiring issues that resulted in the recall of millions of automobiles in the United States to recognize that exporting quality wiring and cables to the automobile industry is serious business. Coficab wiring can be found in many places—from the seating systems provided to Lear Corporation to the actual electrical systems of the Peugeot Citroen line of cars. Their reach extends from Sumitomo Electric in Germany to Japanese assembly of connectors and harnesses in the United States. In fact, they are among the top 10 automotive wiring harness makers as well as the main original equipment manufacturers (OEMs) for companies such as Mercedes, Volkswagen, Renault, Fiat, Ford, and Opel.

Although relatively small and originating in a small African nation (population 10 million), from an export perspective Coficab is a success story. Part of that success has been its ability to tap the closely knit wire market, especially within the Maghreb region and Europe, and take advantage of the opportunities the economic crisis generated. The automobile sector is very sensitive to cost. The crisis brought a need for consolidation in Europe. Coficab lost three competitors during that consolidation. It stepped up to meet the supply demands by expanding its production capabilities. Just as important, the automotive wire and cable market is one that is based not only on the quality of the product but the network of relationships necessary to facilitate the product getting to the customer. In the export business in general—but specifically within the wire and cable business—relationships are critical.

Coficab is part of the Elloumi Group, a family-owned holding company that was started by patriarch Faouzi Elloumi and is now headed by his son Hichem. It is part of an extensive family network that includes brothers as well as sisters. These personal contacts are in turn used to establish the complex system of relationships and trust necessary within the region. And it appears to be working. According to Mohamed Riahi, the sales and marketing manager for Coficab, the company's exports from Tunisia are expected to increase by 50 percent during 2010. Coficab is an example of a great economic recovery during difficult times. ●

Sources: Coficab Web site, www.coficab.com; "Zied Elloumi," *Maghreb Confidential,* 2010; "Coficab," *Maghreb Confidential,* 2010; "Co-operation Agreement Between 'FCI' and 'COFICAB'," *Agency Tunis Afrique Press,* 2010; and H. Saleh, "Tunisia Profits from Crisis," *Financial Times,* 2009.

Introduction

In the previous chapter, we reviewed exporting from a strategic perspective. We considered exporting as just one of a range of strategic options for profiting from international expansion. This chapter is more concerned with the nuts and bolts of exporting (and importing). Here we look at how to export. As the opening case makes clear, exporting is not just for large enterprises; many small entrepreneurial firms such as Vellus Products have benefited significantly from the money-making opportunities of exporting.

 **Another** Perspective

Autarky: Not in the Vocabulary of Globalization!
The word *autarky* refers to the belief that a country should be self-sufficient and avoid trade with other nations. Most economists regard autarky as an idealistic, but impractical, goal. Throughout history, countries have tried to achieve autarky, but soon discovered they could not produce the wide range of goods their population wants *and* make those goods available at competitive prices. In fact, those countries found themselves worse off economically than nations that engage in international trade. Word to the wise: Unless your country can efficiently produce everything it needs, it needs to trade. ("Economics A-Z," www.economist.com)

The volume of export activity in the world economy has increased as exporting has become easier. The gradual decline in trade barriers under the umbrella of GATT and now the WTO (see Chapter 6) along with regional economic agreements such as the European Union and the North American Free Trade Agreement (see Chapter 8) have significantly increased export opportunities. At the same time, modern communication and transportation technologies have alleviated the logistical problems associated with exporting. Firms are increasingly using the World Wide Web, toll-free phone numbers, and international air express services to reduce the costs of exporting. Consequently, it is no longer unusual to find small companies that are thriving as exporters.

Nevertheless, exporting remains a challenge for many firms. Smaller enterprises can find the process intimidating. The firm wishing to export must identify foreign market opportunities, avoid a host of unanticipated problems that are often associated with doing business in a foreign market, familiarize itself with the mechanics of export and import financing, learn where to find financing and export credit insurance, and learn how it should deal with foreign exchange risk. The process can be made more problematic by currencies that are not freely convertible. Arranging payment for exports to countries with weak currencies can be a problem. This brings us to the topic of countertrade, by which payment for exports is received in goods and services rather than money. In this chapter, we will discuss all these issues with the exception of foreign exchange risk, which was covered in Chapter 10. We open the chapter by considering the promise and pitfalls of exporting.

The Promise and Pitfalls of Exporting

LEARNING OBJECTIVE 1
Explain the promises and risks associated with exporting.

The great promise of exporting is that large revenue and profit opportunities are to be found in foreign markets for most firms in most industries. This was true for the company profiled in the opening case. The international market is normally so much larger than the firm's domestic market that exporting is nearly always a way to increase the company's revenue and profit base. By expanding the size of the market, exporting can enable a firm to achieve economies of scale, thereby lowering its unit costs. Firms that do not export often lose out on significant opportunities for growth and cost reduction.[1]

Studies have shown that while many large firms tend to be proactive about seeking opportunities for profitable exporting, systematically scanning foreign markets to find ways to leverage their technology, products, and marketing skills in foreign countries, many medium-sized and small firms are very reactive.[2] Typically, such reactive firms do not even consider exporting until their domestic market is saturated and the emergence of excess productive capacity at home forces them to look for growth opportunities in foreign markets. Also, many small and medium-sized firms tend to wait for the world to come to them, rather than going out into the world to seek opportunities. Even when the world does come to them, they may not respond. An example is MMO Music Group, which makes sing-along tapes for karaoke machines. Foreign sales accounted for about 15 percent of MMO's revenues of $8 million, but the firm's CEO admits that this figure would probably have been much higher had he paid attention to building international sales. Unanswered faxes and phone messages from Asia and Europe often piled up while he was trying to manage the burgeoning domestic side of the business. By the time MMO did turn its attention to foreign markets, other competitors had stepped into the breach and MMO found it tough going to build export volume.[3]

MMO's experience is common, and it suggests a need for firms to become more proactive about seeking export opportunities. One reason more firms are not proactive is that they are unfamiliar with foreign market opportunities; they simply do not know how big the opportunities actually are or where they might lie. Simple ignorance of the potential opportunities is a huge barrier to exporting.[4] Also, many would-be exporters, particularly smaller firms, are often intimidated by the complexities and mechanics of exporting to countries where business practices, language, culture, legal systems, and currency are very different from the home market.[5] This combination of unfamiliarity and intimidation probably explains why exporters still account for only a tiny percentage of U.S. firms, less than 5 percent of firms with fewer than 500 employees, according to the Small Business Administration.[6]

To make matters worse, many neophyte exporters run into significant problems when first trying to do business abroad, and this sours them on future exporting ventures. Common pitfalls include poor market analysis, a poor understanding of competitive

Barokes "Wine in a Can"

In 1996, research began on a packaging system that would permit premium wines to be stored without breaking. Five years later, Vinesafe™ technology was developed and, after a legal battle, finally patented worldwide. With the new technology, the fragile nature of wine transportation and storage began to change. In the process, Barokes Wines was established.

For Australian exporter Barokes Wines, its "Wine-In-A-Can" greatly increases the mobility of wine and therefore its capabilities of being exported. For a number of sectors, the Vinesafe technology is being adopted because it presents a solution rather than being just another wine product. As an example, hotels and airlines are finding the packaging for "wine in a can" advantageous. Cans weigh much less than bottles, an important consideration on aircraft. Because cans are stackable, they take up less room. Shelf life may be as long as five years, and of course, it obviously solves the glass breakage problem.

Barokes wine is sourced from a number of wine-growing regions around Australia, with grapes grown to specification. The wine is carefully matured to achieve its peak and then hermetically sealed in specifically crated, internally lined 250-ml cans. After winning numerous awards and medals for its chardonnay semillon and sparkling chardonnay throughout the world, including the 2008 International Wine Challenge in London and the 2008 San Francisco Wine Competition for the quality of the wines that happen to come in a can, Barokes Wine has set out on an international export drive.

The company has begun exporting its wine and technology to India and Argentina. In India, Managing Director and co-founder Greg Stokes, understanding the idiosyncrasies of the export business, cautioned that Australian exporters need to have patience. "You need to allow for long lead times and, at the moment, India is flooded with companies trying to open markets, so you also have to be sure that you choose the right partner who is able to make your product work for both companies—the Indian and the Australian."

In Argentina, in a partnership with C&M Ship Broker, Barokes Wines focused on the youth market, restaurants, wine bars, and some supermarket and grocery chains. If things progress, the *Maia y K* brand (as it is known in Argentina) will then be subsequently exported with Argentine wines rather than Australian wines. Barokes Wines is finding its way to Japan. Liquor importer Nihon Shurui Hanbai Co. is selling Barokes premium red and white wine and sparkling wine in cans.

But perhaps as the most amazing export, Barokes Wines has managed to penetrate the tradition-bound Spanish wine market, mating the wine connoisseur with practicality. For the Spanish market, Barokes focused on exporting cabernet, syrah, merlot, chardonnay, and semillion wines. If they begin to take off, we can expect perhaps California or French wines to be next.

Sources: Barokes Web site, www.wineinacan.com; "Bodega Australiana Barokes Wines Ingresa a Mercado Argentino," *La Nación*, 2007; "Barokes Wines, the Owner of Wine-In-A-Can, Has Welcomed the Australian Patent," *Foodweek*, 2006; NoticiasFinancieras, "Bodega Australiana Barokes Wines Ingresa a Mercado Argentino," *La Nación*, 2007; K. McGregor, "Canned Wine Makes Progress," *Food Week (ABIX Abstracts)*, 2006; "Business Showroom: Wine in a Can," *Daily Yomiuri*, 2006; and Madrid, *Cinco Días*, "Gastronomía Disfrutar Del Vino En Lata" *Cinco Días*, 2006.

conditions in the foreign market, a failure to customize the product offering to the needs of foreign customers, lack of an effective distribution program, a poorly executed promotional campaign, and problems securing financing.[7] Novice exporters tend to underestimate the time and expertise needed to cultivate business in foreign countries.[8] Few realize the amount of management resources that have to be dedicated to this activity. Many foreign customers require face-to-face negotiations on their home turf. An exporter may have to spend months learning about a country's trade regulations, business practices, and more before a deal can be closed. The accompanying Management Focus documents the experience of Barokes Wines and suggests that it may take years not only to enter foreign markets but also for wine drinkers to become comfortable enough with the concept of "wine in a can" to purchase the product and help companies expand their businesses.

Exporters often face voluminous paperwork, complex formalities, and many potential delays and errors. According to a UN report on trade and development, a typical international trade transaction may involve 30 parties, 60 original documents, and

360 document copies, all of which have to be checked, transmitted, reentered into various information systems, processed, and filed. The United Nations has calculated that the time involved in preparing documentation, along with the costs of common errors in paperwork, often amounts to 10 percent of the final value of goods exported.[9]

Improving Export Performance

Inexperienced exporters have a number of ways to gain information about foreign market opportunities and avoid common pitfalls that tend to discourage and frustrate novice exporters.[10] In this section, we look at information sources for exporters to increase their knowledge of foreign market opportunities, we consider the pros and cons of using export management companies (EMCs) to assist in the export process, and we review various exporting strategies that can increase the probability of successful exporting. We begin, however, with a look at how several nations try to help domestic firms export.

AN INTERNATIONAL COMPARISON   One big impediment to exporting is the simple lack of knowledge of the opportunities available. Often there are many markets for a firm's product, but because they are in countries separated from the firm's home base by culture, language, distance, and time, the firm does not know of them. Identifying export opportunities is made even more complex because more than 200 countries with widely differing cultures compose the world of potential opportunities. Faced with such complexity and diversity, firms sometimes hesitate to seek export opportunities.

The way to overcome ignorance is to collect information. In Germany, one of the world's most successful exporting nations, trade associations, government agencies, and commercial banks gather information, helping small firms identify export opportunities. A similar function is provided by the Japanese Ministry of International Trade and Industry (MITI), which is always on the lookout for export opportunities. In addition, many Japanese firms are affiliated in some way with the *sogo shosha,* Japan's great trading houses. The *sogo shosha* have offices all over the world, and they proactively, continuously seek export opportunities for their affiliated companies large and small.[11]

German and Japanese firms can draw on the large reservoirs of experience, skills, information, and other resources of their respective export-oriented institutions. Unlike their German and Japanese competitors, many U.S. firms are relatively blind when they seek export opportunities; they are information disadvantaged. In part, this reflects historical differences. Both Germany and Japan have long made their living as trading nations, whereas until recently the United States has been a relatively self-contained continental economy in which international trade played a minor role. This is changing; both imports and exports now play a greater role in the U.S. economy than they did 20 years ago. However, the United States has not yet evolved an institutional structure for promoting exports similar to that of either Germany or Japan.

LEARNING OBJECTIVE 2
Identify the steps managers can take to improve their firm's export performance.

Sogo Shosha
Japan's great trading houses.

LEARNING OBJECTIVE 3
Identify information sources and government programs that exist to help exporters.

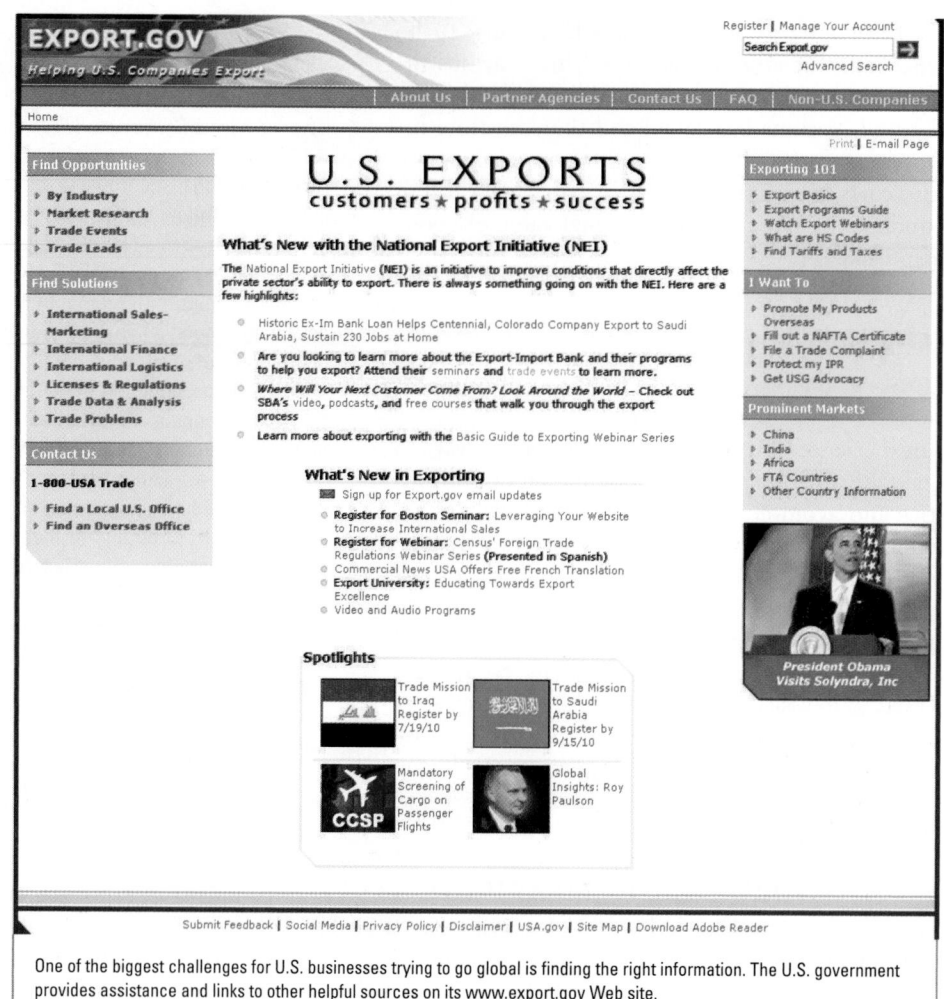

One of the biggest challenges for U.S. businesses trying to go global is finding the right information. The U.S. government provides assistance and links to other helpful sources on its www.export.gov Web site.

INFORMATION SOURCES Despite institutional disadvantages, U.S. firms can increase their awareness of export opportunities. The most comprehensive source of information is the U.S. Department of Commerce and its district offices all over the country. Within that department are two organizations dedicated to providing businesses with intelligence and assistance for attacking foreign markets: the International Trade Administration and the United States and Foreign Commercial Service.

These agencies provide the potential exporter with a "best prospects" list, which gives the names and addresses of potential distributors in foreign markets along with businesses they are in, the products they handle, and their contact person. In addition, the Department of Commerce has assembled a "comparison shopping service" for 14 countries that are major markets for U.S. exports. For a small fee, a firm can receive a customized market research survey on a product of its choice. This survey provides information on marketability, the competition, comparative prices, distribution channels, and names of potential sales representatives. Each study is conducted on-site by an officer of the Department of Commerce.

The Department of Commerce also organizes trade events that help potential exporters make foreign contacts and explore export opportunities. The department

Management FOCUS

Exporting and Governmental Help

For many companies, exporting is the first step taken in an internationalization process. With little or no previous experience, this first step may seem daunting. Business owners or managers, from many countries throughout the world, with little or no experience, especially within the trade finance aspects of exporting, have come to rely on governmental help. For many small- to medium-sized enterprises (SMEs), that help has initially come in the form of the Export–Import (EX–IM) Banks of their respective countries.

Take for example, the Export–Import Bank of Thailand, which recently established a program to provide SMEs with baht-denominated pre-shipment financing facility and forward contract arrangements. The bank also provides U.S. dollar-denominated pre-shipment financing for those seeking to hedge foreign exchange risk as a safety measure to the volatility of the baht.

Similarly, by means of financial guarantees, the Export–Import Bank of Korea provides repayment protection for cofinancing bank's loans to transactions that satisfy the bank's eligibility requirements. The bank guarantees that, in the event of default, it will repay all of the principal and interest on the loan. For the commercial lender, this is good news. Such a guarantee reduces risk exposure for the bank. This in turn facilitates commercial loans being granted to the exporter as they seek to begin to expand markets.

In other countries, such as India, the Export–Import Bank of India also provides working capital loans on a short- or long-term basis, export bills discounting, export packing credit, and cash flow financing. This more advanced form of assistance most certainly caters to those exporters that have more advanced export-driven needs.

Among the more sophisticated export countries is Japan, and the Export–Import Bank of Japan, commonly known as JEXIM, was among the banks at the forefront of export finance and foreign investment. Now, working within a more highly networked environment, JEXIM merged with the Overseas Economic Cooperation Fund and in turn now forms part of the Japanese Bank for International Cooperation (JBIC), which is the international wing of the Japanese Finance Corporation. In this more evolved networked role, the JBIC seeks to promote economic cooperation between Japan and other countries by promoting the overseas development of strategically important natural resources, by providing support to Japanese industry efforts to develop international business operations, and by responding to financial disorder in the international economy, especially those that directly affect Japan. A review of its Web site reveals not only the guarantees, loans, and credit programs found in many EX–IM banks but also a wide variety of programs and services that not only cater to the novice exporter but also to the more sophisticated exporters. In this regard, the coordinated, networked structure of JBIC is most helpful.

As JBIC suggests, this help to exporters makes sense to the country as well. An increase in exports helps in the balance of trade. It brings much needed currency, many times U.S. dollars, into the economy, and it promotes domestic employment. Besides Thailand, India, and Japan, other countries such as Germany, one of the world's leading export nations, and the United States recognize the critical role that EX–IM banks can play in the economic health of a nation and have developed similar programs and services. In this regard EX–IM banks should be looked upon as gateways for export expansion.

Sources: "Thailand: EXIM Thailand Ready to Help SME Exporters Eliminate Exchange Risk," *Thai News Service,* 2010; Export Import Bank of Thailand Web site, http://www.exim.go.th/eng/index.asp; Export Import Bank of Korea Web site, http://www.kexim.co.kr; Export Import Bank of India Web site, http://www.eximbankindia.com; and Export Import Bank of Japan (JEXIM) Web site, http://www.jbic.go.jp.

organizes exhibitions at international trade fairs, which are held regularly in major cities worldwide. The department also has a matchmaker program, in which department representatives accompany groups of U.S. businesspeople abroad to meet with qualified agents, distributors, and customers.

Another government organization, the Small Business Administration (SBA), can help potential exporters. The SBA employs 76 district international trade officers and 10 regional international trade officers throughout the United States as well as a 10-person international trade staff in Washington, D.C. Through its Service Corps of Retired Executives (SCORE) program, the SBA also oversees some 850 volunteers with international trade experience to provide one-on-one counseling to active and new-to-export businesses. The SBA also coordinates the Export Legal Assistance Network (ELAN), a nationwide group of international trade attorneys who provide free initial consultations to small businesses on export-related matters.

In addition to the Department of Commerce and SBA, nearly every state and many large cities maintain active trade commissions whose purpose is to promote exports. Most of these provide business counseling, information gathering, technical assistance, and financing. Unfortunately, many have fallen victim to budget cuts or to turf battles for political and financial support with other export agencies.

A number of private organizations are also beginning to provide more assistance to would-be exporters. Commercial banks and major accounting firms are more willing to assist small firms in starting export operations than they were a decade ago. In addition, large multinationals that have been successful in the global arena are typically willing to discuss opportunities overseas with the owners or managers of small firms.[12]

LEARNING OBJECTIVE 2
Identify the steps managers can take to improve their firm's export performance.

Export Management Company
Export specialists who act as the export marketing department for client firms.

UTILIZING EXPORT MANAGEMENT COMPANIES
One way for first-time exporters to identify the opportunities associated with exporting and to avoid many of the associated pitfalls is to hire an **export management company** (EMC). EMCs are export specialists who act as the export marketing department or international department for their client firms. EMCs normally accept two types of export assignments. They start exporting operations for a firm with the understanding that the firm will take over operations after they are well established. In another type, start-up services are performed with the understanding that the EMC will have continuing responsibility for selling the firm's products. Many EMCs specialize in serving firms in particular industries and in particular areas of the world. Thus, one EMC may specialize in selling agricultural products in the Asian market, while another may focus on exporting electronics products to Eastern Europe. MD International, for example, focuses on selling medical equipment to Latin America.

In theory, the advantage of EMCs is that they are experienced specialists who can help the neophyte exporter identify opportunities and avoid common pitfalls. A good EMC will have a network of contacts in potential markets, have multilingual employees, have a good knowledge of different business mores, and be fully conversant with the ins and outs of the exporting process and with local business regulations. However, the quality of EMCs varies.[13] While some perform their functions very well, others appear to add little value to the exporting company. Therefore, an exporter should review carefully a number of EMCs and check references. One drawback of relying on EMCs is that the company can fail to develop its own exporting capabilities.

LEARNING OBJECTIVE 2
Identify the steps managers can take to improve their firm's export performance.

EXPORT STRATEGY
In addition to using EMCs, a firm can reduce the risks associated with exporting if it is careful about its choice of export strategy.[14] A few guidelines can help firms improve their odds of success. For example, one of the most successful exporting firms in the world, the Minnesota Mining and Manufacturing Co. (3M), has built its export success on three main principles—enter on a small scale to reduce risks, add additional product lines once the exporting operations start to become successful, and hire locals to promote the firm's products (3M's export strategy is profiled in the accompanying Management Focus). Another successful exporter, Red Spot Paint & Varnish, emphasizes the importance of cultivating personal relationships when trying to build an export business (see the Management Focus at the end of this section).

Management FOCUS

Export Strategy at 3M

The Minnesota Mining and Manufacturing Co. (3M), which makes more than 40,000 products including tape, sandpaper, medical products, and the ever-present Post-it Notes, is one of the world's great multinational operations. Today over 60 percent of the firm's revenues are generated outside the United States. Although the bulk of these revenues came from foreign-based operations, 3M remains a major exporter with over $2 billion in exports. The company often uses its exports to establish an initial presence in a foreign market, only building foreign production facilities once sales volume rises to a level that justifies local production.

The export strategy is built around simple principles. One is known as "FIDO," which stands for First In (to a new market) Defeats Others. The essence of FIDO is to gain an advantage over other exporters by getting into a market first and learning about that country and how to sell there before others do. A second principle is "make a little, sell a little," which is the idea of entering on a small scale with a very modest investment and pushing one basic product, such as reflective sheeting for traffic signs in Russia or scouring pads in Hungary. Once 3M believes it has learned enough about the market to reduce the risk of failure to reasonable levels, it adds additional products.

A third principle at 3M is to hire local employees to sell the firm's products. The company normally sets up a local sales subsidiary to handle its export activities in a country. It then staffs this subsidiary with local hires because it believes they are likely to have a much better idea of how to sell in their own country than American expatriates. Because of the implementation of this principle, less than 200 of 3M's 40,000-plus foreign employees are U.S. expatriates.

Another common practice at 3M is to formulate global strategic plans for the export and eventual overseas production of its products. Within the context of these plans, 3M gives local managers considerable autonomy to find the best way to sell the product within their country. Thus, when 3M first exported its Post-it Notes, it planned to "sample the daylights" out of the product, but it also told local managers to find the best way of doing this. Local managers hired office cleaning crews to pass out samples in Great Britain and Germany; in Italy, office products distributors were used to pass out free samples; while in Malaysia, local managers employed young women to go from office to office handing out samples of the product. In typical 3M fashion, when the volume of Post-it Notes was sufficient to justify it, exports from the United States were replaced by local production. Thus, after several years 3M found it worthwhile to set up production facilities in France to produce Post-it Notes for the European market.

Sources: R. L. Rose, "Success Abroad," *The Wall Street Journal,* March 29, 1991, p. A1; T. Eiben, "US Exporters Keep On Rolling," *Fortune,* June 14, 1994, pp. 128–31; 3M Company, *A Century on Innovation,* 3M, 2002; and 2005 10K form archived at 3M's Web site at www.mmm.com.

The probability of exporting successfully can be increased dramatically by taking a handful of simple strategic steps. First, particularly for the novice exporter, it helps to hire an EMC or at least an experienced export consultant to help identify opportunities and navigate the paperwork and regulations so often involved in exporting. Second, it often makes sense to initially focus on one market or a handful of markets. Learn what is required to succeed in those markets before moving on to other markets. The firm that enters many markets at once runs the risk of spreading its limited management resources too thin. The result of such a shotgun approach to exporting may be a failure to become established in any one market. Third, as with 3M, it often makes sense to enter a foreign market on a small scale to reduce the costs of any subsequent failure. Most importantly, entering on a small scale provides the time and opportunity to learn about the foreign country before making significant capital commitments to that market. Fourth, the exporter needs to recognize the time and managerial commitment involved in building export sales and should hire additional personnel to oversee this activity. Fifth, in many countries, it is important to devote a lot of attention to building strong and enduring relationships with local distributors and/or customers (see the Management Focus on Red Spot Paint for an example). Sixth, as 3M often does, it is important to hire local personnel to help the firm establish itself in a foreign market. Local people are likely to have a much greater sense of how to do business in a given

Red Spot Paint & Varnish

Established in 1903 and based in Evansville, Indiana, Red Spot Paint & Varnish Company is in many ways typical of the companies that can be found in the small towns of America's heartland. The closely held company, whose CEO, Charles Storms, is the great-grandson of the founder, has 500 employees and annual sales of close to $90 million. The company's main product is paint for plastic components used in the automobile industry. Red Spot products are seen on automobile bumpers, wheel covers, grilles, headlights, instrument panels, door inserts, radio buttons, and other components. Unlike many other companies of a similar size and location, however, Red Spot has a thriving international business. International sales (which include exports and local production by licensees) now account for between 15 percent and 25 percent of revenue in any one year, and Red Spot does business in about 15 countries.

Red Spot has long had some international sales and once won an export award. To further its international business, Red Spot hired a Central Michigan University professor, Bryan Williams. Williams, who was hired because of his foreign-language skills (he speaks German, Japanese, and some Chinese), was the first employee at Red Spot whose exclusive focus was international marketing and sales. His first challenge was the lack of staff skilled in the business of exporting. He found that it was difficult to build an international business without in-house expertise in the basic mechanics of exporting. According to Williams, Red Spot needed people who understood the nuts and bolts of exporting—letters of credit, payment terms, bills of lading, and so on. As might be expected for a business based in the heartland of America, no ready supply of such individuals was in the vicinity. It took Williams several years to solve this problem. Now Red Spot has a full-time staff of two who have been trained in the principles of exporting and international operations.

A second problem that Williams encountered was the clash between the quarter-to-quarter mentality that frequently pervades management practice in the United States and the long-term perspective that is often necessary to build a successful international business. Williams has found that building long-term personal relationships with potential foreign customers is often the key to getting business. When foreign customers visit Evansville, Williams often invites them home for dinner. His young children started calling one visitor from Hong Kong "Uncle." Even with such efforts, however, the business may not come quickly. Meeting with potential foreign customers yields no direct business 90 percent of the time, although Williams points out that it often yields benefits in terms of competitive information and relationship building. He has found that perseverance pays. For example, Williams and Storms called on a major German automobile parts manufacturer for seven years before finally landing some business from the company.

Sources: R. L. Rose and C. Quintanilla, "More Small U.S. Firms Take Up Exporting with Much Success," *The Wall Street Journal*, December 20, 1996, p. A1, A10; and interview with Bryan Williams of Red Spot Paint.

country than a manager from an exporting firm who has previously never set foot in that country. Seventh, several studies have suggested the firm needs to be proactive about seeking export opportunities.[15] Armchair exporting does not work! The world will not normally beat a pathway to your door. Finally, it is important for the exporter to retain the option of local production. Once exports reach a sufficient volume to justify cost-efficient local production, the exporting firm should consider establishing production facilities in the foreign market. Such localization helps foster good relations with the foreign country and can lead to greater market acceptance. Exporting is often not an end in itself, but merely a step on the road toward establishment of foreign production (again, 3M provides an example of this philosophy).

LEARNING OBJECTIVE 4
Recognize the basic steps involved in export financing.

Export and Import Financing

Mechanisms for financing exports and imports have evolved over the centuries in response to a problem that can be particularly acute in international trade: the lack of trust that exists when one must put faith in a stranger. In this section, we examine the financial devices that have evolved to cope with this problem in the context of international

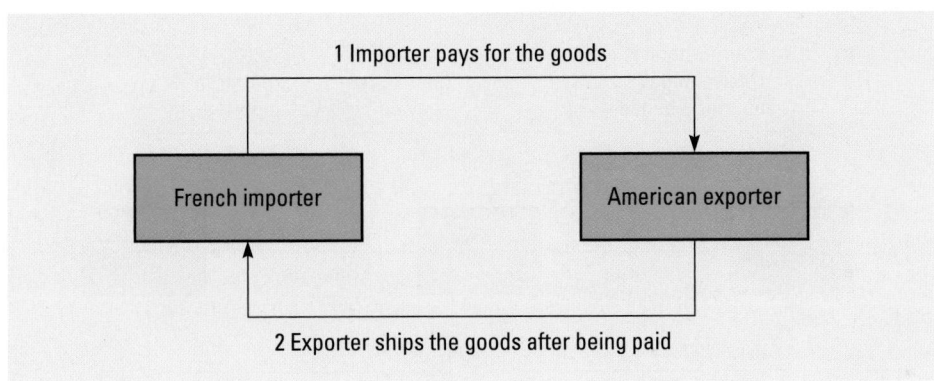

1 Importer pays for the goods

French importer

American exporter

2 Exporter ships the goods after being paid

trade: the letter of credit, the draft (or bill of exchange), and the bill of lading. Then we will trace the 14 steps of a typical export–import transaction.[16]

LACK OF TRUST Firms engaged in international trade have to trust someone they may have never seen, who lives in a different country, who speaks a different language, who abides by (or does not abide by) a different legal system, and who could be very difficult to track down if he or she defaults on an obligation. Consider a U.S. firm exporting to a distributor in France. The U.S. businessman might be concerned that if he ships the products to France before he receives payment from the French businesswoman, she might take delivery of the products and not pay him. Conversely, the French importer might worry that if she pays for the products before they are shipped, the U.S. firm might keep the money and never ship the products or might ship defective products. Neither party to the exchange completely trusts the other. This lack of trust is exacerbated by the distance between the two parties—in space, language, and culture—and by the problems of using an underdeveloped international legal system to enforce contractual obligations.

Due to the (quite reasonable) lack of trust between the two parties, each has his or her own preferences as to how the transaction should be configured. To make sure he is paid, the manager of the U.S. firm would prefer the French distributor to pay for the products before he ships them (see Figure 13.1). Alternatively, to ensure she receives the products, the French distributor would prefer not to pay for them until they arrive (see Figure 13.2). Thus, each party has a different set of preferences. Unless there is some way of establishing trust between the parties, the transaction might never occur.

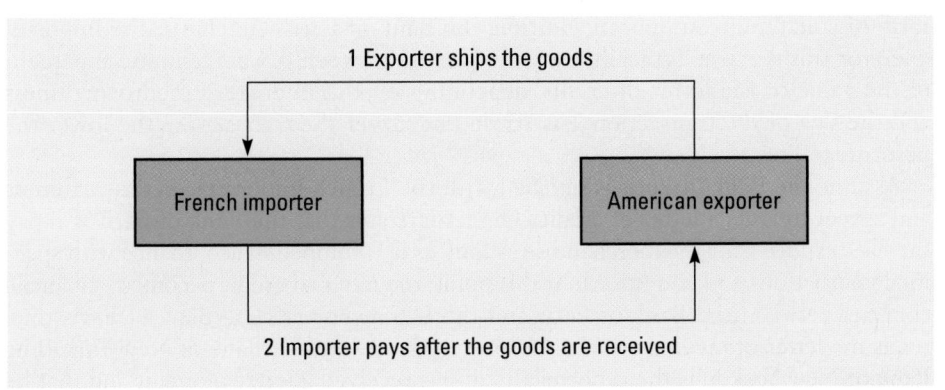

1 Exporter ships the goods

French importer

American exporter

2 Importer pays after the goods are received

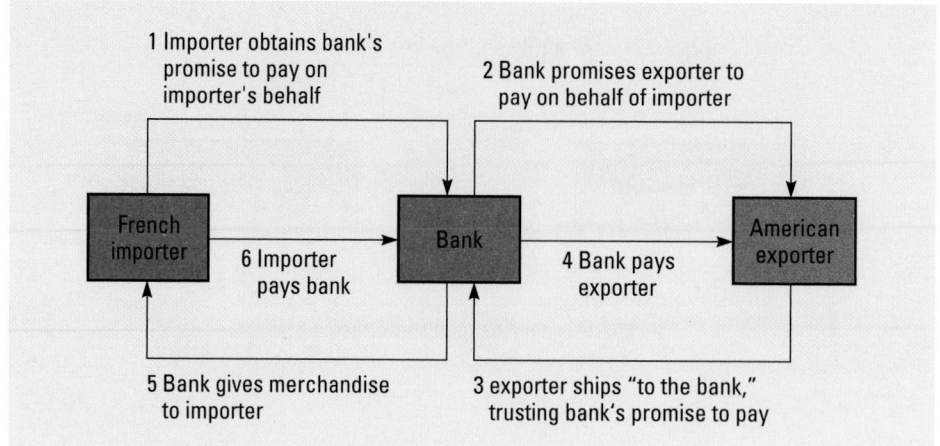

The problem is solved by using a third party trusted by both—normally a reputable bank—to act as an intermediary. What happens can be summarized as follows (see Figure 13.3). First, the French importer obtains the bank's promise to pay on her behalf, knowing the U.S. exporter will trust the bank. This promise is known as a letter of credit. Having seen the letter of credit, the U.S. exporter now ships the products to France. Title to the products is given to the bank in the form of a document called a bill of lading. In return, the U.S. exporter tells the bank to pay for the products, which the bank does. The document for requesting this payment is referred to as a draft. The bank, having paid for the products, now passes the title on to the French importer, whom the bank trusts. At that time or later, depending on their agreement, the importer reimburses the bank. In the remainder of this section, we examine how this system works in more detail.

LETTER OF CREDIT

A letter of credit, abbreviated as L/C, stands at the center of international commercial transactions. Issued by a bank at the request of an importer, the **letter of credit** states that the bank will pay a specified sum of money to a beneficiary, normally the exporter, on presentation of particular, specified documents.

Letter of Credit
Issued by a bank, indicating that the bank will make payments under specific circumstances.

Consider again the example of the U.S. exporter and the French importer. The French importer applies to her local bank, say, the Bank of Paris, for the issuance of a letter of credit. The Bank of Paris then undertakes a credit check of the importer. If the Bank of Paris is satisfied with her creditworthiness, it will issue a letter of credit. However, the Bank of Paris might require a cash deposit or some other form of collateral from her. In addition, the Bank of Paris will charge the importer a fee for this service. Typically this amounts to between 0.5 percent and 2 percent of the value of the letter of credit, depending on the importer's creditworthiness and the size of the transaction. (As a rule, the larger the transaction, the lower the percentage.)

Assume the Bank of Paris is satisfied with the French importer's creditworthiness and agrees to issue a letter of credit. The letter states that the Bank of Paris will pay the U.S. exporter for the merchandise as long as it is shipped in accordance with specified instructions and conditions. At this point, the letter of credit becomes a financial contract between the Bank of Paris and the U.S. exporter. The Bank of Paris then sends the letter of credit to the U.S. exporter's bank, say, the Bank of New York. The Bank of New York tells the exporter that it has received a letter of credit and that he can ship the merchandise. After the exporter has shipped the merchandise, he draws a draft against the Bank of Paris in accordance with the terms of the letter of credit, attaches the required documents, and presents the draft to his own bank, the Bank of New York, for payment. The Bank of New York then forwards the letter of credit and associated documents to the Bank of Paris. If all of the terms and conditions contained in the letter of credit have been complied with, the Bank of Paris will honor the draft and will send payment to the Bank of New York. When the Bank of New York receives the funds, it will pay the U.S. exporter.

As for the Bank of Paris, once it has transferred the funds to the Bank of New York, it will collect payment from the French importer. Alternatively, the Bank of Paris may allow the importer some time to resell the merchandise before requiring payment. This is not unusual, particularly when the importer is a distributor and not the final consumer of the merchandise, since it helps the importer's cash flow. The Bank of Paris will treat such an extension of the payment period as a loan to the importer and will charge an appropriate rate of interest.

The great advantage of this system is that both the French importer and the U.S. exporter are likely to trust reputable banks, even if they do not trust each other. Once the U.S. exporter has seen a letter of credit, he knows that he is guaranteed payment and will ship the merchandise. Also, an exporter may find that having a letter of credit will facilitate obtaining preexport financing. For example, having seen the letter of credit, the Bank of New York might be willing to lend the exporter funds to process and prepare the merchandise for shipping to France. This loan may not have to be repaid until the exporter has received his payment for the merchandise. As for the French importer, she does not have to pay for the merchandise until the documents have arrived and unless all conditions stated in the letter of credit have been satisfied. The drawback for the importer is the fee she must pay the Bank of Paris for the letter of credit. In addition, since the letter of credit is a financial liability against her, it may reduce her ability to borrow funds for other purposes.

DRAFT

A draft, sometimes referred to as a **bill of exchange,** is the instrument normally used in international commerce to effect payment. A **draft** is simply an order written by an exporter instructing an importer, or an importer's agent, to pay a specified amount of money at a specified time. In the example of the U.S. exporter and the French importer, the exporter writes a draft that instructs the Bank of Paris, the French importer's agent, to pay for the merchandise shipped to France. The person or business initiating the draft is known as the maker (in this case, the U.S. exporter). The party to whom the draft is presented is known as the drawee (in this case, the Bank of Paris).

International practice is to use drafts to settle trade transactions. This differs from domestic practice in which a seller usually ships merchandise on an open account, followed by a commercial invoice that specifies the amount due and the terms of payment. In domestic transactions, the buyer can often obtain possession of the merchandise without signing a formal document acknowledging his or her obligation to pay. In contrast, due to the lack of trust in international transactions, payment or a formal promise to pay is required before the buyer can obtain the merchandise.

Drafts fall into two categories, sight drafts and time drafts. A **sight draft** is payable on presentation to the drawee. A **time draft** allows for a delay in payment—normally 30, 60, 90, or 120 days. It is presented to the drawee, who signifies acceptance of it by writing or stamping a notice of acceptance on its face. Once accepted, the time draft becomes a promise to pay by the accepting party. When a time draft is drawn on and

Bill of Exchange
An order written by an exporter instructing an importer, or an importer's agent, to pay a specified amount of money at a specified time; also called a **draft.**

Draft
An order written by an exporter instructing an importer, or an importer's agent, to pay a specified amount of money at a specified time.

Sight Draft
A draft payable on presentation to the drawee.

Time Draft
A promise to pay by the accepting party at some future date.

accepted by a bank, it is called a banker's acceptance. When it is drawn on and accepted by a business firm, it is called a trade acceptance.

Time drafts are negotiable instruments; that is, once the draft is stamped with an acceptance, the maker can sell the draft to an investor at a discount from its face value. Imagine the agreement between the U.S. exporter and the French importer calls for the exporter to present the Bank of Paris (through the Bank of New York) with a time draft requiring payment 120 days after presentation. The Bank of Paris stamps the time draft with an acceptance. Imagine further that the draft is for $100,000.

The exporter can either hold onto the accepted time draft and receive $100,000 in 120 days or he can sell it to an investor, say, the Bank of New York, for a discount from the face value. If the prevailing discount rate is 7 percent, the exporter could receive $97,700 by selling it immediately (7 percent per year discount rate for 120 days for $100,000 equals $2,300, and $100,000 − $2,300 = $97,700). The Bank of New York would then collect the full $100,000 from the Bank of Paris in 120 days. The exporter might sell the accepted time draft immediately if he needed the funds to finance merchandise in transit and/or to cover cash flow shortfalls.

BILL OF LADING
The third key document for financing international trade is the bill of lading. The **bill of lading** is issued to the exporter by the common carrier transporting the merchandise. It serves three purposes: it is a receipt, a contract, and a document of title. As a receipt, the bill of lading indicates that the carrier has received the merchandise described on the face of the document. As a contract, it specifies that the carrier is obligated to provide transportation service in return for a certain charge. As a document of title, it can be used to obtain payment or a written promise of payment before the merchandise is released to the importer. The bill of lading can also function as collateral against which funds may be advanced to the exporter by its local bank before or during shipment and before final payment by the importer.

A TYPICAL INTERNATIONAL TRADE TRANSACTION
Now that we have reviewed the elements of an international trade transaction, let us see how the process works in a typical case, sticking with the example of the U.S. exporter and the French importer. The typical transaction involves 14 steps (see Figure 13.4).

1. The French importer places an order with the U.S. exporter and asks the American if he would be willing to ship under a letter of credit.
2. The U.S. exporter agrees to ship under a letter of credit and specifies relevant information such as prices and delivery terms.
3. The French importer applies to the Bank of Paris for a letter of credit to be issued in favor of the U.S. exporter for the merchandise the importer wishes to buy.
4. The Bank of Paris issues a letter of credit in the French importer's favor and sends it to the U.S. exporter's bank, the Bank of New York.
5. The Bank of New York advises the exporter of the opening of a letter of credit in his favor.
6. The U.S. exporter ships the goods to the French importer on a common carrier. An official of the carrier gives the exporter a bill of lading.
7. The U.S. exporter presents a 90-day time draft drawn on the Bank of Paris in accordance with its letter of credit and the bill of lading to the Bank of New York. The exporter endorses the bill of lading so title to the goods is transferred to the Bank of New York.

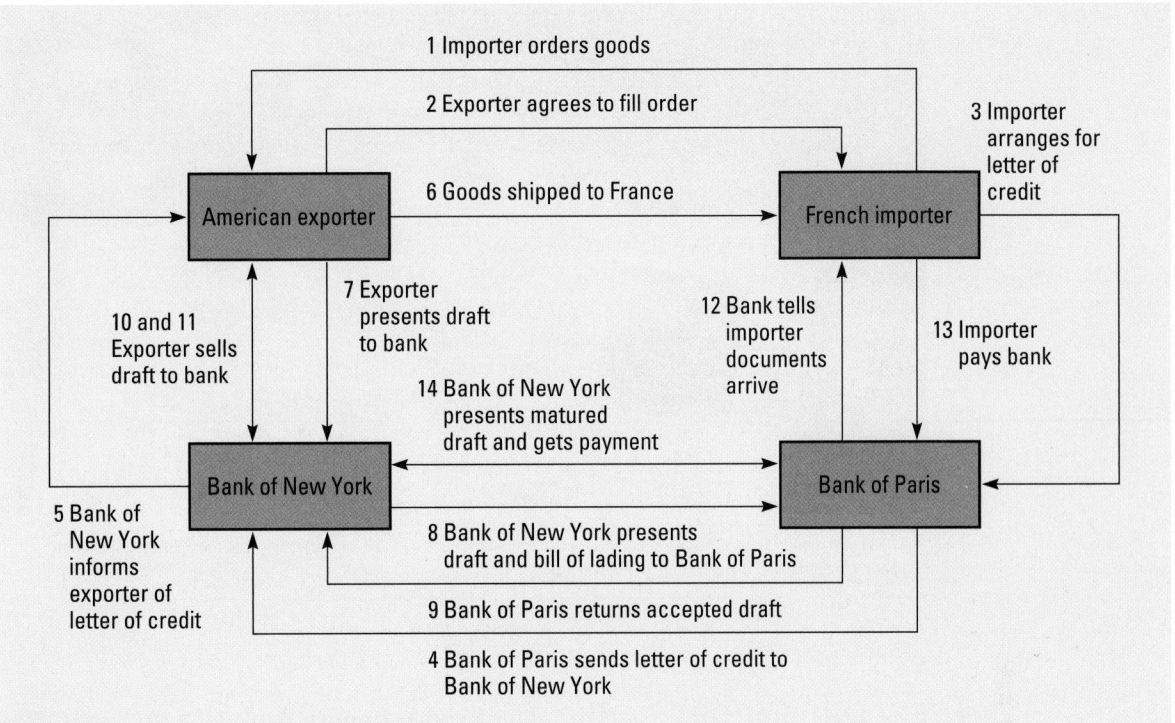

13.4 figure

A Typical International Trade Transaction

8. The Bank of New York sends the draft and bill of lading to the Bank of Paris. The Bank of Paris accepts the draft, taking possession of the documents and promising to pay the now-accepted draft in 90 days.

9. The Bank of Paris returns the accepted draft to the Bank of New York.

10. The Bank of New York tells the U.S. exporter that it has received the accepted bank draft, which is payable in 90 days.

11. The exporter sells the draft to the Bank of New York at a discount from its face value and receives the discounted cash value of the draft in return.

12. The Bank of Paris notifies the French importer of the arrival of the documents. She agrees to pay the Bank of Paris in 90 days. The Bank of Paris releases the documents so the importer can take possession of the shipment.

13. In 90 days, the Bank of Paris receives the importer's payment, so it has funds to pay the maturing draft.

14. In 90 days, the holder of the matured acceptance (in this case, the Bank of New York) presents it to the Bank of Paris for payment. The Bank of Paris pays.

Export Assistance

Prospective U.S. exporters can draw on two forms of government-backed assistance to help finance their export programs. They can get financing aid from the Export–Import Bank and export credit insurance from the Foreign Credit Insurance Association (similar programs are available in most countries).

LEARNING OBJECTIVE 3
Identify information sources and government programs that exist to help exporters.

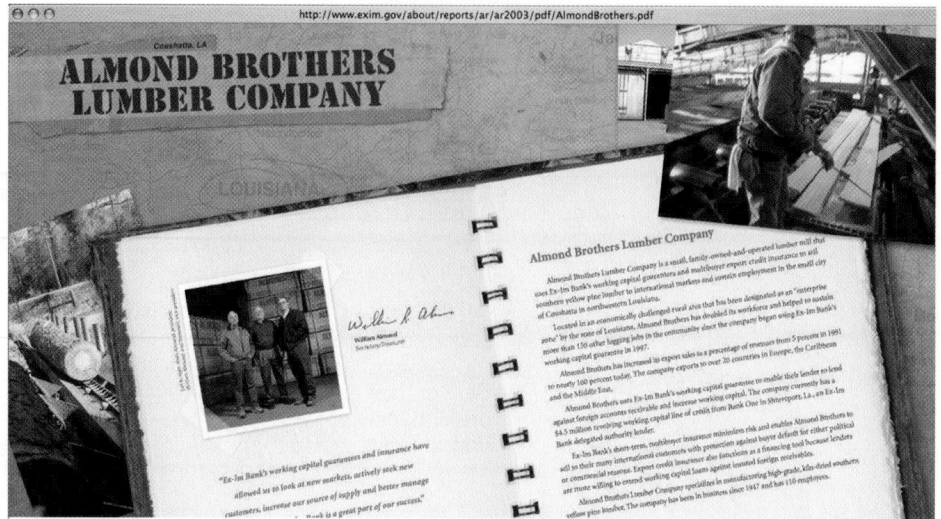

The Export–Import Bank provides financing aid to companies, such as the example above, that require assistance with imports, exports, and the exchange of commodities.

EXPORT–IMPORT BANK

Export–Import Bank
Agency of the U.S. government whose mission is to provide aid in financing and facilitate exports and imports; also referred to as the Ex–Im Bank.

The **Export–Import Bank,** often referred to as Ex–Im Bank, is an independent agency of the U.S. government. Its mission is to provide financing aid that will facilitate exports, imports, and the exchange of commodities between the United States and other countries. In 2010 its financing activities were expanded from $4 billion to $6 billion following a push by the Obama administration to try to create some 2 million new jobs through exports. Ex–Im Bank pursues its mission with various loan and loan-guarantee programs. The agency guarantees repayment of medium and long-term loans U.S. commercial banks make to foreign borrowers for purchasing U.S. exports. The bank guarantee makes the commercial banks more willing to lend cash to foreign enterprises.

Ex–Im Bank also has a direct lending operation under which it lends dollars to foreign borrowers for use in purchasing U.S. exports. In some cases, it grants loans that commercial banks would not if it sees a potential benefit to the United States in doing so. The foreign borrowers use the loans to pay U.S. suppliers and repay the loan to the agency with interest.

EXPORT CREDIT INSURANCE

For reasons outlined earlier, exporters clearly prefer to get letters of credit from importers. However, sometimes an exporter who insists on a letter of credit will lose an order to one who does not require a letter of credit. Thus, when the importer is in a strong bargaining position and able to play competing suppliers against each other, an exporter may have to forgo a letter of credit.[17] The lack of a letter of credit exposes the exporter to the risk that the foreign importer will default on payment. The exporter can insure against this possibility by buying export credit insurance. If the customer defaults, the insurance firm will cover a major portion of the loss.

In the United States, export credit insurance is provided by the Foreign Credit Insurance Association (FCIA), an association of private commercial institutions operating under the guidance of the Export–Import Bank. The FCIA provides coverage against commercial risks and political risks. Losses due to commercial risk result from the buyer's insolvency or payment default. Political losses arise from actions of governments that are beyond the control of either buyer or seller.

Countertrade

Countertrade is an alternative means of structuring an international sale when conventional means of payment are difficult, costly, or nonexistent. We first encountered countertrade in Chapter 10 in our discussion of currency convertibility. A government may restrict the convertibility of its currency to preserve its foreign exchange reserves so they can be used to service international debt commitments and purchase crucial imports.[18] This is problematic for exporters. Nonconvertibility implies that the exporter may not be paid in his or her home currency; and few exporters would desire payment in a currency that is not convertible. Countertrade is a common solution.[19] **Countertrade** denotes a whole range of barterlike agreements; its principle is to trade goods and services for other goods and services when they cannot be traded for money. Some examples of countertrade are:

LEARNING OBJECTIVE 5
Describe how countertrade can be used to facilitate exporting.

Countertrade
The trade of goods or services for other goods or services.

- An Italian company that manufactures power-generating equipment, ABB SAE Sadelmi SpA, was awarded a 720 million baht ($17.7 million) contract by the Electricity Generating Authority of Thailand. The contract specified that the company had to accept 218 million baht ($5.4 million) of Thai farm products as part of the payment.
- Saudi Arabia agreed to buy 10 747 jets from Boeing with payment in crude oil, discounted at 10 percent below posted world oil prices.
- General Electric won a contract for a $150 million electric generator project in Romania by agreeing to market $150 million of Romanian products in markets to which Romania did not have access.
- The Venezuelan government negotiated a contract with Caterpillar under which Venezuela would trade 350,000 tons of iron ore for Caterpillar earthmoving equipment.
- Albania offered such items as spring water, tomato juice, and chrome ore in exchange for a $60 million fertilizer and methanol complex.
- Philip Morris ships cigarettes to Russia, for which it receives chemicals that can be used to make fertilizer. Philip Morris ships the chemicals to China, and in return, China ships glassware to North America for retail sale by Philip Morris.[20]

THE INCIDENCE OF COUNTERTRADE In the modern era, countertrade arose in the 1960s as a way for the Soviet Union and the Communist states of Eastern Europe, whose currencies were generally nonconvertible, to purchase imports. During the 1980s, the technique grew in popularity among many developing nations that lacked the foreign exchange reserves required to purchase necessary imports. Today, reflecting their own shortages of foreign exchange reserves, some successor states to the former Soviet Union and the Eastern European Communist nations periodically engage in countertrade to purchase their imports. Estimates of the percentage of world trade covered by some sort of countertrade agreement range from highs of 8 and 10 percent by value to lows of about 2 percent.[21] The precise figure is unknown but it is probably at the low end of these estimates given the increasing liquidity of international financial markets and wider currency convertibility. However, a short-term spike in the volume of countertrade can follow periodic financial crisis. For example, countertrade activity increased notably after

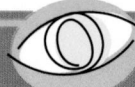

the Asian financial crisis of 1997. That crisis left many Asian nations with little hard currency to finance international trade. In the tight monetary regime that followed the crisis in 1997, many Asian firms found it very difficult to get access to export credits to finance their own international trade. Thus they turned to the only option available to them—countertrade.

Given that countertrade is a means of financing international trade, albeit a relatively minor one, prospective exporters may have to engage in this technique from time to time to gain access to certain international markets. The governments of developing nations sometimes insist on a certain amount of countertrade.[22] For example, all foreign companies contracted by Thai state agencies for work costing more than 500 million baht ($12.3 million) are required to accept at least 30 percent of their payment in Thai agricultural products. Between 1994 and mid-1998, foreign firms purchased 21 billion baht ($517 million) in Thai goods under countertrade deals.[23]

TYPES OF COUNTERTRADE

With its roots in the simple trading of goods and services for other goods and services, countertrade has evolved into a diverse set of activities that can be categorized as five distinct types of trading arrangements: barter, counterpurchase, offset, switch trading, and compensation or buyback.[24] Many countertrade deals involve not just one arrangement, but elements of two or more.

Barter

Barter
The direct exchange of goods and/or services between two parties without a cash transaction.

Barter is the direct exchange of goods and/or services between two parties without a cash transaction. Although barter is the simplest arrangement, it is not common. Its problems are twofold. First, if goods are not exchanged simultaneously, one party ends up financing the other for a period. Second, firms engaged in barter run the risk of having to accept goods they do not want, cannot use, or have difficulty reselling at a reasonable price. For these reasons, barter is viewed as the most restrictive countertrade arrangement. It is primarily used for one-time-only deals in transactions with trading partners who are not creditworthy or trustworthy.

Counterpurchase

Counterpurchase
A reciprocal buying agreement.

Counterpurchase is a reciprocal buying agreement. It occurs when a firm agrees to purchase a certain amount of materials back from a country to which a sale is made. Suppose a U.S. firm sells some products to China. China pays the U.S. firm in dollars, but in exchange, the U.S. firm agrees to spend some of its proceeds from the sale on textiles produced by China. Thus, although China must draw on its foreign exchange reserves to pay the U.S. firm, it knows it will receive some of those dollars back because of the counterpurchase agreement. In one counterpurchase agreement, Rolls-Royce sold jet parts to Finland. As part of the deal, Rolls-Royce agreed to use some of the proceeds from the sale to purchase Finnish-manufactured TV sets that it would then sell in Great Britain.

Offset

Offset
A buying agreement similar to a counterpurchase, but the exporting country can then fulfill the agreement with any firm in the country to which the sale is being made.

An **offset** is similar to a counterpurchase insofar as one party agrees to purchase goods and services with a specified percentage of the proceeds from the original sale. The difference is that this party can fulfill the obligation with any firm in the country to which the sale is being made. From an exporter's perspective, this is more attractive than a straight counterpurchase agreement because it gives the exporter greater flexibility to choose the goods that it wishes to purchase.

Switch Trading   The term **switch trading** refers to the use of a specialized third-party trading house in a countertrade arrangement. When a firm enters a counterpurchase or offset agreement with a country, it often ends up with what are called counterpurchase credits, which can be used to purchase goods from that country. Switch trading occurs when a third-party trading house buys the firm's counterpurchase credits and sells them to another firm that can better use them. For example, a U.S. firm concludes a counterpurchase agreement with Poland for which it receives some number of counterpurchase credits for purchasing Polish goods. The U.S. firm cannot use and does not want any Polish goods, however, so it sells the credits to a third-party trading house at a discount. The trading house finds a firm that can use the credits and sells them at a profit.

In one example of switch trading, Poland and Greece had a counterpurchase agreement that called for Poland to buy the same U.S.-dollar value of goods from Greece that it sold to Greece. However, Poland could not find enough Greek goods that it required, so it ended up with a dollar-denominated counterpurchase balance in Greece that it was unwilling to use. A switch trader bought the right to 250,000 counterpurchase dollars from Poland for $225,000 and sold them to a European sultana (grape) merchant for $235,000, who used them to purchase sultanas from Greece.

Compensation or Buybacks   A **buyback** occurs when a firm builds a plant in a country—or supplies technology, equipment, training, or other services to the country—and agrees to take a certain percentage of the plant's output as partial payment for the contract. For example, Occidental Petroleum negotiated a deal with Russia under which Occidental would build several ammonia plants in Russia and as partial payment receive ammonia over a 20-year period.

THE PROS AND CONS OF COUNTERTRADE   Countertrade's main attraction is that it can give a firm a way to finance an export deal when other means are not available. Given the problems that many developing nations have in raising the foreign exchange necessary to pay for imports, countertrade may be the only option available when doing business in these countries. Even when countertrade is not the only option for structuring an export transaction, many countries prefer countertrade to cash deals. Thus, if a firm is unwilling to enter a countertrade agreement, it may lose an export opportunity to a competitor that is willing to make a countertrade agreement.

In addition, a countertrade agreement may be required by the government of a country to which a firm is exporting goods or services. Boeing often has to agree to counterpurchase agreements to capture orders for its commercial jet aircraft. For example, in exchange for gaining an order from Air India, Boeing may be required to purchase certain component parts, such as aircraft doors, from an Indian company. Taking this one step further, Boeing can use its willingness to enter into a counterpurchase agreement as a way of winning orders in the face of intense competition from its global rival, Airbus. Thus, countertrade can become a strategic marketing weapon.

However, the drawbacks of countertrade agreements are substantial. Other things being equal, firms would normally prefer to be paid in hard currency. Countertrade contracts may involve the exchange of unusable or poor-quality goods that the firm cannot dispose of profitably. For example, a few years ago, one U.S. firm got burned when 50 percent of the television sets it received in a countertrade agreement with Hungary were defective and could not be sold. In addition, even if the goods it receives are of high quality, the firm still needs to dispose of them profitably. To do this, countertrade requires the firm to invest in an in-house trading department dedicated to arranging and managing countertrade deals. This can be expensive and time-consuming.

Given these drawbacks, countertrade is most attractive to large, diverse multinational enterprises that can use their worldwide network of contacts to dispose of goods acquired in countertrading. The masters of countertrade are Japan's giant trading firms, the *sogo shosha*, which use their vast networks of affiliated companies to profitably dispose of goods acquired through countertrade agreements. The trading firm of Mitsui & Company, for example, has about 120 affiliated companies in almost every sector of the manufacturing and service industries. If one of Mitsui's affiliates receives goods in a countertrade agreement that it cannot consume, Mitsui & Company will normally be able to find another affiliate that can profitably use them. Firms affiliated with one of Japan's *sogo shosha* often have a competitive advantage in countries where countertrade agreements are preferred.

Western firms that are large, diverse, and have a global reach (e.g., General Electric, Philip Morris, and 3M) have similar profit advantages from countertrade agreements. Indeed, 3M has established its own trading company—3M Global Trading, Inc.—to develop and manage the company's international countertrade programs. Unless there is no alternative, small and medium-sized exporters should probably try to avoid countertrade deals because they lack the worldwide network of operations that may be required to profitably utilize or dispose of goods acquired through them.[25]

Key Terms

sogo shosha, p. 473

export management company, p. 476

letter of credit, p. 480

bill of exchange, p. 481

draft, p. 481

sight draft, p. 481

time draft, p. 481

bill of lading, p. 482

Export–Import Bank, p. 484

countertrade, p. 485

barter, p. 486

counterpurchase, p. 486

offset, p. 486

switch trading, p. 487

buyback, p. 487

Summary

In this chapter, we examined the steps that firms must take to establish themselves as exporters. The chapter made the following points:

1. One big impediment to exporting is ignorance of foreign market opportunities.
2. Neophyte exporters often become discouraged or frustrated with the exporting process because they encounter many problems, delays, and pitfalls.
3. The way to overcome ignorance is to gather information. In the United States, a number of institutions, most important of which is the Department of Commerce, can help firms gather information in the matchmaking process.

Export management companies can also help identify export opportunities.

4. Many of the pitfalls associated with exporting can be avoided if a company hires an experienced export management company, or export consultant, and if it adopts the appropriate export strategy.

5. Firms engaged in international trade must do business with people they cannot trust and people who may be difficult to track down if they default on an obligation. Due to the lack of trust, each party to an international transaction has a different set of preferences regarding the configuration of the transaction.

6. The problems arising from lack of trust between exporters and importers can be solved by using a third party that is trusted by both, normally a reputable bank.

7. A letter of credit is issued by a bank at the request of an importer. It states that the bank promises to pay a beneficiary, normally the exporter, on presentation of documents specified in the letter.

8. A draft is the instrument normally used in international commerce to effect payment. It is an order written by an exporter instructing an importer, or an importer's agent, to pay a specified amount of money at a specified time.

9. Drafts are either sight drafts or time drafts. Time drafts are negotiable instruments.

10. A bill of lading is issued to the exporter by the common carrier transporting the merchandise. It serves as a receipt, a contract, and a document of title.

11. U.S. exporters can draw on two types of government-backed assistance to help finance their exports: loans from the Export–Import Bank and export credit insurance from the Foreign Credit Insurance Association.

12. Countertrade includes a range of barterlike agreements. It is primarily used when a firm exports to a country whose currency is not freely convertible and may lack the foreign exchange reserves required to purchase the imports.

13. The main attraction of countertrade is that it gives a firm a way to finance an export deal when other means are not available. A firm that insists on being paid in hard currency may be at a competitive disadvantage vis-à-vis one that is willing to engage in countertrade.

14. The main disadvantage of countertrade is that the firm may receive unusable or poor-quality goods that cannot be disposed of profitably.

Critical Thinking and Discussion Questions

1. A firm based in Washington State wants to export a shipload of finished lumber to the Philippines. The would-be importer cannot get sufficient credit from domestic sources to pay for the shipment but insists that the finished lumber can quickly be resold in the Philippines for a profit. Outline the steps the exporter should take to effect this export to the Philippines.

2. You are the assistant to the CEO of a small textile firm that manufactures quality, premium-priced, stylish clothing. The CEO has decided to see what the opportunities are for exporting and has asked you for advice as to the steps the company should take. What advice would you give the CEO?

3. An alternative to using a letter of credit is export credit insurance. What are the advantages and disadvantages of using export credit insurance rather than a letter of credit for exporting (a) a luxury yacht from California to Canada, and (b) machine tools from New York to Ukraine?

4. How do you explain the use of countertrade? Under what scenarios might its use increase further by 2015? Under what scenarios might its use decline?

5. How might a company make strategic use of countertrade schemes as a marketing weapon to generate export revenues? What are the risks associated with pursuing such a strategy?

Use the globalEDGE Resource Desk (http://global
EDGE.msu.edu/resourcedesk/) to complete the
following exercises:

1. The Internet is rich with resources that provide
    guidance for companies wishing to expand their
    markets through exporting. GlobalEDGE
    provides links under a category called *Trade
    Tutorials*. Identify three sources listed by
    globalEDGE and provide a description of
    the services available for new exporters through
    each of these sources.

2. You work for a banking company that hopes to
    provide financial services in India. After searching
    a resource that enumerates the *import and export
    regulations* for a variety of countries, outline the
    most important foreign trade barriers your firm's
    managers must keep in mind while developing a
    strategy for entry into the Indian banking market.

closing case

China's Export and Countertrade Policy

Much has been written about China's export prowess. Yet little attention has been given to its export/countertrade strategy. As a flurry of recent Chinese trade deals worldwide demonstrate, the Chinese are aggressively moving not only to "cut the deal" but also lock up commodities to feed its people, factories, and infrastructure. As may be suspected from a "mixed economy," the state's interests and private commercial interests are many times coordinated to benefit both.

By so doing, the Chinese government is strategically maneuvering to lock up markets for Chinese products and extend the international use of China's currency. Famous for taking a long-term approach, such trade policy can build alliances of trading partners in developing countries with emerging markets that would be separate from the advanced countries, thereby reducing the reliance on U.S. or European markets for its products.

By pursuing this policy, China would be in a strategically advantageous position to sell its products in growing markets such as Latin America or Africa if the United States or Europe was to put up future trade barriers to Chinese products. For example, if Americans stop buying Chinese electronics, perhaps Latin America will. And that's currently a $4.2 billion market for U.S. consumer electronics makers. The U.S.-based Consumer Electronics Association says 15.2 percent of global consumer electronics revenue at the retail level will come from South and Central America this year. By way of another example, U.S. construction machinery exports to Latin

America, Asia, and Africa, totaled $7.5 billion in 2007, according to the Association of Equipment Manufacturers. This would similarly be undercut if China pushes into these markets in a big way.

To the Chinese, this is in response to what they view as anti-Chinese discrimination when Chinese companies try to invest in or sell their products in the United States and Europe. In particular, the "Buy American" campaign is often cited.

In essence China's trade strategy takes the form of long-term countertrade-like deals: China will offer huge amounts of loans and development capital through Chinese institutions, including sovereign funds, banks, and other entities, to nations such as Venezuela to develop port, oil, transport, and power facilities in exchange for long-term supply contracts. The contracts are for commodities like oil, soybeans, iron ore, natural gas, timber, and other resources to feed China's industrial machine. The resources would then be shipped to new decentralized processing and manufacturing centers in rural China that would, in turn, export finished Chinese goods back to countries like Argentina, India, and Ecuador. China will also provide access to Chinese currency and loans to these countries to buy Chinese products. By bartering and establishing countertrade agreements with host countries, the exchange also benefits the Chinese yuan, which has limited convertibility, arguably putting it on the road toward becoming an international currency in competition with the dollar and the euro. For the private commercial sector, such close alliance with the Chinese government will only lead to more direct access to internal markets and companies.

Spearheading much of this drive is the Export–Import Bank of China (China Eximbank), formed in 1994. Much like other export–import banks, its mandate is to support China's balance of payments by providing export buyers' and sellers' credits and also export-credit insurance and guarantees. The bank has taken on a central role in providing export buyers' credit to other developing countries, thus serving as a conduit for the country's bilateral aid programs.

For example, if China is financing a rail system in Nigeria or Brazil, it is in an ideal position to have locals buy Chinese, rather than German, locomotives. Where the United States is concerned, China can demand that the project buy Chinese tractors rather than those made by U.S. companies such as Caterpillar. But by building the railroad with Chinese funds, Nigeria or Brazil is also gaining the much-needed infrastructure and the means by which to finance that infrastructure development.

Whether China will be able to surpass the many hurdles that remain, including being viewed as just another imperialist among many emerging countries, remains to be seen. The benefit it has had to particular regions has also come under heightened scrutiny. Some argue that in fact, as in the case of Latin America, such demand growth is unsustainable. What is clear, however, is that the combination of governmental and private commercial interests, when coordinated, create a formidable expansion strategy.

Sources: "Repelling Borders," *The Economist,* 395, no. 8677 (2010), pp. 75–76; D. Tsuruoka, "China's Shifting Trade Policies Could Hurt U.S. Sales Abroad," *Investor's Business Daily,* 2009; "Trade Financing and Insurance: Countertrade," *The Economist Intelligence Unit: Country Finance;* and K. Gallagher, "The China Syndrome," *Latin Trade* (English), 18, no. 4 (2010), pp. 18–20.

Case Discussion Questions

1. How does China coordinate its national as well as commercial export strategy?

2. From the case, it appears that China has developed a "countertrade-like" approach to trade. How so? What are the advantages and disadvantages of this approach?

3. To what extent are private commercial entities at the mercy of governmental prerogatives? What would happen if commercial interests differed from governmental interests?

4. In your opinion, and from a theoretical position, what would prevent the United States or Europe from taking a similar strategy? Are there structural limitations to the current system of government in the United States and Europe?

part 5 Competing in a Global Marketplace

After you have read this chapter you should be able to:

1 Explain why production and logistics decisions are of central importance to many multinational businesses.

2 Explain how country differences, production technology, and product features all affect the choice of where to locate production activities.

3 Recognize how the role of foreign subsidiaries in production can be enhanced over time as they accumulate knowledge.

4 Identify the factors that influence a firm's decision of whether to source supplies from within the company or from foreign suppliers.

5 Describe what is required to efficiently coordinate a globally dispersed production system.

chapter 14

Global Production, Outsourcing, and Logistics

Embraer: "The *Azul* Skies"

In Portuguese, *Azul,* pronounced "ah-zool," means blue. For the Brazilian aircraft manufacturing industry and global air travel, the skies are most certainly blue.

Brazil's manufacturing industry is the largest and the most diverse in Latin America. One of the most significant is aircraft manufacturing. The biggest is Embraer (***Em**presa **Bra**sileira de **Aer**onáutica, S.A.).* Embraer is the third largest aircraft manufacturer in the world behind Boeing and Airbus. Since its privatization in 1992, the company has embarked on a global production and outsourcing strategy that has come to typify what many are calling "Latin multinationals."

Embraer has been expanding into a number of new markets. Over the next decade, the company expects to realize more than 50 percent of its Asia/Pacific revenues from India and China. As of mid-2010, the company has an order backlog of 40 aircraft from India. China's demand for commercial airliners with 60 to 120 seats is estimated to be around 800 units over the next two decades.

The company also partnered with China Aviation Industry Corporation (AVIC) to form Harbin Embraer Aircraft Industry (HEAI) and establish a plant in China. While Embraer is producing 50-seat ERJ 145s in the country, it is hoping to receive authorization from the Chinese government to manufacture bigger jets seating up to 120 passengers.

Embraer is also looking to manufacture small passenger jets (up to 50 seats) in Russia, marketing them to in-country companies for their regional routes. This is because Russia does not have the capacity to produce these types of jets. The Middle Eastern and Latin American markets are also showing promise for Embraer expansion.

On the Western European and North American fronts, the company entered into a joint venture with EADS in Portugal to form *Indústria Aeronáutica de Portugal* (OGMA), an aeronautics production and maintenance company, in which it holds a 65 percent stake. It is also constructing three industrial units, two in Portugal and one in the United States.

The manufacturing plant in Melbourne, Florida, which will house its U.S.-executive jet operations, is receiving a $50 million investment from the company. Expected to be operational by 2011, this facility includes the final assembly line for its Phenom 100 and 300 executive jets. The new industrial facility also includes a paint shop, customer design center, and delivery center. The company's executive aviation division has been in existence for only a decade—turning out the Phenom and Legacy series, as well as the Lineage 1000.

While executive air travel as a whole was negatively affected during the global recession, it has gotten its "second wind" in 2010. In fact, the company is moving its executive jets and defense aircraft front and center to its commercial jets, which have dominated revenues in the past. The fact that the global market value of business jet aviation is expected to reach $190 billion by 2019 bodes well for Embraer.

By way of example, and as indication of the global nature of the aircraft sector, one of Embraer's customers is Azul Brazilian Airlines. Established in 2008 by Brazilian born David Neeleman, the founder and former CEO of Jet Blue, Azul began service on December 15, 2008, and has ordered 76 Embraer 195 jets. Although considered a risky endeavor, Azul, which got its name from a name contest, is doing well. In its first full year of service, Azul had a 3.82 percent market share of the domestic market. By August 2010, its market share was 6.14 percent. During that same first-year period, Azul also achieved one of the highest load factors in the Brazilian market with 79.71 percent. It became the first airline in the world to load more than 2 million customers in its first year of operations. With revenues of $150 million last year, Azul is projecting that its revenues will more than double this year.

While still too early, observers see the potential for Embraer to develop into a global "regional jet" manufacturer. Although based in Brazil, Embraer has extended its operations and customers worldwide. ●

Sources: Embraer Web site, www.embraer.com; R. Wall and J. Flottau, "Gallois Eyes Working with Embraer," *Aviation Week,* June 9, 2010; "Manufacturing," *Country Profile:. Brazil,* 2007, pp. 33–34; Hoover's Premium: Embraer, accessed at http://premium.hoovers.com/subscribe/co/overview.xhtml?ID=ffffshcyjsrchxrkjs; A. Goldstein, "A Latin American Global Player Goes to Asia: Embraer in China," *International Journal of Technology & Globalization,* 4, no. 1 (2008), p. 4; "Geared for Growth," *Aviation Week & Space Technology,* 172, no. 24 (2010), p. 68; Patricia Sellers, "The Next JetBlue," *Fortune,* July 13, 2010, http://money.cnn.com/2010/07/13/news/companies/azul_neeleman_jetblue.fortune/index.htm; and *"Dados Comparativos Avançados"* (in Portuguese). Agência Nacional de Aviação Civil (ANAC), http://www.anac.gov.br/dadosComparativos/DadosComparativos.asp, retrieved September 26, 2010.

Introduction

As trade barriers fall and global markets develop, many firms increasingly confront a set of interrelated issues. First, where in the world should production activities be located? Should they be concentrated in a single country, or should they be dispersed around the globe, matching the type of activity with country differences in factor costs, tariff barriers, political risks, and the like to minimize costs and maximize value added? Second, what should be the long-term strategic role of foreign production sites? Should the firm abandon a foreign site if factor costs change, moving production to another more favorable location, or is there value to maintaining an operation at a given location even if underlying economic conditions change? Third, should the firm own foreign production activities, or is it better to outsource those activities to independent vendors? Fourth, how should a globally dispersed supply chain be managed, and what is the role of Internet-based information technology in the management of global logistics? Fifth, should the firm manage global logistics itself, or should it outsource the management to enterprises that specialize in this activity?

The rise of the regional aircraft manufacturing industry in Brazil touches on some of these issues. Given that the industry is being driven by global competition with such large players as Boeing and Airbus, global production, outsourcing, and logistics are increasingly important. As the opening case points out, the success of aircraft manufacturing and regional air travel transcends a particular country such as Brazil. From Embraer's view, for example, not only does Brazil's own rapidly growing domestic market make local production attractive with its low labor costs, high quality, and good engineering, but also the growing regional air travel as represented by Azul. In that sense, Azul has taken advantage of this opportunity in its operations and services. From a strategic perspective, the goal of companies such as Embraer and Azul is to turn opportunities and capabilities into a global manufacturing system and successful regional air travel.

Strategy, Production, and Logistics

In Chapter 11, we introduced the concept of the value chain and discussed a number of value creation activities, including production, marketing, logistics, R&D, human resources, and information systems. In this chapter, we will focus on two of these activities—**production** and **logistics**—and attempt to clarify how they might be performed internationally to (1) lower the costs of value creation and (2) add value by better serving customer needs. We will discuss the contributions of information technology to these activities, which has become particularly important in the era of the Internet. In later chapters, we will look at other value creation activities in this international context (marketing, R&D, and human resource management).

In Chapter 11, we defined *production* as "the activities involved in creating a product." We used the term *production* to denote both service and manufacturing activities, since one can produce a service or produce a physical product. Although in this chapter we focus more on the production of physical goods, one should not forget that the term can also be applied to services. This has become more evident in recent years with the trend among U.S. firms to outsource the "production" of certain service activities to developing nations where labor costs are lower (for example, the trend among many U.S. companies to outsource customer care services to places such as India, where English is widely spoken and labor costs are much lower). Logistics is the activity that controls the transmission of physical materials through the value chain, from procurement through production and into distribution. Production and logistics are closely linked since a firm's ability to perform its production activities efficiently depends on a timely supply of high-quality material inputs, for which logistics is responsible.

LEARNING OBJECTIVE 1
Explain why production and logistics decisions are of central importance to many multinational businesses.

Production
Activities involved in creating a product.

Logistics
The procurement and physical transmission of material through the supply chain, from suppliers to customers.

The production and logistics functions of an international firm have a number of important strategic objectives.[1] One is to lower costs. Dispersing production activities to various locations around the globe where each activity can be performed most efficiently can lower costs. Costs can also be cut by managing the global supply chain efficiently so as to better match supply and demand. Efficient supply chain management reduces the amount of inventory in the system and increases inventory turnover, which means the firm has to invest less working capital in inventory and is less likely to find excess inventory on hand that cannot be sold and has to be written off.

A second strategic objective shared by production and logistics is to increase product quality by eliminating defective products from both the supply chain and the manufacturing process.[2] (In this context, *quality* means *reliability*, implying that the product has no defects and performs well.) The objectives of reducing costs and increasing quality are not independent of each other. As illustrated in Figure 14.1, the firm that improves its quality control will also reduce its costs of value creation. Improved quality control reduces costs by:

- Increasing productivity because time is not wasted producing poor-quality products that cannot be sold, leading to a direct reduction in unit costs.
- Lowering rework and scrap costs associated with defective products.
- Reducing the warranty costs and time associated with fixing defective products.

Total Quality Management (TQM)
Management philosophy that takes as its central focus the need to improve the quality of a company's products and services.

The effect is to lower the costs of value creation by reducing both production and after-sales service costs.

The principal tool that most managers now use to increase the reliability of their product offering is the Six Sigma quality improvement methodology. The Six Sigma methodology is a direct descendant of the **total quality management (TQM)** philosophy that was widely adopted, first by Japanese companies and then American companies

figure 14.1

The Relationship between Quality and Costs

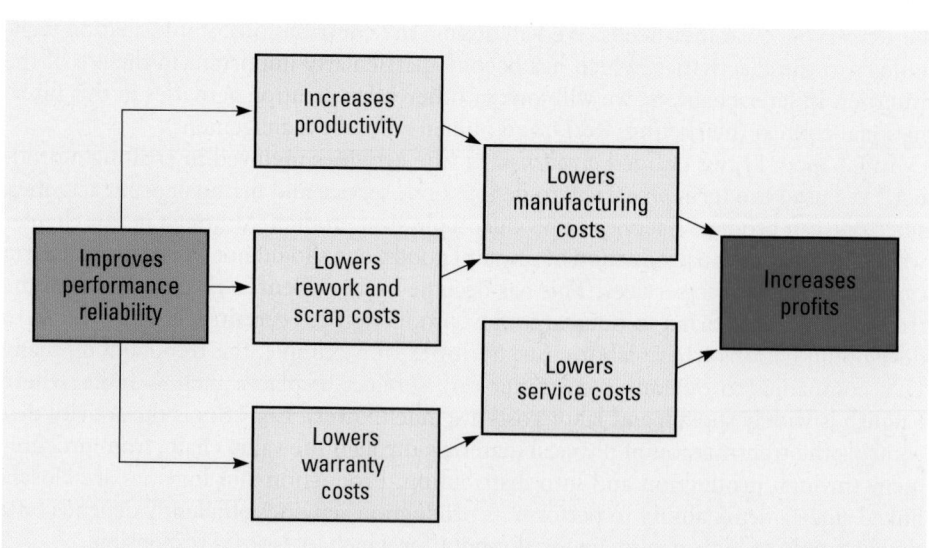

during the 1980s and early 1990s.[3] The TQM philosophy was developed by a number of American consultants such as W. Edward Deming, Joseph Juran, and A. V. Feigenbaum.[4] Deming identified a number of steps that should be part of any TQM program. He argued that management should embrace the philosophy that mistakes, defects, and poor-quality materials are not acceptable and should be eliminated. He suggested that the quality of supervision should be improved by allowing more time for supervisors to work with employees and by providing them with the tools they need to do the job. Deming recommended that management should create an environment in which employees will not fear reporting problems or recommending improvements. He believed that work standards should not only be defined as numbers or quotas, but should also include some notion of quality to promote the production of defect-free output. He argued that management has the responsibility to train employees in new skills to keep pace with changes in the workplace. In addition, he believed that achieving better quality requires the commitment of everyone in the company.

Six Sigma, the modern successor to TQM, is a statistically based philosophy that aims to reduce defects, boost productivity, eliminate waste, and cut costs throughout a company. Six Sigma programs have been adopted by several major corporations, such as Motorola, General Electric, and Allied Signal. Sigma comes from the Greek letter that statisticians use to represent a standard deviation from a mean, the higher the number of "sigmas" the smaller the number of errors. At six sigma, a production process would be 99.99966 percent accurate, creating just 3.4 defects per million units. While it is almost impossible for a company to achieve such perfection, Six Sigma quality is a goal that several strive toward. Increasingly, companies are adopting Six Sigma programs to try to boost their product quality and productivity.[5]

Six Sigma
Statistically based methodology for improving product quality.

The growth of international standards has also focused greater attention on the importance of product quality. In Europe, for example, the European Union requires that the quality of a firm's manufacturing processes and products be certified under a quality standard known as **ISO 9000** before the firm is allowed access to the EU marketplace. Although the ISO 9000 certification process has proved to be somewhat bureaucratic and costly for many firms, it does focus management attention on the need to improve the quality of products and processes.[6]

ISO 9000
Certification process that requires certain quality standards must be met.

Motorola uses the Six Sigma philosophy, which aims to reduce defects, boost productivity, eliminate waste, and cut costs throughout the company.

In addition to the lowering of costs and the improvement of quality, two other objectives have particular importance in international businesses. First, production and logistics functions must be able to accommodate demands for local responsiveness. As we saw in Chapter 12, demands for local responsiveness arise from national differences in consumer tastes and preferences, infrastructure, distribution channels, and host-government demands. Demands for local responsiveness create pressures to decentralize production activities to the major national or regional markets in which the firm does business or to implement flexible manufacturing processes that enable the firm to customize the product coming out of a factory according to the market in which it is to be sold.

Second, production and logistics must be able to respond quickly to shifts in customer demand. In recent years, time-based competition has grown more important.[7] When consumer demand is prone to large and unpredictable shifts, the firm that can adapt most quickly to these shifts will gain an advantage.[8] As we shall see, both production and logistics play critical roles here.

Where to Produce

LEARNING OBJECTIVE 2
Explain how country differences, production technology, and product features all affect the choice of where to locate production activities.

An essential decision facing an international firm is where to locate its production activities to best minimize costs and improve product quality. For the firm contemplating international production, a number of factors must be considered. These factors can be grouped under three broad headings: country factors, technological factors, and product factors.[9]

COUNTRY FACTORS We reviewed country-specific factors in some detail earlier in the book. Political economy, culture, and relative factor costs differ from country to country. In Chapter 5, we saw that due to differences in factor costs, some countries have a comparative advantage for producing certain products. In Chapters 2 and 3, we saw how differences in political economy and national culture influence the benefits, costs, and risks of doing business in a country. Other things being equal, a firm should locate its various manufacturing activities where the economic, political, and cultural conditions, including relative factor costs, are conducive to the performance of those activities (for an example, see the accompanying Management Focus, which looks at the Philips NV investment in China). In Chapter 12, we referred to the benefits derived from such a strategy as location economies. We argued that one result of the strategy is the creation of a global web of value creation activities.

Also important in some industries is the presence of global concentrations of activities at certain locations. In Chapter 7, we discussed the role of location externalities in influencing foreign direct investment decisions. Externalities include the presence of an appropriately skilled labor pool and supporting industries.[10] Such externalities can play an important role in deciding where to locate manufacturing activities. For example, because of a cluster of semiconductor manufacturing plants in Taiwan, a pool of labor with experience in the semiconductor business has developed. In addition, the plants have attracted a number of supporting industries, such as the manufacturers of semiconductor capital equipment and silicon, which have established facilities in Taiwan to be near their customers. This implies that there are real benefits to locating in Taiwan, as opposed to another location that lacks such externalities. Other things being equal, the externalities make Taiwan an attractive location for semiconductor manufacturing facilities.

Of course, other things are not equal. Differences in relative factor costs, political economy, culture, and location externalities are important, but other factors also loom large. Formal and informal trade barriers obviously influence location decisions (see Chapter 6), as do transportation costs and rules and regulations regarding foreign direct investment (see Chapter 7). For example, although relative factor costs may make a

Philips' Presence in China

The Dutch consumer electronics, lighting, semiconductor, and medical equipment conglomerate Philips NV has been operating factories in China since 1985 when the country first opened its markets to foreign investors. Then China was seen as the land of unlimited demand, and Philips, like many other Western companies, dreamed of Chinese consumers snapping up its products by the millions. But the company soon found out that one of the big reasons the company liked China—the low wage rates—also meant that few Chinese workers could afford to buy the products they were producing. Chinese wage rates are currently one-third of those in Mexico and Hungary, and 5 percent of those in the United States or Japan. So Philips hit on a new strategy; keep the factories in China but export most of the goods to the United States and elsewhere.

By the mid-2000s, Philips had invested over $2.5 billion in China. The company now operates 25 wholly owned subsidiaries and joint ventures in China. Together they employ some 30,000 people. Philips exports nearly two-thirds of the $7 billion in products that the factories produce every year. Philips accelerated its Chinese investment in anticipation of China's entry into the World Trade Organization. The company plans to move even more production to China in the future. In 2003, Philips announced it would phase out production of electronic razors in the Netherlands, lay off 2,000 Dutch employees, and move production to China by 2005. A week earlier, Philips had stated it would expand capacity at its semiconductor factories in China, while phasing out production in higher-cost locations elsewhere.

The attractions of China to Philips include low wage rates, an educated workforce, a robust Chinese economy, a stable exchange rate that is pegged to the U.S. dollar, a rapidly expanding industrial base that includes many other Western and Chinese companies that Philips uses as suppliers, and easier access to world markets given China's entry into the WTO. Philips has stated that ultimately its goal is to turn China into a global supply base from which the company's products will be exported around the world. By the mid-2000s more than 25 percent of everything Philips made worldwide came from China, and executives say the figure is rising rapidly. Several products, such as CD and DVD players, are now made only in China. Philips is also starting to give its Chinese factories a greater role in product development. In the TV business, for example, basic development used to occur in Holland but was moved to Singapore in the early 1990s. Now Philips is transferring TV development work to a new R&D center in Suzhou near Shanghai. Similarly, basic product development work on LCD screens for cell phones was recently shifted to Shanghai.

Philips is hardly alone in this process. By the mid-2000s more than half of all exports from China came from foreign manufacturers or their joint ventures in China. China was the source of more than 80 percent of the DVD players sold worldwide, 50 percent of the cameras, 40 percent of all microwave ovens, 30 percent of the air conditioners, 25 percent of the washing machines, and 20 percent of all refrigerators.

But not all operations in China are meant for export. Take, for instance, medical imagers such as CT scanners. At a time when the Chinese government has declared that it will invest $125 billion to build tens of thousands of hospitals and clinics, the business for diagnostic-imaging machines has caused a "feeding frenzy" among General Electric, Siemens, and Philips Healthcare (subsidiary of Philips NV). In fact, according to market research firm Frost Sullivan, China's total medical device and equipment market is expected to roughly double between now and 2015, to $53.7 billion. Internal consumption is now leading much of the health care strategy for ongoing operations. And although some observers worry that many companies are counting on the ongoing political, economic, and social stability of China, continued long-term investment by the Chinese government in the health care infrastructure will go a long way to making a strategic argument for ongoing operations by Philips in the country.

Sources: V. Fuhrmans and P. Glader, "Medical Imagers Scope Out China," *The Wall Street Journal,* July 27, 2010; B. Einhorn. "Philips' Expanding Asia Connections," *BusinessWeek Online,* November 27, 2003; K. Leggett and P. Wonacott, "The World's Factory: A Surge in Exports from China Jolts the Global Industry," *The Wall Street Journal,* October 10, 2002, p. A1; "Philips NV: China Will Be Production Site for Electronic Razors," *The Wall Street Journal,* April 8, 2003, p. B12; "Philips Plans China Expansion," *The Wall Street Journal,* September 25, 2003, p. B13; M. Saunderson, "Eight out of 10 DVD Players Will Be Made in China," *Dealerscope,* July 2004, p. 28; and J. Blau, "Philips Tears Down Eindhoven R&D Fence," *Research Technology Management* 50, no. 6 (2007), pp. 9–11.

country look attractive as a location for performing a manufacturing activity, regulations prohibiting foreign direct investment may eliminate this option. Similarly, a consideration of factor costs might suggest that a firm should source production of a certain component from a particular country, but trade barriers could make this uneconomical.

Another country factor is expected future movements in its exchange rate (see Chapters 9 and 10). Adverse changes in exchange rates can quickly alter a country's attractiveness as a manufacturing base. Currency appreciation can transform a low-cost location into a high-cost location. Many Japanese corporations had to grapple with this problem during the 1990s and early 2000s. The relatively low value of the yen on foreign exchange markets between 1950 and 1980 helped strengthen Japan's position as a low-cost location for manufacturing. Between 1980 and the mid-1990s, however, the yen's steady appreciation against the dollar increased the dollar cost of products exported from Japan, making Japan less attractive as a manufacturing location. In response, many Japanese firms moved their manufacturing offshore to lower-cost locations in East Asia.

TECHNOLOGICAL FACTORS   The type of technology a firm uses to perform specific manufacturing activities can be pivotal in location decisions. For example, because of technological constraints, in some cases it is necessary to perform certain manufacturing activities in only one location and serve the world market from there. In other cases, the technology may make it feasible to perform an activity in multiple locations. Three characteristics of a manufacturing technology are of interest here: the level of fixed costs, the minimum efficient scale, and the flexibility of the technology.

Fixed Costs
As we noted in Chapter 11, in some cases the fixed costs of setting up a production plant are so high that a firm must serve the world market from a single location or from a very few locations. For example, it now costs more than $1 billion to set up a state-of-the-art plant to manufacture semiconductor chips. Given this, other things being equal, serving the world market from a single plant sited at a single (optimal) location can make sense.

Conversely, a relatively low level of fixed costs can make it economical to perform a particular activity in several locations at once. This allows the firm to better accommodate demands for local responsiveness. Manufacturing in multiple locations may also help the firm avoid becoming too dependent on one location. Being too dependent on one location is particularly risky in a world of floating exchange rates. Many firms disperse their manufacturing plants to different locations as a "real hedge" against potentially adverse moves in currencies.

Minimum Efficient Scale
The concept of economies of scale tells us that as plant output expands, unit costs decrease. The reasons include the greater utilization of capital equipment and the productivity gains that come with specialization of employees within the plant.[11] However, beyond a certain level of output, few additional scale economies are available. Thus, the "unit cost curve" declines with output until a certain output level is reached, at which point further increases in output realize little reduction in unit costs. The level of output at which most plant-level scale economies are exhausted is referred to as the **minimum efficient scale** of output. This is the scale of output a plant must operate to realize all major plant-level scale economies (see Figure 14.2).

The implications of this concept are as follows: The larger the minimum efficient scale of a plant relative to total global demand, the greater the argument for centralizing production in a single location or a limited number of locations. Alternatively, when the minimum efficient scale of production is low relative to global demand, it may be economical to manufacture a product at several locations. For example, the minimum efficient scale for a plant to manufacture personal computers is about 250,000 units a year, while the total global demand exceeds 35 million units a year. The low level of minimum efficient scale in relation to total global demand makes it economically feasible for a company such as Dell to manufacture PCs in six locations.

As in the case of low fixed costs, the advantages of a low minimum efficient scale include allowing the firm to accommodate demands for local responsiveness or to hedge against currency risk by manufacturing the same product in several locations.

Minimum Efficient Scale
The level of output at which most plant-level scale economies are exhausted.

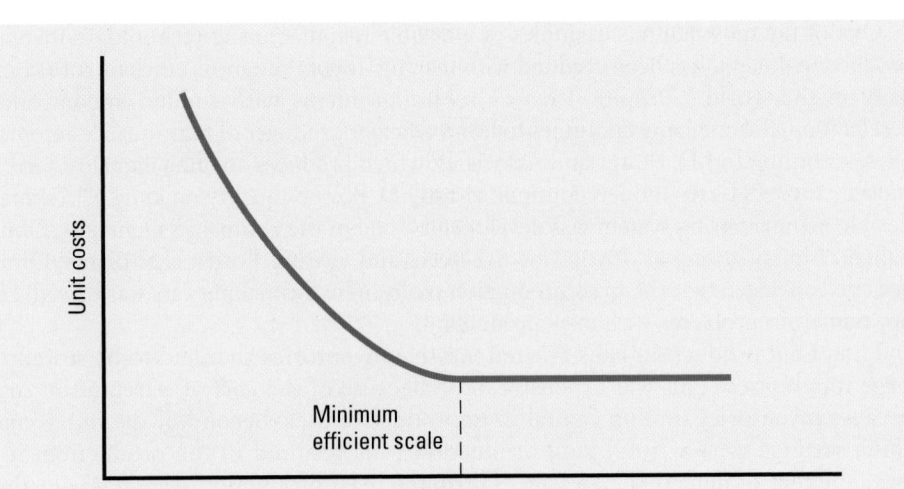

 figure

14.2

A Typical Unit-Cost Curve

Flexible Manufacturing and Mass Customization   Central to the concept of economies of scale is the idea that the best way to achieve high efficiency, and hence low unit costs, is through the mass production of a standardized output. The trade-off implicit in this idea is between unit costs and product variety. Producing greater product variety from a factory implies shorter production runs, which in turn implies an inability to realize economies of scale. That is, wide product variety makes it difficult for a company to increase its production efficiency and thus reduce its unit costs. According to this logic, the way to increase efficiency and drive down unit costs is to limit product variety and produce a standardized product in large volumes.

This view of production efficiency has been challenged by the rise of flexible manufacturing technologies. The term **flexible manufacturing technology**—or **lean production,** as it is often called—covers a range of manufacturing technologies designed to (1) reduce setup times for complex equipment, (2) increase the utilization of individual machines through better scheduling, and (3) improve quality control at all stages of the manufacturing process.[12] Flexible manufacturing technologies allow the company to produce a wider variety of end products at a unit cost that at one time could be achieved only through the mass production of a standardized output. Research suggests the adoption of flexible manufacturing technologies may actually increase efficiency and lower unit costs relative to what can be achieved by the mass production of a standardized output, while at the same time enabling the company to customize its product offering to a much greater extent than was once thought possible. The term **mass customization** has been coined to describe the ability of companies to use flexible manufacturing technology to reconcile two goals that were once thought to be incompatible—low cost and product customization.[13] Flexible manufacturing technologies vary in their sophistication and complexity.

Flexible Manufacturing Technology (Lean Production) Manufacturing technology designed to improve job scheduling, reduce setup time, and improve quality control.

Mass Customization The production of a variety of end products at a unit cost that could once be achieved only through mass production of a standardized output.

Ford Motor Co. uses flexible manufacturing technology at its Louisville, Kentucky, assembly plant.

One of the most famous examples of a flexible manufacturing technology, Toyota's production system, has been credited with making Toyota the most efficient auto company in the world. (Despite Toyota's recent problems with sudden uncontrolled acceleration, the company continues to be an efficient producer of high-quality automobiles, according to J.D. Power and Associates, which produces an annual quality survey. Indeed, Toyota's Lexus models continue to top J.D. Power's quality rankings.)[14] Toyota's flexible manufacturing system was developed by one of the company's engineers, Ohno Taiichi. After working at Toyota for five years and visiting Ford's U.S. plants, Ohno became convinced that the mass production philosophy for making cars was flawed. He saw numerous problems with mass production.

First, long production runs created massive inventories that had to be stored in large warehouses. This was expensive, both because of the cost of warehousing and because inventories tied up capital in unproductive uses. Second, if the initial machine settings were wrong, long production runs resulted in the production of a large number of defects (i.e., waste). Third, the mass production system was unable to accommodate consumer preferences for product diversity.

In response, Ohno looked for ways to make shorter production runs economical. He developed a number of techniques designed to reduce setup times for production equipment (a major source of fixed costs). By using a system of levers and pulleys, he reduced the time required to change dies on stamping equipment from a full day in 1950 to three minutes by 1971. This made small production runs economical, which allowed Toyota to respond better to consumer demands for product diversity. Small production runs also eliminated the need to hold large inventories, thereby reducing warehousing costs. Plus, small product runs and the lack of inventory meant that defective parts were produced only in small numbers and entered the assembly process immediately. This reduced waste and helped trace defects back to their source to fix the problem. In sum, these innovations enabled Toyota to produce a more diverse product range at a lower unit cost than was possible with conventional mass production.[15]

Flexible Machine Cells

Flexible manufacturing technology in which a grouping of various machine types, a common materials handler, and a centralized cell controller produce a family of products.

Flexible machine cells are another common flexible manufacturing technology. A flexible machine cell is a grouping of various types of machinery, a common materials handler, and a centralized cell controller (computer). Each cell normally contains four to six machines capable of performing a variety of operations. The typical cell is dedicated to the production of a family of parts or products. The settings on machines are computer controlled, which allows each cell to switch quickly between the production of different parts or products.

Improved capacity utilization and reductions in work in progress (that is, stockpiles of partly finished products) and in waste are major efficiency benefits of flexible machine cells. Improved capacity utilization arises from the reduction in setup times and from the computer-controlled coordination of production flow between machines, which eliminates bottlenecks. The tight coordination between machines also reduces work-in-progress inventory. Reductions in waste are due to the ability of computer-controlled machinery to identify ways to transform inputs into outputs while producing a minimum of unusable waste material. While freestanding machines might be in use 50 percent of the time, the same machines when grouped into a cell can be used more than 80 percent of the time and produce the same end product with half the waste. This increases efficiency and results in lower costs.

The effects of installing flexible manufacturing technology on a company's cost structure can be dramatic. Ford Motor Co. has been introducing flexible manufacturing technologies into its automotive plants around the world. These new technologies should allow Ford to produce multiple models from the same line and to switch production from one model to another much more quickly than in the past, allowing Ford to take $2 billion out of its cost structure.[16]

Besides improving efficiency and lowering costs, flexible manufacturing technologies also enable companies to customize products to the demands of small consumer groups—at a cost that at one time could be achieved only by mass-producing a standardized output. Thus, the technologies help a company achieve mass customization, which increases its customer responsiveness. Most important for international business, flexible manufacturing technologies can help a firm to customize products for different national markets. The importance of this advantage cannot be overstated. When flexible manufacturing technologies are available, a firm can manufacture products customized to various national markets at a single factory sited at the optimal location. And it can do this without absorbing a significant cost penalty. Thus, firms no longer need to establish manufacturing facilities in each major national market to provide products that satisfy specific consumer tastes and preferences, part of the rationale for a localization strategy (see Chapter 11).

Summary   A number of technological factors support the economic arguments for concentrating production facilities in a few choice locations or even in a single location. Other things being equal, when fixed costs are substantial, the minimum efficient scale of production is high, and/or flexible manufacturing technologies are available, the arguments for concentrating production at a few choice locations are strong. This is true even when substantial differences in consumer tastes and preferences exist between national markets, because flexible manufacturing technologies allow the firm to customize products to national differences at a single facility. Alternatively, when fixed costs are low, the minimum efficient scale of production is low, and flexible manufacturing technologies are not available, the arguments for concentrating production at one or a few locations are not as compelling. In such cases, it may make more sense to manufacture in each major market in which the firm is active if this helps the firm better respond to local demands. This holds only if the increased local responsiveness more than offsets the cost disadvantages of not concentrating manufacturing. With the advent of flexible manufacturing technologies and mass customization, such a strategy is becoming less attractive. In sum, technological factors are making it feasible, and necessary, for firms to concentrate manufacturing facilities at optimal locations. Trade barriers and transportation costs are major brakes on this trend.

PRODUCT FACTORS   Two product features affect location decisions. The first is the product's *value-to-weight* ratio because of its influence on transportation costs. Many electronic components and pharmaceuticals have high value-to-weight ratios; they are expensive and they do not weigh very much. Thus, even if they are shipped halfway around the world, their transportation costs account for a very small percentage of total costs. Given this, other things being equal, there is great pressure to produce these products in the optimal location and to serve the world market from there. The opposite holds for products with low value-to-weight ratios. Refined sugar, certain bulk chemicals, paint, and petroleum products all have low value-to-weight ratios; they are relatively inexpensive products that weigh a lot. Accordingly, when they are shipped long distances, transportation costs account for a large percentage of total costs. Thus, other things being equal, there is great pressure to make these products in multiple locations close to major markets to reduce transportation costs.

The other product feature that can influence location decisions is whether the product serves universal needs, needs that are the same all over the world. Examples include many industrial products (e.g., industrial electronics, steel, bulk chemicals) and modern consumer products (e.g., handheld calculators, personal computers, video game consoles). Because there are few national differences in consumer taste and preference for such products, the need for local responsiveness is reduced. This increases the attractiveness of concentrating production at an optimal location.

LOCATING PRODUCTION FACILITIES   There are two basic strategies for locating production facilities: concentrating them in a centralized location and serving the world market from there, or decentralizing them in various regional or national locations that are close to major markets. The appropriate strategic choice is determined by the various country-specific, technological, and product factors we have discussed in this section and are summarized in Table 14.1.

As can be seen, concentration of production makes most sense when:

- Differences between countries in factor costs, political economy, and culture have a substantial impact on the costs of manufacturing in various countries.
- Trade barriers are low.
- Externalities arising from the concentration of like enterprises favor certain locations.
- Important exchange rates are expected to remain relatively stable.
- The production technology has high fixed costs and high minimum efficient scale relative to global demand, or flexible manufacturing technology exists.
- The product's value-to-weight ratio is high.
- The product serves universal needs.

Alternatively, decentralization of production is appropriate when:

- Differences between countries in factor costs, political economy, and culture do not have a substantial impact on the costs of manufacturing in various countries.
- Trade barriers are high.

table

Location Strategy and Production

	Concentrated Production Favored	Decentralized Production Favored
Country factors		
Difference in political economy	Substantial	Few
Difference in culture	Substantial	Few
Difference in factor costs	Substantial	Few
Trade barriers	Few	Substantial
Location externalities	Important in industry	Not important in industry
Exchange rates	Stable	Volatile
Technological factors		
Fixed costs	High	Low
Minimum efficient scale	High	Low
Flexible manufacturing technology	Available	Not available
Product factors		
Value-to-weight ratio	High	Low
Serves universal needs	Yes	No

- Location externalities are not important.
- Volatility in important exchange rates is expected.
- The production technology has low fixed costs and low minimum efficient scale, and flexible manufacturing technology is not available.
- The product's value-to-weight ratio is low.
- The product does not serve universal needs (that is, significant differences in consumer tastes and preferences exist between nations).

In practice, location decisions are seldom clear cut. For example, it is not unusual for differences in factor costs, technological factors, and product factors to point toward concentrated production while a combination of trade barriers and volatile exchange rates points toward decentralized production. This seems to be the case in the world automobile industry. Although the availability of flexible manufacturing and cars' relatively high value-to-weight ratios suggest concentrated manufacturing, the combination of formal and informal trade barriers and the uncertainties of the world's current floating exchange rate regime (see Chapter 10) have inhibited firms' ability to pursue this strategy. For these reasons, several automobile companies have established "top-to-bottom" manufacturing operations in three major regional markets: Asia, North America, and Western Europe.

The Strategic Role of Foreign Factories

Whatever the rationale behind establishing a foreign production facility, the strategic role of foreign factories can evolve over time.[17] Initially, many foreign factories are established where labor costs are low. Their strategic role typically is to produce labor-intensive products at as low a cost as possible. For example, beginning in the 1970s, many U.S. firms in the computer and telecommunication equipment businesses established factories across Southeast Asia to manufacture electronic components, such as circuit boards and semiconductors, at the lowest possible cost. They located their factories in countries such as Malaysia, Thailand, and Singapore precisely because each of these countries offered an attractive combination of low labor costs, adequate infrastructure, and favorable tax and trade regime. Initially, the components produced by these factories were designed elsewhere and the final product was assembled elsewhere. Over time, however, the strategic role of some of these factories has expanded; they have become important centers for the design and final assembly of products for the global marketplace. For example, Hewlett-Packard's operation in Singapore was established as a low-cost location for the production of circuit boards, but the facility has become the center for the design and final assembly of portable ink-jet printers for the global marketplace (see the accompanying Management Focus). A similar process seems to be occurring at some of the factories that Philips has established in China (see the Management Focus on Philips) and may now be starting to happen in India with regard to the production of small cars.

Such upward migration in the strategic role of foreign factories arises because many foreign factories upgrade their own capabilities.[18] This improvement comes from two sources. First, pressure from the center to improve a factory's cost structure and/or customize a product to the demands of consumers in a particular nation can start a chain of events that ultimately leads to development of additional capabilities at that factory. For example, to meet centrally mandated directions to drive down costs, engineers at HP's Singapore factory argued that they needed to redesign products so they could be manufactured at a lower cost. This led to the establishment of a design center in Singapore. As this design center proved its worth, HP executives realized the importance of co-locating design and manufacturing operations. They increasingly transferred more design

LEARNING OBJECTIVE 3
Recognize how the role of foreign subsidiaries in production can be enhanced over time as they accumulate knowledge.

Hewlett-Packard in Singapore

In the late 1960s, Hewlett-Packard was looking around Asia for a low-cost location to produce electronic components that were to be manufactured using labor-intensive processes. The company looked at several Asian locations and eventually settled on Singapore, opening its first factory there in 1970. Although Singapore did not have the lowest labor costs in the region, costs were low relative to North America. Plus, the Singapore location had several important benefits that could not be found at many other locations in Asia. The education level of the local workforce was high. English was widely spoken. The government of Singapore seemed stable and committed to economic development, and the city-state had one of the better infrastructures in the region, including good communication and transportation networks and a rapidly developing industrial and commercial base. HP also extracted favorable terms from the Singapore government with regard to taxes, tariffs, and subsidies.

At its start, the plant manufactured only basic components. The combination of low labor costs and a favorable tax regime helped to make this plant profitable early. In 1973, HP transferred the manufacture of one of its basic handheld calculators from the United States to Singapore. The objective was to reduce manufacturing costs, which the Singapore factory was quickly able to do. Increasingly confident in the capability of the Singapore factory to handle entire products, as opposed to just components, HP's management transferred other products to Singapore over the next few years including keyboards, solid-state displays, and integrated circuits. However, all these products were still designed, developed, and initially produced in the United States.

The plant's status shifted in the early 1980s when HP embarked on a worldwide campaign to boost product quality and reduce costs. HP transferred the production of its HP41C handheld calculator to Singapore. The managers at the Singapore plant were given the goal of substantially reducing manufacturing costs. They argued that this could be achieved only if they were allowed to redesign the product so it could be manufactured at a lower overall cost. HP's central management agreed, and 20 engineers from the Singapore facility were transferred to the United States for one year to learn how to design application-specific integrated circuits. They then brought this expertise back to Singapore and set about redesigning the HP41C.

The results were a huge success. By redesigning the product, the Singapore engineers reduced manufacturing costs for the HP41C by 50 percent. Using this newly acquired capability for product design, the Singapore facility then set about redesigning other products it produced. HP's corporate managers were so impressed with the progress made at the factory that they transferred production of the entire calculator line to Singapore in 1983. This was followed by the partial transfer of ink-jet production to Singapore in 1984 and keyboard production in 1986. In all cases, the facility redesigned the products and often reduced unit manufacturing costs by more than 30 percent. The initial development and design of all these products, however, still occurred in the United States.

In the late 1980s and 1990s, the Singapore plant assumed added responsibilities, particularly in the ink-jet printer business. The factory was given the job of redesigning an HP ink-jet printer for the Japanese market. Although the initial product redesign was a market failure, the managers at Singapore pushed to be allowed to try again. They were given the job of redesigning HP's DeskJet 505 printer for the Japanese market. This time the redesigned product was a success, garnering significant sales in Japan. Emboldened by this success, the plant has continued to take on additional design responsibilities. Today, it is viewed as a "lead plant" within HP's global network, with primary responsibility not just for manufacturing, but also for the development and design of a family of small ink-jet printers targeted at the Asian market.

Sources: K. Ferdows, "Making the Most of Foreign Factories," *Harvard Business Review,* March–April 1997, pp. 73–88; and "Hewlett-Packard: Singapore," Harvard Business School Case No. 694–035.

responsibilities to the Singapore factory. In addition, the Singapore factory ultimately became the center for the design of products tailored to the needs of the Asian market. This made good strategic sense because it meant products were being designed by engineers who were close to the Asian market and probably had a good understanding of the needs of that market, as opposed to engineers located in the United States.

A second source of improvement in the capabilities of a foreign factory can be the increasing abundance of advanced factors of production in the nation in which the factory is located. Many nations that were considered economic backwaters a generation ago have been experiencing rapid economic development during the past 20 years. Their communication and transportation infrastructures and the education level of the population have improved. While these countries once lacked the advanced infrastructure required to support sophisticated design, development, and manufacturing operations, this is often no longer the case. This has made it much easier for factories based in these nations to take on a greater strategic role.

Because of such developments, many international businesses are moving away from a system in which their foreign factories were viewed as nothing more than low-cost manufacturing facilities and toward one where foreign factories are viewed as globally dispersed centers of excellence.[19] In this new model, foreign factories take the lead role for the design and manufacture of products to serve important national or regional markets or even the global market. The development of such dispersed centers of excellence is consistent with the concept of a transnational strategy, introduced in Chapter 12. A major aspect of a transnational strategy is a belief in **global learning**—the idea that valuable knowledge does not reside just in a firm's domestic operations; it may also be found in its foreign subsidiaries. Foreign factories that upgrade their capabilities over time are creating valuable knowledge that might benefit the whole corporation.

Managers of international businesses need to remember that foreign factories can improve their capabilities over time, and this can be of immense strategic benefit to the firm. Rather than viewing foreign factories simply as sweatshops where unskilled labor churns out low-cost goods, managers need to see them as potential centers of excellence and to encourage and foster attempts by local managers to upgrade the capabilities of their factories and, thereby, enhance their strategic standing within the corporation.

Such a process does imply that once a foreign factory has been established and valuable skills have been accumulated, it may not be wise to switch production to another location simply because some underlying variable, such as wage rates, has changed.[20] HP has kept its facility in Singapore, rather than switching production to a location where wage rates are now much lower, such as Vietnam, because it recognizes that the Singapore factory has accumulated valuable skills that more than make up for the higher wage rates. Thus, when reviewing the location of production facilities, the international manager must consider the valuable skills that may have been accumulated at various locations, and the impact of those skills on factors such as productivity and product design.

Global Learning
The flow of skills and product offerings from foreign subsidiary to home country and from foreign subsidiary and foreign subsidiary.

Outsourcing Production: Make-or-Buy Decisions

International businesses frequently face **make-or-buy decisions,** decisions about whether they should perform a certain value creation activity themselves or outsource it to another entity.[21] Historically, most outsourcing decisions have involved the manufacture of physical products. Most manufacturing firms have done their own final assembly, but have had to decide whether to vertically integrate and manufacture their own component parts or outsource the production of such parts, purchasing them from independent suppliers. Such make-or-buy decisions are an important aspect of the strategy of many firms. In the automobile industry, for example, the typical car contains more than 10,000 components, so automobile firms constantly face make-or-buy decisions. Toyota produces less than 30 percent of the value of cars that roll off its assembly lines. The remaining 70 percent, mainly accounted for by component parts and complex subassemblies, comes from independent suppliers. In the athletic shoe industry, the make-or-buy issue has been taken to an extreme with companies such as Nike and Reebok having no involvement in manufacturing; all production has been outsourced, primarily to manufacturers based in low-wage countries.

LEARNING OBJECTIVE 4
Identify the factors that influence a firm's decision of whether to source supplies from within the company or from foreign suppliers.

Make-or-Buy Decisions
Whether a firm should make or buy component parts.

Nike relies on outsourcing to manufacture its products. The company has received worldwide criticism for turning its back on social responsibility for the sake of profit.

In recent years, the outsourcing decision has gone beyond the manufacture of physical products to embrace the production of service activities. For example, many U.S.-based companies, from credit card issuers to computer companies, have outsourced their customer call centers to India. They are "buying" the customer call center function, while "making" other parts of the product in house. Similarly, many information technology companies have been outsourcing some parts of the software development process, such as testing computer code written in the United States, to independent providers based in India. Such companies are "making" (writing) most of the code in-house, but "buying," or outsourcing, part of the production process—testing—to independent companies. India is often the focus of such outsourcing because English is widely spoken there; the nation has a well-educated workforce, particularly in engineering fields; and the pay is much lower than in the United States (a call center worker in India earns about $200 to $300 a month, about one-tenth of the comparable U.S. wage).[22]

Outsourcing decisions pose plenty of problems for purely domestic businesses but even more problems for international businesses. These decisions in the international arena are complicated by the volatility of countries' political economies, exchange rate movements, changes in relative factor costs, and the like. In this section, we examine the arguments for making products in-house and for buying them, and we consider the trade-offs involved in such a decision. Then we discuss strategic alliances as an alternative to producing all or part of a product within the company.

Specialized Asset
An asset designed to perform a specific task, whose value is significantly reduced in its next-best use.

THE ADVANTAGES OF MAKE
The arguments that support making all or part of a product in-house—vertical integration—are fourfold. Vertical integration may be associated with lower costs, facilitate investments in highly specialized assets, protect proprietary product technology, and ease the scheduling of adjacent processes.

Lowering Costs It may pay a firm to continue manufacturing a product or component part in-house if the firm is more efficient at that production activity than any other enterprise.

Facilitating Specialized Investments Some times firms have to invest in specialized assets in order to do business with another enterprise.[23] A **specialized asset** is an asset whose value is contingent upon a particular relationship persisting. For example, imagine Ford of Europe has developed a new, high-performance, high-quality, and uniquely designed fuel-injection system. The increased fuel efficiency will help sell Ford cars. Ford must decide whether to make the system in-house or to contract out the manufacturing to an independent supplier. Manufacturing these uniquely designed systems requires investments in equipment that can be used only for this purpose; it cannot be used to make fuel injection systems for any other auto firm. Thus, investment in this equipment constitutes an investment in specialized assets. When, as in this situation, one firm must invest in specialized assets to supply another, mutual dependency is created. In such circumstances, each party might fear the other will abuse the relationship by seeking more favorable terms.

To appreciate this, let us first examine this situation from the perspective of an independent supplier who has been asked by Ford to make this investment. The supplier might reason that once it has made the investment, it will become dependent on Ford for business since Ford is the only possible customer for the output of this equipment. The supplier perceives this as putting Ford in a strong bargaining position and worries that once the specialized investment has been made, Ford might use this to squeeze down prices for the systems. Given this risk, the supplier declines to make the investment in specialized equipment.

Now take the position of Ford. Ford might reason that if it contracts out production of these systems to an independent supplier, it might become too dependent on that supplier for a vital input. Because specialized equipment is required to produce the fuel injection systems, Ford cannot easily switch its orders to other suppliers who lack that equipment. (It would face high switching costs.) Ford perceives this as increasing the bargaining power of the supplier and worries that the supplier might use its bargaining strength to demand higher prices.

Thus, the mutual dependency that outsourcing would create makes Ford nervous and scares away potential suppliers. The problem here is lack of trust. Neither party completely trusts the other to play fair. Consequently, Ford might reason that the only safe way to get the new fuel injection systems is to manufacture them itself. It may be unable to persuade any independent supplier to manufacture them. Thus, Ford decides to make rather than buy.

In general, we can predict that when substantial investments in specialized assets are required to manufacture a component, the firm will prefer to make the component internally rather than contract it out to a supplier. Substantial empirical evidence supports this prediction.[24]

Protecting Proprietary Product Technology

Proprietary product technology is unique to a firm. If it enables the firm to produce a product containing superior features, proprietary technology can give the firm a competitive advantage. The firm would not want competitors to get this technology. If the firm outsources the production of entire products or components containing proprietary technology, it runs the risk that those suppliers will expropriate the technology for their own use or that they will sell it to the firm's competitors. Thus, to maintain control over its technology, the firm might prefer to make such products or component parts in-house.

Improving Scheduling

Another argument for producing all or part of a product in-house is that production cost savings result because it makes planning, coordination, and scheduling of adjacent processes easier.[25] This is particularly important in firms with just-in-time inventory systems (discussed later in the chapter). In the 1920s, for example, Ford profited from tight coordination and scheduling made possible by backward vertical integration into steel foundries, iron ore shipping, and mining. Deliveries at Ford's foundries on the Great Lakes were coordinated so well that ore was turned into engine blocks within 24 hours. This substantially reduced Ford's production costs by eliminating the need to hold excessive ore inventories.

For international businesses that source worldwide, scheduling problems can be exacerbated by the time and distance between the firm and its suppliers. This is true whether the firms use their own subunits as suppliers or use independent suppliers. However, ownership of upstream production facilities is not the issue here. By using information technology, firms can attain tight coordination between different stages in the production process.

THE ADVANTAGES OF BUY   Buying component parts, or an entire product, from independent suppliers can give the firm greater flexibility, can help drive down the firm's cost structure, and may help the firm capture orders from international customers.

Strategic Flexibility

The great advantage of buying component parts, or even an entire product, from independent suppliers is that the firm can maintain its flexibility, switching orders between suppliers as circumstances dictate. This is particularly important internationally, where changes in exchange rates and trade barriers can alter the attractiveness of supply sources. One year Hong Kong might offer the lowest cost for a particular component, and the next year, Mexico may. Many firms source the same products from suppliers based in two countries, primarily as a hedge against adverse movements in factor costs, exchange rates, and the like.

Sourcing products from independent suppliers can also be advantageous when the optimal location for manufacturing a product is beset by political risks. Under such circumstances, foreign direct investment to establish a component manufacturing operation in that country would expose the firm to political risks. The firm can avoid many of these risks by buying from an independent supplier in that country, thereby maintaining the flexibility to switch sourcing to another country if a war, revolution, or other political change alters that country's attractiveness as a supply source.

However, maintaining strategic flexibility has its downside. If a supplier perceives the firm will change suppliers in response to changes in exchange rates, trade barriers, or general political circumstances, that supplier might not be willing to make investments in specialized plants and equipment that would ultimately benefit the firm.

Lower Costs

Although making a product or component part in-house—vertical integration—is often undertaken to lower costs, it may have the opposite effect. When this is the case, outsourcing may lower the firm's cost structure. Making all or part of a product in-house increases an organization's scope, and the resulting increase in organizational complexity can raise a firm's cost structure. There are three reasons for this.

First, the greater the number of subunits in an organization, the more problems coordinating and controlling those units. Coordinating and controlling subunits require top management to process large amounts of information about subunit activities. The greater the number of subunits, the more information top management must process and the harder it is to do well. Theoretically, when the firm becomes involved in too many activities, headquarters management will be unable to effectively control all of them, and the resulting inefficiencies will more than offset any advantages derived from vertical integration.[26] This can be particularly serious in an international business, where the problem of controlling subunits is exacerbated by distance and differences in time, language, and culture.

Second, the firm that vertically integrates into component part manufacture may find that because its internal suppliers have a captive customer in the firm, they lack an incentive to reduce costs. The fact that they do not have to compete for orders with other suppliers may result in high operating costs. The managers of the supply operation may be tempted to pass on cost increases to other parts of the firm in the form of higher transfer prices, rather than looking for ways to reduce those costs.

Third, vertically integrated firms have to determine appropriate prices for goods transferred to subunits within the firm. This is a challenge in any firm, but it is even more complex in international businesses. Different tax regimes, exchange rate movements, and headquarters' ignorance about local conditions all increase the complexity of transfer pricing decisions. This complexity enhances internal suppliers' ability to manipulate transfer prices to their advantage, passing cost increases downstream rather than looking for ways to reduce costs.

The firm that buys its components from independent suppliers can avoid all these problems and the associated costs. The firm that sources from independent suppliers has fewer subunits to control. The incentive problems that occur with internal suppliers do not arise when independent suppliers are used. Independent suppliers know they must continue to be efficient if they are to win business from the firm. Also, because independent suppliers' prices are set by market forces, the transfer pricing problem does not exist. In sum, the bureaucratic inefficiencies and resulting costs that can arise when firms vertically integrate backward and produce their own components are avoided by buying component parts from independent suppliers.

Offsets   Another reason for outsourcing some manufacturing to independent suppliers based in other countries is that it may help the firm capture more orders from that country. Offsets are common in the commercial aerospace industry. For example, before Air India places a large order with Boeing, the Indian government might ask Boeing to push some subcontracting work toward Indian manufacturers. This is not unusual in international business. Representatives of the U.S. government have repeatedly urged Japanese automobile companies to purchase more component parts from U.S. suppliers to partially offset the large volume of automobile exports from Japan to the United States.

TRADE-OFFS   Clearly there are trade-offs in make-or-buy decisions. The benefits of making all or part of a product in-house seem to be greatest when highly specialized assets are involved, when vertical integration is necessary for protecting proprietary technology, or when the firm is simply more efficient than external suppliers at performing a particular activity. When these conditions are not present, the risk of strategic inflexibility and organizational problems suggest it may be better to contract out some or all production to independent suppliers. Because issues of strategic flexibility and organizational control loom even larger for international businesses than purely domestic ones, an international business should be particularly wary of vertical integration into component part manufacture. In addition, some outsourcing in the form of offsets may help a firm gain larger orders in the future.

STRATEGIC ALLIANCES WITH SUPPLIERS   Several international businesses have tried to reap some benefits of vertical integration without the associated organizational problems by entering strategic alliances with essential suppliers. For example, there was an alliance between Kodak and Canon, under which Canon built photocopiers for sale by Kodak; an alliance between Microsoft and Flextronics, under which Flextronics built the Xbox for Microsoft; and an alliance between Boeing and several Japanese companies to build its jet aircraft, including the 787. By these alliances, Kodak, Microsoft, and Boeing have committed themselves to long-term relationships with these suppliers, which have encouraged the suppliers to undertake specialized investments. Strategic alliances build trust between the firm and its suppliers. Trust is built when a firm makes a credible commitment to continue purchasing from a supplier on reasonable terms. For example, the firm may invest money in a supplier—perhaps by taking a minority shareholding—to signal its intention to build a productive, mutually beneficial long-term relationship.

This kind of arrangement between the firm and its parts suppliers was pioneered in Japan by large auto companies such as Toyota. Many Japanese automakers have cooperative relationships with their suppliers that go back decades. In these relationships, the auto companies and their suppliers collaborate on ways to increase value added by, for example, implementing just-in-time inventory systems or cooperating in the design of component parts to improve quality and reduce assembly costs. These relationships have been formalized when the auto firms acquired minority shareholdings in many of their essential suppliers to symbolize their desire for long-term cooperative relationships with them. At the same time, the relationship between the firm and each essential supplier remains market mediated and terminable if the supplier fails to perform. By pursuing such a strategy, the Japanese automakers capture many of the benefits of vertical integration, particularly those arising from investments in specialized assets, without suffering the organizational problems that come with formal vertical integration. The parts suppliers also benefit from these relationships because they grow with the firm they supply and share in its success.[27]

The adoption of just-in-time inventory systems (JIT), computer-aided design (CAD), and computer-aided manufacturing (CAM) over the past two decades seem to have increased pressures for firms to establish long-term relationships with their suppliers. JIT, CAD, and CAM systems all rely on close links between firms and their suppliers supported by substantial specialized investment in equipment and information systems hardware. To get a supplier to agree to adopt such systems, a firm must make a credible commitment to an enduring relationship with the supplier—it must build trust with the supplier. It can do this within the framework of a strategic alliance.

Alliances are not all good. Like formal vertical integration, a firm that enters long-term alliances may limit its strategic flexibility by the commitments it makes to its alliance partners. As we saw in Chapter 12 when we considered alliances between competitors, a firm that allies itself with another firm risks giving away key technological know-how to a potential competitor.

Managing a Global Supply Chain

Logistics encompasses the activities necessary to get materials from suppliers to a manufacturing facility, through the manufacturing process, and out through a distribution system to the end user.[28] In the international business, the logistics function manages the global supply chain. The twin objectives of logistics are to manage a firm's global supply chain at the lowest possible cost and in a way that best serves customer needs, thereby lowering the costs of value creation and helping the firm establish a competitive advantage through superior customer service.

The potential for reducing costs through more efficient logistics is enormous. For the typical manufacturing enterprise, material costs account for between 50 and 70 percent of revenues, depending on the industry. Even a small reduction in these costs can have a substantial impact on profitability. According to one estimate, for a firm with revenues of $1 million, a return on investment rate of 5 percent, and materials costs that are 50 percent of sales revenues, a $15,000 increase in total profits could be achieved either by increasing sales revenues 30 percent or by reducing materials costs by 3 percent.[29] In a saturated market, it would be much easier to reduce materials costs by 3 percent than to increase sales revenues by 30 percent.

Just-in-Time (JIT) Inventory
Logistics system designed to deliver parts to a production process as they are needed, not before.

THE ROLE OF JUST-IN-TIME INVENTORY Pioneered by Japanese firms during that country's remarkable economic transformation during the 1960s and 1970s, just-in-time inventory systems now play a major role in most manufacturing firms. The basic philosophy behind **just-in-time (JIT) inventory** systems is to economize on inventory holding costs by having materials arrive at a manufacturing plant just in time to enter the production process and not before. The major cost saving comes from speeding up inventory turnover. This reduces inventory holding costs, such as warehousing and storage costs. It means the company can reduce the amount of working capital it needs to finance inventory, freeing capital for other uses and/or lowering the total capital requirements of the enterprise. Other things being equal, this will boost the company's profitability as measured by return on capital invested. It also means the company is less likely to have excess unsold inventory that it has to write off against earnings or price low to sell.

In addition to the cost benefits, JIT systems can also help firms improve product quality. Under a JIT system, parts enter the manufacturing process immediately; they are not warehoused. This allows defective inputs to be spotted right away.

Another Perspective

Global Supply and Value Chain Trends
In a similar manner, global supply chain management has undergone change and has experienced many of the forces found in other global business sectors, such as globalization, increased cross-border sourcing, collaboration for parts of value chain with low-cost providers, shared service centers for logistical and administrative functions, increasingly global operations (which require increasingly global coordination), and planning to achieve global optimums. Many of these complex problems also involve midsized companies to an increasing degree. These trends have many benefits for manufacturers because they make possible larger lot sizes, lower taxes, and better environments (culture, infrastructure, special tax zones, sophisticated OEM) for their products. ("Supply Chain Management," http://en.wikipedia.org/wiki/Supply_chain_management)

The problem can then be traced to the supply source and fixed before more defective parts are produced. Under a more traditional system, warehousing parts for weeks before they are used allows many defective parts to be produced before a problem is recognized.

The drawback of a JIT system is that it leaves a firm without a buffer stock of inventory. Although buffer stocks are expensive to store, they can help a firm respond quickly to increases in demand and tide a firm over shortages brought about by disruption among suppliers. Such a disruption occurred after the September 11, 2001, attacks on the World Trade Center, when the subsequent shutdown of international air travel and shipping left many firms that relied upon globally dispersed suppliers and tightly managed "just-in-time" supply chains without a buffer stock of inventory. A less pronounced but similar situation occurred again in April 2003 when the outbreak of pneumonia-like SARS (severe acute respiratory syndrome) virus in China resulted in the temporary shutdown of several plants operated by foreign companies and disrupted their global supply chains. Similarly, in late 2004, record imports into the United States left several major West Coast shipping ports clogged with too many ships from Asia that could not be unloaded fast enough, and disrupted the finely tuned supply chains of several major U.S. enterprises.[30]

There are ways of reducing the risks associated with a global supply chain that operates on just-in-time principles. To reduce the risks associated with depending on one supplier for an important input, some firms source these inputs from several suppliers located in different countries. While this does not help in the case of an event with global ramifications, such as September 11, 2001, it does help manage country-specific supply disruptions, which are more common.

THE ROLE OF INFORMATION TECHNOLOGY AND THE INTERNET

Web-based information systems play a crucial role in modern materials management. By tracking component parts as they make their way across the globe toward an assembly plant, information systems enable a firm to optimize its production scheduling according to when components are expected to arrive. By locating component parts in the supply chain precisely, good information systems allow the firm to accelerate production when needed by pulling key components out of the regular supply chain and having them flown to the manufacturing plant.

Firms now typically use electronic data interchange (EDI) via the Internet to coordinate the flow of materials into manufacturing, through manufacturing, and out to customers. Sometimes customers also are integrated into the system. These electronic links are then used to place orders with suppliers, to register parts leaving a supplier, to track them as they travel toward a manufacturing plant, and to register their arrival. Suppliers typically use an EDI link to send invoices to the purchasing firm. One consequence of an EDI system is that suppliers, shippers, and the purchasing firm can communicate with each other with no time delay, which increases the flexibility and responsiveness of the whole global supply system. A second consequence is that much of the paperwork between suppliers, shippers, and the purchasing firm is eliminated. Good EDI systems can help a firm decentralize materials management decisions to the plant level by giving corporate-level managers the information they need for coordinating and controlling decentralized materials management groups.

Before the emergence of the Internet as a major communication medium, firms and their suppliers normally had to purchase expensive proprietary software solutions to implement EDI systems. The ubiquity of the Internet and the availability of Web-based applications have made most of these proprietary solutions obsolete. Less expensive Web-based systems that are much easier to install and manage now dominate the market for global supply chain management software. These Web-based systems have transformed the management of globally dispersed supply chains, allowing even small firms to achieve a much better balance between supply and demand, thereby reducing the inventory in their systems and reaping the associated economic benefits. With many firms now using these systems, those that do not will find themselves at a competitive disadvantage.

Key Terms

production, p. 495

logistics, p. 495

total quality management (TQM), p. 496

Six Sigma, p. 497

ISO 9000, p. 497

minimum efficient scale, p. 500

flexible manufacturing technology (lean production), p. 501

mass customization, p. 501

flexible machine cells, p. 502

global learning, p. 507

make-or-buy decisions, p. 507

specialized asset, p. 508

just-in-time inventory, p. 512

Summary

This chapter explained how efficient production and logistics functions can improve an international business's competitive position by lowering the costs of value creation and by performing value creation activities in such ways that customer service is enhanced and value added is maximized. We looked closely at three issues central to international production and logistics: where to produce, what to make and what to buy, and how to coordinate a globally dispersed manufacturing and supply system. The chapter made the following points:

1. The choice of an optimal production location must consider country factors, technological factors, and product factors.

2. Country factors include the influence of factor costs, political economy, and national culture on production costs, along with the presence of location externalities.

3. Technological factors include the fixed costs of setting up production facilities, the minimum efficient scale of production, and the availability of flexible manufacturing technologies that allow for mass customization.

4. Product factors include the value-to-weight ratio of the product and whether the product serves universal needs.

5. Location strategies either concentrate or decentralize manufacturing. The choice should be made in light of country, technological, and product factors. All location decisions involve trade-offs.

6. Foreign factories can improve their capabilities over time, and this can be of immense strategic benefit to the firm. Managers need to view foreign factories as potential centers of excellence and to encourage and foster attempts by local managers to upgrade factory capabilities.

7. An essential issue in many international businesses is determining which component parts should be manufactured in-house and which should be outsourced to independent suppliers.

8. Making components in-house facilitates investments in specialized assets and helps the firm protect its proprietary technology. It may improve scheduling between adjacent stages in the value chain, also. In-house production also makes sense if the firm is an efficient, low-cost producer of a technology.

9. Buying components from independent suppliers facilitates strategic flexibility and helps the firm avoid the organizational problems associated with extensive vertical integration. Outsourcing might also be employed as part of an "offset" policy, which is designed to win more orders for the firm from a country by pushing some subcontracting work to that country.

10. Several firms have tried to attain the benefits of vertical integration and avoid its associated organizational problems by entering long-term strategic alliances with essential suppliers.

11. Although alliances with suppliers can give a firm the benefits of vertical integration without dispensing entirely with the benefits of a market relationship, alliances have drawbacks. The firm that enters a strategic alliance may find its strategic flexibility limited by commitments to alliance partners.

12. Logistics encompasses all the activities that move materials to a production facility, through the production process, and out through a distribution system to the end user. The logistics function is complicated in an international business by distance, time, exchange rates, custom barriers, and other things.

13. Just-in-time systems generate major cost savings from reducing warehousing and inventory holding costs and from reducing the need to write off excess inventory. In addition, JIT systems help the firm spot defective parts and remove them from the manufacturing process quickly, thereby improving product quality.

14. Information technology, particularly Internet-based electronic data interchange, plays a major role in materials management. EDI facilitates the tracking of inputs, allows the firm to optimize its production schedule, lets the firm and its suppliers communicate in real time, and eliminates the flow of paperwork between a firm and its suppliers.

Critical Thinking and Discussion Questions

1. An electronics firm is considering how best to supply the world market for microprocessors used in consumer and industrial electronic products. A manufacturing plant costs about $500 million to construct and requires a highly skilled workforce. The total value of the world market for this product over the next 10 years is estimated to be between $10 billion and $15 billion. The tariffs prevailing in this industry are currently low. Should the firm adopt a concentrated or decentralized manufacturing strategy? What kind of location(s) should the firm favor for its plant(s)?

2. A chemical firm is considering how best to supply the world market for sulfuric acid. A manufacturing plant costs about $20 million to

construct and requires a moderately skilled workforce. The total value of the world market for this product over the next 10 years is estimated to be between $20 billion and $30 billion. The tariffs prevailing in this industry are moderate. Should the firm favor concentrated manufacturing or decentralized manufacturing? What kind of location(s) should the firm seek for its plant(s)?

3. A firm must decide whether to make a component part in-house or to contract it out to an independent supplier. Manufacturing the part requires a nonrecoverable investment in specialized assets. The most efficient suppliers are located in countries with currencies that many foreign exchange analysts expect to appreciate substantially over the next decade. What are the pros and cons of (*a*) manufacturing the component in-house and (*b*) outsourcing manufacturing to an independent supplier? Which option would you recommend? Why?

4. Reread the Management Focus on Philips' Presence in China then answer the following questions:
   a. What are the benefits to Philips of shifting so much of its global production to China?
   b. What are the risks associated with a heavy concentration of manufacturing assets in China?
   c. What strategies might Philips adopt to maximize the benefits and mitigate the risks associated with moving so much product?

5. Explain how an efficient logistics function can help an international business compete more effectively in the global marketplace.

Research Task  http://globalEDGE.msu.edu

Use the globalEDGE Resource Desk (http://global EDGE.msu.edu/resourcedesk/) to complete the following exercises:

1. You work for a company whose manufacturing operations require a highly skilled labor force. Some executives have recently decided to open a production plant in Europe to serve that market because the high cost of transporting the products from your U.S. plant are making your company's products less attractive for consumers. Using the *Chartbook of International Labor Comparisons*, compare the attractiveness of producing in Spain, Italy, and Portugal based both on labor market indicators and on competitiveness indicators for manufacturing. Prepare an executive summary recommending where your company should produce.

2. The International Association of Outsourcing Professionals (IAOP) ranks the world's best *global outsourcing* service providers. What are the criteria used to rank companies? Identify the 10 best companies. What are the key strengths for each company? Do you notice any trends in the information you have gathered?

Reducing the Cost of Innovation

Over the past two years, several pharmaceutical giants have announced mergers, reorganizations, and job layoffs. British-based GlaxoSmithKline (GSK) recently announced it would shed jobs globally as part of a restructuring program. Merck, Astra Zeneca, and Pfizer have also announced job cuts, and Roche's decision to merge with American biotechnology company Genentech was the third announcement of its kind in the past year. Although one would think that pharmaceutical companies are recession proof, this is not so. And in multiple, cost cutting/ reorganization programs, they are trying to find any means to do so.

In the area of pharmaceuticals, biologics, vaccines, and consumer health care, GSK is the third largest pharmaceutical company in the world, behind Johnson & Johnson and Pfizer based on revenues. GSK's bestsellers include central nervous system therapies, respiratory and cardiovascular drugs, antivirals, and vaccines. The company's top product is the asthma medication, Advair, which combines two of the company's other products, Flovent and Serevent. Other products include herpes treatment, Valtrex; epilepsy treatment, Lamictal; antidepressant, Paxil; prostate enlargement therapy, Avodart; and antibiotic, Augmentin. The company's consumer products include Tums for sour stomachs; dental care products, Aquafresh and Sensodyne; and smoking-cessation products, NicoDerm and Nicorette. The company markets its products directly to hospitals, pharmacies, doctors, and other health care consumers; it also uses wholesale distributors in some markets. Although one-third of GSK's profits are generated in the United States, the company's continued success will depend on maintaining a rich portfolio of global patent-protected products. To keep this edge, GSK must constantly develop new "blockbusters," a process that can be daunting. GSK must focus on continuous research and development in order to satisfy the development efforts that currently include about 150 different clinical stage projects, 30 of which are in late-phase trials.

In 2008, CEO Andrew Witty replaced retiring chief executive Jean-Pierre Garnier. Under its new leadership, the company continued to focus on small strategic acquisitions and expansion in fast-growing markets, including vaccines, biopharmaceuticals, and consumer health products. The company has also been looking to divest non-core assets and to increase its percentage of outsourced R&D operations.

In 2009, the company launched a restructuring program to cut operational costs by 2011 in all areas, including manufacturing, sales, research, and infrastructure. The program includes job cuts, which come on top of previous cost-cutting programs that resulted in an approximate 8 percent workforce reduction during 2007 and 2008. In so doing, GSK is also streamlining its R&D programs to focus on late-stage candidates, and it is eliminating preclinical research in some costlier areas. The restructuring efforts aim to counter the effects of increased generic competition for some products.

As Hoover's Premium database reports, part of the strategy GSK has been using to keep research and development going is to acquire small research firms and form development agreements with other drug companies. For example, in 2008 in the middle of the global recession, GSK acquired Sirtris Pharmaceutical for $720 million, thus adding to its knowledge of metabolism, immunology, inflammation, and neurology. It was such a success that Sirtris is now an independent drug discovery subsidiary.

Also in 2009, GSK widened its offering of dermatology products by acquiring Stiefel Laboratories from the Stiefel family and other investors (including the Blackstone Group) for $2.9 billion. The acquisition added prescription and over-the-counter medications for conditions including acne, psoriasis, dandruff, and fungal infections. Stiefel was combined with the existing GSK dermatology operations into a new business unit under the Stiefel name.

The company is also engaged in several key collaboration projects to grow its pipeline, including a licensing deal worth up to $2.1 billion with biotech firm Genmab to co-develop and market cancer antibody therapies and a $1 billion agreement with Synta Pharmaceuticals to develop a late-stage melanoma candidate. The company has similar development deals with OncoMed (cancer treatments), Galapagos (anti-infectives), and Theravance (gastrointestinal drugs). In 2009, it agreed to work with Pfizer on HIV medications.

In addition, the company is putting some focus on growth in emerging geographical markets. Expansion efforts in 2008 and 2009 included an alliance with South African generic drug maker Aspen Pharmacare and the purchase of pharma operations from Bristol-Myers Squibb and UCB in select Asian, African, Latin American, and Middle Eastern nations. In 2010, the company spent about $250 million to expand in Latin America, with the purchase of Laboratorios Phoenix, an Argentinian drugmaker. Along with a pipeline of branded generic medicines, the purchase gave GSK a factory near Buenos Aires and a primary care sales force.

In this regard, India has taken on a particularly important role in GSK's expansion. Although known for its information technology capabilities, India is also distinguishing itself for outsourced solutions in the area of pharmaceutical research. In the pharmaceutical sector, the Indian economy has the most obvious potential. Drawing on the large pool of graduates created by the country's highly competitive university system, pharmaceutical companies are looking to tap into this efficient source of knowledge. This is particularly true in the areas of chemistry and mathematics. GlaxoSmithKline Pharmaceutical, the Indian subsidiary of GSK, has become India's leading pharmaceutical manufacturer. It is not the lower wages that have proved successful to establishing a GSK subsidiary in India, but rather the lower costs of innovation.

Sources: GSK Web site, www.gsk.com; K. Bartlett, "Jobs Go Down the Tube at Big Drugs Firms: As the Cost of Producing and Licensing New Medicines Soars, the Sector Is Contracting," *The Sunday Times,* March 22, 2009; P. Durman, "India Beats Global Drug Firms at Their Own Game," *The Sunday Times,* 2004; and Hoover's Premium database, GlaxoSmithKline plc.

Case Discussion Questions

1. What are the benefits to GSK of outsourcing so much of the research and development to entities outside the company? What are the potential risks? Do the benefits outweigh the risks?

2. Why should GSK continue with its strategy of outsourcing research and development? What conditions do you think should exist in a particular country that would facilitate outsourcing there?

3. If the largest market for GSK products is in the United States, shouldn't GSK focus its R&D efforts there? If not, why not?

메일 속눈썹
퍼머한듯

라네즈 하이펌 컬링 마스카라

make up stand

LANEíGE

part 5   Competing in a Global Marketplace

After you have read this chapter you should be able to:

1 Explain why it might make sense to vary the attributes of a product from country to country.

2 Recognize why and how a firm's distribution strategy might vary among countries.

3 Identify why and how advertising and promotional strategies might vary among countries.

4 Explain why and how a firm's pricing strategy might vary among countries.

5 Describe how the globalization of the world economy is affecting new-product development within the international business firm.

chapter 15

Global Marketing and R&D

Amore Pacific's Marketing Goes Global

opening case

In a move to become one of the top 10 global players in the cosmetic industry by the year 2015, Amore Pacific, the South Korean cosmetic and personal health care products manufacturer, is focusing on global marketing and research and development (R&D). Currently Amore Pacific offers 14 brands of cosmetics and personal care products, including its flagship line, Laneige, as well as Iope and Hera. Going forward, the company plans to expand Sulwhasoo (its Asian cosmetics line) and Mamonde (its lower-cost brand geared toward the masses). For 2010, the company estimates revenues of 1.95 trillion won ($1.65 billion) and net profits of 330 billion won compared with roughly 1.77 trillion won and 300.6 billion won last year. Most of the products are based on traditional Asian ingredients such as bamboo, red ginseng, green tea, and other Asian botanical plants. Yet, it recognizes that it will need to continue its growth with more research and development.

The company recently completed a brand-new environmentally friendly research center called *Mizium* at its R&D complex (one of the largest of any cosmetic company) in Yongin, Gyeonggi Province. It already has four other research facilities there. According to CEO Suh Kyung-bae, "R&D has been the pillar of our growth during the past 65 years and will be the main driving force for our future sustainable prosperity." "We intend to put a lot of investment and resources into R&D so that we can appeal to global consumers with outstanding products." Amore Pacific plans to increase the number of research fellows at the company's five R&D centers from 330 to 500 by 2015. *"Mi," "zi,"* and *"um"* mean beauty, wisdom, and place, respectively, in Korean. The name symbolizes the company's desire to appeal to customers with uniquely Asian beauty worldwide.

With reinforced R&D, Amore Pacific intends to further expand its overseas business in the long term. "We plan to concentrate on further nurturing our business in the Asian market, mainly with our premium brand Sulwhasoo and mass brand Mamonde. We ultimately want to attract around 3 percent of the total Asian female population, which is around 30 million, as our customers," Suh said.

Suh said that the Asian market was a suitable choice for the company because the market has vast growth potential and good accessibility, which would help save the company logistics costs. The company has rich experience and know-how from operating in the market for 10 years.

The cosmetics maker will increase its marketing efforts in the Chinese and Hong Kong markets, in which it has been doing well with its affordable product lines. It also seeks to make inroads into North America and Japan with high-end lines like the Amore Pacific brand, penetrating Asian markets in North America and Japan.

At present, the company centers on a wide range of research areas, mainly focusing on cosmetics, health products, food and medicine, and medical supplies. It also plans to boost bioscientific research to develop new anti-aging products in the near future.

According to the company's Web site, the firm has been aggressively researching new best-quality products that are the first of their kind in the world with specific patented technology. While studying the processing methods for herbs like red ginseng to rediscover the value of traditional herbal medicine, the company also studies interfacial science and engineering and biotechnology for more innovative studies. Part of the globalization effort also includes the establishment of AGO, the offshore holding company, that will increase management efficiency and facilitate tax shields for future overseas investments. Whether those studies and structures will bear marketable results remains to be seen. ●

Sources: Amore Pacific Web site, www.amorepacific.com; Koh Young-aah, "Amore Pacific Reinforces R&D, Overseas Business" *The Korea Herald,* September 27, 2010; and Lee Jung-yoon, "Amore Pacific Making Global Push," *JoongAng Daily,* September 3, 2010.

Introduction

In the previous chapter, we looked at the roles of global production and logistics in an international business. In this chapter, we continue our focus on specific business functions by examining the roles of marketing and research and development (R&D) in an international business. We focus on how marketing and R&D can be performed so they will reduce the costs of value creation and add value by better serving customer needs.

In Chapter 12 we spoke of the tension existing in most international businesses between the needs to reduce costs and at the same time to respond to local conditions, which tends to raise costs. This tension continues to be a persistent theme in this chapter. A global marketing strategy that views the world's consumers as similar in their tastes and preferences is consistent with the mass production of a standardized output. By mass-producing a standardized output, whether it be soap or semiconductor chips, the firm can realize substantial unit cost reductions from experience curve and other economies of scale. However, ignoring country differences in consumer tastes and preferences can lead to failure. Thus, an international business's marketing function needs to determine when product standardization is appropriate and when it is not, and to adjust the marketing strategy accordingly. Even if product standardization is appropriate, the way in which a product is positioned in a market and the promotions and messages used to sell that product may still have to be customized so that they resonate with local consumers.

As described in the opening case, Amore Pacific is dealing with just these issues. In 2009, the company embarked on an R&D push that recognized that its market for cosmetic products was the entire Asian female population. The goal has been to use traditional Asian botanical plants as the basis for new products that would have a larger market penetration. Amore Pacific has specifically chosen to focus on the Asian population of women, its core competency, for the time being. In so doing, it is establishing common marketing themes that are used throughout the Asian population worldwide. Amore Pacific blends global marketing and R&D in its products.

Likewise, in this chapter, we consider marketing and R&D because of their close relationship. A critical aspect of the marketing function is identifying gaps in the market so that the firm can develop new products to fill those gaps. Developing new products requires R&D—thus, the linkage between marketing and R&D. A firm should develop new products with market needs in mind, and only marketing can define those needs for R&D personnel. Also, only marketing can tell R&D whether to produce globally standardized or locally customized products. Research has long maintained that a major contributor to the success of new-product introductions is a close relationship between marketing and R&D.[1]

In this chapter, we begin by reviewing the debate on the globalization of markets. Then we discuss the issue of market segmentation. Next we look at four elements that constitute a firm's marketing mix: product attributes, distribution strategy, communication strategy, and pricing strategy. The **marketing mix** is the set of choices the firm offers to its targeted markets. Many firms vary their marketing mix from country to country, depending on differences in national culture, economic development, product standards, distribution channels, and so on.

The chapter closes with a look at new-product development in an international business and at the implications of this for the organization of the firm's R&D function.

Marketing Mix
Choices about product attributes, distribution strategy, communication strategy, and pricing strategy that a firm offers its targeted markets.

The Globalization of Markets and Brands

In a now-classic *Harvard Business Review* article, the late Theodore Levitt wrote lyrically about the globalization of world markets. Levitt's arguments have become something of a lightning rod in the debate about the extent of globalization. According to Levitt,

A powerful force drives the world toward a converging commonalty, and that force is technology. It has proletarianized communication, transport, and travel. The result is a new commercial reality—the emergence of global markets for standardized consumer products on a previously unimagined scale of magnitude.

Gone are accustomed differences in national or regional preferences. The globalization of markets is at hand. With that, the multinational commercial world nears its end, and so does the multinational corporation. The multinational corporation operates in a number of countries and adjusts its products and practices to each—at high relative costs. The global corporation operates with resolute consistency—at low relative cost—as if the entire world were a single entity; it sells the same thing in the same way everywhere.

Commercially, nothing confirms this as much as the success of McDonald's from the Champs Élysées to the Ginza, of Coca-Cola in Bahrain and Pepsi-Cola in Moscow, and of rock music, Greek salad, Hollywood movies, Revlon cosmetics, Sony television, and Levi's jeans everywhere.

Ancient differences in national tastes or modes of doing business disappear. The commonalty of preference leads inescapably to the standardization of products, manufacturing, and the institutions of trade and commerce.[2]

This is eloquent and evocative writing, but is Levitt correct? The rise of global media phenomenon from CNN to MTV, and the ability of such media to help shape a global culture, would seem to lend weight to Levitt's argument. If Levitt is correct, his argument has major implications for the marketing strategies pursued by international business. However, many academics feel that Levitt overstates his case.[3] Although Levitt may have a point when it comes to many basic industrial products, such as steel, bulk chemicals, and semiconductor chips, globalization in the sense used by Levitt seems to be the exception rather than the rule in many consumer goods markets and industrial markets. Even a firm such as McDonald's, which Levitt holds up as the archetypal example of a consumer products firm that sells a standardized product worldwide, modifies its menu from country to country in light of local consumer preferences. In the Middle East, for example, McDonald's sells the McArabia, a chicken sandwich on Arabian style bread, and in France, the Croque McDo, a hot ham and cheese sandwich.[4]

On the other hand, Levitt is probably correct to assert that modern transportation and communications technologies are facilitating a convergence of certain tastes and preferences among consumers in the more advanced countries of the world, and this has become even more prevalent since he wrote. The popularity of sushi in Los Angeles, hamburgers in Tokyo, hip-hop music, and global media phenomena such as MTV all support this contention. In the long run, such technological forces may lead to the evolution of a global culture. At present, however, the continuing persistence of cultural and economic differences between nations acts as a brake on any trend toward the standardization of consumer tastes and preferences across nations. Indeed, that may never occur. Some writers have argued that the rise of global culture doesn't mean that consumers share the same tastes and preferences.[5] Rather, people in different nations, often with conflicting viewpoints, are increasingly participating in a shared "global" conversation, drawing upon shared symbols that include global brands from Nike and Dove to Coca-Cola and Sony. But the way in which these brands are perceived, promoted, and used still varies from country to country, depending upon local differences in tastes and preferences. Furthermore, trade barriers and differences in product and technical standards also constrain a firm's ability to sell a standardized product to a global market using a standardized marketing strategy. We discuss the sources of these

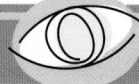

Another Perspective

Sol Meliá in Cuba

According to many, the most beautiful beach in the world is Varadero in Cuba. During a time when the United States has imposed an embargo on the island, Sol Meliá, the largest operator of holiday resorts in the world, has taken advantage of the legal/regulatory restrictions imposed on U.S.-based hotel chains such as Marriott, Hilton, and Starwood Hotels & Resorts. It has marketed itself precisely to those tourists who seek high-class accommodations, especially Canadians. With 15 hotels under management in Cuba, the company is cornering the market. Interestingly, however, it is perhaps because of the U.S. embargo that Cuba is not mentioned on the company's Web site. Instead, you must go to www.solmeliacuba.com to find the hotels. The mystique of the island continues. Is this "anti-marketing" or fear of legal reprisals? (Sol Meliá Web site, www.solmelia.com; S. P. Webber, "Guiding Sol Melia," *Travel Agent* 298, no. 4 [2000]; Sol Meliá Cuba Web site, www.solmeliacuba.com)

differences in subsequent sections when we look at how products must be altered from country to country. In short, Levitt's globally standardized markets seem a long way off in many industries.

Market Segmentation

Market segmentation refers to identifying distinct groups of consumers whose purchasing behavior differs from others in important ways. Markets can be segmented in numerous ways: by geography, demography (sex, age, income, race, education level, etc.), sociocultural factors (social class, values, religion, lifestyle choices), and psychological factors (personality). Because different segments exhibit different patterns of purchasing behavior, firms often adjust their marketing mix from segment to segment. Thus, the precise design of a product, the pricing strategy, the distribution channels used, and the choice of communication strategy may all be varied from segment to segment. The goal is to optimize the fit between the purchasing behavior of consumers in a given segment and the marketing mix, thereby maximizing sales to that segment. Automobile companies, for example, use a different marketing mix to sell cars to different socioeconomic segments. Thus, Toyota uses its Lexus division to sell high-priced luxury cars to high-income consumers, while selling its entry-level models, such as the Toyota Corolla, to lower-income consumers. Similarly, personal computer manufacturers will offer different computer models, embodying different combinations of product attributes and price points, precisely to appeal to consumers from different market segments (e.g., business users and home users).

When managers in an international business consider market segmentation in foreign countries, they need to be cognizant of two main issues: the differences between countries in the structure of market segments and the existence of segments that transcend national borders. The structure of market segments may differ significantly from country to country. An important market segment in a foreign country may have no parallel in the firm's home country, and vice versa. The firm may have to

Market Segmentation
Identifying groups of consumers whose purchasing behavior differs from others in important ways.

Youth around the world have responded to Quiksilver, a company whose products range from clothing to wet suits. Quiksilver uses similar marketing tactics regardless of where stores are located because the popularity of surfing and winter sports transcends international boundaries.

Marketing to Black Brazil

Brazil is home to the largest black population outside of Nigeria. Nearly half of the 160 million people in Brazil are of African or mixed-race origin. Despite this, until recently businesses have made little effort to target this numerically large segment. Part of the reason is rooted in economics. Black Brazilians have historically been poorer than Brazilians of European origin and thus have not received the same attention as whites. But after a decade of relatively strong economic performance in Brazil, an emerging black middle class is beginning to command the attention of consumer product companies. To take advantage of this, companies such as Unilever have introduced a range of skin care products and cosmetics aimed at black Brazilians, and Brazil's largest toy company recently introduced a black Barbie-like doll, Susi Olodum, sales of which quickly caught up with sales of a similar white doll.

But there is more to the issue than simple economics. Unlike the United States, where a protracted history of racial discrimination gave birth to the civil rights movement, fostered black awareness, and produced an identifiable subculture in U.S. society, the history of blacks in Brazil has been very different. Although Brazil did not abolish slavery until 1888, racism in Brazil has historically been much subtler than in the United States. Brazil has never excluded blacks from voting or had a tradition of segregating the races. Historically, too, the government encouraged intermarriage between whites and blacks in order to "bleach" society. Partly due to this more benign history, Brazil has not had a black rights movement similar to that in the United States, and racial self-identification is much weaker. Surveys routinely find that African-Brazilian consumers decline to categorize themselves as either black or white; instead they choose one of dozens of skin tones and see themselves as being part of a culture that transcends race.

This subtler racial dynamic has important implications for market segmentation and tailoring the marketing mix in Brazil. Unilever had to face this issue when launching a Vaseline Intensive Care lotion for black consumers in Brazil. The company learned in focus groups that for the product to resonate with nonwhite women, its promotions had to feature women of different skin tones, excluding neither whites nor blacks. The campaign Unilever devised features three women with different skin shades at a fitness center. The bottle says the lotion is for "tan and black skin," a description that could include many white women considering that much of the population lives near the beach. Unilever learned that the segment exists, but it is more difficult to define and requires more subtle marketing messages than the African-American segment in the United States or middle-class segments in Africa.

Sources: M. Jordan, "Marketers Discover Black Brazil," *The Wall Street Journal,* November 24, 2000, pp. A11, A14. Copyright 2000 by Dow Jones & Co. Inc. Reproduced with permission from Dow Jones & Co. Inc. in the format textbook by the Copyright Clearance Center.

develop a unique marketing mix to appeal to the purchasing behavior of a certain segment in a given country. An example of such a market segment is given in the accompanying Management Focus, which looks at the African-Brazilian market segment in Brazil, which as you will see is very different from the African-American segment in the United States. In another example, a research project identified a segment of consumers in China in the 50-to-60 age range that has few parallels in other countries.[6] Members of this group came of age during China's Cultural Revolution in the late 1960s and early 1970s, and their experiences shaped their value. They tend to be highly sensitive to price and respond negatively to new products and most forms of marketing. Thus, firms doing business in China may need to customize their marketing mix to address the unique values and purchasing behavior of the group. The existence of such a segment constrains the ability of firms to standardize their global marketing strategy.

In contrast, the existence of market segments that transcend national borders clearly enhances the ability of an international business to view the global marketplace as a single entity and pursue a global strategy, selling a standardized product worldwide and using the same basic marketing mix to help position and sell that product in a variety of national markets. For a segment to transcend national borders, consumers in that segment must have some compelling similarities along important dimensions—such as age, values, lifestyle choices—and those similarities must translate into similar purchasing behavior. Although such segments clearly exist in certain industrial markets, they are somewhat rarer in consumer markets. One emerging global segment that is attracting the attention of international marketers of consumer goods is the so-called global youth segment. Global media are paving the way for a global youth segment. Evidence that such a segment exists comes from a study of the cultural attitudes and purchasing behavior of more than 6,500 teenagers in 26 countries.[7] The findings suggest that teens around the world are increasingly living parallel lives that share many common values. It follows that they are likely to purchase the same kind of consumer goods and for the same reasons.

Product Attributes

LEARNING OBJECTIVE 1
Explain why it might make sense to vary the attributes of a product from country to country.

A product can be viewed as a bundle of attributes.[8] For example, the attributes that make up a car include power, design, quality, performance, fuel consumption, and comfort; the attributes of a hamburger include taste, texture, and size; a hotel's attributes include atmosphere, quality, comfort, and service. Products sell well when their attributes match consumer needs (and when their prices are appropriate). BMW cars sell well to people who have high needs for luxury, quality, and performance, precisely because BMW builds those attributes into its cars. If consumer needs were the same the world over, a firm could simply sell the same product worldwide. However, consumer needs vary from country to country, depending on culture and the level of economic development. A firm's ability to sell the same product worldwide is further constrained by countries' differing product standards. In this section, we review each of these issues and discuss how they influence product attributes.

CULTURAL DIFFERENCES   We discussed countries' cultural differences in Chapter 3. Countries differ along a whole range of dimensions, including social structure, language, religion, and education. These differences have important implications for marketing strategy. For example, hamburgers do not sell well in Islamic countries, where the consumption of ham is forbidden by Islamic law. The most important aspect of cultural differences is probably the impact of tradition. Tradition is particularly important in foodstuffs and beverages. For example, reflecting differences in traditional eating habits, the Findus frozen food division of Nestlé, the Swiss food giant, markets fish cakes and fish fingers in Great Britain, but beef bourguignon and coq au vin in France and vitéllo con funghi and braviola in Italy. In addition to its normal range of products, Coca-Cola in Japan markets Georgia, a cold coffee in a can, and Aquarius, a tonic drink, both of which appeal to traditional Japanese tastes.

For historical and idiosyncratic reasons, a range of other cultural differences exist between countries. For example, scent preferences differ from one country to another. SC Johnson, a manufacturer of waxes and polishes, encountered resistance to its lemon-scented Pledge furniture polish among older consumers in Japan. Careful market research revealed that the polish smelled similar to a latrine disinfectant used widely in Japan. Sales rose sharply after the scent was adjusted.[9] In another example, Cheetos, the bright orange and cheesy-tasting snack from

Coca-Cola markets Georgia, a cold coffee in a can, in Japan.

PepsiCo's Frito-Lay unit, do not have a cheese taste in China. Chinese consumers generally do not like the taste of cheese because it has never been part of traditional cuisine and because many Chinese are lactose-intolerant.[10]

There is some evidence of the trends Levitt talked about. Tastes and preferences are becoming more cosmopolitan. Coffee is gaining ground against tea in Japan and Great Britain, while American-style frozen dinners have become popular in Europe (with some fine-tuning to local tastes). Taking advantage of these trends, Nestlé has found that it can market its instant coffee, spaghetti bolognese, and Lean Cuisine frozen dinners in essentially the same manner in both North America and Western Europe. However, there is no market for Lean Cuisine dinners in most of the rest of the world, and there may not be for years or decades. Although some cultural convergence has occurred, particularly among the advanced industrial nations of North America and Western Europe, Levitt's global culture characterized by standardized tastes and preferences is still a long way off.

ECONOMIC DEVELOPMENT   Just as important as differences in culture are differences in the level of economic development. We discussed the extent of country differences in economic development in Chapter 2. Consumer behavior is influenced by the level of economic development of a country. Firms based in highly developed countries such as the United States tend to build a lot of extra performance attributes into their products. These extra attributes are not usually demanded by consumers in less developed nations, where the preference is for more basic products. Thus, cars sold in less developed nations typically lack many of the features found in developed nations, such as air-conditioning, power steering, power windows, radios, and cassette players. For most consumer durables, product reliability may be a more important attribute in less developed nations, where such a purchase may account for a major proportion of a consumer's income, than it is in advanced nations.

Contrary to Levitt's suggestions, consumers in the most developed countries are often not willing to sacrifice their preferred attributes for lower prices. Consumers in the most advanced countries often shun globally standardized products that have been developed with the lowest common denominator in mind. They are willing to pay more for products that have additional features and attributes customized to their tastes and preferences. For example, demand for top-of-the-line four-wheel-drive sport utility vehicles, such as Chrysler's Jeep, Ford's Explorer, and Toyota's Land Cruiser, has been largely restricted to the United States. This is due to a combination of factors, including the high-income level of U.S. consumers, the country's vast distances, the relatively low cost of gasoline, and the culturally grounded "outdoor" theme of American life.

PRODUCT AND TECHNICAL STANDARDS   Even with the forces that are creating some convergence of consumer tastes and preferences among advanced, industrialized nations, Levitt's vision of global markets may still be a long way off because of national differences in product and technological standards.

Differing government-mandated product standards can rule out mass production and marketing of a standardized product. Differences in technical standards also constrain the globalization of markets. Some of these differences result from idiosyncratic decisions made long ago, rather than from government actions, but their long-term effects are profound. For example, DVD equipment manufactured for sale in the United States will not play DVDs recorded on equipment manufactured for sale in Great Britain, Germany, and France (and vice versa). Different technical standards for television signal frequency emerged in the 1950s that require television and video equipment to be customized to prevailing standards. RCA stumbled in the 1970s when it failed to account for this in its marketing of TVs in Asia. Although several Asian countries adopted the U.S. standard, Singapore, Hong Kong, and Malaysia adopted the British standard. People who bought RCA TVs in those countries could receive a picture but no sound![11]

Distribution Strategy

LEARNING OBJECTIVE 2
Recognize why and how a firm's distribution strategy might vary among countries.

A critical element of a firm's marketing mix is its distribution strategy: the means it chooses for delivering the product to the consumer. The way the product is delivered is determined by the firm's entry strategy, discussed in Chapter 12. In this section, we examine a typical distribution system, discuss how its structure varies between countries, and look at how appropriate distribution strategies vary from country to country.

Figure 15.1 illustrates a typical distribution system consisting of a channel that includes a wholesale distributor and a retailer. If the firm manufactures its product in the particular country, it can sell directly to the consumer, to the retailer, or to the wholesaler. The same options are available to a firm that manufactures outside the country. Plus, this firm may decide to sell to an import agent, which then deals with the wholesale distributor, the retailer, or the consumer. Later in the chapter we will consider the factors that determine the firm's choice of channel.

DIFFERENCES BETWEEN COUNTRIES The four main differences between distribution systems are retail concentration, channel length, channel exclusivity, and channel quality.

Retail Concentration In some countries, the retail system is very concentrated, but it is fragmented in others. In a **concentrated retail system,** a few retailers supply most of the market. A **fragmented retail system** is one in which there are many retailers, no one of which has a major share of the market. Many of the differences in concentration are rooted in history and tradition. In the United States, the importance of the automobile and the relative youth of many urban areas have resulted in a retail

Concentrated Retail System
A few retailers supply most of the market.

Fragmented Retail System
Many retailers supply a market with no one having a major share.

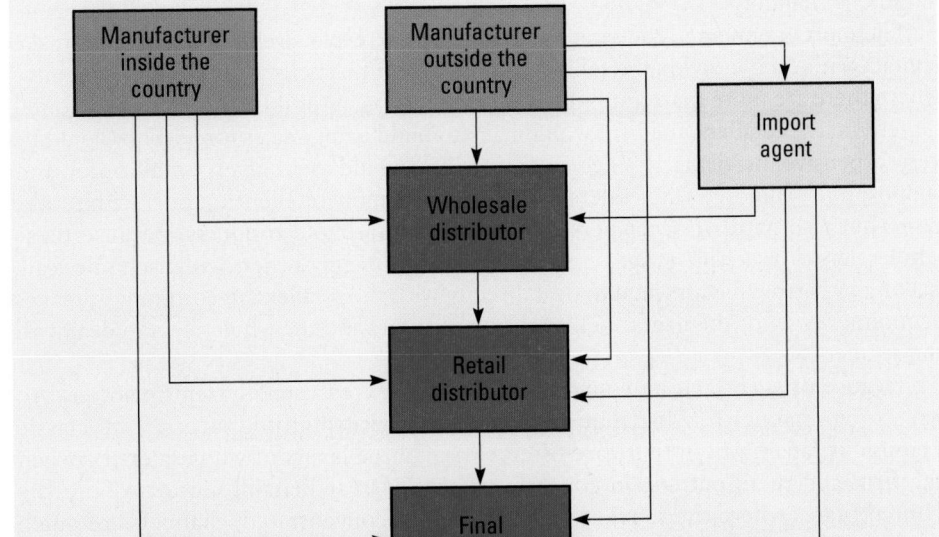

15.1 figure

A Typical Distribution System

system centered on large stores or shopping malls to which people can drive. This has facilitated system concentration. Japan, with a much greater population density and a large number of urban centers that grew up before the automobile, has a more fragmented retail system, with many small stores serving local neighborhoods and to which people frequently walk. In addition, the Japanese legal system protects small retailers. Small retailers can try to block the establishment of a large retail outlet by petitioning their local government.

Developed countries tend toward greater retail concentration. Three factors that contribute to this are the increases in car ownership, number of households with refrigerators and freezers, and number of two-income households. All these factors have changed shopping habits and facilitated the growth of large retail establishments sited away from traditional shopping areas. The last decade has seen consolidation in the global retail industry, with companies such as Walmart and Carrefour attempting to become global retailers by acquiring retailers in different countries. This has increased retail concentration.

In contrast, retail systems are very fragmented in many developing countries, which can make for interesting distribution challenges. In rural China, large areas of the country can be reached only by traveling rutted dirt roads. In India, Unilever has to sell to retailers in 600,000 rural villages, many of which cannot be accessed via paved roads, which means products can reach their destination only by bullock, bicycle, or cart. In neighboring Nepal, the terrain is so rugged that even bicycles and carts are not practical, and businesses rely on yak trains and the human back to deliver products to thousands of small retailers.

Channel Length

Channel Length
The number of intermediaries that a product has to go through before it reaches the final consumer.

Channel length refers to the number of intermediaries between the producer (or manufacturer) and the consumer. If the producer sells directly to the consumer, the channel is very short. If the producer sells through an import agent, a wholesaler, and a retailer, a long channel exists. The choice of a short or long channel is in part a strategic decision for the producing firm. However, some countries have longer distribution channels than others. The most important determinant of channel length is the degree to which the retail system is fragmented. Fragmented retail systems tend to promote the growth of wholesalers to serve retailers, which lengthens channels.

The more fragmented the retail system, the more expensive it is for a firm to make contact with each individual retailer. Imagine a firm that sells toothpaste in a country where there are more than a million small retailers, as in rural India and China. To sell directly to the retailers, the firm would have to build a huge sales force. This would be very expensive, particularly since each sales call would yield a very small order. But suppose a few hundred wholesalers in the country supply retailers not only with toothpaste but also with all other personal care and household products. Because these wholesalers carry a wide range of products, they get bigger orders with each sales call, making it worthwhile for them to deal directly with the retailers. Accordingly, it makes economic sense for the firm to sell to the wholesalers and the wholesalers to deal with the retailers.

Because of such factors, countries with fragmented retail systems also tend to have long channels of distribution, sometimes with multiple layers. The classic example is Japan, where there are often two or three layers of wholesalers between the firm and retail outlets. In countries such as Great Britain, Germany, and the United States where the retail system is far more concentrated, channels are much shorter. When the retail sector is very concentrated, it makes sense for the firm to deal directly with retailers, cutting out wholesalers. A relatively small sales force is required to deal with a concentrated retail sector, and the orders generated from each sales call can be large. Such circumstances tend to prevail in the United States, where large food companies may sell directly to supermarkets rather than going through wholesale distributors.

The rapid development of the Internet in recent years has helped to shorten channel length. For example, the Seattle-based outdoor equipment retailer REI sells its products in Japan via a Japanese-language Web site, thereby eliminating the need for a retail presence on the ground in Japan, which obviously shortens the channel length between REI and its customers. However, there are definite drawbacks with such a strategy. In the case of REI, consumers cannot receive the same level of advice over the Web as in physical retail stores, where salespeople can help customers choose the right gear for their needs. So although REI benefits from a short channel in Japan, it may lose significant sales due to the lack of point-of-sale service.

Another factor that is shortening channel length in some counties is the entry of large discount superstores, such as Carrefour, Walmart, and Tesco. The business model of these retailers is in part based upon the idea that in an attempt to lower prices, they cut out wholesalers and instead deal directly with manufacturers. Thus, when Walmart entered Mexico, its policy of dealing directly with manufacturers, instead of buying merchandise through wholesalers, helped to shorten distribution channels in that nation. Similarly, Japan's historically long distribution channels are now being shortened by the rise of large retailers, some of them foreign owned, such as Toys "R" Us, and some of them indigenous enterprises that are imitating the American model, all of which are progressively cutting out wholesalers and dealing directly with manufacturers.

Channel Exclusivity   An **exclusive distribution channel** is one that is difficult for outsiders to access. For example, it is often difficult for a new firm to get access to shelf space in supermarkets. This occurs because retailers tend to prefer to carry the products of established manufacturers of foodstuffs with national reputations rather than gamble on the products of unknown firms. The exclusivity of a distribution system varies between countries. Japan's system is often held up as an example of a very exclusive system. In Japan, relationships between manufacturers, wholesalers, and retailers often go back decades. Many of these relationships are based on the understanding that distributors will not carry the products of competing firms. In return, the distributors are guaranteed an attractive markup by the manufacturer. As many U.S. and European manufacturers have learned, the close ties that result from this arrangement can make access to the Japanese market difficult. However, it is possible to break into the Japanese market with a new consumer product. Procter & Gamble did during the 1990s with its Joy brand of dish soap. P&G was able to overcome a tradition of exclusivity for two reasons. First, after a decade of lackluster economic performance, Japan is changing. In their search for profits, retailers are far more willing than they have been historically to violate the old norms of exclusivity. Second, P&G has been in Japan long enough and has a broad enough portfolio of consumer products to give it considerable leverage with distributors, enabling it to push new products out through the distribution channel.

Exclusive Distribution Channel
A channel that outsiders find difficult to access.

Channel Quality   **Channel quality** refers to the expertise, competencies, and skills of established retailers in a nation, and their ability to sell and support the products of international businesses. Although the quality of retailers is good in most developed nations, in emerging markets and less developed nations from Russia to Indonesia, channel quality is variable at best. The lack of a high-quality channel may impede market entry, particularly in the case of new or sophisticated products that require significant point-of-sale assistance and after-sales services and support. When channel quality

Channel Quality
The expertise, competencies, and skills of established retailers in a nation, and their ability to sell and support the products of international businesses.

is poor, an international business may have to devote considerable attention to upgrading the channel, for example, by providing extensive education and support to existing retailers, and in extreme cases, by establishing its own channel. Thus, after pioneering its Apple retail store concept in the United States, Apple is opening retail stores in several nations, such as the United Kingdom, to provide point-of-sales education, service, and support for its popular iPod and computer products. Apple believes that this strategy will help it to gain market share in these nations.

CHOOSING A DISTRIBUTION STRATEGY A choice of distribution strategy determines which channel the firm will use to reach potential consumers. Should the firm try to sell directly to the consumer or should it go through retailers; should it go through a wholesaler; should it use an import agent; or should it invest in establishing its own channel? The optimal strategy is determined by the relative costs and benefits of each alternative, which vary from country to country, depending on the four factors we have just discussed: retail concentration, channel length, channel exclusivity, and channel quality.

Because each intermediary in a channel adds its own markup to the products, there is generally a critical link between channel length, the final selling price, and the firm's profit margin. The longer a channel, the greater is the aggregate markup, and the higher the price that consumers are charged for the final product. To ensure that prices do not get too high as a result of markups by multiple intermediaries, a firm might be forced to operate with lower profit margins. Thus, if price is an important competitive weapon, and if the firm does not want to see its profit margins squeezed, other things being equal, the firm would prefer to use a shorter channel.

However, the benefits of using a longer channel may outweigh these drawbacks. As we have seen, one benefit of a longer channel is that it cuts selling costs when the retail sector is very fragmented. Thus, it makes sense for an international business to use longer channels in countries where the retail sector is fragmented and shorter channels in countries where the retail sector is concentrated. Another benefit of using a longer channel is market access—the ability to enter an exclusive channel. Import agents may have long-term relationships with wholesalers, retailers, or important consumers and thus be better able to win orders and get access to a distribution system. Similarly, wholesalers may have long-standing relationships with retailers and be better able to persuade them to carry the firm's product than the firm itself would.

Import agents are not limited to independent trading houses; any firm with a strong local reputation could serve as well. For example, to break down channel exclusivity and gain greater access to the Japanese market, Apple Computer signed distribution agreements with five large Japanese firms, including business equipment giant Brother Industries, stationery leader Kokuyo, Mitsubishi, Sharp, and Minolta. These firms use their own long-established distribution relationships with consumers, retailers, and wholesalers to push Apple computers through the Japanese distribution system. As a result, Apple's share of the Japanese market increased from less than 1 percent to 13 percent in the four years following the signing of the agreements.[12]

If such an arrangement is not possible, the firm might want to consider other, less traditional alternatives to gaining market access. Frustrated by channel exclusivity in Japan, some foreign manufacturers of consumer goods have attempted to sell directly to Japanese consumers using direct mail and catalogs. REI had trouble persuading Japanese wholesalers and retailers to carry its products, so it began a direct-mail campaign and then a Web-based strategy to enter Japan that is proving successful.

Finally, if channel quality is poor, a firm should consider what steps it could take to upgrade the quality of the channel, including establishing its own distribution channel.

Communication Strategy

Another critical element in the marketing mix is communicating the attributes of the product to prospective customers. A number of communication channels are available to a firm, including direct selling, sales promotion, direct marketing, and advertising. A firm's communication strategy is partly defined by its choice of channel. Some firms rely primarily on direct selling, others on point-of-sale promotions or direct marketing, and others on mass advertising; still others use several channels simultaneously to communicate their message to prospective customers. In this section, we will look first at the barriers to international communication. Then we will survey the various factors that determine which communication strategy is most appropriate in a particular country. After that we discuss global advertising.

BARRIERS TO INTERNATIONAL COMMUNICATION   International communication occurs whenever a firm uses a marketing message to sell its products in another country. The effectiveness of a firm's international communication can be jeopardized by three potentially critical variables: cultural barriers, source effects, and noise levels.

Cultural Barriers   Cultural barriers can make it difficult to communicate messages across cultures. We discussed some sources and consequences of cultural differences between nations in Chapter 3 and in the previous section of this chapter. Because of cultural differences, a message that means one thing in one country may mean something quite different in another. For example, when Procter & Gamble first promoted its Camay soap in Japan it ran into unexpected trouble. In a TV commercial, a Japanese man walked into the bathroom while his wife was bathing. The woman began telling her husband all about her new soap, but the husband, stroking her shoulder, hinted that suds were not on his mind. This ad had been popular in Europe, but it flopped in Japan because it is considered bad manners there for a man to intrude on his wife.[13]

Benetton, the Italian clothing manufacturer and retailer, is another firm that has run into cultural problems with its advertising. The company launched a worldwide

UNITED COLORS OF BENETTON.

Clothing retailer Benetton has become famous for advertising that has been deemed offensive or inappropriate in some countries.

advertising campaign with the theme "United Colors of Benetton" that had won awards in France. One of its ads featured a black woman breast-feeding a white baby, and another one showed a black man and a white man handcuffed together. Benetton was surprised when the ads were attacked by U.S. civil rights groups for promoting white racial domination. Benetton withdrew its ads and fired its advertising agency, Eldorado of France.

The best way for a firm to overcome cultural barriers is to develop cross-cultural literacy (see Chapter 3). In addition, it should use local input, such as a local advertising agency, in developing its marketing message. If the firm uses direct selling rather than advertising to communicate its message, it should develop a local sales force whenever possible. Cultural differences limit a firm's ability to use the same marketing message and selling approach worldwide. What works well in one country may be offensive in another.

Source and Country of Origin Effects

Source effects occur when the receiver of the message (the potential consumer in this case) evaluates the message on the basis of status or image of the sender. Source effects can be damaging for an international business when potential consumers in a target country have a bias against foreign firms. For example, a wave of "Japan bashing" swept the United States in the early 1990s. Worried that U.S. consumers might view its products negatively, Honda responded by creating ads that emphasized the U.S. content of its cars to show how "American" the company had become.

Many international businesses try to counter negative source effects by deemphasizing their foreign origins. When the French antiglobalization protestor Jose Bove was hailed as a hero by some in France for razing a partly built McDonald's in 1999, the French franchisee of McDonald's responded with an ad depicting a fat, ignorant American who could not understand why McDonald's France used locally produced food that wasn't genetically modified. The edgy ad worked, and McDonald's French operations are now among the most robust in the company's global network.[14] Similarly, when British Petroleum acquired Mobil Oil's extensive network of U.S. gas stations, it changed its name to BP, diverting attention away from the fact that one of the biggest operators of gas stations in the United States is a British firm.

A subset of source effects is referred to as **country of origin effects,** or the extent to which the place of manufacturing influences product evaluations. Research suggests that the consumer may use country of origin as a cue when evaluating a product, particularly if he or she lacks more detailed knowledge of the product. For example, one study found that Japanese consumers tended to rate Japanese products more favorably than U.S. products across multiple dimensions, even when independent analysis showed that they were actually inferior.[15] When a negative country of origin effect exists, an international business may have to work hard to counteract this effect by, for example, using promotional messages that stress the positive performance attributes of its product. Thus, the South Korean automobile company Hyundai tried to overcome negative perceptions about the quality of its vehicle in the United States by running advertisements that favorably compare the company's cars to more prestigious brands.

Source Effects
When the receiver of the message evaluates the message based on the status or image of the sender.

Country of Origin Effects
The extent to which the place of manufacturing influences product evaluations.

Another Perspective

"Glocal"—Think Globally, Act Locally
Modern global marketing efforts have come to realize that there is a need for multinational corporations to establish local roots. During the 1980s and 1990s, Sony Corporation coined the combined term "glocal" to reflect that need. In Japanese business practices, the term evolved to "glocalization." It comes from the Japanese term, *dochakuka*, which simply means *global localization.* In his book, *The World Is Flat,* Thomas L. Friedman did a variation of "glocalization" by encouraging people to create Web sites in their native language. More recently, the term is being used to describe the local/international context of social media and social networking such as Facebook. In these networks, local and long distance interaction allow for *glocal* relationships. (B. Wellman, "Little Boxes, Glocalization, and Networked Individualism," in *Digital Cities II,* edited by M. Tanabe, P. van den Besselaar, and T. Ishida. [Berlin: Springer-Verlag, 2002], pp. 11–25)

Source effects and country of origin effects are not always negative. French wine, Italian clothes, and German luxury cars benefit from nearly universal positive source effects. In such cases, it may pay a firm to emphasize its foreign origins. In Japan, for example, there is strong demand for high-quality foreign goods, particularly those from Europe. It has become chic to carry a Gucci handbag, sport a Rolex watch, drink expensive French wine, and drive a BMW.

Noise Levels

Noise tends to reduce the probability of effective communication. **Noise** refers to the amount of other messages competing for a potential consumer's attention, and this too varies across countries. In highly developed countries such as the United States, noise is extremely high. Fewer firms vie for the attention of prospective customers in developing countries, thus the noise level is lower.

Noise
The amount of other messages competing for a potential consumer's attention.

PUSH VERSUS PULL STRATEGIES

The main decision with regard to communications strategy is the choice between a push strategy and a pull strategy. A **push strategy** emphasizes personal selling rather than mass media advertising in the promotional mix. Although effective as a promotional tool, personal selling requires intensive use of a sales force and is relatively costly. A **pull strategy** depends more on mass media advertising to communicate the marketing message to potential consumers.

Although some firms employ only a pull strategy and others only a push strategy, still other firms combine direct selling with mass advertising to maximize communication effectiveness. Factors that determine the relative attractiveness of push and pull strategies include product type relative to consumer sophistication, channel length, and media availability.

Push Strategy
A marketing strategy emphasizing personal selling rather than mass media advertising.

Pull Strategy
A marketing strategy emphasizing mass media advertising as opposed to personal selling.

Product Type and Consumer Sophistication

Firms in consumer goods industries that are trying to sell to a large segment of the market generally favor a pull strategy. Mass communication has cost advantages for such firms, thus they rarely use direct selling. Exceptions can be found in poorer nations with low literacy levels, where direct selling may be the only way to reach consumers. Firms that sell industrial products or other complex products favor a push strategy. Direct selling allows the firm to educate potential consumers about the features of the product. This may not be necessary in advanced nations where a complex product has been in use for some time, where the product's attributes are well understood, where consumers are sophisticated, and where high-quality channels exist that can provide point-of-sale assistance. However, customer education may be important when consumers have less sophistication toward the product, which can be the case in developing nations or in advanced nations when a new complex product is being introduced, or where high-quality channels are absent or scarce.

Channel Length

The longer the distribution channel, the more intermediaries there are that must be persuaded to carry the product for it to reach the consumer. This can lead to inertia in the channel, which can make entry difficult. Using direct selling to push a product through many layers of a distribution channel can be expensive. In such circumstances, a firm may try to pull its product through the channels by using mass advertising to create consumer demand—once demand is created, intermediaries will feel obliged to carry the product.

In Japan, products often pass through two, three, or even four wholesalers before they reach the final retail outlet. This can make it difficult for foreign firms to break into the Japanese market. Not only must the foreign firm persuade a Japanese retailer to carry its product, but it may also have to persuade every intermediary in the chain to carry the

Management FOCUS

Subaru's U.S. Marketing Approach: Love

Tim Mahoney is not German, nor is he Japanese. Tim Mahoney is, however, Marketer of the Year 2010 by *Brandweek.* For nine years, Mahoney was chief marketer at Porsche of America; now he is chief marketer at Subaru of America, the automobile manufacturing division of the Japanese transportation conglomerate Fuji Heavy Industries (FHI).

Mahoney is in love with his job, and he has a knack for working with foreign auto makers. Since taking over marketing, Mahoney has increased Subaru of America sales by another 30 percent year to date through July 2010 versus 14 percent for the industry. All this growth has vaulted Subaru passed Volkswagen, Mazda, BMW, and Lexus in sales.

Founded in 1968, Subaru of America Inc. (SOA) is the U.S. Sales and Marketing subsidiary of FHI and is responsible for the distribution, marketing, sales, and service of Subaru vehicles in the United States. It mostly markets and only "manufactures" at the Subaru of Indiana Automotive assembly plant, FHI's only manufacturing operations overseas. From a marketing perspective, SOA should actually be called SOF, Subaru of Fuji. A quintessential Japanese *keiretsu* belonging to Industrial Bank of Japan, FHI involvement in Subaru is a testament to the ability of a large multinational to diversify and market its products in a foreign market—in this case, the United States and Canada. Many times, that success is premised on particular individuals responsible for its marketing. Tim Mahoney was selected to fill that role.

Upon taking over the role, Mahoney fired DDB Advertising and hired Carmichael Lynch. Mahoney's only requirement was that the previous tag line be kept: "It's what makes a Subaru a Subaru." The new ad agency just added one word:

love, the most universal of marketing themes. "Love. It's what makes a Subaru a Subaru" became the tag line. Rather than espousing the rational, technological aspects of the cars, Mahoney sought the emotional content, something that would transcend any potential cultural issue. With adding the word *love,* the emotional content was delivered. Rather than have celebrity spokespersons represent the brand, real Subaru car lovers were featured in their commercials. Rarely, however, does a successful marketing campaign rest on the shoulders of only one person.

Since 2008, Yoshio Hasunuma has been CEO of Subaru of America. But perhaps more telling is that Hasunuma was previously senior vice president of Subaru global marketing in Japan. Because of his Japanese ties, Hasunuma was able to convince FHI to bring the right products to the U.S. market that customers demand—smaller, economically and environmentally friendly products, especially during recessionary times. Another factor that contributed was that the relationships with the 610 dealerships were greatly improved. When asked if dealers were approaching Subaru for franchises, Hasunuma responded: "To appoint a dealer, Subaru and the dealer need to love each other. The dealer needs to understand and agree with Subaru principles and brand strategy. It has to be a good fit." With dealerships eventually around the world, it will be interesting to watch whether such a universal concept will work in other places. It sounds like a "love it or leave it" situation.

Sources: Subaru Web site, *www.subaru.com;* D. Kiley, "Tim Mahoney, Subaru, Marketer of the Year 2010" *Brandweek,* September 13, 2010, accessed at http://www.brandweekmoy.com/2010/09/tim-mahoney-subaru.html; and "Subaru's U.S. Chief: Hot Brand Won't Cool Off," *Automotive News,* June 14, 2010.

product. Mass advertising may be one way to break down channel resistance in such circumstances. However, this is subject to variations (see the Management Focus on Subaru). As an example of a variance of the pull strategy, the culturally acceptable "Love" campaign used by Subaru communicated a marketing message to potential customers. When carefully thought out, pulling on culturally acceptable "heart strings" is a very powerful marketing tool.

Media Availability   A pull strategy relies on access to advertising media. In the United States, a large number of media are available, including print media (newspapers and magazines), broadcasting media (television and radio), and the Internet. The rise of cable television in the United States has facilitated extremely focused advertising (e.g., MTV for teens and young adults, Lifetime for women, ESPN for sports enthusiasts). The same is true of the Internet, with different Web sites attracting different kinds of users, and companies such as Google transforming the ability of companies to do targeted advertising. While this level of media sophistication is now found in many other developed countries, it is still not universal. Even many advanced nations have far fewer electronic media available for advertising than the United States. In Scandinavia, for example, no commercial television or radio stations existed until recently; all electronic media were state owned and carried no commercials, although this has now changed with the advent of satellite television deregulation. In many developing nations, the situation is even more restrictive because mass media of all types are typically more limited. A firm's ability to use a pull strategy is limited in some countries by media availability. In such circumstances, a push strategy is more attractive. For example, Unilever uses a push strategy to sell consumer products in rural India, where few mass media are available.

Media availability is limited by law in some cases. Few countries allow advertisements for tobacco and alcohol products on television and radio, though they are usually permitted in print media. When the leading Japanese whiskey distiller, Suntory, entered the U.S. market, it had to do so without television, its preferred medium. The firm spends about $50 million annually on television advertising in Japan. Similarly, while advertising pharmaceutical products directly to consumers is allowed in the United States, it is prohibited in many other advanced nations. In such cases, pharmaceutical firms must rely heavily upon advertising and direct-sales efforts focused explicitly at doctors in order to get their products prescribed.

The Push–Pull Mix

The optimal mix between push and pull strategies depends on product type and consumer sophistication, channel length, and media sophistication. Push strategies tend to be emphasized

- For industrial products or complex new products.
- When distribution channels are short.
- When few print or electronic media are available.

Pull strategies tend to be emphasized

- For consumer goods.
- When distribution channels are long.
- When sufficient print and electronic media are available to carry the marketing message.

GLOBAL ADVERTISING

In recent years, largely inspired by the work of visionaries such as Theodore Levitt, there has been much discussion about the pros and cons of standardizing advertising worldwide.[16] One of the most successful standardized campaigns in history was Philip Morris's promotion of Marlboro cigarettes. The campaign was instituted in the 1950s, when the brand was repositioned, to assure smokers that the flavor would be unchanged by the addition of a filter. The campaign theme of "Come to where the flavor is: Come to Marlboro country" was a worldwide success. Marlboro built on this when it introduced "the Marlboro man," a rugged cowboy smoking his Marlboro while riding his horse through the great outdoors. This ad proved successful in almost every major market around the world, and it helped propel Marlboro to the top of the world market.

For Standardized Advertising

The support for global advertising is threefold. First, it has significant economic advantages. Standardized advertising lowers the costs of value creation by spreading the fixed costs of developing the advertisements over many countries. For example, Coca-Cola's advertising agency, McCann-Erickson, claims to have saved Coca-Cola $90 million over 20 years by using certain elements of its campaigns globally.

Second, there is the concern that creative talent is scarce and so one large effort to develop a campaign will produce better results than 40 or 50 smaller efforts. A third justification for a standardized approach is that many brand names are global. With the substantial amount of international travel today and the considerable overlap in

National regulations may prevent the use of standardized advertising. For example, Kellogg's tag line "Kellogg's makes their cornflakes the best they have ever been" could not be used in Germany because of a prohibition against competitive claims.

media across national borders, many international firms want to project a single brand image to avoid confusion caused by local campaigns. This is particularly important in regions such as Western Europe, where travel across borders is almost as common as travel across state lines in the United States.

Against Standardized Advertising   There are two main arguments against globally standardized advertising. First, as we have seen repeatedly in this chapter and in Chapter 3, cultural differences between nations are such that a message that works in one nation can fail miserably in another. Cultural diversity makes it extremely difficult to develop a single advertising theme that is effective worldwide. Messages directed at the culture of a given country may be more effective than global messages.

Second, advertising regulations may block implementation of standardized advertising. For example, Kellogg could not use a television commercial it produced in Great Britain to promote its cornflakes in many other European countries. A reference to the iron and vitamin content of its cornflakes was not permissible in the Netherlands, where claims relating to health and medical benefits are outlawed. A child wearing a Kellogg T-shirt had to be edited out of the commercial before it could be used in France, because French law forbids the use of children in product endorsements. The key line "Kellogg's makes their cornflakes the best they have ever been" was disallowed in Germany because of a prohibition against competitive claims.[17] Similarly, American Express ran afoul of regulatory authorities in Germany when it launched a promotional scheme that had proved successful in other countries. The scheme advertised the offer of "bonus points" every time American Express cardholders used their cards. According to the advertisements, these bonus points could be used toward air travel with three airlines and hotel accommodations. American Express was charged with breaking Germany's competition law, which prevents an offer of free gifts in connection with the sale of goods, and the firm had to withdraw the advertisements at considerable cost.[18]

Dealing with Country Differences   Some firms are experimenting with capturing some benefits of global standardization while recognizing differences in countries' cultural and legal environments. A firm may select some features to include in all its advertising campaigns and localize other features. By doing so, it may be able to save on some costs and build international brand recognition and yet customize its advertisements to different cultures.

Nokia, the Finnish cell phone manufacture, has been trying to do this. Historically, Nokia had used a different advertising campaign in different markets. In the mid-2000s, however, the company launched a global advertising campaign that used the slogan "1001 reasons to have a Nokia imaging phone." Nokia did this to reduce advertising costs and capture some economies of scale. In addition, in an increasingly integrated world, the company believes that there is value in trying to establish a consistent global brand image. At the same time, Nokia is tweaking the advertisements for different cultures. The campaign uses actors from the region where the ad runs to reflect the local population, though they will say the same lines. Local settings are also modified when showcasing the phones by, for example, using a marketplace when advertising in Italy or a bazaar when advertising in the Middle East.[19] Another example of this process is given in the accompanying Management Focus feature, which looks at how the Coca-Cola Company built a global brand for its products, while still tweaking the message to take into account local sensibilities.

Coca-Cola

Who does not know Coca-Cola? Regularly considered among the world's most admired companies, in the area of marketing and product standardization Coca-Cola is at the vanguard of brand globalization and global markets. But to say "Coca-Cola" is to utter a wide variety of products carefully crafted to various market segments around the world.

Besides the namesake "Coca-Cola," the Coca-Cola Company offers nearly 400 products and brands in more than 200 countries. Some are highly recognizable, such as Fanta or Sprite, while others cater to particular regions such as Ambasa, a soft drink sold in Japan and Korea; BotaniQ sold in the Ukraine; Chivalry, a fruit drink sold in China; the Turkish drink water Damla; or Yoli, a lemon-lime soda only sold in Acapulco, Guerrero, Mexico. These differences are a result of a carefully formulated marketing strategy that seeks to balance the unique consumer preferences of a particular market segment with the cost efficiencies associated with particularly standardized brands. In fact, for Coca-Cola the simple distinction between standardization and adaptation is much more complex. Here are a few specific examples:

Fanta and the "Work Week": Formulated in the early 1940s in Germany, Fanta came to be known for its refreshing orange taste right after World War II in Europe. In fact, for a considerable time, Fanta sales were mostly associated with Europe. In the United Kingdom in particular, Fanta sales have been in decline since 2005. In response, Coca-Cola did not change the formula as it has done with the flagship brand, Coca-Cola, but rather changed the marketing strategy. They focused on the "end of the working week" with a multimillion pound global ad campaign. "Grab a taste of Friday" is intended to connect drinkers by tapping into the good feelings associated with the end of the working week. Considering that the end of the work week has parallel connotations in other markets, Coca-Cola suggests the campaign might work as well in other areas.

Japan and the Soft Drink Industry: In Japan, the best selling soft drink is not a cola, but rather teas or coffee, many of which are canned. After extensive research, Coca-Cola decided to create and market a tea-flavored Coca-Cola, claiming that not only does it taste good but it is good for health and beauty. It is mainly targeted at health-conscious women in their 20s and 30s. The tea cola contains tea antioxidants. From a product development perspective, the Coca-Cola brand is leveraged with unique local tastes.

Peru and Inca Cola: Inca Cola is a lemon verbena–flavored soft drink, with a sweet fruity flavor sometimes compared to bubblegum, which originated in Peru. To the Latin American palate, it is one of the bestsellers. So much so, that as part of its marketing strategy, Coca-Cola bought 49 percent of Inca Cola. The taste is so unique to Peru and the surrounding area that it used an acquisition as part of its marketing strategy, even in such a small, exotic market.

South Africa, the World Cup, and Digital Marketing: As another example of the sophistication of Coca-Cola's marketing efforts, linking markets and products to sporting events creates a presence for Coca-Cola and its brands. "The World Cup can also work for us in markets with little awareness of Coca-Cola, where the actual per capita consumption of Coke is quite low," suggests Joseph Tripodi, Coca-Cola's chief marketing officer. Coca-Cola uses sponsorship properties such as the World Cup in these markets to put the business on what he calls a "different trajectory." For example, Tripodi claims that the money Coca-Cola spent at Beijing's 2008 Olympic Games transformed its business there. "I wish they were great at football in India," he jokes. (India sales have been notoriously low.)

He continues by further elaborating on the role of the Internet and marketing: "One of the things we're talking about now is how we evolve as a marketing entity around the world. What we're going for more and more will be content management." In doing so, he alludes to a digital marketing campaign that will begin to tap into the ever-growing number of Coca-Cola consumers. As the relationship with consumers develops, says Tripodi, so the number of possibilities grows. "You start to evolve your thinking about how to engage them, beyond giving them a free T-shirt" and presumably a bottle of Coke.

Sources: N. Howell, "Thirsty Work," *New Media Age,* 2010, pp. 14–15; M. Choueke, "Putting Some Fizz into Drinks Marketing," *MarketingWeek,* September 30, 2009; J. Thomas, "Coca-Cola Embarks on Global Fanta Campaign," *Marketing,* December 1, 2009; "Green Tea Coca-Cola to Debut in Japan," retrieved at http://www.msnbc.msn.com/id/31103164/; and Calvin Sims, "Lima Journal; Peru's Pride that Refreshes," *The New York Times, International Herald Tribune,* December 26, 1995, retrieved at http://www.nytimes.com/1995/12/26/world/lima-journal-peru-s-pride-that-refreshes-kola-of-a-local-color.html.

Pricing Strategy

International pricing strategy is an important component of the overall international marketing mix.[20] In this section, we look at three aspects of international pricing strategy. First, we examine the case for pursuing price discrimination, charging different prices for the same product in different countries. Second, we look at what might be called strategic pricing. Third, we review some regulatory factors, such as government-mandated price controls and antidumping regulations, that limit a firm's ability to charge the prices it would prefer in a country.

PRICE DISCRIMINATION

Price discrimination exists whenever consumers in different countries are charged different prices for the same product, or for slightly different variations of the product.[21] Price discrimination involves charging whatever the market will bear; in a competitive market, prices may have to be lower than in a market where the firm has a monopoly. Price discrimination can help a company maximize its profits. It makes economic sense to charge different prices in different countries.

Two conditions are necessary for profitable price discrimination. First, the firm must be able to keep its national markets separate. If it cannot do this, individuals or businesses may undercut its attempt at price discrimination by engaging in arbitrage. Arbitrage occurs when an individual or business capitalizes on a price differential for a firm's product between two countries by purchasing the product in the country where prices are lower and reselling it in the country where prices are higher. For example, many automobile firms have long practiced price discrimination in Europe. A Ford Escort once cost $2,000 more in Germany than it did in Belgium. This policy broke down when car dealers bought Escorts in Belgium and drove them to Germany, where they sold them at a profit for slightly less than Ford was selling Escorts in Germany. To protect the market share of its German auto dealers, Ford had to bring its German prices into line with those being charged in Belgium. Ford could not keep these markets separate.

However, Ford still practices price discrimination between Great Britain and Belgium. A Ford car can cost up to $3,000 more in Great Britain than in Belgium. In this case, arbitrage has not been able to equalize the price, because right-hand-drive cars are sold in Great Britain and left-hand-drive cars in the rest of Europe. Because there is no market for left-hand-drive cars in Great Britain, Ford has been able to keep the markets separate.

The second necessary condition for profitable price discrimination is different price elasticities of demand in different countries. The **price elasticity of demand** is a measure of the responsiveness of demand for a product to change in price. Demand is said to be **elastic** when a small change in price produces a large change in demand; it is said to be **inelastic** when a large change in price produces only a small change in demand. Figure 15.2 illustrates elastic and inelastic demand curves. Generally, a firm can charge a higher price in a country where demand is inelastic.

The elasticity of demand for a product in a given country is determined by a number of factors, of which income level and competitive conditions are the two most important. Price elasticity tends to be greater in countries with low income levels. Consumers with limited incomes tend to be very price conscious; they have less to spend, so they look much more closely at price. Thus, price elasticities for products such as personal computers is greater in countries such as India, where a PC is still a luxury item, than in the United States, where it is now considered a necessity. The same is true of the software that resides on those PCs; thus, to sell more software in India, Microsoft has had to introduce into that market low-priced versions of its products, such as Windows Starter Edition.

In general, the more competitors there are, the greater consumers' bargaining power will be and the more likely consumers will be to buy from the firm that charges the lowest

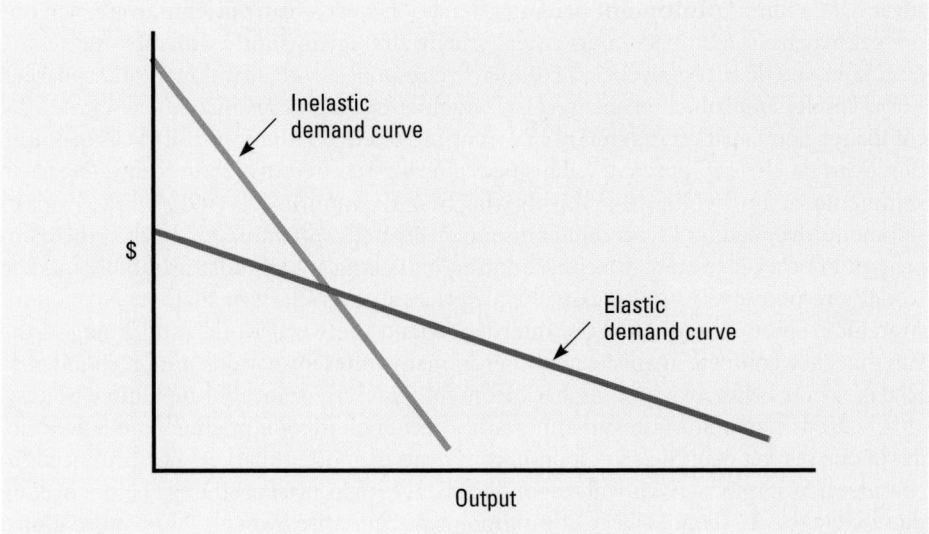

price. Thus, many competitors cause high elasticity of demand. In such circumstances, if a firm raises its prices above those of its competitors, consumers will switch to the competitors' products. The opposite is true when a firm faces few competitors. When competitors are limited, consumers' bargaining power is weaker and price is less important as a competitive weapon. Thus, a firm may charge a higher price for its product in a country where competition is limited than in one where competition is intense.

STRATEGIC PRICING   The concept of **strategic pricing** has three aspects, which we will refer to as predatory pricing, multipoint pricing, and experience curve pricing. Both predatory pricing and experience curve pricing may violate antidumping regulations. After we review predatory and experience curve pricing, we will look at antidumping rules and other regulatory policies.

Strategic Pricing
Pricing aimed at giving a company a competitive advantage over its rivals.

Predatory Pricing   **Predatory pricing** is the use of price as a competitive weapon to drive weaker competitors out of a national market. Once the competitors have left the market, the firm can raise prices and enjoy high profits. For such a pricing strategy to work, the firm must normally have a profitable position in another national market, which it can use to subsidize aggressive pricing in the market it is trying to monopolize. Historically, many Japanese firms were accused of pursuing such a policy. The argument ran like this: Because the Japanese market was protected from foreign competition by high informal trade barriers, Japanese firms could charge high prices and earn high profits at home. They then used these profits to subsidize aggressive pricing overseas, with the goal of driving competitors out of those markets. Once this had occurred, so it is claimed, the Japanese firms then raised prices. Matsushita was accused of using this strategy to enter the U.S. TV market. As one of the major TV producers in Japan, Matsushita earned high profits at home. It then used these profits to subsidize the losses it made in the United States during its early years there, when it priced low to increase its market penetration. Ultimately, Matsushita became the world's largest manufacturer of TVs.[22]

Predatory Pricing
Reducing prices below fair market value as a competitive weapon to drive weaker competitors out of the market ("fair" being cost plus some reasonable profit margin).

Multipoint Pricing Strategy   Multipoint pricing becomes an issue when two or more international businesses compete against each other in two or more national markets. For example, multipoint pricing was an issue for Kodak and Fuji Photo because the companies long competed against each other around the world in the market for

Multipoint Pricing
Occurs when a pricing
strategy in one market
may have an impact on a
rival's pricing strategy in
another market.

silver halide film.[23] **Multipoint pricing** refers to the fact a firm's pricing strategy in one market may have an impact on its rivals' pricing strategy in another market. Aggressive pricing in one market may elicit a competitive response from a rival in another market. For example, Fuji launched an aggressive competitive attack against Kodak in the U.S. company's home market in January 1997, cutting prices on multiple-roll packs of 35mm film by as much as 50 percent.[24] This price cutting resulted in a 28 percent increase in shipments of Fuji color film during the first six months of 1997, while Kodak's shipments dropped by 11 percent. This attack created a dilemma for Kodak; the company did not want to start price discounting in its largest and most profitable market. Kodak's response was to aggressively cut prices in Fuji's largest market, Japan. This strategic response recognized the interdependence between Kodak and Fuji and the fact that they compete against each other in many different nations. Fuji responded to Kodak's counterattack by pulling back from its aggressive stance in the United States.

The Kodak story illustrates an important aspect of multipoint pricing: Aggressive pricing in one market may elicit a response from rivals in another market. The firm needs to consider how its global rivals will respond to changes in its pricing strategy before making those changes. A second aspect of multipoint pricing arises when two or more global companies focus on particular national markets and launch vigorous price wars in those markets in an attempt to gain market dominance. In the Brazil market for disposable diapers, two U.S. companies, Kimberly-Clark Corp. and Procter & Gamble, entered a price war as each struggled to establish dominance in the market.[25] As a result, over three years the cost of disposable diapers fell from $1 per diaper to 33 cents per diaper, while several other competitors, including indigenous Brazilian firms, were driven out of the market. Kimberly-Clark and Procter & Gamble are engaged in a global struggle for market share and dominance, and Brazil is one of their battlegrounds. Both companies can afford to engage in this behavior, even though it reduces their profits in Brazil, because they have profitable operations elsewhere in the world that can subsidize these losses.

Pricing decisions around the world need to be centrally monitored. It is tempting to delegate full responsibility for pricing decisions to the managers of various national subsidiaries, thereby reaping the benefits of decentralization. However, because pricing strategy in one part of the world can elicit a competitive response in another, central management needs to at least monitor and approve pricing decisions in a given national market, and local managers need to recognize that their actions can affect competitive conditions in other countries.

Experience Curve Pricing   We first encountered the experience curve in Chapter 12. As a firm builds its accumulated production volume over time, unit costs fall due to experience effects. Learning effects and economies of scale underlie the experience curve. Price comes into the picture because aggressive pricing (along with aggressive promotion and advertising) can build accumulated sales volume rapidly and thus move production down the experience curve. Firms further down the experience curve have a cost advantage vis-à-vis those further up the curve.

**Experience Curve
Pricing**
Aggressive pricing
designed to increase
volume and help the firm
realize experience curve
economies.

Many firms pursuing an **experience curve pricing** strategy on an international scale will price low worldwide in attempting to build global sales volume as rapidly as possible, even if this means taking large losses initially. Such a firm believes that in several years, when it has moved down the experience curve, it will be making substantial profits and have a cost advantage over its less-aggressive competitors.

REGULATORY INFLUENCES ON PRICES   The ability to engage in either price discrimination or strategic pricing may be limited by national or international regulations. Most important, a firm's freedom to set its own prices is constrained by antidumping regulations and competition policy.

Antidumping Regulations   Both predatory pricing and experience curve pricing can run afoul of antidumping regulations. Dumping occurs whenever a firm sells a product for a price that is less than the cost of producing it. Most regulations, however, define dumping more vaguely. For example, a country is allowed to bring antidumping actions against an importer under Article 6 of GATT as long as two criteria are met: sales at "less than fair value" and "material injury to a domestic industry." The problem with this terminology is that it does not indicate what value is considered fair. The ambiguity has led some to argue that selling abroad at prices below those in the country of origin, as opposed to below cost, is dumping.

Such logic led the Bush administration to place a 20 percent duty on imports of foreign steel in 2001. Foreign manufacturers protested that they were not selling below cost. Admitting that their prices were lower in the United States than some other countries, they argued that this simply reflected the intensely competitive nature of the U.S. market (i.e., different price elasticities).

Antidumping rules set a floor under export prices and limit firms' ability to pursue strategic pricing. The rather vague terminology used in most antidumping actions suggests that a firm's ability to engage in price discrimination also may be challenged under antidumping legislation.

Competition Policy   Most developed nations have regulations designed to promote competition and to restrict monopoly practices. These regulations can be used to limit the prices a firm can charge in a given country. For example, at one time the Swiss pharmaceutical manufacturer Hoffmann-LaRoche had a monopoly on the supply of Valium and Librium tranquilizers. The company was investigated by the British Monopolies and Mergers Commission, which is responsible for promoting fair competition in Great Britain. The commission found that Hoffmann-LaRoche was overcharging for its tranquilizers and ordered the company to reduce its prices 35 to 40 percent. Hoffmann-LaRoche maintained unsuccessfully that it was merely engaging in price discrimination. Similar actions were later brought against Hoffmann-LaRoche by the German cartel office and by the Dutch and Danish governments.[26]

Configuring the Marketing Mix

A firm might vary aspects of its marketing mix from country to country to take into account local differences in culture, economic conditions, competitive conditions, product and technical standards, distribution systems, government regulations, and the like. Such differences may require variation in product attributes, distribution strategy, communications strategy, and pricing strategy. The cumulative effect of these factors makes it rare for a firm to adopt the same marketing mix worldwide. A detailed example is given in the accompanying Management Focus, which looks at how Levi Strauss now varies its marketing mix from country to country. This is a particularly interesting example because Theodore Levitt held up Levi Strauss as an example of global standardization, but as the Management Focus makes clear, the opposite now seems to be the case.

The financial services industry is often thought of as one in which global standardization of the marketing mix is the norm. However, while a financial services company such as American Express may sell the same basic charge card service worldwide, utilize the same basic fee structure for that product, and adopt the same basic global advertising message ("don't leave home without it"), differences in national regulations still mean that it has to vary aspects of its communications strategy from country to country (as pointed out earlier, the promotional strategy it had developed in the United States was illegal in Germany). Similarly, while McDonald's is often thought of as the quintessential

Levi Strauss Goes Local

It's been a tough few years for Levi Strauss, the iconic manufacturer of blue jeans. The company, whose 501 jeans became the global symbol of the baby boom generation and were sold in more than 100 countries, saw its sales drop from a peak of $7.1 billion in 1996 to just $4.0 billion in 2004. Fashion trends had moved on, its critics charged, and Levi Strauss, hamstrung by high costs and a stagnant product line, was looking more faded than a well-worn pair of 501s. Perhaps so, but 2005–2009 brought signs that a turnaround was in progress. Sales increased, and after a string of losses the company started to register profits again.

There were three parts to this turnaround. First, there were cost reductions at home. Levi Strauss closed its last remaining American factories and moved production offshore where jeans could be produced more cheaply. Second, the company broadened its product line, introducing the Levi's Signature brand that could be sold through lower-priced outlets in markets that were more competitive, including the core American market where Walmart had driven down prices. Third, in the late 1990s the company decided to give more responsibility to national managers, allowing them to better tailor the product offering and marketing mix to local conditions. Before this, Levi Strauss had basically sold the same product worldwide, often using the same advertising message. The old strategy was designed to enable the company to realize economies of scale in production and advertising, but it wasn't working.

Under the new strategy, variations between national markets have become more pronounced. Jeans have been tailored to different body types. In Asia, shorter leg lengths are common, whereas in South Africa, more room is needed for the backside of women's jeans, so Levi Strauss has customized the product offering to account for these physical differences. Then there are sociocultural differences: In Japan, tight-fitting black jeans are popular; in Islamic countries, women are discouraged from wearing tight-fitting jeans, so Levi's offerings in countries like Turkey are roomier. Climate also has an effect on product design. In Northern Europe, standard-weight denim jeans are sold, whereas in hotter countries lighter denim is used, along with brighter colors that are not washed out by the tropical sun.

Levi's ads, which used to be global, have also been tailored to regional differences. In Europe, the ads now talk about the cool fit. In Asia, they talk about the rebirth of an original. In the United States, the ads show real people who are themselves originals: ranchers, surfers, great musicians. There are also differences in distribution channels and pricing strategy. In the fiercely competitive American market, prices are as low as $25 and Levi's are sold through mass-market discount retailers, such as Walmart. In India, strong sales growth is being driven by Levi's low-priced Signature brand. In Spain, jeans are seen as higher fashion items and are being sold for $50 in higher-quality outlets. In the United Kingdom, too, prices for 501s are much higher than in the United States, reflecting a more benign competitive environment.

This marketing mix variation seems to be reaping dividends; although demand in the United States and Europe remains sluggish, growth in many other countries is strong. Turkey, South Korea, and South Africa all recorded growth rates in excess of 20 percent a year following the introduction of this strategy in 2005. Looking forward, Levi Strauss expects 60 percent of its growth to come from emerging markets.

Sources: "How Levi Strauss Rekindled the Allure of Brand America," *World Trade,* March 2005, p. 28; "Levi Strauss Walks with a Swagger into New Markets," *Africa News,* March 17, 2005; "Levi's Adaptable Standards," *Strategic Direction,* June 2005, pp. 14–16; A. Benady, "Levi's Looks to the Bottom Line," *Financial Times,* February 15, 2005, p. 14, and R. A. Smith, "At Levi Strauss Dockers Are In," *The Wall Street Journal,* February 14, 2007, p. A14.

example of a firm that sells the same basic standardized product worldwide, in reality it varies one important aspect of its marketing mix—its menu—from country to country. McDonald's also varies its distribution strategy. In Canada and the United States, most McDonald's are located in areas that are easily accessible by car, whereas in more densely populated and less automobile-reliant societies of the world, such as Japan and Great Britain, location decisions are driven by the accessibility of a restaurant to pedestrian traffic. Because countries typically still differ along one or more of the dimensions discussed above, some customization of the marketing mix is normal.

However, there are often significant opportunities for standardization along one or more elements of the marketing mix.[27] Firms may find that it is possible and desirable to standardize their global advertising message or core product attributes to realize substantial cost economies. They may find it desirable to customize their distribution and pricing strategy to take advantage of local differences. In reality, the "customization versus standardization" debate is not an all or nothing issue; it frequently makes sense to standardize some aspects of the marketing mix and customize others, depending on conditions in various national marketplaces.

New-Product Development

Firms that successfully develop and market new products can earn enormous returns. Examples include DuPont, which has produced a steady stream of successful innovations such as cellophane, nylon, Freon, and Teflon (nonstick pans); Sony, whose successes include the Walkman, the compact disk, the PlayStation, the Blu-ray high-definition DVD player; Pfizer, the drug company that during the 1990s produced several major new drugs, including Viagra; 3M, which has applied its core competency in tapes and adhesives to developing a wide range of new products; Intel, which has consistently managed to lead in the development of innovative microprocessors to run personal computers; and Cisco Systems, which developed the routers that sit at the hubs of Internet connections, directing the flow of digital traffic.

LEARNING OBJECTIVE 5
Describe how the globalization of the world economy is affecting new-product development within the international business firm.

In today's world, competition is as much about technological innovation as anything else. The pace of technological change has accelerated since the Industrial Revolution in the eighteenth century, and it continues to do so today. The result has been a dramatic shortening of product life cycles. Technological innovation is both creative and destructive.[28] An innovation can make established products obsolete overnight. But an innovation can also make a host of new products possible. Witness recent changes in the electronics industry. For 40 years before the early 1950s, vacuum tubes were a major component in radios and then in record players and early computers. The advent of transistors destroyed the market for vacuum tubes, but at the same time it created new opportunities connected with transistors. Transistors took up far less space than vacuum tubes, creating a trend toward miniaturization that continues today. The transistor held its position as the major component in the electronics industry for just a decade. Microprocessors were developed in the 1970s, and the market for transistors declined rapidly. The microprocessor created yet another set of new-product opportunities: handheld calculators (which destroyed the market for slide rules), compact disk players (which destroyed the market for analog record players), personal computers (which destroyed the market for typewriters), cell phones (which may ultimately replace landline phones), to name a few.

This "creative destruction" unleashed by technological change makes it critical that a firm stay on the leading edge of technology, lest it lose out to a competitor's innovations. As we explain in the next subsection, this not only creates a need for the firm to invest in R&D, but it also requires the firm to establish R&D activities at those locations where expertise is concentrated. As we shall see, leading-edge technology on its own is not enough to guarantee a firm's survival. The firm must also apply that technology to developing products that satisfy consumer needs, and it must design the product so that it can be manufactured in a cost-effective manner. To do that, the firm needs to build close links between R&D, marketing, and manufacturing.

Another Perspective

New-Product Development—on a Budget
Innovation rises to new heights when companies introduce a product that's truly affordable. Consider the Nano, built by Tata Motors of India and, with the almost unbelievable sticker price of $2,500, dubbed "the world's cheapest car." Tata's introduction of the fuel-efficient, low-emission four-passenger vehicle made car ownership—for the first time—a possibility for millions of Indian families.

For physicians practicing in rural India, GE Healthcare created an ultra-portable electrocardiograph machine. The product's success motivated GE to adapt the design and offer a similar device to U.S. doctors for about $1,000—a fraction of the cost of the traditional machine. (Mark Foster, "New, Improved, and Super Low-Cost," *BusinessWeek*, April 9, 2010, www.businessweek.com)

This is difficult enough for the domestic firm, but it is even more problematic for the international business competing in an industry where consumer tastes and preferences differ from country to country.[29] With all of this in mind, we move on to examine locating R&D activities and building links between R&D, marketing, and manufacturing.

THE LOCATION OF R&D   Ideas for new products are stimulated by the interactions of scientific research, demand conditions, and competitive conditions. Other things being equal, the rate of new-product development seems to be greater in countries where

- More money is spent on basic and applied research and development.
- Underlying demand is strong.
- Consumers are affluent.
- Competition is intense.[30]

Basic and applied research and development discovers new technologies and then commercializes them. Strong demand and affluent consumers create a potential market for new products. Intense competition between firms stimulates innovation as the firms try to beat their competitors and reap potentially enormous first-mover advantages that result from successful innovation.

For most of the post-World War II period, the country that ranked highest on these criteria was the United States. The United States devoted a greater proportion of its gross domestic product to R&D than any other country did. Its scientific establishment was the largest and most active in the world. U.S. consumers were the most affluent, the market was large, and competition among U.S. firms was brisk. Due to these factors, the United States was the market where most new products were developed and introduced. Accordingly, it was the best location for R&D activities; it was where the action was.

Over the past 20 years, things have been changing quickly. The U.S. monopoly on new-product development has weakened considerably. Although U.S. firms are still at the leading edge of many new technologies, Asian and European firms are also strong players, with companies such as Sony, Sharp, Samsung, Ericsson, Nokia, and Philips NV driving product innovation in their respective industries. In addition, both Japan and the European Union are large, affluent markets, and the wealth gap between them and the United States is closing.

As a result, it is often no longer appropriate to consider the United States as the lead market. In video games, for example, Japan is often the lead market, with companies such as Sony and Nintendo introducing their latest video game players in Japan some six months before they introduce them in the United States. In wireless telecommunications, Europe is generally reckoned to be ahead of the United States. Some of the most advanced applications of wireless telecommunications services are being pioneered not in the United States but in Finland, where more than 90 percent of the population has wireless telephones, compared with 65 percent of the U.S. population. However, it is questionable whether any developed nation can be considered the lead market. To succeed in today's high-technology industries, it is often necessary to simultaneously introduce new products in all major industrialized markets. When Intel introduces a new microprocessor, for example, it does not first introduce it in the United States and then roll it out in Europe a year later. It introduces it simultaneously around the world.

Because leading-edge research is now carried out in many locations around the world, the argument for centralizing R&D activity in the United States is now much weaker than it was two decades ago. (It used to be argued that centralized R&D eliminated duplication.) Much leading-edge research is now occurring in Japan and Europe. Dispersing R&D activities to those locations allows a firm to stay close to the center of leading-edge activity to gather scientific and competitive information and to draw on local scientific resources.[31] This may result in some duplication of R&D activities, but the cost disadvantages of duplication are outweighed by the advantages of dispersion.

For example, to expose themselves to the research and new-product development work being done in Japan, many U.S. firms have set up satellite R&D centers in Japan. Kodak's R&D center in Japan employs about 200 people. The company hired about 100 Japanese researchers and directed the lab to concentrate on electronic imaging technology. U.S. firms that have established R&D facilities in Japan include Corning, Texas Instruments, IBM, Digital Equipment, Procter & Gamble, Upjohn, Pfizer, DuPont, Monsanto, and Microsoft.[32] The National Science Foundation (NSF) has documented a sharp increase in the proportion of total R&D spending by U.S. firms that is now done abroad.[33] For example, Motorola now has 14 dedicated R&D facilities located in seven countries, and Bristol-Myers Squibb has 12 facilities in six countries. At the same time, to internationalize their own research and gain access to U.S. talent, many European and Japanese firms are investing in U.S.-based research facilities, according to the NSF.

INTEGRATING R&D, MARKETING, AND PRODUCTION Although a firm that is successful at developing new products may earn enormous returns, new-product development has a high failure rate. One study of product development in 16 companies in the chemical, drug, petroleum, and electronics industries suggested that only about 20 percent of R&D projects result in commercially successful products or processes.[34] Another in-depth case study of product development in three companies (one in chemicals and two in drugs) reported that about 60 percent of R&D projects reached technical completion, 30 percent were commercialized, and only 12 percent earned an economic profit that exceeded the company's cost of capital.[35] Along the same lines, another study concluded that one in nine major R&D projects, or about 11 percent, produced commercially successful products.[36] In sum, the evidence suggests that only 10 to 20 percent of major R&D projects give rise to commercially successful products. Well-publicized product failures include Apple Computer's Newton personal digital assistant, Sony's Betamax format in the video player and recorder market, and Sega's Dreamcast videogame console.

The reasons for such high failure rates are various and include development of a technology for which demand is limited, failure to adequately commercialize promising technology, and inability to manufacture a new product cost effectively. Firms can reduce the probability of making such mistakes by insisting on tight cross-functional coordination and integration between three core functions involved in the development of new products: R&D, marketing, and production.[37] Tight cross-functional integration between R&D, production, and marketing can help a company to ensure that

1. Product development projects are driven by customer needs.
2. New products are designed for ease of manufacture.
3. Development costs are kept in check.
4. Time to market is minimized.

Companies such as Eastman Kodak Co. have R&D centers in both the United States and Japan to stay on the cutting edge of trends in their industries. Here, in a joint research venture with Sanyo Electronics of Japan, Kodak researchers inspect a glass substrate used in the development of next-generation flat-panel displays that enable brighter, thinner, more power-efficient displays for cellular phones, personal data assistants, and computer terminals.

Close integration between R&D and marketing is required to ensure that product development projects are driven by the needs of customers. A company's customers can be a primary source of new-product ideas. Identification of customer needs, particularly unmet needs, can set the context within which successful product innovation occurs. As the point of contact with customers, the marketing function of a company can provide valuable information in this regard. Integration of R&D and marketing is crucial if a new product is to be properly commercialized. Without integration of R&D and marketing, a company runs the risk of developing products for which there is little or no demand.

Integration between R&D and production can help a company design products with manufacturing requirements in mind. Designing for manufacturing can lower costs and increase product quality. Integrating R&D and production can also help lower development costs and speed products to market. If a new product is not designed with manufacturing capabilities in mind, it may prove too difficult to build. Then the product will have to be redesigned, and both overall development costs and the time it takes to bring the product to market may increase significantly. Making design changes during product planning could increase overall development costs by 50 percent and add 25 percent to the time it takes to bring the product to market.[38] Many quantum product innovations require new processes to manufacture them, which makes it all the more important to achieve close integration between R&D and production. Minimizing time to market and development costs may require the simultaneous development of new products and new processes.[39]

CROSS-FUNCTIONAL TEAMS One way to achieve cross-functional integration is to establish cross-functional product development teams composed of representatives from R&D, marketing, and production. Because these functions may be located in different countries, the team will sometimes have a multinational membership. The objective of a team should be to take a product development project from the initial concept development to market introduction. A number of attributes seem to be important for a product development team to function effectively and meet all its development milestones.[40]

First, the team should be led by a "heavyweight" project manager who has high status within the organization and who has the power and authority required to get the financial and human resources the team needs to succeed. The leader should be dedicated primarily, if not entirely, to the project. He or she should be someone who believes in the project (a champion) and who is skilled at integrating the perspectives of different functions and at helping personnel from different functions and countries work together for a common goal. The leader should also be able to act as an advocate of the team to senior management.

Second, the team should be composed of at least one member from each key function. The team members should have a number of attributes, including an ability to contribute functional expertise, high standing within their function, a willingness to share responsibility for team results, and an ability to put functional and national advocacy aside. It is generally preferable if core team members are 100 percent dedicated to the project for its duration. This assures their focus on the project, not on the ongoing work of their function.

Third, the team members should physically be in one location if possible to create a sense of camaraderie and to facilitate communication. This presents problems if the team members are drawn from facilities in different nations. One solution is to transfer key individuals to one location for the duration of a product development project. Fourth, the team should have a clear plan and clear goals, particularly with regard to critical development milestones and development budgets. The team should have incentives to attain those goals, such as receiving pay bonuses when major development milestones are hit.

Fifth, each team needs to develop its own processes for communication and conflict resolution. For example, one product development team at Quantum Corporation, a California-based manufacturer of disk drives for personal computers, instituted a rule that all major decisions would be made and conflicts resolved at meetings that were held every Monday afternoon. This simple rule helped the team meet its development goals. In this case, it was also common for team members to fly in from Japan, where the product was to be manufactured, to the U.S. development center for the Monday meetings.[41]

BUILDING GLOBAL R&D CAPABILITIES   The need to integrate R&D and marketing to adequately commercialize new technologies poses special problems in the international business because commercialization may require different versions of a new product to be produced for various countries.[42] To do this, the firm must build close links between its R&D centers and its various country operations. A similar argument applies to the need to integrate R&D and production, particularly in those international businesses that have dispersed production activities to different locations around the globe in consideration of relative factor costs and the like.

Integrating R&D, marketing, and production in an international business may require R&D centers in North America, Asia, and Europe that are linked by formal and informal integrating mechanisms with marketing operations in each country in their regions and with the various manufacturing facilities. In addition, the international business may have to establish cross-functional teams whose members are dispersed around the globe. This complex endeavor requires the company to utilize formal and informal integrating mechanisms to knit its far-flung operations together so they can produce new products in an effective and timely manner.

While there is no one best model for allocating product development responsibilities to various centers, one solution adopted by many international businesses involves establishing a global network of R&D centers. Within this model, fundamental research is undertaken at basic research centers around the globe. These centers are normally located in regions or cities where valuable scientific knowledge is being created and where there is a pool of skilled research talent (e.g., Silicon Valley in the United States, Cambridge in England, Kobe in Japan, Singapore). These centers are the innovation engines of the firm. Their job is to develop the basic technologies that become new products.

These technologies are picked up by R&D units attached to global product divisions and are used to generate new products to serve the global marketplace. At this level, commercialization of the technology and design for manufacturing are emphasized. If further customization is needed so the product appeals to the tastes and preferences of consumers in individual markets, such redesign work will be done by an R&D group based in a subsidiary in that country or at a regional center that customizes products for several countries in the region.

Hewlett-Packard has four basic research centers located in Palo Alto, California; Bristol, England; Haifa, Israel; and Tokyo, Japan.[43] These labs are the seedbed for technologies that ultimately become new products and businesses. They are the company's innovation engines. The Palo Alto center, for example, pioneered HP's thermal ink-jet technology. The products are developed by R&D centers associated with HP's global product divisions. Thus, the Consumer Products Group, which has its worldwide headquarters in San Diego, California, designs, develops, and manufactures a range of imaging products using HP-pioneered thermal ink-jet technology. Subsidiaries might then customize the product so that it best matches the needs of important national markets. HP's subsidiary in Singapore, for example, is responsible for the design and production of thermal ink-jet printers for Japan and other Asian markets. This subsidiary takes products originally developed in San Diego and redesigns them for the

Asian market. In addition, the Singapore subsidiary has taken the lead from San Diego in the design and development of certain portable thermal ink-jet printers. HP delegated this responsibility to Singapore because this subsidiary has acquired important competencies in the design and production of thermal ink-jet products, so it has become the best place in the world to undertake this activity.

Microsoft offers a similar example. The company has basic research sites in Redmond, Washington (its headquarters); Silicon Valley, California; Cambridge, England; Tokyo, Japan; Beijing, China; and Bangalore, India. Staff at these research sites work on the fundamental problems that underlie the design of future products. For example, a group at Redmond is working on natural language recognition software, while another works on artificial intelligence. These research centers don't produce new products; rather, they produce the technology that is used to enhance existing products or help produce new products. The products are produced by dedicated product groups (e.g., desktop operating systems, applications). Customization of the products to match the needs of local markets is sometimes carried out at local subsidiaries. Thus, the Chinese subsidiary will do some basic customization of programs such as Microsoft Office, adding Chinese characters and customizing the interface, and the R&D group in India has helped to develop products for that market.

Key Terms

marketing mix, p. 521

market segmentation, p. 523

concentrated retail system, p. 527

fragmented retail system, p. 527

channel length, p. 528

exclusive distribution channel, p. 529

channel quality, p. 529

source effects, p. 532

country of origin effects, p. 532

noise, p. 533

push strategy, p. 533

pull strategy, p. 533

price elasticity of demand, p. 538

elastic, p. 538

inelastic, p. 538

strategic pricing, p. 539

predatory pricing, p. 539

multipoint pricing, p. 540

experience curve pricing, p. 540

Summary

This chapter discussed the marketing and R&D functions in international business. A persistent theme of the chapter is the tension that exists between the need to reduce costs and the need to be responsive to local conditions, which raises costs. The chapter made these major points:

1. Theodore Levitt argued that due to the advent of modern communications and transport technologies, consumer tastes and preferences are becoming global, which is creating global markets for standardized consumer products. However, this position is regarded as extreme by many commentators, who argue that substantial differences still exist between countries.

2. Market segmentation refers to the process of identifying distinct groups of consumers whose purchasing behavior differs from each other in important ways. Managers in an international business need to be aware of two main issues relating to segmentation: the extent to which there are differences between countries in the structure of market segments, and the existence of segments that transcend national borders.

3. A product can be viewed as a bundle of attributes. Product attributes need to be varied from country to country to satisfy different consumer tastes and preferences.

4. Country differences in consumer tastes and preferences are due to differences in culture and economic development. In addition, differences in product and technical standards

may require the firm to customize product attributes from country to country.

5. A distribution strategy decision is an attempt to define the optimal channel for delivering a product to the consumer.

6. Significant country differences exist in distribution systems. In some countries, the retail system is concentrated; in others, it is fragmented. In some countries, channel length is short; in others, it is long. Access to distribution channels is difficult to achieve in some countries, and the quality of the channel may be poor.

7. A critical element in the marketing mix is communication strategy, which defines the process the firm will use in communicating the attributes of its product to prospective customers.

8. Barriers to international communication include cultural differences, source effects, and noise levels.

9. A communication strategy is either a push strategy or a pull strategy. A push strategy emphasizes personal selling, and a pull strategy emphasizes mass media advertising. Whether a push strategy or a pull strategy is optimal depends on the type of product, consumer sophistication, channel length, and media availability.

10. A globally standardized advertising campaign, which uses the same marketing message all over the world, has economic advantages, but it fails to account for differences in culture and advertising regulations.

11. Price discrimination exists when consumers in different countries are charged different prices for the same product. Price discrimination can help a firm maximize its profits. For price discrimination to be effective, the national markets must be separate and their price elasticities of demand must differ.

12. Predatory pricing is the use of profit gained in one market to support aggressive pricing in another market to drive competitors out of that market.

13. Multipoint pricing refers to the fact that a firm's pricing strategy in one market may affect rivals' pricing strategies in another market. Aggressive pricing in one market may elicit a competitive response from a rival in another market that is important to the firm.

14. Experience curve pricing is the use of aggressive pricing to build accumulated volume as rapidly as possible to quickly move the firm down the experience curve.

15. New-product development is a high-risk, potentially high-return activity. To build a competency in new-product development, an international business must do two things: disperse R&D activities to those countries where new products are being pioneered, and integrate R&D with marketing and manufacturing.

16. Achieving tight integration among R&D, marketing, and manufacturing requires the use of cross-functional teams.

Critical Thinking and Discussion Questions

1. Imagine you are the marketing manager for a U.S. manufacturer of disposable diapers. Your firm is considering entering the Brazilian market. Your CEO believes the advertising message that has been effective in the United States will suffice in Brazil. Outline some possible objections to this. Your CEO also believes that the pricing decisions in Brazil can be delegated to local managers. Why might she be wrong?

2. Within 20 years, we will have seen the emergence of enormous global markets for standardized consumer products. Do you agree with this statement? Justify your answer.

3. You are the marketing manager of a food products company that is considering entering the Indian market. The retail system in India tends to be very fragmented. Also, retailers and wholesalers tend to have long-term ties with Indian food companies, which makes access to distribution channels difficult. What distribution strategy would you advise the company to pursue? Why?

4. Price discrimination is indistinguishable from dumping. Discuss the accuracy of this statement.

5. You work for a company that designs and manufactures personal computers. Your company's R&D center is in North Dakota.

The computers are manufactured under contract in Taiwan. Marketing strategy is delegated to the heads of three regional groups: a North American group (based in Chicago), a European group (based in Paris), and an Asian group (based in Singapore). Each regional group develops the marketing approach within its region. In order of importance, the largest markets for your products are North America, Germany, Great Britain, China, and Australia. Your company is experiencing problems in its product development and commercialization process. Products are late to market, the manufacturing quality is poor, costs are higher than projected, and market acceptance of new products is less than hoped for. What might be the source of these problems? How would you fix them?

6. Reread the Management Focus, "Levi Strauss Goes Local," and then answer the following questions:

   a. What marketing strategy was Levi Strauss using until the early 2000s? Why did this strategy appear to work for decades? Why was it not working by the 2000s?

   b. How would you characterize Levi Strauss's current strategy? What elements of the marketing mix are now changed from nation to nation?

   c. What are the benefits of the company's new marketing strategy? Is there a downside?

   d. What does the Levi Strauss story tell you about the "globalization of markets"?

Use the globalEDGE Resource Desk (http://global EDGE.msu.edu/resourcedesk/) to complete the following exercises:

1. You are the marketing manager for a diversified food and beveragecompany. Preliminary market research indicates that Chile holds significant opportunities for your products. Using an analysis of the food and beverage industry in Chile used by *Australian suppliers*, prepare a short report identifying the factors that must be considered when formulating the marketing strategy for this country.

2. A. T. Kearney publishes an annual study to help retailers prioritize their global development strategies by ranking the retail expansion attractiveness of emerging countries based on a set of criteria. Find the latest version of this *Global Retail Development Index*. What criteria are used to identify the attractiveness of the retail environment in emerging countries? Are there any countries in the top 10 that surprise you? Why (or, why not)?

closing case

Apple and the Global iPhone and iPad

Whether listening to iTune songs on the iPod, reading the latest novel on the iPad, chatting up a storm on the iPhone, or working remotely on business spreadsheets on the Apple G4 laptop, Apple has come to be associated with some of the most innovative products and a "cool" lifestyle that has engendered "true believers."

Arguably, Apple is one of history's greatest product development companies. But Apple products are also inextricably linked to an Internet/high-technology culture. Whether that culture is at the corporate or user level, Apple has among the highest brand and repurchase loyalty of any "computer" manufacturer. In the home computer repurchase market, Apple has maintained its strong repurchase brand loyalty—outpacing non-Apple PCs across 16 countries.

Perhaps nowhere is this culture/lifestyle assimilation more exemplified than in the 88-country roll-out that Apple ensued with the iPhone 4G, the next generation of iPhones. Having learned from the iPhone 3G, Apple has focused on going global quicker. In fact, prior to the iPhone, Apple struggled as a global player. Having missed the roll-out of the iPhone 3G in Korea and China, two of the fastest growing markets, Apple made sure it would not happen again with the 4G.

According to analysts, iPhone sales have peaked in the United States because Apple limited its association to only one carrier—AT&T. And while Apple does not break down sales by regions, there are indications that Apple got 58 percent of its revenue from outside the Americas region in the latest quarter (2010), excluding sales at Apple stores. The company saw triple-digit growth in Europe and Asia, in part because it began to use multiple carriers in various markets. Tim Bajarin, an analyst at researcher Creative Strategies, estimates that about 55 percent of iPhone sales are now made outside of the United States, up from about 25 percent two years ago. Particularly promising are France, Germany, the United Kingdom, and Japan, where Apple will offer the iPhone 4 simultaneously with its U.S. release.

In Japan, Tokyo-based MM Research Institute Ltd. estimates the iPhone comprised 72 percent of all smartphones sold in the fiscal year ended March 31, though the category is still a small part of the country's phone sales.

Similarly, the iPad is undergoing a more determined international roll-out. Shortly after the April 2010 iPad launch in the United States, Apple launched in nine countries and did so again in July with another nine. Developers for Apple's App Store, which stocks programs that can be downloaded onto the iPhone and iPad, said they are already seeing the strength of international markets in their own businesses. For example, San Francisco game company Ngmoco Inc.'s chief executive, Neil Young, said he saw "a meaningful bump" in downloads when the iPad went on sale outside of the United States. According to Young, 50 to 70 percent of the start-up's iPad game downloads are coming from other countries.

The internationalization of Apple products is helped by the expansion of its "cool" retail stores. Out of a total 283 Apple stores, 62 were located outside the United States. Apple has said that more than half of the 40 to 50 new stores it plans to open in the 2010 fiscal year ending in September will be overseas in cities such as London and Shanghai. "The Apple stores are a key part in major cities. There is a community effect that's quite powerful," said Nick James, an analyst with London bank Panmure Gordon & Co.

The bonds that tie this community may well be Apple products. However, the other part of Apple's success with its global marketing efforts has nothing to do directly with Apple but rather with the increasing availability and importance of the Internet. Consumers in some countries continue to go on the Web for the first time, while those in other regions increase their time online as video and other Web-delivered services become ever more important to the employment, entertainment, and education communities.

Whether that community, culture, or lifestyle will be found throughout the world will become one of the key questions as Apple continues its global marketing efforts.

Sources: Y. I. Kane and Cecilie Rohwedder, "Apple Strives for Global Markets—Electronics Giant Speeds Overseas Rollout of New iPhone to 88 Countries as It Looks for Growth," *The Wall Street Journal,* June 8, 2010; D. Sellers, "Apple Maintains Brand Loyalty and Nears Home Computer Primacy in Two of 16 Countries," *Macsimum News,* January 27, 2010, retrieved at http://www.macsimumnews.com; P. Carson, "Apple's International Rollout," *RCR Wireless News,* May 5, 2008; and A. Z. Cuneo, T. Elkin, H. Kim, and T.L Stanley, "Apple Transcends as Lifestyle Brand," *Advertising Age,* December 15, 2003.

Case Discussion Questions

1. Being as innovative as it is, why do you think Apple did not seek to expand its marketing efforts globally from the beginning?

2. Do you think that Apple will have to adapt its products to the various global markets? Or will its innovative design and its "cool" approach be sufficient to assume adoption?

3. What general lessons can be derived from Apple's experience with the iPhone 3G?

4. Do you foresee the future of Apple, and other "computer companies" inextricably linked to the expanded use of the Internet worldwide?

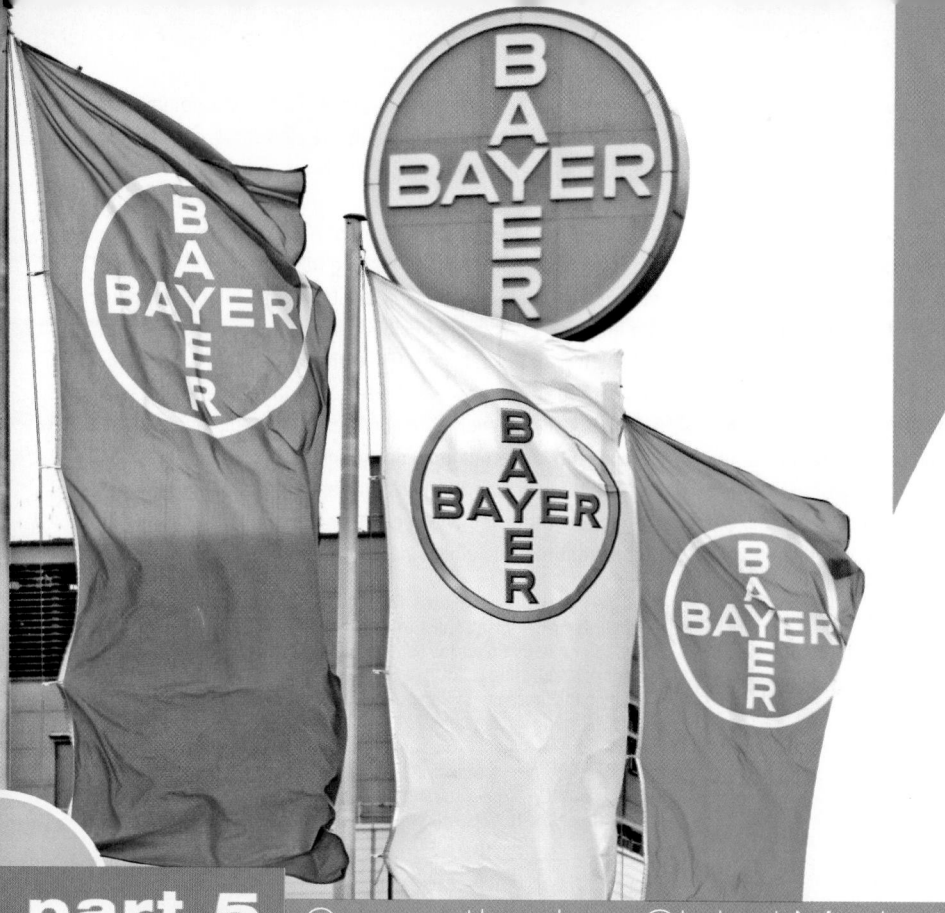

LEARNING OBJECTIVES

After you have read this chapter you should be able to:

1 Summarize the strategic role of human resource management in international business firms.

2 Identify the pros and cons of different approaches to staffing policy in international business firms.

3 Explain why managers may fail to thrive in foreign postings.

4 Recognize how management development and training programs can increase the value of human capital in international business firms.

5 Explain how and why performance appraisal systems might vary across nations.

6 Explain how and why compensation systems might vary across nations.

7 Understand how organized labor can influence strategic choices in international business firms.

chapter

16

Global Human Resource Management

opening case

G one are the days when chemical engineers would work in one facility for their entire career. Increasingly, they have found themselves deployed throughout the world, and their companies' human resource (HR) departments are trying to create the right chemistry. Bayer AG is one of the largest chemical and pharmaceutical corporations in the world. The company has more than 108,000 employees: 24.4 percent from North America; 41.6 percent from Europe; 15.4 percent from Latin America, Africa, and the Middle East; and 18.3 percent from Asia/Pacific. The company is active in more than 60 nations and has annual sales in excess of 31 billion euros. Global competition requires that this multinational build a talented global workforce, led by managers who have a global perspective, are comfortable moving around the world, and are capable of interacting with people from other cultures. This is a difficult task, but Rohm and Haas understands the global challenge.

Rohm and Haas, a U.S.-based, *Fortune* 500 company, specializes in chemical manufacturing and employs more than 17,000 people in 27 countries. Its global reach and human resource management (HRM) challenge were described in 2009 by Chairman and Chief Executive Officer Rajiv L. Gupta: "Ours is a company which has committed itself to a global path and which intends to increase its sales greatly in the world market, and so we have made ourselves a player in the 'world.' This 'world' we play in is a world of multiples. It is multifaceted, multihued, multitextured, multilingual, and multicultural." Similarly, as Giorgio Squinzi, chairman of Italian specialty chemicals company MAPEI, notes, "A strong position or a leadership position in the domestic market is not enough."

In looking for international managers, the HR departments of the three chemical companies searching for strengths and interests that include a good level of comfort in working with people of different races, religions, and customs. Enjoying travel—including very long distance travel—is a must, and chemists interested in foreign assignments must also like, or at least be able to tolerate, the often stressful experience of relocating. The talent search is never ending. At other times, the HR departments require a particular focus on the link between a domestic labor force and global capabilities. This is especially true when a large multinational corporation enters a specific market that needs to integrate the local labor force into the more complex organizational structures of the company.

For example, look at Bayer MaterialScience in China. At its integrated site in Shanghai, Bayer was able to successfully integrate global and local expertise. It serves as an HRM success story of implementing policy that seeks to reduce the number of expatriates by employing more and more local staff. According to Michael Boediger, site general manager, the HR strategy at the site is focused on four aspects: providing excellent training both in China as well as at the overseas facilities, developing the careers of its employees and creating opportunities for higher and cross-functional responsibilities, creating a positive work environment and corporate culture with numerous platforms for staff to engage actively with management, and ensuring fair and competitive remuneration for employees. ●

Sources: Bayer Annual Report 2009 at www.bayer.com; Rohm & Haas Web site, www.rohmhaas.com; "Example of Successful Centralisation of Service Functions," *ICIS Chemical Business,* 1, no. 31 (2006), p. 6; "People as the Strongest Asset," *European Chemical News,* 82, no. 2170 (2005), p. 11; and W. G. Schulz, "Working Abroad," *Chemical and Engineering News,* May 28, 2001, retrieved at http://pubs.acs.org/cen/employment/7922/7922employ.html.

Introduction

Human Resource Management
Activities an organization conducts to use its human resources effectively.

This chapter continues our survey of specific functions within an international business by looking at international human resource management (HRM). **Human resource management** refers to the activities an organization carries out to use its human resources effectively.[1] These activities include determining the firm's human resource strategy, staffing, performance evaluation, management development, compensation, and labor relations. None of these activities is performed in a vacuum; all are related to the strategy of the firm. As we will see, HRM has an important strategic component.[2] Through its influence on the character, development, quality, and productivity of the firm's human resources, the HRM function can help the firm achieve its primary strategic goals of reducing the costs of value creation and adding value by better serving customer.

Irrespective of the desire of managers in many multinationals to build a truly global enterprise with a global workforce, the reality is that HRM practices still have to be modified to national context. The strategic role of HRM is complex enough in a purely domestic firm, but it is more complex in an international business, where staffing, management development, performance evaluation, and compensation activities are complicated by profound differences between countries in labor markets, culture, legal systems, economic systems, and the like (see Chapters 2 and 3). For example,

- Compensation practices may vary from country to country, depending on prevailing management customs.
- Labor laws may prohibit union organization in one country and mandate it in another.
- Equal employment legislation may be strongly pursued in one country and not in another.

If it is to build a cadre of managers capable of managing a multinational enterprise, the HRM function must deal with a host of issues. It must decide how to staff key management posts in the company, how to develop managers so that they are familiar with the nuances of doing business in different countries, how to compensate people in different nations, and how to evaluate the performance of managers based in different countries. HRM must also deal with a host of issues related to expatriate managers. (An **expatriate manager** is a citizen of one country who is working abroad in one of the firm's subsidiaries.) It must decide when to use expatriates, determine whom to send on expatriate postings, be clear about why they are doing it, compensate expatriates appropriately, and make sure that they are adequately debriefed and reoriented once they return home. Take Bayer as an example (see the opening case). This major pharmaceutical firm is trying to become a truly global enterprise. An important component of this is identifying future leaders of the company, and exposing them to the challenges of doing business in different nations, and working in multinational teams, through job transfers.

In this chapter, we will look closely at the role of HRM in an international business. We begin by briefly discussing the strategic role of HRM. Then we turn our attention to four major tasks of the HRM function: staffing policy, management training and development, performance appraisal, and compensation policy. We will point out the strategic implications of each of these tasks. The chapter closes with a look at international labor relations and the relationship between the firm's management of labor relations and its overall strategy.

Another Perspective

Global Literacy

In his book, *Global Literacy: Lessons on Business Leadership and National Cultures,* Robert H. Rosen interviewed CEOs of 78 companies and more than 1,000 senior executives from around the world. From those interviews, two lessons emerged: First, there are leadership universals that every executive and manager need to practice in order to be world class at home and abroad. The second lesson defied conventional wisdom: In the borderless economy, culture doesn't matter *less*, it matters *more*. By way of suggesting a general global HR strategy, Rosen recommends that we learn which are the most globally active, financially successful companies—and countries—in the world, understand how they got there, and apply that learning to our own organizations. He espouses that we must be "business literate"—meaning, personal literacy: understanding and valuing yourself; social literacy: engaging and challenging people; business literacy: focusing and mobilizing your business; and cultural literacy: valuing and leveraging cultural differences. (Robert H. Rosen, *Global Literacy: Lessons on Business Leadership and National Cultures* [New York: Simon & Schuster, 2000])

Expatriate Manager
A national of one country appointed to a management position in another country.

The Strategic Role of International HRM

A large and expanding body of academic research suggests that a strong fit between human resources practices and strategy is required for high profitability.[3] You will recall from Chapter 11 that superior performance requires not only the right strategy, but the strategy must also be supported by the right organization architecture. Strategy is implemented through organization. As shown in Figure 16.1 (which is based on Figure 11.5), people are the linchpin of a firm's organization architecture. For a firm to outperform its rivals in the global market place, it must have the right people in the right postings. Those people must be trained appropriately so that they have the skill sets required to perform their jobs effectively, and so that they behave in a manner that is congruent with the desired culture of the firm. Their compensation packages must create incentives for them to take actions that are consistent with the strategy of the

LEARNING OBJECTIVE 1
Summarize the strategic role of human resource management in international business firms.

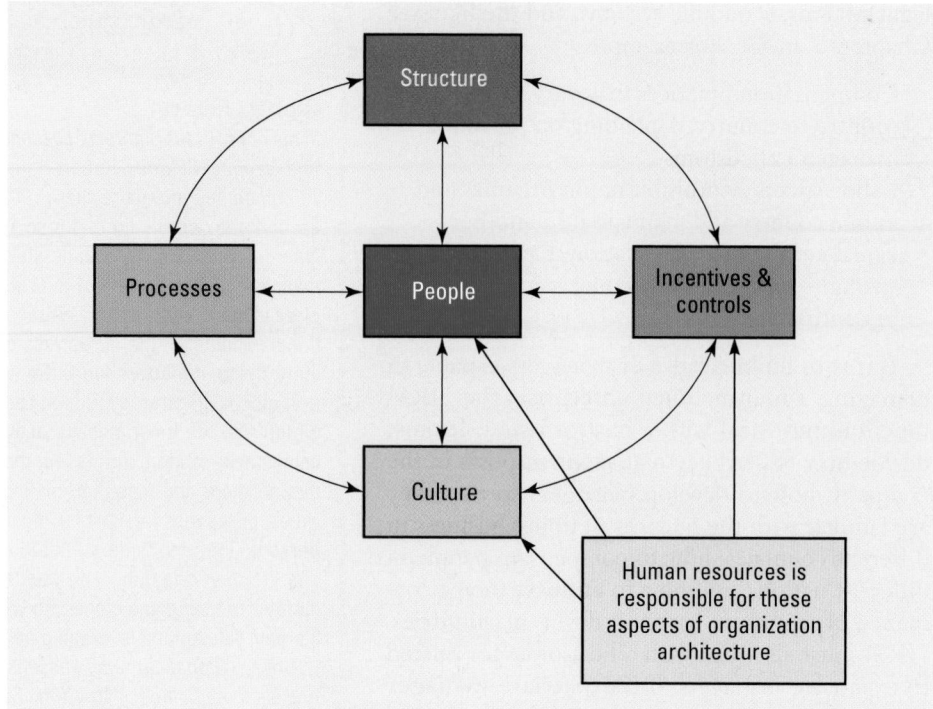

firm, and the performance appraisal systems the firm uses must measure the behavior that the firm wants to encourage.

As indicated in Figure 16.1, the HRM function, through its staffing, training, compensation, and performance appraisal activities, has a critical impact upon the people, culture, incentive, and control system elements of firm's organization architecture (performance appraisal systems are part of the control systems in an enterprise). Thus, HRM professionals have a critically important strategic role. It is incumbent upon them to shape these elements of a firm's organization architecture in a manner that is consistent with the strategy of the enterprise, so that the firm can effectively implement its strategy.

In short, superior human resource management can be a sustained source of high productivity and competitive advantage in the global economy. At the same time, research suggests that many international businesses have room for improving the effectiveness of their HRM function. In one study of competitiveness among 326 large multinationals, the authors found that human resource management was one of the weakest capabilities in most firms, suggesting that improving the effectiveness of international HRM practices might have substantial performance benefits.[4]

In Chapter 11, we examined four strategies pursued by international businesses: localization strategy, international strategy, global standardization strategy, and transnational strategy. Firms that emphasize localization try to create value by emphasizing local responsiveness; international firms, by transferring products and competencies overseas; global firms, by realizing experience curve and location economies; and transnational firms, by doing all these things simultaneously. In this chapter, we will see that success also requires HRM policies to be congruent with the firm's strategy. For example, a transnational strategy imposes different requirements for staffing, management development, and compensation practices than a localization strategy. Firms pursuing a transnational strategy need to build a strong corporate culture and an informal management network for transmitting information and knowledge within the organization (this is one of the things that Bayer is trying to do through managerial transfers; see the opening case). Through its employee selection, management development, performance appraisal, and compensation policies, the HRM function can help develop these things. Thus, as we have noted, HRM has a critical role to play in implementing strategy. In each section that follows, we will review the strategic role of HRM in some detail.

Staffing Policy

Staffing policy is concerned with the selection of employees for particular jobs. At one level, this involves selecting individuals who have the skills required to do particular jobs. At another level, staffing policy can be a tool for developing and promoting the desired corporate culture of the firm.[5] By **corporate culture,** we mean the organization's norms and value systems. A strong corporate culture can help a firm to implement its strategy. General Electric, for example, is not just concerned with hiring people who have the skills required for performing particular jobs; it wants to hire individuals whose behavioral styles, beliefs, and value systems are consistent with those of GE. This is true whether an American is being hired, an Italian, a German, or an Australian and whether the hiring is for a U.S. operation or a foreign operation. The belief is that if employees are predisposed toward the organization's norms and value systems by their personality type, the firm will be able to attain higher performance.

TYPES OF STAFFING POLICY Research has identified three types of staffing policies in international businesses: the ethnocentric approach, the polycentric approach, and the geocentric approach.[6] We will review each policy and link it to the strategy pursued by the firm. The most attractive staffing policy is probably the geocentric approach, although there are several impediments to adopting it.

The Ethnocentric Approach An **ethnocentric staffing policy** is one in which all key management positions are filled by parent-country nationals. This practice was widespread at one time. Firms such as Procter & Gamble, Philips NV, and Matsushita (now called Panasonic) originally followed it. In the Dutch firm Philips, for example, all important positions in most foreign subsidiaries were at one time held by Dutch nationals, who were referred to by their non-Dutch colleagues as the Dutch Mafia. Historically in many Japanese and South Korean firms, such as Toyota, Matsushita, and Samsung, key positions in international operations have often been held by home-country nationals. According to the Japanese Overseas Enterprise Association, only 29 percent of foreign subsidiaries of Japanese companies had presidents who were not Japanese. In contrast, 66 percent of the Japanese subsidiaries of foreign companies had Japanese presidents.[7]

Firms pursue an ethnocentric staffing policy for three reasons. First, the firm may believe the host country lacks qualified individuals to fill senior management positions. This argument is heard most often when the firm has operations in less developed countries. Second, the firm may see an ethnocentric staffing policy as the best way to maintain a unified corporate culture. Many Japanese firms, for example, have traditionally preferred their foreign operations to be headed by expatriate Japanese managers because these managers will have been socialized into the firm's culture while employed in Japan.[8] Procter & Gamble until fairly recently preferred to staff important management positions in its foreign subsidiaries with U.S. nationals who had been socialized into P&G's corporate culture by years of employment in its U.S. operations. Such reasoning tends to predominate when a firm places a high value on its corporate culture.

Staffing Policy
Strategy concerned with selecting employees for particular jobs.

Corporate Culture
An organization's norms and value systems.

Ethnocentric Staffing Policy
A staffing approach within the MNE in which all key management positions are filled by parent-country nationals.

Third, if the firm is trying to create value by transferring core competencies to a foreign operation, as firms pursuing an international strategy are, it may believe that the best way to do this is to transfer parent-country nationals who have knowledge of that competency to the foreign operation. Imagine what might occur if a firm tried to transfer a core competency in marketing to a foreign subsidiary without a corresponding transfer of home-country marketing management personnel. The transfer would probably fail to produce the anticipated benefits because the knowledge underlying a core competency cannot easily be articulated and written down. Such knowledge often has a significant tacit dimension; it is acquired through experience. Just like the great tennis player who cannot instruct others how to become great tennis players simply by writing a handbook, the firm that has a core competency in marketing, or anything else, cannot just write a handbook that tells a foreign subsidiary how to build the firm's core competency anew in a foreign setting. It must also transfer management personnel to the foreign operation to show foreign managers how to become good marketers, for example. The need to transfer managers overseas arises because the knowledge that underlies the firm's core competency resides in the heads of its domestic managers and was acquired through years of experience, not by reading a handbook. Thus, if a firm is to transfer a core competency to a foreign subsidiary, it must also transfer the appropriate managers.

Despite this rationale for pursuing an ethnocentric staffing policy, the policy is now on the wane in most international businesses for two reasons. First, an ethnocentric staffing policy limits advancement opportunities for host-country nationals. This can lead to resentment, lower productivity, and increased turnover among that group. Resentment can be greater still if, as often occurs, expatriate managers are paid significantly more than home-country nationals.

Second, an ethnocentric policy can lead to *cultural myopia*, the firm's failure to understand host-country cultural differences that require different approaches to marketing and management. The adaptation of expatriate managers can take a long time, during which they may make major mistakes. For example, expatriate managers may fail to appreciate how product attributes, distribution strategy, communications strategy, and pricing strategy should be adapted to host-country conditions. The result may be costly blunders. They may also make decisions that are ethically suspect simply because they do not understand the culture in which they are managing.[9] In one highly publicized case in the United States, Mitsubishi Motors was sued by the federal Equal Employment Opportunity Commission for tolerating extensive and systematic sexual harassment in a plant in Illinois. The plant's top management, all Japanese expatriates, denied the charges. The Japanese managers may have failed to realize that behavior that would be viewed as acceptable in Japan was not acceptable in the United States.[10]

Polycentric Staffing Policy
An MNE staffing policy in which host-country nationals are recruited to manage subsidiaries in their own country, while parent-country nationals occupy key positions at corporate headquarters.

The Polycentric Approach   A **polycentric staffing policy** requires host-country nationals to be recruited to manage subsidiaries, while parent-country nationals occupy key positions at corporate headquarters. In many respects, a polycentric approach is a response to the shortcomings of an ethnocentric approach. One advantage of adopting a polycentric approach is that the firm is less likely to suffer from cultural myopia. Host-country managers are unlikely to make the mistakes arising from cultural misunderstandings to which expatriate managers are vulnerable. A second advantage is that a polycentric approach may be less expensive to implement, reducing the costs of value creation. Expatriate managers can be expensive to maintain.

A polycentric approach also has its drawbacks. Host-country nationals have limited opportunities to gain experience outside their own country and thus cannot progress beyond senior positions in their own subsidiary. As in the case of an ethnocentric policy, this may cause resentment. Perhaps the major drawback with a polycentric approach, however, is the gap that can form between host-country managers and parent-country managers. Language barriers, national loyalties, and a range of cultural differences may isolate the corporate headquarters staff from the various foreign subsidiaries. The lack of management transfers from home to host countries, and vice versa, can exacerbate this isolation and lead to a lack of integration between corporate headquarters and foreign subsidiaries. The result can be a "federation" of largely independent national units with only nominal links to the corporate headquarters. Within such a federation, the coordination required to transfer core competencies or to pursue experience curve and location economies may be difficult to achieve. Thus, although a polycentric approach may be effective for firms pursuing a localization strategy, it is inappropriate for other strategies.

The federation that may result from a polycentric approach can also be a force for inertia within the firm. After decades of pursing a polycentric staffing policy, food and detergents giant Unilever found that shifting from a strategic posture that emphasized localization to a transnational posture was very difficult. Unilever's foreign subsidiaries had evolved into quasi-autonomous operations, each with its own strong national identity. These "little kingdoms" objected strenuously to corporate headquarters' attempts to limit their autonomy and to rationalize global manufacturing.[11]

The Geocentric Approach

A **geocentric staffing policy** seeks the best people for key jobs throughout the organization, regardless of nationality. This policy has a number of advantages. First, it enables the firm to make the best use of its human resources. Second, and perhaps more important, a geocentric policy enables the firm to build a cadre of international executives who feel at home working in a number of cultures. Creation of such a cadre may be a critical first step toward building a strong unifying corporate culture and an informal management network, both of which are required for global standardization and transnational strategies.[12] Firms pursuing a geocentric staffing policy may be better able to create value from the pursuit of experience curve and location economies and from the multidirectional transfer of core competencies than firms pursuing other staffing policies. In addition, the multinational composition of the management team that results from geocentric staffing tends to reduce cultural myopia and to enhance local responsiveness.

In sum, other things being equal, a geocentric staffing policy seems the most attractive. Recent years have seen a sharp shift toward the adoption of a geocentric staffing policy by many multinationals. For example, India's Tata Group, now a $20 billion global conglomerate, runs several of its companies with American and British executives. Japan's Sony Corporation broke 60 years of tradition in 2005 when it installed its first non-Japanese chairman and CEO, Howard Stringer, a former CBS president and U.S. citizen who was born and raised in Wales. American companies increasingly draw their managerial talent from overseas. One study found that by the mid-2000s, 24 percent of the managers among the top 100 to 250 people in U.S. companies were from outside the United States. For European companies the average is 40 percent.[13]

However, a number of problems limit the firm's ability to pursue a geocentric policy. Many countries want foreign subsidiaries to employ their citizens. To achieve this goal, they use immigration laws to require the employment of host-country nationals if they are available in adequate numbers and have the necessary skills. Most countries, including the United States, require firms to provide extensive documentation if they wish to hire a foreign national instead of a local national. This documentation can be time consuming, expensive, and at times futile. A geocentric staffing policy also can be expensive to implement. Training and relocation costs increase when transferring

Geocentric Staffing Policy
A staffing policy under which the firm seeks the best people for key jobs throughout the company, regardless of nationality.

Women in International Assignments
According to a report issued by Mercer Human Resource Consulting, employers are sending more women on international assignments than ever before. The trend typifies the ongoing globalization of companies. In the Asia/Pacific region, particularly China, the report highlights the greatest rise in female assignments. Of the respondents, 55 percent said the trend is expected to increase over the next five years. From the women's perspective, they view the acceptance of the assignments as an increasingly important step in the career ladder. Interestingly enough, the report does not mention particularly difficult assignments for women such as Saudi Arabia, Kuwait, Japan, or Korea. (Gina Ruiz, "Employers Sending More Women on International Assignments," *Workforce Magazine,* October 2006, retrieved at http://www.workforce.com/section/recruiting-staffing/feature/employers-sending-more-women-international-assignments/index.html)

managers from country to country. The company may also need a compensation structure with a standardized international base pay level higher than national levels in many countries. In addition, the higher pay enjoyed by managers placed on an international fast track may be a source of resentment within a firm.

Summary The advantages and disadvantages of the three approaches to staffing policy are summarized in Table 16.1. Broadly speaking, an ethnocentric approach is compatible with an international strategy, a polycentric approach is compatible with a localization strategy, and a geocentric approach is compatible with both global standardization and transnational strategies. (See Chapter 11 for details of the strategies.)

While the staffing policies described here are well known and widely used among both practitioners and scholars of international businesses, some critics have claimed that the typology is too simplistic and that it obscures the internal differentiation of management practices within international businesses. The critics claim that within some international businesses, staffing policies vary significantly from national subsidiary to national subsidiary; while some are managed on an ethnocentric basis, others are managed in a polycentric or geocentric manner.[14] Other critics note that the staffing policy adopted by a firm is primarily driven by its geographic scope, as opposed to its strategic orientation. Firms that have a broad geographic scope are the most likely to have a geocentric mind-set.[15]

table 16.1

Comparison of Staffing Approaches

Staffing Approach	Strategic Appropriateness	Advantages	Disadvantages
Ethnocentric	International	Overcomes lack of qualified managers in host nation Unified culture Helps transfer core competencies	Produces resentment in host country Can lead to cultural myopia
Polycentric	Localization	Alleviates cultural myopia Inexpensive to implement	Limits career mobility Isolates headquarters from foreign subsidiaries
Geocentric	Global standardization and transnational	Uses human resources efficiently Helps build strong culture and informal management networks	National immigration policies may limit implementation Expensive

EXPATRIATE MANAGERS

Two of the three staffing policies we have discussed—the ethnocentric and the geocentric—rely on extensive use of expatriate managers. As defined earlier, expatriates are citizens of one country who are working in another country. Sometimes the term *inpatriates* is used to identify a subset of expatriates who are citizens of a foreign country working in the home country of their multinational employer.[16] Thus, a citizen of Japan who moves to the United States to work at Microsoft would be classified as an inpatriate. With an ethnocentric policy, the expatriates are all home-country nationals who are transferred abroad. With a geocentric approach, the expatriates need not be home-country nationals; the firm does not base transfer decisions on nationality. A prominent issue in the international staffing literature is **expatriate failure**—the premature return of an expatriate manager to his or her home country.[17] Here we briefly review the evidence on expatriate failure before discussing a number of ways to minimize the failure rate.

LEARNING OBJECTIVE 3
Explain why managers may fail to thrive in foreign postings.

Expatriate Failure
The premature of an expatriate manager to the home country.

Expatriate Failure Rates

Expatriate failure represents a failure of the firm's selection policies to identify individuals who will not thrive abroad.[18] The consequences include premature return from a foreign posting and high resignation rates, with expatriates leaving their company at about twice the rate of domestic managers.[19] Research suggests that between 16 and 40 percent of all American employees sent abroad to developed nations return from their assignments early, and almost 70 percent of employees sent to developing nations return home early.[20] Although detailed data are not available for most nationalities, one suspects that high expatriate failure is a universal problem. Some 28 percent of British expatriates, for example, are estimated to fail in their overseas postings.[21] The costs of expatriate failure are high. One estimate is that the average cost per failure to the parent firm can be as high as three times the expatriate's annual domestic salary plus the cost of relocation (which is affected by currency exchange rates and location of assignment). Estimates of the costs of each failure run between $250,000 and $1 million.[22] In addition, approximately 30 to 50 percent of American expatriates, whose average annual compensation package runs to $250,000, stay at their international assignments but are considered ineffective or marginally effective by their firms.[23] In a seminal study, R. L. Tung surveyed a number of U.S., European, and Japanese multinationals.[24] Her results, summarized in Table 16.2, show that 76 percent of U.S. multinationals experienced

Recall Rate Percent	Percent of Companies
U.S. multinationals	
20–40%	7%
10–20	69
<10	24
European multinationals	
11–15%	3%
6–10	38
<5	59
Japanese multinationals	
11–19%	14%
6–10	10
<5	76

16.2 table

Expatriate Failure Rates

Source: Data from R. L. Tung, "Selection and Training Procedures of U.S., European, and Japanese Multinationals," pp. 51–71. Copyright © by The Regents of the University of California. Reprinted from the *California Management Review*, Vol. 1.25, No. 1, by permission from The Regents.

expatriate failure rates of 10 percent or more, and 7 percent experienced a failure rate of more than 20 percent. Tung's work also suggests that U.S.-based multinationals experience a much higher expatriate failure rate than either European or Japanese multinationals.

Tung asked her sample of multinational managers to indicate reasons for expatriate failure. For U.S. multinationals, the reasons, in order of importance, were

1. Inability of spouse to adjust.
2. Manager's inability to adjust.
3. Other family problems.
4. Manager's personal or emotional maturity.
5. Inability to cope with larger overseas responsibilities.

Managers of European firms gave only one reason consistently to explain expatriate failure: the inability of the manager's spouse to adjust to a new environment. For the Japanese firms, the reasons for failure were

1. Inability to cope with larger overseas responsibilities.
2. Difficulties with new environment.
3. Personal or emotional problems.
4. Lack of technical competence.
5. Inability of spouse to adjust.

The most striking difference between these lists is that "inability of spouse to adjust" was the top reason for expatriate failure among U.S. and European multinationals but only the number five reason among Japanese multinationals. Tung comments that this difference is not surprising, given the role and status to which Japanese society traditionally relegates the wife and the fact that most of the Japanese expatriate managers in the study were men.

Since Tung's study, a number of other studies have consistently confirmed that the inability of a spouse to adjust, the inability of the manager to adjust, or other family problems remain major reasons for continuing high levels of expatriate failure.[25] One study by International Orientation Resources, an HRM consulting firm, found that 60 percent of expatriate failures occur due to these three reasons.[26] Another study found that the most common reason for assignment failure is lack of partner (spouse) satisfaction, which was listed by 27 percent of respondents.[27] The inability of expatriate managers to adjust to foreign postings seems to be caused by a lack of cultural skills on the part of the manager being transferred. According to one HRM consulting firm, this is because the expatriate selection process at many firms is fundamentally flawed. "Expatriate assignments rarely fail because the person cannot accommodate to the technical demands of the job. Typically, the expatriate selections are made by line managers based on technical competence. They fail because of family and personal issues and lack of cultural skills that haven't been part of the selection process."[28]

The failure of spouses to adjust to a foreign posting seems to be related to a number of factors. Often spouses find themselves in a foreign country without the familiar network of family and friends. Language differences make it difficult for them to make new friends. While this may not be a problem for the manager, who can make friends at work, it can be difficult for the spouse, who might feel trapped at home. The problem is often exacerbated by immigration regulations prohibiting the spouse from taking employment. With the recent rise of two-career families in many developed nations, this issue has become much more important. One survey found that 69 percent of expatriates are married, with spouses accompanying them 77 percent of the time. Of those spouses, 49 percent were employed before an assignment and only

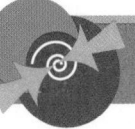

Management FOCUS

Managing Expatriates at Royal Dutch/Shell

Royal Dutch/Shell is a global petroleum company with joint headquarters in both London and The Hague in the Netherlands. The company employs more than 100,000 people, approximately 5,500 of whom are at any one time living and working as expatriates. The expatriates at Shell are a diverse group, made up of over 70 nationalities and located in more than 100 countries. Shell, as a global corporation, has long recognized that the international mobility of its workforce is essential to its success. By the 1990s, however, Shell was finding it harder to recruit key personnel for foreign postings. To discover why, the company interviewed more than 200 expatriate employees and their spouses to determine their biggest concerns. The data were then used to construct a survey that was sent to 17,000 current and former expatriate employees, expatriates' spouses, and employees who had declined international assignments.

The survey registered a phenomenal 70 percent response rate, clearly indicating that many employees thought this was an important issue. According to the survey, five issues had the greatest impact on the willingness of an employee to accept an international assignment. In order of importance, these were (1) separation from children during their secondary education (the children of British and Dutch expatriates were often sent to boarding schools in their home countries while their parents worked abroad), (2) harm done to a spouse's career and employment, (3) failure to recognize and involve a spouse in the relocation decision, (4) failure to provide adequate information and assistance regarding relocation, and (5) health issues. The underlying message was that the family is the basic unit of expatriation, not the individual, and Shell needed to do more to recognize this.

To deal with these issues, Shell implemented a number of programs designed to address some of these problems. To help with the education of children, Shell built elementary schools for Shell employees where there was a heavy concentration of expatriates. As for secondary school education, it worked with local schools, often providing grants, to help them upgrade their educational offerings. It also offered an education supplement to help expatriates send their children to private schools in the host country.

Helping spouses with their careers is a more vexing problem. According to the survey data, half of the spouses accompanying Shell staff on assignment were employed until the transfer. When expatriated, only 12 percent were able to secure employment, while a further 33 percent wished to be employed. Shell set up a spouse employment center to address the problem. The center provides career counseling and assistance in locating employment opportunities both during and immediately after an international assignment. The company also agreed to reimburse up to 80 percent of the costs of vocational training, further education, or re-accreditation, up to $4,400 per assignment.

Shell also set up a global information and advice network known as "The Outpost" to provide support for families contemplating a foreign posting. The Outpost has its headquarters in The Hague and now runs 40 information centers in more than 30 countries. The center recommends schools and medical facilities and provides housing advice and up-to-date information on employment, study, self-employment, and volunteer work.

Sources: E. Smockum, "Don't Forget the Trailing Spouse," *Financial Times*, May 6, 1998, p. 22; V. Frazee, "Tearing Down Roadblocks," *Workforce* 77, no. 2 (1998), pp. 50–54; C. Sievers, "Expatriate Management," *HR Focus* 75, no. 3 (1998), pp. 75–76; and J. Barbian, "Return to Sender," *Training*, January 2002, pp. 40–43.

---

11 percent were employed during an assignment.[29] Research suggests that a main reason managers now turn down international assignments is concern over the impact such an assignment might have on their spouse's career.[30] The accompanying Management Focus examines how one large multinational company, Royal Dutch/Shell, has tried to come to grips with this issue.

Expatriate Selection   One way to reduce expatriate failure rates is by improving selection procedures to screen out inappropriate candidates. In a review of the research on this issue, Mendenhall and Oddou state that a major problem in many firms is that HRM managers tend to equate domestic performance with overseas performance potential.[31] Domestic performance and overseas performance potential are *not* the same thing. An executive who performs well in a domestic setting may not be able to adapt to managing in a different cultural setting. From their review of the research, Mendenhall and Oddou identified four dimensions that seem to predict success in a foreign posting: self-orientation, others-orientation, perceptual ability, and cultural toughness.

1. *Self-orientation.* The attributes of this dimension strengthen the expatriate's self-esteem, self-confidence, and mental well-being. Expatriates with high self-esteem, self-confidence, and mental well-being were more likely to succeed in foreign postings. Mendenhall and Oddou concluded that such individuals were able to adapt their interests in food, sport, and music; had interests outside of work that could be pursued (e.g., hobbies); and were technically competent.

2. *Others-orientation.* The attributes of this dimension enhance the expatriate's ability to interact effectively with host-country nationals. The more effectively the expatriate interacts with host-country nationals, the more likely he or she is to succeed. Two factors seem to be particularly important here: relationship development and willingness to communicate. Relationship development refers to the ability to develop long-lasting friendships with host-country nationals. Willingness to communicate refers to the expatriate's willingness to use the host-country language. Although language fluency helps, an expatriate need not be fluent to show willingness to communicate. Making the effort to use the language is what is important. Such gestures tend to be rewarded with greater cooperation by host-country nationals.

3. *Perceptual ability.* This is the ability to understand why people of other countries behave the way they do; that is, the ability to empathize. This dimension seems critical for managing host-country nationals. Expatriate managers who lack this ability tend to treat foreign nationals as if they were home-country nationals. As a result, they may experience significant management problems and considerable frustration. As one expatriate executive from Hewlett-Packard observed, "It took me six months to accept the fact that my staff meetings would start 30 minutes late, and that it would bother no one but me." According to Mendenhall and Oddou, well-adjusted expatriates tend to be nonjudgmental and nonevaluative in interpreting the behavior of host-country nationals and willing to be flexible in their management style, adjusting it as cultural conditions warrant.

4. *Cultural toughness.* This dimension refers to the relationship between the country of assignment and how well an expatriate adjusts to a particular posting. Some countries are much tougher postings than others because their cultures are more unfamiliar and uncomfortable. For example, many Americans regard Great Britain as a relatively easy foreign posting, and for good reason—the two cultures have much in common. But many Americans find postings in non-Western cultures, such as India, Southeast Asia, and the Middle East, to be much tougher.[32] The reasons are many, including poor health care and housing standards, inhospitable climate, lack of Western entertainment, and language difficulties. Also, many cultures are extremely male-dominated and may be particularly difficult postings for female Western managers.

THE GLOBAL MIND-SET Some researchers suggest that a global mind-set, one characterized by cognitive complexity and a cosmopolitan outlook, is the fundamental attribute of a global manager. Such managers can deal with high levels of complexity and ambiguity and are open to the world. How do you develop these attributes? Often they are gained in early life, from a family that is bicultural, lives in foreign countries, or learns foreign languages as a regular part of family life.

Mendenhall and Oddou note that standard psychological tests can be used to assess the first three of these dimensions, whereas a comparison of cultures can give managers a feeling for the fourth dimension. They contend that these four dimensions, in addition to domestic performance, should be considered when selecting a manager for foreign posting. However, practice does not often conform to Mendenhall and Oddou's recommendations. Tung's research, for example, showed that only 5 percent of the firms in her sample used formal procedures and psychological tests to assess the personality traits and relational abilities of potential expatriates.[33] Research by International Orientation Resources suggests that when selecting employees for foreign assignments, only 10 percent of the 50 *Fortune* 500 firms they surveyed tested for important psychological traits such as cultural sensitivity, interpersonal skills, adaptability, and flexibility. Instead, 90 percent of the time employees were selected on the basis of their technical expertise, not their cross-cultural fluency.[34]

Mendenhall and Oddou do not address the problem of expatriate failure due to a spouse's inability to adjust. According to a number of other researchers, a review of the family situation should be part of the expatriate selection process (see the Management Focus on Royal Dutch/Shell for an example).[35] A survey by Windam International, another international HRM consulting firm, found that spouses were included in preselection interviews for foreign postings only 21 percent of the time, and that only half of them received any cross-cultural training. The rise of dual-career families has added an additional and difficult dimension to this long-standing problem.[36] Increasingly, spouses wonder why they should have to sacrifice their own career to further that of their partner.[37]

Training and Management Development

LEARNING OBJECTIVE 4
Recognize how management development and training programs can increase the value of human capital in international business firms.

Selection is just the first step in matching a manager with a job. The next step is training the manager to do the specific job. For example, an intensive training program might be used to give expatriate managers the skills required for success in a foreign posting. However, management development is a much broader concept. It is intended to develop the manager's skills over his or her career with the firm. Thus, as part of a management development program, a manager might be sent on several foreign postings over a number of years to build his or her cross-cultural sensitivity and experience. At the same time, along with other managers in the firm, the person might attend management education programs at regular intervals. The thinking behind job transfers is that broad international experience will enhance the management and leadership skills of executives. Research suggests this may be the case.[38]

Historically, most international businesses have been more concerned with training than with management development. Plus, they tended to focus their training efforts on preparing home-country nationals for foreign postings. Recently, however, the shift toward greater global competition and the rise of transnational firms have changed this. It is increasingly common for firms to provide general management development programs in addition to training for particular posts. In many international businesses, the explicit purpose of these management development programs is strategic. Management development is seen as a tool to help the firm achieve its strategic goals, not only by giving managers the required skill set, but also by helping to reinforce the desired culture of the firm and by facilitating the

International businesses, such as Caterpillar, are increasingly providing general management development programs in addition to training for particular foreign postings.

creation of an informal network for sharing knowledge within the multinational enterprise.

With this distinction between training and management development in mind, we first examine the types of training managers receive for foreign postings. Then we discuss the connection between management development and strategy in the international business.

TRAINING FOR EXPATRIATE MANAGERS

Earlier in the chapter we saw that the two most common reasons for expatriate failure were the inability of a manager's spouse to adjust to a foreign environment and the manager's own inability to adjust to a foreign environment. Training can help the manager and spouse cope with both these problems. Cultural training, language training, and practical training all seem to reduce expatriate failure. We discuss each of these kinds of training here.[39] Despite the usefulness of these kinds of training, evidence suggests that many managers receive no training before they are sent on foreign postings. One study found that only about 30 percent of managers sent on one- to five-year expatriate assignments received training before their departure.[40]

Cultural Training

Cultural training seeks to foster an appreciation for the host country's culture. The belief is that understanding a host country's culture will help the manager empathize with the culture, which will enhance his or her effectiveness in dealing with host-country nationals. It has been suggested that expatriates should receive training in the host country's culture, history, politics, economy, religion, and social and business practices.[41] If possible, it is also advisable to arrange for a familiarization trip to the host country before the formal transfer, as this seems to ease culture shock. Given the problems related to spouse adaptation, it is important that the spouse, and perhaps the whole family, be included in cultural training programs.

Language Training

English is the language of world business; it is quite possible to conduct business all over the world using only English. Notwithstanding the prevalence of English, however, an exclusive reliance on English diminishes an expatriate manager's ability to interact with host-country nationals. As noted earlier, a willingness to communicate in the language of the host country, even if the expatriate is far from fluent, can help build rapport with local employees and improve the manager's effectiveness. Despite this, one study of 74 executives of U.S. multinationals found that only 23 believed knowledge of foreign languages was necessary for conducting business abroad.[42] Those firms that did offer foreign language training for expatriates believed it improved their employees' effectiveness and enabled them to relate more easily to a foreign culture, which fostered a better image of the firm in the host country.

Practical Training

Practical training is aimed at helping the expatriate manager and family ease themselves into day-to-day life in the host country. The sooner a routine is established, the better are the prospects that the expatriate and his or her family will adapt successfully. One critical need is for a support network of friends for the expatriate. Where an expatriate community exists, firms often devote considerable effort to ensuring the new expatriate family is quickly integrated into that group. The expatriate community can be a useful source of support and information and can be invaluable in helping the family adapt to a foreign culture.

Safety and Security

Global work can, at times, be dangerous. As part of overall training, serious consideration should be given to the issue of personal safety, includ-

Management FOCUS

"K&R" Insurance: Protecting Employees Abroad

Usually, it is simply referred to as "K&R" insurance. It is often not mentioned, and if it is, only in hushed tones. This is because K&R stands for "kidnapping and ransom."

According to Jim Kardaras of Marsh, a global company that issues K&R insurance, global kidnappings are on the rise. According to some experts, 70 percent of kidnappings since 2001 have taken place in Latin American countries such as Colombia, Venezuela, Ecuador, Mexico, Honduras, and Brazil. The list also includes Nigeria, Pakistan, India, Afghanistan, the Philippines, Somalia, and the former Soviet Union—all potentially dangerous places to work.

Kidnappings may be for short periods of time. The term "express kidnapping" is used when a victim is taken for a few hours to make ATM withdrawals. This usually happens right around midnight. The victim is forced to withdraw the maximum amount from the ATM prior to midnight. They are then forced to withdraw a maximum amount again shortly thereafter when the bank resets the limit after the previous day's closing.

Sometimes, the abductions are much more serious. In late December 2009, two Scottish oil workers working in Nigeria for Sparrows Offshore Services (SOS) Ltd., under contract with ExxonMobil, were allegedly kidnapped, tortured, beaten, submerged in swamp water, and forced to lie prone in mud for long periods of time. The oil workers were released after 19 days of captivity. Following these events, SOS removed all expatriate workers from the Nigerian work site.

At other times, kidnappings can be gruesome. While working for Parsons Global Services, an employee was sent to Manila, Philippines, on a long-term assignment as an accountant. Several days after arriving, the employee was abducted by three men who held him captive for approximately three weeks. They chained him to the floor, attempted to hang him, and tortured him. Initially, Parsons' officials allegedly promised the employee's wife they would pay the ransom. However, the company then took the position that paying the ransom would undermine its long-term interests by providing an incentive to kidnap other employees. Parsons paid the ransom the day after it received a videotape of the kidnappers cutting off the employee's ear. It was unclear whether Parsons had K&R insurance on the employee.

As suggested by Parsons, the reason K&R insurance is mentioned in hush tones is obvious: to disclose is to divulge a target. Kidnapping risk increases exponentially when assurances of payment are guaranteed. K&R insurance offers money for the ransom and protection of company personnel and property. Premiums vary based on exposure and can range from a few thousand to millions of dollars annually. Global business and global resource management requires much care. If employees are venturing to hazardous regions, careful consideration should be given to providing K&R insurance in a discrete manner.

Sources: R. Yu, "Fending off Danger Abroad; Companies Step Up Efforts to Train, Protect Staff," *USA Today*, August 24, 2010, p. 1B; P. Berkowitz, "Employment Law Issues: In More Dangerous World, Kidnapping Is a Serious Concern," *New York Law Journal*, 2010; R. Shafer, "On Foreign Ground," *Risk Management*, 56, no. 9 (2009), pp. 48-52; and Control Risks Web site, www.control-risks.com.

ing kidnappings and ransom, especially if employees are traveling in regions that are considered dangerous. See the accompanying Management Focus on protecting employees abroad.

REPATRIATION OF EXPATRIATES A largely overlooked but critically important issue in the training and development of expatriate managers is to prepare them for reentry into their home-country organization.[43] Repatriation should be seen as the final link in an integrated, circular process that connects good selection and cross-cultural training of expatriate managers with completion of their term abroad and reintegration into their national organization. However, instead of having employees come home to share their knowledge and encourage other high-performing managers to take the same international career track, expatriates too often face a different scenario.[44]

Often when they return home after a stint abroad—where they have typically been autonomous, well compensated, and celebrated as a big fish in a little pond—they face an organization that doesn't know what they have done for the past few years, doesn't know how to use their new knowledge, and doesn't particularly care. In the worst cases, reentering employees have to scrounge for jobs, or firms will create standby positions that don't use the expatriate's skills and capabilities and fail to make the most of the business investment the firm has made in that individual.

Research illustrates the extent of this problem. According to one study of repatriated employees, 60 to 70 percent didn't know what their position would be when they returned home. Also, 60 percent said their organizations were vague about repatriation, about their new roles, and about their future career progression within the company; 77 percent of those surveyed took jobs at a lower level in their home organization than in their international assignments.[45] Not surprising, 15 percent of returning expatriates leave their firms within a year of arriving home, and 40 percent leave within three years.[46]

The key to solving this problem is good human resource planning. Just as the HRM function needs to develop good selection and training programs for its expatriates, it also needs to develop good programs for reintegrating expatriates back into work life within their home-country organization, for preparing them for changes in their physical and professional landscape, and for utilizing the knowledge they acquired while abroad.

MANAGEMENT DEVELOPMENT AND STRATEGY Management development programs are designed to increase the overall skill levels of managers through a mix of ongoing management education and rotations of managers through a number of jobs within the firm to give them varied experiences. They are attempts to improve the overall productivity and quality of the firm's management resources.

International businesses increasingly are using management development as a strategic tool. This is particularly true in firms pursuing a transnational strategy, as increasing numbers are. Such firms need a strong unifying corporate culture and informal management networks to assist in coordination and control. In addition, transnational firm managers need to be able to detect pressures for local responsiveness, and that requires them to understand the culture of a host country.

Management development programs help build a unifying corporate culture by socializing new managers into the norms and value systems of the firm. In-house company training programs and intense interaction during off-site training can foster esprit de corps—shared experiences, informal networks, perhaps a company language or jargon—as well as develop technical competencies. These training events often include songs, picnics, and sporting events that promote feelings of togetherness. These rites of integration may include "initiation rites" wherein personal culture is stripped, company uniforms are donned (e.g., T-shirts bearing the company logo), and humiliation is inflicted (e.g., a pie in the face). All these activities aim to strengthen a manager's identification with the company.[47]

Bringing managers together in one location for extended periods and rotating them through different jobs in several countries helps the firm build an informal management network. Such a network can then be used as a conduit for exchanging valuable performance-enhancing knowledge within the organization.[48] Consider the Swedish telecommunications company L. M. Ericsson. Interunit cooperation is extremely important at Ericsson, particularly for transferring know-how and core competencies from the parent to foreign subsidiaries, from foreign subsidiaries to the parent, and between foreign subsidiaries. To facilitate cooperation, Ericsson transfers large numbers of people back and forth between headquarters and subsidiaries. Ericsson sends a team of 50 to 100 engineers and managers from one unit to another for a year or two. This establishes a network of interpersonal contacts. This policy is effective for both solidifying a common culture in the company and coordinating the company's globally dispersed operations.[49]

Performance Appraisal

Performance appraisal systems are used to evaluate the performance of managers against some criteria that the firm judges to be important for the implementation of strategy and the attainment of a competitive advantage. A firm's performance appraisal systems are an important element of its control systems, which is a central component of organization architecture (see Figure 16.1). A particularly thorny issue in many international businesses is how best to evaluate the performance of expatriate managers.[50] In this section, we look at this issue and consider some guidelines for appraising expatriate performance.

LEARNING OBJECTIVE 5
Explain how and why performance appraisal systems might vary across nations.

PERFORMANCE APPRAISAL PROBLEMS Unintentional bias makes it difficult to evaluate the performance of expatriate managers objectively. In many cases, two groups evaluate the performance of expatriate managers—host-nation managers and home-office managers—and both are subject to bias. The host-nation managers may be biased by their own cultural frame of reference and expectations. For example, Oddou and Mendenhall report the case of a U.S. manager who introduced participative decision making while working in an Indian subsidiary.[51] The manager subsequently received a negative evaluation from host-country managers because in India, the strong social stratification means managers are seen as experts who should not have to ask subordinates for help. The local employees apparently viewed the U.S. manager's attempt at participatory management as an indication that he was incompetent and did not know his job.

Home-country managers' appraisals may be biased by distance and by their own lack of experience working abroad. Home-office managers are often not aware of what is going on in a foreign operation. Accordingly, they tend to rely on hard data in evaluating an expatriate's performance, such as the subunit's productivity, profitability, or market share. Such criteria may reflect factors outside the expatriate manager's control (e.g., adverse changes in exchange rates, economic downturns). Also, hard data do not take into account many less-visible soft variables that are also important, such as an expatriate's ability to develop cross-cultural awareness and to work productively with local managers. Due to such biases, many expatriate managers believe that headquarters management evaluates them unfairly and does not fully appreciate the value of their skills and experience. This could be one reason many expatriates believe a foreign posting does not benefit their careers. In one study of personnel managers in U.S. multinationals, 56 percent of the managers surveyed stated that a foreign assignment is either detrimental or immaterial to one's career.[52]

GUIDELINES FOR PERFORMANCE APPRAISAL Several things can reduce bias in the performance appraisal process.[53] First, most expatriates appear to believe more weight should be given to an on-site manager's appraisal than to an off-site manager's appraisal. Due to proximity, an on-site manager is more likely to evaluate the soft variables that are important aspects of an expatriate's performance. The evaluation may be especially valid when the on-site manager is of the same nationality as the expatriate, since cultural bias should be alleviated. In practice, home-office managers often write performance evaluations after receiving input from on-site managers. When this is the case, most experts recommend that a former expatriate who served in the same location should be involved in the appraisal to help reduce bias. Finally, when the policy is for foreign on-site managers to write performance evaluations, home-office managers should be consulted before an on-site manager completes a formal termination evaluation. This gives the home-office manager the opportunity to balance what could be a very hostile evaluation based on a cultural misunderstanding.

Compensation

LEARNING OBJECTIVE 6
Explain how and why compensation systems might vary across nations.

Two issues are raised in every discussion of compensation practices in an international business. One is how compensation should be adjusted to reflect national differences in economic circumstances and compensation practices. The other issue is how expatriate managers should be paid. From a strategic perspective, the important point is that whatever compensation system is used, it should reward managers for taking actions that are consistent with the strategy of the enterprise.

NATIONAL DIFFERENCES IN COMPENSATION Substantial differences exist in the compensation of executives at the same level in various countries. Table 16.3 summarizes the results of a survey undertaken by Towers Perrin. Among other things, this survey looked at average compensation for top human resource executives across 26 countries in the 2005–06 period for companies with annual sales of around

table **16.3**

Compensation in 26 Countries for Top Human Resource Executives

Source: Towers Perrin, *Towers Perrin Worldwide Total Remuneration Study, 2005–2006,* www.towersperrin.com.

Country	HR Executive Average Total Compensation
Argentina	$212,879
Australia	293,782
Belgium	446,624
Brazil	356,733
Canada	307,053
China (Hong Kong)	268,158
China (Shanghai)	85,393
France	384,904
Germany	456,665
India	146,384
Italy	432,569
Japan	278,697
Malaysia	140,587
Mexico	382,334
Netherlands	287,247
Poland	120,410
Singapore	230,281
South Africa	371,781
South Korea	182,716
Spain	305,519
Sweden	302,473
Switzerland	447,563
Taiwan	158,146
United Kingdom	494,519
United States	525,923
Venezuela	225,317

$500 million.[54] The figures include both base compensation and performance-related pay bonuses, but they do not include stock options. As can be seen, wide variations exist across countries. The average compensation for top HR executives in the United States was $525,923, compared with $278,697 in Japan and $158,146 in Taiwan. According to Towers Perrin, similar pay differences can be seen across other job categories, including the CEO and CFO positions. These figures underestimate the true differential because many U.S. executives earn considerable sums of money from stock option grants.

National differences in compensation raise a perplexing question for an international business: Should the firm pay executives in different countries according to the prevailing standards in each country, or should it equalize pay on a global basis? The problem does not arise in firms pursuing ethnocentric or polycentric staffing policies. In ethnocentric firms, the issue can be reduced to that of how much home-country expatriates should be paid (which we will consider later). As for polycentric firms, the lack of managers' mobility among national operations implies that pay can and should be kept country-specific. There would seem to be no point in paying executives in Great Britain the same as U.S. executives if they never work side by side.

However, this problem is very real in firms with geocentric staffing policies. A geocentric staffing policy is consistent with a transnational strategy. One aspect of this policy is the need for a cadre of international managers that may include many different nationalities. Should all members of such a cadre be paid the same salary and the same incentive pay? For a U.S.-based firm, this would mean raising the compensation of foreign nationals to U.S. levels, which could be expensive. If the firm does not equalize pay, it could cause considerable resentment among foreign nationals who are members of the international cadre and work with U.S. nationals. If a firm is serious about building an international cadre, it may have to pay its international executives the same basic salary irrespective of their country of origin or assignment. Currently, however, this practice is not widespread.

Over the past 10 years many firms have moved toward a compensation structure based on consistent global standards, with employees being evaluated by the same grading system and having access to the same bonus pay and benefits structure irrespective of where they work. Some 85 percent of the companies in a recent survey by Mercer Management Consulting have stated that they now have a global compensation strategy.[55] McDonald's, which is featured in the accompanying Management Focus, is one such enterprise. Another survey found that two thirds of multinationals now exercise central control over the benefit plans offered in different nations.[56] However, except for a relative small cadre of internationally mobile executives, base pay in most firms is set with regard to local market conditions.

EXPATRIATE PAY   The most common approach to expatriate pay is the balance sheet approach. According to Organizational Resources Consulting, some 80 percent of the 781 companies it surveyed used this approach.[57] This approach equalizes purchasing power across countries so employees can enjoy the same living standard in their foreign posting that they enjoyed at home. In addition, the approach provides financial incentives to offset qualitative differences between assignment locations.[58] Figure 16.2 shows a typical balance sheet. Note that home-country outlays for the employee are designated as income taxes, housing expenses, expenditures for goods and services (food, clothing, entertainment, etc.), and reserves (savings, pension contributions, etc.). The balance sheet approach attempts to provide expatriates with the same standard of living in their host countries as they enjoy at home plus a financial inducement (i.e., premium, incentive) for accepting an overseas assignment.

The components of the typical expatriate compensation package are a base salary, a foreign service premium, allowances of various types, tax differentials, and benefits. We

Management FOCUS

Global Compensation Practices at McDonald's

With more than 400,000 managers and senior staff employees in 118 countries around the world, by the early 2000s McDonald's had to develop a consistent global compensation and performance appraisal strategy. In 2003, McDonald's launched an initiative that was designed to do just that. After months of consultation with managers all over the world, in 2004 the company began to roll out its new global compensation program.

One important element of this program calls for the corporate head office to provide local-country managers with a menu of business principles to focus on in the coming year. These principles include areas such as customer service, marketing, and restaurant re-imaging. Each country manager then picks three to five areas that they need to focus on for success in their local market. For example, if France is introducing a new menu item, it might create business targets around that for the year. Human resource managers then submit their business cases and targets to senior executives at the headquarters for approval. At the

end of the year, the country's annual incentive pool is based on how the region met its targets, as well as on the business unit's operating income. A portion of individual employees' annual bonus is based on that mix.

The other portion of employees' annual incentives is based on individual performance. McDonald's has always had a performance rating system, but in 2004 the company introduced global guidelines that suggest that 20 percent of employees receive the highest rating, 70 percent the middle, and 10 percent the bottom. By providing guidelines rather than forced ranking, McDonald's hopes to encourage differentiation of performance while allowing for some local flexibility nuances. By providing principles and guidance, and yet allowing local managers to customize their compensation programs to meet local market demands, McDonald's also claims that it has seen a reduction in turnover. The company's own internal surveys suggest that more employees now believe that their compensation is fair and reflects local market conditions.

Source: J. Marquez, "McDonald's Rewards Program Leaves Some Room for Local Flavor," *Workforce Management,* April 10, 2006, p. 26.

shall briefly review each of these components.[59] An expatriate's total compensation package may amount to three times what he or she would cost the firm in a home-country posting. Because of the high cost of expatriates, many firms have reduced their use of them in recent years. However, a firm's ability to reduce its use of expatriates may be limited, particularly if it is pursuing an ethnocentric or geocentric staffing policy.

figure

The Balance Sheet Approach to Expatriate Pay

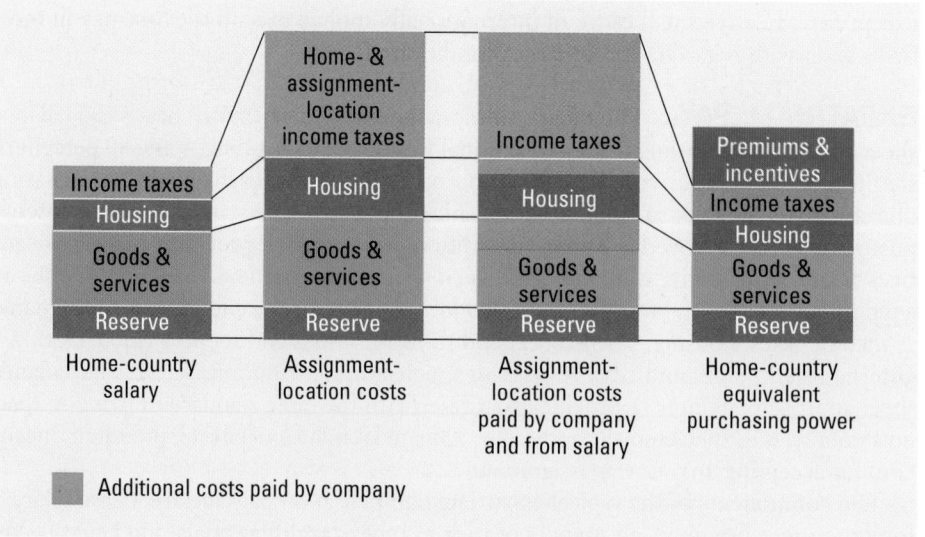

Base Salary   An expatriate's base salary is normally in the same range as the base salary for a similar position in the home country. The base salary is normally paid in either the home-country currency or in the local currency.

Foreign Service Premium   A foreign service premium is extra pay the expatriate receives for working outside his or her country of origin. It is offered as an inducement to accept foreign postings. It compensates the expatriate for having to live in an unfamiliar country isolated from family and friends, having to deal with a new culture and language, and having to adapt to new work habits and practices. Many firms pay foreign service premiums as a percentage of base salary, ranging from 10 to 30 percent after tax, with 16 percent being the average premium.[60]

Allowances   Four types of allowances are often included in an expatriate's compensation package: hardship allowances, housing allowances, cost-of-living allowances, and education allowances. A hardship allowance is paid when the expatriate is being sent to a difficult location, usually defined as one where such basic amenities as health care, schools, and retail stores are grossly deficient by the standards of the expatriate's home country. A housing allowance is normally given to ensure that the expatriate can afford the same quality of housing in the foreign country as at home. In locations where housing is expensive (e.g., London, Tokyo), this allowance can be substantial—as much as 10 to 30 percent of the expatriate's total compensation package. A cost-of-living allowance ensures that the expatriate will enjoy the same standard of living in the foreign posting as at home. An education allowance ensures that an expatriate's children receive adequate schooling (by home-country standards). Host-country public schools are sometimes not suitable for an expatriate's children, in which case they must attend a private school.

Taxation   Unless a host country has a reciprocal tax treaty with the expatriate's home country, the expatriate may have to pay income tax to both the home- and host-country governments. When a reciprocal tax treaty is not in force, the firm typically pays the expatriate's income tax in the host country. In addition, firms normally make up the difference when a higher income tax rate in a host country reduces an expatriate's take-home pay.

Benefits   Many firms also ensure that their expatriates receive the same level of medical and pension benefits abroad that they received at home. This can be costly for the firm, since many benefits that are tax deductible for the firm in the home country (e.g., medical and pension benefits) may not be deductible out of the country.

International Labor Relations

The HRM function of an international business is typically responsible for international labor relations. From a strategic perspective, the key issue in international labor relations is the degree to which organized labor can limit the choices of an international business. A firm's ability to integrate and consolidate its global operations to realize experience

LEARNING OBJECTIVE 7
Understand how organized labor can influence strategic choices in international business firms.

curve and location economies can be limited by organized labor, constraining the pursuit of a transnational or global standardization strategy. Prahalad and Doz cite the example of General Motors, which gained peace with labor unions by agreeing not to integrate and consolidate operations in the most efficient manner.[61] General Motors made substantial investments in Germany—matching its new investments in Austria and Spain—at the demand of the German metalworkers' unions.

One task of the HRM function is to foster harmony and minimize conflict between the firm and organized labor. With this in mind, this section is divided into three parts. First, we review organized labor's concerns about multinational enterprises. Second, we look at how organized labor has tried to deal with these concerns. And third, we look at how international businesses manage their labor relations to minimize labor disputes.

THE CONCERNS OF ORGANIZED LABOR

Labor unions generally try to get better pay, greater job security, and better working conditions for their members through collective bargaining with management. Unions' bargaining power is derived largely from their ability to threaten to disrupt production, either by a strike or some other form of work protest (e.g., refusing to work overtime). This threat is credible, however, only insofar as management has no alternative but to employ union labor.

A principal concern of domestic unions about multinational firms is that the company can counter its bargaining power with the power to move production to another country. Ford, for example, clearly threatened British unions with a plan to move manufacturing to Continental Europe unless British workers abandoned work rules that limited productivity, showed restraint in negotiating for wage increases, and curtailed strikes and other work disruptions.[62]

Another concern of organized labor is that an international business will keep highly skilled tasks in its home country and farm out only low-skilled tasks to foreign plants. Such a practice makes it relatively easy for an international business to switch production from one location to another as economic conditions warrant. Consequently, the bargaining power of organized labor is once more reduced.

A final union concern arises when an international business attempts to import employment practices and contractual agreements from its home country. When these practices are alien to the host country, organized labor fears the change will reduce its influence and power. This concern has surfaced in response to Japanese multinationals that have been trying to export their style of labor relations to other countries. For example, much to the annoyance of the United Auto Workers (UAW), many Japanese auto plants in the United States are not unionized. As a result, union influence in the auto industry is declining.

THE STRATEGY OF ORGANIZED LABOR

Organized labor has responded to the increased bargaining power of multinational corporations by taking three actions: (1) trying to establish international labor organizations, (2) lobbying for national legislation to restrict multinationals, and (3) trying to achieve international regulations on multinationals through such organizations as the United Nations. These efforts have not been very successful.

In the 1960s, organized labor began to establish international trade secretariats (ITSs) to provide worldwide links for national unions in particular industries. The long-term goal was to be able to bargain transnationally with multinational firms. Organized labor believed that by coordinating union action across countries through an ITS, it could counter the power of a multinational corporation by threatening to disrupt production on an international scale. For example, Ford's threat to move production from Great Britain to other European locations would not have been credible if the unions in various European countries had united to oppose it.

The International Labor Organization was set up to seek the promotion of social justice and internationally recognize human and labor rights. *Photo © International Labor Organization*

However, the ITSs have had virtually no real success. Although national unions may want to cooperate, they also compete with each other to attract investment from international businesses, and hence jobs for their members. For example, in attempting to gain new jobs for their members, national unions in the auto industry often court auto firms that are seeking locations for new plants. One reason Nissan chose to build its European production facilities in Great Britain rather than Spain was that the British unions agreed to greater concessions than the Spanish unions did. As a result of such competition between national unions, cooperation is difficult to establish.

A further impediment to cooperation has been the wide variation in union structure. Trade unions developed independently in each country. As a result, the structure and ideology of unions tend to vary significantly from country to country, as does the nature of collective bargaining. For example, in Great Britain, France, and Italy, many unions are controlled by left-wing socialists, who view collective bargaining through the lens of "class conflict." In contrast, most union leaders in Germany, the Netherlands, Scandinavia, and Switzerland are far more moderate politically. The ideological gap between union leaders in different countries has made cooperation difficult. Divergent ideologies are reflected in radically different views about the role of a union in society and the stance unions should take toward multinationals.

Organized labor has also met with only limited success in its efforts to get national and international bodies to regulate multinationals. Such international organizations as the International Labor Organization (ILO) and the Organization for Economic Cooperation and Development (OECD) have adopted codes of conduct for multinational firms to follow in labor relations. However, these guidelines are not as far-reaching as many unions would like. They also do not provide any enforcement mechanisms. Many researchers report that such guidelines are of only limited effectiveness.[63]

APPROACHES TO LABOR RELATIONS   International businesses differ markedly in their approaches to international labor relations. The main difference is the degree to which labor relations activities are centralized or decentralized. Historically, most international businesses have decentralized international labor relations activities to their foreign subsidiaries because labor laws, union power, and the nature of collective bargaining varied so much from country to country. It made sense to decentralize the labor relations function to local managers. The belief was that there was no way central management could effectively handle the complexity of simultaneously managing labor relations in a number of different environments.

Although this logic still holds, there is now a trend toward greater centralized control. This trend reflects international firms' attempts to rationalize their global operations. The general rise in competitive pressure in industry after industry has made it more important for firms to control their costs. Because labor costs account for such a large percentage of total costs, many firms are now using the threat to move production to another country in their negotiations with unions to change work rules and limit wage increases (as Ford did in Europe). Because such a move would involve major new investments and plant closures, this bargaining tactic requires the input of headquarters management. Thus, the level of centralized input into labor relations is increasing.

In addition, the realization is growing that the way work is organized within a plant can be a major source of competitive advantage. Much of the competitive advantage of Japanese automakers, for example, has been attributed to the use of self-managing teams, job rotation, cross-training, and the like in their Japanese plants.[64] To replicate their domestic performance in foreign plants, the Japanese firms have tried to replicate their work practices there. This often brings them into direct conflict with traditional work practices in those countries, as sanctioned by the local labor unions, so the Japanese firms have often made their foreign investments contingent on the local union accepting a radical change in work practices. To achieve this, the headquarters of many Japanese firms bargains directly with local unions to get union agreement to changes in work rules before committing to an investment. For example, before Nissan decided to invest in northern England, it got a commitment from British unions to agree to a change in traditional work practices. By its very nature, pursuing such a strategy requires centralized control over the labor relations function.

Key Terms

human resource management, p. 554

expatriate manager, p. 555

staffing policy, p. 557

corporate culture, p. 557

ethnocentric staffing policy, p. 557

polycentric staffing policy, p. 558

geocentric staffing policy, p. 559

expatriate failure, p. 561

Summary

This chapter focused on human resource management in international businesses. HRM activities include human resource strategy, staffing, performance evaluation, management development, compensation, and labor relations. None of these activities is performed in a vacuum; all must be appropriate to the firm's strategy. The chapter made the following points:

1. Firm success requires HRM policies to be congruent with the firm's strategy and with its formal and informal structure and controls.

2. Staffing policy is concerned with selecting employees who have the skills required to perform particular jobs. Staffing policy can be a tool for developing and promoting a corporate culture.

3. An ethnocentric approach to staffing policy fills all key management positions in an international business with parent-country nationals. The policy is congruent with an international strategy. A drawback is that

ethnocentric staffing can result in cultural myopia.

4. A polycentric staffing policy uses host-country nationals to manage foreign subsidiaries and parent-country nationals for the key positions at corporate headquarters. This approach can minimize the dangers of cultural myopia, but it can create a gap between home- and host-country operations. The policy is best suited to a localization strategy.

5. A geocentric staffing policy seeks the best people for key jobs throughout the organization, regardless of their nationality. This approach is consistent with building a strong unifying culture and informal management network and is well suited to both global standardization and transnational strategies. Immigration policies of national governments may limit a firm's ability to pursue this policy.

6. A prominent issue in the international staffing literature is expatriate failure, defined as the premature return of an expatriate manager to his or her home country. The costs of expatriate failure can be substantial.

7. Expatriate failure can be reduced by selection procedures that screen out inappropriate candidates. The most successful expatriates seem to be those who have high self-esteem and self-confidence, can get along well with others, are willing to attempt to communicate in a foreign language, and can empathize with people of other cultures.

8. Training can lower the probability of expatriate failure. It should include cultural training, language training, and practical training, and it should be provided to both the expatriate manager and the spouse.

9. Management development programs attempt to increase the overall skill levels of managers through a mix of ongoing management education and rotation of managers through different jobs within the firm to give them varied experiences. Management development is often used as a strategic tool to build a strong unifying culture and informal management network, both of which support transnational and global standardization strategies.

10. It can be difficult to evaluate the performance of expatriate managers objectively because of unintentional bias. A firm can take a number of steps to reduce this bias.

11. Country differences in compensation practices raise a difficult question for an international business: Should the firm pay executives in different countries according to the standards in each country or equalize pay on a global basis?

12. The most common approach to expatriate pay is the balance sheet approach. This approach aims to equalize purchasing power so employees can enjoy the same living standard in their foreign posting that they had at home.

13. A key issue in international labor relations is the degree to which organized labor can limit the choices available to an international business. A firm's ability to pursue a transnational or global standardization strategy can be significantly constrained by the actions of labor unions.

14. A principal concern of organized labor is that the multinational can counter union bargaining power with threats to move production to another country.

15. Organized labor has tried to counter the bargaining power of multinationals by forming international labor organizations. In general, these efforts have not been effective.

Critical Thinking and Discussion Questions

1. What are the main advantages and disadvantages of the ethnocentric, polycentric, and geocentric approaches to staffing policy? When is each approach appropriate?

2. Research suggests that many expatriate employees encounter problems that limit both their effectiveness in a foreign posting and their contribution to the company when they return home. What are the main causes and consequences of these problems, and how might a firm reduce the occurrence of such problems?

3. What is the link between an international business's strategy and its human resource management policies, particularly with regard

4. In what ways can organized labor constrain the strategic choices of an international business? How can an international business limit these constraints?

to the use of expatriate employees and their pay scale?

5. Reread the Management Focus on McDonald's global compensation practices. How does McDonald's approach help the company to take local differences into account when reviewing the performance of different country managers and awarding bonus pay?

 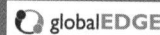
Use the globalEDGE Resource Desk (http://global EDGE.msu.edu/resourcedesk/) to complete the following exercises:

1. The U.S. Department of State prepares quarterly reports for *living costs abroad* to compensate civilian employees working for the U.S. government at various posts worldwide. Using the most current report, identify the posts that are regarded as having a high cost of living as well as those that are perceived as risky (those

receiving a danger pay allowance). What are the living allowances determined by the U.S. Department of State for each post?

2. You work in the human resources department at the headquarters of a multinational corporation. Your company is about to send several American managers to New Zealand as expatriates. Utilize resources available on the globalEDGE Web site regarding *working internationally* to examine the income tax rates in New Zealand.

closing case

Google's HR Department: "People Operations"

Google is the Internet gateway to hundreds of millions of users worldwide, providing searches in languages from Arabic to Zulu. As such, Google is ubiquitous, and its growth has been spectacular.

Yet, Google has not been able to penetrate all corners of the world. As recent events between Google and China demonstrate, there are multiple issues that prohibit the company's global expansion. As the Chinese state-run newspaper *Global Times* said, "The U.S. campaign for uncensored and free flow of information on an unrestricted internet is a disguised attempt to impose its values on other cultures in the name of democracy . . . China's real stake in the 'free flow of information' is evident in its refusal to be victimized by information imperialism." Another example has been South Korea, where Google has not penetrated effectively. Although it has cornered 80 percent of the European search engine market, Google has come under increased regulatory scrutiny.

Most analysts agree that for Google to continue its spectacular growth, it must continue to expand internationally. Given the limited nature of domestic (U.S.) advertising revenues, Google finds itself looking abroad. To secure this

expansion, the identification and recruiting of global talent falls upon identifying and recruiting staff for its HR department.

HR functions at Google fall under the "People Operations" department. Google's HR team is built on what Laszlo Bock, vice president of global people operations, calls the "three-thirds" staffing model.

According to Bock, approximately one-third of the team's employees must have HR backgrounds and bring expertise in client relations as well as in specialty skill areas such as employment law, compensation, and benefits. This group also must have what Bock calls high-level "pattern recognition" skills—or the ability to identify organizational trends and anticipate issues even before they are on the department's radar. An example would be predicting ebbs and flows in hiring and attrition.

The second third comes from nontraditional HR backgrounds, many of which were recruited from strategic consulting firms, such as McKinsey & Co, or Google line functions such as engineering or sales. Most in this group are embedded within business units. Staff in this subgroup have "tremendous problem-solving skills and knowledge about how everything outside of HR works," Bock says. "If you can find people with that skill set, plus an aptitude for people-related issues, we've found they partner very well with traditional HR employees."

The final third is described as a "workforce analytics group," which consists of employees who hold doctorates in statistics, finance, organizational psychology, and other areas. According to Bock, these analysts help make determinations on matters such as setting compensation levels that will retain top talent for maximum periods and conducting the right number of interviews to ensure selection of the best job candidate.

Absent in its staffing model is any specific mention of an international focus. Given its drive for international expansion, it is surprising that Google's HR staffing model does not specifically address an international component. And yet the top executives in its global corporate sales groups demonstrate vast international expertise. In fact, it is curious that a cursory review of Google's Web site demonstrates some of the top sales executives are from Italy, France, Switzerland, Ireland, India, and China. People Operations must have international work in mind.

Sources: Google Web site, www.google.com; D. MacMillan, "Google Undergoes Global Growing Pains," *Bloomberg Businessweek*, February 25, 2010; L. Gordon Crovitz, "Information Age: Google, China and the Shores of Tripoli," *The Wall Street Journal*, January 24, 2010; M. Kimes, "How Do I Groom and Keep Talented Employees?" *Fortune International (Asia)*, November 11, 2008, p. 18; and S. Prasso, and S. Tippu, "Google Goes to India," *Fortune International (Europe)*, October 23, 2007.

Case Discussion Questions

1. What is the staffing policy of the People Operations department at Google?

2. What strategy do you think the company is pursuing? Do you think it is domestic or global strategy? Does the staffing model transcend a specific international focus?

3. What are the strengths of Google's HR department? There is a silence with regard to its international focus, yet has it been able to attract international talent?

4. If Google is to become a truly global enterprise, what should the HR department do to enable the company to attain this goal?

glossary

Absolute advantage A country has an absolute advantage in the production of a product when it is more efficient than any other country at producing it.

Ad valorem tariff A tariff levied as a proportion of the value of an imported good.

Administrative trade policies Administrative policies, typically adopted by government bureaucracies, that can be used to restrict imports or boost exports.

Andean Pact A 1969 agreement between Bolivia, Chile, Ecuador, Colombia, and Peru to establish a customs union.

Antidumping policies Policies designed to punish foreign firms that engage in dumping and thus protect domestic producers from unfair foreign competition.

Arbitrage The purchase of securities in one market for immediate resale in another to profit from a price discrepancy.

Asia-Pacific Economic Cooperation (APEC) Made up of 21 member states whose goal is to increase multilateral cooperation in view of the economic rise of the Pacific nations.

Association of Southeast Asian Nations (ASEAN) An attempt to establish a free trade area between Brunei, Cambodia, Indonesia, Laos, Malaysia, Myanmus, the Philippines, Singapore, Thailand and Vietnam.

Balance-of-payments accounts National accounts that track both payments to and receipts from foreigners.

Balance-of-trade equilibrium Reached when the income a country's residents earn from exports equals the money residents pay for imports.

Bandwagon effect When traders move like a herd, all in the same direction and at the same time, in response to each others' perceived actions.

Banking crisis A loss of confidence in the banking system that leads to a run on banks, as individuals and companies withdraw their deposits.

Barter The direct exchange of goods or services between two parties without a cash transaction.

Bill of exchange An order written by an exporter instructing an importer, or an importer's agent, to pay a specified amount of money at a specified time.

Bill of lading A document issued to an exporter by a common carrier transporting merchandise; it serves as a receipt, a contract, and a document of title.

Bretton Woods A 1944 conference in which representatives of 40 countries met to design a new international monetary system.

Business ethics Accepted principles of right or wrong governing the conduct of businesspeople.

Buyback When a firm builds a plant in a country and agrees to take a certain percentage of the plant's output as partial payment of the contract.

Capital account Records onetime changes in the stock of assets.

Capital flight Residents convert domestic currency into a foreign currency.

Caribbean Single Market and Economy (CSME) Unites six CARICOM members in agreeing to lower trade barriers and harmonize macroeconomic and monetary policies.

CARICOM An association of English-speaking Caribbean states that are attempting to establish a customs union.

Carry trade Involves borrowing in one currency where interest rates are low, and then using the proceeds to invest in another currency where interest rates are high.

Caste system A system of social stratification in which social position is determined by the family into which a person is born, and change in that position is usually not possible during an individual's lifetime.

Central America Free Trade Agreement (CAFTA) The agreement of the member states of the Central American Common Market joined by the Dominican Republic to trade freely with the United States.

Central American Common Market A trade pact between Costa Rica, El Salvador, Guatemala, Honduras, and Nicaragua, which began in the early 1960s but collapsed in 1969 due to war.

Channel length The number of intermediaries that a product has to go through before it reaches the final consumer.

Channel quality The expertise, competencies, and skills of established retailers in a nation, and their ability to sell and support the products of international businesses.

Civil law system A system of law based on a very detailed set of written laws and codes.

Class consciousness A tendency for individuals to perceive themselves in terms of their class background.

Class system A system of social stratification in which social status is determined by the family into which a person is born and by subsequent socioeconomic achievements; mobility between classes is possible.

Code of ethics A business's formal statement of ethical priorities.

Collectivism A political system that emphasizes collective goals as opposed to individual goals.

Command economy An economic system where the allocation of resources, including determination of what goods and services should be produced, and in what quantity, is planned by the government.

Common law A system of law based on tradition, precedent, and custom; when law courts interpret common law, they do so with regard to these characteristics.

Common market A group of countries committed to (1) removing all barriers to the free flow of goods, services, and factors of production between each other and (2) the pursuit of a common external trade policy.

Communist totalitarianism A version of collectivism advocating that socialism can be achieved only through a totalitarian dictatorship.

Communists Those who believe socialism can be achieved only through revolution and totalitarian dictatorship.

Comparative advantage The theory that countries should specialize in the production of goods and services they can produce most efficiently. A country is said to have a comparative advantage in the production of such goods and services.

Concentrated retail system A few retailers supply most of the market.

Confucian dynamism Theory that Confucian teachings affect attitudes toward time, persistence, ordering by status, protection of face, respect for tradition, and reciprocation of gifts and favors. The units of resources required to produce a good are assumed to remain constant no matter where one is on a country's production possibility frontier.

Contract A document that specifies the conditions under which an exchange is to occur and details the rights and obligations of the parties involved.

Contract law The body of law that governs contract enforcement.

Controls The metrics used to measure the performance of subunits and make judgments about how well managers are running those subunits.

Convention on Combating Bribery of Foreign Public Officials in International Business Transactions The convention obliges member states to make the bribery of foreign public officials a criminal offense.

Copyright Exclusive legal rights of authors, composers, playwrights, artists, and publishers to publish and dispose of their work as they see fit.

Core competence Firm skills that competitors cannot easily match or imitate.

Corporate culture Organization's norms and value systems.

Council of the European Union The ultimate decision-making body in the EU.

Counterpurchase A reciprocal buying agreement.

Countertrade The trade of goods and services for other goods and services.

Countervailing duties Antidumping duties.

Country of origin effects The extent to which the place of manufacturing influences product evaluations.

Court of Justice Supreme appeals court for EU law.

Cross-cultural literacy Understanding how the culture of a country affects the way business is practiced.

Cross-licensing agreement An arrangement in which a company licenses valuable intangible property to a foreign partner and receives a license for the partner's valuable knowledge; reduces risk of licensing.

Cultural relativism The belief that ethics are culturally determined and that firms should adopt the ethics of the cultures in which they operate.

Culture A system of values and norms that are shared among a group of people and that when taken together constitute a design for living.

Currency board Means of controlling a country's currency.

Currency crisis Occurs when a speculative attack on the exchange value of a currency results in a sharp depreciation in the value of the currency or forces authorities to expend large volumes of international currency reserves and sharply increase interest rates to defend the prevailing exchange rate.

Currency speculation Involves short-term movement of funds from one currency to another in hopes of profiting from shifts in exchange rates.

Currency swap Simultaneous purchase and sale of a given amount of foreign exchange for two different value dates.

Current account In the balance of payments, records transactions involving the export or import of goods and services.

Current account deficit Occurs when a country imports more good, services, and income than it exports.

Current account surplus Occurs when a country exports more goods, services, and income than it imports.

Customs union A group of countries committed to (1) removing all barriers to the free flow of goods and services between each other and (2) the pursuit of a common external trade policy.

D'Amato Act Act passed in 1996, similar to the Helms-Burton Act, aimed at Libya and Iran.

Democracy Political system in which government is by the people, exercised either directly or through elected representatives.

Deregulation Removal of government restrictions concerning the conduct of a business.

Dirty float A system under which a country's currency is nominally allowed to float freely against other currencies, but in which the government will intervene, buying and selling currency, if it believes that the currency has deviated too far from its fair value.

Draft See **Bill of exchange.**

Dumping Selling goods in a foreign market for less than their cost of production or below their "fair" market value.

Eclectic paradigm Argument that combining location-specific assets or resource endowments and the firm's own unique assets often requires FDI; it requires the firm to establish production facilities where those foreign assets or resource endowments are located.

Economic exposure The extent to which a firm's future international earning power is affected by changes in exchange rates.

Economic risk The likelihood that events, including economic mismanagement, will cause drastic changes in a country's business environment that adversely affect the profit and other goals of a particular business enterprise.

Economic union A group of countries committed to (1) the removal of all barriers to the free flow of goods, services, and factors of production between each other; (2) the adoption of a common currency; (3) the harmonization of tax rates; and (4) the pursuit of a common external trade policy.

Economies of scale Cost advantages associated with large-scale production.

Elastic When a small change in price produces a large change in demand.

Entrepreneurs Those who first commercialize innovations.

Ethical dilemma A situation in which there is no ethically acceptable solution.

Ethical strategy A course of action that does not violate a company's business ethics.

Ethical system A set of moral principles, or values, that are used to guide and shape behavior.

Ethics officer An individual hired by a company to be responsible for making sure that all employees are trained to be ethically aware, that ethical considerations enter the decision-making process, and that employees follow the company's code of ethics.

Ethnocentric staffing policy A staffing approach within the MNE in which all key management positions are filled by parent-country nationals.

Ethnocentrism Behavior that is based on the belief in the superiority of one's own ethnic group or culture; often shows disregard or contempt for the culture of other countries.

European Commission Body responsible for proposing EU legislation, implementing it, and monitoring compliance.

European Council The ultimate controlling authority within the EU.

European Free Trade Association (EFTA) A free trade association including Norway, Iceland, Liechtenstein, and Switzerland.

European Monetary System (EMS) A system to regulate fixed exchange rates before the introduction of the euro.

European Parliament Elected EU body that consults on issues proposed by European Commission.

European Union (EU) An economic group of 27 European nations; established as a customs union, it is moving toward economic union; formerly the European Community.

Exchange rate The rate at which one currency is converted into another.

Exclusive distribution channel A channel that outsiders find difficult to access.

Expatriate failure The premature return of an expatriate manager to the home country.

Expatriate manager A national of one country appointed to a management position in another country.

Experience curve Systematic production cost reductions that occur over the life of a product.

Experience curve pricing Aggressive pricing designed to increase volume and help the firm realize experience curve economies.

Export management company Export specialists who act as an export marketing department for client firms.

Export–Import Bank Agency of the U.S. government whose mission is to provide aid in financing and facilitate exports and imports; also referred to as the Ex–Im Bank.

Exporting Sale of products produced in one country to residents of another country.

External stakeholders Individuals or groups that have some claim on a firm such as customers, suppliers, and unions.

Externalities Knowledge spillovers.

Externally convertible currency Nonresidents can convert their holdings of domestic currency into foreign currency, but the ability of residents to convert the currency is limited in some way.

Factor endowments The extent to which a country is endowed with resources such as land, labor, and capital.

Factors of production Inputs into the productive process of a firm, including labor, management, land, capital, and technological know-how.

Financial account Records transactions that involve the purchase or sale of assets.

First-mover advantages Advantages accruing to the first to enter a market.

First-mover disadvantages Disadvantages associated with entering a foreign market before other international businesses.

Fisher effect Nominal interest rates *(i)* in each country equal the required real rate of interest *(r)* and the expected rate of inflation over the period of time for which the funds are to be lent *(I)*; that is, $i = r - I$.

Fixed exchange rate A system under which the exchange rate for converting one currency into another is fixed.

Flexible machine cells Flexible manufacturing technology in which a grouping of various machine types, a common materials handler, and a centralized cell controller produce a family of products.

Flexible manufacturing technology (lean production) Manufacturing technology designed to improve job scheduling, reduce setup time, and improve quality control.

Floating exchange rate A system under which the exchange rate for converting one currency into another is continuously adjusted depending on the laws of supply and demand.

Flow of foreign direct investment The amount of foreign direct investment undertaken over a given time period (normally one year).

Folkways Routine conventions of everyday life.

Foreign Corrupt Practices Act U.S. law regulating behavior regarding the conduct of international business in the taking of bribes and other unethical actions.

Foreign debt crisis Situation in which a country cannot service its foreign debt obligations, whether private-sector or government debt.

Foreign direct investment (FDI) Direct investment in business operations in a foreign country.

Foreign exchange market A market for converting the currency of one country into that of another country.

Foreign exchange risk The risk that changes in exchange rates will hurt the profitability of a business deal.

Forward exchange When two parties agree to exchange currency and execute a deal at some specific date in the future.

Forward exchange rate The exchange rate governing forward exchange transactions.

Fragmented retail system Many retailers supply a market with no one having a major share.

Franchising A specialized form of licensing in which the franchiser sells intangible property to the franchisee and insists on rules to conduct the business.

Free trade The absence of government barriers to the free flow of goods and services between countries.

Free trade area A group of countries committed to removing all barriers to the free flow of goods and services between each other, but pursuing independent external trade policies.

Freely convertible currency A country's currency is freely convertible when the government of that country allows both residents and nonresidents to purchase unlimited amounts of foreign currency with the domestic currency.

Fundamental analysis Draws on economic theory to construct sophisticated econometric models for predicting exchange rate movements.

Fundamental rights of stakeholders Basic rights of stakeholders, such as the right to information about products and working conditions, that should be considered when business decisions are made.

General Agreement on Tariffs and Trade (GATT) International treaty that committed signatories to lowering barriers to the free flow of goods across national borders and led to the WTO.

Geocentric staffing policy A staffing policy under which the firm seeks the best people for key jobs throughout the company, regardless of nationality.

Global learning The flow of skills and product offerings from foreign subsidiary to home country and from foreign subsidiary to foreign subsidiary.

Global Standardization Strategy A firm focuses on increasing profitability and profit growth by reaping the cost reductions that come from economies of scale, learning effects, and location economies

Global web When different stages of value chain are dispersed to those locations around the globe where value added is maximized or where costs of value creation are minimized.

Globalization Trend away from distinct national economic units and toward one huge global market.

Globalization of markets Moving away from an economic system in which national markets are distinct entities, isolated by trade barriers and barriers of distance, time, and culture, and toward a system in which national markets are merging into one global market.

Globalization of production Trend by individual firms to disperse parts of their productive processes to different locations around the globe to take advantage of differences in cost and quality of factors of production.

Gold par value The amount of currency needed to purchase one ounce of gold.

Gold standard The practice of pegging currencies to gold and guaranteeing convertibility.

Greenfield investment Establishing a new operation in a foreign country.

Gross fixed capital formation Summarizes the total amount of capital invested in factories, stores, office buildings, and the like.

Gross national income (GNI) The yardstick for measuring economic activity of a country, this measures the total annual income of a nation's residents.

Group An association of two or more individuals who have a shared sense of identity and who interact with each other in structured ways on the basis of a common set of expectations about each other's behavior.

Hedging The process of insuring one's business against foreign exchange risk by using forward exchanges or currency swaps.

Helms-Burton Act Act passed in 1996 that allowed Americans to sue foreign firms that use Cuban property confiscated from them after the 1959 revolution.

Human Development Index (HDI) An attempt by the UN to assess the impact of a number of factors on the quality of human life in a country.

Human resource management Activities an organization conducts to use its human resources effectively.

Import quota A direct restriction on the quantity of a good that can be imported into a country.

Incentives The devices used to reward appropriate managerial behavior.

Individualism An emphasis on the importance of guaranteeing individual freedom and self-expression.

Individualism versus collectivism Theory focusing on the relationship between the individual and his or her fellows; in individualistic societies, the ties between individuals are loose and individual achievement is highly valued; in societies where collectivism is emphasized, ties between individuals are tight, people are born into collectives, such as extended families, and everyone is supposed to look after the interests of his or her collective.

Inefficient market One in which prices do not reflect all available information.

Inelastic When a large change in price produces only a small change in demand.

Infant industry argument New industries in developing countries must be temporarily protected from international competition to help them reach a position where they can compete on world markets with the firms of developed nations.

Inflows of FDI Flow of foreign direct investment into a country.

Innovation Development of new products, processes, organizations, management practices, and strategies.

Intellectual property Products of the mind, ideas (e.g., books, music, computer software, designs, technological know-how); intellectual property can be protected by patents, copyrights, and trademarks.

Internal stakeholders People who work for or own the business such as employees, directors, and stockholders.

Internalization theory The argument that firms prefer FDI over licensing in order to retain control over know-how, manufacturing, marketing, and strategy or because some firm capabilities are not amenable to licensing.

International business Any firm that engages in international trade or investment.

International Fisher effect For any two countries, the spot exchange rate should change in an equal amount but in the opposite direction to the difference in nominal interest rates between countries.

International Monetary Fund (IMF) International institution set up to maintain order in the international monetary system.

International monetary system Institutional arrangements countries adopt to govern exchange rates.

International strategy Trying to create value by transferring core competencies to foreign markets where indigenous competitors lack those competencies.

International trade Occurs when a firm exports goods or services to consumers in another country.

ISO 9000 Certification process that requires certain quality standards must be met.

Joint venture Establishing a firm that is jointly owned by two or more otherwise independent firms.

Just distribution A distribution of goods and services that is considered fair and equitable.

Justice theories Ethical approaches that focus on the attainment of a just distribution of economic goods and services.

Just-in-time (JIT) inventory Logistics systems designed to deliver parts to a production process as they are needed, not before.

Kantian ethics The belief that people should be treated as ends and never as means to the ends of others.

Lag strategy Delaying the collection of foreign currency receivables if that currency is expected to appreciate, and delaying payables if that currency is expected to depreciate.

Late-mover disadvantages Handicaps experienced by being a late entrant in a market.

Law of one price In competitive markets free of transportation costs and barriers to trade, identical products sold in different countries must sell for the same price when their price is expressed in the same currency.

Lead strategy Attempting to collect foreign currency receivables early when a foreign currency is expected to depreciate and paying foreign currency payables before they are due when a currency is expected to appreciate.

Lean production Flexible manufacturing technologies pioneered at Toyota and now used in much of the automobile industry.

Learning effects Cost savings from learning by doing.

Legal risk The likelihood that a trading partner will opportunistically break a contract or expropriate intellectual property rights.

Legal system System of rules that regulate behavior and the processes by which the laws of a country are enforced and through which redress of grievances is obtained.

Letter of credit Issued by a bank, indicating that the bank will make payments under specific circumstances.

Licensing Occurs when a firm (the licensor) licenses the right to produce its product, its production processes, or its brand name or trademark to another firm (the licensee); in return for giving the licensee these rights, the licensor collects a royalty fee on every unit the licensee sells.

Licensing agreement Arrangement in which a licensor grants the rights to intangible property to the licensee for a specified period and receives a royalty fee in return.

Local content requirement A requirement that some specific fraction of a good be produced domestically.

Localization strategy Increasing profitability by customizing the firm's goods and services so that they provide a good match to tastes and preferences in different national markets.

Location economies Cost advantages from performing a value creation activity at the optimal location for that activity.

Location-specific advantages Advantages that arise from using resource endowments or assets that are tied to a particular foreign location and that a firm finds valuable to combine with its own unique assets (such as the firm's technological, marketing, or management know-how).

Logistics The procurement and physical transmission of material through the supply chain, from suppliers to customers.

Maastricht Treaty Treaty agreed to in 1991, but not ratified until January 1, 1994, that committed the 12 member states of the European Community to adopt a common currency.

Make-or-buy decisions Whether a firm should make or buy component parts.

Managed-float system System under which some currencies are allowed to float freely, but the majority are either managed by government intervention or pegged to another currency.

Market economy An economic system in which the interaction of supply and demand determines the quantity in which goods and services are produced.

Market segmentation Identifying groups of consumers whose purchasing behavior differs from others in important ways.

Marketing mix Choices about product attributes, distribution strategy, communication strategy, and pricing strategy that a firm offers its targeted markets.

Masculinity versus femininity Theory of the relationship between gender and work roles. In masculine cultures, sex roles are sharply differentiated and traditional "masculine values" such as achievement and the effective exercise of power determine cultural ideals; in feminine cultures, sex roles are less sharply distinguished, and little differentiation is made between men and women in the same job.

Mass customization The production of a variety of end products at a unit cost that could once be achieved only through mass production of a standardized output.

Mercantilism An economic philosophy advocating that countries should simultaneously encourage exports and discourage imports.

Mercosur Pact between Argentina, Brazil, Paraguay, and Uruguay to establish a free trade area.

Minimum efficient scale The level of output at which most plant-level scale economies are exhausted.

Mixed economy Certain sectors of the economy are left to private ownership and free market mechanisms, while other sectors have significant government ownership and government planning.

Moore's law The power of microprocessor technology doubles and its costs of production fall in half every 18 months.

Moral hazard Arises when people behave recklessly because they know they will be saved if things go wrong.

Moral imagination Standing in the shoes of a stakeholder and asking how a proposed decision will affect that stakeholder.

Mores Norms seen as central to the functioning of a society and to its social life.

Multinational enterprise (MNE) A firm that owns business operations in more than one country.

Multipoint competition Arises when two or more enterprises encounter each other in different regional markets, national markets, or industries.

Multipoint pricing Occurs when a pricing strategy in one market may have an impact on a rival's pricing strategy in another market.

Naive immoralism The belief that if a manager of a multinational sees that firm from other nations are not following ethical norms in a host nation, that manager should not either.

New Trade Theory Theory that sometimes countries specialize in the production and export of particular products not because of underlying differences in factor endowments, but because in certain industries the world market can support only a limited number of firms.

Noblesse oblige A French term referring to the honorable and benevolent behavior required of persons of noble birth.

Noise The amount of other messages competing for a potential consumer's attention.

Nonconvertible currency A currency is not convertible when both residents and nonresidents are prohibited from converting their holdings of that currency into another currency.

Norms Social rules and guidelines that prescribe appropriate behavior in particular situations.

North American Free Trade Agreement (NAFTA) Free trade area between Canada, Mexico, and the United States.

Offset A buying agreement similar to counterpurchase, but the exporting country can then fulfill the agreement with any firm in the country to which the sale is being made.

Offshore production FDI undertaken to serve the home market.

Oligopoly An industry composed of a limited number of large firms.

Operations The various value creation activities a firm undertakes.

Optimal currency area One where similarities between the economic structure of countries make it feasible to adopt a single currency.

Organization architecture The totality of a firm's organization, including formal organizational structure, control systems and incentives, organizational culture, processes, and people.

Organization culture The values and norms shared among an organization's employees.

Organizational structure The three-part structure of an organization, including its formal division into subunits such as product divisions, its location of decision-making responsibilities within that structure, and the establishment of integrating mechanisms to coordinate the activities of all subunits.

Outflows of FDI Flow of foreign direct investment out of a country.

Paris Convention for the Protection of Industrial Property International agreement to protect intellectual property.

Patent Grants the inventor of a new product or process exclusive rights to the manufacture, use, or sale of that invention.

Pegged exchange rate Currency value is fixed relative to a reference currency.

People The employees of an organization, its recruiting, compensation, and retention strategies, and the type of people who work at the organization.

Personal ethics The generally accepted principles of right and wrong governing the conduct of individuals.

Pioneering costs Costs an early entrant bears that later entrants avoid, such as the time and effort in learning the rules, failure due to ignorance, and the liability of being a foreigner.

Political economy The political, economic, and legal systems of a country.

Political risk The likelihood that political forces will cause drastic changes in a country's business environment that will adversely affect the profit and other goals of a particular business enterprise.

Political system System of government in a nation.

Political union A central political apparatus that coordinates economic, social, and foreign policy.

Polycentric staffing policy A staffing policy in an MNE in which host-country nationals are recruited to manage subsidiaries in their own country, while parent-country nationals occupy key positions at corporate headquarters.

Power distance Theory of how a society deals with the fact that people are unequal in physical and intellectual capabilities. High power distance cultures are found in countries that let inequalities grow over time into inequalities of power and wealth; low power distance cultures are found in societies that try to play down such inequalities as much as possible.

Predatory pricing Reducing prices below fair market value as a competitive weapon to drive weaker competitors out of the market ("fair" being cost plus some reasonable profit margin).

Price elasticity of demand A measure of how responsive demand for a product is to changes in price.

Private action The theft, piracy, blackmail, and the like by private individuals or groups.

Privatization The sale of state-owned enterprises to private investors.

Processes The manner in which decisions are made and work is performed within any organization.

Product liability Involves holding a firm and its officers responsible when a product causes injury, death, or damage.

Product safety laws Set certain safety standards to which a product must adhere.

Production Activities involved in creating a product.

Production possibility frontier (PPF) The various output possibilities a country can produce from its resource pool.

Profit growth The percentage increase in net profits over time.

Profitability A ratio or rate of return concept.

Property rights Bundle of legal rights over the use to which a resource is put and over the use made of any income that may be derived from that resource.

Public action The extortion of income or resources of property holders by public officials, such as politicians and government bureaucrats.

Pull strategy A marketing strategy emphasizing mass media advertising as opposed to personal selling.

Purchasing power parity (PPP) An adjustment in gross domestic product per capita to reflect differences in the cost of living.

Push strategy A marketing strategy emphasizing personal selling rather than mass media advertising.

Quota rent Extra profit producers make when supply is artificially limited by an import quota.

Regional economic integration Agreements among countries in a geographic region to reduce and ultimately remove tariff and nontariff barriers to the free flow of goods, services, and factors of production between each other.

Relatively efficient market One in which few impediments to international trade and investment exist.

Religion A system of shared beliefs and rituals concerned with the realm of the sacred.

Representative democracy A political system in which citizens periodically elect individuals to represent them in government.

Righteous moralism The belief that a multinational's home-country standards of ethics are the appropriate ones for companies to follow in foreign countries.

Rights theories A 20th-century theory that recognizes that human beings have fundamental rights and privileges that transcend national boundaries and cultures.

Right-wing totalitarianism A political system in which political power is monopolized by a party, group, or individual that generally permits individual economic freedom but restricts individual political freedom, including free speech, often on the grounds that it would lead to the rise of communism.

Sight draft A draft payable on presentation to the drawee.

Single European Act A 1987 act, adopted by members of the European Community, that committed member countries to establishing an economic union.

Six Sigma Statistically based methodology for improving product quality.

Smoot-Hawley Act Enacted in 1930 by the U.S. Congress, this tariff erected a wall of barriers against imports into the United States.

Social democrats Those committed to achieving socialism by democratic means.

Sogo Shosha Japan's great trading houses.

Social mobility The extent to which individuals can move out of the social strata into which they are born.

Social responsibility The idea that businesspeople should consider the social consequences of economic actions when making business decisions.

Social strata Hierarchical social categories often based on family background, occupation, and income.

Social structure The basic social organization of a society.

Socialism A political philosophy advocating substantial public involvement, through government ownership, in the means of production and distribution.

Society Group of people who share a common set of values and norms.

Source effects When the receiver of the message evaluates the message based on the status or image of the sender.

Specialized asset An asset designed to perform a specific task, whose value is significantly reduced in its next-best use.

Specific tariff Tariff levied as a fixed charge for each unit of good imported.

Spot exchange rate The exchange rate at which a foreign exchange dealer will convert one currency into another that particular day.

Staffing policy Strategy concerned with selecting employees for particular jobs.

Stakeholders The individuals or groups that have an interest, stake, or claim in the actions and overall performance of a company.

Stock of foreign direct investment The total accumulated value of foreign-owned assets at a given time.

Strategic alliances Cooperative agreements between two or more firms.

Strategic commitment A decision that has a long-term impact and is difficult to reverse, such as entering a foreign market on a large scale.

Strategic pricing Pricing aimed at giving a company a competitive advantage over its rivals.

Strategic trade policy Government policy aimed at improving the competitive position of a domestic industry or domestic firm in the world market.

Strategy Actions managers take to attain the firm's goals.

Subsidy Government financial assistance to a domestic producer.

Sullivan principles A twofold approach to doing business in apartheid South Africa, comprising passive resistance to apartheid laws and attempts to influence the abolition of apartheid laws.

Switch trading The use of a specialized third-party trading house in a countertrade arrangement.

Tariff A tax levied on imports.

Tariff rate quota The process of applying a lower tariff rate to imports within the import quota than those over the quota.

Technical analysis Uses price and volume data to determine past trends, which are expected to continue into the future.

Theocratic law system A system of law based on religious teachings.

Theocratic totalitarianism A political system in which political power is monopolized by a party, group, or individual that governs according to religious principles.

Time draft A promise to pay by the accepting party at some future date.

Timing of entry Entry is early when a firm enters a foreign market before other foreign firms and late when a firm enters after other international businesses have established themselves.

Total quality management (TQM) Management philosophy that takes as its central focus the need to improve the quality of a company's products and services.

Totalitarianism Form of government in which one person or political party exercises absolute control over all spheres of human life and opposing political parties are prohibited.

Trade creation Trade created due to regional economic integration; occurs when high-cost domestic producers are replaced by low-cost foreign producers in a free trade area.

Trade diversion Trade diverted due to regional economic integration; occurs when low-cost foreign suppliers outside a free trade area are replaced by higher-cost foreign suppliers in a free trade area.

Trademark Designs and names, often officially registered, by which merchants or manufacturers designate and differentiate their products.

Transaction exposure The extent to which income from individual transactions is affected by fluctuations in foreign exchange values.

Translation exposure The extent to which the reported consolidated results and balance sheets of a corporation are affected by fluctuations in foreign exchange values.

Transnational strategy Attempt to simultaneously achieve low costs through location economies, economies of scale, and learning effects while also differentiating product offerings across geographic markets to account for local differences and fostering multidirectional flows of skills between different subsidiaries in the firm's global network of operations.

Treaty of Lisbon Treaty signed in 2007 that made the European Parliament the co-equal legislator for almost all European laws and also created the position of the president of the European Council.

Treaty of Rome The 1957 treaty that established the European Community.

Tribal totalitarianism A political system in which a party, group, or individual that represents the interests of a particular tribe (ethnic group) monopolizes political power.

Turnkey project A project in which a firm agrees to set up an operating plant for a foreign client and hand over the "key" when the plant is fully operational.

Uncertainty avoidance Extent to which cultures socialize members to accept ambiguous situations and to tolerate uncertainty.

United Nations An international organization made up of 191 countries headquartered in New York City, formed in 1945 to promote peace, security, and cooperation.

United Nations Convention on Contracts for the International Sale of Goods (CIGS) A set of rules governing certain aspects of the making and performance of commercial contracts between sellers and buyers who have their places of businesses in different nations.

Universal Declaration of Human Rights A United Nations document that lays down the basic principles of human rights that should be adhered to.

Universal needs Needs that are the same all over the world, such as steel, bulk chemicals, and industrial electronics.

Utilitarian approaches to ethics These hold that the moral worth of actions or practices is determined by their consequences.

Value creation Performing activities that increase the value of goods or services to consumers.

Values Abstract ideas about what a society believes to be good, right, and desirable.

Voluntary export restraint (VER) A quota on trade imposed from the exporting country's side, instead of the importer's; usually imposed at the request of the importing country's government.

Wholly owned subsidiary A subsidiary in which the firm owns 100 percent of the stock.

World Bank International institution set up to promote general economic development in the world's poorer nations.

World Intellectual Property Organization An international organization whose members sign treaties to agree to protect intellectual property.

World Trade Organization (WTO) The organization that succeeded the General Agreement on Tariffs and Trade (GATT) as a result of the successful completion of the Uruguay Round of GATT negotiations.

Zero-sum game A situation in which an economic gain by one country results in an economic loss by another.

endnotes

Chapter 1

1. Trade statistics from World Trade Organization, "Trade to Expand by 9.5% in 2010 after a Dismal 2009," WTO press release, March 26, 2010. Foreign exchange statistics from Bank for International Settlements, www.bis.org/index.htm.

2. Thomas L. Friedman, *The World Is Flat* (New York: Farrar, Straus and Giroux, 2005).

3. Ibid.

4. T. Levitt, "The Globalization of Markets," *Harvard Business Review*, May–June 1983, pp. 92–102.

5. U.S. Department of Commerce, "A Profile of U.S. Exporting Companies, 2000–2001," February 2003; report available at www.census.gov/foreign-trade/aip/index.html#profile.

6. Ibid.

7. C. M. Draffen, "Going Global: Export Market Proves Profitable for Region's Small Businesses," *Newsday*, March 19, 2001, p. C18.

8. B. Benoit and R. Milne, "Germany's Best Kept Secret, How Its Exporters Are Betting the World," *Financial Times*, May 19, 2006, p. 11.

9. See F. T. Knickerbocker, *Oligopolistic Reaction and Multinational Enterprise* (Boston: Harvard Business School Press, 1973); and R. E. Caves, "Japanese Investment in the U.S.: Lessons for the Economic Analysis of Foreign Investment," *The World Economy* 16 (1993), pp. 279–300.

10. I. Metthee, "Playing a Large Part," *Seattle Post-Intelligencer*, April 9, 1994, p. 13.

11. D. Pritchard, "Are Federal Tax Laws and State Subsidies for Boeing 7E7 Selling America Short?" *Aviation Week*, April 12, 2004, pp. 74–75.

12. "Operating Profit," *The Economist*, August 16, 2008, pp. 74–76.

13. R. B. Reich, *The Work of Nations* (New York: A.A. Knopf, 1991).

14. United Nations, "The UN in Brief," www.un.org/Overview/brief.html.

15. J. A. Frankel, "Globalization of the Economy," *National Bureau of Economic Research Working Paper Series*, working paper no. 7858, 2000.

16. J. Bhagwati, *Protectionism* (Cambridge, MA: MIT Press, 1989).

17. F. Williams, "Trade Round Like This May Never Be Seen Again," *Financial Times*, April 15, 1994, p. 8.

18. W. Vieth, "Major Concessions Lead to Success for WTO Talks," *Los Angeles Times*, November 14, 2001, p. A1; and "Seeds Sown for Future Growth," *The Economist*, November 17, 2001, pp. 65–66.

19. Ibid.

20. World Trade Organization, *International Trade Trends and Statistics, 2009* (Geneva: WTO, 2009).

21. World Trade Organization, "Trade to Expand by 9.5% in 2010 after a Dismal 2009."

22. United Nations, *World Investment Report, 2009* (New York: United Nations, 2009); and "Global FFDI Flows continue to slide in 2009," UN Conference on Trade and Development press release, September 17, 2009.

23. World Trade Organization, *International Trade Trends and Statistics, 2008* (Geneva: WTO, 2008); and United Nations, *World Investment Report, 2008* (New York: United Nations, 2008).

24. United Nations, *World Investment Report, 2009*.

25. Moore's law is named after Intel founder Gordon Moore.

26. Frankel, "Globalization of the Economy."

27. J. G. Fernald and V. Greenfield, "The Fall and Rise of the Global Economy," *Chicago Fed Letters*, April 2001, pp. 1–4.

28. Data compiled from various sources and listed at www.internetworldstats.com/stats.htm.

29. From www.census.gov/mrts/www/ecomm.html, accessed May 15, 2009.

30. For a counterpoint, see "Geography and the Net: Putting It in Its Place," *The Economist*, August 11, 2001, pp. 18–20.

31. Frankel, "Globalization of the Economy."

32. Data from Bureau of Transportation Statistics, 2001.

33. Fernald and Greenfield, "The Fall and Rise of the Global Economy."

34. Data located at www.bts.gov/publications/us_ international_trade_and_freight_transportation_ trends/2003/index.html.

35. N. Hood and J. Young, *The Economics of the Multinational Enterprise* (New York: Longman, 1973).

36. United Nations, *World Investment Report, 2009*.

37. Ibid.

38. Ibid.

39. S. Chetty, "Explosive International Growth and Problems of Success among Small and Medium Sized Firms," *International Small Business Journal*, February 2003, pp. 5–28.

40. R. A. Mosbacher, "Opening Up Export Doors for Smaller Firms," *Seattle Times*, July 24, 1991, p. A7.

41. "Small Companies Learn How to Sell to the Japanese," *Seattle Times*, March 19, 1992.

42. Holstein, "Why Johann Can Export, but Johnny Can't."

43. N. Buckley and A. Ostrovsky, "Back to Business—How Putin's Allies Are Turning Russia into a Corporate State," *Financial Times*, June 19, 2006, p. 11.

44. J. E. Stiglitz, *Globalization and Its Discontents* (New York: W. W. Norton, 2003); J. Bhagwati, *In Defense of Globalization* (New York: Oxford University Press, 2004); and Friedman, *The World Is Flat*.

45. See, for example, Ravi Batra, *The Myth of Free Trade* (New York: Touchstone Books, 1993); William Greider, *One World, Ready or Not: The Manic Logic of Global Capitalism* (New York: Simon and Schuster, 1997); and D. Radrik, *Has Globalization Gone Too Far?* (Washington, DC: Institution for International Economics, 1997).

46. James Goldsmith, "The Winners and the Losers," in *The Case against the Global Economy*, eds. J. Mander and E. Goldsmith (San Francisco: Sierra Club, 1996); and Lou Dobbs, *Exporting America* (New York: Time Warner Books, 2004).

47. For an excellent summary, see "The Globalization of Labor," in *World Economic Outlook 2007* (Washington, DC: International Monetary Fund, April 2007), chap. 5. Also see R. Freeman, "Labor Market Imbalances," Harvard University Working Paper, www.bos.frb. org/economic/conf/conf51/papers/freeman.pdf, accessed June 14, 2007.

48. D. L. Bartlett and J. B. Steele, "America: Who Stole the Dream," *Philadelphia Inquirer*, September 9, 1996.

49. For example, see Paul Krugman, *Pop Internationalism* (Cambridge, MA: MIT Press, 1996).

50. For example, see B. Milanovic and L. Squire, "Does Tariff Liberalization Increase Wage Inequality?" *National Bureau of Economic Research Working Paper Series*, working paper no. 11046, January 2005; and B. Milanovic, "Can We Discern the Effect of Globalization on Income Distribution?" *World Bank Economic Review* 19 (2005), pp. 21–44. Also see the summary in "The Globalization of Labor."

51. Jared Bernstein, Elizabeth C. McNichol, Lawrence Mishel, and Robert Zahradnik, "Pulling Apart: A State by State Analysis of Income Trends," *Economic Policy Institute*, January 2000.

52. See "The Globalization of Labor."

53. M. Forster and M. Pearson, "Income Distribution and Poverty in the OECD Area," *OECD Economic Studies* 34 (2002).

54. Bernstein et al., "Pulling Apart."

55. See "The Globalization of Labor."

56. See Krugman, *Pop Internationalism*; and D. Belman and T. M. Lee, "International Trade and the Performance of U.S. Labor Markets," in *U.S. Trade Policy and Global Growth*, ed. R. A. Blecker (New York: Economic Policy Institute, 1996).

57. Freeman, "Labor Market Imbalances."

58. E. Goldsmith, "Global Trade and the Environment," in *The Case against the Global Economy*, eds. J. Mander and E. Goldsmith (San Francisco: Sierra Club, 1996).

59. P. Choate, *Jobs at Risk: Vulnerable U.S. Industries and Jobs under NAFTA* (Washington, DC: Manufacturing Policy Project, 1993).

60. Ibid.

61. B. Lomborg, *The Skeptical Environmentalist* (Cambridge: Cambridge University Press, 2001).

62. H. Nordstrom and S. Vaughan, *Trade and the Environment, World Trade Organization Special Studies No. 4* (Geneva: WTO, 1999).

63. Figures are from "Freedom's Journey: A Survey of the 20th Century. Our Durable Planet," *The Economist*, September 11, 1999, p. 30.

64. For an exhaustive review of the empirical literature, see B. R. Copeland and M. Scott Taylor, "Trade, Growth and the Environment," *Journal of Economic Literature*, March 2004, pp. 7–77.

65. G. M. Grossman and A. B. Krueger, "Economic Growth and the Environment," *Quarterly Journal of Economics* 110 (1995), pp. 353–78.

66. Krugman, *Pop Internationalism*.

67. R. Kuttner, "Managed Trade and Economic Sovereignty," in *U.S. Trade Policy and Global Growth*, ed. R. A. Blecker (New York: Economic Policy Institute, 1996).

68. Ralph Nader and Lori Wallach, "GATT, NAFTA, and the Subversion of the Democratic Process," in *U.S. Trade Policy and Global Growth*, ed. R. A. Blecker (New York: Economic Policy Institute, 1996), pp. 93–94.

69. Lant Pritchett, "Divergence, Big Time," *Journal of Economic Perspectives* 11, no. 3 (Summer 1997), pp. 3–18.

70. Ibid.

71. W. Easterly, "How Did Heavily Indebted Poor Countries Become Heavily Indebted?" *World Development*, October 2002, pp. 1677–96; and J. Sachs, *The End of Poverty* (New York: Penguin Books, 2006).

72. See D. Ben-David, H. Nordstrom, and L. A. Winters, *Trade, Income Disparity and Poverty. World Trade Organization Special Studies No. 5* (Geneva: WTO, 1999).

73. William Easterly, "Debt Relief," *Foreign Policy*, November–December 2001, pp. 20–26.

74. Jeffrey Sachs, "Sachs on Development: Helping the World's Poorest," *The Economist*, August 14, 1999, pp. 17–20.

75. World Trade Organization, *Annual Report 2003* (Geneva: WTO, 2004).

Chapter 2

1. Although as we shall see, there is not a strict one-to-one correspondence between political systems and economic systems. A. O. Hirschman, "The On-and-Off Again Connection between Political and Economic Progress," *American Economic Review* 84, no. 2 (1994), pp. 343–48.

2. For a discussion of the roots of collectivism and individualism, see H. W. Spiegel, *The Growth of Economic Thought* (Durham, NC: Duke University Press, 1991). A discussion of collectivism and individualism can be found in M. Friedman and R. Friedman, *Free to Choose* (London: Penguin Books, 1980).

3. For a classic summary of the tenets of Marxism details, see A. Giddens, *Capitalism and Modern Social Theory* (Cambridge: Cambridge University Press, 1971).

4. J. S. Mill, *On Liberty* (London: Longman's, 1865), p. 6.

5. A. Smith, *The Wealth of Nations, Vol. 1* (London: Penguin Books), p. 325.

6. R. Wesson, *Modern Government—Democracy and Authoritarianism*, 2nd ed. (Englewood Cliffs, NJ: Prentice Hall, 1990).

7. For a detailed but accessible elaboration of this argument, see Friedman and Friedman, *Free to Choose*. Also see P. M. Romer, "The Origins of Endogenous Growth," *Journal of Economic Perspectives* 8, no. 1 (1994), pp. 2–32.

8. T. W. Lippman, *Understanding Islam* (New York: Meridian Books, 1995).

9. "Islam's Interest," *The Economist*, January 18, 1992, pp. 33–34.

10. M. El Qorchi, "Islamic Finance Gears Up," *Finance and Development*, December 2005, pp. 46–50; and S. Timewell, "Islamic Finance—Virtual Concept to Critical Mass," *The Banker*, March, 2008, pp. 10–16.

11. This information can be found on the UN's Treaty Web site at http://untreaty.un.org/ENGLISH/bible/englishinternetbible/partI/chapterX/treaty17.asp.

12. International Court of Arbitration, www.iccwbo.org/index_court.asp.

13. D. North, *Institutions, Institutional Change, and Economic Performance* (Cambridge: Cambridge University Press, 1991).

14. "China's Next Revolution," *The Economist*, March 10, 2007, p. 9.

15. P. Klebnikov, "Russia's Robber Barons," *Forbes*, November 21, 1994, pp. 74–84; C. Mellow, "Russia: Making Cash from Chaos," *Fortune*, April 17, 1995, pp. 145–51; and "Mr Tatum Checks Out," *The Economist*, November 9, 1996, p. 78.

16. K. van Wolferen, *The Enigma of Japanese Power* (New York: Vintage Books, 1990), pp. 100–5.

17. P. Bardhan, "Corruption and Development: A Review of the Issues," *Journal of Economic Literature*, September 1997, pp. 1320–46.

18. K. M. Murphy, A. Shleifer, and R. Vishny, "Why Is Rent Seeking So Costly to Growth?" *American Economic Review* 83, no. 2 (1993), pp. 409–14.

19. Transparency International, "Global Corruption Report, 2009," www.transparency.org, 2009.

20. www.transparency.org.

21. J. Coolidge and S. Rose Ackerman, "High Level Rent Seeking and Corruption in African Regimes," World Bank policy research working paper no. 1780, June 1997; Murphy et al., "Why Is Rent Seeking So Costly to Growth?"; M. Habib and L. Zurawicki, "Corruption and Foreign Direct Investment," *Journal of International Business Studies* 33 (2002), pp. 291–307; J. E. Anderson and D. Marcouiller, "Insecurity and the Pattern of International Trade," *Review of Economics and Statistics* 84 (2002), pp. 342–52; T. S. Aidt, "Economic Analysis of Corruption: A Survey," *The Economic Journal* 113 (November 2003), pp. 632–53;

and D. A. Houston, "Can Corruption Ever Improve an Economy?" *Cato Institute* 27 (2007), pp. 325–43.

22. Details can be found at www.oecd.org/EN/home/0, EN-home-31-nodirectorate-no-nono-31,00.html.

23. Dale Stackhouse and Kenneth Ungar, "The Foreign Corrupt Practices Act: Bribery, Corruption, Record Keeping and More," *Indiana Lawyer*, April 21, 1993.

24. For an interesting discussion of strategies for dealing with the low cost of copying and distributing digital information, see the chapter on rights management in C. Shapiro and H. R. Varian, *Information Rules* (Boston: Harvard Business School Press, 1999). Also see Charles W. L. Hill, "Digital Piracy," *Asian Pacific Journal of Management*, 2007.

25. Douglass North has argued that the correct specification of intellectual property rights is one factor that lowers the cost of doing business and, thereby, stimulates economic growth and development. See North, *Institutions, Institutional Change, and Economic Performance*.

26. International Federation of the Phonographic Industry, *The Commercial Music Industry Global Piracy Report, 2005*, www.ifpi.org.

27. Business Software Alliance, "Sixth Annual BSA and IDC Global Software Piracy Study," May 2009, www.bsa.org, accessed April 5, 2010.

28. Ibid.

29. "Trade Tripwires," *The Economist*, August 27, 1994, p. 61.

30. World Bank, "World Development Indicators Online, 2010."

31. A. Sen, *Development as Freedom* (New York: Alfred A. Knopf, 1999).

32. G. M. Grossman and E. Helpman, "Endogenous Innovation in the Theory of Growth," *Journal of Economic Perspectives* 8, no. 1 (1994), pp. 23–44; and Romer, "The Origins of Endogenous Growth."

33. W. W. Lewis, *The Power of Productivity* (Chicago: University of Chicago Press, 2004).

34. F. A. Hayek, *The Fatal Conceit: Errors of Socialism* (Chicago: University of Chicago Press, 1989).

35. James Gwartney, Robert Lawson, and Walter Block, *Economic Freedom of the World: 1975–1995* (London: Institute of Economic Affairs, 1996).

36. North, *Institutions, Institutional Change, and Economic Performance*. See also Murphy et al., "Why Is Rent Seeking So Costly to Growth?"; and K. E. Maskus, "Intellectual Property Rights in the Global Economy," *Institute for International Economics*, 2000.

37. Hernando de Soto, *The Mystery of Capital: Why Capitalism Triumphs in the West and Fails Everywhere Else* (New York: Basic Books, 2000).

38. Hirschman, "The On-and-Off Again Connection between Political and Economic Progress"; and A. Przeworski and F. Limongi, "Political Regimes and Economic Growth," *Journal of Economic Perspectives* 7, no. 3 (1993), pp. 51–59.

39. Ibid.

40. For details of this argument, see M. Olson, "Dictatorship, Democracy, and Development," *American Political Science Review*, September 1993.

41. For example, see Jarad Diamond's Pulitzer Prize-winning book, *Guns, Germs, and Steel* (New York: W. W. Norton, 1997). Also see J. Sachs, "Nature, Nurture and Growth," *The Economist*, June 14, 1997, pp. 19–22; and J. Sachs, *The End of Poverty* (New York: Penguin Books, 2005).

42. Sachs, "Nature, Nurture and Growth."

43. "What Can the Rest of the World Learn from the Classrooms of Asia?" *The Economist*, September 21, 1996, p. 24.

44. J. Fagerberg, "Technology and International Differences in Growth Rates," *Journal of Economic Literature* 32 (September 1994), pp. 1147–75.

45. See The Freedom House Survey Team, "Freedom in the World: 2010" and associated materials, www.freedomhouse.org.

46. "Russia Downgraded to Not Free," Freedom House press release, December 20, 2004, www.freedomhouse.org.

47. Freedom House, "Democracies Century: A Survey of Political Change in the Twentieth Century, 1999," www.freedomhouse.org.

48. L. Conners, "Freedom to Connect," *Wired*, August 1997, pp. 105–6.

49. F. Fukuyama, "The End of History," *The National Interest* 16 (Summer 1989), p. 18.

50. S. P. Huntington, *The Clash of Civilizations and the Remaking of World Order* (New York: Simon & Schuster, 1996).

51. Ibid., p. 116.

52. United States Department of State, "Country Reports on Terrorism, 2008," archived at www.state.gov/s/ct/rls/crt/2007/103716.htm, accessed April 5, 2010.

53. United States National Counterterrorism Center, "Reports on Incidents of Terrorism, 2005," April 11, 2006.

54. S. Fisher, R. Sahay, and C. A. Vegh, "Stabilization and the Growth in Transition Economies: the Early

Experience," *Journal of Economic Perspectives* 10 (Spring 1996), pp. 45–66.

55. M. Miles et al., *2010 Index of Economic Freedom* (Washington, DC: Heritage Foundation, 2010).

56. International Monetary Fund, *World Economic Outlook: Focus on Transition Economies* (Geneva: IMF, October 2000).

57. J. C. Brada, "Privatization Is Transition—Is It?" *Journal of Economic Perspectives*, Spring 1996, pp. 67–86.

58. See S. Zahra et al., "Privatization and Entrepreneurial Transformation," *Academy of Management Review* 3, no. 25 (2000), pp. 509–24.

59. N. Brune, G. Garrett, and B. Kogut, "The International Monetary Fund and the Global Spread of Privatization," *IMF Staff Papers* 51, no. 2 (2003), pp. 195–219.

60. Fischer et al., "Stabilization and the Growth in Transition Economies."

61. J. Sachs, C. Zinnes, and Y. Eilat, "The Gains from Privatization in Transition Economies: Is Change of Ownership Enough?" CAER discussion paper no. 63 (Cambridge, MA: Harvard Institute for International Development, 2000).

62. J. Nellis, "Time to Rethink Privatization in Transition Economies?" *Finance and Development* 36, no. 2 (1999), pp. 16–19.

63. M. S. Borish and M. Noel, "Private Sector Development in the Visegrad Countries," *World Bank*, March 1997.

64. "Caught between Right and Left, Town and Country," *The Economist*, March 10, 2007, pp. 23–24.

65. For a discussion of first-mover advantages, see M. Liberman and D. Montgomery, "First-Mover Advantages," *Strategic Management Journal* 9 (Summer Special Issue, 1988), pp. 41–58.

66. S. H. Robock, "Political Risk: Identification and Assessment," *Columbia Journal of World Business*, July–August 1971, pp. 6–20.

Chapter 3

1. Mary Yoko Brannen, "When Mickey Loses Face: Recontextualization, Semantic Fit, and the Semiotics of Foreignness," *Academy of Management Review* 29, no. 4 (2004), pp. 593–616.

2. See R. Dore, *Taking Japan Seriously* (Stanford, CA: Stanford University Press, 1987).

3. Data come from J. Monger, "International Comparison of Labor Disputes in 2004," *Labor Market Trends*, April 2006, pp. 117–28.

4. E. B. Tylor, *Primitive Culture* (London: Murray, 1871).

5. Geert Hofstede, *Culture's Consequences: International Differences in Work-Related Values* (Beverly Hills, CA: Sage Publications, 1984), p. 21.

6. J. Z. Namenwirth and R. B. Weber, *Dynamics of Culture* (Boston: Allen & Unwin, 1987), p. 8.

7. R. Mead, *International Management: Cross-Cultural Dimensions* (Oxford: Blackwell Business, 1994), p. 7.

8. Edward T. Hall and M. R. Hall, *Understanding Cultural Differences* (Yarmouth, ME: Intercultural Press, 1990).

9. Edward T. Hall and M. R. Hall, *Hidden Differences: Doing Business with the Japanese* (New York: Doubleday, 1987).

10. "Iraq: Down but Not Out," *The Economist*, April 8, 1995, pp. 21–23.

11. S. P. Huntington, *The Clash of Civilizations* (New York: Simon & Schuster, 1996).

12. M. Thompson, R. Ellis, and A. Wildavsky, *Cultural Theory* (Boulder, CO: Westview Press, 1990).

13. M. Douglas, *In the Active Voice* (London: Routledge, 1982), pp. 183–254.

14. M. L. Dertouzos, R. K. Lester, and R. M. Solow, *Made in America* (Cambridge, MA: MIT Press, 1989).

15. C. Nakane, *Japanese Society* (Berkeley: University of California Press, 1970).

16. Ibid.

17. For details, see M. Aoki, *Information, Incentives, and Bargaining in the Japanese Economy* (Cambridge: Cambridge University Press, 1988); and Dertouzos et al., *Made in America*.

18. E. Luce, *The Strange Rise of Modern India* (Boston: Little Brown, 2006); and D. Pick and K. Dayaram, "Modernity and Tradition in the Global Era: The Re-invention of Caste in India," *International Journal of Sociology and Social Policy* 26, no. 7/8 (2006), pp. 284–301.

19. For an excellent historical treatment of the evolution of the English class system, see E. P. Thompson, *The Making of the English Working Class* (London: Vintage Books, 1966). See also R. Miliband, *The State in Capitalist Society* (New York: Basic Books, 1969), especially Chapter 2. For more recent studies of class in British societies, see Stephen Brook, *Class: Knowing Your Place in Modern Britain* (London: Victor Gollancz, 1997); A. Adonis and S. Pollard, *A Class Act: The Myth of Britain's Classless Society* (London: Hamish Hamilton, 1997); and J. Gerteis and M. Savage, "The Salience of Class in Britain and America: A Comparative Analysis," *British Journal of Sociology*, June 1998.

20. Adonis and Pollard, *A Class Act*.

21. Y. Bian, "Chinese Social Stratification and Social Mobility," *Annual Review of Sociology* 28 (2002), pp. 91–117.

22. N. Goodman, *An Introduction to Sociology* (New York: HarperCollins, 1991).

23. R. J. Barro and R. McCleary, "Religion and Economic Growth across Countries," *American Sociological Review*, October 2003, pp. 760–82.

24. M. Weber, *The Protestant Ethic and the Spirit of Capitalism* (New York: Charles Scribner's Sons, 1958, original 1904–1905). For an excellent review of Weber's work, see A. Giddens, *Capitalism and Modern Social Theory* (Cambridge: Cambridge University Press, 1971).

25. Weber, *The Protestant Ethic and the Spirit of Capitalism*, p. 35.

26. A. S. Thomas and S. L. Mueller, "The Case for Comparative Entrepreneurship," *Journal of International Business Studies* 31, no. 2 (2000), pp. 287–302; and S. A. Shane, "Why Do Some Societies Invent More than Others?" *Journal of Business Venturing* 7 (1992), pp. 29–46.

27. See S. M. Abbasi, K. W. Hollman, and J. H. Murrey, "Islamic Economics: Foundations and Practices," *International Journal of Social Economics* 16, no. 5 (1990), pp. 5–17; and R. H. Dekmejian, *Islam in Revolution: Fundamentalism in the Arab World* (Syracuse, NY: Syracuse University Press, 1995).

28. T. W. Lippman, *Understanding Islam* (New York: Meridian Books, 1995).

29. Dekmejian, *Islam in Revolution.*

30. M. K. Nydell, *Understanding Arabs* (Yarmouth, ME: Intercultural Press, 1987).

31. Lippman, *Understanding Islam.*

32. The material in this section is based largely on Abbasi et al., "Islamic Economics."

33. "Islamic Finance: Calling the Faithful," *The Economist*, December 9ᵗ, 2006, pp. 77–78; and "Savings and Souls," *The Economist*, September 6, 2008, pp. 81–83.

34. "Forced Devotion," *The Economist*, February 17, 2001, pp. 76–77.

35. For details of Weber's work and views, see Giddens, *Capitalism and Modern Social Theory.*

36. See, for example, the views expressed in "A Survey of India: The Tiger Steps Out," *The Economist*, January 21, 1995.

37. See R. Dore, *Taking Japan Seriously*; and C. W. L. Hill, "Transaction Cost Economizing as a Source of Comparative Advantage: The Case of Japan," *Organization Science* 6 (1995).

38. C. C. Chen, Y. R. Chen, and K. Xin, "Guanxi Practices and Trust in Management," *Organization Science* 15, no. 2 (March–April 2004), pp. 200–10.

39. See Aoki, *Information, Incentives, and Bargaining*; and J. P. Womack, D. T. Jones, and D. Roos, *The Machine That Changed the World* (New York: Rawson Associates, 1990).

40. For examples of this line of thinking, see M. W. Peng and P. S. Heath, "The Growth of the Firm in Planned Economies in Transition," *Academy of Management Review* 21 (1996), pp. 492–528; M. W. Peng, *Business Strategies in Transition Economies* (Thousand Oaks, CA: Sage, 2000); and M. W. Peng and Y. Luo, "Managerial Ties and Firm Performance in a Transition Economy," *Academy of Management Journal*, June 2000, pp. 486–501.

41. This hypothesis dates back to two anthropologists, Edward Sapir and Benjamin Lee Whorf. See E. Sapir, "The Status of Linguistics as a Science," *Language* 5 (1929), pp. 207–14; and B. L. Whorf, *Language, Thought, and Reality* (Cambridge, MA: MIT Press, 1956).

42. The tendency has been documented empirically. See A. Annett, "Social Fractionalization, Political Instability, and the Size of Government," *IMF Staff Papers* 48 (2001), pp. 561–92.

43. D. A. Ricks, *Big Business Blunders: Mistakes in Multinational Marketing* (Homewood, IL: Dow Jones-Irwin, 1983).

44. Goodman, *An Introduction to Sociology.*

45. M. E. Porter, *The Competitive Advantage of Nations* (New York: Free Press, 1990).

46. Ibid., pp. 395–97.

47. G. Hofstede, "The Cultural Relativity of Organizational Practices and Theories," *Journal of International Business Studies*, Fall 1983, pp. 75–89; and G. Hofstede, *Cultures and Organizations: Software of the Mind* (New York: McGraw-Hill, 1997).

48. For a more detailed critique, see R. Mead, *International Management: Cross-Cultural Dimensions* (Oxford: Blackwell, 1994), pp. 73–75.

49. For example, see W. J. Bigoness and G. L. Blakely, "A Cross-National Study of Managerial Values," *Journal of International Business Studies*, December 1996, p. 739; D. H. Ralston, D. H. Holt, R. H. Terpstra, and Y. Kai-Cheng, "The Impact of National Culture and Economic Ideology on Managerial Work Values," *Journal of International Business Studies* 28, no. 1 (1997), pp. 177–208; P. B. Smith, M. F. Peterson, and Z. Ming Wang, "The Manager as a Mediator of Alternative Meanings," *Journal of International Business Studies* 27, no. 1 (1996), pp. 115–37; and L. Tang and P. E. Koves, "A Framework to Update Hofstede's

Cultural Value Indices," *Journal of International Business Studies* 39 (2008), pp. 1045–63.

50. G. Hofstede and M. H. Bond, "The Confucius Connection," *Organizational Dynamics* 16, no. 4 (1988), pp. 5–12; and G. Hofstede, *Culture's Consequences: Comparing Values, Behaviors, Institutions and Organizations across Nations* (Thousand Oaks, CA: Sage, 2001).

51. R. S. Yeh and J. J. Lawerence, "Individualism and Confucian Dynamism," *Journal of International Business Studies* 26, no. 3 (1995), pp. 655–66.

52. For evidence of this, see R. Inglehart. "Globalization and Postmodern Values," *The Washington Quarterly*, Winter 2000, pp. 215–28.

53. Mead, *International Management*, chap. 17.

54. "Free, Young, and Japanese," *The Economist*, December 21, 1991.

55. Namenwirth and Weber, *Dynamics of Culture;* and Inglehart, "Globalization and Postmodern Values."

56. G. Hofstede, "National Cultures in Four Dimensions," *International Studies of Management and Organization* 13, no. 1, pp. 46–74; and Tang and Koves, "A Framework to Update Hofstede's Cultural Value Indices."

57. See Inglehart, "Globalization and Postmodern-Values." For updates, go to http://wvs.isr.umich.edu/index.html.

58. Hofstede, "National Cultures in Four Dimensions."

59. Hall and Hall, *Understanding Cultural Differences.*

60. See Aoki, *Information, Incentives, and Bargaining;* Dertouzos et al., *Made in America;* and Porter, *The Competitive Advantage of Nations*, pp. 395–97.

61. For empirical work supporting such a view, see Annett, "Social Fractionalization, Political Instability, and the Size of Government."

Chapter 4

1. S. Greenhouse, "Nike Shoe Plant in Vietnam Is Called Unsafe for Workers," *The New York Times*, November 8, 1997; and V. Dobnik, "Chinese Workers Abused Making Nikes, Reeboks," *Seattle Times*, September 21, 1997, p. A4.

2. Thomas Donaldson, "Values in Tension: Ethics Away from Home," *Harvard Business Review*, September–October 1996.

3. Robert Kinloch Massie, *Loosing the Bonds: The United States and South Africa in the Apartheid Years* (New York: Doubleday, 1997).

4. Not everyone agrees that the divestment trend had much influence on the South African economy. For a counterview see Siew Hong Teoh, Ivo Welch, and

C. Paul Wazzan, "The Effect of Socially Activist Investing on the Financial Markets: Evidence from South Africa," *The Journal of Business* 72, no. 1 (January 1999), pp. 35–60.

5. Andy Rowell, "Trouble Flares in the Delta of Death; Shell Has Polluted More Than Ken Saro Wiwa's Oroniland in Nigeria," *The Guardian*, November 8, 1995, p. 6.

6. H. Hamilton, "Shell's New World Wide View," *Washington Post*, August 2, 1998, p. H1.

7. Rowell, "Trouble Flares in the Delta of Death."

8. Peter Singer, *One World: The Ethics of Globalization.* (New Haven, CT: Yale University Press, 2002).

9. Garrett Hardin, "The Tragedy of the Commons," *Science* 162, no. 1 (1968), pp. 1243–48.

10. For a summary of the evidence see S. Solomon, D. Qin, M. Manning, Z. Chen, M. Marquis, K. B. Avery, M. Tignor, and H. L. Miller, eds., *Contribution of Working Group I to the Fourth Assessment Report of the Intergovernmental Panel on Climate Change* (Cambridge: Cambridge University Press, 2007).

11. J. Everett, D. Neu, and A. S. Rahaman, "The Global Fight Against Corruption," *Journal of Business Ethics* 65 (2006), pp. 1–18.

12. Richard T. De George, *Competing with Integrity in International Business* (Oxford: Oxford University Press, 1993).

13. Details can be found at www.oecd.org/EN/home/0,,EN-home-31-nodirectorate-no-nono-31,00.html.

14. Bardhan Pranab, "Corruption and Development," *Journal of Economic Literature* 36 (September 1997), pp. 1320–46.

15. A. Shleifer and R. W. Vishny, "Corruption," *Quarterly Journal of Economics*, no. 108 (1993), pp. 599–617; and I. Ehrlich and F. Lui, "Bureaucratic Corruption and Endogenous Economic Growth," *Journal of Political Economy* 107 (December 1999), pp. 270–92.

16. P. Mauro, "Corruption and Growth," *Quarterly Journal of Economics*, no. 110 (1995), pp. 681–712.

17. Detailed at www.iit.edu/departments/csep/PublicWWW/codes/coe/Bus_Conduct_Dow_Corning (1996).html.

18. S. A. Waddock and S. B. Graves, "The Corporate Social Performance-Financial Performance Link," *Strategic Management Journal* 8 (1997), pp. 303–19.

19. Daniel Litvin, *Empires of Profit* (New York: Texere, 2003).

20. Details can be found at BP's Web site, www.bp.com.

21. This is known as the "when in Rome perspective." Donaldson, "Values in Tension: Ethics Away from Home."

22. De George, *Competing with Integrity in International Business.*

23. For a discussion of the ethics of using child labor, see J. Isern, "Bittersweet Chocolate: The Legacy of Child Labor in Cocoa Production in Cote d'Ivoire," *Journal of Applied Management and Entrepreneurship* 11 (2006), pp. 115–32.

24. Saul W. Gellerman, "Why Good Managers Make Bad Ethical Choices," in *Ethics in Practice: Managing the Moral Corporation*, ed. Kenneth R. Andrews (Cambridge, MA: Harvard Business School Press, 1989).

25. David Messick and Max H. Bazerman, "Ethical Leadership and the Psychology of Decision Making," *Sloan Management Review* 37 (Winter 1996), pp. 9–20.

26. Robert Bryce, *Pipe Dreams: Greed, Ego and the Death of Enron* (New York: Public Affairs, 2002).

27. Milton Friedman, "The Social Responsibility of Business Is to Increase Profits," *The New York Times Magazine*, September 13, 1970. Reprinted in Tom L. Beauchamp and Norman E. Bowie, *Ethical Theory and Business*, 7th ed. (Upper Saddle River, NJ: Prentice Hall, 2001).

28. Friedman, "The Social Responsibility of Business Is to Increase Profits," p. 55.

29. For example, see Donaldson, "Values in Tension: Ethics Away from Home." See also Norman Bowie, "Relativism and the Moral Obligations of Multination Corporations," in Beauchamp and Bowie, *Ethical Theory and Business.*

30. For example, see De George, *Competing with Integrity in International Business.*

31. Details can be found at www.bp.com/sectiongeneri carticle.do?category1d=79&contentId=2002369 #2014689.

32. This example is often repeated in the literature on international business ethics. It was first outlined by Arthur Kelly in "Case Study—Italian Style Mores." Printed in Thomas Donaldson and Patricia Werhane, *Ethical Issues in Business* (Englewood Cliffs, NJ: Prentice Hall, 1979).

33. See Beauchamp and Bowie, *Ethical Theory and Business.*

34. Thomas Donaldson, *The Ethics of International Business* (Oxford: Oxford University Press, 1989).

35. Found at www.un.org/Overview/rights.html.

36. Donaldson, *The Ethics of International Business.*

37. See Chapter 10 in Beauchamp and Bowie, *Ethical Theory and Business.*

38. John Rawls, *A Theory of Justice*, rev. ed. (Cambridge, MA: Belknap Press, 1999).

39. Found on Unilever's Web site at www.unilever.com/ company/ourprinciples/.

40. Joseph Bower and Jay Dial, "Jack Welch: General Electrics Revolutionary," Harvard Business School Case, Case #9-394-065, April 1994.

41. For example, see R. Edward Freeman and Daniel Gilbert, *Corporate Strategy and the Search for Ethics* (Englewood Cliffs, NJ: Prentice Hall, 1988); Thomas Jones, "Ethical Decision Making by Individuals in Organizations," *Academy of Management Review* 16 (1991), pp. 366–95; and J. R. Rest, *Moral Development: Advances in Research and Theory* (New York: Praeger, 1986).

42. Ibid.

43. See E. Freeman, *Strategic Management: A Stakeholder Approach* (Boston: Pitman Press, 1984); C. W. L. Hill and T. M. Jones, "Stakeholder-Agency Theory," *Journal of Management Studies* 29 (1992), pp. 131–54; and J. G. March and H. A. Simon, *Organizations* (New York: John Wiley & Sons, Inc., 1958).

44. Hill and Jones, "Stakeholder-Agency Theory," and March and Simon, *Organizations.*

45. De George, *Competing with Integrity in International Business.*

46. The code can be accessed at United Technologies Web site, www.utc.com/profile/ethics/index.htm.

47. Colin Grant, "Whistle Blowers: Saints of Secular Culture," *Journal of Business Ethics*, September 2002, pp. 391–400.

48. Found on Unilever's Web site, www.unilever.com/ company/ourprinciples/.

Chapter 5

1. H. W. Spiegel, *The Growth of Economic Thought* (Durham, NC: Duke University Press, 1991).

2. M. Solis, "The Politics of Self-Restraint: FDI Subsidies and Japanese Mercantilism," *The World Economy* 26 (February 2003), pp. 153–70; A. Browne, "China's Wild Swings Can Roil the Global Economy," *The Wall Street Journal*, October 24, 2005, p. A2; S. H. Hanke, "Stop the Mercantilists," *Forbes*, June 20, 2005, p. 164; G. Dyer and A. Balls, "Dollar Threat as China Signals Shift," *Financial Times*, January 6, 2006, p. 1; Tim Annett, "Righting the Balance," *The Wall Street Journal*, January 10, 2007, p. 15; "China's Trade Surplus Peaks," *Financial Times*, January 12, 2008, p. 1; and W. Chong, "China's Trade Surplus to U.S. to Narrow," *China Daily*, December 7, 2009.

3. S. Hollander, *The Economics of David Ricardo* (Buffalo: The University of Toronto Press, 1979).

4. D. Ricardo, *The Principles of Political Economy and Taxation* (Homewood, IL: Irwin, 1967, first published in 1817).

5. For example, R. Dornbusch, S. Fischer, and P. Samuelson, "Comparative Advantage: Trade and Payments

in a Ricardian Model with a Continuum of Goods," *American Economic Review* 67 (December 1977), pp. 823–39.

6. B. Balassa, "An Empirical Demonstration of Classic Comparative Cost Theory," *Review of Economics and Statistics*, 1963, pp. 231–38.

7. See P. R. Krugman, "Is Free Trade Passé?" *Journal of Economic Perspectives* 1 (Fall 1987), pp. 131–44.

8. P. Samuelson, "Where Ricardo and Mill Rebut and Confirm Arguments of Mainstream Economists Supporting Globalization," *Journal of Economic Perspectives* 18, no. 3 (Summer 2004), pp. 135–46.

9. P. Samuelson, "The Gains from International Trade Once Again," *Economic Journal* 72 (1962), pp. 820–29.

10. S. Lohr, "An Elder Challenges Outsourcing's Orthodoxy," *The New York Times*, September 9, 2004, p. C1.

11. Samuelson, "Where Ricardo and Mill Rebut and Confirm Arguments of Mainstream Economists Supporting Globalization," p. 143.

12. See A. Dixit and G. Grossman, "Samuelson Says Nothing About Trade Policy," Princeton University, 2004, accessed from http://www.princeton.edu/~dixitak/home/.

13. J. Bhagwati, A. Panagariya, and T. N. Sirinivasan, "The Muddles over Outsourcing," *Journal of Economic Perspectives* 18, no. 4 (Fall 2004), pp. 93–114.

14. For example, J. D. Sachs and A. Warner, "Economic Reform and the Process of Global Integration," *Brookings Papers on Economic Activity*, 1995, pp. 1–96; J. A. Frankel and D. Romer, "Does Trade Cause Growth?" *American Economic Review* 89, no. 3 (June 1999), pp. 379–99; and D. Dollar and A. Kraay, "Trade, Growth and Poverty," Working Paper, Development Research Group, World Bank, June 2001. Also, for an accessible discussion of the relationship between free trade and economic growth, see T. Taylor, "The Truth about Globalization," *Public Interest*, Spring 2002, pp. 24–44; and D. Acemoglu, S. Johnson, and J. Robinson, "The Rise of Europe: Atlantic Trade, Institutional Change and Economic Growth, *American Economic Review* 95, no. 3 (2005), pp. 547–79.

15. Sachs and Warner, "Economic Reform and the Process of Global Integration."

16. Ibid., pp. 35–36.

17. R. Wacziarg and K. H. Welch, "Trade Liberalization and Growth: New Evidence," *National Bureau of Economic Research Working Paper Series*, working paper no. 10152, December 2003.

18. Frankel and Romer, "Does Trade Cause Growth?"

19. A recent skeptical review of the empirical work on the relationship between trade and growth questions these results. See Francisco Rodriguez and Dani Rodrik, "Trade Policy and Economic Growth: A Skeptics Guide to the Cross-National Evidence," *National Bureau of Economic Research*, working paper no. 7081, April 1999. Even these authors, however, cannot find any evidence that trade hurts economic growth or income levels.

20. B. Ohlin, *Interregional and International Trade* (Cambridge: Harvard University Press, 1933). For a summary, see R. W. Jones and J. P. Neary, "The Positive Theory of International Trade," in *Handbook of International Economics*, eds. R. W. Jones and P. B. Kenen (Amsterdam: North Holland, 1984).

21. W. Leontief, "Domestic Production and Foreign Trade: The American Capital Position Re- Examined," *Proceedings of the American Philosophical Society* 97 (1953), pp. 331–49.

22. R. M. Stern and K. Maskus, "Determinants of the Structure of U.S. Foreign Trade," *Journal of International Economics* 11 (1981), pp. 207–44.

23. See H. P. Bowen, E. E. Leamer, and L. Sveikayskas, "Multicountry, Multifactor Tests of the Factor Abundance Theory," *American Economic Review* 77 (1987), pp. 791–809.

24. D. Trefler, "The Case of the Missing Trade and Other Mysteries," *American Economic Review* 85 (December 1995), pp. 1029–46.

25. D. R. Davis and D. E. Weinstein, "An Account of Global Factor Trade," *American Economic Review*, December 2001, pp. 1423–52.

26. R. Vernon, "International Investments and International Trade in the Product Life Cycle," *Quarterly Journal of Economics*, May 1966, pp. 190–207; and R. Vernon and L. T. Wells, *The Economic Environment of International Business*, 4th ed. (Englewood Cliffs, NJ: Prentice Hall, 1986).

27. For a good summary of this literature, see E. Helpman and P. Krugman, *Market Structure and Foreign Trade: Increasing Returns, Imperfect Competition, and the International Economy* (Boston: MIT Press, 1985). Also see P. Krugman, "Does The New Trade Theory Require a New Trade Policy?" *World Economy* 15, no. 4 (1992), pp. 423–41.

28. M. B. Lieberman and D. B. Montgomery, "First- Mover Advantages," *Strategic Management Journal* 9 (Summer 1988), pp. 41–58; and W. T. Robinson and Sungwook Min, "Is the First to Market the First to Fail?" *Journal of Marketing Research* 29 (2002), pp. 120–28.

29. J. R. Tybout, "Plant and Firm Level Evidence on New Trade Theories," *National Bureau of Economic Research Working Paper Series*, working paper no. 8418, August 2001 (paper available at http://www.nber.org); and S. Deraniyagala and B. Fine, "New Trade Theory Versus Old Trade Policy: A

Continuing Enigma," *Cambridge Journal of Economics* 25 (November 2001), pp. 809–25.

30. A. D. Chandler, *Scale and Scope* (New York: Free Press, 1990).

31. Krugman, "Does the New Trade Theory Require a New Trade Policy?"

32. M. E. Porter, *The Competitive Advantage of Nations* (New York: Free Press, 1990). For a good review of this book, see R. M. Grant, "Porter's Competitive Advantage of Nations: An Assessment," *Strategic Management Journal* 12 (1991), pp. 535–48.

33. B. Kogut, ed., *Country Competitiveness: Technology and the Organizing of Work* (New York: Oxford University Press, 1993).

34. Porter, *The Competitive Advantage of Nations*, p. 121.

35. Lieberman and Montgomery, "First-Mover Advantages." See also Robinson and Min, "Is the First to Market the First to Fail?"; W. Boulding and M. Christen, "First Mover Disadvantage," *Harvard Business Review*, October 2001, pp. 20–21; and R. Agarwal and M. Gort, "First Mover Advantage and the Speed of Competitive Entry," *Journal of Law and Economics* 44 (2001), pp. 131–59.

36. C. A. Hamilton, "Building Better Machine Tools," *Journal of Commerce*, October 30, 1991, p. 8; and "Manufacturing Trouble," *The Economist*, October 12, 1991, p. 71.

37. J. W. Peters, "U.S. Trade Deficit Grew to Another Record in 06," *The New York Times*, February 14, 2007, p. 1.

38. P. Krugman, *The Age of Diminished Expectations* (Cambridge, MA: MIT Press, 1990).

39. D. Griswold, "Are Trade Deficits a Drag on U.S. Economic Growth," *Free Trade Bulletin*, March 12, 2007, Cato Institute; and O. Blanchard, "Current Account Deficits in Rich Countries," *NBER Working Paper Series*, working paper no. 12925, February 2007.

40. S. Edwards, "The U.S. Current Account Deficit: Gradual Correction or Abrupt Adjustment?" *NBER Working Paper Series*, working paper no. 12154, April 2006.

Chapter 6

1. For a detailed welfare analysis of the effect of a tariff, see P. R. Krugman and M. Obstfeld, *International Economics: Theory and Policy* (New York: HarperCollins, 2000), chap. 8.

2. Y. Sazanami, S. Urata, and H. Kawai, *Measuring the Costs of Protection in Japan* (Washington, DC: Institute for International Economics, 1994).

3. J. Bhagwati, *Protectionism* (Cambridge, MA: MIT Press, 1988); and "Costs of Protection," *Journal of Commerce*, September 25, 1991, p. 8A.

4. World Trade Organization, *World Trade Report 2006* (Geneva: WTO, 2006).

5. The study was undertaken by Kym Anderson of the University of Adelaide. See "A Not So Perfect Market," *The Economist; Survey of Agriculture and Technology*, March 25, 2000, pp. 8–10.

6. K. Anderson, W. Martin, and D. van der Mensbrugghe, "Distortions to World Trade: Impact on Agricultural Markets and Farm Incomes," *Review of Agricultural Economics* 28 (Summer 2006), pp. 168–94.

7. R. W. Crandall, *Regulating the Automobile* (Washington, DC: Brookings Institution, 1986).

8. Krugman and Obstfeld, *International Economics*.

9. G. Hufbauer and Z. A. Elliott, *Measuring the Costs of Protectionism in the United States* (Washington, DC: Institute for International Economics, 1993).

10. Bhagwati, *Protectionism;* and "Japan to Curb VCR Exports," *The New York Times*, November 21, 1983, p. D5.

11. Alan Goldstein, "Sematech Members Facing Dues Increase; 30% Jump to Make Up for Loss of Federal Funding," *Dallas Morning News*, July 27, 1996, p. 2F.

12. N. Dunne and R. Waters, "U.S. Waves a Big Stick at Chinese Pirates," *Financial Times*, January 6, 1995, p. 4.

13. B. Tomson, "U.S. Beef Heads Back to China," *Barron's*, December 26, 2005, p. M16.

14. Bill Lambrecht, "Monsanto Softens Its Stance on Labeling in Europe," *St. Louis Post-Dispatch*, March 15, 1998, p. E1.

15. Peter S. Jordan, "Country Sanctions and the International Business Community," *American Society of International Law Proceedings of the Annual Meeting* 20, no. 9 (1997), pp. 333–42.

16. "Waiting for China; Human Rights and International Trade," *Commonwealth*, March 11, 1994; and "China: The Cost of Putting Business First," *Human Rights Watch*, July 1996.

17. For a comprehensive review of the evidence, see B. R. Copeland and M. Scott Taylor, "Trade, Growth and the Environment," *Journal of Economic Literature* 42 (March 2004), pp. 7–71.

18. For accessible summaries of the issues, see T. Flannery, *The Weather Makers* (New York: Grove Press, 2005); and J. Houghton, *Global Warming: The Complete Briefing* (Cambridge: Cambridge University Press, 1994).

19. S. Solomon et al., eds., *Contribution of Working Group I to the Fourth Assessment Report of the Intergovernmental Panel on Climate Change, 2007* (Cambridge: Cambridge University Press, 2007).

20. Ibid.

21. Copeland and Taylor, "Trade, Growth and the Environment."

22. "Brazil's Auto Industry Struggles to Boost Global Competitiveness," *Journal of Commerce*, October 10, 1991, p. 6A.

23. For reviews, see J. A. Brander, "Rationales for Strategic Trade and Industrial Policy," in *Strategic Trade Policy and the New International Economics*, ed. P. R. Krugman (Cambridge, MA: MIT Press, 1986); P. R. Krugman, "Is Free Trade Passé?" *Journal of Economic Perspectives* 1 (1987), pp. 131–44; and P. R. Krugman, "Does the New Trade Theory Require a New Trade Policy?" *World Economy* 15, no. 4 (1992), pp. 423–41.

24. "Airbus and Boeing: The Jumbo War," *The Economist*, June 15, 1991, pp. 65–66.

25. For details see Krugman, "Is Free Trade Passé?"; and Brander, "Rationales for Strategic Trade and Industrial Policy."

26. Krugman, "Is Free Trade Passé?"

27. This dilemma is a variant of the famous prisoner's dilemma, which has become a classic metaphor for the difficulty of achieving cooperation between self-interested and mutually suspicious entities. For a good general introduction, see A. Dixit and B. Nalebuff, *Thinking Strategically: The Competitive Edge in Business, Politics, and Everyday Life* (New York: W. W. Norton & Co., 1991).

28. Note that the Smoot-Hawley Act did not cause the Great Depression. However, the beggar-thy-neighbor trade policies that it ushered in certainly made things worse. See Bhagwati, *Protectionism*.

29. Ibid.

30. World Bank, *World Development Report* (New York: Oxford University Press, 1987).

31. World Trade Organization, *World Trade Report, 2008* (Geneva: WTO, 2008).

32. Frances Williams, "WTO—New Name Heralds New Powers," *Financial Times*, December 16, 1993, p. 5; and Frances Williams, "Gatt's Successor to Be Given Real Clout," *Financial Times*, April 4, 1994, p. 6.

33. W. J. Davey, "The WTO Dispute Settlement System: The First Ten Years," *Journal of International Economic Law*, March 2005, pp. 17–28.

34. Information provided on WTO Web site, www.wto.org/english/tratop_e/dispu_e/dispu_status_e.htm.

35. Frances Williams, "Telecoms: World Pact Set to Slash Costs of Calls," *Financial Times*, February 17, 1997.

36. G. De Jonquieres, "Happy End to a Cliff Hanger," *Financial Times*, December 15, 1997, p. 15.

37. Jim Carlton, "Greens Target WTO Plan for Lumber," *The Wall Street Journal*, November 24, 1999, p. A2.

38. Kari Huus, "WTO Summit Leaves Only Discontent," MSNBC, December 3, 1999, www.msnbc.com.

39. Data at www.wto.org/english/tratop_e/adp_e/adp_e.htm.

40. *Annual Report by the Director General 2003* (Geneva: World Trade Organization, 2003).

41. Ibid.

42. Ibid.

43. Anderson, Martin, and van der Mensbrugghe, "Distortions to World Trade: Impact on Agricultural Markets and Farm Incomes."

44. World Trade Organization, *Annual Report 2002* (Geneva: WTO, 2002).

45. A. Tanzer, "Pill Factory to the World," *Forbes*, December 10, 2001, pp. 70–72.

46. S. C. Bradford, P. L. E. Grieco, and G. C. Hufbauer, "The Payoff to America from Global Integration," in *The United States and the World Economy: Foreign Policy for the Next Decade*, ed. C. F. Bergsten (Washington, DC: Institute for International Economics, 2005).

47. World Bank, *Global Economic Prospects 2005* (Washington, DC: World Bank, 2005).

48. "Doha Development Agenda," *OECD Observer*, September 2006, pp. 64–67.

49. W. Vieth, "Major Concessions Lead to Success for WTO Talks," *Los Angeles Times*, November 14, 2001, p. A1; and "Seeds Sown for Future Growth," *The Economist*, November 17, 2001, pp. 65–66.

50. "The WTO under Fire—The Doha Round," *The Economist*, September 20, 2003, pp. 30–32.

51. "Punitive Tariffs Are Approved on Imports of Japanese Steel," *The New York Times*, June 12, 1999, p. A3.

Chapter 7

1. United Nations, *World Investment Report, 2009* (New York and Geneva: United Nations, 2009).

2. Ibid.; and "Global FFDI Flows Continue to Slide in 2009," UN Conference on Trade and Development press release, September 17, 2009.

3. World Trade Organization, *International Trade Statistics, 2008* (Geneva: WTO, 2008); and United Nations, *World Investment Report, 2008* (New York and Geneva: United Nations, 2008).

4. United Nations, *World Investment Report, 2009*.

5. Ibid.

6. Ibid.

7. Ibid.

8. Ibid.

9. Ibid.

10. Ibid.

11. Ibid.

12. See D. J. Ravenscraft and F. M. Scherer, *Mergers, Sell-offs and Economic Efficiency* (Washington, DC: The Brookings Institution, 1987); and A. Seth, K. P. Song, and R. R. Pettit, "Value Creation and Destruction in Cross-Border Acquisitions," *Strategic Management Journal* 23 (2002), pp. 921–40.

13. For example, see S. H. Hymer, *The International Operations of National Firms: A Study of Direct Foreign Investment* (Cambridge, MA: MIT Press, 1976); A. M. Rugman, *Inside the Multinationals: The Economics of Internal Markets* (New York: Columbia University Press, 1981); D. J. Teece, "Multinational Enterprise, Internal Governance, and Industrial Organization," *American Economic Review* 75 (May 1983), pp. 233–38; C. W. L. Hill and W. C. Kim, "Searching for a Dynamic Theory of the Multinational Enterprise: A Transaction Cost Model," *Strategic Management Journal* 9 (special issue, 1988), pp. 93–104; A. Verbeke, "The Evolutionary View of the MNE and the Future of Internalization Theory," *Journal of International Business Studies* 34 (2003), pp. 498–501; and J. H. Dunning, "Some Antecedents of Internalization Theory," *Journal of International Business Studies* 34 (2003), pp. 108–28.

14. J. P. Womack, D. T. Jones, and D. Roos, *The Machine that Changed the World* (New York: Rawson Associates, 1990).

15. The argument is most often associated with F. T. Knickerbocker, *Oligopolistic Reaction and Multinational Enterprise* (Boston: Harvard Business School Press, 1973).

16. The studies are summarized in R. E. Caves, *Multinational Enterprise and Economic Analysis*, 2nd ed. (Cambridge, UK: Cambridge University Press, 1996).

17. See R. E. Caves, "Japanese Investment in the US: Lessons for the Economic Analysis of Foreign Investment," *The World Economy* 16 (1993), pp. 279–300; B. Kogut and S. J. Chang, "Technological Capabilities and Japanese Direct Investment in the United States," *Review of Economics and Statistics* 73 (1991), pp. 401–43; and J. Anand and B. Kogut, "Technological Capabilities of Countries, Firm Rivalry, and Foreign Direct Investment," *Journal of International Business Studies*, 1997, pp. 445–65.

18. K. Ito and E. L. Rose, "Foreign Direct Investment Location Strategies in the Tire Industry," *Journal of International Business Studies* 33 (2002), pp. 593–602.

19. H. Haveman and L. Nonnemaker, "Competition in Multiple Geographical Markets," *Administrative Science Quarterly* 45 (2000), pp. 232–67; and L. Fuentelsaz and J. Gomez, "Multipoint Competition, Strategic Similarity and Entry into Geographic Markets," *Strategic Management Journal* 27 (2006), pp. 447–57.

20. For the use of Vernon's theory to explain Japanese direct investment in the United States and Europe, see S. Thomsen, "Japanese Direct Investment in the European Community," *The World Economy* 16 (1993), pp. 301–15. Also see Z. Gao and C. Tisdell, "Foreign Investment and Asia, Particularly China's Rise in the Television Industry: The International Product Life Cycle Reconsidered," *Journal of Asia-Pacific Business* 6, no. 3 (2005), pp. 37–50.

21. J. H. Dunning, *Explaining International Production* (London: Unwin Hyman, 1988).

22. P. Krugman, "Increasing Returns and Economic Geography," *Journal of Political Economy* 99, no. 3 (1991), pp. 483–99.

23. J. M. Shaver and F. Flyer, "Agglomeration Economies, Firm Heterogeneity, and Foreign Direct Investment in the United States," *Strategic Management Journal* 21 (2000), pp. 1175–93.

24. J. H. Dunning and R. Narula, "Transpacific Foreign Direct Investment and the Investment Development Path," *South Carolina Essays in International Business*, May 1995.

25. W. Shan and J. Song, "Foreign Direct Investment and the Sourcing of Technological Advantage: Evidence from the Biotechnology Industry," *Journal of International Business Studies* 28, no. 2 (1997), pp. 267–84.

26. For some additional evidence, see L. E. Brouthers, K. D. Brouthers, and S. Warner, "Is Dunning's Eclectic Framework Descriptive or Normative?" *Journal of International Business Studies* 30 (1999), pp. 831–44.

27. For elaboration, see S. Hood and S. Young, *The Economics of the Multinational Enterprise* (London: Longman, 1979); and P. M. Sweezy and H. Magdoff, "The Dynamics of U.S. Capitalism," *Monthly Review Press*, 1972.

28. C. Forelle and G. Hitt, "IBM Discusses Security Measure in Lenovo Deal," *The Wall Street Journal*, February 25, 2005, p. A2.

29. For an example of this policy as practiced in China, see L. G. Branstetter and R. C. Freenstra, "Trade and Foreign Direct Investment in China: A Political Economy Approach," *Journal of International Economics* 58 (December 2002), pp. 335–58.

30. M. Itoh and K. Kiyono, "Foreign Trade and Direct Investment," in *Industrial Policy of Japan*, ed. R. Komiya, M. Okuno, and K. Suzumura (Tokyo: Academic Press, 1988).

31. R. E. Lipsey, "Home and Host Country Effects of FDI," *National Bureau of Economic Research Working Paper Series*, working paper no. 9293, October 2002; and X. Li and X. Liu, "Foreign Direct Investment and Economic Growth," *World Development* 33 (March 2005), pp. 393–413.

32. X. J. Zhan and T. Ozawa, *Business Restructuring in Asia: Cross Border M&As in Crisis Affected Countries* (Copenhagen: Copenhagen Business School, 2000); I. Costa, S. Robles, and R. de Queiroz, "Foreign Direct Investment and Technological Capabilities," *Research Policy* 31 (2002), pp. 1431–43; B. Potterie and F. Lichtenberg, "Does Foreign Direct Investment Transfer Technology across Borders?" *Review of Economics and Statistics* 83 (2001), pp. 490–97; and K. Saggi, "Trade, Foreign Direct Investment and International Technology Transfer," *World Bank Research Observer* 17 (2002), pp. 191–235.

33. K. M. Moden, "Foreign Acquisitions of Swedish Companies: Effects on R&D and Productivity," Stockholm: Research Institute of International Economics, 1998, mimeo.

34. "Foreign Friends," *The Economist*, January 8, 2000, pp. 71–72.

35. A. Jack, "French Go into Overdrive to Win Investors," *Financial Times*, December 10, 1997, p. 6.

36. "Foreign Friends."

37. G. Hunya and K. Kalotay, *Privatization and Foreign Direct Investment in Eastern and Central Europe* (Geneva: UNCTAD, 2001).

38. United Nations, *World Investment Report, 2002* (New York and Geneva: United Nations, 2002).

39. R. Ram and K. H. Zang, "Foreign Direct Investment and Economic Growth," *Economic Development and Cultural Change* 51 (2002), pp. 205–25.

40. United Nations, *World Investment Report, 1998* (New York and Geneva: United Nations, 1997).

41. United Nations, *World Investment Report, 2000* (New York and Geneva: United Nations, 2000).

42. R. B. Reich, *The Work of Nations: Preparing Ourselves for the 21st Century* (New York: Alfred A. Knopf, 1991).

43. This idea has been articulated, although not quite in this form, by C. A. Bartlett and S. Ghoshal, *Managing across Borders: The Transnational Solution* (Boston: Harvard Business School Press, 1989).

44. P. Magnusson, "The Mexico Pact: Worth the Price?" *BusinessWeek*, May 27, 1991, pp. 32–35.

45. C. Johnston, "Political Risk Insurance," in *Assessing Corporate Political Risk*, ed. D. M. Raddock (Totowa, NJ: Rowan & Littlefield, 1986).

46. M. Tolchin and S. Tolchin, *Buying into America: How Foreign Money Is Changing the Face of Our Nation* (New York: Times Books, 1988).

47. S. Rai, "India to Ease Limits on Foreign Ownership of Media and Tea," *The New York Times*, June 26, 2002, p. W1.

48. L. D. Qiu and Z. Tao, "Export, Foreign Direct Investment and Local Content Requirements," *Journal of Development Economics* 66 (October 2001), pp. 101–25.

49. United Nations, *World Investment Report, 2003* (New York and Geneva: United Nations, 2003).

50. See R. E. Caves, *Multinational Enterprise and Economic Analysis* (Cambridge, UK: Cambridge University Press, 1982).

51. For a good general introduction to negotiation strategy, see M. H. Bazerman and M. A. Neale, *Negotiating Rationally* (New York: Free Press, 1992); A. Dixit and B. Nalebuff, *Thinking Strategically: The Competitive Edge in Business, Politics, and Everyday Life* (New York: W. W. Norton, 1991); and H. Raiffa, *The Art and Science of Negotiation* (Cambridge, MA: Harvard University Press, 1982).

Chapter 8

1. Information taken from World Trade Organization Web site and current as of February 2010, www.wto.org.

2. Ibid.

3. The Andean Pact has been through a number of changes since its inception. The latest version was established in 1991. See "Free-Trade Free for All," *The Economist*, January 4, 1991, p. 63.

4. D. Swann, *The Economics of the Common Market*, 6th ed. (London: Penguin Books, 1990).

5. See J. Bhagwati, "Regionalism and Multilateralism: An Overview," Columbia University Discussion Paper 603, Department of Economics, Columbia University, New York; A. de la Torre and M. Kelly, "Regional Trade Arrangements," Occasional Paper 93, Washington, DC: International Monetary Fund, March 1992; J. Bhagwati, "Fast Track to Nowhere," *The Economist*, October 18, 1997, pp. 21–24; Jagdish Bhagwati, *Free Trade Today* (Princeton and Oxford: Princeton University Press, 2002); and B. K. Gordon, "A High Risk Trade Policy," *Foreign Affairs* 82 no. 4 (July/August 2003), pp. 105–15.

6. N. Colchester and D. Buchan, *Europower: The Essential Guide to Europe's Economic Transformation in 1992* (London: The Economist Books, 1990), and Swann, *Economics of the Common Market*.

7. A. S. Posen, "Fleeting Equality, The Relative Size of the EU and US Economies in 2020," The Brookings Institution, September 2004.

8. Swann, *Economics of the Common Market*; Colchester and Buchan, *Europower: The Essential Guide to Europe's Economic Transformation in 1992*; "The European Union: A Survey," *The Economist*, October 22, 1994;

"The European Community: A Survey," *The Economist*, July 3, 1993; and the European Union Web site at http://europa.eu.int.

9. E. J. Morgan, "A Decade of EC Merger Control," *International Journal of Economics and Business*, November 2001, pp. 451–73.

10. "The European Community: A Survey."

11. Tony Barber, "The Lisbon Reform Treaty," *FT.com*, December 13, 2007.

12. "One Europe, One Economy," *The Economist*, November 30, 1991, pp. 53–54; and "Market Failure: A Survey of Business in Europe," *The Economist*, June 8, 1991, pp. 6–10.

13. Alan Riley, "The Single Market Ten Years On," *European Policy Analyst*, December 2002, pp. 65–72.

14. See C. Wyploze, "EMU: Why and How It Might Happen," *Journal of Economic Perspectives* 11 (1997), pp. 3–22; and M. Feldstein, "The Political Economy of the European Economic and Monetary Union," *Journal of Economic Perspectives* 11 (1997), pp. 23–42.

15. "One Europe, One Economy"; and Feldstein, "The Political Economy of the European Economic and Monetary Union."

16. Feldstein, "The Political Economy of the European Economic and Monetary Union."

17. "Time for Europhoria?" *The Economist*, January 4, 2003, p. 58.

18. "The Passing of the Buck?" *The Economist*, December 4, 2004, pp. 78–80.

19. Details regarding conditions of membership and the progression of enlargement negotiations can be found at http:europa.eu.int/comm/enlargement/index.htm.

20. "What Is NAFTA?" *Financial Times*, November 17, 1993, p. 6; and S. Garland, "Sweet Victory," *BusinessWeek*, November 29, 1993, pp. 30–31.

21. "NAFTA: The Showdown," *The Economist*, November 13, 1993, pp. 23–36.

22. N. C. Lustog, "NAFTA: Setting the Record Straight," *The World Economy*, 1997, pp. 605–14; and G. C. Hufbauer and J. J. Scott, *NAFTA Revisited: Achievements and Challenges* (Washington, DC: Institute for International Economics, 2005).

23. W. Thorbecke and C. Eigen-Zucchi, "Did NAFTA Cause a Giant Sucking Sound?" *Journal of Labor Research*, Fall 2002, pp. 647–58; G. Gagne, "North American Free Trade, Canada, and U.S. Trade Remedies: An Assessment after Ten Years," *The World Economy*, 2000, pp. 77–91; Hufbauer and Schott, *NAFTA Revisited*; and J. Romalis, "NAFTA's and Custfa's Impact on International Trade," *Review of Economics and Statistics* 98, no. 3 (2007), pp. 416–35.

24. All trade figures from U.S. Department of Commerce Trade Stat Express Web site at http://tse.export.gov/.

25. J. Cavanagh et al., "Happy Ever NAFTA?" *Foreign Policy*, September–October 2002, pp. 58–65.

26. "The Business of the American Hemisphere," *The Economist*, August 24, 1991, pp. 37–38.

27. "NAFTA Is Not Alone," *The Economist*, June 18, 1994, pp. 47–48.

28. "Murky Mercosur," *The Economist*, July 26, 1997, pp. 66–67.

29. See M. Philips, "South American Trade Pact under Fire," *The Wall Street Journal*, October 23, 1996, p. A2; A. J. Yeats, *Does Mercosur's Trade Performance Justify Concerns about the Global Welfare-Reducing Effects of Free Trade Arrangements? Yes!* (Washington, DC: World Bank, 1996); and D. M. Leipziger et al., "Mercosur: Integration and Industrial Policy," *The World Economy*, 1997, pp. 585–604.

30. "Another Blow to Mercosur," *The Economist*, March 31, 2001, pp. 33–34.

31. "Lula Lays Out Mercosur Rescue Mission," *Latin America Newsletters*, February 4, 2003, p. 7.

32. "A Free Trade Tug of War," *The Economist*, December 11, 2004, p. 54.

33. "CARICOM Single Market Begins," *EIU Views*, February 3, 2006.

34. M. Esterl, "Free Trade Area of the Americas Stalls," *The Economist*, January 19, 2005, p. 1.

35. M. Moffett and J. D. McKinnon, "Failed Summit Casts Shadow on Global Trade Talks," *The Wall Street Journal*, November 7, 2005, p. A1.

36. "Every Man for Himself: Trade in Asia," *The Economist*, November 2, 2002, pp. 43–44.

37. L. Gooch, "Asian Free-Trade Zone Raises Hopes," *The New York Times*, January 1st, 2010, p. B3.

38. "Aimless in Seattle," *The Economist*, November 13, 1993, pp. 35–36.

39. G. de Jonquieres, "APEC Grapples with Market Turmoil," *Financial Times*, November 21, 1997, p. 6; and G. Baker, "Clinton Team Wins Most of the APEC Tricks," *Financial Times*, November 27, 1997, p. 5.

40. M. Turner, "Trio Revives East African Union," *Financial Times*, January 16, 2001, p. 4.

41. P. Davis, "A European Campaign: Local Companies Rush for a Share of EC Market While Barriers Are Down," *Minneapolis-St. Paul City Business*, January 8, 1990, p. 1.

42. "The Business of Europe," *The Economist*, December 7, 1991, pp. 63–64.

43. T. Horwitz, "Europe's Borders Fade," *The Wall Street Journal*, May 18, 1993, pp. A1, A12; "A Singular Market," *The Economist*, October 22, 1994, pp. 10–16; and "Something Dodgy in Europe's Single Market," *The Economist*, May 21, 1994, pp. 69–70.

44. E. G. Friberg, "1992: Moves Europeans Are Making," *Harvard Business Review*, May–June 1989, pp. 85–89.

Chapter 9

1. For a good general introduction to the foreign exchange market, see R. Weisweiller, *How the Foreign Exchange Market Works* (New York: New York Institute of Finance, 1990). A detailed description of the economics of foreign exchange markets can be found in P. R. Krugman and M. Obstfeld, *International Economics: Theory and Policy* (New York: HarperCollins, 1994).

2. "The Domino Effect," *The Economist*, July 5, 2008, p. 85.

3. Bank for International Settlements, *Tri-annual Central Bank Survey of Foreign Exchange and Derivatives Market Activity*, April 2007 (Basle, Switzerland: BIS, December 2007).

4. Ibid.

5. Ibid.

6. M. Dickson, "Capital Gain: How London Is Thriving as it Takes on the Global Competition," *Financial Times*, March 27, 2006, p. 11.

7. For a comprehensive review, see M. Taylor, "The Economics of Exchange Rates," *Journal of Economic Literature* 33 (1995), pp. 13–47.

8. Krugman and Obstfeld, *International Economics: Theory and Policy*.

9. M. Friedman, *Studies in the Quantity Theory of Money* (Chicago: University of Chicago Press, 1956). For an accessible explanation, see M. Friedman and R. Friedman, *Free to Choose* (London: Penguin Books, 1979), chap. 9.

10. Juan-Antino Morales, "Inflation Stabilization in Bolivia," in *Inflation Stabilization: The Experience of Israel, Argentina, Brazil, Bolivia, and Mexico*, ed. Michael Bruno et al. (Cambridge, MA: MIT Press, 1988); and The Economist, *World Book of Vital Statistics* (New York: Random House, 1990).

11. For reviews and recent articles see, H. J. Edison, J. E. Gagnon, and W. R. Melick, "Understanding the Empirical Literature on Purchasing Power Parity," *Journal of International Money and Finance* 16 (February 1997), pp. 1–18; J. R. Edison, "Multi-Country Evidence on the Behavior of Purchasing Parity under the Current Float," *Journal of International Money and Finance* 16 (February 1997), pp. 19–36;

K. Rogoff, "The Purchasing Power Parity Puzzle," *Journal of Economic Literature* 34 (1996), pp. 647–68; D. R. Rapach and M. E. Wohar, "Testing the Monetary Model of Exchange Rate Determination: New Evidence from a Century of Data," *Journal of International Economics*, December 2002, pp. 359–85; and M. P. Taylor, "Purchasing Power Parity," *Review of International Economics*, August 2003, pp. 436–456.

12. M. Obstfeld and K. Rogoff, "The Six Major Puzzles in International Economics," *National Bureau of Economic Research Working Paper Series*, working paper no. 7777, July 2000.

13. Ibid.

14. See M. Devereux and C. Engel, "Monetary Policy in the Open Economy Revisited: Price Setting and Exchange Rate Flexibility," *National Bureau of Economic Research Working Paper Series*, working paper no. 7665, April 2000. Also P. Krugman, "Pricing to Market When the Exchange Rate Changes," in *Real Financial Economics*, ed. S. Arndt and J. Richardson (Cambridge, MA: MIT Press, 1987).

15. For a summary of the evidence, see the survey by Taylor, "The Economics of Exchange Rates."

16. R. E. Cumby and M. Obstfeld, "A Note on Exchange Rate Expectations and Nominal Interest Differentials: A Test of the Fisher Hypothesis," *Journal of Finance*, June 1981, pp. 697–703; and L. Coppock and M. Poitras, "Evaluating the Fisher Effect in Long Term Cross Country Averages," *International Review of Economics and Finance* 9 (2000), pp. 181–203.

17. Taylor, "The Economics of Exchange Rates." See also R. K. Lyons, *The Microstructure Approach to Exchange Rates* (Cambridge, MA: MIT Press, 2002).

18. See H. L. Allen and M. P. Taylor, "Charts, Noise, and Fundamentals in the Foreign Exchange Market," *Economic Journal* 100 (1990), pp. 49–59; and T. Ito, "Foreign Exchange Rate Expectations: Micro Survey Data," *American Economic Review* 80 (1990), pp. 434–49.

19. For example, see E. Fama, "Forward Rates as Predictors of Future Spot Rates," *Journal of Financial Economics*, October 1976, pp. 361–77.

20. L. Kilian and M. P. Taylor, "Why Is It so Difficult to Beat the Random Walk Forecast of Exchange Rates?" *Journal of International Economics* 20 (May 2003), pp. 85–103; and R. M. Levich, "The Efficiency of Markets for Foreign Exchange," in *International Finance*, ed. G. D. Gay and R. W. Kold (Richmond, VA: Robert F. Dane, Inc., 1983).

21. J. Williamson, *The Exchange Rate System* (Washington, DC: Institute for International Economics, 1983); and R. H. Clarida, L. Sarno, M. P. Taylor, and G. Valente, "The Out of Sample Success of Term

Structure Models as Exchange Rate Predictors," *Journal of International Economics* 60 (May 2003), pp. 61–84.

22. Kilian and Taylor, "Why Is It So Difficult to Beat the Random Walk Forecast of Exchange Rates."

23. Rogoff, "The Purchasing Power Parity Puzzle."

24. C. Engel and J. D. Hamilton, "Long Swings in the Dollar: Are They in the Data and Do Markets Know It?" *American Economic Review*, September 1990, pp. 689–713.

25. J. R. Carter and J. Gagne, "The Do's and Don'ts of International Countertrade," *Sloan Management Review*, Spring 1988, pp. 31–37.

26. "Where There Is a Will," *Trade Finance*, October 2003, pp. 1–2.

27. D. S. Levine, "Got a Spare Destroyer Lying Around?" *World Trade* 10 (June 1997), pp. 34–35; and Dan West, "Countertrade," *Business Credit*, April 2001, pp. 64–67.

28. For details on how various firms manage their foreign exchange exposure, see the articles contained in the special foreign exchange issue of *Business International Money Report*, December 18, 1989, pp. 401–12.

29. Ibid.

30. S. Arterian, "How Black & Decker Defines Exposure," *Business International Money Report*, December 18, 1989, pp. 404, 405, 409.

Chapter 10

1. Updates can be found at the IMF Web site: www .imf.org.

2. The argument goes back to 18th century philosopher David Hume. See D. Hume, "On the Balance of Trade," reprinted in *The Gold Standard in Theory and in History*, ed. B. Eichengreen (London: Methuen, 1985).

3. R. Solomon, *The International Monetary System, 1945–1981* (New York: Harper & Row, 1982).

4. International Monetary Fund, *World Economic Outlook, 2005* (Washington, DC: IMF, May 2005).

5. For an extended discussion of the dollar exchange rate in the 1980s, see B. D. Pauls, "US Exchange Rate Policy: Bretton Woods to the Present," *Federal Reserve Bulletin*, November 1990, pp. 891–908.

6. R. Miller, "Why the Dollar Is Giving Way," *BusinessWeek*, December 6, 2004, pp. 36–37.

7. For a feel for the issues contained in this debate, see P. Krugman, *Has the Adjustment Process Worked?* (Washington, DC: Institute for International Economics, 1991); "Time to Tether Currencies," *The Economist*, January 6, 1990, pp. 15–16; P. R. Krugman and M. Obstfeld, *International Economics: Theory and*

Policy (New York: HarperCollins, 1994); J. Shelton, *Money Meltdown* (New York: Free Press, 1994); and S. Edwards, "Exchange Rates and the Political Economy of Macroeconomic Discipline," *American Economic Review* 86, no. 2 (May 1996), pp. 159–63.

8. The argument is made by several prominent economists, particularly Stanford's Robert McKinnon. See R. McKinnon, "An International Standard for Monetary Stabilization," *Policy Analyses in International Economics* 8 (1984). The details of this argument are beyond the scope of this book. For a relatively accessible exposition, see P. Krugman, *The Age of Diminished Expectations* (Cambridge, MA: MIT Press, 1990).

9. A. R. Ghosh, J. D. Ostry, A. M. Gulde, and H.C. Wolf, "Does the Exchange Rate Regime Matter for Inflation and Growth?" *IMF Economic Issues No. 2*, 1997.

10. "The ABC of Currency Boards," *The Economist*, November 1, 1997, p. 80.

11. International Monetary Fund, *World Economic Outlook, 1998* (Washington, DC: IMF, 1998).

12. Ibid.

13. See P. Carroll and C. Torres, "Mexico Unveils Program of Harsh Fiscal Medicine," *The Wall Street Journal*, March 10, 1995, pp. A1, A6; and "Putting Mexico Together Again," *The Economist*, February 4, 1995, p. 65.

14. World Trade Organization, *Annual Report, 1997*, vol. II, table III, p. 69.

15. J. Ridding and J. Kynge, "Complacency Gives Way to Contagion," *Financial Times*, January 13, 1998, p. 8.

16. J. Burton and G. Baker, "The Country That Invested Its Way into Trouble," *Financial Times*, January 15, 1998, p. 8.

17. P. Shenon, "The Suharto Billions," *The New York Times*, January 16, 1998, p. 1.

18. World Bank, *1997 World Development Report* (Oxford: Oxford University Press, 1998), Table 11.

19. Ridding and Kynge, "Complacency Gives Way to Contagion."

20. Burton and Baker, "The Country That Invested Its Way into Trouble."

21. "Bitter Pill for the Thais," *Straits Times*, July 5, 1997, p. 46.

22. World Bank, *1997 World Development Report*, Table 2.

23. International Monetary Fund, press release no. 97/37, August 20, 1997.

24. T. S. Shorrock, "Korea Starts Overhaul; IMF Aid Hits $60 Billion," *Journal of Commerce*, December 8, 1997, p. 3A.

25. See J. Sachs, "Economic Transition and Exchange Rate Regime," *American Economic Review* 86, no. 92 (May 1996), pp. 147–52; and J. Sachs, "Power unto Itself," *Financial Times*, December 11, 1997, p. 11.

26. Sachs, "Power unto Itself."

27. Martin Wolf, "Same Old IMF Medicine," *Financial Times*, December 9, 1997, p. 12.

28. Sachs, "Power unto Itself."

29. "New Fund, Old Fundamentals," *The Economist*, May 2, 2009, p. 78.

30. P. Gumbel and B. Coleman, "Daimler Warns of Severe '95 Loss Due to Strong Mark," *The New York Times*, June 29, 1995, pp. 1, 10; and M. Wolf, "Daimler-Benz Announces Major Losses," *Financial Times*, June 29, 1995, p. 1.

Chapter 11

1. More formally, ROIC = Net profit after tax/Capital, where capital includes the sum of the firm's equity and debt. This way of calculating profitability is highly correlated with return on assets.

2. T. Copeland, T. Koller, and J. Murrin, *Valuation: Measuring and Managing the Value of Companies* (New York: John Wiley & Sons, Inc., 2000).

3. The concept of consumer surplus is an important one in economics. For a more detailed exposition, see D. Besanko, D. Dranove, and M. Shanley, *Economics of Strategy* (New York: John Wiley & Sons, Inc., 1996).

4. However, $P = V$ only in the special case where the company has a perfect monopoly, and where it can charge each customer a unique price that reflects the value of the product to that customer (i.e., where perfect price discrimination is possible). More generally, except in the limiting case of perfect price discrimination, even a monopolist will see most consumers capture some of the value of a product in the form of a consumer surplus.

5. This point is central to the work of Michael Porter, *Competitive Advantage* (New York: Free Press, 1985). See also chap. 4 in P. Ghemawat, *Commitment: The Dynamic of Strategy* (New York: Free Press, 1991).

6. M. E. Porter, *Competitive Strategy* (New York: Free Press, 1980).

7. M. E. Porter, "What Is Strategy?" *Harvard Business Review*, On-point Enhanced Edition article, February 1, 2000.

8. Porter, *Competitive Advantage*.

9. D. Naidler, M. Gerstein, and R. Shaw, *Organization Architecture* (San Francisco: Jossey-Bass, 1992).

10. G. Morgan, *Images of Organization* (Beverly Hills, CA: Sage Publications, 1986).

11. Empirical evidence does seem to indicate that, on average, international expansion is linked to greater firm profitability. For some recent examples, see M. A. Hitt, R. E. Hoskisson, and H. Kim, "International Diversification, Effects on Innovation and Firm Performance," *Academy of Management Journal* 40, no. 4 (1997), pp. 767–98; and S. Tallman and J. Li, "Effects of International Diversity and Product Diversity on the Performance of Multinational Firms," *Academy of Management Journal* 39, no. 1 (1996), pp. 179–96.

12. This concept has been popularized by G. Hamel and C. K. Prahalad, *Competing for the Future* (Boston: Harvard Business School Press, 1994). The concept is grounded in the resource-based view of the firm; for a summary, see J. B. Barney, "Firm Resources and Sustained Competitive Advantage," *Journal of Management* 17 (1991), pp. 99–120; and K. R. Conner, "A Historical Comparison of Resource-Based Theory and Five Schools of Thought within Industrial Organization Economics: Do We Have a New Theory of the Firm?" *Journal of Management* 17 (1991), pp. 121–54.

13. J. P. Womack, D. T. Jones, and D. Roos, *The Machine That Changed the World* (New York: Rawson Associates, 1990).

14. M. E. Porter, *The Competitive Advantage of Nations* (New York: Free Press, 1990).

15. Example is based on C. S. Trager, "Enter the Mini-Multinational," *Northeast International Business*, March 1989, pp. 13–14.

16. See R. B. Reich, *The Work of Nations* (New York: Alfred A. Knopf, 1991); and P. J. Buckley and N. Hashai, "A Global System View of Firm Boundaries," *Journal of International Business Studies*, January 2004, pp. 33–50.

17. D. Barboza, "An Unknown Giant Flexes Its Muscles," *The New York Times*, December 4, 2004, pp. B1, B3.

18. G. Hall and S. Howell, "The Experience Curve from an Economist's Perspective," *Strategic Management Journal* 6 (1985), pp. 197–212.

19. A. A. Alchain, "Reliability of Progress Curves in Airframe Production," *Econometrica* 31 (1963), pp. 697–93.

20. Hall and Howell, "The Experience Curve from an Economist's Perspective."

21. For a full discussion of the source of scale economies, see D. Besanko, D. Dranove, and M. Shanley, *Economics of Strategy* (New York: John Wiley & Sons, Inc., 1996).

22. This estimate was provided by the Pharmaceutical Manufacturers Association.

23. "Matsushita Electrical Industrial in 1987," in *Transnational Management*, eds. C. A. Bartlett and S. Ghoshal (Homewood, IL: Richard D. Irwin, 1992).

24. See J. Birkinshaw and N. Hood, "Multinational Subsidiary Evolution: Capability and Charter Change in Foreign Owned Subsidiary Companies," *Academy of Management Review* 23 (October 1998), pp. 773–95; A. K. Gupta and V. J. Govindarajan, "Knowledge Flows within Multinational Corporations," *Strategic Management Journal* 21 (2000), pp. 473–96; V. J. Govindarajan and A. K. Gupta, *The Quest for Global Dominance* (San Francisco: Jossey Bass, 2001); T. S. Frost, J. M. Birkinshaw, and P. C. Ensign, "Centers of Excellence in Multinational Corporations," *Strategic Management Journal* 23 (2002), pp. 997–1018; and U. Andersson, M. Forsgren, and U. Holm, "The Strategic Impact of External Networks," *Strategic Management Journal* 23 (2002), pp. 979–96.

25. S. Leung, "Armchairs, TVs and Espresso: Is It McDonald's?" *The Wall Street Journal*, August 30, 2002, pp. A1, A6.

26. C. K. Prahalad and Yves L. Doz, *The Multinational Mission: Balancing Local Demands and Global Vision* (New York: Free Press, 1987). Also see J. Birkinshaw, A. Morrison, and J. Hulland, "Structural and Competitive Determinants of a Global Integration Strategy," *Strategic Management Journal* 16 (1995), pp. 637–55; and P. Ghemawat, *Redefining Global Strategy* (Boston: Harvard Business School Press, 2007).

27. J. E. Garten, "Wal-Mart Gives Globalization a Bad Name," *BusinessWeek*, March 8, 2004, p. 24.

28. Prahalad and Doz, *The Multinational Mission: Balancing Local Demands and Global Vision*. Prahalad and Doz actually talk about local responsiveness rather than local customization.

29. T. Levitt, "The Globalization of Markets," *Harvard Business Review*, May–June 1983, pp. 92–102.

30. K. Belson, "In U.S., Cell Phone Users Are Often All Talk," *The New York Times*, December 13, 2004, pp. C1, C4.

31. W. W. Lewis, *The Power of Productivity* (Chicago: University of Chicago Press, 2004).

32. C. J. Chipello, "Local Presence Is Key to European Deals," *The Wall Street Journal*, June 30, 1998, p. A15.

33. Bartlett and Ghoshal, *Managing across Borders*.

34. Ibid. Pankaj Ghemawat makes a similar argument, although he does not use the term *transnational*. See Ghemawat, *Redefining Global Strategy*.

35. T. Hout, M. E. Porter, and E. Rudden, "How Global Companies Win Out," *Harvard Business Review*, September–October 1982, pp. 98–108.

36. See K. Ohmae, "The Global Logic of Strategic Alliances," *Harvard Business Review*, March–April 1989, pp. 143–54; G. Hamel, Y. L. Doz, and C. K. Prahalad, "Collaborate with Your Competitors and Win!" *Harvard Business Review*, January–February 1989, pp. 133–39; W. Burgers, C. W. L. Hill, and W. C. Kim, "Alliances in the Global Auto Industry," *Strategic Management Journal* 14 (1993), pp. 419–32; and P. Kale, H. Singh, H. Perlmutter, "Learning and Protection of Proprietary Assets in Strategic Alliances: Building Relational Capital," *Strategic Management Journal* 21 (2000), pp. 217–37.

37. L. T. Chang, "China Eases Foreign Film Rules," *The Wall Street Journal*, October 15, 2004, p. B2.

38. B. L. Simonin, "Transfer of Marketing Knowhow in International Strategic Alliances," *Journal of International Business Studies*, 1999, pp. 463–91, and J. W. Spencer, "Firms' Knowledge Sharing Strategies in the Global Innovation System," *Strategic Management Journal* 24 (2003), pp. 217–33.

39. C. Souza, "Microsoft Teams with MIPS, Toshiba," *EBN*, February 10, 2003, p. 4.

40. M. Frankel, "Now Sony Is Giving Palm a Hand," *BusinessWeek*, November 29, 2000, p. 50.

41. Kale, Singh, and Perlmutter, "Learning and Protection of Proprietary Assets."

42. R. B. Reich and E. D. Mankin, "Joint Ventures with Japan Give Away Our Future," *Harvard Business Review*, March–April 1986, pp. 78–90.

43. J. Bleeke and D. Ernst, "The Way to Win in Cross-Border Alliances," *Harvard Business Review*, November–December 1991, pp. 127–35.

44. C. H. Deutsch, "The Venturesome Giant," *The New York Times*, October 5, 2007, pp. C1, C8.

45. "Odd Couple," *The Economist*, May 5, 2007, pp. 79–80.

46. W. Roehl and J. F. Truitt, "Stormy Open Marriages Are Better," *Columbia Journal of World Business*, Summer 1987, pp. 87–95.

47. K. McQuade and B. Gomes-Casseres, "Xerox and Fuji-Xerox," *Harvard Business Review*, February 15, 1991.

48. See T. Khanna, R. Gulati, and N. Nohria, "The Dynamics of Learning Alliances: Competition, Cooperation, and Relative Scope," *Strategic Management Journal* 19 (1998), pp. 193–210; and Kale, Singh, Perlmutter, "Learning and Protection of Proprietary Assets."

49. Kale, Singh, Perlmutter, "Learning and Protection of Proprietary Assets in Strategic Alliances."

50. Hamel, Doz, and Prahalad, "Collaborate with Competitors"; Khanna, Gulati, and Nohria, "The Dynamics of Learning Alliances: Competition, Cooperation, and Relative Scope"; and E. W. K. Tang, "Acquiring Knowledge by Foreign Partners from International Joint Ventures in a Transition Economy: Learning by

Doing and Learning Myopia," *Strategic Management Journal* 23 (2002), pp. 835–54.

51. Hamel, Doz, and Prahalad, "Collaborate with Competitors."

52. B. Wysocki, "Cross-Border Alliances Become Favorite Way to Crack New Markets," *The Wall Street Journal*, March 4, 1990, p. A1.

53. Hamel, Doz, and Prahalad, "Collaborate with Competitors," p. 138.

Chapter 12

1. For interesting empirical studies that deal with the issues of timing and resource commitments, see T. Isobe, S. Makino, and D. B. Montgomery, "Resource Commitment, Entry Timing, and Market Performance of Foreign Direct Investments in Emerging Economies," *Academy of Management Journal* 43, no. 3 (2000), pp. 468–84, and Y. Pan and P. S. K. Chi, "Financial Performance and Survival of Multinational Corporations in China," *Strategic Management Journal* 20, no. 4 (1999), pp. 359–74. A complementary theoretical perspective on this issue can be found in V. Govindarjan and A. K. Gupta, *The Quest for Global Dominance* (San Francisco: Jossey-Bass, 2001). Also see F. Vermeulen and H. Barkeme, "Pace, Rhythm and Scope: Process Dependence in Building a Profitable Multinational Corporation," *Strategic Management Journal* 23 (2002), pp. 637–54.

2. This can be reconceptualized as the resource base of the entrant, relative to indigenous competitors. For work that focuses on this issue, see W. C. Bogner, H. Thomas, and J. McGee, "A Longitudinal Study of the Competitive Positions and Entry Paths of European Firms in the U.S. Pharmaceutical Market," *Strategic Management Journal* 17 (1996), pp. 85–107; D. Collis, "A Resource-Based Analysis of Global Competition," *Strategic Management Journal* 12 (1991), pp. 49–68; and S. Tallman, "Strategic Management Models and Resource-Based Strategies among MNEs in a Host Market," *Strategic Management Journal* 12 (1991), pp. 69–82.

3. For a discussion of first-mover advantages, see M. Lieberman and D. Montgomery, "First-Mover Advantages," *Strategic Management Journal* 9 (Summer Special Issue, 1988), pp. 41–58.

4. J. M. Shaver, W. Mitchell, and B. Yeung, "The Effect of Own Firm and Other Firm Experience on Foreign Direct Investment Survival in the United States, 1987–92," *Strategic Management Journal* 18 (1997), pp. 811–24.

5. S. Zaheer and E. Mosakowski, "The Dynamics of the Liability of Foreignness: A Global Study of Survival in the Financial Services Industry," *Strategic Management Journal* 18 (1997), pp. 439–64.

6. Shaver, Mitchell, and Yeung, "The Effect of Own Firm and Other Firm Experience on Foreign Direct Investment Survival in the United States."

7. P. Ghemawat, *Commitment: The Dynamics of Strategy* (New York: Free Press, 1991).

8. R. Luecke, *Scuttle Your Ships before Advancing* (Oxford: Oxford University Press, 1994).

9. Isobe, Makino, and Montgomery, "Resource Commitment, Entry Timing, and Market Performance"; Pan and Chi, "Financial Performance and Survival of Multinational Corporations in China"; and Govindarjan and Gupta, *The Quest for Global Dominance.*

10. Christopher Bartlett and Sumantra Ghoshal, "Going Global: Lessons from Late Movers," *Harvard Business Review*, March–April 2000, pp. 132–45.

11. This section draws on numerous studies, including: C. W. L. Hill, P. Hwang, and W. C. Kim, "An Eclectic Theory of the Choice of International Entry Mode," *Strategic Management Journal* 11 (1990), pp. 117–28; C. W. L. Hill and W. C. Kim, "Searching for a Dynamic Theory of the Multinational Enterprise: A Transaction Cost Model," *Strategic Management Journal* 9 (Special Issue on Strategy Content, 1988), pp. 93–104; E. Anderson and H. Gatignon, "Modes of Foreign Entry: A Transaction Cost Analysis and Propositions," *Journal of International Business Studies* 17 (1986), pp. 1–26; F. R. Root, *Entry Strategies for International Markets* (Lexington, MA: D. C. Heath, 1980); A. Madhok, "Cost, Value and Foreign Market Entry: The Transaction and the Firm," *Strategic Management Journal* 18 (1997), pp. 39–61; K. D. Brouthers and L. B. Brouthers, "Acquisition or Greenfield Start-Up?" *Strategic Management Journal* 21, no. 1 (2000), pp. 89–97; X. Martin and R. Salmon, "Knowledge Transfer Capacity and Its Implications for the Theory of the Multinational Enterprise," *Journal of International Business Studies*, July 2003, p. 356; and A. Verbeke, "The Evolutionary View of the MNE and the Future of Internalization Theory," *Journal of International Business Studies*, November 2003, pp. 498–515.

12. For a general discussion of licensing, see F. J. Contractor, "The Role of Licensing in International Strategy," *Columbia Journal of World Business*, Winter 1982, pp. 73–83.

13. See E. Terazono and C. Lorenz, "An Angry Young Warrior," *Financial Times*, September 19, 1994, p. 11; and K. McQuade and B. Gomes-Casseres, "Xerox and Fuji-Xerox," Harvard Business School Case No. 9-391-156.

14. O. E. Williamson, *The Economic Institutions of Capitalism* (New York: Free Press, 1985).

15. J. H. Dunning and M. McQueen, "The Eclectic Theory of International Production: A Case Study of the International Hotel Industry," *Managerial and Decision Economics* 2 (1981), pp. 197–210.

16. Andrew E. Serwer, "McDonald's Conquers the World," *Fortune*, October 17, 1994, pp. 103–16.

17. For an excellent review of the basic theoretical literature of joint ventures, see B. Kogut, "Joint Ventures: Theoretical and Empirical Perspectives," *Strategic Management Journal* 9 (1988), pp. 319–32. More recent studies include T. Chi, "Option to Acquire or Divest a Joint Venture," *Strategic Management Journal* 21, no. 6 (2000), pp. 665–88; H. Merchant and D. Schendel, "How Do International Joint Ventures Create Shareholder Value?" *Strategic Management Journal* 21, no. 7 (2000), pp. 723–37; H. K. Steensma and M. A. Lyles, "Explaining IJV Survival in a Transitional Economy though Social Exchange and Knowledge Based Perspectives," *Strategic Management Journal* 21, no. 8 (2000), pp. 831–51; and J. F. Hennart and M. Zeng, "Cross Cultural Differences and Joint Venture Longevity," *Journal of International Business Studies*, December 2002, pp. 699–717.

18. D. G. Bradley, "Managing against Expropriation," *Harvard Business Review*, July–August 1977, pp. 78–90.

19. J. A. Robins, S. Tallman, and K. Fladmoe-Lindquist, "Autonomy and Dependence of International Cooperative Ventures," *Strategic Management Journal*, October 2002, pp. 881–902.

20. Speech given by Tony Kobayashi at the University of Washington Business School, October 1992.

21. A. C. Inkpen and P. W. Beamish, "Knowledge, Bargaining Power, and the Instability of International Joint Ventures," *Academy of Management Review* 22 (1997), pp. 177–202; and S. H. Park and G. R. Ungson, "The Effect of National Culture, Organizational Complementarity, and Economic Motivation on Joint Venture Dissolution," *Academy of Management Journal* 40 (1997), pp. 279–307.

22. Inkpen and Beamish, "Knowledge, Bargaining Power, and the Instability of International Joint Ventures."

23. See Brouthers and Brouthers, "Acquisition or Greenfield Start-up?"; and J. F. Hennart and Y. R. Park, "Greenfield versus Acquisition: The Strategy of Japanese Investors in the United States," *Management Science*, 1993, pp. 1054–70.

24. This section draws on Hill, Hwang, and Kim, "An Eclectic Theory of the Choice of International Entry Mode."

25. C. W. L. Hill, "Strategies for Exploiting Technological Innovations: When and When Not to License," *Organization Science* 3 (1992), pp. 428–41.

26. See Brouthers and Brouthers, "Acquisition or Greenfield Start-Up?"; and J. Anand and A. Delios, "Absolute and Relative Resources as Determinants of International Acquisitions," *Strategic Management Journal*, February 2002, pp. 119–34.

27. United Nations, *World Investment Report, 2009* (New York and Geneva: United Nations, 2009).

28. Ibid.

29. For evidence on acquisitions and performance, see R. E. Caves, "Mergers, Takeovers, and Economic Efficiency," *International Journal of Industrial Organization* 7 (1989), pp. 151–74; M. C. Jensen and R. S. Ruback, "The Market for Corporate Control: The Scientific Evidence," *Journal of Financial Economics* 11 (1983), pp. 5–50; R. Roll, "Empirical Evidence on Takeover Activity and Shareholder Wealth," in *Knights, Raiders and Targets*, ed. J. C. Coffee, L. Lowenstein, and S. Rose (Oxford: Oxford University Press, 1989); A. Schleifer and R. W. Vishny, "Takeovers in the 60s and 80s: Evidence and Implications," *Strategic Management Journal* 12 (Winter 1991 Special Issue), pp. 51–60; T. H. Brush, "Predicted Changes in Operational Synergy and Post-Acquisition Performance of Acquired Businesses," *Strategic Management Journal* 17 (1996), pp. 1–24; and A. Seth, K. P. Song, and R. R. Pettit, "Value Creation and Destruction in Cross-Border Acquisitions," *Strategic Management Journal* 23 (October 2002), pp. 921–40.

30. J. Warner, J. Templeman, and R. Horn, "The Case against Mergers," *BusinessWeek*, October 30, 1995, pp. 122–34.

31. "Few Takeovers Pay Off for Big Buyers," *Investors Business Daily*, May 25, 2001, p. 1.

32. S. A. Christofferson, R. S. McNish, and D. L. Sias, "Where Mergers Go Wrong," *The McKinsey Quarterly* 2 (2004), pp. 92–110.

33. D. J. Ravenscraft and F. M. Scherer, *Mergers, Selloffs, and Economic Efficiency* (Washington, DC: Brookings Institution, 1987).

34. See P. Ghemawat and F. Ghadar, "The Dubious Logic of Global Mega-mergers," *Harvard Business Review*, July–August 2000, pp. 65–72.

35. R. Roll, "The Hubris Hypothesis of Corporate Takeovers," *Journal of Business* 59 (1986), pp. 197–216.

36. "Marital Problems," *The Economist*, October 14, 2000.

37. See J. P. Walsh, "Top Management Turnover Following Mergers and Acquisitions," *Strategic Management Journal* 9 (1988), pp. 173–83.

38. B. Vlasic and B. A. Stertz, *Taken for a Ride: How Daimler-Benz Drove Off with Chrysler* (New York: HarperCollins, 2000).

39. See A. A. Cannella and D. C. Hambrick, "Executive Departure and Acquisition Performance," *Strategic Management Journal* 14 (1993), pp. 137–52.

40. P. Haspeslagh and D. Jemison, *Managing Acquisitions* (New York: Free Press, 1991).

41. Ibid.

Chapter 13

1. R. A. Pope, "Why Small Firms Export: Another Look," *Journal of Small Business Management* 40 (2002), pp. 17–26.

2. S. T. Cavusgil, "Global Dimensions of Marketing," in *Marketing*, ed. P. E. Murphy and B. M. Enis (Glenview, IL: Scott, Foresman, 1985), pp. 577–99.

3. S. M. Mehta, "Enterprise: Small Companies Look to Cultivate Foreign Business," *The Wall Street Journal*, July 7, 1994, p. B2.

4. P. A. Julien and C. Ramagelahy, "Competitive Strategy and Performance of Exporting SMEs," *Entrepreneurship Theory and Practice* 27, no. 3 (March 2003), pp. 227–94.

5. W. J. Burpitt and D. A. Rondinelli, "Small Firms' Motivations for Exporting: To Earn and Learn?" *Journal of Small Business Management*, October 2000, pp. 1–14; and J. D. Mittelstaedt, G. N. Harben, and W. A. Ward, "How Small Is Too Small?" *Journal of Small Business Management* 41 (2003), pp. 68–85.

6. Small Business Administration, "The State of Small Business 1999–2000: Report to the President," 2001 (accessed at www.sba.gov/advo/stats/stateofsb99_00.pdf); and D. Ransom, "Obama's Math: More Exports Equals More Jobs," *The Wall Street Journal*, February 5, 2010.

7. A. O. Ogbuehi and T. A. Longfellow, "Perceptions of U.S. Manufacturing Companies Concerning Exporting," *Journal of Small Business Management*, October 1994, pp. 37–59; and U.S. Small Business Administration, "Guide to Exporting," www.sba.gov/oit/info/Guide-toExporting/index.html.

8. R. W. Haigh, "Thinking of Exporting?" *Columbia Journal of World Business* 29 (December 1994), pp. 66–86.

9. F. Williams, "The Quest for More Efficient Commerce," *Financial Times*, October 13, 1994, p. 7.

10. See Burpitt and Rondinelli, "Small Firms' Motivations for Exporting"; and C. S. Katsikeas, L. C. Leonidou, and N. A. Morgan, "Firm Level Export Performance Assessment," *Academy of Marketing Science* 28 (2000), pp. 493–511.

11. M. Y. Yoshino and T. B. Lifson, *The Invisible Link* (Cambridge, MA: MIT Press, 1986).

12. L. W. Tuller, *Going Global* (Homewood, IL: Business One-Irwin, 1991).

13. Haigh, "Thinking of Exporting?"

14. M. A. Raymond, J. Kim, and A. T. Shao. "Export Strategy and Performance," *Journal of Global Marketing* 15 (2001), pp. 5–29; and P. S. Aulakh, M. Kotabe, and H. Teegen, "Export Strategies and Performance of Firms from Emerging Economies," *Academy of Management Journal* 43 (2000), pp. 342–61.

15. J. Francis and C. Collins-Dodd, "The Impact of Firms' Export Orientation on the Export Performance of High-Tech Small and Medium Sized Enterprises," *Journal of International Marketing* 8, no. 3 (2000), pp. 84–103.

16. J. Koch, "Integration of U.S. Small Businesses into the Export Trade Sector Using Available Financial Tools and Resources," *Business Credit* 109, no. 10 (2007), pp. 64–68.

17. For a review of the conditions under which a buyer has power over a supplier, see M. E. Porter, *Competitive Strategy* (New York: Free Press, 1980).

18. *Exchange Agreements and Exchange Restrictions* (Washington, DC: International Monetary Fund, 1989).

19. It's also sometimes argued that countertrade is a way of reducing the risks inherent in a traditional money-for-goods transaction, particularly with entities from emerging economies. See C. J. Choi, S. H. Lee, and J. B. Kim, "A Note of Countertrade: Contractual Uncertainty and Transactional Governance in Emerging Economies," *Journal of International Business Studies* 30, no. 1 (1999), pp. 189–202.

20. J. R. Carter and J. Gagne, "The Do's and Don'ts of International Countertrade," *Sloan Management Review*, Spring 1988, pp. 31–37; and W. Maneerungsee, "Countertrade: Farm Goods Swapped for Italian Electricity," *Bangkok Post*, July 23, 1998.

21. Estimate from the American Countertrade Association at www.countertrade.org/index.htm. See also D. West, "Countertrade," *Business Credit* 104, no. 4 (2001), pp. 64–67; and B. Meyer, "The Original Meaning of Trade Meets the Future of Barter," *World Trade* 13 (January 2000), pp. 46–50.

22. Carter and Gagne, "The Do's and Dont's of International Countertrade."

23. Maneerungsee, "Countertrade: Farm Goods Swapped for Italian Electricity."

24. For details, see Carter and Gagne, "The Do's and Dont's of International Countertrade"; J. F. Hennart, "Some Empirical Dimensions of Countertrade," *Journal of International Business Studies*, 1990, pp. 240–60; and West, "Countertrade."

25. D. J. Lecraw, "The Management of Counter-trade: Factors Influencing Success," *Journal of International Business Studies*, Spring 1989, pp. 41–59.

Chapter 14

1. B. C. Arntzen, G. G. Brown, T. P. Harrison, and L. L. Trafton, "Global Supply Chain Management at Digital Equipment Corporation," *Interfaces* 25 (1995), pp. 69–93; and Diana Farrell, "Beyond Offshoring," *Harvard Business Review*, December 2004, pp. 1–8.

2. D. A. Garvin, "What Does Product Quality Really Mean," *Sloan Management Review* 26 (Fall 1984), pp. 25–44.

3. See the articles published in the special issue of the *Academy of Management Review on Total Quality Management* 19, no. 3 (1994). The following article provides a good overview of many of the issues involved from an academic perspective: J. W. Dean and D. E. Bowen, "Management Theory and Total Quality," *Academy of Management Review* 19 (1994), pp. 392–418. Also see T. C. Powell, "Total Quality Management as Competitive Advantage," *Strategic Management Journal* 16 (1995), pp. 15–37; and S. B. Han et al., "The Impact of ISO 9000 on TQM and Business Performance," *Journal of Business and Economic Studies* 13, no. 2 (2007), pp. 1–25.

4. For general background information, see "How to Build Quality," *The Economist*, September 23, 1989, pp. 91–92; A. Gabor, *The Man Who Discovered Quality* (New York: Penguin, 1990); P. B. Crosby, *Quality Is Free* (New York: Mentor, 1980); and M. Elliot et al., "A Quality World, a Quality Life," *Industrial Engineer*, January 2003, pp. 26–33.

5. G. T. Lucier and S. Seshadri, "GE Takes Six Sigma beyond the Bottom line," *Strategic Finance*, May 2001, pp. 40–46; and U. D. Kumar et al., "On the Optimal Selection of Process Alternatives in a Six Sigma Implementation," *International Journal of Production Economics* 111, no. 2 (2008), pp. 456–70.

6. M. Saunders, "U.S. Firms Doing Business in Europe Have Options in Registering for ISO 9000 Quality Standards," *Business America*, June 14, 1993, p. 7; and Han et al., "The Impact of ISO 9000 on TQM and Business Performance."

7. G. Stalk and T. M. Hout, *Competing against Time* (New York: Free Press, 1990).

8. N. Tokatli, "Global Sourcing: Insights from the Global Clothing Industry—The Case of Zara, a Fast Fashion Retailer," *Journal of Economic Geography* 8, no. 1 (2008), pp. 21–39.

9. Diana Farrell, "Beyond Offshoring," *Harvard Business Review*, December 2004, pp. 1–8; and M. A. Cohen and H. L. Lee, "Resource Deployment Analysis of Global Manufacturing and Distribution Networks," *Journal of Manufacturing and Operations Management* 2 (1989), pp. 81–104.

10. P. Krugman, "Increasing Returns and Economic Geography," *Journal of Political Economy* 99, no. 3 (1991), pp. 483–99; J. M. Shaver and F. Flyer, "Agglomeration Economies, Firm Heterogeneity, and Foreign Direct Investment in the United States," *Strategic Management Journal* 21 (2000), pp. 1175–93; and R. E. Baldwin and T. Okubo, "Heterogeneous Firms, Agglomeration Economies, and Economic Geography," *Journal of Economic Geography* 6, no. 3 (2006), pp. 323–50.

11. For a review of the technical arguments, see D. A. Hay and D. J. Morris, *Industrial Economics: Theory and Evidence* (Oxford: Oxford University Press, 1979). See also C. W. L. Hill and G. R. Jones, *Strategic Management: An Integrated Approach* (Boston: Houghton Mifflin, 2004).

12. See P. Nemetz and L. Fry, "Flexible Manufacturing Organizations: Implications for Strategy Formulation," *Academy of Management Review* 13 (1988), pp. 627–38; N. Greenwood, *Implementing Flexible Manufacturing Systems* (New York: Halstead Press, 1986); J. P. Womack, D. T. Jones, and D. Roos, *The Machine That Changed the World* (New York: Rawson Associates, 1990); and R. Parthasarthy and S. P. Seith, "The Impact of Flexible Automation on Business Strategy and Organizational Structure," *Academy of Management Review* 17 (1992), pp. 86–111.

13. B. J. Pine, *Mass Customization: The New Frontier in Business Competition* (Boston: Harvard Business School Press, 1993); S. Kotha, "Mass Customization: Implementing the Emerging Paradigm for Competitive Advantage," *Strategic Management Journal* 16 (1995), pp. 21–42; J. H. Gilmore and B. J. Pine II, "The Four Faces of Mass Customization," *Harvard Business Review*, January–February 1997, pp. 91–101; and M. Zerenler and D. Ozilhan, "Mass Customization Manufacturing: The Drivers and Concepts," *Journal of American Academy of Business* 12, no. 1 (2007), pp. 262–30.

14. "Toyota Motor Corporation Captures Ten Segment Awards," J. D. Power press release, March 19, 2009. Archived at http://businesscenter.jdpower.com/news/pressrelease.aspx?ID=2009043.

15. M. A. Cusumano, *The Japanese Automobile Industry* (Cambridge, MA: Harvard University Press, 1989); T. Ohno, *Toyota Production System* (Cambridge, MA: Productivity Press, 1990); and Womack, Jones, and Roos, *The Machine That Changed the World*.

16. P. Waurzyniak, "Ford's Flexible Push," *Manufacturing Engineering*, September 2003, pp. 47–50.

17. K. Ferdows, "Making the Most of Foreign Factories," *Harvard Business Review*, March–April 1997, pp. 73–88.

18. This argument represents a simple extension of the dynamic capabilities research stream in the strategic management literature. See D. J. Teece, G. Pisano, and A. Shuen, "Dynamic Capabilities and Strategic Management," *Strategic Management Journal* 18 (1997), pp. 509–33.

19. T. S. Frost, J. M. Birkinshaw, and P. C. Ensign, "Centers of Excellence in Multinational Corporations," *Strategic Management Journal* 23 (November 2002), pp. 997–1018.

20. C. W. L. Hill, "Globalization, the Myth of the Nomadic Multinational Enterprise, and the Advantages of Location Persistence," School of Business working paper, University of Washington, 2001.

21. Anne Parmigiani, "Why Do Firms Both Make and Buy?" *Strategic Management Journal* 29, no. 3 (2007), pp. 285–303.

22. J. Solomon and E. Cherney, "A Global Report: Outsourcing to India Sees a Twist," *The Wall Street Journal*, April 1, 2004, p. A2.

23. The material in this section is based primarily on the transaction cost literature of vertical integration; for example, O. E. Williamson, *The Economic Institutions of Capitalism* (New York: The Free Press, 1985).

24. For a review of the evidence, see Williamson, *The Economic Institutions of Capitalism*. See also L. Poppo and T. Zenger, "Testing Alternative Theories of the Firm: Transaction Cost, Knowledge Based, and Measurement Explanations for Make or Buy Decisions in Information Services," *Strategic Management Journal* 19 (1998), pp. 853–78; and R. Carter and G. M. Hodgson, "The Impact of Empirical Tests to Transaction Cost Economics on the Debate on the Nature of the Firm," *Strategic Management Journal* 27, no. 5 (2006), pp. 461–80.

25. A. D. Chandler, *The Visible Hand* (Cambridge, MA: Harvard University Press, 1977).

26. For a review of these arguments, see C. W. L. Hill and R. E. Hoskisson, "Strategy and Structure in the Multiproduct Firm," *Academy of Management Review* 12 (1987), pp. 331–41.

27. C. W. L. Hill, "Cooperation, Opportunism, and the Invisible Hand," *Academy of Management Review* 15 (1990), pp. 500–13.

28. See R. Narasimhan and J. R. Carter, "Organization, Communication and Coordination of International Sourcing," *International Marketing Review* 7 (1990), pp. 6–20; and Arntzen, Brown, Harrison, and Trafton, "Global Supply Chain Management at Digital Equipment Corporation."

29. H. F. Busch, "Integrated Materials Management," *IJPD & MM* 18 (1990), pp. 28–39.

30. T. Aeppel, "Manufacturers Cope with the Costs of Strained Global Supply Lines," *The Wall Street Journal*, December 8, 2004, p. A1.

Chapter 15

1. See R. W. Ruekert and O. C. Walker, "Interactions between Marketing and R&D Departments in Implementing Different Business-Level Strategies," *Strategic Management Journal* 8 (1987), pp. 233–48; and K. B. Clark and S. C. Wheelwright, *Managing New Product and Process Development* (New York: Free Press, 1993).

2. T. Levitt, "The Globalization of Markets," *Harvard Business Review*, May–June 1983, pp. 92–102. Reprinted by permission of *Harvard Business Review*, an excerpt from "The Globalization of Markets," by Theodore Levitt, May–June 1983. Copyright © 1983 by the President and Fellows of Harvard College. All rights reserved.

3. For example, see S. P. Douglas and Y. Wind, "The Myth of Globalization," *Columbia Journal of World Business*, Winter 1987, pp. 19–29; C. A. Bartlett and S. Ghoshal, *Managing across Borders: The Transnational Solution* (Boston: Harvard Business School Press, 1989); V. J. Govindarajan and A. K. Gupta, *The Quest for Global Dominance* (San Francisco: Jossey Bass, 2001); J. Quelch. "The Return of the Global Brand," *Harvard Business Review*, August 2003, pp. 1–3; and P. J. Ghemawat, *Redefining Global Strategy* (Boston: Harvard Business School Press, 2007).

4. J. Tagliabue, "U.S. Brands Are Feeling Global Tension," *The New York Times*, March 15, 2003, p. C3.

5. D. B. Holt, J. A. Quelch, and E. L. Taylor, "How Global Brands Compete," *Harvard Business Review*, September 2004.

6. J. T. Landry, "Emerging Markets: Are Chinese Consumers Coming of Age?" *Harvard Business Review*, May–June 1998, pp. 17–20.

7. C. Miller, "Teens Seen as the First Truly Global Consumers," *Marketing News*, March 27, 1995, p. 9.

8. This approach was originally developed in K. Lancaster, "A New Approach to Demand Theory," *Journal of Political Economy* 74 (1965), pp. 132–57.

9. V. R. Alden, "Who Says You Can't Crack Japanese Markets?" *Harvard Business Review*, January–February 1987, pp. 52–56.

10. T. Parker-Pope, "Custom Made," *The Wall Street Journal*, September 26, 1996, p. 22.

11. "RCA's New Vista: The Bottom Line," *BusinessWeek*, July 4, 1987, p. 44.

12. N. Gross and K. Rebello, "Apple? Japan Can't Say No," *BusinessWeek*, June 29, 1992, pp. 32–33.

13. "After Early Stumbles P&G Is Making Inroads Overseas," *The Wall Street Journal*, February 6, 1989, p. B1.

14. C. Matlack and P. Gogoi, "What's This? The French Love McDonald's?" *BusinessWeek*, January 13, 2003, pp. 50–51.

15. Z. Gurhan-Cvanli and D. Maheswaran, "Cultural Variation in Country of Origin Effects," *Journal of Marketing Research*, August 2000, pp. 309–17.

16. See M. Laroche, V. H. Kirpalani, F. Pons, and L. Zhou, "A Model of Advertising Standardization in Multinational Corporations," *Journal of International Business Studies*, 32 (2001), pp. 249–66; and D. A. Aaker and E. Joachimsthaler, "The Lure of Global Branding," *Harvard Business Review*, November–December 1999, pp. 137–44.

17. "Advertising in a Single Market," *The Economist*, March 24, 1990, p. 64.

18. D. Waller, "Charged Up over Competition Law," *Financial Times*, June 23, 1994, p. 14.

19. R. G. Matthews and D. Pringle, "Nokia Bets One Global Message Will Ring True in Many Markets," *The Wall Street Journal*, September 27, 2004, p. B6.

20. R. J. Dolan and H. Simon, *Power Pricing* (New York: Free Press, 1999).

21. B. Stottinger, "Strategic Export Pricing: A Long Winding Road," *Journal of International Marketing* 9 (2001), pp. 40–63; S. Gil-Pareja "Export Process Discrimination in Europe and Exchange Rates," *Review of International Economics*, May 2002, pp. 299–312; and G. Corsetti and L. Dedola, "A Macro Economic Model of International Price Discrimination," *Journal of International Economics*, September 2005, pp. 129–40.

22. These allegations were made on a PBS *Frontline* documentary telecast in the United States in May 1992.

23. Y. Tsurumi and H. Tsurumi, "Fujifilm–Kodak Duopolistic Competition in Japan and the United States," *Journal of International Business Studies* 30 (1999), pp. 813–30.

24. G. Smith and B. Wolverton, "A Dark Moment for Kodak," *BusinessWeek*, August 4, 1997, pp. 30–31.

25. R. Narisette and J. Friedland, "Disposable Income: Diaper Wars of P&G and Kimberly-Clark Now Heat Up in Brazil," *The Wall Street Journal*, June 4, 1997, p. A1.

26. J. F. Pickering, *Industrial Structure and Market Conduct* (London: Martin Robertson, 1974).

27. S. P. Douglas, C. Samuel Craig, and E. J. Nijissen, "Integrating Branding Strategy across Markets," *Journal of International Marketing* 9, no. 2 (2001), pp. 97–114

28. The phrase was first used by economist Joseph Schumpeter in *Capitalism, Socialism, and Democracy* (New York: Harper Brothers, 1942).

29. S. Kotabe, S. Srinivasan, and P. S. Aulakh, "Multinationality and Firm Performance: The Moderating Role of R&D and Marketing," *Journal of International Business Studies* 33 (2002), pp. 79–97.

30. See D. C. Mowery and N. Rosenberg, *Technology and the Pursuit of Economic Growth* (Cambridge, UK: Cambridge University Press, 1989); and M. E. Porter, *The Competitive Advantage of Nations* (New York: Free Press, 1990).

31. W. Kuemmerle, "Building Effective R&D Capabilities Abroad," *Harvard Business Review*, March–April 1997, pp. 61–70; and C. Le Bas and C. Sierra, "Location versus Home Country Advantages in R&D Activities," *Research Policy* 31 (2002), pp. 589–609.

32. "When the Corporate Lab Goes to Japan," *The New York Times*, April 28, 1991, sec. 3, p. 1.

33. D. Shapley, "Globalization Prompts Exodus," *Financial Times*, March 17, 1994, p. 10.

34. E. Mansfield, "How Economists See R&D," *Harvard Business Review*, November–December, 1981, pp. 98–106.

35. Ibid.

36. G. A. Stevens and J. Burley, "Piloting the Rocket of Radical Innovation," *Research Technology Management* 46 (2003), pp. 16–26.

37. K. B. Clark and S. C. Wheelwright, *Managing New Product and Process Development* (New York: Free Press, 1993); and M. A. Shilling and C. W. L. Hill, "Managing the New Product Development Process," *Academy of Management Executive* 12, no. 3 (1998), pp. 67–81.

38. O. Port, "Moving Past the Assembly Line," *BusinessWeek Special Issue: Reinventing America*, 1992, pp. 177–80.

39. K. B. Clark and T. Fujimoto, "The Power of Product Integrity," *Harvard Business Review*, November–December 1990, pp. 107–18; Clark and Wheelwright, *Managing New Product and Process Development*; S. L. Brown and K. M. Eisenhardt, "Product Development: Past Research, Present Findings, and Future Directions," *Academy of Management Review* 20 (1995), pp. 348–78; and G. Stalk and T. M. Hout, *Competing against Time* (New York: Free Press, 1990).

40. Shilling and Hill, "Managing the New Product Development Process."

41. C. Christensen. "Quantum Corporation—Business and Product Teams," Harvard Business School case no. 9-692-023.

42. R. Nobel and J. Birkinshaw, "Innovation in Multinational Corporations: Control and Communication Patterns in International R&D Operations," *Strategic Management Journal* 19 (1998), pp. 479–96.

43. Information comes from the company's Web site; also see K. Ferdows, "Making the Most of Foreign Factories," *Harvard Business Review*, March–April 1997, pp. 73–88.

Chapter 16

1. P. J. Dowling and R. S. Schuler, *International Dimensions of Human Resource Management* (Boston: PSW-Kent, 1990).

2. J. Millman, M. A. von Glinow, and M. Nathan, "Organizational Life Cycles and Strategic International Human Resource Management in Multinational Companies," *Academy of Management Review* 16 (1991), pp. 318–39; A. Bird and S. Beechler, "Links Between Business Strategy and Human Resource Management," *Journal of International Business Studies* 26 (1995), pp. 23–47; B. A. Colbert, "The Complex Resource Based View: Implications for Theory and Practice of Strategic Human Resource Management," *Academy of Management Review* 29 (2004), pp. 341–60; and C. J. Collins and K. D. Clark, "Strategic Human Resource Practices, Top Management Team Social Networks, and Firm Performance," *Academy of Management Journal* 46 (2003), pp. 740–60.

3. See Peter Bamberger and Ilan Meshoulam, *Human Resource Strategy: Formulation, Implementation, and Impact* (Thousand Oaks, CA: Sage, 2000); P. M. Wright and S. Snell, "Towards a Unifying Framework for Exploring Fit and Flexibility in Human Resource Management," *Academy of Management Review* 23 (October 1998), pp. 756–72; and B.A. Colbert, "The Complex Resource-Based View: Implications for Theory and Practice in Strategic Human Resource Management," *Academy of Management Review* 29 (July 2004), pp. 341–60.

4. R. Colman, "HR Management Lags behind at World Class Firms," *CMA Management*, July–August 2002, p. 9.

5. E. H. Schein, *Organizational Culture and Leadership* (San Francisco: Jossey-Bass, 1985).

6. H. V. Perlmutter, "The Tortuous Evolution of the Multinational Corporation," *Columbia Journal of World Business* 4 (1969), pp. 9–18; D. A. Heenan and H. V. Perlmutter, *Multinational Organizational Development* (Reading, MA: Addison-Wesley, 1979); D. A. Ondrack, "International Human Resources Management in European and North American Firms," *International Studies of Management and Organization* 15 (1985), pp. 6–32; and T. Jackson, "The Management of People across Cultures: Valuing People Differently," *Human Resource Management* 41 (2002), pp. 455–75.

7. V. Reitman and M. Schuman, "Men's Club: Japanese and Korean Companies Rarely Look Outside for People to Run Their Overseas Operations," *The Wall Street Journal*, September 26, 1996, p. 17.

8. S. Beechler and J. Z. Yang, "The Transfer of Japanese Style Management to American Subsidiaries," *Journal of International Business Studies* 25 (1994), pp. 467–91. See also R. Konopaske, S. Warner, and K. E. Neupert, "Entry Mode Strategy and Performance: The Role of FDI Staffing," *Journal of Business Research*, September 2002, pp. 759–70.

9. M. Banai and L. M. Sama, "Ethical Dilemma in MNCs' International Staffing Policies," *Journal of Business Ethics*, June 2000, pp. 221–35.

10. Reitman and Schuman, "Men's Club."

11. C. A. Bartlett and S. Ghoshal, *Managing across Borders: The Transnational Solution* (Boston: Harvard Business School Press, 1989).

12. S. J. Kobrin, "Geocentric Mindset and Multinational Strategy," *Journal of International Business Studies* 25 (1994), pp. 493–511.

13. F. Hansen, "International Business Machine," *Workforce Management*, July 2005, pp. 36–44.

14. P. M. Rosenzweig and N. Nohria, "Influences on Human Resource Management Practices in Multinational Corporations," *Journal of International Business Studies* 25 (1994), pp. 229–51.

15. Kobrin, "Geocentric Mindset and Multinational Strategy."

16. M. Harvey and H. Fung, "Inpatriate Managers: The Need for Realistic Relocation Reviews," *International Journal of Management* 17 (2000), pp. 151–59.

17. S. Black, M. Mendenhall, and G. Oddou, "Toward a Comprehensive Model of International Adjustment," *Academy of Management Review* 16 (1991), pp. 291–317; J. Shay and T. J. Bruce, "Expatriate Managers," *Cornell Hotel & Restaurant Administration Quarterly*, February 1997, p. 30–40; and Y. Baruch and Y. Altman, "Expatriation and Repatriation in MNCs—A Taxonomy," *Human Resource Management* 41 (2002), pp. 239–59.

18. M. G. Harvey, "The Multinational Corporation's Expatriate Problem: An Application of Murphy's Law," *Business Horizons* 26 (1983), pp. 71–78.

19. J. Barbian, "Return to Sender," *Training*, January 2002, pp. 40–43.

20. Shay and Bruce, "Expatriate Managers." Also see J. S. Black and H. Gregersen, "The Right Way to Manage Expatriates," *Harvard Business Review*, March–April

1999, pp. 52–63; and Baruch and Altman, "Expatriation and Repatriation in MNCs."

21. N. Foster, "The Persistent Myth of High Expatriate Failure Rates," *Journal of Human Resource Management* 8 (1997), pp. 177–205.

22. Barbian, "Return to Sender."

23. Black, Mendenhall, and Oddou, "Toward a Comprehensive Model of International Adjustment."

24. R. L. Tung, "Selection and Training Procedures of U.S., European, and Japanese Multinationals," *California Management Review* 25 (1982), pp. 57–71.

25. H. W. Lee, "Factors That Influence Expatriate Failure," *International Journal of Management* 24 (2007), pp. 403–15.

26. C. M. Solomon, "Success Abroad Depends upon More than Job Skills," *Personnel Journal*, April 1994, pp. 51–58.

27. C. M. Solomon, "Unhappy Trails," *Workforce*, August 2000, pp. 36–41.

28. Solomon, "Success Abroad."

29. Solomon, "Unhappy Trails."

30. M. Harvey, "Addressing the Dual-Career Expatriation Dilemma," *Human Resource Planning* 19, no. 4 (1996), pp. 18–32.

31. M. Mendenhall and G. Oddou, "The Dimensions of Expatriate Acculturation: A Review," *Academy of Management Review* 10 (1985), pp. 39–47.

32. I. Torbiorin, *Living Abroad: Personal Adjustment and Personnel Policy in the Overseas Setting* (New York: John Wiley & Sons, Inc., 1982).

33. R. L. Tung, "Selection and Training of Personnel for Overseas Assignments," *Columbia Journal of World Business* 16 (1981), pp. 68–78.

34. Solomon, "Success Abroad."

35. S. Ronen, "Training and International Assignee," in *Training and Career Development*, ed. I. Goldstein (San Francisco: Jossey-Bass, 1985); and Tung, "Selection and Training of Personnel for Overseas Assignments."

36. Solomon, "Success Abroad."

37. Harvey, "Addressing the Dual-Career Expatriation Dilemma"; and J. W. Hunt, "The Perils of Foreign Postings for Two," *Financial Times*, May 6, 1998, p. 22.

38. C. M. Daily, S. T. Certo, and D. R. Dalton, "International Experience in the Executive Suite: A Path to Prosperity?" *Strategic Management Journal* 21 (2000), pp. 515–23.

39. Dowling and Schuler, *International Dimensions of Human Resource Management*.

40. Ibid.

41. G. Baliga and J. C. Baker, "Multinational Corporate Policies for Expatriate Managers: Selection, Training, and Evaluation," *Advanced Management Journal*, Autumn 1985, pp. 31–38.

42. J. C. Baker, "Foreign Language and Departure Training in U.S. Multinational Firms," *Personnel Administrator*, July 1984, pp. 68–70.

43. A 1997 study by the Conference Board looked at this in depth. For a summary, see L. Grant, "That Overseas Job Could Derail Your Career," *Fortune*, April 14, 1997, p. 166. Also see J. S. Black and H. Gregersen, "The Right Way to Manage Expatriates," *Harvard Business Review*, March–April 1999, pp. 52–63.

44. J. S. Black and M. E. Mendenhall, *Global Assignments: Successfully Expatriating and Repatriating International Managers* (San Francisco: Jossey-Bass, 1992); and K. Vermond, "Expatriates Come Home," *CMA Management*, October 2001, pp. 30–33.

45. Ibid.

46. Figures from the Conference Board study. For a summary, see Grant, "That Overseas Job Could Derail Your Career."

47. S. C. Schneider, "National v. Corporate Culture: Implications for Human Resource Management," *Human Resource Management* 27 (Summer 1988), pp. 231–46.

48. I. M. Manve and W. B. Stevenson, "Nationality, Cultural Distance and Expatriate Status," *Journal of International Business Studies* 32 (2001), pp. 285–303; and D. Minbaeva et al., "MNC Knowledge Transfer, Subsidiary Absorptive Capacity, and HRM," *Journal of International Business Studies* 34, no. 6 (2003), pp. 586–604.

49. Bartlett and Ghoshal, *Managing across Borders.*

50. See G. Oddou and M. Mendenhall, "Expatriate Performance Appraisal: Problems and Solutions," in *International Human Resource Management*, ed. Mendenhall and Oddou (Boston: PWS-Kent, 1991); Dowling and Schuler, *International Dimensions*; R. S. Schuler and G.W. Florkowski, "International Human Resource Management," in *Handbook for International Management Research*, ed. B. J. Punnett and O. Shenkar (Oxford: Blackwell, 1996); and K. Roth and S. O'Donnell, "Foreign Subsidiary Compensation Strategy: An Agency Theory Perspective," *Academy of Management Journal* 39, no. 3 (1996), pp. 678–703.

51. Oddou and Mendenhall, "Expatriate Performance Appraisal."

52. "Expatriates Often See Little Benefit to Careers in Foreign Stints, Indifference at Home," *The Wall Street Journal*, December 11, 1989, p. B1.

53. Oddou and Mendenhall, "Expatriate Performance Appraisal"; and Schuler and Florkowski, "International Human Resource Management."

54. Towers Perrin, *Towers Perrin Worldwide Total Remuneration Study, 2005–2006*, www.towersperrin.com.

55. J. Cummings and L. Brannen, "The New World of Compensation," *Business Finance*, June 2005, p. 8.

56. "Multinational Tighten Control of Benefit Plans," *Workforce Management*, May 2005, p. 5.

57. Organizational Resource Counselors, *2002 Survey of International Assignment Policies and Practices*, March 2003.

58. C. Reynolds, "Compensation of Overseas Personnel," in *Handbook of Human Resource Administration*, ed. J. J. Famularo (New York: McGraw-Hill, 1986).

59. M. Helms, "International Executive Compensation Practices," in *International Human Resource Management*, ed. M. Mendenhall and G. Oddou (Boston: PWS-Kent, 1991).

60. G. W. Latta, "Expatriate Incentives," *HR Focus* 75, no. 3 (March 1998), p. S3.

61. C. K. Prahalad and Y. L. Doz, *The Multinational Mission* (New York: Free Press, 1987).

62. Ibid.

63. Schuler and Florkowski, "International Human Resource Management."

64. See J. P. Womack, D. T. Jones, and D. Roos, *The Machine That Changed the World* (New York: Rawson Associates, 1990).

photo credits

Chapter 14

page 492 © Mauricio Lima/AFP/Getty Images
page 497 © George Steinmetz/Corbis
page 501 © AP Photo/Brian Bohannon
page 508 © AP Photo/Dinda

Chapter 15

page 518 © AP Photo/Ahn Young-joon
page 523 © AP Photo/Ed Bailey
page 525 © AP Photo/David Guttenfelder

page 531 © The McGraw-Hill Companies, Inc./
Andrew Resek, photographer
page 536 © Peter Yates/Corbis
page 545 © AP Photo/Feature Photo Service/Kodak

Chapter 16

page 552 © AP Photo/Eckehard Schulz
page 565 © Reprinted Courtesy of Caterpillar, Inc.
page 575 © International Labour Organization

name index

Nader, Ralph, 60, 592
Naidler, D., 606
Nakane, C., 124, 594
Nalebuff, B., 600, 602
Namenwirth, J. Z., 120, 594, 596
Narasimhan, R., 612
Narisette, R., 613
Narula, R., 601
Nathan, M., 614
Nayef, Prince, 75
Neale, M. A., 602
Neary, J. P., 598
Neeleman, David, 494
Nellis, J., 594
Nemetz, P., 611
Neu, D., 596
Neupert, K. E., 614
Nijissen, E. J., 613
Nixon, Richard M., 377
Nobel, R., 614
Nohria, N., 607, 614
Nonnemaker, L., 601
Nordstrom, H., 591, 592
Norman, P., 314
North, Douglass, 95, 592, 593
Nydell, M. K., 595

Obama, Barack, 51, 59
Obasanjo, Olusegun, 259
Obstfeld, M., 599, 604, 605
Oddou, G., 563–565, 569, 614, 615, 616
O'Donnell, S., 615
Ogbuehi, A. O., 610
Ohlin, Bertil, 189, 203–204, 598
Ohmae, K., 607
Ohno, Taiichi, 502, 611
Okubo, T., 611
Okuno, M., 601
Olson, M., 593
Ondrack, D. A., 614
O'Neill, J., 259
Orane, Douglas, 433
Orban, Viktor, 402
Oshikoya, T., 259
Ostrovsky, A., 591
Ostry, J. D., 605
Owen-Jones, Lindsay, 309
Ozawa, T., 602
Ozilhan, D., 611

Pachauri, R. K., 265
Packard, David, 169
Pan, Y., 608
Panagariya, A., 598
Papandreou, George, 396

Park, S. H., 609
Park. Y. H., 609
Parker, G., 429
Parker-Pope, T., 612
Parmigiani, Anne, 612
Parra-Bernal, G., 188
Parthasarthy, R., 611
Patten, Chris, 165
Pauls, B. D., 605
Pearson, M., 591
Pecoul, B., 256
Peng, M. W., 595
Penty, C., 30
Perlmutter, H., 607
Perlmutter, H. V., 614
Perot, Ross, 321
Peters, J. W., 599
Peterson, M. F., 595
Petrakis, M., 397
Pettit, R. R., 601, 609
Philips, M., 603
Pick, D., 594
Pickering, J. F., 613
Piggott, C., 277
Pimentel, L., 188
Pine, B. J., 611
Pine, B. J., II, 611
Pisano, G., 612
Plamondon, G., 134
Plato, 72, 73
Poitras, M., 604
Polanyi, Karl, 303
Pollard, S., 594
Pons, F., 613
Pope, R. A., 610
Poppo, L., 612
Port, O., 613
Porter, Michael E., 141, 191, 211–213, 215–216, 218, 409, 410, 592, 595, 599, 606, 607, 610, 613
Posen, A. S., 602
Potterie, B., 602
Powell, Colin, 102
Powell, T. C., 611
Prahalad, C. K., 437, 438, 574, 606, 607, 608, 616
Pranab, Bardhan, 596
Prasso, S., 579
Pringle, D., 613
Pritchard, D., 590
Pritchett, Lant, 592
Przeworski, A., 593
Punnett, B. J., 615
Purushothaman, R., 259
Putra, Hutomo Mandala, 390

Qin, D., 596
Qiu, L. D., 602
Quelch, J., 612
Quintanilla, C., 478

Raddock, D. M., 602
Radrik, D., 591
Rahaman, A. S., 596
Rai, S., 602
Raiffa, H., 602
Ralston, D. H., 595
Ram, R., 602
Ramagelahy, C., 610
Randzio-Plath, C., 314
Ransom, D., 610
Rapach, D. R., 604
Rastello, S., 397
Rauwald, C., 398
Ravenscraft, D. J., 461, 601, 609
Rawls, John, 175–176, 179, 180, 183, 597
Raymond, M. A., 610
Rebello, K., 613
Reed, A., 140
Reich, Robert B., 35, 289, 590, 602, 606, 607
Reinking, G., 398
Reitman, V., 614
Reynolds, C., 616
Riahi, Mohamed, 470
Ricardo, David, 189, 190, 193, 195, 247, 248, 249, 283, 597
Richardson, J., 604
Ricks, D. A., 595
Ridding, J., 605
Riley, Alan, 603
Ritter, N., 214
Robins, J. A., 609
Robinson, J., 598
Robinson, W. T., 598, 599
Robles, S., 602
Robock, S. H., 594
Rodriguez, Francisco, 598
Rodrik, Dani, 598
Roehl, W., 607
Roethel, Kathryn, 178
Rogoff, K., 604, 605
Rohwedde, Cecilia, 551
Roll, R., 609
Romalis, J., 603
Romer, David, 203, 598
Romer, P. M., 592
Rondinelli, D. A., 610
Ronen, S., 615
Roos, D., 595, 601, 606, 611, 616
Root, F. R., 608

subject index

Economies of scale
  definition, 208, 420
  global expansion and, 420–421
  minimum efficient scale,
    500–501
  in new trade theory, 209
Economist, 348, 350
Ecuador, rose exports, 43; *see also*
    Andean Community
EDI; *see* Electronic data interchange
Education
  cultural differences and, 140–141
  as factor endowment, 213
  influence on economic
    development, 98
  measures, 213
  role in national competitive
    advantage, 141
  in value chain, 408
Efficiency frontier, 410–411
Efficient markets, 347, 356–357
EFTA; *see* European Free Trade
    Association
ELAN; *see* Export Legal Assistance
    Network
Elastic demand curves, 538–539
Eldorado of France, 532
Electricitie de France, 334
Electricity Generating Authority of
    Thailand, 485
Electronic data interchange
    (EDI), 514
Elloumi Group, 470
E-Mart, 49, 288
Embraer, 493–494, 495
EMCs; *see* Export management
    companies
EMI, 311
Employees; *see* Human resources
    management; Workers
Employment; *see also* Outsourcing
  effects of foreign direct
    investment, 286–287, 290–291
  effects of NAFTA, 303, 307,
    321–322, 323
  effects of regional trade
    agreements, 290–291, 307
  ethical issues, 157–158, 166–167
  slave labor, 264–265
EMS; *see* European Monetary System
Endesa, 334
Enel, 334
Energy, renewable sources,
    212, 214
Enron, 168–169, 177
Entrepreneurs, 94–96, 148, 149

Environmental issues
  arguments against free trade
    agreements, 57–59,
    253–254, 322
  climate change, 59, 162, 244
  deforestation, 46
  fair trade, 178
  mining, 161
  relationship of pollution and
    income levels, 58–59
Environmental safeguards
  countries with lax, 160–162, 245
  globalization debate and, 57–59,
    253–254
  trade and, 243–245
E.ON, 334
Equal Employment Opportunity
    Commission, 558
Ericsson Telecom AB, 288,
    427, 544
Eritrea, human rights violations,
    160, 161
Eritrean National Mining
    Corporation, 161
ESCO Interamerica, 451
Ethanol, 265
Ethical algorithms, 179
Ethical dilemmas, 166–167, 340
Ethical issues; *see also* Business ethics;
    Corruption; Human rights
    issues
  child labor, 166–167, 170, 171
  employment practices, 155–156,
    157–158, 166–167
  environmental pollution,
    160–162
  moral obligations, 164–166
  product safety and product
    liability, 87
  sweatshop labor, 155–156,
    157–158, 170
  totalitarian regimes, 107
Ethical strategies, 156
Ethical systems, 129, 131; *see also*
    Confucianism
Ethics; *see also* Business ethics
  definition, 156
  personal, 167–168, 177
  philosophical approaches
    casuist morality, 176
    cultural relativism, 170–171
    Friedman doctrine, 170
    justice theories, 175–176, 179
    Kantian, 172–174
    naive immoralism, 172
    righteous moralism, 171–172

  rights theories, 174–175
  straw men, 170–172
  utilitarianism, 172–173
Ethics codes, 164, 178–179, 181
Ethics officers, 180–181
Ethnocentric staffing policy,
    557–558, 560
Ethnocentrism, 147
Euro
  benefits, 315–316
  conditions, 396
  costs, 316–317
  EU members not participating,
    307–308, 315, 402
  exchange rates against dollar
    effects on companies, 344, 361,
      362, 398
    trading history, 317, 318,
      339, 344
  experience to date, 317–318
  introduction, 303, 315
  as reserve currency, 317–318
  as vehicle currency, 346
European Aeronautic Defense and
    Space Co.; *see* EADS
European Bank for Reconstruction
    and Development
    (EBRD), 406
European Central Bank (ECB), 307,
    316, 317, 318
European Coal and Steel
    Community, 309
European Commission, 309–311,
    313, 314; *see also* European
    Union
European Community (EC)
  as common market, 305, 309
  as customs union, 305
  establishment, 307, 308–309
  members, 309
European Council, 311–312
European Court of Justice, 312
European Free Trade Association
    (EFTA), 305, 308
European Monetary System
    (EMS), 371, 378
European Parliament, 306, 309,
    312, 314
European Union (EU)
  agricultural subsidies, 233
  ban on hormone-treated beef,
    240, 241
  biofuel subsidies, 265
  candidate members,
    310, 319
  car price differentials, 538

Externalities, 281–282, 498
Externally convertible currencies, 358
Exxon, 50, 159
ExxonMobil, 429, 567

Facebook, 532
Facilitating payments; see also Bribery
    economic effects, 163–164
    legal exceptions for, 83–85, 163,
        164, 171
    zero-tolerance policies, 171, 172
Factor endowments
    Heckscher-Ohlin theory, 203–205
    national competitive advantage
        and, 212, 213
Factors of production, 34
Fagor, 49
Fair trade, 178
Falun Gong, 165
Fascism, 77
FDI; see Foreign direct investment
Federal Express, 237
Federal Reserve, 386
Federal Trade Commission,
    236, 310
Femininity, 142
FHI; see Fuji Heavy Industries
Fiat, 440, 469
Financial account, 223, 225
Financial crises; see also Asian
        financial crisis; Currency
        crises of 2008-09, 39–40, 52,
        229–230, 395, 405–406
    banking, 387–388
    causes, 388
    of Dubai, 134
    European, 317
    frequency, 388
    global effects, 52
    Greek, 54, 70, 318, 396–397
    Hungarian, 402–403
    types, 387–388
Financial services
    banking crises, 387–388
    entry into foreign markets, 448
    global firms, 29–30
    Islamic banking methods, 80, 134,
        135, 381
    marketing mix, 541
    mergers, 314
    microfinance, 426
    single European market, 314
    trade liberalization, 252, 293
Financial statements, translation
    exposure, 361
First Global Bank, 433

First-mover advantages
    definition, 107, 446
    in foreign markets, 446
    in new trade theory, 209, 211, 217
First-mover disadvantages, 446–448
Fisher effect, 353–354
Fitch, 396
Fixed costs, 500
Fixed exchange rates
    Bretton Woods system, 374–375
    case for, 383–384
    definition, 371
    discipline of, 375
Flexible machine cells, 502
Flexible manufacturing
        technology, 501–503
Flextronics, 511
Floating exchange rates
    case for, 382–383
    current regime, 377, 380–382
    definition, 371
    dirty float, 371
    Jamaica Agreement, 378
    managed float, 382, 384
    monetary policy, 382–383
    in practice, 384
    volatility, 378–380, 383–384
Flows of foreign direct
        investment, 269
Fokker, 211
Folkways, 120–121
Food and Agriculture
        Organization, 241
Food prices, 256
Ford Motor Company, 31, 32, 34, 35,
        40, 50, 290, 412, 416, 425, 428,
        430–431, 437, 461, 469, 501,
        502–503, 508–509, 526, 538,
        574, 576
Forecasting; see Exchange rate
        forecasting
Foreign Corrupt Practices Act,
        83–85, 163, 171
Foreign Credit Insurance
        Association, 483, 484–485
Foreign debt crises, 388
Foreign direct investment (FDI),
        269–270; see also Acquisitions;
        Greenfield ventures
    benefits
        balance-of-payments
            effects, 287–288, 290
        effects on competition, 288
        employment effects, 286–287,
            290, 291
        to home countries, 290

        to host countries, 285–288
        resource-transfer effects,
            285–286, 290
    costs
        adverse effects on
            competition, 288–289
        balance-of-payments
            effects, 289, 290
        employment effects, 290–291
        to home countries, 290–291
        to host countries, 288–289
        national sovereignty and
            autonomy, 289
    criticism of, 290
    definition, 38
    direction, 271–274
    explanations of increase, 269–271
    flows, 40, 47–48, 269, 270
    government policies
        encouraging, 269, 291
        of home countries, 283, 291–292
        of host countries, 269–270,
            283–285, 292–293
        impact on investment
            decisions, 296
        incentives, 292
        restrictions on inflows, 110, 270,
            283, 284, 292–293
        restrictions on outflows,
            283, 291–292
    gross fixed capital formation
        percentage, 272–274
    inflows, 269, 271–272
    insurance programs, 291
    liberalization, 39, 293
    local labor and, 429
    outflows, 269, 270, 274–275
    political views, 282–285
    source countries, 274–275
    sources, 45
    stocks, 40, 46–47, 269
    trade theory and, 291
    treaties, 271, 293–294
    trends, 40, 45–48, 269–271
Foreign direct investment
        theories, 275–276
    eclectic paradigm, 276, 280–282
    explanation of patterns, 279–280
    explanations of investment decisions,
        276, 278–280, 294–296
    internalization, 278, 280, 294
    location-specific advantages,
        280–281, 294
    managerial implications, 294–296
    product life-cycle, 280, 296
    strategic behavior, 279–280, 296

InterGenNV, 443
Internal stakeholders, 179
Internalization theory, 278, 280, 294
International Bank for
    Reconstruction or
    Development (IBRD), 376; *see
    also* World Bank
International businesses, 62–63
International Chamber of
    Commerce, 81
International Court of Arbitration, 81
International Development
    Association (IDA), 376
International Federation of the
    Phonographic Industry, 85
International Finance
    Corporation, 433
International Fisher effect, 353–354
International Labor Organization
    (ILO), 265, 575
International Monetary Fund (IMF)
    agricultural protectionism
        study, 256
    crisis management, 387–388
        Asia (1997), 371–372, 389,
            392–394
        global crisis (2008-09), 395
        Greece, 318, 396–397
        Hungary, 402
        Mexico, 388–389
        moral hazard issue, 394–395
        rescue packages, 371–372, 387
        South Korea, 355, 389, 393,
            394, 395
        Thailand, 389, 392
        Turkey, 70
    criticism of, 37, 372, 393–395
    debt relief program, 62
    definition, 36
    establishment, 36, 371, 374
    exchange rate policies of
        members, 384–385
    financial crisis study, 388
    foreign investment
        recommendations, 298
    implications for businesses, 399
    loans, 36–37, 372, 375–376,
        386–387
    mandate, 387
    members, 378, 387
    monetary and fiscal
        conditions, 376, 393–394, 395
    OPEC member spending
        report, 381
    quotas, 378
    role, 375–376, 386–387

International monetary system;
    see also Exchange rate regimes
    Bretton Woods system, 371–372,
        374–375
    definition, 370
    gold standard, 372–374, 377
    history, 372–374
    managerial implications, 397–400
    mixed system, 372
    shocks, 378
International Orientation
    Resources, 562, 565
International strategy, 431–432
International trade; *see also* Exporting;
    Free trade; Trade policies
    definition, 38
    development of system, 248–250
    fair trade, 178
    laws applied in disputes, 81
    relationship to economic
        growth, 203
    theoretical explanations of
        patterns, 190–191, 204–205
    typical transactions, 482–483
    volume, 39–40
International Trade
    Administration, 474
International Trade Commission
    (ITC), 237, 261
International trade
    secretariats, 574–575
Internet
    freedom, 87, 175, 578
    growth, 41
    logistics use, 514
    outsourcing service activities
        via, 34–35, 43
    role in globalization, 34–35, 41
    role in political change, 100
    shopping on, 529
Inventory, just-in-time
    systems, 512–513
Investment; *see* Foreign direct
    investment
Investment treaties, 271
Investor psychology, 354, 356
Iraq
    cultures, 121–122
    oil production, 45
    trade sanctions on, 242
Islam
    banking methods, 80, 134, 135, 381
    culture, 121–122
    economic implications, 133–135
    fundamentalism, 101, 132–133,
        146, 273

number of adherents, 129, 131
    origins, 131
    principles, 131–132
    Shiites and Sunnis, 121–122
Islamic countries
    religious resurgence, 101
    theocratic law systems, 75, 80, 133
    theocratic totalitarianism, 76
Islamic law (*Sharia*), 75, 80, 133
ISO 9000, 497
Isuzu, 290
Italy, banks, 314
ITC; *see* International Trade
    Commission

Jabil Circuit, 158
Jaguar, 443
Jamaica Agreement, 378
Japan
    agricultural subsidies, 233
    bribery scandals, 162–163
    culture
        changes in, 144–145
        condolences, 140
        Confucianism, 137, 139, 148
        economic advantages, 119
        folkways, 121
        group membership, 124–125
        influence on competitive
            advantage, 148
    distribution system, 427, 528, 529,
        530, 533
    economic growth, 106, 366
    education, 141
    entrepreneurs, 148
    exchange rates, 366–367
    Export-Import Bank, 475
    foreign direct investment in, 284,
        291, 293
    Ministry of International Trade
        and Industry, 473
    national competitive
        advantage, 148
    new product development, 544
    nontariff barriers, 236–237,
        249–250
    social structure, 124–125
    trading firms (*sogo shosha*), 473, 488
Japanese Bank for International
    Cooperation (JBIC), 475
Japanese Finance Corporation, 475
Japanese Overseas Enterprise
    Association, 557
JBIC; *see* Japanese Bank for
    International Cooperation
J.D. Power and Associates, 502

Jet Airways, 144
Jet Blue, 494
JEXIM; *see* Export-Import Bank of Japan
JIT; *see* Just-in-time inventory systems
Johnson & Johnson, 516
Joint ventures; *see also* Strategic alliances
  advantages, 456
  definition, 455
  disadvantages, 456–457
  in foreign markets, 455–457
Judaism, 129, 131
Jumeirah Group, 66
Just distribution, 175
Justice theories, 175–176, 179
Just-in-time inventory systems (JIT), 512–513
JVC, 40

K&R insurance, 567
K.A. Associates, 452
Kantian ethics, 172–174
Kellogg, 536
Kemper Corp., 285
KFC, 448, 455
Kia Motors, 390
Kidnappings, 567
Kimberly-Clark, 540
Kirin, 454
Kmart, 447
Knowledge economy, 190, 192
Kodak, 40, 50, 159, 280, 511, 539–540, 545
Kokuyo, 530
Komatsu, 34, 352, 431
Korea; *see* South Korea
KPMG, 461
Kwality, 289
KYE Systems Corporation, 158
Kyrgyzstan, 73

Labor; *see* Workers
Labor policies, globalization debate and, 57–59
Labor relations, international, 573–576
Labor unions; *see* Organized labor
Laboratorios Phoenix, 517
Lafarge Group, 277
Lag strategy, 361–362
Land Rover, 443
Language
  differences, 139–140
  foreign, 566

spoken, 139–140
unspoken, 140
Late-mover disadvantages, 107
Latin America; *see also individual countries*
  Andean Community, 305, 323–324
  culture, 120–121, 140
  democratization, 51
  economic reforms, 51
  foreign direct investment in, 270, 272
  leftist politics, 102
  Mercosur, 304, 305, 324–325
  regional trade agreements, 304
Law of one price, 347, 348
Laws; *see* Legal systems
L/Cs; *see* Letters of credit
Lead strategy, 361–362
Lean production, 278, 501–503
Lear Corporation, 469
Learning
  from alliance partners, 437–438
  global, 507
Learning effects, 420
Legal risk, 109–110
Legal systems; *see also* Property rights
  civil law, 80, 81
  common law, 80, 81
  contract law, 81
  definition, 79
  intellectual property protection, 85–86, 110
  product liability laws, 86–87
  product safety laws, 86–87
  theocratic, 75, 80, 133
  in transition economies, 105–106
Lenovo, 419
Leontief paradox, 204–205
Letters of credit (L/Cs), 480–481
Levi Strauss, 146, 158, 522, 541, 542
Lexus, 534
LG Electronics, 40, 434, 451
LG Semicon, 237
Li & Fung, 155
Libya, countertrade deals, 360
Licensing
  advantages, 453
  compared to foreign direct investment, 278–279
  cross-licensing agreements, 454
  definition, 276
  disadvantages, 453–454
  limitations, 278–279, 294–295
  use of, 295–296
Liebherr Group, 49
Lincoln Electric, 463, 464
Lixi, Inc., 50

Liz Claiborne, 155
Lobbying, 217–218, 399–400
Local content requirements, 236, 261
Local responsiveness
  customer preferences, 425–426, 429, 522
  distribution systems, 427
  host government demands, 427
  infrastructure and practices, 426–427
  pressure for, 423–425
Localization strategy, 429–430, 432
Location economies, 417–419
Location externalities, 281–282, 498
Location selection; *see* Foreign markets; Global production
Location-specific advantages, 280–281, 294
Lockheed, 162–163
Logistics
  definition, 495
  objectives, 512
  strategic objectives, 496, 498
  as support activity, 413
  use of technology, 513–514
Logitech, 221–222
L'Oreal, 309
Lotus, 447
Louvre Accord, 380
Lubricating Systems, Inc., 50

Maastricht Treaty, 315, 316
Macau, 369–370, 371
Mafia, 82
Make-or-buy decisions; *see also* Outsourcing
  advantages of buy, 510–511
  advantages of make, 508–510
  definition, 507
  trade-offs, 511
Malaysia
  ASEAN membership, 326
  currency crisis, 392
  exchange rate policies, 385–386
  investment boom, 389–390
Managed-float system, 382, 384
Management development, 565–566, 568
Management in global markets, 62–63, 564–565; *see also* Expatriate managers
Manufacturing; *see also* Global production; Production
  flexible, 501–503
  lean production, 278, 501–503
  mass customization, 501–503

Protestantism, 129, 131
Proxemics, 180
Pruksa Real Estate, 445
Public action, 82
Pull strategy, 533–535
Purchasing power parity (PPP)
  definition, 89
  explanations of exchange
    rates, 347–348, 351–353
  national differences, 89, 90
Push strategy, 533–535

Qatar Telecom, 273
Qingdao Refrigerator Co., 49
Qinghai Satellite, 165
Quality
  international standards, 497
  relationship to cost reductions, 496
  Six Sigma, 497
  total quality management, 496–497
Quantum Corporation, 547
Quiksilver, 523
Quota rents, 236
Quotas
  import, 234–236
  Multi-Fiber Agreement, 235
  tariff rate, 235

R&D; see Research and development
Radical view of foreign direct
  investment, 282, 284
Rank-Xerox, 206, 280
RCA Corporation, 278, 454, 526–527
Real estate development, 66–67
Red Spot Paint & Varnish
  Company, 476, 478
Reebok, 507
Regional economic integration
  in Africa, 329
  aggregation theory and, 306
  in Americas, 319, 320, 325–326
  in Asia, 326–329
  benefits, 303
  case against, 308
  case for, 306–307
  concerns, 303–304
  definition, 303
  impediments, 307–308
  managerial implications, 329–331
  Roman Empire, 303
Regional trade agreements; see also
    European Union; North
    American Free Trade
    Agreement
  in Africa, 299
  Andean Community, 305, 323–324

in Asia, 326
in Caribbean, 325
gains from trade, 303
in Latin America, 304
Mercosur, 304, 305, 324–325
number of, 303
Regulation; see also Antidumping
    policies; Competition policy
  of advertising, 535, 536
  effects on pricing
    strategies, 540–541
  of human resources practices, 555
  national differences, 427
REI, 529, 530
Relational capital, 437
Relatively efficient markets, 347
Religions; see also Islam
  Buddhism, 129, 136–137
  business implications, 129
  Christianity, 129, 131, 132
  definition, 129
  freedom, 131
  Hinduism, 129, 135–136
  Judaism, 129, 131
  largest, 129
  theocratic law systems, 80, 133
  theocratic totalitarianism, 76
  of world, 130
Renault SA, 79, 461, 469
Renault–Nissan, 440–441
Renewable energy, 212, 214
Repatriation of expatriate
    managers, 567–568
Reporters Without Borders, 175
Representative democracies, 76
Research and development (R&D)
  centralized, 544
  creation of value, 411–412
  foreign investment in, 286
  global capabilities, 547–548
  integrating with marketing and
    production, 545–546
  location, 544–545
  need for, 543
  new product development,
    543–545
  relationship to marketing, 412, 521
RESO, 406
Retail systems; see also Distribution
    systems
  concentrated, 527–528
  fragmented, 527–528
  quality, 529–530
Return on invested capital
    (ROIC), 407–408
Revlon, 522

Righteous moralism, 171–172
Rights; see also Human rights issues;
    Property rights
  of stakeholders, 179–180
  theories of, 174–175
Right-wing totalitarianism, 77
Rio Tinto, 184–185
Risks; see also Foreign exchange risk
  economic, 109
  in foreign markets, 108–110, 463
  legal, 109–110
  political, 108–109
Ritz Carlton, 444
RMC, 277, 289
Roche, 516
Rohm and Haas, 553–554
ROIC; see Return on invested capital
Rolex, 533
Rolls-Royce, 34, 486
Roman Catholic Church, 129, 131;
    see also Christianity
Roman Empire, 303
Romania, countertrade deals, 360, 485
Royal Bank of Scotland, 30
Royal Dutch Shell, 160, 429, 563, 565
Runde Investment Corp., 165
Russia
  bathhouses, 117
  blat relationships, 118, 119
  corruption, 117
  countertrade deals, 485, 487
  distribution system, 427
  doing business in, 117–118
  fall of communism, 50
  Mafia, 82
  McDonald's restaurants, 108
  political system, 50, 98
Rwanda, foreign direct investment
    in, 286
Ryanair Holdings PLC, 311

Safety and security, 566–567
SAIC; see Shanghai Automotive
    Industry Corp.
Sales; see Marketing and sales
    functions
Samsung, 40, 447, 450, 544, 557
Sara Lee, 311
SARS (severe acute respiratory
    syndrome), 513
Saudi Arabia
  countertrade deals, 485
  economic development, 75
  Islamic law, 75
  monarchy, 75
  oil production, 45

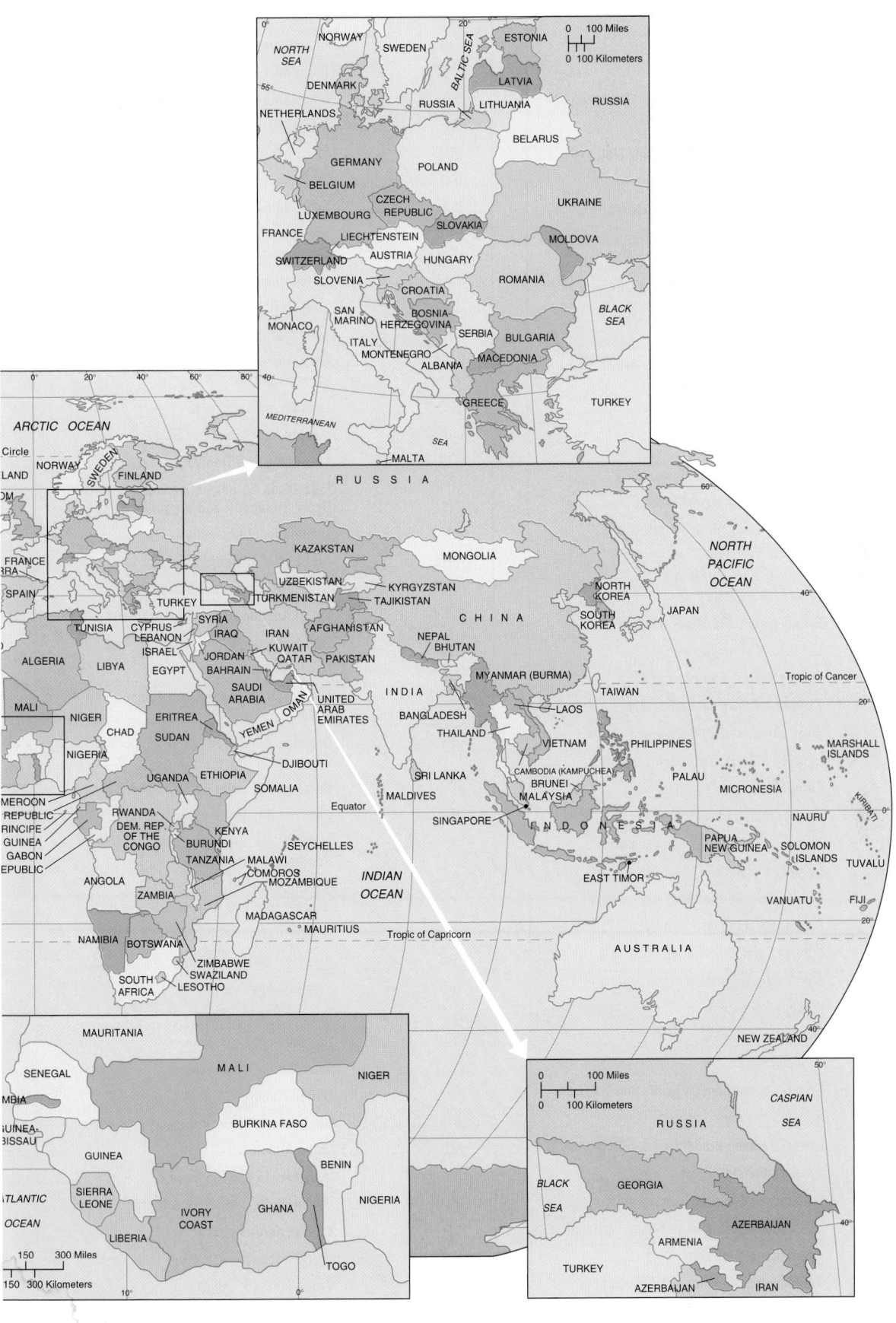

ACRONYM	PROPER NAME
ADB	Asian Development Bank
AfDB	African Development Bank
AFIC	Asian Finance and Investment Corporation
AFTA	Asian Free Trade Agreement
ASEAN	Association of Southeast Asian Nations
ATPA	Andean Trade Preference Act
BIS	Bank for International Settlements
BOP	Balance of Payments
CIM	Computer-Integrated Manufacturing
CIS	Commonwealth of Independent States
CISG	UN Convention on Contracts for the International Sale of Goods
CEMA	Council for Mutual Economic Assistance
CRA	Country Risk Assessment
DB	Development Bank
DC	Developed Country
DFIs	Development Finance Institutions
DISC	Domestic International Sales Corporation
EBRD	European Bank for Reconstruction and Development
ECOWAS	Economic Community of West African States
EMU	Economic and Monetary Union
EEA	European Economic Area
EFTA	European Free Trade Association
EMs	Export Management Companies
EMCF	European Monetary Cooperation Fund
EMS	European Monetary System
EPO	European Patent Organization
ETC	Export Trading Company
ETUC	European Trade Union Confederation
EU	European Union
FCPA	Foreign Corrupt Practices Act
FDI	Foreign Direct Investment
FSC	Foreign Sales Corporation
FTAA	Free Trade Agreement of the Americas
FTZ	Foreign Trade Zone
Fx	Foreign Exchange
G7	Group of Seven
GATT	General Agreement on Tariffs and Trade
GC	Global Company
GDP	Gross Domestic Product
GNP	Gross National Product
GSP	Generalized System of Preferences
IAC	International Anti-counterfeiting Coalition
IC	International Company
IDA	International Development Association

ACRONYM	PROPER NAME
IDB	Inter-American Development Bank
IEC	International Electrotechnical Commission
IFC	International Finance Corporation
IMF	International Monetary Fund
IPLC	International Product Life Cycle
IRC	International Revenue Code
ISA	International Seabed Authority
ISO	International Organization for Standardization
ITA	International Trade Administration
JIT	Just-in-Time
JV	Joint Venture
LAIA	Latin American Integration Association (formerly LAFTA)
LDC	Less Developed Country
LIBOR	London Interbank Offer Rate
LOST	Law of the Sea Treaty
MERCOSUR	Free Trade Agreement between Argentina, Brazil, Paraguay, and Uruguay
MNC	Multinational Company
MNE	Multinational Enterprise
NAFTA	North American Free Trade Agreement
NATO	North Atlantic Treaty Organization
NIC	Newly Industrializing Country
NTBs	Nontariff Barriers
OECD	Organization for Economic Cooperation & Development
OPEC	Organizational of Petroleum Exporting Countries
PPP	Purchasing Power Parity
PRC	People's Republic of China
PTA	Preferential Trade Area for Eastern and Southern Africa
SACC	Southern African Development Coordination Conference
SBA	Small Business Administration
SBC	Strategic Business Center
SBU	Small Business Unit
SDR	Special Drawing Rights
SEZ	Special Economic Zone
TQM	Total Quality Management
UN	United Nations
UNCTAD	UN Conference on Trade and Development
VAT	Value Added Tax
VER	Voluntary Export Restraint
VRAs	Voluntary Restraints Agreements
WEC	World Energy Council
WIPO	World Intellectual Property Organization
WTO	World Trade Organization

COUNTRY	CAPITAL
Afghanistan	Kabul
Albania	Tirana
Algeria	Algiers
Andorra	Andorra la Vella
Angola	Luanda
Antigua and Barbuda	St. John's
Argentina	Buenos Aires
Armenia	Yerevan
Australia	Canberra
Austria	Vienna
Azerbaijan	Baku
Bahamas	Nassau
Bahrain	Manama
Bangladesh	Dhaka
Barbados	Bridgetown
Belarus	Minsk
Belgium	Brussels
Belize	Belmopan
Benin	Porto-Novo
Bhutan	Thimphu
Bolivia	La Paz
Bosnia and Herzegovina	Sarajevo
Botswana	Gaborone
Brazil	Brasilia
Brunei	Bandar Seri Begawan
Bulgaria	Sofia
Burkina Faso	Ouagadougou
Burundi	Bujumbura
Cambodia	Phnom Penh
Cameroon	Yaounde
Canada	Ottawa
Cape Verde	Praia
Central African Republic	Bangui
Chad	N'Djamena
Chile	Santiago
China	Beijing
Colombia	Bogota
Comoros	Moroni
Congo	Brazzaville
Congo (formerly Zaire)	Kinshasa
Costa Rica	San Jose
Cote d'Ivoire	Yamoussoukro
Croatia	Zagreb
Cuba	Havana
Cyprus	Nicosia
Czech Republic	Prague
Denmark	Copenhagen
Djibouti	Djibouti
Dominica	Roseau
Dominican Republic	Santo Domingo
Ecuador	Quito
Egypt	Cairo
El Salvador	San Salvador
Equatorial Guinea	Malabo
Eritrea	Asmara
Estonia	Tallinn
Ethiopia	Addis Ababa
Fiji	Suva
Finland	Helsinki
France	Paris
Gabon	Libreville
The Gambia	Banjul
Georgia	Tbilisi

COUNTRY	CAPITAL
Germany	Berlin
Ghana	Accra
Greece	Athens
Grenada	St. George's
Guatemala	Guatemala City
Guinea	Conakry
Guinea-Bissau	Bissau
Guyana	Georgetown
Haiti	Port-au-Prince
Honduras	Tegucigalpa
Hungary	Budapest
Iceland	Reykjavik
India	New Delhi
Indonisia	Jakarta
Iran	Tehran
Iraq	Baghdad
Ireland	Dublin
Israel	Jerusalem
Italy	Rome
Jamaica	Kingston
Japan	Tokyo
Jordan	Amman
Kazakhstan	Astana
Kenya	Nairobi
Kiribati	Tarawa
Korea, North	Pyongyang
Korea, South	Seoul
Kuwait	Kuwait City
Kyrgyzstan	Bishkek
Laos	Vientiane
Latvia	Riga
Lebanon	Beirut
Lesotho	Maseru
Liberia	Monrovia
Libya	Tripoli
Liechtenstein	Vaduz
Lithuania	Vilnius
Luxembourg	Luxembourg
Macedonia, The Former Yugoslav Republic of	Skopje
Madagascar	Antananarivo
Malawi	Lilongwe
Malaysia	Kuala Lumpur
Maldives	Male
Mali	Bamako
Malta	Valletta
Marshall Islands	Majuro
Mauritania	Nouakchott
Mauritius	Port Louis
Mexico	Mexico City
Micronesia	Palikir
Moldova	Chisinau
Monaco	Monaco
Mongolia	Ulaanbaatar
Montenegro	Podgorica
Morocco	Rabat
Mozambique	Maputo
Myanmar	Rangoon
Namibia	Windhoek
Nauru	Yaren
Nepal	Kathmandu
The Netherlands	Amsterdam
New Zealand	Wellington
Nicaragua	Managua
Niger	Niamey
Nigeria	Abuja
Norway	Oslo
Oman	Muscat

COUNTRY	CAPITAL
Pakistan	Islamabad
Palau	Koror
Panama	Panama City
Papua New Guinea	Port Moresby
Paraguay	Asuncion
Peru	Lima
Philippines	Manila
Poland	Warsaw
Portugal	Lisbon
Qatar	Doha
Romania	Bucharest
Russia	Moscow
Rwanda	Kigali
Saint Kitts and Nevis	Basseterre
Saint Lucia	Castries
Saint Vincent and the Grenadines	Kingstown
San Marino	San Marino
Sao Tome and Principe	Sao Tome
Saudi Arabia	Riyadh
Senegal	Dakar
Serbia	Belgrade
Seychelles	Victoria
Sierra Leone	Freetown
Singapore	Singapore
Slovakia	Bratislava
Slovenia	Ljubljana
Solomon Islands	Honiara
Somalia	Mogadishu
South Africa	Pretoria
Spain	Madrid
Sri Lanka	Colombo
Sudan	Khartoum
Suriname	Paramaribo
Swaziland	Mbabane
Sweden	Stockholm
Switzerland	Bern
Syria	Damascus
Taiwan	Taipei
Tajikistan	Dushanbe
Tanzania	Dar-es-Salaam
Thailand	Bangkok
Togo	Lome
Tonga	Nuku'alofa
Trinidad and Tobago	Port-of-Spain
Tunisia	Tunis
Turkey	Ankara
Turkmenistan	Ashgabat
Tuvalu	Funafuti
Uganda	Kampala
Ukraine	Kiev
United Arab Emirates	Abu Dhabi
United Kingdom	London
United States of America	Washington, DC
Uruguay	Montevideo
Uzbekistan	Tashkent
Vanuatu	Vila
Vatican City	
Venezuela	Caracas
Vietnam	Hanoi
Western Samoa	Apia
Yemen	Sanaa
Zambia	Lusaka
Zimbabwe	Harare